KT-154-256

MILLER'S

2006

PRICE GUIDE 2006

antiques

MILLER'S 2006

PRICE GUIDE 2006

antiques

ELIZABETH NORFOLK *GENERAL EDITOR*

2006
VOLUME XXVII

MILLER'S ANTIQUES PRICE GUIDE 2006

Created and designed by
Miller's Publications
The Cellars, High Street
Tenterden, Kent, TN30 6BN
Tel: +44 (0) 1580 766411
Fax: +44 (0) 1580 766100

First published in Great Britain in 2005
by Miller's, a division of Mitchell Beazley,
imprints of Octopus Publishing Group Ltd,
2–4 Heron Quays, London E14 4JP
Miller's is a registered trademark of
Octopus Publishing Group Ltd

ISBN 1 84533 135 4

A CIP catalogue record for this book is
available from the British Library

Set in Frutiger

Colour origination by 1.13, Whitstable, Kent
Additional colour origination by Ian Williamson
Printed and bound: Rotolito Lombarda, Italy

General Editor: Elizabeth Norfolk
Managing Editor: Valerie Lewis
Production Co-ordinator: Philip Hannath
Editorial Co-ordinator: Deborah Wanstall
Editorial Assistants: Melissa Hall, Joanna Hill
Production Assistants: Caroline Bugeja, Natasha Hamblin,
Charlotte Smith, Mel Smith, Ethne Tragett
Advertising Executives: Emma Gillingham, Jill Jackson,
Michael Webb, Carol Woodcock
Advertising Co-ordinator & Administrator: Melinda Williams
Designer: Nick Harris
Advertisement Designer: Kari Moody
Indexer: Hilary Bird
Production: Jane Rogers
Jacket Design: Alexa Brommer
Additional Photographers: Emma Gillingham, Dennis O'Reilly, Robin Saker

Front cover illustrations:
A Victorian mahogany fire screen, with a Berlinwork panel,
51½in (131cm) high. **£400–480 / €580–700 / $720–870 G(B)**

A *famille rose* bowl, painted with figures in a landscape, c1790,
16in (40.5cm) diam. **£1,500–1,800 / €2,200–2,650 / $2,700–3,250 SWO**

A Bohemian goblet, with a castellated rim and gilt decoration,
mid-19thC, 11¼in (28.5cm) high. **£190–220 / €280–320 / $340–400 SWO**

Half title illustration:
A pottery plate, decorated with a flower, c1820,
7in (18cm) diam. **£270–300 / €390–440 / $490–540 HOW**

Contents illustration:
A bentwood and upholstery chair, by Norman Cherner for Plycraft,
American, Massachusetts, c1955. **£350–420 / €510–610 / $630–760 SK**

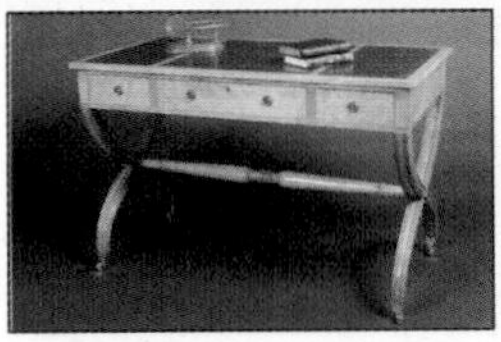

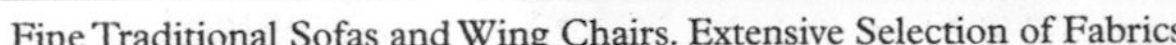

12,000 sq ft of antiques within 10 miles of each other

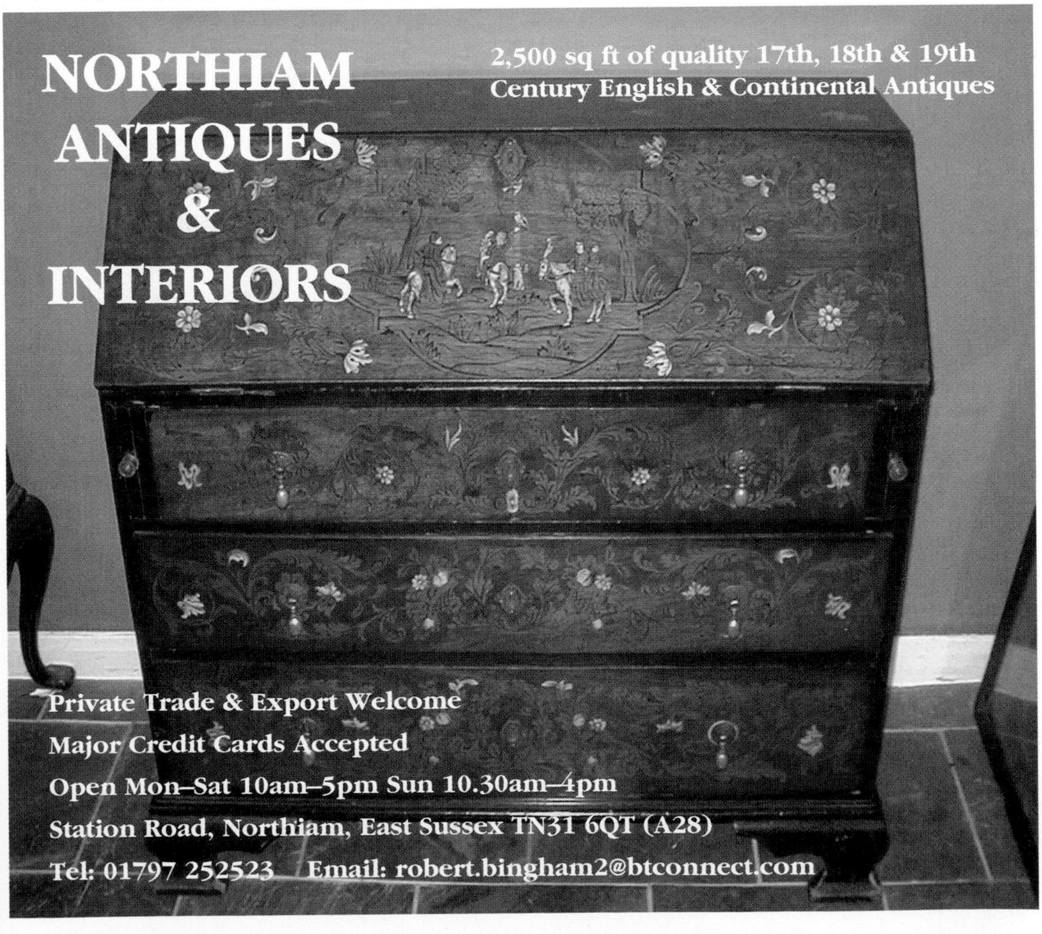

The Antiques
Fairs & Centres Guide
January – June 2005
www.antiquesfairsguide.co.uk

Dates	British Monarch	British Period	French Period
1558–1603	Elizabeth I	Elizabethan	Renaissance
1603–1625	James I	Jacobean	
1625–1649	Charles I	Carolean	Louis XIII (1610–1643)
1649–1660	Commonwealth	Cromwellian	Louis XIV (1643–1715)
1660–1685	Charles II	Restoration	
1685–1689	James II	Restoration	
1689–1694	William & Mary	William & Mary	
1694–1702	William III	William III	
1702–1714	Anne	Queen Anne	
1714–1727	George I	Early Georgian	Régence (1715–1723)
1727–1760	George II	Early Georgian	Louis XV (1723–1774)
1760–1811	George III	Late Georgian	Louis XVI (1774–1793) Directoire (1793–1799) Empire (1799–1815)
1812–1820	George III	Regency	Restauration Charles X (1815–1830)
1820–1830	George IV	Regency	
1830–1837	William IV	William IV	Louis Philippe (1830–1848) 2nd Empire Napoleon III (1848–1870) 3rd Republic (1871–1940)
1837–1901	Victoria	Victorian	
1901–1910	Edward VII	Edwardian	

German Period	U.S. Period	Style	Woods
Renaissance	Early Colonial	Gothic	Oak Period (to c1670)
Renaissance/ Baroque (c1650–1700)		Baroque (c1620–1700)	Walnut period (c1670–1735)
	William & Mary		
	Dutch Colonial	Rococo (c1695–1760)	
Baroque (c1700–1730)	Queen Anne		
Rococo (c1730–1760)	Chippendale (from 1750)		Early mahogany period (c1735–1770)
Neo–classicism (c1760–1800)	Early Federal (1790–1810)	Neo–classical (c1755–1805)	Late mahogany period (c1770–1810)
Empire (c1800–1815)	American Directoire (1798–1804)	Empire (c1799–1815)	
	American Empire (1804–1815)		
Biedermeier (c1815–1848)	Late Federal (1810–1830)	Regency (c1812–1830)	
Revivale (c1830–1880)	Victorian	Eclectic (c1830–1880)	
Jugendstil (c1880–1920)		Arts & Crafts (c1880–1900)	
	Art Nouveau (c1900–1920)	Art Nouveau (c1900–1920)	

contents

Acknowledgments

The publishers would like to acknowledge the great assistance given by our consultants. We would also like to extend our thanks to all auction houses and their press offices, as well as dealers and collectors, who have assisted us in the production of this book.

FURNITURE:	Jonty Hearnden, Dorchester Antiques, The Barn, 3 High Street, Dorchester-on-Thames, Oxon OX1 7HH
OAK & COUNTRY FURNITURE:	Antony Bennett, Bonhams, New House, 150 Christleton Road, Chester CH3 5TD
POTTERY:	John Howard, 6 Market Place, Woodstock, Oxon OX20 1TE
PORCELAIN:	John Sandon, Bonhams, 101 New Bond Street, London W1Y 0AS
ASIAN CERAMICS & WORKS OF ART:	Peter Wain, Anglesey
GLASS:	Brian Watson, Foxwarren Cottage, High Street, Marsham, Nr Norwich, Norfolk NR10 5QA
SILVER & SILVER PLATE:	Hugh Gregory, Thomson, Roddick & Medcalf, Coleridge House, Shaddongate, Carlisle, Cumbria CA2 5TU
CLOCKS:	Richard Garnier, Kent rich.garnier@tinyworld.com
BAROMETERS:	Derek & Tina Rayment, Orchard House, Barton Road, Barton, Nr Farndon, Cheshire SY14 7HT
DECORATIVE ARTS:	Mark Oliver, Bonhams, 101 New Bond Street, London W1Y 0AS
RUGS & CARPETS:	Jonathan Wadsworth, Wadsworth's, Marehill, Pulborough, West Sussex RH20 2DY
PORTRAIT MINIATURES:	Haydn Williams, London
ANTIQUITIES:	Joanna van der Lande, Bonhams, 101 New Bond Street, London W1Y 0AS
TRIBAL ART:	Siobhan Quin, Bonhams, 101 New Bond Street, London W1Y 0AS
SCIENTIFIC INSTRUMENTS & MARINE:	Bill Higgins, Fossack & Furkle, PO Box 733, Abington, Cambridge CB1 6BF

How to use this book

In order to find a particular item, consult the contents list on page 19 to find the main heading – for example, Decorative Arts. Having located your area of interest, you will find that larger sections have been sub-divided. If you are looking for a particular factory, designer or craftsman, consult the index which starts on page 788.

ARTS & CRAFTS METALWARE 449

Arts & Crafts Metalware

A pair of Roycroft copper bookends, American, c1915, 4½in (11.5cm) high.
£250–280 / €370–410
$450–510 ⊞ SHa
The American craft community known as the Roycrofters (1895–1938) was founded by Elbert Hubbard to produce metalwork, textiles and furniture.

A pewter bowl and cover, 1880–1920, 8in (20.5cm) wide.
£135–150 / €195–220
$240–270 ⊞ STRA

A silver-plated box, with inset wooden panel, c1880, 5in (12.5cm) wide.
£440–490 / €640–720
$800–890 ⊞ TDG

Further reading
Miller's Art Nouveau & Art Deco Buyer's Guide, Miller's Publications, 2001

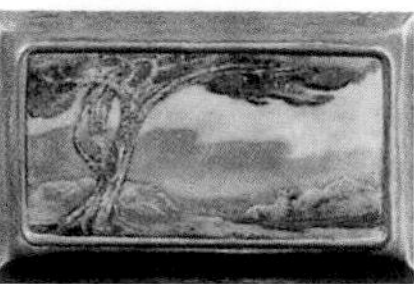

► **A Guild of Handicraft hammered silver box,** by Fleetwood Charles Varley, with inset enamel plaque, signed, London 1903, 6¾in (17cm) wide.
£4,800–5,700 / €7,000–8,300
$8,700–10,300 ⚒ S

A Wiener Werkstätte silver box, designed by Carl Otto Czeschka, made by Josef Hossfeld, decorated with enamelled bird motif medallions, impressed marks, Austrian, Vienna, c1907, 2¾in (7cm) diam.
£5,200–6,200 / €7,600–9,100
$9,400–11,200 ⚒ DORO

DECORATIVE ARTS

Miller's Compares

I. A Liberty & Co Tudric pewter and enamel biscuit box, by Archibald Knox, decorated with stylized leaves, stamped mark, early 20thC, 4¾in (12cm) square.
£1,800–2,150 / €2,650–3,150
$3,250–3,900 ⚒ S(O)

II. A Liberty & Co Tudric pewter biscuit box, by Archibald Knox, decorated with stylized leaves, stamped mark, early 20thC, 4¾in (12cm) square.
£450–540 / €660–790
$810–980 ⚒ S(O)

Item I and Item II are almost identical in design and size but Item I is applied with enamel roundels. These add great value to pewter wares designed by Archibald Knox as they are expensive to produce and more attractive, therefore making them very appealing to collectors.

A Liberty & Co Tudric pewter coupe, with a later glass liner, stamped mark, early 20thC, 7¼in (18.5cm) diam.
£1,000–1,200 / €1,450–1,750
$1,800–2,150 ⚒ S(O)

A pair of Newlyn copper alms dishes, decorated with fish among seaweed, marked, c1898, 12¾in (32.5cm) diam.
£2,350–2,800 / €3,450–4,100
$4,250–5,100 ⚒ LAY

A silver inkwell, by A. E. Jones, Birmingham 1912, 5in (12.5cm) diam.
£1,000–1,150 / €1,450–1,650
$1,800–2,050 ⊞ SHa

A. E. Jones
Albert Edward Jones grew up in Birmingham as part of a large family of blacksmiths. In 1902, he began to produce an extensive range of silver and jewellery items, mostly hand-beaten and often decorated with turquoise stones. His wares are easily identified by an oval maker's mark enclosing the initials A. E. J., and many are typically in the Arts & Crafts style.

Further reading
directs the reader towards additional sources of information.

Page tab
identifies the main heading under which larger sections have been sub-divided, therefore, allowing easy access to the various sections.

Caption
provides a brief description of the item including the maker's name, medium, year it was made and in some cases condition.

Miller's Compares
explains why two items which look similar have realized very different prices.

Price guide
this is based on actual prices realized. Remember that Miller's is a price guide not a price list and prices are affected by many variables such as location, condition, desirability and so on. Don't forget that if you are selling it is quite likely you will be offered less than the price range. Price ranges for items sold at auction tend to include the buyer's premium and VAT if applicable. The exchange rate used in this edition is 1.46 for € and 1.81 for $.

Source code
refers to the Key to Illustrations on page 778 that lists the details of where the item was photographed. The ⚒ icon indicates the item was sold at auction. The ⊞ icon indicates the item originated from a dealer.

Information box
covers relevant collecting information on factories, makers, care and restoration, fakes and alterations.

Introduction

Looking back over my old copies of *Miller's Antiques Price Guide* it is fascinating to see how some of the staple pieces of the auctioneer and dealer have fared. In 1985, a George III mahogany demi-lune card table with tulipwood crossbanding could have been purchased for about £900 / €1,300 / $1,600 at auction. Today the same table would cost 25 per cent less. Conversely, you could have bought a pair of Nantgarw plates for around £500 / €730 / $900 and today would be looking at paying nearer £2,000 / €2,900 / $3,600.

The change in tastes, and attendant change in values for familiar pieces, can be attributed to many factors, most of which are completely beyond our control. International upheaval, economic and demographic changes and people living in smaller houses and flats have all contributed to certain pieces losing their value. Modern developers provide fitted furniture and the George III toilet mirror, once a standard item in many homes, can now be had for as little as £60 / €90 / $110 – less than the price of a piece of 1960s' Whitefriars glass. It is no good imagining that the good old days will return and those dealers and auctioneers who are prepared to ring the changes will reap the rewards. I know of many dealers who now stock modern 'design' items alongside their traditional stock and are very glad they do. The moral of this is simple: start buying designs of the 1960s and '70s while they are still affordable and stick to things you like. If they drop in value at least you will have had fun and will still have objects you can display around you.

These changes in lifestyle have had a marked effect on certain aspects of the silver market as well. A late George III three-piece tea service is worth the same today as it was twenty years ago, but in real terms this shows a significant fall in value. On the other hand the market for early spoons has more than doubled over the same period. These pieces are being eagerly sought by a growing and well-informed group of collectors, and there are now sales devoted just to spoons.

Scarcely ten years ago, the world of antiques began to embrace the internet and none of us could have imagined the ripples that would still be felt today. Any good auctioneer will now have a fully searchable website with current and past sales available and also links to other group sites such as those of the *Antiques Trade Gazette*, Invaluable and Artnet. Strangely, auction catalogue sales are up even though many clients appear in the saleroom clutching a downloaded page from the website, only to buy a catalogue before leaving. The consequence is that there are buyers attending sales in numbers and ways that could never have been dreamt of even a few years ago. In the last year Dreweatt Neate sold a mid-19th century micro-mosaic table for £290,000 / €423,000 / $525,000 to an American bidder who had seen it on the internet. Within two months of the sale a second similar table had been consigned for auction on the strength of a Scottish client seeing the high price achieved and before long a third table was in the saleroom.

The dissemination of academic research and special exhibitions in museums can have a very positive effect on the market, even bringing in new collections. The great rash of TV game shows on the other hand seems to have little positive effect on either the general trade or auctioneers. However, eBay is now a potent force in certain sectors, most notably the world of branded collectables, and has reduced the stock of these items coming forward to traditional auctions and collectors' fairs.

The saleroom discovery is always a great thrill and each travelling valuer, dealer and collector will know how many calls they have to make before the great find turns up. Last year an 18th-century Irish serving table was discovered in a church hall. It was in such a bad state that all the legs had came off and it fitted into a hatchback, rather like an Ikea flat-pack table. After careful gluing and a good photograph in the catalogue it went on to make £49,500 / €72,000 / $90,000. The continued demand for all things Irish and of good quality will bring out fierce competition and result in exceptional prices. This applies equally to Irish pictures, silver, furniture and ceramics and is a reflection on the economic strength of the domestic Irish market and the huge Irish community across the globe.

Collectors and dealers in mainland China have, increasingly, been asking for condition reports and bidding in sales, sight unseen, with considerable success. This new interest has had a significant and positive effect on the values of certain types of Chinese ceramics and works of art, most notably late enamelled ceramics and jades. Conversely those early wares, so beloved by the academic collectors of the mid-1900s, are increasingly difficult to sell, particularly if they were funerary or monochromatic wares. These new buyers are also travelling to the ceramics fairs held in London and the USA, although attempts at restricting the sale of Chinese works of art through international trade agreements threatens to upset this growing market.

Looking back over twenty six years of *Miller's Antiques Price Guides* I realize what a vast array of items have passed through the hands of auctioneers, dealers and collectors and how useful these guides have been in covering new trends and discoveries – happy hunting!

Clive Stewart-Lockhart

Furniture

I have been involved in the world of antiques for 25 years and have witnessed many changes, but none seem greater than the changes that are currently seeping through the world of furniture. In recent years, a now familiar pattern has emerged that not only follows the furniture trade but other disciplines within the business of buying and selling antiques.

Buyers have become much more discerning. Ten years ago, when I first became a dealer, most people who were furnishing their homes were interested only in the antique look. Today's buyer is now bombarded with images and styles from all different sides such as the internet, style television programmes and designers championing the modern contemporary look. This style dominates magazines and the colour supplements.

So what has happened in a market that is being squeezed from so many different directions? Firstly, prices have fallen in many areas including whole swathes of furniture made in the Victorian and Edwardian eras. Furniture of inferior quality or unremarkable design has been particularly badly hit. This fall in interest has allowed buyers the unrivalled opportunity to purchase furniture such as good-quality 19th- and early 20th-century chests of drawers, wardrobes, and many types of dining furniture at prices that have not been seen for many years. So all is not doom and gloom. There are many recent examples of the market for furniture of very good quality being more buoyant than ever, thus proving that there is an even greater divide in the gap between what is popular and what is not.

Paradoxically, many auctioneers have recently had their most successful sales yet. A good example of this is when Gorringes of East Sussex sold a 17th-century *pietra dura* table top for £300,000 / €438,000 / $543,000 and Dreweatt Neate of Newbury sold an Italian micro-mosiac table for £290,000 / €423,000 / $525,000, thus proving once again the old adage that the market loves stock that has a combination of high quality and good provenance. Another example, breaking its own 1990 record as being the most expensive piece of furniture ever sold at auction, the Badminton Cabinet again exchanged hands at Christie's for a staggering £20,000,000 / €.29,000,000 / $36,000,000.

There is a definite sense that the market is treading on shifting sands and, although some may feel uncomfortable with this situation, I for one have never been more excited by the opportunities that will inevitably present themselves in the times ahead.

Jonty Hearnden

Beds

► **A Louis Philippe mahogany bed,** damaged and restored, French, 72¾in (185cm) long.
£820–980 / €1,200–1,400 $1,500–1,750 ⚒ S(P)

◄ **A Regency mahogany four-poster bed,** the baluster posts carved with wheat ears and lotus leaves, with gadrooned terminals and an upholstered footboard, 56in (142cm) wide.
£1,900–2,250 €2,750–3,300 $3,450–4,050 ⚒ HYD

A mahogany four-poster bed, the tester raised on turned posts, the headboard carved with a shell-and-scroll crest over a figured panel, American, mid-19thC, 78in (198cm) wide.
£4,250–5,100 €6,200–7,400 $7,700–9,200 ⚒ NOA

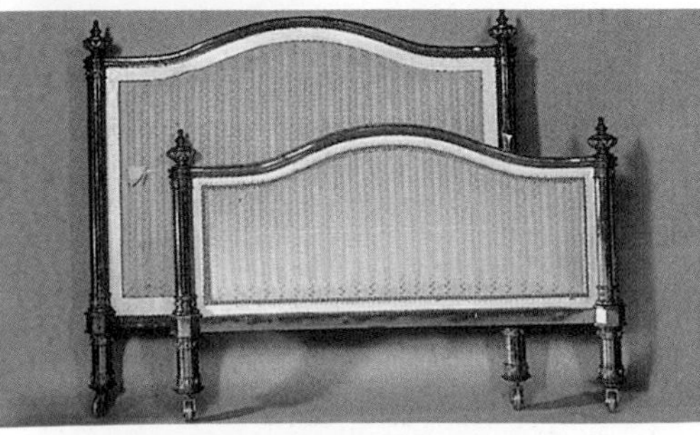

A brass bed, with upholstered head and footboard, Continental, 19thC, 74in (188cm) wide.
£3,450–4,100 / €5,000–6,000 $6,200–7,400 ⚒ S(Am)

◄ **A Victorian mahogany four-poster bed,** with two carved columns, 61in (155cm) wide.
£840–1,000 €1,250–1,450 $1,500–1,800 ⚒ SWO

A Victorian mahogany half-tester bed, the moulded cornice with baluster-turned pendants and roundels, the arched panelled footboard flanked by columns with turned finials, 57in (149cm) wide.
£2,900–3,450 / €4,250–5,000
$5,200–6,200 AH

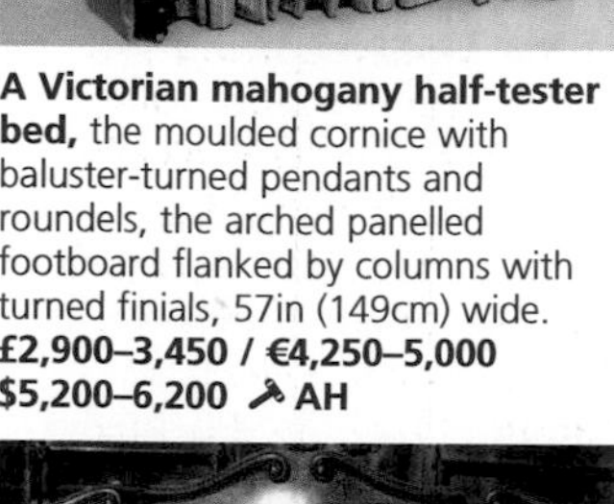

A walnut and marquetry-inlaid *bombé* bed, Italian, 1880s, 62in (157.5cm) wide.
£1,100–1,250 / €1,600–1,850
$2,000–2,250 PUGH

A Victorian painted cast-iron bed, with brass foot rail and finials, 55in (139.5cm) wide.
£420–500 / €610–730
$760–910 DD

A Louis XVI-style mahogany bed, with gilt-metal mounts, the headboard with a Wedgwood-style porcelain plaque, c1890, 58in (147.5cm) wide.
£1,200–1,400 / €1,750–2,050
$2,150–2,550 S(O)

A mahogany *lit en bateau*, with scroll ends and moulded apron, French, 19thC, 53in (134.5cm) wide.
£440–520 / €640–760
$800–940 WW

A Louis XV-style rosewood bed, French, c1900, 60in (152.5cm) wide.
£1,700–1,900 / €2,500–2,750
$3,100–3,450 SWA

A Louis XV-style walnut bed, French, c1900, 60in (152.5cm) wide.
£1,100–1,250 / €1,600–1,800
$2,000–2,250 PUGH

An Empire-style mahogany bed, with quartered veneers, French, c1900, 60in (152.5cm) wide.
£1,050–1,200 / €1,550–1,750
$1,900–2,150 SWA

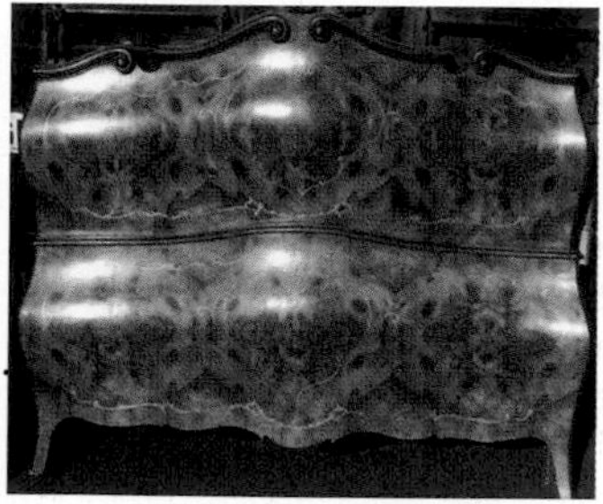

FURNITURE

Benches

A mahogany hall bench, decorated with an armorial panel with the arms of Nicholas Soult, c1820, 54in (137cm) wide.
£10,800–12,000 / €15,800–17,500
$19,500–21,700 ⊞ HA
This bench was given to Soult, who had been one of Napoleon's marshalls and was an ambassador of the French government when he attended Queen Victoria's coronation in 1837.

A carved rosewood and rosewood-veneered bench, c1830, 54in (137cm) wide.
£8,900–9,900 / €13,000–14,500
$16,100–17,900 ⊞ HA

A mahogany bench, with turned columns, 19thC, 45in (114.5cm) wide.
£620–700 / €910–1,000
$1,100–1,250 ⊞ MLL

A walnut hall bench, with bamboo-style handles and turned supports, c1870, 36in (91.5cm) wide.
£850–950 / €1,250–1,400
$1,500–1,700 ⊞ LGr

A late Victorian walnut hall bench, with a moulded rail and scroll arms, 54in (137cm) wide.
£1,000–1,200 / €1,450–1,700
$1,800–2,150 ⚒ SWO

◀ **A Black Forest walnut bench,** the supports in the form of bears, the back carved with grapes, leaves and dancing bears, German, 19thC, 62in (157.5cm) wide.
£8,400–9,400 / €12,300–13,700
$15,200–17,000 ⊞ NART
Furniture carved with bears is very popular at the moment, particularly in America.

Bonheurs du Jour

A George III Sheraton-style mahogany and crossbanded bonheur du jour, with satinwood stringing, the 14 small drawers with turned ivory knobs around three pigeonholes, the fold-out writing surface above two frieze drawers, 30in (76cm) wide.
£1,900–2,250 / €2,800–3,300
$3,450–4,050 ⚒ HYD

A George III mahogany bonheur du jour, with boxwood stringing, the double-arched panelled cupboard doors enclosing three short drawers flanking an aperture, above a hinged flap, with an ebony-strung and satinwood-crossbanded frieze drawer, 40in (101.5cm) wide.
£1,650–1,950 / €2,400–2,850
$3,000–3,550 ⚒ Mit

A rosewood bonheur du jour, with two drawers above a scrolled fall-front enclosing a fitted interior, above a frieze drawer, French, 19thC, 39¾in (101cm) wide.
£230–270 / €330–390
$420–490 ⚒ CHTR

▶ **A rosewood and marquetry-inlaid bonheur du jour,** the upper section with two doors enclosing a fitted compartment flanked by two quadrant shelves and two drawers, the leather-inset writing surface above five drawers, early 20thC, 38in (96.5cm) wide.
£880–1,050 / €1,300–1,550
$1,600–1,900 ⚒ PF

Bookcases

A George I walnut-veneered bookcase, the ogee-moulded cornice above two glazed doors with half-round mouldings enclosing adjustable shelves, on bracket feet, with later additions, 42in (106.5cm) wide.
£3,500–4,200
€5,100–6,100
$6,300–7,500 WW

A George III mahogany bookcase, with two astragal-glazed doors above two short and three long graduated drawers with brass handles, on a plinth base, bracket feet missing, 42in (106.5cm) wide.
£1,650–1,950
€2,400–2,850
$3,000–3,550 HYD

A baroque walnut and burr-walnut parquetry bookcase, the upper section with glazed doors, the inverted breakfront lower section with three drawers, inlaid with foliage and strapwork cartouches, on block feet, damaged, south German, 18thC, 50in (127cm) wide.
£3,700–4,400
€5,400–6,400
$6,700–8,000 S(Am)

A mahogany bookcase, the pediment with turned finials, over two glazed doors enclosing adjustable shelves, the lower section with a central drawer flanked by two drawers, over three graduated long drawers, the legs with bellflower and string inlay, American, c1800, 47½in (120.5cm) wide.
£2,150–2,550
€3,150–3,700
$3,900–4,600 NOA

◄ **A mahogany breakfront library bookcase,** with four astragal-glazed crossbanded doors, each enclosing three shelves, over two central panelled doors enclosing two sliding trays, flanked by three graduating drawers with brass handles, c1825, 100¼in (254.5cm) wide.
£16,600–18,500 / €24,200–27,000
$30,000–33,000 JC

► **A late Georgian mahogany bookcase,** the cornice above a dentil frieze, over two astragal-glazed doors enclosing shelves, the base with fluted decoration above two panelled doors, 58in (147.5cm) wide.
£1,750–2,100 €2,550–3,050
$3,200–3,800 AG

A mahogany bookcase, the upper section with silk-panelled doors, c1850, 77in (195.5cm) high.
£5,400–6,000
€7,900–8,800
$9,800–10,900 GEO

A mahogany breakfront bookcase, c1830, 94in (239cm) high.
£11,200–12,500
€16,400–18,300
$20,300–22,600 GEO

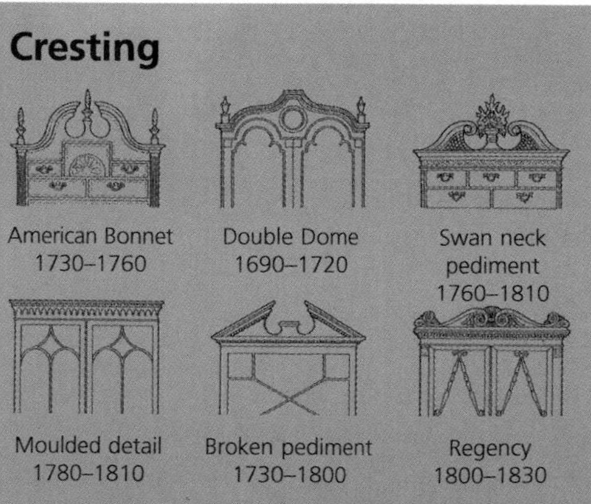

Cresting

Cresting can often be a good indication of date, but remember that copies of earlier styles were prolific in the late 19th and early 20th centuries.

A mahogany library bookcase, the glass and panelled doors enclosing adjustable shelves, French, c1860, 47¼in (120cm) wide.
£900–1,050
€1,300–1,550
$1,650–1,900 S(O)

An ebonized bookcase, by Eastlake, with carved and incised gilt decoration, the upper section with three glazed doors, the base with three drawers, American, c1875, 58in (147.5cm) wide.
£1,000–1,200
€1,450–1,750
$1,800–2,150 JAA

An oak bookcase, late 19thC, 51in (129.5cm) wide.
£2,050–2,300
€3,000–3,350
$3,700–4,150 APO

A Victorian oak breakfront bookcase, the coved cornice and burr-oak frieze above four key-arched glazed doors enclosing shelves, the base with two moulded-panel doors enclosing drawers and trays, flanked by conforming canted cupboards, 72¾in (185cm) wide.
£2,600–3,100
€3,800–4,550
$4,700–5,600 TEN

A mahogany bookcase, c1880, 46½in (118cm) wide.
£1,550–1,750
€2,250–2,550
$2,800–3,150 WiB

A Victorian walnut bookcase, the moulded cornice above glazed doors enclosing four shelves, the base with two drawers above a pair of scrolled urn-carved panelled doors, 43in (109cm) wide.
£490–580 / €720–850
$890–1,050 DD

A Victorian mahogany bookcase, the upper section with glazed doors, the base with a frieze drawer above two panelled doors, 35in (89cm) wide.
£175–210 / €260–310
$320–380 CHTR

▶ **A burr-walnut bookcase,** by John Taylor, the upper section with two glazed doors, the base with two panelled doors, Scottish, c1880, 89in (226cm) high.
£11,200–12,500
€16,400–18,300
$20,300–22,600 GEO
John Taylor & Son were appointed cabinet-makers to Queen Victoria in 1852. The firm also made billiard tables and supplied shop fittings and public house interiors.

A mahogany bookcase, the upper section with glazed doors enclosing shelves over a drawer and panelled doors, c1890, 48in (122cm) wide.
£1,500–1,700
€2,200–2,500
$2,700–3,100 SWA

A mahogany breakfront library bookcase, the upper section with four glazed doors enclosing shelves, the base with three drawers and four cupboard doors, 19thC, 72in (183cm) wide.
£2,800–3,350
€4,100–4,900
$5,100–6,100 E

An Edwardian mahogany bookcase, with inlaid decoration, the upper section with glazed doors, the base with two drawers over two cupboard doors, 34¾in (88.5cm) wide.
£910–1,100
€1,350–1,600
$1,650–1,950 SWO

Bureau Bookcases

A George III Sheraton-style mahogany bureau bookcase, with boxwood stringing and satinwood banding, the swan-neck pediment inlaid with shell and fan motifs, above two mahogany and boxwood-strung astragal-glazed doors enclosing shelves, the base with a fall-front with inlaid paterae and corner spandrels enclosing drawers and pigeonholes, over four graduated drawers, handles later. 41in (104cm) wide.
£1,900–2,250
€2,750–3,300
$3,450–4,050 Mit

A George III mahogany bureau bookcase, the two doors enclosing adjustable shelves and three short drawers, the base with a fall-front enclosing a fitted interior, 46½in (118cm) wide.
£2,700–3,200
€3,950–4,650
$4,900–5,800 L

Further reading

Miller's Antiques Encyclopedia, Miller's Publications, 2003

A George III mahogany bureau bookcase, the broken pediment above two astragal-glazed doors, the base with a fall-front enclosing a leather writing surface and a cupboard flanked by drawers and pigeonholes, the base with two short drawers and three long graduated drawers, later additions, 43in (109cm) wide.
£3,650–4,350
€5,300–6,300
$6,600–7,900 NOA

A mahogany cylinder bureau bookcase, the fall-front enclosing a slide, pigeonholes and ten drawers, bookcase probably associated, c1825, 37¾in (96cm) wide.
£3,100–3,700
€4,500–5,400
$5,600–6,700 S(O)

► **A Victorian mahogany cylinder bureau bookcase,** the breakfront dentil cornice above two glazed doors enclosing shelves, flanked by fruit- and foliate-carved corbals, the fall-front enclosing a slide-out interior with writing slope, pigeonholes and drawers, above two sets of three graduated drawers, 47in (119.5cm) wide.
£1,000–1,200 / €1,450–1,700
$1,800–2,150 Mit

Open Bookcases

◄ **A pair of Regency rosewood open bookcases,** with boxwood stringing, each with a three-quarter gallery above four graduated shelves and a single drawer below, on turned legs, 21in (53.5cm) wide.
£9,100–10,900 / €13,300–15,900
$16,500–19,700 L&T

► **A mahogany open bookcase,** with six shelves, c1825, 64in (162.5cm) high.
£3,350–3,750 €4,900–5,500
$6,100–6,800 SAT

► **A pair of Regency rosewood open bookcases,** with brass quatrefoil three-quarter galleries, reel-moulded borders and fluted columns, on bun feet, 39in (99cm) wide.
£12,000–14,400
€17,500–21,000
$21,700–26,100 HYD

◄ **An ebonized open bookcase,** with a pierced brass gallery and brass carrying handles, 19thC, 31in (78.5cm) wide.
£400–480 / €590–700
$720–860 ⚒ BWL

► **A mahogany open bookcase,** with a glazed cupboard above two drawers and shelves, 19thC, 53½in (136cm) wide.
£770–920 / €1,100–1,300
$1,400–1,650 ⚒ AH

A Victorian mahogany open bookcase, the shelves flanked by turned columns, 57in (145cm) wide.
£880–1,050 / €1,300–1,550
$1,600–1,900 ⚒ SWO

► **A Sheraton-style open bookcase,** with three shelves above two cupboard doors, c1905, 52½in (133.5cm) wide.
£1,650–1,950
€2,400–2,850
$3,000–3,550
⚒ AH

◄ **An oak bookcase,** with four adjustable shelves, 19thC, 26in (66cm) wide.
£940–1,100 / €1,350–1,600
$1,700–2,000 ⚒ WW

Revolving Bookcases

◄ **A mahogany revolving bookcase,** by Maple & Co, with inlaid marquetry and crossbanding, c1880, 35in (89cm) high.
£1,750–1,950
€2,550–2,850
$3,150–3,550 ⊞ WAA

► **A mahogany revolving bookcase,** c1900, 35in (89cm) high.
£1,650–1,850
€2,400–2,700
$3,000–3,350 ⊞ Man

An Edwardian inlaid mahogany revolving bookcase, with a crossbanded top, 20in (51cm) square.
£490–590 / €720–860
$890–1,050 ⚒ DMC

Revolving bookcases were first introduced in the late 18th century. They were cylindrical with two to six tiers of open shelves diminishing in size towards the top and supported by a central pillar rising from the base. They became popular in the Edwardian era, and examples from this period are generally square with two tiers, each side having a solid panel or slats forming the end supports of a central shelf. They are usually constructed of mahogany or rosewood although some Edwardian examples are of oak.

An Edwardian inlaid mahogany revolving bookcase, 33in (84cm) high.
£890–1,050
€1,300–1,550
$1,600–1,900 ⚒ SWO

► **An Edwardian mahogany revolving bookcase,** the top inlaid with a fan medallion, geometric box inlay and crossbanded edges, 19in (48.5cm) wide.
£820–980 / €1,200–1,400
£1,500–1,750 ⚒ Mit

Secretaire Bookcases

A mahogany secretaire bookcase, the upper section with glazed doors, c1790, 36in (91.5cm) wide.
£9,800–10,900
€14,300–15,900
$17,700–19,700 ⊞ GGD

► A George III mahogany secretaire bookcase, the swan-neck pediment above two doors with Gothic glazing bars, the base with a secretaire drawer above two panelled doors, 59½in (151cm) high.
£8,200–9,800
€12,000–14,300
$14,800–17,700 SWO

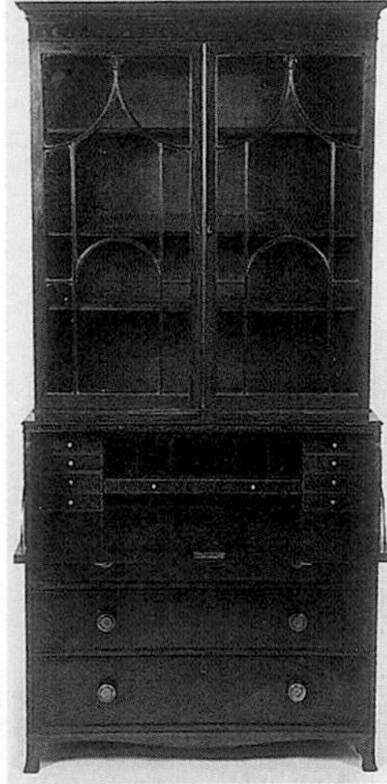

A George III mahogany secretaire bookcase, with two astragal-glazed doors with Prince of Wales feather detailing, enclosing shelves, the base with a secretaire drawer fitted with burrwood drawers and pigeonholes, above three graduated drawers, 41in (104cm) wide.
£5,300–6,300
€7,700–9,200
$9,600–11,400 HYD

A mahogany secretaire bookcase, c1790, 42in (106.5cm) wide.
£3,550–3,950
€5,200–5,750
$6,400–7,100 ⊞ WiB

Items in the Furniture section have been arranged in date order within each sub-section.

A George III mahogany secretaire bookcase, with astragal-glazed doors enclosing shelves, the ebony-strung base with a fall-front enclosing shelves, above two doors enclosing four drawers, 49¾in (126.5cm) wide.
£2,600–3,100
€3,800–4,550
$4,700–5,600 L&T

A mahogany secretaire bookcase, with two glazed doors flanked by columns, the base with a fitted secretaire drawer and three further drawers, early 19thC, 45in (114.5cm) wide.
£1,400–1,650
€2,000–2,400
$2,500–3,000 E

A George III mahogany secretaire bookcase, the astragal-glazed doors enclosing three adjustable shelves, over a secretaire drawer with a fitted interior, above two panelled doors, 43¼in (110cm) wide.
£3,000–3,600
€4,400–5,300
$5,400–6,500 DN(BR)

A mahogany secretaire bookcase, the moulded cornice above two glazed doors, the glazing bars carved as lotus leaves, the base with a fitted secretaire drawer above panelled doors, c1830, 48in (122cm) wide.
£3,000–3,600
€4,400–5,300
$5,400–6,500 HOK

◄ A fiddle-back mahogany secretaire bookcase, the moulded cornice above two glazed doors enclosing three adjustable shelves, the base with a secretaire drawer above two panelled doors, mid-19thC, 49¼in (125cm) wide.
£1,500–1,800 / €2,200–2,650
$2,700–3,250 DN(BR)

Buckets

A George III brass-bound mahogany peat bucket, with a swing handle, 17in (43cm) high.
£4,000–4,800
€5,800–7,000
$7,200–8,700 JAd

A George III brass-bound mahogany bucket, c1780, 13½in (34.5cm) high.
£2,000–2,400
€2,950–3,500
$3,600–4,300 S(O)

A George III brass-bound mahogany peat bucket, with carrying handles, 24¼in (61.5cm) diam.
£4,450–5,300
€6,500–7,700
$8,100–9,600 G(B)

A brass-bound mahogany plate bucket, c1830, 22in (56cm) high.
£3,600–4,000
€5,200–5,800
$6,500–7,200 GGD

Buffets

A Victorian mahogany three-tier buffet, with a three-quarter gallery, 34½in (87.5cm) wide.
£470–560 / €690–820
$850–1,000 DA

A Victorian mahogany three-tier buffet, 41in (104cm) wide.
£700–840 / €1,000–1,200
$1,250–1,500 DMC

A Henri II-style walnut buffet, with a marble top, spindled galleries and two drawers, French, c1890, 49in (124.5cm) wide.
£800–900 / €1,150–1,300
$1,450–1,600 SWA

Bureaux

A George I walnut bureau, 24in (61cm) wide.
£1,800–2,150 / €2,650–3,150
$3,250–3,900 S(O)

A George II walnut and crossbanded bureau, the fall-front opening to reveal pigeonholes and a well, above four graduated drawers, 31½in (80cm) wide.
£1,000–1,200 / €1,500–1,750
$1,800–2,150 DN(BR)

◄ **A William and Mary walnut and burr-walnut bureau,** the fall-front above two short and one long drawer, with an X-stretcher, 30in (76cm) wide.
£2,300–2,750 / €3,350–4,000
$4,150–5,000 S(Am)

A mahogany bureau, with fitted interior, c1745, 36in (91.5cm) wide.
£3,350–3,750 / €4,900–5,500
$6,100–6,800 ⊞ WAA

A walnut bureau, with a stepped interior, 18thC, 41in (104cm) high.
£5,000–5,500 / €7,300–8,100
$9,000–10,000 ⊞ ANAn

A George III walnut and crossbanded bureau, with herrringbone inlay, the fall-front enclosing a fitted interior, above four graduated drawers, some later veneer, 39in (99cm) wide.
£1,300–1,550 / €1,900–2,250
$2,350–2,800 ⚒ G(L)

A walnut and crossbanded bureau, the fall-front enclosing a fitted interior, c1750, 38½in (98cm) wide.
£1,200–1,400 / €1,750–2,050
$2,150–2,550 ⚒ S(O)

A George III mahogany bureau, the fall-front enclosing pigeonholes and drawers, above two short and three long drawers, with later brass handles and escutcheons, 40½in (103cm) wide.
£520–620 / €760–910
$940–1,100 ⚒ WW

A mahogany bureau, with a fitted interior, c1770, 41¾in (106cm) wide.
£2,250–2,700 / €3,300–3,950
$4,100–4,900 ⚒ S(O)

◄ **A Hepplewhite-style burr-yew cylinder bureau,** with line inlay, the top above a frieze drawer, the cylinder enclosing a fitted interior, over a writing slide and two drawers, 1785–90, 33in (84cm) wide.
£2,900–3,450 / €4,250–5,000
$5,200–6,200 ⚒ DN(BR)

► **A George III mahogany bureau,** the fall-front enclosing a fitted interior inlaid with boxwood and holly stringing, the base with four graduated drawers, 39in (99cm) wide.
£2,900–3,250 / €4,250–4,750
$5,200–5,900 ⊞ JC

A walnut bureau, with herringbone crossbanding, the fall-front enclosing a fitted interior, with two short and two long drawers, mid-18thC, 29in (73.5cm) wide.
£800–960 / €1,200–1,400
$1,500–1,750 ⚒ HOLL

A George III mahogany bureau, the fall-front enclosing a fitted interior, over four graduated drawers, 35¾in (91cm) wide.
£280–330 / €410–480
$510–600 ⚒ L&E

A George III mahogany bureau, the fall-front enclosing a fitted interior, above two short and three long graduated cockbeaded drawers, 41in (104cm) wide.
£610–730 / €890–1,050
$1,100–1,300 ⚒ DD

A rococo-style walnut-veneered bureau, inlaid with jacaranda and fruitwood, with gilt-brass mounts, the fall-front enclosing a fitted interior, over four drawers, Swedish, 1750–1800, 42¼in (107.5cm) wide.
£6,300–7,500 / €9,200–11,000 $11,400–13,600 BUK

A Sheraton-style satinwood bureau, the cylinder enclosing a leather-lined writing slope, drawers and pigeonholes, over a drawer above a tambour cupboard, c1795, 24in (61cm) wide.
£17,400–19,300 / €25,400–28,200 $31,000–35,000 GGD

A mulberry bureau, with ebony inlay, the cylinder enclosing a fitted interior, Austrian, c1800, 49¼in (125cm) wide.
£4,800–5,700 / €7,000–8,300 $8,700–10,300 S(O)

A late Regency rosewood bureau, with brass inlay, the top with a later three-quarter brass gallery, the cylinder enclosing satinwood- and line-inlaid veneered drawers, pigeonholes and a pull-out writing surface, above a frieze drawer and a dummy apron drawer, damaged, 36in (91.5cm) wide.
£680–810 / €990–1,200 $1,250–1,500 WW

A mahogany bureau, the roll top enclosing a fitted interior and a sliding writing surface, over three drawers flanked by pilasters, restored, Dutch, 19thC, 37½in (95.5cm) wide.
£1,200–1,400 / €1,750–2,050 $2,150–2,550 S(Am)

A Victorian walnut and marquetry *bureau de dame*, the upper section with a pair of cabinets with three-quarter galleries, flanking a mirror and a single drawer, above a fall-front enclosing a fitted interior, 31½in (80cm) wide.
£1,900–2,250 / €2,750–3,300 $3,450–4,000 LAY

A Victorian inlaid walnut *bureau de dame*, with gilt-metal mounts and mouldings, the central mirror flanked by a pair of cupboards with glazed doors, the fall-front enclosing a fitted interior, 31½in (80cm) wide.
£1,300–1,550 / €1,900–2,250 $2,350–2,800 SWO

A Victorian burr-walnut and marquetry bureau, the gilt-metal three-quarter gallery above three frieze drawers, the inlaid sliding front enclosing a fitted interior with a writing slope and secretaire drawers, over a frieze drawer, 31in (78.5cm) wide.
£1,300–1,550 / €1,900–2,250 $2,350–2,800 HYD

An 18thC-style rosewood bureau, Portuguese, c1880, 39½in (100.5cm) wide.
£2,600–3,100 / €3,800–4,550 $4,700–5,600 S(O)

Cabinets

A baroque walnut, burr-walnut and ebonized cabinet, inlaid with banding, the top fitted with a hidden compartment, above two shaped doors, on a serpentine base, Austrian, 1700–50, 49½in (125.5cm) wide.
£3,100–3,700 / €4,550–5,400
$5,600–6,700 ⚒ S(Am)

A Biedermeier cabinet, with two pairs of doors enclosing a painted interior, north European, 1800–50, 61in (155cm) wide.
£900–1,050 / €1,300–1,550
$1,600–1,900 ⚒ S(Am)

A mahogany *cartonnier*, the two stiles opening to reveal 12 later tooled-leather boxes, above two cupboard doors enclosing two shelves, on a platform base, French, early 19thC, 11¾in (30cm) wide.
£6,000–7,200 / €8,800–10,500
$10,900–13,000 ⚒ S

► **A satinwood cabinet,** c1900, 39in (99cm) high.
£630–700 / €900–1,000
$1,100–1,250 ⊞ QA

A mahogany cabinet, with a moulded breakfront cornice, panelled doors with rosette detail, the base with one long drawer, Dutch, early 19thC, 74¾in (190cm) wide.
£760–910 / €1,100–1,300
$1,400–1,650 ⚒ TRM

An ormolu-mounted kingwood cabinet, in the style of François Linke, with quarter veneers, the marble top above a blind frieze drawer over two glazed and silk-curtained doors with wire grilles, above a drawer and tambour-shuttered cupboard, French, c1900, 24in (61cm) wide.
£1,750–2,100 / €2,550–3,050
$3,200–3,800 ⚒ WW

Bedside Cabinets

A Chippendale-style mahogany tray-top bedside cabinet, the base with a shaped frieze on four sides, c1760, 22in (56cm) wide.
£3,300–3,700 / €4,800–5,400
$6,000–6,700 ⊞ WAA

A mahogany bedside cabinet, with a moulded gallery above two cleated doors, the base with two dummy drawers now converted to a single drawer, c1770, 21in (53.5cm) wide.
£1,650–1,850 / €2,400–2,700
$3,000–3,350 ⊞ JC

A George III mahogany tray-top bedside cabinet, the drawer enclosing a later writing slope, 24in (61cm) wide.
£2,350–2,600 / €3,450–3,800
$4,250–4,700 ⊞ HA

A George III mahogany tray-top bedside cabinet, the pierced handgrips above two doors, with a pull-out base, 23¼in (59cm) wide.
£530–630 / €770–920
$960–1,150 WW

A George III mahogany tray-top bedside cabinet, 22in (56cm) wide.
£2,500–2,800
€3,650–4,100
$4,550–5,100 APO

A George III mahogany tray-top bedside cabinet, the tambour-front cupboard above a pull out dummy drawer front, 19in (48.5cm).
£630–750 / €920–1,100
$1,150–1,350 HYD

A George III mahogany bedside cabinet, with a tambour front, 20in (51cm) wide.
£2,450–2,700
€3,550–3,950
$4,450–4,900 CRU

A mahogany bedside cabinet, some alterations, c1770, 21¼in (54cm) wide.
£1,000–1,200 / €1,450–1,750
$1,800–2,150 S(O)

A Georgian mahogany tray-top bedside cabinet, 21in (53.5cm) wide.
£1,750–1,950 / €2,550–2,850
$3,150–3,550 WAA

Bedside cabinets and commodes were originally called night tables. First made in France c1735, they quickly became fashionable in Britain, replacing the commode chairs that had been in production from the early 18th century. Towards the end of the 1700s they were sometimes supplied in pairs, one to conceal a chamber pot and the other to contain a bowl for washing and shaving. In more modern times the lower pot drawer has often been converted into an ordinary drawer.

A pair of George III mahogany bedside cabinets, each with a cockbeaded frieze drawer over a tambour cupboard, above a pull-out bidet drawer flanked by two drawers, on three front and two rear tapering legs, 30in (76cm) wide.
£2,900–3,450
€4,250–5,000
$5,200–6,200 HYD

◄ **A George III mahogany bedside cabinet,** the galleried top above a tambour door, with carrying handles and a shaped apron, c1780, 17in (43cm) wide.
£1,100–1,250 / €1,600–1,800
$2,000–2,250 JC

A mahogany tray-top bedside cabinet, with line inlay, the drawer conversion with a brass handle, c1790, 21in (53.5cm) wide.
£1,750–1,950
€2,550–2,850
$3,150–3,550 LGr

A mahogany bedside cabinet, the shaped gallery with carrying handles, above a cockbeaded door, the base converted to a drawer, c1790, 21in (53.5cm) wide.
£1,300–1,450
€1,900–2,100
$2,350–2,600 JC

◄ **A brass-mounted mahogany-veneered bedside cabinet,** the limestone top above a pull-out slide, Swedish, late 18thC, 18¾in (47.5cm) wide.
£4,000–4,800 / €5,900–7,000
$7,300–8,700 BUK

A late George III mahogany and boxwood- strung bedside cabinet, the top with a later pierced gallery and fan inlay, above a drawer, over two doors and a further drawer, 21¾in (55.5cm) wide.
£490–580 / €720–850
$890–1,050 DN

► **A mahogany bedside cabinet,** the pierced gallery above a panelled door, on moulded legs, 19thC, 15¾in (40cm) wide.
£470–560 / €690–820
$850–1,000 WW

A neo-classical blond wood bedside cabinet, with a hinged two-part top above a tambour door, Russian, early 19thC, 21¾in (55.5cm) wide.
£1,150–1,350
€1,700–2,000
$2,100–2,450 S(Am)

An inlaid mahogany bedside cabinet, c1900, 29in (73.5cm) high.
£310–350 / €450–510
$560–630 QA

A bedside cabinet, with rope-twist legs, c1815, 35in (89cm) high.
£1,500–1,700
€2,200–2,500
$2,700–3,100 WAA

► **A pair of walnut-veneered bedside cabinets,** with inlaid decoration, c1900, 29in (74cm) high.
£1,250–1,400
€1,850–2,050
$2,250–2,550 WAA

A Louis XV-style walnut bedside cabinet, with a marble top, French, c1900, 15in (38cm) wide.
£360–400 / €520–580
$650–720 SWA

A mahogany bedside cabinet, with a tambour front, Dutch, c1820, 18in (45.5cm) wide.
£810–900 / €1,150–1,300
$1,450–1,650 GGD

A walnut-veneered bedside cabinet, with parquetry and marquetry inlay, the cupboard enclosing a shelf, Italian, early 19thC, 21in (53.5cm) wide.
£370–440 / €540–640
$670–800 WW

◄ **A pair of walnut bedside cabinets,** c1860, 31in (78.5cm) high.
£2,000–2,250
€2,900–3,300
$3,600–4,050 QA

A mahogany bedside cabinet, c1890, 32in (81.5cm) high.
£290–330 / €420–480
$520–600 QA

A pair of Louis XV-style walnut bedside cabinets, with marble tops, French, c1900, 16in (40.5cm) wide.
£1,000–1,150 / €1,450–1,700
$1,800–2,100 SWA

FURNITURE

Bureau Cabinets

◄ **A George I japanned bureau cabinet,** the double-arched cornice over two arched doors with conforming mirrors, enclosing a fitted interior, the base with a slope enclosing a fitted interior and well, over two short and two long drawers, ball feet reduced, 39½in (100.5cm) wide.
£64,000–75,000 / €93,000–110,000
$116,000–136,000 TEN
The top of the lower section of this piece is stamped 'RF'. Only three other pieces with this stamp are known. These are associated with the London furniture maker John Belchier, who was working in the early 1720s. Eighteenth-century japanned furniture in original condition is highly sought after. Purchasers appreciate pieces that have little or no restoration, and the presence of a maker's stamp further enhances the desirability. Moreover, this extremely decorative cabinet with the double-arched feature to the top is very pleasing to the eye.

A baroque walnut and burr-walnut bureau cabinet, the upper section with two doors enclosing compartments, the fall-front enclosing drawers, above three short and three long drawers, north German, c1720, 45in (114.5cm) wide.
£3,700–4,400
€5,400–6,400
$6,700–8,000 S(Am)

◄ **A mahogany bureau cabinet,** the moulded pediment above two fielded panel doors and candle slides, the crossbanded slope enclosing a fitted interior, a long drawer over two short and two graduated long drawers, Irish, 18thC, 39in (99cm) wide.
£3,050–3,650
€4,450–5,300
$5,500–6,600 HOK

► **A mahogany bureau cabinet,** with oak-lined drawers, c1775, 47in (119.5cm) wide.
£13,000–14,500
€19,000–21,200
$23,500–26,200 GGD

► **A walnut and marquetry-inlaid bureau cabinet,** the moulded cornice with a carved cartouche, above mirror doors with carved borders, the interior with reverse marquetry panels and three drawers, above two candle slides, the fall-front enclosing a fitted interior, the *bombé* base with three drawers, marquetry later, Dutch, 18thC, 50in (127cm) wide.
£20,000–24,000 / €29,200–35,000
$36,000–43,000 F&C

Cabinets-on-Chests

◄ **A walnut cabinet-on-chest,** the upper section with a cushion freize drawer and two cupboard doors inlaid with feather-banded panels enclosing a fitted interior, the base with two short over two long drawers, with label inscribed 'Gill & Reigate, London', alterations, early 18thC, 46½in (118cm) wide.
£2,000–2,400
€2,900–3,500
$3,600–4,350 L&T

► **A baroque rosewood and kingwood cabinet-on-chest,** with silvered-brass mounts, the upper section with two doors with mirrors and inlaid decoration, enclosing drawers flanking a central compartment, the base with eight drawers, mirrors replaced, north German, c1720, 37in (94cm) wide.
£5,700–6,800 / €8,300–9,900
$10,300–12,300 S(Am)

A Louis XVI-style cabinet-on-chest, the cornice with a pierced gallery centred by a carved foliate ornament, above a dentil frieze, the two doors enclosing three drawers, damaged, Dutch, 1775–1800, 77¼in (196cm) wide.
£2,100–2,500
€3,050–3,650
$3,800–4,550 S(Am)

Corner Cabinets

A Louis XV-style stained-mahogany corner cabinet, with two panelled doors above a slide, over two doors, Dutch, c1740, 49¾in (126.5cm) wide.
£1,600–1,900
€2,350–2,750
$2,900–3,450 S(Am)

A George III glazed bow-fronted hanging corner cabinet, the swan-neck pediment decorated with inlay and crossbanding, 22½in (57cm) wide.
£700–840 / €1,000–1,200
$1,250–1,500 WilP

A lacquered corner cabinet-on-stand, 18thC, 76in (193cm) high.
£5,200–5,800
€7,600–8,500
$9,400–10,500 ⊞ HA

► A George III mahogany hanging corner cupboard, the moulded cornice above a panelled door enclosing shelves, 32¾in (83cm) wide.
£770–920 / €1,150–1,350
$1,400–1,650 WW

A George III mahogany hanging corner cabinet, the broken-arch pediment with Greek key moulding above a satinwood-crossbanded marquetry frieze, the astragal-glazed door enclosing painted shelves, 27½in (70cm) wide.
£640–760 / €930–1,100
$1,150–1,350 Mit

◄ A George III mahogany cabinet, with boxwood stringing, the two satinwood-banded doors enclosing three shelves and three drawers, 28¾in (73cm) wide.
£800–960 / €1,200–1,400
$1,450–1,750 DN

A japanned corner cabinet, with a single door, 18thC, 39in (99cm) high.
£770–850 / €1,100–1,250
$1,400–1,550 ⊞ DOA

► A George III mahogany-crossbanded satinwood corner cabinet, the two doors inlaid with conch shells enclosing three shelves, 28¼in (72cm) wide.
£460–550 / €670–800
$830–1,000 DD

A George III mahogany corner cabinet, with an astragal-glazed door, c1800, 39¾in (101cm) wide.
£840–1,000
€1,250–1,450
$1,500–1,800 S(O)

A George III mahogany corner cabinet, with boxwood stringing, the swan-neck pediment with brass roundels and a finial, above two astragal-glazed doors enclosing shelves, above two panelled doors, 46½in (118cm) wide.
£1,500–1,800
€2,200–2,650
$2,700–3,250 DN

A late George III mahogany hanging corner cabinet, inlaid with boxwood stringing, the astragal-glazed door enclosing shelves, 26in (66cm) wide.
£1,100–1,300
€1,600–1,900
$2,000–2,400 WW

A late George III mahogany hanging corner cabinet, the swan-neck pediment above an astragal-glazed door enclosing shelves, 34¼in (87cm) wide.
£350–420 / €510–610 $630–760 WW

A walnut corner cabinet, decorated with floral marquetry, with a glazed door above a bowfronted cupboard, Dutch, early 19thC, 77½in (197cm) high.
£2,250–2,700 €3,300–3,950 $4,100–4,900 SWO

◄ **A mahogany corner cabinet,** c1900, 83in (211cm) high.
£1,700–1,900 €2,500–2,750 $3,100–3,450 QA

A mahogany corner cabinet, the two glazed doors enclosing shelves, the base with two inset ogee arch panelled doors, Welsh, 42in (106.5cm) wide.
£700–840 / €1,000–1,200 $1,250–1,500 PF

A Victorian rosewood and ivory-inlaid corner cabinet, the raised mirrored back with a scroll pediment, the base with panelled doors, on baluster turned supports united by an undertier, 36in (91.5cm) wide.
£1,200–1,400 €1,750–2,050 $2,150–2,550 DA

◄ **A mahogany and marquetry-inlaid corner cabinet,** c1905, 28¼in (72cm) wide.
£1,300–1,550 €1,900–2,250 $2,350–2,800 S(O)

Display Cabinets

A walnut display cabinet, the moulded cornice over two glazed doors, the *bombé* base with three drawers, on claw-and-ball feet, Dutch, c1800, 49¾in (126.5cm) wide.
£1,650–1,950 €2,400–2,850 $3,000–3,550 G(B)

A Victorian burr-walnut and marquetry-inlaid vitrine, with gilt-metal mounts and borders to the glazed door and sides, enclosing four boxwood-strung shelves, 32in (81.5cm) wide.
£2,050–2,450 €3,000–3,600 $3,700–4,450 DN

A Louis XV-style rosewood and ebonized display cabinet, with gilt-bronze mounts, a hinged and glazed top above a glazed cupboard door and sides, the front mounted with roundels depicting a young couple, French, c1880, 30in (76cm) wide.
£810–970 / €1,200–1,400 $1,450–1,750 S(Am)

A mahogany display cabinet, with satinwood banding and ebony inlay, the upper section with a raised top above two glazed doors, the breakfront base with a glazed door and sides, late 19thC, 36in (91.5cm) wide.
£880–1,050 €1,300–1,550 $1,600–1,900 E

A mahogany and fruitwood-banded display cabinet, the two glazed doors enclosing a velvet-lined interior with two shelves, above two drawers, c1900, 47¾in (121.5cm) wide.
£900–1,050
€1,300–1,550
$1,650–1,900 ⚒ S(Am)

An Edwardian inlaid mahogany display cabinet, the two doors enclosing a shelf, 48¾in (124cm) wide.
£175–210 / €260–310
$320–380 ⚒ AMB

A Louis XV-style rosewood *bombé* vitrine, with gilt-brass mounts, the glazed door with *vernis Martin* panels of lovers in a landscape, enclosing a lined interior with glass shelves, early 20thC, 43¾in (111cm) wide.
£3,000–3,600
€4,400–5,300
$5,400–6,500 ⚒ L&T

A kingwood-veneered vitrine, the top with an acanthus ormolu mount above two glazed doors and sides enclosing three shelves, the base with *vernis Martin* panels of figures and landscapes, French, 19thC, 28¼in (72cm) wide.
£540–640 / €790–930
$980–1,150 ⚒ L&E

An Edwardian mahogany and boxwood-strung display cabinet, the serpentine cornice above two astragal-glazed doors, the central panel inlaid with a ribbon-tied flower basket, flanked by two fluted Corinthian capped columns, 48in (122cm) wide.
£470–560 / €690–820
$850–1,000 ⚒ DD

A mahogany display cabinet, on claw-and-ball feet, 1920s, 42¼in (107.5cm) wide.
£350–420 / €510–610
$630–760 ⚒ AMB

An Edwardian mahogany and boxwood-inlaid demi-lune display cabinet, the mirrored back with turned finials, above two glazed doors, with an undertier, 36¼in (92cm) wide.
£1,450–1,700
€2,100–2,500
$2,600–3,100 ⚒ DD

An Edwardian Sheraton-style inlaid mahogany display cabinet, with two glazed doors, 37in (94cm) wide.
£270–320 / €390–470
$490–580 ⚒ JM

A mahogany display cabinet, the two glazed doors enclosing three shelves, on claw-and-ball feet, 1920s, 44½in (113cm) wide.
£300–360 / €440–530
$540–650 ⚒ CHTR

An Edwardian mahogany display cabinet, inlaid with boxwood and ebony, with two leaded glass doors, 42½in (108cm) wide.
£260–310 / €380–450
$470–560 ⚒ CHTR

An Edwardian mahogany display cabinet, the moulded frieze over two astragal-glazed doors, 42¼in (107.5cm) wide.
£230–270 / €330–390
$410–490 ⚒ CHTR

A silvered vitrine, carved with flowers and stiff-leaf borders, the frieze centred with a musical trophy, above two glazed doors and glazed sides, the base with a panelled frieze, Continental, early 20thC, 45¼in (115cm) wide.
£1,250–1,500
€1,850–2,200
$2,250–2,700 ⚒ DN

Secretaire Cabinets

A Queen Anne walnut escritoire, with seaweed marquetry, the moulded cornice with a cushion frieze drawer, the interior with pigeonholes and ten drawers flanking a door, above two short and two long drawers, 43¼in (110cm) wide.
£10,800–12,900
€15,800–18,800
$19,500–23,300 S

A walnut secretaire cabinet, with a frieze drawer, above a fall-front veneered with figured quartered walnut within herringbone stringing and crossbanding, enclosing a fitted interior, the base with two short and three long graduated drawers, early 18thC, 38in (96.5cm) wide.
£4,900–5,800
€7,200–8,500
$8,900–10,500 LAY

A Biedermeier satin birch secretaire cabinet, the fall-front enclosing a fitted interior of mahogany-crossbanded drawers, northern European, c1820, 35½in (90cm) wide.
£2,600–3,100
€3,800–4,550
$4,700–5,600 S(O)

A mahogany *secrétaire à abbatant*, the marble top above a drawer, the fall-front enclosing cupboards and a writing surface, over two cupboards, French, 1800–25, 36¼in (92cm) wide.
£700–840 / €1,000–1,200
$1,250–1,500 NOA

A mahogany *secrétaire à abbatant*, with a frieze drawer above a fall-front enclosing a fitted interior and pull-out galleried writing slide, above three drawers, Continental, 18250–50, 44in (112cm) wide.
£940–1,100
€1,350–1,600
$1,700–1,900 G(L)

A mahogany secretaire cabinet, with two panelled doors over three short drawers, the lower section fitted with two concealed drawers, the base with one long drawer over two short drawers flanking a kneehole, American, c1825, 45in (114.5cm) wide.
£760–910 / €1,100–1,300
$1,400–1,650 NOA

A mahogany secretaire cabinet, the upper section containing slides, Scottish, c1830, 51¼in (130cm) wide.
£1,200–1,400
€1,750–2,050
$2,150–2,550 S(O)

A kingwood and marquetry escritoire, with a brass gallery above a fall-front enclosing a fitted interior, over a drawer, French, 19thC, 22in (56cm) wide.
£2,100–2,500
€3,050–3,650
$3,800–4,550 JNic

► **A Louis XVI-style rosewood and parquetry *secrétaire à abbatant*,** early 20thC, 25¼in (64cm) wide.
£1,400–1,650
€2,000–2,400
$2,500–3,000 S(O)

◄ **An ebony and marquetry secretaire cabinet,** by Hunsinger, with two doors above a secretaire drawer, signed, French, c1880, 33½in (85cm) wide.
£9,600–11,500 / €14,000–16,800
$17,400–20,800 S(O)

Charles Hunsinger (1823–93) specialized in furniture made with ebony and ivory marquetry. He became established at 244 rue du Fauborg-Saint-Antoine in 1863, moving to 56 rue de la Roquette in 1867, and 13 rue Sedaine in 1874. In 1872, he formed a business with Charles-Adolphe-Frédéric Wagner. They took part in the Paris Exhibitions of 1865, 1867, 1868 and 1889 and won a gold medal in Brussels in 1881.

Side Cabinets

A mahogany side cabinet, with chequer stringing, the top above a frieze drawer and two cupboard doors centred by shell paterae, Dutch, 18thC, 37½in (95.5cm) wide.
£1,300–1,550 / €1,900–2,250
$2,350–2,800 ⚒ L&T

A Sheraton-style mahogany side cabinet, with boxwood line-inlaid fielded panelled doors, the harewood panels inlaid with classical urns, c1800, 40¼in (102cm) wide.
£1,150–1,350 / €1,650–1,950
$2,100–2,450 ⚒ HOK

► **A rosewood and parcel-gilt side cabinet,** c1810, 54in (137cm) wide.
£16,200–18,000 / €23,700–26,300
$29,300–33,000 ⊞ GDB

A Regency mahogany chiffonier, the base with a frieze drawer above two cupboard doors with pleated silk and brass grille insets, flanked by two pilasters, 41¾in (106cm) wide.
£6,800–8,100 / €9,900–11,800
$12,300–14,700 ⚒ HOLL

A kingwood side cabinet, with a single door, Continental, late 18thC, 22in (56cm) wide.
£1,500–1,800 / €2,200–2,650
$2,700–3,250 ⚒ G(L)

A late George III rosewood and simulated rosewood side cabinet, with satinwood banding, the two doors enclosing a shelf, 70in (178cm) wide.
£10,800–12,900 / €15,800–18,800
$19,500–23,300 ⚒ S

A Regency satinwood side cabinet, the fitted drawer above two doors with pleated silk panels, 25in (63.5cm) wide.
£440–520 / €640–760
$800–940 ⚒ G(B)

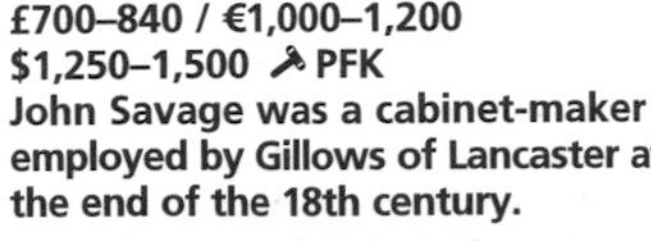

A mahogany side cabinet, in the style of Gillows of Lancaster, the hinged top enclosing divisions and compartments, two cockbeaded dummy drawers over two further drawers, above two panelled cupboard doors enclosing a shelf, signed 'John Savage', 1790–1800, 22½in (57cm) wide.
£700–840 / €1,000–1,200
$1,250–1,500 ⚒ PFK
John Savage was a cabinet-maker employed by Gillows of Lancaster at the end of the 18th century.

A rosewood side cabinet, c1810, 29½in (75cm) wide.
£4,400–4,850 / €6,400–7,100
$8,000–8,800 ⊞ RGa

A Regency rosewood, mahogany and string-inlaid chiffonier, with two frieze drawers, the base with two panelled doors with reeded surrounds and bulls-eye carving, feet replaced, 28in (71cm) wide.
£2,050–2,450 / €3,000–3,600
$3,700–4,450 ⚒ DA

A Regency rosewood chiffonier, with a mirrored back, the pierced brass gallery on turned and carved columns, over a brass-strung frieze drawer and two grille cupboard doors, 34in (86.5cm) wide.
£1,900–2,250 / €2,750–3,300
$3,450–4,050 G(L)

A mahogany-veneered side cabinet, with a marble top, on carved lion-paw feet, c1820, 36in (91.5cm) wide.
£9,900–11,000 / €14,500–16,100
$17,900–19,900 ⊞ HA

- Side cabinets originated in the 18th century but were rather simple affairs and did not become fashionable until the early 19th century.
- Regency designs are generally more refined than many Victorian examples, which by then were being mass-produced.
- French and British makers were the market leaders, the latter being heavily influenced by French and Italian styles.
- Features to look for on good-quality pieces are brass galleries, pleated silk door panels and lyre-shaped shelf supports. Original feet, decoration and glass will usually add to value.

A late Regency side cabinet, the marble top above two panelled doors flanked by turned pilasters, 37in (94cm) wide.
£990–1,100 / €1,450–1,600
$1,800–2,000 ⊞ LGr

A George IV rosewood and brass chiffonier, the back with a pierced gallery above turned supports, the frieze inlaid with shamrocks, over two doors with inset grilles flanked by turned pillars with pineapple finials, 43in (109cm) wide.
£2,900–3,450 / €4,250–5,000
$5,200–6,200 DN

A late Regency mahogany side cabinet, with a brass gallery, the two doors enclosing a divided shelf, the spiral ribbed side pilasters with stiff-leaf capitals, gallery and shelf later, upper section missing, 35¼in (89.5cm) wide.
£1,000–1,200 / €1,450–1,700
$1,800–2,150 WW

An elm and burr-elm side cupboard, French, c1825, 53in (134.4cm) wide.
£2,400–2,850 / €3,500–4,150
$4,350–5,200 S(O)

A mahogany chiffonier, with a two-tier gallery, the grille doors with later silk, c1825, 41in (104cm) wide.
£5,600–6,200 / €8,200–9,100
$10,100–11,200 ⊞ HA

A rosewood chiffonier, with a drawer above two doors, c1830, 36in (91.5cm) wide.
£2,600–2,900 / €3,800–4,250
$4,700–5,200 ⊞ WAA

◄ **A William IV rosewood chiffonier,** the mirrored back with an open shelf, with gilt-metal mounts, on stiff-leaf-carved columns, 32¾in (83cm) wide.
£1,000–1,200 / €1,450–1,700
$1,800–2,150 L&T

◄ **A Louis XVI-style mahogany library cabinet,** the top with a leather writing surface, above two doors flanked by four drawers, Dutch, 19thC, 98½in (250cm) wide.
£4,100–4,900
€6,000–7,200
$7,400–8,900 S(Am)

A rosewood side cabinet, with a mirrored back, c1840, 78in (198cm) wide.
£2,000–2,250 / €2,900–3,300
$3,600–4,050 ⊞ MTay

A boulle-work side cabinet, with gilt-bronze mounts and a marble top, German, c1850, 61¾in (157cm) wide.
£10,200–12,200 / €14,900–17,800
$18,500–22,100 S(O)

An ebonized and burr-walnut-crossbanded credenza, with ebony and boxwood line inlay, ormolu beading and mounts, the panelled door with a Sèvres panel depicting a half-portrait, flanked by two turned and reeded columns and two glazed side cupboards, 19thC, 62in (157.5cm) wide.
£840–1,000 / €1,250–1,450
$1,500–1,800 JM

An ormolu-mounted figured walnut side cabinet, the glazed door with tulipwood crossbanding and boxwood line inlay, c1860, 31in (78.5cm) wide.
£1,500–1,650 / €2,200–2,450
$2,700–3,000 ⊞ LGr

A Victorian amboyna and ebonized pier cabinet, by Gillows & Co, the moulded inverted breakfront top with a brass gallery, the velvet-lined interior enclosed by two glazed doors flanked by turned pilasters with *faux* jewels, stamped and numbered '6050', 42¼in (107.5cm) wide.
£1,650–1,950 / €2,400–2,850
$3,000–3,550 G(B)

Gillows was founded in Lancaster in the 1730s by Robert Gillow. The last family member to be connected with the company was Robert's grandson, Richard, who retired in 1830. The firm was taken over by Redmayne, Whiteside & Ferguson in 1813, but they traded with 'late Gillows' after their names until 1829, when they changed the name back to Gillow & Co. They then reverted to using their own names from 1834–54, before once again becoming Gillow & Co from 1855.

A Victorian walnut side cabinet, the glazed door enclosing three shelves, flanked by gilt-metal cappings, 29½in (75cm) wide.
£300–360 / €440–530
$540–650 CHTR

A Victorian figured walnut credenza, with ormolu and gilt-metal mounts, the central door with a marquetry panel, 73in (185.5cm) wide.
£4,000–4,800 / €5,900–7,000
$7,300–8,700 DMC

A Victorian mahogany chiffonier, the scroll-moulded back with a shelf, above a frieze drawer with two panelled doors below, 48in (122cm) wide.
£330–390 / €480–570
$600–710 DD

► **A walnut and amboyna-crossbanded side cabinet,** with boxwood and ebony stringing and gilt-metal mounts, the two doors with Sèvres-style portrait plaques with ribbon cresting, flanked by glazed doors and ebonized pilasters with Corinthian capitals, 19thC, 72½in (184cm) wide.
£2,350–2,800 / €3,450–4,100
$4,250–5,100 M

A Victorian walnut credenza, the mirrored back above a marble top, over three mirrored doors flanked by leaf-carved corbels, 60¼in (153cm) wide.
£590–700 / €860–1,000
$1,050–1,200 DN(BR)

A Victorian walnut and marquetry pier cabinet, the frieze with gilt-metal beading over a glazed door flanked by pillars with ormolu mounts, above an egg-and-dart moulding, 31in (78.5cm) wide.
£2,100–2,500 / €3,050–3,650
$3,800–4,550 Mit

A Sheraton revival satinwood and marquetry side cabinet, c1890, 27in (68.5cm) wide.
£8,800–9,800 / €12,800–14,300
$15,900–17,700 Che

A mid-Victorian walnut credenza, the marble top above four mirrored doors with flower-carved arches and scrolled bosses, 72½in (184cm) wide.
£1,100–1,300 / €1,600–1,900
$2,000–2,350 DN

A Victorian ebonized pier cabinet, with gilt-metal mounts and Sèvres-style floral panels, 34½in (87.5cm) wide.
£590–700 / €850–1,000
$1,100–1,300 SPF

A mahogany bowfronted side cabinet, with crossbanding and inlay, c1890, 40in (101.5cm) wide.
£2,850–3,200 / €4,150–4,650
$5,200–5,800 DOA

A mid-Victorian burr-walnut credenza, with line and foliate scroll inlay, the frieze with a gilt-metal egg-and-dart band, the panelled door flanked by cast gilt-metal mask mounts and glazed cupboards, 60¼in (153cm) wide.
£1,500–1,800 / €2,200–2,650
$2,700–3,250 RTo

A tulipwood and marquetry side cabinet, with a marble top and gilt-metal mounts, probably Dutch, c1880, 17¼in (44cm) wide.
£840–1,000 / €1,250–1,450
$1,500–1,800 S(O)

An oak side cabinet, by Christopher Pratt of Bradford, the mirrored back with a shelf over an arcaded mirrored recess, above panelled and carved cupboard doors flanked by four drawers and a leaded glazed door, c1900, 82in (208.5cm) wide.
£610–730 / €890–1,050
$1,100–1,300 AH

◄ An Edwardian rosewood and boxwood-strung side cabinet, inlaid with urns and floral scrolls, the mirrored back with a brass gallery above a drawer, the mirrored recess and two mirrored doors flanked by panelled doors, 54in (137cm) wide.
£520–620 / €760–910
$940–1,100 DD

Cabinets-on-Stands

An ebonized and repoussé silver-plated cabinet-on-stand, the central door enclosing small drawers, on a later stand, Dutch, 17thC, 24in (61cm) wide.
£3,600–4,300 / €5,300–6,300 $6,500–7,800 ⚒ S(O)

A pair of Regency ebonized, lacquer and gilt-brass-mounted cabinets-on-stands, with Spanish brocatelle marble tops, the doors incorporating 17thC Japanese panels and enclosing shelves, altered, 19¾in (50cm) wide.
£7,200–8,600 / €10,500–12,600 $13,000–15,600 ⚒ S
These cabinets-on-stands were the property of Viscount Astor and came from Cliveden in Buckinghamshire.

An oyster-veneered and floral marquetry cabinet-on-stand, the cushion-moulded frieze drawer above two doors with central panels of birds and flower-filled urns with stained-bone inlay, enclosing a fitted interior with conforming inlay, on a moulded base over a long drawer, on a later spiral-twist stand, late 17thC, 46¾in (119cm) wide.
£4,750–5,700 / €6,900–8,300 $8,600–10,300 ⚒ HOK

◄ A japanned cabinet-on-stand, with pierced and engraved strapwork mounts, decorated with gilt chinoiseries, the two doors enclosing an arrangement of drawers, late 17thC, 40½in (103cm) wide.
£1,750–2,100 / €2,550–3,050 $3,150–3,800 ⚒ L

A japanned cabinet-on-stand, decorated in relief with gold figures in a wooded landscape, the two doors with engraved lockplate and hinges enclosing ten drawers, with turned legs and X-shaped stretcher, damaged, 18thC and later, 32¾in (83cm) wide.
£2,850–3,400 / €4,150–4,950 $5,200–6,200 ⚒ S(Am)

► An ebonized and painted cabinet-on-stand, the two doors with papier-mâché panels inlaid with mother-of-pearl ivy leaves, on paw feet, the stand with an X-stretcher, mid-19thC, 33in (84cm) wide.
£1,400–1,650 / €2,050–2,400 $2,550–3,000 ⚒ DN

A William and Mary oyster kingwood cabinet-on-stand, the cushion-moulded cornice above two crossbanded doors enclosing 11 drawers flanking a cupboard enclosing four further drawers, with two brass carrying handles, on a later stand, 43¾in (111cm) wide.
£8,200–9,800 / €12,000–14,300 $14,800–17,700 ⚒ DN(BR)

A fruitwood and ebonized cabinet-on-stand, the two doors enclosing a door surrounded by drawers decorated with scrolling foliage, on a later stand, damaged, south German, 18thC, 21¾in (55.5cm) wide.
£2,300–2,750 / €3,350–4,000 $4,150–5,000 ⚒ S(Am)

Table Cabinets

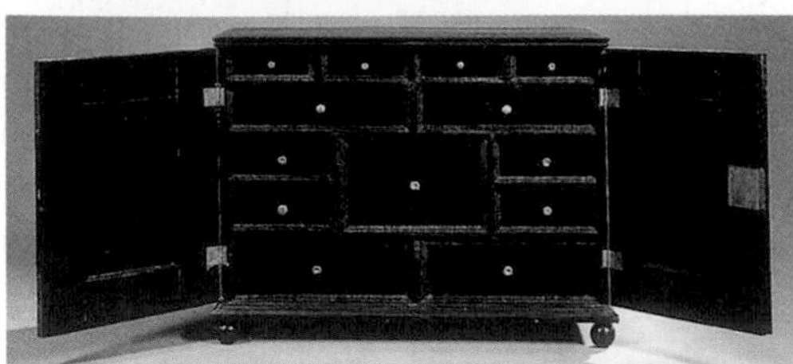

A baroque ebonized table cabinet, the two ripple-moulded doors enclosing a central drawer surrounded by 11 further drawers, on bun feet, German, 17thC, 35¾in (91cm) wide.
£1,950–2,300 / €2,850–3,350
$3,550–4,150 S(Am)

A Regency mahogany stationery cabinet, with a fitted interior, 30in (76cm) wide.
£710–790 / €1,000–1,150
$1,300–1,450 DOA

◀ **A William IV mahogany table cabinet,** the moulded cornice above two doors with glazing bars, flanked by pilasters, on a plinth base, 35½in (90.5cm) wide.
£280–330
€410–480
$510–600 DN

A rosewood jewellery cabinet, 1815–30, 13in (33cm) wide.
£1,450–1,600 / €2,100–2,350
$2,600–2,900 GGD

▶ **A mahogany clubhouse cigar cabinet,** c1910, 18in (45.5cm) high.
£220–250
€320–370
$400–450 WiB

A Victorian coin collector's cabinet, 13in (33cm) wide.
£1,100–1,250 / €1,600–1,800
$2,000–2,250 GEO

A smoker's oak compendium, stamped '1894', 13in (33cm) high.
£810–900 / €1,200–1,350
$1,450–1,650 SAT

Canterburies

A George III mahogany canterbury, with two drawers, 21in (53.5cm) high.
£7,200–8,000 / €10,500–11,700
$13,000–14,500 HWK

A mahogany canterbury, c1810, 19in (48.5cm) high.
£1,650–1,850 / €2,400–2,700
$3,000–3,350 F&F

A Regency mahogany canterbury, 22in (56cm) wide.
£440–520 / €640–760
$800–940 G(L)

A Regency mahogany canterbury, 20in (51cm) wide.
£2,700–3,000 / €3,950–4,400
$4,900–5,400 ⊞ GGD

An early Victorian rosewood canterbury, with carved partitions above a drawer, 20in (51cm) wide.
£2,000–2,200 / €2,900–3,300
$3,600–4,000 ⊞ LGr

A rosewood canterbury, with a drawer, handles replaced, c1820, 19in (48.5cm) wide.
£4,150–4,600 / €6,000–6,700
$7,500–8,300 ⊞ HA

An inlaid walnut whatnot canterbury, c1860, 38in (96.5cm) high.
£2,250–2,500 / €3,300–3,650
$4,050–4,550 ⊞ GEO

◄ **A Victorian rosewood whatnot canterbury,** with turned and carved supports and a drawer, 24in (61cm) wide.
£1,300–1,550 / €1,900–2,250
$2,350–2,800 ⚒ L&T

A Victorian walnut canterbury, with a drawer, 23in (58.5cm) wide.
£1,650–1,850 / €2,400–2,700
$3,000–3,350 ⊞ WAA

► **A late Victorian rosewood and marquetry canterbury,** with a drawer, 22in (56cm) wide.
£590–700 / €860–1,000
$1,050–1,250 ⚒ DN

◄ **A walnut whatnot canterbury,** c1880, 29½in (75cm) wide.
£960–1,150 / €1,450–1,700
$1,750–2,100 ⚒ S(O)

A mahogany canterbury, c1840, 18in (45.5cm) wide.
£2,700–3,000 / €3,950–4,400
$4,900–5,400 ⊞ Man

A Victorian walnut whatnot canterbury, the fitted brass rail above an inlaid top, on turned supports over pierced fretwork and a drawer base, feet missing, 24½in (62cm) wide.
£560–670 / €820–980
$1,000–1,200 ⚒ CHTR

A walnut canterbury, c1870, 22in (56cm) wide.
£1,350–1,500 / €1,950–2,200
$2,450–2,700 ⊞ GEO

Open Armchairs

A Charles II carved walnut armchair, with padded arms.
£1,150–1,300
€1,700–1,900
$2,100–2,350 ⊞ DEB

A William and Mary walnut chair, with a caned back and seat, on turned legs.
£1,000–1,200
€1,500–1,750
$1,800–2,150 ⚒ S(O)

A walnut armchair, with a pierced carved back, on baluster legs, restored, French, late 17thC.
£1,650–1,950
€2,400–2,850
$3,000–3,550 ⚒ S(O)

A walnut armchair, the inlaid cresting with initials 'HC' and 'IB', with a velvet-upholstered back and seat, probably German, c1690.
£960–1,150
€1,450–1,700
$1,750–2,100 ⚒ S(O)

A walnut *fauteuil*, the back upholstered with gros and petit point tapestry, on cabriole legs, French, early 18thC.
£1,900–2,250
€2,750–3,300
$3,450–4,050 ⚒ G(L)

A rococo armchair, the crest rail and apron carved with rocaille, the woodwork decorated with painted grain effect, damaged and repaired, Swedish, mid-18thC.
£2,350–2,800
€3,450–4,100
$4,250–5,100 ⚒ BUK

A George II mahogany open armchair, with upholstered back and seat, on carved cabriole legs.
£1,050–1,250
€1,550–1,850
$1,900–2,250 ⚒ S(O)

A George II mahogany open armchair, the arms with scroll terminals, on cabriole legs and pad feet.
£2,000–2,400
€2,950–3,500
$3,600–4,300 ⚒ L&T

A pair of Louis XV birch *fauteuils*, with shell-capped scroll-carved rests, aprons and legs, Canadian, Quebec, mid-18thC.
£20,800–24,900 / €30,000–36,000
$38,000–45,000 ⚒ RIT
These rare chairs attracted great interest from not only private collectors but also museums, institutions and government officials.

A Gothic Chippendale-style mahogany open armchair, c1760.
£7,200–8,000
€10,500–11,700
$13,000–14,500 ⊞ HWK

A Chippendale-style mahogany open armchair, c1775.
£850–950 / €1,250–1,400
$1,500–1,700 ⊞ GGD

A mahogany splat back open armchair, c1780.
£720–860 / €1,050–1,250
$1,300–1,550 S(O)

A pair of Hepplewhite-style mahogany open armchairs, with line and shell inlay and darkened mahogany splats, c1780.
£3,100–3,450
€4,500–5,000
$5,600–6,200 GEO

A George III Chippendale-style mahogany open armchair, the back with a moulded Gothic splat, over shepherd's crook arms, on chamfered legs, repaired.
£290–340 / €420–500
$520–620 L&E

A George III mahogany open armchair, on chamfered moulded legs with an H-stretcher.
£680–810 / €1,000–1,200
$1,250–1,450 DN

A George III provincial Chinese Chippendale-style mahogany open armchair, the upholstered seat on chamfered legs.
£960–1,150 / €1,450–1,700
$1,750–2,100 WW

A pair of Adam-style carved mahogany open armchairs, with anthemion-carved splats and foliate rails, on moulded legs with florets, reupholstered in leather, c1785.
£3,450–3,850 / €5,000–5,600
$6,200–7,000 RGa

A mahogany open armchair, stamped 'G. Jacob', late 18thC.
£5,000–6,000
€7,400–8,800
$9,100–10,900 S(P)
Georges Jacob (1739–1814), cabinet-maker, was received master in 1765.

◄ A Gustavian open armchair, by Johan Lindgren, painted and gilded, signed 'ILG', Swedish, 1770–1800.
£1,900–2,250
€2,750–3,300
$3,450–4,050 BUK
Johan Lindgren was a master cabinet-maker in Stockholm between 1770 and 1800.

◄ A carved walnut open armchair, Italian, Venetian, c1780.
£650–780 / €950–1,100
$1,200–1,400 S(Mi)

A Regency mahogany open armchair, the back with a carved rope-twist rail, on turned legs.
£130–155 / €190–220
$240–280 DD

A Sheraton-style mahogany open armchair, with moulded arms, on turned legs with a cross stretcher, c1795.
£880–980 / €1,300–1,450
$1,600–1,800 WAA

A mahogany open armchair, c1800.
£810–900 / €1,150–1,300
$1,500–1,650 GGD

A mahogany open armchair, c1815.
£430–480 / €630–700
$780–870 Lfo

A Regency mahogany rocking open armchair, upholstered in leather.
£630–700 / €900–1,000
$1,100–1,250 ⊞ MLL

A mahogany open armchair, c1835.
£400–450 / €600–660
$740–820 ⊞ DY

A pair of walnut open armchairs, French, 1820s–30s.
£3,500–3,900
€5,100–5,700
$6,300–7,100 ⊞ GGD

A rococo-style giltwood open armchair, with scrolling arms and a carved apron, damaged, Italian, 19thC.
£1,950–2,300
€2,850–3,350
$3,550–4,150 ⚒ S(Am)

◄ A carved walnut open armchair, with pictorial leather upholstery, the padded arms carved with putti terminals, the seat rails carved with masks, Italian, 19thC.
£810–900 / €1,200–1,350
$1,450–1,650 ⊞ LGr

A George IV mahogany open armchair, the back with a carved and crested rail, damaged, c1830.
£3,600–4,300
€5,300–6,300
$6,500–7,800 ⚒ S(O)

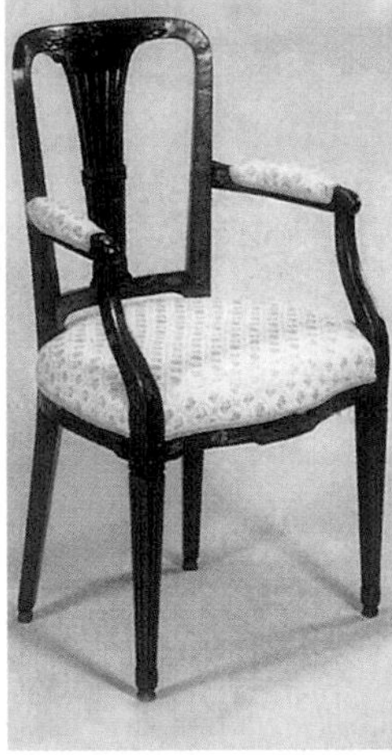

A mahogany open armchair, with floral marquetry and boxwood stringing, the back carved with a patera and garrya above a pierced splat, with padded armrests and seat, on tapering chanelled legs, Dutch, 19thC.
£500–600 / €740–880
$920–1,100 ⚒ DN

A mahogany and sycamore open armchair, in the style of Israel Friedrich Wirth, with scrolled arms, banded and inlaid with trefoils, stylized leaves and scrolls, German, 1800–50.
£530–630 / €770–920
$960–1,150 ⚒ S(Am)

Israel Friedrich Wirth (1806–83) was a leading cabinet-maker in Württemberg. He was highly regarded by King Wilhelm I who made him a *Kommerzienrat*, a title conferred on distinguished businessmen.

A Queen Anne-style carved walnut open armchair, with a petit point tapestry seat, 19thC.
£2,500–2,800
€3,650–4,100
$4,550–5,100 ⊞ GGD

A walnut open armchair, with carved lion-head terminals, c1840.
£840–1,000
€1,250–1,450
$1,500–1,800 ⚒ S(O)

A pair of early Victorian mahogany open armchairs, with applied paterae decoration, scrolling arms and buttoned peg feet.
£850–950 / €1,250–1,400
$1,500–1,700 ⊞ LGr

A walnut open armchair, with a buttoned back, floral carving and cabriole legs, reupholstered, c1850.
£1,700–1,900
€2,500–2,750
$3,100–3,450 ⊞ LGr

A mahogany extending and reclining open armchair, French, mid-19thC.
£2,300–2,750 / €3,350–4,000
$4,150–5,000 S(P)

A Victorian open armchair with an occasional chair *en suite*, with satinwood floral inlay, on turned front legs and casters.
£940–1,100 / €1,350–1,600
$1,700–2,000 BWL

A rococo revival laminated rosewood open armchair, attributed to J. and J. W. Meeks, New York, in the Stanton Hall pattern, with a floral-carved crest, American, 1875–1900.
£2,900–3,450
€4,250–5,000
$5,200–6,200 NOA

J. and J. W. Meeks produced furniture in the rococo style in New York during the 1850s and 1860s.

A pair of Victorian walnut open armchairs, with scroll-carved crests, button-upholstered backs, stuff-over seats and padded arms, on turned legs.
£230–270 / €330–390
$420–490 DA

► **A carved mahogany open armchair,** c1870.
£580–650 / €850–950
$1,050–1,200 CRU

A pair of George I-style walnut open armchairs, with shell-carved knees, on claw-and-ball feet, c1880.
£4,400–4,900
€6,400–7,200
$8,000–8,900 ⊞ GEO

A Louis XIV-style walnut open armchair, carved with acanthus leaves and scallop shells, damaged, French, 19thC.
£530–630 / €770–920
$960–1,150 ⚒ RTo

A pair of painted and gilded open armchairs, French, c1880.
£4,400–4,900
€6,400–7,200
$8,000–8,900 ⊞ CRU

A late Victorian Hepplewhite-style mahogany open armchair, with inlaid decoration, reupholstered.
£810–900 / €1,200–1,350
$1,450–1,650 ⊞ LGr

◄ A pair of Louis XVI-style giltwood and gesso *fauteuils*, French, late 19thC.
£3,100–3,700
€4,550–5,400
$5,600–6,700 ⚒ S(O)

A Hepplewhite-style mahogany open armchair, by Marsh, Jones Cribb & Co, c1900.
£1,200–1,350
€1,750–1,950
$2,150–2,450 ⊞ WAA

Marsh, Jones, Cribb & Co was founded in Leeds in the mid-19th century and they later opened a showroom in Cavendish Square, London. They worked with many of the top designers of the day, including Charles Bevan, Bruce Talbert and William Lethaby.

A walnut open armchair, with ivory stringing, the arms carved with Renaissance-style heads, on dolphin supports, late 19thC.
£2,350–2,800
€3,450–4,100
$4,250–5,100 ⚒ L&E

An inlaid mahogany open armchair, c1900.
£450–500 / €660–730
$810–910 ⊞ QA

An inlaid mahogany open armchair, c1900.
£360–400 / €520–580
$650–720 ⊞ QA

Upholstered Furniture

Before 1828, all upholstered chairs were timber framed and covered in layers of horsehair supported by webbing and covered in fabric. Coiled springs were then introduced for extra comfort and this was to revolutionize the furniture-making industry. From the 1830s onwards, many cabinet-makers incorporated the word 'upholsterer' in their trading details.

When buying an upholstered chair, thoroughly check the condition of the frame – the upholstery can always be replaced, whereas the frame cannot.

An inlaid mahogany open armchair, c1915.
£580–650 / €850–950
$1,050–1,200 ⊞ WAA

A mahogany open armchair, by Gillows, signed, c1920.
£310–350 / €450–510
$560–630 ⊞ QA

Upholstered Armchairs

A George III wing armchair, with leather upholstery.
£1,800–2,150
€2,650–3,150
$3,250–3,900 NSal

A Louis XVI carved and painted armchair, with a ribbon-twist frame, French, late 18thC.
£2,150–2,550
€3,150–3,700
$3,900–4,600 S

A pair of Regency simulated rosewood armchairs, the uprights, rails and legs with gilded decoration.
£4,000–4,800 / €5,900–7,000
$7,200–8,600 L&T

A mahogany armchair, with carved scroll arms, c1830.
£1,450–1,600
€2,100–2,350
$2,600–2,900 GGD

An early Victorian rosewood armchair, with acanthus leaf and rosebud carving, with scroll toes.
£400–480 / €580–700
$720–870 AMB

An early Victorian armchair, with a buttoned back, acanthus-carved arms and lotus-moulded turned legs.
£330–390 / €480–570
$600–710 DD

A Victorian walnut wing armchair, with carved cabriole legs.
£1,700–1,900
€2,550–2,800
$3,100–3,450 LGr

◄ **A Victorian rosewood armchair,** with scroll-carved arms, on turned lobed feet with brass terminals and casters.
£590–700 / €860–1,000
$1,050–1,250 DN

► **A late Victorian armchair.**
£420–470 / €610–690
$760–850 WiB

A pair of Edwardian mahogany armchairs, inlaid with stringing and marquetry, stamped '7848'.
£370–440 / €540–640
$670–800 WW

A carved walnut wing armchair, French, c1890.
£1,050–1,250
€1,550–1,850
$1,900–2,250 S(O)

A walnut wing armchair, early 20thC.
£280–330 / €410–480
$510–600 CHTR

Bergères

A Regency simulated rosewood bergère, on sabre legs with brass terminals and casters, worn, losses.
£230–270 / €340–390
$420–490 DN

In 18th-century France, a fashion developed for more comfortable chairs that could be placed close to one another to encourage conversation, rather than around the sides of a room as had previously been the custom. The most luxurious of these chairs was the bergère, characterized by its deep seat, padded or caned back and sides, and squab cushion. It was very much a rich person's chair and French examples remain relatively expensive today. The style was copied widely throughout Europe, particularly in Regency Britain and again in the late 19th and early 20th centuries.

A mahogany bergère, c1815.
£1,650–1,950 / €2,400–2,850
$3,000–3,550 S(O)

► **A Regency carved mahogany bergère,** with a buttoned leather seat.
£3,150–3,500 / €4,600–5,100
$5,700–6,300 CRU

A late Regency mahogany bergère, the reeded frame with padded arms, on turned legs.
£1,200–1,400 / €1,750–2,050
$2,150–2,550 LAY

◄ **A pair of oak bergères,** with leather-upholstered elbow pads and dentil-carved turned front legs, worn, early 19thC.
£3,600–4,300
€5,300–6,300
$6,500–7,800
TRM(D)

Children's Chairs

◄ **A child's walnut armchair,** with a caned back and seat, c1680.
£2,150–2,550
€3,150–3,700
$3,900–4,600 S(O)

A child's mahogany rocking chair, 19thC.
£230–270 / €330–390
$420–490 AH

◄ **A child's mahogany bergère high chair and table,** c1775.
£670–750 / €980–1,100
$1,200–1,350 WAA

A child's mahogany high chair and table, c1880.
£1,050–1,200
€1,550–1,750
$1,900–2,150 WAA

Corner Chairs

A carved mahogany corner chair, on claw-and-ball feet, Irish, mid-18thC.
£3,200–3,800 / €4,650–5,500
$5,800–6,900 HOK

A pair of upholstered walnut corner chairs, c1860.
£5,900–6,500 / €8,600–9,500
$10,700–11,800 ⊞ CRU

◀ **A Chippendale-style carved mahogany corner chair,** American, New York, c1770.
£7,300–8,700 / €10,700–12,700
$13,200–15,700 S(NY)

Desk Chairs

A mahogany swivel desk chair, c1870.
£540–600 / €790–880
$980–1,100 ⊞ QA

An oak swivel and tilt desk armchair, c1900.
£450–500 / €660–730
$810–910 ⊞ QA

An oak swivel and tilt desk chair, c1900.
£500–550 / €730–800
$910–1,000 ⊞ QA

An oak swivel and tilt desk chair, c1900.
£580–650 / €850–950
$1,050–1,200 ⊞ QA

A mahogany swivel and tilt desk chair, c1900.
£880–980 / €1,300–1,450
$1,600–1,800 ⊞ QA

A walnut swivel desk chair, early 20thC.
£230–270 / €330–390
$420–490 DA

A mahogany swivel desk chair, with leather-upholstered back and seat, c1910.
£1,000–1,150 / €1,450–1,650
$1,800–2,100 ⊞ MTay

Dining Chairs

A set of six baroque stained walnut and carved oak dining chairs, with stuff-over seats, on cabriole legs with carved knees, label inscribed 'DM2 Münster', German, c1720.
£1,950–2,300 / €2,850–3,350
$3,550–4,150 ⚒ S(Am)

A set of six mahogany dining chairs, Irish, c1770.
£1,900–2,250 / €2,750–3,300
$3,450–4,050 ⚒ S(O)

◄ A set of six Chippendale-style carved mahogany dining chairs, with stuff-over leather seats, c1770.
£11,200–12,500 / €16,400–18,300
$20,300–22,600 ⊞ JC

A pair of mahogany rococo-style Chippendale-style dining chairs, c1770.
£1,350–1,500
€1,950–2,200
$2,450–2,700 ⊞ GDB

An inlaid mahogany dining chair, 1780.
£150–165 / €220–250
$270–300 ⊞ QA

A pair of George III mahogany dining chairs, with a pierced splat and drop-in seat.
£590–700 / €860–1,000
$1,100–1,250 ⚒ DN

A set of four George III mahogany dining chairs, with pierced and carved ladder backs above later needlework seats, damaged.
£420–500 / €610–730
$760–910 ⚒ WW

British chair styles

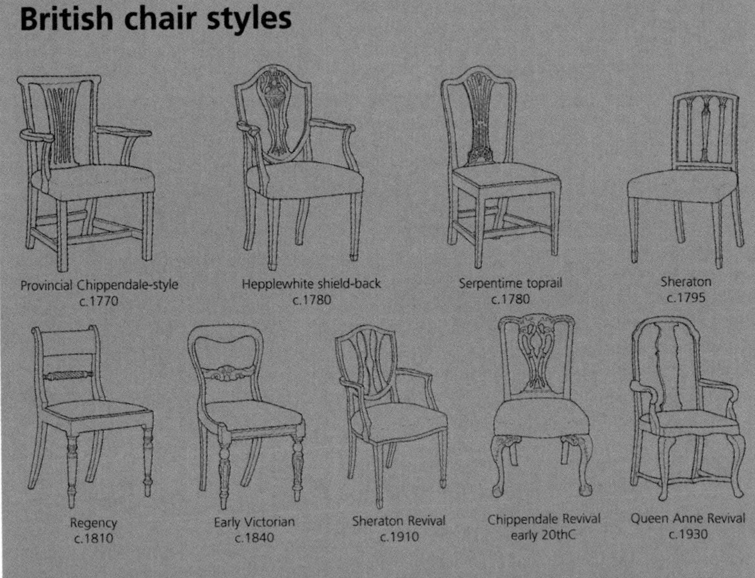

Late 18th-century styles in Britain are dominated by leading cabinet-makers such as George Hepplewhite and Thomas Sheraton. Regency examples are very neo-classical in appearance, while the Victorians favoured sturdier, more ornate designs. The Edwardians returned to the elegance of the late 18th century, although the proportions tended to be slightly narrower.

A set of six George III mahogany dining chairs, the stepped top rails above carved wheat ear splats, with stuff-over seats.
£1,050–1,250
€1,550–1,850
$1,900–2,250 ⚒ DMC

◄ **A set of six rosewood-crossbanded Trafalgar dining chairs,** the centre rails with rope-twist carving above stuff-over seats, on reeded legs, c1810.
£3,600–4,000
€5,300–5,900
$6,500–7,200
⊞ LGr

Valuing sets of chairs

Sets of dining chairs are worth proportionally more the larger the set. For good quality 19th-century copies of Georgian chairs, for example:
2: approx 3 x price of a single
4: approx 6 x price of a single
6: approx 10 x price of a single
8: approx 16 x price of a single
10: approx 25 x price of a single
The reason that the unit price between a pair and four is the same is that the latter are difficult to sell unless looking for chairs for a card table. Pairs and sets of six or more are more desirable.

A pair of Regency mahogany dining chairs, with bar backs and reeded rails, on square tapering legs.
£120–145 / €175–210
$220–260 WW

A set of six Regency mahogany dining chairs, with drop-in seats.
£1,200–1,400 / €1,750–2,050
$2,150–2,550 S(Am)

◄ **A set of six Regency carved mahogany dining chairs,** with cane seats.
£7,000–7,800 / €10,200–11,400
$12,700–14,200 ⊞ CRU

A set of six Regency mahogany dining chairs, including one carver, with ebony-strung cresting rails and drop-in seats, on sabre legs.
£940–1,100 / €1,350–1,600
$1,700–2,000 G(L)

A set of six mahogany dining chairs, the fielded bar rails above saltire cruciform backs with a carved boss, with stuff-over seats, c1825.
£580–650 / €850–950
$1,050–1,200 LGr

A set of eight figured rosewood dining chairs, the moulded top rails with scrolled volutes, the back splats with a cartouche between moulded lotus leaf carved stiles, over buttoned leather seats, on reeded tapering front legs, c1830.
£22,000–24,500
€32,000–36,000
$40,000–44,000 F

The high quality intricate carving on these chairs, and the fact that they were made of solid richly-coloured and figured rosewood, would indicate that they were produced by an eminent maker, probably for an important and wealthy client.

A set of six simulated rosewood dining chairs, inlaid with boxwood, c1830.
£2,700–3,000
€3,950–4,400
$4,900–5,400 GGD

A set of five simulated rosewood dining chairs, c1835.
£850–950 / €1,250–1,400
$1,550–1,750 WAA

A set of six late Regency simulated rosewood dining chairs, with bellflower and rosette-carved bar backs and cane seats, on gadroon-moulded legs.
£560–670 / €820–980
$1,000–1,200 WW

A set of four rosewood dining chairs, with boxwood inlay, c1830.
£2,250–2,500
€3,300–3,650
$4,050–4,550 CRU

► **A set of eight Chippendale-style mahogany dining chairs,** including two carvers, each with pierced splats above stuff-over seats, 19thC.
£2,600–3,100
€3,800–4,550
$4,700–5,600
L&T

A set of six rosewood dining chairs, c1840.
£840–1,000
€1,250–1,450
$1,500–1,800 S(O)

◄ **A set of nine ebonized and gilt-painted dining chairs,** with cane seats and cushions, on turned front legs.
£590–700
€860–1,000
$1,050–1,250
BWL

► **A set of four mahogany dining chairs,** with balloon backs and stuff-over seats, on fluted front legs.
£850–950 / €1,250–1,400
$1,550–1,750 LGr

A set of six mahogany dining chairs, by Gillows, including two carvers, 1850–60.
£1,700–1,900 / €2,500–2,750
$3,100–3,450 ⊞ APO

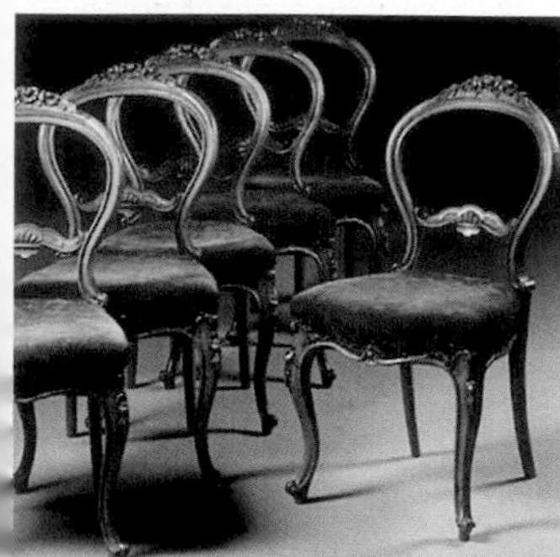

Miller's Compares

I. A set of six Victorian mahogany dining chairs, including a carver, with moulded backs, on turned tapering legs.
£760–910 / €1,100–1,300
$1,400–1,650 ⚒ TRM(E)

II. A set of six Victorian mahogany dining chairs, including a carver, with moulded top rails and scroll-carved splats, above drop-in seats.
£350–420 / €510–610
$640–760 ⚒ TRM(D)

These two sets of dining chairs are very similar in design, but Item I is more elegant than Item II in both size and appearance. The arms of Item I are also more attractive – just a little extra decorative detail or a slightly more stylish shape will make all the difference. Another important factor is that, although both sets are made of mahogany, the quality of the timber of which Item I is constructed is far superior to that of Item II. These days in particular, dealers are looking for pieces that will sell quickly. The chairs shown in Item II had loose frames and pieces missing, as well as non-uniform upholstery, which would necessitate both time and money being spent on them before they could be sold.

◀ **A set of six Victorian French-style carved walnut dining chairs,** c1860.
£960–1,150 / €1,450–1,700
$1,750–2,100 ⚒ S(O)

A set of six Victorian dining chairs, the balloon backs with carved leaf decoration, above stuff-over seats, on cabriole legs.
£330–390 / €480–570
$600–710 HYD

A set of eight Victorian oak dining chairs, with stuff-over seats, on turned and fluted front legs, stamped 'James Winter, 101 Wardour Street, Soho, London'.
£910–1,050 / €1,350–1,550
$1,650–1,900 DMC
James Winter is listed in directories as a 'Furniture broker, appraiser and undertaker'. The company traded until 1870.

A set of six Victorian oak dining chairs, with carved cresting rails and upholstered seats.
£350–420 / €510–610
$640–760 DD

A set of 12 mahogany dining chairs, c1870.
£4,500–5,000 / €6,600–7,300
$8,100–9,100 QA

A set of eight mahogany dining chairs, including two carvers, with shield backs and leather seats, c1870.
£8,100–9,000 / €11,800–13,100
$14,700–16,300 GGD

A set of eight Empire-style stained beech chairs, with drop-in seats, French, late 19thC.
£2,950–3,250 / €4,300–4,750
$5,300–5,900 DOA

A set of 12 mahogany dining chairs, decorated with floral paterae, with stuff-over seats, 1875–1925.
£2,100–2,500
€3,050–3,650
$3,800–4,550 Mit

◀ **A set of six Chippendale-style mahogany dining chairs,** c1900.
£3,150–3,500 / €4,600–5,100
$5,700–6,300 WAA

A set of eight Hepplewhite-style mahogany dining chairs, early 20thC.
£3,850–4,600 / €5,600–6,700
$7,000–8,300 S(O)

► **A set of six walnut banqueting chairs,** with tapestry seats and backs, c1920.
£2,000–2,200
€2,900–3,200
$3,600–4,000 DOA

► **A set of eight Chippendale-style mahogany dining chairs,** including two carvers, c1920.
£5,000–5,500
€7,300–8,100
$9,100–10,000
QA

Hall Chairs

A set of four George III mahogany hall chairs, the backs painted with an armorial of a horse's head, above shaped seats.
£1,750–2,100 / €2,550–3,050
$3,200–3,800 HYD

A Regency mahogany hall chair, with a bar back and panel support.
£230–270 / €350–410
$420–490 DN

A mahogany hall chair, the cabriole legs with claw-and-ball feet, c1830.
£1,150–1,300
€1,700–1,900
$2,100–2,350 ⊞ GEO

A pair of carved mahogany hall chairs, mid-19thC.
£1,450–1,600 / €2,100–2,350
$2,600–2,900 ⊞ GEO

A pair of Victorian oak hall chairs, with pierced backs, on scrolled legs.
£220–260 / €320–380
$400–470 WilP

► **A Gothic revival oak hall chair,** with an ebony-inlaid back panel, c1870.
£360–400 / €520–580
$650–720 ⊞ ANO

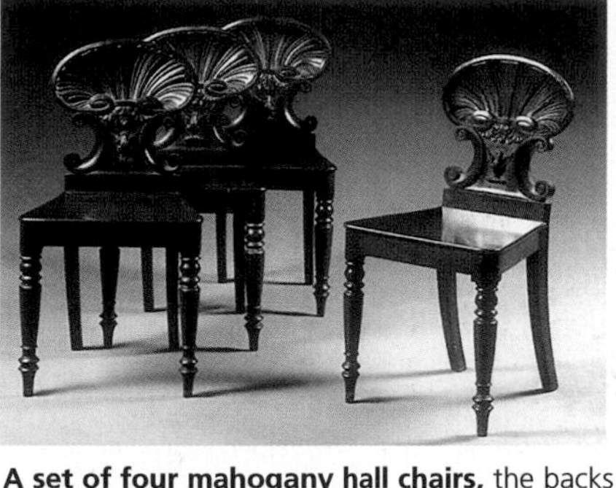

A set of four mahogany hall chairs, the backs carved with an eagle cresting, restored, c1830.
£2,850–3,400 / €4,150–4,950
$5,200–6,200 S(O)

A pair of Victorian mahogany hall chairs, with carved and pierced backs, on turned front legs.
£530–640 / €770–920
$960–1,150 DMC

A Shoolbred-style mahogany hall chair, the brass-mounted back with a brass balustrade, late 19thC.
£1,700–1,900 / €2,500–2,750
$3,100–3,450 CHTR

► **A pair of 16thC-style carved walnut hall chairs,** Italian, late 19thC.
£1,400–1,650 / €2,050–2,400
$2,550–3,000 S(O)

Library Chairs

A Georgian mahogany library armchair, with a rising back mechanism.
£3,300–3,900 / €4,800–5,700
$6,000–7,100 BWL

A walnut library tub chair, with scrolled top rail and down-scrolled arms, on cabriole legs with pad feet, 1825–50.
£470–560 / €690–820
$850–1,000 PFK

A William IV mahogany library chair, on reeded legs.
£820–980 / €1,200–1,400
$1,500–1,750 SWO

A mahogany library chair, on turned legs, stamped 'Straham & Co', c1835.
£520–580 / €760–850
$940–1,050 DEB

A satinwood library chair, with fluted front legs, c1900.
£1,200–1,350 / €1,750–1,950
$2,150–2,450 HA

◄ **An oak-framed library armchair,** with leather upholstery, c1890.
£1,750–1,950 / €2,550–2,850
$3,150–3,550 WAA

Nursing Chairs

A pair of Victorian walnut nursing chairs, with upholstered top rails and seats, on turned and fluted front legs.
£130–155 / €190–220
$240–280 L&E

A pair of inlaid rosewood nursing chairs, c1910.
£310–350 / €450–510
$560–630 WiB

◄ **An Edwardian walnut nursing chair,** with a tapestry seat.
£90–100 / €130–145
$160–180 WiB

Prie-dieux

A giltwood prie-dieu, with tapestry upholstery, c1850.
£900–1,000 / €1,300–1,450
$1,650–1,850 ⊞ GGD

A pair of Victorian walnut prie-dieux, with fretwork back panels, on scrolled legs.
£230–270 / €340–390
$420–490 ⚒ L&E

◀ **A Victorian prie-dieu,** with needlework upholstery, on cabriole legs.
£95–110 / €140–160
$170–200 ⚒ L&E

Salon Chairs

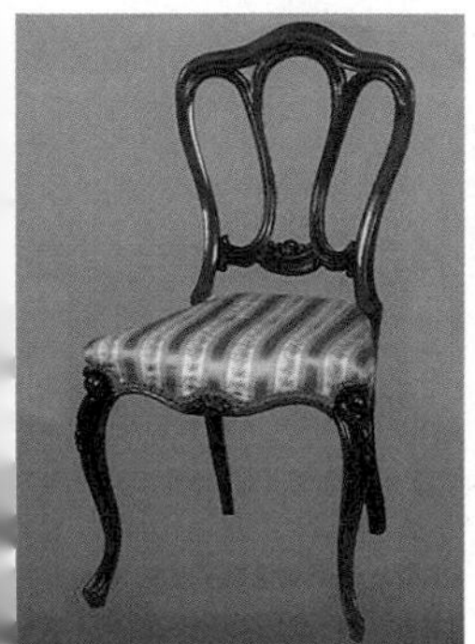

A set of four Victorian walnut salon chairs, with foliate-carved decoration, on cabriole legs.
£440–520 / €640–760
$800–940 ⚒ Mit

A pair of rosewood salon chairs, by Gillows of Lancaster, with ivory and boxwood foliate inlay, on square tapering front legs with spade feet, stamped, c1900.
£330–390 / €480–570
$600–710 ⚒ PFK

◀ **A set of six Victorian walnut salon chairs,** reupholstered,
£2,500–2,800 / €3,650–4,100
$4,550–5,100 ⊞ LGr

Side Chairs

A Queen Anne walnut side chair, c1710.
£2,600–2,900
€3,800–4,250
$4,700–5,200 ⊞ CRU

A George I walnut side chair.
£3,600–4,000
€5,300–5,900
$6,500–7,200 ⊞ HWK

A carved mahogany side chair, c1760.
£3,400–3,800
€4,950–5,500
$6,200–6,900 ⊞ HWK

◀ **A pair of carved walnut side chairs,** on turned legs, 18thC.
£1,700–1,900
€2,500–2,750
$3,100–3,450 ⊞ DEB

A pair of mahogany Chippendale-style side chairs, c1775.
£620–690 / €900–1,000
$1,100–1,250 ⊞ GGD

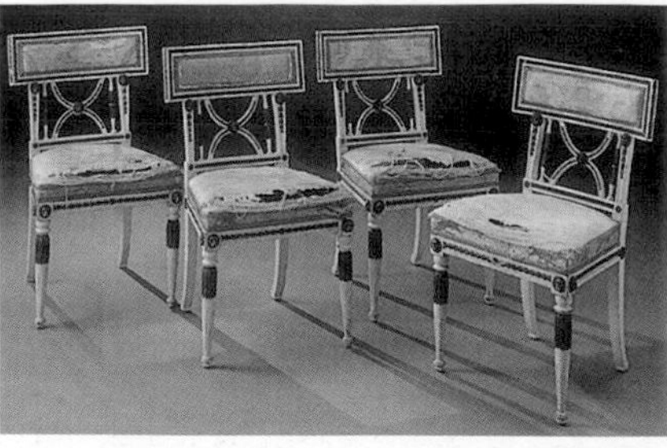

A set of four painted and ebonized side chairs, by Erik Ohrmark, stamped, Swedish, c1800.
£7,300–8,700 / €10,700–12,700
$13,200–15,800 ⚒ S(NY)

Ehrik Ohrmark, active from 1777 to 1813, was the chair-maker to the Royal Swedish Court in Stockholm and provided much of the seat furniture for Gustaf III's pavilion at Haga.

A pair of mahogany side chairs, Russian, c1810.
£7,300–8,700 / €10,700–12,700
$13,200–15,800 ⚒ S(NY)

A pair of William IV painted hardwood side chairs, with carved and polychromed Prince of Wales feathers and rush seats, on turned legs, Canadian.
£1,850–2,200
€2,700–3,200
$3,350–4,000 ⚒ RIT

A pair of Regency mahogany side chairs, in the style of Thomas Hope.
£350–420 / €510–610
$630–760 ⚒ SWO

A set of four late Regency mahogany side chairs, with stuff-over seats, on turned legs.
£300–360 / €440–530
$540–650 ⚒ WW

A rococo revival laminated rosewood side chair, attributed to J. H. Belter, with carved decoration and needlepoint upholstery, American, mid-19thC.
£1,150–1,350
€1,650–1,950
$2,100–2,500 ⚒ NOA

► A set of six Hitchcock-style side chairs, each with a different painted backsplat, attributed to Samuel Bartoll, Salem, American, 1800–50.
£5,100–6,100
€7,500–8,900
$9,200–11,000
⚒ JDJ

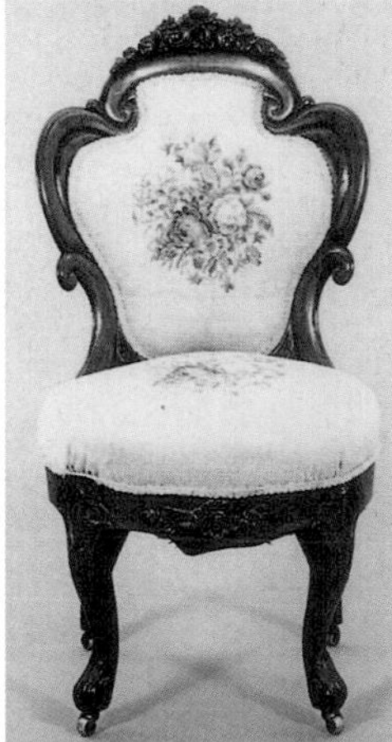

A rococo revival laminated rosewood side chair, attributed to J. H. Belter, with carved decoration, on cabriole legs, American, mid-19thC.
£430–510 / €630–740
$780–920 ⚒ NOA

John Henry Belter was born in Germany in 1804 and emigrated to America in 1833. His furniture is typically of heavy proportions and is sumptuously carved. Intended to grace the houses of the country's nouveaux riches, these pieces were seldom marked and rarely exported.

A carved rosewood side chair, 19thC.
£400–450 / €580–680
$720–850 ⚒ WW

A set of six walnut side chairs, with cane seats, French, c1890.
£810–900 / €1,200–1,350
$1,450–1,650 ⊞ MLL

Chaises Longues

A Regency painted wood chaise longue, on sabre legs with anthemion-moulded brass caps and casters, 81¼in (206.5cm) long.
£1,350–1,600 / €1,950–2,350
$2,450–2,900 WW

► **A rococo revival laminated rosewood chaise longue,** attributed to J. and J. W. Meeks, in the Stanton Hall pattern, on cabriole legs, American, 1850–75, 51½in (131cm) long.
£7,900–9,500
€11,500–13,900
$14,300–17,200
NOA

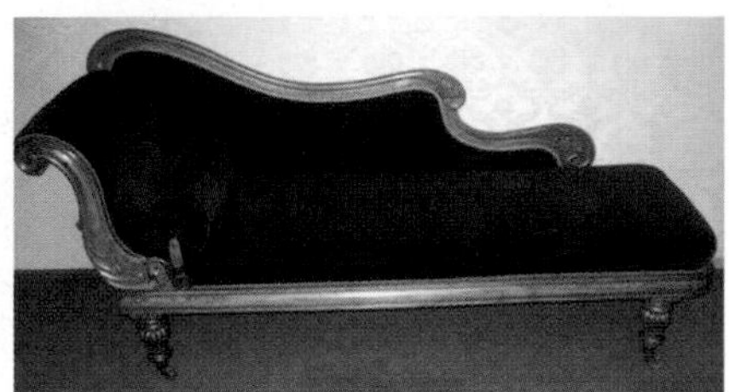

A William IV rosewood chaise longue, on turned and fluted legs, 76in (193cm) long.
£990–1,100 / €1,450–1,600
$1,800–2,000 SWA

A giltwood chaise longue, on carved cabriole legs, with paper label 'Clumber N399', 19thC, 69¾in (177cm) long.
£560–670 / €820–980
$1,000–1,200 WW
Clumber, in Nottinghamshire, was the seat of the Duke of Newcastle. It was demolished in 1938.

Chests & Coffers

◄ **A carved walnut *cassone*,** damaged, Italian, Veneto, 17thC, 67in (170cm) wide.
£2,850–3,400
€4,150–4,950
$5,200–6,200
S(Mi)

A walnut chest, decorated with Masur birch panels, the hinged cover over an arcaded front, feet missing, restored, German, late 17thC, 58in (147.5cm) wide.
£4,450–5,300 / €6,500–7,700
$8,100–9,600 TEN

► **A George III Lancashire-style mahogany mule chest,** the hinged cover above four drawers and two dummy drawers, 65in (165cm) long.
£1,000–1,200 / €1,450–1,750
$1,800–2,150 Mit

A japanned chest-on-stand, with brass carrying handles, lock plate and hinges, damaged, on later stand, probably German, 18th/19thC, 46in (117cm) wide.
£1,300–1,550 / €1,900–2,250
$2,350–2,800 S(Am)

A walnut coffer, the cover with a foliate motif, early 19thC, 52¾in (134cm) wide.
£230–270 / €340–390
$420–490 CHTR

A Biedermeier mahogany chest, the front applied with an embroidered floral panel, northern European, 1800–50, 34¼in (87cm) wide.
£1,400–1,650 / €2,050–2,400
$2,550–3,000 S(Am)

Chests-on-Chests

A walnut-veneered chest-on-chest, the moulded cornice above two short and three long drawers, the base with secretaire drawer above two long drawers and inlaid starburst, restored, c1720, 40½in (103cm) wide.
£22,500–25,000
€33,000–37,000
$41,000–46,000 ⊞ HA

This piece has all the features sought after by collectors: a three-plus-three drawer top section with beautiful finger fluting on canted corners, an original secretaire drawer and the inlaid concave starburst in the bottom drawer.

A Chippendale-style carved mahogany chest-on-chest, with later upper section, damaged and restored, American, Boston, c1770, 42in (106.5cm) wide.
£4,600–5,500
€6,700–8,000
$8,300–10,000 S(NY)

A George III mahogany chest-on-chest, the upper section with two short and three long drawers flanked by blind fret-carved corners, the base with secretaire drawer enclosing a fitted interior, 42½in (108cm) wide.
£3,200–3,800
€4,650–5,500
$5,800–6,900 AG

A walnut chest-on-chest, the upper section with two short and three long feather-banded drawers, the base with three short and two long drawers, 18thC, 42in (106.5cm) wide.
£3,300–3,950
€4,800–5,800
$6,000–7,200 BWL

Further reading

Miller's Late Georgian to Edwardian Buyers Guide, Miller's Publications, 2003

A Regency mahogany bowfronted chest-on-chest, the upper section with a moulded cornice above two short and two long drawers, the base with three long graduated drawers, 47in (119.5cm) wide.
£1,650–1,950
€2,400–2,850
$3,000–3,550 G(L)

Miller's Compares

I. A George III mahogany chest-on-chest, the upper section with a dentil cornice above four long graduated drawers, the base with a brushing slide above four long drawers, 43¼in (110cm) wide.
£4,350–5,200
€6,400–7,600
$7,900–9,400 SWO

II. A late George III mahogany chest-on-chest, the upper section with a moulded dentil cornice above two short and three long drawers, the base with a secretaire drawer enclosing a fitted interior, 46½in (118cm) wide.
£2,350–2,800
€3,450–4,100
$4,250–5,100 SWO

Item I was made c1760. It has an untouched appearance with original pierced brass drop handles, both features sought after by dealers. It is constructed of solid mahogany with decorative reeded canted corners to the upper section, the lower section having a brushing slide and elegant ogee feet. Item II was made c1810 when it was fashionable to veneer mahogany onto cheaper timbers such as oak or even pine. Although the handles look original, there is an overall appearance of it being too square, lacking the elegance of Item I. Secretaire drawers do not necessarily add value to a Georgian mahogany chest-on-chest.

A mahogany chest-on-chest, 1780, 42in (106.5cm) wide.
£3,000–3,300
€4,400–4,850
$5,400–6,000 ⊞ GGD

A Biedermeier mahogany chest-on-chest, with five long drawers above two graduated drawers flanked by spiral-twist pilasters, northern European, 19thC, 39½in (100.5cm) wide.
£1,050–1,250
€1,550–1,850
$1,900–2,250 S(Am)

Chests of Drawers & Commodes

A olive- and kingwood-veneered chest of drawers, with two short drawers over three long drawers, on walnut feet, c1680, 37in (94cm) wide.
£22,500–25,000 / €33,000–37,000 $41,000–46,000 ⊞ HA

The majority of oyster-veneered William and Mary period chests of drawers are oyster walnut. This piece has a mixture of olive and kingwood veneers which is rare. It also has the advantage of beautifully patterned sides using the same oysters.

▶ A Queen Anne walnut and marquetry chest of drawers, 40¼in (102cm) wide.
£4,800–5,700 / €7,000–8,300 $8,700–10,300 ⚒ S(O)

A kingwood and tulipwood commode, with brass-inlaid decoration, with two short and three long drawers, some later mounts, French, early 18thC, 50¾in (129cm) wide.
£18,000–21,600 / €26,500–32,000 $33,000–39,000 ⚒ S

A William and Mary oyster-veneered chest of drawers, the top with geometric stringing above two short and three long drawers, with walnut crossbanding and half-round drawer dividers, 36in (91.5cm) wide.
£4,450–5,300 / €6,500–7,700 $8,100–9,600 ⚒ HYD

A walnut-veneered chest of drawers, with two short over three long drawers, later handles, c1720, 37in (94cm) wide.
£12,200–13,500 / €17,800–19,700 $22,100–24,400 ⊞ HA

A walnut and marquetry chest of drawers, c1690, 38in (96.5cm) high.
£7,600–8,500 / €11,100–12,400 $13,800–15,500 ⊞ GEO

A figured walnut two-part chest of drawers, with two short and three long crossbanded drawers, handles replaced, early 18thC, 39½in (100.5cm) wide.
£1,300–1,550 / €1,900–2,250 $2,350–2,800 ⚒ SWO

A walnut and marquetry serpentine chest of drawers, with three drawers, restored, German, mid-18thC, 36¼in (92cm) wide.
£1,250–1,400 / €1,800–2,050 $2,250–2,600 ⚒ S(O)

A walnut chest of drawers, c1730, 20in (51cm) wide.
£11,200–12,500 €16,400–18,300 $20,300–22,600 ⊞ GDB

A walnut-veneered commode, in the style of Christian Linning, with slide, damaged and restored, Swedish, Stockholm, c1750, 48¾in (124cm) wide.
£4,750–5,700 / €6,900–8,300 $8,600–10,300 ⚒ BUK

A crossbanded mahogany serpentine chest of drawers, with four graduated drawers, c1760, 39in (99cm) wide.
£6,200–6,900 / €9,100–10,100 $11,200–12,500 ⊞ WAA

A maple serpentine chest of drawers, with ash banding and four graduated drawers, c1770, 41¼in (105cm) wide.
£9,600–11,500 / €14,000–16,800 $17,400–20,800 S

A George III mahogany, boxwood and ebony-strung serpentine chest of drawers, the fitted drawer above three long drawers with satinwood stringing, flanked by canted corners, 38½in (98cm) wide.
£2,700–3,200 / €3,950–4,650 $4,900–5,800 DN

A George III mahogany serpentine chest of drawers, 43in (109cm) wide.
£7,600–8,500 / €11,100–12,400 $13,800–15,400 GGD

A walnut serpentine chest of drawers, with three graduated drawers, late 18thC, 41¼in (105cm) wide.
£1,100–1,300 / €1,600–1,900 $2,000–2,350 L&T

A mahogany brass-inlaid bowfronted chest of drawers, with a brushing slide, the top drawer fitted with a writing tray, mirror and lidded compartments, c1770, 44in (112cm) wide.
£7,600–8,500 / €11,100–12,400 $13,800–15,400 YOX

A mahogany and satinwood-crossbanded bowfronted chest of drawers, c1780, 43¼in (110cm) wide.
£2,150–2,550 / €3,150–3,700 $3,900–4,600 S(O)

A mahogany chest of drawers, with two short drawers over three long drawers, handles replaced, c1790, 42in (106.5cm) wide.
£4,300–4,800 / €6,300–7,000 $7,800–8,700 HA

► **A Georgian mahogany bowfronted chest of drawers,** with two short drawers over three long drawers, 42in (106.5cm) wide.
£1,050–1,200 / €1,550–1,750 $1,900–2,150 SWA

A Chippendale-style inlaid and figured mahogany chest of drawers, escutcheons later, American, Pennsylvania, c1770, 39½in (100.5cm) wide.
£2,500–3,000 / €3,650–4,400 $4,550–5,400 S(NY)

◄ **A George III mahogany chest of drawers,** with ebonized banding and three graduated drawers, 19¼in (49cm) wide.
£1,800–2,150 / €2,650–3,150 $3,250–3,900 DD

A George III mahogany chest of drawers, with two short drawers above three long oak-lined graduated drawers flanked by quarter pilasters, 39½in (100.5cm) wide.
£1,050–1,250 / €1,550–1,850 $1,900–2,250 DMC

A mahogany serpentine chest of drawers, attributed to Gillows of Lancaster, with fitted top drawer, c1790, 41in (104cm) wide.
£18,000–20,000 / €26,300–29,200 $33,000–37,000 JeA

A fruitwood commode, with inlaid banding, Austrian, late 18thC, 51¼in (130cm) wide.
£1,500–1,800 / €2,200–2,650
$2,700–3,250 ⚒ S(Am)

A mahogany bowfronted dressing chest, the fitted top drawer above three graduated drawers, Irish, late 18thC, 44in (112cm) wide.
£9,600–11,500 / €14,000–16,800
$17,400–20,800 ⚒ HOK

A Louis XVI-style mahogany and fruitwood chest of drawers, with six long drawers, decorated with later marquetry shell motifs and flowers, damaged, Dutch, c1800, 40¼in (102cm) wide.
£730–870 / €1,050–1,250
$1,300–1,550 ⚒ S(Am)

An ash and burr-ash commode, with a marble top, French, early 19thC, 51in (129.5cm) wide.
£3,150–3,500 / €4,600–5,100
$5,700–6,300 ⊞ DOA

A kingwood and gilt-metal-mounted commode, the later marble top above a frieze drawer with inlaid *faux* fluting, above two quarter-veneered drawers, French, late 18thC, 36½in (92.5cm) wide.
£1,900–2,250 / €2,750–3,300
$3,450–4,050 ⚒ L&T

A walnut, tulipwood and marquetry commode, the crossbanded top inlaid with an urn, above three drawers, north Italian, late 18thC, 50¾in (129cm) wide.
£7,300–8,600 / €10,700–12,600
$13,200–15,600 ⚒ TEN

A Louis XVI-style kingwood commode, with gilt-brass mounts, restored, Russian, late 18thC, 53¼in (135.5cm) wide.
£6,100–7,300 / €8,900–10,700
$11,000–13,200 ⚒ S(Am)

A figured mahogany bowfronted chest of drawers, American, New York, c1810, 37½in (95.5cm) wide.
£3,000–3,600 / €4,400–5,300
$5,400–6,500 ⚒ S(NY)

A walnut and marquetry serpentine *bombé* commode, inlaid with geometric and floral panels, south German, 18thC, 47in (119.5cm) wide.
£6,300–7,500 / €9,200–11,000
$11,400–13,600 ⚒ E

A parquetry serpentine chest of drawers, the crossbanded top inlaid with floral motifs above three long drawers, north Italian, 18thC, 54in (137cm) wide.
£3,500–4,200 / €5,100–6,100
$6,300–7,600 ⚒ HYD

A mahogany chest of drawers, with boxwood and ebony inlay, two short and three long drawers, c1800, 43in (109cm) wide.
£2,450–2,750 / €3,600–4,000
$4,450–5,000 ⊞ WAA

A mahogany and rosewood-crossbanded bowfronted chest of drawers, with satinwood inlay and three graduated drawers, c1820, 39in (99cm) wide.
£1,600–1,800 / €2,350–2,650
$2,900–3,250 ⊞ LGr

A mahogany chest of drawers, with two short and three long drawers, c1820, 42in (106.5cm) wide.
£900–1,000 / €1,300–1,450
$1,600–1,800 ⊞ QA

A mahogany chest of drawers, with five cedar-lined drawers, c1830, 46in (117cm) wide.
£2,400–2,650 / €3,500–3,850
$4,350–4,800 ⊞ SAT

A walnut serpentine commode, French, handles later, c1840, 48in (122cm) wide.
£2,700–3,000 / €3,950–4,400
$4,900–5,400 ⊞ MLL

A mahogany bowfronted chest of drawers, with satinwood inlay, with two short over three long drawers, c1850, 35in (89cm) wide.
£3,150–3,500 / €4,600–5,100
$5,700–6,300 ⊞ CRU

► A mahogany 'Scotch' chest of drawers, with inlaid decoration, the hat drawer flanked by four short drawers over three long drawers, c1850, 43in (109cm) high.
£850–950 / €1,250–1,400
$1,500–1,700 ⊞ GEO

► A mahogany commode, with gilt-bronze mounts, French, c1830, 52½in (133.5cm) wide.
£3,450–4,100
€5,000–6,000
$6,200–7,400
⚒ S(O)

A mahogany-veneered commode, Swedish, 1800–50, 41¾in (106cm) wide.
£4,400–5,300 / €6,400–7,700
$8,000–9,600 ⚒ BUK

A Biedermeier burr-walnut commode, the moulded frieze drawer above three further drawers, marble top missing, damaged, south German, c1840, 50¼in (127.5cm) wide.
£1,550–1,800 / €2,250–2,650
$2,700–3,250 ⚒ S(Am)

A marquetry breakfront commode, decorated with flowers, leaves, birds, scrolls and urns, with a fitted frieze drawer over two deep drawers flanked by four side drawers, Dutch, 19thC, 59in (150cm) wide.
£3,750–4,500 / €5,500–6,600
$6,800–8,100 ⚒ AG

A mahogany bowfronted chest of drawers, with two short over three long drawers, 19thC, 45¼in (115cm) wide.
£800–960 / €1,200–1,450
$1,450–1,750 ⚒ AH

◄ A mahogany chest of drawers, with three drawers, c1850, 36in (91.5cm) wide.
£1,550–1,750 / €2,250–2,550
$2,700–3,100 ⊞ WAA

An oak commode, inlaid with floral marquetry, with three *bombé* drawers, Dutch, 19thC, 36in (91.5cm) wide.
£1,700–2,000 / €2,500–2,900
$3,100–3,600 ⚒ BWL

A Victorian mahogany 'Scotch' chest of drawers, the upper section with two cushion drawers over three long graduated drawers flanked by barley-twist columns, the base with a moulded drawer, 48in (122cm) wide.
£350–420 / €510–610
$630–760 L&E

An Edwardian satinwood bowfronted chest of drawers, with painted decoration and oval vignettes, with two short and three long graduated drawers, 36¾in (93.5cm) wide.
£2,350–2,800 / €3,450–4,100
$4,250–5,100 L&T

A Victorian walnut chest of drawers, 41in (104cm) wide.
£2,200–2,450 / €3,200–3,600
$4,000–4,450 Man

An Edwardian 18thC-style lacquered oak serpentine commode, the marble top above two long graduated drawers, with painted decoration and gilt-metal mounts, 37in (94cm) wide.
£1,450–1,700 / €2,100–2,500
$2,600–3,100 L&T

A Victorian figured mahogany bowfronted chest of drawers, with four drawers flanked by pilasters, 46in (117cm) wide.
£490–590 / €720–860
$890–1,050 DD

◄ **A mahogany chest of drawers,** with a frieze drawer over three further drawers, c1890, 46in (117cm) wide.
£630–700 / €880–1,000
$1,100–1,250 SWA

Items in the Furniture section have been arranged in date order within each sub-section.

An Edwardian mahogany chest of drawers, with two short over three long drawers, 42in (106.5cm) wide.
£1,750–1,950 / €2,550–2,850
$3,150–3,550 Man

Military Chests

An oak secretaire campaign chest, the secretaire drawer fitted with pigeonholes and drawers behind a rising panel, over three long drawers, with Army & Navy label, early 19thC, 39in (99cm) wide.
£1,750–2,100 / €2,550–3,050
$3,150–3,800 TMA

A teak brass-bound military chest, the upper section with three short and one long drawer, the base with two long drawers, 19thC, 39½in (100.5cm) wide.
£700–840 / €1,000–1,200
$1,250–1,500 E

A camphorwood brass-bound campaign chest, with ebony stringing and reeded banding, the carved galleried top over two short and four long drawers, 19thC, 43in (109cm) wide.
£1,400–1,650 / €2,050–2,400
$2,550–3,000 AH

Secretaire Chests

A George III mahogany secretaire chest, with a fitted interior, 41in (104cm) wide.
£630–750 / €920–1,100
$1,150–1,350 ⚒ BWL

► A George III mahogany secretaire chest, with a fitted, strung and inlaid interior over three graduated drawers, 40¼in (102cm) wide.
£1,400–1,650 / €2,050–2,400
$2,550–3,000 ⚒ SWO

A mahogany and walnut secretaire chest, with a fitted drawer, on later bracket feet, c1780, 43¼in (110cm) wide.
£840–1,000 / €1,250–1,450
$1,500–1,800 ⚒ S(O)

◄ A Regency mahogany secretaire chest, the fitted interior over three long graduated drawers, label for Spillman & Co, London, 36¼in (92cm) wide.
£680–810 / €1,000–1,200
$1,250–1,450 ⚒ G(B)

A George III mahogany secretaire chest, the top drawer fitted with a stationery side drawer and a secret drawer, above four short drawers, 32in (81.5cm) wide.
£490–590 / €720–860
$890–1,050 ⚒ SPF

Chests-on-Stands

A Queen Anne walnut chest-on-stand, the moulded cornice above two short and three long drawers, the base with a central drawer flanked by two further drawers, on later cabriole legs, restored, 42in (106.5cm) wide.
£1,700–2,000
€2,500–2,900
$3,100–3,600 ⚒ DN(BR)

A George I walnut chest-on-stand, the top with a cushion drawer, 38½in (98cm) wide.
£1,050–1,250
€1,550–1,850
$1,900–2,250 ⚒ S(O)

Queen Anne

American furniture termed, for example, 'Queen Anne' does not necessarily date from the actual period of Queen Anne. This is because the latest fashions took about 20 years to cross the Atlantic from Britain to America, but the style is nevertheless of that period.

A walnut and veneered chest-on-stand, stand later, c1715, 42in (106.5cm) wide.
£10,800–12,000
€15,800–17,500
$19,500–21,700 ⊞ HA

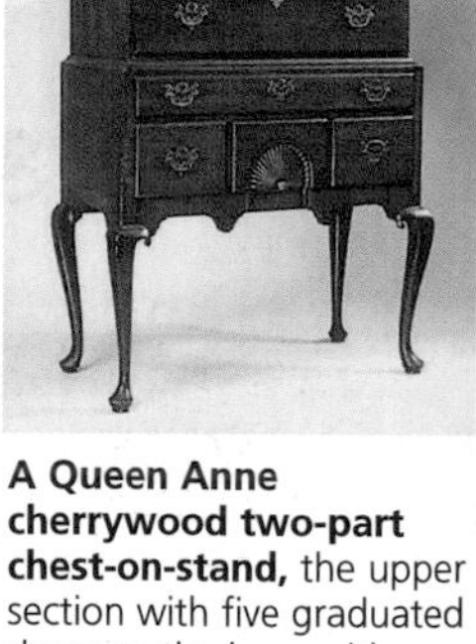

A Queen Anne cherrywood two-part chest-on-stand, the upper section with five graduated drawers, the base with one long drawer over three short drawers, one carved with a fan, American, Massachusetts, 37¼in (94.5cm) wide.
£11,100–13,300
€16,200–19,000
$20,200–23,500 ⚒ JDJ

◄ A Queen Anne figured maple chest-on-stand, with dummy drawers carved with fans, damaged and repaired, American, possibly New Hampshire, c1760, 39½in (100.5cm) wide.
£4,000–4,800
€5,800–7,000
$7,200–8,700 ⚒ S(NY)

Wellington Chests

◄ **An oak Wellington chest,** with eight drawers, 19thC, 24in (61cm) wide.
£640–760 / €930–1,100
$1,200–1,400 ⚒ E

Miller's Compares

I. A Victorian mahogany Wellington chest, with seven graduated drawers and locking action, 22in (56cm) wide.
£1,900–2,250
€2,750–3,300
$3,450–4,050 ⚒ Mit

II. A Victorian walnut-veneered Wellington chest, with seven graduated drawers and locking action, 22in (56cm) wide.
£700–840
€1,000–1,200
$1,250–1,500 ⚒ Mit

Item I has a more substantial and imposing presence than Item II, although some may prefer the more compact proportions of the latter piece. Item I is in better condition as the veneer on the plinth of Item II is lifting and the chest is in what it is known in the trade as an overall 'tired' condition.

A rosewood Wellington chest, with six graduated drawers, brass handles later, 19thC, 26in (66cm) wide.
£730–870 / €1,050–1,250
$1,300–1,550 ⚒ AMB

A Victorian burr-oak Wellington chest, 48in (122cm) high.
£2,900–3,250
€4,250–4,750
$5,200–5,900 ⊞ Man

A Victorian rosewood-veneered Wellington chest, with seven graduated oak-lined drawers and locking action, damaged, 22½in (57cm) wide.
£2,350–2,800
€3,450–4,100
$4,250–5,100 ⚒ WW

Clothes & Linen Presses

◄ **A George III mahogany linen press,** attributed to Thomas Bradshaw, the two doors enclosing three tray shelves, one shelf missing and one later, c1760, 50in (127cm) wide.
£9,600–11,500
€14,000–16,800
$17,400–20,800 ⚒ S

Thomas Bradshaw, who traded from 10 St Paul's Churchyard, London, subscribed to Thomas Chippendale's *Director* (1754) and this influence is evident on this linen press. Bradshaw was declared bankrupt in 1772.

LOCATE THE SOURCE

The source of each illustration in Miller's can be found by checking the code letters below each caption with the Key to Illustrations, pages 778–784.

A George III mahogany linen press, with a carved and inlaid swan-neck pediment, the two panelled doors enclosing slides, the base with two short over three long drawers, damaged, 53in (134.5cm) wide.
£2,350–2,800
€3,450–4,100
$4,250–5,100 ⚒ SWO

A George III mahogany secretaire linen press, the two panelled doors enclosing slides, the secretaire drawer with dummy drawer front enclosing a fitted interior above three long drawers, feet replaced, 82in (208.5cm) wide.
£2,900–3,450
€4,250–5,000
$5,200–6,200 ⚒ AH

A George III mahogany, boxwood- and ebony-inlaid and crossbanded clothes press, the two panelled doors enclosing sliding trays, the base with two short over two long drawers, 51in (129.5cm) wide.
£1,400–1,650
€2,050–2,400
$2,550–3,000 ⚒ E

► A mahogany and inlaid linen press, with four doors, c1795, 55in (139.5cm) wide.
£8,000–8,900
€11,700–13,000
$14,500–16,100 ⊞ Che

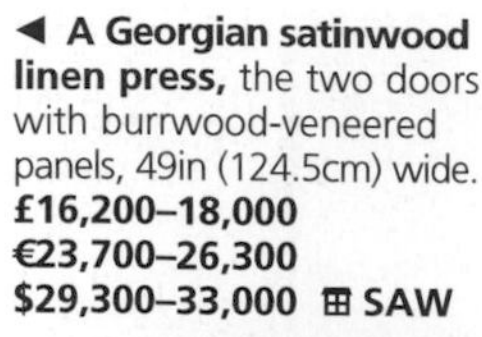

◄ A Georgian satinwood linen press, the two doors with burrwood-veneered panels, 49in (124.5cm) wide.
£16,200–18,000
€23,700–26,300
$29,300–33,000 ⊞ SAW

A George III mahogany linen press, with two panelled doors enclosing slides, the base with two short drawers over one long drawer, 52in (132cm) wide.
£2,250–2,700
€3,300–3,950
$4,050–4,900 ⚒ SWO

A George III mahogany linen press, with two figured panelled doors enclosing one slide and a later hanging rail, the base with two short over two long drawers, 50in (127cm) wide.
£1,500–1,800
€2,200–2,650
$2,700–3,250 ⚒ WW

A mahogany secretaire linen press, the two crossbanded and fielded panelled doors enclosing hanging space, the base with a fitted secretaire drawer above two long drawers, c1800, 49in (124.5cm) wide.
£4,800–5,300
€7,000–7,700
$8,700–9,600 ⊞ JC

A Regency mahogany and ebony-inlaid linen press, with two figured panelled doors, the base with two short over two long graduated drawers, 50in (127cm) wide.
£2,700–3,200
€3,950–4,650
$4,900–5,800 ⚒ LAY

A crossbanded mahogany linen press, c1820, 48in (122cm) wide.
£2,700–3,000
€3,950–4,400
$4,900–5,400 ⊞ GBr

A George III mahogany two-part clothes press, with panelled doors, Isle of Man, c1820, 47¼in (120cm) wide.
£960–1,150
€1,450–1,700
$1,750–2,100 ⚒ S(O)

A George IV mahogany gentleman's press, probably by Gillows, the panelled doors flanked by four drawers to either side, c1825, 87in (221cm) wide.
£2,400–2,850 / €3,500–4,150
$4,350–5,200 ⚒ S(O)

A mahogany linen press, the two panelled doors enclosing slides, the base with two short and two long drawers, 19thC, 56¼in (143cm) wide.
£1,300–1,550
€1,900–2,250
$2,350–2,800 ⚒ CHTR

A mahogany linen press, the two panelled doors enclosing later hanging rails, the base with two short over two long drawers, 19thC, 50in (127cm) wide.
£730–860 / €1,050–1,250
$1,300–1,550 ⚒ WW

A mahogany linen press, the two brass-trimmed panelled and crossbanded doors enclosing slides and flanked by wrythen-turned columns, the base with two short over two long drawers, c1825, 52in (132cm) wide.
£1,350–1,600
€1,950–2,350
$2,400–2,900 AH

A mahogany linen press, the two panelled doors above two short and one long drawer, 19thC, 55in (139.5cm) wide.
£470–560 / €690–820
$850–1,000 CHTR

A mahogany linen press, the two doors over two short and two long drawers, c1840, 54in (137cm) wide.
£3,150–3,500
€4,600–5,100
$5,700–6,300 MHA

► **A rosewood, ebony and ebonized linen press,** with a frieze drawer, the stand also with a frieze drawer, with four extra leaves, Dutch, 19thC, 76in (193cm) wide.
£1,050–1,250 / €1,550–1,850
$1,900–2,250 S(Am)

Davenports

A mahogany davenport, with four drawers, c1790, 32in (81.5cm) high.
£12,100–13,500 / €17,700–19,700
$21,900–24,400 HWK

A rosewood davenport, with a satinwood interior, c1830, 23in (58.5cm) wide.
£2,250–2,500 / €3,300–3,650
$4,050–4,550 QA

► **A rosewood davenport,** the hinged top with a leather writing surface enclosing a mahogany fitted interior with drawers, the base with a door enclosing four graduated mahogany-lined drawers, c1820, 24in (61cm) wide.
£3,750–4,200 / €5,500–6,100
$6,800–7,600 JC

Miller's Compares

I. A Regency rosewood davenport, in the style of Gillows, the sliding upper section with a leather writing surface and brass gallery, the fitted interior with two short and two dummy drawers and a hidden inkwell, above four short and four dummy drawers, 20in (51cm) wide.
£3,500–4,200 / €5,100–6,100
$6,300–7,600 HYD

II. A Regency mahogany davenport, the sliding upper section with a leather writing surface and brass gallery, the fitted interior with five small drawers, above three drawers, 25½in (65cm) wide.
£1,400–1,650 / €2,050–2,400
$2,550–3,000 HYD

Item I is of a design by a very desirable firm of cabinet makers and has the added advantage of being in original condition and having an attractive patina. It is also more compact and stylish than Item II, which is rather cumbersome in appearance. Davenports are currently very good value for money – both these examples would possibly have sold for more ten years ago.

An early Victorian rosewood davenport, the hinged top with a leather writing surface above four drawers and four dummy drawers, 19in (48.5cm) wide.
£590–700 / €860–1,000
$1,050–1,250 G(B)

A Victorian walnut davenport, by T. H. Filmer, the rising stationery compartment with a pierced brass gallery fitted with drawers and pigeonholes, the hinged piano top enclosing a leather-lined writing surface, above four side drawers, maker's label, 21¾in (55.5cm) wide.
£1,750–2,100
€2,550–3,050
$3,150–3,800 G(B)
Thomas Henry Filmer is listed in 1839 directories as a cabinet-maker and undertaker.

A walnut and marquetry-inlaid davenport, c1860, 24in (61cm) wide.
£1,100–1,300
€1,600–1,900
$2,000–2,350 S(O)

A walnut davenport, the hinged top with a leather writing surface, c1880, 21in (53.5cm) wide.
£1,650–1,850
€2,400–2,700
$3,000–3,350 WAA

A burr-walnut davenport, with a hinged piano top, c1860, 36in (91.5cm) high.
£3,800–4,250
€5,500–6,200
$6,900–7,700 GEO

A late Victorian rosewood and boxwood-strung davenport, the hinged top with a gilt-metal gallery above a frieze drawer and brackets, the base with fall-front enclosing shelves, 22¾in (58cm) wide.
£820–980 / €1,200–1,450
$1,500–1,750 DN

◄ **A mahogany davenport,** the hinged top enclosing a fitted interior, c1900, 21in (53.5cm) wide.
£1,350–1,500
€1,950–2,200
$2,450–2,700 DEB

A Victorian walnut davenport, the rising stationery compartment with a pierced brass gallery and fitted with drawers and pigeonholes, the hinged top enclosing a writing surface and two drawers, above four side drawers, 22¾in (58cm) wide.
£2,100–2,500
€3,050–3,650
$3,800–4,550 AH

A burr-walnut and parquetry davenport, the hinged top with a leather writing surface and enclosing a fitted interior, above panelled doors enclosing four short drawers, late 19thC, 25¼in (64cm) wide.
£2,800–3,350
€4,100–4,900
$5,100–6,100 HOK

Daybeds

A carved walnut daybed, restored, late 17thC, 67¼in (171cm) long.
£2,850–3,400 / €4,150–4,950
$5,200–6,200 S(O)

► **A carved walnut daybed,** with a cane back and seat, c1680, 67in (170cm) long.
£810–970
€1,200–1,400
$1,450–1,750
S(O)

◄ **A Victorian daybed,** with carved walnut legs, 75½in (192cm) long.
£640–760
€930–1,100
$1,200–1,400
DN

Desks

A burr-walnut kneehole desk, c1720, 29in (73.5cm) wide.
£8,100–9,000 / €11,800–13,100
$14,700–16,300 ⊞ WAA

A walnut kneehole desk, early 18thC, 29½in (75cm) wide.
£4,350–5,200 / €6,400–7,600
$7,900–9,400 ⚒ G(L)

A George I walnut-veneered kneehole desk, with herringbone stringing and crossbanding, 33in (84cm) wide.
£3,750–4,500 / €5,500–6,600
$6,800–8,100 ⚒ HYD

A rococo-style figured kingwood and ebony-inlaid desk, with a slide, German, 1775–1800 and later, 53in (134.5cm) wide.
£500–600 / €730–880
$910–1,100 ⚒ NOA

◄ A Federal carved and figured-mahogany writing desk, probably by Duncan Phyfe, New York, the two doors enclosing a bookcase, above a fitted interior, American, c1810, 32in (81.5cm) wide.
£4,650–5,500 / €6,800–8,000
$8,400–10,000 ⚒ S(NY)

Duncan Phyfe (1768–1854) drew on the forms and ornament of ancient Greece and Rome to create furniture in the neo-classical style. This type of furniture was made up to the mid-19th century and revived in the late 19th/early 20th century.

A Regency mahogany pedestal desk, with later leather and feet, 72in (183cm) wide.
£7,200–8,600 / €10,500–12,600
$13,000–15,600 ⚒ S

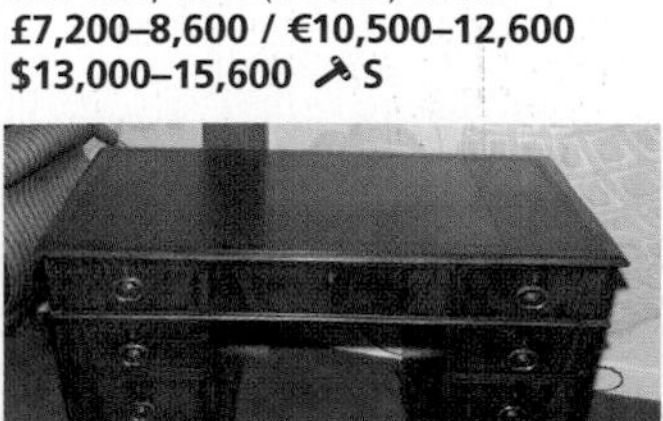

◄ A mahogany pedestal desk, c1825, 49in (124.5cm) wide.
£11,200–12,500
€16,400–18,300
$20,300–22,600
⊞ GGD

► A mahogany pedestal desk, the gilt-leather inset writing surface above a dummy drawer and eight further drawers, 19thC, 52in (132cm) wide.
£410–490
€600–720
$740–890 ⚒ E

◄ **An oak pedestal desk,** 19thC, 60in (152.5cm) wide.
£4,700–5,300
€6,900–7,700
$8,500–9,600
⊞ HA

A mahogany partners' desk, the leatherette-covered writing surface above a frieze fitted with a writing slide, the pedestals with panelled doors enclosing three drawers to one side and three pull-out trays to the other, 19thC, 61in (155cm) wide.
£1,500–1,800 / €2,200–2,650
$2,700–3,250 ⚒ Mit

A mahogany desk, the frieze drawer flanked by two banks of short drawers, 19thC, 54in (137cm) wide.
£210–250 / €310–370
$380–450 ⚒ CHTR

An inlaid rosewood writing desk, c1870, 22in (56cm) wide.
£1,050–1,200
€1,550–1,750
$1,900–2,150 ⊞ MTay

◄ **A Victorian mahogany-veneered pedestal desk,** by T. H. Filmer, each pedestal with three drawers, 48in (122cm) wide.
£470–560 / €690–820
$850–1,000 ⚒ WW

A gilt-bronze-mounted walnut *bombé* kneehole desk, decorated with a European royal coat-of-arms, south German, c1860, 53in (134.5cm) wide.
£4,200–5,000 / €6,100–7,300
$7,600–9,100 ⚒ S(O)

A Victorian burr-walnut marquetry and ebonized pedestal desk, with a leather writing surface, some damage, 50½in (128.5cm) wide.
£1,100–1,300 / €1,600–1,900
$2,000–2,350 ⚒ G(B)

A Victorian mahogany desk, the upper section with a tambour door enclosing pigeonholes flanked by two banks of four drawers, the top with a hinged writing slope above a central drawer flanked by three drawers.
£260–310 / €380–450
$470–560 ⚒ CHTR

A Victorian figured-walnut desk, the mirrored back flanked by short drawers, the top with a hinged writing slope enclosing a fitted interior, the central frieze drawer flanked by three drawers to either side, 58in (147.5cm) wide.
£1,400–1,650 / €2,050–2,400
$2,550–3,000 ⚒ JNic

A Victorian mahogany desk, with marquetry-inlaid rosewood panels, the raised galleried back with a stationery compartment, the top with a leather-inset writing surface above three drawers, with an undershelf, 42½in (108cm) wide.
£2,000–2,400 / €2,900–3,500
$3,600–4,350 ⚒ AH

A Victorian mahogany pedestal desk, in the manner of Gillows, with a cloth-inset top, 54in (137cm) wide.
£1,000–1,200 / €1,450–1,750
$1,800–2,150 ⚒ WW

A Victorian carved oak desk, the upper section with a mirror flanked by two banks of drawers, the base with three frieze drawers above six drawers, 54¼in (138cm) wide.
£210–250 / €310–370
$380–450 ⚒ CHTR

A Victorian mahogany partners' desk, with a leather-inset writing surface, the three frieze drawers above a cupboard and three drawers, 60in (152.5cm) wide.
£2,250–2,700 / €3,300–3,950
$4,050–4,900 HYD

A Sheraton-style mahogany and inlaid desk, by Edwards & Roberts, c1890, 48in (122cm) wide.
£4,250–4,700 / €6,200–6,900
$7,700–8,500 Che

Edwards & Roberts

Edwards & Roberts of London (established 1845) produced furniture of contemporary design as well as reproductions of earlier French and English styles. Their name is associated with high-quality workmanship and materials.

A Georgian-style mahogany partners' desk, c1900, 72in (183cm) wide.
£4,000–4,500 / €5,800–6,600
$7,200–8,100 GEO

An Edwardian oak pedestal desk, the leather-inset top above three frieze drawers, over two banks of three drawers, 41in (104cm) wide.
£230–270 / €340–390
$420–490 CHTR

A Sheraton-style mahogany and inlaid pedestal desk, c1885, 30in (76cm) wide.
£3,000–3,400 / €4,400–4,950
$5,400–6,200 Che

An inlaid mahogany desk, by Maple & Co, with a leather-inset top, c1890, 53in (134.5cm) wide.
£4,300–4,800 / €6,300–7,000
$7,800–8,700 WAA

Maple & Co of Tottenham Court Road, London, became one of Britain's top manufacturers and retailers of the late 19th century and the first half of the 20th century. The company stamped their furniture and it is usually easily identifiable. Their name is associated with good design and quality.

A mahogany and marquetry kidney-shaped desk, in the manner of Edwards & Roberts, c1900, 54¼in (138cm) wide.
£4,300–5,100 / €6,300–7,400
$7,800–9,200 S

An oak desk, the fitted stationery surmount with tambour shutter, the sloping top with a folding writing surface, above a frieze drawer and two side drawers, early 20thC, 31½in (80cm) wide.
£660–790 / €960–1,150
$1,200–1,450 AH

A Victorian walnut partners' pedestal desk, with nine drawers to one side and three drawers with cupboards to the reverse, c1890, 60¼in (153cm) wide.
£1,650–1,950 / €2,400–2,850
$3,000–3,550 S(O)

A Louis XVI-style gilt-bronze and porcelain-mounted mahogany writing desk, by Edmond Poteau, stamped, French, Paris, c1890, 41in (104cm) wide.
£2,650–3,150 / €3,850–4,600
$4,800–5,700 S(NY)

A George III-style satinwood and marquetry Carlton House desk, by Edwards & Roberts, with mahogany banding and stringing, stamped, c1905, 54in (137cm) wide.
£15,600–18,700 / €22,800–27,300
$28,200–34,000 S

An Edwardian inlaid rosewood cylinder desk, 30in (76cm) wide.
£1,800–2,000 / €2,600–2,900
$3,250–3,600 WAA

FURNITURE

Dumb Waiters

A George III mahogany dumb waiter, with three tiers, 45¾in (116cm) high.
£1,050–1,250
€1,500–1,800
$1,900–2,250 DN(BR)

A pair of mahogany three-tier dumb waiters, Irish, c1790, 56in (142cm) high.
£11,700–13,000
€17,100–19,000
$21,200–23,500 GEO

A William IV dumb waiter, with three adjustable tiers, 26in (66cm) diam.
£730–870 / €1,050–1,250
$1,300–1,550 DA

A mahogany dumb waiter, c1900, 30in (76cm) high.
£300–350 / €440–510
$540–630 QA

Etagères

Two japanned *étagères*, with four tiers, decorated with painted lines, repainted, one early 19thC, 60¾in (154.5cm) high.
£9,000–10,800 / €13,100–15,800
$16,300–19,500 S

◄ **A Biedermeier walnut corner *étagère*,** with six tiers, northern European, c1840, 82¾in (210cm) high.
£820–980
€1,200–1,450
$1,450–1,750
S(Am)

A kingwood and fruitwood *étagère*, with gilt-metal mounts, the three tiers inlaid with flowers on an ebonized ground, French, late 19thC, 28in (71cm) high.
£330–390 / €480–570
$600–710 DN

Hall Stands

◄ **A Victorian cast-iron hall stand,** 81in (205.5cm) high.
£760–910 / €1,100–1,300
$1,400–1,650 Mit

► **A Victorian cast-iron hall stand,** by Yates, Haywood & Drabble, with nine coat hooks, two stick/umbrella divisions and a removable drip pan, 71¼in (181cm) high.
£640–760 / €930–1,100
$1,150–1,350 DN

A late Victorian carved oak hall stand, with a central mirror over a shelf, the base with a drawer, shelf and double cupboard flanked by umbrella stands, 97¼in (247cm) high.
£750–900 / €1,100–1,300
$1,350–1,600 RTo

Jardinières

A mahogany jardinière, c1830, 13in (33cm) diam.
£860–1,000
€1,250–1,450
$1,550–1,800 S(O)

A Louis XV-style kingwood jardinière, with a removable top, French, late 19thC, 24in (61cm) wide.
£1,050–1,250
€1,550–1,850
$1,900–2,250 S(O)

An Edwardian giltwood and cane jardinière, 27in (68.5cm) wide.
£1,000–1,150
€1,450–1,700
$1,800–2,100 DEB

◄ **An inlaid mahogany jardinière,** c1900, 36in (91.5cm) high.
£360–400 / €520–580
$650–720 QA

Lowboys

A walnut and crossbanded lowboy, with feather inlay, with three drawers, c1710, 29in (73.5cm) wide.
£1,800–2,000 / €2,600–2,900
$3,250–3,600 DEB

A George III mahogany lowboy, with three drawers, 30in (76cm) wide.
£330–390 / €480–570
$600–710 SWO

A George I walnut lowboy, the quarter-veneered top with herringbone inlay and crossbanded border, above three frieze drawers, on associated legs, 30in (76cm) wide.
£760–910 / €1,100–1,300
$1,400–1,650 HYD

◄ **A George II mahogany lowboy,** with three drawers, 30in (76cm) wide.
£1,050–1,250 / €1,550–1,850
$1,900–2,250 Gam

A Louis XV-style mahogany lowboy, with gilt-bronze flower-cast mounts, Dutch, 18thC, 27½in (70cm) wide.
£2,050–2,450 / €3,000–3,600
$3,700–4,450 S(Am)

A George I walnut and crossbanded lowboy, with herringbone inlay, three drawers, legs replaced, 33½in (85cm) wide.
£1,400–1,650 / €2,050–2,400
$2,550–3,000 G(L)

A George III mahogany lowboy, with three drawers, 28in (71cm) wide.
£820–980 / €1,200–1,450
$1,450–1,750 HYD

Condition

The condition is absolutely vital when assessing the value of an antique. Damaged pieces on the whole appreciate much less than perfect examples. However, a rare desirable piece may command a high price even when damaged.

Miniature Furniture

An oak miniature bureau, with two short over three long drawers, c1830, 20in (51cm) high.
£1,150–1,300 / €1,700–1,900
$2,100–2,350 ⊞ MLL

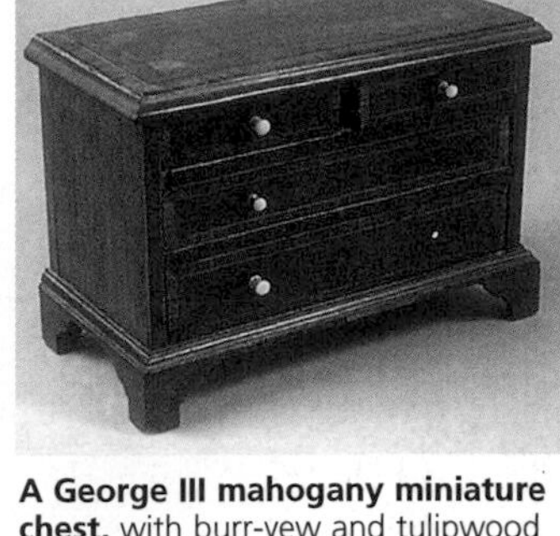

A George III mahogany miniature chest, with burr-yew and tulipwood banding and satinwood spandrels and stringing, lower drawer inscribed 'Coleman 1776', damaged, 8½in (21.5cm) wide.
£760–910 / €1,100–1,300
$1,400–1,650 ⚒ WW

◄ A pine miniature chest of drawers, with two short over three long drawers, c1880, 13in (33cm) high.
£120–135 / €175–195
$220–240 ⊞ Cot

An Edwardian oak and walnut miniature chest, on bun feet, 14in (35.5cm) wide.
£150–165 / €220–250
$270–300 ⊞ DEB

◄ A Sheraton revival miniature inlaid mahogany Wellington chest, the satinwood-crossbanded top with a shell medallion and fan spandrels, above five graduated drawers with brass knobs, late 19thC, 13½in (34.5cm) wide.
£560–670 / €820–980
$1,000–1,200 ⚒ Mit

A mahogany-veneered miniature chest of drawers, with two short over three long drawers, c1820, 14in (35.5cm) wide.
£4,000–4,500 / €5,900–6,600
$7,300–8,100 ⊞ HA

A mahogany and stained pine miniature 'Scotch' chest of drawers, with label inscribed 'These drawers were bought at the Franchise Demonstration which took place at Falkirk on 27 September 1884', inscribed in pencil 'Made by Robert Rae, Falkirk; £1.10s', 15½in (39.5cm) wide.
£1,750–2,100 / €2,550–3,050
$3,150–3,800 ⚒ L&T
Robert Rae was 14, and must therefore have been serving his apprenticeship when he made this chest. In the census of 1891 he was recorded as a chair-maker in Falkirk. The franchise demonstration, organized by the tradesmen of Falkirk, supported the government bill to extend the right of suffrage to all men over 21, which had just been rejected by the House of Lords.

An oak miniature kneehole desk, c1750, 14in (35.5cm) wide.
£990–1,100 / €1,450–1,600
$1,800–2,000 ⊞ SAT

A mahogany teacaddy, in the form of a miniature sideboard, c1880, 15½in (39.5cm) high.
£1,800–2,000 / €2,600–2,900
$3,250–3,600 ⊞ HAA

A mahogany miniature loo table, c1850, 12in (30.5cm) diam.
£1,100–1,250 / €1,600–1,850
$2,000–2,250 ⊞ TIM

Cheval Mirrors

A mahogany cheval mirror, with original mirror plate and brass candle sconces, stamped 'J. J. Byrne, Dublin', Irish, early 19thC, 46in (117cm) wide.
£1,600–1,900
€2,350–2,750
$2,900–3,450 TMA

► **A mahogany cheval mirror,** 19thC, 26¾in (68cm) wide.
£640–760 / €930–1,100
$1,150–1,350 CHTR

The first adjustable dressing mirrors were introduced by the end of the 18th century. The mirror lengths were half or three quarters in size and could be adjusted by either two screw pins situated on the uprights or raised or lowered by concealed straps, similar in design to a louvered window.

Early cheval mirrors reflected the neo-classical taste with urn-shaped finals capping supports that terminated in out swept legs. Later 19th-century versions were heavier in appearance following the taste of the day but by the end of the century the classical style had become fashionable once more. Early frames were made of mahogany but Victorian frames were sometimes constructed of walnut. Edwardian examples often appear with marquetry inlay with rectangular or oval mirror plates.

Original candle sconces will add to the value, as well as mirror plates in good condition and frames with little or no damage.

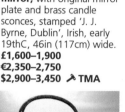

A Victorian mahogany cheval mirror, with original mirror plate, c1845, 30in (76cm) wide.
£1,350–1,500
€1,950–2,200
$2,450–2,700 LGr

◄ **An Edwardian satinwood-inlaid cheval mirror,** 76in (193cm) high.
£1,500–1,800
€2,200–2,650
$2,700–3,250 SWO

Items in the Furniture section have been arranged in date order within each sub-section.

► **An inlaid mahogany cheval mirror,** c1910, 71in (180.5cm) high.
£1,150–1,300
€1,700–1,900
$2,100–2,350 GEO

Dressing Table Mirrors

An early Georgian walnut dressing table mirror, with a later mirror plate, 17¾in (45cm) wide.
£1,650–1,950
€2,400–2,850
$3,000–3,550 TEN

A Hepplewhite-style mahogany dressing table mirror, c1800, 29in (73.5cm) high.
£1,050–1,200 / €1,550–1,750
$1,900–2,150 HA

A mahogany dressing table mirror, in the style of Gillow, c1810, 24in (61cm) wide.
£1,350–1,500 / €1,950–2,200
$2,450–2,700 GGD

A Regency mahogany-veneered dressing table mirror, with tulipwood crossbanding and turned bone finials, handles and feet, 18½in (47cm) wide.
£270–320 / €390–470
$490–580 WW

► **A mahogany-veneered dressing table mirror,** with boxwood edging, early 19thC, 27in (68.5cm) wide.
£230–270 / €340–400
$420–500 WW

A Victorian mahogany dressing table mirror, 25in (63.5cm) high.
£175–195 / €250–280
$310–350 WiB

A mahogany dressing table mirror, c1820, 22in (56cm) wide.
£1,400–1,650 / €2,050–2,400
$2,550–3,000 S(O)

A mahogany dressing table mirror, with boxwood stringing, early 19thC, 17¼in (44cm) wide.
£280–330 / €410–480
$510–600 DN

A mahogany dressing table mirror, c1870, 34in (86.5cm) high.
£360–400 / €520–580
$650–720 QA

◄ **A Victorian mahogany dressing table mirror,** 33in (84cm) high.
£175–195 / €250–280
$310–350 DEB

A walnut dressing table mirror, with gilt-metal mounts, the base inlaid with strapwork marquetry, French, 1850–1900, 28in (71cm) wide.
£1,650–1,950
€2,400–2,850
$3,000–3,550 L&T

◄ **A carved giltwood dressing table mirror,** c1900, 30in (76cm) high.
£610–680 / €890–990
$1,100–1,250 DEB

► **A Queen Anne-style burr-walnut dressing table mirror,** by Whytock & Reid, Scottish, c1920, 43in (109cm) high.
£1,350–1,500
€1,950–2,200
$2,450–2,700 GEO

► **A mahogany dressing table mirror,** c1910, 25in (63.5cm) wide.
£150–165
€210–240
$270–300
WiB

Wall Mirrors

A baroque ebonized and parcel-gilt wall mirror, some damage, German, 17thC, 30¾in (78cm) wide.
£2,600–3,100 / €3,800–4,550
$4,700–5,600 ⚒ S(Am)

► **A William and Mary walnut cushion-framed wall mirror,** with original mirror plate, 12in (30.5cm) wide.
£700–840 / €1,000–1,200
$1,250–1,500 ⚒ G(L)

A japanned mirror, with an etched mirror plate, some damage, Continental, late 17thC, 17¾in (45cm) wide.
£290–340 / €420–500
$520–620 ⚒ SWO

A giltwood wall mirror, pediment replaced, early 18thC, 51in (129.5cm) high.
£4,400–4,900
€6,400–7,200
$8,000–8,900 ⊞ GGD

A Queen Anne walnut wall mirror, the fret-cut pediment over an original plate, 17½in (44.5cm) wide.
£330–390 / €480–570
$600–700 ⚒ G(L)

Miller's Compares

I. A giltwood and gesso wall mirror, with a bevelled mirror plate, regilded, c1730, 24in (61cm) wide.
£7,800–9,300
€11,400–13,600
$14,100–16,800 ⚒ S

II. A giltwood and gesso wall mirror, with a bevelled mirror plate, regilded, c1730, 24½in (62cm) wide.
£3,600–4,300
€5,300–6,300
$6,500–7,800 ⚒ S

Although these two wall mirrors are not identical, they are made in a similar style and are of equally good craftsmanship. However, Item I is a more aesthetically pleasing and well-balanced example of a George II mirror. Another reason that it sold for so much more than Item II could be that more than one prospective purchaser was determined to acquire it.

A George II giltwood wall mirror, in the style of William Kent, with shell and scrolled acanthus leaf cresting and apron with an egg-and-dart border, plate possibly later, candle sconces missing, 28¼in (72cm) wide.
£940–1,100
€1,350–1,600
$1,700–2,000 ⚒ DN(BR)

A carved giltwood mirror, in the style of Abraham Swan, c1740, 35in (89cm) wide.
£16,500–18,500
€24,100–27,000
$29,900–33,000 ⊞ GGD
Abraham Swan was an 18th-century wood carver.

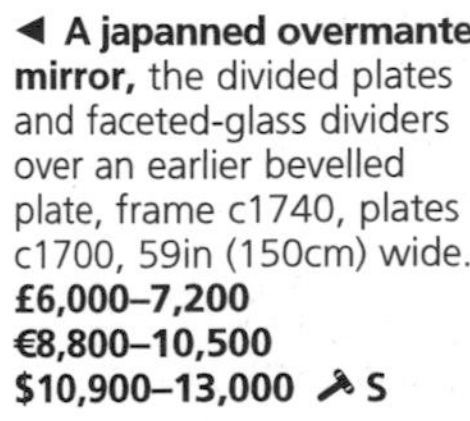

◄ **A japanned overmantel mirror,** the divided plates and faceted-glass dividers over an earlier bevelled plate, frame c1740, plates c1700, 59in (150cm) wide.
£6,000–7,200
€8,800–10,500
$10,900–13,000 ⚒ S

A rococo-style giltwood wall mirror, by Johan Åkerblad, damaged, later mirror plate, signed, Swedish, date stamp for 1774, 16½in (42cm) wide.
£2,250–2,700
€3,300–3,950
$4,050–4,900 ⚒ BUK
Johan Åkerblad was a master cabinet-maker in Stockholm from 1758 to 1799.

A Chippendale-style carved giltwood and gesso wall mirror, with acanthus leaf, C-scroll and rocaille cresting, some restoration, early 19thC, 24in (61cm) wide.
£2,500–2,850
€3,650–4,150
$4,550–5,200 ⊞ JC

A gilt gesso convex wall mirror, with gilt ball decoration within beaded and foliate borders, 19thC, 21½in (54.5cm) diam.
£290–340 / €420–500
$520–620 ⚒ NSal

A Regency giltwood and gesso convex wall mirror, with an eagle surmount flanked by sea serpents, the twin candle sconces with crystal nozzles, 40¼in (102cm) wide.
£3,000–3,600 / €4,400–5,300
$5,400–6,500 ⚒ L&T

A Regency giltwood convex mirror, by Thomas Fentham, with an ebonized slip, the base with carved leaves and pineapple pendant, the reverse with paper label 'Thomas Fentham No. 136, Strand, Nr. Somerset House', surmount missing, painted later, 29¼in (74.5cm) diam.
£940–1,100 / €1,350–1,600
$1,700–2,000 ⚒ WW
Thomas Fentham was a carver, gilder, glass grinder and picture frame maker. He traded from 136 Strand, London, between 1794 and 1820.

A carved giltwood overmantel mirror, 19thC, 65½in (166.5cm) wide.
£3,600–4,300 / €5,300–6,300
$6,500–7,800 ⚒ HOK

A Regency giltwood and gesso overmantel mirror, with three bevelled plates enclosed by acanthus-topped columns, 55½in (141cm) wide.
£520–620 / €760–910
$940–1,100 ⚒ DD

A Regency giltwood overmantel, the moulded and ball-decorated cornice over a triple mirror plate flanked by column pilasters with leaf capitals, 56¼in (143cm) wide.
£610–730 / €890–1,050
$1,100–1,300 ⚒ SWO

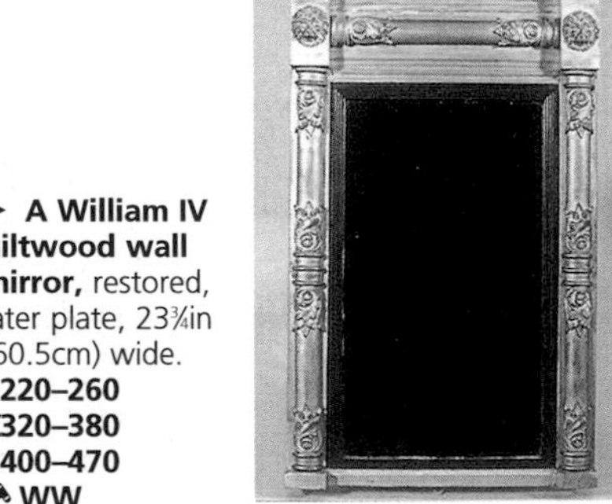

► **A William IV giltwood wall mirror,** restored, later plate, 23¾in (60.5cm) wide.
£220–260
€320–380
$400–470
⚒ WW

◄ **A rococo-style carved giltwood and gesso wall mirror,** the pierced scrolling frame decorated with *ho-o* birds, 19thC, 34¼in (87cm) wide.
£2,000–2,400 / €2,900–3,500
$3,600–4,350 ⚒ S(O)

A gilt gesso and carved wood wall mirror, with flower scroll and foliate decoration, the plate with bevelled glass and flanked by female heads, 19thC, 36in (91.5cm) wide.
£1,300–1,550 / €1,900–2,250
$2,350–2,800 ⚒ E

A giltwood wall mirror, French, 19thC, 21¾in (55.5cm) wide.
£1,300–1,550
€1,900–2,250
$2,350–2,800 S(O)

An ebonized and embossed gilt-metal wall mirror, the crest with foliate scrolls and flowerheads, the bevelled plate enclosed by four smaller plates, Continental, 19thC, 40½in (103cm) wide.
£1,050–1,250
€1,550–1,850
$1,900–2,250 DN

A carved giltwood wall mirror, c1850, 62in (157.5cm) high.
£3,150–3,500
€4,600–5,100
$5,700–6,300 GEO

A rococo-style giltwood wall mirror, the frame decorated with fruit and flora and an open foliate- and scroll-carved crest, probably American, 1850–1875, 43in (109cm) wide.
£890–1,050
€1,300–1,550
$1,600–1,900 NOA

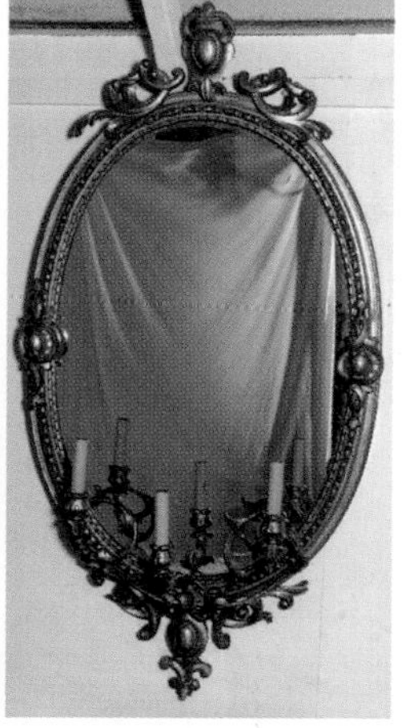

A carved wood and gesso wall mirror, with three candle sconces, c1890, 53in (134.5cm) high.
£1,650–1,850
€2,400–2,700
$3,000–3,350 GEO

► **A carved giltwood and gesso wall mirror,** Italian, Rome, c1880, 19¾in (50cm) wide.
£1,800–2,150
€2,650–3,150
$3,250–3,900 S(O)

A Victorian gilt gesso overmantel mirror, with shell surmount and open scroll corner brackets, 48in (122cm) wide.
£400–480 / €580–700
$720–870 NSal

A Victorian giltwood and gesso overmantel mirror, the frame centred by a heraldic shield, the mirrored side panels with porcelain plaques painted with classical female profile portraits, 84½in (214.5cm) wide.
£2,250–2,700 / €3,300–3,950
$4,050–4,900 M

A wall mirror, with an oil on canvas panel depicting a river landscape above a mirror plate, the frame moulded with leaves and paterae, Continental, late 19thC, 28¾in (73cm) wide.
£880–1,050
€1,300–1,550
$1,600–1,900 DN

A giltwood and gesso overmantel mirror, with a pierced ribbon surmount, the plate with bevelled line decoration, c1900, 72in (183cm) wide.
£230–270 / €340–400
$420–500 PFK

► **A rococo-style carved giltwood wall mirror,** with floral decoration and original bevelled plate, c1930, 22in (56cm) wide.
£810–900 / €1,200–1,350
$1,450–1,650 LGr

Pedestals & Columns

A pair of baroque carved giltwood columns, with Corinthian capitals, Italian, 18thC, 55in (140.5cm) high.
£2,250–2,700
€3,300–3,950
$4,050–4,900 S(Am)

A pair of ormolu-mounted satinwood pedestals, with marble tops, 19thC, 41in (104cm) high.
£2,800–3,350
€4,100–4,900
$5,100–6,100 BWL

A late Victorian Sheraton revival satinwood and chequer-banded pedestal, with painted decoration, 44in (112cm) high.
£530–630 / €770–920
$960–1,150 DN

A carved marble pedestal, late 19thC, 43¾in (111cm) high.
£1,000–1,200
€1,450–1,750
$1,800–2,150 DN

Screens

A japanned leather four-fold screen, decorated with figures in a stylized landscape, 19thC, 78¼in (199cm) high.
£1,050–1,250
€1,550–1,850
$1,900–2,250 S(O)

A canvas six-fold screen, painted with chinoiserie decoration after Pillement, the reverse simulating damask, 19thC, 72in (183cm) high.
£4,900–5,900 / €7,200–8,600
$8,900–10,700 S(NY)
Jean Baptiste Pillement was a French rococo-style painter of the 18th century.

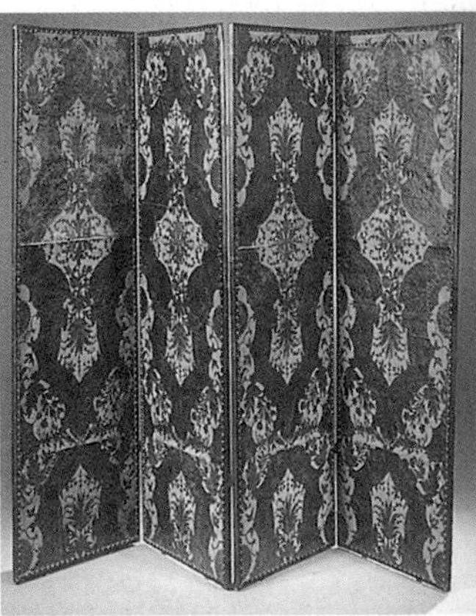

A leather four-fold screen, applied with gilt-leather fragments, Spanish or Dutch, 19thC, 73¾in (187.5cm) wide.
£2,250–2,700 / €3,300–3,950
$4,050–4,900 S(Am)

◄ **A painted four-fold screen,** decorated with a harvest scene, signed 'Espie', c1880, 69in (175.5cm) high.
£660–790 / €960–1,150
$1,200–1,450 BWL

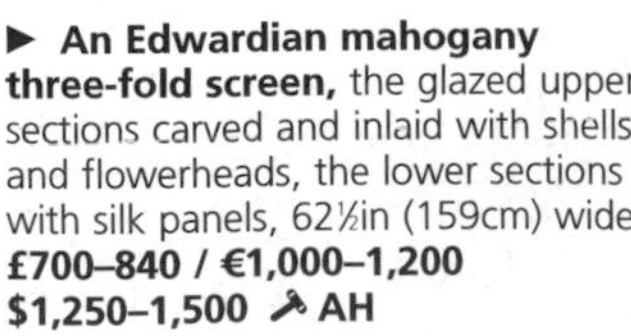

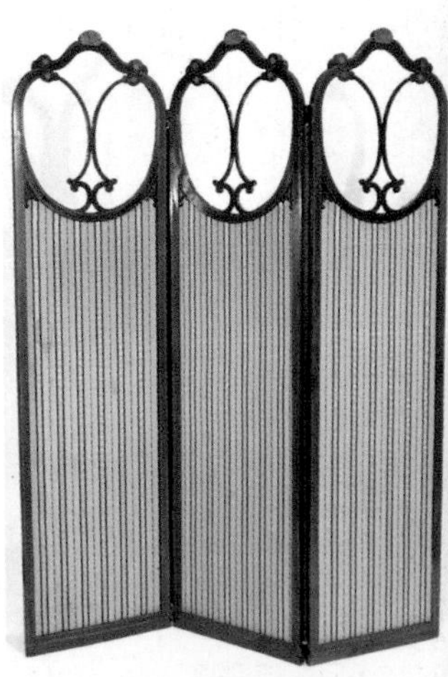

► **An Edwardian mahogany three-fold screen,** the glazed upper sections carved and inlaid with shells and flowerheads, the lower sections with silk panels, 62½in (159cm) wide.
£700–840 / €1,000–1,200
$1,250–1,500 AH

Firescreens

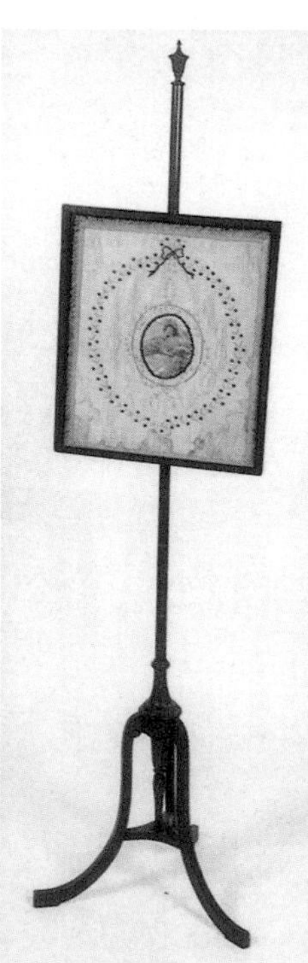

A late George III painted satinwood pole screen, with a silkwork and sarcenet glazed panel, 65in (165cm) high.
£350–420 / €510–610
$630–760 HYD

A walnut pole screen, with a woolwork panel in a scroll-mounted frame, mid-19thC, 68in (172.5cm) high.
£320–380 / €470–550
$580–690 PF

► **A Victorian carved pole screen,** with a brass finial and woolwork panel, 57in (145cm) high.
£3,350–3,700
€4,900–5,400
$6,000–6,700 ⊞ DEB

A carved rosewood pole screen, c1830, 60in (152.5cm) high.
£630–700 / €900–1,000
$1,100–1,250 ⊞ GGD

A Victorian mahogany fire screen, with a Berlinwork panel, the pierced frame on turned columns, 51½in (131cm) high.
£400–480 / €580–700
$720–870 G(B)

A mahogany pole screen, Scottish, c1830, 57in (145cm) high.
£760–850 / €1,100–1,250
$1,400–1,550 ⊞ GEO

A Victorian carved and turned rosewood fire screen, with a tapestry panel, 25½in (65cm) wide.
£300–360 / €440–530
$540–650 WilP

A Victorian mahogany fire screen, with a folding shelf and sliding tapestry panel, 19½in (49.5cm) wide.
£175–210 / €260–310
$320–380 AH

A rosewood pole screen, with a woolwork tapestry panel, c1835, 62in (157.5cm) high.
£630–700 / €900–1,000
$1,100–1,250 ⊞ DEB

A Victorian mahogany fire screen, with a needlework panel within a pierced scroll frame, 56in (142cm) high.
£350–420 / €510–610
$630–760 BWL

A Victorian oak fire screen, with a gros point needlework panel within a pierced scroll-carved frame, 44½in (113cm) wide.
£340–400 / €500–580
$620–720 TRM(E)

Settees & Sofas

A walnut canapé, losses, French, 1700–50, 57in (145cm) wide.
£3,250–3,900 / €4,750–5,700
$5,900–7,100 S(P)

A Gustavian painted and gilt sofa, Swedish, Stockholm, 1780s, 80¼in (204cm) wide.
£4,100–4,900 / €6,000–7,200
$7,400–8,900 BUK

A George III Hepplewhite-style mahogany sofa, the front legs carved with stylized anthemia, 84in (213.5cm) wide.
£1,050–1,250 / €1,550–1,850
$1,900–2,250 HYD

A mahogany sofa, with shaped back and scroll arms, c1800, 85in (216cm) wide.
£6,100–6,800 / €8,900–9,900
$11,000–12,300 HA

A mahogany chair back settee, with a drop-in seat, c1770, 71¼in (181cm) wide.
£7,200–8,600 / €10,500–12,600
$13,000–15,600 S

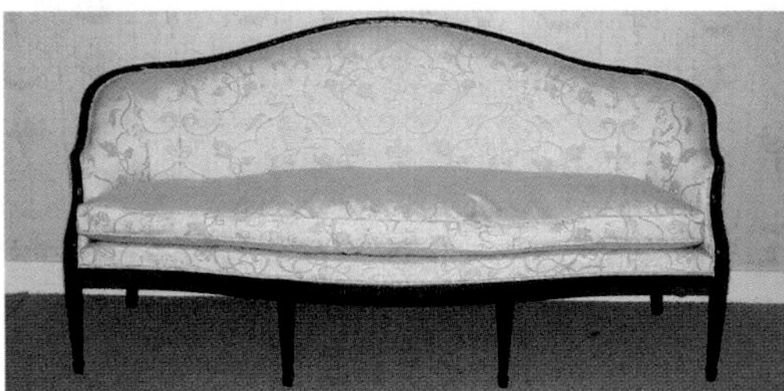

A mahogany sofa, the top rail and arms carved with ribbon and flower decoration, c1780, 80in (203cm) wide.
£17,100–19,000 / €25,000–27,700
$30,000–34,000 HA

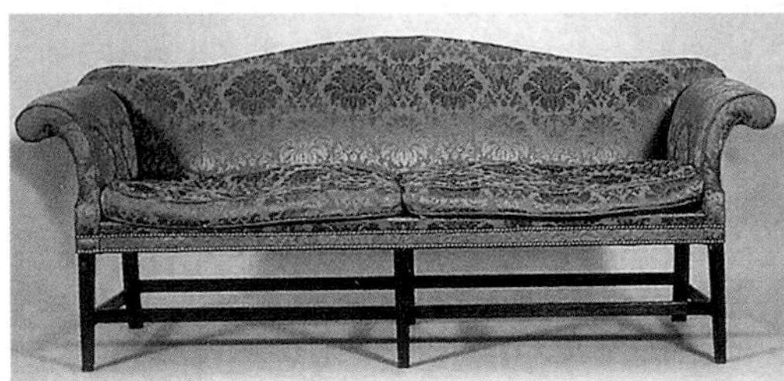

A George III settee, with serpentine back and scroll arms, on mahogany legs, 89in (226cm) wide.
£2,350–2,800 / €3,450–4,100
$4,250–5,100 WW

► **A George III mahogany settee,** upholstered in Berlinwork needlepoint, on acanthus-carved cabriole legs, 46½in (118cm) wide.

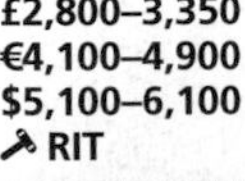

£2,800–3,350
€4,100–4,900
$5,100–6,100
RIT

A mahogany-veneered settee, stamped 'B. B. & Co, Patent', early 19thC, 78in (198cm) wide.
£610–730 / €890–1,050
$1,100–1,300 WW

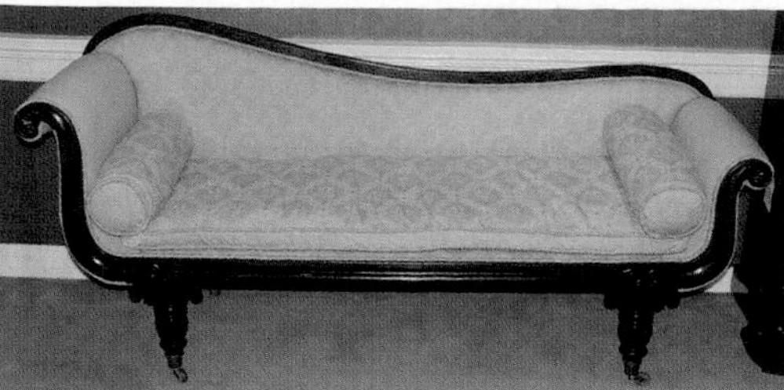

◄ **A mahogany sofa,** c1830, 78in (198cm) wide.
£1,050–1,200 / €1,550–1,750
$1,900–2,150 ⊞ GGD

A Grecian-style giltwood sofa, c1830, 72in (183cm) wide.
£2,150–2,400 / €3,150–3,500
$3,900–4,350 ⊞ Lfo

A William IV mahogany settee, with a stuff-over back and arms, shell-carved knees and reeded legs, 90in (228.5cm) wide.
£470–560 / €690–820
$850–1,000 ⚒ Mit

A Biedermeier mahogany sofa, the padded back carved with a flowerhead and stylized foliage, with scrolling arm rests, Dutch, mid-19thC, 60½in (153.5cm) wide.
£1,300–1,550 / €1,900–2,250
$2,350–2,800 ⚒ S(Am)

◄ **A mahogany settee,** the scroll back carved with acanthus, fruit and foliage, c1850, 78¾in (200cm) wide.
£880–1,050 / €1,300–1,550
$1,600–1,900 ⚒ WL

A mahogany sofa, on cabriole legs, c1860, 72in (183cm) wide.
£2,900–3,250 / €4,250–4,750
$5,200–5,900 ⊞ WAA

A Victorian carved rosewood settee, on cabriole legs, 68in (172.5cm) wide.
£2,250–2,500 / €3,300–3,650
$4,050–4,550 ⊞ HA

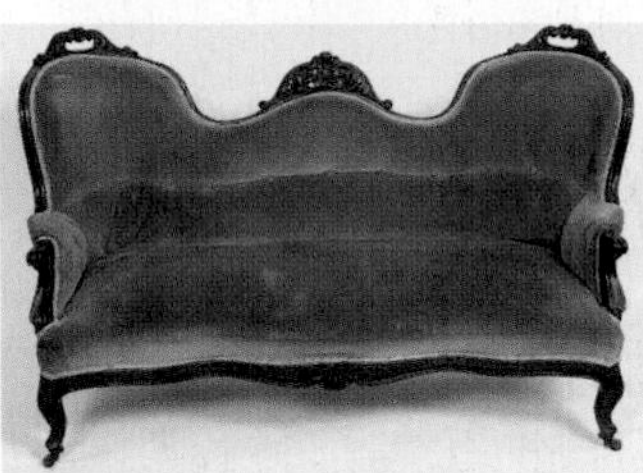

A Victorian carved walnut sofa, with knurled arms and stuff-over seat, 65in (165cm) wide.
£230–270 / €340–390
$420–490 ⚒ CHTR

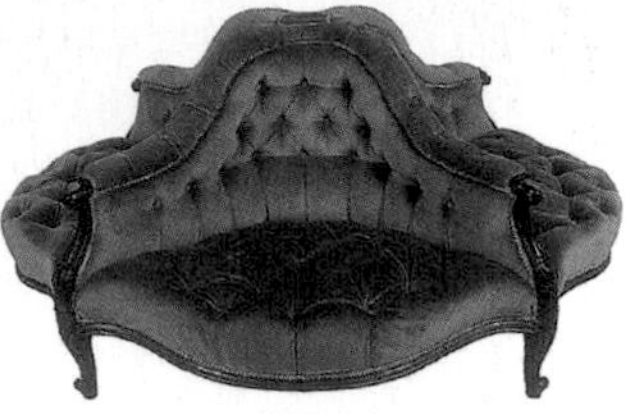

A Victorian rosewood conversation sofa, with buttoned upholstery, the four sections with foliate-carved arm supports and cabriole legs, 72in (183cm) wide.
£1,900–2,250 / €2,750–3,300
$3,450–4,050 ⚒ Bea

A Victorian walnut sofa, with pierced and carved frame and buttoned back, 73in (185.5cm) wide.
£960–1,150 / €1,400–1,650
$1,750–2,100 ⚒ DN

A carved walnut sofa, with buttoned back, c1880, 60in (152.5cm) wide.
£3,150–3,500
€4,600–5,100
$5,700–6,300 ⊞ GEO

A giltwood settee, late 19thC, 51in (129.5cm) wide.
£2,000–2,200 / €2,900–3,200
$3,600–4,000 ⊞ DOA

A pair of walnut chesterfield sofas, by Howard & Sons, Nos. 16287/1269 and 16919/4002, one sofa with fragmentary label, reupholstered with Howard & Sons logo material, late 19thC, 81in (205.5cm) wide.
£9,600–11,500 / €14,000–16,500
$17,400–20,800 ⚒ S

Howard & Sons was a leading firm of London furniture makers, established in 1820. The company exhibited at the Great Exhibition of 1851 and was awarded prize medals at the 1862 and 1878 International Exhibitions and the 1894 Antwerp Exhibition. They also won a gold medal at the Paris Universal Exhibition in 1900.

► **An early 19thC-style walnut and parcel-gilt sofa,** Swedish, late 19thC, 71¾in (182.5cm) wide.
£2,500–3,000
€3,650–4,400
$4,550–5,400 ⚒ S(O)

A Biedermeier-style birchwood sofa, Swedish, 1900–10, 74½in (189cm) wide.
£4,400–4,900 / €6,400–7,200
$8,000–8,900 ⊞ CAV

A mahogany sofa, with serpentine back and scroll-carved cabriole legs, American, early 20thC, 79½in (202cm) wide.
£840–1,000 / €1,250–1,450
$1,500–1,800 ⚒ DN

Shelves

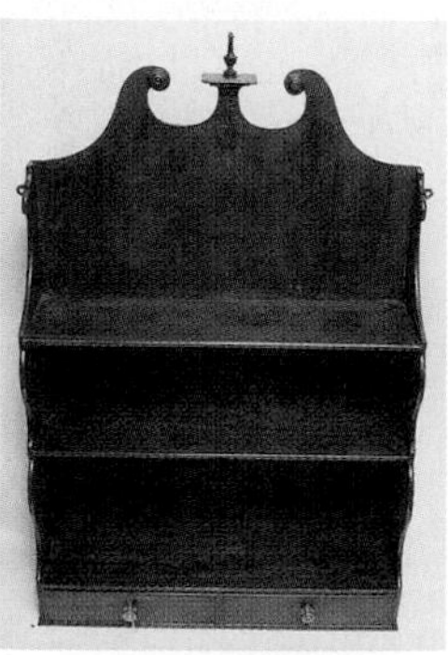

A mahogany hanging shelf, with swan-neck pediment and drawer, c1790, 37½in (95.5cm) high.
£740–830 / €1,050–1,200
$1,350–1,500 ⊞ F&F

► **A George III mahogany three-tier hanging shelf,** with pierced fret-cut sides, 28in (71cm) wide.
£540–640 / €790–930
$980–1,150 ⚒ G(L)

A Regency rosewood shelf, with mirror back, 23in (58.5cm) wide.
£310–350 / €450–510
$560–630 ⊞ GGD

A George IV rosewood hanging shelf, with graduated tiers, 36in (91cm) wide.
£660–790 / €960–1,150
$1,200–1,450 ⚒ L

A walnut hanging shelf, with three tiers, c1840, 20in (51cm) high.
£280–320 / €400–460
$500–570 ⊞ F&F

A Victorian gilt-gesso hanging shelf, with three graduated tiers and a plaque inscribed 'C. Nosett, Carver and Gilder, Oxford St,' 18½in (47cm) wide.
£280–330 / €410–480
$510–600 ⚒ DN

A Victorian mahogany hanging shelf, with three tiers on turned column supports, 30in (76cm) wide.
£260–310 / €380–450
$470–560 ⚒ SWO

Sideboards

A George III boxwood-strung mahogany serpentine sideboard, the stage with tambour drawers above two drawers with inlaid panels, flanked by drawers including a cellaret, 78¾in (200cm) wide.
£1,500–1,800 / €2,200–2,650
$2,700–3,250 ⚒ TRM(E)

Items in the Furniture section have been arranged in date order within each sub-section.

► **A George III mahogany sideboard,** with a frieze drawer, the pot cupboard with a fall-front, 60in (153cm) wide.
£2,250–2,700 / €3,300–3,900
$4,000–4,800 ⚒ L

A George III mahogany breakfront serpentine sideboard, inlaid with harewood banding and satinwood stringing, brass rail missing, 59in (150cm) wide.
£2,100–2,500 / €3,050–3,650
$3,800–4,550 ⚒ F&C

A George III boxwood- and ebony-strung mahogany bowfronted sideboard, the central drawer flanked by a cellaret drawer and two small drawers, 59¾in (152cm) wide.
£3,200–3,800 / €4,650–5,500
$5,800–6,900 ⚒ DN

◄ **A George III boxwood-strung mahogany bowfronted sideboard,** with an arrangement of four crossbanded drawers, one a deep drawer simulating two drawers, 58in (147.5cm) wide.
£2,350–2,800
€3,450–4,100
$4,250–5,100 Bea

A Hepplewhite-style mahogany-veneered sideboard, c1790, 34in (86.5cm) wide.
£2,500–2,800 / €3,650–4,100
$4,550–5,100 ⊞ GGD

► **A mahogany bowfronted sideboard,** inlaid with boxwood and ebony stringing and crossbanded in kingwood, the central drawer above an arched apron, flanked by drawers and a cellaret, c1790, 63in (160cm) wide.
£8,500–9,500
€12,400–13,900
$15,400–17,200 ⊞ JC

A mahogany demi-lune sideboard, with boxwood and ebony stringing, the central drawer flanked by two doors, early 19thC, 48in (122cm) wide.
£660–790 / €960–1,150
$1,200–1,450 G(L)

A late George III mahogany bowfronted sideboard, the frieze drawer flanked by two drawers, each simulating two short drawers, one fitted for bottles, 58in (147.5cm) wide.
£1,650–1,950 / €2,400–2,850
$3,000–3,550 HYD

A George III mahogany bowfronted sideboard, with a short drawer above a cupboard and a deep drawer simulating two drawers, 72in (183cm) wide.
£1,650–1,950 / €2,400–2,850
$3,000–3,550 L

A Regency mahogany barrel-fronted sideboard, with inlaid ebonized stringing, the two frieze drawers flanked by a deep drawer and cupboard door, handles replaced, 60in (152.5cm) wide.
£1,800–2,150 / €2,650–3,150
$3,250–3,900 WW

A mahogany bowfronted sideboard, with ebony stringing and cast-brass lion-paw feet, c1815, 81in (205.5cm) wide.
£30,000–34,000 / €44,000–50,000
$54,000–63,000 ⊞ HA
This substantial sideboard with its magnificent cast-brass lion-paw feet is in original condition, retaining all of its original ebony inlay and brass handles. Such pieces will always command a premium.

► **A mahogany bowfronted sideboard,** the central drawer flanked by two deep drawers, c1815, 54in (137cm) wide.
£3,800–4,250
€5,500–6,200
$6,900–7,700
⊞ WAA

Prices

The price ranges quoted in this book reflect the average price a purchaser might expect to pay for a similar item. The price will vary according to the condition, rarity, size, popularity, provenance, colour and restoration of the item, and this must be taken into account when assessing values. Don't forget that if you are selling it is quite likely that you will be offered less than the price range.

A Regency mahogany sideboard, with stringing, the shaped back with brass appliqués of classical maidens, the two frieze drawers flanked by cupboards, on turned legs with brass paw feet, 93in (236cm) wide.
£3,750–4,500 / €5,500–6,600
$6,800–8,100 ⚒ TEN

A late Regency mahogany sideboard, with a marble top above two frieze drawers, the two doors with grille and fabric panels flanked by turned columns, 62½in (159cm) wide.
£700–840 / €1,050–1,250
$1,250–1,500 ⚒ E

A mahogany sideboard, attributed to Williams & Gibton, with an acanthus-carved scroll-crested back, the central bowed section with two frieze drawers, the pedestals with moulded tops above drawers and doors, Irish, 91¾in (233cm) wide.
£5,200–6,200 / €7,600–9,000
$9,400–11,200 ⚒ HOK

Mack, Williams & Gibton was the leading firm of cabinet-makers in Dublin in the 19th century, and were appointed upholsterers and cabinet-makers to the King in 1806. On the death of John Mack in 1829, the firm traded as Williams & Gibton until 1844 when William Gibton died. The company continued in business under the name Williams & Sons until 1952.

◄ **A William IV flame mahogany breakfront sideboard,** with three *bombé* drawers and three doors, 62in (157.5cm) wide.
£2,700–3,000
€3,950–4,400
$4,900–5,400
⊞ GGD

► **A Regency mahogany sideboard,** the central drawer flanked by two deep drawers, 54in (137cm) wide.
£1,600–1,800
€2,350–2,650
$2,900–3,250
⊞ NAW

◄ **A Regency mahogany and brass-strung sideboard,** with a brass gallery, the upper section with tambour doors and rosewood panels, the base with a frieze drawer flanked by drawers, Scottish, 78¼in (199cm) wide.
£3,400–4,050
€4,950–5,900
$6,200–7,300 ⚒ L&T

► **A George IV mahogany bowfronted sideboard,** with crossbanding and line inlay, the frieze drawer flanked by two deep side drawers, 47in (119.5cm) wide.
£1,200–1,400
€1,750–2,050
$2,150–2,550
⚒ WW

A William IV mahogany pedestal sideboard, the semi-bowed top above a central drawer flanked by two further drawers, each above a panelled door flanked by spiral-carved columns, 66¼in (168.5cm) wide.
£1,900–2,250 / €2,750–3,300
$3,450–4,050 ≯ L&T

A Victorian carved mahogany sideboard, with applied moulding to the panelled back, the breakfront top fitted with a serpentine frieze drawer above two panelled cupboard doors, flanked by panelled doors with applied mouldings enclosing drawers and pull-out trays, 80in (203cm) wide.
£760–910 / €1,100–1,300
$1,400–1,650 ≯ Mit

A late Victorian pollarded oak sideboard, the base with three drawers over cupboards and a recess, stamped 'Waring & Sons, 44 Bold Street, Liverpool', 87½in (222,5cm) wide.
£940–1,100 / €1,350–1,600
$1,700–2,000 ≯ PFK
Waring & Sons merged with Gillows of Lancaster in 1897.

A coromandel and line-inlaid mahogany sideboard, by Gillows of Lancaster, the raised back with a mirror above a shelf and fabric panels, the base with three drawers above a cupboard with two glazed doors, flanked by panelled doors, 19thC, 71in (180.5cm) wide.
£640–760 / €930–1,100
$1,150–1,350 ≯ E

An oak bowfronted sideboard, with applied carving, 1850–1900, 59in (150cm) wide.
£500–600 / €730–880
$910–1,100 ≯ JAA

A carved oak sideboard, with a marble top, c1870, 62in (157.5cm) wide.
£4,250–4,750 / €6,200–6,900
$7,700–8,600 ⊞ MTay

A Classical revival mahogany sideboard, the panelled raised back flanked by scroll supports, the base with moulded drawers over cupboard doors flanked by scroll columns, American, mid-19thC, 56¾in (144cm) wide.
£600–720 / €880–1,050
$1,100–1,300 ≯ NOA

A Gothic revival oak sideboard, in the style of Bruce Talbert, 19thC, 77in (195.5cm) wide.
£2,700–3,000 / €3,950–4,400
$4,900–5,400 ⊞ APO

A Victorian mahogany sideboard, the canopy top above a mirrored back with a shelf, the base with two drawers above two doors flanked by panelled doors, 66½in (169cm) wide.
£440–520 / €640–760
$800–940 ≯ DA

A pollarded oak sideboard, c1890, 73in (185.5cm) wide.
£990–1,100 / €1,450–1,600
$1,800–2,000 ⊞ QA

► **An Edwardian inlaid mahogany sideboard,** with two frieze drawers above two panelled doors, 59¾in (152cm) wide.
£220–260
€320–380
$400–470
≯ CHTR

Boot & Whip Stands

◄ **A mahogany boot and whip stand,** with a brass handle, c1800, 40in (101.5cm) high.
£580–650 / €850–950
$1,050–1,200 ⊞ WAA

A mahogany boot and whip stand, with a brass handle, c1850, 26in (66cm) wide.
£900–1,000 / €1,300–1,450
$1,600–1,850 ⊞ WAA

◄ **A mahogany boot and whip stand,** 19thC, 30in (76cm) wide.
£450–500 / €660–730
$820–910 ⊞ Lfo

Hat, Coat & Stick Stands

◄ **A coat, hat and stick stand,** probably stained pine, carved in the form of a bear holding a tree, damaged, German, Bavarian, c1900, 76¼in (193.5cm) high.
£3,650–4,350
€5,300–6,400
$6,600–7,900 ⚒ DN

► **A lacquered wood coat stand,** 19thC, 67in (170cm) high.
£2,300–2,750
€3,350–4,000
$4,150–5,000 ⚒ S(P)

An Edwardian brass corner stick stand, with a lift-out tray, 25½in (65cm) high.
£190–220 / €280–320
$340–400 ⚒ WW

A Black Forest walnut hat and umbrella stand, carved with a bear holding a tree, German, 19thC, 74in (188cm) high.
£9,200–10,200
€13,400–14,900
$16,700–18,500 ⊞ NART

An antler stick stand, c1890, 39in (99cm) high.
£2,700–3,000
€3,950–4,400
$4,900–5,400 ⊞ MSh

► **A Victorian mahogany revolving stick stand,** on a turned column, 29½in (75cm) high.
£440–520 / €640–760
$800–940 ⚒ SWO

► **A William IV mahogany coat stand,** with five cast-iron branches, 61¾in (157cm) high.
£500–600 / €730–880
$910–1,100 ⚒ SWO

Kettle & Urn Stands

A George III mahogany urn stand, crossbanded with stringing and parquetry banding, alterations, 13in (33cm) wide.
£1,050–1,250
€1,550–1,850
$1,900–2,250 AH

A rosewood kettle stand, in the style of Gillows, on an acanthus-carved tripod base, 19thC, 28¾in (73cm) high.
£800–960 / €1,200–1,400
$1,450–1,750 G(B)

A walnut kettle stand, with inlaid stringing, with a brass liner and handle, on ball feet, liner and kettle associated, Dutch, 19thC, 17in (43cm) high.
£470–560 / €690–820
$850–1,000 WW

A burr-walnut kettle stand, with boxwood stringing, the top inlaid with a conch shell over a rosewood-crossbanded frieze inset with a candle slide, 19thC, 14in (35.5cm) wide.
£590–700 / €860–1,000
$1,050–1,250 GH

Music Stands

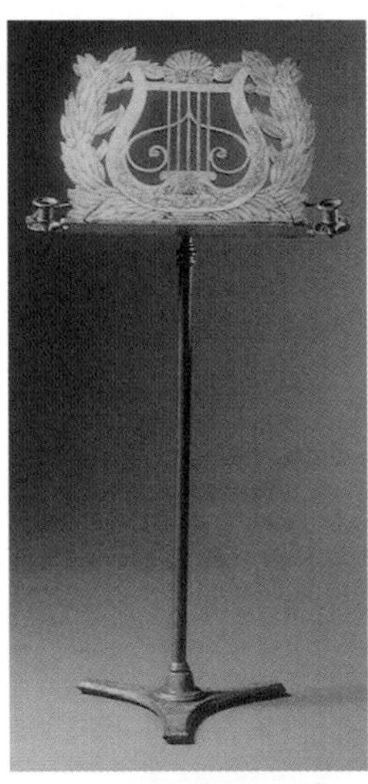

◄ **A simulated maple and parcel-gilt music stand,** attributed to Pierre Erard, the adjustable stand with brass candle arms, c1820, 44½in (113cm) high.
£5,000–6,000
€7,300–8,800
$9,100–10,900 S
Pierre Erard was a pianoforte and music stand maker who traded from 17 Great Marlborough Street, London, between 1826 and 1827, before moving to nearby Little Portland Street in 1837.

A mahogany music stand, the adjustable top with fold-out candle stands, 19thC, top 18in (46cm) square.
£1,150–1,350
€1,700–2,000
$2,100–2,500 HOLL

A rosewood adjustable duet stand, c1840, 43¼in (110cm) high.
£1,300–1,550
€1,900–2,250
$2,350–2,800 S(O)

Miscellaneous Stands

◄ **A Victorian Georgian-style mahogany reading stand,** the line-inlaid top above an adjustable column, 45in (114.5cm) high.
£1,300–1,450
€1,900–2,100
$2,350–2,600 ⊞ LGr

► **A walnut shaving stand,** with a mirror, c1880, 59in (150cm) high.
£2,150–2,400
€3,150–3,500
$3,900–4,350 ⊞ SAW

An inlaid mahogany cake stand, c1900, 30in (76cm) high.
£310–350 / €450–510
$560–630 ⊞ QA

Steps

A set of late George III mahogany steps, 19½in (49.5cm) wide.
£1,300–1,550 / €1,900–2,250
$2,350–2,800 L

A set of mahogany library steps, the treads inset with leather, formerly a step commode, 29in (73.5cm) wide.
£840–1,000 / €1,250–1,450
$1,500–1,800 DN

A set of Regency giltwood bed steps, 25in (63.5cm) wide.
£8,400–10,000 / €12,300–14,600
$15,200–18,100 S
The design of these bed steps derives from an antique marble seat believed to have been supplied by Charles Heathcote Tatham to the Earl of Yarborough at Brocklesby Park, Lincolnshire.

Stools

A George I walnut stool, upholstered in petit point needlework, 22in (56cm) wide.
£7,400–8,900 / €10,800–13,000
$13,400–16,100 S

A mahogany stool, c1720, 21in (53.5cm) wide.
£8,800–9,800 / €12,800–14,300
$15,900–17,700 HWK

A mahogany stool, with needlework upholstery, c1775, 20in (51cm) wide.
£300–330 / €440–490
$540–600 GGD

A mahogany stool, the legs carved with ancanthus-leaf motifs, c1790, 20in (51cm) wide.
£630–700 / €900–1,000
$1,150–1,300 F&F

A Regency giltwood and gesso stool, c1820, 22in (56cm) wide.
£1,300–1,550 / €1,900–2,250
$2,350–2,800 S(O)

◀ **A Georgian mahogany stool,** 21in (53.5cm) wide.
£1,550–1,750 / €2,250–2,550
$2,800–3,150 CRU

A pair of mahogany stools, each with damask upholstery and a scalloped apron, 1825–50, 25½in (65cm) wide.
£310–370 / €450–540
$560–670 NOA

A pair of William IV rosewood footstools, with tapestry upholstery, 12½in (32cm) square.
£350–420 / €510–610
$630–760 DN(BR)

An early Victorian walnut stool, carved with chevron shields, scrolling foliage and berries, the drop-in seat upholstered in floral needlework, 29in (73.5cm) wide.
£880–1,050 / €1,300–1,550
$1,600–1,900 NSal

A pair of early Victorian japanned papier-mâché stools, 19in (48.5cm) high.
£900–1,000 / €1,300–1,450
$1,600–1,800 Lfo

A rococo revival rosewood dressing stool, with an upholstered seat, the carved cross stretcher with a finial, c1850, 36in (91.5cm) wide.
£2,200–2,450 / €3,200–3,600
$4,000–4,450 LGr

A rosewood stool, with woolwork upholstery, 19thC, 21in (53.5cm) wide.
£190–220 / €280–320
$350–400 DEB

A Victorian rosewood stool, with needlework upholstery, 39in (99cm) wide.
£1,750–2,100 / €2,500–3,000
$3,150–3,800 L

A Victorian carved rosewood footstool, 16¼in (41.5cm) wide.
£170–200 / €250–290
$310–360 WW

► **A pair of Victorian rosewood footstools,** each with woolwork upholstery and John Kendell & Co label, 17½in (44.5cm) wide.
£1,750–2,100 / €2,550–3,050
$3,150–3,800 Mit
John Kendell & Co traded in Leeds from 1783 and included the Earl of Harewood among their patrons. They began the practice of labelling their furniture in the 1830s, leaving spaces on the label for a serial number and the names of the craftsmen who produced the piece. The firm was taken over by Martin & Jones in 1863.

A Victorian walnut stool, on carved cabriole legs, 43¼in (110cm) wide.
£1,600–1,900 / €2,350–2,750
$2,900–3,450 SWO

A walnut stool, with carved and moulded cabriole legs, c1860, 37in (94cm) wide.
£2,300–2,600 / €3,350–3,800
$4,150–4,700 HA

◄ **A Victorian walnut dressing stool,** with tapestry upholstery, 32in (81.5cm) wide.
£330–390 / €480–570
$600–710 G(L)

► **A Victorian walnut stool,** with tapestry upholstery, 38in (96.5cm) wide.
£800–960 / €1,200–1,400
$1,450–1,750 AH

A Victorian giltwood stool, with an X-frame, upholstered seat and arms, 30in (76cm) wide.
£760–910 / €1,100–1,300
$1,400–1,650 ⚒ HYD

► **A Queen Anne-style mahogany stool,** the upholstered seat above carved cabriole legs on claw-and-ball feet, c1880, 20in (51cm) wide.
£580–650 / €850–950
$1,050–1,200 ⊞ WAA

◄ **A pair of walnut footstools,** c1870, 11in (28cm) diam.
£310–350 / €450–510
$560–630 ⊞ QA

A pair of upholstered mahogany footstools, c1880, 11in (28cm) wide.
£270–300 / €390–440
$490–550 ⊞ HEM

A painted wood stool, French, c1920, 46½in (118cm) wide.
£1,350–1,500 / €1,950–2,200
$2,450–2,700 ⊞ HA

Music Stools

A Victorian mahogany adjustable piano stool, 12in (30.5cm) diam.
£130–155 / €190–220
$240–280 ⚒ CHTR

A Victorian ebonized and parcel-gilt adjustable piano stool, 18in (45.5cm) high.
£270–300 / €390–440
$490–540 ⊞ DOA

A mahogany and leather piano stool, c1880, 17in (43cm) wide.
£175–200 / €260–290
$320–360 ⊞ HEM

A late Victorian mahogany adjustable piano stool, with Brooks patent mechanism, reupholstered, 20in (51cm) wide.
£490–550 / €720–800
$890–1,000 ⊞ LGr

An inlaid mahogany piano stool, c1900, 22in (56cm) wide.
£240–270 / €350–390
$430–480 ⊞ QA

An Edwardian oak adjustable piano stool, 14in (35.5cm) wide.
£75–85 / €110–125
$135–155 ⊞ WiB

Bedroom Suites

◄ **A Victorian inlaid mahogany bedroom suite,** comprising dressing table with swing mirror, wardrobe with slides and drawers, and washstand with a marble top, dressing table 60in (152.5cm) wide.
£3,500–4,200
€5,100–6,100
$6,300–7,600
BWL

A late Victorian rosewood and marquetry part bedroom suite, comprising triple wardrobe, dressing table, washstand, bedside cabinet and a pair of carved chairs, with label for T. Simpson & Sons, Halifax, wardrobe 76½in (194.5cm) wide.
£3,750–4,500 / €5,500–6,600
$6,800–8,100 AH

◄ **An Edwardian mahogany bedroom suite,** comprising combination wardrobe and kneehole dressing table, wardrobe 69¾in (177cm) wide.
£590–700 / €860–1,000
$1,050–1,250 DA

► **A rosewood bedroom suite,** comprising wardrobe, dressing table and a pair of bedside cabinets, c1890, wardrobe 83in (211cm) high.
£5,400–6,000 / €7,900–8,800
$9,800–10,900 QA

Salon Suites

A carved rosewood salon suite, comprising settee, two armchairs and six side chairs, c1860.
£2,850–3,400 / €4,150–4,950
$5,200–6,200 S(O)

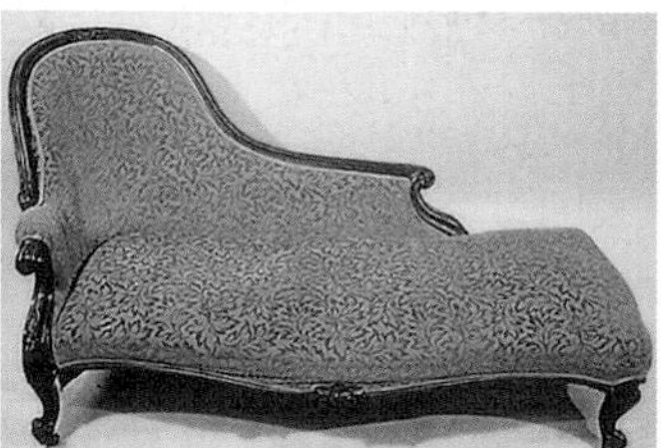

A Victorian walnut upholstered salon suite, comprising chaise longue, one side chair and one armchair, chaise longue 59in (150cm) long.
£760–910 / €1,100–1,300
$1,350–1,600 E

A late Victorian carved mahogany salon suite, comprising two-seater settee, two side chairs, a nursing chair and an open armchair.
£770–920 / €1,100–1,300
$1,400–1,650 AMB

An Edwardian Chippendale-style mahogany salon suite, comprising a settee, two armchairs and four side chairs.
£350–420 / €510–610
$630–760 L&E

A walnut salon suite, with ivory and boxwood inlay, comprising settee, two armchairs and four side chairs, c1905.
£730–870 / €1,050–1,250
$1,300–1,550 WL

Architects' Tables

A mahogany architect's table, with later candle slides and restoration, c1740, 34½in (87.5cm) wide.
£2,750–3,300 / €4,000–4,800
$5,000–6,000 ⚒ S(O)

A mahogany architect's table, the later top inset with leatherette, above two slides and a long frieze drawer, early 19thC, 31¾in (80.5cm) wide.
£260–310 / €380–450
$470–560 ⚒ CHTR

◀ **A Louis XVI mahogany architect's table,** by C. J. Petit, with a drawer and two slides, stamped, 31½in (80cm) wide.
£4,900–5,800 / €7,200–8,500
$8,900–10,500 ⚒ S(P)
Claude Jean Petit, carpenter and cabinet-maker, was working in the late 18th and early 19th centuries.

Breakfast Tables

A George III mahogany breakfast table, the top crossbanded with satinwood and partridgewood, on a gunbarrel pillar and sabre-leg tripod base, 42in (106.5cm) wide.
£2,100–2,500 / €3,050–3,650
$3,800–4,550 ⚒ TEN

A Regency mahogany and satinwood-crossbanded breakfast table, the top later inlaid with a shell, 49½in (125.5cm) wide.
£470–560 / €690–820
$850–1,000 ⚒ DN

A William IV mahogany breakfast table, Irish, possibly Cork, 55in (139.5cm) wide.
£890–1,050 / €1,300–1,550
$1,600–1,900 ⚒ MEA

▶ **A mahogany and tulipwood-crossbanded breakfast table,** c1810, 54¼in (138cm) wide.
£3,450–4,100 / €5,000–6,000
$6,200–7,400 ⚒ S(O)

A Sheraton-style inlaid mahogany breakfast table, with maple crossbanding, late 18thC, 46in (117cm) wide.
£4,300–4,800 / €6,300–7,000
$7,800–8,700 ⊞ HA

A George IV mahogany breakfast table, the tilt top with a figured and crossbanded veneer, damaged, 51½in (131cm) diam.
£770–920 / €1,100–1,300
$1,400–1,650 ⚒ WW

▶ **A Victorian burr-walnut breakfast table,** the quarter-veneered tilt-top above a carved base, 54in (137cm) diam.
£2,450–2,750 / €3,600–4,000
$4,450–5,000 ⊞ LGr

A Federal carved and figured mahogany drop-leaf breakfast table, attributed to Duncan Phyfe, American, New York, c1810, 25in (63.5cm) wide.
£5,900–7,100 / €8,600–10,400
$10,700–12,900 ⚒ S(NY)

Card Tables

Miller's Compares

I. A mahogany serpentine card table, the concertina-action top inset with baize, c1780, 36¼in (92cm) wide.
£2,000–2,400 / €2,900–3,500
$3,600–4,350 ⚒ S(O)

II. A George III mahogany serpentine card table, 31½in (80cm) wide.
£1,050–1,250 / €1,500–1,800
$1,900–2,250 ⚒ S(O)

Item I is of a far superior colour to Item II, and also has attractive egg-and-dart carving to the edge. The legs are also more impressive in appearance. The concertina action of Item I is a sign of quality – when the table is opened out it has legs at each corner rendering it more solid and decorative to look at, whereas Item II has a simple gateleg action.

An inlaid satinwood card table, with a fold-over top, c1790, 29in (73.5cm) high.
£6,300–7,000 / €9,200–10,200
$11,400–12,700 ⊞ HWK

► A Regency mahogany card table, 36in (91.5cm) wide.
£3,150–3,500 / €4,600–5,100
$5,700–6,300 ⊞ GGD

A rosewood card table, c1820, 26in (66cm) wide.
£3,350–3,750 / €4,900–5,500
$6,100–6,800 ⊞ WAA

► A mahogany card table, with a fold-over top, c1820, 36in (91.5cm) wide.
£1,650–1,850 / €2,400–2,700
$3,000–3,350 ⊞ LGr

A mahogany card table, with ebony stringing, the fold-over top with a baize-lined interior, c1810, 36in (91.5cm) wide.
£1,650–1,850 / €2,400–2,700
$3,000–3,350 ⊞ JC

A George III mahogany demi-lune card table, on reeded legs, 37in (94cm) wide.
£2,250–2,500 / €3,300–3,650
$4,050–4,550 ⊞ DOA

A George III satinwood card table, the fold-over top line-inlaid and crossbanded with painted rosewood, damaged, 35¾in (91cm) wide.
£1,050–1,250 / €1,550–1,850
$1,900–2,250 ⚒ G(B)

A Regency mahogany card table, with a fold-over and swivel top, 35¾in (91cm) wide.
£660–790 / €960–1,150
$1,200–1,450 ⚒ AH

A George IV oak card table, the swivel top with bead-and-reel edge over a panelled frieze carved with poppy-head brackets, 36¼in (92cm) wide.
£1,050–1,250 / €1,550–1,850
$1,900–2,250 ⚒ TEN

A William IV mahogany card table, with a fold-over swivel top, 36in (91.5cm) wide.
£700–840 / €1,000–1,200
$1,250–1,500 AH

A Victorian walnut loo table, the burr-walnut top with inlaid decoration and stringing, 58¼in (148cm) wide.
£1,000–1,200 / €1,450–1,750
$1,800–2,150 SWO

A Victorian figured walnut card table, with a fold-over top, 36¼in (92cm) wide.
£410–490 / €600–720
$740–890 L&E

A late Victorian mahogany envelope card table, the hinged top with boxwood stringing, the interior lined with tooled leather, the counter wells above a frieze with one long drawer, 22in (56cm) wide.
£410–490 / €600–720
$740–890 Mit

► **An inlaid walnut card table,** c1890, 36in (91.5cm) wide.
£1,850–2,100 / €2,700–3,050
$3,350–3,800 WAA

A rosewood card table, by T. & G. Seddon, with a fold-out and swivel top, with label, c1840, 36¼in (92cm) wide.
£7,200–8,600 / €10,500–12,600
$13,000–15,600 S(O)

T. & G. Seddon were descendants of the well-reputed cabinet-maker George Seddon. Originally based at the two-acre family site in Aldersgate Street, London, they later moved to Gray's Inn Road.

A pair of Louis Philippe mahogany card tables, each with a fold-over top, French, c1850, 33in (84cm) wide.
£3,000–3,600 / €4,400–5,300
$5,400–6,500 S(O)

A Sheraton revival satinwood parquetry envelope card table, with counter wells, c1870, 23in (58.5cm) wide.
£3,150–3,500 / €4,600–5,100
$5,700–6,300 CRU

A rosewood card table, with a fold-over top and carved lion-paw feet, c1845, 35in (89cm) wide.
£1,200–1,350 / €2,400–2,700
$3,000–3,350 WAA

A rosewood card table, c1850, 34in (86.5cm) wide.
£3,250–3,650 / €4,750–5,300
$5,900–6,600 Man

An inlaid walnut card table, c1880, 34in (86.5cm) wide.
£1,050–1,200 / €1,550–1,750
$1,900–2,150 QA

An inlaid mahogany envelope card table, c1900, 31in (78.5cm) wide.
£800–900 / €1,150–1,300
$1,450–1,650 QA

Centre Tables

◄ **A carved oak centre table,** the marble top above a pierced frieze, the sides carved with stylized scallop shells and bearded masks, joined by an X-stretcher centred by a basket of flowers, French or Belgian, mid-18thC, 44½in (113cm) wide.
£9,000–10,800 / €13,100–15,800
$16,300–19,500 ⚒ S

► **A Regency mahogany centre table,** with a bead-and-reel frieze, 50¾in (129cm) diam.
£1,650–1,950 / €2,400–2,850
$3,000–3,550 ⚒ L&T

A Regency yew-wood centre table, c1815, 28in (71cm) high.
£10,800–12,000 / €15,800–17,500
$19,500–21,700 ⊞ HWK

A mahogany and parcel-gilt centre table, Russian, 1800–25, 45¾in (116cm) diam.
£4,950–5,900 / €7,200–8,600
$9,000–10,700 ⚒ S(NY)

A mahogany tilt-top centre table, with rosewood crossbanding, on four reeded legs, 19thC, 60in (152.5cm) wide.
£1,950–2,300 / €2,850–3,350
$3,550–4,150 ⚒ JM

A satinwood and parquetry centre table, attributed to Ralph Turnbull, the tilt top with mahogany, ebony and palmwood veneers, Jamaican, 1825–50, 53½in (136cm) diam.
£24,000–28,000 / €35,000–41,000
$43,000–51,000 ⚒ S

This type of idiosyncratic furniture, with its unusual exotic veneers, is typical of the work of Ralph Turnbull of Jamaica. Born in 1788 in Scotland, he moved to Jamaica with his two brothers, Thomas and Cuthbert, in the early 19th century. Ralph is the only Turnbull known to have labelled his furniture and he carried out commissions for the Governor of Jamaica, the Marquis of Sligo. By the 1830s, Turnbull had received a grant from the House of Assembly and was employing over 60 journeymen and apprentices. The firm was still operating in the 1870s.

A Gothic revival oak fold-over table, the crossbanded top above a panelled frieze, mid-19thC, 48in (122cm) wide.
£2,350–2,800 / €3,450–4,100
$4,250–5,100 ⚒ L&T

A Regency rosewood centre table, with two drawers, 42in (106.5cm) wide.
£350–420 / €510–610
$630–760 ⚒ AMB

A tigerwood centre table, by Gillingtons of Dublin, with a crossbanded top, stamped, Irish, early 19thC, 35in (89cm) diam.
£2,350–2,800 / €3,450–4,100
$4,250–5,100 ⚒ HOK

Gillingtons were one of the foremost Dublin cabinet-makers from the late 18th century. It was run by John Gillington in partnership with his two sons, George and Samuel. John retired from the company in 1814 and George apparently continued in business alone from 1820 to 1838.

An Empire-style mahogany and parcel-gilt centre table, the stem carved with palm leaves, on winged claw feet, Dutch, c1830, 45in (114.5cm) diam.
£650–780 / €950–1,100
$1,200–1,450 ⚒ S(Am)

A pollarded oak centre table, 19thC, 54in (137cm) wide.
£8,900–9,900 / €13,000–14,500
$16,100–17,900 ⊞ SAW

A mahogany and rosewood-banded centre table, by Strahan of Dublin, stamped, Irish, mid-19thC, 48¾in (124cm) diam.
£1,950–2,300 / €2,850–3,350
$3,550–4,150 HOK

The Dublin cabinet-makers Robert Strahan & Co are listed at various addresses in the city between 1811 and 1867, before finally settling at 135 St Stephen's Green from 1869 to 1969. The company exhibited walnut, marquetry and gilded furniture at the Dublin Great Industrial Exhibition in 1853.

A kingwood marquetry and gilt-bronze centre table, in the manner of Cremer, French, c1860, 63in (160cm) wide.
£6,600–7,900 / €9,600–11,500
$11,900–14,300 S(O)

The marquetry on this centre table bears strong resemblance to the style of Joseph Cremer (1839–78). Cremer was a specialist *marqueteur* who developed a highly distinctive style of inlaid decoration in the middle of the 19th century, drawing upon the late 17th-century and early 18th-century tradition of the Boulle workshops and the emergent naturalistic style of the 1840s. Cremer supplied furniture to Louis Philippe in 1844 and also the King of Holland, exhibiting at the 1852, 1855 and the 1862 International Exhibitions. He also worked in conjunction with André Lemoine who had a Royal Warrant from Napoleon III.

► **A Louis XV-style tulipwood centre table,** probably by Linke, with two drawers and two slides, stamped '6258', French, c1900, 33¾in (86cm) diam.
£2,150–2,550 / €3,150–3,700
$3,900–4,600 S(O)

François Linke had a workshop in the Faubourg Saint Antoine, the centre of the Parisian furniture trade, from c1875. He specialized in the production of luxury furniture, especially in the Louis XVI style.

A giltwood and micromosiac centre table, the marble top centred with a roundel of Romulus and Remus, surrounded by eight views of Italian cities, damaged and restored, with later support, Italian, 1850–75, 45¾in (116cm) diam.
£111,500–134,000
€163,000–196,000
$202,000–243,000 DN

This table would have taken a long time to make and consequently would have been a prestige item even when new. Featuring views of Italian cities that were 'musts' to visit on the Grand Tour, and remain so today.

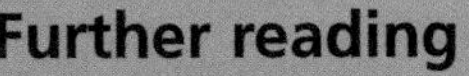

Further reading

Miller's Furniture Antiques Checklist, Miller's Publications, 2001

An ebonized drop-leaf centre table, decorated with floral marquetry and ormolu mounts, Continental, c1860, 22in (56cm) square, folded.
£1,350–1,500 / €1,950–2,200
$2,450–2,700 LGr

A Renaissance revival walnut centre table, with a marble top, American, 1850–75, 35½in (90cm) diam.
£820–980 / €1,200–1,450
$1,500–1,750 NOA

A carved walnut centre table, the leather-inset writing surface above a frieze drawer, Continental, late 19thC, 48¾in (124cm) wide.
£640–760 / €930–1,100
$1,200–1,400 CHTR

A burr-walnut centre table, c1890, 23in (58.5cm) wide.
£1,150–1,300 / €1,700–1,900
$2,100–2,350 Man

An Edwardian inlaid rosewood centre table, 32in (81.5cm) wide.
£1,350–1,550 / €1,950–2,250
$2,450–2,800 MTay

FURNITURE

Console & Pier Tables

A silvered and painted console table, Italian, Parma, 1750–75, 43¾in (111cm) wide.
£4,600–5,500 / €6,700–8,000
$8,300–10,000 S(NY)

A carved oak console table, with a marble top, 19thC, 31½in (80cm) wide.
£1,400–1,650 / €2,050–2,400
$2,500–3,000 S(O)

A carved giltwood console table, with a marble top, Italian, 19thC, 53in (134.5cm) wide.
£3,350–4,000 / €4,900–5,800
$6,100–7,200 S(O)

A George III Sheraton-style mahogany and satinwood pier table, the top inlaid with a fan motif within a crossbanded border, 37in (94cm) wide.
£760–910 / €1,100–1,300
$1,400–1,650 HYD

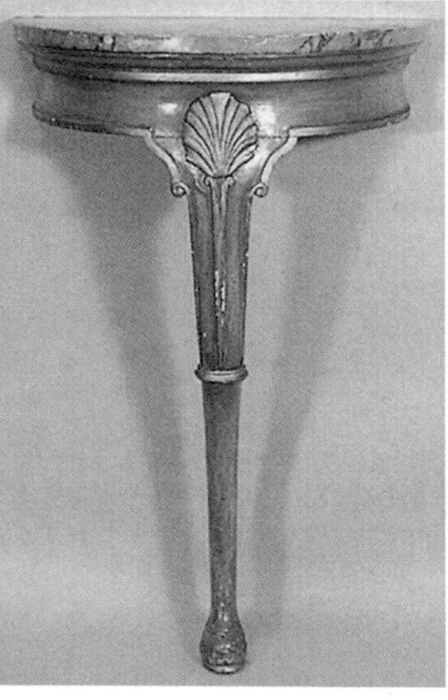

A painted wood demi-lune console table, the simulated marble top above a cabriole leg, 19thC, 22in (56cm) wide.
£220–260 / €320–380
$400–470 WW

A Victorian carved rosewood console table, with a marble top, 36in (91.5cm) wide.
£330–390 / €480–570
$600–710 BWL

◄ **A carved pine and gilt console table,** with a later marble top, Continental, 19thC, 26¾in (68cm) wide.
£400–480 / €580–700
$720–870 SWO

An Empire mahogany pier table, the marble top above a frieze drawer with gilt-metal mounts, French, early 19thC, 41in (104cm) wide.
£1,100–1,300 / €1,600–1,900
$2,000–2,350 HYD

A painted wood console table, with a marble top, French, 19thC, 53in (134.5cm) wide.
£1,400–1,650 / €2,050–2,400
$2,500–3,000 S(O)

A rococo-style ebonized and parcel-gilt console table, the marble top decorated with scrolling leaves, Italian, 19thC, 41in (104cm) wide.
£8,200–9,800 / €12,000–14,300
$14,800–17,700 S(Am)

A gilt and composition pier table, in the manner of Robert Adam, the marble top inlaid with anthemia and scrolling foliage, the frieze with an inset jasper ware panel, c1900, 59½in (151cm) wide.
£3,800–4,550 / €5,500–6,600
$6,900–8,200 S(O)

Dining Tables

A George II mahogany dining table, the turned legs with leaf-carved knees and claw-and-ball feet, 50in (127cm) wide.
£1,650–1,950 / €2,400–2,850
$3,000–3,550 ⚒ HYD

A George III mahogany dining table, with concertina action and three extra leaves, on turned tapering legs, 90¼in (229cm) wide.
£6,300–7,500 / €9,200–11,000
$11,400–13,600 ⚒ SWO

A Louis XVI-style mahogany extending dining table, with three extra oak leaves and three extra mahogany leaves, on fluted tapering legs, Dutch, c1800, 52¾in (134cm) wide.
£1,600–1,900 / €2,350–2,750
$2,900–3,450 ⚒ S(Am)

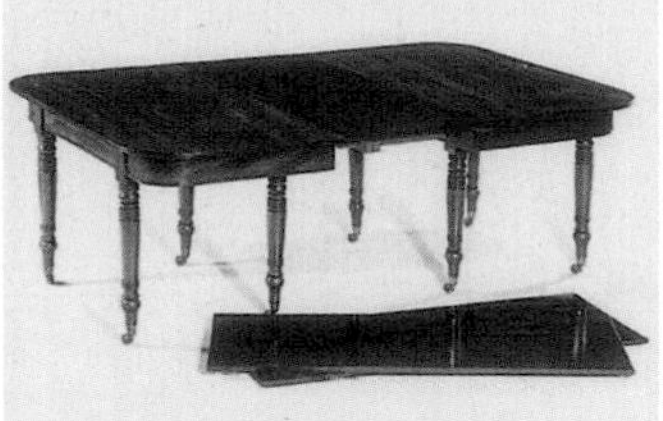

A late George III mahogany extending dining table, with three extra leaves, on turned tapering legs with brass caps and casters, 121¼in (308cm) wide.
£4,700–5,600 / €6,800–8,100
$8,500–10,100 ⚒ DN

► A mahogany gateleg drop-leaf dining table, on scroll-carved cabriole legs with hoof feet, mid-18thC, 62½in (159cm) extended.
£540–640 / €790–940
$980–1,150 ⚒ JM

◄ A Regency mahogany dining table, with telescopic action, one later leg and four later extra leaves, 104¾in (266cm) extended.
£3,350–4,000 / €4,900–5,800
$6,100–7,200 ⚒ S(O)

FURNITURE

A Regency mahogany extending dining table, the centre section with gateleg action, on ring-turned tapering legs, 111in (282cm) extended.
£3,300–3,950 / €4,800–5,700
$6,000–7,200 NSal

A Regency mahogany extending dining table, with one extra leaf, on turned and reeded tapering legs, 139¾in (355cm) extended.
£4,000–4,800 / €5,800–7,000
$7,200–8,700 L&T

A late Regency mahogany extending dining table, with two extra leaves, on turned and reeded legs, 93in (236cm) extended.
£1,300–1,550 / €1,900–2,250
$2,350–2,800 E

◄ **A mahogany extending dining table,** with two extra leaves, on foliate-moulded turned tapering legs, early 19thC, 85in (216cm) extended.
£2,000–2,400 / €2,900–3,500
$3,600–4,300 PF

► **A mahogany dining table,** early 19thC, 167in (420cm) extended.
£1,250–1,500
€1,850–2,200
$2,250–2,700
L

A mahogany extending dining table, with two extra leaves, early 19thC, 121½in (308.5cm) wide.
£2,400–2,850 / €3,500–4,150
$4,350–5,200 S(O)

A George IV mahogany extending dining table, with extra leaves, on fluted tapering legs, 94in (239cm) wide.
£2,600–3,100 / €3,800–4,450
$4,700–5,600 HYD

A William IV mahogany extending dining table, with two extra leaves, on reeded tapering legs, 56¼in (143cm) wide.
£3,750–4,500 / €5,500–6,600
$6,800–8,200 DN(BR)

An early Victorian mahogany extending dining table, with three extra leaves, on turned faceted tapering legs, 122¼in (310.5cm) wide.
£3,500–4,200 / €5,100–6,100
$6,300–7,600 AH

◄ **A mahogany extending dining table,** 19thC, 96¾in (246cm) extended.
£1,050–1,250 / €1,550–1,800
$1,900–2,250 S(O)

A walnut and marquetry-inlaid drop-leaf dining table, with two frieze drawers, with 'Hewetson, Milner & Thexton, House Furnishers, London' brass plaque, Dutch, 19thC, 58½in (148.5cm) wide.
£1,200–1,400 / €1,700–2,000
$2,200–2,600 WW

Extending dining tables were introduced towards the end of the 18th century to enable the Georgian upper and middle classes to entertain a varying number of guests. Tables from this period have square tapering legs or central supports with outswept legs. Early 19th-century examples have slender ring-turned legs, and those from the later 19th-century have a more bulbous and heavier turned leg. Towards the end of the Victorian period and into the Edwardian era a revival of earlier Georgian designs became fashionable.

Always look on the underside of a table for restoration or signs of a marriage, which will naturally affect the value.

◀ **A mahogany extending dining table,** with two extra leaves, on lappet-moulded baluster turned legs, mid-19thC, 83in (211cm) wide.
£1,450–1,700
€2,100–2,500
$2,600–3,100
PF

A mahogany dining table, with rosewood crossbanding and three extra leaves, on splayed legs with brass paw caps and casters, mid-19thC and later, 143in (363cm) wide.
£2,100–2,500 / €3,050–3,650
$3,800–4,550 Bea

► **A mahogany extending dining table,** with two extra leaves, c1860, 91in (231cm) wide.
£3,300–3,700
€4,800–5,400
$6,000–6,700
⊞ QA

A walnut extending dining table, with rosewood crossbanding, leaves missing, c1860, 74¾in (190cm) wide.
£9,600–11,500 / €14,000–16,800
$17,400–20,800 S(O)

◀ **A mahogany extending dining table,** c1870, 97in (246.5cm) wide.
£3,600–4,000
€5,300–5,900
$6,500–7,200
⊞ QA

◀ **A Victorian rosewood tilt-top dining table,** the base on carved paw feet with acanthus leaf brackets, 55in (139.5cm) wide.
£2,200–2,600
€3,200–3,800
$4,000–4,700
SWO

A Victorian mahogany extending dining table, with two extra leaves, on lotus-leaf carved baluster legs, 90in (228.5cm) extended.
£1,400–1,650 / €2,050–2,400
$2,500–3,000 HYD

► **A Victorian mahogany extending dining table,** by John Taylor & Son, stamped, extra leaves missing, Scottish, 157in (400cm) extended.
£1,500–1,800
€2,200–2,650
$2,700–3,250
DD

A Victorian mahogany extending dining table, with three extra leaves, on reeded turned legs, 95in (241.5cm) wide.
£1,300–1,550 / €1,900–2,250
$2,350–2,800 DN

A Victorian mahogany extending dining table, with three extra leaves, on turned tapering legs, 107in (272cm) wide.
£1,400–1,650 / €2,050–2,400
$2,500–3,000 DN

A mahogany dining table, with telescopic mechanism, on turned legs, c1880, 58in (147.5cm) wide.
£1,150–1,300 / €1,700–1,900
$2,100–2,350 ⊞ HEM

◄ **A late Victorian mahogany extending dining table,** with a telescopic mechanism and one extra leaf, on tapering reeded legs, 71¼in (179.5cm) extended.
£960–1,150
€1,450–1,700
$1,700–2,000 ⚒ WW

► **A mahogany extending dining table,** with three extra leaves, Continental, late 19thC, 94½in (240cm) extended.
£1,650–1,950 / €2,400–2,850
$3,000–3,550 ⚒ DN

Display Tables

A Sheraton-style satinwood display table, the frieze printed with roses and foliage, stretcher missing, 19thC, 17in (43cm) wide.
£630–750 / €920–1,100
$1,150–1,350 ⚒ BWL

A satinwood and mahogany display table, c1890, 18in (45.5cm) wide.
£2,050–2,300
€3,000–3,350
$3,700–4,150 ⊞ GGD

A walnut display table, with gilt-metal mounts, French, late 19thC, 25½in (65cm) wide.
£1,350–1,600
€1,950–2,350
$2,450–2,900 ⚒ DN

An Edwardian mahogany and marquetry display table, the top with a border of leaf and hop inlay, 25in (63.5cm) wide.
£1,400–1,650
€2,050–2,400
$2,550–3,000 ⚒ HYD

An Edwardian inlaid mahogany display table, the legs with boxwood stringing, 25¼in (64cm) wide.
£220–260 / €320–380
$400–470 ⚒ TRM(D)

An Edwardian mahogany display table, the platform stretcher with a fretwork Gothic border, 20in (51cm) wide.
£330–390 / €480–570
$600–710 ⚒ HYD

A mahogany display table, on carved cabriole legs with an X-stretcher and claw-and-ball feet, early 20thC, 31in (78.5cm) wide.
£560–670 / €820–980
$1,000–1,200 ⚒ DN

Dressing Tables

A mahogany kneehole dressing table, with an oak-lined drawer above three conforming graduated drawers flanking a central door with an apron drawer above, c1770, 30¼in (77cm) wide.
£3,350–3,750 / €4,900–5,500
$6,100–6,800 ⊞ JC

A mahogany dressing table, with three drawers, c1800, 39in (99cm) wide.
£2,500–2,800 / €3,650–4,100
$4,550–5,100 ⊞ WAA

A William IV mahogany dressing table, the frieze drawer flanked by deep drawers, 42in (106.5cm) wide.
£440–520 / €640–760
$800–940 ⚒ Mit

A mahogany bowfronted dressing table, with five drawers, on tapering legs, 19thC, 40in (101.5cm) wide.
£1,300–1,550 / €1,900–2,250
$2,350–2,800 ⚒ BWL

A Rudd's dressing table, with three frieze drawers, the central drawer with a box and lidded compartments and a sliding tray, flanked by two swivelling pull-out drawers fitted with a box and open compartments, late 18thC, 49¼in (125cm) wide.
£4,450–5,300 / €6,500–7,700
$8,100–9,600 ⚒ CHTR

A Rudd's table was a variant of a bureau dressing table, but with a row of three deep fitted drawers. The central drawer had a writing slide; the flanking drawers, each with a swivel mirror, could be swung out on quadrants so that they could be used in combination for viewing one's back or profile.

A George IV mahogany kneehole dressing table, the frieze drawer above a cupboard door, flanked by three drawers each side, brass handles later, 44in (112cm) wide.
£610–730 / €890–1,050
$1,100–1,300 ⚒ WW

A carved mahogany dressing table, c1870, 48in (122cm) wide.
£810–900 / €1,200–1,350
$1,450–1,650 ⊞ SWA

A Louis XVI mahogany, kingwood and harewood-banded *poudreuse*, the top with a hinged mirror flanked by a dummy drawer and a small drawer above a frieze drawer, French, 32in (81.5cm) wide.
£680–810 / €1,000–1,200
$1,250–1,450 ⚒ DN

A Regency mahogany dressing table, by T. & G. Seddon, the frieze drawer flanked by two side drawers moulded as four dummy drawers, stamped and labelled, 48in (122cm) wide.
£940–1,100 / €1,350–1,600
$1,700–2,000 ⚒ HYD

A stained beech dressing table, in the style of Gabriel Viardot, inlaid with mother-of-pearl, French, Paris, c1890.
£13,200–15,800 / €19,300–23,100
$23,900–28,600 ⚒ S(O)

Gabriel Viardot specialized in exotic furniture of Chinese and Japanese inspiration.

Drop-leaf Tables

A walnut drop-leaf table, with shell-carved cabriole legs, c1750, 48in (122cm) wide.
£1,200–1,400 / €1,750–2,050
$2,150–2,550 S(O)

A George III mahogany drop-leaf table, with a frieze drawer, on cabriole legs with hoof feet, 49¼in (125cm) wide.
£1,000–1,200 / €1,500–1,750
$1,800–2,150 Bea

A mahogany, rosewood, walnut and burr-walnut drop-leaf table, by B. Molitor, stamped, French, c1790, 45¾in (116cm) wide.
£13,200–15,800 / €19,300–23,100
$23,900–28,600 S
One of the greatest cabinet-makers of his time, Bernard Molitor was born in Luxemborg. He moved to Paris c1776, where he established himself in the Faubourg Saint Antoine. He is thought to have received training in the J. H. Riesener workshop. Distinguished both by his business sense and artistic skill, he executed various royal commissions, including one for Marie-Antoinette in 1787. His strong monarchist links caused him problems during the Revolution, but served him very well at the restoration of the Bourbon monarchy in 1814. Molitor was fascinated by English cabinet making, which he reinterpreted for the French market, exemplified by the table shown here.

A mahogany drop-leaf table, the four cabriole legs on hoof feet, mid-18thC, 54in (137cm) wide.
£410–490 / €600–720
$740–890 PF

A walnut drop-leaf table, c1930, 36in (91.5cm) wide.
£1,150–1,300 / €1,700–1,900
$2,100–2,350 Man

Drum Tables

A late George III mahogany drum table, the leather-inset top above four drawers and four dummy drawers, on a turned column and tripod base, 38½in (98cm) diam.
£3,650–4,350 / €5,300–6,400
$6,600–7,900 DN

A Regency rosewood drum table, the frieze with alternating dummy drawers and real drawers, restored, 38½in (98cm) diam.
£9,600–11,500 / €14,000–16,800
$17,400–20,800 S

A Regency mahogany drum table, the frieze fitted with boxwood-strung drawers and panels, the triform base with carved brackets, 45in (114.5cm) diam.

£1,050–1,250 / €1,550–1,850
$1,900–2,250 Mit

► **A George IV mahogany drum table,** the revolving leather-inset top above alternating drawers and dummy drawers, 54in (137cm) diam.
£3,400–4,050
€4,950–5,900
$6,200–7,300 L

A William IV mahogany drum table, the revolving top with rosewood and marquetry inlay, above four frieze drawers and four dummy drawers, damaged, 43in (109cm) diam.
£1,900–2,250 / €2,750–3,300
$3,450–4,050 JM

Games Tables

A mahogany games table, the tilt top with needlework depicting playing cards and gaming tokens in a stylized foliate surround, damaged, mid-18thC, 33½in (85cm) wide.
£6,000–7,200 / €8,800–10,500
$10,900–13,000 S

A George III mahogany and burrwood-crossbanded games table, the frieze with two dummy drawers, on tapering legs with spade feet on barrel casters, 25½in (65cm) wide.
£2,050–2,450 / €3,000–3,600
$3,700–4,450 HYD

A George III mahogany triple-top games/tea table, with an end drawer, on tapering legs with spade feet, 32½in (82.5cm) wide.
£700–840 / €1,000–1,200
$1,250–1,500 Mit

A baroque walnut games table, the top with games boards, enclosing a backgammon board, on later tapering legs, south German, 18thC, 41¼in (105cm) wide.
£2,600–3,100 / €3,800–4,550
$4,700–5,600 S(Am)

A rosewood games table, converted from a pole screen, c1815, 17in (43cm) diam.
£1,050–1,200 / €1,550–1,750
$1,900–2,150 DOA

A George IV rosewood and parcel-gilt games/work table, the reversible slide inlaid with a draughts and backgammon board, on twin supports and scroll legs, bag missing, 30¼in (77cm) wide.
£800–960 / €1,200–1,400
$1,450–1,750 WW

A rosewood-veneered games table, c1830, 30in (76cm) wide.
£6,400–7,200 / €9,300–10,500
$11,600–13,000 HA

A rosewood-veneered games table, with brass inlay, 1830–40, 36in (91.5cm) wide.
£1,650–1,850 / €2,400–2,700
$3,000–3,350 WAA

A rosewood games table, the inlaid chequered top with a marquetry border above two slide-out counter wells, c1850, 23in (58.5cm) wide.
£2,600–2,900 / €3,800–4,250
$4,700–5,200 HA

◄ **A rosewood and penwork games table,** the top inlaid with a chess board, on a cluster column and platform base, with moulded scroll feet, Continental, mid-19thC, 22in (56cm) wide.
£940–1,100 / €1,350–1,600
$1,700–2,000 PF

► **A walnut games table,** on a carved tripod base, c1860, 23in (58.5cm) diam.
£810–900 / €1,200–1,350
$1,450–1,650 GGD

FURNITURE

A walnut games/work table, with a hinged top, c1860, 30in (76cm) wide.
£1,100–1,300 / €1,600–1,900
$2,000–2,350 ⚒ S(O)

A Victorian mahogany games table, the quatrefoil top with four counting dials and later baize, over four drawers and eight counter wells, on reeded turned supports, 34¼in (84cm) square.
£350–420 / €510–610
$630–760 ⚒ L&E

An inlaid walnut games table, c1880, 26in (66cm) wide.
£3,100–3,450 / €4,500–5,000
$5,600–6,200 ⊞ WAA

Library Tables

A Regency rosewood library table, the carved end supports with an upholstered cross stretcher, on claw-and-ball feet, 51in (129.5cm) wide.
£1,750–2,100 / €2,550–3,000
$3,200–3,800 ⚒ G(L)

A William IV mahogany library table, with a leather-inset top above a frieze with a long drawer opposing dummy drawers, handles replaced, 49¾in (126.5cm) wide.
£14,400–17,200 / €21,000–25,100
$26,100–31,000 ⚒ S
This table was made for the Home Office, when the Secretaries in charge were the future Prime Ministers, Lord Melbourne and Lord John Russell.

A mahogany library table, by Mack, Williams & Gibton, with a long drawer opposing a dummy drawer, the supports with roundel-carved brackets, with a turned stretcher on bar bases with bun feet, drawers stamped 'D6444', with paper label, Irish, c1825, 35in (90cm) wide.
£3,600–4,300 / €5,300–6,300
$6,500–7,800 ⚒ HOK

A rosewood library table, with a label for 'G. Seddon, Gray's Inn Road, London', c1835, 57½in (146cm) wide.
£840–1,000 / €1,250–1,500
$1,500–1,800 ⚒ S(O)

◄ **An early Victorian mahogany library table,** the leather-inset top above two pairs of frieze drawers, with gilt-brass label for 'Druce & Co, Upholsterers & Cabinet Makers, Baker Street, Portland Square', 54¼in (138cm) wide.
£1,200–1,400 / €1,750–2,050
$2,150–2,550 ⚒ CHTR

A maplewood library table, c1830, 36in (91.5cm) wide.
£1,050–1,200 / €1,550–1,750
$1,900–2,150 ⊞ MLL

A rosewood library table, c1835, 46½in (118cm) wide.
£840–1,000 / €1,250–1,500
$1,500–1,800 ⚒ S(O)

A Victorian Gothic-style oak library table, with a frieze drawer, on pierced and carved end supports with claw-and-ball feet, 39in (99cm) wide.
£480–570 / €700–830
$870–1,050 ⚒ BWL

Nests of Tables

A nest of three sabicu and kingwood tables, c1810, largest, 29in (73.5cm) high.
£9,000–10,000 / €13,100–14,600
$16,300–18,100 ⊞ HWK

A nest of three mahogany tables, 19thC, largest 29¼in (74.5cm) high.
£940–1,100 / €1,350–1,600
$1,700–2,000 ⚒ DN

An Edwardian nest of four chequer-strung tables, largest 27½in (70cm) high.
£610–730 / €890–1,050
$1,100–1,300 ⚒ DN

Occasional Tables

A baroque japanned occasional table, the S-shaped supports joined by an X-stretcher, German, c1700.
£3,100–3,700 / €4,550–5,400
$5,600–6,700 ⚒ S(Am)

A George III satinwood, ebonized-harewood and mahogany occasional table, on tapering legs, 24in (61cm) wide.
£4,400–4,900 / €6,400–7,200
$8,000–8,900 ⊞ HA

A partridge-wood-veneered occasional table, decorated with boxwood stringing, with two drawers, c1790, 20in (51cm) wide.
£2,600–2,900 / €3,800–4,250
$4,700–5,200 ⊞ HA

A mahogany occasional table, the platform base on hipped sabre legs with turned paterae, c1810, 24in (61cm) wide.
£1,650–1,850 / €2,400–2,700
$3,000–3,350 ⊞ JC

◄ **A Regency mahogany occasional table,** the tilt top on a turned column above four hipped and swept legs with brass terminals and casters, 33½in (85cm) wide.
£280–330 / €410–480
$510–600 ⚒ WW

► **A Regency rosewood drop-leaf occasional table,** with a drawer, 20½in (52cm) wide.
£1,400–1,650 / €2,050–2,400
$2,550–3,000 ⚒ G(L)

A rosewood occasional table, early 19thC, 31½in (80cm) diam.
£1,050–1,250 / €1,550–1,850
$1,900–2,250 ⚒ TRM(E)

A George IV calamander and rosewood-veneered occasional table, the frieze drawer above a turned and petal-carved stretcher, the moulded scroll-capped splay legs with brass leaf-chased sabots on casters, 19¾in (50cm) wide.
£1,200–1,400 / €1,750–2,050
$2,150–2,550 ⚒ NSal

An ormolu-mounted marquetry and ebonized occasional table, inlaid with cranes and foliate decoration, the cross stretcher centred with a brass finial, on casters, 19thC, 34¾in (88.5cm) wide.
£1,450–1,700 / €2,100–2,500
$2,600–3,100 ⚒ DA

A William IV mahogany occasional table, 30in (76cm) wide.
£2,550–2,850 / €3,700–4,150
$4,600–5,200 ⊞ GGD

A gilt-metal and kingwood *table ambulante*, the top inset with a porcelain dish, on four curved supports united by an undertier, French, 19thC, 20½in (52cm) wide.
£3,000–3,600 / €4,400–5,300
$5,400–6,500 ⚒ TEN

▶ **A Victorian inlaid walnut occasional table,** 35¾in (91cm) wide.
£400–480 / €580–700
$720–870 ⚒ CHTR

A Biedermeier walnut occasional table, the frieze drawer above lyre-shaped supports joined by a baluster stretcher, Austrian, probably Vienna, c1835, 47¼in (120cm) wide.
£610–730 / €890–1,050
$1,100–1,300 ⚒ S(Am)

A Victorian figured walnut occasional table, with a hinged top, 36in (91.5cm) wide.
£680–810 / €1,000–1,200
$1,250–1,450 ⚒ PF

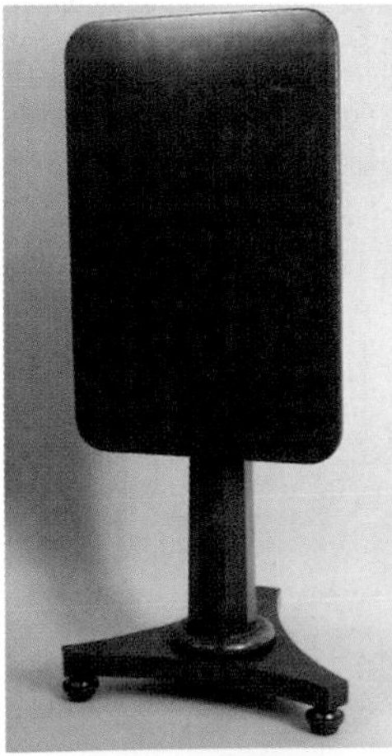

A Victorian mahogany tilt-top occasional table, 29½in (75cm) wide.
£150–180 / €220–260
$270–320 ⚒ DA

A mahogany occasional table, the top inset with a glazed tapestry panel, c1870, 18in (45.5cm) diam.
£400–450 / €580–660
$720–810 ⊞ HA

A papier-mâché occasional table, with mother-of-pearl inlay, c1870, 19in (48.5cm) diam.
£600–660 / €880–970
$1,050–1,200 ⊞ HA

A Victorian ebonized-beech occasional table, with a velvet-covered top, on turned legs, 18in (45.5cm) diam.
£110–125 / €160–185
$200–230 ⊞ MLL

◄ **A rosewood occasional table,** attributed to William Watt, c1880, 27¼in (69cm) diam.
£960–1,150 / €1,450–1,700
$1,750–2,100 ⚒ S(O)
The firm of William Watt was established in 1857 in Grafton Street, London, and from 1867 until the death of Watt in 1885 it was responsible for producing many of the designs of Edward William Godwin (1833–86).

A Victorian walnut occasional table, with turned cross stretchers, 21in (53.5cm) diam.
£230–270 / €340–400
$420–490 ⚒ CHTR

A mahogany occasional table, c1880, 27in (68.5cm) wide.
£810–900 / €1,200–1,350
$1,450–1,650 ⊞ Man

A walnut and ebonized occasional table, with gilt-metal mounts, the top decorated with floral marquetry and parquetry with scagliola insets, above a frieze drawer and undertier, on outswept feet, French, late 19thC, 22½in (57cm) wide.
£880–1,050 / €1,300–1,550
$1,600–1,900 ⚒ DN

A mahogany revolving occasional table, the top with a brass gallery and handle, on brass legs, c1900, 18in (45.5cm) wide.
£610–680 / €890–990
$1,100–1,250 ⊞ GGD

A mahogany occasional table, with four drop-leaf sides, c1900, 22in (56cm) wide.
£450–500 / €660–730
$810–910 ⊞ QA

A pair of Edwardian Sheraton revival inlaid mahogany occasional tables, the crossbanded tops inlaid with satinwood and olivewood paterae, above a frieze drawer, 16in (40.5cm) wide.
£940–1,100 / €1,350–1,600
$1,700–2,000 ⚒ HYD

An Edwardian mahogany occasional table, with satinwood stringing, 29½in (75cm) diam.
£650–780 / €950–1,100
$1,200–1,400 ⚒ SWO

An inlaid mahogany occasional table, c1910, 30½in (77.5cm) high.
£470–530 / €690–770
$850–960 ⊞ PGO

◄ **A painted occasional table,** with an antler base, Continental, c1920, 23in (58.5cm) diam.
£810–900 / €1,200–1,350
$1,450–1,650 ⊞ SAW

FURNITURE

Pembroke Tables

A George III mahogany and satinwood-banded Pembroke table, attributed to Young & Trotter, Edinburgh, the top with canted corners above a drawer opposing a dummy drawer, on tapering legs with brass caps and casters, Scottish, 38½in (98cm) wide.
£1,300–1,550 / €1,900–2,250
$2,350–2,800 L&T

A George III mahogany and ebonized Pembroke table, the frieze drawer decorated with stringing, 29¾in (75.5cm) wide.
£990–1,150 / €1,450–1,700
$1,800–2,150 AH

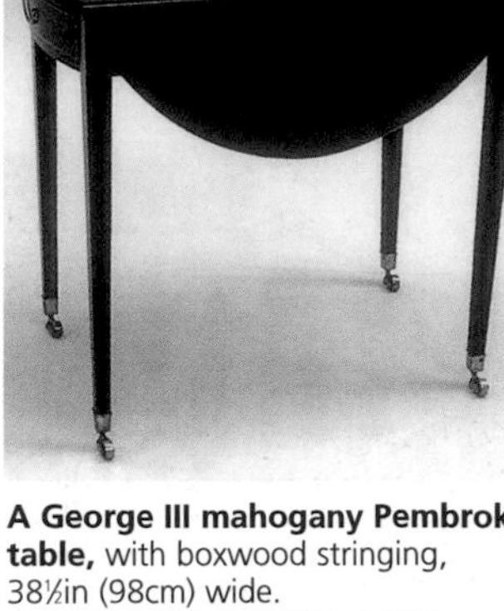

A George III mahogany Pembroke table, with boxwood stringing, 38½in (98cm) wide.
£1,500–1,800 / €2,200–2,650
$2,700–3,250 DD

A Sheraton-style mahogany Pembroke table, the top with mahogany inlay with tulipwood crossbanding, above a bowed drawer, late 18thC, 29¼in (74.5cm) diam closed.
£700–840 / €1,000–1,200
$1,250–1,500 DN(BR)

A George III mahogany Pembroke table, with a single drawer, 31in (78.5cm) wide.
£880–1,050 / €1,300–1,550
$1,600–1,900 G(L)

A Sheraton-style mahogany Pembroke table, the drop-leaf top crossbanded with tulipwood and inlaid stringing, with a bowed frieze drawer and a dummy drawer, late 18thC, 30in (76cm) wide.
£890–1,050 / €1,300–1,550
$1,600–1,900 NSal

A mahogany pedestal Pembroke table, with boxwood and ebony beading and a full-length drawer, c1790, 30in (76cm) wide.
£2,550–2,850 / €3,700–4,150
$4,600–5,200 GGD

A mahogany Pembroke table, c1790, 39in (99cm) wide.
£2,450–2,750 / €3,600–4,000
$4,450–5,000 WAA

A mahogany Pembroke table, with a drawer, c1790, 39in (99cm) wide.
£1,300–1,450 / €1,900–2,100
$2,350–2,600 LGr

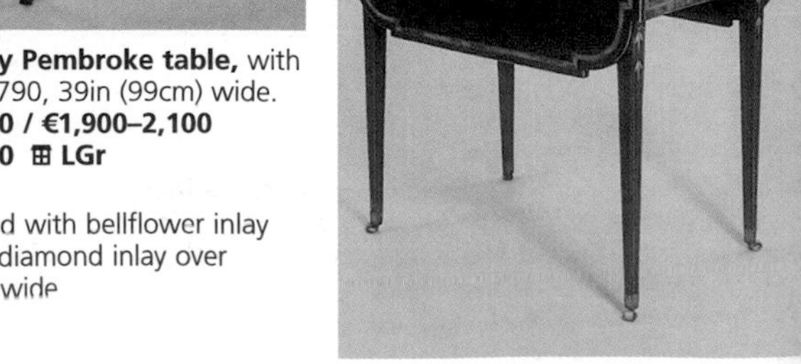

► **A Federal mahogany Pembroke table,** decorated with bellflower inlay and line stringing, with a frieze drawer, the legs with diamond inlay over bellflowers, restored, American, c1800, 32¼in (82cm) wide.
£700–840 / €1,000–1,200
$1,250–1,500 NOA

A Federal inlaid and figured mahogany Pembroke table, with a drawer, American, New York, c1810, 32in (81.5cm) wide.
£1,500–1,800 / €2,200–2,600
$2,700–3,250 S(NY)

Pembroke tables were used for occasional use in drawing rooms to serve tea or light meals. These tables were introduced in the mid-18th century and were named after the Countess of Pembroke, who reputedly ordered the first of its type. They have rectangular, circular or serpentine tops with a pair of drop flap extensions and were often made in mahogany or satinwood.

► **A satinwood Pembroke table,** c1905, 33in (84cm) wide.
£1,050–1,250 / €1,550–1,850
$1,900–2,250 S(O)

► **A mahogany Pembroke table,** with a drawer, dummy drawer and brass casters, later painted decoration, 19thC, 37in (94cm) wide.
£1,100–1,250 / €1,700–1,900
$2,000–2,250 HA

Serving Tables

A George III mahogany serpentine serving table, the fluted frieze carved with rosettes, on tapering legs with block feet, 67in (170cm) wide.
£12,000–14,400 / €17,500–21,000
$21,700–26,100 L&T

A George III mahogany serving table, the recessed frieze with a boxwood- and ebony-strung and satinwood-banded tablet to the centre, on turned tapering reeded legs, 71in (180.5cm) wide.
£4,000–4,800 / €5,800–7,000
$7,200–8,700 Mit

► **A mahogany serpentine serving table,** the frieze inlaid with paterae, with two drawers, on tapering legs with scroll brackets and spade feet, probably Dutch, 19thC, restored, 59in (150cm) wide.
£2,800–3,350 / €4,100–4,900
$5,100–6,100 Bea

A George III mahogany serpentine serving table, the fluted frieze carved with a rosette, on tapering legs, damaged and repaired, 30½in (76cm) wide.
£1,500–1,800 / €2,200–2,650
$2,700–3,250 WW

A Regency mahogany serving table, altered, 51½in (131cm) wide.
£10,200–12,200 / €14,900–17,800
$18,500–22,100 S

Side Tables

A William and Mary walnut side table, with a frieze drawer above an X-stretcher, 38¼in (97cm) wide.
£3,500–4,200 / €5,100–6,100
$6,300–7,600 ⚒ TEN

A George II walnut side table, with an oak-lined drawer, on turned legs and pad feet, some damage, 30in (76cm) wide.
£540–640 / €790–930
$980–1,150 ⚒ F&C

A carved mahogany side table, with three frieze drawers, on leaf-capped cabriole legs with stepped claw feet, Irish, mid-18thC, 45¾in (116cm) wide.
£6,400–7,600 / €9,300–11,100
$11,600–13,800 ⚒ HOK

A kingwood and marquetry serpentine side table, with a drawer, probably Maltese, mid-18thC, 38½in (98cm) wide.
£1,550–1,850 / €2,250–2,700
$2,800–3,350 ⚒ S(O)

A William and Mary seaweed marquetry side table, the top banded and divided into a shaped central reserve and four quadrants, over a frieze drawer, on spiral-turned legs joined by a shaped cross stretcher, on ball feet, altered, 47¾in(121.5cm) wide.
£2,150–2,550 / €3,150–3,700
$3,900–4,600 ⚒ S(O)

A George II mahogany serpentine side table, on tapering legs, 25in (63.5cm) wide.
£370–440 / €540–640
$670–800 ⚒ HYD

► **A walnut and mahogany side table,** with rococo carving, top later, restored, Irish, mid-18thC, 72¾in (185cm) wide.
£20,400–24,400 / €29,800–36,000
$37,000–44,000 ⚒ S

A mahogany side table, with a frieze drawer, on leaf-capped cabriole legs with faceted pad feet, Irish, 18thC, 29½in (75cm) wide.
£2,400–2,850 / €3,500–4,150
$4,350–5,200 ⚒ HOK

A George II carved giltwood and gesso side table, 30¼in (77cm) wide.
£4,800–5,700 / €7,000–8,300
$8,700–10,300 ⚒ S(O)

A walnut side table, c1740, 30in (76cm) wide.
£2,000–2,200 / €2,900–3,200
$3,600–4,000 ⊞ DEB

LOCATE THE SOURCE

The source of each illustration in Miller's can be found by checking the code letters below each caption with the Key to Illustrations, pages 778–784.

An early George III mahogany side table, with a frieze drawer, on cabriole legs, 33in (84cm) wide.
£1,650–1,950 / €2,400–2,850
$3,000–3,550 ⚒ L

A Georgian mahogany side table, with a drawer, on turned legs, 24in (61cm) wide.
£120–140 / €175–200
$220–250 AMB

A George III mahogany bowfronted side table, with satinwood and tulipwood crossbanding, c1790, 36¼in (92cm) wide.
£1,900–2,250 / €2,750–3,300
$3,450–4,050 S(O)

A Regency rosewood-veneered and crossbanded side table, with inlaid stringing, the frieze drawer with slope missing, the end supports united by a high stretcher, the splay legs with brass caps and casters, 25¾in (65.5cm) wide.
£700–840 / €1,000–1,200
$1,250–1,500 WW

◄ A rosewood and *pietra dura* side table, with a drawer, c1820, 24¾in (63cm) wide.
£2,600–3,100
€3,800–4,550
$4,700–5,600
S(O)

A late George IV bowfronted mahogany side table, with three frieze drawers, on ring-turned legs, 48in (122cm) wide.
£560–670 / €820–980
$1,000–1,200 MEA

A cast-iron side table, with later-painted marble top, stamped 'James Yates, Rotherham, registered 22 March 1842, No. 1148', c1845, 63¾in (162cm) wide.
£6,600–7,900 / €9,600–11,500
$11,900–14,300 S

James Yates, the founder of the firm Yates & Hayward, is known for his high-quality domestic ironware. He initially trained with the Walker family, but by 1823 was working on his own account. Running works in Rotherham, Yorkshire, he continued to remain active in the company Yates, Hayward & Co until 1874.

A Napoleon III painted and giltwood side table, inlaid with mother-of-pearl, with a drawer, damaged, French, 29½in (75cm) wide.
£1,550–1,850
€2,250–2,700
$2,800–3,350 S(P)

A mahogany side table, c1850, 19in (48.5cm) wide.
£3,400–3,800
€4,950–5,500
$6,200–6,900 HA

FURNITURE

◀ **A Victorian walnut side table,** the fretwork supports united by a spiral-twist stretcher, with scroll fretwork-carved legs, 22in (56cm) wide.
£230–270 / €340–400
$420–490 ⚒ Mit

An inlaid mahogany side table, possibly Irish, c1860, 48in (122cm) wide.
£900–1,000 / €1,300–1,450
$1,600–1,800 ⊞ QA

A Victorian oak side table, with gadrooned border, on scrolled front supports, 36¼in (92cm) wide.
£220–260 / €320–380
$400–470 ⚒ WilP

◀ **A mahogany and gilt side table,** with a drawer, French, c1890, 33in (84cm) high.
£1,100–1,250 / €1,600–1,850
$2,000–2,250 ⊞ Man

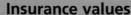

A late Victorian rosewood side table, inlaid with harewood, satinwood and boxwood, the top with marquetry inlay, the supports united by an inlaid cross stretcher, 18in (45.5cm) wide.
£630–700 / €900–1,000
$1,100–1,250 ⊞ LGr

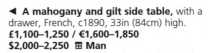

A rosewood side table, stamped 'Edwards & Roberts', c1895, 35in (89cm) wide.
£5,400–6,000 / €7,900–8,800
$9,800–10,900 ⊞ Man

◀ **A mahogany demi-lune side table,** with chequer-banded floral marquetry and a drawer, on tapering legs, Dutch, late 19thC, 26in (66cm) wide.
£410–490 / €600–720
$740–890 ⚒ DN(BR)

Silver Tables

A mahogany silver table, with a drawer, on cabriole legs, 18thC, 31in (78.5cm) wide.
£2,000–2,250 / €2,900–3,300
$3,600–4,050 ⊞ DEB

Insurance values

Always insure your valuable antiques for the cost of replacing them with similar items, regardless of the original price paid. Both dealers and auctioneers can provide a valuation service for a fee.

▶ **A George III mahogany silver table,** the cabriole legs carved with scallop shells and scrolls, on trefid feet, Irish, 30¾in (78cm) high.
£9,200–11,000 / €13,400–16,100
$16,700–19,900 ⚒ JAd

A George II mahogany silver table, in the style of John Channon, with a frieze drawer, 30in (76cm) wide.
£21,000–25,200 / €31,000–37,000
$38,000–45,000 ⚒ HYD

From a family of Exeter cabinet-makers, John Channon had established his own business in St Martin's Lane, London by 1733. This table, with its rare inset brass key escutcheon with engraved decoration, is in original condition from a private source and therefore highly desirable.

Sofa Tables

A Regency rosewood sofa table, with two drawers, 52¾in (134cm) wide.
£900–1,050 / €1,300–1,550
$1,650–1,900 ⚒ S(O)

A Regency mahogany and ebony-lined sofa table, with two drawers and two dummy drawers, on curved reeded legs with brass caps and casters, 45¼in (115cm) wide.
£1,000–1,200 / €1,450–1,750
$1,800–2,150 ⚒ L&T

A Regency rosewood sofa table, with two drawers and two dummy drawers, on a quadriform base with four legs with brass stringing and brass leaf cap casters, 38in (96.5cm) wide.
£2,000–2,400 / €2,900–3,500
$3,600–4,350 ⚒ HYD

A Regency sofa table, with a drawer, 33in (84cm) wide.
£420–500 / €610–730
$760–910 ⚒ SWO

A mahogany sofa table, with two drawers, possibly Scottish, c1820, 62¼in (158cm) wide.
£4,200–5,000 / €6,100–7,300
$7,600–9,100 ⚒ S(O)

A late Regency ebony-inlaid mahogany sofa table, with two drawers and two dummy drawers, the legs with brass caps and casters, 35in (89cm) wide.
£1,500–1,800 / €2,200–2,650
$2,700–3,250 ⚒ WW

A mahogany sofa table, with two drawers and dummy drawers, the tapering supports united by a block stretcher, on reeded splay legs with brass casters, 19thC, 42¼in (107.5cm) wide.
£1,250–1,500 / €1,850–2,200
$2,250–2,700 ⚒ WW

A rosewood and parquetry-inlaid sofa table, with a drawer, Continental, 19thC, 28¾in (73cm) wide.
£730–870 / €1,050–1,250
$1,300–1,550 ⚒ SWO

A mahogany sofa table, with two drawers, the trestle end supports united by a block stretcher, on reeded scroll legs with brass caps and casters, 19thC, 28¾in (73cm) wide closed.
£750–900 / €1,100–1,300
$1,350–1,600 ⚒ WW

A mahogany sofa table, with a drawer and a dummy drawer, north European, c1820, 61½in (156cm) wide.
£1,050–1,250 / €1,550–1,850
$1,900–2,250 ⚒ S(O)

A mahogany and parcel-gilt sofa table, with applied gilt-metal mounts and a drawer, Baltic, 1900–50, 53½in (136cm) wide.
£1,050–1,250 / €1,550–1,850
$1,900–2,250 ⚒ S(O)

Sutherland Tables

An inlaid walnut two-tier Sutherland table, c1860, 31in (78.5cm) high.
£1,750–1,950 / €2,550–2,850
$3,150–3,550 ⊞ WAA

An inlaid mahogany Sutherland table, c1900, 23in (58.5cm) wide.
£540–600 / €790–880
$980–1,100 ⊞ QA

► **A Victorian burr-walnut Sutherland table,** 31¾in (80.5cm) wide.
£590–700 / €880–1,000
$1,050–1,250 ⚒ AH

A Victorian walnut-veneered Sutherland table, the fluted, turned and lobed legs on sledge supports united by a stretcher, 35in (89cm) wide.
£440–520 / €640–770
$800–940 ⚒ Mit

A Victorian oak Sutherland table, on chamfered columns, stamped 'Gillows', 32in (81.5cm) wide.
£490–580 / €720–850
$890–1,050 ⚒ SWO

◄ **An Edwardian mahogany and satinwood-banded Sutherland table,** inlaid with fan paterae, on tapered supports, 29½in (75cm) wide.
£480–570 / €700–830
$870–1,050 ⚒ DD

Tea Tables

A mahogany tea table, with carved cabriole legs and pad feet, c1740, 31in (78.5cm) wide.
£2,400–2,700 / €3,500–3,950
$4,350–4,900 ⊞ GGD

► **A George III mahogany tea table,** the crossbanded top on moulded tapering legs, 36in (91.5cm) wide.
£350–420 / €510–610
$630–760 ⚒ HYD

A George III demi-lune fold-over tea table, the shaped frieze above cabriole legs with hoof feet, 33in (84cm) wide.
£1,350–1,600 / €1,950–2,350
$2,450–2,900 ⚒ SWO

◄ **A mahogany fold-over tea table,** c1770, 28in (71cm) high.
£4,750–5,300 / €6,900–7,700
$8,600–9,600 ⊞ HWK

A Louis XVI-style mahogany tea table, Dutch, 1775–1800, 39in (99cm) wide.
£1,100–1,300 / €1,600–1,900
$2,000–2,350 ⚒ S(Am)

A demi-lune fold-over tea table, with inlay and stringing, the double gateleg on tapered collared supports, c1790, 34in (86.5cm) wide.
£1,800–2,000 / €2,600–2,900
$3,250–3,600 ⊞ LGr

A Regency mahogany fold-over tea table, the frieze with boxwood and ebony stringing, above turned tapered and reeded legs with brass caps and casters, 36in (91.5cm) wide.
£1,500–1,800 / €2,200–2,650
$2,700–3,250 ⚒ Mit

A figured oak fold-over tea table, c1820, 36in (91.5cm) wide.
£3,000–3,350 / €4,400–4,900
$5,400–6,100 ⊞ GEO

A mahogany fold-over tea table, with ebony and satinwood stringing and a drawer, c1830, 36in (91.5cm) wide.
£2,700–3,000 / €3,950–4,400
$4,900–5,400 ⊞ HA

A William IV plum pudding mahogany fold-over tea table, the swivel top above a leaf- and scroll-carved frieze, the collared stem carved with a band of lotus leaves, the base on lion-paw feet and casters, 36in (91.5cm) wide.
£910–1,050 / €1,350–1,550
$1,650–1,900 ⚒ AH

A mahogany demi-lune tea table, with inlaid stringing, the legs with floral marquetry panels, frieze drawer later, 19thC, 40¼in (102cm) wide.
£590–700 / €860–1,000
$1,050–1,250 ⚒ WW

Tripod Tables

A mahogany tilt-top tripod table, with birdcage mechanism, 1740, 36in (91.5cm) diam.
£3,150–3,500 / €4,600–5,100
$5,700–6,300 ⊞ GGD

A mahogany tilt-top tripod table, 18thC, 29in (73.5cm) diam.
£1,350–1,550 / €1,950–2,250
$2,450–2,800 ⊞ CRU

A Cuban mahogany tilt-top tripod table, 18thC, 32in (81.5cm) diam.
£3,600–4,000 / €5,200–5,800
$6,500–7,200 ⊞ Man

Birdcage mechanism

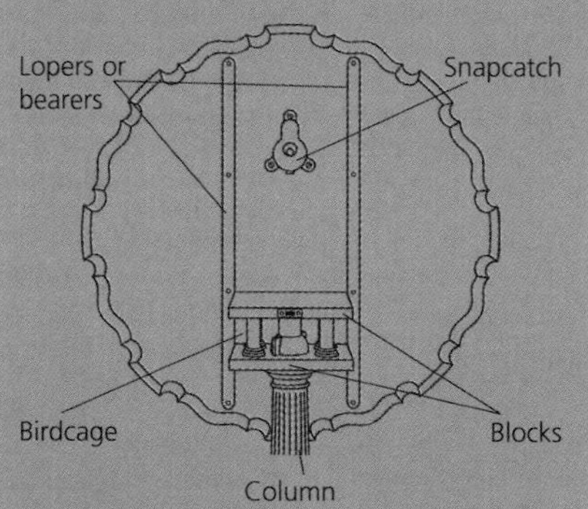

Most tripod tables have tilt-tops, but more sophisticated examples have a 'birdcage' fixed to the underside of the table top which enabled the top to turn well. The top and bottom blocks of the birdcage have holes cut into them through which the column of the table passes. A hole was also cut into the column so that the birdcage could be attached to it by means of a wooden wedge.

A mahogany tripod table, with birdcage mechanism, mid-18thC, 21¼in (54cm) diam.
£2,000–2,400
€2,900–3,500
$3,600–4,300 ⚒ S

A mahogany tilt-top tripod table, the edge carved with rosettes, the fluted support carved with an acanthus collar, c1760, 38½in (98cm) diam.
£3,400–4,050 / €5,000–5,900
$6,100–7,300 ⚒ HOK

► A mahogany tripod table, c1775, 26in (66cm) diam.
£810–900 / €1,150–1,300
$1,450–1,650 ⊞ GGD

A George III mahogany tilt-top tripod table, the baluster column with spiral-twist carving, damaged, 28in (71cm) diam.
£470–560 / €690–820
$850–1,000 ⚒ WW

A mahogany tripod table, on a double vase and ring-turned column, c1795, 19¾in (50cm) diam.
£1,100–1,250 / €1,600–1,850
$2,000–2,250 ⊞ JC

A tripod tilt-top table, with dished top, c1800, 19in (48.5cm) diam.
£440–490 / €640–720
$800–890 ⊞ DEB

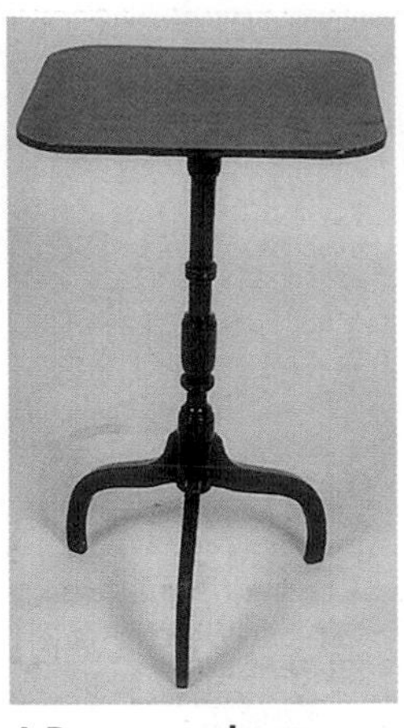

A Regency mahogany tilt-top tripod table, with baluster column and scroll legs, 16in (40.5cm) wide.
£370–440 / €540–640
$670–800 HYD

A mahogany tripod table, with turned stem and Gothic-style carved scroll legs, c1835, 28in (71cm) high.
£1,000–1,150
€1,450–1,700
$1,800–2,100 WAA

A Regency-style mahogany tripod table, with carved spiral stem and splay legs on ball feet, 19thC, 30in (76cm) high.
£1,500–1,700
€2,200–2,500
$2,700–3,050 WAA

An olivewood tripod table, with reeded legs and ball feet, Continental, 19thC, 18in (45.5cm) diam.
£1,600–1,800
€2,350–2,650
$2,900–3,250 HA

A mahogany tilt-top tripod table, c1850, 19in (48.5cm) wide.
£360–400 / €520–580
$650–720 GGD

◄ A mahogany tilt-top tripod table, with barley-twist column, c1860, 22in (56cm) diam.
£720–800 / €1,050–1,200
$1,300–1,450 GGD

► A Victorian walnut tripod table, the top with an ebonized edge and floral marquetry panel on a turned column, three scroll legs with floral marquetry and scroll feet, 23in (58.5cm) diam.
£760–910 / €1,150–1,350
$1,400–1,650 Mit

► A Victorian walnut tripod table, on a turned and reeded column, 20in (51cm) wide.
£760–910 / €1,150–1,350
$1,400–1,650 Mit

A carved mahogany tripod table, c1880, 17in (43cm) diam.
£145–165 / €210–240
$260–300 WiB

A carved mahogany tripod table, c1900, 26in (66cm) high.
£1,100–1,250
€1,600–1,850
$2,000–2,250 Man

Two-Tier Tables

A rosewood and amboyna-crossbanded two-tier table, by Gillows, stamped, c1870, 42½in (108cm) wide.
£4,200–5,000 / €6,100–7,300
$7,600–9,100 ⚒ S(O)

A painted papier-mâché two-tier table, Italian, c1880, 29in (73.5cm) high.
£800–880 / €1,150–1,300
$1,450–1,600 ⊞ GGD

A satinwood two-tier table, with a drawer, c1880, 15in (38cm) wide.
£1,500–1,700 / €2,200–2,500
$2,700–3,100 ⊞ WAA

An inlaid satinwood two-tier table, c1890, 35in (89cm) wide.
£1,850–2,100 / €2,700–3,050
$3,350–3,800 ⊞ MTay

A mahogany two-tier table, c1890, 22in (56cm) wide.
£250–280 / €370–410
$450–510 ⊞ QA

A pair of kingwood and gilt-bronze two-tier tables, c1890, 17¾in (45cm) wide.
£3,100–3,700 / €4,550–5,300
$5,600–6,700 ⚒ S(O)

An inlaid mahogany two-tier table, c1900, 27in (68.5cm) wide.
£360–400 / €520–580
$650–720 ⊞ QA

A walnut two-tier table/jardinière stand, c1900, 30in (76cm) high.
£450–500 / €660–730
$810–910 ⊞ Man

A mahogany two-tier table, inlaid in holly with musical instruments and trailing foliage, with satinwood stringing, c1900, 29in (73.5cm) wide.
£480–540 / €700–790
$870–980 ⊞ HA

An inlaid mahogany two-tier table, c1900, 27in (68.5cm) wide.
£310–350 / €450–510
$560–630 ⊞ QA

► **An Edwardian satinwood and purple heart two-tier table,** with chequered inlay and crossbanding, the top with two brass handles, 27½in (70cm) wide.
£540–640 / €790–930
$980–1,150 ⚒ TRM(D)

An Edwardian inlaid mahogany and brass two-tier table, with a glass tray top, 31¾in (80.5cm) wide.
£1,700–2,000 / €2,500–2,900
$3,100–3,600 SWO

► **An Edwardian inlaid mahogany and boxwood-strung two-tier table,** the crossbanded top with two leaves above a frieze drawer, on tapered legs with boxwood stringing, 24in (61cm) wide.
£300–360 / €440–530
$540–650 DD

An Edwardian rosewood two-tier table, the top inlaid with a roundel and boxwood stringing, 15in (38cm) wide.
£220–260 / €320–380
$400–470 DD

◄ **An Edwardian Sheraton revival satinwood two-tier table,** with ebonized crossbanding and quarter-veneered stained harebell ovals, with a tray top, 33½in (85cm) wide.
£1,650–1,950 / €2,400–2,850
$3,000–3,550 DD

A pair of mahogany two-tier tables, each with a leather top and mirrored back, c1920, 35in (89cm) wide.
£1,000–1,150 / €1,450–1,700
$1,800–2,100 Che

Work Tables

◄ **A Sheraton-style satinwood work table,** c1775, 32in (81.5cm) high.
£1,600–1,800
€2,350–2,650
$2,900–3,250 WAA

A mahogany and satinwood-crossbanded work table, with boxwood and ebony stringing, c1790, 21in (53.5cm) wide.
£3,300–3,700
€4,800–5,400
$6,000–6,700 GGD

◄ **A satinwood and banded work table,** c1790, 29in (73.5cm) high.
£6,300–7,000
€9,200–10,200
$11,400–12,700 HWK

A George III mahogany Pembroke work table, the reeded top with two leaves above two boxwood-banded drawers, 20in (51cm) wide.
£1,200–1,400
€1,750–2,050
$2,150–2,550 DD

A George III satinwood and ebony-veneered work table, the top with a drawer above a sliding work bag, the back with a face screen, 17in (43cm) wide.
£1,300–1,550
€1,900–2,250
$2,350–2,800 S(O)

◄ **A Federal figured mahogany work table,** attributed to Duncan Phyfe, the hinged top enclosing a writing surface with a fitted interior, above two drawers and a writing slide, American, New York, c1810, 20½in (52cm) wide.
£3,950–4,700
€5,800–6,900
$7,200–8,500 S(NY)

A mahogany drop-leaf work table, with two real and two dummy drawers, c1810, 20½in (52cm) wide.
£2,250–2,700 / €3,300–3,950
$4,050–4,900 ⚒ S(O)

A Regency mahogany drop-leaf work table, with a writing drawer and a short drawer, c1820, 20in (51cm) wide.
£3,150–3,500 / €4,600–5,100
$5,700–6,300 ⊞ GGD

► A William IV rosewood work table, with a frieze drawer, 18in (45.5cm) wide.
£210–250 / €310–370
$380–450 ⚒ HYD

A William IV rosewood work table, with a drawer and sliding wool bag, 24in (61cm) wide.
£730–870 / €1,050–1,250
$1,300–1,500 ⚒ DN

► A kingwood and marquetry work table, 19thC, 27in (68.5cm) wide.
£2,250–2,500 / €3,300–3,650
$4,050–4,550 ⊞ CRU

A rosewood and gilt-brass-mounted work table, in the style of Gillows, with a frieze drawer, work bag missing, c1815, 24½in (62cm) wide.
£5,200–6,200 / €7,600–9,100
$9,400–11,200 ⚒ S

A rosewood work table, c1820, 18in (45.5cm) wide.
£1,800–2,000 / €2,600–2,900
$3,250–3,600 ⊞ GGD

A Regency mahogany work table, the rosewood-banded top with brass inlay and a rising screen, above a drawer with a baize-lined slope, a pull-out pen drawer and bag, 21in (53.5cm) wide.
£1,650–1,950 / €2,400–2,850
$3,000–3,550 ⚒ WW

A George IV yew-wood sewing table, the hinged cover inlaid with stringing, enclosing a lift-out tray, on a moulded walnut stem, slight damage, 17in (43cm) wide.
£3,000–3,600 / €4,400–5,300
$5,400–6,300 ⚒ WW

A rosewood work table, with a screen, c1835, 30in (76cm) wide.
£2,250–2,500 / €3,300–3,650
$4,050–4,550 ⊞ WAA

A mahogany work table, the lifting top with figured veneers, c1845, 20in (51cm) wide.
£1,350–1,500
€1,950–2,200
$2,450–2,700 ⊞ WAA

A rosewood drop-leaf work table, with two drawers, French, Paris, mid-19thC, 28in (71cm) high.
£660–730 / €950–1,050
$1,150–1,300 ⊞ DEB
This table bears the maker's signature (possibly Swartz), in pencil on the inside, followed by 'Paris, September 1856'.

A satin-birch work table, with traces of gilding, c1860, 18in (45.5cm) wide.
£2,600–2,900
€3,800–4,250
$4,700–5,200 ⊞ CRU

A Victorian rosewood sewing table, attributed to W. Smee & Sons, the lappet gallery above a pull-out bag, 19¾in (50cm) wide.
£820–980
€1,200–1,400
$1,450–1,750 ⚒ WW
William Smee & Sons, of Finsbury Pavement, London, was established in 1817.

A Victorian inlaid walnut sewing table, 18in (45.5cm) diam.
£690–770 / €1,000–1,100
$1,250–1,400 ⊞ MLL

A Victorian walnut work table, 17¾in (45cm) wide.
£330–390 / €480–570
$600–710 ⚒ AMB

A Victorian walnut and marquetry-inlaid work/games table, 17¾in (45cm) wide.
£420–500 / €610–730
$760–910 ⚒ L&E

A Victorian mahogany work table, with floral inlay, the hinged top enclosing a fitted interior, 16½in (42cm) wide.
£330–390 / €480–570
$600–710 ⚒ DA

► **A burr-walnut and boxwood-inlaid work table,** with a fitted interior, c1880, 24in (61cm) wide.
£1,450–1,650
€2,100–2,400
$2,600–3,000 ⊞ WAA

A mahogany sewing table, by Maple & Co, c1900, 19in (48.5cm) wide.
£900–1,000
€1,300–1,450
$1,600–1,800 ⊞ QA
When the two side flaps of this sewing table are opened, the central compartment rises. Maples also made cocktail cabinets to a similar design.

A rosewood sewing table, c1890, 27in (68.5cm) wide.
£540–600 / €790–880
$980–1,100 ⊞ QA

◄ **A Sheraton revival mahogany work table,** the satinwood-crossbanded and harewood-inlaid top enclosing a fitted interior and a work bag, 16in (40.5cm) wide.
£230–270 / €340–400
$420–500 ⚒ G(B)

A coromandel and boxwood work table, with a fitted silver interior, 1900–20, 14in (35.5cm) wide.
£2,300–2,600
€3,350–3,800
$4,150–4,700 ⊞ GGD

FURNITURE

Writing Tables

A Sheraton-style satinwood writing table, the inset leather top with buttons releasing a rising screen and two pen and ink compartments, with a frieze drawer, late 18thC, 30¼in (77cm) wide.
£13,200–15,800 / €19,300–23,100
$23,900–28,600 ⚒ S
This piece follows Thomas Sheraton's design for a lady's writing table in his *Cabinet Maker and Upholsterer's Drawing Book*, published in 1793.

A satinwood and rosewood-crossbanded writing table, the tambour shutter enclosing a ratchet, with a baize-lined interior, c1790, 28in (71cm) wide.
£1,800–2,150 / €2,650–3,150
$3,250–3,900 ⚒ S(O)

A mahogany and ebony-strung writing table, by Tatham, Bailey & Saunders, marked 'T. B. & S. / 5 June 1815', c1815, 35¾in (91cm) wide.
£3,100–3,700 / €4,550–5,400
$5,600–6,700 ⚒ S
The firm of Tatham, Bailey & Saunders, throughout various name changes, produced furniture for the Pavilion in Brighton and the Regent's household generally throughout the early part of the 19th century. Founded around 1785 with premises at 14 Mount Street, the firm was originally the partnership of George Elward and William Marsh. Edward Bailey joined in 1793 and Thomas Tatham – brother to the designer C. H. Tatham – five years later. From 1803 to 1811 the firm styled itself Marsh & Tatham or Tatham & Bailey and, after the arrival of Richard Saunders in 1811, Tatham, Bailey & Saunders.

◀ **A mahogany library writing table,** c1815, 38in (96.5cm) wide.
£4,500–5,000 / €6,600–7,300
$8,200–9,100 ⊞ WAA

A mahogany writing table, stamped M. Willson, c1835, 42in (106.5cm) wide.
£1,400–1,650 / €2,050–2,400
$2,550–3,000 ⚒ S(O)
Furniture stamped 'M. Willson' was either made or retailed through Mary and Thomas Willson's furniture broking and cabinet-making business.

▶ **A mahogany partners' writing table,** the leather-inset top above two frieze drawers opposing frieze drawers, stamped 'Jenks & Wood', London, 19thC, 54in (137cm) wide.
£2,900–3,450
€4,250–5,000
$5,200–6,200
⚒ DMC

A mahogany writing table, with two drawers and panelled decoration, c1840, 42in (106.5cm) wide.
£1,250–1,400 / €1,850–2,050
$2,250–2,550 ⊞ LGr

A satin-birch writing table, in the style of Gillows, the top inset with a writing surface and ebony stringing, above a frieze drawer, mid-19thC, 44½in (113cm) wide.
£1,700–2,050 / €2,500–3,000
$3,100–3,700 ⚒ L&T

A boulle marquetry writing table, 1850–75, 30in (76cm) wide.
£3,300–3,950 / €4,800–5,800
$6,000–7,200 ⚒ S(NY)

◀ **A burr-walnut work/writing table,** c1860, 27in (68.5cm) wide.
£2,700–3,000 / €3,950–4,400
$4,900–5,400 ⊞ WAA

A Victorian mahogany writing table, the hinged central section above four drawers, 47½in (120.5cm) wide.
£280–330 / €410–480
$510–600 ⚒ AMB

A Victorian oak writing table, the leather-inset writing surface above two frieze drawers, with a William and Mary-style X-stretcher, 51in (129.5cm) wide.
£420–500 / €610–730
$760–910 ⚒ PFK

A Victorian mahogany writing table, with two frieze drawers opposing four dummy drawers, stamped 'Heal & Son', 42in (106.5cm) wide.
£630–750 / €920–1,100
$1,150–1,350 ⚒ WW

A Victorian walnut writing table, the tooled leather-inset top with a gilt-metal three-quarter gallery, above a frieze drawer, damaged, 43in (109cm) wide.
£610–730 / €890–1,050
$1,100–1,300 ⚒ DN

A Milanese-style ebony-veneered and ivory-inlaid writing table, with two drawers, stamped 'Jackson & Graham, London', c1880, 59in (150cm) wide.
£7,200–8,600 / €10,500–12,600
$13,000–15,600 ⚒ S(O)
Jackson & Graham (1836–40) specialized in the manufacture of high-quality reproduction boulle and other French furniture.

A Pembroke-style drop-leaf mahogany writing table, the hinged leather-inset top enclosing an ink and pen tray, above a frieze drawer, late 19thC, 17in (43cm) wide.
£350–420 / €510–610
$630–760 ⚒ G(L)

A rosewood writing table, French, late 19thC, 39½in (100.5cm) wide.
£2,250–2,700 / €3,300–3,950
$4,050–4,900 ⚒ E

A mahogany writing table, with a leather-inset top above two drawers, c1900, 58in (147.5cm) wide.
£500–570 / €730–830
$910–1,050 ⊞ MLL

Miscellaneous Tables

A mahogany hunt table, c1810, 69½in (176.5cm) wide.
£6,600–7,300 / €9,600–10,700
$11,900–13,200 ⊞ RGa

A mahogany coaching table, with a folding top, c1820, 35in (89cm) wide.
£1,450–1,650 / €2,100–2,400
$2,600–2,950 ⊞ JC

An Edwardian mahogany reading table, with a ratcheted slope, 37in (94cm) wide.
£140–165 / €200–240
$250–300 ⚒ WW

Teapoys

A William IV mahogany teapoy, the hinged top enclosing a fitted interior, two lidded caddies and bowl apertures, 18¼in (46.5cm) wide.
£700–840 / €1,000–1,200
$1,250–1,500 AH

A William IV carved oak teapoy, with a hinged top, 42in (106.5cm) high.
£220–260 / €320–380
$400–470 MAR

A thuya wood teapoy, c1840, 31in (78.5cm) high.
£3,150–3,500
€4,600–5,100
$5,700–6,300 CRU

Teapoys were introduced at the very end of the 18th century for the storage and mixing of teas in the drawing room. They are effectively tea caddies on stands and were made in mahogany, rosewood and satinwood and sometimes tortoiseshell. Examples retaining the original zinc linings and glass mixing bowls in good condition will sell for a premium. A recognized maker's stamp on a teapoy will also add to value.

Torchères

A pair of carved giltwood torchères, each in the form of a male figure, Italian, regessoed and regilded, c1700, 48¾in (124cm) high.
£7,200–8,600
€10,500–12,600
$13,000–15,600 S

◄ **A pair of walnut torchères,** the knopped baluster columns on outswept legs with scroll knop feet, 19thC, 42in (106.5cm) high.
£880–1,050
€1,300–1,550
$1,600–1,900
WILK

► **An Edwardian mahogany torchère,** 37in (94cm) high.
£890–990
€1,300–1,450
$1,600–1,800
Man

Towel Rails

A turned mahogany double-gate towel rail, 19thC, 40½in (103cm) wide.
£110–130 / €160–190
$200–240 WW

An early Victorian turned mahogany towel rail, 31in (78.5cm) wide.
£200–240 / €290–350
$360–430 WW

A mahogany towel rail, c1910, 33in (84cm) wide.
£110–125 / €160–180
$200–220 HEM

Trays

A tôle tray, the central panel after Morland, on a later *faux* bamboo and ebonized stand, c1790, 30in (76cm) wide.
£2,250–2,500 / €3,300–3,650
$4,050–4,550 ⊞ HA

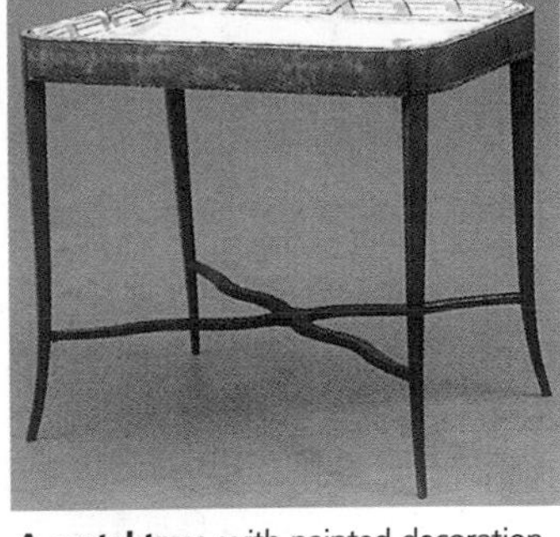

A metal tray, with painted decoration, on a mahogany stand, X-stretcher possibly later, Swedish, c1790, 22½in (57cm) wide.
£1,650–1,950 / €2,400–2,850
$3,000–3,550 ⚒ BUK

A mahogany and marquetry tray, on a later stand, c1810, 27in (68.5cm) wide.
£1,350–1,500 / €1,950–2,200
$2,450–2,700 ⊞ GGD

A japanned pâpier-maché tray, on a later stand, c1815, 17in (43cm) wide.
£2,900–3,250 / €4,250–4,750
$5,200–5,900 ⊞ HWK

A mahogany butler's tray, on a later stand, 19thC, 39¾in (101cm) wide.
£1,400–1,650 / €2,050–2,400
$2,550–3,000 ⚒ S(O)

An oak tray, on a later stand, c1900, 24in (61cm) wide.
£210–240 / €310–350
$380–430 ⊞ MLL

Wall Brackets

A pair of baroque giltwood wall brackets, south German, c1720, 9¾in (25cm) wide.
£1,300–1,550
€1,900–2,250
$2,350–2,800 ⚒ S(Am)

A Victorian Black Forest-style stained wood wall bracket, the support carved as a winged eagle flanked by birds, 29in (73.5cm) wide.
£230–270 / €340–400
$420–500 ⚒ HYD

A pair of carved walnut wall brackets, one in the form of a hound, the other a fox, German, c1880, 11½in (29cm) wide.
£1,000–1,200 / €1,450–1,750
$1,800–2,150 ⚒ S(O)

Wardrobes

A Louis XV kingwood armoire, by Pierre Denizot, with two quarter-veneered doors, gilt-bronze escutcheons and sabots, French, 1700–50, 37¾in (96cm) wide.
£7,700–9,200 / €11,200–13,400 $13,900–16,700 ⚒ S(Am)
Pierre Denizot, cabinet-maker, was received master in 1740.

A mahogany wardrobe, the central panelled doors enclosing trays, c1820, 96¾in (246cm) wide.
£9,600–11,500 / €14,000–16,800 $17,400–20,800 ⚒ S(O)

A William IV mahogany breakfront wardrobe, the central doors enclosing trays, flanked by two further doors enclosing hanging space and a drawer, c1835, 94½in (240cm) wide.
£1,550–1,850 / €2,250–2,700 $2,800–3,350 ⚒ S(O)

A mahogany wardrobe, the two panelled boxwood doors with ebony stringing, over two dummy drawers, above one base drawer, c1770, 51in (129.5cm) wide.
£940–1,100 / €1,350–1,600 $1,700–2,000 ⚒ DMC

A Regency mahogany wardrobe, the two panelled doors enclosing pull-out trays, over two short and two long graduated drawers flanked by two further doors enclosing hanging space, 90in (228.5cm) wide.
£1,900–2,250 / €2,750–3,300 $3,450–4,050 ⚒ Mit

A mahogany wardrobe, the two panelled doors inlaid with shell and paterae, with a drawer, 19thC, 51¼in (130cm) wide.
£1,400–1,650 / €2,050–2,400 $2,550–3,000 ⚒ SWO

A Georgian flame mahogany wardrobe, with two dummy drawers, 48in (122cm) wide.
£760–850 / €1,100–1,250 $1,400–1,550 ⊞ NAW

A mahogany wardrobe, the two fielded panelled doors enclosing hanging space and a removable shelf, Jersey, c1830, 50½in (128.5cm) wide.
£4,000–4,500 / €5,800–6,700 $7,200–8,100 ⊞ JC

A mahogany and crossbanded breakfront wardrobe, the moulded cornice with boxwood stringing, the central panelled doors above two short and two long graduated drawers, flanked by further doors enclosing hanging space, 19thC, 80in (203cm) wide.
£2,000–2,400 / €2,900–3,500 $3,600–4,350 ⚒ L&T

A mahogany and satinwood-crossbanded wardrobe, with ebony marquetry motifs and two panelled doors, slight damage, Continental, 19thC, 83¾in (212.5cm) wide.
£2,100–2,500
€3,050–3,650
$3,800–4,550 DN

A mahogany breakfront wardrobe, the four doors enclosing drawers and shelves, c1850, 76in (193cm) wide.
£4,000–4,400
€5,800–6,400
$7,200–8,000 HA

A mahogany wardrobe, with figured mahogany veneers, with three doors, c1870, 75in (190.5cm) wide.
£1,600–1,800
€2,350–2,650
$2,900–3,250 SWA

► **A walnut wardrobe,** with three doors and a mirror, c1890, 88in (223.5cm) wide.
£1,500–1,700
€2,200–2,500
$2,700–3,100 HEM

A mahogany wardrobe, with two panelled doors enclosing three drawers, American, New Orleans, mid-19thC, 68in (172.5cm) wide.
£2,500–3,000
€3,650–4,400
$4,550–5,400 NOA

A mahogany-veneered wardrobe, with two doors, c1860.
£2,000–2,200
€2,900–3,200
$3,600–4,000 HA

A Victorian mahogany wardrobe, the mirrored door flanked by two panelled doors, enclosing slides and drawers, 70½in (179cm) wide.
£260–310 / €380–450
$470–560 L&E

A walnut-veneered wardrobe, the mirrored doors flanked by pillars, French, late 19thC, 50in (127cm) wide.
£540–640 / €790–930
$980–1,150 JAA

Originally clothes were laid flat on sliding drawers and stored in cabinets known as linen presses. It was not until the mid-19th century that clothes were stored vertically on hangers in wardrobes, which were originally designed as individual pieces of bedroom furniture maintaining the quality of the earlier Georgian linen press. By the end of the 19th century, wardrobes were often produced as part of a bedroom suite, which sometimes resulted in a decline in the quality of craftsmanship.

Due to the curent popularity of built-in bedroom storage units, prices for free-standing wardrobes have become extremely reasonable.

A mahogany and inlaid wardrobe, the two panelled doors enclosing hanging space and a drawer, c1900, 79in (200.5cm) high.
£810–900 / €1,200–1,350
$1,450–1,650 DEB

A mahogany and inlaid wardrobe, with three doors, c1900, 72in (183cm) wide.
£3,600–4,000 / €5,200–5,800
$6,500–7,200 Man

An inlaid walnut wardrobe, c1900, 84in (213.5cm) high.
£540–600 / €790–880
$980–1,100 QA

A mahogany wardrobe, the mirrored door flanked by two doors over two drawers, c1905, 70in (178cm) wide.
£990–1,100 / €1,450–1,600
$1,800–2,000 HEM

An inlaid mahogany wardrobe, the central door enclosing shelves, above three short drawers flanked by two mirrored doors enclosing hanging space, c1910, 69in (175.5cm) wide.
£1,250–1,400 / €1,850–2,050
$2,250–2,550 HEM

An Empire-style mahogany wardrobe, the three doors with quarter-veneer and marquetry panels, with a central mirror, above drawers, c1910, 70in (178cm) wide.
£1,500–1,700 / €2,200–2,500
$2,700–3,100 SWA

A Sheraton revival inlaid mahogany wardrobe, the panelled central door inlaid with laurel wreaths and bellflowers and enclosing a shelf, above two short and three long chequer-strung drawers, flanked by chequer-strung mirrored doors, early 20thC, 75in (191cm) wide.
£470–560 / €690–820
$850–1,000 PFK

Washstands

A mahogany washstand, with a drawer, c1740, 31in (78.5cm) high.
£2,000–2,250 €2,900–3,300 $3,600–4,050 ⊞ HWK

A George III mahogany washstand, with ebony stringing, the hinged top enclosing a mirror, a Wedgwood bowl and jug printed with Willow pattern and a Copeland beaker, above a dummy drawer, two doors and two further drawers, adapted, 18¾in (47.5cm) wide.
£350–420 / €510–610 $630–760 ⚒ DN

A George III mahogany washstand, the hinged top enclosing a rising mirror, above a cockbeaded cupboard and drawer, 16in (40.5cm) wide.
£110–130 / €160–190 $200–240 ⚒ TRM(E)

A George III mahogany corner washstand, with ebony stringing, the splash-back with a shelf, above a shelf with dummy drawers, 26in (66cm) wide.
£590–700 / €850–1,000 $1,050–1,250 ⚒ Mit

A George III mahogany washstand, with two drawers, 30½in (77.5cm) high.
£230–270 / €340–400 $420–500 ⚒ SWO

An inlaid mahogany corner washstand, the two doors above a drawer flanked by dummy drawers, c1780, 28in (71cm) wide.
£600–720 / €880–1,050 $1,100–1,300 ⚒ S(O)

A mahogany washstand, with bowls and dishes above a drawer, c1790, 14in (35.5cm) wide.
£400–450 / €580–660 $720–810 ⊞ DEB

A mahogany corner washstand, with a drawer, c1790, 47in (119.5cm) wide.
£810–900 / €1,200–1,350 $1,400–1,600 ⊞ GGD

A mahogany corner washstand, with holly stringing, the splash-back with a quarter shelf, the later top enclosing spaces for a jug and basin above a shelf with a lined drawer, the stretcher with a space for a ewer, c1800, 24¾in (63cm) wide.
£880–980 / €1,300–1,450 $1,600–1,800 ⊞ JC

A mahogany washstand, c1820, 31in (78.5cm) high.
£630–700 / €900–1,000 $1,100–1,250 ⊞ GGD

◄ **A George IV mahogany corner washstand,** the splash-back above a tier with a drawer and two dummy drawers, 23in (58.5cm) wide.
£175–210 / €260–310 $320–380 ⚒ WW

► **A mahogany washstand,** the shelved marble top above two short drawers, altered, 19thC, 48¼in (122.5cm) wide.
£740–880 / €1,100–1,300 $1,350–1,600 ⚒ S(Am)

A mahogany washstand, with a bowl, the shelf with a drawer, c1880, 23in (58.5cm) wide.
£450–500 / €660–730 $810–910 ⊞ DEB

Whatnots

A Federal mahogany five-tier whatnot, the base with a drawer, American, c1800, 63½in (161.5cm) high.
£1,050–1,250
€1,550–1,850
$1,900–2,250 SGA

► **A George IV rosewood four-tier whatnot,** with a drawer, 59in (150cm) high.
£1,750–2,100
€2,550–3,050
$3,150–3,800 DN(BR)

A Victorian walnut four-tier corner whatnot, the shelves inlaid with anthemia, on turned and fluted supports, 49in (124.5cm) high.
£630–750 / €920–1,100
$1,150–1,350 AH

A George IV mahogany three-tier whatnot, the lower tier with a drawer, 56in (142cm) high.
£820–980 / €1,200–1,450
$1,500–1,700 BWL

A Victorian rosewood three-tier whatnot, with a carved pediment and barley-twist supports, with a drawer, 29½in (75cm) wide.
£1,000–1,200
€1,450–1,750
$1,800–2,150 AH

A mahogany four-tier whatnot, with a satinwood-banded drawer, damaged, early 19thC, 19¼in (49cm) wide.
£230–270 / €340–400
$420–500 DD

A burr-walnut whatnot, by Clear of Wolverhampton, with a brass gallery, c1860, 41in (104cm) wide.
£1,800–2,000
€2,600–2,900
$3,250–3,600 MTay

A Victorian rosewood whatnot, with three tiers, pierced gallery and scroll and twist supports, the base with a drawer, 30¼in (77cm) wide.
£470–560 / €690–820
$850–1,000 WW

A George IV mahogany four-tier whatnot, with a fitted drawer, 24in (61cm) wide.
£630–750 / €920–1,100
$1,150–1,350 G(B)

A Victorian rosewood four-tier corner whatnot, with barley-twist supports, 24in (61cm) wide.
£800–900 / €1,150–1,300
$1,450–1,650 LGr

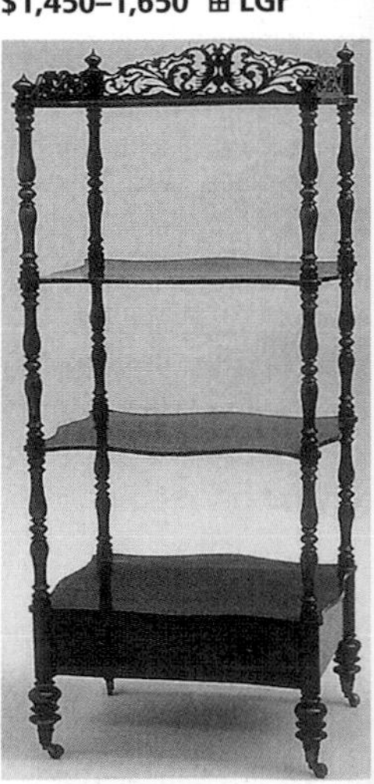

A Victorian rosewood four-tier whatnot, with a drawer, 19¾in (50cm) wide.
£820–980 / €1,200–1,450
$1,500–1,800 DD

Window Seats

An 18thC-style giltwood window seat, Italian, 19thC, 39½in (100.5cm) wide.
£1,200–1,400 / €1,750–2,050
$2,150–2,550 S(O)

A simulated-rosewood window seat, with gilt-brass mounts and loose cushions, 19thC, 47¾in (121.5cm) wide.
£3,300–3,950
€4,800–5,800
$6,000–7,200 WW

A carved hardwood window seat, late 19thC, 32in (81.5cm) wide.
£770–920 / €1,100–1,300
$1,400–1,650 WW

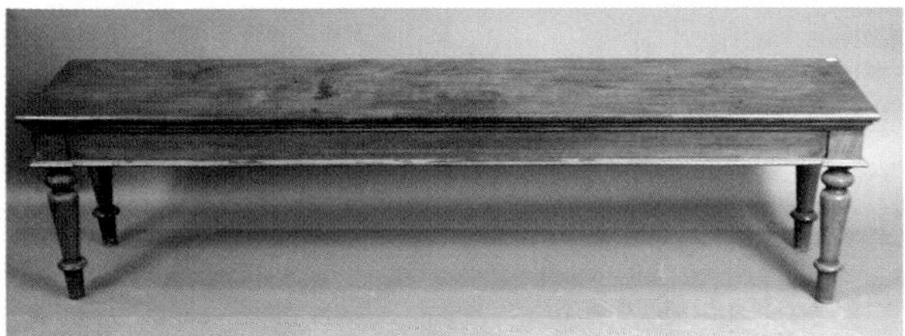

A Victorian mahogany window seat, with turned legs, 72¾in (185cm) wide.
£350–420 / €510–610
$630–760 SWO

An 18thC-style mahogany window seat, with damask upholstery and claw-and-ball feet, early 20thC, 43½in (110.5cm) wide.
£210–250 / €310–370
$380–450 PFK

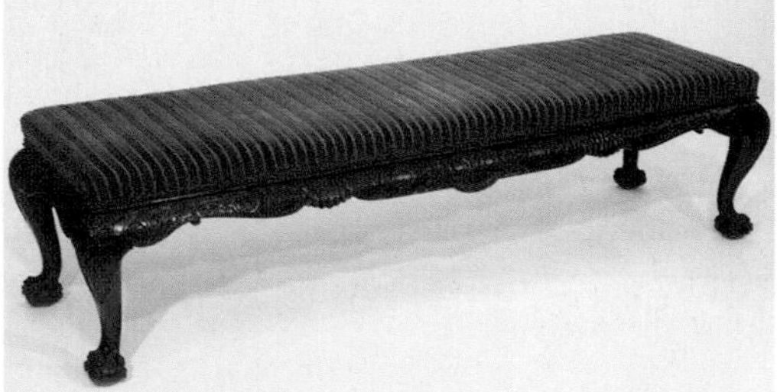

A mahogany window seat, carved with shells and scrolling foliage, with velvet upholstery and claw-and-ball feet, early 20thC, 73in (185.5cm) wide.
£980–1,150 / €1,450–1,700
$1,750–2,100 AH

A Queen Anne-style walnut window seat, c1920, 60in (152.5cm) wide.
£2,000–2,200 / €2,900–3,200
$3,600–4,000 DOA

Wine Coolers & Cellarets

A George III mahogany and boxwood-inlaid wine cooler, 18in (45.5cm) wide.
£2,050–2,300
€3,000–3,350
$3,700–4,100 DOA

A mahogany and brass wine cooler, c1780, 23in (58.5cm) high.
£17,000–19,000
€25,000–27,700
$31,000–35,000 HWK

A George III mahogany cellaret, the interior formerly divided, with brass carrying handles, 23in (58.5cm) wide.
£820–980 / €1,200–1,450
$1,500–1,800 DMC

A George III brass-bound mahogany cellaret, with satinwood banding and lead-lined interior, Scottish, 18in (45.5cm) wide.
£1,900–2,250
€2,750–3,300
$3,450–4,100 L&T

Miller's Compares

I. A George III brass-bound wine cooler, with lion-mask handles, interior missing, 18in (45.5cm) diam.
£2,100–2,500 / €3,050–3,650 $3,800–4,550 TEN

II. A George III brass-bound mahogany wine cooler, with a metal liner, repaired and restored, 23¼in (59cm) wide.
£880–1,050 / €1,300–1,550 $1,600–1,900 TEN

Item I is of good proportions and this octagonal design is always popular with collectors. The lion-mask drop handles on Item I, as found on quality 18th-century classical furniture, are more desirable than the plain bale handles of Item II. The elegant stand of Item I, with its square tapering legs and brass-cupped casters, is more attractive than that of Item II. Although Item I is missing its interior, it appears to be in original condition, while Item II has been repaired and restored.

An inlaid mahogany cellaret, the interior with compartments, c1800, 24in (61cm) high.
£1,000–1,200 / €1,450–1,700 $1,800–2,150 DEB

A mahogany cellaret, c1815, 24in (61cm) wide.
£1,800–2,000 / €2,600–2,900 $3,250–3,600 WAA

A Regency mahogany cellaret, with a fitted interior, 15in (38cm) wide.
£440–520 / €640–760 $800–940 Mit

A Regency mahogany wine cooler, in the style of George Smith, 28¼in (72cm) wide.
£1,500–1,800 / €2,200–2,650 $2,700–3,250 LAY

George Smith (active 1786–1828) was a cabinet-maker, upholsterer and designer in the Regency style.

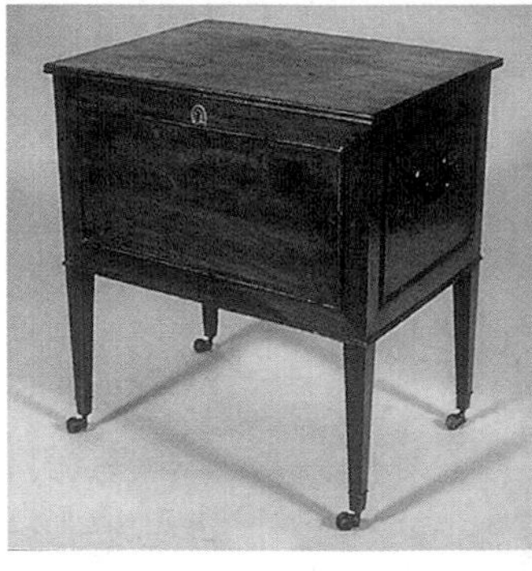

A Regency mahogany cellaret, with a partly fitted interior, 23in (58.5cm) wide.
£420–500 / €610–730 $760–910 WW

A brass-lined mahogany wine cooler, Dutch, c1820, 19in (48.5cm) high.
£900–1,000 / €1,300–1,450 $1,600–1,800 GGD

A bird's-eye maple sarcophogus-shaped cellaret, with mahogany stringing and a mother-of-pearl escutcheon in the form of a butterfly, Scandinavian, late 19thC, 26in (66cm) wide.
£1,200–1,400 / €1,750–2,100 $2,150–2,550 G(L)

A George III-style mahogany cellaret, c1900, 21in (53.5cm) high.
£1,000–1,150 / €1,450–1,700 $1,800–2,100 GEO

Oak & Country Furniture

Looking back over the last twelve months of trading in oak and country furniture, it seems as if this market has weathered the ever-changing fashions comparatively well, the higher value items are still very much in demand, and mostly maintaining their prices. Perhaps one reason for this is that the really good items seem to be coming onto the market less often, as rarer pieces find more permanent homes in long-established collections. This scarcity at the upper end of the market is keeping prices more buoyant.

While the middle market in the UK is a little flat and prices have not changed much, there is still a passionate demand for oak and country furniture. The situation seems to be similar in America where country furniture sells well if there are no problems with its condition and if, with painted pieces, the paint is original. Early American furniture has a small but devoted following, and pieces that retain much of their original components usually sell easily. The huge variety and distinct characteristics of oak and country furniture find great appeal to collectors living in all types of houses, collecting within all levels of budget. Anyone can appreciate the distinct charm that this type of furniture adds to a home. It is worth noting that quite often oak and country furniture surpasses the basic function for which it was made and has to be viewed as a work of art. This point is well illustrated when considering some of the fine carved and inlaid furniture from the 17th century. The obvious planning, effort and artistic skill required to make an inlaid and carved panelled coffer must surely blur the line between cabinet-maker and artist.

It is widely agreed that the lower end of the market, defined as items of poor quality or objects that have been badly restored or damaged, has dropped in price. By definition these pieces will always have been inexpensive, but increasingly they are becoming harder to sell, being squeezed out of the market as the trade and collectors' market focuses on what is 'right' and on modern furniture, which now offers interesting styles at modest prices.

In conclusion, the market trends of the last twelve months have followed the pattern of the previous year. If one can try and predict the market pattern for next year, the same trends are set to continue, with the upper market trading well, the middle market remaining stable and offering remarkable value and the lower market items remaining difficult to sell.

Antony Bennett

Beds

An oak tester bed, with a carved headboard, the canopy with 12 panels carved with relief strapwork and enclosed by later mouldings, supported by fluted pedestals and columns, late 16thC and later, 65in (165cm) wide.
£7,800–9,300 / €11,400–13,600
$14,100–16,800 S(Am)

► A baroque stained oak four-poster bed, the panelled canopy within a moulded cornice, the headboard decorated with panels flanked and divided by pilasters, alterations, German, dated 1697, late 17thC, 60¼in (153cm) wide.
£4,500–5,400 / €6,600–7,900
$8,100–9,800 S(Am)

An oak tester bed, the canopy with a carved floral tablet flanked by panels, 1625–50, 58in (147.5cm) wide.
£8,400–10,000 / €12,300–14,600
$15,200–18,100 S

An oak cradle, the hood above panels carved with stylized tulips and scroll motifs within marquetry-inlaid borders, c1640, 37in (94cm) wide.
£4,900–5,900 / €7,200–8,600
$8,900–10,700 HYD
This is an exceptional piece in good condition with attractive carving, colour and patination.

A spool-turned maple bed frame, mid-19thC, 54in (137cm) wide.
£140–165 / €200–240
$250–300 JAA

Benches

A carved oak hall bench, c1880, 48in (122cm) wide.
£790–880 / €1,150–1,300
$1,450–1,600 ⊞ MTay

A Victorian Gothic revival oak hall bench, 52in (132cm) wide.
£540–640 / €790–940
$980–1,150 ⚒ S(O)

An Edwardian oak hall bench, the back carved with warriors' heads and jousting knights, hinged seat, the front carved with acanthus scrolls, 54½in (138cm) wide.
£1,000–1,200 / €1,450–1,750
$1,800–2,150 ⚒ DD

Bookcases

An oak bookcase, with two astragal-glazed doors above two panelled doors, 19thC, 55¼in (140.5cm) wide.
£560–670 / €820–980
$1,000–1,200 ⚒ SWO

A late Victorian carved oak library bookcase, the cornice with a relief-carved female bust flanked by cherubs, the three glazed arched doors enclosing shelves, above a central aperture flanked by two carved and panelled doors, 85in (216cm) wide.
£2,000–2,400 / €2,900–3,500
$3,600–4,350 ⚒ Mit

◄ **An oak bookcase,** with glazed doors above two carved doors, c1880, 42in (106.5cm) wide.
£2,000–2,250 / €2,900–3,300
$3,600–4,000 ⊞ MTay

Boxes

A walnut salt box, with carved geometric decoration, 17thC, 7¼in (18.5cm) wide.
£1,000–1,200 / €1,450–1,750
$1,800–2,150 ⚒ S

► **An oak collection box,** with painted decoration and iron straps, Dutch, dated 1645, 6½in (16.5cm) wide.
£1,600–1,900 / €2,350–2,750
$2,900–3,450 ⚒ S(Am)

An oak Bible box, on a later stand, c1650, 27in (68.5cm) wide.
£810–900 / €1,200–1,350
$1,450–1,650 ⊞ DEB

An oak desk box, carved with roundels and geometric motifs, the top with iron hinges, mid-17thC, 20½in (52cm) wide.
£300–360 / €440–530
$540–650 DN

An oak box, with carved decoration, c1660, 16½in (42cm) wide.
£900–1,000 / €1,300–1,450
$1,600–1,800 HWK

A carved oak candle box, with brass fittings and carved initials, c1780, 16¼in (41.5cm) wide.
£1,600–1,800 / €2,300–2,600
$2,900–3,250 RYA

Candle boxes, an everyday necessity before the advent of gas and electricity, were frequently made and offered as betrothal gifts and love tokens, often incorporating the recipient's initials and occasionally a date. Suitors traditionally enjoyed the symbolism of the candles 'lighting up' the lives of their loved ones.

Collecting Boxes

One of the interesting aspects of collecting boxes is that they have been made from earliest times to the present day. Most surviving 17th-century boxes are made of oak: examples made from or veneered in other woods are rare and desirable. Boxes dating from the 18th and 19th centuries are found in a variety of timbers and their colour and patination can add considerably to their charm and value.

◄ **An oak candle box,** c1780, 19in (48.5cm) high.
£390–440 / €570–640
$710–800 PeN

OAK & COUNTRY FURNITURE

Buffets

A fruitwood buffet, with a short drawer over two panelled doors, French, late 18thC, 56in (142cm) wide.
£1,750–2,100 / €2,550–3,050
$3,150–3,800 NOA

An oak buffet, with three frieze drawers above two carved and panelled doors, Continental, late 18thC, 53½in (136cm) wide.
£880–1,050 / €1,300–1,550
$1,600–1,900 SWO

A walnut and beech buffet, with later paint, French, 1775–1825, 48in (122cm) wide.
£1,550–1,750 / €2,250–2,550
$2,800–3,150 MMA

◄ **An oak buffet,** the raised back on turned columns, above two carved doors, c1870, 42in (106.5cm) wide.
£900–1,000 / €1,300–1,450
$1,600–1,800 HEM

► **A carved oak *buffet à deux corps*,** Flemish, c1900, 48in (122cm) wide.
£720–800 / €1,000–1,150
$1,300–1,450 MIN

Bureaux

Miller's Compares

I. An oak and walnut-banded bureau, the refitted interior with a well, c1750, 39in (99cm) wide.
£1,650–1,950 / €2,400–2,850
$3,000–3,550 S

II. An oak bureau, the fall-front enclosing a fitted interior, c1750, 36¼in (92cm) wide.
£840–1,000 / €1,200–1,450
$1,500–1,800 S

An attractive feature of Item I is the walnut crossbanding. More importantly, the colour is better than Item II – a major factor when valuing country furniture. Item I also has a well in the interior of the upper part which provides access to the lower section – although Item II has four drawers of useful size, the top drawer cannot be accessed if the slope is down. Additionally, two short drawers, as seen in Item I, are generally more desirable in a bureau than one long drawer.

A George III oak bureau, the fall-front enclosing a fitted interior above a drawer, c1760, 39in (99cm) wide.
£1,300–1,550 / €1,900–2,250
$2,350–2,800 S(O)

Eighteenth-century bureaux

Very few bureaux were made prior to the reign of Charles II, but once the design was established in the early 18th century it changed very little. Bureaux from the first half of the 18th century tend to be slightly smaller in size and are often veneered in walnut or burrwood. Their age, quality of craftsmanship and more compact size make them generally more desirable today. Features to look for that often suggest high quality are feather-banded drawers, stepped interiors, often fitted around a central well, and secret compartments.

A George III oak bureau, the fall-front enclosing a fitted interior, 37½in (95.5cm) wide.
£350–420 / €510–610
$630–760 TRM(D)

OAK & COUNTRY FURNITURE

Bureau Cabinets

A George III oak and mahogany-crossbanded bureau cabinet, the fall-front enclosing a fitted interior, c1760, 42½in (108cm) wide.
£1,050–1,250 / €1,550–1,850
$1,900–2,250 S

A George III oak bureau cabinet, the fall-front enclosing a fitted interior, with later Renaissance-style carving, 46½in (118cm) wide.
£350–420 / €510–610
$630–760 DD
The price for this piece was low because of the later carving.

A George III oak, mahogany-crossbanded and inlaid bureau cabinet, the two doors enclosing three shelves, above a fall-front enclosing a fitted interior, 45in (114.5cm) wide.
£820–980 / €1,200–1,450
$1,500–1,800 L&E

Chairs

An oak armchair, with a panelled back, c1640.
£8,100–9,000
€11,800–13,100
$14,700–16,300 ⊞ HWK

An oak armchair, with panelled sides and back, carved with initials, c1650.
£11,200–12,500
€16,400–18,300
$20,300–22,600 ⊞ RYA

An oak table chair, with carved arms, with a later Georgian top, 17thC.
£1,250–1,400
€1,850–2,050
$2,250–2,550 ⊞ DEB

A carved oak wainscot chair, late 17thC.
£2,900–3,250
€4,250–4,750
$5,200–5,900 ⊞ REF

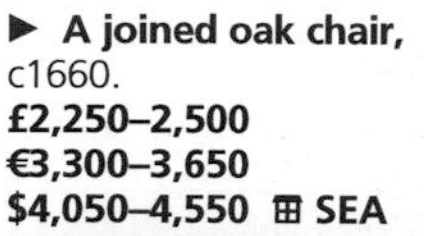

► **A joined oak chair,** c1660.
£2,250–2,500
€3,300–3,650
$4,050–4,550 ⊞ SEA

A carved oak armchair, with a panelled back, arms probably later, c1680.
£1,550–1,850
€2,250–2,700
$2,800–3,350 ⚒ S(O)

A joined oak wainscot chair, the panelled and carved back above twist supports, restored, late 17thC and later.
£1,750–2,100
€2,550–3,050
$3,150–3,800 ⚒ Mit

◄ **An oak chair,** with a later pine seat, restored, c1700.
£100–110 / €145–160
$180–200 ⊞ CHAC

◄ **A pair of oak side chairs,** with fielded panelled backs, late 17thC.
£490–580 €720–850
$890–1,050 ⚒ WW

◄ **An oak armchair,** the panelled back above a seat with a drawer, c1700.
£11,200–12,500
€16,400–18,300
$20,300–22,600 ⊞ HWK

► **An oak chair,** with a panelled back, c1710.
£480–540 / €700–790
$870–980 ⊞ PeN

A joined oak wainscot chair, the panelled back carved with 'WRH' and '1712', early 18thC.
£2,100–2,500
€3,100–3,700
$3,800–4,500 ⚒ TEN

An oak chair, c1720.
£1,000–1,200
€1,550–1,750
$1,900–2,150 ⊞ HWK

A pair of oak side chairs, with pierced panelled backs, c1720.
£1,700–1,900
€2,500–2,750
$3,100–3,450 ⊞ PeN

A pair of oak side chairs, North Country, c1725.
£2,250–2,500
€3,300–3,650
$4,050–4,550 ⊞ PeN

An oak hall porter's chair, with two side drawers, c1760.
£4,650–5,200
€6,800–7,600
$8,400–9,400 ⊞ KEY

► **A set of six oak dining chairs,** each with a splat back, 18thC.
£840–1,000
€1,200–1,450
$1,500–1,800
TRM(C)

North Country Furniture

The term North Country is used to describe furniture with unique features, decoration or proportions that originate from the north of England. For example, virtually all rush-seated chairs from the 18th and early 19th century are from the northwest of England. Oak furniture that is crossbanded in mahogany tends to be from the north. North Country dressers from Yorkshire can often be recognized by a two-colour inlaid stella star. Cheshire dresser bases can be distinguished by their robust low form, ogee bracket feet and turned fluted corner pilasters.

The range of North Country regional vernacular furniture extends beyond country furniture to include more traditional mahogany pieces and clock cases.

A pair of Chippendale-style cherrywood chairs, c1770.
£1,000–1,100
€1,450–1,600
$1,800–2,000 ⊞ WAA

An oak wing-back armchair, with tapestry upholstery, 18thC.
£700–840 / €1,000–1,200
$1,250–1,500 AH

A fruitwood ladder-back armchair, with a rush seat, c1790.
£630–700 / €930–1,050
$1,100–1,250 ⊞ PeN

A fruitwood and elm stick-back armchair, c1800
£1,550–1,750
€2,250–2,550
$2,800–3,150 ⊞ HWK

◄ **A set of eight painted wood Windsor chairs,** American, New England, c1810.
£3,300–3,950 / €4,800–5,800
$6,000–7,200 S(NY)

A set of six ash and elm chairs, with splat backs, probably Shropshire or Staffordshire, early 19thC.
£320–380 / €470–560
$580–680 ⚒ RTo

A matched pair of oak wainscot chairs, with satinwood and mahogany inlay, probably Flemish, 19thC.
£2,050–2,300 / €3,000–3,350
$3,700–4,150 ⊞ REF

A set of eight painted wood Windsor chairs, with simulated bamboo turning and stencilled decoration, American, New England, some restoration, 1800–50.
£1,100–1,300 / €1,600–1,900
$2,000–2,350 ⚒ JDJ

An elm and ash Windsor chair, c1840.
£400–450 / €580–660
$720–810 ⊞ MIN

► An oak bathing chair, with a copper bowl, 19thC.
£420–480 / €610–700
$760–870 ⊞ MLL

A fruitwood chair, with a rush seat, c1860.
£710–800 / €1,000–1,150
$1,300–1,450 ⊞ MLL

► An elm and beech Windsor armchair, 19thC.
£380–430 / €550–620
$700–780 ⊞ CHAC

A yew-wood Windsor armchair, with a crinoline stretcher, c1850.
£620–690 / €900–1,000
$1,100–1,250 ⊞ PeN

A stained wood rocking chair, one spindle missing, American, Boston, 19thC.
£175–195 / €250–280
$310–350 ⚒ SWO

An ash Windsor chair, 19thC.
£490–550 / €720–800
$890–1,000 ⊞ GGD

◄ A Gothic revival carved oak armchair, the pierced back above padded arms and seat, with velvet upholstery, damaged, German, mid-19thC.
£2,100–2,500
€3,050–3,650
$3,800–4,550 ⚒ S(Am)

An ash and elm Windsor chair, c1860.
£580–650 / €850–950
$1,050–1,200 ⊞ MIN

◄ An elbow chair, with a rush seat, Lancashire, c187
£290–330 / €410–480
$540–600 ⊞ WiB

An ash and oak ladder-back armchair, c1870.
£1,350–1,500
€1,950–2,200
$2,450–2,700 ⊞ HWK

► **An ash and elm chair,** c1880.
£75–85 / €110–125
$135–155 ⊞ MIN

A beech and elm Windsor elbow chair, c1880.
£165–185 / €240–270
$300–330 ⊞ WiB

► **A Carolean-style oak armchair,** with carved and incised decoration, late 19thC.
£350–420 / €510–610
$630–760 ⚒ Mit

A beech and elm Windsor chair, c1880.
£120–135 / €175–195
$220–250 ⊞ WiB

A beech smoker's bow chair, with an ash or elm seat, c1870.
£250–280 / €370–410
$450–510 ⊞ WiB

A walnut chair, with a rush seat, French, c1870.
£400–450 / €580–660
$720–810 ⊞ MLL

A beech and elm chair, c1880.
£70–80 / €100–115
$125–140 ⊞ WiB

A set of eight carved oak dining chairs, including two armchairs, carved with heraldic beasts, with barley-twist supports and upholstered back panels and seats, late 19thC.
£1,300–1,550
€1,900–2,250
$2,350–2,800 ⚒ DMC

◄ **A carved and turned oak armchair,** with an upholstered seat and back, early 20thC.
£140–165 / €200–240
$250–300 ⚒ WilP

A beech and elm chair, c1880.
£70–80 / €100–115
$125–140 ⊞ WiB

A set of four ash dining chairs, with rush seats, c1880.
£360–400 / €520–580
$650–720 ⊞ WiB

An oak lambing chair, c1890.
£600–680 / €880–990
$1,100–1,250 ⊞ DEB

Children's Chairs

A child's oak high chair, c1670.
£5,300–6,300
€8,300–9,200
$10,300–11,400 ⊞ HWK

A child's ash and elm Windsor high chair, c1820.
£650–730 / €950–1,050
$1,150–1,300 ⊞ F&F

A child's beech Windsor chair, c1860.
£135–150 / €195–220
$240–270 ⊞ MLL

A child's oak elbow chair, with a splat back, restored, mid-18thC.
£280–330 / €410–480
$510–600 ⚒ DN(BR)

A child's ash and elm chair, with a saddle seat, 19thC.
£140–165 / €200–240
$250–300 ⚒ DA

A child's Windsor armchair, with traces of original paint, 18thC.
£530–630 / €770–920
$960–1,150 ⚒ AH

A child's ash and elm Windsor rocking chair, 19thC.
£370–440 / €540–640
$670–800 ⚒ AH

◄ **A child's ash chair,** 19thC.
£85–95 / €125–140
$150–170 ⊞ Cot

A child's Chippendale-style oak chair, c1880.
£420–480 / €610–700
$760–870 ⊞ PeN

◄ **A child's oak Orkney chair,** with a rush drop-in seat, Scottish, early 20thC.
£560–670 / €820–980
$1,000–1,200 ⚒ DN

A fruitwood correction chair, with box seat, c1820.
£810–900 / €1,150–1,300
$1,450–1,650 ⊞ PeN

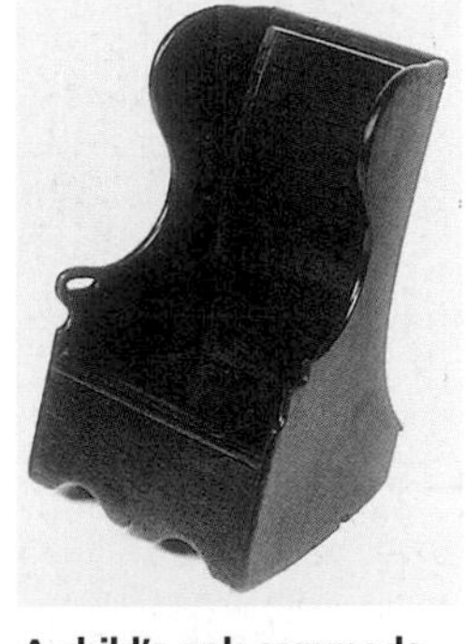

A child's oak commode chair, with a hinged seat, Welsh, 19thC.
£300–360 / €430–520
$540–650 ⚒ HYD

A child's beech Windsor armchair, c1890.
£310–350 / €450–510
$560–630 ⊞ SAT

Chests & Coffers

An oak coffer, with linen-fold panelling, probably German, c1500, 28in (71cm) wide.
£2,400–2,700 / €3,500–3,950
$4,350–4,900 ⊞ HWK

An oak coffer, with carved panels, 16thC, 45¼in (115cm) wide.
£2,350–2,800 / €3,450–4,100
$4,250–5,100 ⚒ PFK

A carved elm chest, probably by James Griffin, the front carved with lozenges, beasts, strapwork and 'The 24 of Mai Ano 1646 James Griffin', 1646, 57in (145cm) wide.
£12,000–14,400 / €17,500–21,000
$21,700–26,100 ⚒ S
This chest shares many similarities with a chest in the Victoria & Albert Museum, London, and is almost certainly by the same hand. Both examples have the same hippocampus and lozenge motifs to the front but, more tellingly, both bear the name of James Griffin. It has been suggested that Griffin may in fact be the maker and the owner. The example at the V&A is dated 1639, seven years prior to the manufacture of this chest, but despite this gap there is little stylistic variation to the carving.

An oak chest, with linen-fold panels, early 16thC, 60in (152.5cm) wide.
£4,900–5,500 / €7,200–8,000
$8,900–10,000 ⊞ REF

An oak coffer, the front with carved decoration, 17thC, 51½in (131cm) wide.
£700–840 / €1,000–1,200
$1,250–1,500 ⚒ SWO

◄ **A carved oak coffer,** 17thC, 51in (129.5cm) wide.
£1,600–1,800 / €2,350–2,650
$2,900–3,250 ⊞ DOA

An oak six-plank coffer, 17thC, 37in (94cm) wide.
£1,300–1,450 / €1,900–2,100
$2,350–2,600 ⊞ MMA

An oak chest, the top with four panels enclosing a lidded till, c1670, 59½in (151cm) wide.
£1,100–1,300 / €1,600–1,900
$2,000–2,350 ⚒ S(O)

A carved oak chest, with a lead-lined interior, north German, c1560, 32in (81.5cm) wide.
£2,700–3,000 / €3,950–4,400
$4,900–5,400 ⊞ DEB
The carving on the front and side panels of this chest is of particularly good quality.

An oak coffer, with a hinged top, 17thC, 36in (91.5cm) wide.
£470–560 / €690–820
$850–1,000 ⚒ MAR

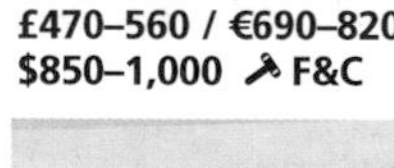

An oak coffer, the base enclosing a long drawer, with pierced iron strapwork and wrought-iron carrying handles, repaired, German, 17thC, 46in (117cm) wide.
£470–560 / €690–820
$850–1,000 ⚒ F&C

An oak coffer, with chip-carved decoration, c1675, 25in (63.5cm) wide.
£1,500–1,700 / €2,200–2,500
$2,700–3,100 ⊞ PeN

◄ **An oak coffer,** the panelled top and sides with guilloche and lozenge carving, c1680, 44in (112cm) wide.
£1,600–1,800 / €2,350–2,650
$2,900–3,250 ⊞ KEY

An oak chest, the plank top enclosing a candle box, the arcaded front with carved pilasters, late 17thC, 43¾in (111cm) wide.
£470–560 / €690–820
$850–1,000 WW

An oak coffer, the base with a drawer, Welsh, early 18thC, 27in (68.5cm) wide.
£620–700 / €900–1,000
$1,100–1,250 DEB

A George III oak Lancashire mule chest, the hinged top above three dummy drawers and a panelled door flanked by six crossbanded drawers, 78¾in (200cm) wide.
£1,700–2,000 / €2,500–3,000
$3,000–3,600 L&T

Coffers & Mule Chests

Coffers are among the earliest pieces of British case furniture and, remarkably, examples from the late 16th and early 17th century can be bought relatively inexpensively. Virtually all coffers are made from oak, which hardens with time and resists woodworm infestation. Coffers of simple construction are often known as 'six plank coffers', the six planks forming the lid, base, front, back and sides. These primitive examples were practical but, with time and changes in temperature and humidity, the planks often cracked or split. Using panelled construction solved this problem. The panels fitted loosely into a frame allowing shrinkage and expansion without damage.

The problem of retrieving items from the bottom of large coffers was solved by the addition of drawers at the base. This type of coffer is often known as a 'mule chest'.

By the mid-18th century coffers were becoming a thing of the past and were being replaced by chests of drawers. When buying coffers dated examples are always desirable. Inlay and carving usually add to both the appeal and price.

An oak coffer, the plank top above a fielded panelled front, 18thC, 34in (86.5cm) wide.
£300–360 / €440–530
$540–650 BWL

An oak mule chest, the panelled front above two drawers, c1760, 55in (139.5cm) wide.
£2,700–3,000 / €4,000–4,400
$4,900–5,400 WAA

◄ **An oak and mahogany-crossbanded Lancashire mule chest,** the hinged top above three dummy drawers, three short drawers and two long drawers, flanked by quadrant pillars, late 18thC, 55in (139.5cm) wide.
£700–840 / €1,000–1,200
$1,250–1,500 PF

Chests-on-Chests

A George II oak chest-on-chest, the moulded cornice above two short and three long drawers, the lower section with three long drawers, on a later base, 42in (106.5cm) wide.
£440–520 / €640–760
$800–940 HYD

A George III oak chest-on-chest, the moulded dentil cornice above two short and three long drawers, the base with three drawers, 44¾in (113.5cm) wide.
£1,200–1,450
€1,750–2,050
$2,150–2,550 CHTR

An oak chest-on-chest, the moulded cornice above three short and three long drawers, the lower section with two long deep drawers, handles replaced, back feet later, 18thC, 42in (106.5cm) wide.
£760–910 / €1,100–1,300
$1,400–1,650 WW

An oak chest-on-chest, the moulded dentil cornice above two short and four long drawers flanked by quarter-turned reeded pilasters, the lower section with three long drawers, 18thC, 43in (109cm) wide.
£2,350–2,800
€3,450–4,100
$4,250–5,100 TRM(C)

Chests of Drawers

An oak chest of drawers, with mother-of-pearl, bone and ebony inlay, the frieze drawer above a deep drawer and two doors enclosing three further drawers, 1675–1700, 46in (117cm) wide.
£14,400–17,200 / €21,000–25,100
$26,000–31,000 S

Percy Macquoid in *A History of English Furniture – The Age of Oak* suggests that the use of these exotic materials and inlay in the Moorish taste is derived from work on caskets and furniture imported from Spain as a result of the betrothal and then marriage of Catherine of Braganza to Charles II in 1662.

An oak chest of drawers, with moulded decoration, on later bun feet, c1690, 30in (76cm) wide.
£3,300–3,650 / €4,800–5,300
$6,000–6,600 PeN

An oak chest of drawers, with two short over three long drawers with geometric panelling, on bun feet, c1700, 41in (104cm) wide.
£760–910 / €1,100–1,300
$1,400–1,650 L&T

An oak and walnut chest of drawers, c1690, 41in (104cm) high.
£10,800–12,000 / €15,800–17,600
$19,600–21,700 HWK

An oak chest of drawers, with geometric moulding, 17thC, 34¼in (87cm) wide.
£730–870 / €1,050–1,250
$1,300–1,550 SWO

An oak chest of drawers, the four drawers with moulded decoration, on later bun feet, late 17thC, 33½in (85cm) wide.
£1,050–1,250 / €1,550–1,850
$1,900–2,250 SWO

An oak chest of drawers, with moulded decoration, c1700, 34in (86.5cm) wide.
£1,650–1,850 / €2,400–2,700
$3,000–3,350 REF

An oak chest of drawers, in two sections, c1690, 40in (101.5cm) wide.
£2,050–2,300 / €3,000–3,350
$3,700–4,150 GGD

An oak chest of drawers, with later bracket feet, late 17thC, 37½in (95.5cm) wide.
£1,900–2,250 / €2,750–3,300
$3,450–4,050 S

An oak chest of drawers, with eight drawers, four drawers with geometric moulded decoration, late 17thC, 34in (86.5cm) wide.
£1,650–1,850 / €2,400–2,700
$3,000–3,350 REF

A Queen Anne oak chest of drawers, with two short above three long graduated drawers, 38in (96.5cm) wide.
£420–500 / €620–730
$760–910 HYD

An inlaid oak chest of drawers, with moulded decoration, c1710, 36in (91.5cm) wide.
£2,300–2,600 / €3,350–3,800
$4,150–4,700 ⊞ REF

A George III fruitwood chest of drawers, the crossbanded top above a slide over two short and three long drawers, handles later, 31¼in (79.5cm) wide.
£1,500–1,800 / €2,200–2,600
$2,700–3,250 ⚒ DN

► **A fruitwood commode,** with four long graduated drawers, French, early 19thC, 48in (122cm) wide.
£760–910 / €1,100–1,300
$1,400–1,650 ⚒ NOA

An oak and mahogany-crossbanded chest of drawers, with two short drawers over three long drawers, c1800, 43in (109cm) wide.
£1,750–1,950 / €2,550–2,850
$4,150–4,700 ⊞ WAA

An oak chest of drawers, with two short drawers over three long drawers, with panelled sides, early 18thC, 40¼in (102cm) wide.
£440–520 / €640–760
$800–940 ⚒ SWO

An oak chest of drawers, with two short drawers over three long drawers, 18thC, 36in (91.5cm) wide.
£530–630 / €770–920
$960–1,150 ⚒ BWL

An oak 'Scotch' chest of drawers, the frieze drawer above a deep central drawer flanked by two short drawers, above three long drawers, with a secret drawer, early 19thC, 24½in (62cm) wide.
£410–490 / €600–720
$740–890 ⚒ CHTR

A George III oak chest of drawers, with two short drawers over three long drawers, 37in (94cm) wide.
£520–620 / €760–910
$940–1,100 ⚒ L

A cherrywood commode, with three long drawers, French, 18thC, 40½in (102cm) wide.
£2,850–3,400 / €4,150–4,950
$5,200–6,200 ⚒ S(O)

An oak chest of drawers, with ebony stringing, c1820, 40½in (103cm) wide.
£700–780 / €1,000–1,100
$1,250–1,400 ⊞ WiB

An oak chest of drawers, the two panelled doors enclosing 31 small drawers, probably Spanish, 19thC, 42½in (108cm) wide.
£1,450–1,700 / €2,100–2,500
$2,600–3,100 ⚒ PFK

◄ **A George IV oak chest of drawers,** with two short over three long mahogany-crossbanded and cockbeaded drawers, 40¼in (102cm) wide.
£270–320 / €390–470
$490–580 ⚒ DD

Chests-on-Stands

A George II fruitwood chest-on-stand, with two short over three long drawers, 31¼in (79.5cm) wide.
£2,000–2,400
€2,900–3,500
$3,600–4,350 S(O)

An oak chest-on-stand, c1740, on cabriole legs, 37in (94cm) wide.
£2,150–2,550
€3,150–3,700
$3,900–4,600 S

A yew-wood chest-on-stand, the six drawers with oak cockbeading, restored, c1760, 37¾in (96cm) wide.
£4,200–5,000
€6,100–7,300
$7,600–9,100 S

A George III oak chest-on-stand, with two short and three graduated long drawers, the stand with five drawers, 55in (139.5cm) wide.
£2,350–2,800
€3,450–4,100
$4,250–5,100 G(L)

Clothes & Linen Presses

An oak clothes press, the two panelled doors enclosing pegs and hanging space, 1675–1700, 48½in (123cm) wide.
£6,000–7,200
€8,800–10,500
$10,900–13,000 S

A rosewood and oak linen press, the two panelled doors enclosing two pierced cupboard doors, a sliding panel enclosing three secret drawers, open shelves and a long drawer, above a further long drawer, Dutch, c1700, 74¾in (190cm) wide.
£3,600–4,300
€5,300–6,300
$6,500–7,800 S(O)

An oak clothes press, the two panelled doors above a base with two drawers, Welsh, 18thC, 51¼in (130cm) wide.
£820–980 / €1,200–1,450
$1,500–1,800 DN

A George III oak clothes press, the two doors with applied panelling enclosing hanging space, above two long drawers, 54¼in (138cm) wide.
£960–1,150
€1,400–1,650
$1,750–2,100 AH

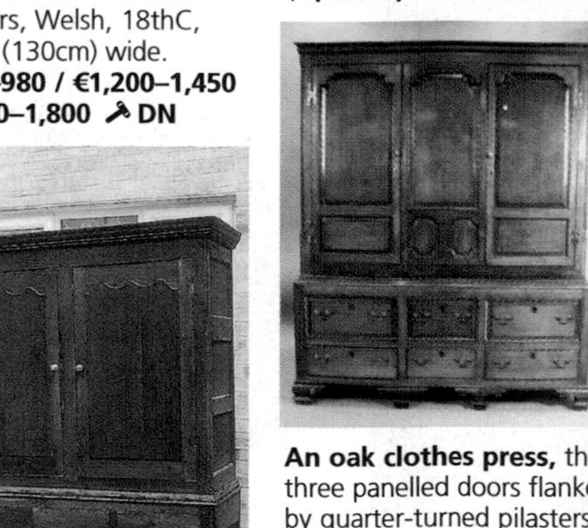

An oak clothes press, the three panelled doors flanked by quarter-turned pilasters, above an arrangement of six drawers, altered, late 18thC, 72in (183cm) wide.
£1,200–1,400
€1,750–2,050
$2,150–2,550 SWO

A George III oak and mahogany-crossbanded clothes press, the moulded dentil cornice above two panelled doors enclosing hanging space, above three short drawers, 64in (162.5cm) wide.
£1,200 1,400
€1,750–2,050
$2,150–2,550 Mit

► **An oak linen press,** the panelled doors enclosing slides, two short and one long drawer, Welsh, c1780 54in (137cm) wide.
£2,300–2,600
€3,350–3,800
$4,150–4,700 REF

◄ **An oak clothes press,** the two panelled doors enclosing hanging space and two shelves, flanking a further panelled door enclosing three shelves, the base with six drawers, mid 18thC, 74¾in (190cm) wide.
£1,300–1,550 / €1,900–2,250
$2,350–2,800 PFK

Cupboards

A carved oak cupboard, the raised back on two turned pillars with chip-carved capitals, the base inscribed 'Except A Man Be Borne A Gain He Cannot Se The Kingdom Of God' and 'W. S.', above a panelled door, probably Lancashire, dated 1654, 52in (132cm) wide.
£15,600–18,700 / €22,800–27,300
$28,200–34,000 ⚒ S
This piece forms part of a well-documented group of furniture attributed to the same hand. All the pieces share comparable characteristics and it is likely that they formed part of a commission for William Stanley (1640–70). Stanley, to whom the initials 'W. S.' probably relate, was a younger son of the Earl of Derby.

A joined oak livery cupboard, with Westmorland carving, c1658, 49in (124.5cm) wide.
£22,500–25,000 / €33,000–37,000
$40,000–45,000 ⊞ KEY
This piece is in totally original condition and is therefore highly desirable.

◀ **An oak cupboard,** the two doors flanked and divided by carvings, above two further doors, German, 17thC, 34¼in (88.5cm) wide.
£2,100–2,500 / €3,050–3,650
$3,800–4,550 ⚒ S(Am)

▶ **An oak hanging cupboard,** with central recessed drawer, c1670, 42in (106.5cm) wide.
£3,500–3,900
€5,100–5,700
$6,300–7,100
⊞ PeN

Miller's Compares

I. An oak press cupboard, the projecting frieze supported by baluster pillars, above two recessed cupboards, the lower section with two short drawers above two panelled doors enclosing a shelf, 1650–1700, West Country, 62½in (159cm) wide.
£12,000–14,400 / €17,500–21,000
$21,700–26,100 S

II. An oak press cupboard, the projecting frieze above two cupboards, the lower section with two panelled doors enclosing a shelf, inscribed '1669' and 'I. A. T.', late 17thC, 60¼in (153cm) wide.
£3,000–3,600 / €4,400–5,300
$5,400–6,500 S

Item I is more expensive that Item II because it is a well-documented piece and is known to have come from a particular village in Devon. In recent years information such as this has become very important to specialist collectors and dealers. Item I is also well-carved with a variety of different regional motifs. The carving on Item II is more restrained and of a more standard nature, although it is worth noting that the addition of a date is always a desirable feature. Item I also has two drawers making it a more useful piece of furniture.

An oak cupboard, c1680, 54in (137cm) wide.
£2,250–2,500 / €3,250–3,650
$4,000–4,500 ⊞ REF

A William and Mary oak cupboard, the two panelled doors enclosing 15 small drawers, 49¾in (126.5cm) wide.
£960–1,150 / €1,400–1,650
$1,750–2,050 S(O)

An oak livery cupboard, with a spindle front, possibly Welsh, c1695, 21in (53.5cm) wide.
£7,600–8,500 / €11,000–12,400
$13,800–15,400 ⊞ RYA

An oak cupboard, the fielded panelled door enclosing two shelves, the top branded 'I. G.', late 17thC, 23in (58.5cm) wide.
£230–270 / €340–400
$420–500 WW

An oak *tridarn*, the canopied top above a carved lunette frieze and two panelled cupboards and a central panel, the base with three frieze drawers and a double cupboard, with Victorian carving, altered and repaired, dated 1735, 18thC, 50¾in (129cm) wide.
£700–840 / €1,000–1,200
$1,250–1,500 RTo

A fruitwood corner cupboard, c1740, 38in (96.5cm) high.
£850–950 / €1,250–1,400
$1,550–1,750 ⊞ DEB

◄ **An oak cupboard,** with two panelled doors, French, 18thC, 73in (185.5cm) high.
£2,700–3,000 / €3,900–4,400
$4,900–5,400 ⊞ DOA

An elm bowfronted corner cupboard, c1790, 36in (91.5cm) high.
£1,400–1,600 / €2,000–2,200
$2,500–2,800 ⊞ MMA

A late George III oak and mahogany-crossbanded food cupboard, the panelled doors with vents, the lower section with two drawers over two doors, on bracket feet, Welsh, Caernarvonshire, 41¾in (106cm) wide.
£2,250–2,700 / €3,300–3,900
$4,100–4,900 ⚒ SWO

A cherrywood cupboard, the two doors with full-length steel hinges, brass studs and locks, French, Châteauneuf du Faou, dated 1899, late 19thC, 51in (129.5cm) wide.
£2,000–2,250 / €2,900–3,300
$3,600–4,100 ⊞ GD

A fruitwood cabinet, the domed and moulded cornice with foliate-carved crest above panelled doors, the base with two further drawers, French, late 18thC, 52¾in (134 cm) wide.
£2,000–2,400 / €2,900–3,500
$3,600–4,350 ⚒ DN

A Victorian oak corner cupboard, the two glazed doors with applied moulding enclosing shelves, the lower doors with similar moulding, with canted angles, on bracket feet, Welsh, 39in (99cm) wide.
£820–980 / €1,200–1,400
$1,500–1,800 ⚒ PF

A maple kitchen cupboard, with nine glass canisters, American, 19thC, 70in (178cm) high.
£270–320 / €390–470
$490–580 ⚒ JAA

An oak press cupboard, c1800, 55in (139.5cm) wide.
£4,350–4,850 / €6,400–7,100
$7,900–8,800 ⊞ MTay

A walnut cupboard, the two panelled doors enclosing a shelved interior, French, c1880, 50in (127cm) wide.
£2,100–2,350 / €3,050–3,450
$3,800–4,250 ⊞ ARCA

A cherrywood corner cupboard, with two panelled doors over a drawer and two dummy drawers, over two further panelled doors, on bracket feet, American, late 19thC, 48in (122cm) wide.
£950–1,100 / €1,400–1,650
$1,700–2,000 ⚒ NOA

Dressers

An oak dresser, the upper section with shelves over two drawers and two cupboards, the base with three drawers and two cupboards, possibly a marriage, 18thC, 52in (132cm) wide.
£1,900–2,250 / €2,750–3,300
$3,450–4,050 E

An oak dresser, with three shelves above three drawers and a pot board, Welsh, c1800, 66½in (169cm) wide.
£2,350–2,800 / €3,450–4,100
$4,250–5,100 SWO

An oak dresser, with associated rack, c1780, 66in (167.5cm) wide.
£3,600–4,000 / €5,200–5,800
$6,500–7,200 REF

An oak dresser, with three frieze drawers and a pot board, shelf hooks missing, handles replaced, the back later, Welsh, mid-18thC, 76½in (194.5cm) wide.
£3,500–4,200 / €5,100–6,100
$6,300–7,600 WW

An oak dresser, with five drawers above a pierced fretwork apron, Welsh, c1780, 69¾in (177cm) wide.
£2,750–3,300 / €4,000–4,800
$5,000–6,000 S

► **An oak dresser,** with five drawers, c1790, 63¾in (160.5cm) wide.
£960–1,150 / €1,400–1,650
$1,750–2,100 S

An oak dresser, with mahogany-crossbanded doors and drawers, late 18thC, 73½in (186.5cm) wide.
£3,850–4,600 / €5,600–6,700
$7,000–8,300 S

An oak dresser, with three shelves above three drawers and an undertier, c1760, 58¼in (148cm) wide.
£2,250–2,700 / €3,300–3,950
$4,100–4,900 S

An oak dresser, with three drawers, Welsh, c1780, 70in (178cm) wide.
£4,500–5,000 / €6,600–7,300
$8,100–9,100 HEM

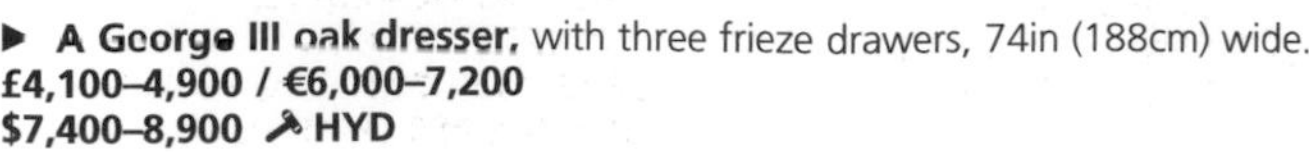
► **A George III oak dresser,** with three frieze drawers, 74in (188cm) wide.
£4,100–4,900 / €6,000–7,200
$7,400–8,900 HYD

An oak dresser, the base with three drawers above two panelled doors flanking dummy drawers, Welsh, early 19thC, 61½in (156cm) wide.
£1,500–1,800 / €2,200–2,650
$2,700–3,250 ⚒ E

An oak dresser, the rack with two shelves above three short frieze drawers, with a pot board, Welsh, Cardiganshire, early 19thC, 60in (152.5cm) wide.
£1,650–1,950 / €2,400–2,850
$3,000–3,550 ⚒ PF

► **An oak dresser,** with three drawers above two doors flanking dummy drawers, with bone escutcheons, Welsh, c1840, 63in (160cm) wide.
£4,400–4,900 / €6,400–7,200
$8,000–8,900 ⊞ HEM

An oak dresser, with a deep drawer flanked by four short drawers, over a pot board, 19thC, 70in (178cm) wide.
£3,000–3,600 / €4,400–5,300
$5,400–6,500 ⚒ AH

An oak dresser, with three frieze drawers and two panelled doors, early 19thC, 65in (165cm) wide.
£4,000–4,800 / €5,800–7,000
$7,200–8,700 ⚒ TEN

An oak dresser, with six drawers and two cupboards, Welsh, c1820, 61in (155cm) wide.
£4,650–5,200 / €6,800–7,600
$8,400–9,400 ⊞ PICA

An oak dresser, with two drawers above a pot board, Welsh, early 19thC, 55in (139.5cm) wide.
£1,800–2,150 / €2,650–3,150
$3,250–3,900 ⚒ PF

An oak dresser, with six short drawers and two panelled doors, cornice missing, Welsh, 19thC, 61½in (156cm) wide.
£1,350–1,600 / €1,950–2,350
$2,450–2,900 ⚒ Bea

A Victorian oak dresser, the shelves flanked by glazed cupboards, the base with three drawers above two cupboards, 63¾in (160.5cm) wide.
£230–270 / €340–400
$420–490 ⚒ L&E

◄ **An oak dresser,** the shelves flanked by two cupboards, the base with three drawers flanked by two panelled doors, with geometric moulding, early 20thC, 74¾in (190cm) wide.
£640–760 / €930–1,100
$1,150–1,350 ⚒ CHTR

Low Dressers

A Charles II oak low dresser, with three drawers, handles replaced, 82in (208.5cm) long.
£4,450–5,300 / €6,500–7,700
$8,100–9,600 JNic

An oak low dresser, with three frieze drawers above a pot board, altered, 18thC, 63¾in (162cm) wide.
£2,700–3,200 / €3,950–4,650
$4,900–5,800 RTo

A willow low dresser, with original paint, c1770, 68in (172.5cm) wide.
£8,500–9,500 / €12,400–13,900
$15,400–17,200 RYA

A George III oak low dresser, the plank top above seven drawers and a cupboard, North Country, 82¼in (209cm) wide.
£1,400–1,650 / €2,050–2,400
$2,500–3,000 DN(BR)

► **An oak low dresser,** Welsh, c1740, 48in (122cm) wide.
£5,400–6,000
€7,900–8,800
$9,800–10,900
REF

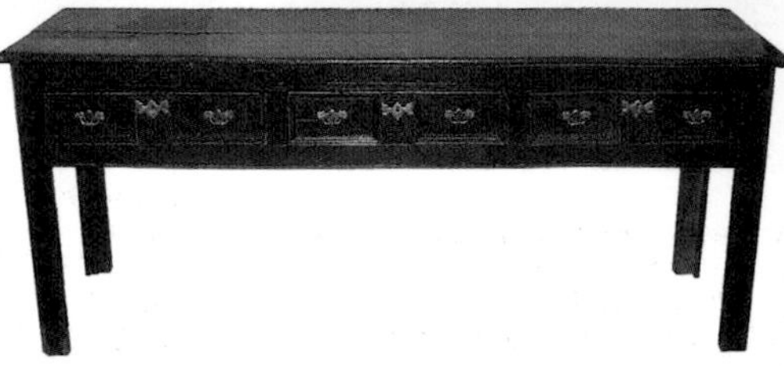

A cherrywood low dresser, c1760, 72in (183cm) wide.
£2,850–3,200 / €4,150–4,650
$5,200–5,800 MMA

Low dressers originated in the late 17th century and had moulded decoration, 18th-century English examples tend to have an open base, normally with three drawers. Early examples have turned legs but by the late 18th century they were often given cabriole legs linked by shaped aprons.

The majority of low dressers are made of oak – those constructed from other timbers are particularly desirable and command a premium.

Low dressers are often referred to as dresser bases. Although they were not originally made with a rack they have often acquired one in the passage of time. Sometimes the rack has been made in the late 19th or early 20th century. These racks rarely damage the base but can make it look a little out of proportion. Equally, dressers often lose their racks and also become known as dresser bases. These are often difficult to spot, but tell-tale marks where the rack has once been give them away. When buying a low dresser seek expert advice as these alterations can significantly affect the price.

◄ **A George III oak and chequer-banded low dresser,** with three panelled doors flanked by two doors, 74in (188cm) wide.
£1,400–1,650
€2,050–2,400
$2,500–3,000
DN

► **An oak low dresser,** with five drawers and an undertier, shelf back missing, c1800, 68¾in (174.5cm) wide.
£2,150–2,550
€3,150–3,700
$3,900–4,600
S

OAK & COUNTRY FURNITURE

Lowboys

An oak lowboy, with three drawers and an arcaded apron, late 17thC, 33in (84cm) wide.
£2,400–2,850 / €3,500–4,150
$4,350–5,200 ⚒ S

An oak lowboy, with three drawers, on turned legs, c1700, 30in (76cm) wide.
£1,550–1,750 / €2,250–2,550
$2,800–3,150 ⊞ DEB

An oak lowboy, with three drawers, on cabriole legs, c1730.
£3,000–3,300 / €4,350–4,800
$5,400–6,000 ⊞ PeN

An oak lowboy, with one long above two short drawers, on carved cabriole legs, 18thC, 33in (84cm) wide.
£590–700 / €860–1,000
$1,050–1,250 ⚒ E

An elm and oak lowboy, with three drawers, on cabriole legs, early 18thC, 42in (106.5cm) wide.
£540–640 / €790–930
$980–1,150 ⚒ TRM(E)

An oak lowboy, the plank top above a short drawer, on tapering legs, c1750, 27¼in (69cm) wide.
£850–1,000 / €1,250–1,450
$1,550–1,800 ⚒ WL

► A George III mahogany-crossbanded oak lowboy, with three short drawers, on cabriole legs, 30½in (77.4cm) high.
£1,750–2,100 / €2,550–3,050
$3,150–3,800 ⚒ AH

Racks & Shelves

An early George III oak dresser rack, the three shelves flanked by two cupboards each enclosing three shelves, 54½in (138.5cm) wide.
£530–630 / €770–920
$960–1,150 ⚒ PFK

► An oak hanging plate rack, the three tiers with spindle-turned galleries, with wrought-iron hooks, Flemish, late 18thC, 41¾in (106cm) wide.
£840–1,000 / €1,250–1,450
$1,500–1,800 ⚒ S

◄ An oak plate rack, with moulded stiles and arcaded friezes, early 19thC, 48½in (123cm) wide.
£490–580 / €720–850
$890–1,050 ⚒ WW

OAK & COUNTRY FURNITURE

Settles & Settees

An oak settee, with turned legs and stretchers, c1800, 64¼in (163cm) wide.
£2,600–3,100 / €3,800–4,550
$4,700–5,600 ⚒ S(Am)

An oak settle, the moulded top rail above a panelled back, the rope seat with a loose cushion, mid-18thC, 72in (183cm) wide.
£530–630 / €770–920
$960–1,150 ⚒ PF

A yew-wood settle table, with a hinged top, early 18thC, 66in (167.5cm) wide.
£7,800–9,300 / €11,400–13,600
$14,100–16,800 ⚒ S
The use of yew- wood for this piece is particularly unusual as most examples from this period are made from oak.

► **An oak and mahogany-crossbanded bacon settle,** the seat with a drawer, with rear doors, c1790, 28in (71cm) wide.
£8,000–8,900 / €11,700–13,000
$14,500–16,100 ⊞ PeN
This settle would have been used to hang bacon to be cured after it had been smoked on a fire.

◄ **An elm, beech and oak settle,** with a panelled back, end of one arm rest missing, the base with later skirting, 18thC, 48¾in (124cm) wide.
£700–840 / €1,000–1,200
$1,250–1,500 ⚒ DN(BR)

► **An oak settle,** with a panelled back, 19thC, 72in (183cm) wide.
£560–670 / €820–980
$1,000–1,200 ⚒ SWO

A George II oak settle, with a panelled back, 55in (139.5cm) wide.
£1,050–1,250 / €1,550–1,850
$1,900–2,250 ⚒ G(B)

Stands

◄ **An oak candle stand,** with a birdcage mechanism, c1690, 24in (61cm) high.
£6,600–7,300
€9,600–10,700
$11,900–13,200 ⊞ HWK
The birdcage mechanism allowed the top to revolve.

For further information on
Birdcage mechanism see page 132

► **An ash, oak and sycamore candle stand,** mid-19thC and earlier, 27in (68.5cm) high.
£1,300–1,450
€1,900–2,100
$2,350–2,600 ⊞ MMA

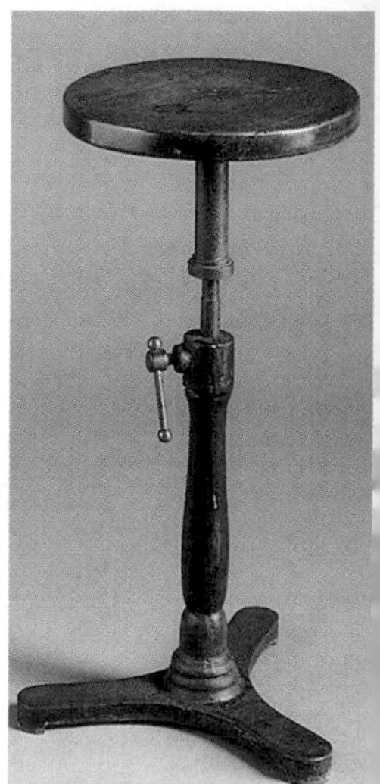

A sculptor's walnut and cast-iron adjustable stand, c1850, 24in (61cm) wide.
£1,250–1,500
€1,850–2,200
$2,250–2,700 ⚒ RYA

Stools

A joined oak stool, c1600, 21in (53.5cm) high.
£10,800–12,000 / €15,800–17,500
$19,500–21,700 ⊞ HWK

A joined oak stool, the moulded frieze above turned tapering legs, damaged, 17thC, 21½in (54.5cm) high.
£440–520 / €640–760
$800–940 ⚒ WW

A joined oak stool, restored, c1675, 42in (106.5cm) high.
£1,600–1,800 / €2,350–2,600
$2,900–3,250 ⊞ REF

A beech stool, c1830, 7in (18cm) high.
£240–270 / €350–390
$440–490 ⊞ PeN

A joined oak stool, with carved rails and original paint, c1640, 19½in (49.5cm) high.
£3,150–3,500 / €4,600–5,100
$5,700–6,300 ⊞ RYA

A joined oak stool, with a later seat, 17thC, 16in (40.5cm) wide.
£530–630 / €770–920
$960–1,150 ⚒ TMA

A joined oak stool, the moulded top above shaped and moulded rails, late 17thC, 18in (45.5cm) wide.
£820–980 / €1,200–1,450
$1,500–1,750 ⚒ TEN

► **An ash stool,** late 19thC, 10in (25.5cm) high.
£110–125 / €160–180
$200–220 ⊞ NEW

A joined oak stool, on four ring-turned legs, with later stretchers, top repaired, 17thC and later, 17in (43cm) wide.
£350–420 / €510–610
$630–760 ⚒ Mit

A child's joined oak stool, on turned baluster legs, c1670, 12in (30.5cm) high.
£2,500–2,800 / €3,650–4,100
$4,550–5,100 ⊞ PeN

A joined oak stool, on turned baluster legs, c1680, 24in (61cm) wide.
£2,500–2,800 / €3,650–4,100
$4,550–5,100 ⊞ PeN

Tables

A carved oak table, dated 1640, 29in (73.5cm) wide.
£3,400–3,800 / €4,950–5,500
6,200–6,900 ⊞ REF

An oak refectory table, the boarded top on four baluster and ring-turned legs, the feet united by moulded stretchers, mid-17thC, 96in (244cm) wide.
£15,000–18,000 / €21,900–26,300
$27,300–33,000 ⚒ S

An oak side table, 17thC, 33½in (85cm) wide.
£850–1,000 / €1,250–1,500
$1,500–1,800 ⚒ L

An oak side table, the frieze with a panel-moulded drawer above spiral-twist legs and stretchers, late 17thC, 36in (91.5cm) wide.
£7,400–8,800 / €10,800–12,800
$13,400–15,900 ⚒ S

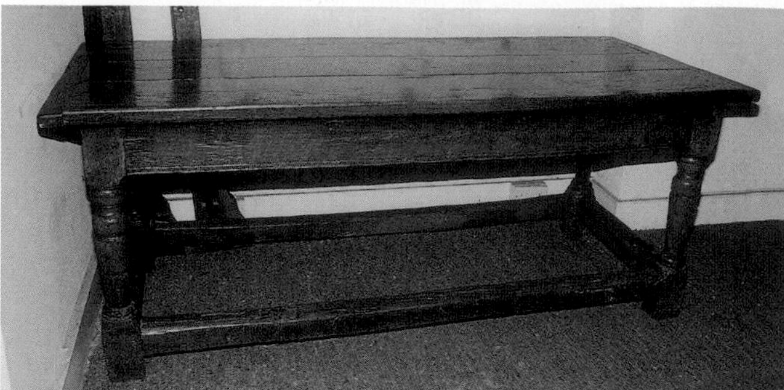

An oak refectory table, c1645, 78in (198cm) wide.
£5,400–6,000 / €7,900–8,800
$9,800–10,900 ⊞ REF

An oak table, the top above a carved frieze, on four legs united by stretchers, 17thC, 71in (180.5cm) wide.
£2,300–2,750 / €3,350–4,000
$4,150–5,000 ⚒ S(Am)

A joined oak stool table, 1650–80, 26in (66cm) diam.
£7,200–8,000 / €10,500–11,700
$13,000–14,500 ⊞ KEY

Prices

The price ranges quoted in this book reflect the average price a purchaser might expect to pay for a similar item. The price will vary according to the condition, rarity, size, popularity, provenance, colour and restoration of the item, and this must be taken into account when assessing values. Don't forget that if you are selling it is quite likely that you will be offered less than the price range.

An oak gateleg table, 17thC, 32½in (82.5cm) wide.
£350–420 / €510–610
$630–760 ⚒ L

An oak bobbin-turned side table, c1660, 28in (71cm) high.
£9,000–10,000 / €13,100–14,600
$16,300–18,100 ⊞ HWK

A Charles II oak side table, with bobbin-turned legs, 33½in (85cm) wide.
£4,150–4,600 / €6,000–6,700
$7,500–8,300 ⊞ KEY

▶ **An oak gateleg table,** with barley-twist legs, gates and stretchers, c1680, 42¾in (108.5cm) diam.
£2,250–2,500 / €3,300–3,650
$4,050–4,550 ⊞ JC

An oak side table, with a drawer, on turned legs, c1680, 31in (78.5cm) wide.
£2,500–2,800 / €3,650–4,100
$4,550–5,100 ⊞ KEY

An oak side table, with a drawer, on bobbin-turned legs and stretchers, c1680, 33in (84cm) wide.
£3,750–4,200 / €5,500–6,100
$6,800–7,600 ⊞ KEY

An oak centre table, on bobbin-turned legs united by stretchers, c1680, 31½in (80cm) wide.
£1,650–1,950 / €2,400–2,850
$3,000–3,550 ⚒ S

A walnut side table, with a frieze drawer, on bobbin-turned legs and stretchers, c1680, 33in (84cm) wide.
£2,000–2,250 / €2,900–3,300
$3,600–4,050 ⊞ DEB

An oak side table, the plank-moulded top over a frieze drawer, on bobbin-turned legs united by a bobbin-turned stretcher, c1685, 36in (91.5cm) wide.
£1,750–1,950 / €2,550–2,850
$3,150–3,550 ⊞ DEB

An oak side table, with a drawer, late 17thC, 29in (73.5cm) high.
£2,250–2,500 / €2,550–2,850
$3,150–3,550 ⊞ DOA

A Charles II oak gateleg table, on bobbin-turned legs and block stretchers, 28in (71cm) wide.
£760–910 / €1,100–1,300
$1,400–1,650 ⚒ HYD

A fruitwood side table, late 17thC, 29½in (75cm) wide.
£590–700 / €850–1,000
$1,050–1,250 ⚒ L

A joined oak gateleg table, with a drawer, above turned legs, c1690, 39in (99cm) wide.
£10,800–12,000 / €15,800–17,500
$19,500–21,700 ⊞ RYA

An oak side table, with baluster legs, c1690, 32in (81.5cm) wide.
£2,900–3,250 / €4,250–4,750
$5,200–5,900 ⊞ PeN

A cherrywood side table, c1690, 25¾in (65.5cm) wide.
£3,750–4,200 / €5,500–6,100
$6,800–7,600 ⊞ RYA

An oak side table, the hinged top enclosing a well, restored, c1690, 20½in (52cm) wide.
£1,200–1,400 / €1,750–2,050
$2,150–2,550 ⚒ S(O)

A turned oak tripod table, c1690, 16in (40.5cm) diam.
£2,500–2,800
€3,650–4,100
$4,550–5,100 ⊞ KEY

An oak gateleg table, c1700, 25in (63.5cm) diam.
£760–910 / €1,100–1,300
$1,400–1,650 ⚒ Mit

► **An oak gateleg table,** with a drawer, c1700, 37in (94cm) extended.
£1,800–2,150
€2,650–3,150
$3,250–3,900 ⚒ S

An oak side table, the plank top above a long drawer and an X-stretcher, c1690, 36in (91.5cm) wide.
£2,000–2,200 / €2,900–3,200
$3,600–4,000 ⊞ DEB

An oak side table, with an X-stretcher, Flemish, c1690, 28in (71cm) high.
£5,700–6,300 / €8,300–9,200
$10,300–11,400 ⊞ HWK

◄ **A yew-wood and oak side table,** with a drawer and an X-stretcher, c1700, 27¼in (69cm) wide.
£4,200–5,000 / €6,100–7,300
$7,600–9,100 ⚒ S

An oak extending table, with a carved frieze, damaged, German, 17thC, 44in (112cm) wide.
£1,200–1,400 / €1,750–2,050
$2,150–2,550 ⚒ S(Am)

An oak centre table, the top inlaid with a marble slab, above a drawer, the sides inlaid with parquetry, with applied mouldings, the legs carved with eagles' claws, German, 17thC and later, 47¾in (121.5cm) wide.
£4,900–5,800 / €7,100–8,500
$8,900–10,500 ⚒ S(Am)

An oak refectory-style table, c1700 and later, 67in (170cm) wide.
£760–910 / €1,100–1,300
$1,400–1,650 ⚒ HYD

Further reading

Miller's Pine & Country Furniture Buyer's Guide, Miller's Publications, 2001

An oak table, with a drawer and a single drop leaf, c1710, 34in (86.5cm) wide.
£7,200–8,000 / €10,500–11,700
$13,000–14,500 ⊞ HWK

An oak tripod table, c1720, 22in (56cm) diam.
£2,600–2,900 / €3,800–4,250
$4,700–5,200 ⊞ PeN

An elm and fruitwood cricket table, c1740, 37in (94cm) diam.
£2,900–3,250 / €4,250–4,750
$5,200–5,900 ⊞ HWK

An oak and fruitwood cricket table, c1740, 24in (61cm) diam.
£1,750–1,950 / €2,550–2,850
$3,150–3,550 ⊞ KEY

An oak gateleg table, the plank top above a drawer, 18thC, 51¼in (130cm) wide.
£700–840 / €1,000–1,200
$1,250–1,500 ⚒ DN

► **An oak tripod table,** with a birdcage mechanism, 18thC, 24in (61cm) diam.
£450–500 / €660–730
$810–910 ⊞ HEM

An oak side table, with a drawer, 18thC, 30in (76cm) wide.
£770–920 / €1,100–1,300
$1,400–1,650 ⚒ BWL

A walnut centre table, 18thC, Spanish, 82in (208.5cm) wide.
£6,900–8,200 / €10,100–12,000
$12,500–14,800 ⚒ S

A George II oak table, with a drawer, 27in (68.5cm) wide.
£540–600 / €790–880
$980–1,100 ⊞ Lfo

An oak gateleg table, 18thC, 47in (119.5cm) wide.
£200–240 / €290–350
$360–430 ⚒ PF

An oak tripod table, c1760, 14in (35.5cm) wide.
£2,700–3,000 / €3,950–4,400
$4,900–5,400 ⊞ KEY

A walnut table, with a plank top, Spanish, 18thC, 46in (117cm) wide.
£260–310 / €380–450
$470–560 ⚒ CHTR

An oak side table, with a frieze drawer, 18thC, 33¼in (84.5cm) wide.
£260–310 / €380–450
$470–560 ⚒ CHTR

An oak gateleg table, with a drawer, 18thC, 46in (117cm) wide.
£860–950 / €1,250–1,400
$1,550–1,750 ⊞ HEM

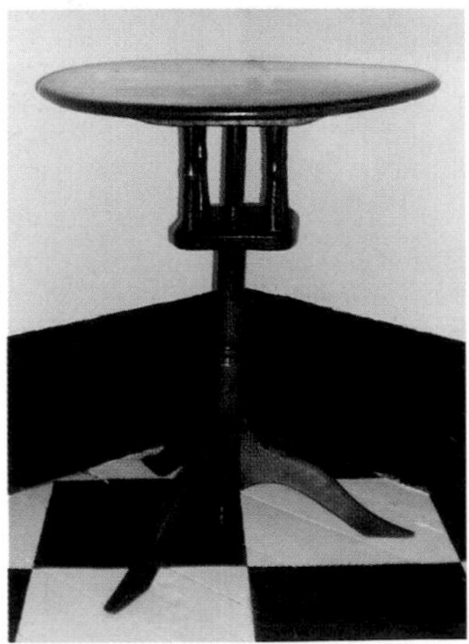

An oak tripod table, c1780, 19in (48.5cm) diam.
£1,650–1,850 / €2,400–2,700
$3,000–3,350 ⊞ MMA
This table has an unusually high birdcage mechanism.

An elm side table, with three drawers, c1790, 37½in (95.5cm) wide.
£1,200–1,350 / €1,750–1,950
$2,150–2,450 ⊞ DEB

An elm cricket table, with a shaped frieze, c1800, 27in (68.5cm) diam.
£1,200–1,350 / €1,750–1,950
$2,150–2,450 ⊞ DEB

A sycamore and ash cricket table, early 19thC, 27¼in (69cm) diam.
£870–1,000 / €1,200–1,450
$1,500–1,800 ⚒ SWO

A yew-wood drop-leaf table, 19thC, 54¼in (138cm) wide.
£2,000–2,400 / €2,900–3,500
$3,600–4,350 ⚒ S

An ash and elm two-tier cricket table, c1790, 27in (68.5cm) diam.
£3,350–3,750 / €4,900–5,500
$6,100–6,800 ⊞ HWK

An elm and oak Windsor tavern table, c1800, 20¾in (52.5cm) diam.
£3,600–4,000 / €5,200–5,800
$6,500–7,200 ⊞ RYA

A burr-elm and elm tavern table, with a plank top, c1830, 39in (99cm) wide.
£4,000–4,500 / €6,000–6,600
$7,400–8,200 ⊞ RYA
It is most unusual to find a broad single plank of burr-elm with such fine and tight figuring.

An oak and pine refectory table, with carved frieze and drawer, 19thC, 33½in (85cm) wide.
£210–250 / €310–370
$380–450 ⚒ CHTR

A walnut side table, with a drawer, French, 18thC, 34in (86.5cm) wide.
£1,050–1,250 / €1,550–1,850
$1,900–2,250 ⚒ S(O)

An oak tripod wine table, with two inlaid stars, c1820, 16in (40.5cm) diam.
£1,000–1,150 / €1,500–1,700
$1,800–2,000 ⊞ PeN

A cherrywood table, the plank top above two frieze drawers, French, early 19thC, 65½in (166.5cm) wide.
£760–910 / €1,100–1,300
$1,400–1,650 ⚒ WW

A fruitwood side table, the plank top above a divided frieze drawer, 19thC, 30¾in (78cm) wide.
£440–520 / €640–760
$800–940 ⚒ WW

◄ **A chestnut table,** with a plank top and a drawer, French, 19thC, 99¾in (253.5cm) wide.
£1,900–2,250
€2,750–3,300
$3,450–4,050 S

► **A sycamore and ash cricket table,** c1840, possibly Welsh, 26½in (67.5cm) diam.
£3,400–3,800
€4,950–5,500
$6,200–6,900 ⊞ **RYA**

A cherrywood wine table, French, Burgundy, c1870, 42in (106.5cm) wide.
£690–770 / €1,000–1,100
$1,250–1,400 ⊞ **MLL**

A Victorian Gothic-style oak centre table, with an ebonized top, 48in (122cm) wide.
£800–960 / €1,200–1,450
$1,450–1,750 L

Insurance values

Always insure your valuable antiques for the cost of replacing them with similar items, regardless of the original price paid. Both dealers and auctioneers can provide a valuation service for a fee.

OAK & COUNTRY FURNITURE

A 17thC-style oak trestle table, c1890, 136¼in (346cm) wide.
£1,900–2,250 / €2,750–3,300
$3,450–4,050 S(O)

An oak cricket table, c1920, 28in (71cm) diam.
£145–165 / €210–240
$270–300 ⊞ **WiB**

An oak two-leaf table, with barley-twist legs, 1920s, 41in (104cm) wide.
£350–390 / €510–570
$630–710 ⊞ **MTay**

Washstands

A George III oak two-tier washstand, with a drawer, 14in (35.5cm) wide.
£210–240 / €310–350
$380–430 ⊞ **MLL**

An elm washstand, with a drawer, c1800, 32in (81.5cm) high.
£700–780 / €1,000–1,150
$1,250–1,400 ⊞ **WAA**

A beech and oak washstand, c1900, 24in (61cm) wide.
£90–100 / €130–145
$160–180 ⊞ **DFA**

Pine Furniture

Beds

A painted pine marriage bed, paint refreshed, with later mattress, Austrian, late 18thC, 49¼in (125cm) wide.
£5,200–6,200 / €7,600–9,100
$9,400–11,200 DORO

A pair of pine beds, converts to a larger bed, European, c1880, 36in (91.5cm) wide.
£360–400 / €520–580
$650–720 B2W

A pine bed, Continental, c1920, 72in (183cm) wide.
£1,350–1,500 / €1,950–2,200
$2,450–2,700 COF

Bookcases

A George III Chippendale-style pine library bookcase, the upper section with astragal-glazed doors enclosing adjustable shelves, the lower section with four panelled doors, 72in (183cm) wide.
£9,400–11,200
€13,700–16,400
$17,000–20,300 HYD

► **A pine bookcase,** the four glazed doors enclosing shelves, c1860, 88in (223.5cm) wide.
£760–850
€1,100–1,250
$1,400–1,550
TPC

A painted pine bookcase, c1860, 40in (101.5cm) wide.
£490–550 / €720–800
$890–1,000 ARCA

► **A pine bookcase,** American, c1860, 40in (101.5cm) wide.
£410–490 / €600–720
$740–890 DuM

◄ **A pine bookcase,** with adjustable shelves, Czechoslovakian, c1900, 50in (127cm) wide.
£420–470 / €600–690
$740–850 ERA

Boxes

A pine box, with carved decoration, c1820, 28in (71cm) wide.
£220–250 / €320–360
$400–450 TPC

A pine box, c1880, 19in (48.5cm) wide.
£70–80 / €100–110
$125–140 MLL

◄ **A set of four Shaker pine boxes,** American, 19thC, largest 9¼in (23.5cm) diam.
£1,100–1,300 / €1,600–1,900
$2,000–2,350 DuM

Chairs

A pine rocking chair, late 17thC.
£1,300–1,450
€1,900–2,100
$2,350–2,600 ⊞ NAW

A pair of painted pine open armchairs, American, New England, early 19thC.
£6,600–7,900 / €9,600–11,500
$11,900–14,300 ⚒ S(NY)

A pair of painted pine chairs, French, c1830.
£310–350 / €450–510
$560–630 ⊞ Lfo

Chests & Coffers

A pine mule chest, with two drawers, interior altered, early 18thC, 43¾in (111cm) wide.
£900–1,050 / €1,300–1,550
$1,600–1,900 ⚒ S

► A painted pine coffer, paint refreshed, altered, Austrian, Salzburg, dated 1753, 61½in (156cm) wide.
£1,300–1,550
€1,900–2,250
$2,350–2,800 ⚒ DORO

A Georgian pine coffer, with original paint, 46in (117cm) wide.
£450–500 / €660–730
$810–910 ⊞ TPC

A pine mule chest, with two drawers and original paint, Welsh, c1760, 40in (101.5cm) wide.
£1,250–1,400 / €1,850–2,050
$2,250–2,550 ⊞ MMA

A Federal stained pine blanket chest, the hinged top above two drawers, American, c1800, 41¼in (105cm) wide.
£145–175 / €210–250
$250–300 ⚒ SGA

A pine trunk, with original paint, eastern European, dated 1826, 44in (112cm) wide.
£220–250 / €320–360
$400–450 ⊞ NWE

A painted pine chest, the interior with a candle box, Scottish, c1840, 34in (86.5cm) wide.
£450–500 / €660–730
$810–910 ⊞ Lfo

◄ A pine travelling trunk, with original paint, Russian, c1850, 26in (66cm) wide.
£90–100 / €130–145
$160–180 ⊞ ERA

► A pine blanket chest, with a drawer, c1880, 42in (106.5cm) wide.
£220–250 / €320–360
$400–450 ⊞ WiB

Chests of Drawers

A painted pine chest of drawers, the three drawers flanked by half columns, paint refreshed, Continental, 1800–50, 46¾in (119cm) wide.
£1,500–1,800 / €2,200–2,650
$2,700–3,250 DORO

A simulated bamboo pine chest of drawers, with two short over two long drawers, 19thC, 39in (99cm) wide.
£630–700 / €900–1,000
$1,100–1,250 ⊞ Lfo

A Victorian pine chest of drawers, with two short over two long drawers, 38in (96.5cm) wide.
£450–500 / €660–730
$810–910 ⊞ TPC

A Victorian pine miniature chest of drawers, with mahogany handles, 13in (33cm) wide.
£200–220 / €290–320
$360–400 ⊞ LGr

A pine chest of drawers, with a galleried top, c1870, 40in (101.5cm) wide.
£380–430 / €550–630
$690–780 ⊞ ERA

A pine chest of drawers, with two short over two long drawers, c1880, 33in (84cm) wide.
£270–300 / €390–440
$490–540 ⊞ MLL

A pine chest of drawers, c1880, 33in (84cm) wide.
£260–290 / €380–420
$470–520 ⊞ WiB

A pine chest of drawers, with painted decoration, eastern European, c1880, 41in (104cm) wide.
£270–300 / €390–440
$490–540 ⊞ NWE

A painted pine chest of drawers, with two short over two long drawers, c1890, 35in (89cm) wide.
£220–250 / €320–360
$400–450 ⊞ NWE

A painted pine chest of drawers, eastern European, c1890, 38in (96.5cm) wide.
£270–300 / €390–440
$490–540 ⊞ NWE

A 'Scotch' pine chest of drawers, with carved pillars, c1900, 40in (101.5cm) high.
£450–500 / €660–730
$810–910 ⊞ B2W

A pine chest of drawers, c1930, central European, 31in (78.5cm) wide.
£400–450 / €580–660
$720–810 ⊞ COF

Cupboards

A pine cupboard, European, late 17thC, 68in (172.5cm) high.
£380–430 / €550–620
$700–780 ⊞ B2W
This cupboard can be split into two down the middle.

A pine cupboard, with four doors, European, c1900, 76in (193cm) high.
£480–530 / €700–790
$870–980 ⊞ B2W

A painted pine clothes press, with carved decoration, the interior with a later hanging rail, restored, German, 18thC, 61¾in (157cm) wide.
£840–1,000
€1,250–1,450
$1,500–1,800 ⚒ S

A George III pine corner cupboard, with open shelves above a panelled door, 42in (106.5cm) wide.
£540–640 / €790–950
$980–1,150 ⚒ S(O)

A George III pine hanging corner cupboard, the astragal-glazed door enclosing five painted shelves, 27½in (70cm) wide.
£1,150–1,350 / €1,700–2,000
$2,100–2,500 ⚒ DN(BR)

A painted pine cupboard, with a paper label inscribed 'Staatliche Kunstsammlungen Dresden' the side restored, with later shelves, Tyrolean, dated 1792, 55in (139.5cm) wide.
£3,350–4,000 / €4,900–5,800
$6,100–7,200 ⚒ S

A pine cupboard, the four doors with wrought-iron mounts, with carved decoration, Austrian or Bavarian, 18thC, 57in (145cm) wide.
£1,250–1,500 / €1,850–2,200
$2,250–2,700 ⚒ DN

A pine barrel-back corner cupboard, with some original paint, the three shelves above two panelled doors, American, c1780, 52in (132cm) wide.
£4,450–5,300
€6,500–7,700
$8,100–9,600 ⚒ JDJ

A pine corner cupboard, American, Pennsylvania, c1800, 37in (94cm) wide.
£1,900–2,250
€2,750–3,300
$3,450–4,050 ⚒ DuM

A Georgian pine food cupboard, Irish, 48in (122cm) wide.
£1,800–2,000
€2,600–2,900
$3,250–3,600 ⊞ TPC

A painted pine cupboard, East Anglian, c1825, 48in (122cm) wide.
£5,800–6,500
€8,500–9,500
$10,500–11,800 ⊞ RYA

A pine cupboard, with two doors enclosing shelves, c1820, 50in (127cm) wide.
£720–800 / €1,000–1,150
$1,300–1,450 ⊞ TPC

A painted pine cupboard, with two arched doors above a base with two doors, early 19thC, 40¼in (102cm) wide.
£700–840 / €1,000–1,200
$1,250–1,500 ⚒ SWO

A pine corner cupboard, with four doors, c1830, 80in (203cm) high.
£630–700 / €900–1,000
$1,100–1,250 ⊞ NWE

A pine standing corner cabinet, 1830–60, 86in (218.5cm) high.
£710–800 / €1,000–1,150
$1,300–1,450 ⊞ B2W

A painted pine marriage cupboard, central European, c1830, 54¼in (138cm) wide.
£3,150–3,500
€4,600–5,100
$5,700–6,300 ⊞ RYA

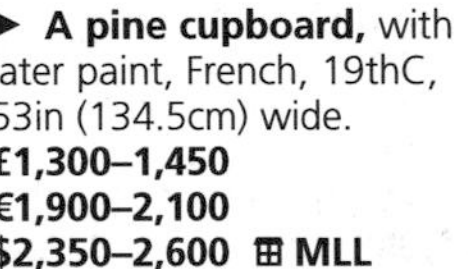

◄ **A pine cupboard,** with a moulded cornice, the open shelves above two panelled doors, 19thC, 48in (122cm) wide.
£2,200–2,600
€3,200–3,800
$4,000–4,700 ⚒ SWO

► **A pine cupboard,** with later paint, French, 19thC, 53in (134.5cm) wide.
£1,300–1,450
€1,900–2,100
$2,350–2,600 ⊞ MLL

◄ **A stained pine display cabinet,** applied with carved panels, German, 19thC, 79¼in (201.5cm) wide.
£1,450–1,700 / €2,100–2,500
$2,600–3,100 ⚒ S(Am)

A pine cupboard, with two panelled doors enclosing shelves, c1840, 52in (132cm) wide.
£540–600 / €790–880
$980–1,100 ⊞ TPC

A painted pine cupboard, with two doors over a drawer, Austrian, c1850, 52in (132cm) wide.
£1,550–1,750 / €2,250–2,550
$2,800–3,150 ⊞ Lfo

◄ **A pine cupboard,** with four doors, c1850, 41in (104cm) wide.
£900–1,000 / €1,300–1,450
$1,600–1,800 ⊞ TPC

A painted pine housekeeper's cupboard, c1860, 88in (223.5cm) high.
£2,850–3,200 / €4,150–4,650
$5,200–5,800 ⊞ ARCA

PINE FURNITURE

A pine corner cupboard, c1860, 41in (104cm) wide.
£450–500 / €660–730
$810–910 ⊞ Lfo

A pine hanging corner cupboard, c1860, 32in (81.5cm) wide.
£220–250 / €320–360
$400–450 ⊞ NWE

A painted pine cupboard, American, c1860, 56in (142cm) wide.
£380–450 / €550–660
$690–810 ⚒ DuM

◄ A painted pine corner cupboard, with floral decoration, Transylvanian, c1875, 31in (78.5cm) wide.
£450–500
€660–730
$810–910
⊞ ERA

► A painted pine cupboard, c1860, 78in (198cm) high.
£1,550–1,750
€2,250–2,550
$2,800–3,150
⊞ Lfo

A pair of painted pine corner cupboards, each with two glazed doors, c1880, 44in (112cm) wide.
£2,050–2,300 / €3,000–3,350
$3,700–4,150 ⊞ ARCA

◄ A pine food cupboard, with a door and four drawers, Dutch, c1900, 37½in (95.5cm) wide.
£390–440 / €570–640
$710–800 ⊞ B2W

A Victorian pine pot cupboard, vith a galleried top, 16in (40.5cm) wide.
£180–200 / €260–290
$320–360 ⊞ TPC

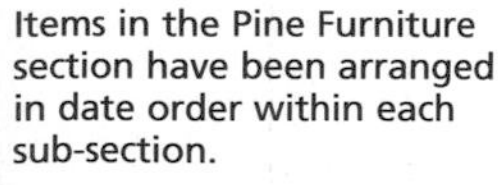

Items in the Pine Furniture section have been arranged in date order within each sub-section.

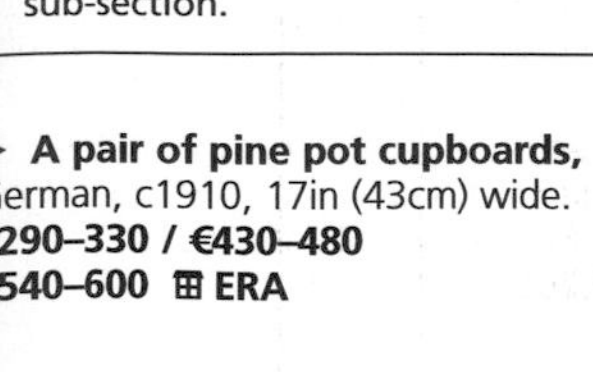

► A pair of pine pot cupboards, German, c1910, 17in (43cm) wide.
£290–330 / €430–480
$540–600 ⊞ ERA

A pine bedside cupboard, central European, c1920, 24in (61cm) high.
£175–195 / €260–290
$320–360 ⊞ COF

PINE FURNITURE

Desks & Bureaux

◀ **A painted pine bureau,** with 'Farmer's Marbling', the fall-front enclosing a fitted interior, stamped maker's mark, Swedish, c1770, 42in (106.5cm) wide.
£10,800–12,000 / €15,800–17,500 $19,500–21,700 ⊞ RYA
'Farmer's Marbling' is a technique associated with the traditional painting of Swedish folk art. It was based loosely on real marble patterns and was sometimes painted on the walls of rooms.

A late Georgian pine kneehole desk, 34in (86.5cm) wide.
£1,600–1,800 / €2,350–2,650 $2,900–3,250 ⊞ TPC

A pine pedestal desk, with original paint, c1900, 53in (134.5cm) wide.
£720–800 / €1,000–1,150 $1,300–1,450 ⊞ TPC

A painted pine clerk's desk, eastern European, c1900, 48in (122cm) wide.
£200–230 / €290–330 $360–420 ⊞ NWE

A pine school desk, c1930, 24in (61cm) wide.
£350–390 / €510–570 $630–710 ⊞ MLL

Dressers

◀ **A pine dresser,** the upper section with two shelves with plate grooves, above a door enclosing a shelf, slight damage, early 18thC, 42in (106.5cm) wide.
£1,000–1,200 / €1,450–1,750 $1,800–2,150 ⚒ JDJ

▶ **A pine dresser,** American, Pennsylvania, 18thC, 54½in (138.5cm) wide.
£1,800–2,100 €2,600–3,050 $3,250–3,800 ⚒ DuM

A pine dresser, the upper section with two glazed cupboards flanking three shelves, the base with six drawers and two doors, with original paint, Welsh, c1820, 70in (178cm) wide.
£4,000–4,500 / €5,800–6,600 $7,200–8,100 ⊞ NWE

A pine dresser, with traces of original paint, west country, c1830, 64¾in (160.5cm) wide.
£8,500–9,500 / €12,400–13,900 $15,400–17,200 ⊞ RYA

A Georgian pine dresser, the base with three deep drawers, 68in (172.5cm) wide
£1,600–1,800 €2,350–2,650 $2,900–3,250 ⊞ TPC

A painted pine dresser, c1870, 55in (139.5cm) wide
£1,550–1,750 €2,250–2,500 $2,800–3,150 ⊞ ARCA

PINE FURNITURE

◄ **A painted pine dresser,** c1870, 56in (142cm) wide.
£1,550–1,750 / €2,250–2,500
$2,800–3,150 ⊞ ARCA

A pine dresser, the upper section with glazed doors and spice drawers, c1870, 52in (132cm) wide.
£1,250–1,400 / €1,850–2,050
$2,250–2,500 ⊞ TPC

A pine dog kennel dresser, the rack above a drawer and two doors flanking a recess, Welsh, Pembrokeshire, 19thC, 54in (137cm) wide.
£1,000–1,200 / €1,450–1,750
$1,800–2,150 ⚒ PF

A pine dresser, the base with three drawers above four doors, c1870, 86in (218.5cm) wide.
£2,000–2,200 / €2,850–3,200
$3,550–4,000 ⊞ TPC

Painted pine furniture

Antique pine furniture was almost always painted. The techniques used for decorating were often inventive and included scumble (softening the painted finish by applying an opaque top coat of a different shade) and *faux* marbling. When pine furniture became popular again from the 1960s the fashion was to strip and wax it in imitation of the clean, light appearance of Scandinavian furniture, but in recent years there has been an increased demand for pieces with their original finish and they generally command a premium.

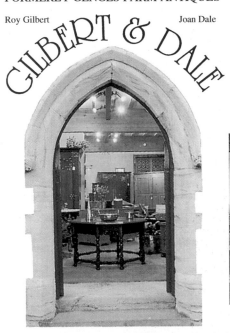

PINE FURNITURE

A painted pine dresser, with two drawers above two doors, Irish, c1870, 51in (129.5cm) wide.
£1,100–1,250
€1,600–1,800
$2,000–2,250 ⊞ ARCA

A pine dog kennel dresser, the upper section with two glazed doors, c1880, 40in (101.5cm) wide.
£900–1,000 / €1,300–1,450
$1,600–1,800 ⊞ TPC

A painted pine dresser, the base with four drawers flanked by two doors, c1880, 60in (152.5cm) wide.
£1,550–1,750
€2,250–2,550
$2,800–3,150 ⊞ ARCA

A painted pine dresser, with three drawers over three doors, Welsh, c1880, 59in (150cm) wide.
£1,550–1,750
€2,250–2,550
$2,800–3,150 ⊞ ARCA

A painted pine dresser, c1890, 51in (129.5cm) wide.
£1,500–1,700
€2,200–2,500
$2,750–3,100 ⊞ ARCA

A painted pine dresser, the rack above six spice drawers, the base with three drawers flanked by two doors, c1890, 64in (162.5cm) wide.
£1,900–2,100
€2,750–3,050
$3,450–3,800 ⊞ ARCA

A painted pine dresser, the base with two doors, Irish, c1890, 82in (208.5cm) high.
£580–650 / €850–950
$1,050–1,200 ⊞ NWE

A pine dresser, the upper section with glazed doors supported on turned columns, the base with two frieze drawers and two panelled doors, Continental, late 19thC, 44in (112cm) wide.
£300–360 / €440–530
$540–650 🔨 L&E

A George III-style pine dresser, with a fretwork frieze, 19thC and later, 110¼in (280cm) wide.
£840–1,000 / €1,250–1,500
$1,500–1,800 🔨 S

◄ **A pine dresser,** with two drawers and four doors, Hungarian, c1900, 77in (195.5cm) high.
£460–520 / €670–760
$830–940 ⊞ B2W

◄ **A pine dresser,** with three drawers and three doors, European, c1900, 77½in (197cm) high.
£1,200–1,350
€1,750–1,950
$2,150–2,450 ⊞ B2W

► **A pine dresser,** with three drawers and seven doors, Dutch, c1900, 72in (183cm) high.
£630–700 / €900–1,000
$1,100–1,250 ⊞ B2W

A pine dresser, with two drawers and four drawers, European, c1900, 75in (190.5cm) wide.
£520–580 / €760–850
$940–1,050 ⊞ B2W

Racks & Shelves

A pine wall shelf, with original paint, c1880, 31in (78.5cm) wide.
£120–135 / €175–195
$220–250 ⊞ MLL

◀ **A pine wall shelf,** with bird finials and original paint, mid-19thC, 13in (33cm) wide.
£700–780 / €1,000–1,150
$1,250–1,400 ⊞ MMA

▶ **A pine wall rack,** with four spice drawers, c1900, 40in (101.5cm) wide.
£135–150 / €195–220
$240–270 ⊞ TPC

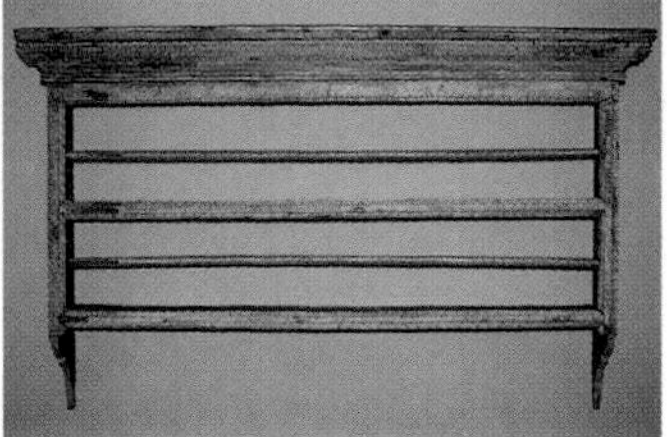

A painted pine dresser rack, c1890, 67in (170cm) wide.
£600–670 / €880–980
$1,100–1,250 ⊞ ARCA

Settles & Seats

. late Georgian ash and pine ettle, the back with four panels bove a hinged seat, the arms on ırned supports, the base with two anels, 49in (124.5cm) wide.
370–440 / €540–640
670–800 ⚒ PFK

A stained pine settle, with a panelled back, the arms on turned supports, the base with a lift-up seat, Welsh, Pembrokeshire, 19thC, 52in (132cm) wide.
£290–340 / €420–500
$520–620 ⚒ PF

A pine wing settle, painted to simulate oak, with a panelled back, the base with a lift-up seat, Welsh, Pembrokeshire, 19thC, 43in (109cm) wide.
£610–730 / €890–1,050
$1,100–1,300 ⚒ PF

◀ **A pine settle,** with lift-up seat and original paint, c1880, 78in (198cm) wide.
£540–600
€790–880
$980–1,100
⊞ TPC

A pine seat, c1880, 42in (106.5cm) wide.
£220–250 / €320–370
$400–450 ⊞ MTay

Side Cabinets & Low Dressers

A Regency pine low dresser, with six drawers flanking a door, 63in (160cm) wide.
£1,350–1,500 / €1,950–2,200
$2,450–2,700 ⊞ TPC

► A pine low dresser, with original paint, c1820, 49in (124.5cm) wide.
£4,000–4,500 / €5,800–6,600
$7,200–8,100 ⊞ RYA

A Victorian pine side cabinet, with a drawer above a door, 38in (96.5cm) wide.
£200–230 / €290–340
$360–420 ⊞ WiB

◄ A Victorian pine side cabinet, with a drawer above two doors, 32in (81.5cm) wide.
£450–500 / €660–730
$810–910 ⊞ TPC

A Victorian painted pine side cabinet, with original crackled paint, the galleried top above two doors, 48in (122cm) wide.
£540–600 / €790–880
$980–1,100 ⊞ TPC

◄ A painted pine low dresser/ serving table, with turned legs, Dutch, c1860, 79½in (202cm) wide.
£1,500–1,700 / €2,200–2,500
$2,700–3,100 ⊞ ARCA

◄ A pine dresser base, with six drawers and two doors, Welsh, c1870, 61in (155cm) wide.
£580–650
€850–950
$1,050–1,200
⊞ NWE

A pine side cabinet, the upper section with two short drawers flanking a mirror, the base with a long drawer above two doors, European, c1890, 70in (178cm) high.
£470–530 / €690–770
$850–960 ⊞ B2W

► A painted pine low dresser, c1890, 70in (178cm) wide.
£940–1,050 / €1,350–1,550
$1,700–1,900 ⊞ ARCA

A pine side cabinet, with three drawers and a door, European, c1900, 26in (66cm) wide.
£200–220 / €290–320
$360–400 ⊞ B2W

◄ A pine side cabinet, with three short drawers over three doors, European, early 20thC, 33in (84cm) high.
£370–420 / €540–610
$670–760 ⊞ B2W

Tables

pine table, with original paint, 18thC, 42in (106.5cm) wide.
£540–600 / €790–880
$980–1,100 ⊞ MLL

► **A pine table,** with a drawer, on turned legs with brass casters, c1820, 48in (122cm) wide.
£540–600 / €790–880
$980–1,100 ⊞ TPC

A Regency pine Pembroke table, 43in (109cm) wide.
£360–400 / €520–580
$650–720 ⊞ TPC

A Georgian pine gateleg table, 42in (106.5cm) wide.
£360–400 / €520–580
$650–720 ⊞ TPC

► **A pine cricket table,** c1830, 21in (53.5cm) diam.
£880–980 / €1,300–1,450
$1,600–1,800 ⊞ PeN

A Federal-style stained pine bedside table, with two drawers, American, 1786–1810, 18in (45.5cm) wide.
£260–310 / €380–450
$470–560 ⚒ SGA

A pine kitchen table, with three frieze drawers, 19thC, 82in (208.5cm) long.
£1,250–1,500 / €1,850–2,200
$2,250–2,700 ⚒ SWO

A pine farmhouse table, the base with two end drawers and original paint, c1840, 72in (183cm) long.
£800–900 / €1,150–1,300
$1,450–1,650 ⊞ TPC

A pine communion table, with Gothic-style end supports, c1850, 42in (106.5cm) wide.
£105–120 / €155–175
$190–220 ⊞ ERA

A pine farmhouse table, on a painted base, c1850, 90in (228.5cm) long.
£1,050–1,200 / €1,550–1,750
$1,900–2,200 ⊞ ARCA

◄ **A pine table,** c1850, 39in (99cm) wide.
£220–250 / €320–370
$400–450 ⊞ TPC

◄ **A pine serving table,** with two drawers, c1860, 56in (142cm) long.
£310–350 / €450–510
$560–630 ⊞ NWE

► **A Victorian pine library table,** with two drawers, 42in (106.5cm) wide.
£360–400
€520–580
$650–720
⊞ TPC

◄ **A Gothic-style pine table/stool,** on fruitwood supports and stretchers, c1860, 30in (76cm) wide.
£70–80 / €100–115
$125–145 ⊞ ERA

A pine and ash lowboy, c1860, 35in (89cm) wide.
£430–480 / €630–700
$780–870 ⊞ Lfo

► **A Victorian pine extending table,** 56in (142cm) wide.
£540–600 / €790–880
$980–1,100 ⊞ TPC

A Victorian pine table, with a drawer, 46in (117cm) wide.
£360–400 / €520–580
$650–720 ⊞ TPC

A pine side table, Irish, c1870, 32in (81.5cm) wide.
£155–175 / €230–260
$280–320 ⊞ MLL

A Victorian pine cricket table, 22in (56cm) diam.
£180–200 / €260–290
$320–360 ⊞ TPC

A pine extending table, Hungarian, c1880, 45½in (115.5cm) wide.
£310–350 / €450–510
$560–640 ⊞ B2W

A pine side table, with a drawer, Spanish, c1880, 40in (101.5cm) wide.
£510–570 / €740–830
$920–1,050 ⊞ MLL

A pine farmhouse table, European, c1880, 47in (119.5cm) wide.
£220–250 / €320–370
$400–450 ⊞ B2W

A pine table, with a drawer, c1890, 40½in (103cm) wide.
£270–300 / €390–440
$490–540 ⊞ B2W

A pine table, European, c1890, 39in (99cm) wide.
£220–250 / €320–370
$400–450 ⊞ B2W

Wardrobes

A pine wardrobe, with two doors, the base with two drawers, c1780, 45in (114.5cm) wide.
£1,050–1,200
€1,550–1,750
$1,900–2,150 ⊞ TPC

A pine wardrobe, with two doors and original paint, eastern European, c1820, 48in (122cm) wide.
£500–550 / €730–810
$900–1,000 ⊞ NWE

A painted pine wardrobe, Austrian, dated 1827, early 19thC, 50¾in (129cm) wide.
£780–930 / €1,150–1,350
$1,450–1,700 ⚒ L

A pine wardrobe, with two doors and original paint, eastern European, dated 1834, 76in (176cm) high.
£580–650 / €850–950
$1,050–1,200 ⊞ NWE

A pine wardrobe, the two doors flanked by columns, with original paint, eastern European, dated 1847, 65in (165cm) high.
£400–450 / €580–660
$720–810 ⊞ NWE

A pine miniature wardrobe, French, c1860, 30in (76cm) high.
£290–320 / €420–470
$520–580 ⊞ Lfo

A pine wardrobe, with two doors above two drawers, Continental, c1870, 66in (167.5cm) wide.
£1,650–1,850
€2,400–2,700
$3,000–3,350 ⊞ COF

◄ **A pine wardrobe,** with carved corbels, with a single drawer, altered, German, 19thC, 61in (155cm) high.
£350–390 / €510–570
$630–710 ⊞ ERA

A pine cupboard, with two doors above a drawer, Czechoslovakian, c1875, 42in (106.5cm) wide.
£540–600 / €790–880
$980–1,100 ⊞ ERA

A pine wardrobe, with two doors above two drawers, European, c1880, 79in (200.5cm) high.
£760–850 / €1,100–1,250
$1,400–1,550 ⊞ B2W

A pine wardrobe, German, c1880, 42in (106.5ccm) wide.
£450–500 / €660–730
$810–910 ⊞ ERA

A late Victorian pine wardrobe, with two doors, one short and one long drawer, 46in (117cm) wide.
£1,050–1,200
€1,550–1,750
$1,900–2,150 ⊞ TPC

◄ **A pine wardrobe,** with two doors, European, c1890, 67in (170cm) high.
£620–690 / €900–1,000
$1,100–1,250 ⊞ B2W

A pine wardrobe, decorated with gesso, c1900, 76in (193cm) high.
£380–430 / €550–630
$690–780 ⊞ B2W

A pine wardrobe, with two doors flanked by turned columns, over one drawer, Hungarian, c1900, 71½in (181.5cm) high.
£470–530 / €690–770
$850–960 ⊞ B2W

LOCATE THE SOURCE

The source of each illustration in Miller's can be found by checking the code letters below each caption with the Key to Illustrations, pages 778–784.

A pine wardrobe, with three doors, Dutch, c1900, 78in (198cm) high.
£870–970 / €1,250–1,400
$1,550–1,750 ⊞ B2W

► **A pine wardrobe,** with three doors and two drawers, German, c1910, 64in (162.5cm) wide.
£780–870 / €1,150–1,300
$1,400–1,550 ⊞ ERA

Wash Stands

A Victorian pine washstand, 36in (91.5cm) wide.
£270–300 / €390–440
$490–540 ⊞ TPC

A painted pine washstand, c1880, 32in (81.5cm) high.
£165–185 / €240–270
$300–330 ⊞ WiB

A pine washstand, Hungarian, c1900, 30in (76cm) high.
£250–280 / €370–410
$450–510 ⊞ B2W

Miscellaneous

A pair of *faux* bamboo pine bedside cabinets, c1900, 34in (86.5cm) high.
£440–490 / €640–720
$800–890 ⊞ MLL

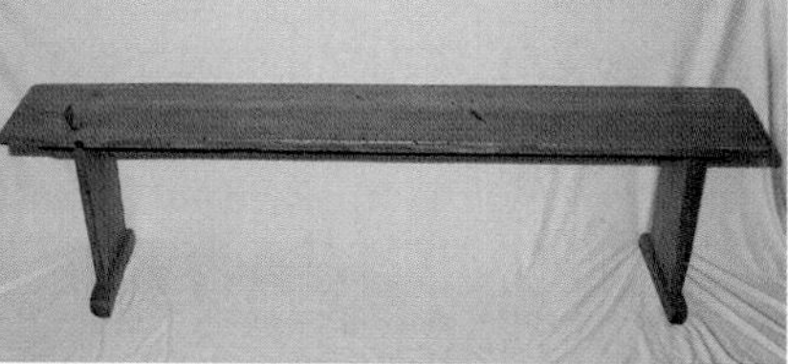

A pine bench, c1890, 27¼in (69cm) long.
£250–280 / €370–410
$450–510 ⊞ COF

A pine bank of drawers, 19thC, 76½in (194.5cm) wide.
£1,400–1,650 / €2,050–2,400
$2,550–3,000 ⚒ CHTR

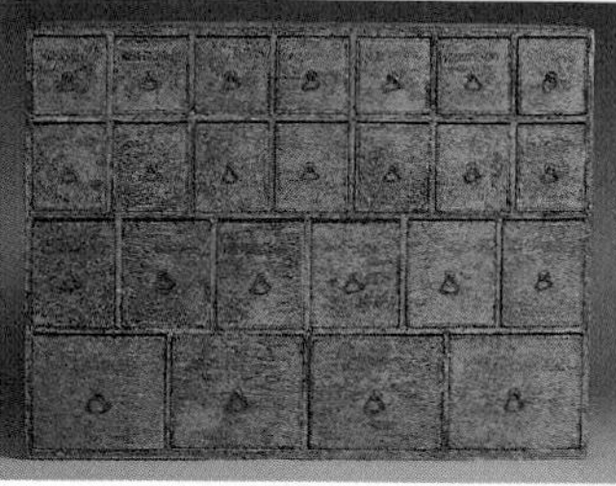

A pine bank of seed drawers, with iron handles and original paint, c1780, 47½in (120.5cm) wide.
£2,900–3,200 / €4,250–4,700
$5,200–5,800 ⊞ RYA

A pine dough bin, eastern European, c1880, 31in (78.5cm) wide.
£40–45 / €55–65
$70–80 ⊞ NWE

Items in the Pine Miscellaneous section have been arranged in alphabetical order.

A late Victorian pine dressing table, with gesso decoration, 45in (114.5cm) wide.
£630–700 / €920–1,050
$1,150–1,300 ⊞ TPC

A painted pine dog kennel, c1870, 27in (68.5cm) long.
£250–280 / €370–410
$450–510 ⊞ ARCA

A pair of painted pine bargeware stools, c1860, 14in (35.5cm) wide.
£540–600 / €790–880
$980–1,100 ⊞ SMI

PINE FURNITURE

Bamboo, Cane & Wicker Furniture

A bamboo cabinet, with four doors enclosing shelves, late 19thC, 35½in (90cm) wide.
£2,450–2,900
€3,600–4,250
$4,450–5,200 ⚒ S(P)

A cane and giltwood canterbury, 19thC, 28in (71cm) high.
£380–430 / €550–630
$690–780 ⊞ Lfo

A parcel-gilt and cane daybed, late 19thC, 53½in (136cm) long.
£500–600 / €730–870
$910–1,050 ⚒ DN(BR)

A beech and wicker chair, with a lined interior, Dutch, early 20thC, 58¾in (149cm) high.
£1,800–2,150
€2,650–3,150
$3,250–3,900 ⚒ S(Am)

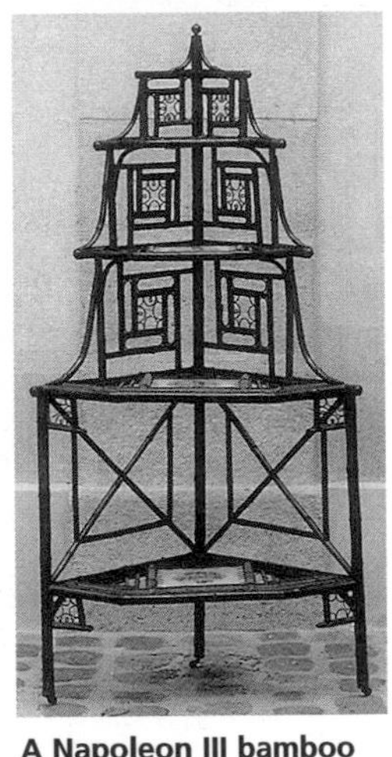

A Victorian bamboo dressing table, with three drawers, 30in (76cm) wide.
£1,200–1,400
€1,750–2,050
$2,150–2,550 ⚒ S(Am)

A Napoleon III bamboo corner *étagère*, French, mid-19thC, 30¾in (78cm) wide.
£1,600–1,900
€2,350–2,750
$2,900–3,450 ⚒ S(P)

A wicker jardinière, c1930, 27in (68.5cm) high.
£55–65 / €80–95
$100–115 ⊞ MLL

◄ **A beech *faux* bamboo three-tier tray stand,** with cane trays, c1920, 22in (56cm) wide.
£220–250
€320–370
$400–450
⊞ MLL

◄ **A bamboo and japanned *secrétaire à abattant*,** decorated with birds and foliage, the fall-front enclosing a fitted interior, above two shelves, 1875–1900, 25½in (65cm) wide.
£1,200–1,400 / €1,750–2,050
$2,150–2,550 ⚒ S(Am)

A bamboo and papier-mâché three-tier whatnot, c1880, 36in (91.5cm) high.
£220–250 / €320–370
$400–450 ⊞ DOA

Kitchenware

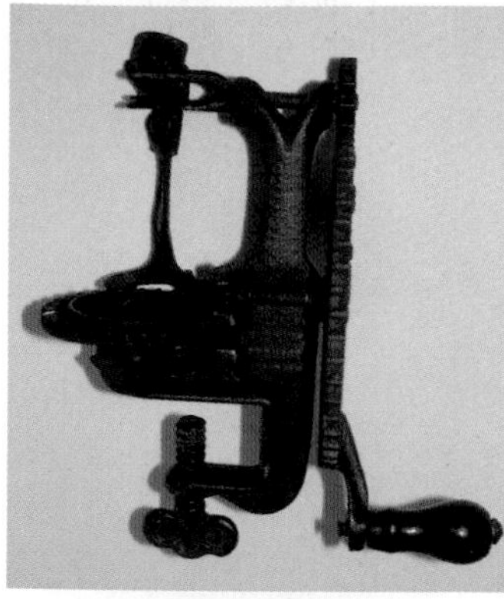

A metal apple peeler, American, Baltimore, late 19thC, 7in (18cm) long.
£155–175 / €230–260
$280–320 ⊞ WeA

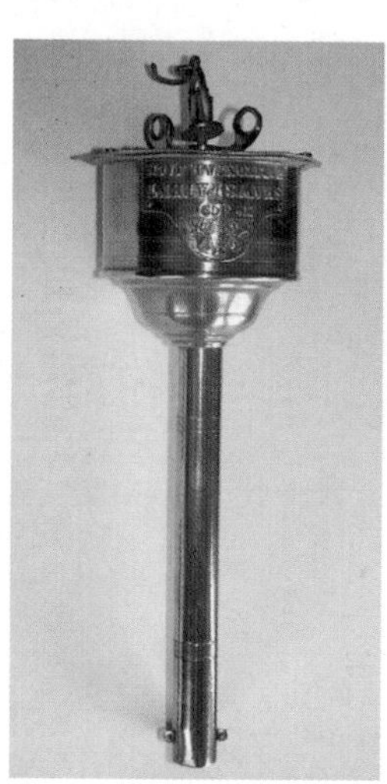

A ceramic bowl, by Parnall, inscribed 'New Laid Eggs', c1850, 10in (25.5cm) diam.
£450–500 / €660–730
$810–910 ⊞ SMI

◄ **A Shaw's brass bottlejack,** with a clockwork spit, late 19thC, 13¾in (35cm) long.
£180–200 / €260–290
$320–360 ⊞ WeA

A sycamore bread board, with carved decoration, c1910, 12in (30.5cm) wide.
£105–120 / €155–175
$200–220 ⊞ SMI

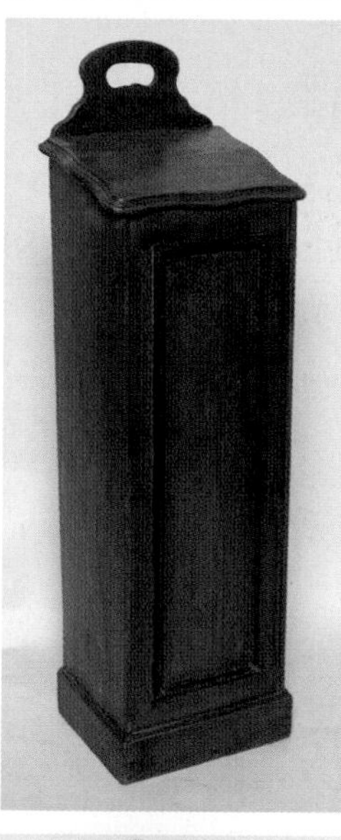

► **A fruitwood bread box,** French, c1900, 36in (91.5cm) high.
£90–100 / €130–145
$160–180 ⊞ MLL

A Canadian maple and beech butcher's block, c1920, 48in (122cm) wide.
£1,100–1,250 / €1,600–1,800
$2,000–2,250 ⊞ COF

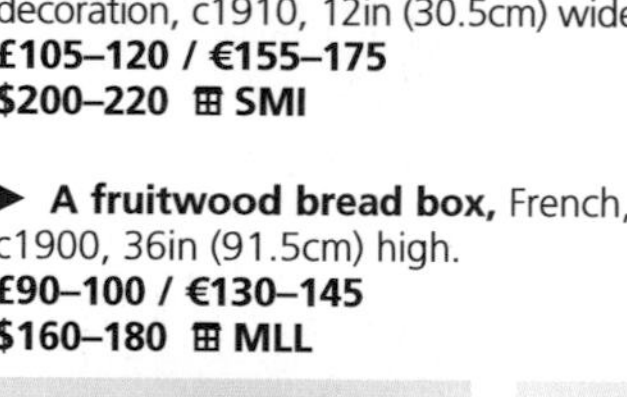

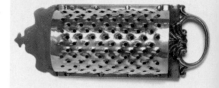

A brass cheese grater, c1820, 13in (33cm) high.
£270–300 / €390–440
$490–540 ⊞ SMI

◄ **A pine and iron coconut shredder,** by L. Collier, Rochdale, c1850, 13in (33cm) high.
£165–185
€240–270
$300–330 ⊞ HEM

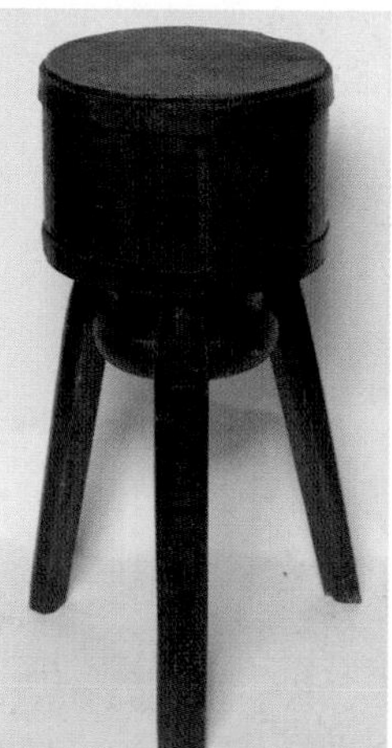

An oak chopping block, c1850, 13in (33cm) wide.
£270–300 / €390–440
$490–540 ⊞ MLL

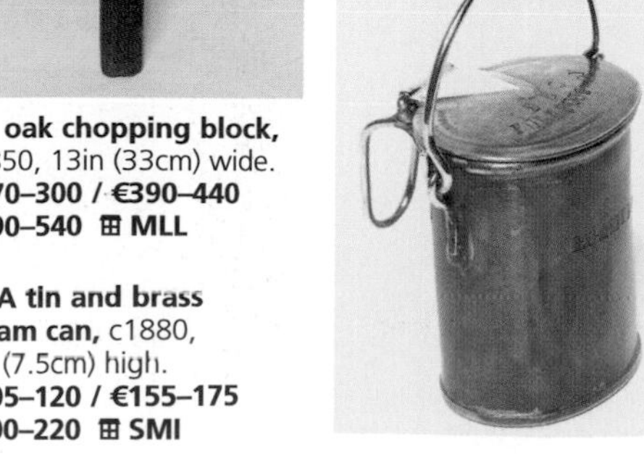

► **A tin and brass cream can,** c1880, 3in (7.5cm) high.
£105–120 / €155–175
$200–220 ⊞ SMI

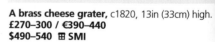

A cast-iron and brass coffee grinder, by Clark, c1840, 5in (12.5cm) wide.
£220–250 / €320–360
$400–450 ⊞ SMI

◄ **A salt-glazed crock,** Canadian, Ontario, 19thC, 14¾in (37.5cm) high.
£380–450 / €560–660
$690–810 ⚒ DuM

A pine cutlery tray, carved with hearts, c1860, 15in (38cm) wide.
£180–200 / €260–290
$320–360 ⊞ SMI

◀ **A butcher's ceramic dripping pot,** c1850, 5in (12.5cm) diam.
£105–120 / €155–175
$200–220 ⊞ SMI

A wooden egg timer, early 19thC, 13½in (34.5cm) high.
£220–260 / €320–380
$400–480 ⚒ SWO

A copper goffering iron, 19thC, 12in (30.5cm) long.
£450–500 / €660–730
$810–910 ⊞ SEA

A cast-iron and brass gas iron and trivet, by Otto, the iron with a wooden handle, c1880, 8in (20.5cm) wide.
£135–150 / €195–220
$240–270 ⊞ SMI

◀ **A brass ox tongue iron,** c1880, Austrian, 8in (20.5cm) long.
£670–750 / €980–1,100
$1,200–1,350 ⊞ SEA

A ceramic jar, inscribed 'Pl. Barley', Scottish, c1890, 12in (30.5cm) high.
£105–120 / €155–175
$200–220 ⊞ B&R

A ceramic hot water jug, c1910, 10in (25.5cm) high.
£310–350 / €450–510
$560–630 ⊞ SMI

A brass lemon squeezer, on an oak base, c1880, 14in (35.5cm) wide.
£440–490 / €640–720
$800–890 ⊞ SMI

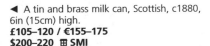

A creamware mould, in the form of a fish, c1850, 8in (20.5cm) wide.
£135–150 / €195–220
$240–270 ⊞ SMI

◀ A tin and brass milk can, Scottish, c1880, 6in (15cm) high.
£105–120 / €155–175
$200–220 ⊞ SMI

▶ **A steel and copper ice cream mould,** with raised decoration of fruit, 19thC, 7in (18cm) high.
£200–220 / €290–320
$360–400 ⊞ BS

A copper jelly mould, by Benham & Froud, 19thC, 4½in (11.5cm) high.
£130–145 / €190–210
$240–270 ⊞ BS

A Victorian copper jelly mould, by Benham & Froud, in the form of Prince of Wales feathers, 5½in (14cm) wide.
£420–500 / €610–730
$760–910 ⚒ SWO

A tin chocolate mould, in the form of a bear, Continental, c1910, 8in (20.5cm) wide.
£55–65 / €80–95
$145–170 ⊞ B&R

A cast-iron heating stove, French, c1900, 19in (48.5cm) wide.
£220–250 / €340–380
$420–470 ⊞ B&R
This stove was used for heating irons.

A copper jelly mould, damaged, maker's mark, 19thC, 7in (18cm) diam.
£270–320 / €390–470
$490–580 ⚒ DORO

► A tin and copper jelly mould, with raised turkey decoration, c1880, 8in (20.5cm) diam.
£135–150 / €195–220
$240–270 ⊞ SMI

A ceramic jelly mould, with raised decoration of a cockerel and chicks, c1880, 8in (20.5cm) wide.
£115–130 / €170–190
$210–240 ⊞ SMI

A white metal nutmeg grater, in the form of a heart, early 19thC, 1in (2.5cm) wide.
£165–195 / €240–290
$300–360 ⚒ G(L)

A brass strainer, Dutch, c1730, 15in (38cm) diam.
£520–580 / €760–850
$940–1,050 ⊞ SEA

A copper jelly mould, in the form of a hedgehog, c1850, 9in (23cm) wide.
£360–400 / €520–580
$650–720 ⊞ SMI

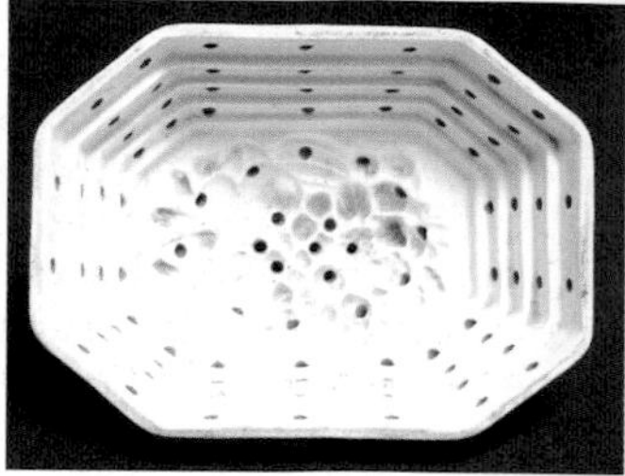

A ceramic curd mould, with raised fruit decoration, c1880, 7in (18cm) high.
£115–130 / €170–190
$210–240 ⊞ SMI

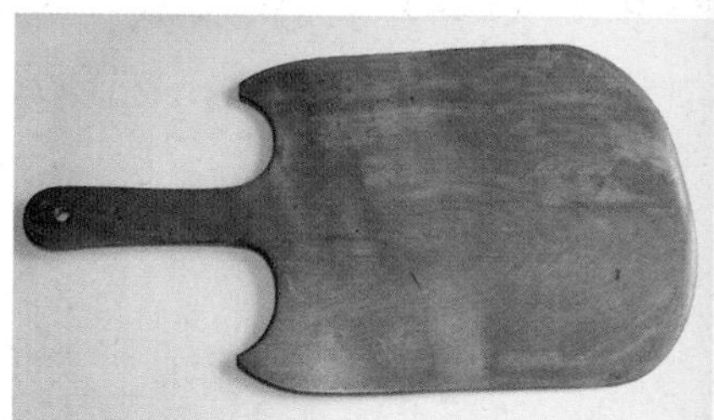

A sycamore pie peel, 1825–75, 17¼in (44cm) wide.
£220–250 / €340–380
$420–470 ⊞ WeA

Items in the Kitchenware section have been arranged in alphabetical order.

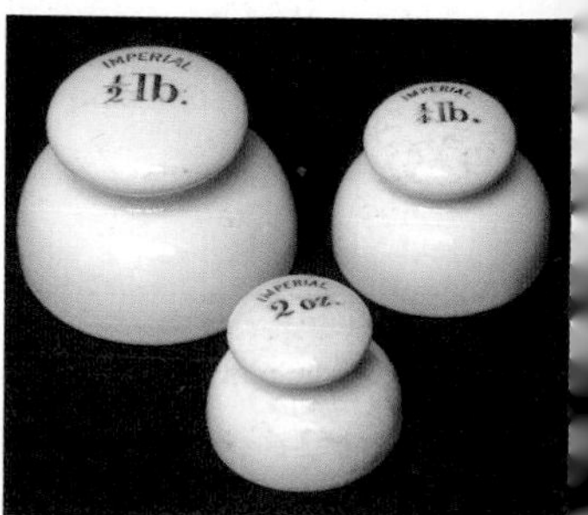

A set of three ceramic weights, c1910, largest 2½in (6.5cm) diam.
£220–250 / €340–380
$420–470 ⊞ B&R

Pottery

The English pottery market has seen a further polarization in the past year, a trend that has been noticeable for three years or so. The bottom and mid-range of the market has seen a drop in values while the top end has remained very stable and is continuing to rise. The home market is coupled with a vibrant interest from the USA and, broadly speaking, is split about 50/50 per cent between the UK and the USA.

To a large extent, it is still the collectors who maintain the market levels although the interior design influence, mainly from the USA, is a growing factor. As a generalization it is quality, rarity and condition that dictate prices, although decorative appeal is especially relevant to interior designers. The traditional collector's market tends to consist of people who have collected for many years, and there is very little interest from younger buyers. The experienced collectors are discriminating in their buying and, generally, only the very rare and best examples are considered.

Mid-19th century Staffordshire portrait figures have continued to drop in value due to lack of interest and the market has most likely bottomed out. The weakness of the US dollar will continue to keep the middle and lower end of the market somewhat depressed, making them very affordable and this is a good time to buy. Meanwhile models of animals, particularly jungle animals, have continued to rise in price. This is due to the ongoing universal appeal of animals and the decline of the popularity of British historical celebrities relating to religion, the theatre, war and royalty, the exception being the keen interest in the 200th anniversary of Admiral Lord Nelson's victory at the Battle of Trafalgar in 2005.

Currently a large area of the British pottery market is significantly under-valued. For example, creamware plates with painted decoration, some examples of English delftware and Jackfield pottery from the 18th century are for the most part very affordable and can be found for under £200 / €290 / $360.

One can only speculate on whether collecting as a passion will ever grip a new generation. It seems that the 35 to 50 age group has missed the collecting bug but there are signs that there is growing interest from the 20-somethings who are beginning to discover the magic and romance of owning a piece of history. The scarcity and desirability of the best items will as always attract the serious buyers and prices in this area are likely to continue to rise. For the time being, it is this level that is sustaining the British antique pottery trade.

John Howard

Animals & Birds

A pair of Ansbach faïence models of horses, one restored, German, c1740, 8in (20.5cm) wide.
£2,600–3,100 / €3,800–4,550
$4,700–5,600 ⚒ S(Am)

For further information on
Staffordshire animals see pages 232–240

▶ A creamware model of a bear, with sponged decoration, c1790, 3in (7.5cm) high.
£1,050–1,200 / €1,550–1,750
$1,900–2,150 ⊞ TYE

A Dutch Delft model of a cow, restored, c1760, 5¾in (14.5cm) high.
£430–480 / €630–700
$780–870 ⊞ G&G

An agate salt-glazed stoneware model of a pug dog, 1745–50, 2¾in (7cm) high.
£3,650–4,350 / €5,300–6,400
$6,600–7,900 ⚒ WW

A Prattware model of a cockerel, c1790, 4in (10cm) high.
£400–440 / €580–640
$720–800 ⊞ DAN

A pearlware model of a lion, c1790, 4in (10cm) wide.
£400–440 / €580–640
$720–800 ⊞ TYE

A Prattware model of a camel, 1810–20, 2¾in (7cm) wide.
£730–870 / €1,050–1,250
$1,300–1,550 ⚒ WW

A Kirkaldy Pottery model of a goat, Scottish, c1835, 7in (18cm) high.
£1,250–1,400 / €1,850–2,050
$2,250–2,550 ⊞ HOW

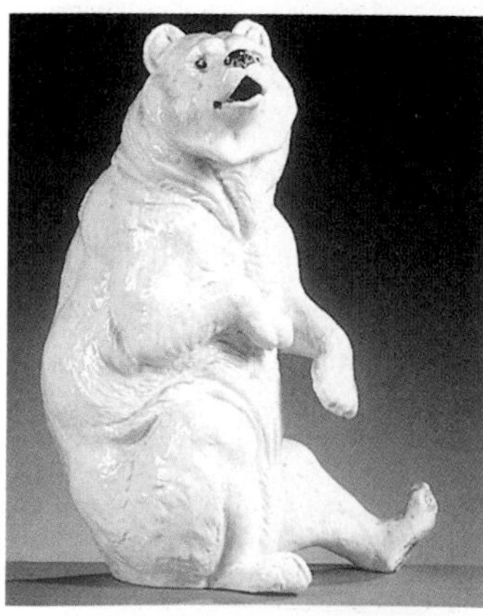

A glazed terracotta model of a polar bear, 19thC, 22½in (57cm) high.
£450–540 / €660–790
$810–980 ⚒ S(Am)

A creamware stirrup cup, in the form of a fox's mask, decorated with slip, late 18thC, 5in (12.5cm) high.
£1,300–1,550 / €1,900–2,250
$2,350–2,800 ⚒ SJH

A Walton pearlware model of a stag, with bocage, some damage, marked, c1820, 4in (10cm) high.
£210–250 / €310–370
$380–450 ⚒ DN

A treacle-glazed stirrup cup, in the form of a trout's head, c1840, 5in (12.5cm) high.
£340–380 / €500–550
$620–690 ⊞ TYE

A pair of sponge-decorated models of cats, one restored, c1850, 3¾in (9.5cm) high.
£260–310 / €380–450
$470–560 ⚒ DN

A Prattware stirrup cup, in the form of a dog's head, c1800, 3in (7.5cm) wide.
£1,000–1,150 / €1,500–1,700
$1,900–2,100 ⊞ HOW

A model of a horse, Scottish, c1820, 6in (15cm) high.
£3,000–3,300 / €4,400–4,800
$5,400–6,000 ⊞ HOW

A pottery model of a spaniel, Scottish, c1845, 10in (25.5cm) high.
£2,250–2,500 / €3,300–3,650
$4,000–4,500 ⊞ HOW

A Brownfield model of a begging terrier, seated on a cushion with a basket in its mouth, c1870, 7¾in (19.5cm) high.
£130–155 / €190–220
$240–280 ⚒ L&E

A Holdcroft majolica posy vase, in the form of a bear with a barrel, c1870, 4in (10cm) high.
£430–480 / €630–700
$780–870 ⊞ BRT

Joseph Holdcroft

Joseph Holdcroft established the Sutherland Pottery at Daisy Bank, Longton, Staffordshire in 1870. The factory produced fine examples of majolica. Some of Holdcroft's work was inspired by Minton, where he worked before setting up on his own, as well as George Jones and Wedgwood, who were major producers of fashionable majolica during the last quarter of the 19th century. Holdcroft's work was often inspired from nature and his use of colours was exceptional. Many of the items produced were unmarked and can only be attributed by the reference to the pattern and colouring of the piece. Some items, however, are marked with a JH logo which may be printed or impressed.

A majolica model of a duck, c1900, 9in (23cm) wide.
£155–175 / €230–260
$290–320 ⊞ MLL

A majolica tobacco jar, in the form of a pug dog, 19thC, 8in (20.5cm) high.
£590–700 / €840–1,000
$1,050–1,250 ⚒ F&C

A pair of models of dogs, with glass eyes, Scottish, c1900, 12in (30.5cm) high.
£500–550 / €720–800
$900–1,000 ⊞ HOW

◄ A Wemyss model of a pig, Scottish, c1900, 7in (18cm) wide.
£540–600 / €790–880
$980–1,100 ⊞ GLB

A Wemyss Plichta model of a pig, painted with flowers, c1930, 6in (15cm) wide.
£700–780 / €1,000–1,100
$1,250–1,400 ⊞ RdeR
The buttercup painting is a very rare variety

Baskets

A Bayreuth faïence basket, the centre painted with a flower spray, some damage, marked 'B.P.' in blue, German, Pfeiffer period, 1761–88, 7¼in (18.5cm) wide.
£720–860 / €1,050–1,250
$1,300–1,550 ⚒ S

A Wedgwood flower basket and cover image:

A Wedgwood flower basket and cover, with two leaf handles, impressed mark, c1790, 10in (25.5cm) diam.
£680–810 / €1,000–1,200
$1,250–1,450 ⚒ G(L)

A pearlware pierced basket and stand, 1810–20, 11in (28cm) wide.
£450–500 / €660–730
$810–910 ⊞ TYE

◄ A Wedgwood creamware pierced basket and stand, c1830, 8in (20.5cm) diam.
£210–240 / €310–350
$380–430 ⊞ AUC

A Wemyss basket, decorated with branches of fruiting cherries, damaged, Scottish, c1905, 12in (30.5cm) wide.
£880–980 / €1,300–1,450
$1,600–1800 ⊞ GLB

POTTERY

Bough Pots

A pair of delft flower bowls and covers, probably London or Bristol, with sponged and painted decoration, damaged, c1730, 5in (12.5cm) high.
£4,200–5,000 / €6,100–7,300
$7,600–9,100 S(O)

A Wedgwood caneware bough pot, with jasper ware bas relief, c1800, 7½in (19cm) high.
£720–800 / €1,000–1,150
$1,300–1,450 LGr

► **A creamware bough pot,** bat-printed with a hunting scene, c1820, 7in (18cm) high.
£450–500 / €660–730
$810–910 TYE

Bat printing is a type of transfer printing used to produce fine detail on ceramics by English factories in the early 19th century. The design was conveyed from an engraved copper plate to a glazed surface by means of slabs of glue or gelatin (bats). Tiny dots of oil were transferred to the porcelain and a fine coloured powder was then dusted on to the surface of the glaze. This powder stuck to the oil, rendering the design onto the article.

Bowls

◄ **An English delft bowl,** painted with a pagoda within a foliage surround, c1750, 6in (15cm) diam.
£280–320 / €410–470
$510–580 KEY

A pearlware commemorative bowl, the interior inscribed 'Long Live the King' within a cartouche surmounted by a crown with a scallop shell below the banded rim, damaged, c1789, 6¼in (16cm) diam.
£1,000–1,200 / €1,450–1,750
$1,800–2,150 S

In October 1788, King George III contracted an illness which failed to improve by November and sparked a major political crisis. In an effort to prevent the opposition from gaining strength, the Tories, supported by the Prince of Wales, issued a number of items advocating health to the King.

An English delft bowl, c1770, 9in (23cm) diam.
£540–600 / €790–880
$980–1,100 HOW

A delft bowl, the interior painted with a two-masted ship, restored, Continental, possibly Dutch, 18thC, 9¾in (25cm) diam.
£470–560 / €690–820
$850–1,000 WW

A Staffordshire salt-glazed stoneware punch bowl, the interior inscribed 'Mary Orm' and decorated with flowers and insects, restored, c1760, 9in (23cm) diam.
£680–810 / €1,000–1,200
$1,250–1,450 DN

A pair of Dutch Delft bowls, each painted with a riverside scene, 18thC, 12½in (32cm) diam.
£560–670 / €820–980
$1,000–1,200 LAY

A London delft bowl, inscribed 'Success to Trade', c1790, 9in (23cm) diam.
£1,050–1,200 / €1,550–1,750
$1,900–2,150 JHo

A Llanelli Pottery bowl, decorated with Amherst Japan pattern, Welsh, c1850, 7in (18cm) diam.
£220–250 / €320–370
$400–450 ⊞ WeW

► **A Minton majolica cistern,** the rim moulded with grapes, the two handles modelled as mythological figures, with Paris Exhibition label for T. Goode & Co, impressed marks, late 19thC, 22in (56cm) diam.
£1,750–2,100 / €2,550–3,050
$3,150–3,800 ⚒ GIL

A Wemyss bowl, painted with roses by Karel Nekola, Scottish, 1890–1900, 12in (30.5cm) diam.
£580–650 / €850–950
$1,050–1,200 ⊞ RdeR

◄ **A spongeware porringer,** commemorating the Gordon Highlanders, inscribed 'We'll Fight and We'll Conquer Again and Again', Scottish, c1915, 7in (18cm) diam.
£140–155 / €200–230
$250–280 ⊞ GAU

A Wedgwood caneware bough pot, with jasper ware bas relief,
c1800, 7½in (19cm) high.
800 / €1,000–1,150
LGr

A Pountney bowl, by Louis Wain, decorated with a dog and a cat, inscribed 'How dare you', some damage, signed, maker's marks, impressed retailer's stamp, early 20thC, 5in (12.5cm) high.
£105–120 / €155–175
$190–220 ⚒ PFK

Buildings

A Staffordshire pastille burner, in the form of a house, early 19thC, 5¼in (13.5cm) high.
£165–195 / €240–280
$300–360 ⚒ GIL

A Staffordshire money box, in the form of a cottage flanked by a male and a female figure, 1800–50, 5¼in (13.5cm) high.
£440–520 / €640–760
$800–940 ⚒ AH

A Staffordshire model of Euston Station, c1850, 11in (28cm) high.
£850–950 / €1,250–1,400
$1,500–1,700 ⊞ HOW

A model of a thatched house, c1860, 9¼in (23.5cm) high.
£230–270 / €330–390
$410–490 ⚒ SWO

Cow Creamers

A Whieldon-style cow creamer and cover, decorated with a running glaze, restored, 18thC, 7½in (19cm) wide.
£640–760 / €930–1,100
$1,150–1,350 ⚒ WW

A pearlware cow creamer, slight damage to associated cover, c1815, 7in (18cm) wide.
£730–870 / €1,050–1,250
$1,300–1,550 ⚒ DN

A Swansea Pottery cow creamer, Welsh, c1840, 7in (18cm) wide.
£300–340 / €440–500
$540–620 ⊞ WeW

POTTERY

Dishes

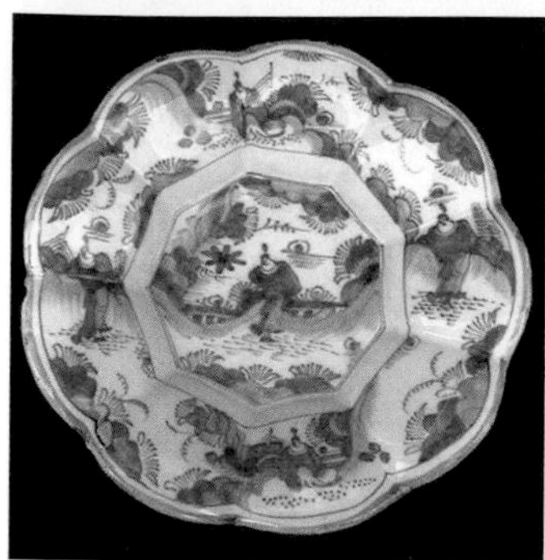

A faïence dish, decorated in Chinese Transitional style in underglaze blue, damaged, German, c1700, 13½in (34.5cm) diam.
£580–650 / €850–950
$1,050–1,200 ⊞ G&G

A Dutch Delft dish, painted with willow and stylized flowers, c1750, 14½in (37cm) diam.
£270–320 / €390–470
$490–580 ⚒ DN(BR)

A Strasbourg faïence dish, by Joseph Hannong, with a pierced border, the centre decorated with a floral spray, some damage, restored, signed, German, 1762–81, 11¾in (30cm) wide.
£680–750 / €1,000–1,100
$1,250–1,350 ⊞ G&G

POTTERY

A slipware dish, late 18thC, 16in (40.5cm) wide.
£1,800–2,000 / €2,600–2,900
$3,250–3,600 ⊞ KEY

► A set of three pearlware leaf pickle dishes, with lustre decoration, early 19thC, 5½in (14cm) wide.
£230–270 / €340–390
$420–490 ⚒ PFK

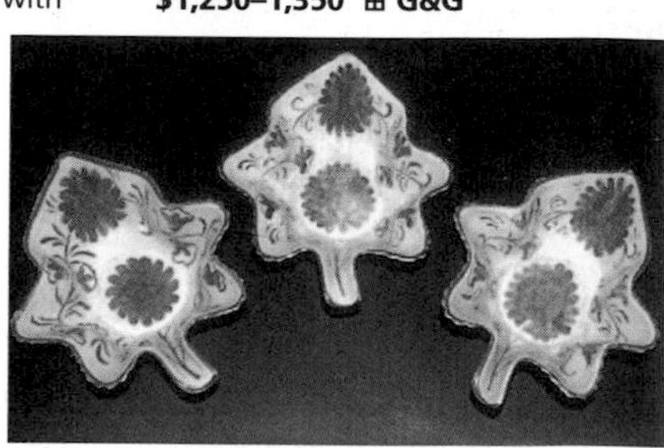

A creamware dish, possibly Swansea Pottery, c1820, 8in (20.5cm) wide.
£360–400 / €520–580
$650–720 ⊞ ReN
The floral decoration on this dish was taken from an original in *Curtis's Botanical Magazine*.

Miller's Compares

I. A George Jones majolica nut dish, c1860, 9in (23cm) wide.
£1,250–1,400 / €1,850–2,050
$2,250–2,550 ⊞ BRT

II. A Holdcroft majolica nut dish, c1870, 8in (20.5cm) wide.
£540–600 / €790–880
$980–1,100 ⊞ BRT

These nut dishes are both very appealing but Item I is more desirable because it is by George Jones, who is considered by most people to be the premier maker of majolica wares. Jones's attention to detail is easily seen on Item I – features such as the fine execution of the twigs and the veining on the leaves are clear indications of a master craftsman. Item II does not have this wealth of detail, and the squirrel is not as well observed as the one in Item I. Holdcroft is also keenly collected, but his pieces lack the intricacy of George Jones's wares. For more information on Joseph Holdcroft see page 205.

◄ A Minton majolica dish, in the form of a blue tit on an oak leaf, impressed mark No. 1331, damaged, date mark for 1869, 8in (20.5cm) wide.
£260–310 / €380–450
$470–560 ⚒ PF

► An artichoke drainer and dish, French, c1890, 13in (33cm) diam.
£340–380 / €500–550
$620–690 ⊞ MLL

Covered Dishes

A Staffordshire tureen and cover, in the form of a hen on a nest, c1870, 8in (20.5cm) wide.
£450–500 / €650–730
$810–900 ⊞ RdeR

A pair of Staffordshire tureens and covers, in the form of pigeons, late 19thC, 8¾in (22cm) wide.
£770–920 / €1,150–1,350
$1,400–1,650 ⚒ SWO

A Minton majolica pie dish and cover, the knop modelled as a dog, the handles as twigs, the base with a relief-moulded panel to either side of a hare and pheasant, with a liner, on paw feet, impressed factory and number marks, cypher mark for 1874, 14¼in (36cm) wide.
£2,350–2,800 / €3,450–4,100
$4,250–5,100 ⚒ L&T

POTTERY

Figures

A creamware figural group, of a man and a woman beneath a tree with birds, Italian, c1800, 13¾in (35cm) high.
£900–1,050
€1,300–1,550
$1,650–1,900 ⚒ S

A pearlware figural group, in the form of birds in a tree above a man and a woman each holding a bird, above a hat with chicks, losses, c1820, 10¼in (26cm) high.
£590–700 / €860–1,000
$1,050–1,250 ⚒ DN(BR)

An Enoch Wood figure of a boy in a tree, some damage, 1820–30, 6in (15cm) high.
£165–185 / €240–270
$300–330 ⊞ SER

A Minton majolica figure of a man with a wheelbarrow, c1851, 13in (33cm) high.
£4,400–4,900
€6,400–7,200
$8,000–8,900 ⊞ BRT

For further information on
Staffordshire figures see pages 232–240

Flasks

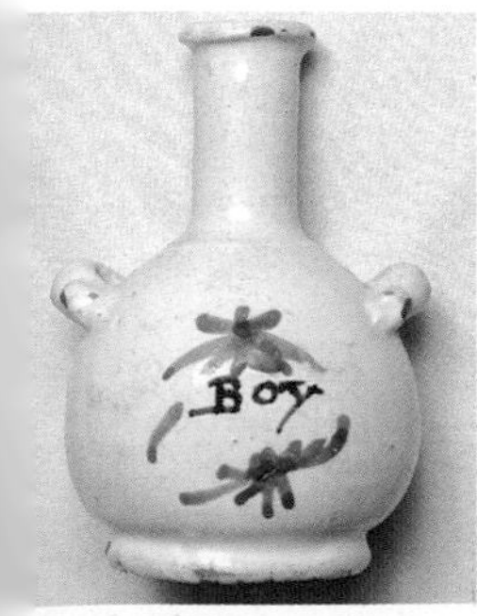

A delft flask, inscribed 'Boy', 1680–1700, 6in (15cm) high.
£1,300–1,450
€1,900–2,100
$2,350–2,600 ⊞ KEY

A pearlware spirit flask, in the form of a heart, c1820, 6in (15cm) high.
£450–500 / €660–730
$810–910 ⊞ HOW

LOCATE THE SOURCE
The source of each illustration in Miller's can be found by checking the code letters below each caption with the Key to Illustrations, pages 778–784.

► **A Fulham Pottery salt-glazed stoneware flask,** c1835, 6½in (16.5cm) high.
£610–680 / €890–990
$1,100–1,250 ⊞ JHo

POTTERY

Flatware

A Hispano-Moresque dish, Spanish, late 16thC, 10¾in (27.5cm) diam.
£760–850 / €1,100–1,250
$1,400–1,550 ⊞ G&G

Hispano-Moresque ware is Spanish tin-glazed earthenware that used techniques and designs introduced by the Moorish invaders in the eighth century. The most notable wares are decorated with lustre, introduced from the 13th century and used especially in Malaga and the Valencia area in the 15th century. The ware inspired the development of Italian majolica and was arguably the first pottery of any artistic value to be produced in Europe since the ancient civilizations.

A De Grieksche A factory Dutch Delft doré plate, by Adriaaen van Rijsselbergh, painted and gilt with a dragon in a quatrefoil reserve, damaged, restored, factory mark, 1701–35, 8¾in (22cm) diam.
£820–980 / €1,200–1,450
$1,500–1,750 ⚒ S(Am)

A Nuremberg faïence dish, painted with a peacock on rocks within a flower-panelled border, slight damage, Hi monogram mark, German, c1730, 13in (33cm) diam.
£740–880 / €1,100–1,300
$1,350–1,600 ⚒ S(Am)

A Bristol delft charger, decorated with tulips and chrysanthemums, 17thC, 13¼in (33.5cm) diam.
£3,600–4,300 / €5,300–6,300
$6,500–7,800 ⚒ SWO

A Savona charger, decorated in underglaze blue with a cherub, restored, marked, Italian, late 17thC, 14¼in (36cm) diam.
£670–750 / €980–1,100
$1,200–1,350 ⊞ G&G

A Frankfurt delft dish, decorated in Chinese Transitional style, damaged, German, c1720, 13in (33cm) diam.
£680–760 / €990–1,100
$1,250–1,400 ⊞ G&G

► A Castelli *istoriato* dish, painted with the Procession of Venus, later suspension holes, early 18thC, 13¾in (35cm) diam.
£4,250–5,100 / €6,200–7,400
$7,700–9,200 ⚒ RTo

***Istoriato* is a school of maiolica painting dating from the beginning of the 16th century in which the artist used the dish or vessel as a canvas on which to represent a narrative subject derived from biblical, allegorical, mythological or genre sources, usually via an engraving. The most important centres were Urbino, Castel Durante and Faenza.**

A tin-glazed armorial dish, decorated with the arms of a cardinal, Spanish, 17thC, 10¼in (26cm) diam.
£370–440 / €540–640
$670–800 ⚒ WW

A Dutch Delft dish, painted with a stylized hare or dog within a border of flowers, damaged, c1800, 13¾in (35cm) diam.
£630–750 / €920–1,100
$1,150–1,350 ⚒ WW

A Castelli dish, painted by Grue with figures within classical ruins and a wooded landscape, Italian, c1720, 6¾in (17cm) diam.
£1,600–1,800 / €2,350–2,650
$2,900–3,250 ⊞ G&G

A Pavia maiolica dish, damaged, Italian, 1700–50, 16¼in (41.5cm) diam.
£1,950–2,300 / €2,850–3,350
$3,550–4,150 ⚒ S(Mi)

A Savona faïence tazza, painted with a couple in a landscape flanked by rockwork, flowers and insects, damaged and restored, Italian, 1700–50, 11¼in (28.5cm) diam.
£1,050–1,250 / €1,550–1,850
$1,900–2,250 ⚒ S

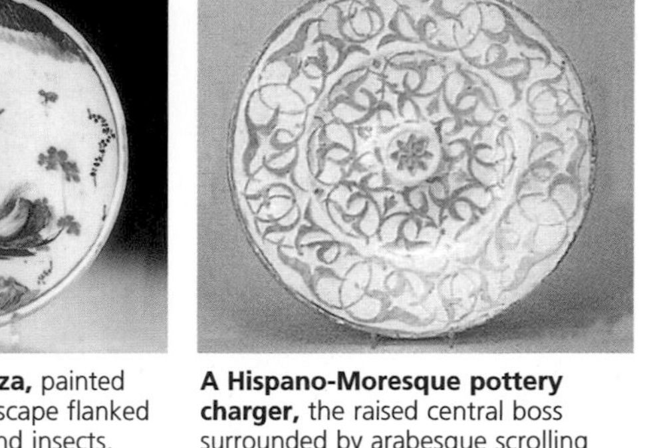

A Hispano-Moresque pottery charger, the raised central boss surrounded by arabesque scrolling foliage, restored, Spanish, 18thC, 15¾in (40cm) diam.
£280–330 / €410–480
$510–600 ⚒ DN

◄ A Bristol delft blue dash charger, decorated with Adam and Eve, c1740, 12½in (32cm) diam.
£4,900–5,900 / €7,200–8,600
$8,900–10,700 ⚒ WW
Blue dash is a simple blue on white decoration of oblique, regularly spaced, cobalt blue dashes. This decoration is particularly found on the rims of 17th- and 18th-century London and Bristol chargers.

A Bristol delft charger, decorated with an Oriental landscape, c1740, 14in (35.5cm) diam.
£1,400–1,600 / €2,050–2,350
$2,550–2,900 ⊞ KEY

► A pair of Whieldon-style mottled-glaze plates, 18thC, 10in (25.5cm) diam.
£490–580
€720–850
$890–1,050
⚒ PF

An English delft dish, painted with flowers, 18thC, 10½in (26.5cm) diam.
£180–200 / €260–290
$320–360 ⊞ G&G

An English delft dish, painted with a rat peering through a window at a figure, 18thC, 8¾in (22cm) diam.
£490–580 / €720–850
$890–1,050 ⚒ WW

An English delft charger, possibly Liverpool, painted with cockerels under a blossoming tree, 18thC, 14in (35.5cm) diam.
£360–430 / €530–630
$650–780 ⚒ AH

A maiolica dish, depicting Aragon Castle, damaged, repaired, Spanish, 18thC, 12½in (32cm) diam.
£850–950 / €1,250–1,400
$1,500–1,700 ⊞ G&G

A set of four English delft plates, painted with a Chinese pagoda in a landscape, c1750, 9in (23cm) diam.
£430–480 / €630–700
$780–870 ⊞ KEY

A pair of Bristol delft plates, painted with stylized flowers, slight damage, 18thC, 8¾in (22cm) diam.
£630–750 / €920–1,100
$1,150–1,350 ⚒ WW

An English delft plate, decorated with a tree in a pot, c1750, 9in (23cm) diam.
£820–980 / €1,200–1,450
$1,500–1,750 WW

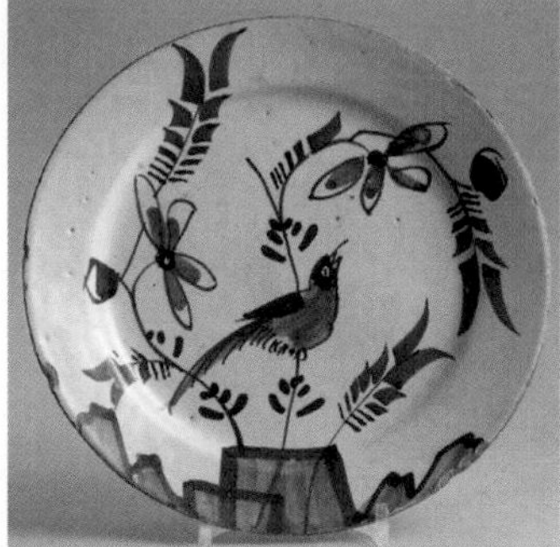

A delft plate, painted with a bird and flower stems, c1750, 9in (23cm) diam.
£420–500 / €610–730
$760–910 WW

A maiolica dish, slight damage, Italian, Lodi, c1750, 15in (38cm) diam.
£1,950–2,300 / €2,850–3,350
$3,550–4,150 S(Mi)

A London delft dish, painted with chrysanthemums, restored, c1760, 12in (30.5cm) diam.
£520–620 / €760–910
$940–1,100 WW

A Liverpool delft plate, painted with two cockerels beneath a prunus branch, damaged, c1760, 14¼in (36cm) diam.
£370–440 / €540–640
$670–800 WW

A Liverpool delft plate, c1760, 8¾in (22cm) diam.
£360–400 / €520–580
$650–720 KEY

An English delft charger, damaged, c1760, 13½in (34.5cm) diam.
£220–250 / €320–370
$400–450 G&G

A set of five English delft plates, decorated with a Chinese man in a garden landscape, c1760, 9in (23cm) diam.
£370–420 / €540–610
$670–760 KEY

A faïence dish, possibly Bayreuth, the centre decorated with a rose, German, c1760, 13½in (34.5cm) diam.
£900–1,050 / €1,300–1,550
$1,650–1,900 S(Am)

A Dutch Delft plate, painted with a floral design, c1760, 9¼in (23.5cm) diam.
£360–400 / €520–580
$650–720 KEY

A pair of Wiesbaden faïence plates, painted with roses and scattered flowers, one damaged, German, c1760, 9¾in (24.5cm) diam.
£900–1,050 / €1,300–1,550
$1,650–1,900 S(Am)

A Liverpool delft dish, painted with birds, a figure and buildings in a landscape, damaged, c1780, 11¾in (30cm) diam.
£350–420 / €510–610
$630–760 SWO

Fourteen creamware pierced dessert plates, Yorkshire or Staffordshire, 1780–90, 9½in (24cm) diam.
£2,500–2,800 / €3,650–4,100
$4,550–5,100 ⊞ KEY

A creamware dish, printed with a rural scene and a monogram, slight damage, 18thC, 18¼in (46.5cm) diam.
£280–330 / €410–480
$510–600 ⚒ WW

A Dutch Delft plate, painted with flowers and corn sheaves, 18thC, 8¾in (22cm) diam.
£300–360 / €440–530
$540–650 ⚒ WW

A Swansea Pottery plate, with an arcaded border, the centre painted with a heron, Welsh, c1815, 8in (20.5cm) diam.
£850–950 / €1,250–1,400
$1,500–1,700 ⊞ HOW

A pearlware plate, decorated with an American eagle, c1815, 8in (20.5cm) diam.
£630–700 / €920–1,050
$1,150–1,300 ⊞ HOW

A Mason's Ironstone meat plate and drainer, decorated with Japan pattern, c1820, 16½in (42cm) wide.
£1,150–1,300 / €1,700–1,900
$2,100–2,350 ⊞ RdV

A Staffordshire pearlware plate, decorated with a transfer print of an owl, c1820, 6in (15cm) diam.
£270–300 / €390–440
$490–540 ⊞ ReN

A pearlware plate, decorated with a peacock, c1820, 17in (43cm) wide.
£1,250–1,400 / €1,850–2,050
$2,250–2,550 ⊞ HOW

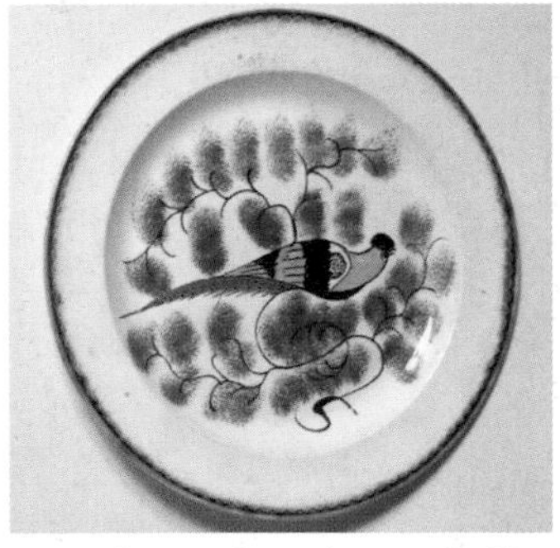

A pearlware plate, decorated with a peacock, c1820, 10in (25.5cm) diam.
£450–500 / €660–730
$810–910 ⊞ HOW

A pottery plate, decorated with a flower, c1820, 7in (18cm) diam.
£270–300 / €390–440
$490–540 ⊞ HOW

A pottery plate, decorated with pink lustre, c1820, 7in (18cm) diam.
£450–500 / €660–730
$810–910 ⊞ HOW

A Swansea Pottery nursery plate, decorated with a rural scene, Welsh, c1830, 6in (15cm) diam.
£110–125 / €160–185
$200–230 ⊞ WeW

A pair of nursery plates, each entitled 'The Milkmaid', with raised flower borders, Welsh, c1830, 7in (18cm) diam.
£270–300 / €390–440
$490–540 ⊞ RdeR

A pair of nursery alphabet clock plates, c1840, 6½in (16.5cm) diam.
£450–500 / €660–730
$810–910 ⊞ RdeR

A set of six artichoke and asparagus plates, French, c1890, 10in (25.5cm) diam.
£420–470 / €610–690
$760–850 ⊞ MLL

A Llanelli Pottery plate, painted by Shufflebotham with cockerels, Welsh, c1900, 7in (18cm) diam.
£990–1,100 / €1,450–1,600
$1,800–2,000 ⊞ WeW

A nursery plate, commemorating the coronation of William IV, the border moulded with animals, hair crack, 1831, 5in (12.5cm) diam.
£165–195 / €240–280
$300–350 ⚒ SAS

A set of four John Carr & Co nursery plates, the centres printed with statues entitled 'Fidelity', 'Gratitude', 'Massacre of the Innocents' and 'Boy with Broken Drum', each marked '1851 Exhibition', impressed marks, c1851, largest 7¼in (18.5cm) diam.
£280–330 / €410–480
$510–600 ⚒ DN

These depictions are all sculptures that featured in the Great Exhibition of 1851. 'Innocence' and 'Gratitude' were by G. M. Benzoni, 'Massacre of the Innocents' by Henry Wiles, and 'Boy with Broken Drum' (more correctly called 'The Unhappy Child') was by Simonis.

A Wemyss Gordon plate, painted with iris, Scottish, c1895, 8¼in (21cm) diam.
£400–450 / €580–660
$720–810 ⊞ RdeR

► **A Wemyss plate,** decorated with thistles, Scottish, c1905, 5½in (14cm) diam.
£230–260 / €340–380
$420–470 ⊞ GLB

A Swansea Pottery plate, depicting the church of St Austell, Cornwall, Welsh, c1835, 6in (15cm) diam.
£95–105 / €140–155
$170–190 ⊞ WeW

A majolica plate, by George Jones, moulded with butterflies and flowers, c1860, 11in (28cm) wide.
£1,450–1,650 / €2,100–2,400
$2,600–3,000 ⊞ BRT

A pair of maiolica chargers, the centres decorated with biblical scenes, the borders painted with putti and grotesque masks, Italian, late 19thC, 20in (51cm) diam.
£760–910 / €1,100–1,300
$1,400–1,650 ⚒ HYD

Inkstands & Inkwells

A faïence powdered-manganese inkstand, with ink pot and pounce pot, c1750, south German, 6in (15cm) wide.
£740–880 / €1,100–1,300
$1,350–1,600 S(Am)

Further reading
Miller's Pens & Writing Equipment: A Collector's Guide, Miller's Publications, 1999

A Wemyss inkwell, painted with strawberries, Scottish, c1895, 7in (18cm) wide.
£450–500 / €660–730
$810–910 RdeR

► **A Wemyss inkwell,** with dolphins flanking a shell, painted with wild roses, Scottish, c1900, 8in (20.5cm) wide.
£900–1,000 / €1,300–1,450
$1,600–1,800 RdeR

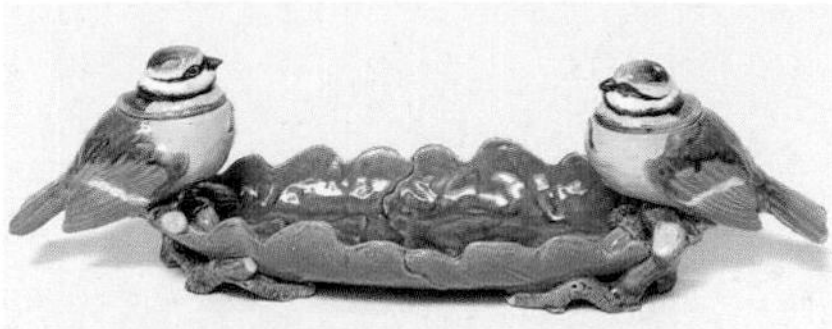

A Minton majolica inkwell, c1860, 13in (33cm) wide.
£1,400–1,600 / €2,050–2,350
$2,550–2,900 BRT

Jardinières

A jardinière and stand, c1820, 5in (12.5cm) high.
£490–550 / €720–800
$890–1,000 HOW

A Minton majolica jardinière, c1860, 21in (53.5cm) wide.
£3,500–3,900 / €5,100–5,700
$6,300–7,100 BRT

► **A Delphin Massier majolica jardinière and stand,** French, c1880, 36in (91.5cm) high.
£1,800–2,000 / €2,600–2,900
$3,250–3,600 MLL

A Wemyss Coombe jardinière, painted with daffodils, Scottish, c1880, 13in (33cm) wide.
£1,600–1,800 / €2,350–2,650
$2,900–3,250 ⊞ SDD

A pair of Wedgwood jasper ware jardinières, decorated in relief with nine muses presiding over the arts and sciences, surmounted by lion's-head masks and swags, slight damage, c1900, 10in (25.5cm) wide.
£490–550 / €720–800
$890–1,000 ⊞ LGr

A Wemyss jardinière, by Karol Nekola, decorated with roses, impressed mark, Scottish, c1900, 6in (15cm) diam.
£270–300 / €390–440
$490–540 ⊞ RdeR

Jars

An *albarello*, decorated with stylized leaves, Italian, 16th–17thC, 7in (18cm) high.
£990–1,100 / €1,450–1,600
$1,800–2,000 ⊞ G&G

A maiolica *albarello*, painted with a boy in a landscape, inscribed 'Dianisum', Italian, 17thC, 8in (20.5cm) high.
£1,750–2,100
€2,550–3,050
$3,150–3,800 ⚒ WW

► **A Caltagirone maiolica wet drug jar,** painted with flowers, Sicilian, mid-17thC, 8¾in (22cm) high.
£490–580
€720–850
$890–1,050
⚒ SWO

◄ **A London delft jar,** painted with a Chinese figure in a rocky landscape, with a C-scroll handle, restored, c1685, 2in (5cm) high.
£3,000–3,600
€4,400–5,300
$5,400–6,500
⚒ WW

A maiolica *albarello*, painted with pine kernels, Sicilian, c1700, 11¼in (28.5cm) high.
£1,150–1,350
€1,650–1,950
$2,050–2,450 ⚒ S(Am)

A maiolica *albarello*, probably Castelli, damaged, Italian, dated 1701, 4¾in (12cm) high.
£440–520 / €640–760
$800–950 ⚒ SWO

◄ **A Lambeth delft wet drug jar,** inscribed 'S:Caryoph', early 18thC, 7¼in (18.5cm) high.
£1,250–1,500
€1,850–2,200
$2,250–2,700
⚒ SWO
The full inscription would be *syrupus caryophullata* (*herba Benedicta*) or *caryophilli*, meaning syrup of cloves.

A maiolica wet drug jar, painted with scrolling foliage, repaired, Italian, 18thC, 8¼in (21cm) high.
£260–310 / €380–450
$470–560 ⚒ DN

A Gerace maiolica drug jar, painted with a warrior, Italian, mid-19thC, 9½in (24cm) high.
£370–440 / €540–640
$670–800 ⚒ SWO

Jugs & Ewers

A stoneware jug, with a 'tigerware' glaze, German, c1600, 6in (15cm) high.
£340–380 / €500–550
$620–690 ⊞ PeN

A Westerwald flagon, with a pewter cover, German, c1740, 5½in (14cm) high.
£720–800 / €1,000–1,150
$1,300–1,450 ⊞ PeN

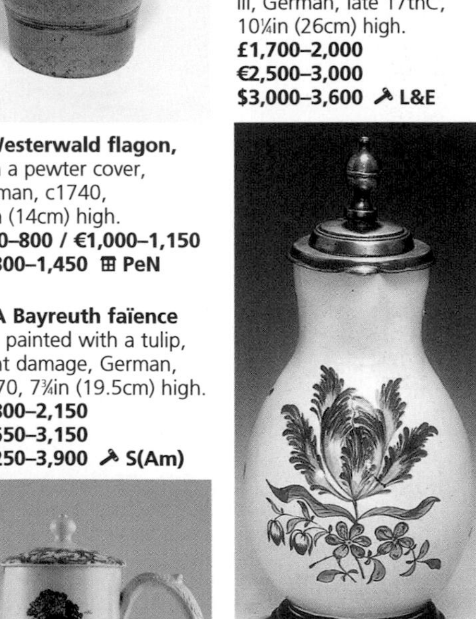

► A Bayreuth faïence jug, painted with a tulip, slight damage, German, c1770, 7¾in (19.5cm) high.
£1,800–2,150
€2,650–3,150
$3,250–3,900 ⚒ S(Am)

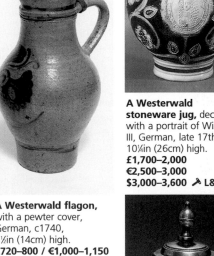

A stoneware bellarmine, c1600, 5in (12.5cm) high.
£720–800 / €1,000–1,150
$1,300–1,450 ⊞ PeN

A Westerwald stoneware jug, decorated with a portrait of William III, German, late 17thC, 10¼in (26cm) high.
£1,700–2,000
€2,500–3,000
$3,000–3,600 ⚒ L&E

◄ A creamware milk jug and cover, possibly Wedgwood, painted with Harlequin, Columbine and Pierrot, restored, c1765, 6in (15cm) high.
£300–360 / €440–530
$540–650 ⚒ WW

A Dutch Delft ewer, painted with Chinese figures, slight damage and losses, marked '8', early 18thC, 9in (23cm) high.
£440–520 / €640–760
$800–940 ⚒ DN

A creamware jug, transfer-printed with Mr Macklin as Shylock and Mr Woodward as Boradil, 18thC, 8in (20.5cm) high.
£1,450–1,700
€2,100–2,500
$2,600–3,100 ⚒ HYD

► A creamware jug, applied with female heads joined by garlands, a mask below the spout, the handle with a figure, c1780, 6½in (16.5cm) high.
£1,500–1,700
€2,200–2,500
$2,700–3,100
⊞ AUC

A faïence jug, with central tunnel, inscribed 'I. C. R.', south German, 1725–50, 11¼in (28.5cm) high.
£320–380 / €470–550
$580–690 ⚒ S(Am)

A jug, transfer-printed with rural scenes, with a silver lustre band, inscribed 'William Rudge Born March 7 1757', 18thC, 5¾in (14.5cm) high.
£280–330 / €410–480
$510–600 ⚒ SJH

◄ A pearlware 'agate' jug, decorated with a marbled slip, slight damage, c1790, 4¾in (12cm) high.
£680–810
€1,000–1,200
$1,200–1,450
⚒ DN

POTTERY

A Turner stoneware jug, decorated with classical figures, impressed mark, 1790–1810, 7in (18cm) high.
£210–250 / €310–370
$380–450 ⚒ DN

A pearlware jug, painted with Masonic emblems and flowers, inscribed 'Hold Justice, Use Oeconomy' and 'Frances & Jane Wragg 1801', restored, 8¾in (22cm) high.
£1,050–1,250
€1,550–1,850
$1,900–2,250 ⚒ LFA

◀ **A caneware jug,** decorated with Admiral Lord Nelson, Neptune, Britannia and Victory, slight damage, 1805–10, 7in (18cm) high.
£590–700 / €850–1,000
$1,050–1,250 ⚒ DN

▶ **A pearlware jug,** dated 1811, 7in (18cm) high.
£1,400–1,600
€2,050–2,350
$2,550–2,900 ⊞ HOW

Sunderland Lustre

There were several potteries in the Sunderland area manufacturing pink lustre wares in the early 19th century. The main factories were Ball, Dawson, Moore, Scott and the Garrison Pottery. The Sunderland pink lustre often has a distinctive splash application.

Pink lustre was used in all the main pottery-producing regions of the UK, but the Sunderland production can easily be identified by its use of transfer designs with verses, mottoes and pictures relating to mariners, religion, trade and politics and, of course, the Wear Bridge. The shapes produced also help the attribution of Sunderland wares such as ovoid jugs with loop handles and the classic rectangular plaque, often with a strong Methodist message such a 'Prepare to Meet thy God'.

A Sunderland pottery lustre jug, transfer-printed with a view of the Iron Bridge over the river Wear and a verse, c1820, 8in (20.5cm) high.
£720–800 / €1,050–1,200
$1,300–1,450 ⊞ HOW

A lustre jug, commemorating the death of Princess Charlotte, daughter of the Prince Regent, c1817, 5in (12.5cm) high.
£880–980 / €1,300–1,450
$1,600–1,800 ⊞ RdV

A pearlware jug, printed and painted with a shield for the Society of Forresters, inscribed 'Marcula Fundus Argua', and a short verse, early 19thC, 6in (15cm) high.
£530–630 / €770–920
$960–1,150 ⚒ WW

A lustre jug, decorated with an armorial, c1820, 5in (12.5cm) high.
£630–700 / €900–1,000
$1,100–1,250 ⊞ HOW

A lustre jug, painted with a vignette of a hound chasing a fox, inscribed 'Joseph Lewis, Woodworth Green, 1817', 6½in (16.5cm) high.
£300–360 / €440–530
$540–650 ⚒ HYD

A lustre jug, painted with a rural landscape, early 19thC, 11in (28cm) high.
£490–580 / €720–850
$890–1,050 ⚒ PFK

A jug, commemorating the life of Admiral Lord Nelson, depicting Britannia and the ashes of Nelson, c1820, 8¼in (21cm) high.
£2,000–2,400 / €2,900–3,500
$3,600–4,350 ⚒ SJH

POTTERY

A jug, with silver resist decoration, c1820, 5in (12.5cm) high.
£400–450 / €580–650
$720–810 ⊞ HOW

A Mochaware jug, c1820, 8in (20.5cm) high.
£1,200–1,400 / €1,750–2,000
$2,200–2,500 ⊞ HOW

A lustre jug, commemorating Queen Caroline, inscribed 'Success to Queen Caroline', slight damage and repair, 1820–21, 5¼in (13.5cm) high.
£280–330 / €410–480
$510–600 ⚒ DN
Queen Caroline was the estranged wife of King George IV.

A pearlware jug, painted with a crown and thistles, restored, 1822, 5in (12.5cm) high.
£300–360 / €440–530
$540–650 ⚒ SAS

A Sunderland lustre jug, decorated with Masonic emblems, c1830, 9in (23cm) high.
£990–1,100 / €1,450–1,600
$1,800–2,000 ⊞ HOW

A Mason's Ironstone jug, the handle in the form of a dragon, early 19thC, 8in (20.5cm) high.
£170–200 / €250–300
$310–370 ⚒ TRM(E)

POTTERY

A set of three moulded stoneware jugs, decorated with floral sprays and figures, sprigged scroll mark containing 'model No. 47' and 'A', 1825–40, largest 9½in (24cm) high.
£320–380 / €470–550
$580–690 ⚒ DN
The scroll mark on these jugs is very similar to a Minton mark except for the initial A instead of M. The maker may have been Samuel Alcock & Co.

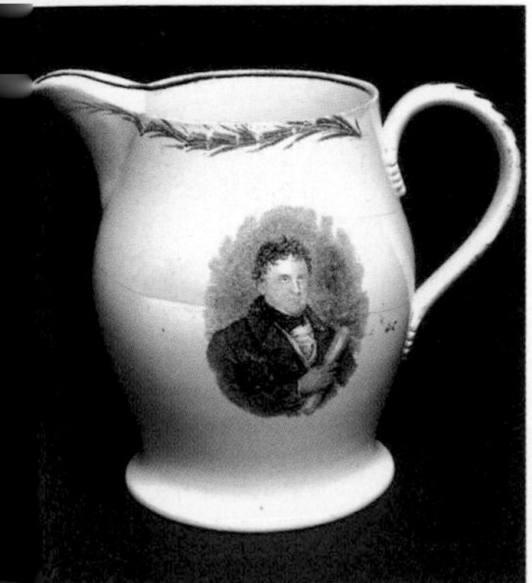

◄ **A Swansea Pottery jug,** depicting Father O'Connell, Welsh, c1830, 7in (18cm) high.
£150–170
€220–250
$270–300
⊞ WeW

An earthenware jug, transfer-printed with named portraits entitled 'Napoleon Polka', and 'Victoria Albert Polka' restored, 1844, 3¼in (8.5cm) high.
£350–420 / €510–610
$630–760 SAS

A jug, with transfer-printed decoration, inscribed 'Priscilla Palmer, born August 3rd 1847', 9in (23cm) high.
£220–260 / €320–380
$400–470 GH

◄ **A set of four Samuel Alcock & Co Camel jugs,** with relief-moulded decoration, printed maker's mark, model No. 240, restored, 1853-59, largest 9in (23cm) high.
£165–195 / €240–280
$270–320 DN

A stoneware milk jug, moulded in relief with scenes from *Uncle Tom's Cabin*, marked 'published by E. Ridgway & Abingdon, Hanley, 1 June, 1853', 7in (18cm) high.
£440–520 / €640–760
$800–940 PFK

◄ **A jug,** possibly Llanelli Pottery, commemorating the death of Prince Albert, transfer-printed with Britannia and the Prince, Welsh, c1861, 9¼in (23.5cm) high.
£220–260
€320–380
$400–470
HOLL

A Minton majolica jug, decorated with medieval characters, c1860, 14in (35.5cm) high.
£1,700–1,900 / €2,500–2,750
$3,100–3,450 BRT

A palissy-style ewer, by Manuel Mafra, decorated with lizards and moss, Portuguese, Caldras, 19thC, 11¾in (30cm) high.
£230–270 / €340–400
$420–500 DD

► **A pair of Minton majolica Renaissance revival ewers,** painted with putti, one rivetted, impressed mark, year mark for 1862, 14¼in (36cm) high.
£1,300–1,550 / €1,900–2,250
$2,350–2,800 TEN

A Mochaware jug, c1865, 10in (25.5cm) high.
£630–700 / €920–1,050
$1,150–1,300 HOW

A stoneware jug, relief-moulded with a Crimean War battle scene, c1880, 10¼in (26cm) high.
£120–145 / €175–210
$220–260 SWO

► **A Staffordshire majolica jug,** relief-moulded with a child and a dog, with a pewter cover, c1900, 9in (23cm) high.
£60–70 / €90–100
$110–130
WL

Loving Cups & Tygs

◄ **A Newcastle-upon-Tyne pearlware loving cup,** painted with tulips, inscribed 'William Boothby Born March 19th, 1807', early 19thC, 5½in (14cm) high.
£300–360 / €440–530
$540–650 PFK

► **A Hartshorne loving cup,** transfer-printed with figures and landscapes, impressed 'John Coates, Loughborough', c1840, 6¼in (16cm) high.
£200–240 / €290–350
$360–430 SWO

A Ewenny loving cup, commemorating the General Election in South Glamorgan, Welsh, c1895, 6in (15cm) high.
£220–250 / €320–360
$400–450 WeW

► **A Wemyss tyg,** painted with lilac, Scottish, c1900, 9½in (24cm) high.
£1,800–2,000 / €2,600–2,900
$3,250–3,600 RdeR

◄ **A Wemyss tyg,** painted with cockerels, impressed mark, Scottish, c1900, 4½in (11.5cm) high.
£580–650 / €850–950
$1,050–1,200 RdeR

Mugs & Tankards

A faïence manganese-ground tankard, mounts replaced, incised marks, German, Berlin, c1740, 7½in (19cm) high.
£740–880 / €1,100–1,300
$1,350–1,600 S(Am)

A stoneware tankard, with a pewter cover, German, cover dated 1770, 9¾in (25cm) high.
£490–550 / €720–800
$890–1,000 G&G

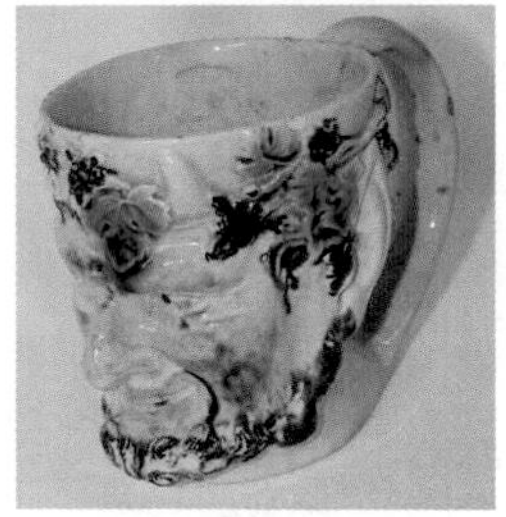

► **A Whieldon-style mug,** moulded with a bacchic satyr face, c1780, 3½in (9cm) high.
£145–165 / €210–240
$270–300 SER

POTTERY

A mug, with silver resist decoration, c1820, 4in (10cm) high.
£360–400 / €520–580
$650–720 ⊞ HOW

A Mochaware tankard, c1820, 6in (15cm) high.
£1,100–1,250 / €1,600–1,800
$2,000–2,250 ⊞ HOW

A Swansea Pottery mug, Welsh, c1850, 3½in (9cm) high.
£95–105 / €140–155
$170–190 ⊞ WeW

A Wemyss mug, decorated with branches of cherries, Scottish, c1900, 6in (15cm) high.
£410–460 / €600–670
$740–830 ⊞ GLB

A Staffordshire mug, with lustre rim and transfer-printed decoration, c1820, 2½in (6.5cm) diam.
£250–280 / €370–410
$450–510 ⊞ ReN

A Staffordshire mug, transfer-printed with 'A Present For A Good Girl', c1840, 2½in (6.5cm) diam.
£180–200 / €260–290
$320–360 ⊞ ReN

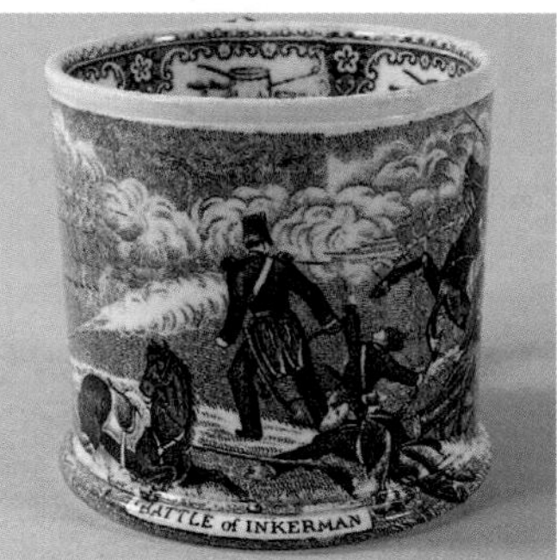

An earthenware mug, transfer-printed with a Crimean battle scene entitled 'Battle of Inkerman', restored, 1854, 3¼in (8.5cm) high.
£350–420 / €510–610
$630–760 ⚒ SAS

A Wemyss mug, painted with roses, impressed mark, Scottish, 1900–20, 5½in (14cm) high.
£670–750 / €980–1,100
$1,200–1,350 ⊞ RdeR

A Sunderland creamware frog tankard, by Dixon & Co, c1820, 5in (12.5cm) high.
£360–400 / €520–580
$650–720 ⊞ HOW

A Staffordshire mug, painted with Billy Butler's journey to Brentford, 1840, 2½in (6.5cm) diam.
£310–350 / €450–510
$560–630 ⊞ ReN

A Wemyss mug, painted with goldfinches, Scottish, c1880, 5½in (14cm) high.
£760–850 / €1,100–1,250
$1,400–1,550 ⊞ SDD

A T. G. Green Mochaware mug, 1910–20, 3in (7.5cm) high.
£135–150 / €195–220
$240–270 ⊞ CAL

Plaques

A Prattware plaque, moulded with a hunting scene, slight damage, c1790, 6 x 9in (15 x 23cm).
£2,700–3,200 / €3,950–4,650
$4,900–5,800 WW

A pair of Wedgwood jasper ware portrait plaques, depicting Louis XVI and Queen Marie Antoinette, in gilt frames, early 19thC, 2½in (6.5cm) high.
£460–510 / €670–740
$830–920 MCA

A maiolica plaque, slight damage, Sicilian, 18th–19thC, 13¼ x 10½in (33.5 x 26.5cm).
£1,600–1,900
€2,350–2,750
$2,900–3,450 S(Mi)

► A Sunderland lustre plaque, printed with a three-masted frigate, 1840–60, 8¾in (22cm) wide.
£220–260 / €320–380
$400–480 DN

A wall plaque, commemorating Adam Clarke, slight damage, 1815–40, 7½in (19cm) diam.
£175–210 / €260–310
$320–380 DN

POTTERY

Pots

A Bristol delft two-handled posset pot, painted with stylized leaf motifs, slight damage, c1720, 6½in (16.5cm) wide.
£840–1,000 / €1,250–1,500
$1,500–1,800 WW

► A Mochaware pot, cover and stand, c1820, 6in (15cm) high.
£630–700 / €900–1,000
$1,100–1,250 HOW

A Bristol delft posset pot and cover, slight damage, 18thC, 9½in (24cm) wide.
£1,350–1,600 / €1,950–2,350
$2,450–2,900 WW

◄ A Wemyss jam pot, decorated with roses, Scottish, c1900, 5in (12.5cm) high.
£400–450 / €580–660
$720–810 GLB

► A Wemyss honey pot, painted with a skep and bees, impressed mark, Scottish, c1900, 6in (15cm) high.
£450–500 / €660–730
$810–910 RdeR

Pot Lids

'Alas Poor Bruin No Lantern', Ball No. 1, mid-19thC, 3in (7.5cm) diam.
£220–260 / €320–380
$400–480 ⚒ SAS

'Arctic Expedition in Search of Sir John Franklin', Ball No. 19, restored, c1855, 3in (7.5cm) diam.
£230–270 / €330–390
$410–490 ⚒ SAS

'Bear, Lion and Cock', after Jesse Austin's original drawing, mid-19thC, 3in (7.5cm) diam.
£55–65 / €80–95
$100–120 ⚒ PFK

'Belle Vue Tavern', by S. Banger, Ball No. 29, some damage, 19thC, 4in (10cm) diam, framed.
£490–580 / €720–850
$890–1,050 ⚒ SAS

Pot lid numbers

The numbers in the captions refer to the system used by A. Ball in his reference work *The Price Guide to Pot Lids*, Antique Collectors Club, 1980.

◄ **'New St Thomas's Hospital',** Ball No. 203, 19thC, 4in (10cm) diam.
£150–180 / €220–260
$270–320 ⚒ SAS

'The Queen! God Bless Her!', Ball No. 319, with matching base, c1860, 4in (10cm) diam.
£230–270 / €330–390
$410–490 ⚒ SAS

Dessert & Dinner Services

An ironstone part dinner service, comprising seven pieces, decorated with Japan pattern, some damage and repair, printed marks, 1815–35.
£370–440 / €540–640
$670–800 ⚒ DN

A Wedgwood creamware part dessert service, comprising 13 pieces, decorated with Greek key borders, restored, impressed marks, 19thC.
£640–760 / €930–1,100
$1,150–1,350 ⚒ WW

An ironstone dessert service, comprising 17 pieces, decorated with Chinoiserie flower pattern, mid-19thC.
£700–840 / €1,000–1,200
$1,250–1,500 ⚒ PF

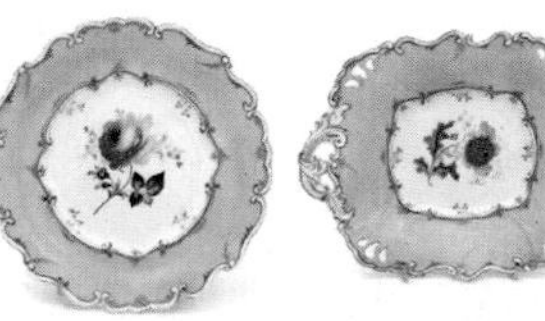
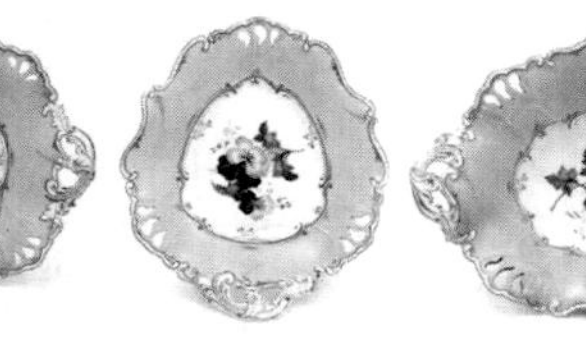

A Wedgwood dessert service, comprising 25 pieces, each painted in enamels with a botanical specimen, impressed marks, mid-19thC.
£1,250–1,500 / €1,800–2,150
$2,250–2,700 ⚒ GIL

A Victorian Imperial Stone dinner service, comprising 102 pieces, transfer-printed and hand-painted with floral sprays, printed and impressed marks.
£350–420 / €510–610
$630–760 ⚒ Mit

Creamware

The creamware pottery manufactured by Josiah Wedgwood in the 1760s replaced the use of tin-glazed (delft) and salt-glazed pottery in the late 18th century. Wedgwood's creamware, sometimes referred to as Queen's ware, was a truly significant step as it brought together beauty with lightness and strength. Other major producers of creamware were the Leeds Pottery, Staffordshire and Swansea. The designs used often replicated silver items and the classic shapes, often with intricate and finely executed moulding and attention to detail, have never been surpassed.

Stands

A Dutch Delft stand, some damage, c1750, 4½in (11.5cm) diam.
£470–520 / €690–760
$850–940 ⊞ G&G

A Choisy le Roi comport, decorated with strawberries, French, c1880, 9in (23cm) wide.
£145–165 / €210–240
$270–300 ⊞ MLL

A Llanelli Pottery cabaret set tray, painted by Shufflebotham, decorated with Wild Rose pattern, Welsh, c1900, 12in (30.5cm) wide.
£400–450 / €580–660
$720–810 ⊞ WeW

Tea & Coffee Pots

◄ **A Staffordshire Redware teapot,** applied with Oriental figures, impressed mark, damaged and restored, early 18thC, 4in (10cm) high.
£430–480 / €630–700
$780–870 ⊞ G&G

A Staffordshire stoneware teapot, on three feet, restored, 18thC, 6½in (16.5cm) wide.
£300–360 / €440–530
$540–650 ⚒ WW

◄ **A salt-glazed miniature teapot,** c1740, 3in (7.5cm) high.
£950–1,050 / €1,400–1,550
$1,700–1,900 ⊞ KEY

A salt-glazed stoneware teapot, slipcast with panels of figures and beasts, restored, c1745, 5¼in (13.5cm) wide.
£1,050–1,250 / €1,550–1,850
$1,900–2,250 ⚒ WW

Salt-glazed pottery

In the late 17th century John Dwight of Fulham, London, began experiments to produce a pottery body that would rival the whiteness and delicacy of porcelain. By 1719, the Staffordshire potters were also making stoneware whitened with calcined flint. White clay from Dorset and Devon was the preferred clay and remained the staple ingredient for all white-bodied pottery. It is extremely difficult to attribute salt-glazed pottery to any particular area as there is an absence of potters marks. Although traditionally associated and certainly made in some quantity in Staffordshire, there were potteries producing salt-glazed wares in other centres including Yorkshire and Liverpool until the end of the 1770s when, for finer products, creamware took over in popularity.

◄ **An Elers-style stoneware teapot,** with engine-turned decoration, damaged, seal mark, mid-18thC, 7in (18cm) wide.
£520–620 / €760–910
$940–1,100 ⚒ SWO

A Staffordshire salt-glazed stoneware teapot, painted in enamels with figures, restored, c1760, 7¼in (18.5cm) wide.
£1,050–1,250 / €1,550–1,850
$1,900–2,250 ⚒ WW

A Staffordshire salt-glazed stoneware teapot, with applied decoration, c1765, 5in (12.5cm) wide.
£1,550–1,750 / €2,250–2,550
$2,800–3,150 ⊞ JHo

A Derbyshire coffee pot, c1770, 9in (23cm) high.
£1,650–1,850 / €2,400–2,700
$3,000–3,350 ⊞ JHo

POTTERY

◄ **A Höchst faïence teapot,** painted with floral sprays and branches, damaged, German, c1770, 4¾in (12cm) high.
£2,300–2,750
€3,350–4,000
$4,150–5,000 S(Am)

► **A Staffordshire/ Yorkshire coffee pot,** c1775, 7in (18cm) high.
£1,200–1,350
€1,750–1,950
$2,150–2,450 JHo

A creamware teapot, decorated with a shepherd and a tea party, some damage, 1770–80, 6¾in (17cm) wide.
£330–390 / €480–570
$600–710 WW

A creamware teapot, c1780, 4in (10cm) high.
£490–550 / €720–800
$890–990 HOW

A creamware teapot, painted with a verse, damaged, 18thC, 5¼in (13.5cm) wide.
£730–870 / €1,050–1,250
$1,300–1,550 G(L)

A creamware teapot, with floral decoration, c1780, 6in (15cm) high.
£630–700 / €920–1,050
$1,100–1,250 HOW

A Regency black basalt coffee pot, commemorating the Duke of Wellington, inscribed 'Vittoria 21 June 1813', impressed marks, 7¾in (19.5cm) high.
£820–980 / €1,200–1,450
$1,500–1,800 PFK

A William Baddeley black basalt teapot, commemorating the Duke of Wellington, c1815, 6in (15cm) high.
£400–450 / €580–660
$720–810 AUC

◄ **A Wedgwood stoneware coffee pot,** embossed with foliate scrolls and flowerheads, the cover with a lion knop, impressed mark, 1815–30, 9in (23cm) high.
£200–240 / €290–350
$360–430 DN

A Prattware miniature teapot and creamer, c1815, 3in (7.5cm) high.
£220–250 / €320–360
$400–450 ReN

A George Jones majolica teapot, c1860, 9in (23cm) wide.
£3,500–3,900 / €5,100–5,700
$6,300–7,100 BRT

A bargeware teapot and stand, c1870, 13in (33cm) high.
£400–450 / €580–660
$720–810 JBL

A Cumnock Pottery teapot, Scottish, c1883, 7½in (19cm) high.
£220–250 / €320–360
$400–450 SDD

Tiles

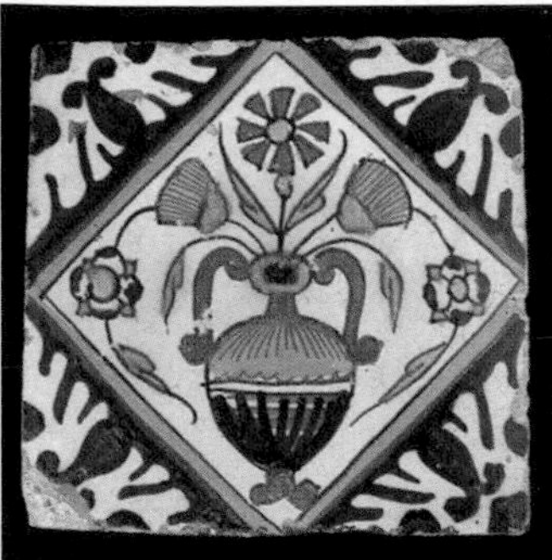

A Dutch Delft tile, damaged, 17thC, 5in (12.5cm) square.
£65–75 / €95–110
$120–135 ⊞ G&G

A London delft tile, depicting a bowl of flowers, c1750, 5in (12.5cm) square.
£85–95 / €125–140
$150–170 ⊞ JHo

A Dutch Delft tile picture, comprising 20 tiles, decorated with a vase of flowers, damaged and restored, 18thC, 26½ x 21½in (67.5 x 54.5cm).
£3,250–3,900 / €4,750–5,700
$5,900–7,100 S(Am)

A delft tile, decorated in manganese, c1760, 5¼in (13.5cm) square.
£35–40 / €50–60
$65–70 ⊞ F&F

Items in the Pottery section have been arranged in date order within each sub-section.

◄ **A Liverpool delft tile,** c1770, 5in (12.5cm) square.
£55–65 / €80–95
$100–120 ⊞ JHo

A Dutch Delft tile, depicting figures and a horse-drawn cart, 18thC, 5in (12.5cm) square.
£100–110 / €145–160
$180–200 ⊞ JHo

A delft tile, transfer-printed with 'The Boar and the Ass', from *Aesop's Fables*, 1750–75, 5in (12.5cm) square.
£90–100 / €130–145
$165–185 PFK

A set of six Davis & Co tiles, depicting scenes of Greek mythology, c1835, 12in (30.5cm) square.
£1,600–1,800 / €2,350–2,650
$2,900–3,250 ⊞ OLA

..n early Victorian pottery tile, ..ansfer-printed with 'Manchester Unity ..f Independent Order of Oddfellows', ..in (15cm) square, in a wooden frame.
..60–70 / €85–95
..105–125 PFK

A Minton, Hollins & Co tile, from the Water Birds series, with transfer-printed decoration, c1875, 6in (15cm) square.
£130–145 / €190–210
$240–270 ⊞ ReN

A set of four Victorian tiles, designed by Randoph Caldecott, with transfer-printed and hand-painted decoration, 6in (15cm) square.
£280–330 / €410–480
$510–600 PFK

Toby & Character Jugs

A Wood family creamware toby jug, with measure, damaged and restored, late 18thC, 9½in (24cm) high.
£1,300–1,500
€1,900–2,200
$2,350–2,700 S

The Wood family of Burslem were important potters in the late 18th and early 19th centuries.

A creamware Toby jug, smoking a pipe, some restored, late 18thC, 9½in (24cm) high.
£3,800–4,550
€5,500–6,600
$6,900–8,200 S

A Prattware Martha Gunn Toby jug, with a pearlware glaze, c1790, 10in (25.5cm) high.
£1,150–1,300
€1,700–1,900
$2,100–2,350 JBL

A pearlware Toby jug, c1800, 10in (25.5cm) high.
£1,800–2,000
€2,600–2,900
$3,250–3,600 JBL

A Staffordshire Toby jug, handle repaired, c1840, 9¾in (25cm) high.
£370–440 / €540–640
$670–800 SWO

A Prattware-style Toby jug, c1800, 9¾in (25cm) high.
£720–860 / €1,050–1,250
$1,300–1,550 S

A Toby jug, slight damage, 19thC, 10¼in (26cm) high.
£350–420 / €510–610
$630–760 WW

◄ **A Staffordshire Toby jug,** early 19thC, 10in (25.5cm) high.
£350–420 / €510–610
$630–760 SJH

Tureens

A Marieberg faïence tureen, painted with Meadow pattern, the cover with a pomegranate knop, damaged and repaired, signed, Swedish, 1758–66, 15¾in (40cm) diam.
£1,300–1,550 / €1,900–2,250
$2,350–2,800 BUK

A Stralsund faïence tureen, painted with hops and vines, the cover with a pear knop, marked 'B', German, c1770, 11¾in (30cm) wide.
£2,600–3,100 / €3,800–4,550
$4,700–5,600 BUK

A creamware tureen, stand and ladle, transfer-printed with birds, c1780, 8in (20.5cm) wide.
£720–800 / €1,050–1,150
$1,300–1,450 HOW

For further information on
Transfer-printed wares see pages 241–246

Vases & Urns

◀ **A Palermo maiolica vase,** painted with a portrait of a woman, repaired, Sicilian, dated 1625, 13¼in (33.5cm) high.
£4,800–5,700
€7,000–8,300
$8,700–10,300 ⚒ S

▶ **A Frankfurt faïence urn,** with chinoiserie decoration, cover repaired, slight damage, German, 1650–1700, 21½in (54.5cm) high.
£1,750–2,100
€2,550–3,050
$3,150–3,800 ⚒ BUK

A Dutch Delft vase, with floral decoration, damaged, early 18thC, 12¾in (32.5cm) high.
£550–620 / €800–910
$1,000–1,100 ⊞ G&G

A maiolica vase, slight damage, Sicilian, 18thC, 11in (28cm) high.
£1,050–1,250
€1,550–1,850
$1,900–2,250 ⚒ S(Mi)

A Staffordshire pearlware quintal, c1820, 7in (18cm) high.
£630–700 / €900–1,000
$1,100–1,250 ⊞ HOW

◀ **A Minton majolica vase,** c1860, 9in (23cm) high.
£2,150–2,400
€3,150–3,500
$3,900–4,350 ⊞ BRT

◄ **A pair of Minton majolica vases,** decorated with male and female masks, year cypher for 1860, 14¼in (36cm) high.
£1,650–1,950
€2,400–2,850
$3,000–3,550 **WilP**

A Minton majolica vase, c1865, 6in (15cm) high.
£1,700–1,900
€2,500–2,750
$3,100–3,450 **BRT**

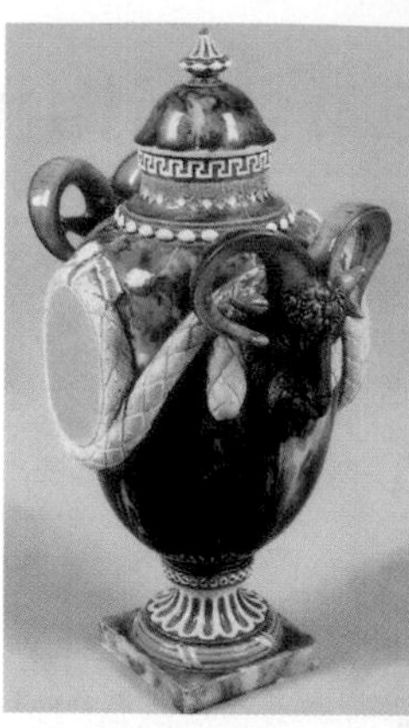

A Victorian majolica urn and cover, with ram's head handles, 25¼in (64cm) high.
£480–560 / €700–820
$870–1,000 **JAd**

A Minton majolica urn, restored, impressed marks and No. 1009, 1874, 17in (43cm) high.
£590–700 / €840–1,000
$1,050–1,250 **BWL**

A majolica vase, decorated with water lilies, impressed marks, Continental, late 19thC, 12¾in (32.5cm) high.
£130–155 / €195–230
$240–280 **HOLL**

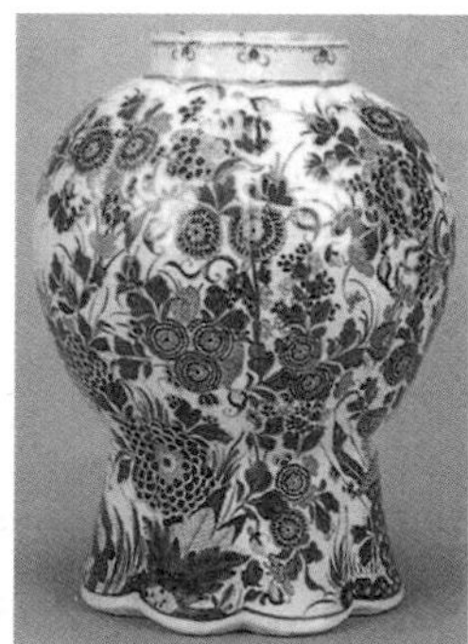

◄ **A delft vase,** with floral decoration, script marks, late 19thC, 13¾in (35cm) high.
£610–730 / €880–1,050
$1,100–1,300 **DN**

A Wemyss spill vase, painted with heather, Scottish, c1880, 3in (7.5cm) high.
£580–650 / €850–950
$1,050–1,200 **SDD**

A Wemyss brush vase, painted with honeysuckle and bees, impressed mark, Scottish, c1900, 4½in (11.5cm) high.
£630–700 / €900–1,000
$1,100–1,250 **RdeR**

A Robert Heron & Son vase, moulded with a cockerel, marked, Scottish, Fife, c1900, 15¼in (38.5cm) high.
£1,250–1,500
€1,850–2,200
$2,250–2,700 **TEN**

A Wemyss Grosvenor vase, painted with roses, Scottish, c1901, 8in (20.5cm) high.
£380–430 / €550–620
$690–780 **GLB**

Wall Pockets

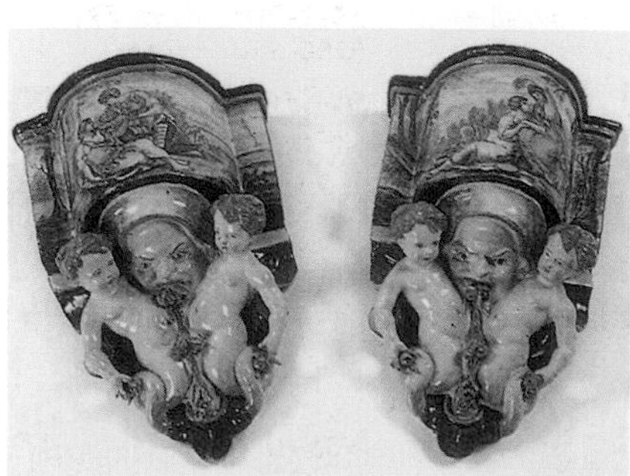

A pair of majolica wall pockets, painted in Castelli style with a scene of lovers, 19thC, 14in (35.5cm) high.
£1,650–1,950 / €2,400–2,850
$3,000–3,550 **JNic**

A wall pocket, French, Gien, c1890, 12in (30.5cm) high.
£165–185 / €240–270
$300–330 **SER**

A Quimper wall pocket, French, c1920, 11in (28cm) high.
£220–250 / €320–360
$400–450 **MLL**

POTTERY

Miscellaneous

◀ **A creamware barrel,** surmounted by a figure of Silenus, c1820, 7in (18cm) high.
£1,300–1,450 / €1,900–2,100
$2,350–2,600 ⊞ AUC

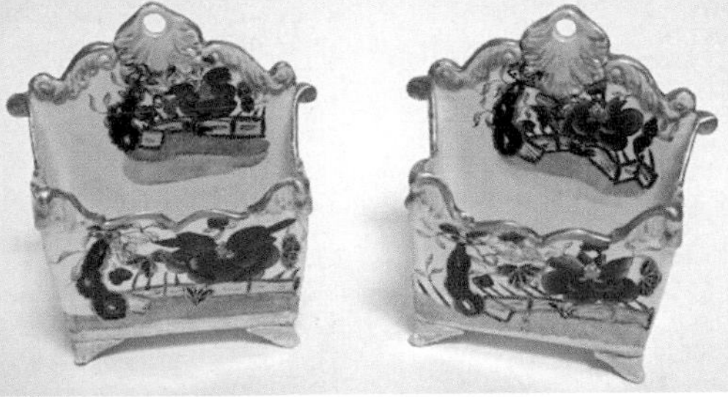

A pair of Mason's Ironstone card racks, c1820, 7in (18cm) high.
£1,700–1,900 / €2,500–2,750
$3,100–3,450 ⊞ ReN

A Turner bulb pot and cover, with claw-and-ball feet, cover restored, c1785, 7in (18cm) high.
£800–890 / €1,150–1,300
$1,450–1,600 ⊞ TYE

A Bovey Pottery earthenware crib, slight damage, late 18thC, 4¾in (12cm) long.
£640–760 / €930–1,100
$1,200–1,400 ⚒ Bea

A delft flower brick, with floral decoration, restored, c1760, 6in (15cm) wide.
£640–760 / €930–1,100
$1,200–1,400 ⚒ WW

A maiolica guglet, decorated with fruit, flowers and scrolling leaves, restored, Italian, probably Caltagirone, c1700, 9¼in (23.5cm) high.
£290–340 / €420–500
$520–620 ⚒ WW

A pair of Leeds creamware pastille burners, c1900, 3in (7.5cm) high.
£310–350 / €450–510
$560–630 ⊞ TYE

▶ **A pair of Maw & Co majolica pedestals,** c1860, 28in (71cm) high.
£1,250–1,400
€1,850–2,050
$2,250–2,550 ⊞ ReN

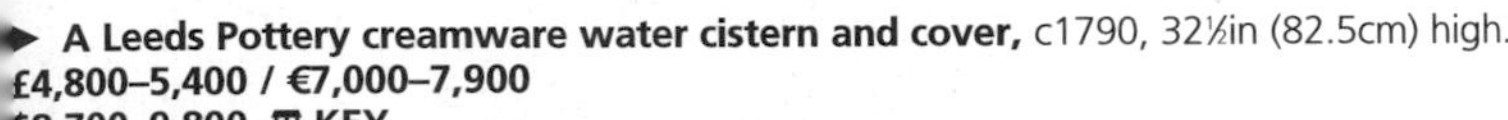

A delft pipkin, painted in manganese with a monogram of William III, slight damage, possibly Dutch, late 17thC, 3in (7.5cm) high.
£420–500 / €610–730
$760–910 ⚒ WW
A pipkin is a small earthenware or metal vessel.

A pair of Wedgwood potpourri jars, decorated with bands of roses, damaged, impressed marks, 19thC, 13in (33cm) high.
£420–500 / €610–730
$760–910 ⚒ Bea

▶ **A Leeds Pottery creamware water cistern and cover,** c1790, 32½in (82.5cm) high.
£4,800–5,400 / €7,000–7,900
$8,700–9,800 ⊞ KEY
There were several designs of water cisterns made by the Leeds Pottery and it is believed that they were made for a local market. Although they were frequently referred to as filters this is in fact erroneous as there is no arrangement in them for filtering. The water supply in Leeds when these cisterns were made was of extremely poor quality and there was a great demand for Holbeck Spa Water, particularly for the very fashionable occupation of tea drinking. These immensely elaborate and refined cisterns would no doubt take pride of place in the homes of the wealthier classes in Leeds.

POTTERY

Staffordshire Animals & Figures

With over 300 factories in and around Stoke-on-Trent in the 19th century, countless Staffordshire pottery figures were produced. The popularity of these figures is largely due to timing. The industrial revolution had increased the spending power of the working classes and small luxuries such as ornamental figures could be afforded. Moreover, the vast social changes during the reign of Queen Victoria were a rich source of inspiration for the entrepreneurial pottery manufacturer. In the mid-19th century, the British Empire was at the height of its glory and spanned half the world. The thirst for representations of this glory, both social and historical, produced a massive home market to commemorate and acknowledge the great events of the times.

Figures from this period fall into several categories, including Royalty, Military, Political, Theatrical, Crime, Jungle and Domestic Animals. Factories are another specific collecting area, such as those of Thomas Parr & Co or Lloyd Shelton. Another focus is the object itself, for the Staffordshire potters often combined a functional use for their figures. Spill vases, candlesticks, pastille burners and watch-holders were among the most popular and are now keenly collected.

However, one does not have to be constrained by a category or a theme and many collectors acquire the figures for the pure delight of their decorative impact. They can look stunning as an assemblage or as an individual feature, their strong lines and colours looking equally at home in a town house or a country cottage. The classic period for figures was between 1840 and 1870. After this the quality deteriorated dramatically as the potters simplified the manufacturing techniques in an effort to reduce production costs. Features to look for in figures are crisp modelling, well-executed painting and general condition. Look for humour and charm as well, as this will often add to the appeal. Some restoration is acceptable, providing it has been carried out professionally. The figures and models produced in Staffordshire pottery figures give a unique 'snap-shot' of the Victorian period. The history of the time with its stories of triumph, heroism, defeat, pomp, grandeur and tragedy are all there, represented by figures that were mass-produced for the ordinary people. It has been described as the 'Last Tribal Art of Britain' which is a fitting description, as it is unlikely we will never see the like of this pottery phenomenon again.

John Howard

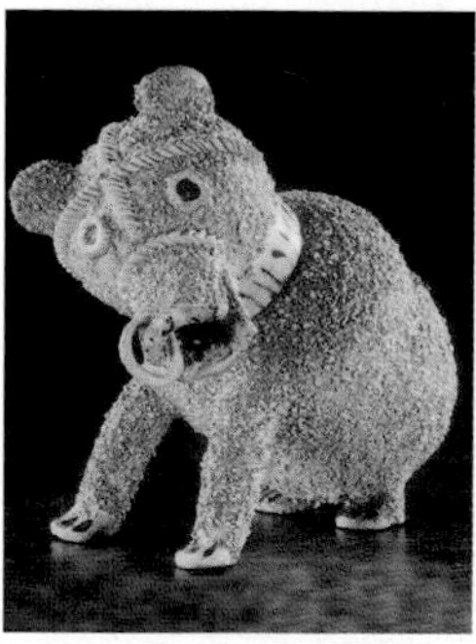

A Staffordshire salt-glazed stoneware bear jug and cover, damaged, c1760, 10¼in (26cm) wide.
£4,500–5,400
€6,600–7,900
$8,200–9,800 ⚒ S

A Staffordshire figure of a lady holding a watering can, late 18thC, 5½in (14cm) high.
£200–220 / €290–320
$360–400 ⊞ G&G

A Staffordshire porcellaneous figure of a lady, entitled 'Winter', c1790, 5in (12.5cm) high.
£220–250 / €320–370
$400–450 ⊞ LBr

A Staffordshire pearlware group of a stag and birds, c1810, 6in (15cm) high.
£720–800 / €1,050–1,200
$1,300–1,450 ⊞ HOW

◄ **A Staffordshire group of three sheep,** seated before bocage, c1815, 4¾in (12cm) high.
£260–290
€380–420
$470–520 ⊞ SER

A Staffordshire model of a leopard, c1815, 8in (20.5cm) wide.
£3,150–3,500 / €4,600–5,100
$5,700–6,300 ⊞ HOW

A Staffordshire model of a girl holding a piglet in a box, decorated with enamels, restored, early 19thC, 8in (20.5cm) high.
£95–110 / €140–160
$170–200 WW

A Staffordshire pearlware figural group, entitled 'Lost Sheep', slight damage, c1820, 8¾in (22cm) high.
£800–960 / €1,200–1,400
$1,450–1,750 DN

► **A Staffordshire model of a leopard,** c1820, 4in (10cm) high.
£1,250–1,400
€1,850–2,050
$2,250–2,550
HOW

A pair of Staffordshire treacle-glazed models of lions, 19thC, 12in (30.5cm) wide.
£730–870 / €1,050–1,250
$1,300–1,550 AH

A Staffordshire model of a deer, seated before bocage, c1820, 4½in (11.5cm) high.
£165–195 / €240–280
$300–350 SJH

A Staffordshire pearlware model of a cow, with bocage, c1820, 7in (18cm) high.
£900–1,000
€1,300–1,450
$1,600–1,800 HOW

Bocage figures

Bocage is a French term for a grove or copse, and it is a mystery why the French rather than the English term was adopted. The bocage are press-moulded leaves applied to the backs of figural groups. Bocage figures were produced by several factories in Staffordshire, such as Walton, Sherratt and Salt. The figures often depict a romantic rural theme such as a ewe and ram with lambs or a shepherd and lady gardener. Rarer examples are often quite complex and expensive, sometimes showing an entire flock of sheep or depicting jungle animals. Bocage items are decorated in bright enamel colours in pearlware glaze that can be identified by its pale blue colour. The production of bocage figures ceased c1840, probably as a result of the time-consuming nature of their production.

◄ **A pair of Staffordshire pearlware figures of a sheherd and a shepherdess,** slight damage, early 19thC, 8in (20.5cm) high.
£370–440
€540–640
$670–800
WW

A pair of Staffordshire figural groups, by Walton, entitled 'Flight to Egypt' and 'Return from Egypt', marked, c1820, 9in (23cm) high.
£3,450–3,850 / €5,000–5,600
$6,200–7,000 JHo

A pair of Staffordshire pearlware figures of musicians, slight restoration, c1820, 6in (15cm) high.
£720–800 / €1,050–1,200
$1,300–1,450 TYE

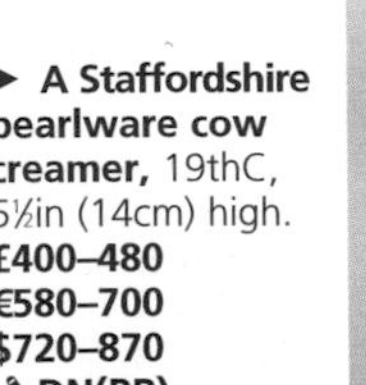

► **A Staffordshire pearlware cow creamer,** 19thC, 5½in (14cm) high.
£400–480
€580–700
$720–870
DN(BR)

A Staffordshire pepper pot, in the form of Roger Giles, c1825, 5in (12.5cm) high.
£540–600 / €790–880
$980–1,100 ⊞ DAN

Roger Giles is always depicted as a seated gentleman relieving himself. He was a Devonshire schoolteacher who placed an advertisement in his local newspaper for his fresh egg 'new laid' by himself every day. Always looking for interesting news items to pot, the Staffordshire factories potted him laying his own eggs.

A Staffordshire pearlware figure of Elijah and the Raven, decorated with enamels, marked '27' in red, slight damage, early 19thC, 9½in (24cm) high.
£150–180 / €220–260
$270–320 ⚒ DN

A Staffordshire porcellaneous figure of Dr Syntax landing at Calais, c1830, 6in (15cm) high.
£410–460 / €600–670
$740–830 ⊞ DAN

A Staffordshire pearlware figural group of Vicar and Moses, c1830, 10¼in (26cm) high.
£230–270 / €340–390
$420–490 ⚒ SWO

A Staffordshire porcellaneous model of a begging poodle, c1840, 4in (10cm) high.
£360–400 / €520–580
$650–720 ⊞ DAN

Religious figures

The Victorian era saw the rise of evangelism particularly in Wales and the north of England including Staffordshire. Figures of Wesley, Spurgeon and Christmas Evans found a ready demand from non-conformists.

A Staffordshire model of a Dalmation, on a scrolled base, 19thC, 4in (10cm) wide.
£175–195 / €250–280
$310–350 ⊞ TYE

A Staffordshire stoneware model of a lop-eared rabbit, c1840, 3in (7.5cm) high.
£450–500 / €660–730
$810–910 ⊞ HOW

◄ **A Staffordshire model of Punch and his dog Toby,** c1840, 12in (30.5cm) high.
£2,500–2,800 / €3,650–4,100
$4,550–5,100 ⊞ HOW

A pair of Staffordshire models of spaniels, by Alcock & Co, c1840, 5in (12.5cm) high.
£900–1,000 / €1,300–1,450
$1,650–1,800 ⊞ HOW

A Staffordshire model of a cat, c1840, 7in (18cm) high.
£1,800–2,000 / €2,600–2,900
$3,250–3,600 ⊞ HOW

A Staffordshire porcellaneous model of a dog, c1845, 4in (10cm) long.
£250–280 / €370–410
$450–510 ⊞ DAN

A Staffordshire model of a spaniel, c1845, 7in (18cm) high.
£630–700 / €920–1,050
$1,150–1,300 ⊞ HOW

A Staffordshire foxhunting group, mid-19thC, 10½in (26.5cm) wide.
£330–390 / €480–570
$600–710 ⚒ DN

A Staffordshire porcellaneous Toby vinegar jug and cover, c1845, 5in (12.5cm) high.
£320–360 / €470–530
$580–650 ⊞ DAN

Political figures

Politicians were more popular in the 19th century than they are today, and ceramic figures such as Benjamin Disraeli and Robert Peel were given pride of place in the home.

A pair of Staffordshire models of ponies, c1850, 5in (12.5cm) high.
£500–550 / €730–810
$900–1,000 ⊞ HOW

A Staffordshire model of Sir Robert Peel on horseback, c1850, 11in (28cm) high.
£720–800 / €1,050–1,200
$1,300–1,450 ⊞ HOW

A pair of Staffordshire models of lions, each standing above a lamb, mid-19thC, 4in (10cm) high.
£300–360 / €440–530
$540–650 DN

A pair of Staffordshire models of greyhounds, c1850, 11in (28cm) high.
£1,050–1,200 / €1,550–1,750
$1,900–2,150 HOW

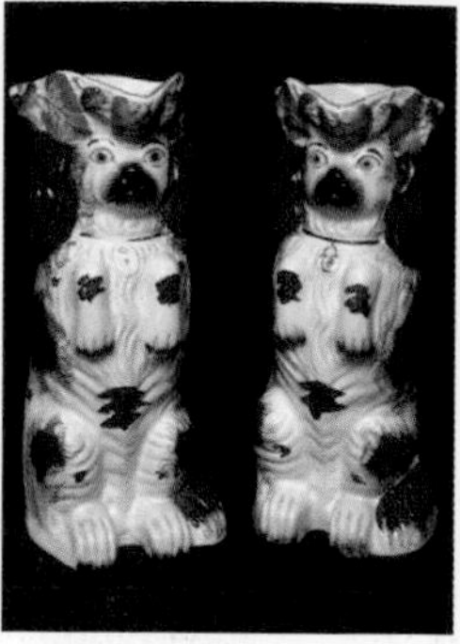

A pair of Staffordshire jugs, in the form of begging King Charles spaniels, c1850, 10in (25.5cm) high.
£1,200–1,350
€1,750–1,950
$2,150–2,450 RdeR

Royalty

The public have always had a strong interest in the events surrounding the Royals. The wedding of Queen Victoria and Prince Albert, the birth of their children and visits from foreign dignitaries were all represented by the Staffordshire potters. Even the iconic Staffordshire spaniels were probably inspired by the Queen's fondness for Dash, her beautiful King Charles spaniel. As a result, tens of thousands of pairs of Staffordshire spaniels have graced the mantelpieces of the general public.

◄ **A Staffordshire model of a dog smoking a pipe,** c1850, 10in (25.5cm) high.
£1,250–1,400
€1,850–2,050
$2,250–2,550 HOW

A pair of Staffordshire porcellaneous models of poodles, holding baskets in their mouths, mid-19thC, 3¼in (8.5cm) high.
£200–240 / €290–350
$360–430 WW

A pair of Staffordshire models of spaniels, c1850, 5in (12.5cm) high.
£1,300–1,450 / €1,900–2,100
$2,350–2,700 HOW

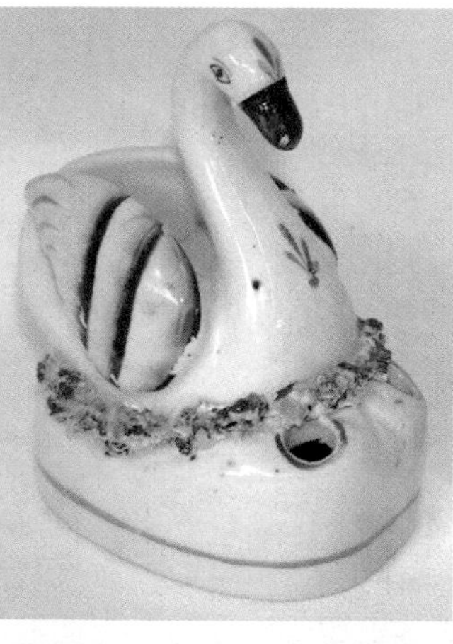

◄ **A Staffordshire model of a swan,** c1860, 4in (10cm) high.
£110–125 / €160–185
$200–230 SER

A pair of Staffordshire models of exotic birds, c1850, 9in (23cm) high.
£670–750 / €980–1,100
$1,200–1,350 HOW

► **A Staffordshire figural group of a girl with a baby in a crib,** mid-19thC, 6¼in (16cm) high.
£165–195 / €240–280
$300–350 DN

A Staffordshire spill vase group, of a couple with a cat at their feet, mid-19thC, 9in (23cm) high.
£90–105 / €130–155
$165–190 DN

A set of four Staffordshire figures of the seasons, Spring depicted as a girl with a flower garland, Summer as a boy with a sheaf of corn, Autumn as a girl with a basket of fruit and Winter as a boy carrying a game basket, slight damage, mid-19thC, 9¾in (25cm) high.
£560–670 / €810–970
$1,000–1,200 GIL

◄ A Staffordshire figure of Admiral Sir Deans Dundas, entitled 'Dundas', with a flag to one side and a cannon to the other, some damage, 1854–56, 11½in (29cm) high.
£165–195 / €240–280
$300–350 DN
Sir James Deans Dundas was in charge of the transport of the army to the Crimea. He was also involved in the Battle of Alma and the engagement with the sea forts of Sebastopol.

A pair of Staffordshire spill vases, with cows and milkmaids, c1855, 9in (23cm) high.
£580–650 / €850–950
$1,050–1,200 HOW

A pair of Staffordshire models of sheep with flags, c1855, 3in (7.5cm) high.
£340–380 / €500–550
$620–690 HOW

POTTERY

A pair of Staffordshire spill vases, with foxes, c1855, 9in (23cm) high.
£720–800 / $1,050–1,200
€1,300–1,450 HOW

A pair of Staffordshire models of lions with lambs, c1855, 10in (25.5cm) high.
£3,400–3,800 / €4,950–5,500
$6,200–6,900 HOW

A pair of Staffordshire models of St Bernard dogs with royal children, c1855, 9in (23cm) high.
£2,250–2,500 / €3,300–3,650
$4,050–4,550 HOW

A Staffordshire group of a dog with a child riding on its back, the dog carrying a basket in its mouth, c1855, 10in (25.5cm) high.
£580–650 / €850–950
$1,050–1,200 HOW

Animals

Ceramic models of dogs such as spaniels, greyhounds, poodles, pugs, setters and many other breeds were produced by the Staffordshire potteries. Nostalgia for life in the countryside was catered for by models of sheep, rabbits, cows with milkmaids and farm hands. Exotic birds and animals such as lions, giraffes, camels and zebras were a novelty in the mid-19th century as few people had seen these animals before.

A pair of Staffordshire models of spaniels, each with a puppy, c1855, 6in (15cm) high.
£1,200–1,350 / €1,750–1,950
$2,150–2,450 HOW

Further reading

Miller's Staffordshire Figures of the 19th & 20th Centuries: A collector's Guide,
Miller's Publications, 2000

A Staffordshire model of Billy the rat-catcher, c1855, 6in (15cm) high.
£580–650 / €850–950
$1,050–1,200 ⊞ HOW

A pair of Staffordshire models of spaniels, carrying baskets of flowers in their mouths, c1855, 8in (20.5cm) high.
£1,000–1,100 / €1,450–1,600
$1,800–2,000 ⊞ HOW

◄ A Staffordshire spill vase, with a cow, c1860, 13in (33cm) high.
£1,050–1,200 / €1,550–1,750
$1,900–2,150 ⊞ HOW

A Staffordshire model of a cat, with sponged decoration, c1860, 4¾in (12cm) high.
£130–155 / €190–220
$240–280 ⚒ SJH

A pair of Staffordshire figures of a milkmaid and a cowherd, slight damage, c1860, 9in (23cm) wide.
£700–840 / €1,000–1,200
$1,250–1,500 ⚒ WW

A Staffordshire tobacco box, in the form of a spaniel's head, c1860, 5in (12.5cm) high.
£540–600 / €790–880
$1,000–1,100 ⊞ HOW

A Staffordshire pen stand, in the form of spaniels, c1860, 5½in (14cm) wide.
£420–500 / €610–730
$760–910 ⚒ LF

◄ A pair of Staffordshire models of spaniels, c1860 13in (33cm) high.
£450–500 / €660–730
$810–910 ⊞ HOW

► A pair of Staffordshire spill vases, with poodles and kennels, c1860, 8in (20.5cm) high.
£720–800 / €1,050–1,200
$1,300–1,450 ⊞ HOW

A pair of Staffordshire models of spaniels, each with a puppy, c1860, 8in (20.5cm) high.
£540–600 / €790–880
$1,000–1,100 ⊞ HOW

◄ A pair of Staffordshire models of greyhounds, c1860, 13in (33cm) high.
£1,000–1,100
€1,450–1,600
$1,800–2,000
⊞ HOW

A pair of Staffordshire spill vases, with sporting dogs with game, c1860, 9in (23cm) high.
£720–800 / €1,050–1,200
$1,300–1,450 HOW

A pair of Staffordshire models of hares, one cracked, c1860, 3in (7.5cm) wide.
£270–300 / €390–440
$490–540 WW

A Staffordshire spill vase, with an elephant, c1860, 7in (18cm) high.
£540–600 / €790–880
$1,000–1,100 HOW

A Staffordshire spill vase, with a fox and a wheatsheaf, c1860, 5in (122.5cm) high.
£350–390 / €510–570
$630–710 HOW

A Staffordshire spill vase, with a lion, c1860, 5in (12.5cm) high.
£310–350 / €450–510
$560–630 HOW

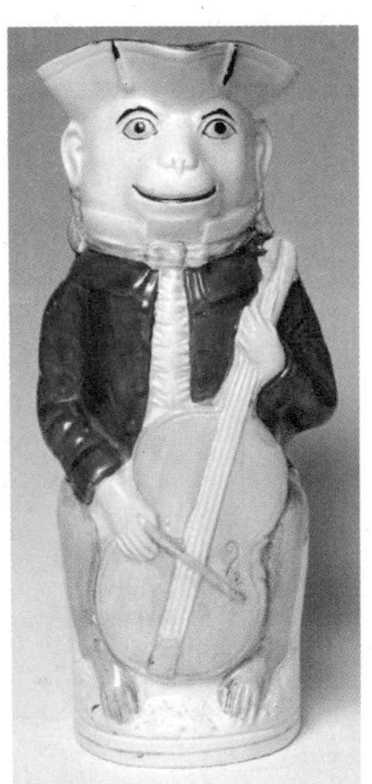

A Staffordshire jug, modelled as a monkey with a cello, c1860, 11in (28cm) high.
£360–400 / €520–580
$650–720 HOW

POTTERY

Military subjects

Many historical naval and military battles such as the Crimean War and Indian Mutiny gave rise to interest in the generals and heroes who took part. Napoleon and Garibaldi are among many famous names that were commemorated by pottery figures.

◄ **A Staffordshire figure of Garibaldi,** by Thomas Parr, c1860, 9in (23cm) high.
£430–480 / €630–700
$780–870 HOW

A Staffordshire figural group of Jenny Jones and Ned Morgan, c1860, 11in (28cm) high.
£810–900 / €1,200–1,350
$1,450–1,650 HOW
This group is also known as 'The Legless Mother'.

A pair of Staffordshire models of roosters, c1860, 4in (10cm) high.
£430–480 / €630–700
$780–870 HOW

A Staffordshire figure of a rifle volunteer NCO, probably by Thomas Parr, slight damage, c1860, 11½in (29cm) high.
£440–520 / €640–760
$800–940 DN

◄ **A pair of Staffordshire spill vases,** with cows, calves and milkmaids, c1870, 11in (28cm) high.
£470–560 / €690–820
$850–1,000 WW

A Staffordshire spill vase, with a horse and foal, c1870, 13in (33cm) high.
£500–550 / €720–800
$900–1,000 ⊞ HOW

A Staffordshire spill vase, with a cow, entitled 'Milk Sold Here', c1870, 15in (38cm) high.
£1,800–2,000 / €2,600–2,900
$3,200–3,600 ⊞ HOW

A pair of Staffordshire models of King Charles spaniels, c1870, 12in (30.5cm) high.
£400–450 / €580–660
$720–810 ⊞ RdeR

A pair of Staffordshire models of zebras, c1870, 9in (23cm) high.
£430–480 / €630–700
$780–870 ⊞ SER

A pair of Staffordshire models of pug dogs, c1880, 7in (18cm) high.
£500–550 / €730–810
$900–1,000 ⊞ HOW

A pair of Staffordshire models of pug dogs, c1880, 11in (28cm) high.
£1,000–1,150 / €1,450–1,700
$1,800–2,100 ⊞ HOW

A pair of Staffordshire models of elephants, c1880, 8in (20.5cm) high.
£1,800–2,000 / €2,600–2,900
$3,200–3,600 ⊞ HOW

► **A pair of Staffordshire models of spaniels,** with separated forelegs, c1880, 9½in (24cm) high.
£450–540
€660–790
$810–980 ⚒ PF

A Staffordshire model of a smiling cat, with glass eyes, 1890–1900, 14in (35.5cm) high.
£810–900 / €1,200–1,350
$1,450–1,650 ⊞ RdeR

A Staffordshire porcellaneous candle snuffer, in the form of Pierre Moule, c1900, 3½in (9cm) high.
£165–185 / €240–270
$300–330 ⊞ GGD

A pair of Staffordshire models of camels, c1900, 6in (15cm) high.
£1,450–1,600 / €2,100–2,350
$2,600–3,000 ⊞ HOW

Transfer-Printed Pottery

A baby's bottle, transfer-printed with a romantic scene, c1825, 7in (18cm) high.
£670–750 / €980–1,100
$1,200–1,350 ⊞ GN

A coffee pot, transfer-printed with One Man Chinoiserie pattern, the cover with a flowerhead knop, restored, 1805–15, 10½in (26.5cm) high.
£80–95 / €120–140
$145–170 ⚒ DN

A Minton coffee pot, transfer-printed with Farmyard pattern, c1820, 8in (20.5cm) high.
£400–450 / €580–660
$720–810 ⊞ GN

A Beamaster coffee pot, with transfer-printed decoration, c1820, 11in (28cm) high.
£2,300–2,600
€3,350–3,800
$4,150–4,700 ⊞ SCO
This is a very rare shape in this pattern.

Items in this section have been arranged in alphabetical order.

A Ridgway comport, transfer-printed with a view of Osterley Park, c1820, 12in (30.5cm) wide.
£280–320 / €410–470
$510–580 ⊞ SCO

► **A comport/footed bowl,** transfer-printed with British Cattle pattern, slight damage, 1830–35, 10¾in (27.5cm) wide.
£150–180
€220–260
$270–320 ⚒ DN

A cruet set, with transfer-printed decoration, c1830, pepper 4in (10cm) high.
£360–400 / €520–580
$650–720 ⊞ GN

A dinner service, comprising 31 pieces, transfer-printed with Fence pattern, Royal Arms mark, c1820.
£1,900–2,250 / €2,750–3,300
$3,450–4.050 ⚒ G(L)

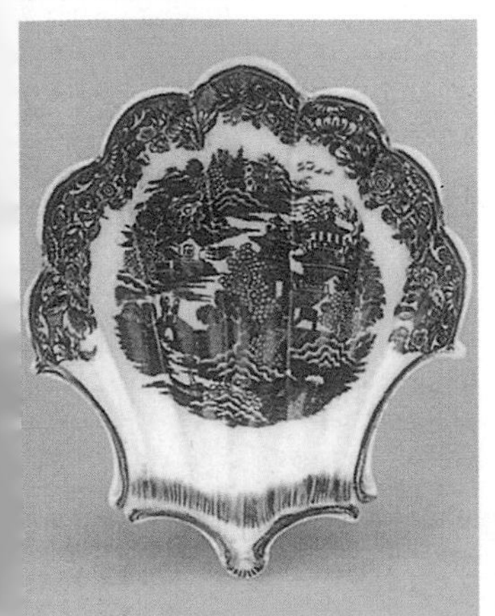

A Mason's dish, transfer-printed with a view of Richmond, Yorkshire, from the Beaded Frame series, c1820, 11in (28cm) wide.
£350–390 / €510–570
$630–700 ⊞ GRe

◄ **A dessert dish,** transfer-printed with Conversation pattern, on three feet, one foot repaired, 1790–1800, 8¼in (21cm) wide.
£130–155 / €190–220
$240–280 ⚒ DN

A Hicks & Meigh dish, with transfer-printed decoration, c1820, 6in (15cm) wide.
£100–115 / €150–170
$180–200 ⊞ SCO

A leaf-shaped pickle dish, transfer-printed with Jupiter pattern, slight damage, 1820–30, 5½in (14cm) wide.
£190–220 / €280–320
$340–400 DN

An egg cup, transfer-printed with Village Church pattern, 1820–30, 2½in (6.5cm) high.
£280–330 / €410–480
$510–600 DN

A Spode garden seat, transfer-printed with Willow pattern, 19thC, 19in (48.5cm) high.
£1,700–2,000 / €2,500–2,900
$3,100–3,600 IM

A William Mason pearlware dessert dish, transfer-printed with a scene of Lynmouth, north Devon, c1830, 11¼in (28.5cm) wide.
£440–490 / €640–720
$800–890 ⊞ RdV

A Spode eggstand, transfer-printed with sarcophagi and sepulchres at the Head of the harbour at Cacamo, from the Caramanian series, 1810, 7¼in (18.5cm) diam.
£500–550 / €720–800
$900–1,000 ⊞ GRe

A Spode water jug, transfer-printed with Chinese of Rank pattern, c1820, 8in (20.5cm) high.
£1,550–1,750 / €2,250–2,550
$2,800–3,150 ⊞ GN

An Adams jug, transfer-printed with Beehive pattern, c1835, 4in (10cm) wide.
£155–175 / €230–260
$280–320 ⊞ GN

◄ **A jug,** transfer-printed with a scene of boys fishing, c1835, 8in (20.5cm) high.
£720–800 / €1,000–1,150
$1,300–1,450 ⊞ GN

A drainer, transfer-printed with an Alpine scene, impressed mark, 1835–45, 10¾in (27.5cm) wide.
£175–210 / €260–310
$320–380 DN

A pilgrim flask, with transfer-printed flow-blue decoration, c1840, 8in (20.5cm) high.
£450–500 / €660–730
$810–910 ⊞ GN

A jug, transfer-printed with Sportsman's Inn pattern, 1820–30, 7½in (19cm) high.
£680–810 / €1,000–1,200
$1,250–1,450 DN

A commemorative jug, transfer-printed with Queen Victoria on the balcony of Windsor Castle, with an inscription, c1838, 9½in (24cm) high.
£850–950 / €1,250–1,400
$1,500–1,700 ⊞ RdV

A Pountney & Allies jug, transfer-printed with a rural scene, c1840, 6in (15cm) high.
£200–230 / €290–320
$360–400 ⊞ GN

A Stevenson jug, transfer-printed with the Royal Cottage, Windsor, from the British Palaces series, c1840, 6in (15cm) high.
£200–230 / €290–320
$360–400 ⊞ GN

A Swansea Pottery jug, transfer-printed with Oriental Basket pattern, Welsh, c1840, 6in (15cm) high.
£115–130 / €165–190
$200–220 ⊞ WeW

A commemorative mug, transfer-printed and entitled 'His Royal Highness Frederick Duke of York', c1793, 4¾in (12cm) high.
£1,100–1,300 / €1,600–1,900
$2,000–2,350 ⚒ DN

A Staffordshire loving cup, transfer-printed with Charity pattern, marked 'J.W.' to base, damaged, 19thC, 6in (15cm) high.
£100–120 / €145–175
$185–210 ⊞ G&G

A mug, transfer-printed with a rural scene, slight damage, 1820–30, 3¼in (8.5cm) high.
£130–155 / €190–220
$240–280 ⚒ DN

◄ **A Staffordshire mug,** titled and transfer-printed with The Sower, c1825, 2½in (6.5cm) diam.
£200–230
€290–340
$360–420
⊞ ReN

► **A mug,** transfer-printed with Albion pattern, inscribed 'Success to the rail', 19thC, 4¾in (12cm) high.
£490–580
€720–850
$890–1,050
⚒ TRM(E)

A John and Richard Riley plate, transfer-printed with a flower arrangement, 1815–25, 7in (18cm) diam.
£145–165 / €210–240
$260–300 ⊞ GRe

A Minton plate, transfer-printed with Monk's Rock pattern, c1820, 9½in (24cm) diam.
£130–155 / €190–220
$240–280 ⚒ SJH

A plate, designed by Carey, transfer-printed with a view of Lichfield Cathedral, from the Cathedral Series, c1830, 10in (25.5cm) diam.
£130–145 / €190–210
$230–260 ⊞ GN

A child's plate, titled and transfer-printed with 'The Old Hound' from *Aesop's Fables*, within an alphabet border, c1840, 7in (18cm) diam.
£290–330 / €420–480
$520–600 ⊞ GN

A dinner plate, attributed to Ridgway, transfer-printed with Blind Boy pattern, 1815–25, 9¾in (24.5cm) diam.
£90–105 / €130–155
$160–190 ⚒ DN

A Stevenson tea plate, transfer-printed with The Rookery, Surrey within a border of acorns and oak leaves, printed mark, 1820–30, 6½in (16.5cm) diam.
£120–140 / €175–200
$220–250 ⚒ DN

A Herculaneum plate, transfer-printed with Archery pattern, c1830, 10in (25.5cm) diam.
£175–195 / €250–280
$310–350 ⊞ GN

An Enoch Wood & Sons platter, transfer-printed with Lime House Dock and Regent's Canal, from the London Views series, c1820, 15in (38cm) wide.
£720–800 / €1,000–1,150
$1,300–1,450 ⊞ GN

A Clews pearlware plate, transfer-printed with The Miller pattern within a raised floral border, c1820, 6in (15cm) diam.
£210–240 / €310–350
$380–430 ⊞ ReN

A Jones & Son plate, transfer-printed with the signing of the Magna Carta, from the British History series, printed mark, 1826–28, 9¾in (25cm) diam.
£240–270 / €350–390
$430–490 ⊞ GRe

A Swansea Pottery plate, transfer-printed with Cows Crossing the Stream pattern, Welsh, c1835, 10in (25.5cm) diam.
£105–120 / €155–175
$200–220 ⊞ WeW

An Enoch Wood & Sons meat platter, transfer-printed with Rochester Castle, from the Grapevine Border series, printed mark, 1820–30, 17in (43cm) wide.
£590–700 / €860–1,000
$1,050–1,250 ⚒ DN

A meat platter, transfer-printed with a stag and deer in a landscape, the border decorated with a stag hunt, early 19thC, 18½in (47cm) wide.
£440–520 / €640–760
$800–940 TRM(E)

A meat platter, attributed to Minton, transfer-printed with a view of Monk's Rock at Tenby, 1820–30, 19¾in (47.6cm) wide.
£1,250–1,500 / €1,850–2,200
$2,250–2,700 DN

► **A Lockett & Hulme meat platter,** transfer-printed with Ponte Rotto pattern, printed mark, 1822–26, 21in (53.5cm) wide.
£300–360 / €440–530
$540–650 G(L)

A Davenport meat platter, transfer-printed with The Villagers pattern, impressed mark, 1820–30, 17¾in (45cm) wide.
£870–970 / €1,250–1,400
$1,550–1,750 GRe

A Swansea Pottery meat platter, transfer-printed with Ladies of Llangollen pattern, Welsh, c1830, 12in (30.5cm) wide.
£450–500 / €660–730
$810–910 WeW

A John & William Ridgway meat platter, transfer-printed with a view of Raby Castle, Durham, from the Angus Seats series, the border with four landscape cartouches and wild flowers, damaged, early 19thC, 19½in (49.5cm) wide.
£105–125 / €155–180
$190–220 PFK

A Ridgway meat platter, transfer-printed with a view of St Peter's College, c1820, 15in (38cm) wide.
£630–700 / €900–1,000
$1,100–1,250 SCO

A Samuel & John Burton meat platter, transfer-printed with The Shield pattern, printed mark, 1832–45, 18¾in (47.5cm) wide.
£175–210 / €260–310
$320–380 DN

A Spode fish platter, transfer-printed with a chinoiserie pattern, c1815, 22in (56cm) wide.
£630–700 / €900–1,000
$1,100–1,250 SCO

A meat platter, transfer-printed with Durham Ox pattern, c1820, 20in (51cm) wide.
£3,150–3,500 / €4,600–5,100
$5,700–6,300 SCO

An Andrew Stevenson meat platter, transfer-printed with Rural pattern, 1825, 16in (40.5cm) wide.
£400–450 / €580–660
$720–810 GN

A Stevenson soup dish, transfer-printed with a view of Windsor Castle, from the Lace Border series, c1830, 10in (25.5cm) diam.
£145–165 / €210–240
$260–300 GN

◄ **A Turner strainer,** transfer-printed with Stag pattern, with a moulded lug handle, 1790–1805, 3¼in (8.5cm) diam.
£200–240 / €290–350
$360–430 DN

A teabowl and saucer, transfer-printed with Time Clipping the Wings of Love pattern, Welsh, 1790–1800, saucer 5¼in (13.5cm) diam.
£145–165 / €210–240
$260–300 ⊞ GRe

► **A teapot,** transfer-printed with a chinoiserie scene, damaged and repaired, 1795–1810, 8¾in (22cm) wide.
£150–180
€220–260
$270–320 ⚒ DN

A pair of Wedgwood tiles, transfer-printed with Helena and Mustard from Shakespeare's *Midsummer Night's Dream*, moulded marks, 1878–85, 8in (20.5cm) diam.
£220–260 / €320–380
$400–470 ⚒ DN

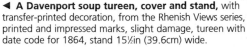

A Woods & Brettle supper set centrepiece and cover, transfer-printed with The Bird's Nest pattern, impressed mark, c1820, 9in (23cm) diam.
£1,000–1,150 / €1,450–1,700
$1,800–2,100 ⊞ GN

A soup tureen and cover, transfer-printed with The Wine Makers pattern, c1820, 16in (40.5cm) wide.
£1,550–1,750 / €2,250–2,550
$2,800–3,150 ⊞ GN

A Clews soup tureen and cover, transfer-printed with a view of Fonthill Abbey, Wiltshire, the lid with a view of Lumley Castle, Durham, from the Bluebell Border series, impressed mark, slight damage, 1820–30, 14in (35.5cm) wide.
£800–960 / €1,200–1,400
$1,450–1,750 ⚒ DN

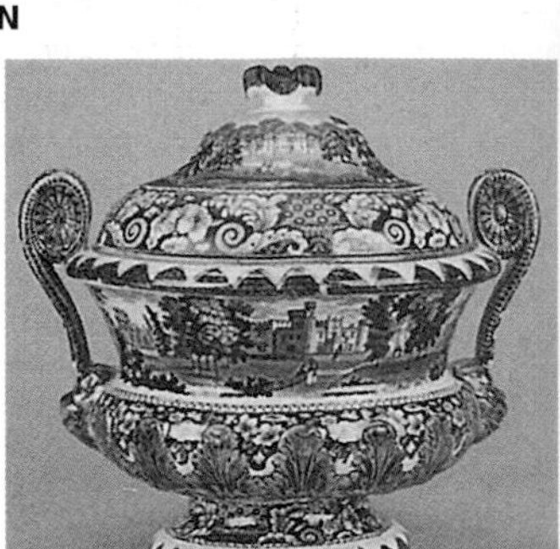

A John & Richard Riley soup tureen and cover, transfer-printed with a view of Balloch Castle, Dumbartonshire, the cover possibly associated, damaged, printed mark, 1820–30, 12¾in (32.5cm) wide.
£280–330 / €410–480
$510–600 ⚒ DN

◄ **A Davenport soup tureen, cover and stand,** with transfer-printed decoration, from the Rhenish Views series, printed and impressed marks, slight damage, tureen with date code for 1864, stand 15½in (39.6cm) wide.
£230–270 / €340–390
$420–490 ⚒ DN

◄ **A pair of vases,** probably by Riley or Pountney, transfer-printed with Camel pattern, restored, covers and one liner missing, 1815–30, larger 11¾in (30cm) high.
£270–320
€390–470
$490–580 ⚒ DN

A Staffordshire pearlware group of vases, comprising three baluster vases with covers and two trumpet vases, each transfer-printed with the Boy on Buffalo pattern, restored, early 19thC, baluster vases 8¾in (22cm) high.
£520–620 / €760–910
$940–1,100 ⚒ RTo

Porcelain

Driven by pure obsession, some porcelain collectors have been paying twice as much for pieces as they paid a year ago. Minton *pâte-sur-pâte* and rare Russian porcelain has doubled in price, for instance, so it is clear that some sectors of the porcelain market are really on a roll, while others are in the doldrums. However, it is not just a question of quality. All collectors are biased and believe their own favourite factory is better than the rest, but is Lowestoft (which is doing well) really better than Liverpool (which is not)? Is Sèvres (which is very costly) really better than Vienna (which strikes me as ridiculously cheap)? Nineteenth-century Meissen rides higher and higher, while 18th-century Meissen remains static.

There are many micro-markets within the porcelain-collecting world and the number of active collectors in each sector determines the price levels. Some smaller porcelain factories have collectors' clubs promoting interest and encouraging competition among members. Caughley and New Hall have been the subjects of new books and exhibitions, and anything unusual from these makers sells quite easily and at a premium. However, because the main buyers have moved beyond the beginner stage, ordinary New Hall cups and saucers have never been cheaper.

New research into the Welsh porcelain factories has led to sell-out conferences, fresh publications and many new collectors with deep pockets. Swansea and Nantgarw have enjoyed a spectacular leap in interest and demand far outstrips supply. As a result, prices have gone through the roof. Derby, on the other hand, benefited from a similar wave of interest and dramatic price-rise 15 years ago. Values escalated in the short term, but this prevented new collectors from entering the field. The past decade has seen prices for classic Derby drop significantly in real terms, to the point where some attractive pieces seem undervalued today.

Markets are cyclical. The connoisseurs who bought early Meissen 20 years ago have not been replaced by a new generation of collectors. Superb 18th-century pieces are still very expensive, but a lot of wonderful Meissen tableware is worth the same today as it was in the 1970s and '80s. Late 19th-century Minton has shot up in value, and so has artist-signed Royal Worcester and Royal Crown Derby. By contrast, early Minton and Regency Worcester have not moved in price for several years. These fields presently offer great opportunities. It is all a question of waiting for the cycles to come around again.

John Sandon

Animals

A Samuel Alcock model of a poodle, c1835, 3in (7.5cm) high.
£230–260 / €340–380
$420–470 ⊞ DAN

◄ **A Samuel Alcock model of a wolf,** impressed '192', c1840, 7in (18cm) high.
£610–680 / €890–990
$1,100–1,250 ⊞ TYE

► **A J. & T. Bevington group,** entitled 'The Monkey, the Dog and the Rat', from *Aesop's Fables*, 1865–1877, 4in (10cm) high.
£105–125
€155–175
$190–210 ⊞ JAK

Items in the Porcelain section have been arranged alphabetically in factory order, with non-specific pieces appearing at the end of each sub-section.

► **A pair of Bow models of goldfinches,** perched among leaves and flowers, restored, 1760–70, 3½in (9cm) high.
£420–500
€610–730
$760–910
WW

A Derby model of a ram, 1760–65, restored, 4½in (11.5cm) wide.
£610–730 / €890–1,050
$1,100–1,300 LFA

PORCELAIN

A Derby model of a ewe, standing before bocage, losses, c1765, 7in (18cm) high.
£490–550 / €720–800
$890–1,000 ⊞ TYE

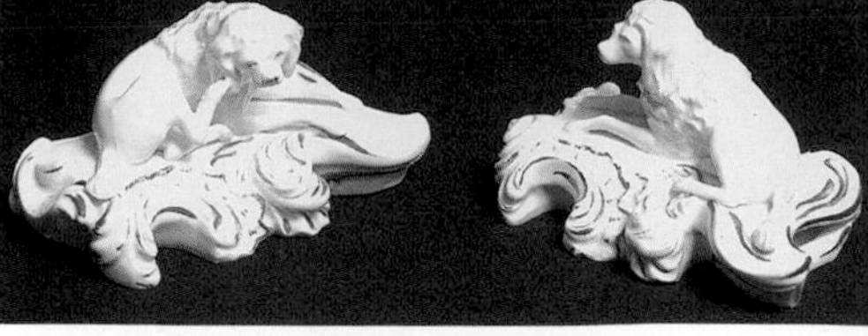

A pair of Derby models of poodles, with gilt decoration, marked, c1845, 4in (10cm) wide.
£610–680 / €890–990
$1,100–1,250 ⊞ TYE

◄ **A Derby model of a cow and a sucking calf,** standing before bocage, c1800, 6in (15cm) high.
£700–780 / €1,000–1,100
$1,200–1,350 ⊞ TYE

A Meissen model of two Breton spaniels and a pug, impressed '23' and incised 'VCH', slight damage, cancelled mark, German, c1880, 5½in (14cm) high.
£820–980 / €1,200–1,450
$1,500–1,800 ⚒ TEN
The cancelled mark (lines cut through the factory mark) refers to this being a factory 'second' due to the firing crack and this has affected the price.

► **A pair of Meissen models of golden oriels,** perched on tree stumps, decorated with enamels, restored, German, 1850–1900, 10in (25.5cm) high.
£1,300–1,550
€1,900–2,250
$2,350–2,800 ⚒ WW

► **A Meissen model of a parrot,** perched on a tree stump, slight damage, German, late 19thC, 16¼in (41.5cm) high.
£1,200–1,450 / €1,750–2,100
$2,150–2,600 ⚒ S(Am)

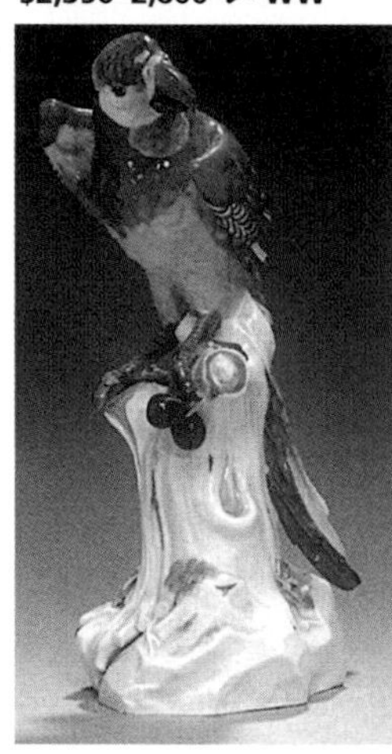

A Meissen model of a turkey, by Paul Walther, model number F275, crossed swords mark, German, c1920, 14in (35.5cm) high.
£2,900–3,200 / €4,200–4,650
$5,200–5,800 ⊞ DAV

◄ **A Minton Parian model of a Spaniel,** c1850, 4in (10cm) wide.
£250–280 / €370–410
$450–510 ⊞ TYE

◄ **A Meissen model of a bear,** model number H244, crossed swords mark, c1923, 11in (28cm) high.
£2,450–2,750
€3,600–4,000
$4,450–5,000
⊞ DAV

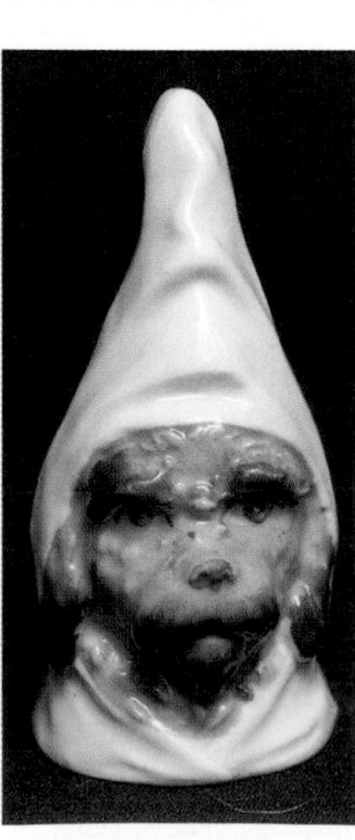

A pug dog tobacco jar, German, c1870, 11in (28cm) high.
£700–800 / €1,000–1,100
$1,250–1,400 ⊞ RdeR

◄ **A dog's head candle snuffer,** German, c1870, 3½in (9cm) high.
£200–220 / €290–320
$360–400 ⊞ TH

Baskets

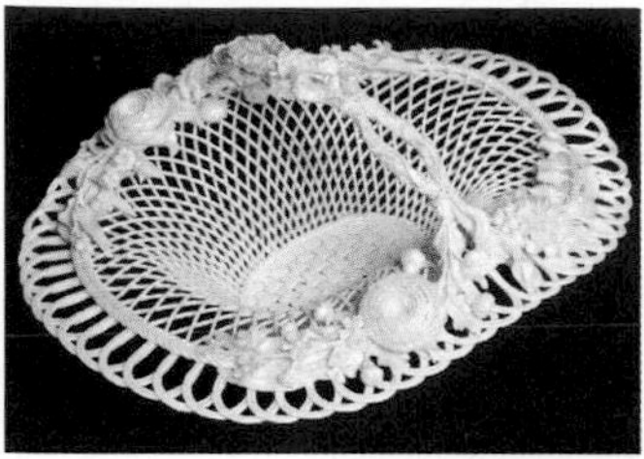

◄ **A Belleek basket,** Irish, First Period, 1863–90, 11in (28cm) wide.
£1,800–2,000
€2,600–2,900
$3,250–3,600
⊞ DeA

A Copeland Parian trug, c1880, 14in (35.5cm) wide.
£130–150 / €195–220
$240–270 ⊞ JAK

► **A Höchst latticework basket,** decorated with flowers and moulded with gadroons, German, 18thC, 7in (18cm) wide.
£550–650
€800–950
$1,000–1,200
⚒ WW

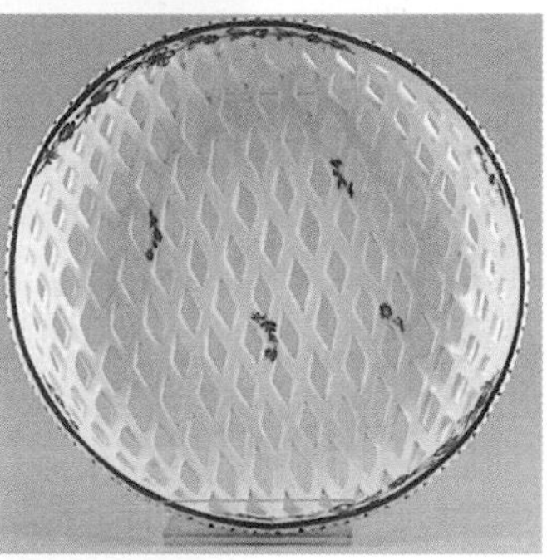

A Meissen basket of flowers, German, c1840, 7in (18cm) diam.
£1,750–1,950 / €2,550–2,850
$3,150–3,550 ⊞ BROW

◄ **A Meissen basket,** applied with flowers, gilt decoration, crossed swords mark, incised Y5, slight damage, German, c1850, 15½in (39.5cm) long.
£950–1,100
€1,400–1,650
$1,700–2,000
⚒ JAA

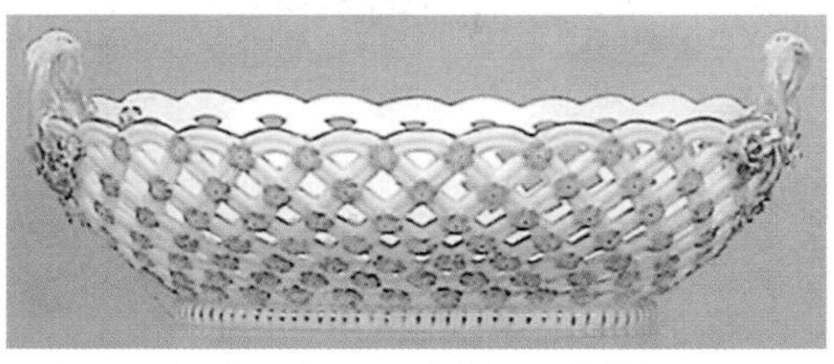

A Meissen basket, decorated with applied flowers, restored, crossed swords mark, German, 1850–1900, 10¼in (26cm) wide.
£320–380 / €470–550
$580–690 ⚒ DORO

► **A Paris basket,** the base with lion-paw feet, slight damage, French, 19thC, 8½in (21.5cm) high.
£350–410
€510–600
$630–740
⚒ WW

► **A Worcester pierced basket,** of flared form, with pierced interlocking rings, c1765, 5in (13cm) diam.
£1,500–1,650 / €2,150–2,400
$2,700–3,000 ⊞ GIR

A Worcester basket, cover and stand, decorated with flowers and enamels, damaged, handles missing from stand, seal mark, c1770, 10in (25.5cm) wide.
£1,100–1,300 / €1,600–1,900
$2,000–2,350 ⚒ BWL

A pair of Worcester pierced baskets, decorated with flowers, one repaired, square seal mark, c1770, 7½in (19cm) diam.
£2,250–2,650 / €3,300–3,900
$4,100–4,800 ⚒ JNic

Bowls

A Caughley junket bowl, decorated with Fisherman pattern, c1785, 10in (25.5cm) diam.
£900–1,000 / €1,300–1,450
$1,600–1,800 ⊞ JUP

A Lowestoft bowl, printed with birds among flowering branches, slight damage, c1770, 8¼in (21cm) diam.
£210–250 / €310–370
$380–450 ⚒ WW

A slop bowl, probably Christian's Liverpool or Lowestoft, decorated with The Dragon pattern, slight damage, 1765–70, 6in (15cm) diam.
£390–460 / €570–670
$700–830 ⚒ RBB

A Liverpool Gilbody bowl, decorated with rockwork and a bird, damaged, c1758, 5in (12.5cm) diam.
£1,500–1,700 / €2,200–2,500
$2,700–3,100 ⊞ JUP

► **A Miles Mason punch bowl,** painted with landscapes, slight damage, c1820, 18in (45.5cm) diam.
£3,600–4,000 / €5,200–5,800
$6,500–7,200 ⊞ JP
This punch bowl is unusually large.

◄ **A Worcester bowl,** painted with Cormorant pattern, slight damage, c1758, 6in (15cm) diam.
£540–600
€790–880
$980–1,100
⊞ JUP

◄ **A Worcester bowl,** painted with Jabberwocky pattern, c1765, 6¼in (16cm) diam.
£470–560 / €690–820
$850–1,000 ⚒ SWO

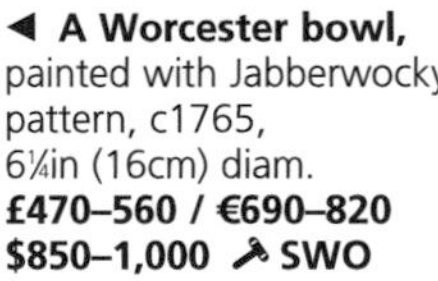

► **A Worcester bowl,** decorated with Japan pattern, c1775, 5in (12.5cm) diam.
£75–85 / €110–125
$135–155 ⊞ NAW

PORCELAIN

Covered Bowls

◄ **A Berlin ormolu-mounted pedestal punch bowl and cover,** the finial in the form of the infant Bacchus raising a glass of wine, c1860, 18¼in (46.5cm) high.
£4,100–4,900 / €6,000–7,100
$7,400–8,900 ⚒ TEN
This punch bowl realized a high price because of the ormolu mounts.

A Sèvres-style *écuelle*, cover and stand, decorated with classical bands of scrolls, foliage and beasts, printed and incised marks, French, late 19thC, 9in (23cm) diam.
£520–620 / €760–910
$940–1,100 ⚒ WW

◄ **A Coalport sugar bowl and cover,** decorated with fruiting vines and gilt, early 19thC, 6in (15cm) high
£290–340 / €420–500
$520–620 ⚒ DN(BR)

A Meissen sucrier and cover, painted with flowers, slight damage, German, mid-18thC, 4½in (11.5cm) diam.
£760–850 / €1,100–1,250
$1,400–1,550 ⊞ G&G

A Meissen sucrier and cover, German, Marcolini period, 1774–1813, 4¾in (12cm) diam.
£330–390 / €480–570
$600–710 ⚒ WW

A Meissen bowl, cover and stand, applied with flowers, German, mid-19thC, 8in (20.5cm) diam.
£1,450–1,650 / €2,100–2,400
$2,650–3,000 ⊞ BROW

► A Spode sugar bowl and cover, painted and decorated in relief with flowers, the gilt handles in the form of fruiting branches, c1820, 6in (15cm) wide.
£370–420 / €540–610
$670–760 ⊞ G&G

A Minton Munster Globe potpourri bowl and cover, decorated with a view of Near Blurton, Staffordshire, crossed swords mark, c1835, 9in (23cm) diam.
£410–490 / €600–720
$740–890 ⚒ JNic
This is a copy of a Meissen bowl. Minton gave it a German-sounding name to reflect this and even copied Meissen's crossed swords mark. In books of Minton factory shapes it is given the name 'Globe Potpourri' or 'Munster Potpourri'.

Further reading
Miller's Collecting Porcelain,
Miller's Publications, 2003

A Worcester Barr, Flight & Barr hot water dish and cover, probably by William Billingsley, 1808–13, 13in (33cm) diam.
£2,500–2,800 / €3,650–4,100
$4,550–5,100 ⊞ JOR
William Billingsley was at the Worcester factory from 1808 to 1813 and influenced the flower painting.

◄ A Worcester Flight, Barr & Barr muffin dish, printed with rustic scenes, 1814–40, 8in (20.5cm) diam.
£870–980
€1,250–1,400
$1,550–1,750
⊞ JOR

PORCELAIN

Boxes

A Chelsea rose box and cover, restored, c1755, 3½in (9cm) high.
£1,550–1,850 / €2,200–2,650
$2,800–3,350 ⚒ S

► A metal-mounted snuff box, painted with vignettes of figures and animals, the inside cover decorated with two gentlemen and a lady playing backgammon, German, 1850–1900, 3¼in (8.5cm) wide.
£840–1,000 / €1,250–1,500
$1,500–1,800 ⚒ S

◄ A Meissen silver-gilt-mounted sugar box and cover, painted in the manner of J. G. Höroldt, maker's mark and crossed swords mark, German, 1723–24, 4¾in (12cm) diam.
£8,400–10,100 / €12,300–14,700
$15,200–18,300 ⚒ S
The silver mounts carry the marks of a well-known maker and add to the value of this piece.

Busts

A W. H. Goss Parian bust of Queen Victoria, 1886, 6½in (16.5cm) high.
£180–200 / €260–290
$330–370 ⊞ JAK

A biscuit porcelain bust of the Countess Dubary, with inscription, French, late 19thC, 20¾in (52.5cm) high.
£470–560 / €690–820
$850–1,000 ⚒ BERN
This is a copy of a Sèvres original.

► A biscuit porcelain bust of Palissy, by Jean Gille, marked, c1855, 13½in (34.5cm) high.
£230–270 / €340–400
$420–500 ⚒ SWO

A bust of woman, repaired, Italian, late 18thC, 2½in (6.5cm) high.
£140–165 / €200–240
$250–300 ⚒ WW

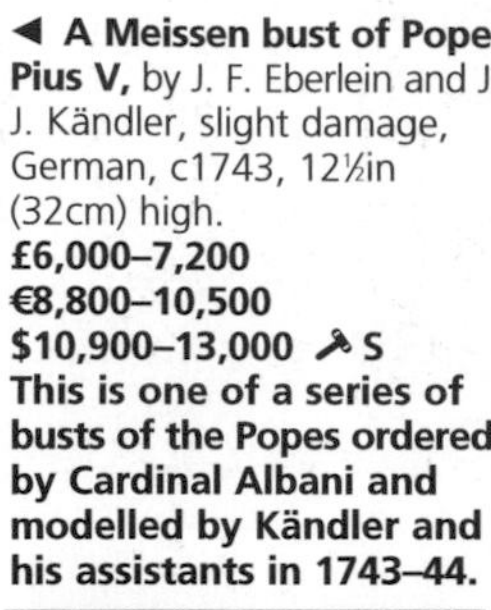

◄ A Meissen bust of Pope Pius V, by J. F. Eberlein and J. J. Kändler, slight damage, German, c1743, 12½in (32cm) high.
£6,000–7,200
€8,800–10,500
$10,900–13,000 ⚒ S
This is one of a series of busts of the Popes ordered by Cardinal Albani and modelled by Kändler and his assistants in 1743–44.

A Robinson & Leadbeater Parian bust of O. W. Holmes, 1880, 8in (20.5cm) high.
£200–220 / €290–320
$360–400 ⊞ JAK
Oliver Wendell Holmes (1809–94) was a professor of Anatomy and Physiology at Harvard University, USA, later becoming Dean of Harvard Medical School. He is best known, however, for his humorous essays and comic verse.

◄ A Parian bust of Napoleon Eugène, the Prince Imperial, impressed marks, 1879, 9¾in (25cm) high.
£260–310 / €380–450
$470–560 ⚒ SAS
Son of Napoleon III of France, the Prince Imperial was a guest of the British forces during the Zulu wars but was killed on a reconnoitering party.

Candlesticks & Chambersticks

A pair of Berlin candlesticks, each in the form of a putto, repaired, German, 19thC, 11in (28cm) high.
£190–220 / €270–320
$340–400 ⚒ DN(BR)

A Derby candlestick, applied with a figure of spring, c1770, 7in (18cm) high.
£440–490 / €640–720
$800–890 ⊞ TYE

A Meissen candelabra, applied with Bacchic figures, slight damage, crossed swords mark, German, 1850–1900, 30¾in (78cm) high.
£2,650–3,000 / €3,850–4,400
$4,800–5,400 ⚒ S

PORCELAIN

A pair of Meissen candelabra, applied with figures, German, c1880, 19½in (49.5cm) high.
£4,500–5,000 / €6,600–7,300
$8,100–9,100 ⊞ BROW

◄ A pair of Minton candlesticks, crossed swords mark, c1840, 11in (28cm) high.
£900–1,000 / €1,300–1,450
$1,600–1,800 ⊞ HKW

A Minton 'Henri Deux' candlestick, by Charles Toft, in the form of a tower supported by putti, signed, c1873, 13in (33cm) high.
£4,500–5,400 / €6,600–7,900
$8,100–9,800 ⚒ S

This candlestick is a reproduction of the early French pottery made at St Porchaire, France during the reign of Henry II and is much prized by Victorian collectors. Charles Toft made superb copies.

◄ A pair of Spode chambersticks, decorated in the Imari palette with panels of flowers and leaves, script marks, 1815–20, 3in (7.5cm) high.
£1,200–1,400
€1,750–2,050
$2,150–2,550
⚒ LFA

◄ A pair of Royal Worcester candlesticks, by James Hadley, in the form of children resting in trees, No. 1125, date mark for 1892, 8½in (21.5cm) high.
£1,300–1,550 / €1,900–2,250
$2,350–2,800 ⚒ AH

A Worcester chamberstick, painted with a landscape, c1805, 5in (12.5cm) diam.
£1,350–1,500 / €1,950–2,200
$2,450–2,700 ⊞ JOR

◄ A chamberstick, 1825–30, 4in (10cm) diam.
£270–300 / €390–440
$490–540 ⊞ TYE

Centrepieces

A Mason's fruit comport, hand-painted with flowers, marked 'Felt Spar', 1815–20, 6in (15cm) high.
£670–750 / €900–1,000
$1,200–1,350 ⊞ JP

A pair of Derby comports, decorated in the Imari palette, printed marks and date mark, 1885, 9in (23cm) diam.
£125–150 / €185–220
$230–270 ⚒ GAK

A pair of Moore Brothers centrepieces, in the form of putti carrying bowls, one damaged, 1880s, 8¾in (22cm) high.
£290–340 / €420–500
$520–620 ⚒ DN(BR)

Clocks

◀ **A Dresden clock,** with two putto-head handles, surmounted by an urn, slight damage and repairs, stamped 'Rollin à Paris', Berlin marks, German, late 19thC, 15¾in (40cm) high.
£760–910 / €1,100–1,300
$1,400–1,650 ⚒ DN

▶ **A table clock,** dial marked 'Aubert à Paris', slight damage, French, mid-19thC, 13¼in (33.5cm) high.
£930–1,100 / €1,350–1,600
$1,700–2,000 ⚒ BUK

A mantel clock and stand, painted and gilded with floral sprays, French, mid-19thC, 14¼in (36cm) high.
£530–630 / €770–920
$960–1,150 ⚒ DN(BR)

Cream & Sauce Boats

A Bow *famille rose*-style sauce boat, the handle in the form of a serpent, 1752–55, 5in (12.5cm) wide.
£760–850 / €1,100–1,250
$1,400–1,550 ⊞ GIR

A Derby sauce boat, painted with landscapes, damaged, handle missing, incised 'D', c1752, 3¾in (9.5cm) wide.
£840–1,000 / €1,250–1,450
$1,500–1,800 ⚒ S
The incised 'D' is a rare feature and accounts for the high price of this damaged specimen.

A Worcester sauce boat, moulded with cos lettuce leaves, painted with flowers, the handle in the form of a branch, slight damage, 1754–55, 9in (23cm) wide.
£270–320 / €390–470
$490–580 ⚒ RBB

▶ **A Chelsea sauce boat,** painted with flowers, repaired, anchor mark, c1755, 7½in (19cm) wide.
£410–490 / €600–720
$740–890 ⚒ WW

A Derby sauce boat, painted with flowers, c1765, 6½in (16.5cm) wide.
£540–600 / €790–880
$980–1,100 ⊞ GIR

A Worcester sauce boat, transfer-printed with a squirrel, pheasant and herdsman, c1755, 8in (20.5cm) wide.
£1,000–1,150 / €1,450–1,700
$1,800–2,100 ⊞ JUP
The earliest transfer prints at Worcester are known as 'smoky primitives' because of their characteristically smudged appearance, caused by imperfect printing.

A Worcester sauce boat, the moulded reserves decorated with flowers, crescent mark, c1775, 7½in (19cm) wide.
£280–330 / €410–480
$510–600 ⚒ RBB

A Plymouth cream boat, painted in the *famille verte* palette with flowers and leaves, c1770, 5½in (14cm) wide.
£2,000–2,400 / €2,900–3,500
$3,600–4,350 ⚒ LFA
William Cookworthy closed the Plymouth factory in 1770 and moved to Bristol. It is difficult to distinguish between Cookworthy's Bristol and Plymouth wares. All are rare and sought after.

A Worcester cream boat, printed with Obelisk Fisherman pattern, disguised numeral mark, slight damage, c1780, 4¼in (11cm) wide.
£820–980 / €1,200–1,450
$1,500–1,750 ⚒ WW
This cream boat bears a mark of a numeral concealed by mock Chinese characters which are found on Worcester porcelain c1780 to give the impression of Chinese origin. However, not all the patterns are Chinese, as in this case.

Cups

A Belleek Artichoke cup and saucer, Irish, First Period, 1863–90.
£810–900 / €1,200–1,350
$1,450–1,650 ⊞ MLa
The price reflects the rarity of this particular moulded pattern.

A Bow coffee can, painted with Chinese figures, c1750.
£490–580 / €720–850
$890–1,050 ⚒ WW

A Coalport cup and saucer, painted by John Randall with birds, c1860.
£580–650 / €850–950
$1,050–1,200 ⊞ JAK

A Derby cup and saucer, decorated with playing cards, marked, c1830.
£1,050–1,200 / €1,550–1,750
$1,900–2,150 ⊞ ReN

► A Liverpool Chaffers cup and saucer, painted with Jumping Boy pattern, c1758.
£2,600–2,900 / €3,800–4,250
$4,700–5,200 ⊞ JUP

A Berlin cup and saucer, decorated with bouquets of flowers, sceptre mark, German, c1798.
£560–670 / €820–980
$1,000–1,200 ⚒ DORO

A Coalport cup and saucer, painted with botanical studies based on illustrations from *Curtis's Botanical Magazine*, c1812.
£720–800 / €1,050–1,200
$1,300–1,450 ⊞ JOR
The decoration on this cup and saucer is attributed to Thomas Pardoe while working at his Bristol studio.

A Berlin coffee can and saucer, painted with a medallion of flowers within vine-leaf borders, sceptre mark and painter's mark, German, 1800–10.
£1,050–1,250 / €1,550–1,850
$1,900–2,250 ⚒ S(Am)

Prices

The price ranges quoted in this book reflect the average price a purchaser might expect to pay for a similar item. The price will vary according to the condition, rarity, size, popularity, provenance, colour and restoration of the item, and this must be taken into account when assessing values. Don't forget that if you are selling it is quite likely that you will be offered less than the price range.

A Coalport coffee can and saucer, c1890.
£400–450 / €580–650
$720–820 ⊞ HKW

◄ A Fürstenberg cup, painted in the manner of Pillement with Oriental figures in a landscape, marked, German, c1760.
£350–420 / €510–610
$630–760 ⚒ WW
Jean Pillement was a French artist whose work was copied by porcelain makers on the Continent as well as in England, at Chelsea and Worcester.

A Longton Hall coffee cup, decorated in the *famille rose* palette, 1755–58.
£1,100–1,250 / €1,600–1,850
$2,000–2,250 ⊞ GIR

◄ A Lowestoft tea bowl and saucer, painted with flowers, slight damage, c1770.
£260–310 / €380–450
$470–560 WW

A Meissen cabinet cup and saucer, encrusted with forget-me-nots, crossed swords mark, German, 1850–1900.
£240–290 / €350–410
$430–510 RBB

Cabinet porcelain

Most cups and saucers formed parts of tea services and were made to be used. Fine china factories also made exceptional pieces as art objects in their own right, intended to be displayed in a china cabinet. Cabinet cups were enamelled with finely painted panels and the richest gilding. The best china painters treated display plates in the same way, as fine canvases framed with their own fancy jewelled and gilded borders. Lavish plates from costly dessert services are often sold as cabinet plates, an appropriate term for nobody would dream of eating off them anymore.

A Minton *pâte-sur-pâte* coffee cup and saucer, by Lawrence Birks, decorated with panels of birds within rocaille panels, the cup with a heron and a frog, the saucer with a cockerel, impressed marks, 1879.
£1,000–1,200 / €1,450–1,750
$1,800–2,150 DN

► A Nymphenburg cabinet cup, decorated with a named view of Munich, lozenge shield mark, German, c1830.
£680–810 / €1,000–1,200
$1,250–1,500 DORO

A Ludwigsburg tea cup and saucer, painted by Philipp Jacob Ihle with man and a woman in a landscape, impressed and painted marks, German, 1770–75.
£1,900–2,250 / €2,750–3,300
$3,450–4,000 S
The painter Philipp Jacob Ihle is recorded at Ludwigsburg between 1763 and 1781.

A Minton tea cup and saucer, painted with panels of landscapes, with gilt borders, c1810.
£300–360 / €440–530
$540–650 WW

A New Hall cup and saucer, c1820.
£190–220 / €280–320
$340–400 JAK

A Meissen tea bowl, decorated in the manner of J. G. Höroldt with a duck hunting scene, the reverse decorated in Kakiemon style with branches, slight damage, marked, German, 1723–24.
£1,200–1,400 / €1,750–2,050
$2,150–2,550 S
This tea bowl belongs to a rare group of early Meissen services decorated with hunting scenes and figures.

A Minton cabinet cup and stand, painted by Joseph Bancroft with feathers, the handle in the form of a butterfly, c1830.
£1,450–1,650 / €2,100–2,400
$2,600–3,000 JOR

A Minton cup and saucer, decorated in relief with paste gilding, on paw feet, c1830.
£550–620 / €800–920
$1,000–1,100 JOR

A Paris coffee can and saucer, painted with a bird perched on a branch, painted mark, French, c1800
£150–180 / €220–260
$270–320 SWO

PORCELAIN

A pair of tea bowls and saucers, probably Le Nove, painted with flower sprays, incised marks, Italian, c1780.
£230–270 / €340–390
$420–490 WW

A Ridgway cup and saucer, pattern No. 414, c1810.
£270–300 / €390–440
$490–540 JOR

A Schlaggenwald cup and saucer, the cup decorated with Cupid, the saucer with a butterfly, underglaze mark, Bohemian, c1825.
£600–720 / €880–1,050
$1,100–1,300 DORO

A Sèvres coffee cup and saucer, decorated with rosettes, laurel wreaths and diaper panels, damaged, painted mark, French, c1763.
£330–390 / €480–570
$600–710 DN(BR)

A Sèvres cup and saucer, painted by Claude Couturier with flower sprays, marked, French, c1773.
£2,150–2,550 / €3,150–3,700
$3,900–4,600 S

A Worcester miniature coffee cup and saucer, painted with Prunus Root pattern, c1760, saucer 3in (7.5cm) diam.
£900–1,000 / €1,300–1,450
$1,600–1,800 JUP

Miller's Compares

I. A Worcester cup, painted with Chinese figures, c1753.
£2,000–2,250 / €2,900–3,300
$3,600–4,050 JUP

II. A Worcester coffee cup, painted with Pu Tai pattern, c1765.
£530–600 / €770–880
$960–1,100 JUP

Items I and II both copy Chinese porcelain. Both are First Period, but Item II is 12 years later than Item I. Item I is Worcester's own invention, a spirited depiction of Chinese figures in the palette of the first few years of the factory. Item II is a laboured, direct copy of a Chinese original. It is still fun, but lacks the spontaneity of the earliest Worcester pieces, hence its lower price.

A Worcester tea cup and saucer, painted with Mansfield pattern, c1768.
£330–380 / €480–550
$600–690 JUP

A Worcester tea cup and saucer, c1785.
£220–250 / €320–370
$400–450 LGr

A Worcester tea bowl and saucer, decorated with Cannonball pattern, c1770.
£100–120 / €145–175
$180–210 CHTR

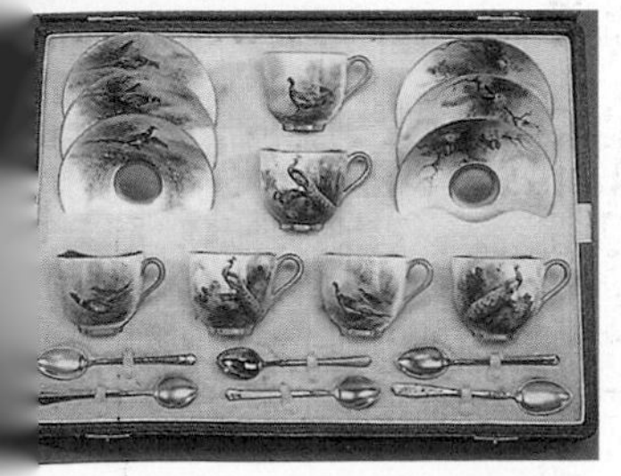

◄ **A set of six Royal Worcester coffee cups and saucers,** comprising three painted by James Stinton and three by Reginald Harry Austin, signed, crown and wheel mark, c1925, together with six gilt white metal and enamelled coffee spoons, in original Finnigans fitted case.
£2,250–2,700 / €3,300–3,950
$4,100–4,900 TEN

Dessert & Dinner Services

A Coalport dessert service, comprising 49 pieces, decorated with scrolling foliage, 1810–20.
£9,100–10,900 / €13,300–15,900
$16,500–19,700 WW

A Coalport part dessert service, comprising 33 pieces, printed with flowers, damaged, c1820.
£1,000–1,200 / €1,450–1,750
$1,800–2,150 S

A Coalport part dessert service, comprising 35 pieces, painted with buildings and foliage, slight damage, c1815.
£1,750–2,100 / €2,550–3,050
$3,150–3,800 DN

Coalport

For the first 50 years of the 19th century the Coalport factory rarely marked its porcelain, and as a result it is hard to identify early productions. Much early Coalport was enamelled in London and can be highly decorative. As it is located away from Staffordshire, near Ironbridge in Shropshire, one would expect Coalport to be very individual, but most 19th-century Coalport is derivative, especially from Meissen. Coalport is famous for its flower-encrusted porcelain known as Coalbrookdale. Later productions are frequently marked 'Coalport AD 1750' after the date they erroneously claimed to have been founded. This mark does confuse many people who think they own a piece of mid-18th century porcelain.

A Derby dinner service, comprising 95 pieces, painted and gilt with cornflowers and foliage, damaged, c1820.
£1,300–1,550 / €1,900–2,250
$2,350–2,800 M

A Pirkenhammer dessert service, comprising 29 pieces, decorated with flowers within pierced and gilt borders, crossed hammers mark, Bohemian, late 19thC.
£780–930 / €1,150–1,350
$1,400–1,650 S(Am)

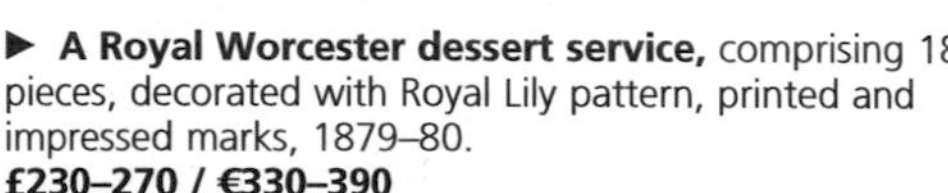

► **A Royal Worcester dessert service,** comprising 18 pieces, decorated with Royal Lily pattern, printed and impressed marks, 1879–80.
£230–270 / €330–390
$410–490 SWO

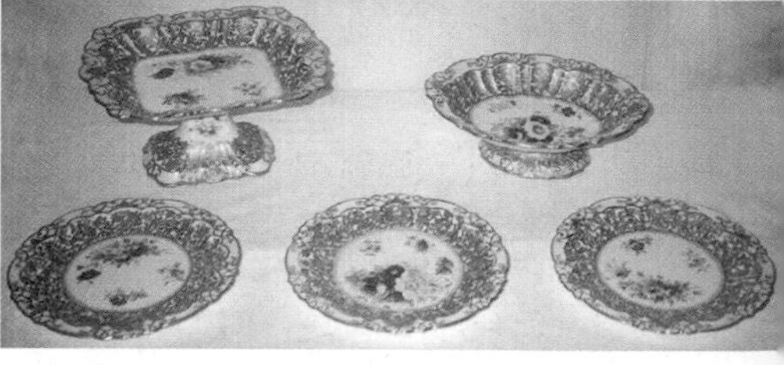

A Staffordshire dessert service, comprising 16 pieces, painted with flowers within gilt leaf scroll and floral borders, 1850–1900.
£610–730 / €890–1,050
$1,100–1,300 LF

A dessert service, comprising 14 pieces, each piece enamel-painted with a flower, c1830.
£1,750–2,100 / €2,550–3,050
$3,150–3,800 PF

► **A part dessert service,** comprising 26 pieces, with painted and gilt floral decoration, slight damage, c1840.
£1,300–1,550 / €1,900–2,250
$2,350–2,800 RTo

Dishes

◄ **A Bow dish,** painted and moulded with leaves, damaged, c1765, 11¼in (28.5cm) wide.
£350–420
€510–610
$630–760 WW

A pair of Bow pickle dishes, each decorated with flowers and a fence, 1756–58, 4in (10cm) long.
£910–1,100 / €1,350–1,600
$1,650–1,950 CHTR

\ Caughley butter boat, printed vith Fisherman pattern, c1780, ¾in (7cm) wide.
130–155 / €190–220
240–280 WW

A Chelsea peony dish, stilt marks, c1755, 8in (20.5cm) wide.
£3,100–3,700 / €4,550–5,400
$5,600–6,700 S

A Chelsea dish, moulded with vine leaves, red anchor mark, c1755, 9¼in (23.5cm) wide.
£2,000–2,400 / €2,900–3,500
$3,600–4,350 S

Chelsea dish, in the form of a af, incised with veins, painted with ower sprigs, slight damage, c1755, ⁄in (21.5cm) wide.
350–420 / €510–610
630–760 WW

A pair of Chelsea Derby dishes, painted and gilded with garlands of flowers, c1770, 9in (23cm) wide.
£1,800–2,000 / €2,600–2,900
$3,250–3,600 JUP

A H. & R. Daniel dessert dish, pattern No. 3785, c1824, 9in (23cm) wide.
£220–250 / €320–370
$400–450 JAK

Bloor Derby dish, from the Earl rrers service, painted and gilt, obably by John Hancock Jnr, with wers and the Ferrers armorial, printed arks, c1830, 10¾in (27.5cm) wide.
,700–2,000 / €2,500–2,900
,100–3,600 LFA

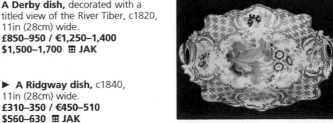

A Derby dish, decorated with a titled view of the River Tiber, c1820, 11in (28cm) wide.
£850–950 / €1,250–1,400
$1,500–1,700 JAK

A Derby dish, decorated with a titled view of Yorkshire, c1825, 11in (28cm) wide.
£360–400 / €520–580
$650–720 JAK

► **A Ridgway dish,** c1840, 11in (28cm) wide.
£310–350 / €450–510
$560–630 JAK

PORCELAIN

◀ **A Spode dish,** pattern No. 2004, c1820, 11in (28cm) wide.
£360–400 / €520–580
$650–720 ⊞ JAK

A Worcester dish, painted with sprays of European flowers and leaves, slight damage, 1772–75, 8¾in (22cm) wide.
£1,350–1,600 / €1,950–2,350
$2,450–2,900 ⚒ LFA

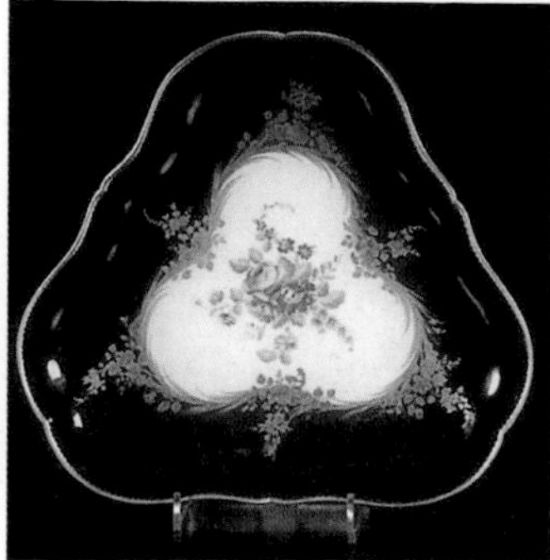

A Vincennes dish, painted with a floral spray, gilt dentil border, interlaced 'LL' monogram and date letter 'B', incised 'T', French, c1754, 8¾in (22cm) wide.
£1,550–1,850 / €2,250–2,700
$2,800–3,350 ⚒ S

▶ **A Royal Worcester shell dish,** painted with flowers, supported on three smaller shells, c1912, 9½in (24cm) wide.
£470–560 / €690–820
$850–1,000 ⚒ WW

A Worcester pickle dish, painted with Two Peony Rock Bird pattern, c1758, 3in (7.5cm) diam.
£620–700 / €900–1,000
$1,100–1,250 ⊞ JUP

Figures

◀ **A pair of Belleek figures of boy and girl basket-carriers,** Irish, First Period, 1863–90, 9in (23cm) high.
£3,550–3,950
€5,200–5,800
$6,400–7,200
⊞ DeA

A Bow figure of Autumn, modelled as a boy holding grapes, damaged, 1755–60, 5½in (14cm) high.
£900–1,050 / €1,350–1,550
$1,650–1,900 ⚒ S

A J. & T. Bevington Parian figure of The Reading Girl, c1865, 12in (30.5cm) high.
£400–450 / €580–660
$720–810 ⊞ JAK

◀ **A Chelsea figure of a carter,** by Joseph Williams, red anchor mark, 1754–55, 5in (12.5cm) high.
£4,800–5,300
€7,000–7,700
$8,700–9,600 ⊞ DMa

▶ **A Copeland Parian figure of Storm,** c1870, 18in (45.5cm) high.
£540–600 / €790–880
$980–1,100 ⊞ JAK

A Bow figure of a cheru holding a fruiting vine, restored, c1750, 7in (18cm) high.
£1,300–1,550 / €1,900–2,2
$2,350–2,800 ⚒ WW

PORCELAIN

A Copeland Parian group, entitled 'The Prodigal's Return', inscribed 'Father I Have Sinned', slight damage, c1855, 19¾in (50cm) high.
£290–340 / €420–500
$520–620 Bea

A Derby figure of a girl with a guitar, c1770, 6in (15cm) high.
£380–430 / €550–630
$690–780 TYE

A pair of Derby figures of musicians, a bagpipe player with a dog and a girl with a mandolin and sheep, slight damage, c1770, 7½in (19cm) high.
£560–670 / €820–980
$1,000–1,200 LAY

A pair of Derby figures of Shakespeare and Milton, painted in enamels and gilt, each standing beside a plinth and resting on literary tomes, 1770–80, 12¼in (31cm) high.
£1,500–1,800 / €2,200–2,600
$2,700–3,250 WW

A pair of Derby figures of an Austrian woodcutter and his wife, c1820, 6in (15cm) high.
£1,150–1,300 / €1,700–1,900
$2,100–2,350 HKW

A Doccia figure, Italian, losses, 1750–1800, 5¾in (14.5cm) high.
£1,300–1,550
€1,900–2,250
$2,350–2,800 S(Mi)

Miller's Compares

I. A Meissen figure of a seated female hurdy-gurdy player, by J. J. Kändler, slight damage, crossed swords mark, German, 1736–40, 4¾in (12cm) high.
£4,550–5,400
€6,600–7,900
$8,200–9,800 S

II. A Meissen figure of a seated female hurdy-gurdy player, possibly by J. F. Eberlein after an earlier model by J. J. Kändler, slight damage, crossed swords mark, German, c1745, 5in (12.5cm) high.
£840–1,000
€1,250–1,450
$1,500–1,800 S

Item I, an old woman, may not be to everyone's taste, but it is by the master modeller J. J. Kändler, whose work is full of character. Item II was based on Kändler's model but reworked by his pupil, J. F. Eberlein, and simplified for large-scale production. Although this piece is prettier than Item I, it is not as rare, nor as dramatic.

A Meissen figure of a Parisian trinket salesman, by J. J. Kändler, German, c1740, 7in (18cm) high.
£3,150–3,500
€4,600–5,100
$5,700–6,300 ⊞ BHa

A Meissen figural group of child musicians, by J. J. Kändler, restored, German, c1755, 7in (18cm) high.
£7,100–7,900
€10,400–11,500
$12,900–14,300 ⊞ BHa

A Meissen figure of Minerva, by J. J. Kändler, restored, German, 1750–1800, 12in (30.5cm) high.
£4,000–4,500
€5,800–6,600
$7,200–8,100 ⊞ BHa

A Meissen figure of The London Courtesan, by J. J. Kändler, German, restored, c1750, 5in (12.5cm) high.
£5,300–5,900
€7,700–8,600
$9,600–10,700 ⊞ BHa

A Meissen figure of a court gentleman, by J. J. Kändler and Peter Reinicke, restored, German, 1755–60, 5½in (14cm) high.
£2,600–2,900
€3,800–4,250
$4,700–5,200 ⊞ BHa

► A pair of Meissen figures of a lady and gentleman, German, c1860, 7in (18cm) high.
£1,800–2,000
€2,600–2,900
$3,250–3,600
⊞ HKW

A Meissen figure of a girl flute player, by J. J. Kändler, German, c1750, 5in (12.5cm) high.
£2,600–2,900
€3,800–4,250
$4,700–5,200 ⊞ BHa

A Meissen Commedia dell'Arte figure of a child, by J. J. Kändler, from the *Komödienkinder* series, restored, incised '24', German, c1765, 5in (12.5cm) high.
£1,150–1,350
€1,700–1,950
$2,100–2,450 ⚒ S

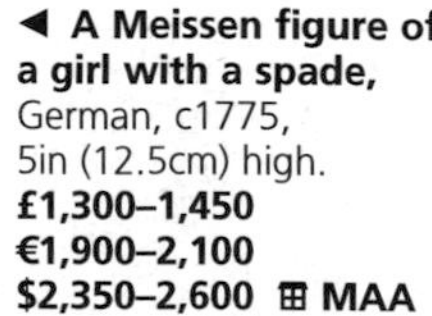

◄ A Meissen figure of a girl with a spade, German, c1775, 5in (12.5cm) high.
£1,300–1,450
€1,900–2,100
$2,350–2,600 ⊞ MAA

A Meissen figure of the Carp Seller, by Peter Reinicke, from the *Cris de Paris* series, crossed swords mark, impressed '13', German, c1754, 5¼in (13.5cm) high.
£3,800–4,550
€5,500–6,600
$6,900–8,200 ⚒ S

A Meissen figure of a girl feeding a cat, after a model by Acier in 1767, model No. B94, crossed swords mark, German, c1850, 5½in (14cm) high.
£1,050–1,200
€1,550–1,750
$1,900–2,150 ⊞ DAV

A Meissen figural group of lovers, after a model by Acier in 1774, model No. E65, crossed swords mark, German, c1860, 7½in (19cm) high.
£1,600–1,800
€2,350–2,650
$2,900–3,250 ⊞ DAV

A pair of Meissen figures of a lady and gentleman, German, c1870, 7in (18cm) high.
£2,200–2,500
€3,200–3,650
$4,000–4,550 ⊞ MAA

A Meissen figural group of The Broken Eggs, German, c1880, 9in (23cm) high.
£2,700–3,000
€3,950–4,400
$4,900–5,400 ⊞ HKW
This figural group is a pair to 'The Broken Bridge'.

A Meissen figural group of a mother and daughter playing with a dog, German, c1890, 5in (12.5cm) high.
£2,550–2,850
€3,700–4,150
$4,600–5,200 ⊞ BROW

► A Meissen figure of a girl with vegetables and a dog, first modelled by Jakob Ungerer in 1902, model No. T.62, crossed swords mark, c1908, 9in (23cm) high.
£1,950–2,200
€2,850–3,200
$3,550–4,000 ⊞ DAV

A Meissen figural group of Summer, after the model by Schönheit in 1782, from the Four Seasons series, model No. G92, crossed swords mark, German, c1870, 6½in (16.5cm) high.
£1,700–1,900
€2,500–2,750
$3,100–3,450 ⊞ DAV

A Meissen figure of a boy with a shuttlecock, German, c1880, 6in (15cm) high.
£1,000–1,150
€1,450–1,700
$1,800–2,100 ⊞ BROW

A Meissen figural group depicting Sculpture, from the Arts series, German, c1870, 8in (20.5cm) high.
£3,100–3,450
€4,500–5,000
$5,600–6,200 ⊞ BROW

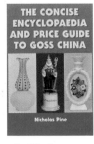

A Meissen figural group of The Broken Bridge, German, c1880, 10in (25.5cm) high.
£2,700–3,000
€3,950–4,400
$4,900–5,400 ⊞ HKW

◄ A Meissen figure of Cupid carrying a shoe, probably modelled by Professor Schwabe, crossed swords mark, incised model No. L.117, impressed and painted marks, German, late 19thC, 6½in (16.5cm) high.
£900–1,050
€1,300–1,550
$1,650–1,900 ⚒ S

A Minton Parian figure of Miranda, by John Bell, signed, date mark for 1865, 15½in (39.5cm) high.
£330–390 / €480–570
$600–710 AH

► A Minton Parian figure of Whistler's Mother, 1872, 11in (28cm) high.
£630–700 / €920–1,050
$1,100–1,250 JAK

Parian

This uniquely British porcelain was named after the famous Roman marble mined in the Greek island of Paros. Both the Minton and Copeland factories claimed to have invented Parian during the 1840s. Their work is the most famous and valuable, although many other makers produced this refined bisque porcelain that contained its own built-in-glaze and did not require a glass dome to keep it clean. Copies of classical subjects and the most famous Victorian sculptures were perfectly reproduced and extremely popular.

A Robinson & Leadbeater tinted Parian figure of a lady on a lily pad, on a gilded base, late 19thC, 15in (38cm) high.
£320–380 / €470–550
$580–690 AH

◄ A Nymphenburg biscuit porcelain figure of a woman with a lyre, her right foot resting on a dolphin, foot restored, German, c1800, 15in (38cm) high.
£1,100–1,300 / €1,600–1,90
$2,000–2,350 DORO

A Vienna figure of a man with a parasol and dog, damaged and restored, shield mark, impressed and inscribed marks, Austrian, 1755–60, 7in (18cm) high.
£840–1,000 / €1,250–1,450
$1,500–1,800 S

A Vienna figure of a mother and daughter with a doll, restored, marked, Austrian, c1765, 6in (15cm) high.
£820–980 / €1,200–1,450
$1,500–1,750 DORO

A Volkstedt figural group of bird nesters, slight damage and restoration, German, c1770, 10¾in (27.5cm) high.
£1,400–1,650
€2,050–2,400
$2,550–3,000 S

A figure of John Liston, in the role of Paul Pry, c1830, 5¾in (14.5cm) high.
£370–440 / €540–640
$670–800 SJH
John Liston, the leading comic actor of the first hal of the 19th century, created the character of Paul Pry in 1820. Pry was an interfering busybody and was Liston's masterpiece character. Images of Pry were extremely popular and appeared on inn signs, snuff boxes and butter stamps. The Staffordshire Rockingham and Derby factories all produced figures of Pry.

A Royal Worcester figure of The Irishman, by James Hadley, from the Countries of the World series, c1892, 7in (18cm) high.
£310–350 / €450–510
$560–630 WAC

A Royal Worcester candle snuffer, entitled 'Budge', c1880, 4in (10cm) high.
£2,450–2,750 / €3,600–4,000
$4,450–5,000 TH
Budge is a character from the Victorian bestseller *Helen's Babies* by John Habberton, published in 1876.

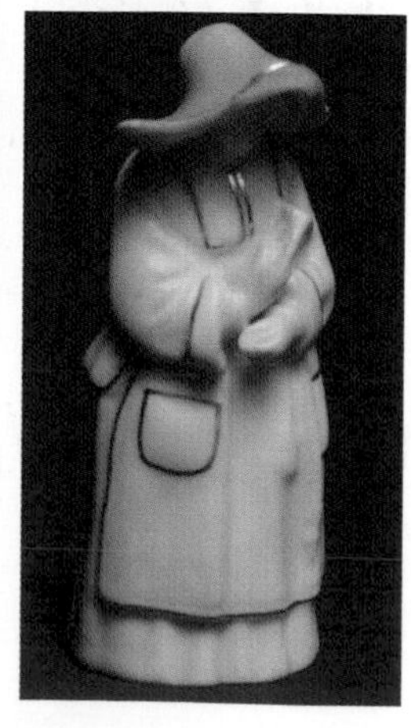

◄ A Royal Worcester candle snuffer, entitled 'The Abbess', c1902, 4in (10cm) high.
£290–330 / €420–480
$520–600 TH

◄ **A Royal Worcester candle snuffer,** in the form of a witch, c1922, 4in (10cm) high.
£270–300 / €390–440
$490–540 ⊞ GGD

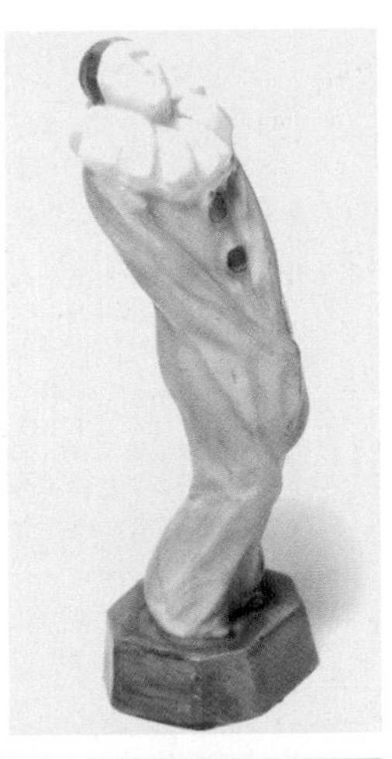

► **A Royal Worcester figure of a Pierrot,** by Doris Lindner, 1933, 6in (15cm) high.
£380–430 / €550–630
$690–780 ⊞ WAC

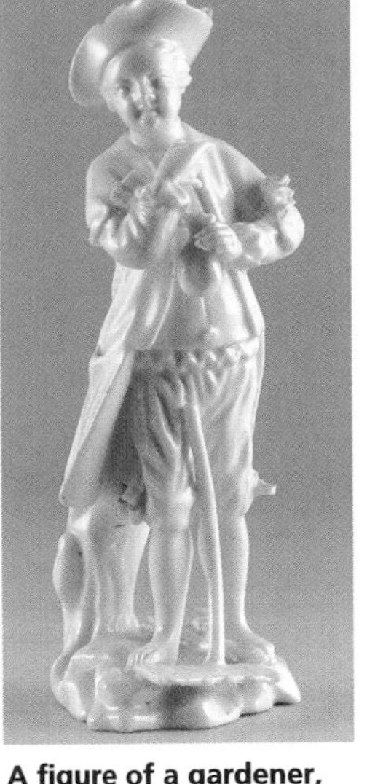

A figure of a gardener, slight damage, French, 18thC, 6¼in (16cm) high.
£590–700 / €860–1,000
$1,050–1,250 ⚒ WW

► **A figure of a tisane/lemonade seller,** after the Meissen model by Peter Reinicke, slight damage, impressed mark, German, mid-18thC, 6¼in (16cm) high.
£640–760
€930–1,100
$1,200–1,400
⚒ DN(BR)

◄ **A pair of figures of a gallant and his lady,** with encrusted decoration, incised 'JG', French, late 19thC, 19in (48.5cm) high.
£1,000–1,200
€1,450–1,750
$1,800–2,150 ⚒ TEN
'JG' is probably Jean Gille of Paris, who made large figures, often in biscuit porcelain.

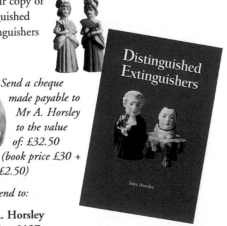

Flatware

A Berlin dish, painted with a bird on a branch, slight damage, sceptre mark, German, c1770, 15½in (39.5cm) diam.
£450–540 / €660–790
$810–980 S(Am)

► **A set of 12 Bodley plates,** each hand-painted with a roundel enclosing a fish within a riverscape background, printed and impressed marks and No. 3987, c1870, 9¼in (23.5cm) diam.
£420–500 / €610–730
$760–910 SWO

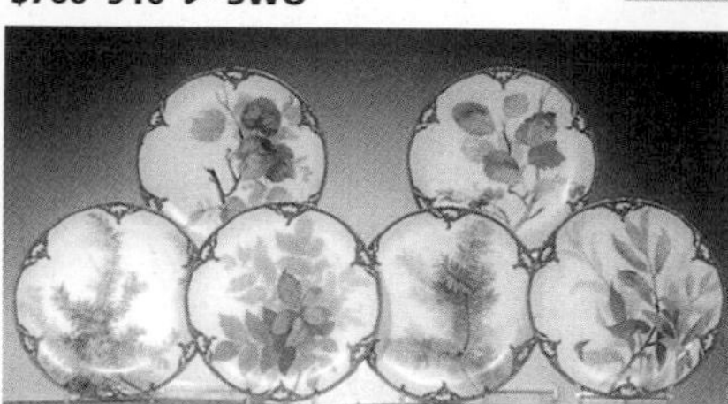

◄ **A set of six Berlin botanical plates,** painted with named studies of leafy branches within gilt low-relief scrolling borders, sceptre marks, impressed and inscribed marks, German, c1910, 8¾in (22cm) diam.
£740–880 / €1,100–1,300
$1,350–1,600 S(Am)

► **A Bow dish,** painted with peonies, bamboo and stylized rockwork, slight damage, c1750, 10½in (26.5cm) wide.
£530–630
€770–920
$960–1,150
WW

A Bow botanical plate, painted with a peony spray and insects, damaged, c1755, 8½in (21.5cm) diam.
£300–360 / €440–530
$540–650 WW

◄ **A pair of Bow plates,** painted with birds among foliage, the borders painted with winged insects, slight damage, red anchor and dagger marks, c1770, 8in (20.5cm) diam.
£1,200–1,400 / €1,750–2,050
$2,150–2,550 WW

A Chelsea serving dish, painted with bouquets and scattered sprigs, red anchor mark, c1755, 11¼in (28.5cm) wide.
£1,000–1,200 / €1,450–1,750
$1,800–2,150 TEN

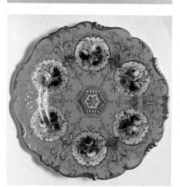

A pair of Cauldon plates, by Harrison, c1900, 9½in (24cm) diam.
£900–1,000 / €1,300–1,450
$1,600–1,800 HKW

A Chelsea 'Hans Sloane' plate, painted with an exotic plant, seed pods and insects, restored, red anchor mark, No. 15, c1755, 9¼in (23.5cm) diam.
£2,600–3,100 / €3,800–4,550
$4,700–5,600 S
The decoration on this plate is said to represent botanical specimens from Sir Hans Sloane's Chelsea Physic Garden. It is based on engravings by the curator, Philip Miller and Georg Dionysus Ehret.

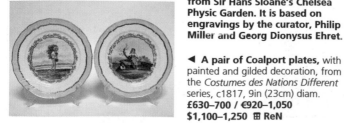

◄ **A pair of Coalport plates,** with painted and gilded decoration, from the *Costumes des Nations Different* series, c1817, 9in (23cm) diam.
£630–700 / €920–1,050
$1,100–1,250 ReN

A Davenport dessert plate, the centre painted with a water rail in a landscape, marked, c1840, 9in (23cm) diam.
£290–330 / €420–480
$520–600 JOR

A Derby botanical plate, entitled 'Senecio Elegans, Purple Groundsell, or Ragwort', pattern No. 115, marked '21', late 18thC, 8½in (21.5cm) diam.
£350–420 / €510–610
$630–760 WW

A Royal Crown Derby plate, painted by J. P. Wale with an English country garden, signed, c1911, 8½in (21.5cm) diam.
£1,600–1,800 / €2,350–2,650
$2,900–3,250 ⊞ BP

A Dresden charger, painted in Meissen style after Wouwerman with a scene of figures and animals, surrounded by vignettes of river landscapes and sprays of flowers, German, 19thC, 20¾in (52.5cm) diam.
£630–750 / €920–1,100
$1,150–1,350 F&C

◄ **A pair of Meissen saucers,** one painted with 'The Death of General Wolfe', after the painting by Benjamin West, the other with a soldier by a river, slight damage, crossed swords mark, impressed and inscribed marks, German, Marcolini period, late 18thC, 5¼in (13.5cm) diam.
£1,550–1,850 / €2,250–2,700
$2,800–3,350 S

► **A Minton plate,** by James Rouse, signed, c1860, 9in (23cm) diam.
£450–500
€660–730
$810–910
⊞ JAK

► **A Minton plate,** entitled 'Strawberry Hill', c1861, 9in (23cm) diam.
£70–80
€100–110
$125–140
⊞ LGr

◄ **A Minton plate,** by Antonin Boullemier, painted with figures in a classical landscape, with a pierced border, signed, c1880, 10in (25.5cm) diam.
£1,900–2,150
€2,750–3,150
$3,450–3,900
⊞ JOR

► **A pair of Minton cabinet plates,** each hand-painted with an English butterfly, c1871, 9¼in (23.5cm) diam.
£270–300
€390–440
$490–540
⊞ LGr

A Minton plate, decorated with raised enamelled flowers and a butterfly, c1880, 9½in (24cm) diam.
£180–200 / €260–290
$320–360 ⊞ JAK

A Minton cabinet plate, by F. Bellanger, with an Arabian butcher, signed, impressed marks and date code,1887, 9¾in (25cm) diam.
£190–220 / €280–330
$340–400 ⚒ SWO

A New Hall saucer dish, after Adam Buck, c1820, 8in (20.5cm) diam.
£180–200 / €260–290
$320–360 ⊞ JAK
Adam Buck was an artist and illustrator. Prints of his work were published and copied widely.

A Ridgway plate, decorated with an armorial, c1830, 10in (25.5cm) diam.
£270–300 / €390–440
$490–540 ⊞ ReN

A Sèvres-style cabinet plate, titled and painted with a portrait of Louis XVI, with a fleur-de-lys 'jewelled' and gilt border, damaged, marked, 19thC, 9¾in (25cm) diam.
£350–420 / €510–610
$630–760 ⚒ DN(BR)

A cabinet plate, painted with a portrait of the Duchesse du Maine, the border decorated with flowers and gilt, signed 'Morin', printed and painted marks, French, date codes for 1837 and 1846, c1880, 9½in (24cm) diam.
£90–105 / €130–155
$165–195 ⚒ SWO

PORCELAIN

A Staffordshire plate, painted with an armorial within a border decorated with vignettes of flowers and gilding, c1830, 10in (25.5cm) diam.
£175–195 / €250–280
$310–350 ⊞ ReN

A Vienna-style plate, by C. Yung, entitled 'Die Kinder von Vogel', painted with two children reading a book, the border decorated with panels of raised gilt flowers and leaves, 19thC, 10¼in (26cm) diam.
£490–580 / €720–850
$890–1,050 ⚒ WW

A Worcester dessert plate, painted with Kangxi Lotus pattern, the reverse with a Buddhistic symbol, c1770, 7½in (19cm) diam.
£300–360 / €440–530
$540–650 ⚒ G(L)

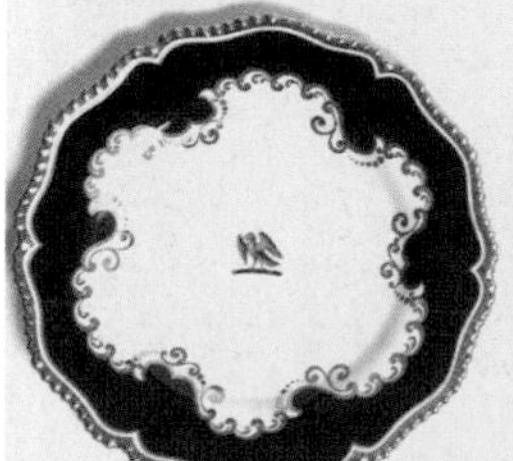

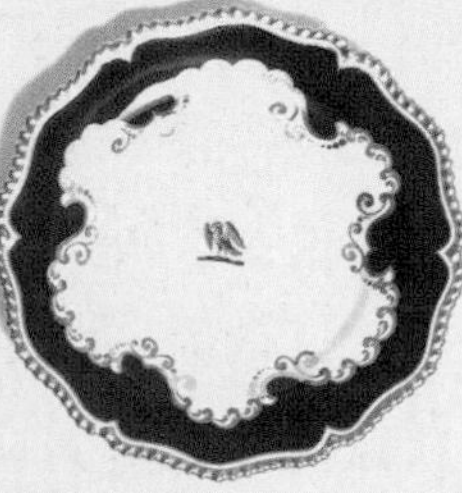

A pair of Worcester Flight, Barr & Barr plates, impressed mark, 1825–40, 10½in (26.5cm) diam.
£720–800 / €1,000–1,150
$1,300–1,450 ⊞ TYE

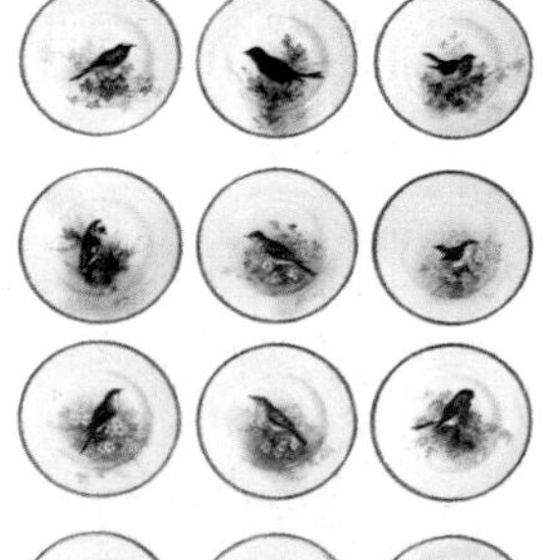

► **A set of 12 Royal Worcester plates,** by William Powell, each painted with a named British bird, slight damage, signed, marked, date code for 1918, 4½in (11.5cm) diam.
£1,750–2,100
€2,550–3,050
$3,150–3,800
⚒ F&C

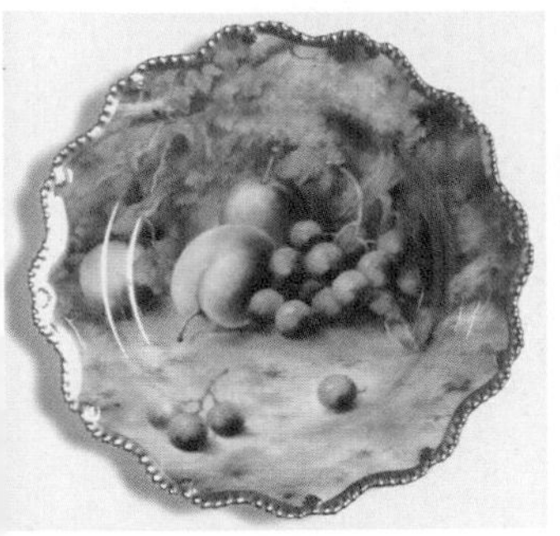

A Royal Worcester plate, by Frank Roberts, painted with fruit, c1919, 9in (23cm) diam.
£630–700 / €900–1,000
$1,100–1,250 ⊞ JUP

◄ A pair of Yates plates, with hand-painted and gilded decoration, c1820, 9¼in (23.5cm) diam.
£360–400 / €520–580
$650–720 ⊞ LGr

► A pair of Staffordshire plates, one entitled 'Dr Syntax Reading', the other 'Dr Syntax Losing his Wig', with gilt moulded borders, painted marks, early 19thC, 8¼in (21cm) diam.
£520–620 / €760–910
$940–1,100 ⚒ SWO

Ice Pails & Wine Coolers

An ice pail and cover, robably Coalport, of Warwick vase shape, each ide painted with a floral ouquet flanked by a gilt ruiting vine, with ntwined branch handles, he cover with a pine cone inial, liner missing, c1825, 1¾in (30cm) high.
1,300–1,550
1,900–2,250
2,350–2,800 ⚒ S(O)

Chelsea wine cooler, oulded and painted with uiting vines and flower prigs, with rococo handles, amaged, red anchor mark, 1755, 8in (20.5cm) high.
940–1,100
1,350–1,600
1,700–2,000 ⚒ WW

An ice pail, probably by Coalport, of Warwick vase shape, the beaded rim above a moulded fruiting vine and a band of painted moulded flowers, with entwined rope handles, cover missing, early 19thC, 10¾in (27.5cm) high.
£470–560 / €690–820
$850–1,000 ⚒ SJH

► A Vienna wine cooler, with gilt and painted decoration, applied with festoons and two biscuit medallions depicting bacchants, with ram's-head handles, restored, slight damage, marked, c1780, 8in (20.5cm) high.
£4,000–4,800 / €5,800–7,000
$7,200–8,700 ⚒ DORO

A pair of Chantilly wine coolers, each side decorated with an armorial, painted and incised marks, slight damage, French, 1765–70, 7½in (19cm) high.
£2,150–2,550 / €3,150–3,700
$3,900–4,600 ⚒ S

A pair of Minton wine coolers, each painted with four flower garlands, with gilt ram's-head handles, restored, printed mark, shape No. 750, c1900, 8½in (21.5cm) high.
£3,000–3,600 / €4,400–5,300
$5,400–6,500 ⚒ S

◄ A pair of Doccia wine coolers, slight damage and losses, Italian, c1770, 7¾in (19.5cm) high.
£2,450–2,900 / €3,600–4,250
$4,400–5,200 ⚒ S(Mi)

◄ A pair of Sèvres glass coolers, by Nicolas Catrice, from the Du Barry service, each decorated with the 'DB' monogram below a border of urns and floral swags, with gilt-edge foliate scroll handles, slight damage, marked, one with incised marks, c1771, 4¼in (11cm) high.
£13,200–15,800 / €19,300–23,100
$23,900–28,600 ⚒ S

Inkstands & Inkwells

A Meissen desk set, decorated with *Fels und Vogel* pattern, slight damage, blue crossed swords mark, No. 7, German, 19thC.
£600–720 / €880–1,050
$1,100–1,300 ⚒ S(Am)

A Worcester inkwell, with a beaded rim, enamel-painted with rose sprigs, c1830, 4¼in (10.5cm) diam.
£290–340 / €420–500
$520–620 ⚒ DN(BR)

An ink stand, in the form of a shell on the back of a dolphin, painted with floral sprays and gilt, damaged, early 19thC, 4¼in (10.5cm) wide.
£165–195 / €240–280
$300–360 ⚒ Bea

For further information on
Inkstands & Inkwells
see page 215

Jardinières

A Belleek jardinière, Irish, Second Period, 1891–26, 7in (18cm) high.
£890–990 / €1,300–1,450
$1,600–1,800 ⊞ DeA

A pair of Coalport jardinières and saucers, painted with flower panels and gilt decoration, c1830, 5in (12.5cm) high.
£1,350–1,500 / €1,950–2,200
$2,450–2,700 ⊞ ReN

A pair of jardinières, possibly Coalport, decorated with flowering prunus, c1880, 4¼in (10.5cm) high.
£230–270 / €340–400
$420–500 ⚒ WW

A pair of Sèvres-style jardinières, with gilt-metal mounts, the reserves painted with figures in garden settings and floral sprays, the double-scroll handles with mask heads, 1850–1900, 13¾in (35cm) high.
£6,200–7,400 / €9,100–10,800
$11,200–13,400 ⚒ GIL

A Worcester Flight Barr & Barr Sèvres-style jardinière, decorated with a view of Windsor Castle, flower sprigs and gilding, c1835, 9in (23cm) wide.
£3,350–3,750 / €4,900–5,500
$6,100–6,800 ⊞ JOR

A Royal Worcester Metallic Patent Lotus jardinière, in the form of a le[af] trumpet with an insect, the base modelled as lotus leaves and a rhizome with a frog, impressed and painted marks, 1884, 13¼in (33.5cm) high.
£940–1,100 / €1,350–1,600
$1,700–2,000 ⚒ TEN

◀ **A Royal Worcester jardinière,** by Walter Powell, painted with peafowl roosting in pine trees, slight damage, printed marks, date code for 1907, 9¾in (25cm) diam.
£1,350–1,600 / €1,950–2,350
$2,450–2,900 ⚒ DN

▶ **A Locke & Co Worcester jardinière,** by James Henry Lewis, painted with birds among pine branches, with two handles, on three legs, repaired, printed and painted marks, early 20thC, 8in (20.5cm) high.
£290–340 / €420–500
$520–620 ⚒ RTo

Jugs & Ewers

A Belleek jug, with a harp handle, First Period, 1863–90, 6½in (16.5cm) high.
£1,000–1,150
€1,450–1,650
$1,800–2,000 ⊞ DeA

◄ A Ludwigsburg hot water jug and cover, painted with three birds perched on branches, the cover with a bird and surmounted by an apple finial, slight damage, German, c1760, 6¾in (17cm) high.
£3,100–3,700
€4,550–5,400
$5,600–6,700
S

A Meissen milk jug and cover, painted with the Two Quail pattern, crossed swords mark, German, c1730, 6½in (16.5cm) high.
£2,800–3,350 / €4,100–4,900
$5,100–6,100 WW

A Meissen jug and cover, from the Münchhausen service, painted in the manner of A. F. von Löwenfinck with an armorial, animals, trees, flowers and insects, the spout with a bearded-mask terminal, restored, crossed swords mark, German, c1745, 7in (18cm) high.
£6,100–7,300
€8,900–10,700
$11,000–13,200 S
This jug is from the service completed in 1745 for Gerlach Adolf von Münchhausen, apparently as a gift from Augustus III of Saxony, patron of the Meissen factory.

A Meissen cream jug, painted with flowers, crossed swords mark, German, late 19thC, 3¼in (8.5cm) high.
£150–180 / €220–260
$270–320 SWO

A Minton Parian jug, moulded with bacchanalian cherubs, c1855, 8½in (21.5cm) high.
£150–170 / €220–250
$270–310 ⊞ JAK

A Rockingham jug, c1838, 5in (12.5cm) high.
£230–260 / €340–380
$420–470 ⊞ TYE

A Worcester mask jug, moulded with cabbage leaves and decorated with Parrot and Fruit pattern, disguised numeral mark, c1780, 8in (20.5cm) high.
£400–450 / €580–660
$720–810 ⊞ LGr

A Worcester milk jug, decorated with Temple pattern, disguised numeral mark, 1780–90, 4¾in (12cm) high.
£130–155 / €190–220
$240–280 WW

◄ A set of three graduated jugs, each moulded as a female head, the handle in the form of a branch, Continental, late 19thC, largest 5½in (14cm) high.
£165–195
€240–280
$300–360
SWO

A Royal Worcester ewer, painted by Harry Chair with swags of roses, the body pierced with honeycomb banding by George Owen, shape No. 1144, 1908, 6½in (16.5cm) high.
£4,000–4,800
€5,800–7,000
$7,200–8,700 AH

Mugs & Tankards

A Caughley mug, printed with Thorny Rose pattern, printed mark, c1775, 4¾in (12cm) high.
£1,250–1,500 / €1,850–2,200
$2,250–2,700 Bea

A Caughley miniature mug, painted with Island pattern, 1780–85, 1½in (4cm) high.
£1,000–1,200 / €1,450–1,750
$1,800–2,150 LFA

A Meissen silver-mounted tankard, painted with a chinoiserie scene in the manner of P. E. Schindler, engraved with a monogram, the silver-gilt cover and mount possibly later, German, c1730, 8½in (21.5cm) high.
£4,550–5,400 / €6,500–7,900
$8,200–9,800 S

A Lowestoft mug, moulded with a concentric ring and leaf border, painted with a fisherman in an Oriental landscape, painter's mark, 1765–68, 3¾in (9.5cm) high.
£4,250–5,100 / €6,200–7,400
$7,700–9,200 RBB

A New Hall-style mug, painted with flowers, c1785, 4¼in (11cm) high.
£520–620 / €760–910
$940–1,100 WW

A Vauxhall mug, decorated in the Chinese Imari style, 1755–60, 4in (10cm) high.
£1,350–1,500 / €1,950–2,200
$2,450–2,700 GIR

A Worcester mug, painted with The Walk in the Garden pattern, 1751–74, 5in (12.5cm) high.
£840–1,000 / €1,250–1,500
$1,500–1,800 RBB

◄ **A Worcester mug,** depicting the King of Prussia, signed, marked, dated 1757, 4½in (11.5cm) high.
£1,000–1,150 / €1,500–1,700
$1,850–2,100 JUP

► **A Worcester Flight tankard,** decorated with Royal Lily pattern, c1790, 4½in (11.5cm) high.
£550–620 / €800–910
$1,000–1,100 JOR
The Royal Lily pattern is so-called because a set of this standard pattern was ordered by George III and Queen Charlottte when they visited Worcester in 1788.

A loving cup, painted with flowers and a gilded inscription to Charles Blackhurst, 1858, 5½in (14cm) high.
£250–300 / €370–440
$450–540 JAd

PORCELAIN

Plaques

A Berlin plaque, after Gainsborough, depicting a young man in a landscape, impressed KPM and sceptre mark, decorated in Dresden, German, late 19thC, 9¼ x 6¼in (23.5 x 16cm).
£1,000–1,200
€1,450–1,750
$1,800–2,150 ⚒ S

Berlin plaques are usually better painted than other examples because they were bought by the best china painters. Lesser painters economized and bought plaques from smaller German factories.

Skilled china painters regarded plaques as an opportunity to move into the realms of fine art. Very few china factories could make perfectly flat slabs of porcelain. Instead specialist manufacturers supplied plaques to china painters: of these, Berlin (KPM) made the finest, and the best artists in Dresden and Vienna painted them. In England the Davenport factory patented a method of making very thin examples. These were painted by artists of very different abilities and it is therefore important to consider the quality of the painting, as this is just as important as the subject.

A pair of Royal Worcester plaques, by John Stinton, c1917, 4¼in (11cm) square.
£7,200–8,000 / €10,500–11,700
$13,000–14,800 ⊞ HKW

A Berlin plaque, after Rubens, painted with child bacchants, signed and dated, impressed eagle mark, German, 1844–47, 7 x 8in (18 x 20.5cm).
£1,150–1,350 / €1,700–2,000
$2,100–2,450 ⚒ DORO

A pair of plaques, depicting Milton and Shakespeare, c1810, 9 x 8in (23 x 20.5cm).
£1,200–1,350 / €1,750–1,950
$2,150–2,450 ⊞ TYE

◄ **A plaque,** painted with a farmyard scene, signed 'C. J. Weaver 1879', 6¼ x 8½in (16 x 21.5cm).
£280–330 / €410–480
$510–600 ⚒ WW

► **A Limoges *pâte-sur-pâte* plaque,** French, early 20thC, 7in (18cm) square.
£220–250 / €320–360
$400–450 ⊞ SER

Potpourri Vases

A Grainger's Worcester potpourri bowl and cover, moulded with flowers, on three feet, printed mark, c1900, 8in (20.5cm) diam.
£120–145 / €170–200
$210–250 ⚒ WW

◄ **A Fürstenberg potpourri vase and cover,** painted with flowers, the finial in the form of a cherub holding fruit, slight damage, 'F' mark, German, 19thC, 21¼in (54cm) high.
£560–670 / €810–980
$1,000–1,200 ⚒ WW

A Royal Worcester potpourri vase, by Harry Davis, painted with sheep in a highland landscape, shape No. 1428, 1911, 13½in (34.5cm) high.
£13,500–16,200
€19,700–23,700
$24,400–29,300 ⚒ AH

Tea Canisters

A Bow tea canister and cover, painted with flower sprays, butterflies and insects, cover damaged, 1755–60, 5½in (14cm) high.
£700–840 / €1,000–1,200
$1,250–1,500 WW

► A pair of Worcester tea canisters and covers, painted with Kylin pattern, damaged, square seal marks, c1770, 5½in (14cm) high.
£610–730 / €890–1,050
$1,100–1,300 WW

◄ A Meissen tea canister, painted with flowers and a pastoral scene, cover missing, crossed swords mark with star, German, Marcolini period, 1774–1813, 4in (10cm) high.
£300–360 / €440–530
$540–650 DORO

Tea & Coffee Pots

A Belleek tea kettle and cover, decorated with Grass pattern, Irish, First Period, 1863–90, 6½in (16.5cm) high.
£740–830 / €1,050–1,200
$1,350–1,500 DeA

A Beleek Bamboo teapot, Irish, First Period, 1863–90, 6in (15cm) high.
£580–650 / €850–950
$1,050–1,200 DeA

A Coalport teapot and cover, painted with panels of roses and cornflowers in gilt geometric panels, slight damage, c1810, 10in (25.5cm) wide.
£530–630 / €770–920
$960–1,150 WW

For further information on
Tea & Coffee Pots
see pages 225–226

A Coalport teapot, c1820, 6in (15cm) high.
£400–450 / €580–660
$720–810 JAK

A Coalport teapot, cover and stand, c1820, 6in (15cm) high.
£580–650 / €850–950
$1,050–1,200 JAK

A Copeland Spode teapot, c1884, 5in (12.5cm) high.
£220–250 / €320–360
$400–450 JAK

► A Höchst teapot and cover, probably painted by Johann Melchior Schöllhammer with figures, butterflies and insects, the finial in the form of a rose, wheel mark, German, c1765, 4½in (11.5cm) high.
£4,800–5,700
€7,000–8,300
$8,700–10,300
S

PORCELAIN

A Liverpool Christian's teapot and cover, painted in the Imari style with flowers and leaves, slight damage, c1770, 8in (20.5cm) high.
£210–250 / €310–370
$380–450 ⚒ WW

A Meissen gilt-metal-mounted tea kettle, painted with two Watteausque panels, with a swing handle, restored, crossed swords mark, German, late 19thC, 9in (23cm) high.
£260–310 / €380–450
$470–560 ⚒ DN

A Rockingham miniature teapot and cover, applied with flowers and leaves, marked, c1835, 3in (7.5cm) wide.
£900–1,000 / €1,300–1,450
$1,600–1,800 ⊞ JOR

A Worcester teapot and cover, painted with Waiting Chinaman pattern, slight damage, open crescent mark, c1770, 5½in (14cm) high.
£640–760 / €930–1,100
$1,200–1,400 ⚒ DN

A Liverpool Christian's teapot and cover, moulded and painted with Palm Tree pattern, slight damage, c1770, 7¼in (18.5cm) high.
£1,000–1,200 / €1,450–1,750
$1,800–2,150 ⚒ LFA

A miniature coffee pot and cover, possibly New Hall, painted with scattered flowers, damaged, c1785, 3¼in (8.5cm) high.
£1,500–1,800 / €2,200–2,650
$2,700–3,250 ⚒ TEN

A Sèvres teapot and cover, with gilt flowers and leaves, restored, crowned interlaced 'LL' mark, French, late 18thC, 6½in (16.5cm) wide.
£230–270 / €340–400
$420–500 ⚒ WW

A Worcester Barr, Flight & Barr teapot, cover and stand, c1810, 6in (15cm) high.
£1,750–1,950 / €2,550–2,850
$3,150–3,550 ⊞ JOR

A Meissen coffee pot and cover, the spout in the form of a putto tipping a ewer, painted with putti and scattered flowers, the foot with a coiled serpent, restored, impressed marks, German, Marcolini period, 1774–1813, 8½in (21.5cm) high
£1,850–2,200 / €2,700–3,200
$3,350–4,000 ⚒ LFA

A New Hall teapot, cover and stand, decorated with Tobbaco Leaf pattern No. 856, c1815, 5in (12.5cm) high.
£500–550 / €720–800
$900–1,000 ⊞ JAK

A Worcester teapot and cover, painted with Prunus Root pattern, c1753, 5in (12.5cm) wide.
£2,500–2,800 / €3,650–4,100
$4,550–5,100 ⊞ JUP

A Grainger, Lee & Co Worcester teapot, cover and stand, marked, 1812–20, 7in (18cm) high.
£400–450 / €580–660
$720–810 ⊞ TYE

Tea & Coffee Services

◀ **A Caughley tea service,** comprising 18 pieces, decorated with a gilt dot pattern, c1780.
£800–960
€1,200–1,400
$1,450–1,750 **RTo**

A Caughley part tea service, comprising five pieces, decorated with a Nankin pattern, c1790.
£200–240 / €290–350
$360–430 **WL**

A Coalport tea service, comprising 17 pieces, decorated with flowers and gilded cartouches, early 19thC.
£290–340 / €420–500
$520–620 **GAK**

A Coalport tea service, decorated with prunus blossom, slight damage, c1883.
£260–310 / €380–450
$470–560 **SWO**

▶ **A Copeland Parian coffee service,** comprising four pieces, c1880.
£270–300 / €390–440
$490–540 **JAK**

◀ **A Meissen coffee service,** comprising ten pieces, decorated with medallions of flowers, slight damage, crossed swords mark, German, c1800.
£560–670 / €820–980
$1,000–1,200 **DORO**

▶ **A Rockingham tea and coffee service,** comprising 44 pieces, the sugar bowl and teapot with finials in the form of crowns, some pieces with printed griffin mark, 1830–35.
£1,900–2,250 / €2,750–3,300
$3,350–4,000 **TEN**

A Rockingham part tea service, comprising 27 pieces, painted with leaves and berries, slight damage, printed griffin mark, 1838–42.
£840–1,000 / €1,200–1,450
$1,500–1,800 **S**

▶ **A Thuringian coffee service,** comprising 11 pieces, painted with flowers, damaged, flowerhead mark, German, late 18thC.
£370–440 / €540–640
$670–800 **S(Am)**

PORCELAIN

► **A Worcester Flight part tea service,** comprising 18 pieces, with spiral-moulded decoration, c1790.
£220–260 / €320–380
$400–470 ⚒ SWO

◄ **A Wedgwood tea service,** transfer-printed with birds and foliage, damaged, late 19thC.
£165–195 / €240–280
$300–360 ⚒ CHTR

A Worcester Flight & Barr part tea service, comprising 21 pieces, decorated with bands of gilt fruit and foliage, slight damage, incised marks, 1792–1804.
£180–210 / €260–310
$320–380 ⚒ WW

A Chamberlain's Worcester part tea service, comprising 38 pieces, decorated in the Imari palette, damaged, script marks, c1805.
£3,100–3,700 / €4,600–5,400
$5,600–6,600 ⚒ S

A Chamberlain's Worcester part tea service, comprising 41 pieces, decorated with Old Gadroon Chinese Figures pattern, slight damage, some printed marks, c1820.
£700–840 / €1,000–1,200
$1,250–1,500 ⚒ DN

Trays

A Bloor Derby tray, gilded with flowers and birds, c1830, 9½in (24cm) wide.
£310–350 / €450–510
$560–630 ⊞ TYE

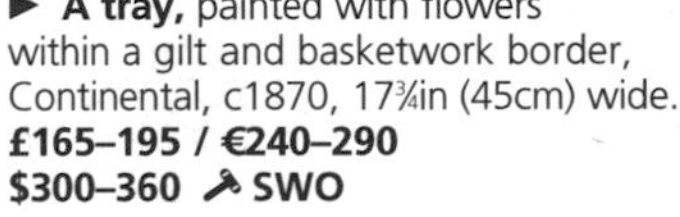

► **A tray,** painted with flowers within a gilt and basketwork border, Continental, c1870, 17¾in (45cm) wide.
£165–195 / €240–290
$300–360 ⚒ SWO

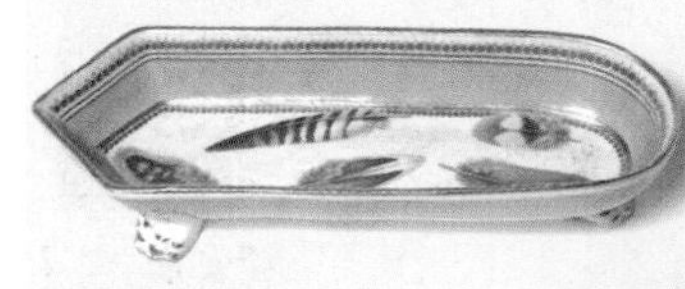

◄ **A Chamberlain's Worcester pen tray,** painted with feathers, c1810, 9in (23cm) long.
£1,900–2,150 / €2,750–3,150
$3,450–3,900 ⊞ JOR

PORCELAIN

Tureens

A pair of H. & R. Daniel cream tureens, covers and stands, painted with roses, the finials in the form of butterflies, c1824, 7in (18cm) high.
£2,000–2,250 / €2,900–3,300
$3,600–4,050 ⊞ JOR

► **A pair of Davenport tureens, covers and stands,** decorated in an Imari palette, early 19thC, 4¾in (12cm) high.
£350–420 / €510–610
$630–760 ⚒ HYD

◄ **A pair of Grainger's Worcester dessert tureens, covers and stands,** with swan knops and feet, 1815–20, 9in (23cm) diam.
£1,100–1,250
€1,600–1,800
$2,000–2,250 ⊞ JAK

Vases

A Samuel Alcock vase, c1840, 11in (28cm) high.
£200–220 / €290–320
$360–400 ⊞ TYE

A Belleek vase, in the form of a hand holding a shell, Irish, Second Period, 1891–1926, 8in (20.5cm) high.
£1,250–1,400
€1,850–2,050
$2,250–2,550 ⊞ MLa

A pair of Belleek Bird Tree Stump vases, Irish, Second Period, 1891–1926, 8in (20.5cm) high.
£1,700–1,900
€2,500–2,750
$3,100–3,450 ⊞ DeA

A Belleek Lily of the Valley vase, Irish, Third Period, 1926–46, 6in (15cm) high.
£270–300 / €390–440
$490–540 ⊞ WAA

A Bow vase, painted with a pavilion and a willow tree, damaged, incised mark, c1750, 6¼in (16cm) high.
£1,750–2,100
€2,550–3,050
$3,150–3,800 ⚒ WW

A Bow vase, painted in Meissen style, c1758, 6in (15cm) high.
£1,550–1,750
€2,250–2,550
$2,800–3,150 ⊞ GIR

A Chelsea Derby vase, decorated with flowers, gold anchor mark, c1770, 7in (18cm) high.
£190–220 / €280–320
$340–400 ⚒ SWO

A pair of Chelsea-style Coalport vases, painted with panels of flowers and classical figures, c1830, 11in (28cm) high.
£3,950–4,400
€5,750–6,400
$7,100–8,000 ⊞ JOR

A Coalport vase and cover, painted by Frederick Chivers with fruit, c1900, 16in (40.5cm) high.
£3,600–4,000
€5,200–5,800
$6,500–7,200 ⊞ JUP
Known as Ramshead vases, these came in several sizes. The size of the vase is significant.

◄ **A pair of Coalport vases,** decorated with flowers, damaged and repaired, early 20thC, 9in (23cm) high.
£440–520
€640–760
$800–940
⚒ DN(BR)

► **A pair of Copeland & Garrett vases,** painted with floral bouquets, 1840–45, 5in (12.5cm) high.
£240–280
€350–410
$430–510 ⚒ BWL

A Davenport vase, 1813–30, 9in (23cm) high.
£630–700 / €900–1,000
$1,100–1,250 ⊞ JAK

PORCELAIN

A pair of Davenport vases, painted with insects, the handles in the form of butterflies, late 19thC, 9½in (24cm) high.
£190–220 / €280–320
$340–400 DA

◄ **A pair of Derby miniature vases,** c1820, 3in (7.5cm) high.
£400–450
€580–660
$720–810 ⊞ TYE

A Derby vase, painted with a continuous band of flowers within gilt borders, c1815, 13in (33cm) high.
£2,700–3,000
€3,950–4,400
$4,900–5,400 ⊞ JOR

A Royal Crown Derby vase and cover, by Albert Gregory, painted with a band of flowers, restored, signed, 1903, 6¾in (17.5cm) high.
£940–1,100 / €1,350–1,600
$1,700–2,000 WW

Three Royal Crown Derby vases, painted with flowers within gilt borders, painted marks, c1908, largest 6½in (16.5cm) high.
£680–810 / €1,000–1,200
$1,250–1,450 SWO

► **A Royal Crown Derby vase and cover,** painted by Désiré Leroy with a panel of flowers within a gilt and jewelled frame, printed and painted marks, c1904, 6in (15cm) high.
£6,800–8,100 / €9,900–11,800
$12,300–14,500 HYD

A pair of Dresden vases, covers and pedestals, painted with lovers in landscapes within flowering trelliswork, one knop restored, painted marks, German, c1900, 16½in (42cm) high.
£900–1,050 / €1,300–1,550
$1,600–1,900 S(O)

A pair of Dresden double gourd vases, decorated with two gilt vignettes of figures on horseback, marked, German, c1910, 8in (20.5cm) high.
£175–210 / €250–300
$320–380 WL

A Ludwigsburg baluster vase and cover, painted with a flower bouquet, the cover surmounted by two putti, cover repaired, marked, German, 1770–75, 13¼in (33.5cm) high.
£5,000–6,000
€7,300–8,800
$9,100–10,900 S

Items in the Porcelain section have been arranged alphabetically in factory order, with non-specific pieces appearing at the end of each sub-section.

◄ **A Meissen vase and cover,** slight damage, crossed swords and star mark, German, 1814, 13½in (34.5cm) high.
£760–910 / €1,100–1,300
$1,400–1,650 JAA

◄ **A Meissen vase and cover,** encrusted with flowers, German, c1860, 24in (61cm) high.
£5,400–6,000
€7,900–8,800
$9,800–10,900 ⊞ BROW

A pair of Minton vases, with Sèvres-style decoration, c1850, 11in (28cm) high.
£1,050–1,200 / €1,550–1,750
$1,900–2,150 ⊞ TYE

◄ A Sèvres-style Minton vase, painted by Antonin Boullemier with panels representing Summer and Winter, with a later gilt-metal foot, c1873, 11in (28cm) high.
£1,600–1,850
€2,350–2,700
$2,900–3,350
⊞ JOR

A Minton vase, by Alboin Birks, with a *pâte-sur-pâte* panel, late 19thC, 14in (35.5cm) high.
£4,500–5,000
€6,600–7,300
$8,100–9,100 ⊞ HKW

A twin-handled Minton vase, with enamel decoration, c1902, 5in (12.5cm) high.
£220–250 / €320–360
$400–450 ⊞ TYE

► A Sèvres-style ormolu-mounted vase and cover, painted with a continuous scene of a maiden and cupids in a woodland, signed 'Schilt de Sèvres', French, late 19thC, 21½in (54.5cm) high.
£1,650–1,950
€2,400–2,850
$3,000–3,600
⚒ S(NY)

A Sèvres-style gilt-bronze-mounted vase, painted with musical emblems and putti, French, Paris, c1890, 34¾in (88.5cm) high.
£5,000–6,000
€7,300–8,800
$9,100–10,900 ⚒ S(O)

A pair of Spode vases, enamelled and gilded in an Imari palette, slight damage, painted marks, c1810, 9½in (24cm) high.
£820–980 / €1,200–1,450
$1,500–1,800 ⚒ Bea

A Spode vase, decorated in Imari style, script mark, c1815, 14½in (37cm) high.
£2,900–3,450
€4,250–5,000
$5,200–6,200 ⚒ LFA

A set of three Spode vases, decorated in the Imari palette, 1815–20, 7¾in (19.5cm) high.
£2,800–3,350 / €4,100–4,900
$5,100–6,100 ⚒ LFA

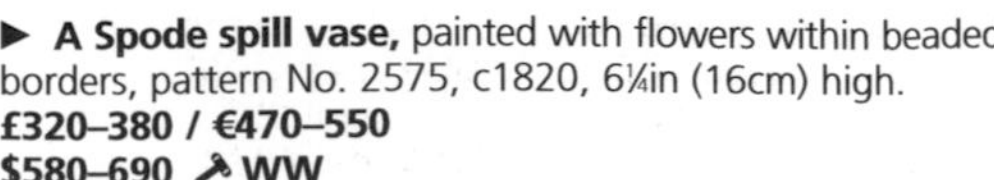

► A Spode spill vase, painted with flowers within beaded borders, pattern No. 2575, c1820, 6¼in (16cm) high.
£320–380 / €470–550
$580–690 ⚒ WW

A Worcester Flight, Barr & Barr urn, decorated with a portrait of Gaston de Foix after Giorgio Franco, flanked by horse-head ring handles, 1820–25, 19¾in (50cm) high.
£4,650–5,500
€6,800–8,000
$8,400–10,000 ⚒ JAd

◄ **A Royal Worcester vase,** painted after Thomas Sidney Cooper with a panel depicting cattle within a gilded cartouche, printed mark, 1865, 13in (33cm) high.
£700–840
€1,000–1,200
$1,250–1,500
PF

A pair of Royal Worcester vases, moulded and painted with birds and foliage, marked, date code for 1873, 8in (20.5cm) high.
£760–910 / €1,100–1,300
$1,400–1,650 GIL

A Worcester vase, by Boullemier, c1895, 8in (20.5cm) high.
£1,600–1,800
€2,350–2,650
$2,900–3,250 HKW

A Royal Worcester vase, painted with flowers, printed marks, 1895, 10½in (26.5cm) high.
£370–440 / €540–640
$670–800 SWO

A Locke & Co Worcester *pâte-sur-pâte* vase, with two handles, c1900, 7½in (19cm) high.
£360–400 / €520–580
$650–720 JUP

A Royal Worcester vase and cover, painted with a band of flowers, slight damage, printed mark, 1919, 14½in (37cm) high.
£410–490 / €600–710
$740–880 RTo

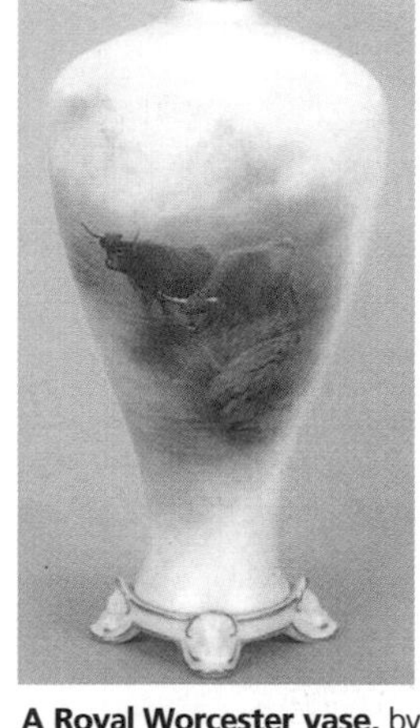

A Royal Worcester vase, by John Stinton, painted with Highland cattle, marked, 1923, 9¾in (25cm) high.
£2,350–2,800
€3,450–4,100
$4,250–5,100 DN

◄ **A pair of spill vases,** painted with follies and river landscapes within gilt borders, c1825, 4¾in (12cm) high.
£260–310 / €380–450
$470–560 PFK

A pair of vases, decorated with panels depicting shepherds and shepherdesses, slight damage, covers missing, Bohemian, c1850, 12½in (32cm) high.
£1,200–1,450 / €1,750–2,100
$2,150–2,600 DORO

A Sèvres-style vase, decorated with cherub cartouches, interlaced 'LL' mark, c1860, 5½in (14cm) high.
£420–500 / €610–730
$760–910 SWO

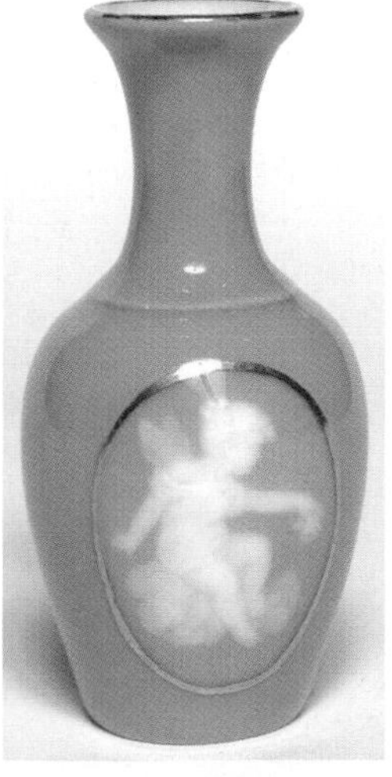

A miniature *pâte-sur-pâte* vase, Continental, c1900, 3in (7.5cm) high.
£200–220 / €290–320
$360–400 ANO

PORCELAIN

Wall Pockets

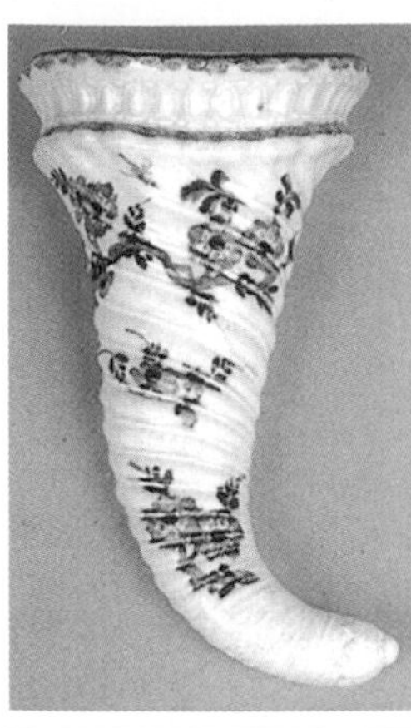

► **A pair of Royal Worcester wall pockets,** in the form of cornucopiae, printed marks, 1885, 11in (28cm) high.
£490–580 €720–850 $890–1,050 WL

◄ **A Worcester wall pocket,** decorated with Cornucopia Prunus pattern, marked, c1756, 9¾in (25cm) high.
£1,900–2,250 / €2,750–3,300 $3,400–4,000 L

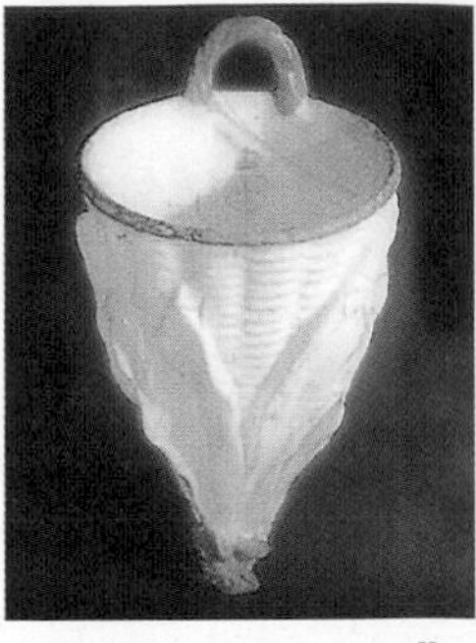

A Royal Worcester wall pocket, in the form of a pannier, moulded with leaves and tied with a ribbon, printed mark, c1880, 6½in (16.5cm) high.
£95–110 / €140–160 $170–200 PFK

Miscellaneous

◄ **A Chamberlain's Worcester bough pot,** with botanical decoration and satyr-mask handles, marked, c1810, 8in (20.5cm) wide.
£700–840 / €1,000–1,250 $1,250–1,500 TEN

► **A Bow *blanc-de-Chine* egg cup,** decorated with raised rose sprays, c1755, 3in (7.5cm) high.
£2,350–2,650 / €3,450–3,850 $4,250–4,800 GIR

A Chelsea Derby jar and cover, painted with spiral garrya swags, the knop in the form of a flower, marked, c1775, 3in (7.5cm) high.
£210–250 / €310–370 $380–450 WW

◄ **A Dresden mirror,** encrusted with flowers and cherubs, German, late 19thC, 11¾in (30cm) high.
£190–220 / €270–320 $340–400 DN(BR)

A Mennecy mustard pot and cover, damaged French, c1740, 5¾in (14.5cm) high.
£400–480 / €580–700 $720–870 WW

A Royal Worcester miniature pot and cover, decorated with floral sprays, printed mark, 1909, 1¾in (4.5cm) diam.
£105–125 / €155–185 $200–230 PFK

A Coalport scent bottle, enamelled with a waterside scene, c1881, 4in (10cm) high.
£340–380 / €500–550 $620–690 TYE

A Chelsea tureen stand, moulded with leaves, feathers and ears of wheat on a basketwork ground, red anchor mark, c1755, 11½in (29cm) wide.
£4,800–5,700 / €7,000–8,300 $8,700–10,300 S

PORCELAIN

Welsh Porcelain

The porcelain of Swansea and Nantgarw is widely acknowledged to be the most beautiful made in Britain, and it is not just diehard Welshmen who hold this view. The genius behind Welsh porcelain was the skilled china painter William Billingsley, who arrived in South Wales at the end of 1813 and carried out experiments at Nantgarw. Progress was slow but eventually, thanks to financial backing from Llewelyn Dillwyn, the first successful Welsh porcelain was made at nearby Swansea later the following year. Full production began in 1815 and for two years much remarkable porcelain was made, heavily influenced by French taste. Billingsley encouraged many talented painters to join him, including the floral artists David Evans, Henry Morris and William Pollard. Ascribing pieces to individual painters is often controversial, but a firm attribution always adds to the value.

By 1818, Billingsley had returned to Nantgarw where this time he successfully produced fine white porcelain to rival the celebrated pre-Revolutionary Sèvres. The best China-painting workshops in London eagerly bought undecorated Nantgarw plates and dishes. Most Nantgarw porcelain was enamelled in London rather than South Wales, and some Swansea likewise bears London decoration, although attributing painting to individual London workshops is far from easy.

In spite of the great beauty of their productions, the two Welsh factories were surprisingly short-lived, as the porcelain proved difficult and costly to produce. Nantgarw ceased production around 1820, leaving a large stock of undecorated white plates. Some of these were painted anything up to a decade later, and as a result dating Welsh porcelain is always problematic. In these pages, the date range given refers to the making of the porcelain rather than the decoration.

Swansea and Nantgarw porcelain has always been expensive, for this pinnacle of Welsh artistic achievement has universal appeal. Many collectors prefer locally-decorated Welsh porcelain, and the value of such pieces has doubled – trebled even – in the last three or four years. A plate from the most famous service from the Nantgarw factory, decorated in London for the marriage of the Mackintosh of Mackintosh, illustrated on page 287, sold recently for £20,400 / €30,000 / $37,000. Six years earlier, I had sold four similar plates from the Major Guy Dawnay collection for around £2,300–2,530 / €3,350–3,700 / $4,150–4,600 each. This remarkable leap in value has had one inevitable effect. Several more Mackintosh service plates have come onto the market recently, resulting in lower prices. Meanwhile, other fine Welsh porcelain looks set to go from strength to strength.

John Sandon

A Swansea bowl, decorated with Paris Flute pattern, with gilt borders, Welsh, 1815–17, 6½in (16.5cm) diam.
£340–380 / €500–550
$620–690 ⊞ DAP

A Swansea bowl, Welsh, 1815–17, 6in (15cm) diam.
£270–300 / €390–440
$490–540 ⊞ WeW

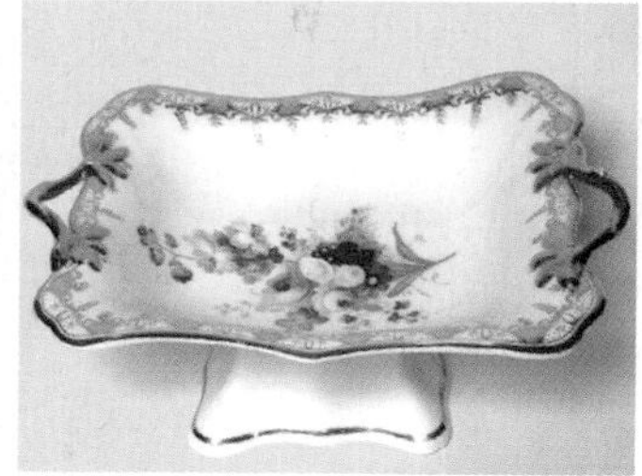

A Swansea centrepiece, by William Pollard, Welsh, 1815–17, 13in (33cm) wide.
£4,500–5,000 / €6,600–7,300
$8,100–9,100 ⊞ DMa

A Swansea cabinet cup and saucer, by William Pollard, slight restoration, Welsh, 1815–17.
£1,800–2,000 / €2,600–2,900
$3,250–3,600 ⊞ DAP

A Swansea cup and saucer, decorated with an osier-moulded border, marked, Welsh, 1815–17.
£630–700 / €900–1,000
$1,100–1,250 ⊞ DAP

A Swansea cup and saucer, with Paris Flute moulding and gilt borders, Welsh, 1815–17.
£175–195 / €250–280
$310–350 ⊞ DAP

◀ **A Swansea cup and saucer,** painted with panels of flowers, 1815–17.
£640–760 / €930–1,100
$1,200–1,400 ⚒ CAu

Items in the Welsh Porcelain section have been arranged in alphabetical order.

▶ **A Swansea cabaret cup,** attributed to Henry Morris, from the Clyne Castle service, Welsh, 1815–17.
£450–500 / €660–730
$810–910 ⊞ WeW

◀ **A Nantgarw tea cup and saucer,** London decorated with Dog Rose pattern within gilt borders, Welsh, 1818–20.
£900–1,000
€1,300–1,450
$1,600–1,800
⊞ DAP

A Nantgarw shell dish, from the Marquis of Bute service, Cardiff Castle, Welsh, 1818–20, 8in (20.5cm) diam.
£1,550–1,750 / €2,250–2,550
$2,800–3,150 ⊞ WeW

A Swansea part dessert service, comprising 14 pieces, painted with flowers, damaged, marked, Welsh, 1815–17.
£6,100–7,300 / €8,900–10,700
$11,000–13,000 ⚒ DN(BR)

A pair of Nantgarw dishes, London decorated, Welsh, 1818–20, 11in (28cm) wide.
£1,500–1,700 / €2,200–2,500
$2,700–3,100 ⊞ WeW

A Swansea dish, by William Pollard, the two handles in the form of twigs, Welsh, 1815–17, 12in (30.5cm) wide.
£1,350–1,500 / €1,950–2,200
$2,350–2,700 ⊞ WeW

A Swansea dish, attributed to William Pollard, Welsh, 1815–17, 10in (25.5cm) wide.
£1,700–1,900 / €2,500–2,750
$3,100–3,450 ⊞ WeW

A Swansea dish, decorated in gilt with the Venn family crest within gilt and moulded borders, marked, Welsh, 1815–17, 10in (25.5cm) wide.
£750–850 / €1,100–1,250
$1,350–1,550 ⊞ DAP

A Swansea cruciform dish, Welsh, 1815–17, 9in (23cm) diam.
£790–880 / €1,150–1,300
$1,450–1,600 ⊞ DMa

A Swansea cruciform dish, painted with flowers, within a gilt border, Welsh, 1815–17, 9in (23cm) diam.
£900–1,000 / €1,300–1,450
$1,600–1,800 ⊞ DAP

A Swansea cruciform dish, London decorated, Welsh, 1815–17, 9in (23cm) diam.
£760–850 / €1,100–1,250
$1,400–1,550 ⊞ WeW

A Swansea saucer dish, painted by Henry Morris, Welsh, 1815–17, 7in (18cm) diam.
£280–320 / €410–470
$510–580 ⊞ WeW

A Llanelli lithophane plaque, Welsh, mid-19thC, 8in (20.5cm) high.
£560–630 / €820–920
$1,000–1,150 ⊞ WeW

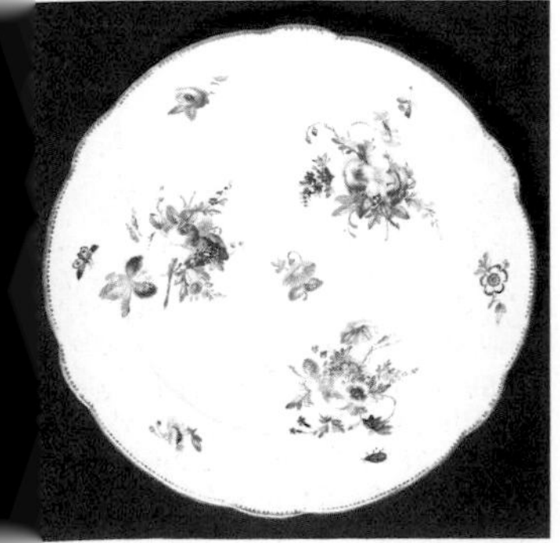

A Swansea dish, from the Princess Margaret service, Welsh, 1815–17, 12in (30.5cm) wide.
£1,350–1,500 / €1,950–2,200
$2,350–2,700 ⊞ WeW

A Swansea plate, printed with Mandarin pattern, Welsh, 1815–17, 8in (20.5cm) diam.
£800–900 / €1,150–1,300
$1,450–1,650 ⊞ WeW

A Nantgarw plate, attributed to William Billingsley, Welsh, 1818–20, 7½in (19cm) diam.
£1,000–1,100 / €1,450–1,600
$1,800–2,000 ⊞ DAP
This plate is from a service that once belonged to Canon William Duncombe of Hereford Cathedral. He married Isobel Twyning, granddaughter of Edward Edmunds, William Billingsley's landlord.

◄ **A Nantgarw plate,** Welsh, 1818–20, 8in (20.5cm) diam.
£2,550–2,850 / €3,700–4,150
$4,600–5,200 ⊞ DMa

► **A Nantgarw plate,** London decorated with flowers, fruit and birds, slight damage, Welsh, 1818–20, 8½in (21.5cm) diam.
£780–930 / €1,150–1,350
$1,400–1,700 ⚒ S

A Swansea dish, London decorated, the two handles in the form of twigs, Welsh, 1815–17, 13in (33cm) wide.
£2,000–2,200 / €2,900–3,200
$3,600–4,000 ⊞ WeW

A Swansea jug, pattern No. 231, marked, Welsh, 1815–17, 6in (15cm) wide.
£880–980 / €1,300–1,450
$1,600–1,850 ⊞ DAP

William Billingsley

Arguably the most influential figure in the whole history of British porcelain, Billingsley's genius was as a painter of flowers and landscapes and also as a maker of fine porcelain. He began as a painter at Derby in 1774, leaving in 1796 to establish his own china factory at Pinxton. After a period working independently at Torksey and Mansfield, he joined Barr, Flight & Barr in Worcester in 1808. Between 1813 and 1820 Billingsley is associated with the Welsh factories of Swansea and Nantgarw where he is credited with developing the superb Welsh porcelain bodies and glazes. He ended his days at Coalport where he died in 1826. Attributing porcelain painting to Billingsley's hand is not easy, for he influenced so many other china painters.

A Swansea plate, London decorated with flowers within a gilt border, Welsh, 1815–17, 8in (20.5cm) diam.
£1,350–1,500 / €1,950–2,200
$2,450–2,700 ⊞ DAP

A Swansea plate, attributed to Henry Morris, Welsh, 1815–17, 9in (23cm) diam.
£2,550–2,850 / €3,700–4,150
$4,600–5,200 ⊞ DMa

A Sèvres-style Nantgarw plate, London decorated, Welsh, early 19thC, 9½in (24cm) diam.
£670–750 / €980–1,100
$1,200–1,350 ⊞ WeW

A Nantgarw plate, attributed to de Junic, decorated with Bearded Tulip pattern, Welsh, 1818–20, 8in (20.5cm) diam.
£900–1,000 / €1,300–1,450
$1,600–1,800 ⊞ WeW

Miller's Compares

I. A Swansea plate, attributed to William Pollard, with floral decoration within moulded borders, Welsh, 1815–17, 8in (20.5cm) diam.
£2,850–3,200 / €4,150–4,650
$5,200–5,800 ⊞ WeW

II. A Swansea plate, attributed to William Pollard, with floral decoration within moulded borders, Welsh, 1815–17, 8in (20.5cm) diam.
£1,150–1,300 / €1,700–1,900
$2,100–2,350 ⊞ WeW

Items I and II are identical in size and moulding and are both attributed to the same painter, William Pollard. Both have borders that include his favourite sprigs of heather and strawberries but they have very different decoration to the centres. Item II, bearing a small spray of roses, is typically Welsh, but the full bouquet of wild flowers adorning Item I is very decorative and more sought after by Swansea collectors.

◄ **A Swansea plate,** by William Pollard, with floral decoration within moulded borders, Welsh, 1815–17, 8in (20.5cm) diam.
£1,350–1,500 / €1,950–2,200
$2,350–2,700 ⊞ DAP

A Swansea plate, London decorated with a view of The Wrekin from Buildwas, Welsh, 1815–17, 8in (20.5cm) diam.
£1,400–1,600 / €2,050–2,350
$2,550–2,900 ⊞ WeW
The Wrekin is a large hill on the Shropshire plain which can be seen from the village of Buildwas.

A Swansea plate, 1815–17, Welsh, 8in (20.5cm) diam.
£580–650 / €850–950
$1,050–1,200 ⊞ WeW

A Swansea plate, 1815–17, Welsh, 8in (20.5cm) diam.
£400–450 / €580–660
$720–810 ⊞ WeW

A Swansea plate, decorated with flowers, painted mark, Welsh, 1815–17, 8in (20.5cm) diam.
£940–1,100 / €1,350–1,600
$1,700–2,000 G(L)

A Swansea plate, from the Burdett Coutts service, Welsh, 1815–17, 9in (23cm) diam.
£1,400–1,600 / €2,050–2,350
$2,500–2,850 WeW

A Nantgarw plate, London decorated, attributed to Mortlocks, impressed mark, Welsh, 1818–20, 9½in (24cm) diam.
£3,150–3,500 / €4,600–5,100
$5,700–6,300 DAP

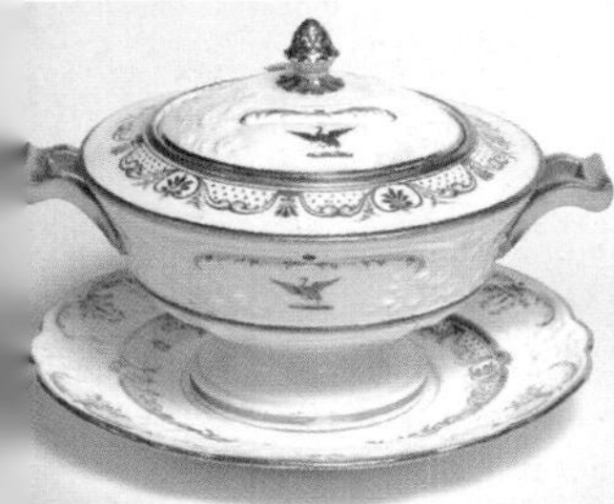

A Swansea sugar bowl, cover and stand, decorated in gilt with the Penn family crest within gilt and moulded panels, Welsh, 1815–17, 6in (15cm) high.
£2,250–2,500 / €3,300–3,650
$4,000–4,500 WeW

A Swansea plate, Welsh, 1815–17, 9in (23cm) diam.
£180–200 / €260–290
$320–360 WeW

A Swansea plate, from the Marino Ballroom service, Welsh, 1815–17, 9in (23cm) diam.
£380–430 / €550–630
$690–780 WeW
This was a service of over 200 pieces ordered from the Swansea factory by Mr J. Vivian of Marino, Swansea, whose home was decorated in the latest fashion.

A Nantgarw plate, London decorated, impressed mark, Welsh, 1818–20, 9in (23cm) diam.
£2,000–2,200 / €2,900–3,200
$3,600–4,000 DAP

A Swansea teapot, cover and stand, painted with flower sprays and gilt, repaired, stencil mark, Welsh, 1815–17, 10¾in (27.5cm) wide.
£1,800–2,150 / €2,650–3,150
$3,250–3,900 S

A Swansea plate, transfer-printed with Yellow Jasmine, from the Botanical series, Welsh, 1815–17, 8in (20.5cm) diam.
£450–500 / €660–730
$810–910 WeW

A Nantgarw soup plate, from the Mackintosh service, London decorated with a bird on a tree stump, impressed mark, Welsh, 1818–20, 10in (25.5cm) diam.
£20,400–24,400 / €29,800–36,000
$37,000–44,000 S
This price reflects the strength of the market for Welsh porcelain and the fact that few Mackintosh pieces have been sold for some time.

A Nantgarw dessert tureen, cover and stand, from the Mackintosh service, painted with birds on tree stumps, finial restored, impressed mark, Welsh, 1818–20, stand 7¼in (18.5cm) wide.
£25,200–30,000 / €37,000–44,000
$46,000–54,000 S
The Mackintosh dessert service, comprising 40 pieces, was originally owned by the Richards family. Edward Priest Richards of St Nicholas was agent to the Marquis of Bute. His only child, Ella, married into the Mackintosh family in 1880 and the service was given as a wedding present. The bird subjects for the service were taken from the bird books of François Levaillant, issued in Paris between 1801 and 1806. The service is likely to have been painted at the London workshops of Thomas Martin Randall.

A Selection of Chinese Dynasties & Marks

Early Dynasties

Neolithic	10th – early 1st millennium BC
Shang Dynasty	16th century–c1050 BC
Zhou Dynasty	c1050–221 BC
Warring States	480–221 BC
Qin Dynasty	221–206 BC
Han Dynasty	206 BC–AD 220
Six Dynasties	222–589
Wei Dynasty	386–557
Sui Dynasty	581–618
Tang Dynasty	618–907
Five Dynasties	907–960
Liao Dynasty	907–1125
Song Dynasty	960–1279
Northern Song	960–1127
Southern Song	1127–1279
Xixia Dynasty	1038–1227
Jin Dynasty	1115–1234
Yuan Dynasty	1279–1368

Ming Dynasty Marks

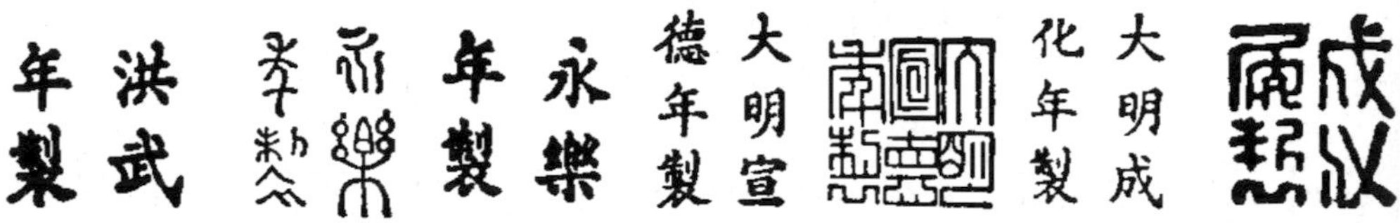

Hongwu 1368–1398

Yongle 1403–1424

Xuande 1426–1435

Chenghua 1465–1487

Hongzhi 1488–1505

Zhengde 1506–1521

Jiajing 1522–1566

Longqing 1567–1572

Wanli 1573–1619

Tianqi 1621–1627

Chongzhen 1628–1644

Qing Dynasty Marks

Shunzhi 1644–1661

Kangxi 1662–1722

Yongzheng 1723–1735

Qianlong 1736–1795

Jiaqing 1796–1820

Daoguang 1821–1850

Xianfeng 1851–1861

Tongzhi 1862–1874

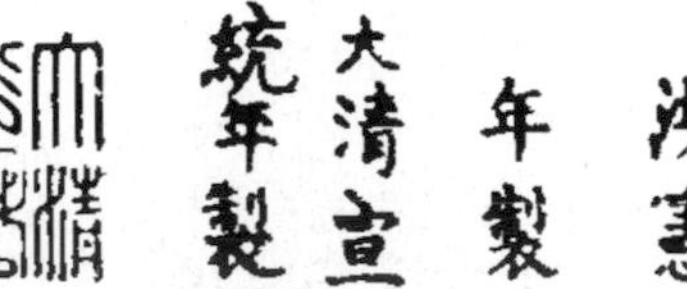

Guangxu 1875–1908

Xuantong 1909–1911

Hongxian 1916

Chinese Ceramics

Animals

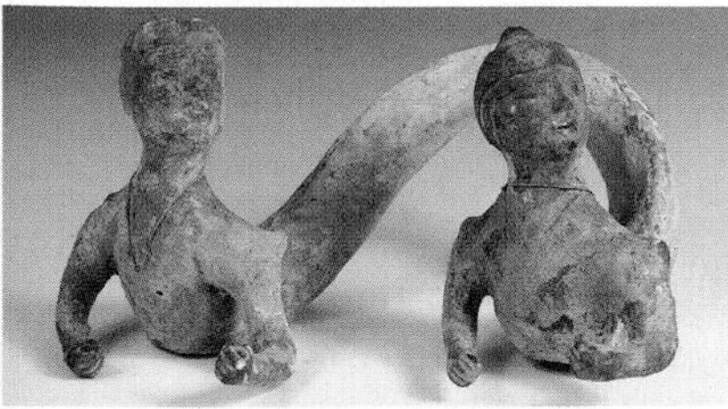

A pottery model of a mythical beast, damaged, Wei Dynasty, AD 386–557, 8½in (21.5cm) high.
£230–270 / €340–400
$420–500 SWO

Tang tomb figures

During the Tang Dynasty (AD 618–907) the Chinese created new styles in ceramics and metalwork, influenced by central Asian styles. A colourful type of pottery known as three-colour ware (*sancai*) became very popular and many figures in this style have been excavated from tombs, providing a vivid picture of the Tang lifestyle.

A *sancai*-glazed model of a camel, Oxford T/L tested, Tang Dynasty, AD 618–907, 23½in (59.5cm) high.
£7,900–8,800
€11,500–12,800
$14,300–15,900 GLD

A pottery model of a horse, with original slip coating, restored, Tang Dynasty, AD 618–907, 24in (61cm) high.
£4,100–4,600 / €6,000–6,700
$7,400–8,300 SOO

A *famille rose* porcelain pillow, in the form of a cat, the bronze stopper in the form of a rat, c1820, 9½in (24cm) wide.
£1,450–1,750 / €2,100–2,500
$2,600–3,100 DN

A pair of *famille verte* models of parrots, Jiaqing period, 1796–1820, 7in (18cm) high.
£970–1,150 / €1,400–1,650
$1,750–2,100 BUK

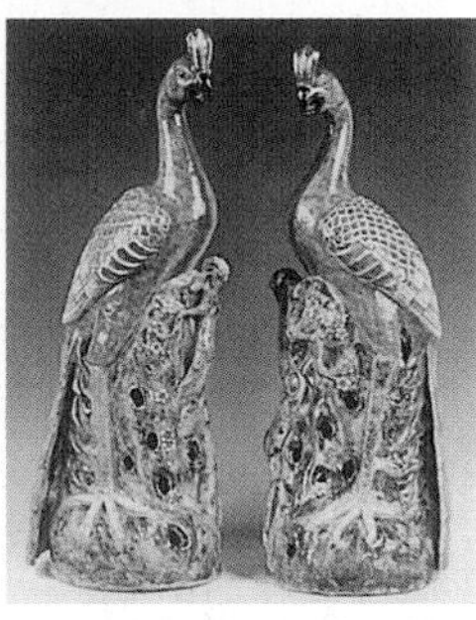

A pair of Chinese export porcelain models of peacocks, slight restoration, mid-19thC, 23½in (59.5cm) high.
£6,300–7,500
€9,200–11,000
$11,400–13,600 RTo

Baskets

A Chinese export porcelain pierced basket and stand, decorated with landscapes, Qianlong period, 1736–95, 11¾in (30cm) wide.
£440–520 / €640–760
$800–940 BUK(F)

Condition

The condition is absolutely vital when assessing the value of an antique. Damaged pieces on the whole appreciate much less than perfect examples. However, a rare desirable piece may command a high price even when damaged.

A Chinese export reticulated basket and stand, decorated in the *famille-rose* palette with Pseudo Cabbage Leaf pattern, mid-19thC, 5in (12.5cm) high.
£310–370 / €450–540
$560–670 WcH

A *famille rose* pierced basket and stand, decorated with flowers, handles missing, damaged, c1770, 11in (28cm) wide.
£1,750–2,100 / €2,550–3,050
$3,150–3,800 BUK
This basket and stand was made for Claes Alströmer (1736–94) who was a pupil of the Swedish botanist Carl von Linné. Alströmer discovered the flower depicted on the stand in Cadiz and gave it to Carl von Linné, who named it Alstroemeria after its donor. Alströmer's porcelain was decorated with the flower instead of a coat-of-arms.

Bowls

A pottery bowl, with painted decoration, Majiayao, 3200–2700 BC, 12¾in (32.5cm) wide.
£2,750–3,300 / €4,000–4,800
$5,000–6,000 ⚒ S(O)

A bowl, depicting Shou Lau and other Immortals, marked, Jiajing period, 1522–66, 4½in (11.5cm) wide.
£540–640 / €790–930
$980–1,150 ⚒ SWO

A *klapmuts* bowl, painted with *taotie* masks, Wanli period, 1573–1619, 5¾in (14.5cm) wide.
£850–950 / €1,250–1,400
$1,500–1,700 ⊞ G&G

A *famille verte* punch bowl, slight damage, Kangxi period, 1662–1722, 13½in (34.5cm) wide.
£800–960 / €1,200–1,400
$1,450–1,750 ⚒ LAY

► **A pair of bowls,** painted with Sanskrit characters and floral sprays, 17thC, 7¼in (18.5cm) wide.
£1,050–1,250
€1,550–1,850
$1,900–2,250 ⚒ S(O)

► **A Chinese Imari bowl,** with floral decoration, slight damage, Kangxi period, c1710, 12in (30.5cm) diam.
£730–870 / €1,050–1,250
$1,300–1,550 ⚒ S(Am)

A glazed bowl, marked, Yongzheng period, 1723–35, 4in (10cm) diam.
£1,650–1,950 / €2,400–2,850
$3,000–3,550 ⚒ S(O)

Miller's Compares

I. A *famille rose* bowl, painted with figures in a landscape, the interior painted with a figural panel and floral and gilt border, restored, c1790, 16in (40.5cm) diam.
£1,500–1,800 / €2,200–2,650
$2,700–3,250 ⚒ SWO

II. A *famille rose* bowl, painted with figures and birds in a landscape, restored, c1750, 14in (35.5cm) diam.
£440–520 / €640–760
$800–940 ⚒ SWO

Item I is larger than Item II and is much more richly decorated, the panels being larger and containing many more figures. The gilt background, which usually rubs and fades, is in much better condition. Furthermore, Item I has only minor restoration, whereas Item II is heavily restored.

A bowl, 18thC, 9¾in (25cm) diam.
£360–400 / €520–580
$650–720 ⊞ G&G

◄ **A *famille rose* bowl,** painted with figures, inscribed 'John Miller', 18thC, 11¾in (30cm) diam.
£820–980 / €1,200–1,400
$1,450–1,700 ⚒ WW

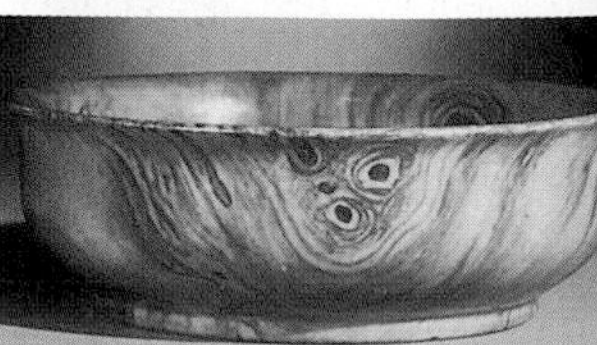

A *famille rose faux-bois* bowl, marked, Qianlong period, 1736–95, 5½in (14cm) diam.
£8,500–10,200 / €12,400–14,900
$15,400–18,500 ⚒ S(HK)
This bowl has been meticulously painted to imitate wood.

A Chinese export punch bowl, enamelled with the arms of Wakefield impaling Christie, Qianlong period, 1736–95, 13¾in (35cm) diam.
£2,800–3,350 / €4,100–4,900
$5,100–6,100 HYD

A *famille rose* bowl, decorated with fruit, marked, Qianlong period, 1736–95, 4½in (11.5cm) diam.
£6,800–8,100 / €9,900–11,800
$12,300–14,700 S(HK)

A glazed lotus stem bowl, the exterior incised with lotus flowers, the interior with lotus scrolls and mark, Qianlong period, 1736–95, 5¾in (14.5cm) diam.
£9,300–11,100 / €13,600–16,200
$16,800–20,100 S(HK)

A *famille rose* marriage bowl, painted with stylized lotus flowers, marked, Daoguang period, 1821–50, 8½in (21.5cm) diam.
£3,550–4,250 / €5,200–6,200
$6,400–7,700 S(NY)

A *famille rose* porcelain fish bowl, painted with dogs of *Fo*, mid-19thC, 12¼in (31cm) high.
£800–960 / €1,200–1,400
$1,450–1,750 RTo

► **A Chinese export bowl,** decorated with urns, restored, Qianlong period, 1736–95, 10¼in (26cm) diam.
£340–380 / €500–550
$620–690 G&G

◄ **A *famille rose* punch bowl,** painted *en grisaille* with a riverscape, slight damage, Qianlong period, 1736–95, 15in (38cm) diam.
£1,250–1,500
€1,850–2,200
$2,250–2,700
BUK

A *famille rose* barber's bowl, painted with exotic birds and a tree, inscribed 'Sir Your Quaters Up', Qianlong period, 1736–95, 11¾in (30cm) diam.
£4,900–5,900 / €7,200–8,600
$8,900–10,700 L
This inscription relates to the general practice of regular clients paying once a quarter. This dish would have been proffered as a tactful reminder.

A *famille rose* Baragon Tumed-style bowl, decorated with six dignitaries and the Eight Precious Things, marked, Qing Dynasty, Daoguang period, 1821–50, 6¼in (16cm) diam.
£960–1,150 / €1,450–1,700
$1,750–2,100 S(O)
This is a marriage bowl from the service that the Emperor Daoguang commissioned for the wedding of one of his daughters to a Tumed Mongol prince. Decorated with the Eight Precious Things of the Bhuddist religion, it bears its four-character Baragon Tumed mark: 'Mark of the West Wing of the Tumed Mongolian Banner'.

► **A porcelain fish bowl,** decorated with dragons, c1900, 11¾in (30cm) high.
£590–700 / €850–1,000
$1,050–1,250 TEN

A punch bowl, decorated with figures on a terrace, c1760, 11½in (29cm) diam.
£1,000–1,200 / €1,450–1,750
$1,800–2,150 SWO

A *famille rose* bowl, restored, c1770, 15¾in (40cm) diam.
£730–870 / €1,050–1,250
$1,300–1,550 SWO

A Canton punch bowl, with gilt decoration, c1860, 15½in (39.5cm) diam.
£1,500–1,800 / €2,200–2,650
$2,700–3,250 DN

Covered Bowls

A Yingqing bowl and cover, Song Dynasty, 960–1279, 3½in (9cm) high.
£580–650 / €860–950
$1,050–1,200 ⊞ G&G

A bowl and cover, with gilt decoration, restored, Kangxi period, 1662–1722, 9in (23cm) diam.
£120–145 / €170–200
$210–250 ⚒ WW

A pair of tripod spice bowls and covers, one cover restored, Kangxi period, 1662–1722, 2¼in (5.5cm) high.
£1,600–1,900 / €2,350–2,750
$2,900–3,450 ⚒ S(Am)

Brushpots

◄ **A porcelain brushpot,** depicting the scholar Fu Yijian, slight damage, inscribed with a poem and dated 'Yihai, 1635', 9in (23cm) high.
£13,000–15,600 / €19,000–22,800
$23,500–28,200 ⚒ Bea
This superbly painted brushpot has smoke damage to the glaze and in particular a large stain on the reverse. It was therefore given a low estimate. However, it was still the subject of keen interest because of the quality of the decoration and the fact that it is dated which is very rare in porcelain of this period. Had it been in perfect condition it could have realized considerably more.

A brushpot, Kangxi period, 1662–1722, 5¼in (13.5cm) high.
£2,850–3,400
€4,150–4,950
$5,200–6,200
⚒ S(O)

A brushpot, 18thC, 4¾in (12cm) high.
£840–1,000
€1,250–1,450
$1,500–1,800 ⚒ S(O)

Censers

A Wentang censer, decorated with a stylized landscape, Ming Dynasty, 15thC, 3in (7.5cm) high.
£2,400–2,850 / €3,500–4,150
$4,350–5,200 ⚒ S(O)
This type of censer was made for a scholar's studio, and often also used as a brushpot.

A porcelain *blanc-de-Chine* censer, damaged, 17thC, 7in (18cm) diam.
£630–700 / €900–1,000
$1,100–1,250 ⊞ G&G

A *blanc-de-Chine* censer, the central band with *anhua* decoration, on three feet, damaged, Kangxi period 1662–1722, 4¾in (12cm) diam, with a wooden stand
£1,250–1,400
€1,850–2,050
$2,250–2,550 ⊞ G&G

► **A censer,** decorated with the eight Daoist Immortals, some damage, Kangxi period, 1662–1722, 8in (20.5cm) diam.
£700–840 / €1,000–1,200
$1,250–1,500 ⚒ WW

An enamelled censer, with 'tea-dust' glaze, marked, 19thC, 7½in (19cm) wide.
£2,850–3,400 / €4,150–4,950
$5,200–6,200 ⚒ S(O)

Cups

A stem cup, decorated with three boys in a garden, damaged, Kangxi period, 1662–1722, 3¾in (9.5cm) high.
£590–700 / €850–1,000
$1,050–1,250 ⚒ JNic

A double-walled cup, the outer wall with pierced decoration, slight damage, Kangxi period, 1662–1722, 3¼in (8.5cm) diam.
£640–760 / €930–1,100
$1,200–1,400 ⚒ S(Am)

A pair of cups, painted with lotus flowers, marked, Yongzheng period, 1723–35, 2¾in (7cm) diam.
£5,900–7,000 / €8,600–10,200
$10,700–12,700 ⚒ S(HK)

► **A set of five tea bowls,** decorated with magpies, marked, Qing Dynasty, 19thC, 3½in (9cm) high.
£6,000–7,200 / €8,800–10,500
$10,900–13,000 ⚒ S(O)
These tea bowls are marked on the base 'Juewu Lu Zhi' – a rare mark from a private studio.

A pair of *famille verte* tea bowls and saucers, decorated with cherry blossom, slight damage, Kangxi period, 1662–1722, saucers 4¾in (12cm) diam.
£490–550 / €720–800
$890–1,000 ⊞ G&G

A set of four porcelain tea bowls and saucers, decorated with fish and cranes, slight damage, Yongzheng period, 1723–35.
£370–440 / €540–640
$670–800 ⚒ WW

Ewers & Jugs

ewer, carved with peonies, Liao Dynasty, 10thC, 9in (23cm) high.
£1,200–1,400
€1,750–2,050
$2,150–2,550 ⚒ S(O)

A pair of jugs, decorated with stylized foliage, slight damage, 17thC, 7¾in (19.5cm) high.
£2,400–2,850 / €3,500–4,150
$4,350–5,200 ⚒ S(Am)

A *famille rose* jug, painted with ribbon-tied flower sprays, 18thC, ½in (14cm) high.
£120–145 / €170–200
$210–250 ⚒ WW

A Chinese Imari ewer, painted with flowers, slight damage, Kangxi period, 1662–1722, 7¾in (19.5cm) high.
£1,200–1,350
€1,750–1,950
$2,150–2,450 ⊞ G&G

◄ **A ewer,** with a later metal cover, painted with fruit and flowers, seal mark, damaged, Qianlong period, 1736–95, 11in (28cm) high.
£2,800–3,350
€4,100–4,900
$5,100–6,100 ⚒ WW

An armorial sparrowbeak jug, depicting a cobbler, inscribed 'I'm...a work for leather...dear', Qianlong period, 1736–95, 5in (12.5cm) high.
£1,650–1,950
€2,400–2,850
$3,000–3,550 HYD

An *encre-de Chine* milk jug and cover, painted *en grisaille* with a medallion depicting a view of Middleburg city church, slight damage, inscribed 'Nieuwe Kerk Abtdy Tooren en Munt', 1780–90, 5¼in (13.5cm) high.
£1,450–1,700
€2,100–2,500
$2,600–3,100 S(Am)

A pair of Canton *famille rose* jugs and covers, painted with figures, flowers and insects, some damage, early 19thC, 8¾in (22cm) high.
£2,600–3,100 / €3,800–4,550
$4,700–5,600 WW
These jugs, often referred to as cider jugs, are particularly desirable because they are a pair, of good quality, with original covers and in good condition.

Further reading

Miller's Chinese & Japanese Antiques Buyer's Guide, Miller's Publications, 2004

Figures

A set of nine figures of musicians and dancers, Han Dynasty, 206 BC–AD 220, largest 12in (30.5cm) high.
£2,400–2,850 / €3,500–4,150
$4,350–5,200 S(O)

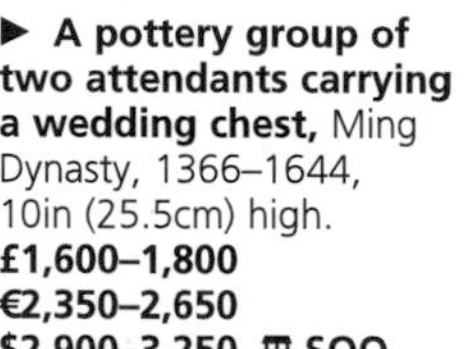

► **A pottery group of two attendants carrying a wedding chest,** Ming Dynasty, 1366–1644, 10in (25.5cm) high.
£1,600–1,800
€2,350–2,650
$2,900–3,250 SOO

blanc-de-Chine

Literally meaning white china, the name *blanc-de-Chine* is given to undecorated white porcelain from Dehua county in the southeastern Chinese province of Fujian. Porcelain has been made in Dehua for more than 1,000 years. It became extremely popular during the Ming Dynasty (1368–1644) and was exported to the west in large quantities during the 17th and 18th centuries.

A glazed pottery figure, holding a fan, damaged, Ming Dynasty, early 17thC, 9¾in (25cm) high.
£470–560 / €690–820
$850–1,000 WW

A *blanc-de-Chine* figure of Guanyin with acolytes traces of enamel decoration Kangxi period, 1662–1722 8in (20.5cm) high.
£2,000–2,200
€2,900–3,200
$3,600–4,000 GLD
Guanyin is the Bodhisattva of Compassion. A Bodhisattva is an attendant of Bhudda who has achieved enlightenment but who has remained in the human world to help others achieve it.

A biscuit porcelain figure of Li Bo, restored, Kangxi period, 1662–1722, 6¾in (17cm) wide.
£610–730 / €890–1,050
$1,100–1,300 SWO
Li Bo was an 8th century Chinese poet, one of the great figures of Chinese literature.

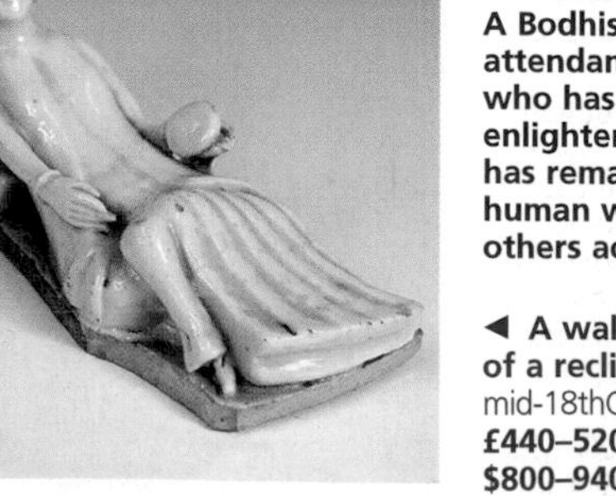

◄ **A wall-hanging figure of a reclining woman,** mid-18thC, 5½in (14cm) long.
£440–520 / €640–760
$800–940 SWO

Flatware

A Qinqbai porcelain saucer, moulded with fish, slight damage, Song Dynasty, 960–1280, 4¼in (11cm) diam.
£490–550 / €720–800
$890–1,000 ⊞ G&G

A *kraak porselein* dish, decorated with birds, flowers and emblems, Wanli period, 1573–1619, 11¼in (28.5m) diam.
£410–490 / €600–720
$740–890 ⚒ DN

A pair of *famille verte* plates, painted with the eight horses of Mu Wang, damaged, Fang mark, Kangxi period, 1662–1722, 8½in (21.5cm) diam.
£420–500 / €610–730
$760–910 ⚒ SWO

Mu Wang was a mythical 10th-century BC king who loved horses. Eight horses are normally depicted in various poses and colours.

◀ **A set of six moulded plates,** decorated with flowers, the reverse with Precious Objects, some damage, marked 'Precious object of rare jade among treasured vessels', Kangxi period, 1662–1722, 8¾in (22cm) diam.
£890–1,050 / €1,300–1,550
$1,600–1,900 ⚒ S(Am)

A celadon dish, 15thC, 10½in (26.5cm) diam.
£400–450 / €580–660
$720–810 ⊞ G&G

► **A *kraak porselein* saucer dish,** decorated with birds and flowers, Wanli period, 1573–1619, 8in (20.5m) diam.
£1,050–1,200 / €1,550–1,750
$1,900–2,150 ⊞ G&G

A set of five saucer dishes, enamelled with ten birds, slight damage, Cheng Hua six character mark, 1600–50, 6¼in (16cm) diam.
£1,250–1,500 / €1,850–2,200
$2,250–2,700 ⚒ S(Am)

A *famille verte* dish, painted with a basket of flowers, restored, Kangxi period, 1662–1722, 10¾in (27.5cm) diam.
£550–620 / €800–910
$1,000–1,100 ⊞ G&G

A *kraak porselein* dish, painted with geese, emblems and asters, Wanli period, 1573–1619, 12½in (32cm) diam.
£540–640 / €790–930
$980–1,150 ⚒ L

A dish, decorated with swallows, Tianqi period, 1621–27, 8¼in (21cm) diam.
£1,000–1,200 / €1,450–1,750
$1,800–2,150 ⚒ S(O)

A *famille verte* dish, painted with lotus blooms and a butterfly, Kangxi period, 1662–1722, 6¼in (16cm) diam.
£1,200–1,400 / €1,750–2,050
$2,150–2,550 ⚒ S(O)

A *famille verte* dish, decorated with a basket of flowers, restored, Kangxi period, 1662–1722, 10¾in (27.5cm) diam.
£165–195 / €240–280
$300–350 WW

Famille verte

The term *famille verte* applies to Chinese porcelain of the Kangxi period (1661–1722). The *famille verte* enamels were painted over the glaze with vivid green, strong rust-red, yellow, manganese, purpe and violet enamels, the green predominating. As the pink/rose enamel had yet to be introduced, the red of the decoration was obtained by the use of a flat iron-red. *Famille verte* was used to great effect in copying Japanese export ceramics, known as Chinese Imari.

A pair of *famille verte* plates, decorated with figures and pavilions, restored, Kangxi period, 1662–1722, 10¾in (27.5cm) diam.
£990–1,100 / €1,450–1,600
$2,000–2,200 G&G

A dish, decorated with fruit trees, marked, Kangxi period, 1662–1722, 13in (33cm) diam.
£820–980 / €1,200–1,450
$1,500–1,800 S(O)

A dish, with floral decoration, slight damage, Kangxi period, 1662–1722, 12¼in (31cm) diam.
£580–650 / €850–950
$1,000–1,150 G&G

A plate, painted with figures in a landscape, damaged, Kangxi period, 1662–1722, 10¾in (27.5cm) diam.
£210–240 / €310–350
$380–430 G&G

A *famille verte* plate, c1700, 13in (33cm) diam.
£2,550–2,850 / €3,700–4,150
$4,600–5,200 McP

A dish, entitled 'Cuckoo in the House', Kangxi period, early 18thC, 15½in (39.5cm) diam.
£1,050–1,200 / €1,550–1,750
$1,900–2,150 G&G

A *famille rose* plate, decorated with ladies on a terrace within a silvered border, Yongzheng period, 1723–35, 11¼in (28.5cm) diam.
£730–870 / €1,050–1,250
$1,300–1,550 S(Am)

A baptism plate, depicting Christ being baptized by John the Baptist below a stylized dove representing the Holy Spirit, inscribed 'Mat.3.16', c1735, 10in (25.5cm) diam.
£2,800–3,350 / €4,100–4,900
$5,100–6,100 S(Am)

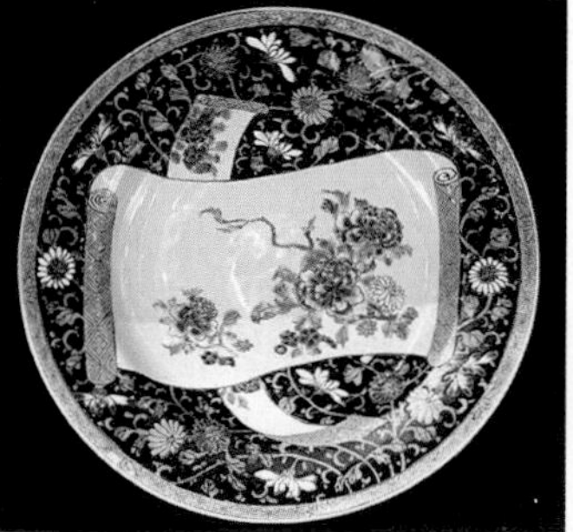

A *famille noire* plate, decorated with scrolls, Yongzheng period, 1723–35, 8¾in (22cm) diam.
£790–880 / €1,150–1,300
$1,450–1,600 G&G

A *famille rose* plate, decorated with a basket of flowers and goldfis within an *encre-de-Chine* band, 1700–50, 15¼in (38.5cm) diam.
£1,100–1,300 / €1,600–1,900
$2,000–2,350 S(Am)

A pair of Chinese export dishes, painted with a mother and a child in a garden, 18thC, 10¾in (27.5cm) wide.
£300–360 / €440–530
$540–650 ⚒ G(L)

A *famille rose* plate, painted with two birds, c1740, 8¾in (22cm) diam.
£260–310 / €380–450
$470–560 ⚒ SWO

Famille rose

During the Yongzheng period (1723–35) the new *famille rose* enamels became the main style for decorating porcelains. The colour is derived from colloidal gold and varied in tone from pale pink to deep ruby. It is thought that this technique was probably adopted from European painted enamels on gold and copper, introduced into China by Jesuit missionaries. The term *famille rose* denotes a style change and just the smallest amount of pink enamel is required for it to be described as such.

A Chinese export porcelain serving dish, with European decoration, repaired, Qianlong period, 1736–95, 11½in (29cm) long.
£610–730 / €890–1,050
$1,100–1,300 ⚒ BUK

A *famille rose* charger, painted with a basket of flowers and Precious Objects, 18thC, 21¾in (55.5cm) diam.
£680–810 / €990–1,150
$1,250–1,450 ⚒ L&T

A Chinese export *famille rose* serving plate, enamelled with peonies and blossom, 18thC, 14½in (37cm) wide.
£490–580 / €720–850
$890–1,050 ⚒ G(L)

An armorial dinner plate, with the Swedish arms of Grill, slight damage, c1740, 9in (23cm) diam.
£1,300–1,550 / €1,900–2,250
$2,350–2,800 ⚒ BUK

A pair of Chinese export platters, each decorated with a coat-of-arms, c1770, 6½in (16.5cm) wide.
£2,800–3,350 / €4,100–4,900
$5,100–6,100 ⚒ JAA

A *famille rose* plate, decorated with Tsar Peter working as a carpenter in Zaandam, slight damage, c1740, 8¾in (22cm) diam.
£1,200–1,400 / €1,750–2,050
$2,150–2,550 ⚒ S(Am)

A pair of *famille rose* meat plates, painted with floral sprays, Qianlong period, 1736–95, 13¼in (33.5cm) wide.
£490–580 / €720–840
$890–1,050 ⚒ L

◄ **A pair of *famille rose* plates,** decorated with Tobacco Leaf pattern, slight damage, c1760, 8½in (21.5cm) wide.
£130–145
€190–210
$230–260
⊞ LGr

► **A pair of Chinese export porcelain meat dishes,** painted with coastal landscapes, one damaged, Qianlong period, 1736–95, 15in (38cm) wide.
£350–420
€510–610
$630–760 ⚒ RTo

A plate, painted *en grisaille* with Venus and Cupid and other mythological figures, Qianlong period, 1736–95, 9in (23cm) diam.
£350–420 / €510–610
$630–760 WW

A Chinese export plate, decorated with peonies, Qianlong period, 1736–95, 13¼in (33.5cm) diam.
£280–330 / €410–480
$510–600 HYD

A *famille rose* saucer dish, decorated with lotus flowers, Qianlong period, 1736–95, 11¾in (30cm) diam.
£1,350–1,500 / €1,950–2,200
$2,450–2,700 G&G

A Canton dish, painted with figures in a landscape, the reverse with a flaming pearl, mid-19thC, 13½in (34.5cm) diam.
£590–700 / €860–1,000
$1,050–1,250 G(L)

A Chinese export *famille rose* armorial platter, damaged, Qianlong period, 1736–95, 16¼in (41.5cm) wide.
£560–670 / €820–980
$1,000–1,200 WcH

A Chinese export armorial plate, decorated with the arms of Livingstone impaling Kennedy, slight damage, Qianlong period, 1736–95, 9in (23cm) diam.
£260–310 / €380–450
$470–560 DN

A set of 12 *famille rose* dinner plates and 12 dessert plates, decorated with European flowers and inscribed 'Anna', slight damage, c1800, dinner plate 9¾in (24.5cm) diam.
£1,750–2,100 / €2,550–3,050
$3,150–3,800 BUK

LOCATE THE SOURCE

The source of each illustration in Miller's can be found by checking the code letters below each caption with the Key to Illustrations, pages 778–784.

A plate, Guangxu period, 1875–1905, 6in (15cm) diam.
£105–120 / €150–175
$190–220 SOO

A set of ten plates, each painted with a riverscape, together with 12 matching soup plates, Qianlong period, 1736–95.
£490–580 / €720–850
$890–1,050 L

A set of six *famille rose* plates, painted with a peacocks, Qianlong period, 1736–95, 9¼in (23.5cm) diam.
£470–560 / €690–820
$850–1,000 L

A porcelain charger, 19thC, 16in (40.5cm) diam.
£195–220 / €280–320
$350–400 SAT

A Canton export dish, decorated with panels depicting figures and flowers, with gilt inscription, made for the Persian market, dated 1878, 6¾in (17cm) diam.
£840–1,000 / €1,250–1,450
$1,500–1,800 SWO

Jars

A glazed jar, with four lug handles, Sui Dynasty, 6thC AD, 8¾in (22cm) high.
£1,900–2,250 / €2,750–3,300
$3,450–4,050 S(O)

A glazed jar, with two loop handles, Song Dynasty, 12th–13thC, 4½in (11.5cm) high.
£1,100–1,300 / €1,600–1,900
$2,000–2,350 S(O)

► A porcelain jar, 1620–44, 5in (12.5cm) high.
£75–85 / €110–1250
$135–155 ⊞ SOO

A jar and cover, from the Hatcher cargo, cover damaged, Ming Dynasty, c1643, 12in (30.5cm) high.
£1,050–1,200 / €1,550–1,750
$1,900–2,150 ⊞ McP
This was one of the pieces salvaged by Captain Hatcher from a shipwreck that occurred in the South China Sea c1643. Hatcher later discovered the Nanking cargo.

A stoneware funery jar, Oxford T/L tested, Song Dynasty, AD 960–1279, 20in (51cm) high.
£7,200–8,000 / €10,500–11,700
$13,000–14,500 ⊞ GLD

T/L test

Oxford T/L test refers to a test certificate awarded by Oxford Authentication Ltd to those genuine pieces of ceramics which have passed their thermoluminescence test which is accurate to plus or minus 200 years.

A jar, with a later wooden cover, Transitional period, c1650, 7in (18cm) high.
£2,000–2,200 / €2,900–3,200
$3,600–4,000 ⊞ GLD

A glazed jar, with two lug handles, Oxford T/L tested, Song Dynasty, 11th–12thC, 11in (28cm) high.
£1,400–1,600 / €2,050–2,350
$2,550–2,900 ⊞ GLD

A jar and cover, decorated with slip, with *fu shou* mark, Wanli period, 1573–1619, 4½in (11.5cm) high.
£1,900–2,250 / €2,750–3,300
$3,450–4,050 S(O)

Two jars and covers, from the Nanking cargo, Transitional period, c1650, 11in (28cm) high.
£1,900–2,250 / €2,750–3,300
$3,450–4,050 BUK

A *wucai* jar and cover, with painted decoration, *fu* character mark, Transitional/Shunzi period, 17thC, 16in (40.5cm) high.
£4,600–5,500 / €6,700–8,000
$8,300–10,000 S(NY)

A jar, Kangxi period, 1662–1722, 6½in (16.5cm) high.
£800–960 / €1,200–1,400
$1,450–1,750 S(Am)

A Chinese Imari jar and cover, cover damaged, Kangxi period, 1662–1722, 9½in (24cm) high.
£350–420 / €510–610
$630–760 Bea

A jar and cover, from the Vung Tau cargo, Kangxi period, 1662–1722, 6½in (16.5cm) high.
£990–1,100
€1,450–1,600
$1,800–2,000 G&G

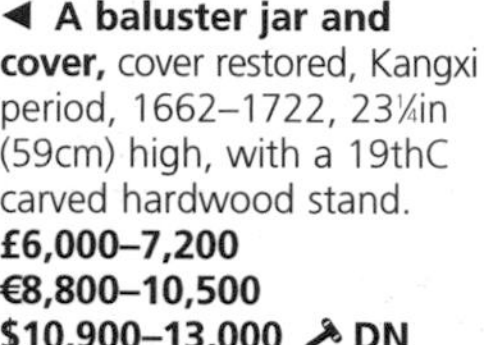

◀ **A baluster jar and cover,** cover restored, Kangxi period, 1662–1722, 23¼in (59cm) high, with a 19thC carved hardwood stand.
£6,000–7,200
€8,800–10,500
$10,900–13,000 DN

A jar and cover, Kangxi period, 1662–1722, 17in (43cm) high.
£2,150–2,400
€3,150–3,500
$3,900–4,350 G&G

A jar and cover, Kangxi period, 1662–1722, 8in (20.5cm) high.
£2,000–2,200
€2,900–3,200
$3,600–4,000 G&G

A *famille verte* porcelain jar and cover, cover damaged, Kangxi period, 1662–1722, 10¾in (27.5cm) high.
£270–320 / €390–470
$490–580 Bea

◀ **A jar and cover,** with crackle glaze and gilt relief decoration, the cover knop modelled as a dog of *Fo*, restored, 18thC, 16½in (42cm) high.
£700–840
€1,000–1,200
$1,250–1,500
BUK

◀ **A Chinese Imari ginger jar,** painted with *ho-o* birds and *qilin*, Qianlong period, 1736–95, 8in (20.5cm) diam.
£590–700 / €860–1,000
$1,050–1,250 L

A *famille rose* jar, Jiaqing period, 1796–1820, 3½in (9cm) high.
£2,600–3,100 / €3,800–4,550
$4,700–5,600 S(O)

A jar, decorated with the Eight Daoist Immortals, applied with two lion-head masks, Cai Hua Tang mark, 19thC, 5in (12.5cm) high.
£3,400–4,050 / €5,000–5,900
$6,200–7,300 S(HK)
This jar bears an Imperial Palace mark which makes it very desirable.

A *famille verte* baluster jar and cover, 19thC, 16½in (42cm) high.
£500–600 / €730–880
$910–1,100 DN(BR)

Mugs & Tankards

A *famille rose* mug, decorated with a lady at a window, birds, peaches and flowers, 18thC, 5¼in (13.5cm) high.
£210–250 / €310–370
$380–450 WW

A Chinese Imari mug, from the Nanking cargo, decorated with a rock terrace and trailing flowers, c1750, 5in (12.5cm) high.
£670–750 / €980–1,100
$1,200–1,350 RBA

A Chinese export mug, with clobbered decoration, the handle moulded as a branch, Qianlong period, late 18thC, 6¼in (16cm) high.
£640–760 / €930–1,100
$1,150–1,350 HYD
Clobbering is the technique of applying coloured enamel glazes over blue and white underglaze colours.

Sauce boats

A pair of sauce boats, decorated with a peony and bamboo pattern, minor damage, Qianlong period, 1736–95, 6¾in (17cm) high.
£1,100–1,250 / €1,600–1,850
$2,000–2,250 G&G

► **A pair of *encre-de-Chine* and gilt sauce boats,** slight damage, Qianlong period, 1736–95, 8¾in (22cm) wide.
£810–970
€1,200–1,400
$1,450–1,750
S(Am)

► **A Canton *famille rose* sauce boat,** decorated with a pheasant and chrysanthemum pattern, 18thC, 8in (20.5cm) wide.
£120–140
€175–200
$220–250
G(L)

A pair of sauce boats, each decorated with an armorial to the interior, late 18thC, 7½in (19cm) wide.
£230–270 / €340–390
$420–490 SWO

Spoon Trays

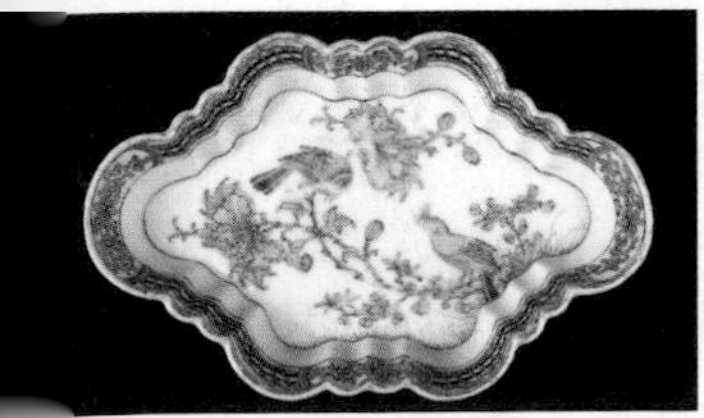

***famille rose* spoon tray,** decorated with two birds on a peony branch, Qianlong period, 1736–95, 5¼in (13.5cm) wide.
£500–560 / €730–820
$900–1,000 G&G

A spoon tray, c1760, 5in (12.5cm) wide.
£310–350 / €450–510
$560–630 DAN

A Chinese export porcelain spoon tray, c1770, 5in (12.5cm) wide.
£200–220 / €290–320
$360–400 DAN

Tea Canisters

◄ **A tea canister,** painted with birds and willow trees, 18thC, 4in (10cm) high.
£165–195
€240–280
$300–350
WW

◄ **A tea canister,** with a later silver cover, Kangxi period, 1662–1722, 5½in (14cm) high.
£520–580 / €760–850
$940–1,050 G&G

A pair of tea canisters, each decorated with figures and a phoenix in a garden above moulded scrolls, with later silver mounts and covers, Kangxi period, 1662–1722, 5⅓in (13.5cm) high.
£2,100–2,500 / €3,050–3,650
$3,800–4,550 S(Am)

Tea, Coffee & Chocolate Pots

A teapot, decorated with two vignettes of people in a garden, silver cover later, Chenghua mark, Transitional period, 1628–44, 4½in (11.5cm) high.
£760–850 / €1,100–1,250
$1,400–1,550 G&G

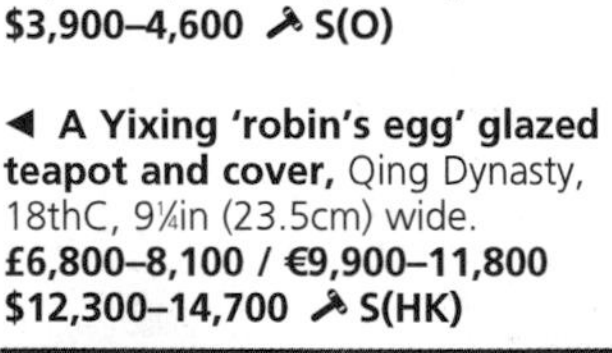

A *famille verte* teapot and cover, the body painted with tree peonies, chrysanthemums, camellias and morning glories, Kangxi period, 1662–1722, 4¼in (11cm) high.
£2,150–2,550 / €3,150–3,700
$3,900–4,600 S(O)

A *famille verte* teapot and cover, decorated with flower sprays, finial restored, Kangxi period, 1662–1722, 6in (15cm) wide.
£1,300–1,550 / €1,900–2,250
$2,350–2,800 WW

◄ **A Yixing 'robin's egg' glazed teapot and cover,** Qing Dynasty, 18thC, 9¼in (23.5cm) wide.
£6,800–8,100 / €9,900–11,800
$12,300–14,700 S(HK)

A Chinese export teapot and cover, painted with a chinoiserie scene, the entwined handle with leaf terminals, slight damage, 18thC, 5½in (14cm) wide.
£165–195 / €240–280
$300–350 TMA

A *famille rose* teapot and cover, decorated with two panels, one with a cockerel and peonies, the other with a Chinese dog, cover restored, Yongzheng period, 1723–35, 4½in (11.5cm) high.
£4,450–5,300 / €6,500–7,700
$8,100–9,600 S(Am)

◄ **A chocolate pot and cover,** Qianlong period, 1736–95, 7in (18cm) high.
£850–950 / €1,250–1,400
$1,550–1,700 G&G

► **A painted porcelain miniature coffee pot,** c1855, 5in (12.5cm) high.
£125–140 / €180–200
$220–250 SOO

Tea & Coffee Services

A porcelain part tea and coffee service, comprising 15 pieces, each decorated with a monogram and a crest, Qianlong period, 1736–95.
£1,400–1,650 / €2,050–2,400
$2,550–3,000 Gam

A *famille rose* part tea service, comprising six pieces, decorated with panels of flowers and birds, Qianlong period, 1736–95.
£2,400–2,850 / €3,500–4,150
$4,350–5,200 S(Am)

A *famille rose* miniature part tea service, comprising 13 pieces, each painted with figures at play, Qianlong period, 1736–95, teapot and cover 3¼in (8.5cm) high.
£440–520 / €640–760
$800–940 L

Tureens

A tureen, cover and stand, all decorated with sprays of flowers, the tureen with hare-head handles and rococo finial, 18thC, tureen 13½in (34.5cm) wide.
£3,100–3,700 / €4,550–5,400
$5,600–6,700 S(O)

A *famille rose* tureen, with rabbit-mask handles, painted with flowering plants, cover missing, Qianlong period, 1736–95, 9in (23cm) diam.
£105–125 / €155–185
$190–220 L

A tureen and cover, decorated with pagodas in a river landscape, damaged, Qianlong period, 1736–95, 9¾in (25cm) diam.
£730–870 / €1,050–1,250
$1,300–1,550 S(Am)

◄ **A *famille rose* tureen and cover,** slight damage to cover, Qianlong period, 1736–95, 8¾in (22cm) diam.
£1,750–2,100
€2,550–3,050
$3,150–3,800
S(Am)

A *famille rose* sauce tureen and cover, decorated with an armorial, late 18thC, 9in (23cm) wide.
£200–240 / €290–350
$360–430 L

Vases

◄ **A vase and cover,** with painted decoration and relief-moulded *taotie* mask handles, Han Dynasty, 206 BC – AD 220, 21½in (54.5cm) high.
£1,300–1,550
€1,900–2,250
$2,350–2,800 S(O)

► **A vase,** decorated with incised bands, with applied mask ring handles, Han Dynasty, 206 BC – AD 220, 18in (45.5cm) high.
£540–640 / €790–930
$980–1,150 WW

A vase, decorated with two carved peony sprays, Liao Dynasty, 10thC, 15½in (39.5cm) high.
£2,400–2,850
€3,500–4,150
$4,350–5,200 S(O)

A bottle vase, painted with stylized foliage, 16thC, 4½in (11.5cm) high.
£350–420 / €510–610
$630–760 L

A bottle vase, painted with dragons among clouds and waves, c1650, 23in (58.5cm) high.
£1,550–1,850
€2,250–2,700
$2,800–3,350 S(O)

A *meiping*, the body decorated with sprays of flowers and stiff leaves, slight damage, Kangxi period, 1662–1722, 7in (18cm) high.
£2,800–3,350
€4,100–4,900
$5,100–6,100 S(Am)

A vase, decorated with two flower-filled vases beneath a *ruyi* head and pearl-drop border, Wanli period, 1573–1619, 10½in (26.5cm) high.
£2,150–2,550
€3,200–3,700
$3,900–4,600 S(O)

A *wucai* baluster vase, decorated with magnolia and peony among birds and insects in flight, slight damage, c1650, 11in (28cm) high.
£1,400–1,650
€2,050–2,400
$2,550–3,000 WW

An 'egg and spinach' glazed double gourd vase, slight damage, Kangxi period, 1662–1722, 4¼in (11cm) high.
£220–260 / €320–380
$400–470 SWO

A *kraak porselein* double-gourd bottle vase, painted with chrysanthemum sprays and fruit, Wanli period, 1573–1619, 10in (25.5cm) high.
£1,200–1,400
€1,750–2,050
$2,150–2,550 S(O)

A *wucai* vase and cover, decorated with ladies playing instruments, the cover painted with jumping boys, neck repaired, Transitional period, mid-17thC, 18½in (47cm) high.
£5,200–6,200
€7,600–9,100
$9,400–11,200 SWO

A vase, decorated with panels filled with an interlace pattern, Kangxi period, 1662–1722, 13¼in (33.5cm) high.
£840–1,000
€1,250–1,450
$1,500–1,800 S(O)
This vase was possibly made for the Japanese market.

A trumpet vase, enamel-painted with a Daoist Immortal and his attendants, above bands of peonies and pomegranates, mid-17thC, 16¾in (42.5cm) high.
£6,800–8,100
€9,900–11,800
$12,300–14,700 SWO

A baluster vase and cover, decorated with scrolling lotus, damaged, 17thC, 15¾in (40cm) high.
£940–1,100
€1,350–1,600
$1,700–2,000 DN

A *sang de boeuf* glazed vase, early 18thC, 6¼in (16cm) high.
£230–270 / €340–390
$420–490 SWO

LOCATE THE SOURCE

The source of each illustration in Miller's can be found by checking the code letters below each caption with the Key to Illustrations, pages 778–784.

A crackle-glazed biscuit porcelain vase, 18thC, 8¼in (21cm) high.
£5,300–6,300
€7,700–9,200
$9,600–11,400 S(NY)

A bottle vase, restored, 18thC, 8in (20.5cm) high.
£350–420 / €510–610
$630–760 WW

A crackle-glazed vase, Qing Dynasty, 18thC, 9in (23cm) high, with a wooden stand.
£3,800–4,550
€5,500–6,600
$6,900–8,200 S(O)

A soft-paste porcelain vase, moulded with stylized flowers and decorated with a crackle glaze, rim with later silver mount, 18thC, 12¼in (31cm) high.
£2,650–3,150
€3,850–4,600
$4,800–5,700 S(NY)

◄ **A pair of vases,** moulded with panels depicting domestic objects against a scroll ground, 18thC, 16½in (42cm) high.
£2,000–2,400
€2,900–3,450
$3,600–4,350
G(L)

A bottle vase, 18thC, 12½in (32cm) high.
£1,800–2,150
€2,650–3,150
$3,250–3,900 S(NY)

A flambé bottle vase, Qianlong period, 1736–95, 17in (43cm) high.
£1,600–1,800
€2,350–2,600
$2,900–3,250 GLD

► **A pair of ormolu-mounted *famille rose* beaker vases,** decorated with flowering peonies, damaged, mounts later, 18thC, 9in (23cm) high.
£490–580
€720–850
$890–1,050
S(Am)

◄ **A pair of *famille rose* wall vases,** each applied with two boys beneath animal-mask handles, one vase restored, Qianlong period, 1736–95, 6¼in (16cm) high.
£890–1,050 / €1,300–1,550

$1,600–1,900 S(Am)

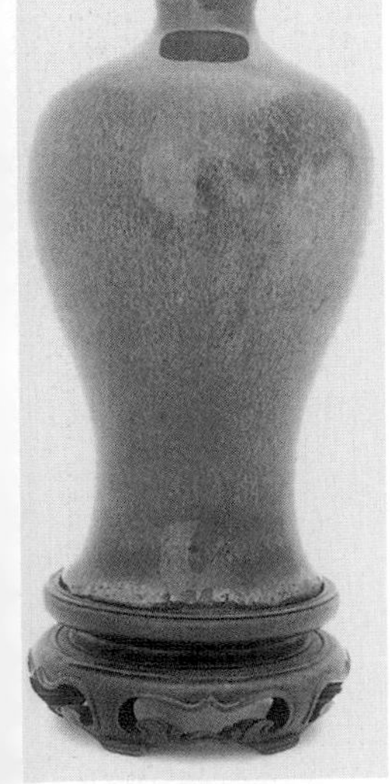

◄ **A *meiping,*** early 19thC, 8½in (22cm) high.
£220–260 / €320–380
$400–470 GIL

A pair of *famille verte* bottle vases, each painted with Hohsien-Gu, 19thC, 8in (20.5cm) high.
£210–250 / €310–370
$380–450 SWO
Hohsien-Gu was one of the Eight Immortals.

A pair of Canton *famille verte* vases, decorated with reserve panels of domestic scenes, with flowers, birds and insects, 19thC, 17½in (44.5cm) high.
£420–500 / €610–730
$760–910 JM

A *famille noir* vase, painted with prunus branches, 19thC, 16in (40.5cm) high.
£440–520 / €640–760 $800–940 G(L)

A vase, decorated with panels of foliage and birds, 19thC, 17¼in (44cm) high.
£400–480 / €580–700 $720–870 SWO

► **A pair of Canton vases,** with painted and gilt panels of figures, birds and insects, late 19thC, 10in (25.5cm) high.
£150–180 €220–260 $270–320 Mit

◄ **A pair of vases,** decorated with birds, flowers and rocks, 19thC, 9½in (24cm) high.
£530–630 €770–920 $960–1,150 WW

A vase, painted in enamels with bands of chintz decoration, 19thC, 18¼in (46.5cm) high.
£470–560 / €690–820 $850–1,000 HOK

A pair of Canton *famille rose* vases, decorated with Samurai warriors, 25¼in (64cm) high.
£270–320 / €390–470 $490–580 JAd

► **A Chinese export *famille verte* vase,** fitted as a lamp on a pierced hardwood stand, Guangxu period, 1875–1908, 17½in (44.5cm) high.
£470–560 / €690–820 $850–1,000 WcH

A pair of *famille rose* vases, with dragon handles, painted *en grisaille* with horses grazing beneath a weeping willow, Hongxian marks, early 20thC, 6¼in (16cm) high.
£4,200–5,000 €6,100–7,300 $7,600–9,100 S(HK)

Miscellaneous

A Neolithic amphora, Oxford T/L tested, 5,000–4,000 BC, 13in (33cm) high.
£3,600–4,000 €5,200–5,800 $6,500–7,200 GLD

A silver-mounted perfume bottle, painted with scrolls and flowers, Kangxi period, c1680, 7½in (19cm) high.
£410–490 / €600–720 $740–890 SWO

► **A Canton *famille rose* bough pot and cover,** with two handles, enamelled with birds, butterflies and flowers on a gilt ground and painted with panels of figures in interior settings, slight damage, mid-19thC, 9in (23cm) high.
£730–870 / €1,050–1,250 $1,300–1,550 RTo

◄ **A pair of *blanc-de-Chine* dishes,** impressed mark, early 18thC, 9in (23cm) wide, with stands.
£610–730 €890–1,050 $1,100–1,300 SWO

A glazed terracotta model of a goat farm, Han Dynasty, AD 89–198, 8in (20.5cm) wide.
£660–740 / €960–1,050
$1,200–1,350 ⊞ SOO

A pair of Canton *famille rose* garden seats, painted with panels enclosing pheasants and flowers alternating with figural panels, 19thC, 18½in (47cm) high.
£2,250–2,700 / €3,300–3,950
$4,050–4,900 ⚒ S(O)

A *famille rose* jardinière, decorated with figures in various pursuits, c1925, 18¼in (46.5cm) high.
£1,300–1,550 / €1,900–2,250
$2,350–2,800 ⚒ WW
This bowl is very large in size and appeals to the Chinese taste.

A glazed pottery opium pillow, Guangxu period, 1875–1908, 19in (48.5cm) wide.
£175–195 / €250–280
$310–350 ⊞ SOO

► A pair of salts, the tops painted with a lady and a child, the sides with panels of flowers, one restored, Kangxi period, 1662–1722, 3in (7.5cm) wide.
£810–970 / €1,200–1,400
$1,450–1,750 ⚒ S(Am)

◄ A porcelain snuff bottle, painted with a lakeside scene, 19thC, 3¾in (9.5cm) high.
£1,000–1,100 / €1,450–1,600
$1,800–2,000 ⊞ RHa

A pottery scoop, Han Dynasty, AD 206–221, 8in (20.5cm) wide.
£270–300 / €390–440
$490–540 ⊞ SOO

A spoon, from the *Tek Sing* cargo, c1822, 4in (10cm) long.
£45–50 / €65–75
$80–95 ⊞ McP

A silver-mounted rosewater sprinkler and cover, decorated with scrolling foliage and flowers, silver mounts 19thC, slight damage, Kangxi period, 1662–1722, 9in (23cm) high.
£1,500–1,800
€2,200–2,650
$2,700–3,250 ⚒ S(Am)

A stick stand, decorated with a dragon among flowers, c1900, 23¾in (60.5cm) high.
£280–330 / €410–480
$510–600 ⚒ WW

► A *famille rose* teapot stand, c1760, 5½in (14cm) diam.
£280–330
€410–480
$510–600
⊞ DAN

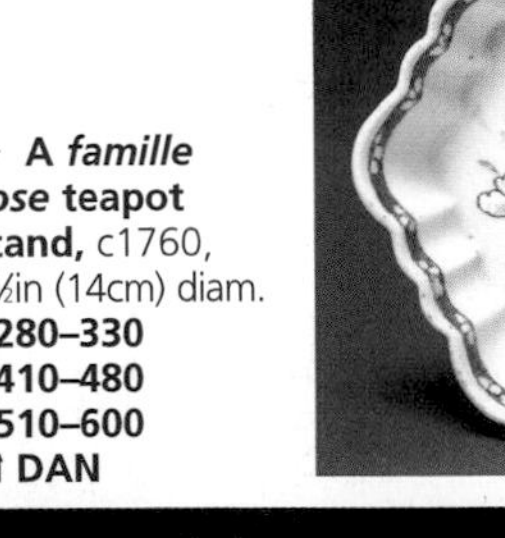

A pair of *famille rose* wine coolers, with gilt-decorated scroll handles, each painted with figures in a garden, Qianlong period, 1736–95, 6in (15cm) high.
£4,050–4,850 / €5,900–7,100
$7,300–8,800 ⚒ S(O)

Japanese Ceramics

Bowls

An Arita Imari bowl, slight damage, c1700, 4¾in (12cm) diam.
£520–580 / €760–850
$940–1,050 ⊞ G&G

A Satsuma bowl, painted with a cockerel and a hen, gilt signature and paper label for S. Kinkozan, Kyoto, Meiji period, 1868–1911, 4¾in (12cm) diam.
£640–760 / €940–1,100
$1,150–1,350 ⚒ RTo

A Nabeshima bowl, painted with cloud scrolls, with a silver handle, 18thC, 11¾in (30cm) wide.
£430–510 / €630–750
$780–930 ⚒ WW

An Imari porcelain bowl, decorated with cranes and stylized foliage, Meiji period, 1868–1911, 11½in (29cm) diam.
£320–380 / €470–550
$580–690 ⚒ Bea

A Kutani bowl, painted with peacocks and flowers, character marks, Meiji period, 1868–1911, 10½in (26.5cm) high.
£165–195 / €240–280
$300–350 ⚒ G(L)

An Imari bowl, decorated with panels of birds and Samurai warriors, late 19thC, 5in (12.5cm) diam.
£140–165 / €200–240
$250–300 ⚒ CHTR

Dishes

An Imari basin, decorated with blossoming branches and crabs, early 18thC, 14¾in (37.5cm) diam.
£260–310 / €380–450
$470–560 ⚒ HYD

An earthenware dish, decorated with a procession of dancers, signed 'Dai Nihon Kinkozan', Meiji period, 1868–1911, 9½in (24cm) diam.
£1,400–1,650 / €2,050–2,400
$2,550–3,000 ⚒ S

A set of five Kutani dishes, probably by Yoshidaya, each decorated with a spray of chrysanthemum, Fuku mark, 19thC, 8¾in (22cm) diam.
£3,100–3,700 / €4,550–5,400
$5,600–6,700 ⚒ S
Yoshidaya, a wealthy merchant, re-established the Kutani kiln in 1810.

Japanese chronology chart

Jomon (Neolithic) period	c10,000–100 BC
Yayoi period	c200 BC–AD 200
Tumulus (Kofun) period	200–552
Asuka period	552–710
Nara period	710–794
Heian period	794–1185
Kamakura period	1185–1333
Muromachi (Ashikaga) period	1333–1568
Momoyama period	1568–1600
Edo (Tokugawa) period	1600–1868
Genroku period	*1688–1703*
Meiji period	1868–1911
Taisho period	1912–1926
Showa period	1926–1989

Flatware

An Imari charger, decorated with cranes and pine trees, c1700, 21¾in (55.5cm) diam.
£2,850–3,400 / €4,150–4,950
$5,200–6,200 ⚒ S

An Imari charger, the domed centre decorated with a woman and a man in a landscape, c1720, 14¼in (36cm) diam.
£1,450–1,700 / €2,100–2,500
$2,600–3,100 ⚒ S(Am)

A pair of Kakiemon-style saucers, 18thC, 5½in (14cm) diam.
£2,250–2,500 / €3,300–3,650
$4,050–4,550 ⊞ McP

A pair of plates, by Kinkozan, each decorated with a woman in a garden, gilt and impressed marks, Meiji period, 1868–1911, 26¾in (68cm) diam.
£590–700 / €860–1,000
$1,050–1,250 ⚒ SWO

An Imari charger, Meiji period, 1868–1911, 26¾in (68cm) diam.
£2,750–3,300 / €4,000–4,800
$5,000–6,000 ⚒ LJ

A pair of Imari dishes, decorated with flowers and birds, late 19thC, 12¾in (32.5cm) diam.
£350–420 / €510–610
$630–760 ⚒ WW

◄ **A pair of Arita chargers,** c1880, 18in (45.5cm) diam.
£210–250 / €310–370
$380–450 ⚒ SWO

◄ **A set of eight plates,** decorated with butterflies and convolvulus, c1900, 8½in (21.5cm) diam.
£120–140 / €175–200
$220–250 ⚒ WW

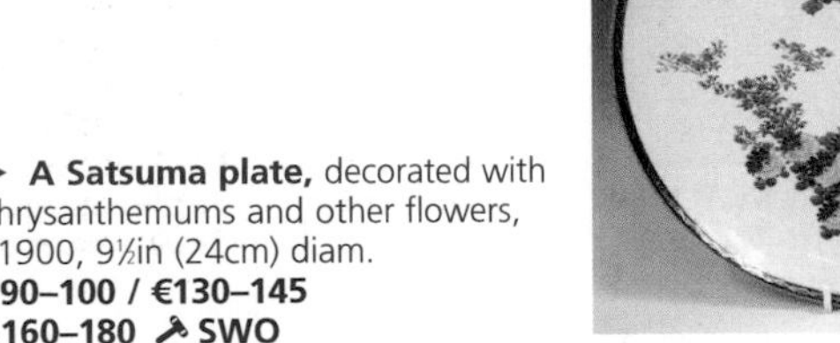

► **A Satsuma plate,** decorated with chrysanthemums and other flowers, c1900, 9½in (24cm) diam.
£90–100 / €130–145
$160–180 ⚒ SWO

Koros

A Satsuma *koro* and cover, decorated with warriors and a maiden, with *shishi* handles, finial and feet, signed, c1875, 6¾in (17cm) wide.
£350–420 / €510–610
$630–760 ⚒ SWO

A Satsuma tripod *koro* and cover, by Yabu Meizan, painted with a shipping scene, on elephant-head feet, cover restored, gilt four character mark, Meiji period, 1868–1911, 4¾in (12cm) high.
£2,800–3,350
€4,100–4,900
$5,100–6,100 ⚒ RTo

A Makuzu Kozan *koro*, in the form of a lotus pod on a lotus leaf, applied with a kingfisher, signed, impressed seal, late Meiji Period, 1868–1911, 4¾in (12cm) high.
£4,800–5,700
€7,000–8,300
$8,700–10,300 ⚒ S

A pair of Kutani *koros* and covers, painted with birds among flowers, with lion finials, ten character mark, Meiji period, 1868–1911, 13in (33cm) high.
£590–700 / €860–1,000
$1,050–1,250 ⚒ GIL

Vases

◄ An Imari vase and cover, decorated with pine trees, peonies and a temple among clouds, slight damage 17thC, 29in (73.5cm) high.
£2,350–2,800
€3,450–4,100
$4,250–5,100 ⚒ DORO

An Imari vase, painted with flowers, slight damage, converted for electricity, 19thC, 21in (53.5cm) high.
£190–220 / €270–320
$340–400 ⚒ G(L)

A pair of Imari vases, each decorated with panels of birds and flowers, restored, 18thC, 12½in (32cm) high.
£700–840 / €1,000–1,200
$1,250–1,500 ⚒ DN

A pair of Imari vases, painted with fruiting foliage, 19thC, 17¼in (44cm) high, on later mahogany stands.
£1,000–1,200
€1,450–1,750
$1,800–2,150 ⚒ DN(BR)

A pair of Seto porcelain vases, by Gawamoto, signed, dated 1881, 12¼in (31cm) high.
£230–270 / €340–390
$420–490 ⚒ SWO

A Hirado Mikawachi vase and cover, painted with panels of landscapes, the cover surmounted with a *shishi*, Meiji period, 1868–1911, 19½in (49.5cm) high.
£1,000–1,200
€1,450–1,750
$1,800–2,150 ⚒ RTo
Mikawachi is a famous Hirado factory. It is still in production today.

◄ A pair of Seto vases, painted with birds and flowers, c1890, 19¾in (50cm) high.
£820–980
€1,200–1,450
$1,500–1,750
⚒ SWO

Seto

The town of Seto has had a long tradition of ceramic manufacture. By the end of the 19th century there were 434 kilns operating, with 109 of these producing porcelain. Large numbers of stoneware plates were produced in the 'Shino' style, with very sketchy painting in iron brown. Seto also became famous for its celadon wares and green-glazed pottery, but porcelain remained the major part of Seto's production.

◄ **A Satsuma vase,** decorated with butterflies above wild flowers, signed 'Hododa Satsuma Yaki' four character mark, Meiji period, 1868–1911, 6¼in (16cm) high.
£470–560 / €690–820
$850–1,000 WW

► **A pair of porcelain vases,** painted with birds and flowers, Meiji period, 1868–1911, 22in (56cm) high.
£210–250 / €310–370
$380–450 RTo

A Kutani vase, applied with three phoenix, c1900, 14½in (36.5cm) high, on a metal stand.
£165–195 / €240–280
$300–350 WW

A pair of Kutani porcelain vases, decorated with birds and flowers, c1900, 11¾in (30cm) high.
£175–210 / €260–310
$320–380 DMC

► **A pair of Kutani vases,** painted with figures, birds and flowers, character marks, c1900, 11¾in (30cm) high.
£210–250 / €310–370
$380–450 WW

Miscellaneous

◄ **A Kakiemon-style figure of a lady,** late 17thC, 9½in (24cm) high.
£6,200–7,400
€9,100–10,800
$11,200–13,400 S

► **An Imari water filter,** decorated with the Seven Lucky Gods, slight damage, late 17thC, 16¾in (42.5cm) high.
£2,250–2,700
€3,300–3,950
$4,050–4,900 S(Am)

An Arita mug, applied with discs, handle missing, c1700, 5½in (14cm) high.
£120–140 / €175–200
$220–250 WW

An Arita teapot and cover, decorated with birds and flowers, slight damage, c1700, 4in (10cm) high.
£1,050–1,200 / €1,550–1,750
$1,900–2,150 G&G

A Satsuma tea service, comprising nine pieces, with handles and finials in the form of dragons, slight damage, Meiji period, 1868–1911, teapot 7in (18cm) high.
£560–670 / €820–980
$1,000–1,200 DORO

Arita

The town of Arita on Honshu Island is famous for being the centre of Japanese porcelain production. Most Japanese export porcelain was made here during the 17th, 18th and 19th centuries but was usually known in the west as Imari, after the port from where it was shipped.

East Asian Ceramics

◀ **A celadon bowl,** Korean, Koryo Dynasty, 11th–12thC, 7¼in (18.5cm) diam.
£2,850–3,400
€4,150–4,950
$5,200–6,200
S(O)

A *punchong* bowl, Korean, Choson Dynasty, 15th–16thC, 7¼in (18.5cm) diam.
£5,400–6,500 / €7,900–9,500
$9,800–11,800 S(O)

A celadon box and cover, incised with a floral medallion, Korean, Koryo Dynasty, 12thC, 1½in (4cm) diam.
£9,000–10,800 / €13,100–15,800
$16,300–19,500 S(O)

◀ **A porcelain brush holder,** carved and pierced with overlapping leaves, Korean, Choson Dynasty, c1800, 5in (12.5cm) high.
£12,000–14,000 / €17,500–21,000
$21,700–26,100 S

A *punchong* dish, inlaid with a central medallion of florets, Korean, Chosun Dynasty, 15th–16thC, 6¾in (17cm) diam.
£2,000–2,400 / €2,900–3,500
$3,600–4,350 S(O)

A glazed jar and cover, Korean, Chosun Dynasty, 16th–17thC, 7¼in (18.5cm) high.
£3,100–3,700 / €4,550–5,400
$5,600–6,700 S(O)

A *punchong* Cocoon vase, Korean, Choson Dynasty, 15th–16thC, 10½in (26.5cm) diam.
£2,150–2,550 / €3,150–3,700
$3,900–4,600 S(O)

The items in this section have been arranged in alphabetical order by country.

A vase, decorated with a dragon among clouds, Korean, Choson Dynasty, c1800, 7¾in (19.5cm) high.
£1,400–1,650 / €2,050–2,400
$2,550–3,000 S

◀ **A pair of vases,** painted with dragons and clouds, Korean, 19thC, 20½in (52cm) high.
£2,850–3,400 / €4,150–4,950
$5,200–6,200 S

▶ **A *wucai* bowl,** painted with peonies, Vietnamese, possibly 17thC, 14¾in (37.5cm) diam.
£760–910 / €1,100–1,300
$1,400–1,650 L

A pot, from the Hoi An hoard, Vietnamese, 1450–1500, 1½in (4cm) high.
£50–55 / €75–85
$90–100 ⊞ McP

Glass

With changing attitudes towards decoration and collecting, lack of confidence in the market and the consequences of the World Trade Center attacks in New York, the antiques trade has changed during the last ten years. Times are now difficult for many dealers and auction houses and this, in turn, affects collectors.

During the early 1990s, it was normal for the major English auction houses to hold several glass sales each year which meant there was a lot of choice, perhaps not as much as twenty years before, but more than today.

Recently, however, the number of London sales with a glass section has been for the most part very small as has the number of glasses offered in them. With such a dearth of items it is inevitable that the hunt should be widened which means that some people may be looking to the Continent to satisfy their requirements. Sales in Amsterdam have attracted English clients for years and some have even been prepared to make longer journeys to Germany, Spain and Italy. Now Paris seems to be exerting an influence, presumably because the journey on Eurostar is so direct and, relatively speaking, short.

Some interesting pieces have appeared in general sales there, notably an early 18th-century Moghul glass vase which sold for more than £69,000 / €100,000 / $125,000.

Catalogued sales in Paris regularly offer Roman and Islamic as well as early Continental glass, although good 19th-century pieces can also be found. Those searching for English glass would in general be disappointed but this may change.

There were two important sales of glass in Paris recently where rare items, including a few English pieces, were sold. There was international interest and high prices were achieved, with only a very small percentage of lots unsold.

It will be interesting to see if the trend continues, if it does, it could influence a change in direction in English collecting, which has been dominated for many years by English glass. Most collectors have tended to regard foreign glass with some caution and certainly the less important items do not sell easily. However, early pieces that are striking, well engraved and highly complex do. Collectors are prepared to pay for something rare. In the past it had to be English, but now it seems that some collectors may be looking for quality and rarity regardless of where it originates.

Brian Watson

Ale, Spirit & Wine Glasses

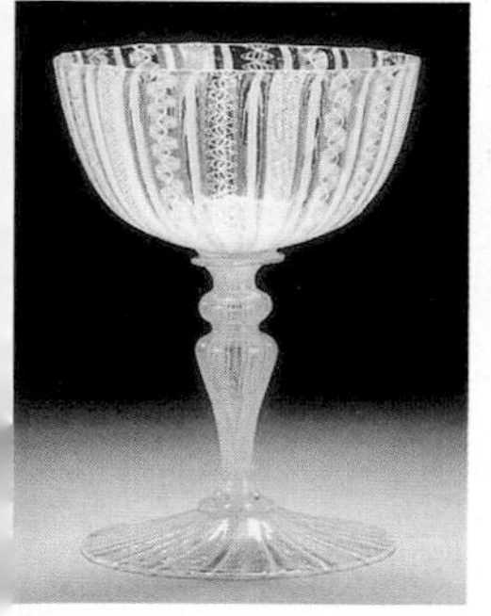

A *façon de Venise* *latticinio* goblet, the bowl above a hollow knop and inverted baluster stem, with a basal collar over a conical foot, Italian/Lowlands, 16th–17thC, 5½in (14cm) high.
£2,150–2,550
€3,150–3,700
$3,900–4,600 ⚒ S

◄ **A *façon de Venise* wine glass,** the bowl with an everted rim, on an oviform stem with a basal collar and conical foot, Italian/Lowlands, 16th–17thC, 6¾in (17cm) high.
£1,050–1,250
€1,550–1,850
$1,900–2,250 ⚒ S

► **A *façon de Venise* ice-glass drinking vessel,** the bell bowl with lobes to the lower half, on a wrythen-ribbed multi-knopped stem with a flared rib-moulded foot, Italian/Lowlands, 16th–17thC, 5½in (14cm) high.
£3,100–3,700
€4,550–5,400
$5,600–6,700 ⚒ S

► **A Bohemian enamelled and gilt graduated goblet,** the waisted upper section with an everted rim above five graduated bulbs over a collar, on a folded conical foot, 1575–1625, 8in (20.5cm) high.
£3,000–3,600
€4,400–5,300
$5,400–6,500 ⚒ S

Façon de Venise

The term *façon de Venise,* meaning 'in the style of Venice', is applied to high-quality glassware made throughout Europe during the 16th and 17th centuries, often by emigrant Venetian glassmakers. Generally it refers to thin soda metal drinking glasses and other vessels, some of which are patterned with white *lattimo* threads. Elaborate handles were sometimes applied. Goblets with such handles are known as winged.

◄ A *façon de Venise* **wine glass,** the bowl with an everted rim, on a flattened knop above an oviform stem with a basal knop on a conical foot, Spanish/ north Italian, 16th–17thC, 4¾in (12cm) high.
£1,200–1,400
€1,750–2,050
$2,150–2,550 ⚒ **S**

A ***façon de Venise*** **wine glass,** the flared bowl with a folded rim, on an inverted baluster stem flanked by a ball knop and basal knop, over a conical foot, Italian, c1600, 5¼in (13.5cm) high.
£3,000–3,600
€4,400–5,300
$5,400–6,500 ⚒ **S**

A wine glass, the bowl inset with *lattimo* threads, Spanish, probably Barcelona, c1600, 7¼in (18.5cm) high.
£2,600–3,100
€3,800–4,550
$4,700–5,600 ⚒ **S**

A Bonhomme Glassworks ***façon de Venise*** **wine glass,** the bell bowl on a stem with three knops and three rings, on a folded foot, Belgian, Liège, 1650–1700, 17in (28cm) high.
£12,300–14,700
€18,000–21,500
$22,300–26,600 ⚒ **SLh**
This rare early wine glass is very fragile – few have survived.

A baluster goblet, the funnel bowl with a solid base on an inverted baluster stem with a basal knop and a folded conical foot, slight damage, c1700, 8¾in (22cm) high.
£4,200–5,000
€6,100–7,300
$7,600–9,100 ⚒ **S**

A ***façon de Venise*** **goblet,** the rib-moulded conical bowl with an everted rim, on a basal collar and conical foot, the multi-knopped stem applied with scrolls, probably Lowlands, 17thC, 6¼in (16cm) high.
£1,550–1,850
€2,250–2,700
$2,800–3,350 ⚒ **S**

A toastmaster's glass, the conical bowl on a ball knop, with a tear and folded foot, c1710, 4½in (11.5cm) high.
£1,650–1,850
€2,400–2,700
$3,000–3,350 ⊞ **BrW**

A baluster wine glass, the bowl above a triple-annular knop and teared section, with a basal knop and folded conical foot, c1715, 6¼in (16cm) high.
£1,650–1,950
€2,400–2,850
$3,000–3,550 ⚒ **S**

Condition

The condition is absolutely vital when assessing the value of an antique. Damaged pieces on the whole appreciate much less than perfect examples. However, a rare desirable piece may command a high price even when damaged.

◄ **A baluster wine glass,** the trumpet bowl on a knopped stem, 1720–30, 6¾in (17cm) high.
£590–700 / €860–1,000
$1,050–1,250 ⚒ **WW**

A Bohemian glass goblet, the facet-cut bowl with an engraved border, the knop and stem with coloured twists, 1720–25, 5½in (14cm) high.
£290–340 / €420–500
$520–620 ⚒ **DORO**

GLASS

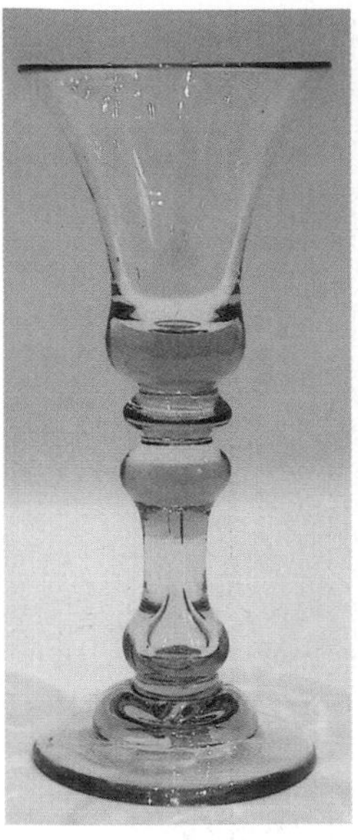

A baluster wine glass, the bell bowl on an annular knop above a teared dumbbell section and domed foot, c1725, 6¼in (16cm) high.
£1,350–1,500
€1,950–2,200
$2,450–2,700 ⊞ GS

A Kit-Kat baluster wine glass, on a folded foot, c1730, 6in (15cm) high.
£450–500 / €660–730
$810–900 ⊞ JHa
These glasses are so-called as they are somewhat similar to those in Sir Geoffrey Kneller's early 18th-century paintings of the Kit-Kat club in London.

► A lead glass toasting flute, c1730, 8in (20.5cm) high.
£310–350 / €450–510
$560–630 ⊞ JHa

A Potsdam cut goblet and cover, with gilt and engraved decoration, the faceted stem with air beads between a gilt knop and a plain section, the cover with a faceted finial between gilt knops, German, 1725–35, 10½in (26.5cm) high.
£3,350–4,000
€4,900–5,800
$6,100–7,200 ⚒ S

► A baluster cordial glass, the bell bowl above a collar, the stem with a central swelling and tear extending into a basal knop and conical foot, c1730, 5¾in (14.5cm) high.
£1,050–1,250
€1,550–1,850
$1,900–2,250 ⚒ S

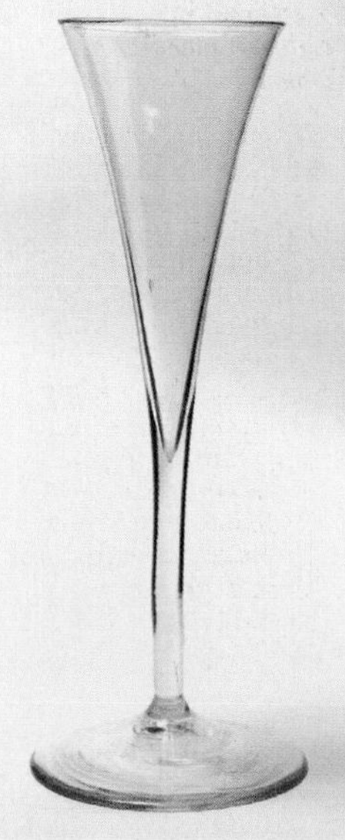

A baluster wine glass, the bell bowl above a double-inverted stem and a plain foot, c1730, 7in (18cm) high.
£830–930 / €1,200–1,350
$1,500–1,700 ⊞ BrW

A baluster wine glass, the bell bowl on a teared inverted stem and folded foot, c1730, 6in (15cm) high.
£720–800 / €1,000–1,150
$1,300–1,450 ⊞ GS

A Newcastle light baluster glass, with floral engraving, c1740, 7in (18cm) high.
£1,150–1,300
€1,700–1,900
$2,050–2,350 ⊞ JHa
This type of glass was originally believed to have been made in the northeast of England around 1730 to 1755. It is distinguished by the lightness of the glass from which it is made. The stems often had knops with tears in them to create the impression of light within the stem. They may well have been made in Holland where high-quality engraving was carried out at this time.

◄ A baluster wine glass, the stem with three knops, on a folded foot, c1730, 5in (12.5cm) high.
£270–300 / €390–440
$490–540 ⊞ JHa

An ale glass, with a ribbed bowl and folded foot, c1730, 8in (20.5cm) high.
£190–210 / €270–300
$340–380 ⊞ JHa

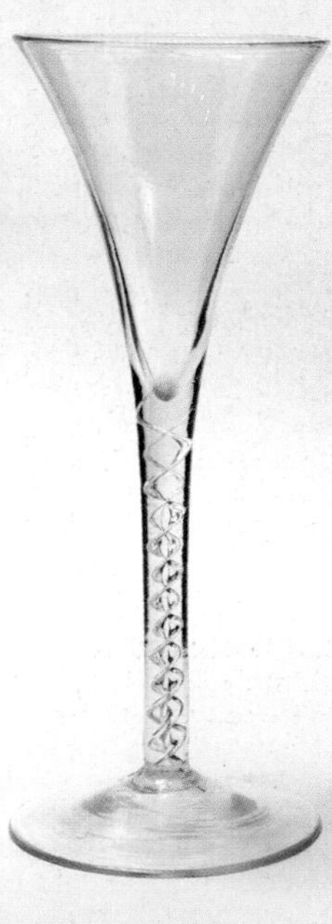

A wine glass, the drawn trumpet bowl on a mercury twist stem, c1740, 8in (20.5cm) high.
£500–550 / €720–800
$900–1,000 ⊞ JHa

► A soda glass, with a drawn trumpet and multi-spiral air-twist stem, c1745, 7in (18cm) high.
£170–190 / €250–280
$300–350 ⊞ JHa
If made in lead glass, this type of glass would cost around £350 €500 / $630.

A wine glass, the drawn trumpet bowl above a basal knop on a folded foot, c1740, 3½in (9cm) high.
£155–175 / €230–260
$280–320 ⊞ BrW

A wine glass, the bowl engraved with a flower and a bird, on a plain stem, c1740, 6in (15cm) high.
£190–210 / €270–300
$340–380 ⊞ JHa

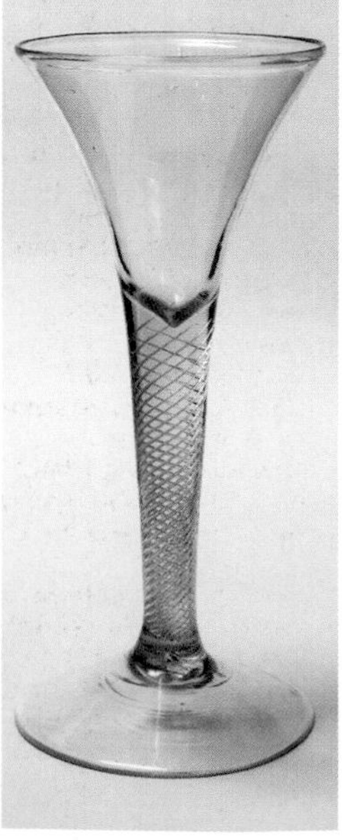

A baluster wine glass, the bell bowl on a plain stem with a basal knop, above a teared knop and domed foot, c1740, 6½in (16.5cm) high.
£1,400–1,600
€2,050–2,350
$2,550–2,900 ⊞ GS

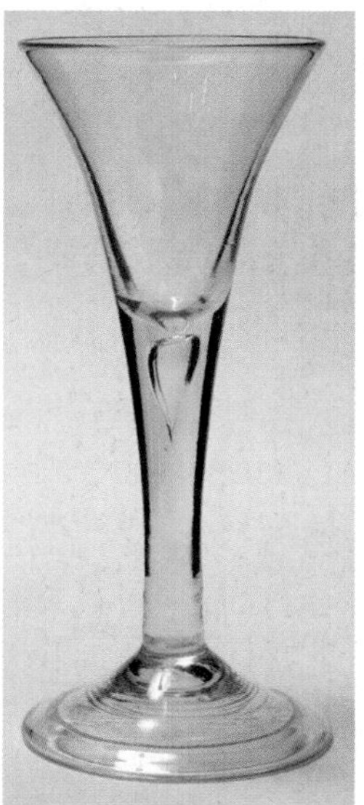

A wine glass, with a drawn trumpet bowl, the stem with a tear, on a folded foot, c1740, 6in (15cm) high.
£190–210 / €270–300
$340–380 ⊞ JHa

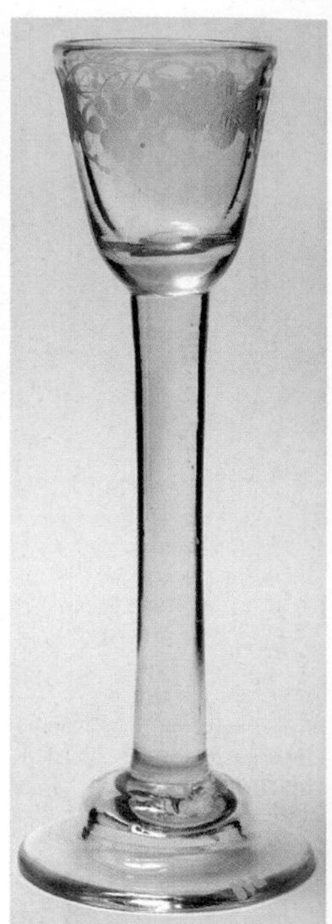

A cordial glass, with grape and vine engraving, on a helmet domed foot, Irish, c1740, 7in (18cm) high.
£1,600–1,800
€2,350–2,600
$2,900–3,250 ⊞ JHa

A goblet, the bell bowl on a moulded stem and a domed folded foot, 18thC, 7½in (19cm) high.
£590–700 / €860–1,000
$1,050–1,250 ⚒ WW

Soda metal and lead glass

Examples of most styles of 18th-century English drinking glasses can be found in soda metal, but they are less popular among collectors than those made of lead glass because of their lightness and, to some people, 'wrong' feel. Soda glass was produced in Holland, but was also made in England in the 19th and 20th centuries and sold as Dutch. Such pieces are consequently cheaper than their lead counterparts.

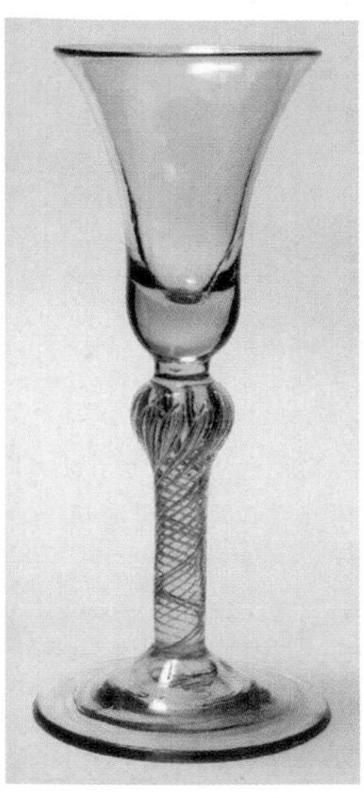

A wine glass, the bell bowl on a multi-spiral air-twist stem with shoulder knop, c1745, 7in (18cm) high.
£450–500 / €660–730
$810–900 ⊞ JHa

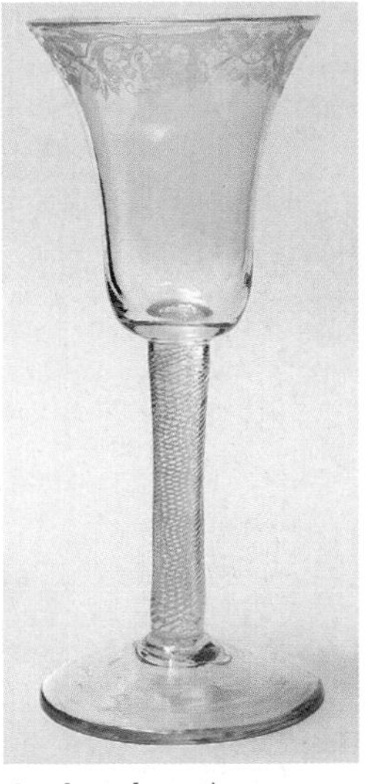

A wine glass, the engraved bell bowl on a multi-spiral air-twist stem, c1745, 8in (20.5cm) high.
£540–600 / €790–880
$980–1,100 ⊞ JHa

A wine glass, the bell bowl on a multi-spiral air-twist stem, c1745, 6in (15cm) high.
£300–340 / €440–500
$540–610 ⊞ JHa

A wine glass, the dimple-moulded bowl on a double series air-twist stem, 18thC, 6¼in (16cm) high.
£590–700 / €860–1,000
$1,050–1,250 ⚒ WW

◄ **A wine glass,** the bowl with engraved diaper decoration on a facet-cut stem, 18thC, 4in (10cm) high.
£105–120 / €155–175
$190–220 ⊞ KET

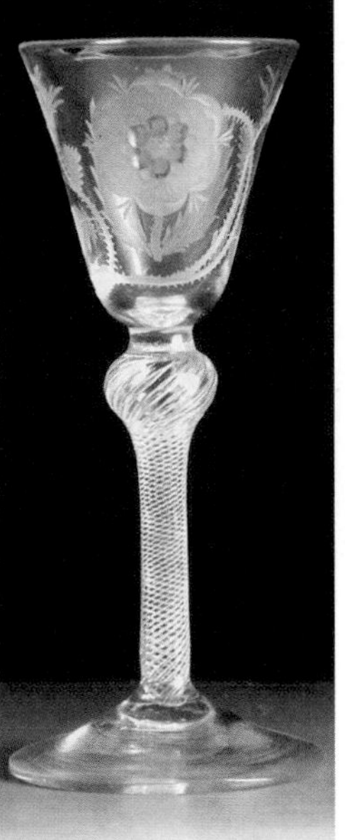

A Jacobite-style wine glass, engraved with a rose and thistle, on a knopped multi-spiral air-twist stem, 18thC, 6¼in (16cm) high.
£1,300–1,550
€1,900–2,250
$2,350–2,800 ⚒ WW

◄ **A goblet,** one side engraved with a motto and dated 1720, the reverse with a medallion and a recumbent stag, German, 18thC, 10in (25.5cm) high.
£520–620 / €760–900
$940–1,100 ⚒ DORO

Miller's Compares

I. A Jacobite wine glass, the funnel bowl engraved with a portrait of a woman, set on a double-knopped multi-spiral air-twist stem and conical foot, c1750, 6in (15cm) high.
£8,400–10,000
€12,300–14,600
$15,200–18,100 ⚒ S

This portrait is ascribed to Betty Burke, the name adopted by Prince Charles Edward Stuart while in disguise as Flora MacDonald's maidservant – or as Flora MacDonald herself – on his journey from the Outer Hebrides to the island of Skye pursued by the forces of George II.

II. A Jacobite wine glass, the funnel bowl engraved with a portrait of Prince Charles Edward Stuart in Highland dress, inscribed 'Audentior Ibo', the reverse with a rose, bud and thistle spray, on a double-knopped multi-spiral air-twist stem, c1750, 6in (15cm) high.
£4,800–5,700
€7,000–8,300
$8,700–10,300 ⚒ S

Both Item I and Item II are very rare glasses and would be highly sought after by collectors. However, Item I is more appealing owing to the subject matter of the portrait, and it also has a more desirable conical foot rather than a flat foot as in Item II.

A goblet, the drawn trumpet bowl on a stem with a tear, on a folded conical foot, mid-18thC, 9in (23cm) high.
£290–340 / €420–500
$520–620 ⚒ DN

A wine glass, with a cut bowl and facet-cut stem, c1750, 5in (12.5cm) high.
£500–550 / €730–810
$900–1,000 ⊞ JHa

Bowl shapes

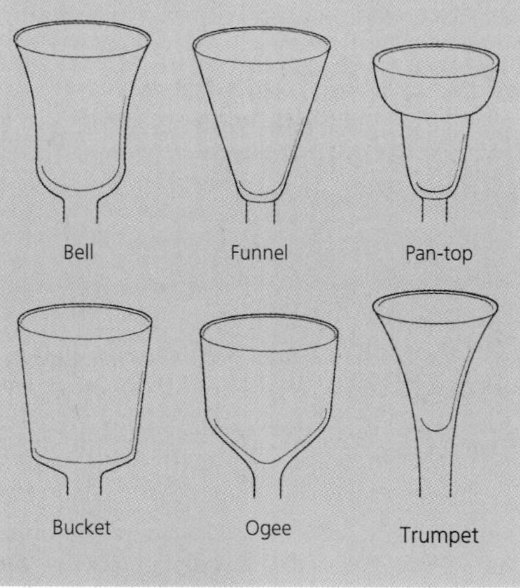

A wine glass, the part cushion-moulded bowl on an incised twist stem, mid-18thC, 6¼in (16cm) high.
£540–640 / €790–930
$980–1,150 ⚒ WW

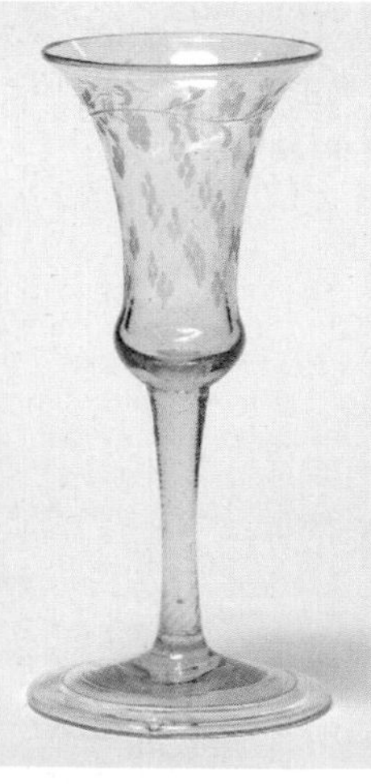

A wine glass, the bell bowl engraved with flowers, the incised stem on a conical and folded foot, Continental, c1750, 6½in (16.5cm) high.
£440–490 / €640–720
$800–890 ⊞ GLAS

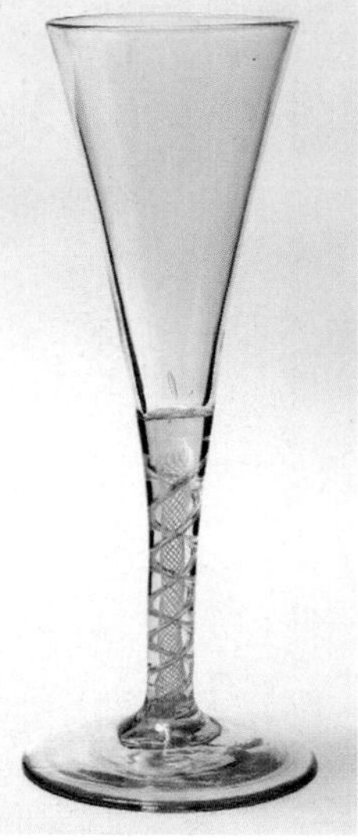

A wine flute, the mixed-twist stem with air and opaque twists, c1750, 7½in (19cm) high.
£720–800 / €1,050–1,200
$1,300–1,450 ⊞ JHa

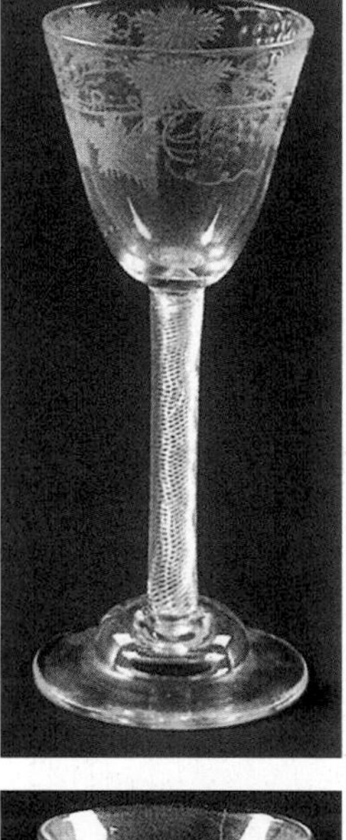

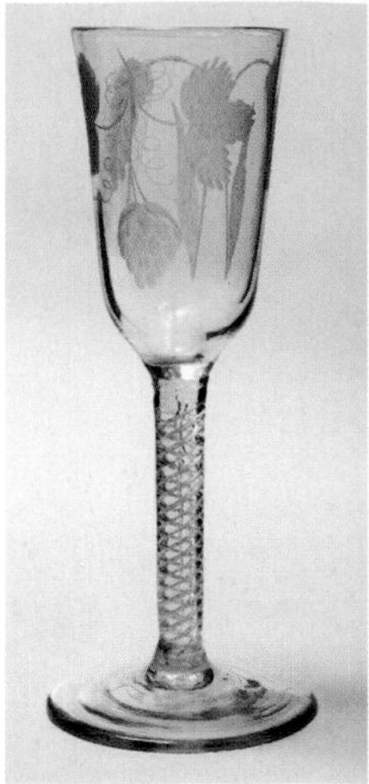

An ale glass, the ogee bowl engraved with hops and barley, on a double-series air-twist stem, c1750, 8in (20.5cm) high.
£800–900 / €1,150–1,300
$1,450–1,600 ⊞ JHa

◄ **A wine glass,** the funnel bowl polished and engraved with a fruiting vine, on a spiral-twist stem and domed foot, mid-18thC, 6in (15cm) high.
£440–520 / €640–760
$800–940 ⚒ DN

A wine glass, the funnel bowl engraved with a fruiting vine border, on a multi-spiral air-twist stem with a swollen knop, c1750, 5½in (14cm) high.
£610–680 / €890–990
$1,100–1,250 ⊞ BrW

◄ **A wine glass,** the bell bowl over a double-knopped spiral twist stem and conical foot, c1750, 6½in (16.5cm) high.
£370–440 / €540–640
$670–800 ⚒ DN

GLASS

A cordial glass, the funnel bowl on a multi-spiral air-twist stem and domed foot, c1750, 6¼in (16cm) high.
£1,300–1,550
€1,900–2,250
$2,350–2,800 S
This is a rare glass with an unusually broad stem.

► **A wine glass,** the bell bowl on a multi-spiral air-twist stem with a teared basal knop, on a domed and folded foot, c1755, 6½in (16.5cm) high.
£850–950 / €1,250–1,400
$1,500–1,700 GS

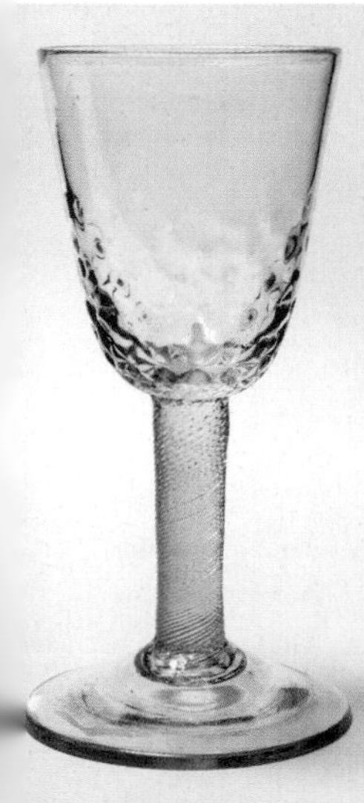

A wine glass, the hammer-moulded bowl on an incised twist stem, c1760, 6in (15cm) high.
£800–900 / €1,150–1,300
$1,450–1,600 JHa

► **A wine glass,** the ogee bowl with basal moulded flutes and engraved with fruiting vine, on a double-series opaque twist stem, c1760, 5in (12.5cm) high.
£380–430 / €550–630
$690–780 BrW

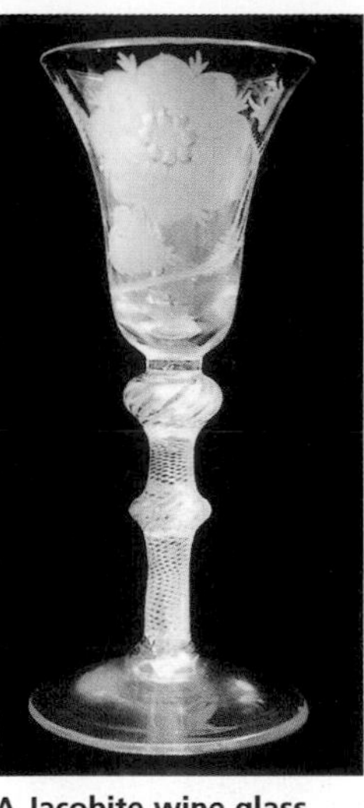

A Jacobite wine glass, the bowl engraved with a rose and two buds, the reverse with a moth, on a multi-spiral air-twist stem with two knops, on a conical foot, c1755, 7in (18cm) high.
£1,550–1,750
€2,250–2,550
$2,800–3,150 GS

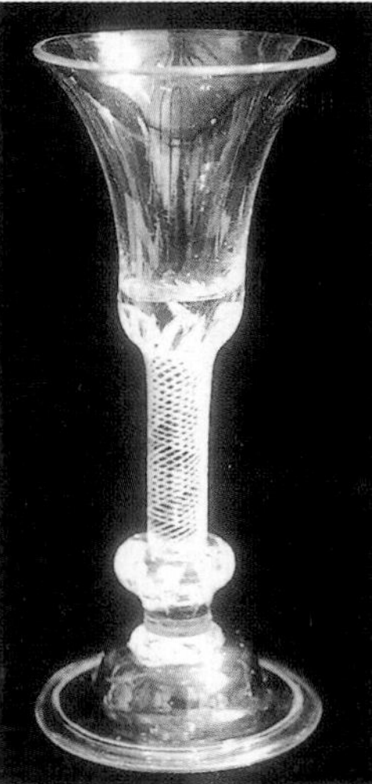

18th-century twisted stems

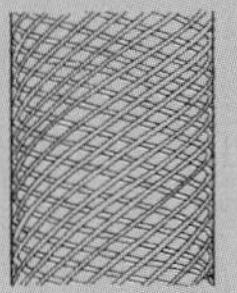

Multi-spiral

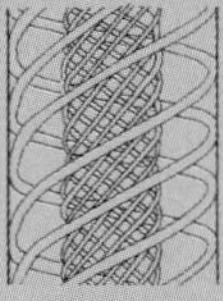

Double-series twist

Multi corkscrew

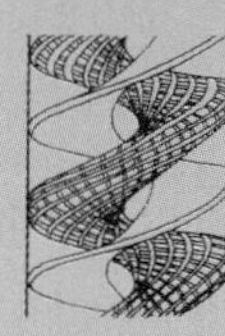

Spiral gauze & flat tape

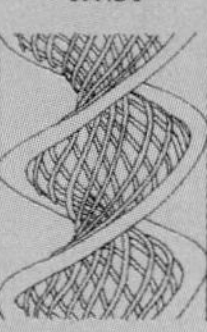

Lace-twist outline

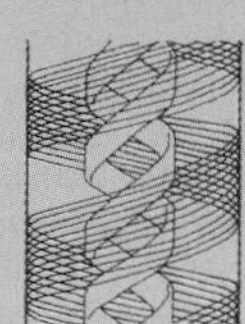

Double-series twist with 12-ply band

A tinted wine glass, the cup-shaped bowl on a wrythen-moulded stem and conical foot with trailed threading, c1760, 5¼in (13.5cm) high.
£1,200–1,400
€1,750–2,050
$2,150–2,550 S

A wine glass, the ogee bowl on a knopped multi-spiral twist stem and a conical foot, c1760, 6¼in (16cm) high.
£410–490 / €600–720
$740–890 DN

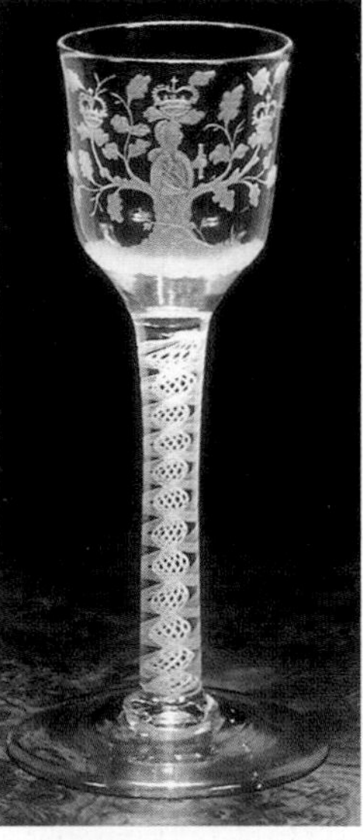

A Jacobite 'Boscobel Oak' wine glass, the ogee bowl engraved with a portrait of a man portrayed as the trunk of an oak tree, the branches supporting three crowns, on a double-series opaque-twist stem and conical foot, c1760, 6in (15cm) high.
£7,800–9,300
€11,400–13,600
$14,100–16,800 S
The tree probably represents the so-called Boscobel Oak in the hollow trunk of which King Charles II hid from the Parliamentarian forces after the Battle of Worcester in 1651.
The trunk of the oak may represent the Church as the foundation of the state, supported by three crowns representing the kingdoms of England, Scotland and Ireland.
The oak tree, and in particular the oak leaf, remained a popular symbol of the Stuart cause.

A wine glass, the bowl engraved with a tulip border, on an incised twist stem, c1760, 5in (12.5cm) high.
£630–700 / €930–1,050 $1,100–1,250 ⊞ JHa

A Beilby enamelled goblet, the bucket bowl painted in opaque enamel with a vine, the reverse with a butterfly, on a later opaque twist stem and folded and domed foot, c1765, 8in (20.5cm) high.
£900–1,050 / €1,300–1,500 $1,650–1,900 ⚒ S
This is a good example of the reduction in value of a piece that is not completely original. The appeal of this goblet is its beautiful decoration – the stem and foot are now merely there for support.

A wine glass, on a double-series opaque-twist stem with a knop, c1765, 7in (18cm) high.
£400–450 / €580–660 $720–820 ⊞ JHa

A wine glass, the funnel bowl on a stem with a canary-yellow core and an opaque white enamel gauze within two spiral opaque white threads, on a conical foot, c1770, 6in (15cm) high.
£13,000–15,600 €19,300–22,800 $23,900–28,200 ⚒ S
The combination of the canary-yellow and opaque white threads forming the gauze core is a particularly rare feature and accounts for the high price of this wine glass.

◀ **A set of six wine flutes,** each with an opaque-twist gauze within a pair of air-twist spirals, slight damage, c1770, 7½in (19cm) high.
£1,200–1,400 €1,750–2,050 $2,150–2,550 ⚒ S

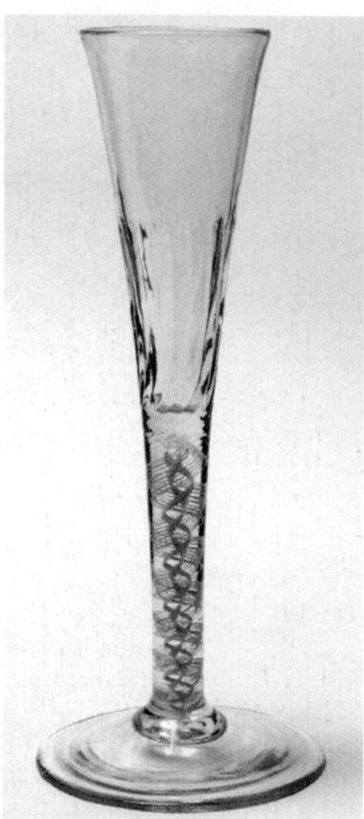

A ratafia glass, on a double-series opaque-twist stem, c1765, 7in (18cm) high.
£1,700–1,900 €2,500–2,750 $3,050–3,450 ⊞ JHa

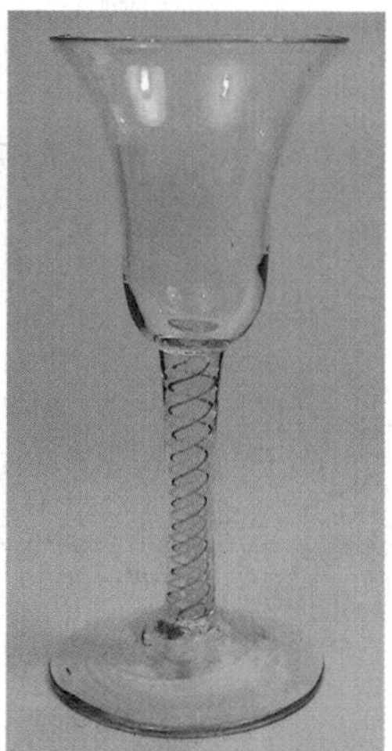

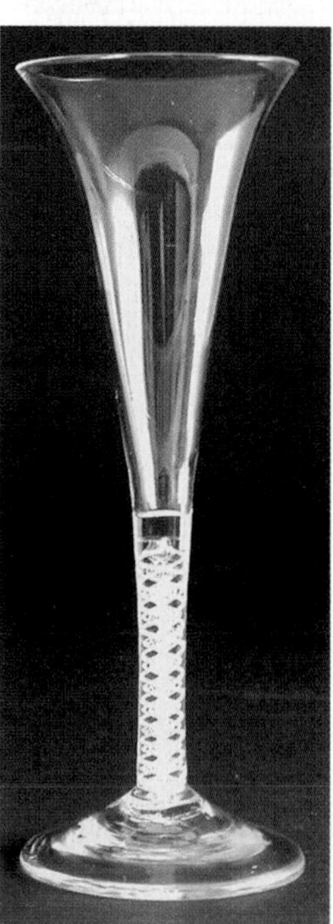

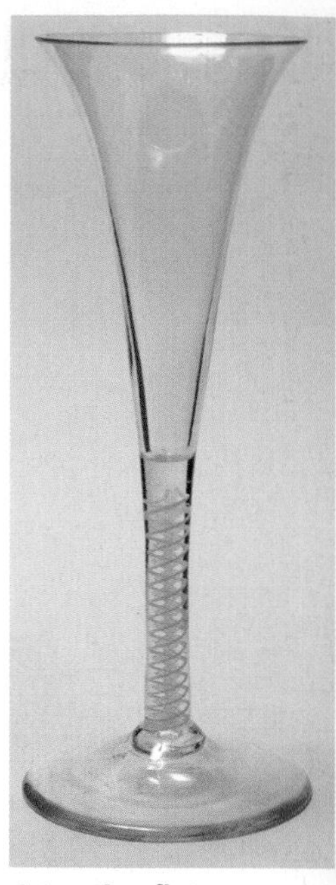

A toasting flute, on a double-series opaque-twist stem, c1765, 8in (20.5cm) high.
£670–750 / €980–1,100 $1,200–1,350 ⊞ JHa

◀ **A wine glass,** the bell bowl on a stem with two blue and one white opaque threads, c1770, 6¼in (16cm) high.
£3,550–3,950 €5,200–5,800 $6,400–7,100 ⊞ GS

A goblet, the part moulded bowl on a double-series opaque twist stem, c1770, 8in (20.5cm) high.
£290–340 / €450–500 $520–620 ⚒ WW

◀ **A wine flute,** the drawn trumpet bowl on a double-series opaque-twist stem, c1770, 7¾in (19.5cm) high.
£350–420 / €510–610 $630–760 ⚒ WW

A ship's glass, the funnel bowl on a facet-cut stem with a heavy foot, c1770, 5½in (14cm) high.
£270–300 / €390–440
$490–540 ⊞ BrW

A wine glass, the bowl engraved with a bellflower, on a double-series opaque-twist stem, 1770–80, 5¾in (14.5cm) high.
£420–500 / €610–730
$760–910 ⚒ WW

◄ **An ale glass,** the funnel bowl engraved and polished with an 'oxo' band, on a double-series opaque-twist stem, c1770, 6¾in (17.5cm) high.
£330–390 / €480–570
$600–710 ⚒ DN

An ale glass, the funnel bowl engraved with hops and barley, on a double-knopped stem and a conical foot, c1770, 8in (20.5cm) high.
£530–630 / €770–920
$960–1,150 ⚒ DN

◄ **A wine glass,** with a facet-cut bowl and stem, c1770, 6in (15cm) high.
£800–900 / €1,150–1,300
$1,450–1,600 ⊞ JHa

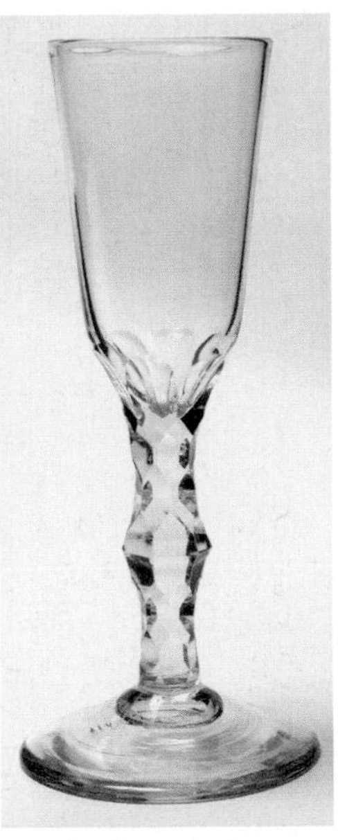

An ale glass, the facet-cut stem with a central knop, c1770, 7½in (19cm) high.
£340–380 / €500–550
$610–690 ⊞ JHa

An ale flute, the ogee bowl engraved with hops and barley, on a double-knopped multi-spiral air-twist stem and conical foot, c1770, 7½in (19cm) high.
£280–330 / €410–480
$510–600 ⚒ DN

◄ **A memorial wine glass,** the bowl engraved with lily-of-the valley and a bee, on a facet-cut stem, c1770, 6in (15cm) high.
£500–550 / €730–810
$900–1,000 ⊞ JHa

A soda glass, the bell bowl on an opaque-twist stem with shoulder knop, Dutch, c1770, 6½in (16.5cm) high.
£140–160 / €200–230
$260–290 ⊞ JHa

◄ **A wine glass,** the engraved bowl on a facet-cut stem, c1770, 6in (15cm) high.
£400–450 / €580–660
$720–820 ⊞ JHa

A wine glass, with facet-cut bowl and stem, c1770, 5in (12.5cm) high.
£170–190 / €250–280
$310–350 ⊞ JHa

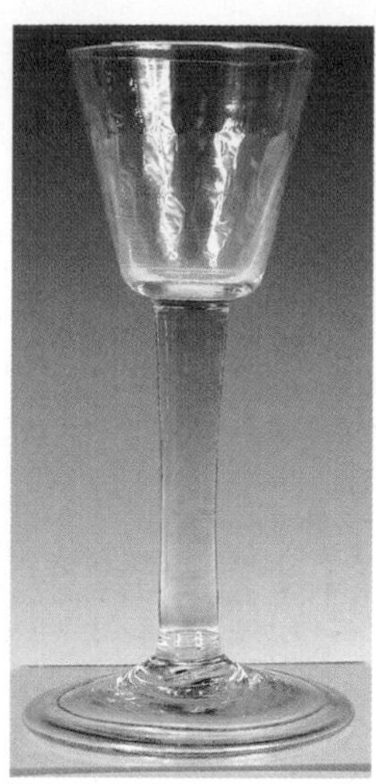

A wine glass, the funnel bowl on a plain stem and folded foot, c1790, 6in (15cm) high.
£120–140
€175–200
$220–250
⚒ SWO

A rummer, the petal-moulded bowl on a capstan stem, 1800–10, 5in (12.5cm) high.
£70–80
€100–115
$125–140 ⊞ JHa

LOCATE THE SOURCE
The source of each illustration in Miller's can be found by checking the code letters below each caption with the Key to Illustrations, pages 778–784.

A pair of rummers, with engraved ship decoration and lemon-squeezer feet, c1810, 4in (10cm) high.
£310–350 / €450–510
$560–630 ⊞ KET

A cut-glass rummer, with a barrel bowl, c1810, 5in (12.5cm) high.
£80–90 / €115–130
$145–160 ⊞ JHa

A goblet, the bowl engraved with hops and barley, on a square foot, c1810, 9in (23cm) high.
£720–800
€1,000–1,150
$1,300–1,450
⊞ KET

A rummer, with a petal-moulded bowl, c1810, 5in (12.5cm) high.
£60–70
€85–100
$110–125 ⊞ JHa

An amethyst wine glass, the stem with a central bladed knop, c1820, 5in (12.5cm) high.
£145–160 / €210–240
$260–290 ⊞ JHa

Auction or dealer?

All the pictures in our price guides originate from auction houses ⚒ and dealers ⊞. When buying at auction, prices can be lower than those of a dealer, but a buyer's premium and VAT will be added to the hammer price. Equally, when selling at auction, commission, tax and photography charges must be taken into account. Dealers will often restore pieces before putting them back on the market. Both dealers and auctioneers can provide professional advice, so it is worth researching both sources before buying or selling your antiques.

A stirrup glass, with cut lapidary knops, c1830, 7in (18cm) high.
£260–290 / €380–420
$470–520 ⊞ BrW

A rummer, with engraved decoration, dated 1836, 6in (15cm) high.
£180–200 / €260–290
$320–360 ⊞ KET

A Baccarat armorial goblet, the double-ogee bowl cut with six printies, on a faceted knopped stem and star-cut base, French, c1850, 6in (15cm) high.
£900–1,050
€1,300–1,550
$1,650–1,900 ⚒ S

A water globlet, with acid-etched decoration, c1870, 8in (20.5cm) high.
£90–100 / €130–145
$160–180 ⊞ JHa

A rummer, wheel-cut with Masonic emblems, text and initials 'W. O.', on a lemon-squeezer foot, 19thC, 5½in (14cm) high.
£430–510 / €630–740
$780–920 ⚒ Bea

A Bohemian goblet, with a castellated rim and gilt decoration, mid-19thC, 11¼in (28.5cm) high.
£190–220 / €280–320
$340–400 ⚒ SWO

A rummer, engraved with a sailing ship and monogram flanked by clover and barley, on a lemon-squeezer foot, 19thC, 4¾in (12cm) high.
£240–280 / €350–410
$430–510 ⚒ WW

A water goblet, the bowl with engraved decoration, c1860, 8in (20.5cm) high.
£120–140 / €175–200
$220–250 ⊞ JHa

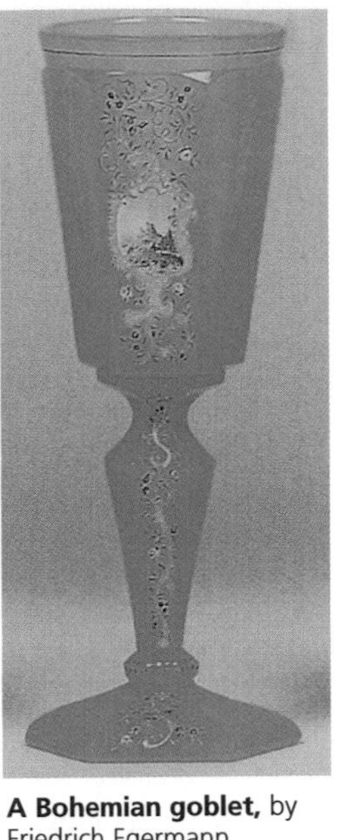

A Bohemian goblet, by Friedrich Egermann, decorated with three landscape cartouches, anchor mark and '4' to foot, c1850, 7¾in (19.5cm) high.
£640–760 / €930–1,100
$1,200–1,400 ⚒ DORO

A port glass, with engraved decoration, c1870, 4in (10cm) high.
£35–40 / €50–60
$65–75 ⊞ JHa

GLASS

A pair of Bohemian Persian-style römers, probably J. & L. Lobmeyr, each painted with flower sprays, the trumpet feet applied with prunts and painted with rosettes, crack to one base, c1880, 6½in (16.5cm) high.
£1,400–1,650 / €2,050–2,400
$2,550–3,000 ⚒ S

A Bohemian goblet, by J. & L. Lobmeyr, decorated in enamels with a coat-of-arms, applied with prunts, marked, late 19thC, 7¾in (19.5cm) high.
£600–720 / €880–1,050
$1,100–1,300 ⚒ DORO

Beakers & Tumblers

A beaker, engraved with an armorial and inscription, German, dated 1698, 5in (12.5cm) high.
£740–880 / €1,100–1,300
$1,350–1,600 ⚒ S(Am)

An opaline tumbler, decorated in enamels with Castle Howard, marked 'Richardson Vitrified', c1840, 4in (10cm) high.
£900–1,000 / €1,300–1,450
$1,600–1,800 ⊞ CB

A pair of wedding beakers, possibly by Kungsholm Glassworks, engraved with a coat-of-arms, slight damage, Swedish, 1750–1800, 3¾in (9.5cm) high.
£520–620 / €760–910
$940–1,100 ⚒ BUK

Anton Kothgasser

Anton Kothgasser (1769–1851) is best-known for his enamelled decoration of glass *Ranftbecher*, a German low beaker with its base in the form of a cogwheel, often decorated with gilding and/or enamelling. He worked as a painter and gilder at the Vienna Imperial Porcelain Factory from 1784 to 1840 and painted glass from 1812 to 1830. His meticulously painted pieces, which are usually signed, include flowers, portraits and buildings. His work is often imitated.

◄ **A Bohemian beaker,** cut with leaf and knot motifs, c1840, 4¾in (12cm) high.
£290–340
€420–500
$520–620
⚒ DORO

A beaker, by Anton Kothgasser, decorated with a band of pansies and an inscription, Austrian, Vienna, c1820, 4in (10cm) high.
£4,750–5,700
€6,900–8,300
$8,600–10,300 ⚒ DORO

A Bohemian beaker, decorated with a cartouche depicting Cupid in a parkland landscape, signed 'A. V. S.', c1900, 5in (12.5cm) high.
£470–560 / €690–820
$850–1,000 ⚒ DORO

Bottles, Carafes & Decanters

◄ **A decanter,** possibly by George Ravenscroft, with trailed 'nipt diamond waies', Anglo-Dutch, c1680, 7¼in (18.5cm) high.
£3,600–4,300 / €5,300–6,300
$6,500–7,800 ⚒ S
Several very similar part-lead flasks have survived, one of which is in the Ashmolean Museum, Oxford. Two others are in the Victorian and Albert museum in London. All three are considered to be English and attributed to the Savoy Glasshouse of George Ravenscroft. R. Charleston in *English Glass* argued that stylistically these lead glass bottles have a strong claim to being English-made but conceded that they may have Dutch origin.

A carafe, moulded with ribs, the neck with a string rim, slight damage, Dutch, late 17thC, 9¾in (25cm) high.
£2,250–2,700
€3,300–3,950
$4,050–4,900 ⚒ S

A mallet-shaped wine bottle, applied with a seal inscribed 'Henry Venn Payhembury' and dated 1735, slight damage, 8¾in (22cm) high
£2,350–2,800
€3,450–4,100
$4,250–5,100
⚒ Bea

GLASS

◀ **A mallet-shaped wine bottle,** applied with a seal inscribed 'G. Cooke Langley' and dated 1766, slight damage, 7¾in (19.5cm) high.
£2,800–3,350
€4,100–4,900
$5,100–6,100 ⚒ DN
Bottles with named and dated seals are always popular with collectors.

A decanter, with tulip cutting, c1780, 10in (25.5cm) high.
£270–300 / €390–440
$490–540 ⊞ KET

A club-shaped decanter, inscribed 'Brandy', c1780, 11in (28cm) high.
£560–630 / €820–920
$1,000–1,150 ⊞ BrW

◀ **A cruciform decanter,** the neck with a single rim, slight damage, 18thC, 11in (28cm) high.
£390–460 / €570–670
$710–830 ⚒ WW

A mallet-shaped decanter, engraved with a simulated wine label inscribed 'Claret', stopper possibly associated, c1770, 11in (28cm) high.
£1,200–1,400
€1,750–2,050
$2,150–2,550 ⚒ S

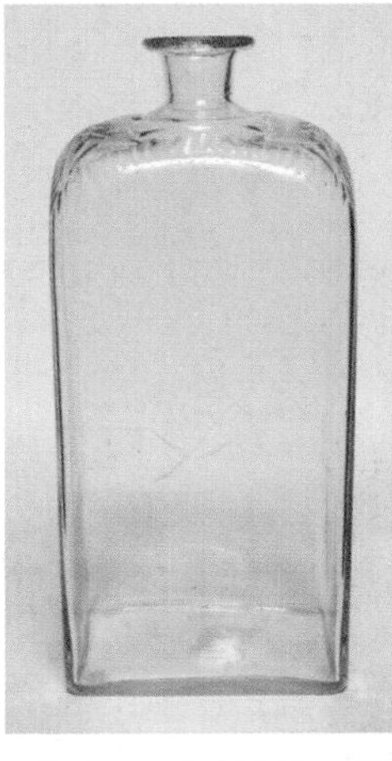

◀ **A glass spirit bottle,** with engraved decoration, Continental, late 18thC, 11in (28cm) high.
£180–200 / €260–290
$320–360 ⊞ KET

A pair of decanters, with diamond-cut decoration, c1820, 10½in (26.5cm) high.
£720–800 / €1,000–1,150
$1,300–1,450 ⊞ KET

A pair of decanters, with diamond-cut and fan-cut decoration, 19thC, 9¾in (25cm) high.
£210–250 / €310–370
$380–450 ⚒ WW

A pair of decanters, with cut decoration, c1860, 9¾in (25cm) high.
£900–1,000
€1,300–1,450
$1,600–1,800 ⊞ CB

Two pairs of decanters, with cut and moulded decoration, c1860, larger 11in (28cm) high.
£120–140 / €175–200
$220–250 ⚒ SWO
These decanters would have been part of a large suite of glass.

A ribbed bottle, c1840, 7in (18cm) high.
£220–250 / €320–370
$400–450 ⊞ KET

A set of spirit decanters, with engraved decoration, in a silver-plated stand, c1880, 16in (40.5cm) high.
£1,300–1,450
€1,900–2,100
$2,350–2,600 ⊞ BrW
The engraving on these decanters is of particularly high quality.

◄ **A pair of decanters,** decorated with raspberry prunts, c1820, 10½in (26.5cm) high.
£3,600–4,000 / €5,200–5,800
$6,500–7,200 ⊞ CB

A set of four carafes, cut with diamond bands, c1820, 7½in (19cm) high.
£200–240 / €290–350
$360–430 ⚒ G(L)

◄ **A pair of painted bottles,** decorated with ships and portraits of two admirals, damaged, Dutch, 19thC, 15½in (39.5cm) high.
£980–1,150 / €1,450–1,700
$1,750–2,100 ⚒ S(Am)
These bottles commemorate two 17th-century Dutch admirals, Egbert Kortenaar and Jan Evertsen.

A Bohemian carafe, decorated with flowers and rocaille, c1840, 10in (25.5cm) high.
£600–720 / €880–1,050
$1,100–1,300 ⚒ DORO

A Thomas Webb & Sons decanter, with lion-mask prunts above the feet, c1880, 11in (28cm) high.
£300–350 / €440–510
$540–630 ⊞ JHa

A pair of bottles, each applied with a seal inscribed 'Inner Temple', mid-19thC, 11½in (29cm) high.
£140–165 / €200–240
$250–300 ⚒ PFK

A James Powell Whitefriars decanter, c1880, 11in (28cm) high.
£300–350 / €440–510
$540–630 ⊞ JHa

Bowls

A *façon de Venise* navette-shaped coupe, gilded, on a ladder stem and folded foot, possibly Italian, Venice, late 16thC, 4¼in (11cm) high.
£26,700–32,000 / €39,000–47,000
$48,000–58,000 ⚒ SLh
This coupe is of early date and therefore highly sought after by collectors of Continental glass.

A pedestal bowl, with cut-glass decoration on a cushion-knopped stem and lemon-squeezer foot, probably Irish, c1820, 11½in (29cm) diam.
£590–700 / €860–1,000
$1,050–1,250 ⚒ TEN

A pair of dishes, with shaped Van Dyke rims, late 18thC, 9in (23cm) wide.
£630–700 / €900–1,000
$1,100–1,250 ⊞ KET

A cream bowl, with folded rim, mid-19thC, 11in (28cm) diam.
£135–150 / €195–220
$240–270 ⊞ KET

A pedestal bowl, with dentil rim and diamond-cut decoration, on a lemon-squeezer foot, Irish, c1810, 9in (23cm) diam.
£1,350–1,500 / €1,950–2,200
$2,450–2,700 ⊞ KET

An Edwardian pedestal bowl, with castellated rim and diamond-cut decoration, 14¼in (36cm) diam.
£105–125 / €155–185
$190–220 ⚒ G(L)

◄ **A set of glass ice cream bowls,** each with aventurine or *latticinio* decoration and cherub-head handles, Italian, Venice, early 20thC, 4in (10cm) diam.
£360–430 / €530–630
$650–780 ⚒ SWO

Covered Bowls & Dishes

A cut-glass covered punch bowl, stand and ladle, damaged, 19thC, bowl 10in (25.5cm) diam.
£890–1,050 / €1,300–1,550
$1,600–1,900 ⚒ BUK

◄ **A Bohemian bowl, cover and stand,** with gilt-edged rims, decorated with enamels, the stand with a rose-cut base, slight damage. c1770, 9in (23cm) diam.
£1,900–2,250 / €2,750–3,300
$3,450–4,050 ⚒ S

A cheese dish and cover, with a star-cut base, 19thC, 9in (23cm) diam.
£150–180 / €220–260
$270–320 ⚒ WW

► **A Bohemian alabaster glass bowl, cover and stand,** decorated with gilt and enamels, slight damage, c1850, 7¼in (18.5cm) diam.
£320–380 / €470–550
$580–690 ⚒ DORO

A Bohemian enamelled *milchglas* tureen, cover and stand, with a gilt rim, painted with vignettes of courting couples, slight damage, c1770, stand 12¼in (31cm) wide.
£1,550–1,850 / €2,250–2,700
$2,800–3,350 ⚒ S

GLASS

Candlesticks & Candelabra

◀ A ***façon de Venise*** **candlestick,** with diamond-point engraving, possibly Venetian, early 17thC, 5¼in (13.5cm) high.
£16,700–20,000
€24,400–29,200
$30,000–36,000 ⚒ SLh

A pair of facet-cut candlesticks, rim chips, 19thC, 8¼in (21cm) high.
£440–520 / €640–760
$800–960 ⚒ WW

A pair of candlesticks, damaged, c1850, 10in (25.5cm) high.
£110–125 / €160–185
$200–230 ⊞ GLAS

Centrepieces

A *façon de Venise craquelé* glass tazza, the stem applied with lions' masks and other motifs, Spanish, Catalonia, 1550–1600, 5¼in (13.5cm) high.
£26,000–31,000 / €38,000–45,000
$47,000–56,000 ⚒ SLh
This rare tazza is sought after by collectors of Continental glass.

▶ **A tazza,** on a Silesian stem with a folded foot, late 18thC, 9in (23cm) diam.
£360–400 / €520–580
$650–720 ⊞ KET

A tazza, on a baluster stem and folded foot, c1740, 8½in (21.5cm) high.
£470–560 / €690–820
$850–1,000 ⚒ WW

A tazza, on a Silesian stem and domed foot, 18thC, 11½in (29cm) diam.
£340–380 / €500–550
$620–690 ⊞ G&G

A cut-glass comport, on a hollow blown stem, c1870, 10in (25.5cm) diam
£220–250 / €320–370
$400–450 ⊞ KET

Flasks

◀ **A *façon de Venise* pilgrim flask,** with gilt and enamelled decoration, slight damage, Italian, Venice, late 15thC, 13in (33cm) high.
£21,200–25,500
€31,000–37,000
$56,000–46,000 ⚒ SLh
This rare and early Continental flask is desirable to collectors.

▶ **A Bohemian flask,** decorated with a lady and an inscription, 18thC, 6¼in (16cm) high.
£370–420 / €540–610
$670–760 ⊞ G&G

A gilt-metal-mounted flask, possibly by Christian Gottfried Schneider, with engraved decoration of a man and a woman among *rocailles* with diaper and foliate scrolls and a monogram, Silesian, c1760, 8½in (21.5cm) high.
£780–930 / €1,150–1,350
$1,450–1,700 ⚒ S

GLASS

Jars

A pair of jars and covers, with moulded feet, Irish, c1800, 8in (20.5cm) high.
£630–700 / €920–1,000
$1,100–1,250 ⊞ KET

A pair of Gothenburg jars and covers, Swedish, c1800, 16¼in (41.5cm) high.
£3,400–4,050 / €4,950–5,900
$6,200–7,300 ⚒ BUK

A glass storage jar, c1800, 13in (33cm) high.
£200–220 / €290–320
$360–400 ⊞ JHa

Jugs & Ewers

A Nailsea-style jug, with opaque inclusions and applied loop handle, 1800–25, 4¾in (12cm) high.
£260–310 / €380–450
$470–560 ⚒ DN

A shaft and globe claret jug, c1880, 12in (30.5cm) high.
£145–160 / €210–240
$260–290 ⊞ JHa

► A claret jug and stopper, engraved with a monogram flanked by two herons, on a domed and folded foot, Scottish, dated 1888, 14in (35.5cm) high.
£1,650–1,950
€2,400–2,850
$3,000–3,550
⚒ S

Lustres

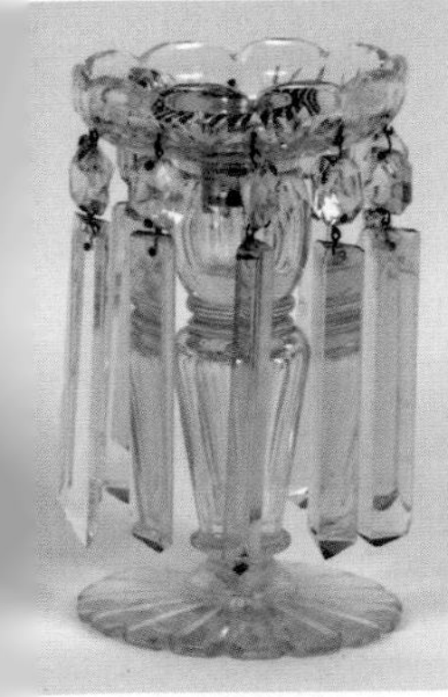

A pair of lustres, on faceted knopped tapering stems and spreading feet, damaged, 19thC, 7¾in (19.5cm) high.
£130–155 / €200–230
$240–280 ⚒ CHTR

An opaque glass lustre, gilded and enamelled with floral garlands, with clear lustre drops, c1880, 12½in (32cm) high.
£120–140 / €175–200
$220–260 ⚒ G(L)
Lustres are usually found in pairs, and as such will command a higher price.

A pair of opaline glass lustres, with gilt decoration and clear lustre drops, c1880, 10¾in (27.5cm) high.
£175–210 / €260–310
$320–380 ⚒ DA
The gilding on these lustres is very worn and this has adversely affected the price.

A pair of lustres, with gilded rims, painted with floral garlands, with clear glass drops, on spreading bases, c1890, 14½in (37cm) high.
£500–600 / €730–880
$910–1,100 ⚒ GAK

Paperweights

A Baccarat concentric mushroom paperweight, French, 1845–60, 3in (7.5cm) diam.
£3,450–3,850 / €5,000–5,600
$6,200–7,000 ⊞ SWB

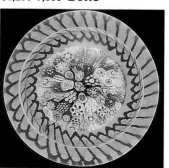

A Baccarat close-pack millefiori mushroom paperweight, the canes on a spiralling *latticinio* torsade, with a star-cut base, French, c1850, 3in (7.5cm) diam.
£960–1,150 / €1,450–1,700
$1,750–2,100 ⚒ S

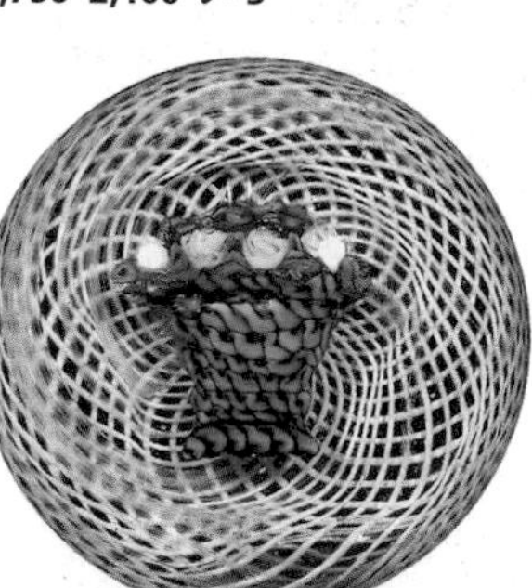

A Boston & Sandwich Glass Co paperweight, with a basket on a spiral filigree cushion, American, c1860, 2¾in (7cm) diam.
£800–880 / €1,150–1,300
$1,450–1,600 ⊞ DLP

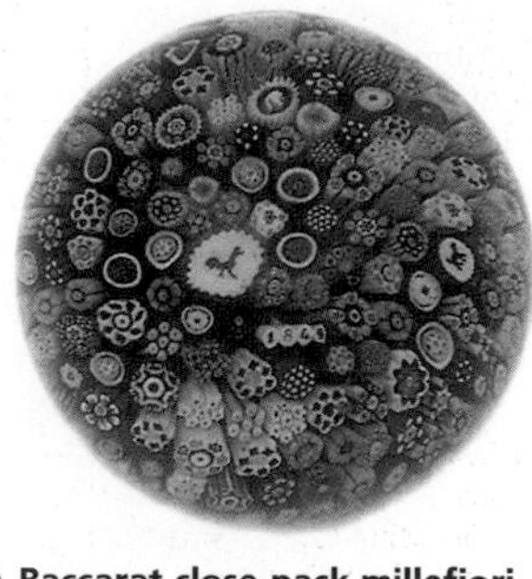

A Baccarat close-pack millefiori paperweight, French, dated 1849, 2½in (6.5cm) diam.
£1,000–1,200 / €1,450–1,750
$1,800–2,150 ⚒ Bea

A Baccarat paperweight, French, c1850, 3in (7.5cm) diam.
£600–670 / €880–980
$1,100–1,250 ⊞ G&G

A Clichy scrambled paperweight, with a white rose, slight damage, inscribed 'Lich', French, c1845, 3in (7.5cm) wide.
£2,000–2,400 / €2,900–3,500
$3,600–4,350 ⚒ WW

◄ **A Clichy millefiori paperweight,** the canes on an 'upset muslin' ground, French, c1850, 2½in (6.5cm) diam.
£720–860 / €1,050–1,250
$1,300–1,550 ⚒ DORO

A Baccarat 'fireworks' paperweight, French, c1850, 3in (7.5cm) diam.
£2,900–3,300 / €4,200–4,800
$5,200–5,900 ⊞ DLP

A Baccarat paperweight, the canes on an 'upset muslin' ground, French, mid-19thC, 3in (7.5cm) diam.
£270–320 / €390–470
$490–580 ⚒ G(L)

◄ **A Clichy concentric paperweight,** with roses, French, 1845–60, 3in (7.5cm) diam.
£900–1,000 / €1,300–1,450
$1,600–1,800 ⊞ SWB

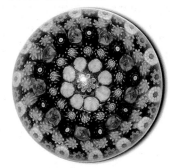

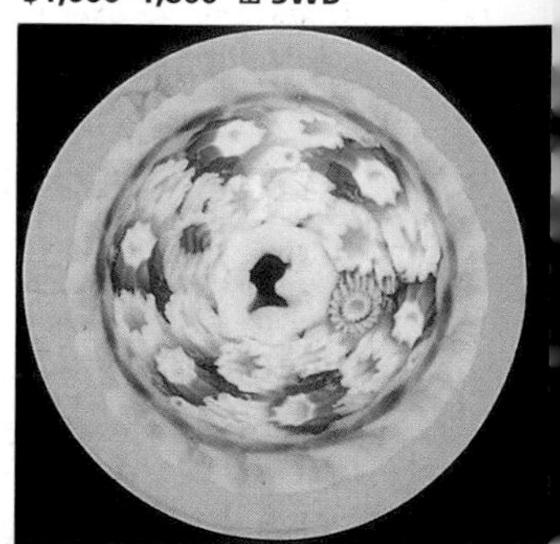

A Gillinder concentric millefiori paperweight, with a silhouette profile bust of Queen Victoria within two rows of canes and a basket, repolished, American, 19thC, 3¼in (8.5cm) diam.
£1,600–1,900 / €2,350–2,750
$2,900–3,450 ⚒ S

William Gillinder was born in England in 1823 but moved to America in 1845. After working first for the New England Glass Co he eventually set up Gillinder & Sons in Philadelphia in 1861. He died in 1871, but his three sons continued the firm which closed in 1930. However, a glass-making company trading as Gillinder Brothers survives to this day at Port Jervis, New York.

GLASS

A Pantin paperweight, with cherries, French, c1878, 2¾in (7cm) diam.
£2,500–2,800 / €3,650–4,100
$4,500–5,000 ⊞ DLP

A St Louis paperweight, with a nosegay within a garland, French, 1845–60, 2¼in (5.5cm) diam.
£670–750 / €980–1,100
$1,200–1,350 ⊞ SWB

A St Louis miniature concentric paperweight, French, 1845–60, 1¾in (4.5cm) diam.
£880–980 / €1,300–1,450
$1,600–1,800 ⊞ SWB

A St Louis cased paperweight, the overlay cut with seven windows, on a star-cut base, French, c1850, 3in (7.5cm) diam.
£1,500–1,800 / €2,200–2,650
$2,700–3,250 ⚒ S

A St Louis paperweight, with a fuchsia, French, 1845–60, 3in (7.5cm) diam.
£2,150–2,400 / €3,150–3,800
$3,900–4,350 ⊞ SWB

A St Louis paperweight, with a dahlia, on a star-cut base, French, c1850, 2½in (6.5cm) diam.
£960–1,150 / €1,450–1,700
$1,700–2,000 ⚒ S

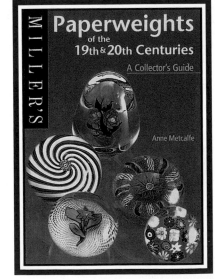

GLASS

A St Louis scrambled paperweight, French, c1850, 2½in (6.5cm) diam.
£230–270 / €330–390
$420–490 WW

A faceted paperweight, the canes on a lace ground, damaged, French, mid-19thC, 2¾in (7cm) diam.
£130–155 / €190–220
$240–280 WW

A sulphide paperweight, with a head-and-shoulders portrait of Prince Albert, French, late 19thC, 3¾in (9.5cm) diam.
£130–155 / €190–220
$240–280 DA

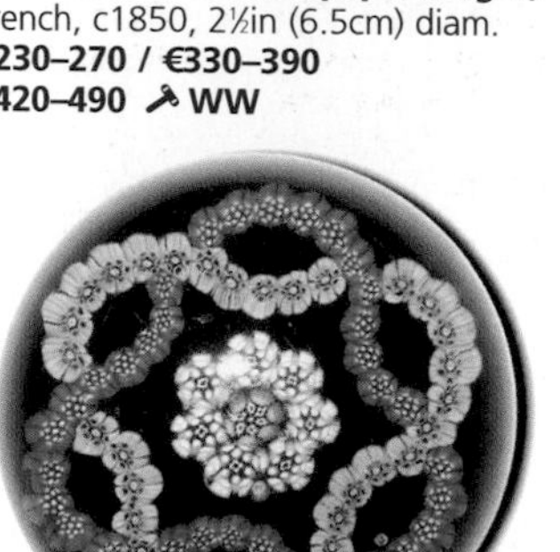

◄ **A Paul Ysart paperweight,** with interlaced trefoils and a PY cane, Scottish, 1930s, 3in (7.5cm) diam.
£1,000–1,100 / €1,450–1,600
$1,800–2,000 SWB

► **A Paul Ysart paperweight,** with a butterfly and a PY cane, Scottish, 1930s, 3in (7.5cm) diam.
£760–850 / €1,100–1,250
$1,400–1,550 SWB

Scent Bottles

A Bohemian scent bottle and stopper, decorated with gilding, gilt rubbed, c1830, 4in (10cm) high.
£360–430 / €530–630
$650–780 DORO

◄ **A Thomas Webb & Sons silver-mounted cameo glass scent bottle,** the silver mount by Sampson Mordan and with maker's mark, c1880, 4in (10cm) high, with original case.
£2,450–2,750
€3,600–4,000
$4,450–5,000
LBr

A Thomas Webb & Sons silver-mounted cameo glass scent bottle, mount London 1894, 5¼in (13.5cm) high.
£2,250–2,500 / €3,300–3,650
$4,050–4,500 VK

GLASS

Sets & Services

A pair of cut-glass carafes, with terrace-cut necks and vertical hobnail bands, with matching tumblers, damaged, 19thC, 6½in (16.5cm) high.
£120–140 / €175–200
$220–250 WW

A Bohemian amber overlay cut-glass spirit decanter, decorated with foliate gilding, with six matching glasses, late 19thC, 10¼in (26cm) high.
£960–1,150 / €1,450–1,700
$1,750–2,100 F&C

A pair of Victorian water sets, comprising two ewers and four glasses *en suite*, the ewers engraved with lilies, on star-cut bases, the glasses engraved with flowers, on hollow stems with star-cut bases, ewers 7in (18cm) high.
£680–810 / €1,000–1,200
$1,250–1,500 DN(BR)

Sweetmeat Glasses & Dishes

A Bohemian cut-glass sweetmeat dish, the handle in the form of a horn, the stem with a colour twist, c1740, 5¾in (14.5cm) high.
£360–430 / €530–630
$650–780 ⚒ DORO

A pair of bonnet glasses, c1760, 2¾in (7cm) high.
£105–120 / €155–175
$190–220 ⊞ G&G
In America these glasses are known as salts.

A sweetmeat glass, on a pedestal stem and domed and folded foot, c1760, 6in (15cm) high.
£360–400 / €520–580
$650–720 ⊞ JHa

◄ Six Bohemian cut-glass sweetmeat dishes, with turnover rims, engraved with bands of oval facets, on scalloped feet, slight damage,19thC, largest 7¼in (18.5cm) high.
£960–1,150 / €1,400–1,650
$1,750–2,050 ⚒ S(O)

Tankards

◄ A tankard, the collar engraved 'A Bird in the Hand is Worth Two in the Bush', above figures, hounds, trees and birds, c1800, 6¼in (16cm) high.
£210–250 / €310–370
$380–450 ⚒ GIL

► A Bohemian silver-mounted tankard, damaged, c1860, 7½in (19cm) high.
£290–340 / €420–500
$520–620 ⚒ DORO

A Bohemian pewter-mounted tankard, engraved with a coach and horses, c1875, 6¾in (17cm) high.
£290–340 / €420–500
$520–620 ⚒ DORO

GLASS

Vases & Urns

A Bohemian *milchglas* vase, decorated with flowers and fruit, with Venetian-style scrolling handles, c1760, 4¼in (11cm) high.
£400–450 / €580–660
$720–810 ⊞ G&G

Milchglas

Milchglas is the German name for opaque white glass usually produced by the addition of tin oxide. It became popular in the 17th and 18th centuries, along with the demand for Chinese porcelain. It was, however, produced all over Europe including France, England, Bohemia, Spain and Germany. It is usually associated with small objects such as tea bowls, saucers and beakers and is often enamelled.

A glass vase, decorated with birds and flowers, French, c1850, 12½in (32cm) high.
£1,750–2,100
€2,550–3,050
$3,150–3,800 ⚒ DORO

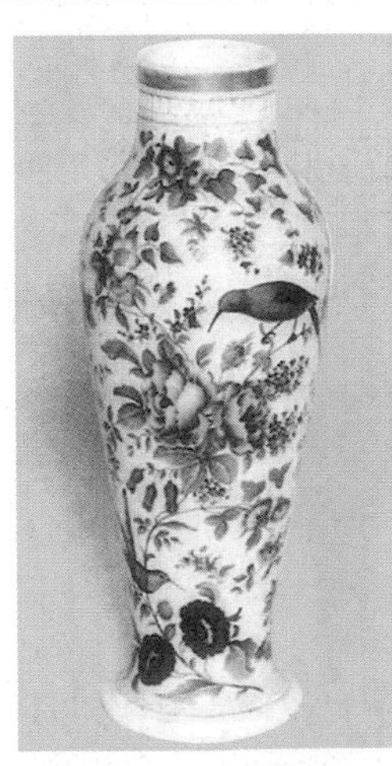

An opaline baluster vase, probably by Richardson, Stourbridge, decorated with birds and flowering tendrils, mid-19thC, 10¾in (27.5cm) high.
£260–310 / €380–450
$470–560 ⚒ LAY

A pair of Victorian overlaid glass vases, with painted gilt decoration, 14in (35.5cm) high.
£175–210 / €260–310
$320–380 HYD

A Thomas Webb & Sons Chinese-style cameo glass vase, carved with songbirds and blossom, on an everted foot, c1890, 10¼in (26cm) high.
£14,400–17,200
€21,000–25,100
$26,100–31,000 S
The unusual Chinese-style carving on this vase is very high quality.

► **A late Victorian acid-etched glass vase,** gilded with blossom and insects, 4in (10cm) high.
£140–165
€200–240
$250–300
HOLL

A Bohemian Moser bottle vase, enamel-painted and gilt with flowers and foliage, on an everted foot, with two applied gilt handles, c1890, 9in (23cm) high.
£840–1,000 / €1,250–1,450
$1,500–1,800 S

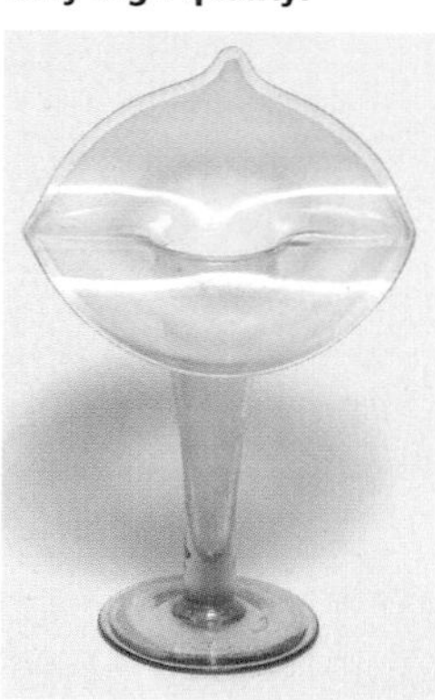

A pair of satin glass Jack-in the-Pulpit vases, c1890, 12in (30.5cm) high.
£155–175 / €230–260
$280–320 GLAS

A vase and cover, enamel-painted with a knight on horseback, on a flared foot, German, late 19thC, 23¾in (60.5cm) high.
£210–250 / €310–370
$380–450 DN(BR)

◄ **A vaseline glass posy vase,** c1900, 9in (23cm) high.
£80–90 / €115–130
$145–165 HTE

Miscellaneous

A pair of glass door handles, probably Baccarat, each decorated with a clematis, slight damage, French, mid-19thC, 2in (5cm) diam, with original brass lock.
£2,100–2,500 / €3,050–3,650
$3,800–4,550 Bea

◄ **A Nevers glass figure of a lady,** French, late 18thC, 3in (7.5cm) high.
£330–370
€480–540
$600–670
BrW

An oil lamp, on an incised stem, early 19thC, 3¼in (8.5cm) high.
£120–140 / €170–200
$210–250 WW

Further reading

Miller's Glass Buyer's Guide, Miller's Publications, 2001

◄ **A tray,** probably Baccarat or St Louis, the rim engraved with leaf scrolls, inset with three rows of spaced millefiori canes within a row of stars and polished circlets, with a star-cut base, French, c1850, 11in (28cm) diam.
£1,800–2,150
€2,650–3,150
$3,250–3,900 S

A pair of cut-glass rinsers, 1820–40, 4¾in (12cm) diam.
£150–165 / €210–240
$270–300 LGr

GLASS

Silver

Animals

A silver pepper pot, by Alexander Crichton, in the form of a rat, with glass eyes, London 1880, 2½in (6.5cm) high, 1½oz.
£1,300–1,550
€1,900–2,250
$2,350–2,800 ⚒ DN

A silver pepperette, in the form of a bird, London 1881, 5in (12.5cm) high.
£500–600 / €730–880
$910–1,100 ⚒ SWO

► **A silver inkwell,** in the form of a cockerel, the hinged neck revealing a recess, inkwell missing, London 1900, 6½in (16.5cm) high, 26½oz.
£1,000–1,200 / €1,450–1,750
$1,800–2,150 ⚒ PFK

A silver centrepiece, by Berthold Müller, in the form of a baying stag, import marks for London 1901, 14in (35.5cm) high, 83oz.
£11,500–13,800 / €16,800–20,100
$20,800–25,000 ⚒ NSal

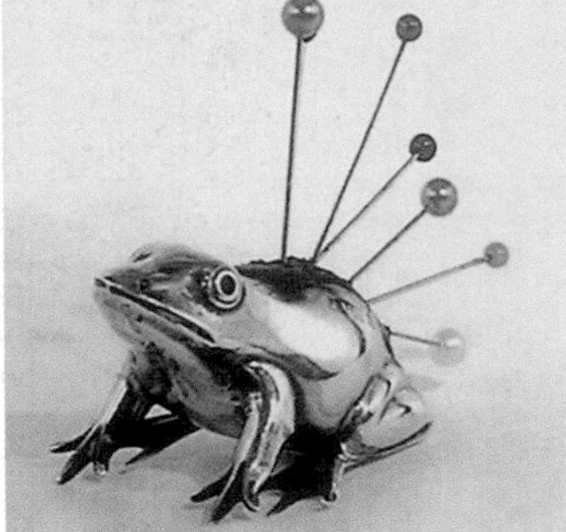

A silver pincushion, in the form of a frog, Birmingham 1907, 1in (2.5cm) high.
£370–440 / €540–640
$670–800 ⚒ LFA

An Edwardian silver pincushion, in the form of an elephant, 1¼in (3cm) high.
£85–100 / €125–145
$150–180 ⚒ G(L)

Baskets

A silver sweetmeat basket, by Parker & Wakelin, the handle entwined with flowers, with pierced sides and rococo decoration, London 1761, 7in (18cm) wide, 9oz.
£2,400–2,850 / €3,500–4,150
$4,350–5,200 ⚒ S

Items in the Silver section have been arranged in date order within each sub-section.

A silver pedestal sugar basket, by Peter and Anne Bateman, with reeded and bright-cut engraved bands, engraved crests, London 1795, 6¾in (17cm) wide, 6½oz.
£520–620 / €760–910
$940–1,100 ⚒ GIL

► **A silver basket,** by Johan Orenius, with a gilt interior, Estonian, Tartu, c1820, 11½in (29cm) wide, 23oz.
£930–1,100 / €1,350–1,600
$1,700–2,000 ⚒ BUK

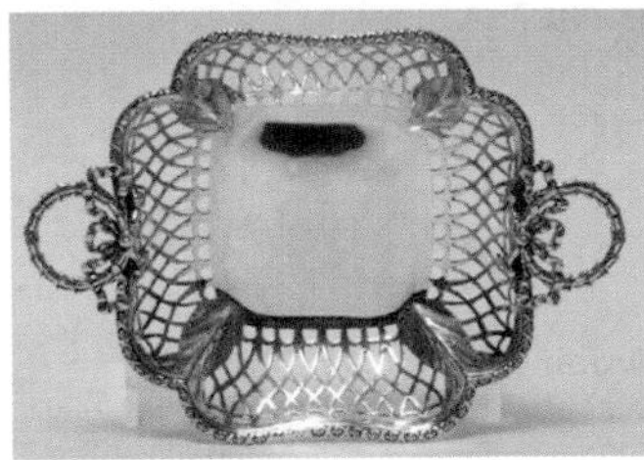

A pair of pierced silver sweetmeat dishes, with ribbon-leaf handles, Birmingham 1811, 6in (15cm) wide.
£280–330 / €410–480
$510–600 ⚒ CHTR

A silver cake basket, by Houle & Houle, with a pierced hinged handle, pierced and moulded floral decoration, on four supports, London 1863, 15in (38cm) wide, 35oz.
£880–1,050 / €1,300–1,550
$1,600–1,900 TEN

A silver basket, by Thomas Bradbury & Sons, with pierced and embossed decoration, Sheffield 1907, 10¼in (26cm) wide.
£300–360 / €440–530
$540–650 RTo

A silver basket, by Elkington & Co, Birmingham 1900, 11in (28cm) wide.
£500–560 / €730–820
$900–1,000 GRe

A silver fruit basket, with pierced sides, Birmingham 1911, 4½in (11.5cm) high.
£300–350 / €440–510
$540–630 BLm

► A silver sugar bowl, by Tiffany & Co, with original glass liner, American, c1930, 5in (12.5cm) high.
£750–850 / €1,100–1,250
$1,350–1,550 SHa

A pierced silver fruit basket, possibly by Elkington & Co, the rim cast with masks, with an openwork base, Sheffield 1903, 8in (20.5cm) wide, 14½oz.
£350–420 / €510–610
$630–760 GIL

Beakers

A silver-gilt beaker, by Jakob Kraer, German, Nuremberg, 1650–60, 3¾in (9.5cm) high, 4oz.
£1,000–1,200
€1,450–1,750
$1,800–2,150 BUK

A silver beaker, by Olaf Norling, Swedish, Orebro, 1764, 4in (10cm) high.
£380–430 / €550–630
$690–780 GRe

A silver-gilt beaker, with snakeskin-effect embossing, maker's mark HP, Polish, Gdansk, c1680, 3½in (9cm) high, 5¾oz.
£1,900–2,250
€2,750–3,300
$3,450–4,050 DORO

Further reading

Miller's Collecting Silver: The Facts at Your Fingertips, Miller's Publications, 1999

► A silver beaker, by Jos Jackson, with a flared rim, chased with a crest, Irish, Dublin, c1780, 3¾in (9.5cm) high.
£370–440 / €540–640
$670–800 SPF

A parcel-gilt silver beaker, by Carl Such, with engraved decoration, on a gadrooned foot, German, Augsburg, 1716, 4in (10cm) high, 4¾oz.
£840–1,000
€1,200–1,450
$1,500–1,800 S

A silver beaker, chased with two cartouches, one with a huntsman on horseback, the other with a pair of lovebirds, maker's mark CG, Russian, Moscow, c1740, 3¼in (8.5cm) high, 2½oz.
£290–340 / €420–500
$520–620 WW

A silver beaker, with a reeded foot and rim, maker's mark TS&S, Scottish, Edinburgh 1904, 4in (10cm) high.
£210–250 / €310–370
$380–450 WW

Biscuit Barrels

A silver-mounted cut-glass biscuit barrel, by Dominick & Haff, London 1899, 6in (15cm) high.
£310–350 / €450–510
$560–630 ⊞ GRe

A silver biscuit barrel, by The Goldsmiths & Silversmiths Co, half-fluted with leaf-mounted handles, on scrolled foliate feet, the cover with a fruit finial, one foot damaged, London 1902, 7½in (19cm) high, 23oz.
£300–360 / €440–530
$540–650 ⚒ PF

A silver-mounted glass biscuit barrel, by William Hutton & Sons, Sheffield 1919, 8in (20.5cm) high.
£400–450 / €580–650
$720–810 ⊞ BEX

Bowls

A silver sugar bowl, by Matthew West, the punched rim embossed with rural figures, animals and buildings, on three shell-capped feet, Irish, Dublin, c1780, 5¼in (13.5cm) diam.
£560–670 / €820–980
$1,000–1,200 ⚒ HOK

A silver monteith-style punch bowl, with a shaped rim, decorated with repoussé foliate motifs, on a stepped base, London 1892, 8½in (21.5cm) diam, 28oz.
£440–520 / €640–760
$800–940 ⚒ JAd

► **A pierced silver pedestal bowl,** decorated with husks, swags and medallions, London 1898, 6in (15cm) wide.
£200–240 / €290–350
$360–430 ⚒ CHTR

A silver sugar bowl, chased and embossed with a musician and a lady among scrollwork and waves, the handles cast in the form of Mandarins, London 1820, 8¼in (21cm) wide.
£175–210 / €260–310
$320–380 ⚒ TMA

A silver punch bowl, by Gibson & Langman, with a detachable pierced band, London 1897, 9¾in (25cm) diam, 40oz, with plinth.
£540–640 / €790–930
$980–1,150 ⚒ TRM(E)

A parcel-gilt bowl, chased with flowers and acanthus leaves in panels, on a spreading foot, indistinct maker's mark, London 1836, 8¼in (21cm) diam, 18oz.
£590–700 / €850–1,000
$1,050–1,250 ⚒ DN

A silver rose bowl, by Richard Martin and Ebenezer Hall, embossed with floral and scroll decoration, the beaded rim above a pierced band of flowerheads and foliage, on scroll feet, Sheffield 1898, 16in (40.5cm) wide, 71½oz, with presentation plaque.
£1,250–1,500 / €1,850–2,200
$2,250–2,700 ⚒ Bea

A silver bowl, by Tiffany & Co, with fluted decoration, American, late 19thC, 9½in (24cm) diam, 19oz.
£280–330 / €410–480
$510–600 ⚒ WW

A silver bowl, by Graff, Washbourne & Dunn, the pierced rim embossed with poppies, daisies and clover, monogrammed HHJ, American, New York, c1900, 14½in (37cm) diam, 32¾oz.
£600–720 / €880–1,050
$1,100–1,300 ⚒ NOA

A silver rose bowl, by The Goldsmiths & Silversmiths Co, with a pierced everted rim, on three scroll feet, London 1903, 11in (28cm) diam, 31oz.
£350–420 / €510–610
$630–760 ⚒ WW

► **A silver rose bowl,** by Neresheimer, the bowl engraved with armorials, German, Hanau, early 20thC, import marks for Chester 1912, 14½in (37cm) diam, 54oz.
£980–1,150 / €1,450–1,700
$1,750–2,100 ⚒ WW

A silver bowl, with two handles, German, c1900, 4½in (11.5cm) diam, 4oz.
£200–230 / €290–330
$360–410 ⊞ BEX

A silver rose bowl, by Elkington & Co, with half-reeded decoration beneath ribbon-tied laurel festoons, London 1904, 12¼in (31cm) diam.
£840–1,000 / €1,250–1,450
$1,500–1,800 ⚒ RTo

A silver pedestal bowl, the rim cast with stylized vases and foliage scrolls, on a fluted foot, Sheffield 1902, 12in (30.5cm) diam, 25oz.
£400–480 / €580–700
$720–870 ⚒ HOLL

A silver monteith, with a strap-cast rim, the fluted body with two scroll and foliage cartouches and lion-mask handles, London 1908, 10¼in (26cm) diam, 34oz.
£700–840 / €1,000–1,200
$1,250–1,500 ⚒ HOLL

A silver quaich, by Nathan & Hayes, Birmingham 1916, 4in (10cm) diam.
£165–185 / €240–270
$300–330 ⊞ GRe

Covered Bowls

A silver sugar bowl, by Carl Anton Carlborg, Finnish, Turku 1819, 9½in (24cm) high.
£1,900–2,250 / €2,750–3,300
$3,450–4,050 ⚒ BUK(F)

A silver sugar urn, by Josef Kern, with a pierced cover and ring handles, Austrian, Vienna, assay mark for 1820, 7in (18cm) high, 18½oz.
£760–910 / €1,100–1,300
$1,400–1,650 ⚒ DORO

► **A silver sugar bowl and cover,** decorated with swirl fluting, with twin handles and four cast feet, French, c1890, 3½in (9cm) high, 10oz.
£120–140 / €175–200
$220–250 ⚒ WW

A silver sugar bowl, by Anders Lundqvist, the cover with a recumbant dog, Swedish, Stockholm 1825, 7½in (19cm) diam.
£890–1,050 / €1,300–1,550
$1,600–1,900 ⚒ BUK

Boxes

A silver box, engraved with an armorial, the cover with a later falcon finial, maker's mark, German, Cologne, 1633–64, 6in (15cm) diam, 9¼oz.
£650–780 / €950–1,100
$1,200–1,400 S(Am)

A silver presentation box, commemorating being awarded the Freedom of the City of Cork, Irish, c1750, 3in (7.5cm) diam.
£2,900–3,250 / €4,250–4,750
$5,200–5,900 WELD

An agate and silver patch box, the hinged cover decorated with a scroll design, 18thC, 3in (7.5cm) wide.
£450–500 / €660–730
$810–910 LBr

A silver taper/wax box, hinged and chased with fruit and vegetables, on four leaf feet, German, probably Dresden, c1770, 3¼in (8.5cm) high, 4½oz.
£350–420 / €510–610
$630–760 WW

A silver-gilt box, with floral decoration, the cover decorated with a scene of putti in a boat, Dutch, late 19thC, 5¾in (14.5cm) wide.
£120–140 / €175–200
$220–250 G(L)

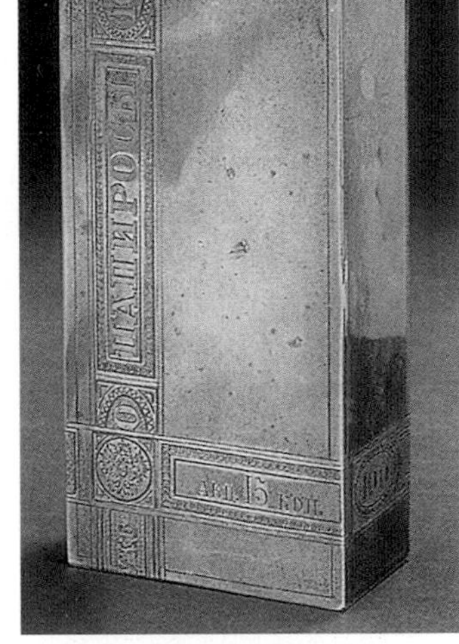

▶ **A silver table cigarette box,** engraved with tax bands and Imperial arms, Russian, St Petersburg, dated 1893, 6¼in (16cm) wide, 13¾oz.
£1,200–1,400 / €1,750–2,050
$2,150–2,550 S(Am)

A silver box, by H. Matthews, Birmingham 1902, 7in (18cm) wide.
£340–380 / €500–550
$620–690 GRe

A silver potpourri box, by W. Comyns, London 1907, 2in (5cm) wide.
£310–350 / €450–510
$560–630 ANO

A silver-gilt box, decorated with gems and enamels and applied wirework roundels, marked NBS, Birmingham 1910, 2¼in (5.5cm) wide.
£210–250 / €310–370
$380–450 WW

Caddy Spoons

A silver caddy spoon, by Joseph Taylor, Birmingham 1798, 2in (5cm) long.
£220–250 / €330–370
$400–450 SAT

▶ **A silver caddy spoon,** by Samuel Pemberton, the bowl bright-cut with Greek key pattern, with a pierced centre, Birmingham 1806, 5½in (14cm) long.
£280–330 / €410–480
$510–600 G(L)

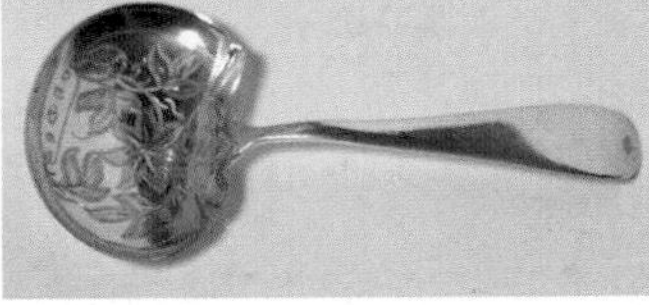

A silver caddy spoon, by Joseph Willmore, Birmingham 1828, 4in (10cm) long.
£80–90 / €115–130
$145–165 SAT

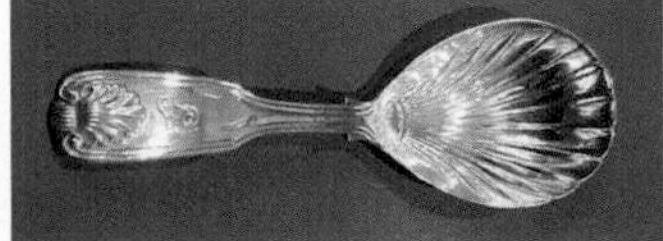

A silver caddy spoon, by William Eaton, London 1843, 4¼in (11cm) long.
£290–330 / €420–480
$520–600 BEX

Candle Snuffers & Trays

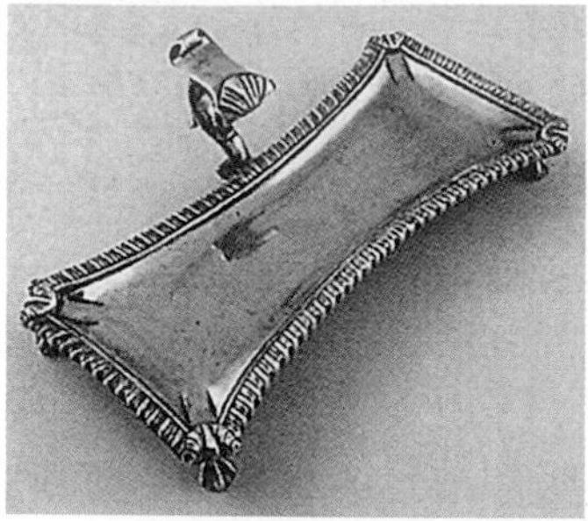

A silver snuffer tray, by William Cafe, with a gadrooned border, on claw-and-ball feet, London 1767, 7¼in (18.5cm) wide, 7½oz.
£470–560 / €690–820
$850–1,000 WW

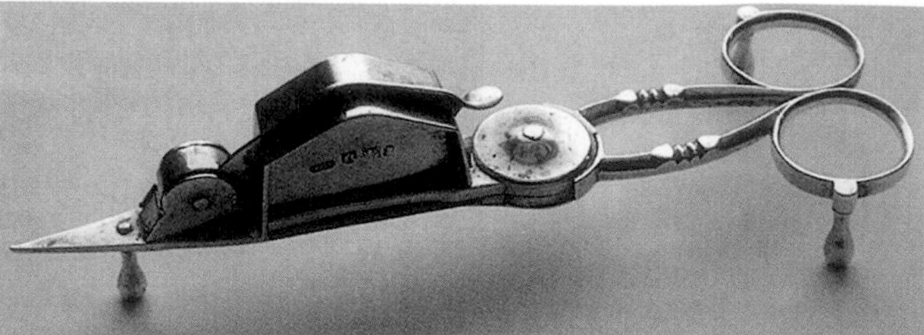

A pair of silver candle snuffers, by George McHattie, engraved with a crest, on three baluster feet, Scottish, Edinburgh 1811, 6in (15cm) long.
£350–420 / €510–610
$630–760 TRM(E)

LOCATE THE SOURCE
The source of each illustration in Miller's can be found by checking the code letters below each caption with the Key to Illustrations, pages 778–784.

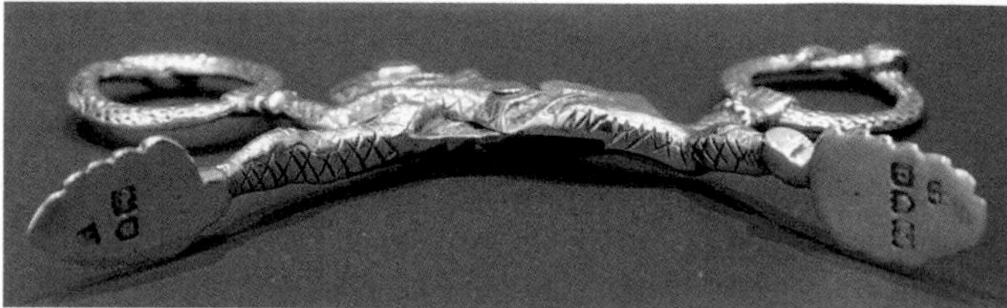

A silver candle snuffer, by John and Frank Pairpoint, in the form of a harlequin, London 1899, 4½in (11.5cm) long.
£400–440 / €580–640
$720–800 BEX

Candlesticks & Chambersticks

A silver taperstick, by Richard Green, on a moulded base, London 1747, 4in (10cm) high.
£590–700 / €850–1,000
$1,050–1,250 TMA

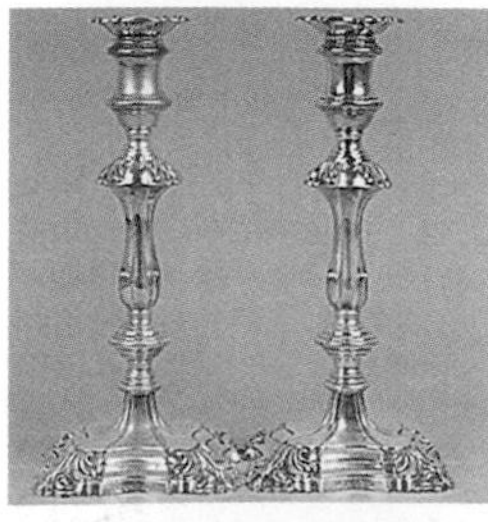

A pair of silver candlesticks, by I. Watson, each with shell corners and conforming knops and nozzles, Sheffield 1844, 12½in (31.5cm) high.
£760–910 / €1,100–1,300
$1,400–1,650 L

A pair of silver candlesticks, by Gustaf Folcker, in the form of lyres on columns, marked, Swedish, Stockholm 1830, 9½in (24cm) high.
£1,750–2,100
€2,550–3,050
$3,150–3,800
BUK

► **A pair of silver chambersticks,** with snuffers and flying scroll handles, London 1905, 7in (18cm) diam, 17oz.
£590–700
€850–1,000
$1,050–1,250
DA

A silver chamberstick, by Henry Wilkinson & Co, Sheffield 1833, 3in (7.5cm) diam.
£540–600 / €790–880
$980–1,100 SAT

A silver candlestick, French, c1880.
£290–330 / €420–480
$520–600 BEX

A silver five-light candelabrum, Portuguese, 19thC, 20in (51cm) high, 119oz.
£1,650–1,950
€2,400–2,850
$3,000–3,500 WILK

A pair of cast-silver candle sticks, Sheffield 1930, 12½in (32cm) high, 49oz.
£2,450–2,750
€3,600–4,000
$4,450–5,000 BLm

SILVER

Card Cases

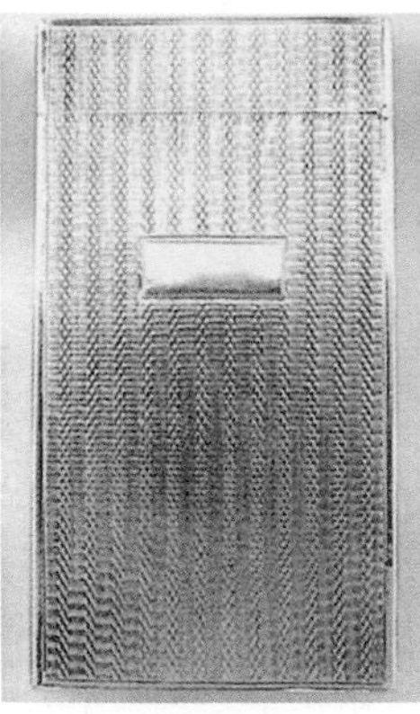

A silver card case, by Taylor & Perry, with engine-turned decoration and a hinged cover, Birmingham 1832, 3in (7.5cm) high, 1½oz.
£190–220 / €270–320
$340–400 WW

A silver castle top card case, by Nathaniel Mills, depicting the Walter Scott Memorial monument, Edinburgh, Birmingham 1844, 4in (10cm) high.
£1,300–1,450
€1,900–2,100
$2,350–2,600 SiA

A silver card case, by Yapp & Woodward, Birmingham 1849, 4in (10cm) high.
£400–450 / €580–660
$720–810 SiA

A silver card case, by Edward Smith, Birmingham 1853, 4in (10cm) high, 2¼oz.
£1,200–1,350
€1,750–1,950
$2,150–2,450 BEX

A silver card case, by George Unite, Birmingham 1879, 3in (7.5cm) high, 1oz.
£360–400 / €520–580
$650–720 BEX

A silver card case, repoussé-decorated with a border collie within a cartouche, maker's mark C&N, Birmingham 1903, 4in (10cm) high.
£280–330 / €410–480
$510–600 AMB

A silver card case, by Spurrier & Co, Birmingham 1904, 3in (7.5cm) wide, 1oz.
£360–400 / €520–580
$650–720 BEX

A silver card case, by William Hornby, London 1904, 2½in (6.5cm) high.
£140–155 / €200–220
$250–280 BEX

A silver card case, by H. Matthews, Birmingham 1907, 3¼in (8.5cm) high.
£430–480 / €630–700
$780–870 SHa

◄ **A silver card case,** by I. S. Greenberg, Birmingham 1908, 3¾in (9.5cm) high.
£340–380 / €500–550
$610–690 BEX

SILVER

Casters

A pair of silver casters, by Francis Garthorne, with pierced bayonet covers and gadrooned banding, London 1693, 5½in (14cm) high, 9oz.
£5,400–6,400
€7,900–9,300
$9,800–11,600 ⚒ G(L)

A silver caster, with a moulded girdle and borders and a pierced cover, maker's mark WC, London 1712, 5½in (14cm) high, 4½oz.
£560–670 / €820–980
$1,000–1,200 ⚒ DN

A late baroque-style silver caster, by Olof Söderman, engraved with initials, Swedish, Lidköping 1732, 7in (18cm) high.
£1,750–2,100
€2,550–3,050
$3,150–3,800 ⚒ BUK

A silver caster, by Samuel Wood, engraved with a crest, London 1748, 7½in (19cm) high.
£200–240 / €290–350
$360–430 ⚒ DN(BR)

A set of three silver casters, by Daniell and Mince, two with pierced covers and one for mustard, with gadrooned borders, London 1770, tallest 7½in (19cm) high, 17½oz.
£1,150–1,350 / €1,700–2,000
$2,100–2,500 ⚒ DN

A silver caster, by Thomas Leddiard, London 1775, 5in (12.5cm) high.
£310–350 / €450–510
$560–630 ⊞ GRe

A pair of silver sugar casters, by William Hutton & Son, London and Sheffield, 1906–07, 6in (15cm) high.
£400–450 / €580–660
$720–810 ⊞ GRe

Centrepieces

A silver cake stand, by Martin & Hall, with engraved ribbon and husk decoration and a beaded edge, the pedestal foot with chased foliate decoration, Sheffield 1886, 11½in (29cm) diam, 23oz.
£330–390 / €480–570
$600–710 ⚒ TEN

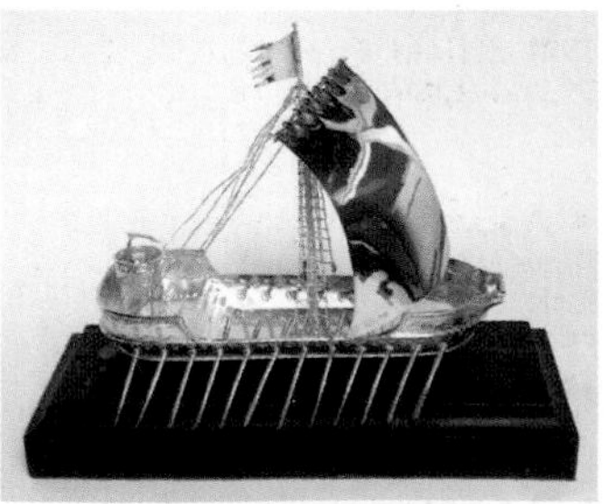

A silver ship centrepiece, by Henry Frazer, London 1903, 11½in (29cm) wide, 21oz.
£500–550 / €720–800
$900–1,000 ⊞ GRe

A silver epergne, the central vase flanked by two smaller vases and two suspended baskets, all with moulded borders, Birmingham 1918, 12¼in (31cm) high.
£1,100–1,300 / €1,600–1,900
$2,000–2,350 ⚒ WilP

Cigar & Cigarette Cases

A silver presentation cigarette case, in the form of an envelope inscribed with the address of H.R.H. Prince of Wales at Sandringham with a lilac enamel penny stamp and a London postmark for 8 November 1881, the reverse with an embossed ducal coronet seal and a Sandringham postmark for 9 November 1881, the interior inscribed 'Very many happy returns of the day', maker's mark LD, London 1881, 2¾in (7cm) wide.
£1,300–1,550 / €1,900–2,250
$2,350–2,800 ⚒ G(B)

► **A silver cigarette case,** the hinged lid set with a gold coin of Tsar Nicholas II, a match holder to one side, Russian, St Petersburg, c1900, 4in (10cm) high, 6oz.
£740–880 / €1,100–1,300
$1,350–1,600 ⚒ S(Am)

A silver and niello cheroot case, maker's mark OA, Russian, Moscow, c1890, 4in (10cm) wide.
£880–980 / €1,300–1,450
$1,600–1,800 ⊞ SHa

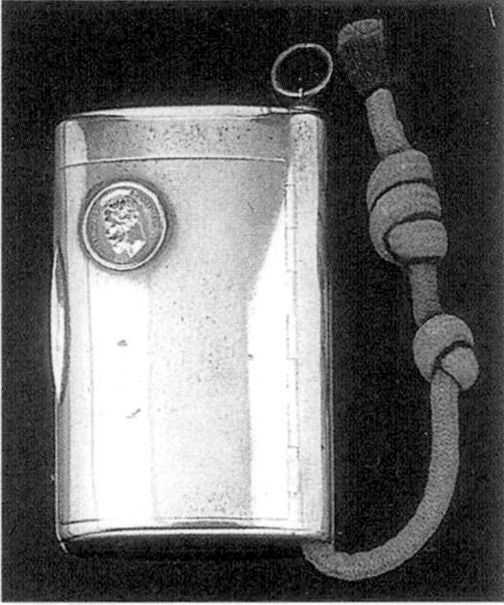

A silver cigarette case, with reeded decoration and applied with an Imperial crest, with a lapis lazuli thumbpiece, Russian, early 20thC, 4in (10cm) wide.
£330–390 / €480–570
$600–710 ⚒ G(L)

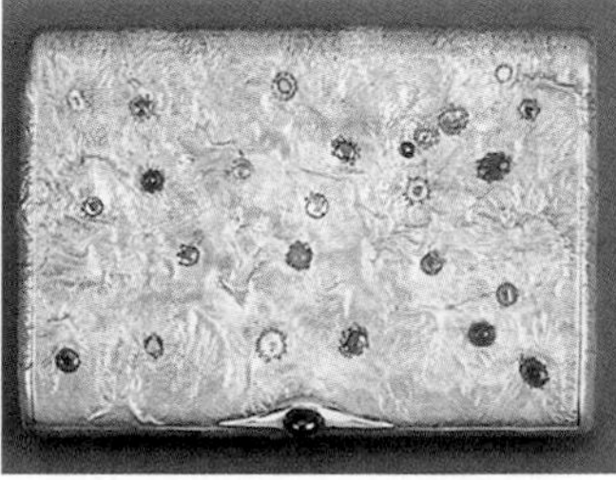

A jewelled silver cigarette case, by A. Kusmichev, the lid inset with gemstones, with a gold and cabochon sapphire clasp, Russian, St Petersburg, 1908–17, 4in (10cm) wide.
£1,550–1,850 / €2,250–2,700
$2,800–3,350 ⚒ S

Coffee & Teapots

A silver coffee pot, with a double-scroll wooden handle, later chased decoration, maker's mark ER, London 1762, 11in (28cm) high, 30½oz.
£880–1,050 / €1,300–1,550
$1,600–1,900 ⚒ TEN

A silver coffee pot, by William Grundy, with an urn finial and a double-scroll handle, London 1775, 11½in (29cm) high, 28oz.
£940–1,100 / €1,350–1,600
$1,700–2,000 ⚒ TEN

◄ **A silver coffee pot,** by René-Pierre Ferrier, handle restored, French, Paris, 1776–77, 8in (20.5cm) high.
£900–1,050 / €1,300–1,550
$1,650–1,900 ⚒ S(P)

► **A silver coffee pot,** by John Lambe, with a ball finial and carved ebony handle, London 1784, 9in (23cm) high, 16oz.
£700–840 / €1,000–1,200
$1,250–1,500 ⚒ TMA

A silver coffee pot, by John Swift, embossed with floral and fabric swags suspended from paterae and a cartouche with an engraved coat-of-arms, with a fruitwood handle, London 1776, 11½in (29cm) high.
£1,400–1,650 / €2,050–2,400
$2,550–3,000 ⚒ WW

A silver coffee pot, the body by Fuller White, with later chased decoration and contemporary crest, repaired, London 1754, cover hallmarked London 1780, 9¾in (25cm) high, 29½oz.
£760–910 / €1,100–1,300
$1,400–1,650 F&C

A silver teapot and stand, the teapot by George Smith II, engraved with a shield and initial and decorated with reeded bands and engraving, with an ebonized finial and handle, teapot 5½in (14cm) wide, the associated stand by John Crouch I and Thomas Hannam, London 1790, 13½oz, stand 6¾in (17cm) wide, 5oz.
£680–810 / €1,000–1,200
$1,250–1,500 DN

A silver teapot, by Gustavus Byrne, with later chased foliate scrolling, Irish, Dublin 1807, 12¼in (31cm) wide, 23½oz.
£370–440 / €540–640
$670–800 TEN

A silver teapot, by J. B. Verbeckt, chased with a band of palmettes and pendant stylized flowers, Belgian, Antwerp, 1814–31, 7in (18cm) high, 17½oz.
£1,050–1,250 / €1,550–1,850
$1,900–2,250 S(P)

A silver coffee pot, by John Nicolson, with embossed rococo decoration and a crest, with a cone finial, Irish, Cork, c1780, 12in (30.5cm) high, 32oz.
£15,500–18,600 / €22,600–27,200
$28,100–34,000 HYD
Irish silver is currently very sought after and pieces from smaller centres such as Cork are particularly desirable.

► **A late Gustavian-style silver teapot,** by Håkan Holmqvist, engraved with Medusa's head, with an ebonized handle, Swedish, Borås, 1800–18, 7½in (19cm) high.
£1,800–2,150 / €2,650–3,150
$3,250–3,900 BUK

A silver teapot, by I. B. or J. B., Irish, Dublin 1808, 11½in (29cm) wide, 20oz.
£1,750–1,950 / €2,550–2,850
$3,150–3,500 ⊞ BEX

A silver coffee pot, by William Bennett, with a tongue-and-dart border and reeded decoration, engraved with initials, London 1811, 12in (30.5cm) high, 35oz.
£330–390 / €480–570
$600–710 WW

► **A silver percolator coffee pot,** by François-Nicolas Boulenger, with an ebonized wood handle, French, Paris, 1819–38, 7¾in (19.5cm) high, 13½oz.
£780–930 / €1,150–1,350
$1,450–1,700 S(P)

A silver teapot, by Pierre-Joseph Dehanne, with an ebonized wood handle, French, Paris, 1787–88, rehallmarked in Paris 1809 and 1819, 7¾in (19.5cm) wide, 13½oz.
£1,150–1,350 / €1,700–2,000
$2,100–2,500 S(P)

A silver teapot, by Solomon Hougham, with a pineapple finial, London 1796, 7½in (19cm) high, 14oz.
£280–330 / €410–480
$510–600 WW

A silver coffee biggin, by William Burwash, on a tripod stand with a detachable burner, London 1814, 10¾in (27.5cm) high, 37oz.
£1,200–1,400 / €1,750–2,050
$2,150–2,550 WW

silver coffee pot, by Rebecca
nes and Edward Barnard, London
323, 9in (23cm) high.
1,150–1,300 / €1,700–1,900
2,100–2,350 ⊞ GRe

silver miniature/herb teapot, by
T. Heath & J. H. Middleton, with a
ll finial and scroll handle, Birmingham
900, 2½in (6.5cm) high, 3oz.
190–220 / €280–330
340–400 ⚒ WW

◄ **A silver coffee pot,** by Sasikov, with a gilt interior and bone handle and knop, slight damage to footrim, Russian, Moscow 1836, 8¾in (22cm) high.
£700–840 / €1,000–1,200
$1,250–1,500 ⚒ BUK

A silver coffee pot, by J. Smyth, embossed with flowers and scrolls and a scroll cartouche with inscription, the cover with a bird and leaf finial, on four scroll feet, Irish, Dublin 1856, 7in (18cm) high, 15oz.
£350–420 / €510–610
$630–760 ⚒ DN

◄ **A silver coffee pot,** by Geoffrey Payne, London 1905, 9in (23cm) high.
£480–540 / €700–790
$870–980 ⊞ GRe

Coffee & Tea Services

silver three-piece tea service, by Joseph Angell, decorated with
aves, on anthemion and paw feet, teapot with ivory handle and
nial, 1818, teapot 5in (15cm) high, 46oz.
680–810 / €1,000–1,200
1,250–1,450 ⚒ L

A silver three-piece
a service, by William
unter, embossed with
gnettes of floral motifs
d thistles and two
cant cartouches,
ndon 1839, 42oz.
490–580 / €720–850
890–1,050 ⚒ WW

silver three-piece tea service,
S. Hayne & D. Cater, decorated
th vignettes of floral sprays,
tialled M, London 1847, 43oz.
560–670 / €820–980
,000–1,200 ⚒ WW

A silver three-piece tea service, by William Eley, the teapot with ebonized handle, London 1821, 45¾oz, in a fitted and baize-lined oak case with brass handles.
£610–730 / €890–1,050
$1,100–1,300 ⚒ PFK

A silver four-piece tea service, by W. H., embossed with leaf bands, the covers with bud finials, London 1839, teapot 10¾in (27.5cm) wide.
£1,500–1,800 / €2,200–2,650
$2,700–3,250 ⚒ AH

► **A silver three-piece tea service,** by G. G., engraved with scrolling floral and foliate motifs, on scroll feet, maker's mark, London, 1853–54, teapot 7½in (19cm) high.
£350–420
€510–610
$630–760 ⚒ SJH

► **A silver three-piece tea service,** by W.H., engraved with foliate scrolls, on scroll feet, teapot with ivory insulators, London 1854, teapot 10¼in (26cm) wide, 41oz.
£540–640 / €790–930
$980–1,150 ⚒ TEN

◄ **A silver three-piece tea service,** by Robert Garrard, engraved with foliate decoration, teapot with ivory handle, London 1853, teapot 7½in (19cm) high, 44oz.
£560–670 / €820–980
$1,000–1,200 ⚒ HYD

A silver six-piece coffee and tea service, by Bailey & Co, chased with landscapes and initialled G within rococo cartouches, the handles in the form of branches, American, Philadelphia, c1860, 214½oz.
£2,750–3,300 / €4,000–4,800
$5,000–6,000 ⚒ S

A silver three-piece tea service, by Martin & Hall, decorated with foliate scrolls, with leaf-capped double scroll handles, teapot with ivory insulators, Sheffield 1863, teapot 7¾in (19.5cm) high, 48oz.
£610–730 / €890–1,050
$1,100–1,300 ⚒ TEN

► **A silver four-piece coffee and tea service,** by Martin & Hall, Sheffield 1873, coffee pot 12in (30.5cm) high, 97oz.
£4,250–4,750 / €11,800–13,100
$14,600–16,300 ⊞ BEX

A silver four-piece coffee and tea service, by Harry Atkin, Sheffield, 1888–89, coffee pot 10in (25.5cm) high, 60½oz.
£3,800–4,250 / €5,500–6,200
$6,900–7,700 ⊞ BEX

A silver three-piece tea service, decorated with engraved and repoussé floral motifs, on scroll feet, Sheffield 1897, 43oz.
£350–420 / €510–610
$630–760 ⚒ G(L)

A silver seven-piece coffee and tea service, by Tiffany & Co, chased with bands of ivy leaves, maker's marks, American, hot water pot 14in (35.5cm) high, late 19thC, 171½oz.
£4,100–4,900 / €6,000–7,200
$7,400–8,900 ⚒ JAA

◄ **A silver three-piece tea service,** with ribbed lower section, Birmingham 1901, 21oz.
£260–310
€380–450
$470–560 ⚒ D

Condiment Pots

A silver mustard pot, by Barthélémy Samson, engraved JG, French, Toulouse, 1764–65, 4½in (11cm) high, 4¾oz.
£3,250–3,900 / €4,750–5,700
$5,900–7,100 ⚒ S(P)

A pair of silver salts, by William Bateman and Daniel Ball, London 1840, 2in (5cm) diam.
£360–400 / €520–580
$650–720 ⊞ GRe

A pair of silver-gilt salt cellars, by . Saltykov, in the form of thrones, with inscribed hinged covers, on four bracket feet, Russian, Moscow 1873 and 1874, 3in (7.5cm) high.
£880–1,050 / €1,300–1,550
$1,600–1,900 ⚒ HYD

pair of silver pepper mills, by eath & Middleton, in the form of lb weights with loop handles, scribed '2lb', Birmingham 1893, n (10cm) high, 11¼oz.
560–670 / €820–980
,000–1,200 ⚒ DN

A silver mustard pot, by Robert Hennell, decorated with two pierced bands, with a crested cover and blue glass liner, London 1784, 3in (7.5cm) high, 3½oz.
£590–700 / €850–1,000
$1,050–1,250 ⚒ DN

A silver mustard pot, by John Figg, London 1855, 2½in (6.5cm) high.
£250–280 / €370–410
$450–510 ⊞ CoHA

A silver pepper mill, by Vincenz Carl Dub, marked, Austrian, Vienna, 1872–1922, 4¼in (11cm) high.
£890–1,050 / €1,300–1,550
$1,600–1,900 ⚒ DORO

A pair of silver salt cellars, by Nathan & Hayes, Chester 1896, 3in (7.5cm) wide.
£165–185 / €240–270
$300–330 ⊞ GRe

A silver mustard pot, by C. Reily & G. Storer, with chased decoration and gilt interior with a glass liner, London 1828, 3in (7.5cm) high, 5½oz.
£370–440 / €540–640
$670–800 ⚒ WW

A pair of silver-gilt salts, by Robert Garrard, in the form of Poseidon holding a trident and steering a shell being pulled by a pair of dolphins, the base formed as waves, with spoons, London 1863, 5¾in (14.5cm) high, 56oz.
£12,000–14,400 / €17,500–21,000
$21,700–26,100 ⚒ JNic
Finely-crafted figural pieces such as this are very popular.

A silver pepper pot, by George Unite, Birmingham 1898, 4in (10cm) high.
£125–140 / €180–200
$220–250 ⊞ CoHA

Cruets

A silver cruet, probably by Samuel Wood, with two silver-mounted cut-glass bottles, London 1752, and an associated silver caster, London 1747, 27¾oz.
£960–1,150 / €1,450–1,700
$1,750–2,100 Bea

A silver Warwick cruet frame, by R. Peaston, engraved with a coat-of-arms, London 1762, 8¼in (21cm) high, 14oz.
£175–210 / €260–310
$320–380 WW

A silver cruet, by Jean-François Balzac, French, Paris, 1765–66, 10¼in (26cm) wide, 23½oz.
£410–490 / €600–720
$740–890 S(P)

Warwick cruets

Warwick cruets are named after the model made by Anthony Nelme in 1715 for William Greville, Earl of Warwick. They are of open design and usually contain three silver casters and two silver-mounted glass bottles.

◄ **A silver Warwick cruet,** by John Delmester, London 1767, 10in (25.5cm) high.
£11,200–12,500 / €16,400–18,300
$20,300–22,400 TSC

A silver cruet, by John Brashier, with five cut-glass bottles, London 1879, 6in (15cm) high.
£300–330 / €430–480
$540–600 GRe

Cups & Goblets

Niello

Niello is often referred to as an enamel but it is actually a mixture of sulphur, lead, silver and copper fused at 1200°C (2200°F) which produces a strong blue/black colour. It has been used in the Middle East from ancient times and is still much used today. Niello was particularly favoured in Russia in the late 18th and early 19th centuries and is often found on spoons, beakers, trays, salts and snuff boxes. An attractive contrast is created when combined with parcel gilding.

► **A silver-gilt and niello vodka cup,** by A. Storozhenko, Russian, Moscow 1871, 2¼in (5.5cm) high, in a gilt-tooled morocco case.
£240–280
€350–410
$430–510 PFK

► **A silver goblet,** by Tiffany & Co, with chased decoration, monogrammed NW, American, c1880, 6½in (16.5cm) high, 8oz.
£220–260 / €320–380
$400–470 JAA

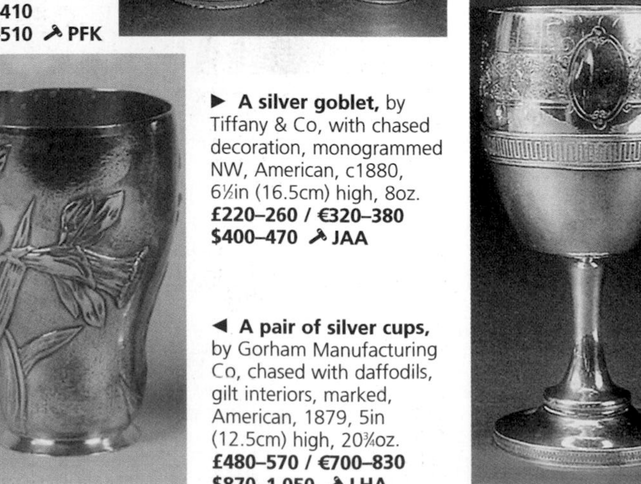

◄ **A pair of silver cups,** by Gorham Manufacturing Co, chased with daffodils, gilt interiors, marked, American, 1879, 5in (12.5cm) high, 20¾oz.
£480–570 / €700–830
$870–1,050 LHA

A silver font cup, by A. E. Jones, 1922, 6in (15cm) high.
£580–650 / €850–950
$1,050–1,200 EXC
This item was modelled after a font cup from Corpus Christi College, Oxford.

Cutlery

A silver laceback trefid spoon, probably by Nicholas Brassey, the reverse with a crest, London 1679, 7½in (19cm) long, 1½oz.
£910–1,050 / €1,350–1,600
$1,650–1,950 ⚒ WW

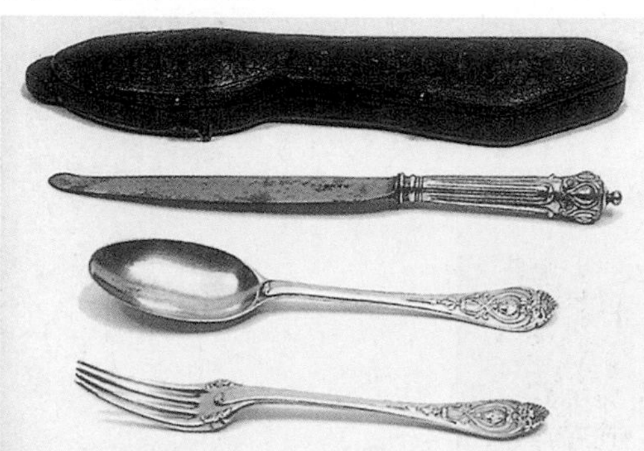

A silver-gilt travelling cutlery set, comprising a knife, fork and spoon, chased with a mask head, foliage and strapwork, French, 1723–74, in a gilded leather fitted case.
£1,300–1,550 / €1,900–2,250
$2,350–2,800 ⚒ Bea

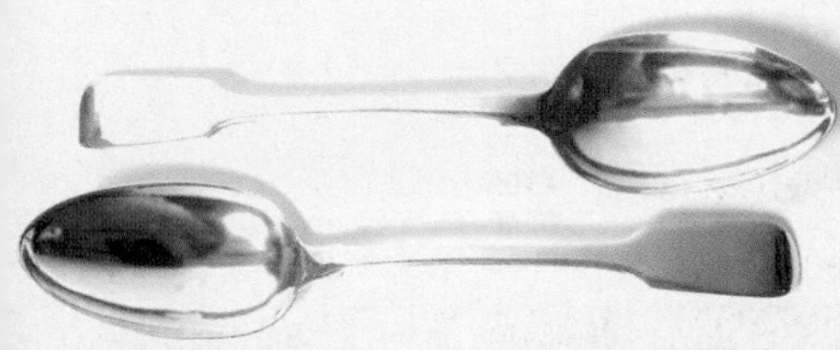

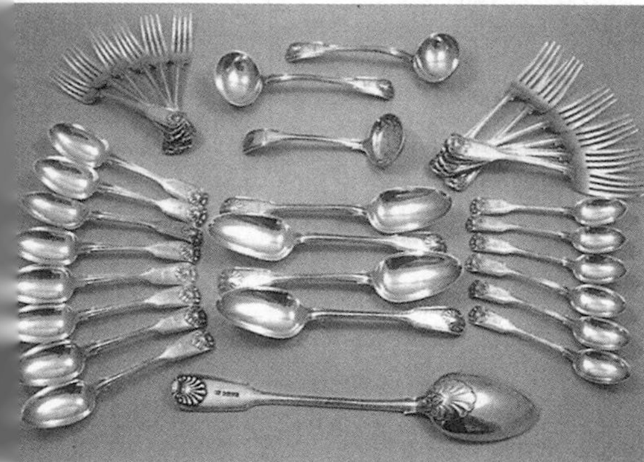

A silver Fiddle, Shell and Husk pattern part table service, by John Stone, comprising 34 pieces engraved with a boar's head crest, Exeter 1856, 78oz.
£940–1,100 / €1,350–1,600
$1,700–2,000 ⚒ DN(BR)

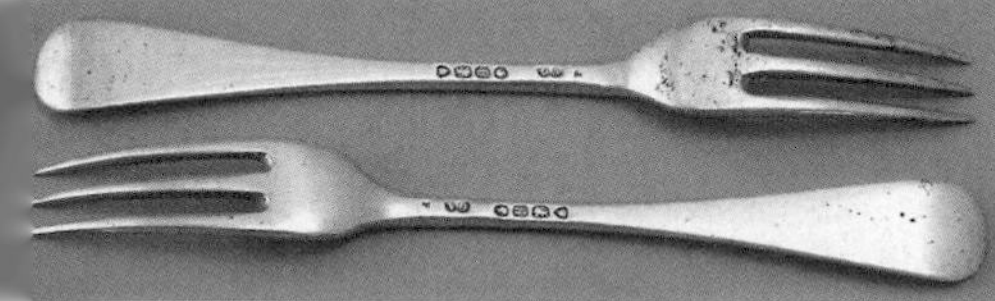

A set of six silver Old English pattern dessert forks, by George Adams, London 1872, 8oz.
£175–210 / €260–310
$320–380 ⚒ G(L)

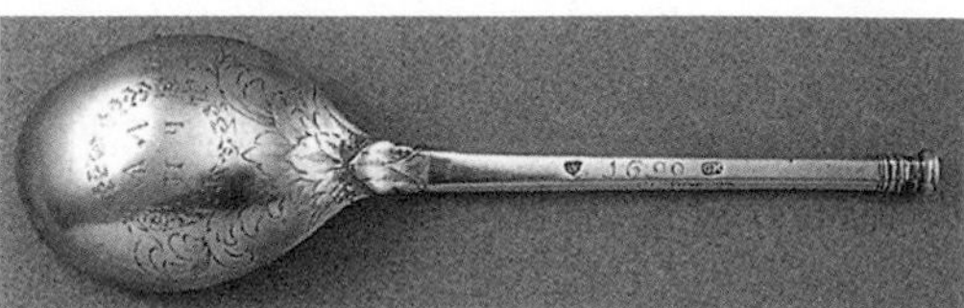

A silver seal top spoon, by Christian Mentzel Breslau, the reverse engraved with foliage and a wreath, the stem dated 1690, German, 7½in (19cm) long, 2½oz.
£610–730 / €890–1,050
$1,100–1,300 ⚒ WW

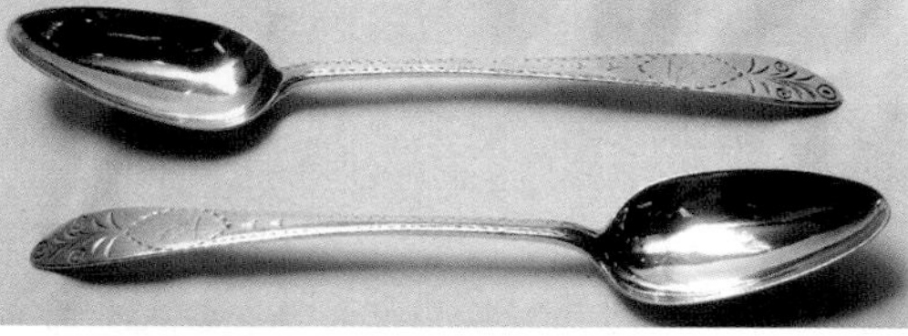

A pair of silver spoons, by John Warner, with bright-cut decoration, Irish, Cork, c1790, 10in (25.5cm) long.
£900–990 / €1,300–1,450
$1,600–1,800 ⊞ WELD

A silver Shell and Thread pattern table service, by Charles Eley, comprising 69 pieces, crested, London, 1827–28, four salt spoons by William Traies, 1833, 161oz.
£2,150–2,550 / €3,150–3,700
$3,900–4,600 ⚒ S

◄ **A pair of silver spoons,** by Barber & North, York 1844, 8½in (21.5cm) long.
£220–250 / €320–370
$400–450 ⊞ CoHA

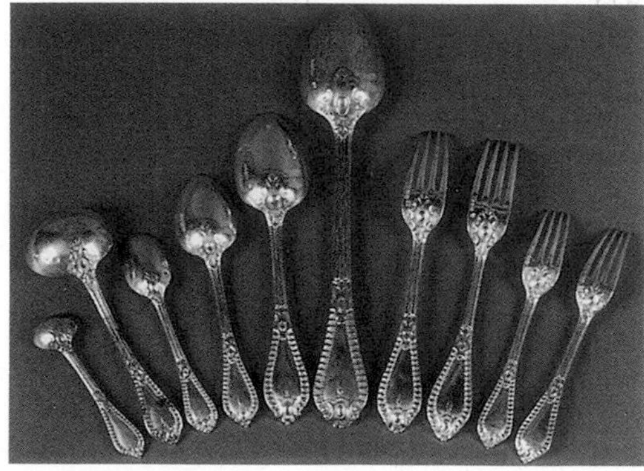

A silver Grecian pattern table service, by Edward and John Barnard, comprising 33 monogrammed pieces, London 1847, one fork London 1976, 82oz.
£820–980 / €1,200–1,450
$1,500–1,750 ⚒ HYD

► **A set of six silver-gilt and niello spoons,** each decorated with a different view of Moscow, Russian, 1887, 5in (12.5cm) long.
£500–560
€730–820
$900–1,000
⊞ GRe

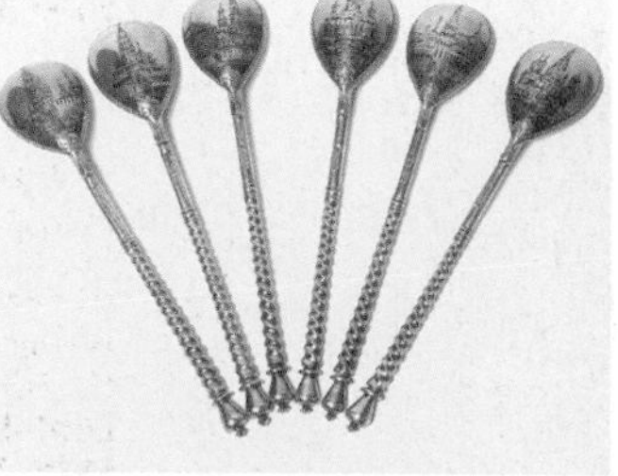

SILVER

Dishes

A silver dish, by Henning Petri, the centre decorated with a chased basket of flowers, Swedish, Nyköping 1694, 11¾in (30cm) wide.
£3,400–4,050 / €4,950–5,900
$6,200–7,300 ⚒ BUK

A silver dish, by William Moering, with embossed decoration, London 1894, 7in (18cm) wide.
£120–135 / €175–195
$210–240 ⊞ GRe

A silver dish, by Dominik Storr, with pierced sides, Austrian, Vienna 1816, 9in (23cm) wide, 25½oz.
£1,200–1,400 / €1,750–2,050
$2,150–2,550 ⚒ DORO

A silver dish, by Richard Martin and Ebenezer Hall, with shell and foliate-cast borders, Sheffield 1894, 11½in (29cm) diam, 37oz.
£470–560 / €690–820
$850–1,000 ⚒ L&T

◀ **A set of three silver nut dishes,** with thread-cast borders, Sheffield 1906, largest 9½in (24cm) wide.
£220–260 / €320–380
$400–470 ⚒ TMA

A silver bonbon dish, by Joseph Willmore, the fluted rim chased with flowers, the centre chased with a view of York Minster, the reverse gilt, Birmingham 1843, 6½in (16.5cm) diam.
£120–140 / €170–200
$210–250 ⚒ PFK

A silver bonbon dish, by Atkins Bros, Sheffield 1900, 5½in (14cm) wide.
£105–120 / €155–175
$200–220 ⊞ CoHA

A silver bonbon dish, by James Dixon & Sons, with pierced and embossed decoration, Sheffield 1909, 8½in (21.5cm) diam, 8oz.
£105–125 / €155–185
$200–230 ⚒ WW

Covered Dishes

A silver vegetable dish and cover, by Jacques-Henri Fauconnier, engraved with a monogram, slight damage, French, Paris, 1809–19, 10½in (26.5cm) wide, 42oz.
£1,150–1,350 / €1,700–2,000
$2,100–2,500 ⚒ S(P)

A pair of silver vegetable dishes and covers, engraved with initials MK, Austrian, Vienna 1840, 6¼in (16cm) wide, 25¼oz.
£570–680 / €830–990
$1,050–1,250 ⚒ S(P)

◀ **A silver vegetable dish and cover,** by S. Kirk & Son, relief-decorated with rural scenes and a country house, the finial in the form of a lion, monogrammed, American, c1900, 12in (30.5cm) wide, 57¾oz.
£1,350–1,600 / €1,950–2,350
$2,450–2,900 ⚒ DORO

A Victorian silver entrée dish and cover, the cover with a detachable handle, Sheffield 1894, 10in (25.5cm) wide, 41oz.
£300–360 / €440–530
$540–650 ⚒ L&E

A pair of silver entrée dishes, by Martin & Hall, Sheffield 1908, 12in (30.5cm) long, 149oz.
£5,400–6,000 / €7,900–8,800
$9,800–11,000 ⊞ BEX

Dish Rings

A pierced silver dish ring, by The Goldsmiths & Silversmiths Co, with a vacant rococo cartouche, maker's mark, Irish, Dublin 1903, 8in (20.5cm) diam.
£1,550–1,850 / €2,250–2,700 $2,800–3,350 WILK

A silver dish ring, by Wakely and Wheeler, the pierced sides decorated with pastoral figures and flowers, with a central vacant cartouche, Irish, Dublin 1908, 7in (18cm) diam, 8½oz.
£800–960 / €1,200–1,400 $1,450–1,750 L&T

A pierced silver dish ring, by Weir & Sons, Irish, Dublin 1910, 9½in (24cm) diam.
£1,650–1,850 / €2,400–2,700 $3,000–3,350 BEX

Further reading
Miller's Silver & Plate Buyer's Guide, Miller's Publications, 2002

Dish Warmers

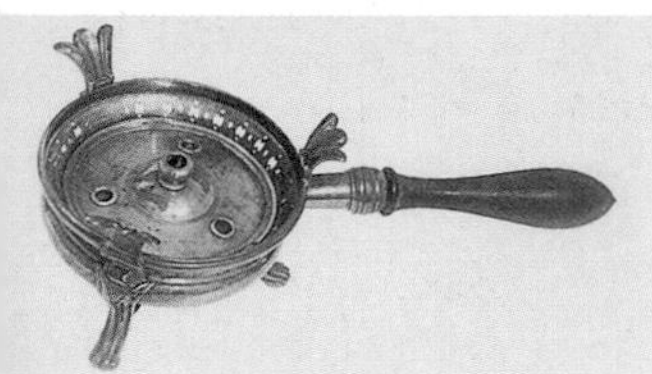

A silver dish warmer, with a pearwood handle, French, Paris, 1732–38, 8¼in (21cm) long, 10½oz.
£520–620 / €760–910 $940–1,100 F&C

A silver dish warmer, by Thomas Heming, London 1765, 8½in (21.5cm) diam, 26oz.
£1,800–2,150 / €2,650–3,150 $3,250–3,900 S

A silver dish warmer, the burner engraved with a crest, maker's mark BD, London 1773, 11¾in (30cm) wide, 15¾oz.
£900–1,050 / €1,300–1,550 $1,650–1,900 S(P)

Items in the Silver section have been arranged in date order within each sub-section.

Flatware

A silver meat dish, by Paul Crespin, with later engraved crests, London 1732, 14½in (37cm) wide.
£540–640 / €790–930 $980–1,150 DN

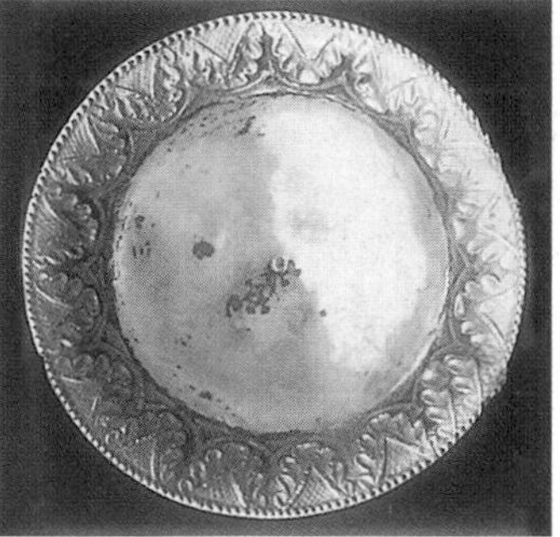

A silver-gilt dish, the border stamped with leaves, marked, 18thC, Dutch, 5¾in (14.5cm) diam.
£175–210 / €260–310 $320–380 HOLL

◄ **A silver entrée dish,** by Odiot, with an engraved armorial above a motto, French, Paris, 1875–1900, 11½in (29cm) diam, 23oz.
£210–250 / €310–370 $380–450 WW

► **A set of eight silver dessert plates,** engraved W, American, c1890, 10in (25.5cm) diam, 125oz.
£2,300–2,750 / €3,350–4,000 $4,150–5,000 S(NY)

A silver plate, decorated with a count's shield-of-arms, maker's mark, Austrian, Vienna 1817, 14½in (37cm) wide, 41oz.
£1,200–1,400 / €1,750–2,050 $2,150–2,550 DORO

Frames

A silver double frame, by John Septimus Beresford, the central boss with trailing floral decoration, London 1886, 15in (38cm) wide.
£1,050–1,200 / €1,550–1,750
$1,900–2,150 ⊞ RICC

A silver-mounted double frame, by William Comyns, embossed with cherub heads, London 1897, 12in (30.5cm) wide.
£470–560 / €690–820
$850–1,000 ⚒ HYD

◀ **A silver frame,** decorated with a cherub, import marks for London, 1892, 4in (10cm) high.
£195–220 / €280–320
$350–400 ⊞ SAT

A silver frame, with chased, embossed and pierced decoration of cherubs, birds and animals within leaves, Chester 1901, 9¼in (23.5cm) high.
£150–180 / €220–260
$280–330 ⚒ TMA

A silver frame, by W. Jackson & Son, in the form of a Greco-Romano portico, London 1908, 5¼in (13.5cm) wide.
£650–730 / €950–1,050
$1,100–1,300 ⊞ RICC

A silver frame, with an embossed gadrooned border, Birmingham 1912, 11in (28cm) wide.
£230–270 / €340–400
$420–500 ⚒ TMA

Inkwells & Inkstands

A silver inkstand, by Messrs Barnard, the two ink pots in the form of melons, with glass liners and detachable taperstick, slight damage, London 1840, 15in (38cm) wide, 49oz.
£2,700–3,200 / €3,950–4,650
$4,900–5,800 ⚒ WW

A silver inkstand, by George Fox, with pierced scrollwork decoration, the two ink pots and sand pot with glass liners, London 1866, 10½in (26.5cm) wide, 19½oz.
£760–910 / €1,100–1,300
$1,400–1,650 ⚒ TEN

A Victorian silver inkstand, with two silver-mounted cut-glass ink pots flanking a wafer pot surmounted by a taperstick, maker's mark SWS, 12in (30.5cm) wide, 19oz.
£420–500 / €610–730
$760–910 ⚒ AH
Wafers were gummed tabs used to stick envelopes down. Alternatively, sealing wax could be kept in wafer pots and melted using the taperstick.

◀ **A silver and glass inkwell and letter holder,** by E. Finley & H. Taylor, London 1886, 5in (12.5cm) wide.
£700–770 / €1,000–1,100
$1,250–1,4000 ⊞ BEX

▶ **A silver inkwell,** by Messrs Emanuel, London 1898, liner missing, 6in (15cm) wide, 10oz, with an associated dip pen.
£230–270 / €340–400
$420–500 ⚒ WW

Jugs

A silver cream jug, by David Hennel, with a contemporary crest, on hoof feet, London 1757, 4¼in (11cm) high, 5oz.
£210–250 / €310–370
$380–450 ⚒ F&C

A silver jug, converted from a tankard, with chased decoration, the spout later assayed, London 1767, 7¾in (19.5cm) high.
£440–520 / €640–760
$800–940 ⚒ CHTR

A silver milk jug, Assay Master's mark IWK for Jakob Wilhelm Kolb, Augsberg assay mark, German, 1777–79, 15in (38cm) high, 8¼oz.
£960–1,150
€1,450–1,700
$1,750–2,100 ⚒ DORO

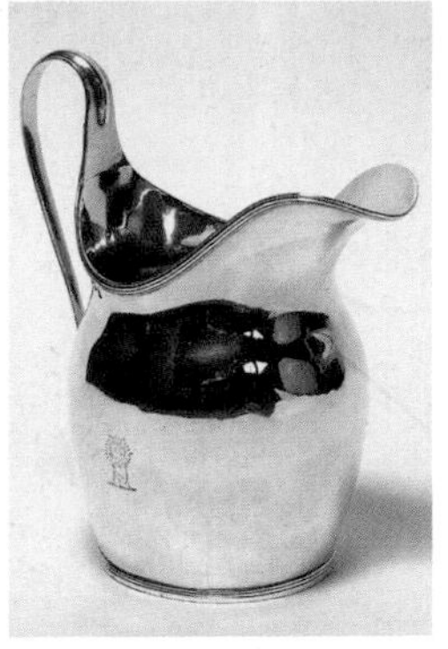

A silver cream jug, by Crispin Fuller, London 1794, 4in (10cm) high.
£340–380 / €500–550
$620–690 ⊞ GRe

► **A silver cream jug,** by Ann Robertson, Newcastle, c1800, 4in (10cm) high.
£580–650
€850–950
$1,050–1,200
⊞ BEX

► **A coin silver jug,** by A. & G. Welles, the hinged cover with a grasshopper finial, American, Boston, 1800–10, 8in (20.5cm) high.
£8,400–10,100
€12,300–14,700
$15,200–18,300 ⚒ JDJ

A silver cream jug, by Thomas Watson, Newcastle 1801, 5in (12.5cm) wide.
£320–360 / €470–530
$580–650 ⊞ GRe

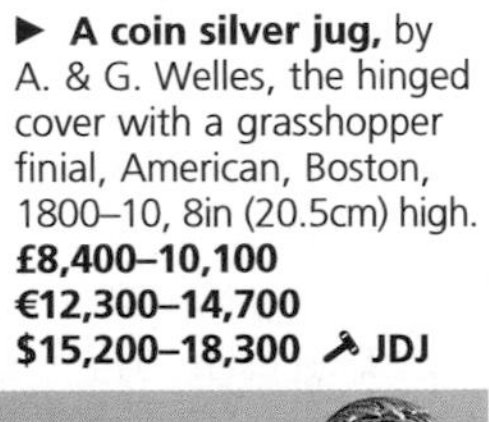

► **A silver cream jug,** with a leaf-moulded rim, crested, London 1833, 6¼in (16cm) wide, 10oz.
£200–240
€290–350
$360–430 ⚒ DA

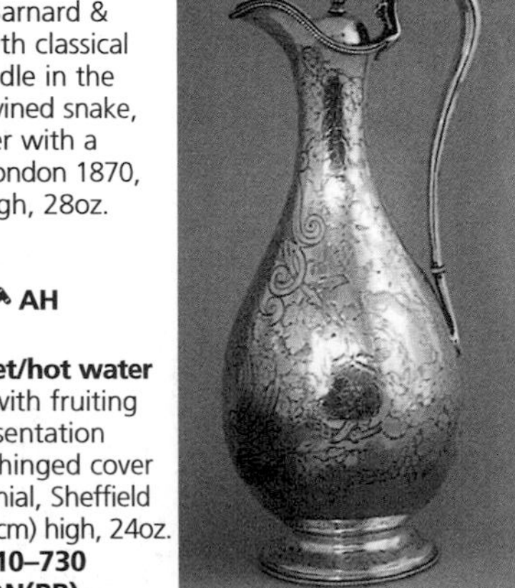

A silver-mounted glass claret jug, by Rupert Favell & Co, London 1886, 9in (23cm) high.
£165–195 / €240–280
$300–350 ⚒ G(L)

A silver-gilt-mounted glass claret jug, by W. G. Sissons, with engraved decoration, Sheffield 1868–69, 10in (25.5cm) high.
£2,450–2,750
€3,600–4,000
$4,450–5,000 ⊞ NS

A silver-mounted glass claret jug, by Barnard & Sons, the glass engraved with a floral festoon, with a scroll handle, London 1870, 12¼in (31cm) high.
£1,750–2,100
€2,550–3,050
$3,150–3,800 ⚒ RTo

A silver presentation claret jug, by Barnard & Sons, chased with classical figures, the handle in the form of an entwined snake, the hinged cover with a butterfly finial, London 1870, 13¾in (35cm) high, 28oz.
£1,150–1,350
€1,700–2,000
$2,100–2,500 ⚒ AH

► **A silver claret/hot water jug,** engraved with fruiting vines and a presentation inscription, the hinged cover with an acorn finial, Sheffield 1887, 12½in (32cm) high, 24oz.
£420–500 / €610–730
$760–910 ⚒ DN(BR)

A silver cream jug, by Nathan & Hayes, Chester 1895, 7in (18cm) high.
£200–230 / €290–340
$360–420 ⊞ GRe

A silver-mounted glass chota-peg, Birmingham 1908, 4in (10cm) high.
£110–125 / €160–180
$200–220 ⊞ EXC

A chota-peg is a jug used for individual servings of alcohol, originating from British colonial India at the end of the 19th century. Chota is Hindi for 'small measure'.

A silver-mounted cut-glass claret jug, by Walker & Hall, Sheffield 1908, 9in (23cm) high.
£480–570 / €700–830
$870–1,050 ⚒ NSal

A silver jug, by Wakely & Wheeler, marked, 1910, 7in (18cm) high.
£155–175 / €230–260
$280–320 ⊞ CoHA

Kettles

A silver tea kettle, stand and burner, by Paul Storr, on three feet, crested, London 1837, 11½in (29cm) high, 37¾oz.
£640–760 / €930–1,100
$1,200–1,400 ⚒ Bea

A silver kettle, stand and burner, by Robert Hennell, decorated with scrollwork, London 1865, 17½in (44.5cm) high, 85½oz.
£2,000–2,400
€2,900–3,500
$3,600–4,350 ⚒ TEN

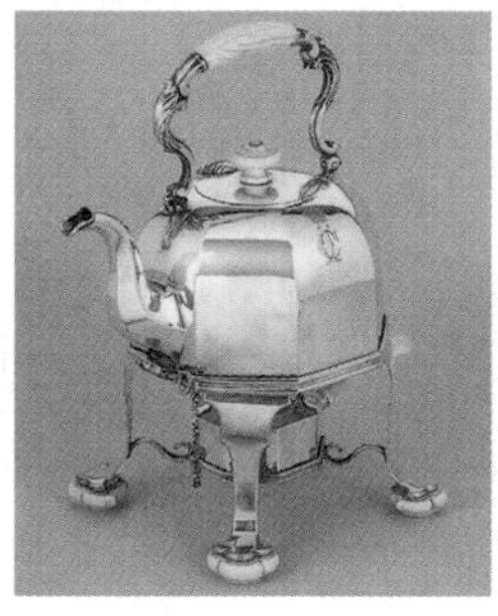

A silver kettle, stand and burner, with an ivory finial, handle and feet, crowned monogram, Master's mark for Stefan Mayerhofer & Klinkosch, Austrian, Vienna, 1867–72, 10½in (26½cm) high.
£1,750–2,100
€2,550–3,050
$3,150–3,800 ⚒ DORO

A George I-style silver spirit kettle and burner, by Harmans, London 1910, 7½in (19cm) high, 42oz.
£540–640 / €790–930
$980–1,150 ⚒ HOLL

Cross Reference
Kitchenware
see pages 200–202

Ladles

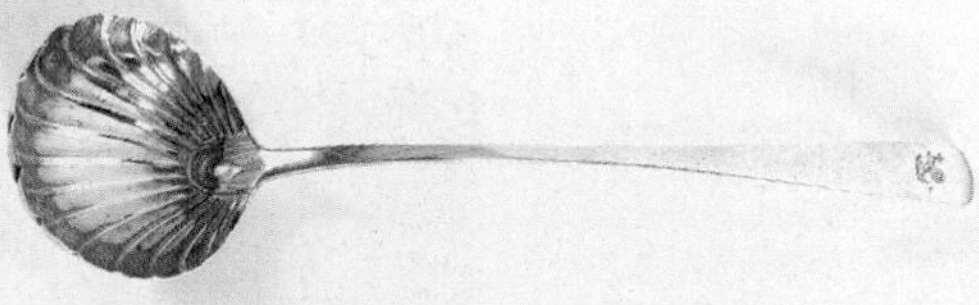

A silver Old English pattern soup ladle, by John King, with a lion crest, Irish, Dublin 1736, 14in (35.5cm) long.
£410–490 / €600–720
$740–890 ⚒ GAK

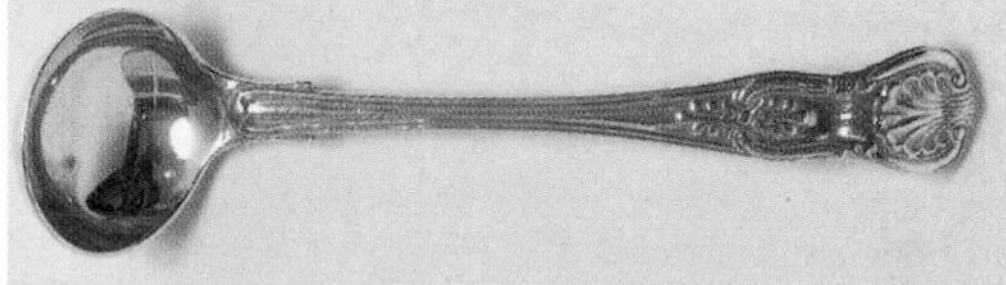

A silver cream ladle, Irish, Dublin 1841, 5½in (14cm) long.
£85–95 / €125–140
$150–170 ⊞ GRe

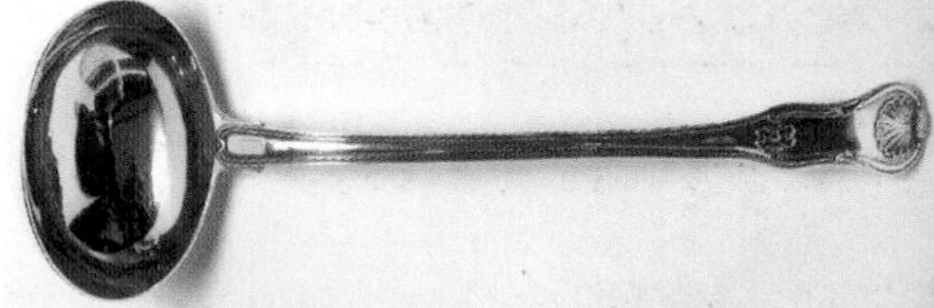

A silver soup ladle, by John Lias, London 1817, 13in (33cm) long, 9oz.
£310–350 / €450–510
$560–630 ⊞ GRe

A pair of silver sauce ladles, London 1900, 7in (18cm) long.
£150–165 / €210–240
$270–300 ⊞ CoHA

Menu Holders

◀ **A silver menu holder,** by William Comyns, London 1896, 1¾in (4.5cm) wide.
£150–165
€210–240
$270–300 ⊞ BEX

A set of four silver owl menu holders, with glass eyes, Chester 1905, 1¼in (3cm) high.
£610–730 / €900–1,050
$1,100–1,300 ⚒ G(L)

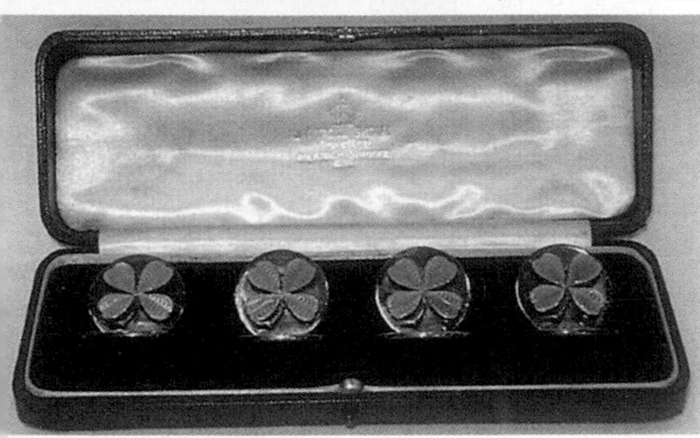

◀ **A set of four silver menu holders,** by Sampson Mordan & Co, each applied with an enamel shamrock, Chester 1909, in a fitted case.
£470–560
€690–820
$850–1,000
⚒ HYD

A silver menu holder, by Stokes & Ireland, Chester 1909, 1½in (4cm) high.
£150–165 / €210–240
$270–300 ⊞ BEX

Mirrors

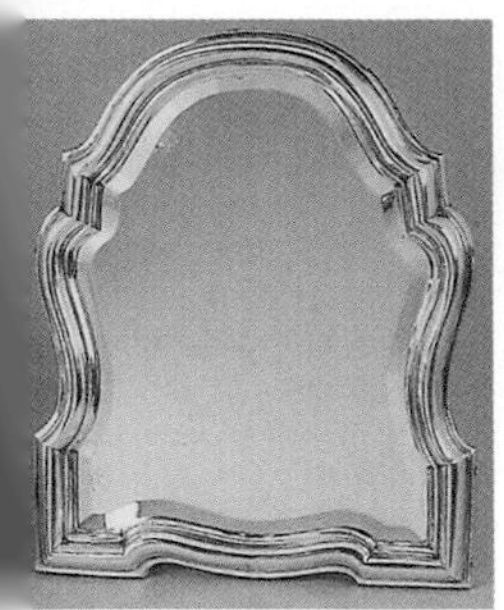

silver mirror, with
laster's mark AFH for
nton Franz Halder,
ustrian, Vienna 1756,
0¼in (26cm) wide.
1,300–1,550
1,900–2,250
2,350–2,800 ⚒ DORO

A silver dressing table mirror, by William Comyns, decorated with scrollwork, birds and flowers, the plate damaged, Birmingham 1893, 11in (28cm) high.
£150–180 / €220–260
$270–320 ⚒ PFK

A silver easel mirror, with a vacant cartouche and scrolling flowers and foliage, London 1896, 32in (81.5cm) high.
£1,750–2,100
€2,550–3,050
$3,150–3,800 ⚒ WILK

A silver mirror, by William Comyns, London 1899, 11in (28cm) high.
£1,450–1,650
€2,100–2,400
$2,600–3,000 ⊞ BEX

Items in the Silver section have been arranged in date order within each sub-section.

Mugs & Tankards

silver tankard, the hinged
over with a corkscrew
umbpiece, London 1685,
¾in (17cm), 18oz.
1,900–2,250
2,750–3,300
3,450–4,050 ⚒ HYD

A silver tankard, by Jonathan French, Newcastle 1720, 6in (15cm) high.
£4,050–4,500
€5,800–6,600
$7,200–8,100 ⊞ NS

A silver tankard, by Richard van Dyck, engraved with a cypher and ship, the handle with rat-tail, marked, spout and some engraving later, American, New York, c1740, 7¾in (19.5cm) high, 42oz.
£4,950–5,900
€7,200–8,600
$9,000–10,700 ⚒ S(NY)

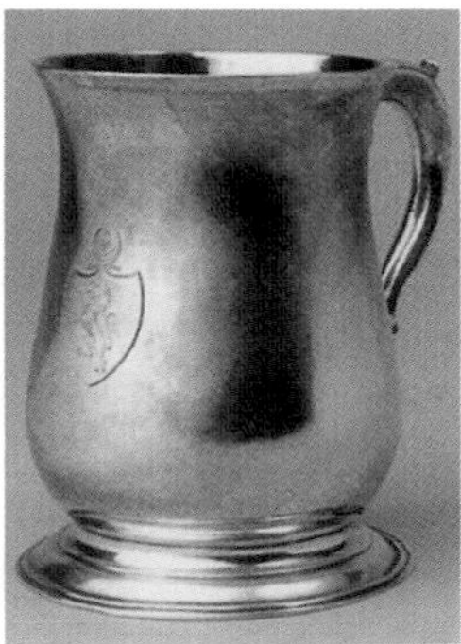

A silver mug, by Robert Albin Cox, engraved with a crescent crest within an armorial shield, London 1758, 4¾in (12cm) high, 11oz.
£640–760 / €930–1,100
$1,150–1,350 ⚒ NSal

A silver christening mug, embossed with acanthus leaves and flowers, with a gilt interior, London 1839, 3in (7.5cm) high.
£210–250 / €310–370
$380–450 GAK

► A silver tankard, with two bands of beadwork and engraved floral decoration, maker's mark rubbed, London 1872, 4in (10cm) high, 7½oz, with a fitted case.
£230–270 / €330–390
$420–490 TEN

A silver mug, by Benjamin Smith, London 1846, 3½in (9cm) high.
£260–290 / €380–420
$470–520 GRe

A silver christening mug, by E. Kerr Reid, with an embossed floral swag and scroll handle, London 1860, 3¾in (9.5cm) high, 4½oz.
£140–165 / €200–240
$250–300 G(L)

A silver mug, possibly by John Carrington, with chased bead and scroll decoration, monogrammed, London 1872, 3in (7.5cm) high, 3½oz.
£120–140 / €175–200
$220–250 HYD

LOCATE THE SOURCE

The source of each illustration in Miller's can be found by checking the code letters below each caption with the Key to Illustrations, pages 778–784.

Napkin Rings

◄ A set of four silver-gilt and enamel napkin rings, by Frederick Elkington, Birmingham 1871, 2in (5cm) diam.
£400–450 / €580–660
$720–810 GRe

A silver napkin ring, by David and George Edward, decorated with the signs of the zodiac, Scottish, Glasgow 1905, 1¼in (3cm) diam.
£130–145 / €190–210
$230–260 BEX

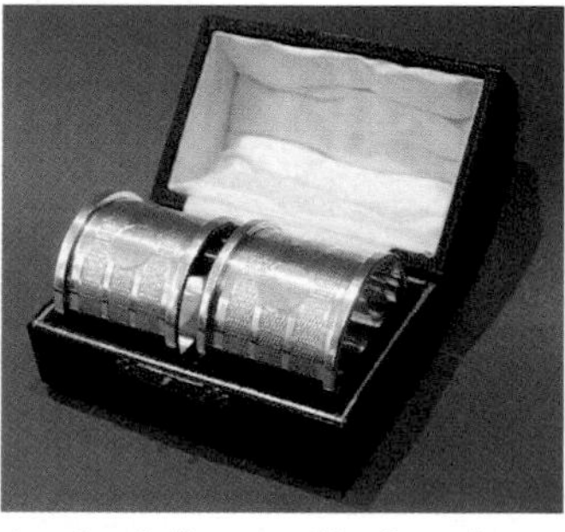

A pair of silver napkin rings, by Levi & Salaman, Birmingham 1926, 1½in (4cm) diam, in a fitted case.
£200–230 / €290–330
$360–420 BEX

A set of six silver napkin rings, by G. F., with monogrammed cartouches, London 1877, in a Mappin Brothers presentation case, 7in (18cm) square.
£360–430 / €530–630
$650–780 SWO

Pails

A silver cream pail, by Richard Meach, pierced and embossed, London, c1775, 2¼in (5.5cm) high, 2½oz.
£330–390 / €480–570
$600–710 WW

◄ A silver-framed pail, with a Royal Worcester liner, Birmingham 1907, 3¾in (9.5cm) high.
£185–220
€280–330
$340–400 SPF

► A silver cream pail, London 1912, 6in (15cm) high.
£220–250
€320–360
$400–450 HTE

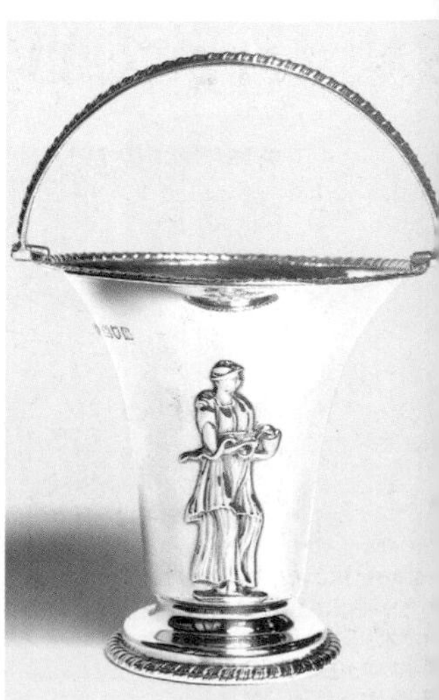

SILVER

Porringers

A silver porringer, the central reserve inscribed 'DS 1715', London 1637, 3¼in (8.5cm) high.
£2,350–2,800 / €3,450–4,100
$4,250–5,100 ⚒ CHTR

A silver porringer, by Katharine Stevens, chased with acanthus leaves, initialled RB ME, London 1675, 4in (10cm) diam.
£1,250–1,500 / €1,850–2,200
$2,250–2,700 ⚒ S

A silver porringer, by Elias Pelletreau, initialled, American, Southampton, Long Island, 1770–80, 5½in (14cm) diam, 8oz.
£4,950–5,900 / €7,200–8,600
$9,000–10,700 ⚒ S(NY)

◄ **A silver porringer,** with fluted and foliate decoration, with two handles, London 1900, 4½in (11.5cm) high.
£280–330 / €410–480
$510–600 ⚒ G(L)

Rattles

A silver rattle, by Carl Magnus Ryberg, with a bone handle, slight damage, Swedish, Stockholm 1812, 5in (12.5cm) long.
£390–460 / €570–670
$700–830 ⚒ BUK

A silver rattle, by Hilliard & Thomason, with a whistle and coral teether, hung with six bells, Birmingham 1904, 5¼in (13.5cm) long.
£260–310 / €380–450
$470–560 ⚒ DN

A silver rattle, with a bone teething ring and mother-of-pearl handle, Birmingham 1908, 5in (12.5cm) long.
£40–45
€55–65
$70–80 ⚒ AMB

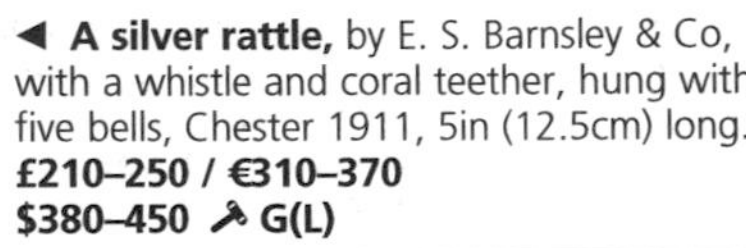

◄ **A silver rattle,** by E. S. Barnsley & Co, with a whistle and coral teether, hung with five bells, Chester 1911, 5in (12.5cm) long.
£210–250 / €310–370
$380–450 ⚒ G(L)

Salvers & Waiters

A silver salver, by Robert Abercromby, on three hoof feet, London 1738, 8in (20.5cm) diam, 11½oz.
£400–480 / €580–700
$720–870 ⚒ DN

A silver waiter, by William Peaston, engraved with an armorial, London 1755, 6in (15cm) diam, 7½oz.
£330–390 / €480–570
$600–710 ⚒ G(L)

A silver waiter, by Charles Wood, engraved with a coat-of-arms, with three hoof feet, marked CW and with an alligator's head, Jamaican, c1760, 8in (20.5cm) wide.
£3,750–4,500 / €5,500–6,600
$6,800–8,100 ⚒ TRM(E)

A silver salver, by Richard Rugg, on claw-and-ball feet, London 1773, 13in (33cm) wide, 31oz.
£560–670 / €820–980
$1,000–1,200 ⚒ DN(BR)

A silver salver, by James Le Bass, with an engraved floral border and later inscription, Irish, Dublin 1818, 15in (38cm) wide, 44oz.
£350–420 / €510–610
$630–760 ⚒ L

◄ **A silver salver,** by Pearce & Sons, engraved with a presentation inscription, Birmingham 1892, 16¼in (41.5cm) wide, 57oz.
£410–490 / €600–720
$740–890 ⚒ TEN

A salver is a flat dish, sometimes with feet, which is used for serving food or drink. It is similar to a tray but without handles, and often has a moulded border. Waiters are smaller and often come in pairs or sets.

A silver salver, with chased and embossed decoration, on three shell feet, London 1903, 12½in (32cm) wide.
£240–290 / €350–420
$420–500 ⚒ GAK

Sauce & Cream Boats

A silver sauce/cream boat, by Charles Chesterman, London 1752, 4in (10cm) wide.
£380–430 / €550–630
$690–780 ⊞ GRe

Items in the Silver section have been arranged in date order within each sub-section.

A silver cream boat, by Daniel Lundström, the handle and feet in the form of leaves, with a gilt interior, Swedish, Stockholm 1775, 7¼in (18.5cm) wide.
£1,750–2,100 / €2,550–3,050
$3,150–3,800 ⚒ BUK

► **A silver sauce boat,** decorated with foliate scrolls, French, c1880, 8½in (21.5cm) wide, 12oz.
£300–360 / €440–530
$540–650 ⚒ WW

A silver sauce boat, with a punched rim, leaf-capped scrolled handle, on three shell and hoof feet, 1778, 5¼in (13.5cm) high.
£390–460 / €570–670
$710–830 ⚒ GAK

Scent Bottles

◄ **A silver scent bottle,** by Sampson Mordan, London 1875, 2in (5cm) diam.
£1,100–1,250
€1,600–1,850
$2,000–2,250
⊞ SHa

► **A silver-mounted glass scent bottle,** Birmingham 1899, 3in (7.5cm) high.
£220–250
€320–360
$400–450 ⊞ SAT

A silver-mounted glass scent bottle, 1929, 4in (10cm) high.
£110–125 / €160–180
$200–230 ⊞ CoHA

SILVER

Serving Implements

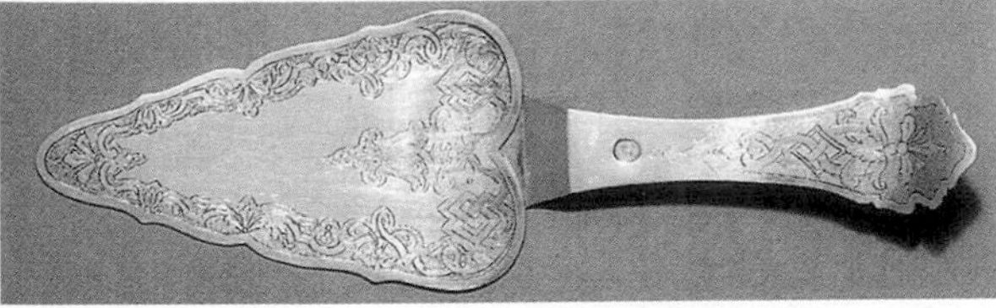

A silver cake slice, by Jürgen Friedrich Sickman, monogram stamp, Swedish, Stockholm 1747, 10¾in (27.5cm) long.
£16,500–19,500 / €24,000–28,500
$30,000–35,000 ⚒ BUK

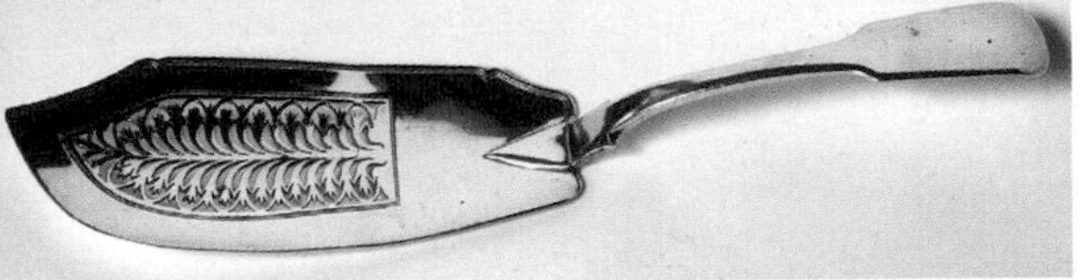

A silver fish slice, London 1820, 12in (30.5cm) long.
£85–95 / €125–140
$155–170 ⊞ SAT

► **A pair of silver sugar nips,** by John and Henry Lias, London 1865, 4in (10cm) long.
£140–160 / €200–230
$250–290 ⊞ SAT

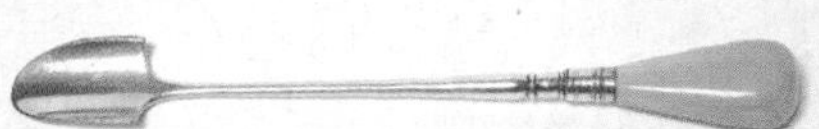

A silver cheese scoop, by John Shekleton, with an ivory handle, London 1800, 10in (25.5cm) long.
£220–250 / €320–360
$400–450 ⊞ GRe

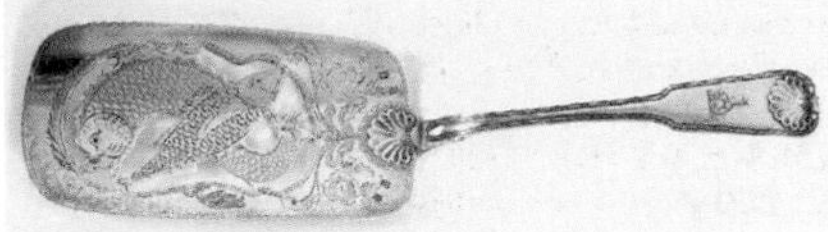

A silver fish slice, by P. W., engraved with a fish, Irish, Dublin 1818, 10in (25.5cm) long, 4½oz.
£590–700 / €860–1,000
$1,050–1,250 ⊞ GAK

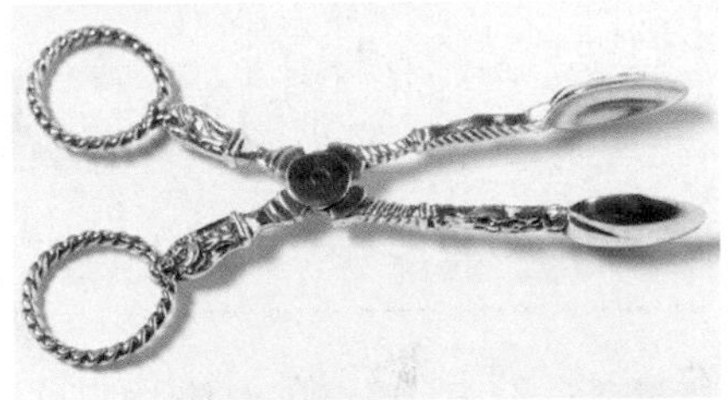

Snuff Boxes

► **A silver navette-shaped snuff box,** by Aeneus Ryan, Irish, Dublin 1789, 3¼in (8.5cm) wide.
£2,000–2,250 / €2,900–3,300
$3,600–4,050 ⊞ WELD

A silver-gilt snuff box, by Joseph Ash, London 1805, 2¾in (7cm) wide.
£175–210 / €260–310
$320–380 ⚒ HYD

A silver and niello snuff box, with a gilt interior, the cover engraved with a summerhouse surrounded by trees, maker's mark SES for Stephan Eduard Starkloff, Austrian, Vienna 1831, 3¼in (8.5cm) long, 4oz.
£1,300–1,550 / €1,900–2,250
$2,350–2,800 ⚒ DORO

◄ **A silver snuff box,** by Nathaniel Mills, the cover chased in relief with a view of Windsor Castle, slight damage, Birmingham 1838, 2¼in (5.5cm) wide.
£400–480 / €580–700
$720–870 ⚒ RTo

Stands

A silver teapot stand, by William Bateman, with a wreath cartouche, London 1802, 2½in (6.5cm) wide, 4½oz.
£175–210 / €250–300
$320–380 ⚒ WW

► **A set of four silver dessert stands,** by Hunt & Roskell, London 1874, 8½in (21.5cm) high, 86oz, with four damaged glass dishes.
£3,600–4,300 / €5,300–6,300
$6,500–7,800 ⚒ S

◄ **A silver teapot stand,** by T. Bradbury, on reeded feet, London 1901, 7in (18cm) wide, 5oz.
£120–140 / €175–210
$210–250 ⚒ WW

Table Bells

A silver table bell, by Peter and William Bateman, London 1813, 4½in (11.5cm) high, 3¾oz.
£2,000–2,250
€2,900–3,300
$3,600–4,050 ⊞ BEX

A silver table bell, by R. Mellin, Finnish, Helsinki 1882, 4¾in (12cm) high.
£1,200–1,400
€1,750–2,050
$2,150–2,550 ⚒ BUK(F)

A silver table bell, by Joseph Septimus Beresford, London 1886, 5in (12.5cm) high, 5½oz.
£540–640 / €790–930
$980–1,150 ⚒ WW

A silver table bell, with an ivory handle, Birmingham 1906, 4¼in (11cm) high.
£200–240 / €290–350
$360–430 ⚒ TEN

Tea Caddies

◀ **A set of three silver tea caddies,** by John Newton, chased with floral decoration, London c1737, largest 5½in (14cm) high, 30oz.
£4,000–4,800
€5,800–7,000
$7,200–8,700
⚒ TEN

A silver tea caddy, monogrammed AL, London 1781, 4¾in (12cm) high.
£1,400–1,650
€2,050–2,400
$2,550–3,000 ⚒ AMB

A George III silver tea caddy, by Charles Aldridge and Henry Green, with beaded decoration, 4in (10cm) wide, 8¾oz.
£1,000–1,200
€1,450–1,750
$1,800–2,150 ⚒ Bea

A silver tea caddy, by George Unite, with spiral-moulded decoration, Birmingham 1884, 3¾in (9.5cm) high, 3½oz.
£105–125 / €155–185
$190–220 ⚒ WW

A silver tea caddy, by Nathan & Hayes, embossed with a stag hunt, Birmingham 1893, 3¾in (9.5cm) high, 4½oz.
£290–340 / €420–500
$520–620 ⚒ DN

A silver and mother-of-pearl tea caddy, London 1895, 3in (7.5cm) high.
£1,450–1,650
€2,100–2,400
$2,600–3,000 ⊞ JTS

A silver tea caddy, with two lion-mask handles, Chester 1902, 4in (10cm) high.
£140–165 / €200–240
$250–300 ⚒ G(L)

▶ **A silver tea caddy,** Birmingham 1903, 4½in (11.5cm) high.
£540–600 / €790–880
$980–1,100 ⊞ BLm

▶ **A silver tea caddy,** Chester 1905, 4in (10cm) high.
£145–165 / €210–240
$260–300 ⊞ EXC

Toast Racks

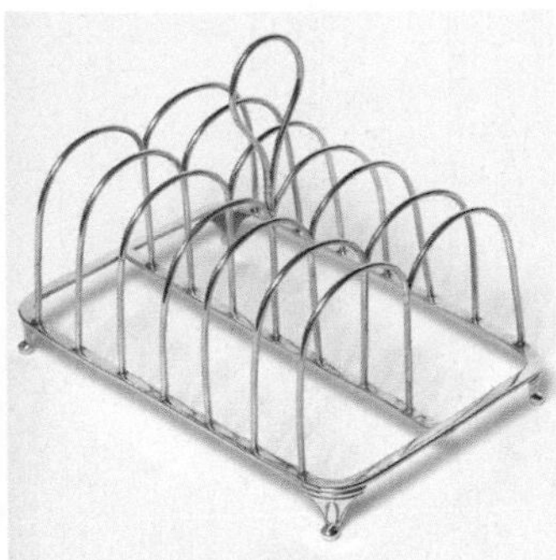

A silver toast rack, by John Tweedie, London 1784, 6in (15cm) wide.
£520–580 / €760–850
$940–1,050 SAT

A silver toast rack, Sheffield 1898, 9in (23cm) wide.
£180–200 / €260–290
$320–360 HO

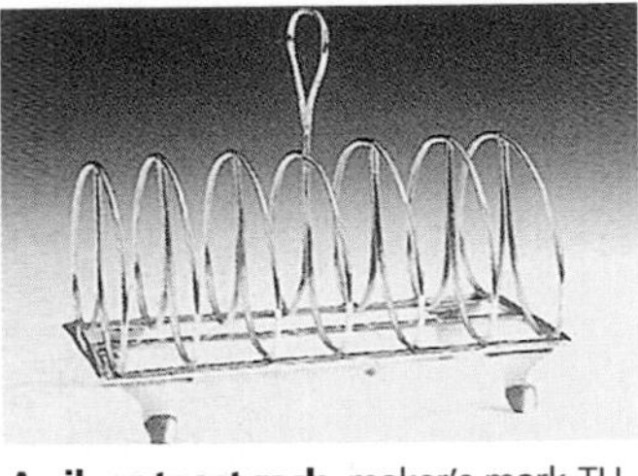

A silver toast rack, maker's mark TH, London 1795, 6in (15cm) wide, 6¾oz.
£440–520 / €640–760
$800–940 TEN

A silver-gilt toast rack, by C. Saunders & F. Shepherd, London 1910, 4in (10cm) wide, 2½oz.
£580–650 / €850–950
$1,050–1,200 BEX

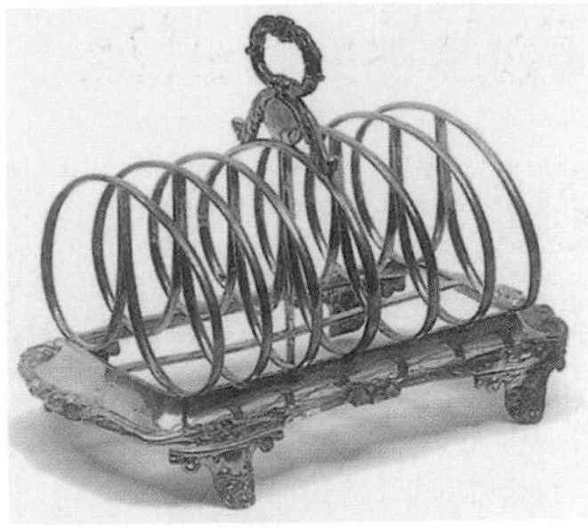

A silver toast rack, by Joseph and John Angell, London 1835, 8in (20.5cm) wide, 13¾oz.
£530–630 / €770–920
$960–1,150 Bea

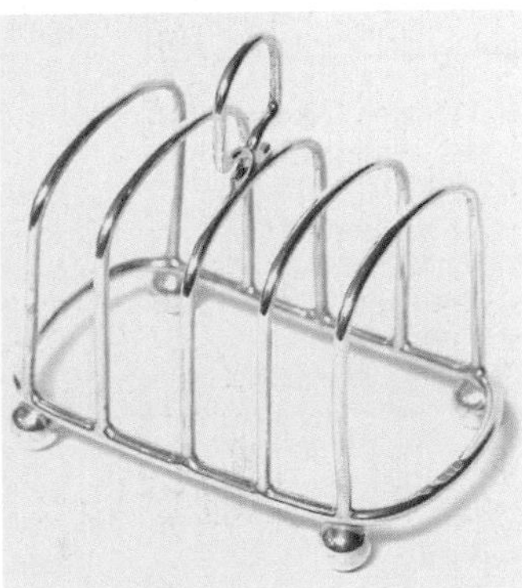

A silver toast rack, Chester 1911, 4in (10cm) wide.
£115–130 / €170–190
$210–240 SAT

Tureens

A pair of silver sauce tureens and covers, by John Carter, applied with paterae and husks, the pedestal supports chased with acanthus leaves, London 1775, 9in (23cm) wide, 48¼oz.
£3,100–3,700 / €4,550–5,400
$5,600–6,700 S

A pair of silver tureens and covers, with entwined loop handles and leaf-cast terminals, French, 19thC, 10¾in (27.5cm) high.
£590–700 / €860–1,000
$1,050–1,250 TEN

A pair of silver sauce tureens and covers, probably by Robert Gainsford, with foliate-chased scrolled handles, marked, Sheffield 1797, 7in (18cm) wide, 38¼oz.
£1,450–1,750 / €2,100–2,500
$2,650–3,150 DN

A silver soup tureen and cover, by R. Garrard, the cover with a later handle, London 1834, 13½in (34.5cm) high.
£1,400–1,650 / €2,050–2,400
$2,550–3,000 G(L)

A silver soup tureen and cover, by Lebrun, with a gilt interior, the cover with a later finial in the form of a grape, French, Paris, 1819–38, 11in (28cm) high.
£2,500–3,000 / €3,650–4,400
$4,550–5,400 S

A silver tureen and cover, engraved with a coat-of-arms, Master's mark BMF for Alexander Schöller, Austrian, Vienna 1852, 11in (28cm) high, 60oz.
£2,250–2,700 / €3,300–3,950
$4,100–4,900 DORO

Vases

A silver openwork vase holder, decorated with masks, vines and serpents, liner and cover missing, maker's mark NRM, French, Paris, 1798–1809, 8in (20.5cm) high, 17oz.
£150–180 / €220–260
$270–320 ⚒ WW

A silver-gilt-mounted cut-crystal vase, in the form of a cornucopia supported by a child, slight damage, French, Paris, c1890, 7¾in (19.5cm) high, 27½oz.
£1,800–2,150
€2,650–3,150
$3,250–3,900 ⚒ S(P)

A pair of silver vases, by Alexander Clark & Co, Birmingham 1899, 6in (15cm) high.
£220–250 / €320–370
$400–450 ⊞ SAT

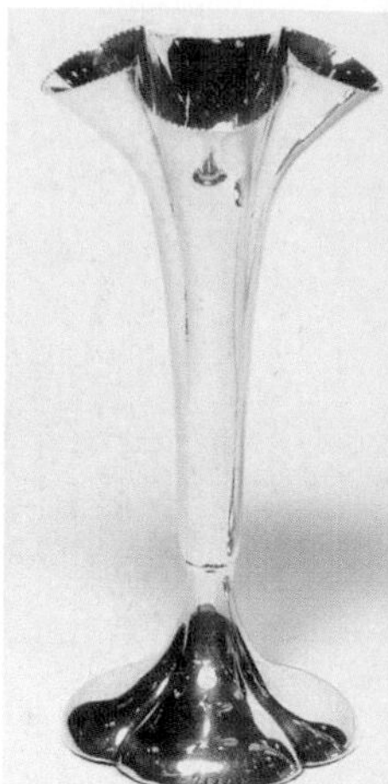

A pair of silver vases, London 1908, 4¼in (11cm) high.
£145–165 / €210–240
$260–300 ⊞ BLm

Vesta Cases

A silver vesta case, by Deakin & Francis, Birmingham 1893, 2in (5cm) high.
£200–230 / €290–330
$360–410 ⊞ BEX

► **A silver vesta case,** decorated in relief with a portrait of Queen Victoria, Chester 1900, 2in (5cm) wide.
£175–210 / €250–300
$320–380 ⚒ G(L)

A silver and enamel vesta case, Birmingham 1898, 2in (5cm) wide.
£760–850 / €1,100–1,250
$1,400–1,550 ⊞ SHa

Silver vesta cases are usually of a rounded rectangular shape in order to fit easily into the waistcoat pocket. Rare designs that are greatly sought after include railway and opera tickets that are invariably accurate copies of the originals with enamel detail.

◄ **A silver vesta case,** by Horace Woodward, Birmingham 1912, 1in (2.5cm) wide.
£65–75 / €95–11
$120–135 ⊞ GR

Vinaigrettes

A silver vinaigrette/pomander, c1695, 1¼in (3cm) diam.
£1,650–1,850 / €2,400–2,700
$3,000–3,350 ⊞ BEX

A silver vinaigrette, by Thomas Willmore, engraved with flower and leaf sprays, Birmingham 1804, 1¼in (3cm) wide.
£190–220 / €280–320
$340–400 ⚒ DN

A silver vinaigrette, by Matthew Linwood, the cover engraved with a horn player leaning against a tree, the pierced grille with a central heart, Birmingham 1810, 1¼in (3cm) wide.
£760–910 / €1,100–1,300
$1,400–1,650 ⚒ G(L)

◄ **A silver-gilt vinaigrette,** by John Shaw, Birmingham 1813, 1½in (4cm) wide.
£210–240 / €310–350
$380–430 ⊞ SAT

A silver vinaigrette, by Joseph Taylor, engraved with wrigglework, the grille pierced with a heart, London 1821, 1½in (4cm) wide.
£230–270 / €340–390
$420–490 ⚒ DN

A silver vinaigrette, by Thomas Shaw, Birmingham 1823, 1½in (4cm) wide.
£155–175 / €230–260
$280–320 ⊞ SAT

A cast-silver vinaigrette, by William Simpson, Birmingham 1835, 1¾in (4.5cm) wide, 1oz.
£1,450–1,650 / €2,100–2,400
$2,600–3,000 ⊞ BEX

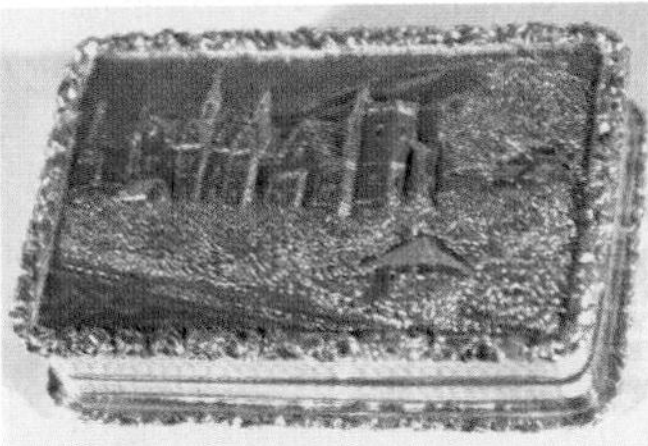

A silver-gilt vinaigrette, by Taylor & Perry, moulded with a view of Abbotsford House, Scotland, with a foliate-pierced grille, Birmingham 1835, 1¾in (4.5cm) wide.
£1,800–2,150 / €2,650–3,150
$3,250–3,900 ⚒ AH

A silver vinaigrette, by Thomas Shaw, the cover engraved with trailing flowers and leaves, the base with acorns within a wrigglework border, the grille pierced with trailing flowers and leaf scrolls, Birmingham 1835, 1¼in (3cm) wide.
£190–220 / €280–320
$340–400 ⚒ DN

A silver vinaigrette, by Nathaniel Mills, Birmingham 1837, 2½in (6.5cm) wide.
£1,250–1,500 / €1,850–2,200
$2,250–2,700 ⚒ BWL

A silver vinaigrette, by Thomas Shaw, with engine-turned decoration, with a pierced and engraved scrolling foliate grille, Birmingham 1838, 1½in (4cm) wide.
£175–210 / €250–300
$320–380 ⚒ DN

A silver vinaigrette, by John Tongue, the cover engraved with fishermen in a boat, Birmingham 1846, 2in (5cm) wide.
£440–520 / €640–760
$800–940 ⚒ WW

◄ **A silver vinaigrette,** by George Unite, engraved with acanthus leaves, with a pierced and engraved grille, on a curb-link chain, Birmingham 1856, 1¼in (3cm) wide.
£150–180 / €220–260
$270–320 ⚒ G(L)

◄ **A silver vinaigrette,** with engine-turned decoration, with a pierced grille, maker's mark D&M, Birmingham 1864, 3in (7.5cm) wide, 3½oz.
£200–240
€290–350
$360–430 ⚒ TEN

A silver vinaigrette, by Nathaniel Mills, depicting the Albert Memorial, with a pierced grille, Birmingham 1883, 2in (5cm) wide.
£670–750 / €980–1,100
$1,200–1,350 ⊞ CoHA

Miscellaneous

A silver model of a WWI biplane, by JSB, London 1916, 5½in (14cm) wide.
£1,650–1,950 / €2,400–2,850
$3,000–3,550 ⚒ RTo

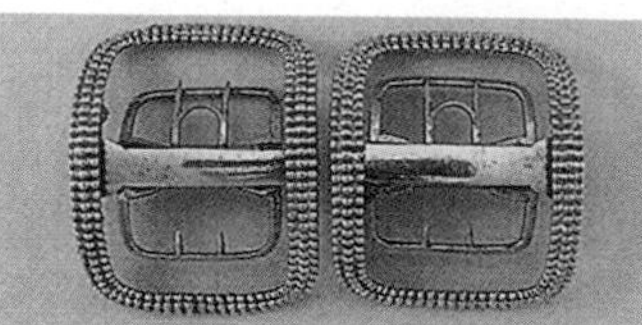

A pair of silver shoe buckles, by Eley, Fearn & Chawner, with steel spring clasps and beaded borders, London 1811, 2½in (6.5cm) wide, 3oz.
£150–180 / €220–260
$270–320 ⚒ WW

A silver filigree casket, containing eight glass scent bottles, decorated with jewels, c1680, 4in (10cm) wide.
£3,150–3,500 / €4,600–5,100
$5,700–6,300 ⊞ LBr

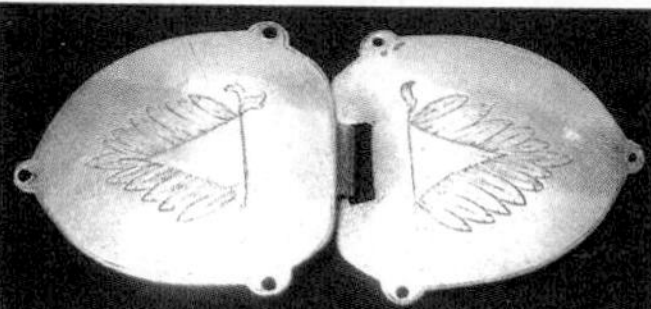

A silver cloak clasp, by George Hodder, Irish, Cork 1765, 4in (10cm) wide.
£1,850–2,050 / €2,700–3,000
$3,350–3,700 ⊞ WELD

A silver clasp, by SMD, London 1907, 5in (12.5cm) wide.
£80–90 / €115–130
$145–165 ⊞ GRe

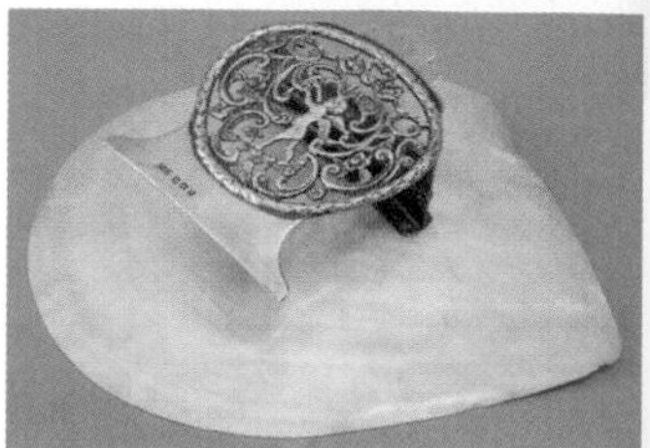

A silver and mother-of-pearl desk clip, pierced and decorated with a cherub and scrolling motifs, Birmingham 1906, 7in (18cm) wide.
£120–140 / €175–200
$220–250 ⚒ G(L)

A silver-mounted tortoiseshell desk folder, Birmingham 1894, 10½in (26.5cm) high.
£440–520 / €640–760
$800–940 ⚒ SWO

A dressing case, enclosing 12 silver-mounted jars and containers, a tortoiseshell and silver manicure set, brushes, an ivory shoe horn and a tortoiseshell comb, in a rosewood case, c1875, 12in (30.5cm) wide.
£3,600–4,000 / €5,200–5,800
$6,500–7,200 ⊞ JTS

A silver double egg cup, with gilt bowls, marked, probably German, 1770–1800, 2in (5cm) high, 1½oz.
£290–340 / €420–500
$520–620 ⚒ WW

Items in the Miscellaneous section have been arranged in alphabetical order.

A silver étui, with embossed floral decoration, 18thC, 3½in (9cm) high.
£810–900 / €1,150–1,300
$1,450–1,650 ⊞ LBr

A silver spirit flask, by James Fraser, with a removable drinking cap, Canadian, Quebec, c1810, 5½in (14cm) high, 9oz.
£300–360 / €440–530
$540–650 ⚒ WW

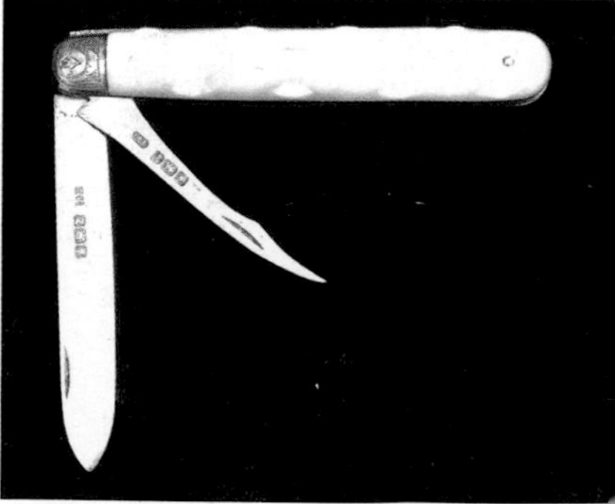

A silver and mother-of-pearl fruit knife and pipper, by Thomas Millington, Sheffield 1892, 3½in (9cm) long.
£135–150 / €195–220
$240–270 ⊞ CoHA

► **A pair of grape scissors,** by John Bridge, London 1824, 6in (15cm) long.
£470–530
€690–770
$850–960 ⊞ GRe

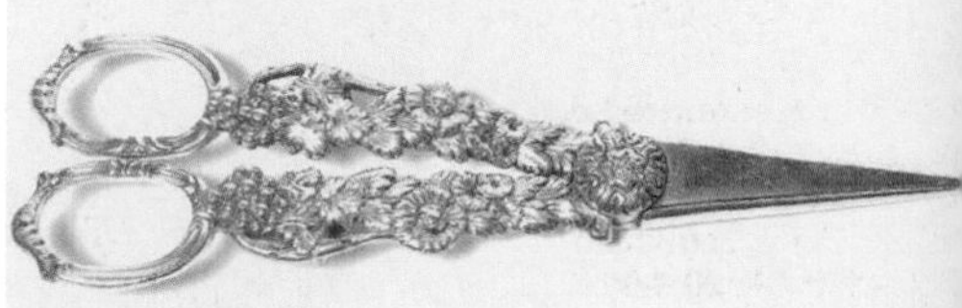

A silver lemon strainer, by George Smith II, London 1766, 5½in (14cm) long, 2½oz.
£165–195 / €240–280
$300–350 WW

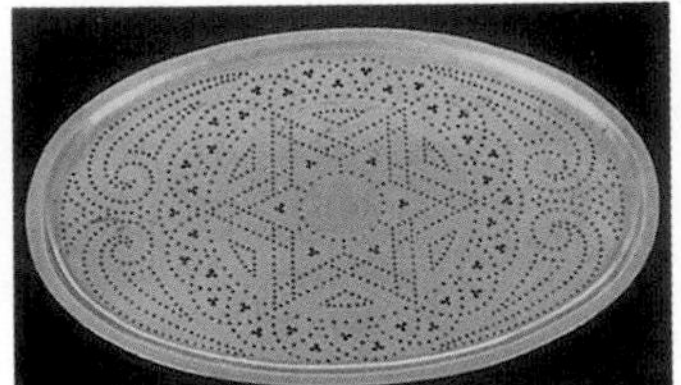

A silver mazarine, pierced with scrolls and stars, engraved with an armorial, early 19thC, 15¾in (40cm) wide, 24½oz.
£280–330 / €410–480
$510–600 DN

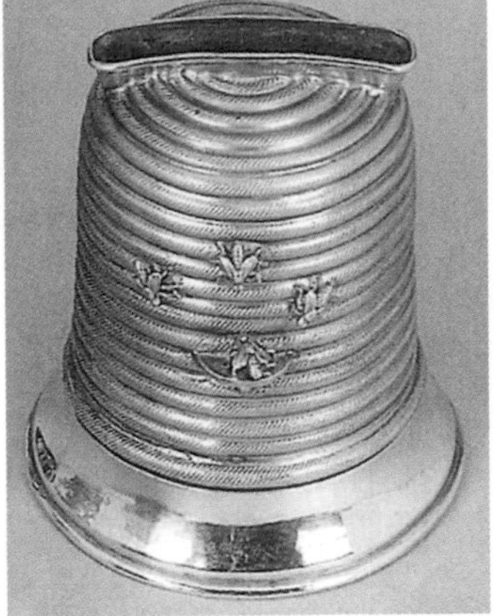

A silver money box, in the form of a beehive, maker's mark AB for Albert Böhr, Austrian, Vienna 1852, 3in (7.5cm) high, 2¼oz.
£1,350–1,600 / €1,950–2,350
$2,450–2,900 DORO

A silver and ivory paper knife, by Horton & Allday, Birmingham 1892, 18in (45.5cm) long.
£240–270 / €350–390
$430–490 GRe

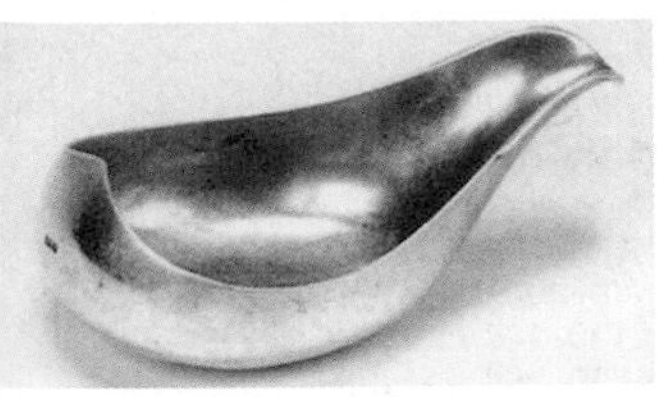

A silver pap boat, by James Le Bass, Irish, Dublin 1816, 4¼in (11cm) wide.
£640–760 / €930–1,100
$1,150–1,350 DN

A silver playing card case, with engine-turned decoration, Birmingham 1921, 3¾in (9.5cm) long.
£230–270 / €340–390
$420–490 DN(BR)

A silver pomander, with three sections, c1740, 1½in (4cm) high.
£400–450 / €580–660
$720–810 LBr

◀ **A silver and niello purse,** decorated with a city scene, Russian, late 19thC, 3in (7.5cm) wide.
£330–390 / €480–570
$600–710 G(L)

A silver-gilt-mounted cut-glass smelling salts bottle, with a mirror to the base, 1872, 3¾in (9.5cm) high.
£490–550 / €720–800
$890–1,000 FOF

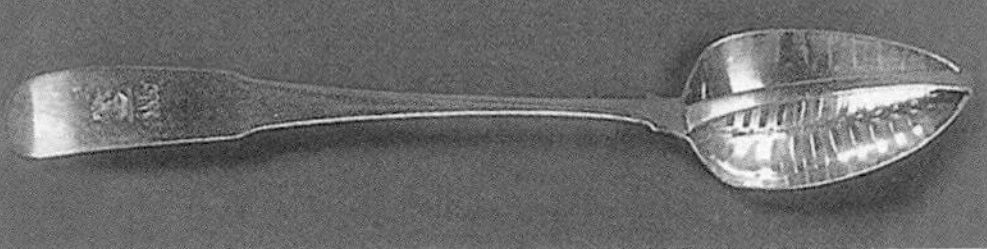

A silver Fiddle pattern straining spoon, by Samuel Neville, engraved with a crested monogram, Irish, Dublin, c1810, 12¾in (32.5cm) long, 4oz.
£350–420 / €510–610
$630–760 HYD

A silver toasting fork, by Nathan Hayes, with a wooden handle, Chester 1902, 15in (38cm) long.
£200–230 / €290–340
$360–420 GRe

A silver model of a wishing well, c1880, 3in (7.5cm) high.
£250–280 / €370–410
$450–510 BLm

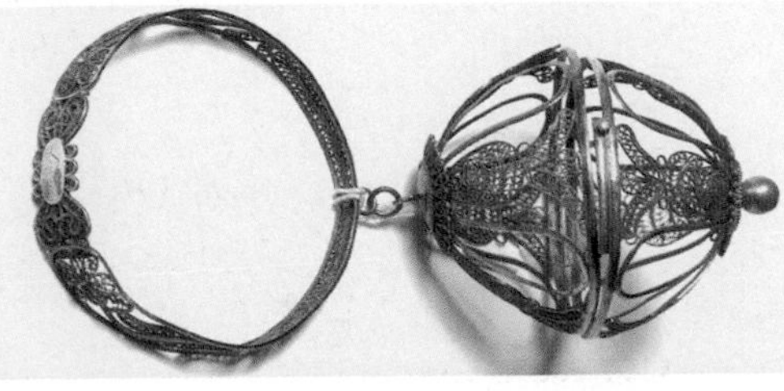

◀ **A silver wool/silk holder,** c1800, 7½in (19cm) high.
£450–500 / €660–730
$810–910 ANGE

Silver Plate

A Victorian silver-plated argyle, 7in (18cm) high.
£120–140 / €175–200
$220–250 ⚒ WW

A pair of silver-plated candle snuffers, by J. Gilbert, with tray, c1810, 10in (25.5cm) wide.
£135–150 / €195–220
$240–270 ⊞ GRe

A pair of silver-plated candlesticks, French, c1720, candlesticks 6¾in (17cm) high, with later glass shades.
£3,700–4,400 / €5,400–6,400
$6,700–8,000 ⚒ S(P)

◄ **A set of six silver-plated candlesticks,** with glass shades, the tapering fluted acanthus-wrapped stems on triform bases with claw feet, 19thC, 22¾in (58cm) high.
£7,600–9,100 / €11,100–13,300
$13,800–16,500 ⚒ HOK

A pair of Sheffield plate Mortons Patent two-drawer telescopic candlesticks, c1800, 9½in (24cm) extended.
£90–105 / €130–155
$165–190 ⚒ WW

A pair of silver-plated candlesticks, by Walker & Hall, 19thC, 12½in (32cm) high.
£65–75 / €95–110
$120–135 ⚒ CHTR

A pair of Victorian Sheffield plate candlesticks, 10in (25.5cm) high.
£165–185 / €240–270
$300–330 ⊞ LGr

A Victorian silver-plated table centrepiece, with four branches and cut-glass dishes, 15in (38cm) high.
£640–760 / €930–1,100
$1,150–1,350 ⚒ WW

A late Victorian silver-plated table centrepiece, possibly by Thomas Bradbury & Sons, in the form of two greyhounds standing by palm trees, 18¼in (46.5cm) high.
£420–500 / €610–730
$760–910 ⚒ GIL

A silver-plated cheese scoop, with an ivory handle, 19thC, 10in (25.5cm) long.
£80–90 / €115–130
$145–165 ⊞ GRe

◄ **A silver-plated cruet set,** in the form of a dairy cart, c1880, 2in (5cm) high.
£310–350 / €450–510
$560–630 ⊞ SMI

► **A Sheffield plate cruet frame,** for three bottles, with chased and repoussé decoration, 19thC, 12½in (32cm) high.
£60–70 / €90–100
$110–125 ⚒ JAA

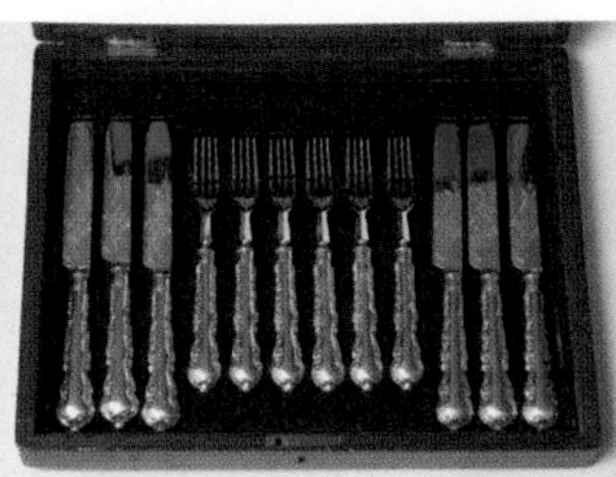

A set of 12 silver-plated fruit knives and forks, with engraved decoration, c1870, knives 8½in (21.5cm) long.
£130–145 / €190–210
$230–260 ⊞ FOX

A Sheffield plate jug, by Matthew Boulton, with an ivory finial and wooden handle, stamped sun marks, c1800, 8in (20.5cm) high.
£250–300 / €370–440
$450–540 ⚒ JAA

A silver-plate-mounted glass claret jug, etched with the archangel Gabriel, early 20thC, 11½in (29cm) high.
£260–310 / €380–450
$470–560 ⚒ DN(BR)

A Sheffield plate tureen and cover, engraved with a regimental badge of the Royal Horse Guards, early 19thC, 15½in (39.5cm) wide.
£800–960 / €1,200–1,400
$1,450–1,750 ⚒ F&C

A silver-plated canteen of cutlery, comprising 12 place settings, with an oak case, c1930, 18in (45.5cm) wide.
£1,650–1,850 / €2,400–2,700
$3,000–3,350 ⊞ Man

A silver-plate-mounted etched-glass claret jug, c1900, 11in (28cm) high.
£260–290 / €380–420
$470–520 ⊞ GRe

A Sheffield plate mustard pot, with a glass liner, c1800, 3in (7.5cm) high.
£70–80 / €100–115
$125–145 ⚒ WW

A silver-plated soup tureen and cover, probably Sheffield plate, engraved with cartouches with two coats-of-arms, one liner handle missing, c1820, 17¾in (45cm) wide.
£1,600–1,900 / €2,350–2,750
$2,900–3,450 ⚒ S(P)

A Sheffield plate four-piece entrée dish, with a detachable handle, marked, c1850, 13½in (34.5cm) long.
£380–450 / €550–660
$690–810 ⚒ JAA

Further reading

Miller's Silver & Plate Antiques Checklist,
Miller's Publications, 2001

A silver-plate-mounted hobnail cut-glass Pimms jug, by Mappin & Webb, with an ice container, c1900, 10in (25.5cm) high.
£420–470 / €610–690
$760–850 ⊞ LGr

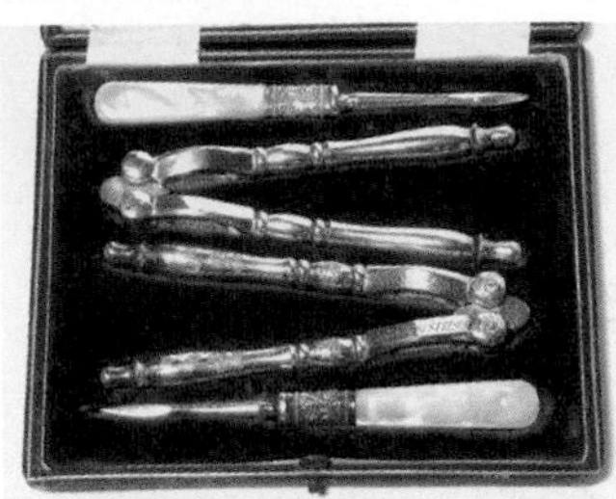

A set of silver-plated nut crackers and walnut picks, with mother-of-pearl handles, in a fitted case, c1900, 6in (15cm) wide.
£65–75 / €95–110
$120–135 ⊞ GRe

A silver-plated wine cooler, in the form of a 17thC porringer, c1850, 9in (23cm) diam.
£430–480 / €630–700
$780–870 ⊞ GRe

Wine Antiques

A copper ale mull, with a brass seam, c1840, 13in (33cm) high.
£70–80 / €100–110
$125–140 ⊞ F&F

This was used to warm ale by pushing it down into the hot coals or ashes of a fire and then immersing it in the pot of ale.

An oak wine bottle corker, French, 1775–1825, 45in (114.5cm) high.
£450–500 / €660–730
$810–910 ⊞ SAT

Items in the Wine Antiques section have been arranged in alphabetical order.

A pair of pierced silver coasters, with turned wood bases, maker's mark 'AI', possibly London 1765, 4¼in (11cm) diam.
£1,750–2,100 / €2,550–3,050
$3,150–3,800 ⚒ GIL

A pair of silver coasters, by Christopher Haines, with pierced and bright-cut decoration, on turned wood bases, Irish, Dublin 1785, 5¼in (13.5cm) diam.
£1,300–1,550 / €1,900–2,250
$2,250–2,700 ⚒ HOK

► A pierced silver wine coaster, with an applied floral rim, Birmingham 1838, 6¼in (16cm) diam.
£210–250 / €310–370
$380–450 ⚒ CHTR

A pair of William IV silver wine coasters, the sides chased and pierced with fruiting vine, the turned wood bases with an escutcheon engraved with a crest, 5½in (14cm) diam.
£1,600–1,900 / €2,350–2,750
$2,900–3,400 ⚒ PFK

A silver bottle coaster, by James Dixon & Sons, pierced with vignettes of foliage, Sheffield 1909, 5¾in (14.5cm) high, 17oz.
£300–360 / €440–530
$540–650 ⚒ WW

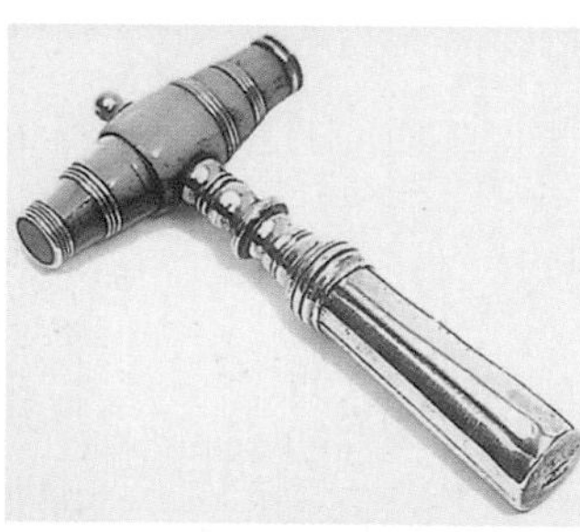

A George III silver miniature corkscrew, possibly by John Robins, with a mother-of-pearl handle, maker's mark JR, 6¾in (17cm) long.
£610–730 / €890–1,050
$1,100–1,300 ⚒ Bea

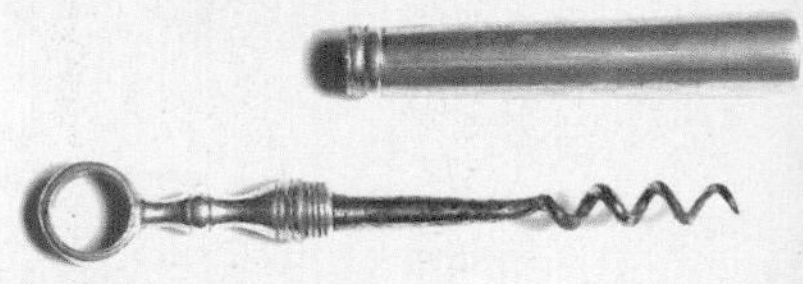

A silver pocket corkscrew, London 1787, 3½in (9cm) long.
£135–150 / €195–220
$240–270 ⊞ CS

Further reading

Miller's Corkscrews & Wine Antiques: A Collector's Guide,
Miller's Publications, 2001

◄ A silver corkscrew, by Joseph Taylor, the stem and sheath with engraved decoration, green-stained ivory grip, Birmingham, c1790, 3in (7.5cm) long.
£250–280 / €360–400
$450–500 ⊞ CS

A Heeley & Son bronze King's-type corkscrew, with a bone handle and a brush, early 19thC, 7in (18cm) long.
£210–250 / €310–370
$380–450 ⚒ G(L)

A brass and steel King's-type corkscrew, with a bone handle and a brush, c1830, 9in (23cm) long.
£480–540 / €700–790
$870–980 ⊞ WAA

A nickel-plated Original Bacchus corkscrew, with a speed worm, 19thC, 6in (15cm) long.
£110–125 / €160–180
$200–220 ⊞ SAT

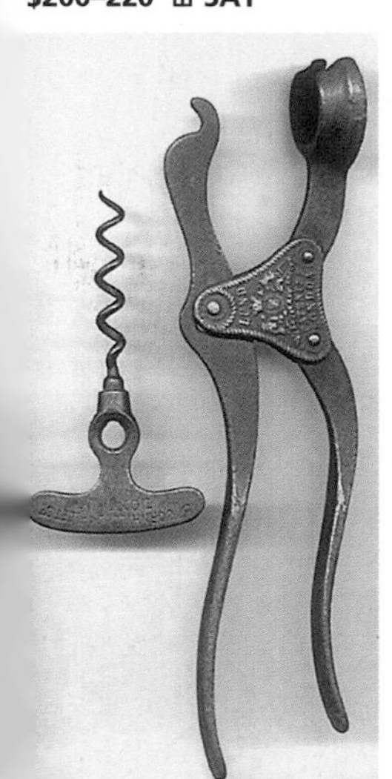

A Lund's steel lever corkscrew, with detachable corkscrew, marked 'Lund Patentee London', with a royal coat-of-arms, c1880, 8in (20.5cm) long.
£55–65 / €80–90
$100–110 ⊞ CS

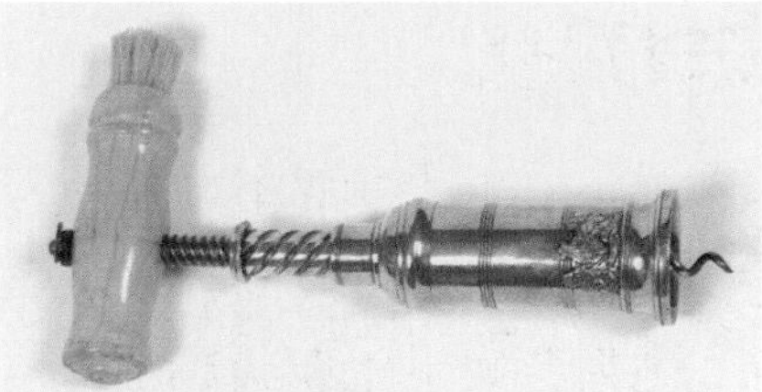

A brass and steel Thomason-type corkscrew, with a bone handle and a brush, c1830, 8in (20.5cm) long.
£400–440 / €580–640
$720–800 ⊞ WAA

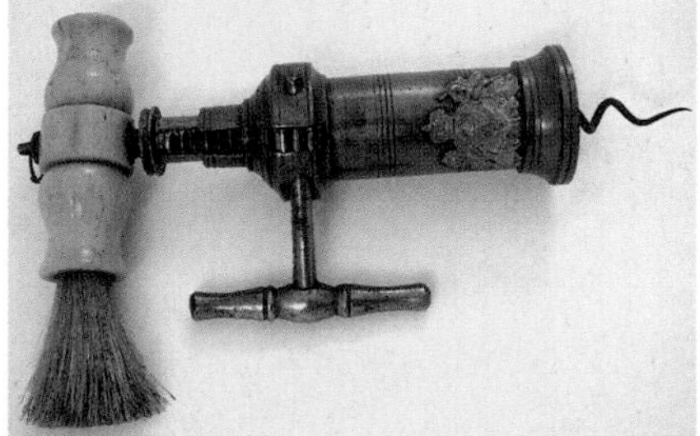

A bronze King's-type corkscrew, with a bone handle and a brush, the barrel applied with a coat-of-arms, 19thC, 7½in (19cm) high.
£190–220 / €280–330
$340–400 ⚒ G(L)

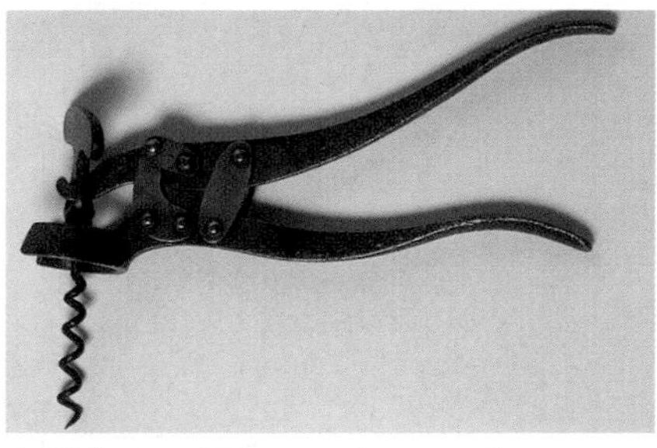

A Wolverson's Tangent lever corkscrew, c1870, 7in (18cm) long.
£175–195 / €250–280
$310–350 ⊞ SAT

A celluloid corkscrew, in the form of a mermaid, the scales with metallic paint, marked 'Ges Geschultz', German, c1900, 4½in (11.5cm) long.
£360–400 / €520–580
$650–720 ⊞ CS

A silver pocket corkscrew, the handle and sheath with embossed decoration, the base with pipe tamper and pricker, Dutch, c1850, 3in (7.5cm) long.
£400–450 / €580–650
$720–810 ⊞ CS

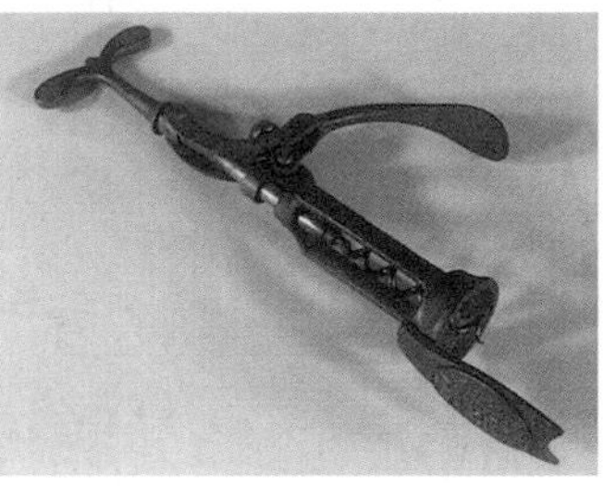

A Charles Hull Patent Royal Club-type single lever corkscrew, stamped 'E. Barrett, 166 Oxford Street, London', traces of bronze paint, 19hC, 10in (25.5cm) long.
£2,100–2,500 / €3,050–3,650
$3,800–4,550 ⚒ Hal

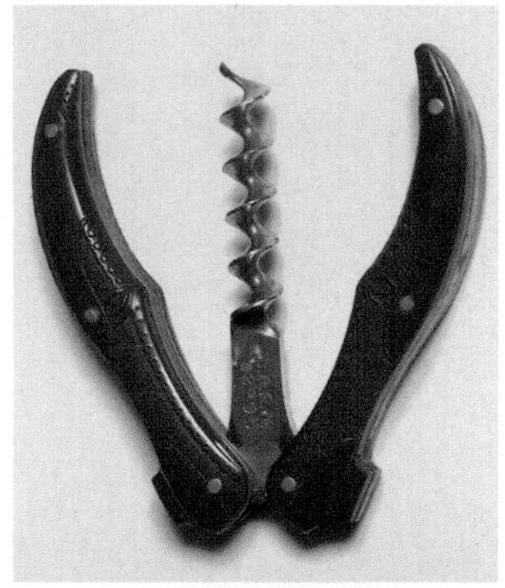

► A celluloid pocket corkscrew, German, c1900, 3in (7.5cm) wide.
£200–220
€290–320
$360–400 ⊞ CS

A silver two-part wine funnel, by Joseph Scammell, London 1795, 4¾in (12cm) high, 2½oz.
£1,150–1,300 / €1,650–1,900
$2,050–2,350 ⊞ BEX

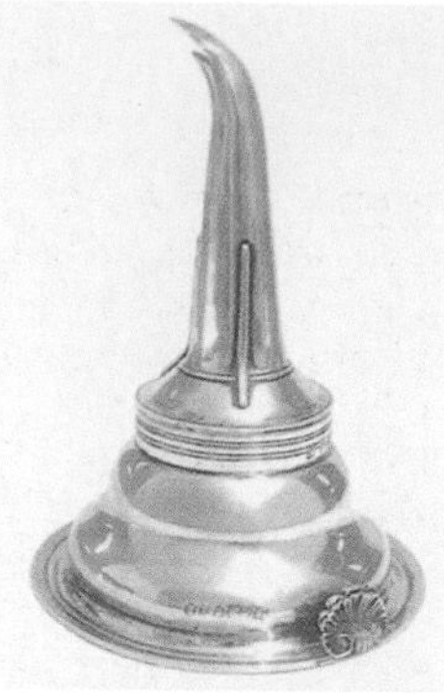

A silver wine funnel, by Edward, John and William Barnard, with a shell terminal and reeded borders, London 1831, 5¼in (13.5cm) high, 3½oz.
£590–700 / €850–1,000
$1,050–1,250 F&C

A silver-plated wine funnel, 19thC, 6in (15cm) high.
£130–145 / €190–210
$230–260 SAT

A coopered oak scrumpy jug, with copper banding, c1830, 11in (28cm) high.
£100–115 / €145–170
$180–210 F&F

LOCATE THE SOURCE

The source of each illustration in Miller's can be found by checking the code letters below each caption with the Key to Illustrations, pages 778–784.

A glass spirit measure, c1850, 6¾in (17cm) high.
£50–60 / €80–90
$95–105 GAU

A pierced silver wine label, by Rebecca Emes and Edward Barnard, the border stamped with fruiting vines, roses and a shell motif, London 1824.
£140–165 / €200–240
$250–300 WW

A silver brandy label, by Taylor & Perry, Birmingham 1827, 1¾in (4.5cm) wide.
£150–165 / €210–240
$270–300 BEX

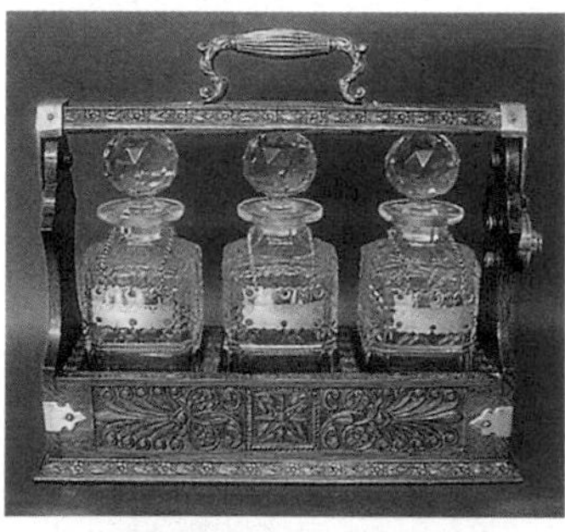

A Victorian carved oak tantalus, with silver-plated mounts and a reeded handle, the three hobnail-cut-glass decanters with silver-plated labels for whisky, port and gin, 14¼in (36cm) wide.
£410–490 / €600–720
$740–890 DD

An oak tantalus, with compartments for glasses, cigars, cards and a cribbage board, c1905, 12½in (32cm) wide.
£610–680 / €890–990
$1,100–1,250 PEZ

A silver-mounted glass toddy lifter/pourer, Birmingham 1912, 6in (15cm) high.
£95–105 / €140–155
$170–190 CoHA

A cut-glass whisky barrel, by Mappin & Webb, on a silver stand, Birmingham 1902, 9in (23cm) high.
£2,200–2,450
€3,200–3,600
$4,000–4,400 JTS

A pair of Sheffield plate wine coolers, in the form of barrels with gadrooned outlines and concentric bands, with loose ring lion-mask handles and liners, 19thC, 8¼in (21cm) high.
£2,000–2,400 / €2,900–3,500
$3,600–4,300 GIL

A silver wine taster, embossed with dimples and fluting, French, c1840, 3in (7.5cm) diam.
£180–200 / €260–290
$320–360 CS

Clocks

The top end of the clock market is booming as are other areas of antiques, but a closer study of individual collecting areas reveals a far more complicated scenario. Skeleton clocks are currently popular but carriage clocks are both up and down: those with porcelain panels or enamel case decoration have fallen back a little in the last year, but engraved gorge cased clocks, which were always the readiest sellers, are holding to previous levels or have even advanced somewhat.

The best British bracket and mantel clocks find a ready market, and are not really affected by the single-purchase mentality since it could not be regarded as excessive to have more than one in the house. However, in the middle to lower price ranges it is really only attractive examples that are doing well.

A similarly selective picture emerges with longcase clocks. The best Victorian three-train, quarter-striking, mahogany examples, especially those with the more attractive cases, are selling well. They have substantial high-quality movements, often of fantastic regulator quality with deadbeat escapement and tubular chimes. Georgian longcases, both London-made and provincial, are normally bought as single-purchase furnishing items and so have to be attractive, of good proportions and ready to go straight into the home, otherwise they will suffer from the doldrums that have affected the English brown furniture market. Prices have not necessarily dropped back but the speed of sales has slowed somewhat. It must be appreciated that the cost of restoration to movement and case makes up the greater part of their value, so a ten per cent drop in wholesale auction prices does not really affect their retail price.

London mahogany longcase clocks have been somewhat less popular in recent years, but they may now be making something of a comeback. However, the days when painted-dial longcase clocks were considered the poor country cousins of those that have dials with metal mounts, and therefore made less money, are seemingly gone for ever. Often a provincial longcase clock with a stunningly attractive polychrome-decorated painted dial is more sought after these days than a country-made example with a metal dial.

That was one of the shifts that happens in the market every now and again and illustrates the potential perils of crystal-ball gazing. Many people were arguing 20 years ago that French 18th-century boulle mantel clocks were underpriced and due for a revival. However, that has still not happened and they are making no more now than then, so in real terms they are much cheaper now.

Richard Garnier

British Bracket, Mantel & Table Clocks

A George I ebony-veneered and gilt-brass-mounted bracket clock, by Joseph Windmills, the engraved brass dial with silvered chapter ring and subsidiary date dial, the twin fusee movement with verge escapement striking on six bells, in a double repoussé basket top case, signed, 24¼in (61.5cm) high.
£23,000–27,600
€34,000–40,000
$42,000–50,000 ⚒ WW
This clock is by one of the more sought-after makers.

A George II ebonized bracket clock, the brass dial with a date aperture and false bob, with strike/silent dial to the arch and silvered chapter ring, the twin-train fusee movement by Gardner, London, in an inverted bell-top case, movement converted to anchor escapement, repeat mechanism removed, 21in (53.5cm) high.
£3,200–3,800
€4,700–5,600
$5,800–6,900 ⚒ Mit

An ebonized bracket/table clock, by John Smallwood, Lichfield, the brass dial with separate silvered-brass chapter ring with rise-and-fall regulator and date, the eight-day five-pillar latched movement with tic-tac escapement, striking the hours on a bell, in a bell-top case, mid-18thC, 18in (45.5cm) high.
£8,900–9,900
€13,000–14,500
$16,100–17,900 ⊞ PAO
This clock is particularly desirable because of the rare tic-tac escapement.

A George III brass-mounted mahogany bracket clock, by Marmaduke Storr, London, the engraved silvered dial with strike/silent selector, the twin fusee five-pillar movement with verge escapement, in an inverted bell-top case, 18in (45.5cm) high.
£3,500–4,200
€5,100–6,100
$6,300–7,600 ⚒ HYD

A brass-mounted mahogany bracket/table clock, by Robert Clidsdale, Edinburgh, the engraved silvered-brass dial with two subsidiary dials, the eight-day five-pillar movement with verge escapement striking the hours on a bell, in a bell-top case, Scottish, c1775, 20in (51cm) high.
£10,300–11,500
€15,000–16,800
$18,600–20,800 ⊞ PAO

An ebonized bracket clock, by Thomas Hill, London, the signed and engraved silvered-brass dial with date aperture and strike/silent, the five-pillar movement with verge escapement and rack striking on a bell, in an inverted bell-top case, finials later, c1780, 21in (53.5cm) high.
£2,100–2,500
€3,050–3,650
$3,800–4,550 ⚒ TEN

A mahogany bracket clock, by Brothers Melly & Martin, the silvered-brass chapter disc with subsidiary strike/silent dial, the eight-day five-pillar movement with verge escapement striking the hour and half-hour on a bell with repeat, in a concave bell-top case, c1780, 18in (45.5cm) high.
£11,500–12,800
€16,800–18,700
$20,800–23,200 ⊞ PAO

An ebonized pear wood-veneered bracket clock, by Kenneth MacLennan, London, the silvered dial with strike/silent dial and calendar aperture, the eight-day twin fusee movement with verge escapement striking on a bell, in a break-arch case, c1785, 14in (35.5cm) high.
£3,300–3,950
€4,800–5,800
$6,000–7,000 ⚒ NSal

A figured mahogany bracket clock, by Thomas Field, Bath, the engraved silvered dial with strike/silent dial, the twin fusee movement with verge escapement and repeat, in a bell-top case, c1790, 16½in (42cm) high.
£7,100–7,900
€10,400–11,500
$12,900–14,300 ⊞ ALS

A gilt-brass-mounted walnut bracket clock, by George Aitken, Edinburgh, with silvered chapter ring, subsidiary seconds and strike/silent dials, going and date apertures, the eight-day twin-train fusee movement with anchor escapement striking on a bell, in a bell-top case, Scottish, c1790, 20½in (52cm) high.
£3,000–3,600
€4,400–5,300
$5,400–6,500 ⚒ L&T

A George III mahogany bracket clock, by Thomas McConnell, Dublin, the mounted dial with silvered chapter ring, the eight-day fusee movement with verge escapement, in a break-arch case, backplate signed, altered and restored, Irish, 16¼in (41.5cm) high.
£1,050–1,250
€1,550–1,850
$1,900–2,250 ⚒ RTo

Items in the Clock section have been arranged in date order.

A brass-mounted mahogany bracket clock, by William Seymour, London, the mounted dial with strike/silent dial, the twin-train fusee movement with verge escapement striking on a bell, in a bell-top case, c1790, 20in (51cm) high.
£12,600–14,000
€18,400–20,400
$22,800–25,200 ⊞ DRA
William Seymour, son of John, worked from Hoxton and Chelsea in London and was a member of the Clockmakers' Company from 1766 to 1825.

◀ **An ebonized bracket clock,** by George Margetts, London, with enamel dial, the twin-train five-pillar gut-fusee movement with verge escapement, in a break-arch case, signed, c1790, 15¾in (40cm) high.
£8,100–9,000 / €11,800–13,100
$14,700–16,300 ⊞ DRA
George Margetts was a member of the Clockmakers' Company from 1779 to 1808. He was noted as a famous maker of complex watches and worked firstly from Cheapside and finally from Hatton Garden in London. In addition to his watches a number of fine, and often complex, clocks are known to be made by him. It is probably because of Margetts' watchmaking connection that this clock has an early example of an enamel dial.

A gilt and bronze mantel clock, by Thompson, London, with enamel dial surrounded by a band of paste stones, the signed single fusee movement with double virgule escapement, c1800, 23in (58.5cm) high.
£5,400–6,000
€7,900–8,800
$9,800–10,900 ⊞ DRA

A flame mahogany bracket clock, by Samuel Marsh, London, with signed and painted dial, the eight-day twin fusee movement with anchor escapement striking on a bell, in a break-arch case, c1810, 16in (40.5cm) high.
£3,600–4,000
€5,200–5,800
$6,500–7,200 ⊞ K&D

A George III mahogany bracket clock, by Langford, Southampton, with enamel dial and eight-day twin-train fusee movement with anchor escapement, in a break-arch case, signed, 16in (40.5cm) high.
£2,900–3,450
€4,250–5,000
$5,200–6,200 ⚒ HYD

A Regency ebonized and brass-inlaid bracket clock, by George Younge, London, with painted dial, the Thwaites movement with anchor escapement, in a lancet case, 16in (40.5cm) high.
£5,300–5,900
€7,700–8,600
$9,600–10,700 ⊞ JIL

The prices realized at auction may reflect the fact that the clocks have sometimes undergone alterations to their movements, or are in unrestored condition.

An ebony-veneered bracket clock, by Grimaldi & Johnson, London, engraved silvered-brass dial with strike/silent dial, the eight-day twin fusee movement with anchor escapement striking on a bell, in a single-pad top case, signed, c1820, 9½in (24cm) high.
£11,700–13,000
€17,100–19,000
$21,200–23,500 ⊞ DRA

Peter Grimaldi was working at 431 Strand, London, from about 1800 and proposed a weight-driven chronometer to the Board of Longitude in 1812. He went into partnership with Johnson between 1815 and 1825. Grimaldi and Johnson were noted for not only making these wonderful small bracket clocks but also for their chronometer work. This expertise is reflected in all their work.

◄ **A mahogany table/bracket clock,** by Desbois & Wheeler, London, the painted dial with strike/silent subsidiary dial, the eight-day five-pillar twin fusee movement with anchor escapement striking on a bell, in a break-arch case, c1810, 15in (38cm) high.
£7,400–8,300 / €10,800–12,100
$13,400–15,000 ⊞ PAO

A marble and ormolu gilded mantel timepiece, by James McCabe, London, with engine-turned gilded dial and eight-day fusee timepiece movement, the drum-shaped case surmounted by an eagle, signed, c1820, 10in (25.5cm) high.
£6,300–7,000
€9,200–10,200
$11,400–12,700 ⊞ DRA

CLOCKS

A Regency mahogany bracket clock, by William Moon, London, with painted enamel dial, the repeating eight-day movement with anchor escapement striking on a bell, in a champfered-top case, 19in (48.5cm) high.
£2,900–3,450
€4,250–5,000
$5,200–6,200 ⚒ DN(BR)

A mahogany table/bracket clock, by James Pike, Eltham, with painted dial, the eight-day twin fusee movement with anchor escapement striking on a bell, in a brass-inlaid lancet case, c1820, 16in (40.5cm) high.
£6,500–7,300
€9,500–10,700
$11,800–13,200 ⊞ PAO

A mahogany table/bracket clock, by Thwaites & Reed, London, the painted brass dial with strike/silent dial, with deadbeat escapement and maintaining power, the eight-day twin fusee movement with regulator escapement striking and repeating the hours on a bell, the lancet case with chamfered front angles, No. 5633, c1820, 19½in (49.5cm) high.
£7,400–8,300
€10,800–12,100
$13,400–15,000 ⊞ PAO

A mahogany bracket clock, by R. Walker, Beverley, with painted enamel dial, the eight-day chain fusee movement with anchor escapement striking on a bell, in a chamfered-top case, c1820, 19½in (49.5cm) high.
£2,000–2,400
€2,900–3,500
$3,600–4,350 ⚒ DA

◀ **A mahogany table/bracket clock,** by Beaumont, Margate, with painted dial, the eight-day twin fusee movement with anchor escapement striking and repeating on a bell, in a lancet case, c1825, 18in (45.5cm) high.
£6,100–6,800
€8,900–9,900
$11,000–12,300 ⊞ PAO

A late Regency ormolu and marble mantel timepiece, by 'V.B.', London, with enamel dial, the fusee movement with anchor escapement, 11in (28cm) high.
£6,700–7,500 / €9,800–11,000
$12,100–13,600 ⊞ DRA

A rosewood and brass-inlaid miniature table clock, with silvered dial, the twin fusee striking movement with anchor escapement, in a chamfered-top case, c1820, 11in (28cm) high.
£10,800–12,000
€15,800–17,500
$19,500–21,700 ⊞ TUR

A mahogany and satinwood-inlaid bracket clock, by John Farmer, London, with painted dial, the movement with repeat mechanism and anchor escapement, c1825, 9¼in (23.5cm) high.
£6,300–7,000
€9,200–10,200
$11,400–12,700 ⊞ GDB

A Gothic-style rosewood bracket clock, by Robert Smith, North Berwick, with engraved silvered dial, the twin fusee movement with anchor escapement striking on a bell, signed, Scottish, c1825, 28¾in (73cm) high.
£1,750–2,100
€2,550–3,050
$3,150–3,800 ⚒ CHTR

A brass-inlaid rosewood bracket clock, by Heckle, Liverpool, with painted dial, the striking movement with anchor escapement, c1825, 17¼in (44cm) high.
£940–1,100
€1,350–1,600
$1,700–2,000 ⚒ WilP

CLOCKS

A mahogany mantel clock, by Steber, Dover, with painted dial, the fusee movement with anchor escapement and trip repeat striking on a bell, in a break-arch case, signed, c1825, 24½in (62cm) high.
£2,400–2,850
€3,500–4,150
$4,350–5,200 S

A brass-inlaid rosewood bracket clock, by Webster, London, the painted dial with subsidiary seconds dial, the single-fusee movement with anchor escapement, in a drum-head case, c1830, 17¾in (45cm) high, with associated brass-inlaid rosewood wall bracket.
£1,650–1,950
€2,400–2,850
$3,000–3,550 TEN
The subsidiary seconds dial on this clock is unusual as it is situated below the XII.

A William IV brass-inlaid flame mahogany bracket clock, by Thomas King, London, with painted dial, the eight-day twin fusee movement with anchor escapement striking on a bell, in an arched case, signed, 16in (40.5cm) high.
£2,900–3,250
€4,250–4,750
$5,200–5,900 K&D

A mahogany bracket clock, the painted dial with dummy winding hole, the single fusee movement with anchor escapement, in a pagoda-top case, c1835, 21in (53.5cm) high.
£940–1,100 / €1,350–1,600
$1,700–2,000 TEN

◄ **A bracket clock,** by Samuel Marsh, London, with a painted dial, the eight-day movement with anchor escapement striking on a bell, in a break-arch case, early 19thC, 18½in (47cm) high.
£2,000–2,400
€2,900–3,500
$3,600–4,350 CHTR

A mahogany mantel timepiece, by William Peck Coales, North Crawley, with engraved silvered dial, in a chamfered-top case, stamped mark, c1830, 15½in (39.5cm) high.
£760–910 / €1,100–1,300
$1,400–1,650 WW

◄ **A late Regency mahogany bracket clock,** by Richards, Cheltenham, with painted dial, the twin-train fusee movement with anchor escapement, 17¾in (45cm) high.
£1,900–2,250
€2,750–3,300
$3,450–4,050 L&T

A brass-inlaid mahogany bracket clock, with painted dial, the twin fusee movement with anchor escapement striking on a bell, in a break-arch case, c1830, 18¼in (46.5cm) high, with associated mahogany and ebony-inlaid wall bracket.
£1,950–2,350
€2,850–3,350
$3,550–4,200 TEN

CLOCKS

A walnut miniature bracket clock, by Thomas Simpson, London, with silvered dial, the triple fusee movement with anchor escapement striking the quarter-hours on eight bells and the hours on a single bell, in a Gothic ogee-arched case, c1840, 10in (25.5cm) high.
£9,900–11,000
€14,500–16,100
$17,900–19,900 TUR

A Gothic revival brass mantel clock, by W. H. Young, Swaffham, with engraved silvered dial, the fusee movement with anchor escapement striking on a bell, c1840, 15¾in (40cm) high.
£1,050–1,250
€1,550–1,850
$1,900–2,250 S

A rosewood mantel timepiece, with silvered dial, the fusee movement with anchor escapement, in a four-glass case, c1840, 12in (30.5cm) high.
£1,000–1,200
€1,450–1,750
$1,800–2,150 WILK

A Gothic revival oak bracket clock, by J. W. Benson, London, the silvered dial with strike/silent dial, the movement with anchor escapement and striking the quarter-hours on eight gongs, c1845, 41½in (105.5cm) high, with conforming bracket.
£1,200–1,400
€1,750–2,050
$2,150–2,550 WW

A cast strut timepiece, by Hunt & Roskell, London, in the manner of Thomas Cole, with engraved silvered dial, the movement with lever escapement, signed, c1845, 6¼in (16cm) high, in original fitted case.
£3,750–4,500 / €5,500–6,600
$6,800–8,100 L

A satinwood library timepiece, by Newall Hart & Sons, London, with engraved gilt dial, the chain fusee movement with anchor escapement, in a four-glass case, c1845, 9in (23cm) high.
£7,600–8,500
€11,100–12,400
$13,800–15,400 DRA
Napthall Hart & Son are listed as working from 77 Cornhill, London between 1839 and 1847.

A mahogany bracket clock, by Langford, Bristol, with painted dial, the eight-day twin-train movement with anchor escapement striking on two bells, in a scroll-top case, c1845, 25in (63.5cm) high.
£530–630 / €770–920
$960–1,150 E

A mahogany-veneered bracket clock, with painted dial, the twin fusee movement with anchor escapement striking on a bell, in an arched case, c1850, 19in (48.5cm) high.
£940–1,100
€1,350–1,600
$1,700–2,000 TEN

A flame mahogany bracket clock, by Brockbank & Atkins, London, with painted dial, the chiming and repeating movement with anchor escapement, c1850, 17in (43cm) high.
£1,750–2,100
€2,550–3,050
$3,200–3,800 WILK

A mahogany mantel clock, by Barraud & Lunds, London, with engraved silvered dial, the movement with anchor escapement, in a four-glass case, c1850, 16¼in (41.5cm) high.
£2,100–2,500
€3,100–3,650
$3,800–4,550 SWO

A bird's-eye maple mant timepiece, by Viners & Co London, with engine-turne gilt-brass dial, the single train movement with anch escapement, c1850, 6¾in (17cm) high.
£700–840 / €1,050–1,250
$1,250–1,500 DMC

◀ **A rosewood table clock,** by James McCabe, London, the gilt dial with subsidiary strike/silent dial and engine-turned decoration, the five-pillar twin-chain fusee movement with anchor escapement striking the quarters on two bells, in a Gothic-style case, c1850, 9¾in (25cm) high.
£8,800–9,800 / €12,800–14,300
$15,900–17,700 ⊞ DRA

James McCabe was born into a watch and clockmaking family in Belfast. He came to London in the 1770s, settling at Royal Exchange in 1804. He gained his Freedom of the Clockmakers' Company in 1786 and became a Warden in 1811, the year he died. James McCabe was succeeded by his son, also James, and it is he who must be regarded as one of the most successful English clock and watchmakers of the 19th century. He was apprenticed to Reid & Auld and was made free of the Clockmakers' Company in 1822. Robert Jeremy McCabe, James's nephew, continued the business until he retired in 1883. Quarter-striking clocks of this size are rare.

An ebonized bracket clock, by Barraud & Lund, London, with engraved silvered dial, the movement with anchor escapement, in an architectural-top four-glass case, 1860, 11½in (29cm) high.
£6,400–7,200
€9,300–10,500
$11,600–13,000 ⊞ JeF

An engraved and gilded strut clock, by Thomas Cole, London, with engraved silvered dial and eight-day movement, c1860, 6½in (16.5cm) high.
£5,400–6,000
€7,900–8,800
$9,800–10,900 ⊞ DRA

Thomas Cole (1800–64), was the son of James Cole, a clockmaker. Thomas went into partnership with his brother James Ferguson Cole around 1823 until 1829. The Great Exhibition of 1851 has Thomas listed as 'Inventor, Designer and Maker'. He was elected to the Royal Society of Arts in 1861 and was also admitted to the British Horological Institute, in which his brother played a leading role.

A Victorian Egyptian revival polished slate mantel clock, with engraved gilt dial, the single train fusee movement with anchor escapement engraved 'Arnold, Charles Frodsham, 84 Strand', 12½in (32cm) high.
£330–390 / €480–570
$600–710 ⚒ HYD

◀ **A mahogany bracket clock,** with painted dial, the twin fusee movement with anchor escapement striking on a bell, in an arch-topped case, c1860, 15¾in (40cm) high.
£1,050–1,250
€1,550–1,850
$1,900–2,250 ⚒ CHTR

A brass-inlaid and mock tortoiseshell table clock, by J. C. Jennens, London, the brass dial with silvered chapter ring and chime/silent dial, the triple-train fusee movement with anchor escapement striking the quarters on eight bells and the hour on a single bell, c1870, 20½in (52cm) high.
£3,000–3,600
€4,400–5,300
$5,400–6,500 ⚒ TEN

LOCATE THE SOURCE

The source of each illustration in Miller's can be found by checking the code letters below each caption with the Key to Illustrations, pages 778–784.

A Sheraton revival mahogany bracket clock, by James Parson, Birmingham, the engraved silvered dial with strike/silent dial, the twin fusee eight-day movement with anchor escapement, in a bell-top case, c1890, 22in (56cm) high.
£3,600–4,000
€5,200–5,800
$6,500–7,200 ⊞ SOS

A Sheraton revival inlaid mahogany and brass-strung bracket clock, with silvered dial, the twin fusee movement with anchor escapement, c1900, 18¾in (47.5cm) high.
£4,200–4,700
€6,100–6,900
$7,600–8,500 ⊞ TUR

A late Victorian ebonized and ormolu-mounted director's clock, the silvered chapter ring beneath chime/silent and slow/fast subsidiary dials, the movement with anchor escapement striking on eight bells and quarter-chime gong, 25½in (65cm) high.
£1,400–1,650
€2,050–2,400
$2,550–3,000 ⚒ HYD

A late Victorian Sheraton revival rosewood and marquetry bracket clock, by F. T. Depree, Exeter, the brass dial with silvered chapter ring and three subsidiary dials for chime/silent, slow/fast and eight bells/Westminster chimes, the triple-fusee movement with anchor escapement striking on eight bells and a gong, with a presentation plaque dated 1900, 21¾in (55.5cm) high.
£2,100–2,500
€3,050–3,650
$3,800–4,550 ⚒ WW

◄ **An Edwardian mahogany table clock,** the brass dial with silvered chapter ring with subsidiary dials for chime/silent, fast/slow and eight bells/Westminster chime, the triple-train movement with anchor escapement, quarter-chiming on eight bells and striking the hour on a gong, in a break-arch case, 30in (76cm) high, with associated wall bracket.
£2,250–2,700
€3,300–3,950
$4,100–4,900 ⚒ TEN

A gilt-metal-mounted and ebonized bracket clock, the engraved silvered dial with subsidiary Cambridge/Westminster chimes and chime/silent dials, the triple-fusee movement with anchor escapement striking on eight bells and a gong, c1890, 29in (73.5cm) high.
£2,600–3,100
€3,800–4,550
$4,700–5,600 ⚒ WILK

► **A silver mantel clock,** the French movement with lever escapement, London 1904, 7½in (19cm) high.
£1,900–2,150
€2,750–3,150
$3,450–3,900
⊞ BLm

► **A silver *guilloche*-enamelled travelling alarm clock,** the engine-turned silvered dial with subsidiary alarm dial, the movement with lever escapement, on a lapis lazuli base, Swiss, c1915, 3in (7.5cm) high, with original tooled leather carrying case.
£5,500–6,200
€8,000–9,100
$10,000–11,200 ⊞ DRA

A Sheraton revival inlaid mahogany boxwood-strung mantel timepiece, with enamel dial, c1890, 7½in (19cm) high.
£210–250 / €310–370
$380–450 ⚒ L&E

For further information on Clocks see page 474

◄ **An Edwardian Sheraton revival mahogany mantel clock,** with enamel dial, the eight-day movement striking on a gong, the case with satinwood scrolls and brass pillars, 14¼in (36cm) high.
£290–340 / €420–500
$520–620 ⚒ RTo

Continental Bracket, Mantel & Table Clocks

A gilt-brass table clock, the brass dial engraved with a biblical scene and flowers, the iron and brass-plated movement with brass pillars, going train with fusee and chain, verge escapement striking on a bell, restored, German, c1700 and later, 3¼in (8.5cm) high.
£3,700–4,400
€5,400–6,400
$6,700–8,000 ⚒ S(Am)

An ormolu and patinated-bronze mantel clock, by Cronier, Paris, the enamel dial on a model of a horse, French, c1765, 15in (38cm) high.
£14,400–16,000
€21,000–23,400
$26,100–29,000 ⊞ JIL
This animal clock is rare and highly sought after by collectors. The gilding and patination are original and in good condition.

An ormolu-mounted boulle-inlaid bracket clock, the movement with five pillars signed 'Albert Baillon, Paris', the verge escapement striking on a bell, slight damage, possible alterations, finial missing, French, c1720, 28¼in (72cm) high.
£2,150–2,550
€3,100–3,700
$3,900–4,600 ⚒ S(Am)

A brass-mounted ebonized table clock, by Johannes Flaschge, the verge escapement striking the quarter hours, restored, Austrian, c1770, 18½in (47cm) high.
£2,400–2,850
€3,500–4,150
$4,350–5,200 ⚒ DORO

◀ **A Biedermeier mahogany mantel clock,** with enamel dial and pendulum escapement, probably Finnish, c1810, 16½in (42cm) high.
£640–760 / €930–1,100
$1,200–1,400 ⚒ BUK(F)

A boulle table timepiece, by P. Perret, with enamel dial, the movement with verge escapement repeating the quarters and hours on three bells, signed, the case surmounted with figures, French, c1720, 30¾in (78cm) high.
£1,900–2,250
€2,750–3,300
$3,450–4,100 ⚒ S

A Neuchâtel bracket clock, by Fc. LS. Huguenin, Chaux-de-Fonds, with ripple enamel dial and verge escapement, restored, Swiss, c1750, 33in (84cm) high.
£7,600–8,500
€11,100–12,400
$13,800–15,400 ⊞ JIL

CLOCKS

An ormolu mantel clock, by Jn Panset, Brussels, with enamel dial, Belgian, c1825, 12in (30.5cm) high.
£4,650–5,200
€6,800–7,600
$8,400–9,400 ⊞ JIL

A painted wood timepiece, with enamel dial and pendulum escapement, 19thC, 13¾in (35cm) high.
£900–1,050 / €1,300–1,550
$1,600–1,900 ⚒ S(P)

A Biedermeier gilt and silvered musical mantel clock, the silvered chapter ring with a pierced foliate centre, the movement with anchor escapement and rack striking on a gong, Austrian, c1830, 19in (48.5cm) high.
£1,300–1,550
€1,900–2,250
$2,350–2,800 ⚒ S(Am)

An ormolu-mounted and ebonized clock, by Le Roy & Fils, the silvered dial with engine-turned decoration and subsidiary moonphase and calender dials, month and day apertures, the movement with pinwheel escapement striking the half-hours on a gong, marked, French, c1840, 23¼in (59cm) high.
£1,250–1,500
€1,850–2,200
$2,250–2,700 ⚒ DN(BR)

An ormolu mantel clock, with enamel dial, the twin barrel movement with pendulum escapement striking on a bell, French, c1840, 11¾in (30cm) high.
£530–630 / €770–920
$960–1,150 ⚒ TEN

An ormolu mantel clock, by Howell & James, Paris, the chiming movement with pendulum escapement, the case surmounted with figures and inset with porcelain panels, French, 19thC, 10½in (26.5cm) high.
£630–750 / €920–1,100
$1,150–1,350 ⚒ BWL

◄ **A gilt-bronze mantel clock,** the enamel dial with strike/silent above a painted porcelain plaque depicting wild boar hunt, the case decorated with hunting trophies and stags' heads, French, c1845, 15¾in (40cm) high.
£1,350–1,600
€1,950–2,350
$2,450–2,900
⚒ SWO

CLOCKS

► **A bronze figural mantel clock,** the enamel dial restored, the Marti et Cie twin-train brass drum movement with pendulum escapement striking on a bell, surmounted by a figure of a Greek philosopher and his student, French, c1850, 21¼in (54cm) high.
£440–520 / €640–760
$800–950 ⚒ DN(BR)

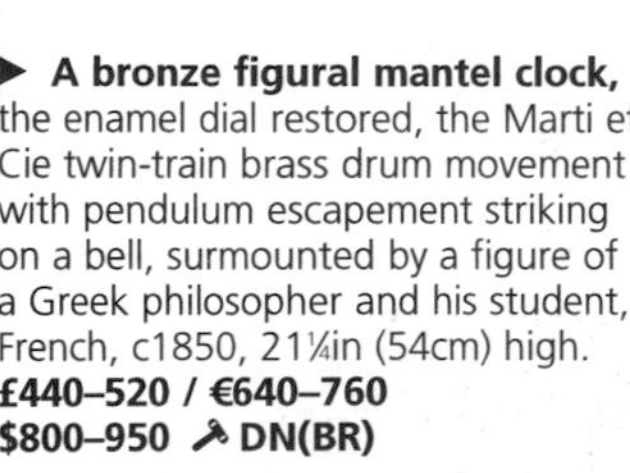

A gilt-brass and marble mantel clock, by Leroy, Paris, with enamel dial, the eight-day movement with outside countwheel, pendulum escapement and striking on a bell, the case surmounted by a putto, French, c1850, 9½in (24cm) high.
£350–420 / €510–610
$630–760 ⚒ WW

A gilt figural clock, with enamel dial, pendulum escapement, surmounted by a mounted crusader, French, 19thC, 18½in (47cm) high.
£300–360 / €440–530
$540–650 ⚒ JAA

◄ **A gilt-bronze mantel clock,** the movement by Japy Frères, surmounted by a scholar and a young boy, French, 19thC, 15¼in (38.5cm) high.
£880–1,050 / €1,300–1,550
$1,600–1,900 ⚒ JNic

◀ **A gilt-spelter figural mantel clock,** with porcelain dial, the movement with countwheel striking on a bell, surmounted by a figure of a classical maiden, on a giltwood base,glass dome damaged, French, mid-19thC, 21in (53.5cm) high.
£640–760 / €930–1,100
$1,200–1,400 ⚒ TMA

▶ **A marble mantel clock,** with enamel dial, pendulum escapement, French, 1850–1900, 14in (35.5cm) wide.
£165–195
€240–290
$300–360
⚒ Mal(O)

◀ **A porcelain mantel clock,** with eight-day striking movement, Austrian, Vienna, c1870, 18in (45.5cm) high.
£4,400–4,900
€6,400–7,200
$8,000–8,900 ⊞ SOS

A biscuit porcelain mantel clock, the enamel dial by Dubuisson, the eight-day movement striking the hour and half-hour, French, c1870, 15in (38cm) high.
£7,100–7,900
€10,400–11,500
$12,900–14,300 ⊞ JIL

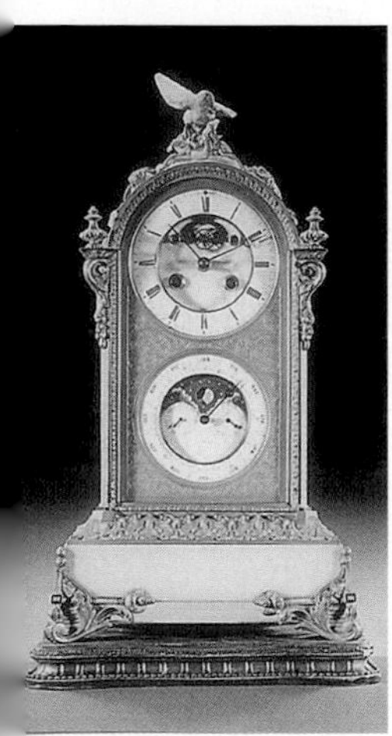

An ormolu and marble perpetual calendar mantel clock, the enamel dial with Brocot escapement, the bell-striking movement signed 'Lee & Son, Belfast', above a calendar dial indicating month, date, day of the week and moonphase, the case surmounted with a bird and a snake, on a giltwood stand, French, 1875, 22½in (57cm) high.
£3,800–4,550
€5,500–6,600
$6,900–8,200 ⚒ S

A gilt-brass 'temple' clock, with an enamel dial, the twin-barrel movement striking on a steel gong, the case with pierced decoration, French, late 19thC, 15¾in (40cm) high.
£330–390 / €440–490
$600–710 ⚒ TEN

A boulle mantel clock, the arched dial with enamel cartouche numerals, the bell-striking movement by Japy Frères, French, c1870, 13in (33cm) high.
£3,150–3,500
€4,600–5,100
$5,700–6,300 ⊞ TUR

A gorge-style brass four-glass year duration mantel clock, with enamel dial, the Brocot escapement with a mercury pendulum, signed 'Susse Frères, Paris', French, c1870, 17½in (44.5cm) high.
£7,600–8,500
€11,100–12,400
$13,800–15,400 ⊞ DRA

◀ **An ormolu and porcelain mantel clock,** by Victor Asselin, Paris, enamel dial, pendulum escapement, surmounted by a cherub and a goat, decorated with Sèvres-style panels, French, c1870, 17in (43cm) high.
£820–980 / €1,200–1,450
$1,500–1,800 ⚒ HYD

CLOCKS

A marble mantel clock, with Fahrenheit and aneroid barometer dials, the case with malachite-style decoration, French, c1875, 18in (45.5cm) high.
£440–520 / €640–760
$800–950 GAK

An ormolu mantel clock, the eight-day movement with pendulum escapement, the case surmounted by a pair of doves flanking a flaming torch and musical and military trophies, on a marble base, French, c1880, 10½in (26.5cm) high.
£760–910 / €1,100–1,300
$1,400–1,650 AH

A slate and variegated marble mantel clock, the twin-train movement with visible Brocot escapement, Continental, late 19thC, 16½in (42cm) wide.
£230–270 / €340–400
$420–500 Mit

► **A boulle clock,** the cast dial with enamel cartouches, the eight-day movement striking the half-hours on a bell, the case surmounted by a cherub, signed 'Miroy Frères, Paris', French, c1880, 5in (12.5cm) high.
£1,450–1,600
€2,100–2,350
$2,600–2,900 K&D

An ormolu mantel clock, the Sèvres-style porcelain dial and sides painted with romantic scenes after Boucher, striking on a gong, signed 'John Bennett, London', in a four-glass case, French, c1875, 6in (15cm) high.
£2,250–2,700
€3,300–3,950
$4,100–4,900 G(L)

A bronze and marble mantel timepiece, signed 'Festau Le Jeune à Paris', in the form of a cherub with a drum, French, c1880, 11½in (29cm) high.
£760–910 / €1,100–1,300
$1,400–1,650 G(L)

An ormolu-mounted boulle bracket clock, the cast dial with enamel numeral cartouches, the eight-day movement with pendulum escapement and striking on a bell, the case surmounted by an angel, the glazed door applied with a putto, French, late 19thC, 29½in (75cm) high.
£1,750–2,100
€2,550–3,050
$3,150–3,800 RTo

An ormolu mantel clock, the Sèvres-style porcelain dial painted with a cherub, the twin-train movement with pendulum escapement, French, 19thC, 14in (35.5cm) high.
£290–340 / €420–500
$520–620 DMC

A gilt-bronze and champlevé enamel mantel clock, the eight-day moveme striking the hours, French, c1880, 18in (45.5cm) high.
£2,250–2,500 / €3,300–3,65
$4,100–4,550 SOS

◄ **An ormolu mantel clock,** with a Paris porcelain dial and panels, pendulum escapement, French, 19thC, 15¾in (40cm) high.
£350–420 / €510–610
$630–760 SWO

An ormolu-mounted and porcelain mantel clock, by Hry Marc, Paris, with enamel dial, the eight-day movemer striking on a bell, the drum case surmounted with flower flanked by a figure of a classical maiden, the porcelain panels painted with a cherub and musical instruments, damaged, French, late 19thC, 12¼in (31cm) high.
£420–500 / €610–730
$760–910 RTo

A gilt-metal mantel clock, the silvered chapter ring signed 'W. Marshall & Co, Paris', the twin-barrel movement striking on a bell, the case with chinoiserie decoration, French, late 19thC, 16¼in (41.5cm) high.
£440–520 / €640–760
$800–950 Bea

A brass and marble mantel clock, the eight-day movement with platform lever escapement striking on a gong, the case surmounted by a lion, French, late 19thC, 9in (23cm) high.
£1,650–1,950
€2,400–2,850
$3,000–3,550 LHA

walnut four-glass antel clock, the gilded ial signed 'Camerer Cuss, ondon', the eight-day ovement striking the hours nd half-hours on a gong, e case with gilt-bronze ecoration, French, early 0thC, 13in (33cm) high.
80–980 / €1,300–1,450
,600–1,800 K&D

A bronze and gilt mantel clock, with an enamel dial, the twin-train movement with platform escapement, the case in the form of a drum being played by a putto, the marble plinth cast with figural panels, French, late 19thC, 12¼in (31cm) high.
£1,000–1,200
€1,450–1,750
$1,800–2,150 L&T

A gilt-bronze and marble mantel clock, with marble dial, the twin-train striking movement by E. White, Paris, the case surmounted by a pagoda, French, late 19thC, 22in (56cm) high.
£800–960 / €1,200–1,400
$1,450–1,750 Mit

A gilt-brass, nickel and marble mantel clock, with gilt dial, the bell-striking movement stamped 'GLT' for Guilmet, the bar-bell handle connected to the escapement, French, c1895, 13in (33cm) high.
£4,550–5,400
€6,600–7,900
$8,200–9,800 S

A four-glass mantel clock, by Japy Frères, with enamel dial, the twin-train movement with mercury compensated balance, French, late 19thC, 12in (30.5cm) high.
£470–560 / €690–820
$850–1,000 DMC

A gilt-bronze mantel clock, by Barbedienne, Paris, with enamel, pendulum escapement, French, late 19thC, 17¾in (45cm) high.
£1,550–1,850
€2,250–2,700
$2,800–3,350 BUK(F)

A four-glass mantel clock, the visible Brocot escapement with mercury compensated pendulum striking the half-hours on a gong, French, late 19thC, 13½in (34.5cm) high.
£2,850–3,200
€4,150–4,650
$5,200–5,800 TUR

A slate, marble and bronze mantel clock, the case surmounted by a figure of a Greek lady, signed 'J. Pradier', French, late 19thC, 20½in (52cm) high.
£440–520 / €640–760
$800–950 CHTR

An ebonized bracket clock, by W. & H., Preston, the silvered dial with subsidiary seconds and strike/silent dials, the eight-day twin-train movement with anchor escapement striking the quarters on a gong, dial signed 'S. Lyon, Preston', German, c1890, 29in (73.5cm) high.
£1,000–1,200
€1,450–1,750
$1,800–2,150 M

A pewter-inlaid tortoiseshell balloon timepiece, with enamel dial, the single-train movement with platform lever escapement, French, late 19thC, 8¼in (21cm) high.
£165–195 / €240–280
$300–360 TMA

A brass-mounted tortoiseshell mantel clock, the enamel dial painted with floral garlands, the twin-drum movement striking on a gong, stamped 'J. Masti', French, late 19thC, 14½in (37cm) high.
£1,800–2,150
€2,650–3,150
$3,250–3,900 Bea

An ebonized bracket clock, the brass dial with fast/slow dial above a silvered chapter ring, the eight-day movement striking on a gong, German, c1900, 15¾in (40cm) high.
£350–420 / €510–610
$630–760 RTo

A rosewood mantel clock, the silvered dial with engraved decoration, with anchor escapement, the case with marquetry inlay, German, c1905, 15½in (39.5cm) high.
£370–440 / €540–640
$670–800 BWL

An ormolu-mounted porcelain clock, the enamel dial painted with floral garlands, the pendulum set with brilliants, the case surmounted by a sunburst with a mask, c1900, 19in (48.5cm) high.
£3,400–4,050
€4,950–5,900
$6,100–7,300 HYD

A gilt portico timepiece, with eight-day movement, German, c1900, 17in (43cm) high.
£165–185 / €240–270
$300–330 DEB

► **A walnut bracket clock,** by Winterhalder & Hofmeier, the eight-day movement striking the quarters on a gong, German, c1910, 13in (33cm) high.
£1,350–1,500 / €1,950–2,200
$2,450–2,700 PTh

A marble and gilt-metal mantel clock, decorated with a frieze of warriors, signed 'H. Ashton, Paris', French, c1900, 20in (51cm) high, with glass dome.
£700–840 / €1,000–1,200
$1,250–1,500 HYD

An ormolu-mounted bronze mantel timepiece, the enamel dial painted with floral garlands and surrounded by diamantés, the eight-day movement with platform escapement, French, c1900, 7in (18cm) high.
£570–640 / €830–930
$1,000–1,150 K&D

◄ **A walnut table clock,** the brass dial with silvered chapter ring, the arch with subsidiary dials for fast/slow and chime/silent, the triple going barrel movement with anchor escapement striking the quarters on four gongs, German, c1910, 17¾in (45cm) high.
£1,050–1,250
€1,550–1,850
$1,900–2,250 TEN

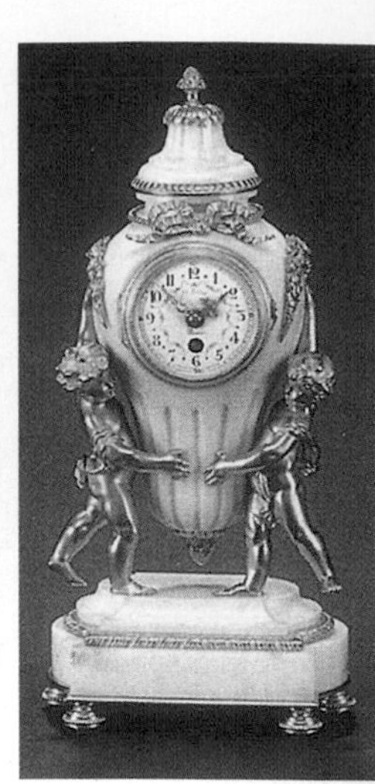

A gilt-bronze-mounted marble mantel timepiece, the enamel dial painted with floral garlands and signed 'La Sieur à Paris', the movement with platform cylinder escapement, the case supported by two gilt putti, altered, French, c1900, 11in (28cm) high.
£820–980 / €1,200–1,450
$1,500–1,800 S(Am)

A walnut Vienna table clock, the eight-day movement striking the half-hours on a gong, German, c1900, 30in (76cm) high.
£400–450 / €580–660
$720–810 DEB

CLOCKS

Carriage Clocks

A gilt-brass carriage clock, by James McCabe, London, with enamel dial and maintaining power, the twin-train fusee and chain repeating movement with lever escapement striking on a gong, c1840, 4½in (11.5cm) high.
£4,800–5,700 / €7,000–8,300
$8,700–10,300 ⚒ S

carriage clock, the enamel dial
th alarm dial signed 'Aubert &
ffenburger', the eight-day repeating
ovement striking the quarter hours
a bell, in an engraved gilded gorge
e, French, c1870, 5¼in (13.5cm) high.
400–6,000 / €7,900–8,800
800–10,900 ⊞ DRA

A gilt-brass *petite sonnerie* carriage clock, by Paul Garnier, Paris, with engine-turned silvered dial, the eight-day movement with alarm and chaffcutter escapement striking the hours and quarter-hours on two bells, French, c1840, 7in (18cm) high.
£12,600–14,000 / €18,400–20,400
$22,800–25,300 ⊞ DRA

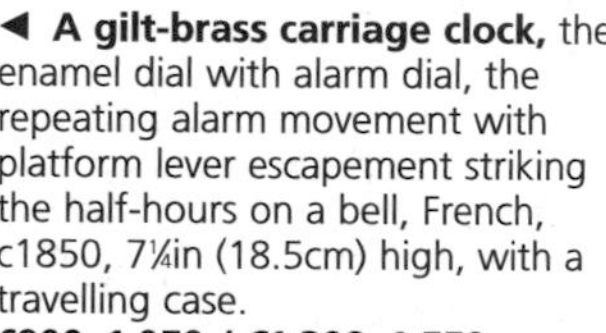

◄ **A gilt-brass carriage clock,** the enamel dial with alarm dial, the repeating alarm movement with platform lever escapement striking the half-hours on a bell, French, c1850, 7¼in (18.5cm) high, with a travelling case.
£900–1,050 / €1,300–1,550
$1,600–1,900 ⚒ S(Am)

An engraved gilt-metal carriage clock, with painted Paris porcelain dial and side panels, the repeating movement with half-hour strike and hour repeat, case damaged, late 19thC, 6in (15cm) high, with a travelling case.
£2,800–3,350 / €4,100–4,900
$5,100–6,100 ⚒ CHTR

► **A carriage clock,** the Paris porcelain dial painted with cherubs, with eight-day movement striking the hours and half-hours on a gong, in a gilded gorge case, the panels decorated with couples and enamelled 'jewels', French, c1880, 7½in (19cm) high.
£6,000–6,700 / €8,800–9,800
$10,900–12,100 ⊞ DRA

An engraved brass carriage clock, the enamel dial with alarm dial, the alarm movement and escapement by Gordon of Paris, with Jules-type platform lever escapement striking the hours and half hours, French, c1840, 7in (18cm) high, with original travelling case.
£2,000–2,200 / €2,900–3,200
$3,600–4,000 ⊞ ROH

A Victorian brass carriage clock, by Howell James & Co, London, with enamel dial, the repeating movement with platform lever escapement striking on a bell, 6in (15cm) high, with a leather travelling case.
£490–580 / €720–850
$890–1,050 ⚒ WW

A gilt-brass *grande sonnerie* carriage clock, by Drocourt, Paris, the enamelled dial with alarm dial, striking the quarter hours on bells, restored, French, c1880, 7½in (19cm) high.
£4,300–4,750
€6,300–7,000
$7,800–8,600 ⊞ CPC

A gilt-brass *grande sonnerie* carriage clock, by Drocourt, Paris, the enamelled dial with alarm dial, striking the quarter-hours on bells, in a gorge case, French, c1880, 7½in (19cm) high.
£4,400–4,900
€6,400–7,100
$8,000–8,900 ⊞ CPC

A gilt-brass *grande sonnerie* carriage clock, by Henri Jacot, with enamel dial, in a gorge case, French, c1880, 7½in (19cm) high.
£3,250–3,600
€4,750–5,300
$5,900–6,500 ⊞ BELL

A gilt *petite sonnerie* carriage clock, by Henri Jacot, with enamel dial, in a gorge case, French, c1885, 5⅓in (13.5cm) high.
£2,950–3,300
€4,300–4,800
$5,400–6,000 ⊞ JeF

A brass miniature carriage clock, with ivorine dial and cylinder escapement, the case with entwined floral decoration, 1885–95, 3¼in (8.5cm) high.
£150–180 / €220–260
$270–320 ⚒ AMB

A gilt-brass miniature carriage timepiece, with enamel dial, French, late 19thC, 3¾in (9.5cm) high, with travelling case.
£370–440 / €540–640
$670–800 ⚒ L&E

An *anglaise riche* carriage clock, the enamel dial with alarm dial, the movement with lever platform escapement striking the hours and half-hours on a bell, with repeat button, in a *champlevé* enamel case French, c1890, 8½in (215cm) high.
£5,000–5,500 / €7,300–8,100
$9,000–10,000 ⊞ DRA

A silvered-bronze carriage clock, attributed to Margaine, the enamel dial with alarm dial, the eight-day movement striking the hours and half-hours, French, c1890, 8in (20.5cm) high.
£2,200–2,450 / €3,200–3,600
$4,000–4,450 ⊞ CPC

A brass *anglaise riche* carriage clock, by J. Brunelot, Paris, the enamel dial with alarm dial, the twin-barrel movement with silvered platform, striking the hours and half-hours, French, c1890, with original leather travelling case and key.
£2,000–2,200 / €2,900–3,200
$3,600–4,100 ⊞ ROH

► **A brass carriage timepiece,** by E. M. & Co, the enamel dial with alarm dial, the lever escapement with silvered platform and bimetallic balance, in a corniche case, French, c1890, 7½in (19cm) high.
£620–690 / €900–1,000
$1,100–1,250 ⊞ ROH

CLOCKS

A brass *anglaise riche* carriage clock, by E. M. & Co, the enamel dial with pierced mask, the lever escapement with silvered platform and bimetallic balance, with strike and repeat, the case with *champlevé* enamel decoration, French, c1890, 8in (20.5cm) high, with original travelling case and key.
£3,500–3,900
€5,100–5,700
$6,300–7,000 ⊞ ROH

A gilded *anglaise riche* carriage clock, the dial with glass chapter ring and alarm dial and gilt pierced mask, striking the hours and half hours, the case with *champlevé* enamel decoration, c1890, 7in (18cm) high.
£3,050–3,400
€4,450–4,950
$5,500–6,100 ⊞ BELL

A brass miniature carriage clock, the enamel dial with silver-gilt mask, the twin-train movement with silvered platform escapement, striking the hours and half-hours on a gong, French, c1890, 3¾in (9.5cm) high.
£2,000–2,200
€2,900–3,200
$3,600–4,000 ⊞ ROH

A brass carriage timepiece, with enamel dial, the eight-day movement striking the hours and half-hours on a gong, with lever platform escapement, French, c1895, 5in (12.5cm) high.
£530–590 / €770–860
$960–1,000 ⊞ K&D

A brass miniature carriage timepiece, by Henri Jacot, with enamel dial, in a corniche case, restored, French, 1890–1900, 3¾in (9.5cm) high, with original travelling case.
£1,300–1,450 / €1,900–2,100
$2,350–2,600 ⊞ CPC

A brass carriage clock, the dial with ivorine chapter ring and silvered mask, with lever platform escapement, striking the hours and half hours on a bell, French, late 19thC, 7½in (19cm) high, with leather travelling case and key.
£680–810 / €990–1,150
$1,250–1,450 ⚒ Bea

A *champlevé* enamel carriage timepiece, with ivorine dial, French, late 19thC, 6¼in (16cm) high.
£630–750 / €920–1,100
$1,150–1,350 ⚒ L&E

A brass carriage timepiece, the enamel dial marked 'R. S. Rowell, Oxford and Paris', with cylinder escapement, French, c1900, 5¼in (13.5cm) high, with original tooled leather travelling case.
£230–270 / €330–390
$410–490 ⚒ WilP

A brass carriage timepiece, by Couaillet, with enamel dial, French, c1900, 6in (15cm) high.
£490–550 / €710–800
$880–990 ⊞ CPC

A brass carriage timepiece and barometer, with enamelled chapter rings and a thermometer, the top with a compass, French, c1900, 7in (18cm) high, with a fitted morocco case.
£770–920 / €1,150–1,350
$1,400–1,650 ⚒ GIL

Electric Clocks

A Sheraton revival mahogany electric mantel clock, by Eureka Clock Co, London, with enamel dial, with 1,000 day duration, the case with marquetry, crossbanding and stringing, c1900, 14¼in (36cm) high.
£730–870 / €1,050–1,250
$1,300–1,550 AH

A gilt-brass four-glass electric mantel clock, by Eureka Clock Co, London, with signed enamel dial, c1910, 15in (38cm) high.
£1,650–1,950
€2,400–2,850
$2,900–3,500 S

A brass electric timepiece, by Tiffany & Co, battery renewed, coil assembly cover missing, American, c1911, 10in (20.5cm) high.
£135–160
€195–230
$240–290 ROSc

A mahogany electric wall clock, by L. Leroy et Cie, Paris, the porcelain dial with ormolu bezel, marble backplate, French, c1920, 21¾in (55.5cm) high.
£2,250–2,500
€3,250–3,650
$4,050–4,500 ET

Garnitures

An ormolu mantel clock garniture, the clock with anchor escapement, the countwheel striking on a bell, surmounted by flowers with a dove and two putti, French, c1840, clock 14½in (37cm) high.
£1,600–1,900 / €2,350–2,750
$2,900–3,450 S(Am)

An ormolu clock garniture, the clock with Sèvres-style porcelain dial, J. Marti et Cie twin-train brass drum movement with anchor escapement and outside countwheel striking on a bell, surmounted by a two-handled urn, French, c1860, 14¾in (37.5cm) high.
£1,750–2,100 / €2,550–3,050
$3,150–3,800 DN(BR)

The prices realized at auction may reflect the fact that the clocks have sometimes undergone alterations to their movements, or are in unrestored condition.

A Napoleon III gilt-metal mantel clock garniture, with porcelain dial, the movement with anchor escapement and countwheel striking on a bell, the case with Sèvres-style porcelain mounts, 19¾in (50cm) high.
£890–1,050 / €1,300–1,550
$1,600–1,900 S(Am)

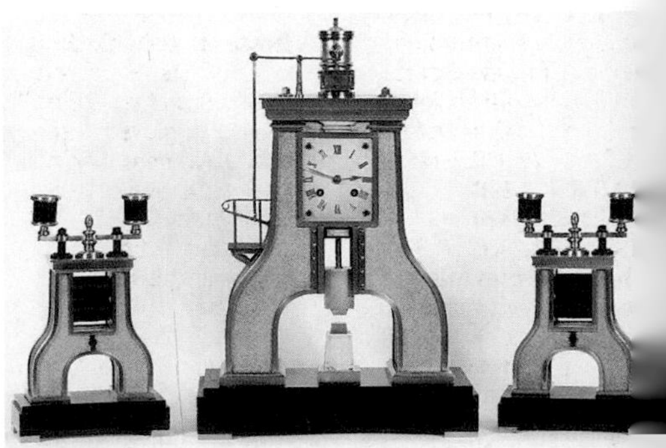

A gilt and silvered 'steam hammer' clock garniture, by Guilmet, the clock with silver dial and gilt hands, the Japy movement rack-striking on a bell, the steam hamm rising and falling with the pendulum, on marble bases, French, c1800, clock 18in (45.5cm) high.
£7,000–7,800 / €10,200–11,400
$12,700–14,100 DRA

A Black Forest carved limewood clock garniture, German, c1880, 25in (63.5cm) high.
£2,700–3,000 / €3,950–4,400
$4,900–5,400 ⊞ MSh

A rococo-style bronze clock garniture, with enamel dial, the Japy Frères eight-day movement striking the hours and half-hours on a bell, French, c1885, clock 14in (35.5cm) high.
£890–990 / €1,300–1,450
$1,600–1,800 ⊞ K&D

A patinated-metal clock garniture, the clock movement with anchor escapement and countwheel striking on a bell, the case surmounted by a chariot with Nike and Cupid pulled by two winged horses, French, c1885, clock 31¼in (79.5cm) high.
£1,100–1,300 / €1,600–1,900
$2,000–2,350 ⚒ S(Am)

A brass and porcelain clock garniture, the clock with porcelain dial and eight-day movement, the case with fruit surmount, 19thC, clock 17in (43cm) high.
£940–1,100 / €1,350–1,600
$1,700–2,000 ⚒ RTo

A Louis XV-style gilt-brass clock garniture, the clock with enamel dial and eight-day half-hour striking movement with outside countwheel, the case with *vernis Martin*-style decoration, movement stamped 'H. & F., Paris', French, late 19thC, clock 19½in (49.5cm) high.
£300–360 / €440–520
$540–650 ⚒ PFK

A gilt-mounted marble clock garniture, the clock with floral swagged enamel dial, with eight-day movement striking the hours and half-hours on a bell, French, Paris, c1900, clock 15in (38cm) high.
£760–850 / €1,100–1,250
$1,350–1,550 ⊞ K&D

Lantern Clocks

A brass lantern clock, by John Wise, London, with silvered chapter ring, dial plate engraved with tulips, the movement converted to tic-tac escapement, external locking plate striking on the bell, the case pierced and engraved with foliate scrolls and dolphin frets, c1670, 15½in (39.5cm) high
£10,500–12,600
€15,300–18,400
$19,000–22,800 ⚒ S

John Wise was made a Free Brother of the Clockmakers' Company in 1646. Although the tic-tac escapement has been reinstated, this clock is thought to be one of the earliest clocks to have been fitted with this type of escapement. It has been suggested that John Wise may have invented the tic-tac rather than Joseph Kribb.

A brass lantern clock, by Henry Webster, Aughton, with silvered chapter ring, dial plate engraved with tulips, movement with anchor escapement and outside countwheel striking on the bell, the Lancashire frame with dolphin frets, bell strap and top finial replaced, c1690, 14in (35.5cm) high.
£2,500–3,000
€3,650–4,350
$4,500–5,400 ⚒ S

A brass lantern clock, the posted movement with anchor escapement and outside countwheel striking on a bell, side doors, the case with urn finials and dolphin frets, frets and part of movement later, c1720, 15in (38cm) high.
£1,500–1,800
€2,200–2,600
$2,700–3,250 ⚒ TEN

A brass lantern clock, by William Hulbert, Bristol, with silvered chapter ring, the 30-hour movement with verge escapement, early 18thC, 15in (38cm) high.
£2,700–3,250
€3,950–4,750
$4,900–5,900 ⚒ WEBB

A brass lantern clock, with silvered chapter ring, the eight-day fusee movement with anchor escapement striking on a bell, the case with urn finials and foliate frets, late 19thC, 13in (33cm) high.
£960–1,150 / €1,400–1,650
$1,750–2,050 ⚒ S

Longcase Clocks

An ebonized longcase clock, by Thomas Stubbs, London, the dial with silvered-brass chapter ring, seconds dial and date ring, the 30-hour rope-wind movement with countwheel striking the hours, the lift-up hood with a blind sound fret top over spiral-twist pillars, the case with a lenticle, c1685, 63in (160cm) high.
£10,600–11,800
€15,500–17,200
$19,200–21,300 ⊞ PAO

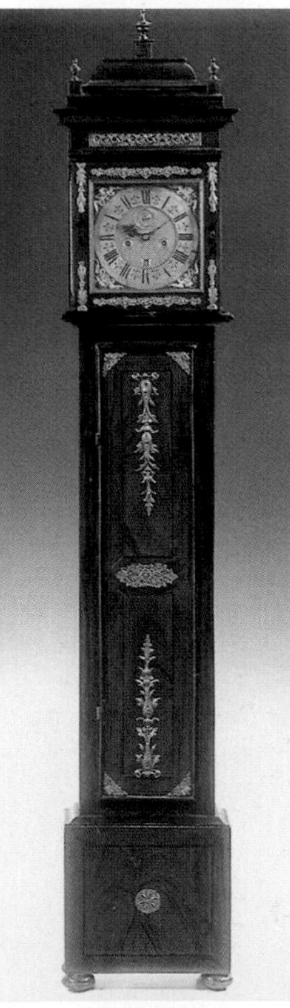

A brass-mounted longcase clock, by Ignatio Huggeford, dial inscribed 'Ignatio Huggeford, Inglese in Firenze', Italian, Florence, c1700, 65in (165cm) high.
£9,800–11,700
€14,300–17,000
$17,700–21,200 ⚒ S(Mi)

An olivewood, oyster-veneered and marquetry longcase clock, by W. Skilmore, London, the dial with silvered chapter ring, half-hour marks and quartering, seconds dial and date aperture, the month-going movement with external countwheel, the case banded with fruitwood and boxwood, with a lenticle, hood now slides forward, c1690, 77½in (197cm) high.
£30,000–34,000
€44,000–49,000
$54,000–61,000 ⊞ DRA

A walnut-veneered and marquetry longcase clock, by Isaac Lownds, London, the brass dial with silvered chapter ring and date aperture, the partially latched month-going movement with outside countwheel striking the hours on a bell, the caddy-top hood with brass finials, c1690, 89in (226cm) high.
£38,000–42,000
€54,000–63,000
$69,000–76,000 ⊞ DRA
This clock is in fine original condition.

◀ **A Queen Anne walnut longcase clock,** by John Free, Oxford, the brass dial with chapter ring, second hand and date aperture, the hood with blind fretwork cornice, the panel door with herringbone crossbanding, 87in (221cm) high.
£5,900–7,100
€8,600–10,300
$10,700–12,800 ⚒ Mal(O)
John Free was apprentice to John Knibb from 1696–1705.

A walnut and marquetry longcase clock, by Daniel Quare, London, the chased dial with chapter ring, seconds ring and date aperture, with eight-day movement, the hood surmounted by carved cresting above spiral-twist columns, the case with stringing and cross-grain veneers, decorated with panels of marquetry, the door with a brass lenticle, c1695, 89in (226cm) high
£67,000–75,000
€98,000–109,000
$121,000–136,000 ⊞ DRA
Daniel Quare (1647–1724) was one of the most eminent makers of the 17th and early 18th centuries. He worked at St Martin le Grand, London and became a Brother of the Clockmakers' Company in 1671 and Master in 1708. As well as being very fine craftsman, he had an inventive mind and, by 1680, had made repeating watches to his own design. In 1690 he applied for a patent for a portable weatherglass. Quare made clocks and watches for the Royal Family and examples may still be seen in their collections.

CLOCKS

◀ **A chinoiserie-decorated longcase clock,** by Cornelius Herbert, London, with eight-day movement, c1715, 82in (208.5cm) high.
£10,200–11,300
€14,900–16,500
$18,500–20,500 ⊞ ALS
Cornelius Herbert was apprenticed to his father of the same name in 1690. He joined the Clockmakers' Company in 1700 and became Master in 1727.

A *faux* tortoiseshell and gilt chinoiserie-decorated longcase clock, by John Smorthwait, Colchester, with eight-day movement, case restored, c1725, 86¼in (218.5cm) high.
£9,200–10,300
€13,400–15,000
$16,600–18,500 ⊞ ALS

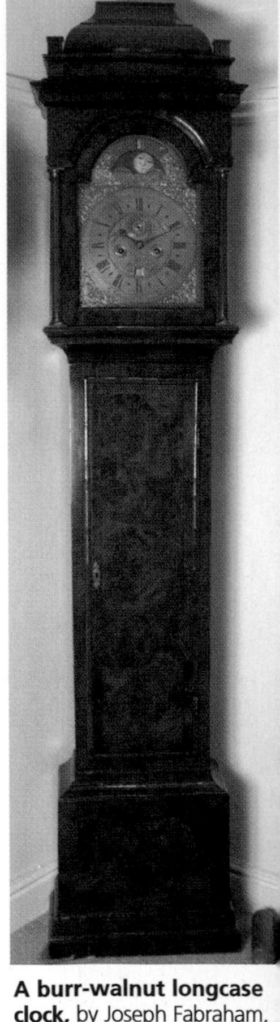

A burr-walnut longcase clock, by Joseph Fabraham, Waltham Abbey, the brass dial with moonphase, with eight-day movement, the case with a caddy top, c1725, 115in (292cm) high.
£20,600–22,900
€30,000–34,000
$37,000–41,000 ⊞ SOS

A japanned longcase clock, by Edward Cockey, Warminster, with 12-month calendar to dial arch, the eight-day movement with countwheel striking, c1730, 98in (249cm) high.
£8,000–9,000
€11,700–13,100
$14,500–16,300 ⊞ TUR

A flame mahogany longcase clock, by John Bryan, London, the brass dial with an automaton of a rocking ship, with eight-day movement, 1727–81, 90in (228.5cm) high.
£14,400–16,000
€21,000–23,300
$26,100–29,000 ⊞ SOS

▶ **An oak longcase clock,** by James Smyth, Saxmundham, the brass dial with single hand supporting 30-hour striking movement, 18thC, dial 10in (25.5cm) diam.
£840–1,000
€1,200–1,450
$1,500–1,800 ⚒ SWO

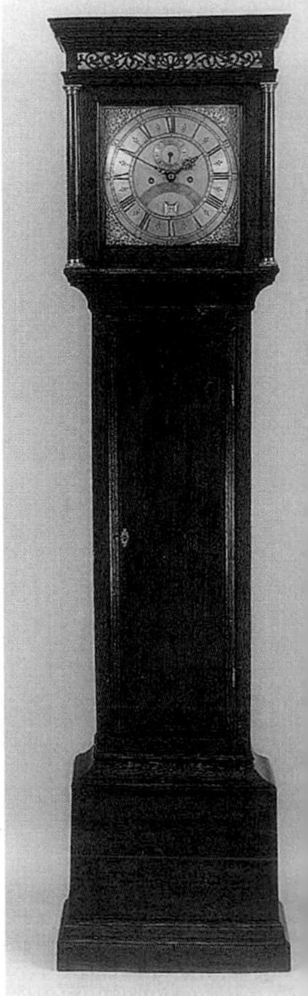

▶ **An oak longcase clock,** by D. Lockwood, Swaffham, the brass dial with seconds dial, date aperture and strike/silent, with eight-day, five-pillar movement striking the hours on a bell, the hood with Doric capitals, c1745, 82in (208.5cm) high.
£7,400–8,300 / €11,000–12,100
$13,400–15,000 ⊞ PAO

CLOCKS

A walnut longcase clock, by Benjamin Stretch, Bristol, the arched brass dial with moonphase, seconds dial and calendar aperture, the eight-day movement striking on a bell, with arched hood, the door inlaid with stringing, the door with later mother-of-pearl label and key plate, base with later skirting, mid-18thC, 96in (244cm) high.
£2,100–2,500
€3,050–3,650
$3,800–4,500 PF

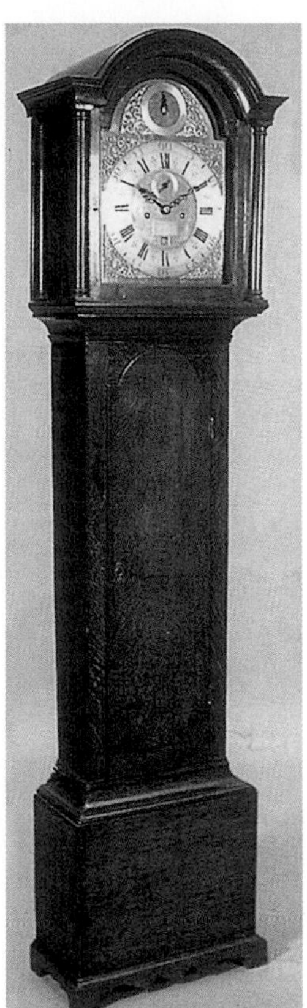

An oak longcase clock, by James Tanqueray, London, the brass dial with silvered chapter ring, subsidiary seconds dial, date aperture and strike/silent, the eight-day movement striking on a bell, mid-18thC, 79in (200.5cm) high.
£1,500–1,800
€2,200–2,600
$2,700–3,250 WW

Condition

The condition is absolutely vital when assessing the value of an antique. Damaged pieces on the whole appreciate much less than perfect examples. However, a rare desirable piece may command a high price even when damaged.

◄ **A walnut longcase clock,** by Thomas Eastland, London, the break-arch dial with silvered chapter ring, subsidiary seconds dial, date aperture and strike/silent, with eight-day movement striking on a bell, the case with arched hood, damaged, base reduced, mid-18thC, 76in (193cm) high.
£1,050–1,250
€1,550–1,850
$1,900–2,250 RTo

Miller's Compares

I A figured walnut longcase clock, by Andrew Hewlett, Bristol, the brass dial with moonphase and High Water at Bristol Key, eight-day movement, c1740, 89in (225cm) high.
£20,200–22,500
€29,500–33,000
$37,000–41,000 ALS

II An oak longcase clock, by Thomas Beeching, Rye, the engraved brass dial with date aperture and moonphase, eight-day movement with pull hour repeat, c1730, 84¼in (214cm) high.
£7,600–8,500
€11,100–12,400
$13,800–15,400 ALS

These clocks are of similar age with slender cases of excellent proportions and attractive breakarch 12-inch (30.5cm) dials with moonphases. Although Item II is earlier than Item I and has the addition of well executed wheatear edge engraving to the dial, Item I is more desirable because of the high tide indication and, more importantly, its superb well figured walnut case with ogee caddy top and brass mounts to the hood. This case was much more expensive to produce and is considerably rarer than the plainer oak design of Item II.

CLOCKS

An oak longcase clock, by John Nash, Bridge, the brass dial with silvered chapter ring, seconds and date rings, the arch with automaton of Father Time, the hood with broken-arch top, blind sound fret and angle pillars, c1745, 86in (218.5cm) high.
£7,600–8,500
€11,100–12,400
$13,800–15,400 ⊞ PAO

► **An oak longcase clock,** by William Walters, the brass dial with penny moon, c1750, 78½in (199.5cm) high.
£6,500–7,300
€9,500–10,700
$11,800–13,200 ⊞ ALS

An oak longcase clock, by David Collier of Gatley, the brass dial with penny moon, eight-day movement, the hood with brass finials and blind fret, c1755, 89½in (227.5cm) high.
£7,600–8,500
€11,100–12,400
$13,800–15,400 ⊞ ALS

A mahogany longcase clock, by Daye Barker, London, the brass dial with strike/silent, eight-day movement, case with later inlay, c1760, 91in (231cm) high.
£17,500–19,500
€25,500–28,500
$31,000–35,000 ⊞ SOS

► **An oak longcase clock,** by Thomas Watts, Lavenham, the brass dial with maker's name in a cartouche, with silvered chapter ring, seconds dial and date aperture, the hood with reeded pillars and broken-arch top, c1755, 82in (208.5cm) high.
£6,100–6,800
€8,900–9,900
$11,000–12,300 ⊞ PAO

A burr-walnut-veneered longcase clock, by Claas Kroon, Leeuwarden, the brass dial with silvered chapter ring, subsidiary seconds dial, date and day apertures and moonphase with high tide in the arch, the movement striking the half-hours, the case surmounted by a giltwood figure of Atlas and two angels above a moulded corniche with carved cresting, front and side frets and brass-capped three-quarter columns, the base with chequered inlaid banding, the door with a lenticle, Dutch, mid-18thC, 111½in (283cm) high.
£6,900–8,300
€10,100–12,100
$12,500–15,000 ⚒ S(Am)
Class Kroon is recorded working in Leeuwarden in 1755. He is also known to have produced and repaired turret clocks.

A George III oak longcase clock, by Jno Ettry, Hortor the square brass dial with silvered chapter ring, 30-hour movement strikin on a bell, base reduced, 75½in (192cm) high.
£960–1,150 / €1,400–1,65
$1,750–2,050 ⚒ WW

CLOCKS

Cornelius Herbert, London Bridge. A superbly proportioned early 18thC classic London blue/green chinoiserie lacquered 8-day longcase clock, with 12in square brass dial, five pillar movement and inside countwheel striking. Circa 1715. 82in (208cm).
Note: Born circa 1676, apprenticed to his father Cornelius Senior 1690/91–97, freed 1700/01.

Peter Garon, London. A superbly proportioned, late 17thC classic London walnut bird and flower marquetry 8-day longcase clock, with 11in square brass dial, five pillar movement and inside countwheel striking. 81in (206cm).
Note: Born 1673, apprenticed to Richard Baker until 1694 when he was granted Freedom of the City by the Lord Mayor and then granted Freedom of the Clockmakers Company in the same year.

A George III mahogany longcase clock, by Thomas Cackett, Cranbook, the brass dial with silvered chapter ring, subsidiary seconds dial, date aperture and turned winding holes, the arch with a silvered boss engraved with a sunburst, five-pillar movement with anchor escapement striking on a bell, the hood with arched cornice above stop-fluted columns and fretted panels, movement altered, dial associated, base reduced, plinth later, in need of restoration, 78¾in (200cm) high.
£2,000–2,400
€2,900–3,500
$3,600–4,350 DN(BR)

Anchor v Verge escapement

The anchor escapement was developed c1670. It was commonly used in longcase clocks from shortly thereafter, being seen as an improvement on the much earlier verge escapement. The latter, however, continued to be used until c1800 for spring-driven bracket or table clocks because they were often carried from room to room. Having a verge escapement meant they did not need to be set up dead level as with a clock with an anchor escapement, which also needed to be in top condition to continue working. Once clocks proliferated in homes and did not need constant moving, many verge bracket clocks were converted to anchor escapements, supposedly giving greater accuracy but in truth necessitating frequent overhauls. Today, an original verge is greatly prized, and even those that have been reconverted to a verge are worth more than one that retains its conversion to anchor escapement. However, early 19th-century bracket clocks with an original anchor escapement are collectable and, if they are attractive and of a small size, they can be worth more than an earlier verge clock. Originality is important, but attractiveness more so.

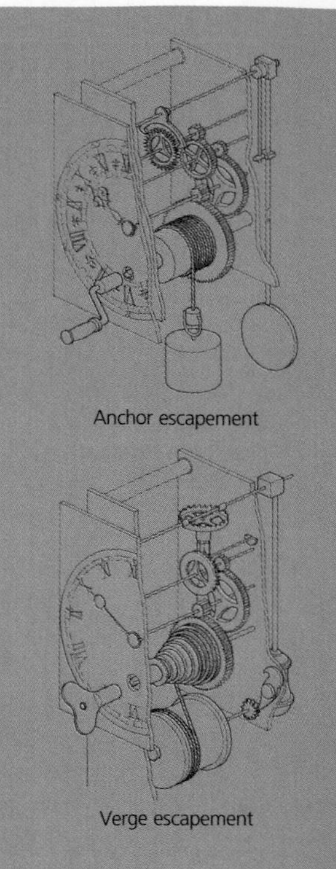

Anchor escapement

Verge escapement

A walnut-veneered longcase clock, by Thomas Gardner, London, the brass dial with silvered chapter ring, seconds ring, date ring and strike/silent, eight-day five-pillar movement striking the hours on a bell, the hood with brass-capped angle pillars and caddy top with brass finials, c1760, 104in (264cm) high.
£15,200–16,900
€22,200–24,700
$27,500–31,000 ⊞ PAO

A George III oak longcase clock, by Edward Blowers, Beccles, the brass break-arch dial with silvered chapter ring, the 30-hour movement striking on a bell, the arched hood with fluted pilasters, altered and restored, 84in (213cm) high.
£800–960 / €1,200–1,400
$1,450–1,700 RTo

An oak longcase clock, by Major Schoffield, Rochdale, the brass dial with silvered chapter ring and calendar aperture, eight-day movement striking on a bell, the hood with painted frieze, movement and dial associated, 18thC, 88¼in (224cm) high.
£1,050–1,250
€1,550–1,850
$1,900–2,250 WW

A burr-elm longcase clock, by Wainwright, the brass dial with moonphase, eight-day movement, 1760–80, 86in (218.5cm) high.
£18,700–20,800
€27,300–30,000
$34,000–38,000 ⊞ SOS

A flame mahogany longcase clock, by Thurston Lassell, Liverpool, the brass dial with moonphase, with eight-day movement, the case with reeded columns, c1760, 92in (233.5cm) high.
€10,100–11,300
€14,700–16,500
$18,300–20,500 ⊞ SOS

An oak longcase clock, by Thomas Farrer, Saxmundham, with arched brass dial, c1765, 86in (218.5cm) high.
£4,500–5,000
€6,600–7,300
$8,100–9,000 ⊞ SOS

A mahogany longcase clock, by Thomas Foden, Congleton, the arched dial with moonphase, c1765, 89in (226cm) high.
£12,500–13,900
€18,200–20,300
$22,600–25,200 ⊞ JeF

A mahogany longcase clock, by James Aikin, Cork, the arched brass dial with subsidiary seconds dial and date aperture, eight-day movement, the hood with swan-neck pediment centred with an urn finial, Irish, 18thC, 92in (233.5cm) high.
£1,950–2,300
€2,850–3,400
$3,600–4,250 ⚒ MEA

mahogany longcase ock, by Thomas Johnson, ndon, with eight-day ovement, mid-18thC, in (228.5cm) high.
,200–8,000
0,500–11,700
3,000–14,500 ⊞ JIL

A mahogany longcase clock, by William Stapleton, London, the brass dial with strike/silent, the hood and case inlaid with brass, c1770, 83in (211cm) high.
£12,900–14,400
€18,800–21,000
$23,400–26,000 ⊞ SOS

An oak longcase clock, by William Davies, Chester, the brass dial with silvered chapter ring and date ring, the arch with moonphase, the eight-day four-pillar movement with anchor escapement rack striking on a bell, the case with mahogany crossbanding, the hood with swan-neck pediment, the trunk with canted corners, c1770, 92½in (235cm) high.
£3,000–3,600
€4,400–5,300
$5,400–6,500 TEN

A George III mahogany longcase clock, by Robertson, Glasgow, the painted break-arch dial with subsidiary seconds dial, the arch with a scene of Britannia accompanied by three men with a galleon, the corners with maidens representing England, Wales, Ireland and Scotland, with eight-day movement striking on a bell, inlaid case, the hood with swan-neck pediment and pierced fret panels, altered and restored, Scottish, 88¼in (224cm) high.
£1,300–1,550
€1,900–2,250
$2,350–2,800 RTo

► **A mahogany longcase clock,** by Wyke, Liverpool, the brass dial with moonphase, eight-day movement, the case with reeded columns, c1775, 89in (226cm) high.
£9,400–10,500
€13,700–15,300
$17,000–19,000 SOS

◄ **A mahogany longcase clock,** by William Hughes, London, the dial with silvered-brass chapter ring, seconds dial and date aperture, the arch with dials for strike/silent and repeat/silent, eight-day five-pillar movement with anchor escapement striking the hour on a bell and the quarters on eight bells, the hood with double domed top with sound fret, surmounted by brass finials, the trunk with reeded and brass-inlaid quarter pillars, c1775, 91in (231cm) high.
£23,800–26,500
€35,000–39,000
$43,000–48,000 PAO

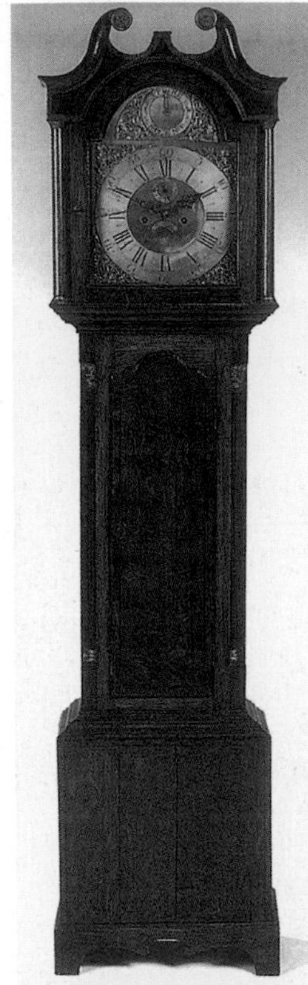

◄ **A George III oak longcase clock,** by Charles Barclay, Montrose, the brass dial with subsidiary seconds dial, date aperture and strike/silent, the twin-train eight-day movement with anchor escapement striking on a gong, the hood with swan-neck pediment and columns, the case with boxwood and ebony stringing and reeded quarter columns, Scottish, 80¾in (205cm) high.
£1,100–1,300
€1,600–1,900
$2,000–2,350 L&T

A George III figured mahogany longcase clock, the break-arch dial with subsidiary seconds and calendar dials, painted with scene entitled 'The May Queen', the corners with figures representing England, Scotland, Ireland and Wales, the eight-day movement striking on a bell, the hood with swan-neck pediment and turned columns, the trunk with fielded panel door, faults, Scottish, 87½in (222cm) high
£700–840 / €1,000–1,200
$1,250–1,500 RTo

◄ **A George III oak longcase clock,** with brass dial inscribed 'Boot of Sutton', 30-hour movement, the case with mahogany crossbanding, the hood with a swan-neck pediment, 88½in (225cm) high.
£900–1,050
€1,300–1,550
$1,600–1,900 DD

CLOCKS

A flame mahogany longcase clock, by John Middleton, Lancs, the brass dial with moonphase, eight-day movement, trunk and hood with reeded pillars, 1775–80, 90in (228.5cm) high.
£7,600–8,500
€11,100–12,400
$13,800–15,400 ⊞ SOS

An oak longcase clock, by John Christian, Aylsham, the brass dial with silvered brass chapter ring, seconds dial and date aperture, eight-day movement with five-plate pillars and anchor escapement striking the hours on a bell, the hood with removable East Anglian cresting, brass-capped and reeded angle pillars, c1780, 96in (244cm) high.
£6,700–7,500
€9,800–11,000
$12,100–13,600 ⊞ PAO

A mahogany-veneered longcase clock, by Wyke & Green, Liverpool, c1780, 92in (233.5cm) high.
£11,200–12,500
€16,400–18,300
$20,300–22,600 ⊞ JeF

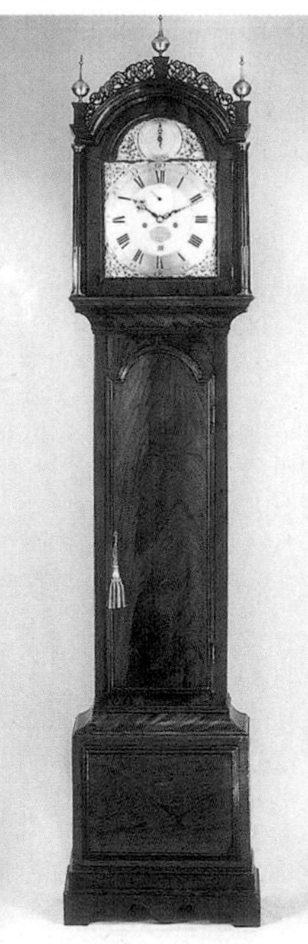

A mahogany longcase clock, by Edmund Prideaux, London, with eight-day movement, the pierced and fretted top with brass finials, c1780, 94in (239cm) high.
£14,200–15,800
€20,700–23,100
$20,700–28,600 ⊞ ALS

An oak and crossbanded longcase clock, the brass dial with centre-sweep seconds, date dial, penny moon and Father Time automaton to arch, the twin-train eight-day rack-striking movement with deadbeat escapement, striking the hours and quarter-hours on two bells, the hood with moulded dentil cornice, blind fret and double baluster columns, 18thC, 81½in (207cm) high.
£4,450–5,300
€6,500–7,700
$8,100–9,600 ⚒ JM

► A mahogany musical longcase clock, by Paul Rimbault, London, the painted dial with chapter ring and date ring, the corners with subsidiary dials, the arch with automaton of Adam and Eve, the eight-day triple-train movement with anchor escapement, 15 hammers striking on eight bells and a further bell for the hour, the top with swan-neck pediment and pierced fretwork, the trunk with stop-fluted pilasters, c1780, 96½in (245cm) high.
£30,000–36,000
€44,000–53,000
$54,000–65,000 ⚒ TEN

The Rimbaults were among the finest clock makers in 18th-century London. Paul Rimbault was a maker of high repute from 1760, and he carried on making highly specialized clocks until his death in 1785.

An oak longcase clock, by J. Lees, Bury, the brass dial with painted centre and moonphase, eight-day movement, with caddy top and mahogany fretwork and quarter columns to hood and trunk, 1730–85, 73in (185cm) high.
£8,100–9,000
€11,800–13,100
$14,700–16,300 ⊞ SOS

A flame mahogany-veneered longcase clock, by Daniel de St Leu, London, the brass dial with silvered chapter ring, date, seconds and strike/silent to the arch, eight-day five-pillar movement striking the hours on a bell, the hood with pagoda pediment, gilt-bronze fretwork and brass stop-fluted columns, c1780, 101in (256.5cm) high.
£8,200–9,200
€12,000–13,400
$14,800–16,700 ⊞ K&D

Daniel de St Leu was a fine watch maker. He was watchmaker to George III and made a watch for the Queen in 1765. Examples of his work are in renowned collections worldwide.

A mahogany longcase clock, by John Morgan, Bristol, the silvered dial with moonphase and High Water at Bristol Quay, with eight-day movement, 1773–98, 91in (231cm) high.
£11,300–12,600
€16,500–18,400
$20,500–22,800 ⊞ SOS

► An oak longcase clock, by William Cuff, Shepton Mallett, the brass dial with seconds dial and date aperture, the 30-hour movement with countwheel striking on a bell, the hood with swan-neck pediment and brass eagle finial, c1780, 84in (213.5cm) high.
£3,900–4,350
€5,700–6,400
$7,100–7,900 ⊞ PAO

A George III oak longcase clock, by Edmund Wills, Sarum, with brass dial and 30-hour birdcage movement, 79¾in (202.5cm) high.
£820–980 / €1,200–1,450
$1,500–1,800 ⚒ WW

A flame mahogany-veneered longcase clock, by James Smith, London, the brass dial with seconds dial and date aperture, the eight-day five-pillar movement striking the hours on a bell, the hood with brass-inlaid and reeded angle pillars and pagoda top surmounted by three brass finials, c1780, 94in (239cm) high.
£15,200–16,900
€22,200–24,700
$27,500–31,000 ⊞ PAO

An oak and marquetry-inlaid longcase clock, by John Nevill, Norwich, the brass dial with silvered-brass chapter ring, seconds dial and date aperture, with strike/silent to the arch, the eight-day five-pillar movement striking the hours on a bell, the hood with brass-capped reeded angle pillars and broken-arch top surmounted by a detachable Norfolk cresting, c1780, 92in (233.5cm) high.
£8,000–8,800
€11,700–12,900
$14,400–15,900 ⊞ PAO

Valuing an antique clock

The value of an antique clock is dependent upon a number of factors:

- the type of clock – for example longcase, wall, bracket, mantel, table, carriage clocks, turret, skeleton, etc
- the driving force – for example weight-, spring-driven or electric
- the type of mechanism – for example precision clocks, mystery clocks, mechanically complicated clocks, striking clocks or timepieces
- the escapement, or timekeeping regulator of the mechanism, and whether it is pendulum or balance controlled
- the case – what the clock is made of and its general appearance. Although an aesthetically pleasing example will have a ready market and can command a high price, a complicated or pioneering example that is less attractive to the eye can also be highly valuable.
- the maker – the best makers will naturally command the highest prices. Beware – names can be changed or faked

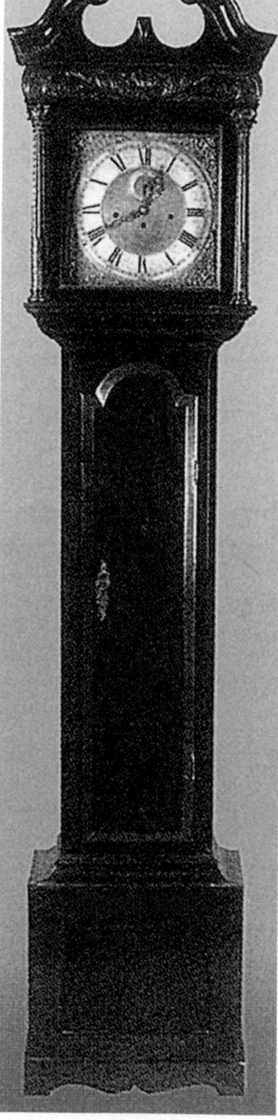

A George III mahogany longcase clock, with silvered-brass dial and eight-day striking musical movement, the top with swan-neck pediment with carved terminals, movement later, Irish, 94in (239cm) high.
£1,100–1,300
€1,600–1,900
$2,000–2,350 ⚒ Mit

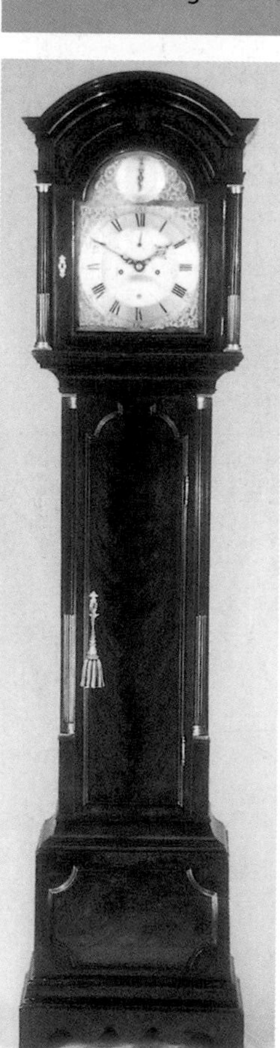

A flame mahogany-veneered longcase clock, by Isaac Floyd, London, with eight-day movement, c1780, 90in (228.5cm) high.
£15,100–16,800
€22,000–24,500
$27,000–30,000 ⊞ ALS

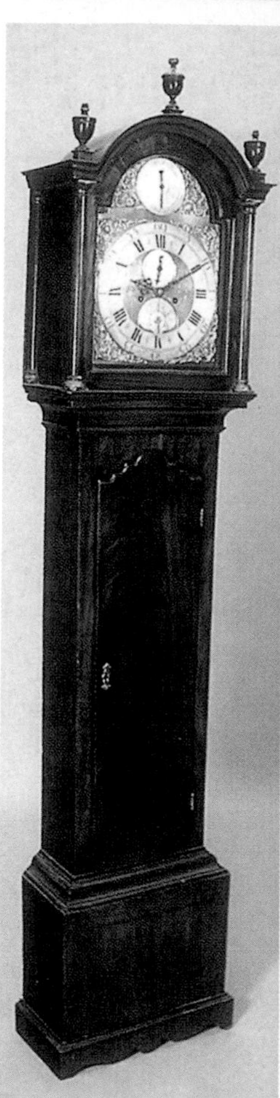

A George III mahogany longcase clock, by William Evill, Bath, the brass dial with silvered chapter ring, subsidiary seconds and date dials, eight-day movement striking on a bell, hood finials replaced, with stained pine sides, 85in (215cm) high.
£3,200–3,800
€4,650–5,500
$5,800–6,900 ⚒ WW

A mahogany longcase clock, by John Buttall, Plymouth, the silvered dial with calendar arch, the arch with automaton of Adam and Eve, with eight-day striking movement, the hood with detachable architectural dentil pediment with brass finials, late 18thC, 93in (236cm) high.
£4,350–5,200 / €6,400–7,600
$7,900–9,400 ⚒ NSal

A mahogany longcase clock, by John Grindall, Dumfries, the brass dial with rocking ship automaton in the arch, eight-day movement, the top with swan-neck pediment, Scottish, c1785, 83in (211cm) high.
£5,400–6,000
€7,900–8,800
$9,800–10,900 ⊞ SOS

A George III mahogany longcase clock, the arched painted dial with moonphase, eight-day movement, the hood with swan-neck pediment and painted panels, the trunk with fluted quarter columns, 93in (236cm) high.
£1,850–2,200
€2,700–3,200
$3,350–4,000 ⚒ Mit

A George III oak longcase clock, by John Stoakes, Fareham, the silvered and brass dial with subsidiary seconds dial, date aperture and strike/silent, eight-day five-pillar movement striking on a bell, the arched hood surmounted by gilt acorn finials and flanked by turned columns, the trunk door inlaid with a dragon, 86in (218.5cm) high.
£1,400–1,650
€2,050–2,400
$2,550–3,000 ⚒ HYD

▶ A George III oak longcase clock, by J. Lighter, Lambeth, with painted dial and eight-day striking movement, 126in (320cm) high.
£1,400–1,650
€2,050–2,400
$2,550–3,000 ⚒ SWO

CLOCKS

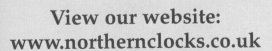

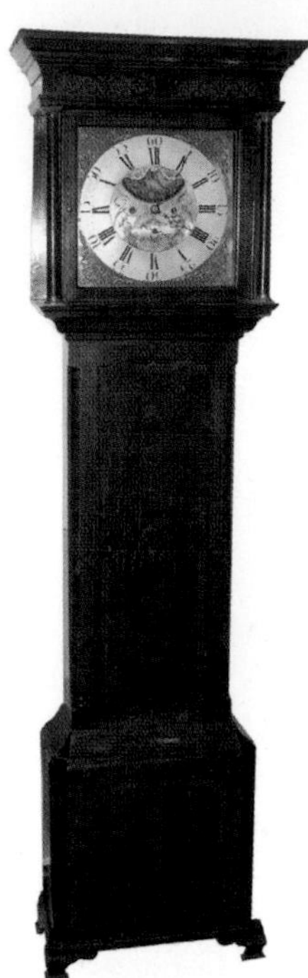

◄ **An oak longcase clock,** by James Whitworth, Lussley, the brass dial with moonphase, with eight-day movement, the case crossbanded with mahogany and walnut, 1770–85, 81in (205.5cm) high.
£6,100–6,800
€8,900–9,900
$11,000–12,300 ⊞ SOS

A George III mahogany longcase clock, by John Dickman, Leith, the painted dial with subsidiary seconds and date dials, the top with fret-carved broken swan-neck pediment over Corinthian pilasters, trunk door inlaid with a shell, flanked by quarter Corinthian columns, Scottish, 85¾in (218cm) high.
£2,350–2,800
€3,450–4,050
$4,250–5,000 ⚒ G(B)

Items in the Clock section have been arranged in date order within each sub-section.

A flame mahogany-veneered longcase clock, by Peter Amyot, Norwich, the dial with seconds and date dials, eight-day five-pillar movement striking the hours on a bell, the pagoda-top hood with Norfolk cresting and reeded angle pillars, the base crossbanded, c1785, 96in (244cm) high.
£8,700–9,700
€12,700–14,200
$15,700–17,500 ⊞ PAO

An oak longcase clock, by Gilbert Bannerman, Banff, the brass dial with chapter ring showing date and seconds, eight-day movement striking the hours on a bell, the hood with broken-arch top with brass finial, Scottish, c1785, 85in (216cm) high.
£5,700–6,300
€8,300–9,200
$10,300–11,400 ⊞ PAO

► **A flame mahogany-veneered longcase clock,** by Emanuel Evans, Winterbourne, the brass dial with subsidiary seconds and date aperture, eight-day movement, c1785, 90in (228.5cm) high.
£8,800–9,800
€12,800–14,300
$15,900–17,700 ⊞ ALS

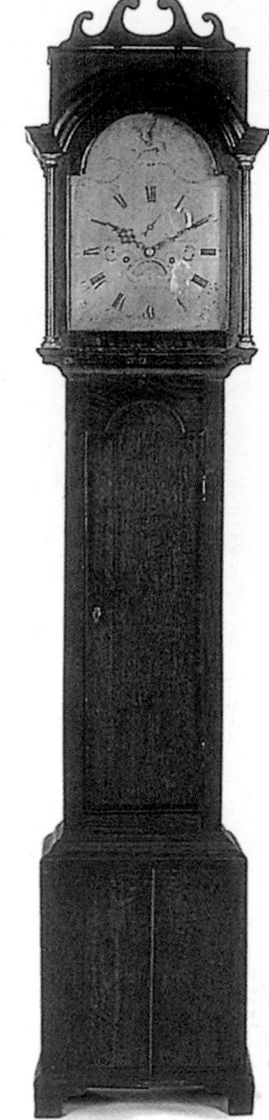

An oak and mahogany longcase clock, by Henry Strawbridge, Chudleigh, the brass dial with subsidiary seconds and date aperture, engraved griffin to arch, the twin-train movement striking on a bell, the arched hood with square top and turned columns, the trunk door with crossbanding, late 18thC, 87in (221cm) high
£1,450–1,700
€2,100–2,500
$2,600–3,050 ⚒ Bea

A mahogany longcase clock, by Grindal, Dumfries, the brass dial with engraved sunburst boss, eight-day movement, Scottish, c1790, 82¼in (209cm) high.
£8,800–9,800
€12,800–14,300
$15,900–17,100 ⊞ ALS

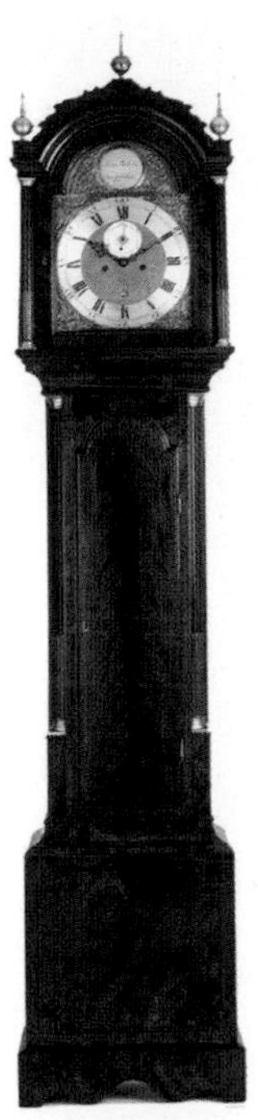

A flame mahogany longcase clock, by Peter Nichols, Newport, the dial with signed boss, the hood and trunk with reeded columns, brass stringing and capitals, late 18thC, 90¼in (229cm) high.
£11,200–12,500
€16,400–18,300
$20,300–22,600 ⊞ TUR

A mahogany longcase clock, by Thomas Bettars, London, with brass dial and eight-day movement, the case with shell and fan inlay, reeded columns and break-arch hood, c1790, 89in (226cm) high.
£17,800–19,800
€26,000–28,900
$32,000–36,000 ⊞ SOS

A George III oak longcase clock, by W. Clark, Kendal, the brass dial with silvered chapter ring, date and lunar apertures, eight-day movement, case mahogany-crossbanded, the hood with turned fluted pilasters, trunk with fluted quarter pilasters, 80in (203cm) high.
£1,900–2,250
€2,750–3,250
$3,450–4,050 ⚒ G(B)

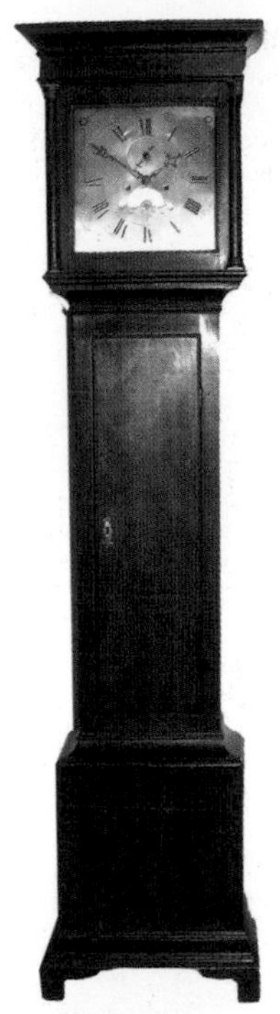

An oak longcase clock, the brass dial with date aperture and subsidiary seconds dial, the hood with moulded pediment and gilded columns, c1790, 82in (208.5cm) high.
£2,100–2,350
€3,050–3,450
$3,800–4,250 ⊞ K&D

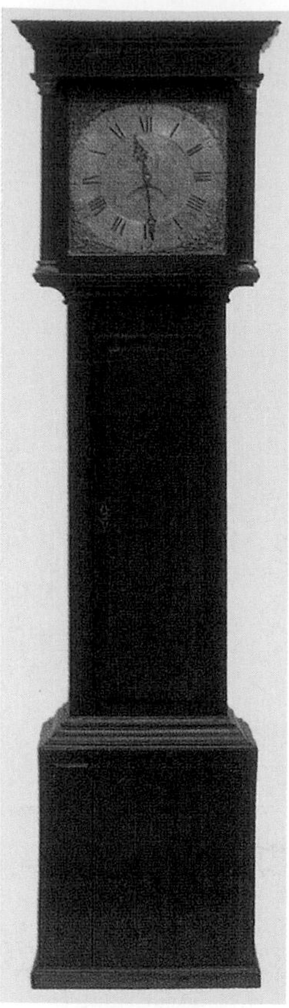

An oak longcase clock, by James Webb, Frome, the brass dial with calendar aperture, the 30-hour movement with outside countwheel, the hood with gilt-capped reeded pillars, trunk and pillars with sycamore banding, late 18thC, 74in (188cm) high.
£940–1,100 / €1,350–1,600
$1,700–2,000 ⚒ NSal

► **A carved and painted musical longcase clock,** the brass dial with subsidiary seconds and tune selection in arch, the triple-train movement with four pillars, anchor escapement, trip repeating, hour striking and chiming one of six tunes with 24 hammers on 12 bells, with break-arch moulded hood, faults, German, movement 18thC, case 19thC, 104¾in (266cm) high.
£2,450–2,950 / €3,600–4,300
$4,450–5,300 ⚒ S(Am)

A George III mahogany longcase clock, by James McCulloch, Aucherarder, the painted dial with subsidiary seconds and date dials, the twin-train eight-day movement with anchor escapement, the hood with swan-neck pediment with brass finials above turned columns, the trunk door with boxwood stringing, Scottish, 85¾in (218cm) high.
£2,800–3,350
€4,100–4,900
$5,100–6,100 ⚒ L&T

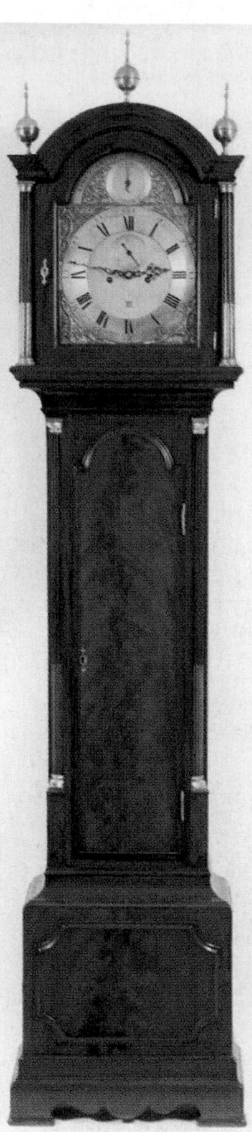

A flame mahogany longcase clock, by James Smith, London, the brass dial with subsidiary seconds dial, date aperture and strike/silent, eight-day striking movement, the breakarch top with brass finials, c1790, 93in (236cm) high.
£13,000–14,500
€19,000–21,200
$23,500–26,200 ⊞ DRA

► **A longcase clock,** by Donaldson, Langholm, the dial with moonphase and date calendar, 30-hour movement striking on a bell, c1790, 90in (228.5cm) high.
£3,300–3,700 / €4,800–5,400
$6,000–6,700 ⊞ JIL

◄ **A George III oak longcase clock,** by Alex MacFarlane, Perth, the silvered dial with subsidiary seconds and calendar dials, eight-day movement with repeat strike on a bell, the hood with swan-neck pediment above blind fret panels and reeded pilasters, Scottish, 82in (208.5cm) high.
£1,100–1,300 / €1,600–1,900
$2,000–2,350 ⚒ M

A George III oak and mahogany longcase clock, by William Snow, Otley, the brass dial with calendar aperture, eight-day movement striking on a bell, 85in (216cm) high.
£1,100–1,300
€1,600–1,900
$2,000–2,350 DD

A Louis XVI oak longcase clock and corner cupboard, by H. Gros Jean à Leuve, the trunk door carved with a bird and foliage, the bowfronted cupboard with two panelled doors and carved with lozenges, altered, Liègeois, 1775–1800 and later, 98¾in (251cm) high.
£2,600–3,100
€3,800–4,500
$4,700–5,600 S(Am)

An oak longcase clock, by James Northwood, Newport, the painted dial with calendar aperture, eight-day movement, the hood with dentil cornice and turned corners, trunk door inlaid with a shell, late 18thC, 81in (205.5cm) high.
£760–900 / €1,100–1,300
$1,350–1,600 PF

An inlaid mahogany longcase clock, by Joseph Fell, Ulverston, the silvered dial with subsidiary seconds and hour dials, rack-and-bell striking movement, hood with swan-neck cresting and fluted pillars, the trunk door flanked by fluted pilasters, inlay later, c1790, 86in (218.5cm) high.
£3,600–4,300
€5,300–6,300
$6,500–7,800 S

An oak and mahogany longcase clock, by William Ashmole, Repton, with painted dial and eight-day movement, c1795, 87in (221cm) high.
£3,150–3,500
€4,600–5,100
$5,700–6,300 SOS

A George III oak longcase clock, by William Porter, Burton, the brass dial with date aperture, 30-hour movement, the later carved case with stepped pediment above turned pilasters, the trunk door carved with roundels, altered and restored, 74½in (189cm) high.
£470–560 / €670–810
$850–1,000 RTo

An oak longcase clock, by D. Jones, Bullfa Lane, the painted dial with moonphase, eight-day movement, case ebony-inlaid, Welsh, c1795, 88in (223.5cm) high.
£5,400–6,000
€7,900–8,700
$9,800–10,900 ⊞ SOS

A mahogany-veneered longcase clock, by James. Lomax, Blackburn, the painted dial with subsidiary seconds and date dials, moonphase and raised gilt corners, eight-day movement striking the hours on a bell, the hood with swan-neck pediment with brass-capped fluted Corinthian columns, c1795, 89in (226cm) high.
£3,550–3,950
€5,200–5,800
$6,400–7,200 ⊞ K&D

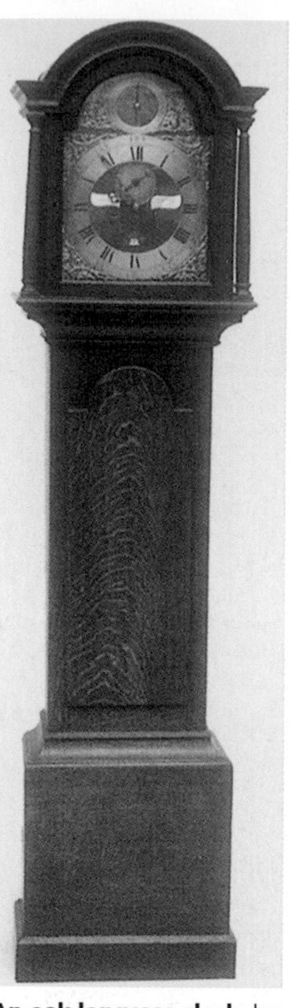

An oak longcase clock, by David Field, Luton, the brass dial with silvered chapter ring, subsidiary seconds dial and calendar aperture, eight-day five-pillar movement with a strike, later converted to a gong, later name plates, the hood with turned walnut side pillars, late 18thC, 78in (198cm) high.
£1,000–1,200
€1,450–1,750
$1,800–2,150 ⚒ NSal

A stripped pine longcase clock, by William West, Helston, with painted dial and eight-day movement, c1800, 80in (203cm) high.
£2,700–3,000
€3,950–4,400
$4,900–5,400 ⊞ SOS

◄ A mahogany longcase clock, with later painted dial by Robert Boylan, Dublin, eight-day movement, the hood with broken swan-neck pediment above a scroll flask centred by a lion mask, above fluted Corinthian columns, Irish, 18thC, 98½in (250cm) high.
£4,800–5,700
€7,000–8,300
$8,700–10,300 ⚒ HOK

► An oak and mahogany-crossbanded longcase clock, by J. Pearson, Atherstone, the enamel dial with date aperture and gilt swan spandrels, with 30-hour movement, c1800, 83in (211cm) high.
£760–910 / €1,100–1,300
$1,400–1,650 ⚒ WL

A George III mahogany longcase clock, by Gard, Exon, the brass dial with date aperture, with eight-day movement, 80¼in (204cm) high.
£2,000–2,400
€2,900–3,500
$3,600–4,350 ⚒ G(B)

A George III Lancashire oak and mahogany longcase clock, by Halliwell, Blackburn, the painted dial with subsidiary seconds dial and date aperture, the restored twin-train brass and steel movement with anchor escapement striking on a bell, 85in (216cm) high.
£1,700–2,000
€2,500–2,900
$3,100–3,600 DN(BR)

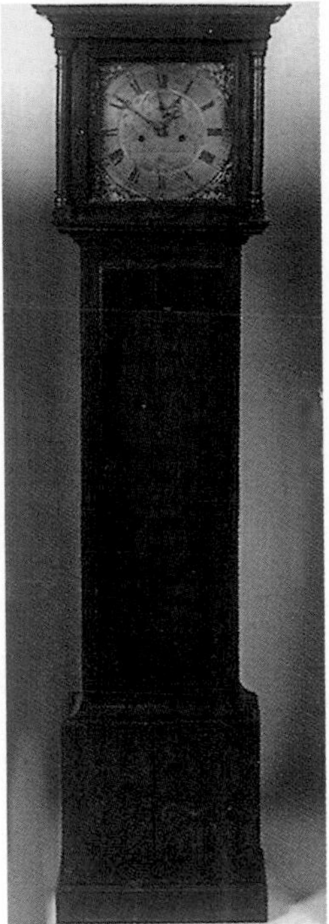

A George III oak longcase clock, by John Price, Chichester, the brass dial with subsidiary seconds dial and date aperture, the eight-day movement striking on a bell, 78in (198cm) high.
£1,300–1,550
€1,900–2,250
$2,350–2,800 HYD

A George III oak and mahogany-crossbanded longcase clock, by Stevenson, Nottingham, the painted break-arch dial surrounded by allegorical scenes, the eight-day movement striking on a bell, the hood with swan-neck pediment, 89in (226cm) high.

£880–1,050 / €1,300–1,550
$1,600–1,900 RTo

A figured mahogany longcase clock, by Lomax, Blackburn, the painted dial with subsidiary dials and moonphases, eight-day movement, c1805, 92in (233.5cm) high.
£6,700–7,500
€9,800–11,000
$12,100–13,600 ALS

An oak and mahogany longcase clock, by John Heselton, Bridlington, the dial with subsidiary seconds and date dials, the eight-day movement striking on a bell, the hood with scroll pediment, early 19thC, 86½in (219.5cm) high.
£2,100–2,500
€3,050–3,650
$3,800–4,550 DA

A George III oak and mahogany longcase clock, the painted dial with subsidiary seconds and date dials, date aperture and moonphase, and High Water at Bristol Quay, the eight-day movement striking on a bell, the case with fruitwood and ebony banding and boxwood stringing, 86¾in (220.5cm) high.
£3,750–4,500
€5,500–6,600
$6,800–8,100 GIL

An oak longcase clock, by John Booth, Aberdeen, the painted dial with subsidiary seconds and date dials, the eight-day movement striking the hours on a bell, the hood with brass-capped pillars, Scottish, c1805, 85in (216cm) high.
£4,700–5,300
€6,900–7,700
$8,500–9,600 PAO

► A George III figured mahogany longcase clock, by Le Fortier, Jersey, the painted dial with subsidiary seconds and calendar dial, the eight-day movement striking on a bell, the hood with applied brass ball-and-eagle finials, slight damage, 91¼in (232cm) high.
£1,200–1,400
€1,750–2,050
$2,150–2,550 RTo

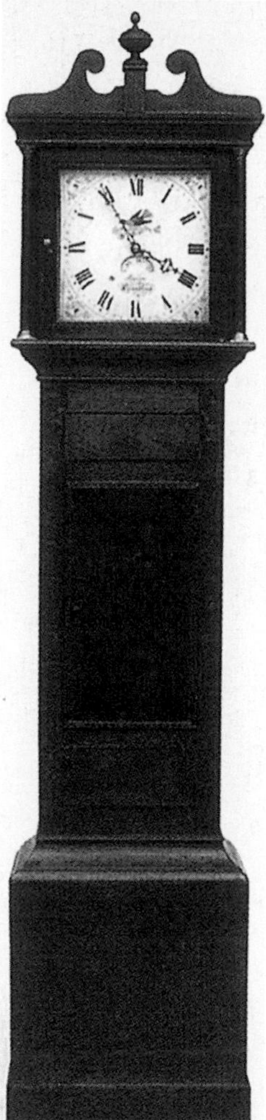

An oak longcase clock, by Barrett, Blandford, the dial painted with a bird above a calender aperture, with 30-hour movement striking on a bell, the case with a mahogany-veneered panel, early 19thC, 82in (208.5cm) high.
£590–700 / €860–1,000
$1,050–1,250 NSal

◄ A mahogany longcase clock, by Rishton, Rochdale, the dial with moonphase and painted with a young boy fishing, the eight-day movement striking the hours on a bell, c1810, 93in (236cm) high.
£7,500–8,400
€11,000–12,300
$13,600–15,200 PAO

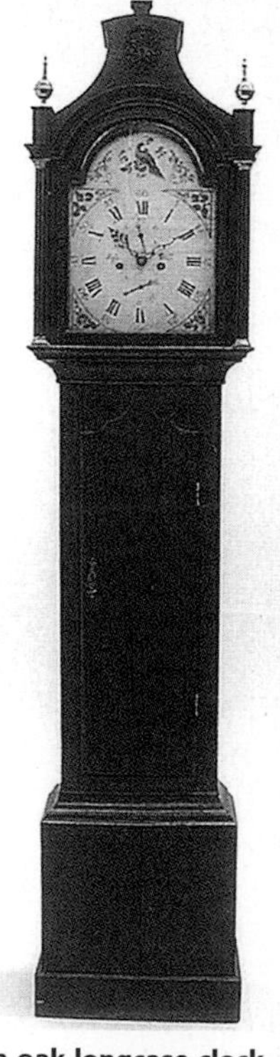

An oak longcase clock, by Ross, Hull, the painted enamel dial with subsidiary seconds and date dials, eight-day movement, the hood crossbanded in mahogany, early 19thC, 84½in (214cm) high.
£1,250–1,500
€1,850–2,200
$2,250–2,700 DD

◄ **An oak longcase clock,** by William Mills, Gloucester, the painted dial with date aperture, the 30-hour movement striking the hours on a bell, early 19thC, 77in (195.5cm) high.
£1,450–1,650
€2,100–2,400
$2,600–3,000 ⊞ K&D

LOCATE THE SOURCE
The source of each illustration in Miller's can be found by checking the code letters below each caption with the Key to Illustrations, pages 778–784.

A pine longcase clock, with traces of original paint, Swedish, c1810, 78in (198cm) high.
£1,700–1,900
€2,500–2,750
$3,100–3,450 ⊞ Lfo

An oak longcase clock, by Fox, Beverley, the arched painted dial with subsidiary seconds and calendar dials, with eight-day striking movement, early 19thC, 94in (239cm) high.
£1,350–1,600
€1,950–2,350
$2,450–2,900 ⚒ PF

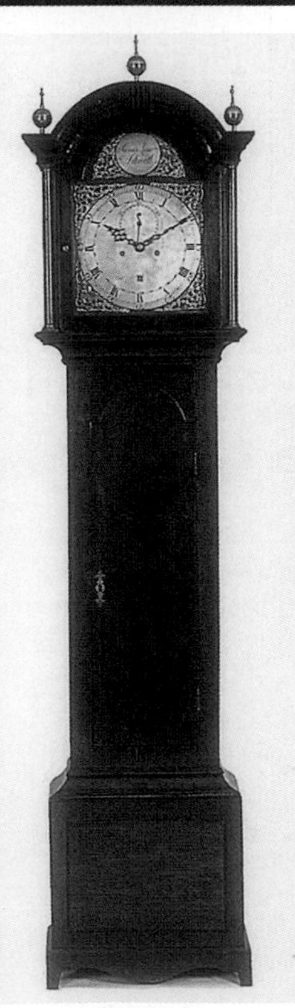

A mahogany longcase clock, by James Low, Arbroath, the brass dial with silvered chapter ring, subsidiary seconds dial and date aperture, with twin-train movement striking on a bell, the arched hood with ball and spire finials, Scottish, early 19thC, 85¾in (218cm) high.
£1,600–1,900
€2,350–2,750
$2,900–3,450 ⚒ Bea

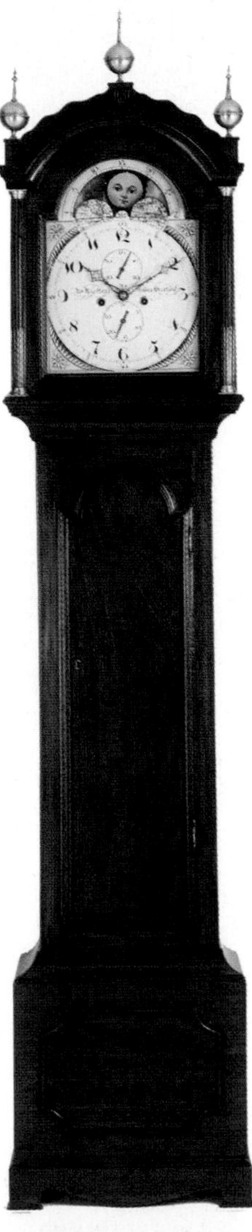

A mahogany longcase clock, by W. Yardley, Bishops Stortford, the painted dial with moonphase, 1813, 91in (231cm) high.
£7,600–8,500
€11,100–12,400
$13,800–15,400 ⊞ TUR

◄ **A mahogany longcase clock,** by Whitehurst & Son, Derby, dated 1818, 81in (205.5cm) high.
£10,800–12,000
€15,800–17,500
$19,500–21,700 ⊞ JIL

An oak and mahogany-crossbanded longcase clock, by William Ewbank, Elland, the break-arch dial with subsidiary seconds dial and moonphase, with twin-train movement, the hood with swan-neck pediment, early 19thC, 93½in (237.5cm) high.
£3,300–3,950
€4,800–5,800
$6,000–7,200 ⚒ DMC

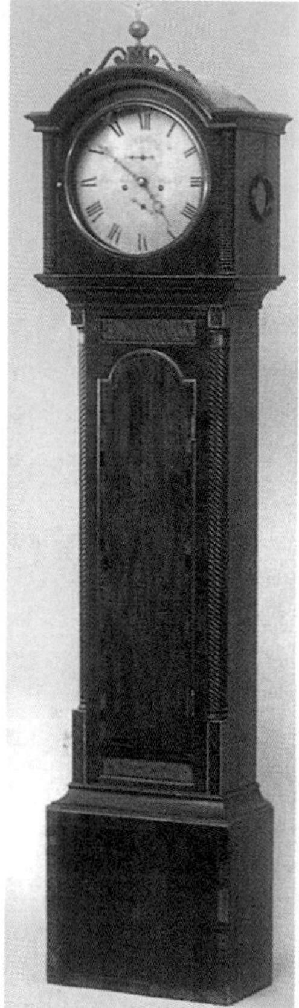

◄ **A mahogany, rosewood-banded and line-inlaid longcase clock,** by John Mearns, Aberdeen, the silvered dial with subsidiary seconds and date dials, the twin-train brass movement with anchor escapement striking on a bell, Scottish, early 19thC, 86¼in (219cm) high.
£890–1,050
€1,300–1,550
$1,600–1,900 ⚒ DN(BR)

A Regency mahogany, rosewood-crossbanded and line-inlaid longcase clock, by John Barron, Aberdeen, the enamel dial with subsidiary seconds and date dials, with eight-day movement, Scottish, 84in (213.5cm) high.
£1,400–1,650
€2,050–2,400
$2,550–3,000 ⚒ G(B)

CLOCKS

A Regency mahogany longcase clock, the painted dial with subsidiary seconds and date dials, with eight-day striking movement, 82in (208.5cm) high.
£1,200–1,400
€1,750–2,050
$2,150–2,550 ⚒ Mit

An oak longcase clock, by David King, Montrose, the arched painted dial with subsidiary seconds and date dials, the eight-day movement striking the hours on a bell, Scottish, c1825, 88in (223.5cm high).
£3,750–4,150
€5,500–6,100
$6,800–7,500 ⊞ PAO

◄ **A flame mahogany longcase clock,** by Thomas Hartnell, Cirencester, the painted dial with moonphase, with eight-day movement, c1830, 82in (208.3cm) high.
£7,200–8,000
€10,500–11,700
$13,000–14,500 ⊞ SOS

A flame mahogany longcase clock, by Upjohn, Exeter, with painted dial and eight-day striking movement, c1830, 79in (200.5cm) high.
£7,600–8,500
€11,100–12,400
$13,800–15,400 ⊞ JIL

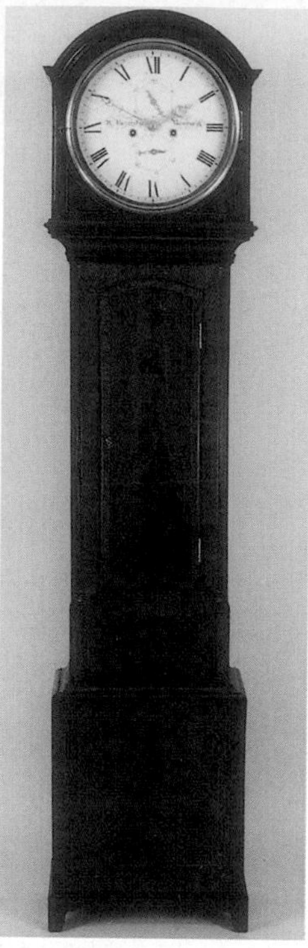

A mahogany longcase clock, by Robert Beveridge, Newburgh, the painted dial with subsidiary seconds and date dials, the eight-day movement striking the hours on a bell, the case with flame mahogany veneers and boxwood stringing, Scottish, c1830, 77in (195.5cm) high.
£7,400–8,300
€10,800–12,100
$13,400–15,000 ⊞ PAO

A mahogany-veneered longcase clock, by Osmond, Tisbury, the painted dial with subsidiary seconds dial, with 30-hour movement striking on a bell, the case with inlaid stringing, second hand missing, 19thC, 78½in (199.5cm) high.
£610–730 / €890–1,050
$1,100–1,300 ⚒ WW

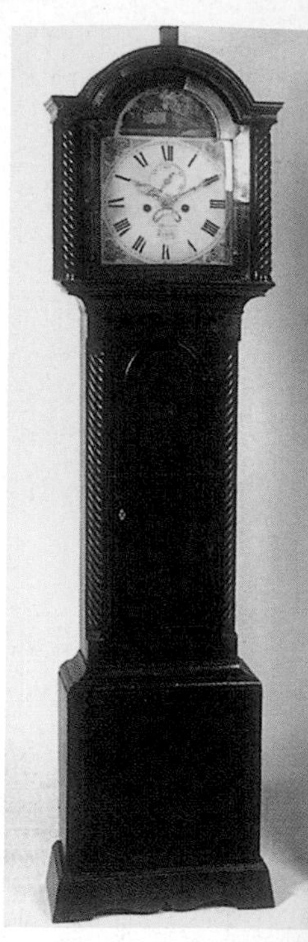

A William IV mahogany longcase clock, by Harris, Truro, the arched painted dial with date aperture and subsidiary seconds dial, the twin-train eight-day movement striking on a bell, the case inlaid with satinwood stringing, 84in (213.5cm) high.
£1,050–1,250
€1,550–1,850
$1,900–2,250 ⚒ HYD

CLOCKS

◄ **A mahogany longcase clock,** by B. R. Hennessy, Swansea, the dial with subsidiary seconds dial, the eight-day movement with deadbeat escapement and striking on a bell, the case with inlaid stringing, the hood with later urn finials, Welsh, 19thC, 83in (211cm) high.
£2,350–2,800
€3,450–4,100
$4,250–5,100 ⚒ M

Further reading

Miller's Antiques Checklist: Clocks, Miller's Publications, 2000

► **A mahogany longcase clock,** by Leddall & Sons, Edinburgh, the silvered brass dial with subsidiary seconds and date dials, the eight-day movement striking the hours on a bell, Scottish, c1840, 78in (198cm) high.
£6,200–6,900
€9,100–10,100
$11,200–12,500 ⊞ PAO

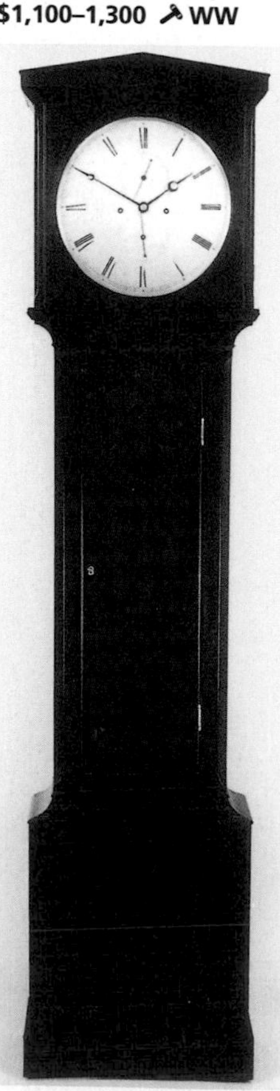

A mahogany longcase clock, by Blackburn, possibly Gateshead, the arched dial painted with romantic scenes, with subsidiary seconds and date dials, the eight-day movement striking on a bell, 19thC, 90¼in (229cm) high.
£1,050–1,250
€1,550–1,850
$1,900–2,250 ⚒ DD

A Victorian mahogany longcase clock, by F. Birckley, Manchester, the arched painted dial with moonphase, subsidiary seconds and calendar dials, the eight-day movement striking on a bell, the case with rosewood banding, 91in (231cm) high.
£1,100–1,300
€1,600–1,900
$2,000–2,350 WW

A mahogany longcase clock, by James Low, Arbroath, the arched dial depicting Mary Queen of Scots and the four seasons, with subsidiary seconds and date dials, the eight-day movement striking the hours on a bell, the case with flame-veneered panels, Scottish, c1845, 76in (193cm) high.
£5,800–6,500
€8,500–9,500
$10,500–11,800 PAO

A boulle longcase clock, decorated with floral motifs and dancing figures, surmounted by the figure of Father Time, French, late 19thC, 89¾in (228cm) high.
£4,000–4,800
€5,800–7,000
$7,200–8,700 BERN

A mahogany longcase clock, the arched silvered dial with engraved floral decoration and subsidiary seconds dial, Whittington/Westminster chimes and chime/silent, the triple-train movement with anchor escapement and eight hammers striking on nine bells and a further one for the hour, c1890, 107in (272cm) high.
£5,900–7,000
€8,600–10,200
$10,700–12,700 TEN

CLOCKS

◄ **A mahogany longcase clock,** by Maple & Co, London, with silvered dial, the case with a pagoda top, c1900, 80in (203cm) high.
£9,700–10,800
€14,200–15,800
$17,600–19,500 ⊞ SOS

A mahogany longcase clock, by John Hall & Co, Manchester, the dial with subsidiary seconds dial, the triple-train movement with deadbeat escapement and maintaining power, chiming and striking on nine tubular bells, early 20thC, 90½in (230cm) high.
£4,900–5,800
€7,200–8,500
$8,900–10,500 ⚒ S(O)

An Edwardian mahogany longcase clock, the break-arch brass dial with silvered chapter ring, with strike/silent and slow/fast dials, the eight-day movement striking on two gongs, the case marquetry-inlaid with husks, swags, cornucopiae and urns, with ormolu columns, 44½in (113cm) high.
£2,250–2,700
€3,300–3,950
$4,050–4,900 ⚒ G(B)

A mahogany longcase clock, the brass dial with silvered chapter ring and subsidiary seconds dial and date aperture, eight-day movement striking on a bell, the case inlaid with shell paterae, early 20thC, 84½in (214cm) high.
£610–730 / €890–1,050
$1,100–1,300 ⚒ RTo

Further reading

Miller's Clocks & Barometers Buyers Guide, Miller's Publications, 2001

◄ **A mahogany longcase clock,** with silvered dial, the eight-day movement chiming the quarters with Westminster/Whittington and St Michaels tunes on nine tubular bells, the trunk with a glazed door, c1910, 77in (195.5cm) high.
£7,200–8,000
€10,500–11,700
$13,000–14,500 ⊞ SOS

Novelty Clocks

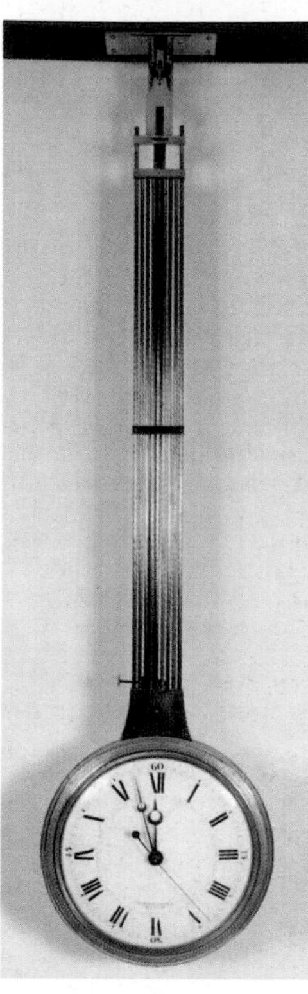

A shop window clock, in the form of a gridiron pendulum, with two enamel dials signed 'Gaston Jolly, Paris', the eight-day French movement with pinwheel escapement, c1820, 50½in (128.5cm) high.
£7,000–7,800
€10,200–11,400
$12,700–14,100 DRA

A satinwood miniature longcase clock, with marquetry fan inlay, c1890, 14in (35.5cm) high.
£2,400–2,650
€3,500–3,850
$4,350–4,800 TIM

A brass timepiece, the engraved brass dial with Breguet hands, the movement with verge escapement and balance forming the wheel of a wheelbarrow carried by an engraved figure, in a glazed case, signed 'Sandhaas, Wien', Austrian, Vienna, c1820, 5½in (14cm) high.
£2,900–3,450
€4,250–5,000
$5,200–6,200 S(Am)

A brass tripod clock, by Thomas Cole, London, the engraved dial with subsidiary seconds dial, with deadbeat escapement, the stepped and engraved base with a barometer and thermometer, 1882, 20in (51cm) high.
£7,000–8,400
€10,200–12,300
$12,700–15,200 WW

► **An ormolu-mounted porcelain and marble urn timepiece,** the two horizontal chapter rings with a gilt coiled serpent indicating time, the eight-day movement with lever escapement signed 'P. Grenon', French, c1900, 9½in (24cm) high.
£3,350–4,000
€4,900–5,800
$6,100–7,200 S

► **A gilt-metal-mounted bronze mystery clock,** by Robert-Houdin, Paris, with a glass dial, French, c1840, 16in (40.5cm) high.
£18,000–20,000
€26,300–29,200
$32,000–36,000 DRA

A Black Forest cuckoo clock, the fusee movement striking on a gong, the case carved with foliage and a bird, slight damage, German, c1860, 22½in (57cm) high.
£560–670 / €820–980
$1,000–1,200 CHTR

A Victorian bronze easel clock, in the form of an owl perched on a branch with a rat, 6¼in (16cm) high.
£210–250 / €310–370
$380–450 SWO

A brass timepiece, in the form of a lighthouse, with silvered chapter ring and eight-day movement, with cylinder platform escapement, two thermometers and an aneroid barometer, with silvered doors and windows, on a marble base, French, c1880, 17½in (44.5cm) high.
£4,200–4,700
€6,100–6,900
$7,600–8,500 DRA

A bronze 'Empire' clock, with a printed globe, moon attachment missing, French, c1900, 16in (40.5cm) high.
£1,150–1,350
€1,700–1,950
$2,100–2,450 JAA

CLOCKS

Skeleton Clocks

An ormolu skeleton mantel clock, with enamel dial, French, c1795, 18in (45.5cm) high.
£7,600–8,500
€11,100–12,400
$13,800–15,400 ⊞ JIL

A brass skeleton clock, the brass dial with engine-turned decoration, with fusee movement, on a brass base and an ebonized stand, chapter ring missing, 19thC, 13½in (34.5cm) high.
£640–760 / €930–1,100
$1,150–1,350 ⚒ DA

A skeleton timepiece, by Craike, Dalkeith, the chronometer escapement with a helical spring of Earnshaw-type spring detent, bi-metallic balance with heat compensation weights, on a velvet stand and ebonized base, Scottish, c1840, 15¾in (40cm) high, with replacement glass dome.
£9,900–11,000
€14,500–16,100
$17,900–19,900 ⊞ DRA

A brass skeleton clock, attributed to Smiths, Clerkenwell, the silvered chapter ring engraved with crowns and foliage, with chain fusee, six-spoke wheels and deadbeat escapement, chiming and pull repeat on eight bells and striking on a gong, on a rosewood base, gong missing, requires restoration, mid-19thC, 21½in (54.5cm) high.
£17,500–21,000
€26,000–31,000
$32,000–38,000 ⚒ GH

The prices realized at auction may reflect the fact that the clocks have sometimes undergone alterations to their movements, or are in unrestored condition.

◄ A brass skeleton clock, by James Condliff, Liverpool, with deadbeat escapement, chiming the quarters on eight bells and the hours on a gong, with a signed plaque, on a walnut base, with a glass dome, c1860, 20in (51cm) high.
£61,000–68,000
€89,000–99,000
$110,000–123,000 ⊞ DRA
John Condliff was perhaps one of the most well-known and admired makers of this type of clock in the 19th century.

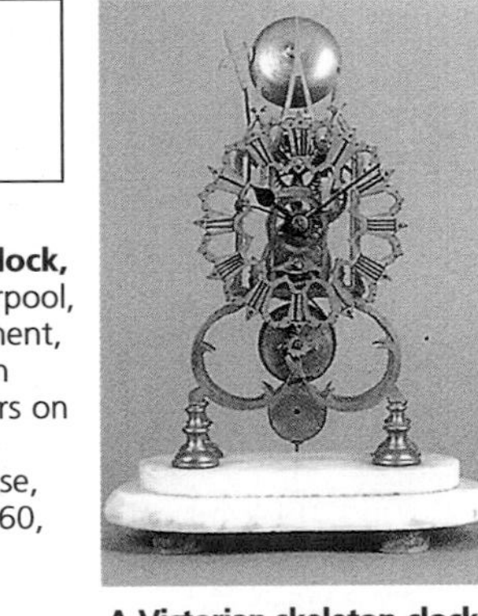

A Victorian skeleton clock, with pierced chapter ring and fusee movement, on a marble base, 15½in (39.5cm) high, glass dome missing.
£470–560 / €690–820
$850–1,000 ⚒ PFK

A brass skeleton clock, with silvered chapter ring, the single fusee movement with anchor escapement striking on a bell, on an ebonized base, glass dome cracked, c1880, 17¾in (45cm) high.
£560–670 / €820–980
$1,000–1,200 ⚒ TEN

Wall Clocks

A brass wall timepiece, with copper chapter ring, the movement signed 'Christoph Scherer', with verge escapement and pendulum, with an iron dust cover, German, c1740, 14½in (37cm) high.
£740–880 / €1,100–1,300
$1,350–1,600 ⚒ S(Am)

◄ An ormolu cartel clock, by Le Doux, Paris, with enamel dial, the movement striking on a bell, French, mid-18thC, 31in (78.5cm) high.
£31,000–35,000
€45,000–51,000
$56,000–64,000 ⊞ JIL
This clock has a superb ormolu case attributed to the bronzier St Germain. The movement is totally original with a verge escapement. Clocks of this type from the transitional period between rococo and classical styles of decoration are particularly sought after.

An ormolu cartel clock, by Lebeuf, Paris, with enamel dial and eight-day movement, French, c1750, 23in (58.5cm) high.
£8,500–9,500
€12,400–13,900
$15,400–17,200 ⊞ JIL

A lacquer tavern clock, signed 'Jas. Williams, London', c1780, dial 22in (56cm) diam.
£13,400–14,900
€19,600–21,800
$24,300–27,000 ⊞ TUR

A carved giltwood wall clock, Swedish, Stockholm, c1780, 35in (89cm) high.
£2,100–2,500
€3,050–3,650
$3,800–4,550 ⚒ BUK

A gilt-bronze cartel clock, by Van der Cruse L'lejeune, Paris, with an eight-day movement, French, c1780, 30in (76cm) high.
£9,900–11,000
€14,500–16,100
$17,900–19,900 ⊞ JIL

A carved giltwood cartel clock, by F. L. Dupuis, Amsterdam, with enamel dial, the movement with verge escapement striking the half-hours on alternating bells, the case surmounted by an urn hung with flowers, signed, Dutch, c1780, 28in (71cm) high.
£3,400–4,050
€4,950–5,900
$6,200–7,300 ⚒ S(Am)

► A mahogany wall timepiece, with painted dial, signed 'Joseph Bramble, London', the gut fusee movement with four pillars and an anchor escapement, c1810, dial 12in (30.5cm) diam.
£3,750–4,300
€5,500–6,100
$6,800–7,600
⊞ DRA

◄ A George III oak wall clock, by Richard Comber, Lewes, the arched brass dial with silvered chapter ring, with alarm, damaged, 19¾in (50cm) high.
£2,600–3,100
€3,800–4,550
$4,700–5,600 ⚒ DN(BR)

A mahogany brass-mounted wall clock, by Handley & Moore, London, with enamel dial, the five-pillar twin-train chain fusee movement striking on a bell, c1815, 18in (45.5cm) high.
£10,300–11,500
€15,000–16,800
$18,600–20,800 ⊞ DRA

Handley and Moore were both apprentices of John Thwaites at 39 Clerkenwell Close, London at the end of the 18th century and, in 1802, formed the well-known partnership of Handley & Moore. G. Handley died in 1824, leaving Moore to continue the business under the name of Jno. Moore & Sons.

A carved and painted wood oscillating wall timepiece, the spring-driven movement signed 'B. Berghys, Deventer', with pinwheel escapement, the case surmounted by griffins, Dutch, c1820, 66½in (169cm) high.
£2,900–3,450
€4,250–5,000
$5,200–6,200 ⚒ S(Am)

► An ebonized and painted miniature *Dachluhr* timepiece, with enamel dial and eight-day movement, Austrian, Vienna, c1830, 24½in (62cm) high.
£5,400–6,000
€7,900–8,800
$9,800–10,900 ⊞ DRA

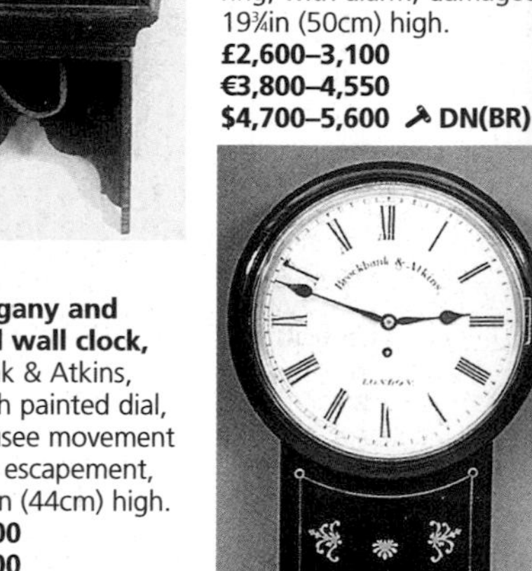

► A mahogany and brass-inlaid wall clock, by Brockbank & Atkins, London, with painted dial, the single fusee movement with anchor escapement, c1830, 17¼in (44cm) high.
£2,350–2,800
€3,450–4,100
$4,250–5,100 ⚒ TEN

A mahogany and brass-inlaid wall clock, with enamel dial and a single fusee movement, 19thC, 12¼in (31cm) high.
£1,350–1,600
€1,950–2,350
$2,450–2,900 ⚒ SWO

A Black Forest carved wood cuckoo clock, German, 19thC, 27½in (70cm) high.
£290–340 / €420–500 $520–620 ⚒ SWO

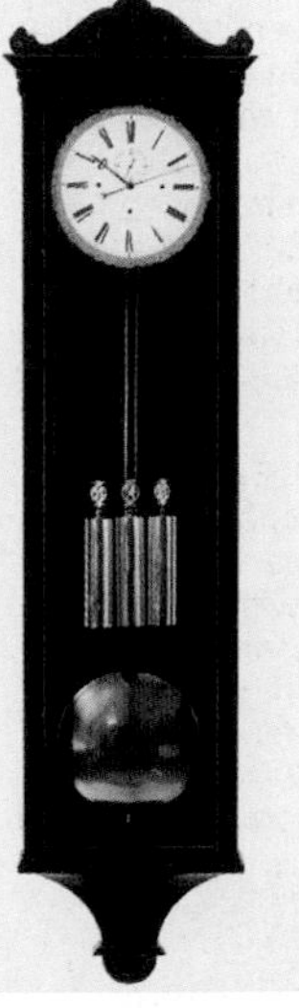

A Biedermeier mahogany and maplewood-strung *grande sonnerie* wall clock, by Schonberg, Vienna, with enamel dial, month-going movement, Austrian, c1850, 63in (160cm) high.
£25,200–28,000 €37,000–41,000 $45,000–50,000 ⊞ DRA
Schonberg was an excellent clockmaker. The fineness of the wheel-work and pivots required to give the clock month duration on relatively small weights is exceptional.

A Victorian walnut wall clock, by J. Scott, Kendal, with painted dial, single fusee movement, the case with eight panes of glass with painted foliate scrollwork, damaged, base associated, 24½in (62cm) high.
£370–440 / €540–640 $670–800 ⚒ PFK

A Louis XV-style gilt-bronze cartel clock, by Barat, Choisy-Le-Roy, with enamel dial, the movement with anchor escapement and countwheel striking on a bell, the case surmounted by a seated figure, French, 1850–1900, 23¼in (59cm) high.
£2,000–2,400 €2,900–3,500 $3,600–4,350 ⚒ S(Am)

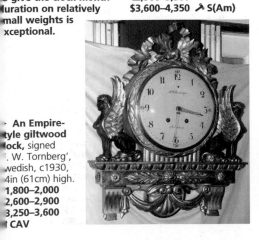

◄ **An Empire-style giltwood clock,** signed 'F. W. Tornberg', Swedish, c1930, 24in (61cm) high.
£1,800–2,000 €2,600–2,900 $3,250–3,600 ⊞ CAV

A mahogany wall clock, the dial signed 'Richard Francis, Wymondham', with a weight-driven movement, 57in (145cm) high.
£4,200–4,700 €6,100–6,900 $7,600–8,500 ⊞ SOS
Richard Francis is recorded working 1812–32.

► **A gilt-metal cartel clock,** with enamel dial and eight-day movement, French, 19thC, 23½in (59.5cm) high.
£1,050–1,250 €1,550–1,850 $1,900–2,250 ⚒ AH

A pollarded oak wall clock, by Monk, Bolton, with painted dial, single fusee movement with anchor escapement, c1850, 22½in (57cm) high.
£1,500–1,800 €2,200–2,650 $2,700–3,250 ⚒ TEN

CLOCKS

American Clocks

A figured walnut longcase clock, by Augustin Neisser, Germantown, Pennsylvania, damaged and restored, c1770, 97½in (247.5cm) high.
£8,000–9,600
€11,700–14,000
$14,500–17,400 S(NY)

A mahogany and parcel-gilt banjo clock, by Simon Willard, with painted tin dial, the case with *verre églomisé* panel, 1800–25, 35in (89cm) high.
£3,600–4,300
€5,300–6,300
$6,500–7,800 SGA

A painted pine longcase clock, Pennsylvania, early 19thC, 83in (211cm) high.
£2,250–2,700
€3,300–3,950
$4,050–4,900 DuM

A shelf clock, by New Haven Clock Co, with 30-hour movement, the case with a reverse-painted glass panel depicting Greenwood Cemetery, damaged, c1835, 26in (66cm) high.
£60–70 / €85–100
$110–125 JAA

A mahogany drop octagon clock, by Seth Thomas Clock Co, eight-day movement, c1885, 22in (56cm) high.
£145–175 / €210–250
$260–310 ROSc

A Victorian iron Imogene mantel clock, by Ansonia Clock Co, the case surmounted by a spelter figure, 20in (51cm) high.
£120–140 / €175–200
$220–250 JAA

A walnut-veneered table clock, the movement by E. N. Welch, Connecticut, 1880–1900, 27in (68.5cm) high.
£610–680 / €890–990
$1,100–1,250 DEB

A figured ash Grecian clock, by E. Ingraham, with eight-day striking movement, dial repapered, hands replaced, case refinished, with original label, c1880, 15in (38cm) high.
£240–280 / €350–400
$430–500 ROSc

An oak Seneca mantel clock, by Ansonia Clock Co, with applied and turned decoration, c1890, 15½in (39.5cm) high.
£60–70 / €85–100
$110–125 JAA

◄ **A cast-iron and painted spelter Shakespeare clock,** by Ansonia Clock Co, with eight-day striking movement, c1894, 15in (38cm) high.
£260–310
€380–450
$470–560
ROSc

◄ **A mahogany alarm mantel clock,** by Welch, late 19thC, 18½in (47cm) high.
£95–110 / €140–160
$170–200 JAA

CLOCKS

British Regulators

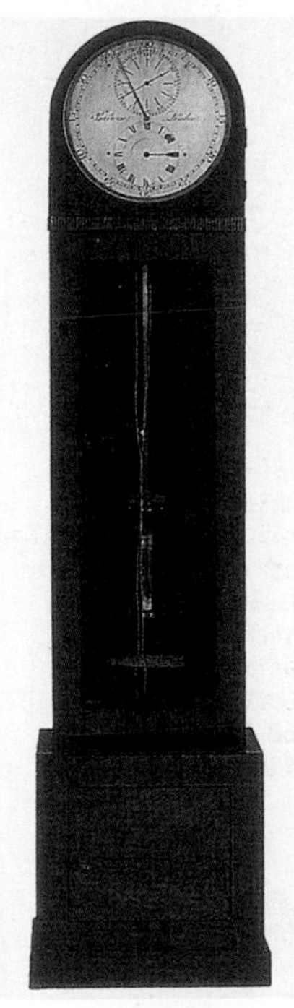

A Regency mahogany longcase regulator, by Barwise, London, with silvered dial, the movement with six pillars, deadbeat escapement and maintaining power, 71¾in (182.5cm) high.
£8,000–9,600
€11,700–14,000
$14,500–17,400 Bea

A Regency mahogany regulator, by Lormier & Edwards, London, the silvered dial with subsidiary seconds and hour dials, single-train movement, with brass inlay and ebony mouldings, 86½in (219.5cm) high.
£9,400–11,200
€13,700–16,400
$17,000–20,300 F&C

A Regency figured mahogany longcase regulator, by Thomas Smith, London, the silvered dial with subsidiary seconds and hour dials, the six-pillar movement with deadbeat escapement and maintaining power, the case with ebony banding, weight missing, 78½in (199.5cm) high.
£6,100–7,300
€8,900–10,700
$11,000–13,200 GH

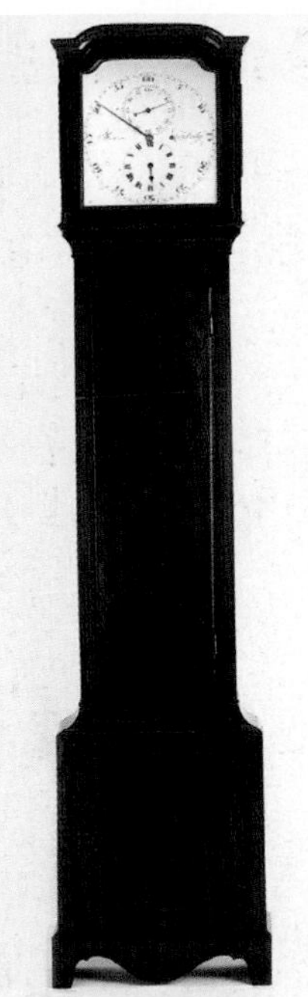

A mahogany longcase regulator, by Thomas Revis, the six-pillar movement with deadbeat escapement and maintaining power, early 19thC, 77¼in (196cm) high.
£14,400–16,000
€21,000–23,400
$26,100–29,000 TUR

◀ **A mahogany domestic regulator,** by A. Whytock, Dundee, the silvered dial with subsidiary seconds and date dials, the eight-day movement with deadbeat escapement, maintaining power and striking on a bell, the case surmounted by a brass stag's head, Scottish, c1850, 85in (216cm) high.
£6,000–6,700 / €8,800–9,800
$10,900–12,100 K&D

A mahogany regulator, by John Fletcher, London, c1850, 71in (180.5cm) high.
£15,300–17,100
€22,300–25,000
$27,700–31,000 SOS

A Victorian oak wall regulator, by Stewart, Glasgow, with enamel dial, the eight-day single-train fusee movement with deadbeat escapement, within a wreath-carved frame, Scottish, 15½in (39.5cm) diam.
£400–480 / €580–700
$720–870 L&T

An oak regulator timepiece, the painted dial signed 'R. Richardson, Middlesbrough', the single fusee movement with deadbeat escapement, c1870, 40¼in (102cm) high.
£880–1,050 / €1,300–1,550
$1,600–1,900 TEN

A walnut-veneered longcase regulator, by Charles Frodsham & Co, London, the silvered dial with subsidiary seconds and hours dials, the five-pillar movement with deadbeat escapement, c1875, 73in (185.5cm) high.
£12,600–15,100
€18,400–22,000
$22,800–27,300 S

Continental Regulators

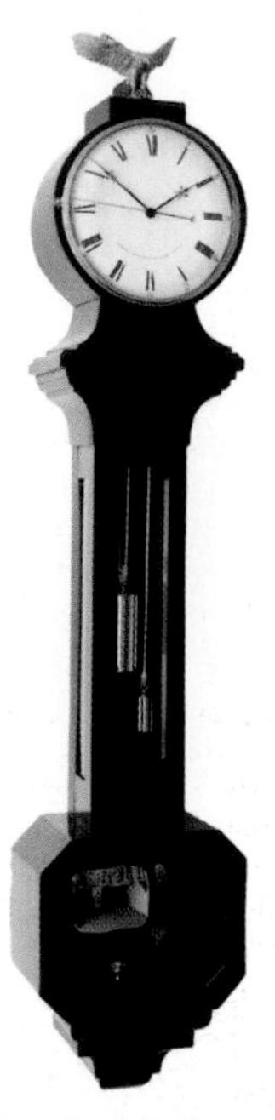

An ebonized-fruitwood *Laterndluhr*, the enamel dial signed 'Simon Felber in Klagenfurt', the movement with pinwheel escapement, Austrian, c1795, 52in (132cm) high.
£25,200–28,000
€37,000–41,000
$46,000–51,000 DRA

A Vienna-style walnut and ebonized regulator, the eight-day movement striking on a gong, c1880, 49in (124.5cm) high.
£2,150–2,400
€3,150–3,500
$3,900–4,350 JIL

A mahogany-veneered wall regulator, with week-long duration, the case with sycamore inlay, probably Austrian, Vienna, 1825–50, 34in (86.5cm) high.
£2,750–3,300
€4,000–4,800
$5,000–6,000 DORO

A gorge-cased four-glass table regulator, with perpetual calendar and moonphase, French, c1865, 15½in (39.5cm) high.
£6,700–7,500
€9,800–11,000
$12,100–13,600 TUR

A gilt and marble table regulator, by Joseph Lechner, Peston, the eight-day movement with pinwheel escapement, Austrian, c1830, 22¼in (54cm) high.
£17,100–19,000
€25,000–28,000
$45,000–51,000 DRA
The pendulum in this regulator is based on the Ellicot principal but with the addition of an adjustable bob which, when moved further along the arm, increases the amount of compensation for a given rise in temperature.

A Vienna regulator, the two-part dial with subsidiary seconds dial, Continental, late 19thC, 55¼in (140.5cm) high.
£500–600 / €730–880
$910–1,100 SWO

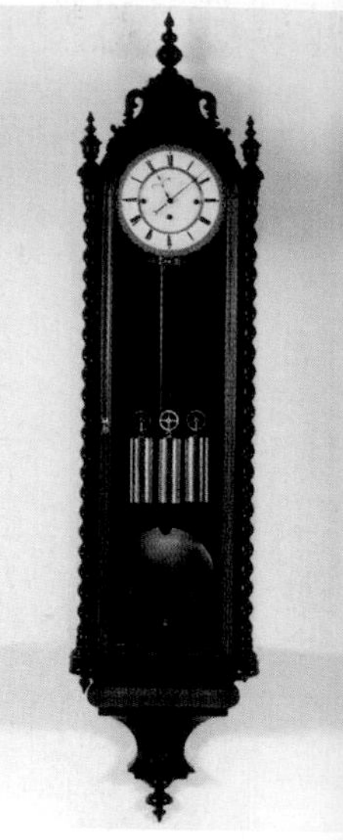

A Biedermeier rosewood and ebonized *grande sonnerie* regulator, with enamel dial, the eight-day weight-driven movement with deadbeat escapement and striking the quarters on gongs, Austrian, probably Vienna, c1850, 53in (134.5cm) high.
£7,200–8,000
€10,500–11,700
$13,000–14,500 DRA

A walnut and ebonized Vienna regulator, the two part enamel dial with subsidiary seconds dial, the eight-day movement with brass weights and pendulum the case with pierced foliate cresting and turned decoration, Continental, late 19thC, 51in (129.5cm) high.
£12,000–14,400
€17,500–21,000
$21,700–26,100 HYD

◄ **A walnut *grande sonnerie* wall regulator,** the triple train weight-driven movement quarter-striking and chiming on a coil, Continental, late 19thC, 57in (145cm) high.
£1,300–1,550 / €1,900–2,250
$2,350–2,800 PF

Watches

Pocket Watches

◄ **An 18ct gold and enamel fusee cylinder watch,** by Musson of Orléans, hand-painted enamel scene to reverse, with ruby jewelled brass coquette and silver Tompion regulator, French, c1750, 1½in (3.5cm) diam.
£1,600–1,800
€2,250–2,550
$2,900–3,250 ⊞ FOF

A 22ct gold pair-cased pocket watch, with watch paper, Irish, 1795, 2½in (6.5cm) diam.
£3,100–3,450 / €4,500–5,000
$8,100–9,000 ⊞ WELD

A gold pocket watch, by Lindquist, Stockholm, slight enamel damage, signed, Swedish, mid-18thC, 2in (5cm) diam.
£1,450–1,700 / €2,100–2,500
$2,600–3,050 ⚒ BUK
Johan Lindquist was working between 1754 and 1779.

► **An 18ct gold pocket watch,** by B. Glasscott, London, the dial decorated with a floral border, with fusee movement and verge escapement, 1818.
£350–420 / €510–610
$630–760 ⚒ SWO

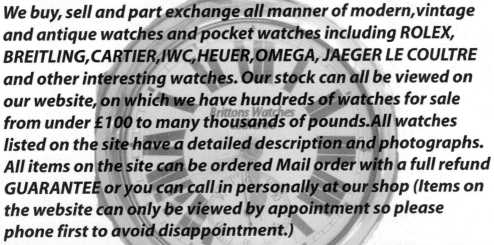

A doctor's silver pair-cased verge watch, by J. Roberts, London, with enamel dial, maker's mark, c1790, 2¼in (5.5cm) diam.
£630–700 / €920–1,050
$1,150–1,300 ⊞ PT

◄ **A gold and champlevé enamel open-faced pocket watch,** by Le Roi, Paris, with silver engine-turned dial, French, c1825, 1¾in (4.5cm) diam.
£540–600 / €790–880
$980–1,100 ⊞ PT

Items in the Pocket Watch section have been arranged in date order.

A silver verge hunter pocket watch, by Haley & Milner, inscribed 'Wm Collier, Labourer in Trust, Windsor Castle, 1826' with enamel dial, London, 1824–25, 2¼in (5.5cm) diam.
£950–1,050 €1,400–1,550
$1,700–1,900 ⊞ FOF

An 18ct gold open-faced pocket chronometer, by James McCabe, with fusee movement, casemaker's initials 'TW', signed, hallmarked, 1830.
£4,000–4,700
€5,800–6,900
$7,200–8,500 ⚒ G(B)

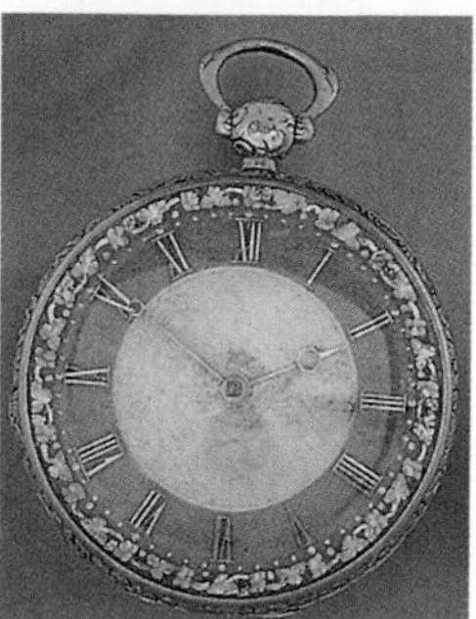

An 18ct gold open-faced lever pocket watch, the gilt dial engraved with fishermen and with applied floral border, the case with chased and engine-turned decoration, signed 'Fras Abbott, Manchester', maker's mark 'CAP', London 1835, 1¾in (4.5cm) diam.
£370–440 / €540–640
$670–800 ⚒ TEN

An 18ct gold hunter pocket watch, by Barraud & Lunds, London, plain polished yellow gold case, fire-gilt movement, London 1879, 2in (5cm) diam.
£1,350–1,500 €1,950–2,200
$2,450–2,700 ⊞ FOF

◄ **A silver hunte pocket watch,** by Waltham, Massachusetts, wi an enamel dial and fusee movement, maker's mark, American, c1885, 2¼in (5.5cm) diam
£540–600
€790–880
$980–1,100 ⊞ PT

A silver open-faced pocket watch, by Cortebert Watch Mfg Co, the enamel dial decorated with polychrome flowers, Swiss, c1890, 2in (5cm) diam.
£1,000–1,100 / €1,450–1,600
$1,800–2,000 ⊞ PT

► **An 18ct gold open-faced pocket watch,** with an enamel dial and keyless movement, the hinged back with engraved monogram and presentation inscription, numbered case and maker's mark 'FT', Chester, c1895, 2¼in (5.5cm) wide.
£230–270 / €330–390
$420–490 ⚒ TEN

An 18ct gold hunter chronograph, by Joseph Hargreaves & Co, Liverpool, with signed enamel dial, Chester 1896, 2¼in (5.5cm) diam.
£1,000–1,150 / €1,450–1,650
$1,800–2,050 ⊞ FOF

A Cartier gold and enamel fob watch, set with diamonds, French, c1910, 1¼in (3cm) diam.
£3,550–4,000
€5,200–5,800
$6,400–7,200 ⊞ SGr

A nickel open-faced lever pocket watch, with enamel dial, the eight-day keyless movement with bimetallic balance and visible club foot lever escapement, Swiss, c1910, 2in (5cm) diam.
£270–300 / €390–440
$490–540 ⊞ PT

A Tiffany & Co 18ct gold open-faced chronograph, the enamel dial with subsidiary seconds, with nickel lever movement, bimetallic compensation balance and micrometer regulator, movement and dial signed, c1905, 1¾in (4.5cm) diam.
£2,150–2,550
€3,150–3,750
$3,900–4,600 ⚒ S(NY)

A Patek Philippe 18ct gold open-faced pocket watch, retailed by A. B. Griswold & Co, New Orleans, the engine-turned gold dial with subsidiary seconds, nickel level movement, the case chased with stylized flowers and two griffins, case, cuvette, dial and movement signed, Swiss, c1910, 1¾in (4.5cm) diam.
£4,300–5,100
€6,300–7,400
$7,800–9,200 ⚒ S(NY)

◀ **An 18ct gold pocket watch,** by Spaulding & Co, the enamel dial with subsidiary seconds, with a Patek Philippe & Co stem-set movement, in a monogrammed case, early 20thC.
£1,100–1,300
€1,600–1,900
$2,000–2,350 ⚒ LHA

Wristwatches

An Autorist chrome-plated automatic wristwatch, with a silvered dial, the signed adjustable lever movement wound by a moving flexible lug, Swiss, c1931, 1in (2.5cm) wide.
£300–360 / €440–520
$540–640 ⚒ TEN

A Cartier 18ct gold tank wristwatch, with silvered dial, nickel lever movement and mono-metallic compensation balance, movement signed 'European Watch and Clock Co Inc', French/Swiss, c1950, 1¼in (3cm) long.
£3,350–4,000 / €4,900–5,900
$6,100–7,200 ⚒ S

◀ **An Eberhard 18ct gold wristwatch,** the silvered dial with subsidiary seconds, the case with stepped lugs, and engraved initials, case, movement and dial signed, c1955, 1½in (3.5cm) diam.
£260–310 / €380–450
$470–560 ⚒ TEN

An International Watch Co stainless steel wristwatch, with silvered dial, nickel lever movement and mono-metallic compensation balance, case, dial and movement signed, Swiss, c1950, 1¼in (3.5cm) diam.
£360–430 / €530–630 $650–770 ⚒ S(Am)

A Longines stainless-steel Conquest automatic wristwatch, with a two-tone silvered dial, marked, Swiss, 1956.
£310–350 / €450–510 $560–630 ⊞ Bns

An Omega 18ct gold Constellation chronometer watch, Swiss, 1967, with later detachable 18ct rose-gold bracelet.
£1,050–1,200 €1,550–1,750 $1,900–2,150 ⊞ Bns

A Patek Philippe 18ct gold wristwatch, the silvered dial with subsidiary seconds, nickel lever movement with mono-metallic compensation balance, dial and movement signed, Swiss, c1955, 1in (2.5cm) long.
£3,350–4,000 €4,900–5,900 $6,100–7,200 ⚒ S

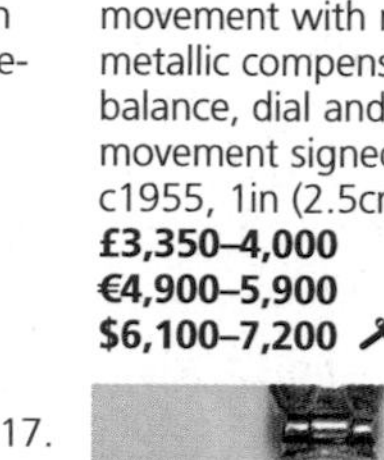

◄ A Rolex silver wristwatch, with an enamelled dial, Swiss, 1917.
£190–220 / €280–320 $340–400 ⚒ G(L)

► A Rolex 9ct gold wristwatch, Swiss, c1920.
£370–440 / €540–640 $670–800 ⚒ G(L)

► A Rolex 9ct gold wristwatch, the engine-turned silvered dial with subsidiary seconds, case and movement signed, later crown, import marks for Glasgow 1934, Swiss.
£280–330 €410–480 $510–600 ⚒ DN

A Rolex 9ct gold wristwatch, the silvered dial with subsidiary seconds, case, dial and movement signed, import marks for Glasgow 1935, Swiss, with associated bracelet.
£140–165 / €200–240 $250–300 ⚒ DN

Further reading

Miller's Watches: A Collector's Guide, Miller's Publications, 1999

A Rolex 9ct gold wristwatch, Swiss, 1950s.
£1,000–1,150 €1,450–1,650 $1,800–2,100 ⊞ TEM

◄ A Rolex 18ct gold Oyster 6285 Perpetual Bubble-back chronometer wristwatch, with silvered dial, early 1950s, Swiss.
£1,600–1,800 €2,350–2,650 $2,900–3,250 ⊞ Bns

A Rolex gold automatic wristwatch, 1950s.
£1,450–1,600 €2,100–2,350 $2,600–2,900 ⊞ TEM

WATCHES

◄ **A Sleda Watch Co sapphire and diamond-set 14ct white gold wristwatch,** with a silvered dial, c1930, ¾in (2cm) wide, with an associated bracelet.
£210–250 / €310–370
$380–450 ⚒ TEN

A Syren diamond-set 18ct white gold wristwatch, with an engine-turned silvered dial, one diamond missing, import marks for Glasgow 1929, Swiss, with a leather case.
£160–190 / €230–270
$290–340 ⚒ DN

◄ **A Tiffany diamond-set platinum wristwatch,** the 60 diamonds set into 9ct white gold bands, c1920, ½in (1cm) wide.
£930–1,100
€1,350–1,600
$1,700–2,000 ⚒ LJ

A Smiths 9ct gold wristwatch, Birmingham 1946.
£220–250 / €320–370
$400–450 ⊞ WAC

A Waltham 18ct pink gold and platinum Maximus wristwatch, the silvered dial with subsidiary seconds, dial and movement signed, American, 1919, 1½in (4cm) wide.
£1,800–2,150
€2,650–3,150
$3,300–3,900 ⚒ S

A diamond-set platinum wristwatch, with a silvered dial, glass missing, Swiss, c1918, on a mesh-cordette bracelet stampet '9ct'.
£190–220 / €280–320
$340–400 ⚒ DN

Barometers

Stick Barometers

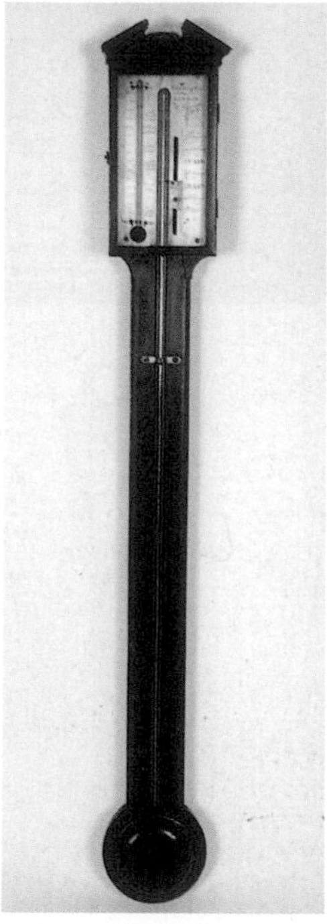

A George III mahogany stick barometer, by John Barelli & Co, London, the silvered engraved scale with vernier and thermometer, 38in (96.5cm) high.
£1,650–1,950
€2,400–2,850
$3,000–3,550 HYD

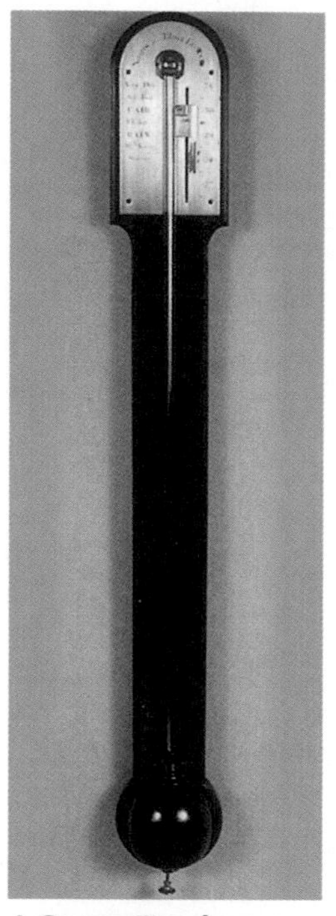

A George III mahogany stick barometer, by Nairne & Blunt, the silvered plate above a vernier scale, well cover replaced, 36½in (92.5cm) high.
£2,000–2,400
€2,900–3,500
$3,600–4,350 WW

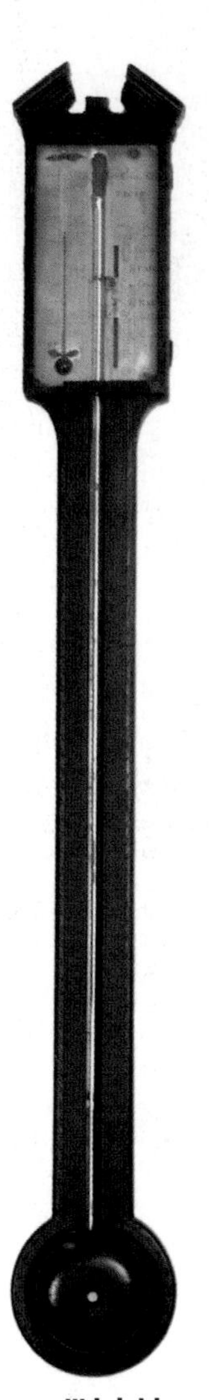

A George III inlaid mahogany stick barometer, by D. Poncia & Co, with a brass dial, the cistern cover with mother-of-pearl inlay, 38¼in (97cm) high.
£1,650–1,950
€2,400–2,850
$3,000–3,550 GIL

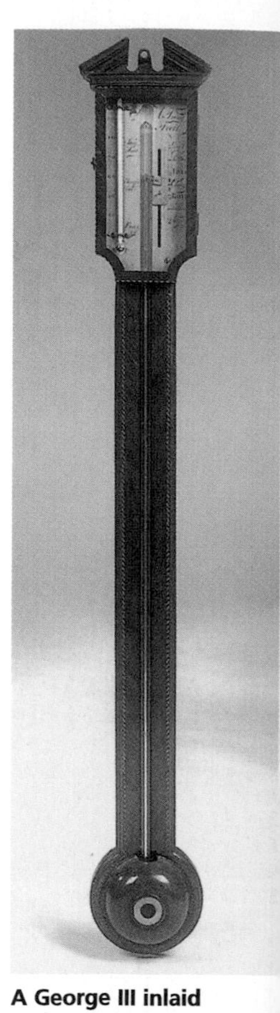

A George III inlaid mahogany stick baromete by A. Taroni, with vernier, th case with chequer stringing 38¼in (97cm) high.
£1,100–1,300
€1,600–1,900
$2,000–2,350 L&T

The prices realized at auction may reflect the fact that some barometers have undergone alterations, or are in unrestored condition.

A mahogany stick barometer, by J. & W. Watkins, London, the silvered-brass engraved scale with vernier and seven weather notations, signed, c1760, 40in (101.5cm) high.
£4,150–4,650
€6,100–6,800
$7,500–8,400 PAO

◄ **A mahogany stick barometer,** by Adams, London, c1780, 39in (99cm) high.
£7,600–8,500
€11,100–12,400
$13,800–15,400 RAY

► **A George III inlaid mahogany stick barometer,** with a silvered scale, the reservoir cover inlaid with a shell patera, 38¼in (97cm) high.
£1,200–1,400
€1,750–2,050
$2,100–2,500 L&T

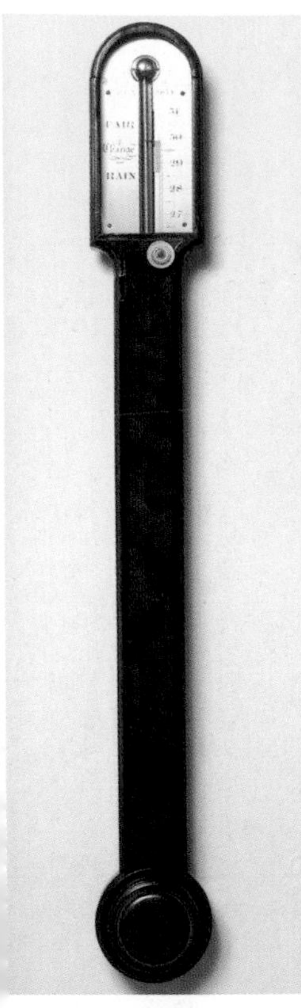

A mahogany stick barometer, by W. S. Jones, London, c1800, 37in (94cm) high.
£4,300–4,800
€6,300–7,000
$7,800–8,700 ⊞ RAY

A mahogany stick barometer, by John Bleuler, London, with ebony banding, c1800, 39½in (100.5cm) high.
£4,300–4,800
€6,300–7,000
$7,800–8,700 ⊞ AW

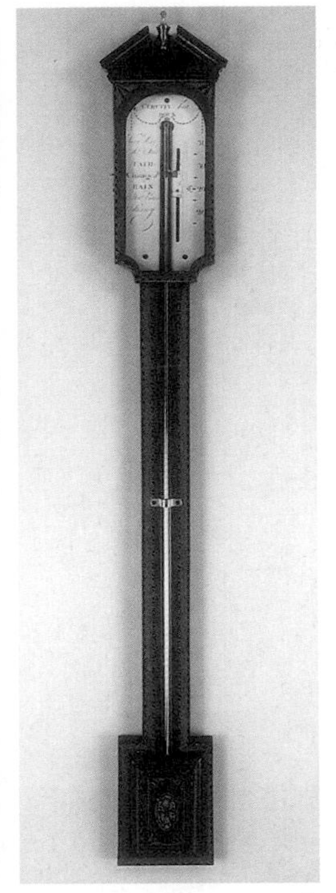

An inlaid mahogany and satinwood stick barometer, by Cerutty, the silvered-brass scale with vernier and engraved weather indicators, signed, c1820, 40in (101.5cm) high.
£3,600–4,000
€5,200–5,800
$6,500–7,200 ⊞ PAO

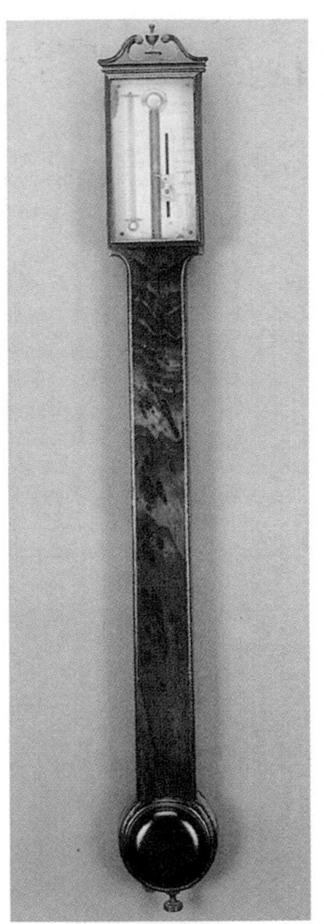

A mahogany stick barometer, by Dollond, London, the silvered plate with vernier and mercury thermometer, c1820, 39¼in (99.5cm) high.
£2,150–2,550
€3,150–3,700
$3,900–4,600 ⚒ S

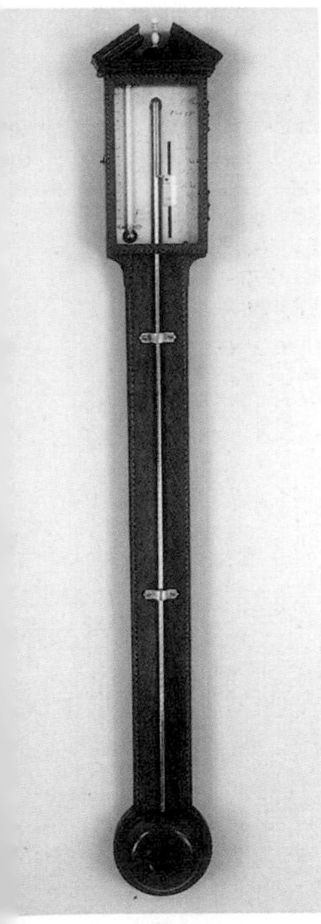

\n inlaid mahogany tick barometer, by James illia, the silvered-brass dial vith sliding vernier and nermometer, c1820, 0in (101.5cm) high.
3,150–3,550
4,600–5,200
5,700–6,400 ⊞ PAO

A mahogany stick barometer, by Luisety, c1820, 39in (99cm) high.
£4,050–4,500
€5,900–6,600
$7,300–8,100 ⊞ RAY

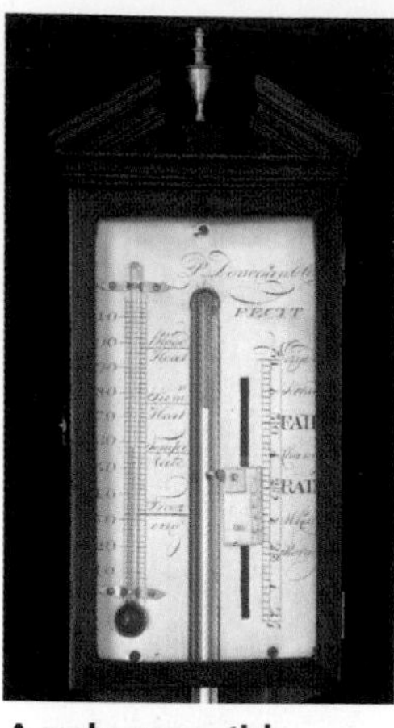

A mahogany stick barometer, by Peter Donegan, London, with silvered-brass plate, signed, the case with rosewood stringing, c1820, 38¾in (98.5cm) high.
£2,500–2,800
€3,650–4,100
$4,550–5,100 ⊞ AW

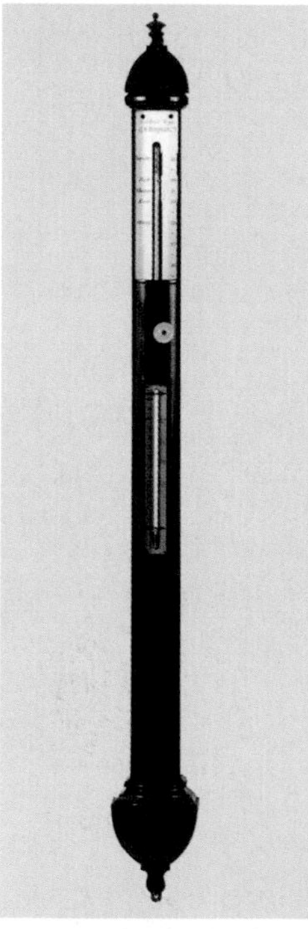

A mahogany bowfronted stick barometer, by Adie & Son, Edinburgh, the silvered and engraved scale with vernier and mercury thermometer, Scottish, c1835, 41in (104cm) high.
£11,700–13,000
€17,100–19,000
$21,200–23,500 ⊞ DRA

Alexander Adie (1774–1858) was a noted Scottish barometer maker. In 1835 he took his son John into the business and from then on signed his barometers Adie & Son. They were particularly noted for making fine and extremely thin stick barometers.

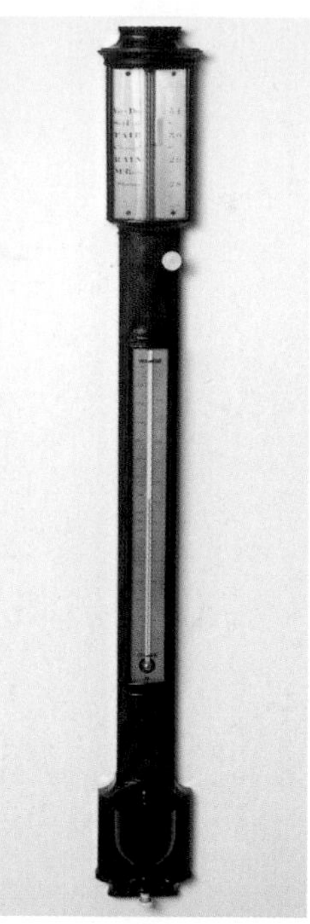

A mahogany bowfronted stick barometer, by Worthington & Allen, London, c1825, 39in (99cm) high.
£8,100–9,000
€11,800–13,100
$14,700–16,300 ⊞ RAY

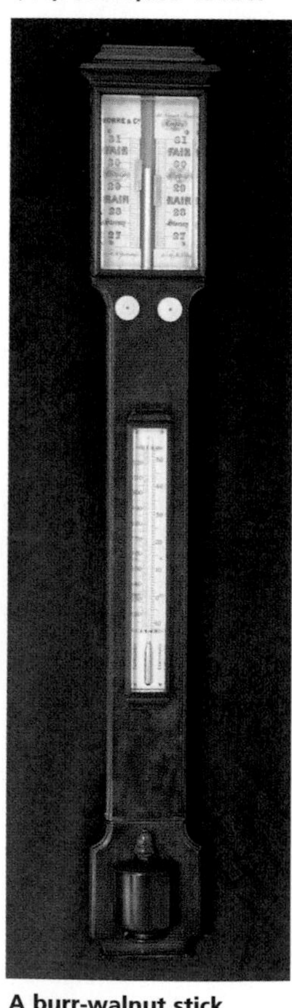

A burr-walnut stick barometer, by Edmund Horne, London, with ivory register plates, c1850, 39in (99cm) high.
£2,500–2,800
€3,650–4,100
$4,550–5,100 ⊞ AW

A mahogany stick barometer, by Knie, Edinburgh, Scottish, c1830, 40in (101.5cm) high.
£5,800–6,500
€8,500–9,500
$10,500–11,800 ⊞ RAY

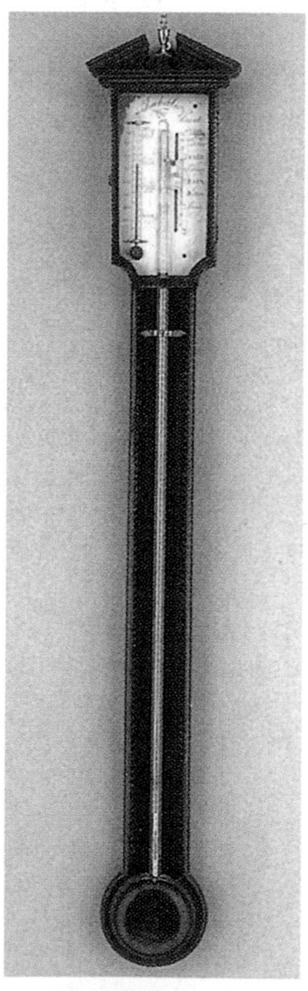

An inlaid mahogany stick barometer, by Rabalio, with silver plates and vernier, thermometer to the side and behind a glazed door, signed, 19thC, 38¼in (97cm) high.
£1,300–1,550
€1,900–2,250
$2,350–2,800 ⚒ TEN

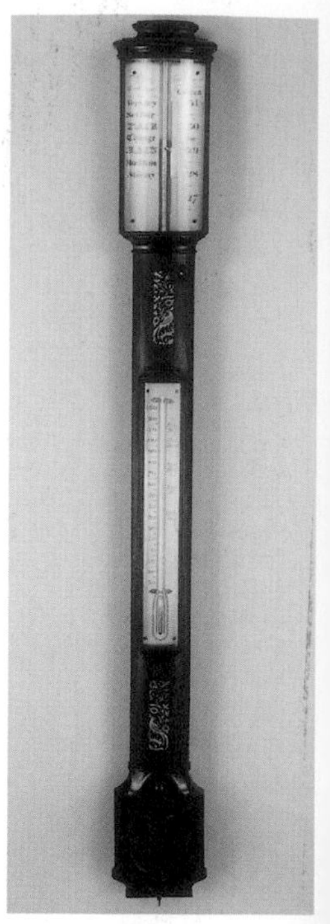

A rosewood bowfronted stick barometer, by Harris & Son, London, the silvered-brass scale with vernier, engraved weather indicators and silvered-brass thermometer, c1835, 39in (99cm) high.
£7,200–8,000
€10,500–11,700
$13,000–14,300 ⊞ PAO

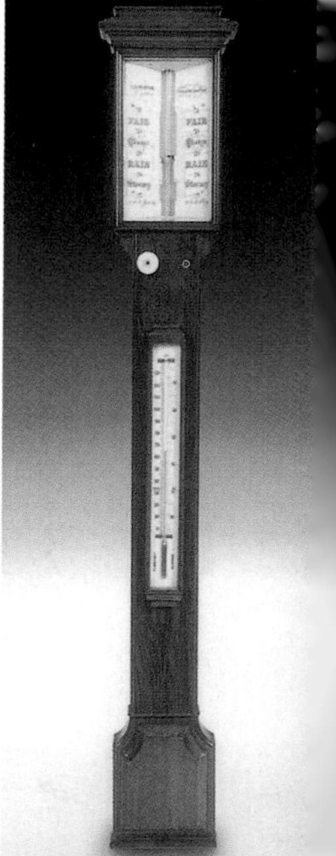

A rosewood stick barometer, by T. B. Winter, Newcastle-upon-Tyne, the ivory scales enclosed within bevelled glass, with thermometer, 19thC, 39½in (100.5cm) high.
£880–1,050
€1,300–1,550
$1,600–1,900 ⚒ L&T

◄ **An oak stick barometer,** by Negretti & Zambra, London, with ivory vernier, the plinth with a carved mask, fahrenheit thermometer, signed, c1860, 42½in (108cm) high.
£2,350–2,800
€3,450–4,100
$4,250–5,100 TEN

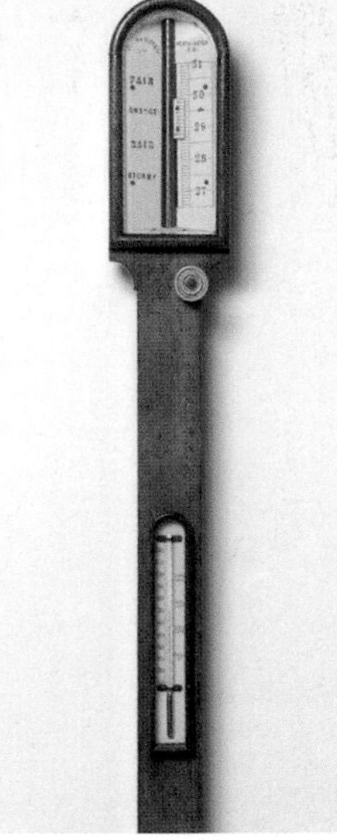

An oak stick barometer, by Sugg, London, signed, c1860, 36in (91.5cm) high.
£1,350–1,500
€1,950–2,200
$2,450–2,700 RAY

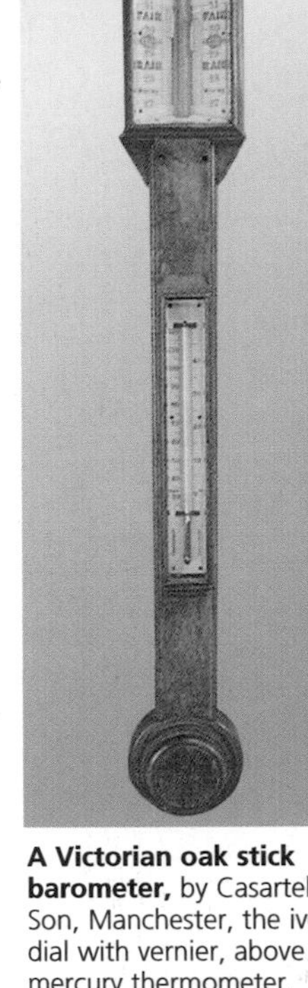

A Victorian oak stick barometer, by Casartelli & Son, Manchester, the ivory dial with vernier, above a mercury thermometer, 38½in (98cm) high.
£410–490 / €600–720
$740–890 RTo

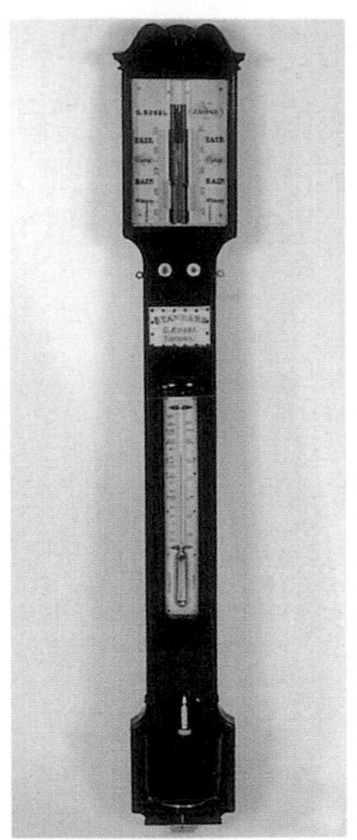

A Victorian mahogany stick barometer, by G. Rossi, Norwich, the mercury-filled tube with engraved ivory dial with twin adjustable gauges, the ebony reservoir case with a turned ivory adjuster, with label, 41in (104cm) high.
£2,700–3,200
€3,950–4,650
$4,900–5,800 HYD

An oak Admiral Fitzroy Storm stick barometer, by Negretti & Zambra, London, with single vernier, c1880, 41in (104cm) high.
£2,150–2,400
€3,150–3,500
$3,900–4,350 RTW

A late Victorian oak stick barometer, by Bailey, Birmingham, with ivory vernier and shield-carved reservoir bell, 38½in (98cm) high.
£750–900 / €1,100–1,300
$1,350–1,600 DN

An oak stick barometer, by Horne & Thornwaite, London, with engraved and silvered dials, 19thC, 36in (91.5cm) high.
£780–930 / €1,150–1,350
$1,400–1,650 BWL

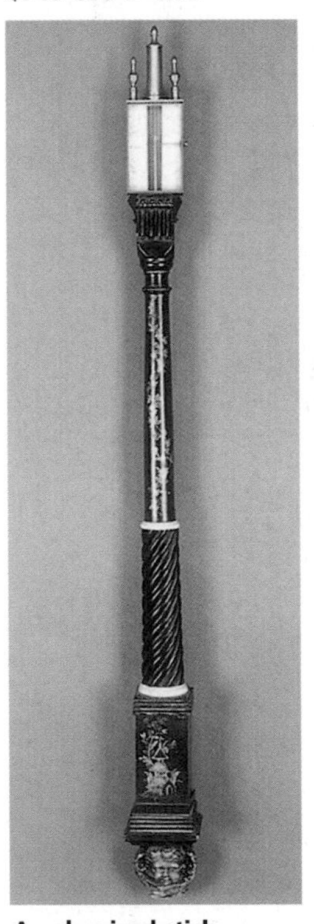

An ebonized stick barometer, in the manner of Daniel Quare, the concealed tube with silvered plates, decorated with japanned flowers, with later giltwood cherub finial, late 19thC, 41¼in (105cm) high.
£4,800–5,700
€7,000–8,300
$8,700–10,300 S

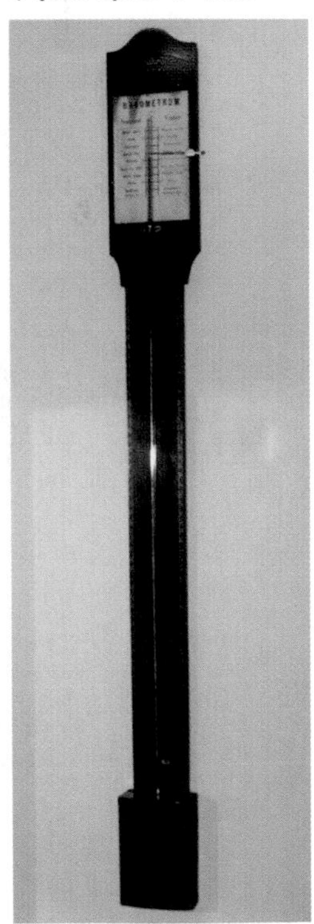

A mahogany stick barometer, with marquetry inlays and chequered edgings, the paper scale inscribed in Danish and English with a note of low air pressure in Martinique 1902, c1910, 38in (96.5cm) high.
£780–870 / €1,150–1,300
$1,400–1,550 K&D

Wheel Barometers

Miller's Compares

I. An inlaid mahogany wheel barometer, by Gally, London, signed, c1785, 37in (94cm) high.
£3,150–3,500
€4,600–5,100
$5,700–6,300 ⊞ RAY

II. An inlaid mahogany wheel barometer, by Cetti, London, signed, c1810, 37in (94cm) high.
£990–1,100
€1,450–1,600
$1,800–2,000 ⊞ RAY

Item I is more expensive than Item II because it is an early example of an inlaid wheel barometer. These were usually individually made, and this means that they are of higher quality and more difficult to find than examples made after 1800,which were mass-produced, making them less desirable to collectors.

A mahogany wheel barometer, by Pellegrino, London, with silvered dial and vernier, with a boxwood and ebonized hatched border, inlaid with Sheraton-style foliate panels, late 18thC, 36½in (92.5cm) high.
£2,250–2,700
€3,300–3,950
$4,050–4,900 ⚒ GAK

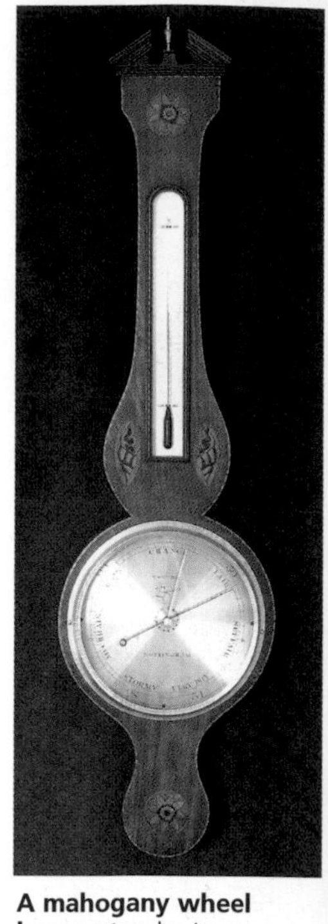

A mahogany wheel barometer, by James Vecchio, Nottingham, inlaid with shells and flowerheads, with rope stringing, c1800, 38¼in (97cm) high.
£1,700–1,900
€2,500–2,800
$3,100–3,450 ⊞ AW

A mahogany wheel barometer, by L. Sioli, Norwich, with silvered-brass dial and thermometer, brass bezel, inlaid with shells and flowers, signed, c1810, dial 8in (20.5cm) diam.
£1,300–1,450
€1,900–2,100
$2,350–2,600 ⊞ PAO

A mahogany wheel barometer, by A. Monti, Canterbury, with silvered dials, inlaid with shell and floral marquetry, c1820, 37in (94cm) high.
£680–750 / €990–1,100
$1,200–1,350 ⊞ K&D

A Sheraton-style inlaid mahogany wheel barometer, by John Maver, London, with silvered-brass dials, signed, c1820, 37¾in (96cm) high.
£1,150–1,300
€1,700–1,900
$2,100–2,350 ⊞ AW

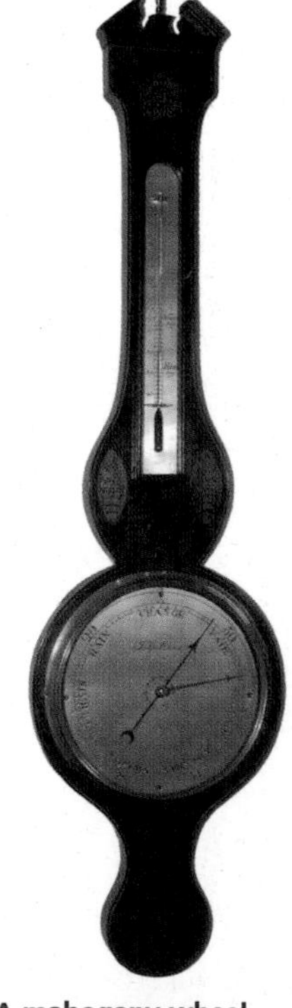

A mahogany wheel barometer, by Spelzini, Cirencester, with silvered and engraved dials, inlaid with shells and fan marquetry, signed, c1820, 38in (96.5cm) high.
£700–780 / €1,000–1,100
$1,250–1,400 ⊞ K&D

An inlaid mahogany wheel barometer, by Cattelly & Co, Worcester, with thermometer, dial 8¼in (21cm) diam.
£420–500 / €610–730
$760–910 CHTR

A mahogany wheel barometer, by Molton, Norwich, c1830, 38in (96.5cm) high.
£1,550–1,750
€2,250–2,550
$2,800–3,150 RAY

A mahogany wheel barometer, by Solomon, Newcastle, the silvered dial with brass and steel hands, with hygrometer, mirror and level, c1830, dial 10in (25.5cm) diam.
£1,250–1,400
€1,850–2,000
$2,250–2,550 PAO

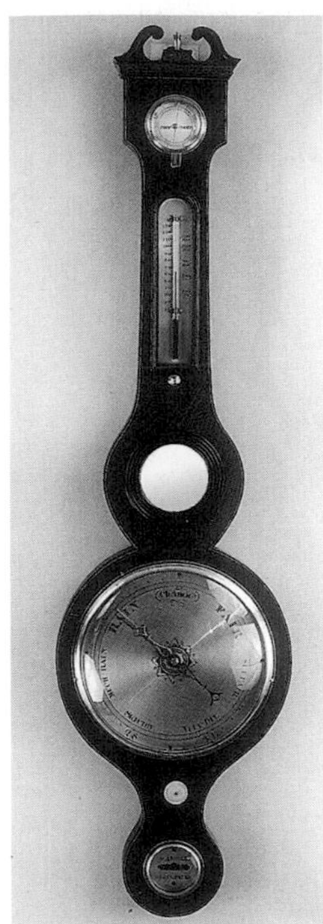

A mahogany wheel barometer, by Donato Arnoldi, Gloucester, with silvered-brass dial and thermometer, hygrometer, mirror and level, signed, c1835, dial 8in (20.5cm) diam.
£880–980 / €1,300–1,450
$1,600–1,800 PAO

A William IV rosewood wheel barometer, by A. Boggia, Plymouth, with silvered dial, hygrometer, alcohol thermometer and level, the case inlaid with mother-of-pearl, signed, dial 8in (20.5cm) diam.
£800–960 / €1,200–1,400
$1,450–1,750 Bea

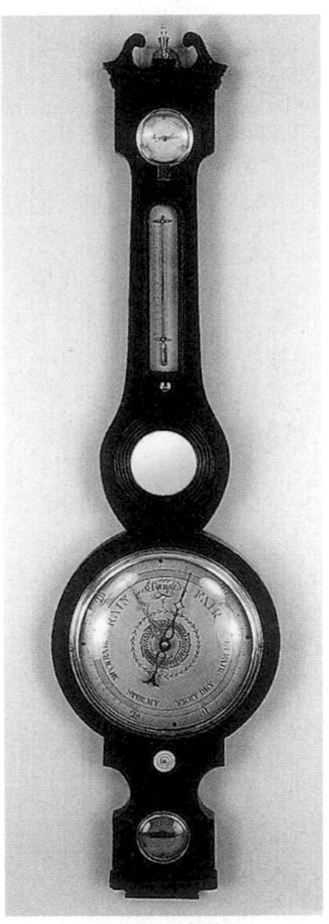

A mahogany wheel barometer, by Galli, Rotherham, with silvered-brass dial, thermometer, hygrometer, mirror and level, the case with ebony stringing, c1835, dial 8in (20.5cm) diam.
£950–1,050
€1,400–1,550
$1,700–1,900 PAO

A rosewood-veneered wheel barometer, by D. Fagioli & Son, London, c1840, dial 12in (30.5cm) diam.
£470–560 / €690–820
$850–1,000 Mit

A rosewood wheel barometer, with clock, thermometer, hydrometer and level, crossbanded in satinwood with boxwood and ebony stringing, signed 'L. Dixey, Brighton', 19thC, 51½in (131cm) high.
£2,500–3,000
€3,650–4,400
$4,550–5,400 CHTR

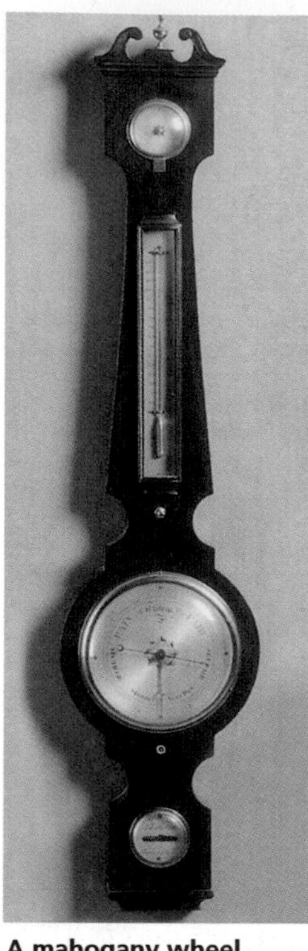

A mahogany wheel barometer, with silvered dial, hygrometer and thermometer, signed 'Shaldrake', c1840, dial 5½in (14cm) diam.
£960–1,150
€1,450–1,700
$1,750–2,100 S

► A rosewood barometer, by Edwards & Son, Glasgow, inlaid with mother-of-pearl, brass wire and stone, Scottish, signed, c1850, 37in (94cm) high.
£1,350–1,500
€1,950–2,200
$2,450–2,700 ⊞ RAY

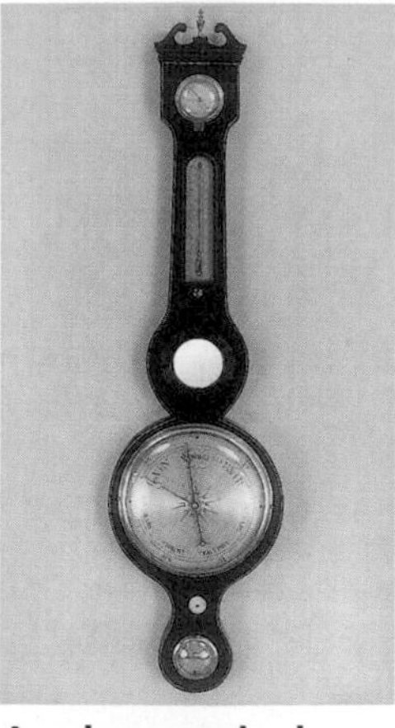

A mahogany wheel barometer, by W. Tanner, Lewes, with silvered-brass dial, thermometer, hygrometer, mirror and level, signed, the case with double edge stringing, c1840, dial 8in (20.5cm) diam.
£850–950 / €1,250–1,400
$1,500–1,700 ⊞ PAO

A rosewood wheel barometer, with mother-of-pearl inlay, signed 'McNab, Perth', Scottish, c1845, 41in (104cm) high.
£1,450–1,650
€2,100–2,400
$2,650–3,000 ⊞ RAY

A Victorian burr-walnut wheel barometer, by A. Casartelli, Liverpool, with silvered dial and a thermometer, signed, damaged, 44¼in (112.5cm) high.
£400–480 / €580–700
$720–870 RTo

◄ A Victorian flame figured mahogany wheel barometer, by J. A. Madio, London, with thermometer, dial 8in (20.5cm) diam.
£280–330 / €410–480
$510–600 NSal

Continental Barometers

An inlaid burr-walnut barometer, by P. Wast, Amsterdam, the thermometer with engraved silvered plate, the barometer with altered engraved silvered plates and brass vernier, Dutch, c1760, 48in (122cm) high.
£3,650–4,350
€5,300–6,400
$6,600–7,900 S(Am)

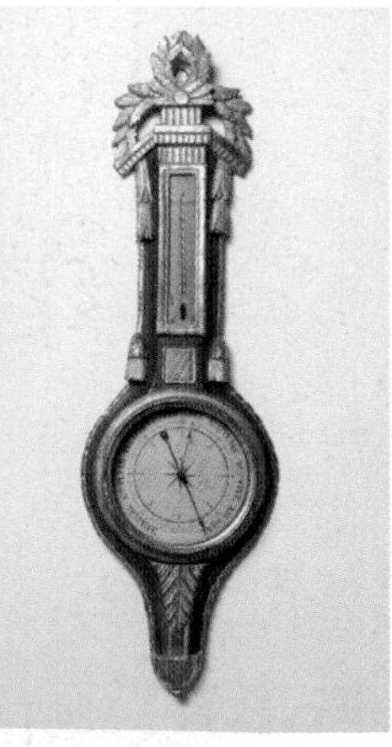

A painted giltwood barometer, by Polino, signed, French, c1780, 40in (101.5cm) high.
£2,250–2,500
€3,300–3,650
$4,050–4,500 ⊞ RAY

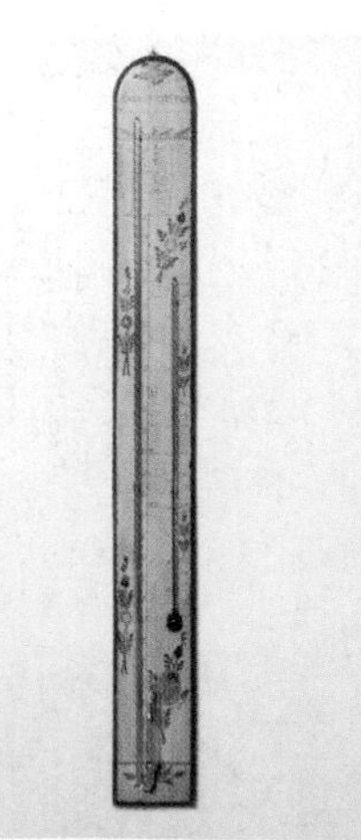

A painted stick barometer, French, c1800, 38in (96.5cm) high.
£1,550–1,750
€2,250–2,550
$2,800–3,150 ⊞ RAY

An inlaid mahogany bakbarometer, by J. Solaro, with signed pewter plates, Dutch, c1800, 46½in (118cm) high.
£1,450–1,700
€2,100–2,500
$2,600–3,100 S(Am)

A giltwood wheel barometer, the thermometer above a *verre églomisé* barometer dial, French, c1820, 41in (1104cm) high, in a mahogany display case with a glazed door.
£1,050–1,250
€1,550–1,850
$1,900–2,250 S(Am)

A giltwood barometer, by Quintapace, Paris, signed, French, c1820, 38in (96.5cm) high.
£4,050–4,500
€5,900–6,600
$7,300–8,100 ⊞ RAY

A giltwood barometer, with a *verre églomisé* dial, French, c1825, 36in (91.5cm) high.
£2,700–3,000
€3,950–4,400
$4,900–5,400 ⊞ RAY

A giltwood barometer, French, early 19thC, 34in (86.5cm) high.
£2,250–2,500
€3,300–3,650
$4,050–4,550 ⊞ RAY

Aneroid Barometers

A mahogany and brass portable aneroid barometer, by E. P. Dent, Paris, the silvered dial with a revolving magnifying glass, French, 19thC, case 6½in (16.5cm) wide.
£470–560 / €690–820
$850–1,000 Mit

◄ A carved mahogany aneroid barometer, by James White, Glasgow, with a silvered dial, signed, Scottish, c1880, 40¼in (102cm) high.
£330–390 / €480–570
$600–710 TEN

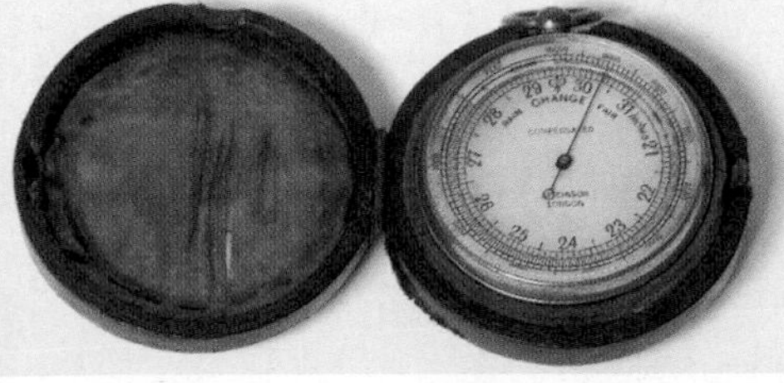

A brass pocket aneroid barometer, by Atchison, London, with a silvered dial, c1900, 2in (5cm) diam, in original morocco case.
£230–260 / €340–380
$420–470 ⊞ SAT

► An aneroid barometer, mounted between two ivory tusks, c1900, 17½in (45cm) high, with two similar candlesticks.
£1,650–1,950
€2,400–2,850
$3,000–3,550 TEN

A bronze aneroid barometer, the column support in the form of a knight in armour, c1900, 12½in (32cm) high.
£150–180 / €220–260
$280–330 BWL

► A carved oak aneroid barometer, by J. Hicks, the engraved silvered dial with subsidiary thermometer, early 20thC, 8in (20.5cm) diam.
£210–240 / €310–350
$380–430 ⊞ RTW

A lacquered-metal pocket aneroid barometer, the silvered dial with swivelling altimeter bezel and subsidiary mercury thermometer, late 19thC, 3in (7.5cm) high.
£175–210 / €260–310
$320–380 PFK

A brass aneroid barometer, with silvered dial and mercury thermometer, c1900, 3in (7.5cm) diam.
£360–400 / €520–580
$650–720 ⊞ HOM

Barographs

An oak-cased barograph, with chart drawer, late 19thC, 17½in (44.5cm) wide.
£1,150–1,350 / €1,650–1,950
$2,050–2,450 ⚒ BWL

An Edwardian oak-cased barograph, by Negretti & Zambra, London, with seven-tier vacuum, single recording arm and chart drawer, 15in (38cm) wide.
£450–540 / €660–790
$810–980 ⚒ Bea

An oak-cased barograph, by Short & Mason, London, with chart drawer, c1910, 15½in (39.5cm) wide.
£1,700–1,900 / €2,500–2,800
$3,100–3,450 ⊞ AW

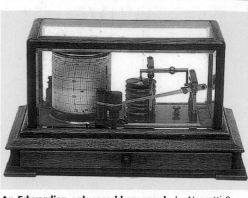

An oak-cased barograph, with a barometer face and chart drawer, early 20thC, 15in (38cm) wide.
£2,150–2,400 / €3,150–3,500
$3,900–4,350 ⊞ RTW

◄ **A mahogany-cased barograph,** by Short & Mason, London, with chart drawer, c1920, 14½in (37cm) wide.
£800–900
€1,150–1,300
$1,450–1,600
⊞ AW

► **An oak-cased barograph,** with chart drawer, c1930, 15in (38cm) wide.
£810–900
€1,200–1,350
$1,450–1,650
⊞ RTW

◄ **A mahogany-cased baro-thermograph,** by Negretti & Zambra, London, with chart drawer, c1950, 14in (35.5cm) wide.
£1,400–1,600
€2,050–2,350
$2,500–2,800
⊞ RTW

Decorative Arts

Aesthetic Movement Ceramics

A Bretby vase, by David Ash, with impasto decoration of flowers, fan-shaped handles, one inscribed and signed 'A. T.', the other dated, 1891, 9¾in (25cm) high.
£360–400 / €520–580
$650–720 ⊞ HUN

A Dunmore Pottery planter, Scottish, c1880, 5¼in (13.5cm) high.
£430–480 / €630–700
$780–870 ⊞ GLB

► A Minton majolica teapot, attributed to Christopher Dresser, 1860, 8in (20.5cm) high.
£4,400–4,900 / €6,400–7,200
$8,000–8,900 ⊞ BRT

A Brown-Westhead Moore & Co charger, painted with a bird among foliage, slight damage, late 19thC, 24½in (62cm) diam.
£230–270 / €340–400
$420–500 ⚒ MAR

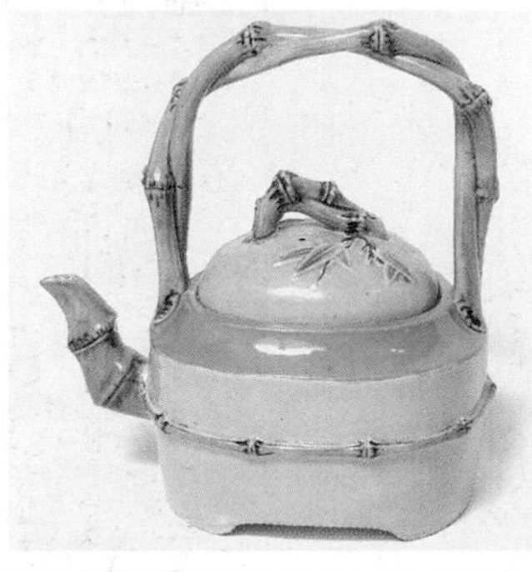

A Helen Paxton Brown cup and saucer, Scottish, c1930.
£200–230 / €290–330
$360–420 ⊞ SDD
Helen Paxton Brown shared a studio at the Glasgow School of Art with Jessie Marion King, the famous illustrator, and the two became close friends.

◄ A Linthorpe jardinière, attributed to Christopher Dresser, with fan-shaped handles, c1885, 8in (20.5cm) high.
£350–390 / €510–570
$630–710 ⊞ HUN

A William De Morgan Isnik-style tile panel, comprising 16 tiles decorated with stylized flowers, impressed factory mark, c1880, each tile 6in (15.5cm) square.
£4,000–4,800 / €5,800–7,000
$7,200–8,700 ⚒ TEN

Aesthetic Movement Furniture

A pair of walnut and parquetry side cabinets, by Herter Brothers, each with side opening and frieze drawer, stamped, American, c1870, 135¾in (91cm) wide.
£4,950–5,900 / €7,200–8,600
$8,900–10,700 ⚒ S(NY)

A mirrored and porcelain-mounted ebonized folio cabinet, inlaid with floral motifs, American, c1875, 37in (94cm) wide.
£1,950–2,300 / €2,850–3,350
$3,450–4,150 ⚒ S(NY)

A Victorian oak hall seat, the back with a brass spindled panel, the sides with brass mounts, on sabre legs.
£1,400–1,650 / €2,050–2,400
$2,550–3,000 ⚒ TEN

An oak sideboard, the shelf above three frieze drawers, the cupboard doors enclosing a shelf, c1880, 59¾in (152cm) wide.
£480–570 / €700–830
$870–1,050 S(O)

A Victorian walnut sideboard, decorated with spindle turning and leaf-carving, with a mirror back, the four cupboard doors and bottom drawer with flower-carved panels, 87in (221cm) wide.
£2,350–2,800 / €3,450–4,100
$4,250–5,100 BWL

◄ **A brass occasional table,** by Charles Parker, with a copper fish-scale top, on spindle legs united by bird and flower stretchers suspending a velvet panel applied with a bird, paper label for Charles Parker & Co, American, Connecticut, c1860, 19in (48.5cm) wide.
£4,050–4,850 / €5,900–7,100
$7,300–8,800 SGA

An ebonized and gilt three-tier stand, the sides and front inset with four Minton tiles above a pierced apron, the bottom tier with a pierced gallery, c1875, 18in (45.5cm) wide.
£490–580 / €720–850
$890–1,050 M

Aesthetic Movement Metalware

A silver claret jug, by the Barnards, engraved with butterflies and insects in a foliate surround, a crest and motto, stylized scroll handle, London 1874, with original fitted case, 11in (28cm) high, 16oz.
£1,900–2,250 / €2,750–3,300
$3,450–4,050 HYD

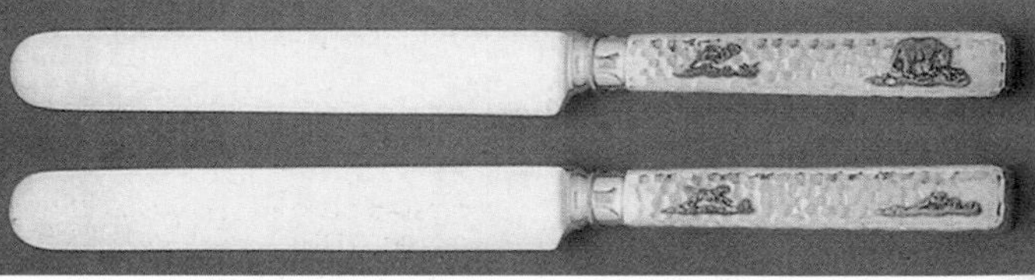

A pair of silver and copper salad servers, by Whiting Manufacturing Co, American, New York, 1880–90, 12¼in (31cm) long, 10oz.
£2,450–2,900 / €3,600–4,250
$4,400–5,200 S(NY)

A set of eight silver and copper Japanese-style table knives, by Gorham Manufacturing Co, the handles with spot-hammered decoration, applied with copper birds, animals, plants and insects, marked, American, Rhode Island, 1884.
£2,650–3,150 / €3,850–4,600
$4,800–5,700 S(NY)

A silver coffee service, by Wood & Hughes, with engraved and repoussé decoration, stamped, American, New York, c1865, 12½in (32cm) high, 71oz.
£600–720 / €880–1,050
$1,100–1,300 JAA

A silver-plated four-piece tea and coffee set, designed by Christopher Dresser for Hukin & Heath, engraved with Japaneze-style floral *mons*, maker's and designer's marks, design kite mark for 8 October 1897, coffee pot 7in (18cm) high.
£2,600–3,100 / €3,800–4,550
$4,700–5,600 DN

A silver five-piece tea and coffee service, by Frederick Elkington, engraved with birds and prunus, London, 1879–80, together with matching sugar tongs, Birmingham 1881.
£1,800–2,150 / €2,650–3,150
$3,250–3,900 DN

Arts & Crafts Ceramics

A pottery vase, attributed to Ault, c1895, 10in (25.5cm) high.
£110–125 / €160–180
$200–220 ⊞ HUN

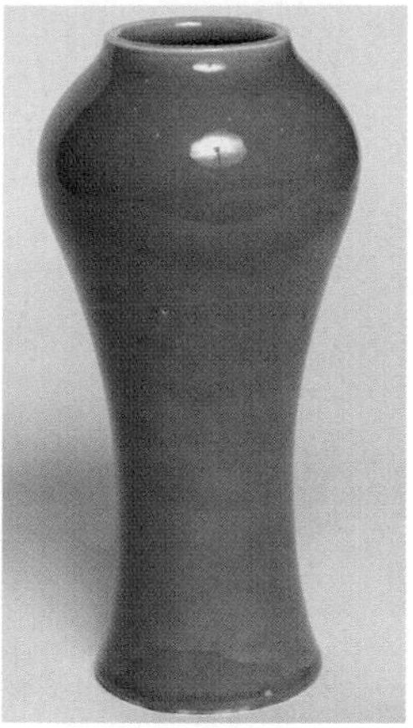

A pair of Ault pottery vases, c1900, 8¼in (21cm) high.
£250–280 / €370–410
$450–510 ⊞ SHa

A Brannam Pottery political pitcher, damaged, c1900, 5½in (14cm) high.
£670–750 / €980–1,100
$1,200–1,350 ⊞ MMc

◄ **A Carter & Co flambé vase,** with streaked glazing, c1904, 15½in (39.5cm) high.
£1,350–1,500
€1,950–2,200
$2,450–2,700 ⊞ MMc

► **A Brannam Pottery vase,** incised with fish and plants, with three strap handles, slight damage, inscribed marks, 1902, 9¾in (25cm) high.
£490–580 / €720–850
$890–1,050 ⚒ F&C

Brannam ware

Charles Brannam established his pottery in Barnstaple, north Devon, in 1879. The pottery is often referred to as Barum ware after the Roman name for Barnstaple. Much of it is sgraffito-decorated, meaning that coloured slips were laid over the red clay and carved through by the artist. Popular Brannam subjects include fish and birds, often by key designers such as James Dewdney, Frederick Braddon and William Baron. They were also responsible for a number of animal and political caricature models which are much sought after by collectors today. The brittle nature of the Devon clay makes the wares subject to damage and collectors should be wary of restoration.

A Brannam Pottery tyg, incised with fish, incised signature and date 1906, 5in (12.5cm) high.
£130–155 / €190–220
$240–290 ⚒ BWL

A Della Robbia plate, signed 'Violet', 1894–1906, 8in (20.5cm) diam.
£200–230 / €290–330
$360–420 ⊞ HABA

► **A Burmantofts faïence vase,** painted and incised with Viking boats, impressed mark and shape No. 2200, 1880–90, 13¼in (33.5cm) high.
£1,650–1,950 / €2,400–2,850
$3,000–3,550 ⚒ AH

A Foley miniature jardinière, with *intarsio* decoration of chickens, c1890, 4in (10cm) high.
£500–550 / €720–800
$900–1,000 ⊞ RH
***Intarsio* is a dramatic form of underglaze decoration featured on wares designed and decorated by Frederick Rhead.**

► **A Grueby Pottery vase,** by Wilhelmina Post, decorated with narcissus, impressed mark and artist's signature, American, Boston, 1898–1907, 10in (25.5cm) high.
£9,000–10,700 / €13,100–15,600
$16,300–19,400 ⚒ SK

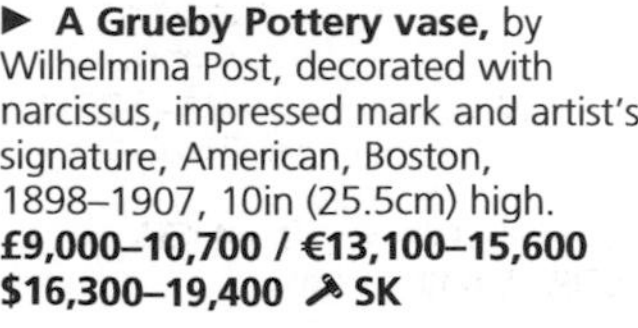

A Lauder pottery vase, applied with a grotesque creature, c1895, 13in (30.5cm) high.
£990–1,100 / €1,400–1,600
$1,700–2,000 ⊞ MMc

A Minton Art Pottery Studio plaque, by W. S. Coleman, decorated with a naked girl, impressed marks and year cipher for 1872, 19¼in (49cm) diam.
£5,900–7,000 / €8,600–10,200
$10,700–12,700 ⚒ TEN

Minton opened a studio in Kensington Gore, London c1870 specifically for producing art pottery. It was only in production for three years before being burnt down. W. S. Coleman was their leading artist. He frequently depicted naked or scantily-clad children, as well as fantastic or mythological worlds, typically in a palette of vivid enamels. Pieces bear a printed circular mark.

A Pilkington's Royal Lancastrian vase, 1914–23, 4in (10cm) high.
£100–110 / €145–160
$180–200 ⊞ SAT

Lauder ware

Lauder ware is very similar in style to Brannam ware. Alexander Lauder was headmaster of the Barnstaple School of Art, north Devon, when Charles Brannam was a pupil there in the mid-1870s. In 1876, he established the Lauder pottery and produced a range of decorative sgraffito wares, as well as tiles and architectural ornaments. Collectors used to consider Lauder ware to be inferior to Brannam ware, but since the 1990s, there has been growing interest in Lauder and today his pieces are regarded as having equal merit. This is reflected in the high prices they can now command.

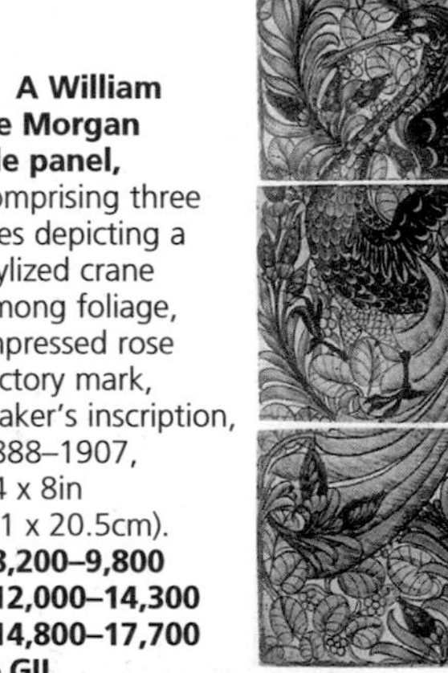

► **A William De Morgan tile panel,** comprising three tiles depicting a stylized crane among foliage, impressed rose factory mark, maker's inscription, 1888–1907, 24 x 8in (61 x 20.5cm).
£8,200–9,800
€12,000–14,300
$14,800–17,700
⚒ GIL

A Rookwood pottery vase, by E. T. Hurley, decorated with fish, impressed marks, c1907, 6½in (16.5cm) high.
£1,800–2,100 / €2,600–3,000
$3,200–3,800 ⚒ LHA

► **A Stump Longniddry pot and cover,** Scottish, 1927–39, 3½in (9cm) high.
£220–250 / €320–370
$400–450 ⊞ SDD

William John Watt (1890–1960) was a disabled veteran of WWI who lived in Longniddry, near Edinburgh. Although he had no hands, he was able to paint his pottery by attaching his brush with two strong elastic bands to his one forearm, hence his work was marked Stump Longniddry. He worked from 1927 to 1939 and his pieces were widely exported.

A pair of Linthorpe glazed terracotta vases, decorated with slip-painted flowers, restored, c1887, 4in (10cm) high.
£180–200 / €260–290
$320–360 ⊞ HUN

A Newcomb College lamp base, by Joseph Meyer, with line and broad leaf decoration, three handles, impressed marks, American, New Orleans, c1907, 4¼in (11cm) high.
£2,250–2,700 / €3,300–3,950
$4,050–4,850 ⚒ SK

A Ruskin Pottery ginger jar and cover, decorated with vines and tendrils, crossed swords mark, dated 1910, 7in (18cm) high.
£400–480 / €580–700
$720–870 ⚒ GIL

Arts & Crafts Clocks

A Guild of Handicraft silver-plated clock, with a tree design surrounding the face, the top with a truncated pyramid and an amethyst, c1904, 8¾in (22cm) high.
£7,800–9,100
€11,400–13,300
$14,100–16,500 S

A Liberty & Co silver and enamel clock, in the style of C. F. A. Voysey, the numerals replaced with the motto 'Festina Lente', Birmingham, c1905, 3¾in (9.5cm) high.
£8,600–10,300
€12,600–15,000
$15,600–18,600 S

A Liberty Tudric pewter and enamel clock, early 20thC, 6¼in (16cm) high.
£1,800–2,100
€2,600–3,000
$3,200–3,800 S(O)

A Liberty Tudric pewter and enamel clock, marked, early 20thC, 9in (23cm) high.
£1,300–1,550
€1,900–2,250
$2,350–2,800 S(O)

Further reading
Miller's Art Nouveau & Art Deco Buyer's Guide, Miller's Publications, 2001

DECORATIVE ARTS

Arts & Crafts Furniture

A Liberty & Co oak bookcase, with leaded glass doors and cantilevered side shelves, with the motto 'Judge Not a Book by the Cover', 1880–1920, 74in (188cm) high.
£2,900–3,500
€4,200–4,700
$5,200–5,900 ⊞ STRA

A mahogany bookcase, c1890, 52in (132cm) wide.
£2,900–3,250
€4,250–4,800
$5,250–5,800 ⊞ MTay

An oak bureau, with floral decoration, c1900, 48in (122cm) high.
£900–1,000
€1,300–1,450
$1,600–1,800 ⊞ TDG

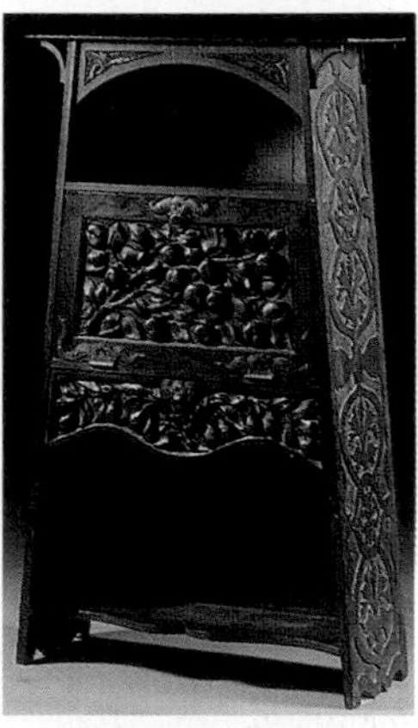

An oak fall-front bureau, carved with apples, pears and foliate motifs, possibly Lake District, early 20thC, 32¾in (83cm) wide.
£2,250–2,700
€3,300–3,950
$4,050–4,850 S(O)

A mahogany cabinet, 1880–1920, 60in (152.5cm) high.
£990–1,100 / €1,450–1,600
$1,800–2,000 ⊞ STRA

An oak cabinet, the four doors enclosing a fitted interior, American, early 20thC, 43in (109cm) wide.
£650–780 / €950–1,100
$1,200–1,400 SK

► **An inlaid mahogany secretaire cabinet,** by George Montague Ellwood for J. S. Henry of London, with brass strapwork hinges, on square legs, stamped 'J. S. Henry', early 20thC, 68in (172.5cm) high.
£1,500–1,700
€2,200–2,500
$2,700–3,100 G(L)

London cabinet-makers J. S. Henry were known for their 'Quaint' furniture – a trade version of Art Nouveau that combined elements of the Glasgow School with European Art Nouveau and Arts and Crafts.

A stained pine side cabinet, by Charles Rennie Mackintosh, Scottish, c1906, 61in (155cm) wide.
£9,000–10,000 / €13,100–14,600
$16,300–18,100 ⊞ JSG
This piece was designed for the Scotland Street School, Glasgow, which has since become the Glasgow Museum of Education.

A child's oak chair, by Charles Limbert, American, Michigan, c1900.
£430–480 / €630–700
$780–870 ⊞ TDG

A set of six oak side chairs, by L. & J. G. Stickley, model number 800, marked, American, c1914.
£2,400–2,850 / €3,500–4,150
$4,350–5,200 ⚒ SK

An oak wall cabinet, 1880–1920, 26in (71cm) wide.
£310–350 / €450–510
$560–630 ⊞ STRA

► **A pair of oak chairs,** by E. A. Taylor, in the Glasgow style, Scottish, c1900.
£900–1,000 / €1,300–1,450
$1,600–1,800 ⊞ JSG

An ebonized oak chair, by Frank Lloyd Wright, with leather upholstery, American, c1903.
£1,800–2,150 / €2,600–3,100
$3,250–3,900 ⚒ S(NY)

An oak chest of drawers, by Shapland & Petter, 1880–1920, 32½in (82.5cm) high.
£380–420 / €550–610
$690–760 ⊞ STRA

◄ **An oak dresser cupboard,** with wrought-iron strapwork, c1905, 59in (150cm) wide.
£1,750–1,950 / €2,550–2,850
$3,150–3,550 ⊞ TDG

► **An oak dresser,** with three frieze drawers above a central fall-front cupboard, two further doors, early 20thC, 70in (178cm) high.
£2,400–2,850 / €3,500–4,150
$4,350–5,200 ⚒ S(O)

A Byrdcliffe Arts & Crafts Colony cherrywood chair, by Zulma Steele, the back panel carved with a lily, marked, American, c1904, 37¾in (96cm) high.
£23,200–27,800 / €34,000–40,000
$42,000–50,000 ⚒ S(NY)
The Byrdcliffe Arts and Crafts Colony was established in Woodstock, New York, at the end of the 19th century. Their simple hand-crafted furniture is suggestive of the more commonly known style of the Stickleys, but because output was much smaller there is strong competition among American collectors for any pieces that find their way to auction, particularly if the provenance is good.

A pine and copper fire surround, embossed with scrolling foliage, early 20thC, 69in (175.5cm) wide.
£4,800–5,700 / €7,000–8,300
$8,700–10,300 S(O)

A Liberty & Co oak sideboard, attributed to Leonard Wyburd, with ironwork ring handles and hinges, on splayed bracket feet, retailer's trade label to reverse, c1900, 75in (190.5cm) wide.
£2,100–2,500 / €3,100–3,650
$3,800–4,550 E

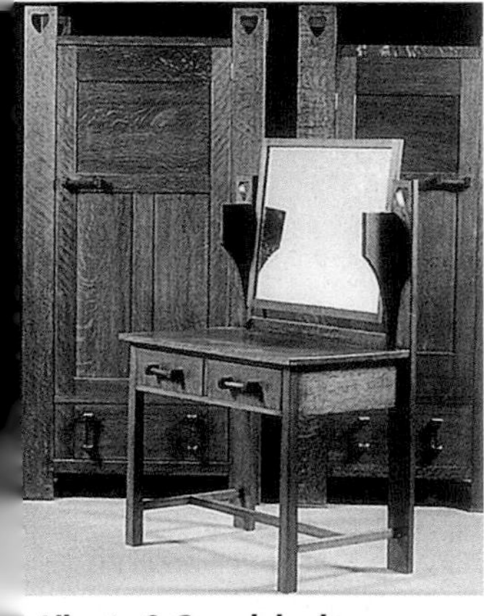

A Liberty & Co oak bedroom suite, comprising a double and single wardrobe and dressing table, marked, early 20thC, double wardrobe 59½in (151cm) high.
£2,100–2,500 / €3,100–3,650
$3,800–4,550 S(O)

An oak overmantel mirror, inset with Ruskin tiles, inscribed 'Well before hearth and hall', dated 1878, 43in (109cm) wide.
£1,800–2,000 / €2,600–2,900
$3,250–3,600 ASP

An oak stool, carved with Celtic symbols and 'Wed 1929', c1929, 13in (33cm) high.
£75–85 / €110–125
$135–155 CCO

A mahogany occasional table, in the style of Liberty & Co, with turned tapered supports joined by a balustrade stretcher, 19thC, 24in (61cm) high.
£190–220 / €280–320
$340–400 CHTR

An inlaid mahogany occasional table, c1900, 27in (68.5cm) wide.
£650–730 / €950–1,050
$1,150–1,300 APO

◄ **An oak table,** with fret-carved apron, c1890, 22in (56cm) diam.
£300–330 / €430–480
$540–600 ANO

A Victorian sideboard back, inset with a mirror, carved and tooled decoration, 42in (106.5cm) high.
£175–210 / €250–300
$320–380 JAA

A late Victorian walnut bedroom suite, with boxwood and ebony stringing, comprising dressing table and wardrobe, wardrobe 54in (137cm) wide.
£1,150–1,300 / €1,700–1,900
$2,100–2,350 SWA

A Georgian-style oak cricket table, c1890, 24in (61cm) diam.
£490–540 / €720–800
$890–980 WAA

An oak dining table, with two later additional leaves, brass trade label for Russell & Sons, Broadway, c1930, 35in (89cm) wide.
£440–520 / €640–760
$800–940 NSal

Arts & Crafts Jewellery

◄ **A silver and moonstone brooch,** marked 'C. R.' and 'S', c1900, 2in (5cm) wide.
£75–85
€110–125
$135–155 ⊞ TDG

A Liberty & Co silver and enamel brooch, by Jessie M. King, marked, Birmingham 1906, 1½in (4cm) wide.
£1,600–1,800 / €2,350–2,650
$2,900–3,250 ⊞ JSG

An enamelled brooch, by George Hunt, depicting a pierrot with female companion, the wirework mount set with pastes, signed, dated 1922, 2in (5cm) diam.
£760–910 / €1,100–1,300
$1,400–1,650 ⚒ DN

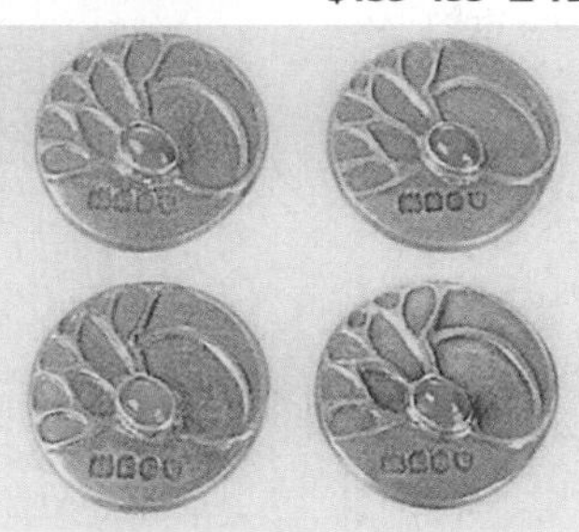

A set of six silver buttons, by Theodor Fahrner, each with stylized motifs and set with a chalcedony cabochon, maker's marks, German, London import marks for 1902, ½in (1.5cm) diam.
£640–760 / €930–1,100
$1,150–1,400 ⚒ DN

A pair of earrings, by Dorrie Nossiter, 1895, ¾in (2cm) long.
£610–680 / €890–990
$1,100–1,250 ⊞ ANO

A silver and enamel pendant, by Pearce & Sons, Birmingham 1908.
£45–55 / €70–80
$85–100 ⚒ CHTR

◄ **A Liberty & Co 9ct gold pendant,** set with a cabochon moonstone and three amethysts, dated 1913, moonstone ¾in (2cm) high, in original fitted case.
£560–670 / €820–980
$1,000–1,200 ⚒ M

► **A silver ring,** set with a chrysoprase, opal and chalcedony, c1890.
£620–700 / €900–1,000
$1,100–1,250 ⊞ TDG

Arts & Crafts Lighting

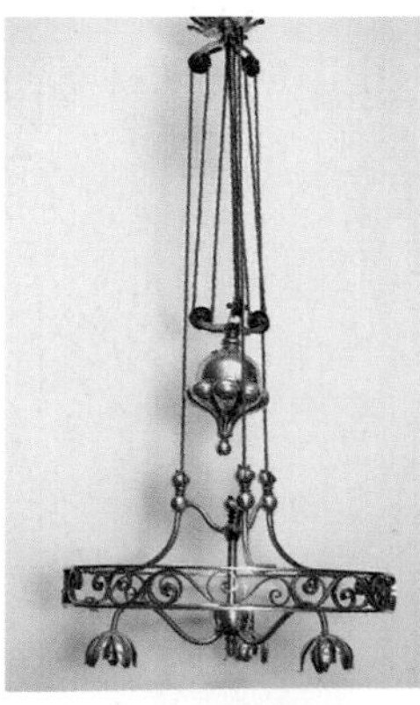

A silver-plated three-branch rise and fall lamp, 1880–1900, 21in (53.5cm) diam.
£620–700 / €900–1,000
$1,100–1,250 ⊞ EAL

A copper and brass table lamp, attributed to W. A. S. Benson, with a James Powell of Whitefriars glass shade, c1895, 12in (30.5cm) high.
£540–600 / €790–880
$980–1,100 ⊞ TDG

A brass three-branch chandelier, in the manner of W. A. S. Benson, with glass shades, c1900, 15¾in (40cm) high.
£2,400–2,850
€3,500–4,150
$4,350–5,200 ⚒ S(O)

A vaseline glass pendant lamp, c1900, 14in (35.5cm) high.
£400–450 / €580–660
$720–810 ⊞ JeH

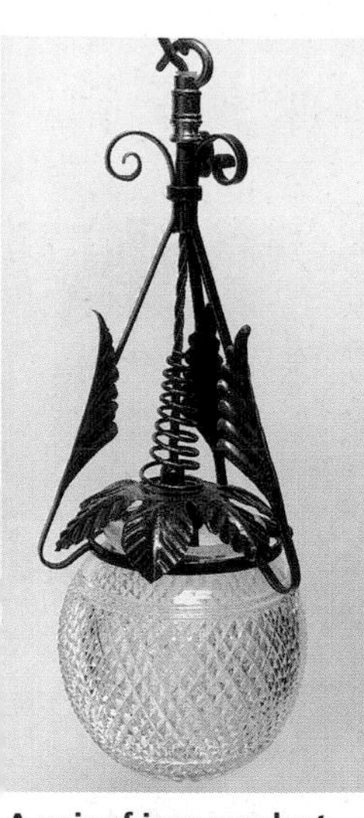

A pair of iron pendant lamps, with crystal lights, c1900, 12in (30.5cm) high.
£340–380 / €500–550
$620–690 ⊞ JeH

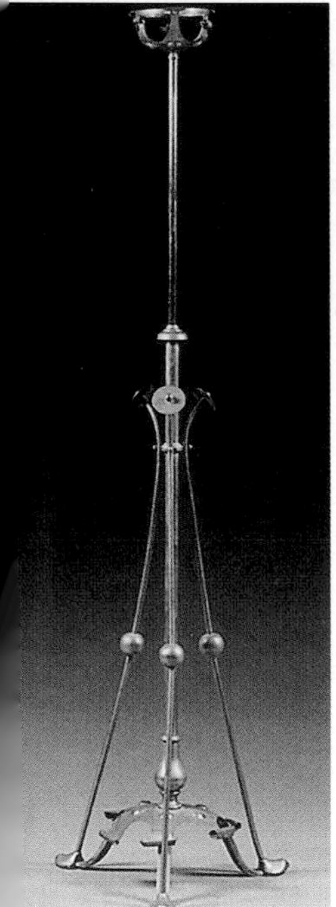

\ brass telescopic tandard oil lamp, c1900, 2in (183cm) extended.
240–290 / €350–420
430–520 ⚒ S(O)

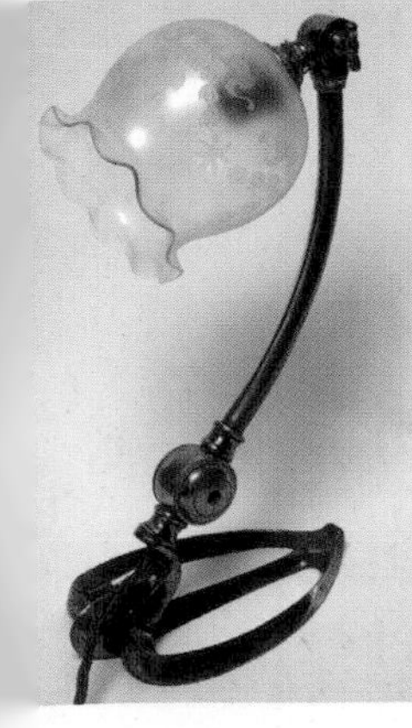

A brass ceiling light, with vaseline glass shades, c1900, 17in (43cm) high.
£990–1,100
€1,450–1,600
$1,800–2,000 ⊞ JeH

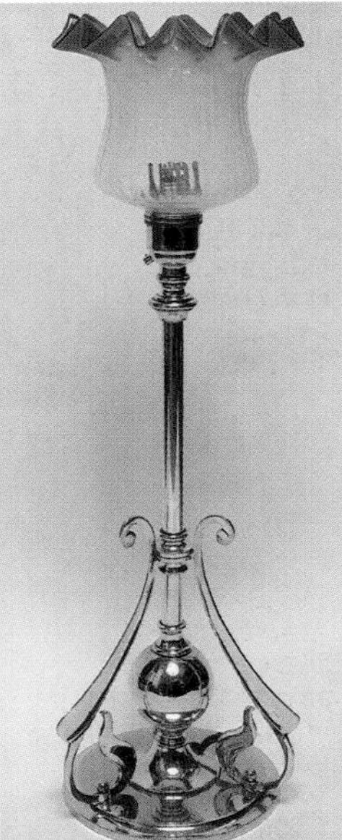

A brass table lamp, with an opaline cranberry glass shade, 1900–10, 18in (45.5cm) high.
£250–280 / €370–410
$450–510 ⊞ JeH

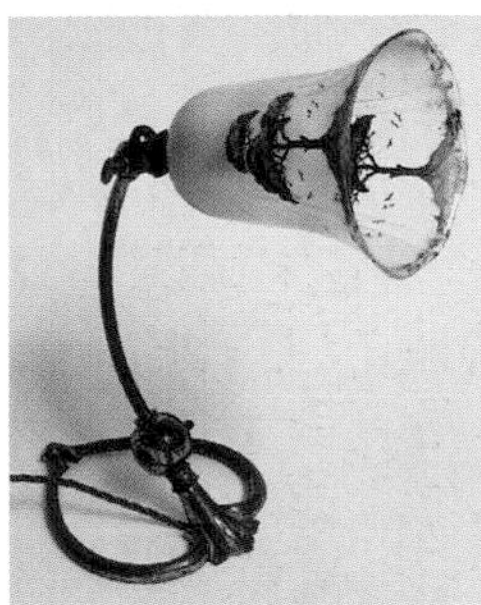

A brass table lamp, by W. A. S. Benson, with a hand-painted vaseline glass shade, c1910, 12in (30.5cm) high.
£760–850 / €1,100–1,250
$1,400–1,550 ⊞ CHA

◄ **A brass table/wall lamp,** in the style of W. A. S. Benson, with an etched-glass shade, c1910, 12in (30.5cm) high.
£350–400 / €510–580
$640–720 ⊞ JeH

A pair of copper wall sconces, c1900, 18in (45.5cm) high.
£670–750 / €980–1,100
$1,200–1,350 ⊞ SHa

A brass three-branch chandelier, with frosted glass shades, early 20thC, 43in (109cm) high.
£840–1,000
€1,250–1,450
$1,500–1,800 ⚒ S(O)

► **An iridescent glass table lamp,** by Victor Durand, on gilt-metal mounts, American, c1920, 14½in (37cm) high.
£250–300 / €370–440
$450–540 ⚒ JAA

Victor Durand (1870–1931) produced art glass at the Vineland Glass Manufacturing Company, New Jersey from 1897 until his death. Typical wares are vases of neo-classical form in gold or blue iridescence. He employed Quezal artists and therefore many of his products resemble Quezal glass.

A hammered copper four-branch ceiling light, c1900, 32in (81.5cm) diam.
£810–900 / €1,200–1,350
$1,450–1,650 ⊞ EAL

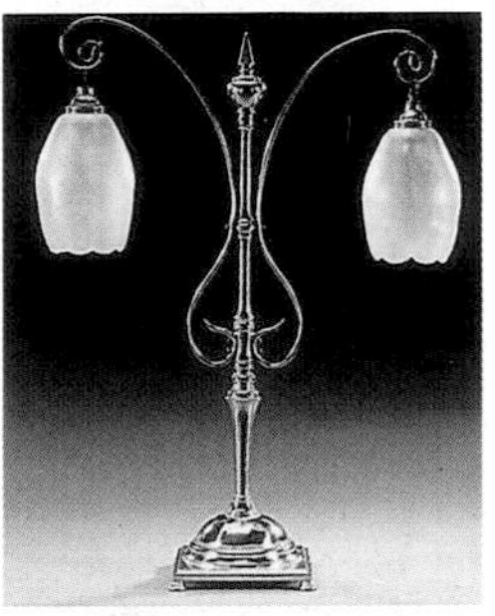

A copper and brass two-branch table lamp, by W. A. S. Benson, with glass shades, early 20thC, 19¼in (49cm) high.
£2,500–3,000
€3,650–4,400
$4,550–5,400 ⚒ S(O)

An oxidized copper ceiling lamp, with vaseline glass shades, c1910, 15in (38cm) diam.
£1,200–1,350
€1,750–1,950
$2,150–2,450 ⊞ CHA

Arts & Crafts Metalware

A pair of Roycroft copper bookends, American, c1915, 4½in (11.5cm) high.
£250–280 / €370–410
$450–510 ⊞ SHa

The American craft community known as the Roycrofters (1895–1938) was founded by Elbert Hubbard to produce metalwork, textiles and furniture. The Roycroft Metalwork Shop was opened c1908.

A silver-plated box, with inset wooden panel, c1880, 5in (12.5cm) wide.
£440–490 / €640–720
$800–890 ⊞ TDG

A pewter bowl and cover, 1880–1920, 8in (20.5cm) wide.
£135–150 / €195–220
$240–270 ⊞ STRA

▶ A Wiener Werkstätte silver box, designed by Carl Otto Czeschka, made by Josef Hossfeld, decorated with enamelled bird motif medallions, impressed marks, Austrian, Vienna, c1907, 2¾in (7cm) diam.
£5,200–6,200 / €7,600–9,100
$9,400–11,200 ⚒ DORO

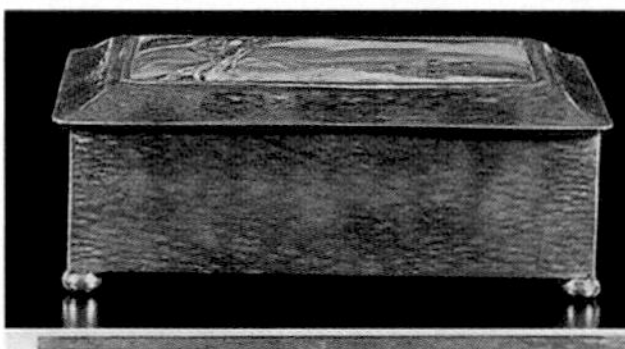

A Guild of Handicraft hammered silver box, by Fleetwood Charles Varley, with inset enamel plaque, signed, London 1903, 6¾in (17cm) wide.
£4,800–5,700 / €7,000–8,300
$8,700–10,300 ⚒ S

A hammered silver bowl, by Ollivant & Botsford, the supports in the form of dolphins, maker's mark, London 1907, 6½in (16.5cm) high.
£450–500 / €660–730
$810–910 ⊞ DAD

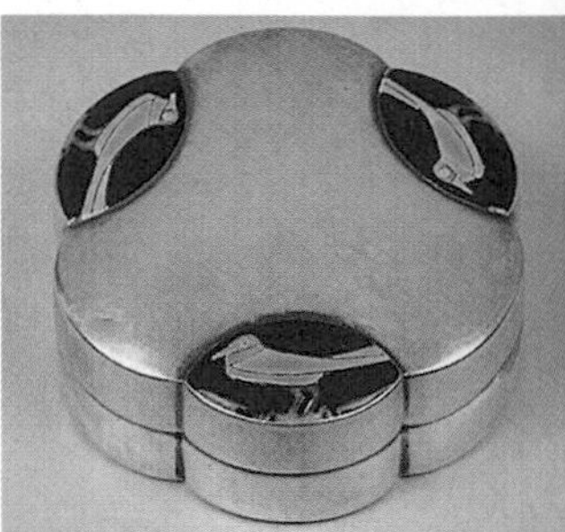

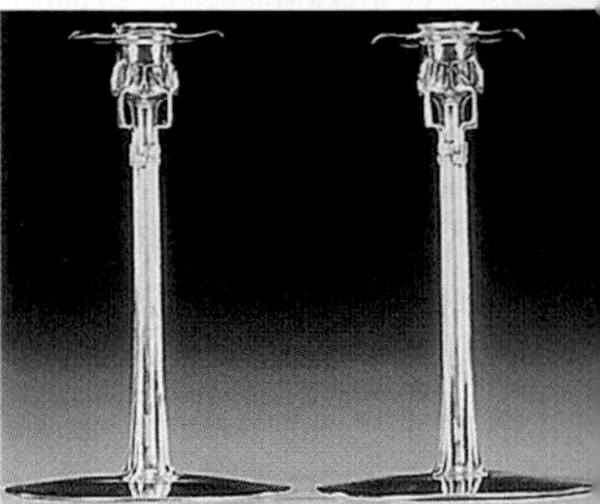

A pair of Liberty & Co Cymric silv Conister candlesticks, by Rex Silver, the detachable nozzles with waved dr pans, Birmingham 1903, 9¾in (25cm) high.
£15,000–18,000 / €21,900–26,300
$27,200–32,000 ⚒ S(O)

These candlesticks cross over into the Art Nouveau style with their sinuous lines, and therefore appea to collectors of both markets.

A pair of silver candlesticks, by Jan Dixon & Sons, the dished drip pans tapering columns and flared bases w riveted banding, maker's mark, Sheffield 1910, 8¾in (22cm) high.
£2,350–2,800 / €3,450–4,100
$4,100–4,900 ⚒ DA

Miller's Compares

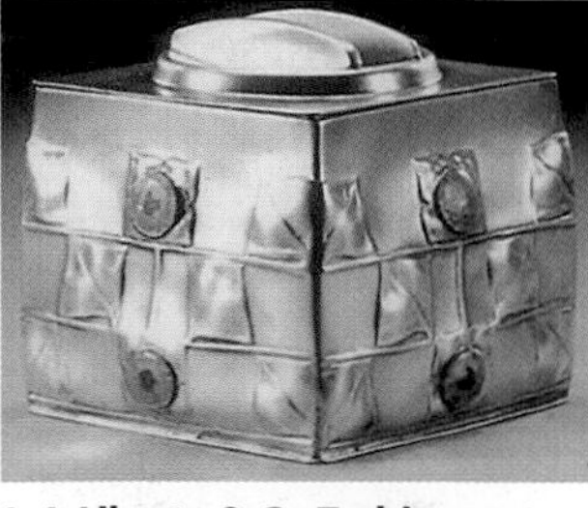

I. A Liberty & Co Tudric pewter and enamel biscuit box, by Archibald Knox, decorated with stylized leaves, stamped mark, early 20thC, 4¾in (12cm) square.
£1,800–2,150 / €2,650–3,150
$3,250–3,900 ⚒ S(O)

II. A Liberty & Co Tudric pewter biscuit box, by Archibald Knox, decorated with stylized leaves, stamped mark, early 20thC, 4¾in (12cm) square.
£450–540 / €660–790
$810–980 ⚒ S(O)

Item I and Item II are almost identical in design and size but Item I is applied with enamel roundels. These add great value to pewter wares designed by Archibald Knox as they are expensive to produce and more attractive, therefore making them very appealing to collectors.

A pair of hammered silver candlesticks, by A. E. Jones, with oak stems, maker's mark, Birmingham 1924, 7in (18cm) high.
£810–900 / €1,150–1,300
$1,450–1,650 ⊞ DAD

A Newlyn copper charger, c1890, 14½in (37cm) diam.
£430–480 / €630–700
$780–870 ⊞ SHa

A hammered silver cigarette case, by Omar Ramsden and Alwyn Carr, embossed with a trailing leaf roundel, Birmingham 1913, 3½in (9cm) wide.
£230–270 / €340–400
$420–500 ⚒ DN

A Liberty & Co Tudric pewter coupe, with a later glass liner, stamped mark, early 20thC, 7¼in (18.5cm) diam.
£1,000–1,200 / €1,450–1,750
$1,800–2,150 ⚒ S(O)

A silver centrepiece, with two removable brass trays, surmounted by a figure of a woman holding a torch, a sickle and a sheaf, marked, German, c1900, 28¾in (73cm) high.
£3,000–3,600 / €4,400–5,300
$5,300–6,300 ⚒ DORO

A Liberty & Co silver desk set, by Archibald Knox, chased and pierced with Celtic knot motifs, Birmingham 1910, 9½in (24cm) wide.
£5,400–6,400 / €7,900–9,300
$9,800–11,600 ⚒ S

A WMF silver-plated chamberstick, c1910, 7in (18cm) wide.
£85–95 / €125–140
$150–170 ⊞ SAT

A set of oak and brass Westminster chimes, by Tocsin, on an oak frame, c1890, 22in (56cm) wide.
£310–350 / €450–510
$560–630 ⊞ ASP

◄ An anodized metal coal bin, with Ruskin Pottery roundels, 1880–1900, 20in (51cm) high.
£450–500 / €660–730
$810–910 ⊞ MRW

A Guild of Handicraft silver comport, the stem pierced with stylized foliage and applied with enamelled panels, 1903, 9in (23cm) diam, 21oz.
£22,500–27,000 / €33,000–39,000
$41,000–49,000 ⚒ Gam
This comport would have been designed by C. R. Ashbee, the key designer at the Guild of Handicraft. It was probably a one-off commission and is a superb piece of craftsmanship.

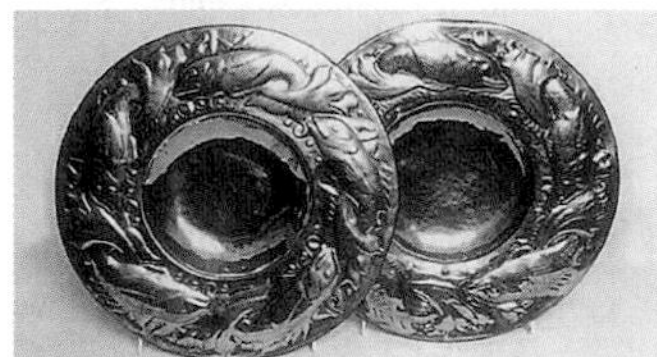
A pair of Newlyn copper alms dishes, decorated with fish among seaweed, marked, c1898, 12¾in (32.5cm) diam.
£2,350–2,800 / €3,450–4,100
$4,250–5,100 ⚒ LAY

◄ A pair of hammered silver dishes, by Omar Ramsden, each applied with a pierced Tudor rose boss over an enamel roundel, maker's mark, London 1930, 6in (15cm) diam.
£2,650–2,950 / €3,850–4,300
$4,800–5,300 ⊞ DAD

A pair of brass fire dogs, by Benham & Froud, c1890, 7in (18cm) high.
£180–200 / €260–290
$320–360 ⊞ NAW
Benham & Froud (1873–93) produced mainly household, utility and kitchen wares.

A copper inkwell, the hinged cover inset with an enamel plaque, c1910, 3in (7.5cm) high.
£190–220 / €280–330
$340–410 ⚒ WL

A brass inkwell, attributed to Russell Workshops, Broadway, liner missing, c1920, base 4½in (11.5cm) wide.
£200–220 / €290–320
$360–400 ⊞ HABA

A Liberty & Co pewter jardinière, 1880–1920, 10in (25.5cm) diam.
£310–350 / €450–510
$560–630 ⊞ STRA

A copper fire screen, c1900, 33in (84cm) high.
£340–390 / €500–570
$620–710 ⊞ TDG

A brass inkwell and pen tray, by Margaret Gilmour, monogrammed 'M.G.', Scottish, c1910, 9in (23cm) wide.
£990–1,100 / €1,450–1,600
$1,800–2,000 ⊞ JSG

A. E. Jones

Albert Edward Jones grew up in Birmingham as part of a large family of blacksmiths. In 1902, he began to produce an extensive range of silver and jewellery items, mostly hand-beaten and often decorated with turquoise stones. His wares are easily identified by an oval maker's mark enclosing the initials A. E. J., and many are typically in the Arts & Crafts style.

A Birmingham Guild of Handicraft silver cream jug, maker's mark 'BGHLd', Birmingham 1903, 3in (7.5cm) high.
£530–600 / €780–880
$1,000–1,100 ⊞ DAD

◀ **A copper jardinière,** set with three Ruskin Pottery glazed ceramic roundels, early 20thC, 7¼in (18.5cm) high.
£150–180 / €220–260
$280–330 ⚒ HOLL

A silver photograph frame, set with turquoise roundels, maker's mark 'E.M.&S.', Birmingham 1901, 4¾in (12cm) diam.
£140–165 / €200–230
$250–290 ⚒ CHTR

A silver inkwell, by A. E. Jones, Birmingham 1912, 5in (12.5cm) diam.
£1,000–1,150 / €1,450–1,650
$1,800–2,050 ⊞ SHa

A copper jardinière, by John Pearson with banded decoration of mythical birds and fish, signed, dated 1891, 10¼in (26cm) high.
£2,450–2,900 / €3,600–4,250
$4,400–5,200 ⚒ Bea

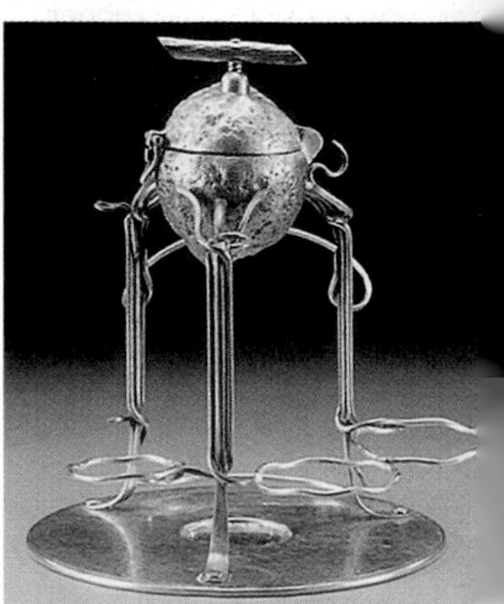

A silver-plated lemon squeezer, b Hukin & Heath, stamped mark, c1880, 11¼in (28.5cm) high.
£720–860 / €1,050–1,250
$1,300–1,550 ⚒ S(O)

A pewter mirror, with embossed floral decoration, c1900, 11 x 9in (28 x 23cm).
£460–520 / €770–870
$1,000–1,100 ⊞ AFD

A hammered-brass wall mirror, attributed to Margaret Gilmour, decorated in high relief with roses, Scottish, early 20thC, 33 x 24in (84 x 61cm).
£350–420 / €510–610
$630–760 ⚒ PFK

A Newlyn copper mirror, decorated with fish and shells, impressed mark, c1908, 27¼ x 14¾in (69 x 37.5cm).
£3,000–3,600
€4,400–5,300
$5,400–6,500 ⚒ LAY
Good-quality mirrors such as this Newlyn example can make ten times as much as those with only an attribution to an artist.

A hammered silver mug, by A. E. Jones, decorated with stylized flower stems set with stones, Birmingham 1904, 3¼in (8.5cm) high.
£960–1,150
€1,450–1,700
$1,750–2,100 ⚒ S(O)

► A Newlyn silver and enamel napkin ring, by Reginald Dick, with a pierced panel centred with an enamel stud, stamped 'Newlyn', maker's mark, London 1911, 2in (5cm) diam.
£410–490
€600–720
$740–890 ⚒ DN

Items in this section have been arranged in alphabetical order.

A silver and glass patch pot and cover, by Spurrier & Co, Birmingham 1909, 1½in (4cm) diam.
£105–120 / €155–175
$200–220 ⊞ ANO

An Artificers' Guild hammered silver quaich, by Edward Spencer, with pierced and entwined fruiting vine handles, maker's mark, signed, London 1931, 7in (18cm) wide.
£810–900 / €1,150–1,300
$1,450–1,650 ⊞ DAD
This London firm of metalworkers was founded by the artist Nelson Dawson in 1901. Its most famous designer was Edward Spencer who became chief designer in 1903. He oversaw production of a wide range of silver and copper wares that were retailed through the Fordham Gallery in Maddox Street, London. Pieces can be identified by a shield-shaped monogram and have a strong flavour of the Arts & Crafts style.

▼ A Liberty & Co Tudric pewter tea caddy, c1905, 5in (12.5cm) high.
£200–230 / €290–340
$360–410 ⊞ NAW

Three silver-plated spoons, by Charles Rennie Mackintosh, Scottish, c1900, 7in (18cm) long.
£720–800 / €1,000–1,150
$1,300–1,450 ⊞ JSG

◄ A WMF copper and brass tea service, stamped marks, German, c1910, stand 16in (40.5cm) high.
£1,250–1,400 / €1,850–2,050
$2,250–2,550 ⊞ TDG

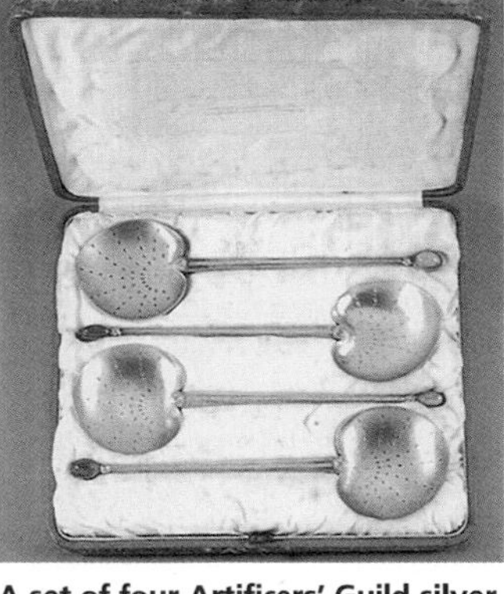

A set of four Artificers' Guild silver spoons, the handles applied with wirework decoration, the terminals set with stones, inscribed, c1900, in a fitted case, 9½in (24cm) wide.
£720–860 / €1,050–1,250
$1,300–1,550 ⚒ S(O)

A Liberty & Co Tudric pewter tea and coffee service, by Archibald Knox, comprising six pieces, with strap-work and enamel decoration, stamped mark, c1900, tray 19¼in (49cm) wide.
£2,700–3,200 / €3,950–4,650
$4,900–5,800 ⚒ TEN
Without the enamel decoration this set would typically make £1,000–1,200 / €1,450–1,750 $1,800–2,100.

Doulton

A Doulton Lambeth silver-mounted stoneware bowl, by Frank Butler, relief-decorated with a continuous frieze, impressed marks, incised monogram, London 1891, 8in (20.5cm) diam.
£330–390 / €480–570
$600–710 SWO

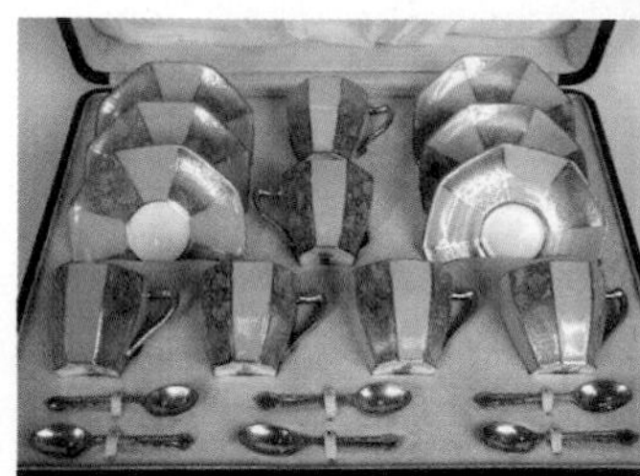

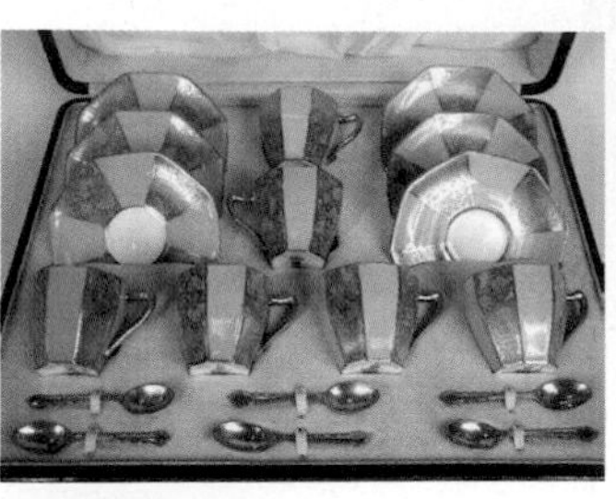

A Royal Doulton coffee service, printed marks, pattern No. H3924, 1937, in a fitted Mappin & Webb presentation case with silver teaspoons.
£330–390 / €480–570
$600–710 SWO

A Doulton Burslem coffee service, comprising nine pieces, painted with a bird among branches, printed Vernon's Patent, maker's initials 'R.A.', late 19thC, tray 22½in (57cm) wide.
£1,400–1,650 / €2,050–2,400
$2,550–3,000 S(O)

The initials 'R. A.' are for Robert Allen who was head of the Art Department at Burslem where, in addition to designing, he oversaw the decoration of the finest pieces produced at the factory. Vernon's Patent refers to the application of rubber to the foot of each piece to prevent the damaging of furniture.

A Doulton Lambeth ewer, by George Tinworth, decorated with Seaweed pattern, c1878, 8in (20.5cm) high.
£450–500 / €660–730
$810–910 JE

A Doulton Lambeth silver-mounted ewer, sgraffito decorated by Hannah Barlow, the borders by Lucy Barlow, 1883, 8in (20.5cm) high.
£2,150–2,400
€3,150–3,500
$3,900–4,350 POW

A Doulton Burslem ewer, 1891–92, 15in (38cm) high.
£620–700
€900–1,000
$1,100–1,250
WAC

A pair of Royal Doulton ewers, by Frank Butler, assisted by Bessie Newbury, 1906, 15in (38cm) high.
£2,400–2,750 / €3,550–4,000
$4,400–5,000 CANI

◄ **A Royal Doulton honey pot,** by Vera Huggins, impressed mark, initialled 'EP' and 'VH', c1923, 3¼in (8.5cm) high.
£340–380
€500–550
$620–690
EHCS

A Royal Doulton figure, by Leslie Harradine, entitled 'Lido Lady', model No. HN1220, impressed date 1928, 7in (18cm) high.
£870–1,000
€1,250–1,450
$1,500–1,800 DN

A pair of Doulton Lambeth stoneware jardinières, moulded with masks, leaves and grapes, c1890, 7¼in (18.5cm) wide.
£370–440 / €540–640
$670–800 SWO

A Doulton Lambeth menu holder, by George Tinworth, entitled 'Quack Doctor' c1886, 4½in (11.5cm) high.
£2,850–3,200
€4,150–4,650
$5,200–5,800 POW

A Doulton Lambeth jardinière and stand, th jardinière on stylized feet in the form of griffins, c1890, 37in (94cm) high.
£1,150–1,300
€1,700–1,900
$2,100–2,350 MMc

A Doulton Lambeth silver-mounted stoneware tea caddy, entitled 'Honest Tea is The Best Policy', Chester 1895, 6¼in (16cm) high.
£350–420 / €510–610
$630–760 ⚒ DD

◄ **A Doulton stoneware vase,** by Hannah Barlow, incised with deer in a landscape, incised mark, dated 1879, 7½in (19cm) high.
£680–810 / €960–1,150
$1,250–1,500 ⚒ HOLL

A pair of Doulton faïence tile panels, painted by J. McLennan, decorated with classical figures, restored, c1880, 63 x 30in (160 x 76cm).
£3,200–3,800
€4,650–5,500
$5,800–6,900 ⚒ S(O)

A Doulton tyg, by Alice Cooke and Elisabeth Shelley, 1912–20, 6in (15cm) high.
£340–390 / €500–560
$620–700 ⊞ CANI

A pair of Doulton Lambeth vases, by Hannah Barlow, c1880, 11in (28cm) high.
£1,650–1,850
€2,400–2,700
$3,000–3,350 ⊞ JE

A Doulton Lambeth stoneware vase, by Louisa E. Edwards, incised monogram, dated 1876, 8¼in (21cm) high.
£560–670 / €810–970
$1,000–1,200 ⚒ G(L)

A pair of Doulton Lambeth vases and covers, by Hannah Barlow, with sgraffito decoration, one cover repaired, impressed wheel mark, incised maker's mark, dated 1887, 5¾in (14.5cm) high.
£1,650–1,950
€2,400–2,850
$3,000–3,550 ⚒ TEN

DECORATIVE ARTS

A Royal Doulton vase, by Mark Marshall and Rosina Brown, decorated with stylized scrolling foliage, impressed marks, dated 1882, 12in (30.5cm) high.
£190–220 / €290–340
$340–400 ⚒ GAK

Mark Marshall is better known for depicting outlandish and grotesque designs which invariably command a higher price.

A Doulton faïence vase, by Margaret Thompson, c1890, 16in (40.5cm) high.
£2,900–3,200
€4,200–4,650
$5,200–5,800 ⊞ JE

Pieces by Margaret Thompson are very collectable and command high prices.

A pair of Doulton Lambeth vases, by Eliza Simmance, incised and tube-lined with panels of stylized flowers, impressed mark, artist's mark, c1884, 11in (28cm) high.
£590–700 / €840–1,000
$1,050–1,250 ⚒ RTo

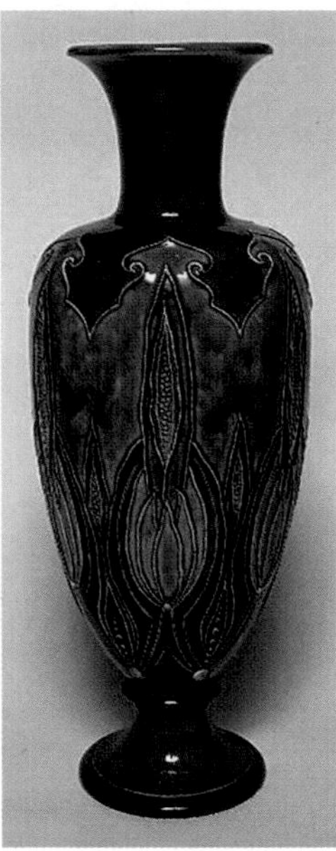

A pair of Doulton Lambeth vases, by Eliza Simmance, 1891–1902, 15½in (39.5cm) high.
£2,350–2,650
€3,450–3,850
$4,250–4,800 ⊞ JE

► A Royal Doulton vase, by Harry Simeon, c1922, 10in (25.5cm) high.
£1,700–1,900
€2,500–2,750
$3,100–3,450 ⊞ POW

► A pair of Doulton stoneware vases, by Florence Barlow and Bessie Newberry, decorated with panels of ducks, impressed marks and incised artist's initials, 1890s, 11in (28cm) high.
£1,500–1,800
€2,200–2,650
$2,700–3,250
⚒ S(O)

A pair of Royal Doulton vases, by Mark Marshall, Bessie Newberry and Nellie Harrison, c1905, 6in (15cm) high.
£2,200–2,450
€3,200–3,600
$4,000–4,450 ⊞ CANI

A Royal Doulton miniature vase, by Maud Bowden and Minnie Forster, c1906, 4in (10cm) high.
£130–145 / €190–210
$230–260 ⊞ CANI

◄ A Royal Doulton vase, by Eliza Simmance, c1910, 9½in (24cm) high.
£430–480 / €630–700
$780–870 ⊞ JE

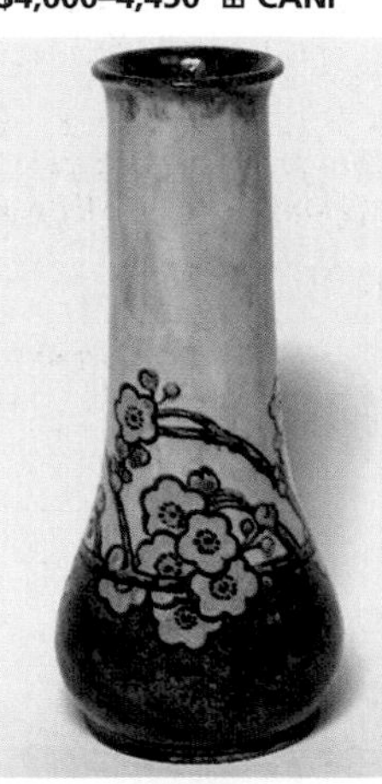

A Royal Doulton vase, b
Florrie Jones, moulded wit
panels of flowering foliag
impressed marks, early
20thC, 12in (30.5cm) hig
£175–210 / €260–310
$320–380 ⚒ GAK

◄ A Royal Doulton vase, by Maud Bowden, 1924–27, 15in (38cm) hig
£270–300 / €390–440
$490–540 ⊞ PGO

Martin Brothers

A Martin Brothers stoneware jar and cover, in the form of a grotesque bird, on an ebonized base, slight damage, incised marks, head dated 1898, base 1899, 13½in (34.5cm) high.
£14,000–16,800
€20,400–24,500
$25,300–30,000 TEN

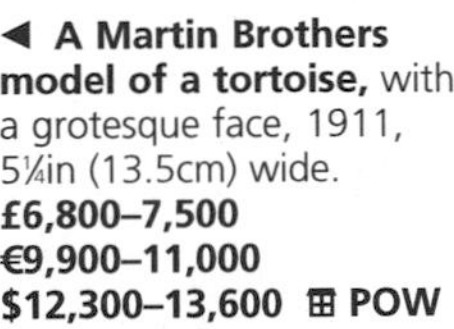

A Martin Brothers jardinière, incised with grotesque birds, 1893, 10in (25.5cm) diam.
£15,700–17,500
€22,900–25,600
$28,400–32,000 POW

Collectors will pay large sums for Martin Brothers wares that are decorated with grotesque imagery. Those with floral designs are not as popular.

◄ **A Martin Brothers stoneware tobacco jar and cover,** decorated with griffins' heads, restored, signed, dated 1892, 5½in (14cm) high.
£820–980 / €1,200–1,450
$1,500–1,800 DN

◄ **A Martin Brothers model of a tortoise,** with a grotesque face, 1911, 5¼in (13.5cm) wide.
£6,800–7,500
€9,900–11,000
$12,300–13,600 POW

► **A Martin Brothers stoneware ewer,** incised with scrolling foliage, incised marks, dated 1881, 8¾in (22cm) high.
£210–250 / €310–370
$380–450 WW

◄ **A Martin Brothers figure,** entitled 'Mr Pickwick', 1914, 2in (5cm) high.
£2,050–2,300
€3,000–3,350
$3,700–4,150
POW

A Martin Brothers vase, decorated with grotesque fish, 1889, 6½in (16.5cm) diam.
£5,400–6,000
€7,900–8,800
$9,800–10,900 POW

A Martin Brothers stoneware vase, incised with stylized leaves and daisies, slight damage, incised marks, 1879–82, 9½in (24cm) high.
£200–240 / €290–350
$360–430 RTo

DECORATIVE ARTS

Moorcroft

Moorcroft flambé erfume bottle, designed by Villiam Moorcroft, decorated vith Orchid pattern, c1935, n (15cm) high.
990–1,100
1,450–1,600
1,800–2,000 GOv

A Moorcroft Macintyre bowl, designed by William Moorcroft, decorated with floral motifs and tulips, painted and impressed marks, late 1890s, 7in (18cm) high.
£1,300–1,550 / €1,900–2,250
$2,350–2,800 S(O)

► **A Moorcroft humidor,** designed by William Moorcroft, decorated with Pomegranate pattern, c1925, 7in (18cm) high.
£810–900
€1,200–1,350
$1,450–1,650
GOv

A Moorcroft bowl, designed by William Moorcroft, decorated with Pansy pattern, 1920s, 6in (15cm) diam.
£350–400 / €440–490
$540–610 PGO

A Moorcroft jardinière, designed by William Moorcroft, decorated with Pomegranate pattern, marked, dated 1923, 6¾in (17cm) high.
£590–700 / €840–1,000
$1,050–1,250 TEN

A Moorcroft Florian Ware vase, decorated with butterflies and stylized flowers, c1900, 8in (20.5cm) high.
£990–1,100
€1,450–1,600
$1,800–2,000 ⊞ HABA

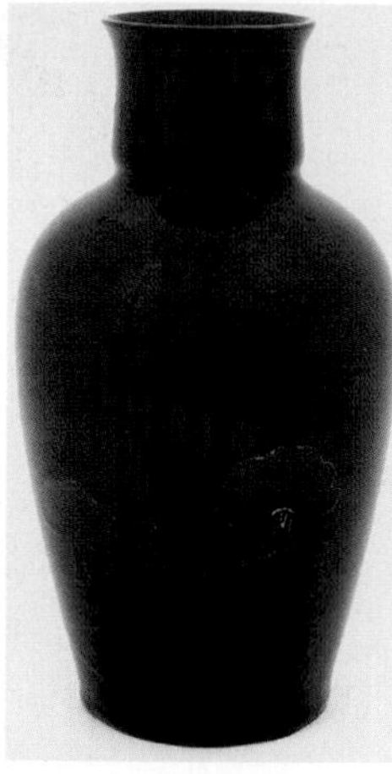

A Moorcroft flambé vase, decorated with a landscape, inscribed 'Made for Liberty & Co', impressed mark, 1902, 6¾in (17cm) high.
£950–1,150
€1,450–1,700
$1,700–2,050 ⚒ GIL

A pair of Moorcroft vases, decorated with Hazledene pattern, printed 'Made for Liberty & Co', painted signature, c1910, 4¾in (12cm) high.
£4,600–5,500 / €6,700–8,000
$8,300–10,000 ⚒ SWO

Sets/pairs

Unless otherwise stated, any description which refers to 'a set' or 'a pair' includes a guide price for the entire set or the pair, even though the illustration may show only a single item.

A pair of Moorcroft Flamminian ware vases, inscribed 'Made for Liberty & Co', incised signature, c1910, 11¾in (30cm) high.
£470–560 / €690–820
$850–1,000 ⚒ SWO

A Moorcroft Macintyre vase, designed by William Moorcroft, decorated with Revived Cornflower pattern, printed and painted marks, 1912–13, 9in (23cm) high.
£1,900–2,250
€2,750–3,300
$3,450–4,100 ⚒ S(O)

A Moorcroft vase, decorated with Wisteria pattern, impressed mark and painted signature, 1914–16, 12½in (32cm) high.
£1,200–1,400
€1,750–2,100
$2,150–2,550 ⚒ RTo

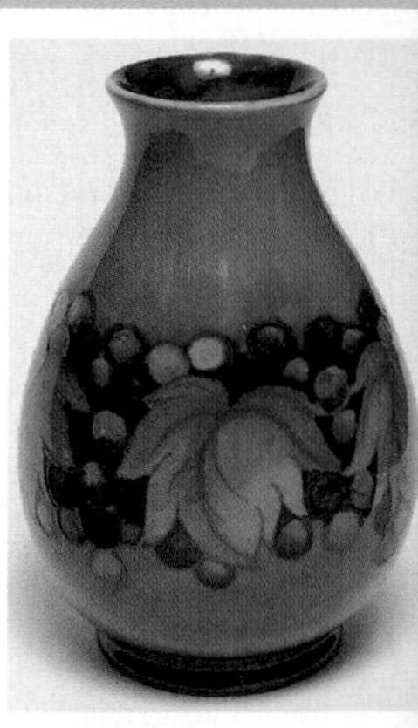

A Moorcroft vase, designed by William Moorcroft, decorated with Grape and Leaf pattern, c1928, 9½in (24cm) high.
£900–1,000
€1,300–1,450
$1,600–1,800 ⊞ GOv

A Moorcroft flambé vase, decorated with Leaves and Fruit pattern, c1930, 4in (10cm) high.
£390–430 / €570–630
$700–780 ⊞ PGO

A Moorcroft flambé vase, designed by William Moorcroft, decorated with Anemone pattern, c1933, 5½in (14cm) high.
£900–1,000
€1,300–1,450
$1,600–1,800 ⊞ GOv

A Moorcroft vase, designed by William Moorcroft, decorated with Big Poppy pattern, c1933, 6¼in (16cm) high.
£670–750 / €980–1,100
$1,200–1,350 ⊞ GOv

A Moorcroft vase, designe by Walter Moorcroft, decorated with Spring Flowers pattern, impressec and painted marks, dated 1954, 13in (33cm) high.
£1,000–1,200
€1,450–1,750
$1,800–2,150 ⚒ S(O)

Art Nouveau Ceramics

A Brannam Pottery vase, by Thomas Liverton, decorated with stylized flowers and leaves, marked, dated 1903, 9½in (24cm) high.
£300–360 / €440–530
$540–650 ⚒ DN

A Hancock & Sons Morris ware bowl, by George Cartlidge, tube-lined with flowers and berries, printed mark, painted signature, early 20thC, 5¼in (13.5cm) diam.
£190–220 / €270–320
$340–400 ⚒ PFK

A Meissen Saxonia cabaret service, designed by Otto E. Voigt, comprising 11 pieces, slight damage, crossed swords and cancelled crossed swords mark, German early 20thC, tray 18¾in (47.5cm) wide.
£3,000–3,600 / €4,400–5,300
$5,400–6,500 ⚒ S(NY)

\ Minton Secessionist jardinière, lecorated with stylized floral motifs, lo. 616446, printed marks, c1900, ¾in (22cm) high.
:230–270 / €340–400
;420–500 ⚒ SWO

Miller's Compares

I. An Emile Gallé faïence model of a cat, wearing a dog cameo, c1900, 14in (35.5cm) high.
£1,800–2,000 / €2,600–2,900
$3,250–3,600 ⊞ RdeR

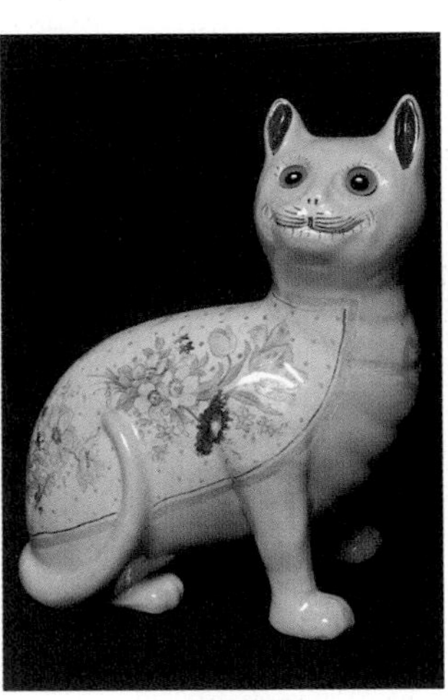

II. A faïence model of a cat, c1870, 9in (23cm) high.
£810–900 / €1,200–1,350
$1,450–1,650 ⊞ RdeR

These cats are similar in style but Item I is by the French master-craftsman Emile Gallé, a name that is important to collectors of art pottery. Pieces that bear the dog cameo such as Item I are particularly desirable. Item II is quaint and will appeal to collectors of such items but will never command the price of a genuine Gallé example.

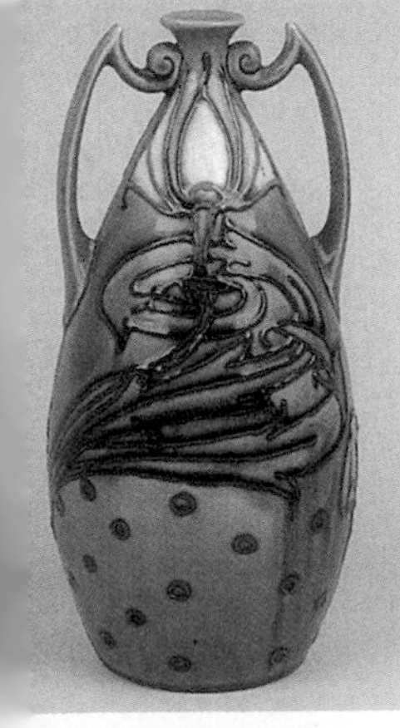

Minton Secessionist ase, with slip-trail ecoration, No. 3736, arked, 1902–14, n (23cm) high.
300–360 / €440–530
540–650 ⚒ L

◄ A Royal Worcester vase, restored, printed and impressed marks, c1890, 16¼in (41.5cm) high.
£120–140 / €170–200
$210–250 ⚒ SWO

A tile, decorated with three stylized flowerheads, c1905, 6in (15cm) square.
£35–40 / €50–55
$65–75 ⊞ DAD

A vase, with silver overlay, Continental, c1900, 4in (10cm) high.
£85–95 / €125–140
$150–170 ⊞ ANO

Art Nouveau Clocks

An oak and marquetry-inlaid mantel clock, with an enamel dial, the Vincent twin-train brass drum movement with anchor escapement striking on a gong, the case inlaid with stylized flowers and scrolling tendrils, slight damage, c1900, 11½in (29cm) high.
£350–420 / €510–610
$630–760 DN(BR)

A mahogany balloon clock, with eight-day movement, 1900–10, 10in (25.5cm) high.
£360–400 / €520–580
$650–720 DEB

◄ **A mahogany longcase clock,** the brass dial with a subsidiary second dial, the twin-barrel movement striking on a bell, Continental, c1900, 81¼in (206.5cm) high.
£960–1,150 / €1,450–1,700
$1,750–2,100 S(O)

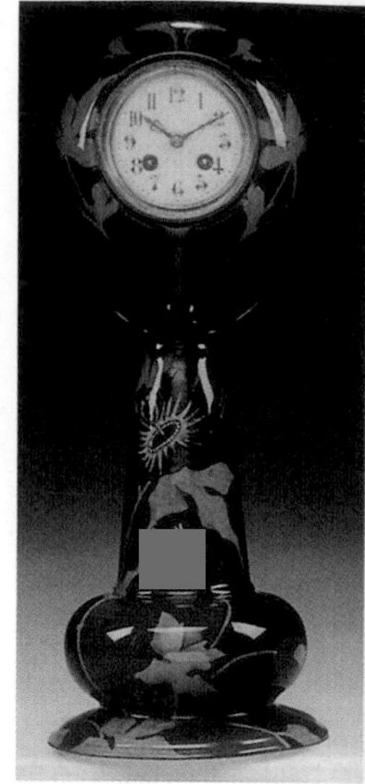

A Zuid Holland earthenware mantel clock, slight damage, restored, painted factory mark, c1910, 20½in (52cm) high.
£970–1,150
€1,450–1,700
$1,750–2,100 S(Am)

Art Nouveau Figures & Busts

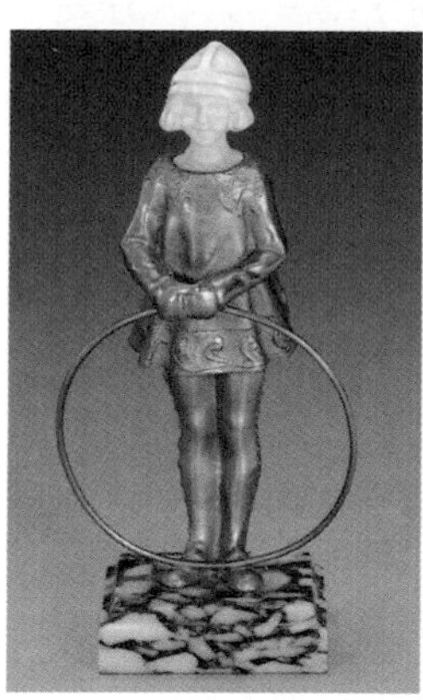

A gilt-bronze and ivory figure of a girl, on a marble base, inscribed 'Bertrand', French, c1920, 6¼in (16cm) high.
£1,100–1,250
€1,600–1,800
$2,000–2,200 MI

A gilt-bronze figure of a maiden, by Maurice Bouval, entitled 'Femme Fleur', holding a casket inscribed '1900', signed, stamped and engraved marks, French, 1900, 13½in (34.5cm) high.
£6,600–7,900
€9,600–11,500
$11,900–14,300 S(O)

◄ **A bronze figure of a nude,** in the manner of Gurschner, early 20thC, 10¼in (26cm) high.
£840–1,000 / €1,200–1,450
$1,500–1,800 S(O)

Gustav Gurschner was a Bavarian sculptor and metalworker.

A bronze figure of Loïe Fuller, by Rupert Carabin, marked, 1896–97, 7¼in (18.5cm) high.
£6,000–7,200
€8,800–10,500
$10,900–13,000 S

Loïe Fuller, the American dancer, was perhaps the greatest source of inspiration for Art Nouveau artists and designers, and the movement's living embodiment. Her repertoire was a theatrical extravaganza performed on a stage with a glass floor lit from below, surrounded by mirrors, incorporating coloured lights and billowing silk drapery.

► **A bronze figure of a maiden,** by Luca Madrassi, signed, Italian, c1900, 32in (81.5cm) high.
£7,400–8,800
€10,800–12,800
$13,400–15,900 S(O)

A bronze figure of a nymph reading a poem by Virgil, by Amadée Charron, entitled 'Génie des Sciences', on a marble pedestal with gilt-bronze mounts, signed, French, c1900, 16¼in (41.5cm) high.
£4,200–5,000
€6,100–7,300
$7,600–9,100 S(O)

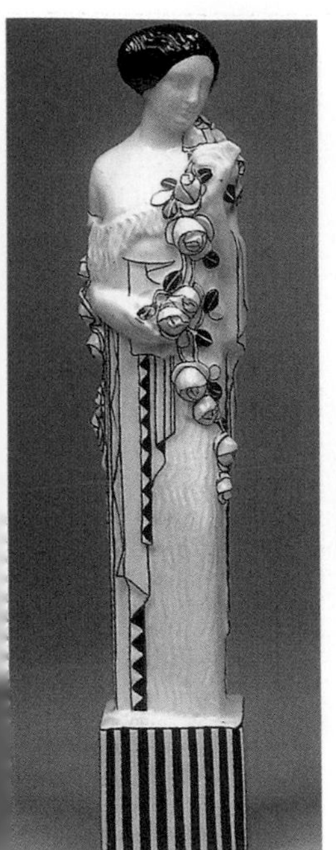

A Wiener Keramik ceramic figure, by Michael Powolny, entitled 'Girl with Roses', slight damage, impressed marks, Austrian, c1910, 11½in (29cm) high.
£6,400–7,600
€9,400–11,100
$11,600–13,800 DORO
Michael Powolny was the founder of the Wiener Keramik factory.

◄ A Reissner, Stellmacher & Kessel porcelain figure of a girl, sitting on a lilypad, Austrian, c1910, 8in (20.5cm) high.
£900–1,000
€1,300–1,450
$1,600–1,800
ASP

A bronze figure of a girl sewing seed, signed 'Schrok', on a marble base, early 20thC, 33in (84cm) high.
£1,100–1,300
€1,600–1,900
$2,000–2,400 BERN

A Royal Dux vase, in the form of a shell and two figures, Austrian, c1900, 14in (35.5cm) high.
£900–1,000 / €1,300–1,450
$1,600–1,800 HKW

◄ A bronze bust of a maiden, by Emmanuel Villanis, entitled 'Dalila', signed, stamped, French, early 20thC, 16¾in (42.5cm) high.
£1,900–2,250
€2,750–3,300
$3,450–4,050 S(O)

► A gilt-bronze figure of a fairy, c1900, 4in (10cm) long.
£400–450 / €580–660
$720–810 ANO

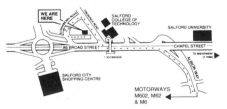

DECORATIVE ARTS

Art Nouveau Furniture

◀ **A mahogany and upholstered banquette,** by Gustave Serrurier-Bovy, with brass mounts and a mirror, Belgian, c1910, 56¼in (143cm) wide.
£4,800–5,700 / €7,000–8,300
$8,700–10,300 S
Gustave Serrurier-Bovy (1858–1910) was one of Belgium's leading Art Nouveau designers and he was greatly influenced by William Morris and the English Arts & Crafts Movement. His early furniture tends to be made of mahogany and is symmetrical in design with restrained curves. Solid in form, pieces are often enhanced with brass fittings.

A bentwood rocking chair, by Thonet, with paper label, Austrian, Vienna, late 19thC.
£840–1,000
€1,200–1,450
$1,500–1,800 S(O)

An oak chair, by Cornelius Smith, c1900.
£850–950 / €1,250–1,400
$1,500–1,700 ⊞ STRA

An oak chair, by Richard Riemerschmid, slight damage, German, Nuremburg, c1905.
£1,600–1,900
€2,350–2,750
$2,900–3,450 SK

An Edwardian inlaid mahogany display cabinet, 52½in (133.5cm) wide.
£1,600–1,900
€2,350–2,750
$2,900–3,450 DMC

◀ **A stained beechwood *étagère*,** by Thonet, restored, Austrian, Vienna, c1900, 23½in (59.5cm) wide.
£950–1,100
€1,400–1,650
$1,700–2,000 DORO

A Secessionist mahogany desk, with brass strapwork and a secret drawer, possibly Austrian, c1905, 75in (190.5cm) high.
£2,700–3,000
€3,950–4,400
$4,900–5,400 ⊞ TDG

An oak sideboard, with a Voysey-style frieze, c1900, 60in (152.5cm) wide.
£2,300–2,600
€3,350–3,800
$4,150–4,700 ⊞ SAT
The architect Charles Annesley Voysey (1847–1941) applied his design expertise to furniture as well as buildings. His work was greatly influenced by the Arts & Crafts movement.

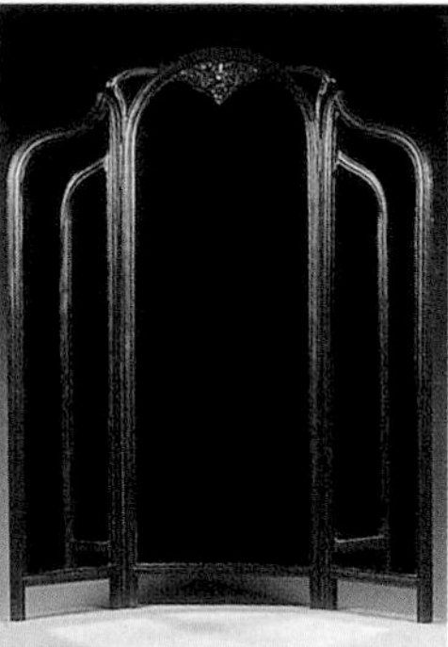

A carved mahogany mirror, attributed to Louis Majorelle, French, early 20thC, 73¾in (187.5cm) wide.
£6,000–7,200
€8,800–10,500
$10,900–13,000 S

▶ **A walnut and marquetry-inlaid two-tier table,** by Emile Gallé, inlaid with irises, marked, signed, French, early 20thC, 32in (81.5cm) wide.
£1,600–1,900
€2,350–2,750
$2,900–3,450 S(O)

A mahogany fire surround, in the the Glasgow School style, the mirror flanked by recesses, inlaid with marquetry and mother-of-pearl panels, c1900, 61in (155cm) wide.
£2,700–3,000
€3,950–4,400
$4,900–5,400 ⊞ DAD

An inlaid mahogany umbrella stand, by Emile Gallé, inlaid with fruit and exotic woods, with brass compartments and iron tray, marked, French, Nancy, c1900, 27½in (70cm) high.
£1,200–1,400
€1,750–2,050
$2,150–2,550 DORO

Art Nouveau Glass

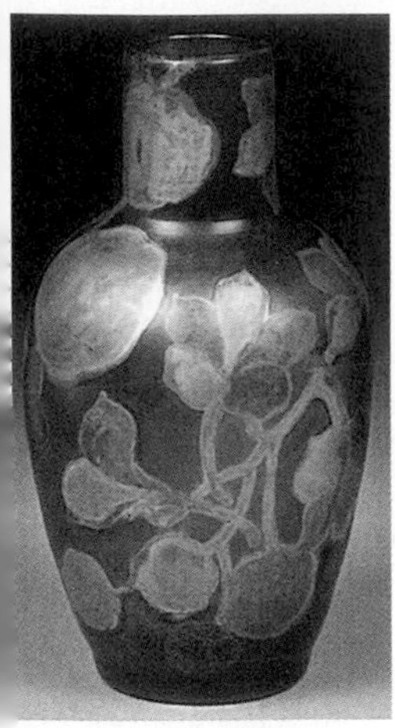

A glass vase, by Amédée de Caranza, with metal oxide painted floral motifs, signed, French, Noyon, c1905, 8in (20.5cm) high.
£760–910 / €1,100–1,300
$1,400–1,650 ⚒ DORO

◄ A Daum silver-mounted and enamelled glass perfume bottle, French, Nancy, c1895, 8in (20.5cm) high.
£2,400–2,700
€3,500–3,950
$4,300–4,900
⊞ MI

A Daum silver-mounted glass bowl, signed, French, Nancy, c1905, 7in (18cm) diam.
£940–1,050 / €1,400–1,550
$1,700–1,900 ⊞ TDG

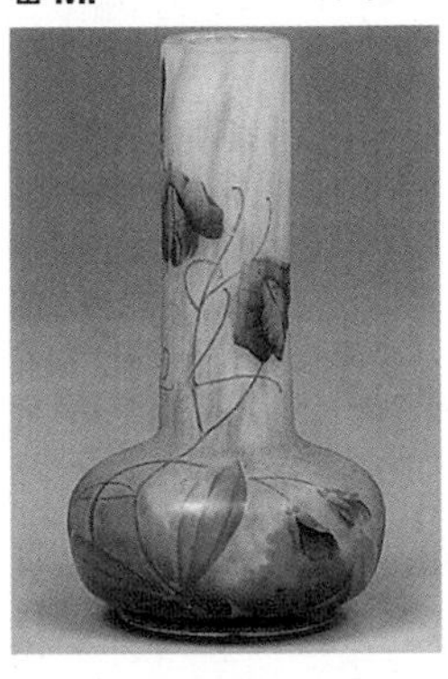

► A Daum glass vase, acid-etched and painted with sweet peas, signed, marked, French, Nancy, c1900, 4¾in (12cm) high.
£1,400–1,650
€2,050–2,400
$2,500–3,000 ⚒ DORO

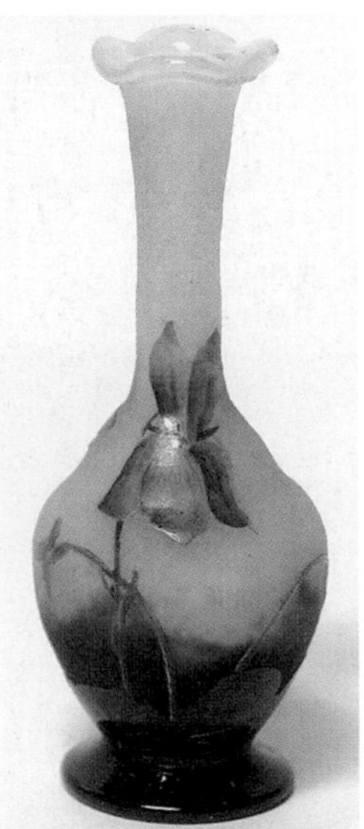

► A Daum miniature glass vase, with acid-etched and enamelled decoration, signed, French, Nancy, c1905, 4in (10cm) high.
£2,450–2,750
€3,600–4,000
$4,450–5,000 ⊞ MI

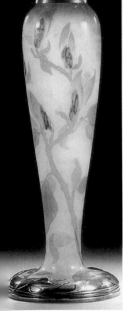

‹n Emile Gallé silver-‹ounted glass vase, ‹arved with magnolia ‹oughs, etched mark, ‹rench, Nancy, late 19thC, ‹8¼in (46.5cm) high.
‹1,250–1,500
‹1,850–2,200
‹2,250–2,700 ⚒ S(O)

An Emile Gallé glass vase, moulded with cherries and leaves, signed, French, c1900, 11½in (29cm) high.
£5,200–6,200
€7,600–9,100
$9,400–11,200 ⚒ JAA

An Emile Gallé glass ‹ase, overlaid with a tree ‹nd a landscape, signed, ‹ench, c1900, 6½in ‹6.5cm) high.
‹80–1,150
‹,450–1,700
‹,750–2,100 ⚒ Bea

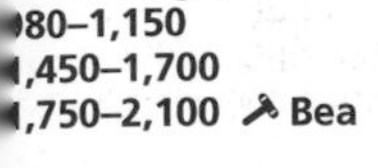

An Emile Gallé cameo glass vase, decorated with ferns, French, c1900, 4in (10cm) high.
£640–720 / €930–1,050
$1,150–1,300 ⊞ SAT

An Emile Gallé glass vase, decorated with ferns, signed, French, Nancy, 1908–14, 5in (12.5cm) high.
£560–670 / €820–980
$1,000–1,200 ⚒ DORO

An Emile Gallé glass vase, carved with trees and a landscape, signed, French, early 20thC, 7in (18cm) high.
£730–870 / €1,050–1,250
$1,300–1,550 ⚒ SWO

A Lamartine glass vase, etched and enamelled with rose trees, painted mark, French, early 20thC, 10¾in (27.5cm) high.
£780–930 / €1,150–1,350
$1,450–1,700 ⚒ S(O)

A pair of Lötz iridescent glass vases, decorated with Creta Papillon pattern, with silver overlay, Austrian, c1900, larger 9in (23cm) high.
£4,300–5,100
€6,300–7,400
$7,800–9,200 ⚒ S
The silver overlay has added greatly to the value. Without it the vases would have been less popular because mottled iridescent Lötz glass is commonly found.

A Lötz iridescent glass vase, decorated with Phänomen pattern, signed, Austrian, c1900, 5¼in (13.5cm) high.
£1,600–1,900
€2,300–2,750
$2,900–3,450 ⚒ DORO

A Muller Frères cameo glass vase, overlaid with blossoms and leaves, signed, c1910, 6¼in (16cm) high.
£1,100–1,300
€1,600–1,900
$2,000–2,350 ⚒ JAA

A Muller Frères glass vase with etched decoration, signed, French, c1920, 14in (35.5cm) high.
£4,300–4,800
€6,300–7,000
$7,800–8,700 ⊞ MI

A Quezal iridescent glass vase, after the Tiffany model 'Jack in the Pulpit', engraved mark, American, early 20thC, 9½in (24cm) high.
£2,000–2,400
€2,900–3,500
$3,600–4,350 ⚒ S(O)

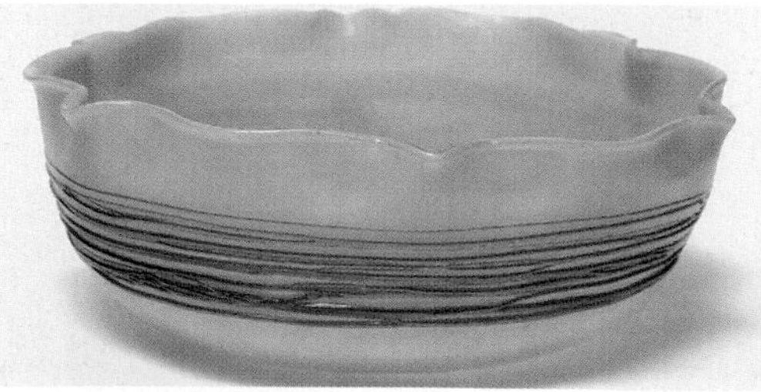

A Palme-König glass bowl, Bohemian, c1910, 11in (28cm) wide.
£230–260 / €340–380
$420–470 ⊞ WAC
Palme-König was established in Bohemia in 1786. From c1900 they produced good-quality Art Nouveau iridescent glass wares using forms pioneered by Lötz. A distinctive feature of Palme-König wares is the use of trailing raised decoration as seen on this bowl.

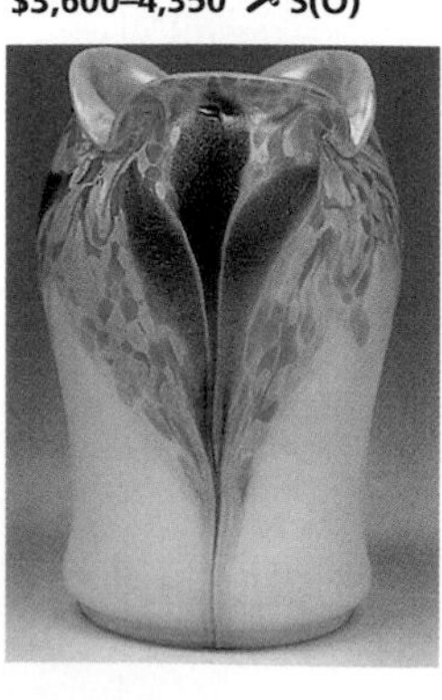

► **An iridescent glass vase,** with applied decoration, Bohemian, c1905, 6¼in (16cm) high.
£950–1,100 / €1,350–1,600
$1,700–2,000 ⚒ DORO

A glass vase, etched and enamelled with lilies, early 20thC, 6in (15cm) high.
£720–860 / €1,050–1,25[illegible]
$1,300–1,550 ⚒ S(O)

Art Nouveau Jewellery

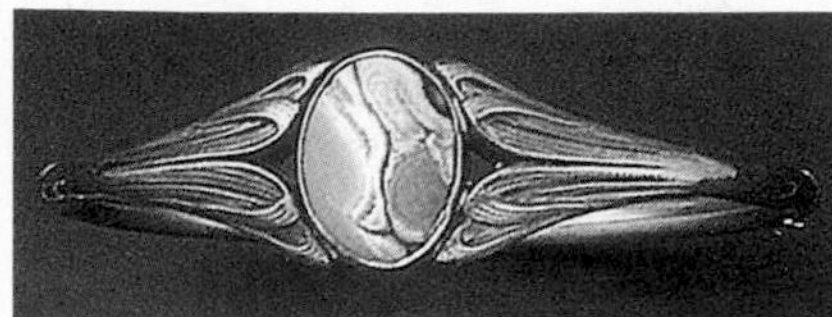

A 14ct gold bangle, by Sloan & Co, set with a turquoise cabochon flanked by stylized lotus blossoms, American, dated 1887.
£580–690 / €850–1,000
$1,050–1,250 ⚒ SK(B)

A silver brooch, by William Haseler, set with an amethyst, 1900, 1½in (4cm) wide.
£220–250 / €320–360
$400–450 ⊞ ANO

A 18ct gold and platinum brooch/pendant, set with diamonds, c1905, in a fitted velvet box.
£2,100–2,500
€3,050–3,650
$3,800–4,550 ⚒ L

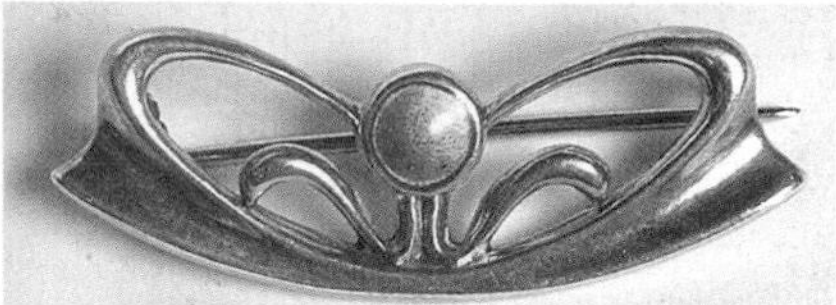

An enamel and silver brooch, by Charles Horner, Chester 1908, 2in (5cm) wide.
£130–145 / €190–210
$230–260 ⊞ HTE

Charles Horner worked in Halifax and specialized in relatively inexpensive, mass-produced jewellery in simple geometric designs, similar to those produced by Liberty & Co.

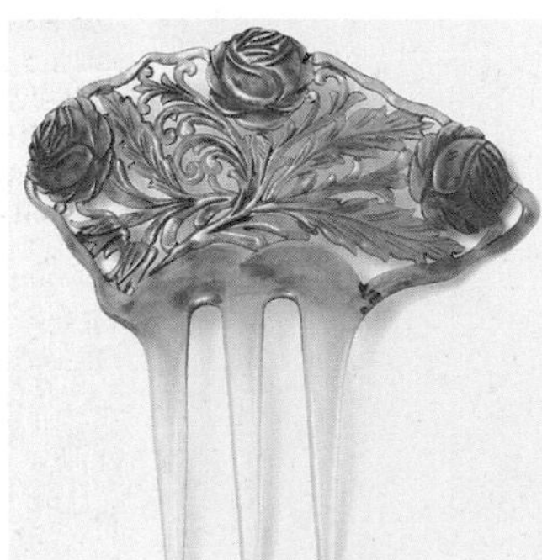

◄ A horn hair comb, carved with roses, c1900, 6in (15cm) high.
£165–185 / €240–270
$300–330 ⊞ TDG

► A *plique-à-jour* and enamel pendant, German, 1900–05, 1¾in (4.5cm) long.
£610–680 / €890–990
$1,100–1,250 ⊞ ANO

A gold and *plique-à-jour* pendant, by Lalique, in the form of a female head with long hair, set with a sapphire, slight damage, signed, French, c1900, 2½in (6.5cm) long.
£35,900–43,000
€53,000–63,000
$65,000–78,000 ⚒ BUK

Lalique began his career as a jewellery designer. For Lalique glassware please see our special feature on pages 478–480.

A silver and enamel pendant, by Murrle Bennet, designed by Archibald Knox, maker's mark, c1905, 1½in (4cm) long, with original chain.
£850–950 / €1,250–1,400
$1,500–1,700 ⊞ DAD

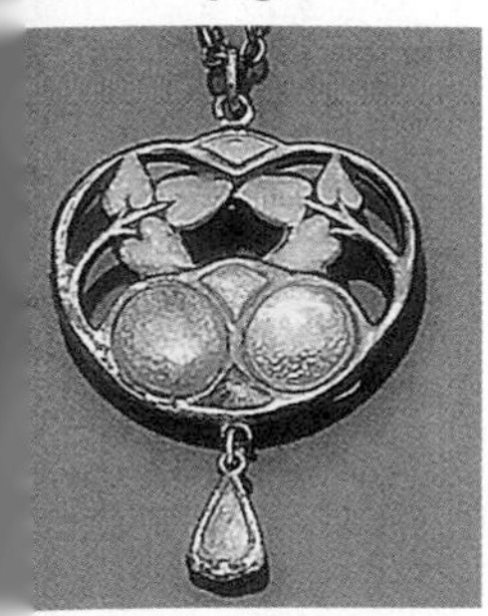

An enamel and silver pendant, by Charles Horner, with pierced decoration, Chester 1909.
£280–330 / €400–480
$500–600 ⚒ TEN

A silver and enamel pendant, by Charles Horner, Chester 1909, 1¾in (4.5cm) long.
£180–200 / €260–290
$320–360 ⊞ ANO

DECORATIVE ARTS

Art Nouveau Lighting

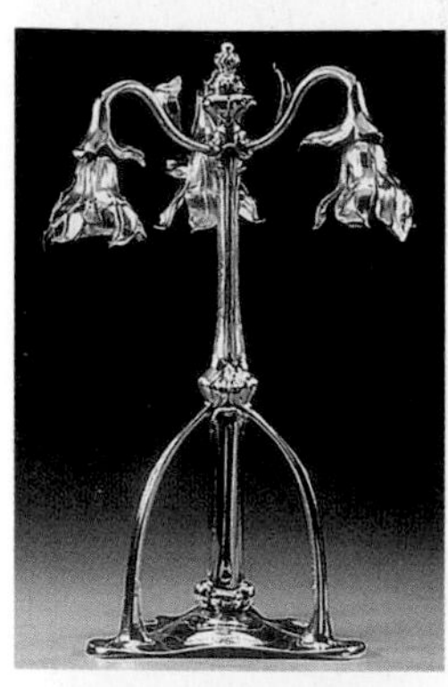

◄ **An Argentor pewter table lamp,** with brass arms, stamped mark, German, c1900, 21in (53.5cm) high.
£3,600–4,300
€5,300–6,300
$6,500–7,800 ⚒ S(O)

A Daum glass and iron table lamp, signed, cross of Lorraine to shade, French, Nancy, c1910, 13½in (34.5cm) high.
£4,400–5,200
€6,400–7,600
$8,000–9,400 ⚒ DORO

A bronze figural lamp, by Maurice Bouval, in the form of a naked maiden, signed, French, c1900, 10¾in (27.5cm) high.
£2,850–3,400
€4,150–4,950
$5,200–6,200 ⚒ S(O)
Maurice Bouval is best known for his figural lamps and busts of women, in a style very similar to that of Alphonse Mucha. His subjects give the impression of merging with nature and are often entwined or draped in foliage, and typically have closed eyes. Bouval also produced inkwells, covered boxes, pin trays and other useful objects, usually in bronze.

A glass table lamp, by Moe Bridges, reverse-painted with a forest scene, signed, American, Milwaukee, c1925, 20¼in (51.5cm) high.
£900–1,050 / €1,300–1,550
$1,600–1,900 ⚒ SK

A bronze and glass table lamp, by Jefferson, decorated with hollyhocks, shade No. 1884, maker's stamp, American, west Virginia, c1915, 21¼in (54cm) high.
£1,600–1,900
€2,300–2,750
$2,900–3,450 ⚒ SK

A de Vez glass and metal lamp, decorated with acid-etched flowering twigs, signed, French, c1910, 14¾in (37.5cm) high.
£2,900–3,450
€4,200–5,000
$5,200–6,200 ⚒ DORO
De Vez produced a wide range of cameo glass at the turn of the last century, much of it less expensive to buy than Gallé pieces.

◄ **A pair of gilt-bronze and glass figural wall lights,** by G. de Kervéguen, entitled 'Boule de Savon', each in the form of a young boy blowing bubbles, signed, French, c1900, 9in (23cm) wide.
£8,600–10,300 / €12,600–15,000
$15,600–18,600 ⚒ S

Further reading

Miller's Art Nouveau & Art Deco Buyer's Guide, Miller's Publications, 1999

A Louis Majorelle/Daum glass and gilt-bronze five-arm chandelier, signed, cross of Lorraine, French, Nancy, c1900, 29¾in (75.5cm) wide.
£5,200–6,200 / €7,600–9,100
$9,400–11,200 ⚒ DORO

► **A Wiener Werkstätte silver-plated brass and glass hanging lamp,** by Koloman Moser, Austrian, Vienna, designed 1903, shade 8in (20.5cm) high.
£8,200–9,800 / €12,000–14,300
$14,800–17,700 ⚒ DORO

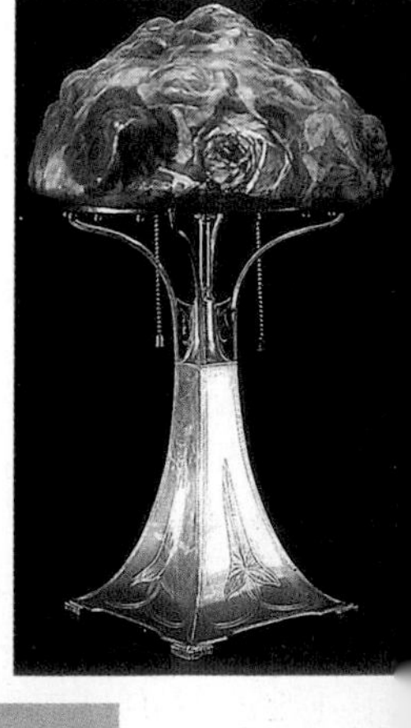

► **A Pairpoint glass and silvered lamp,** reverse-painted with roses, stamped mark, American, c1910, 20in (51cm) high.
£5,800–6,900
€8,500–10,100
$10,500–12,500 ⚒ JAA

◄ **A brass and vaseline glass hanging lamp,** possibly by James Powell of Whitefriars, c1900, 11in (28cm) high.
£640–760
€930–1,100
$1,200–1,400
⚒ DN(BR)

DECORATIVE ARTS

A spelter lamp, by Scotte, foundry mark, French, c1900, 12in (30.5cm) high.
£540–600 / €790–880
$980–1,100 ⊞ ASP

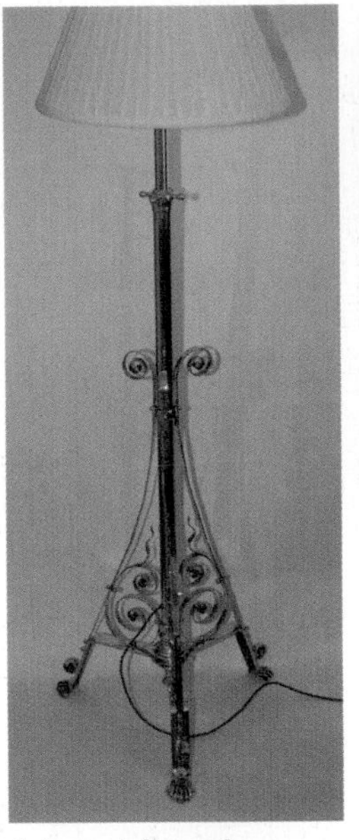

A brass telescopic standard lamp, 1900–10, 58in (147.5cm) high.
£175–195 / €260–290
$310–350 ⊞ JeH

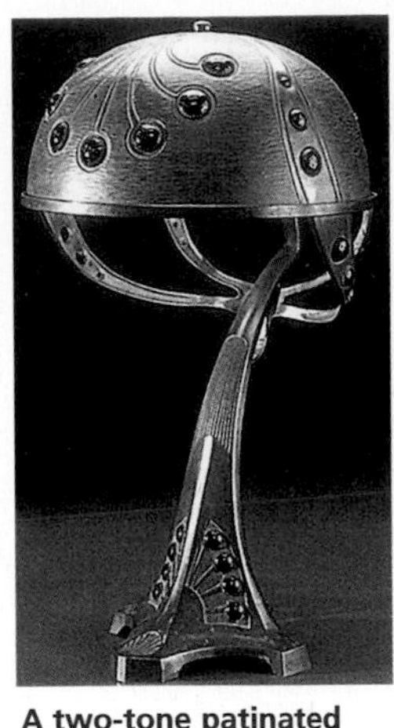

A two-tone patinated bronze table lamp, inset with ruby glass cabochons, one missing, probably Austrian, c1900, 22in (56cm) high.
£1,900–2,250
€2,750–3,300
$3,400–4,050 ⚒ JAA

A brass table lamp, the glass shade above a stem wrapped with a tendril, shade reduced, c1900, 22in (56cm) high.
£1,050–1,250
€1,550–1,850
$1,900–2,250 ⚒ S(O)

DECORATIVE ARTS

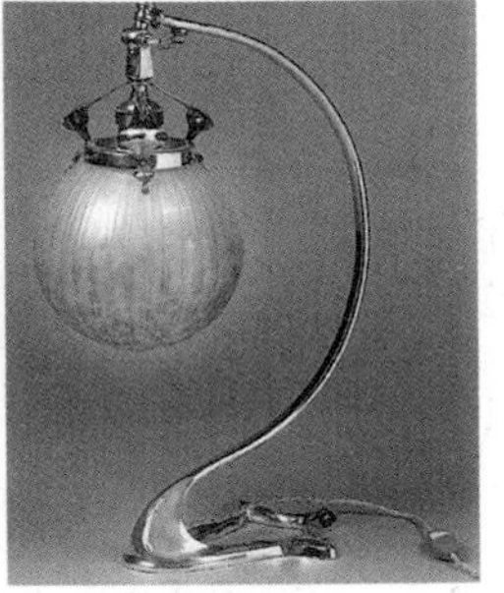

A brass and opalescent glass table lamp, Bohemian, 1900–10, 17in (43cm) high.
£950–1,100
€1,350–1,600
$1,700–2,000 ⚒ DORO

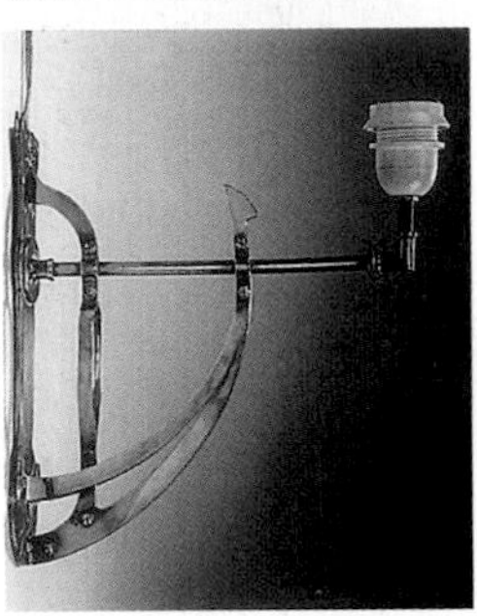

◄ A brass gas wall lamp, fitted for electricity, Dutch, shade missing, c1905, 12in (30.5cm) high.
£1,100–1,300
€1,600–1,900
$2,000–2,350
⚒ S(Am)

A pair of brass twin-branch wall lights, c1910, 14in (35.5cm) high.
£1,100–1,250 / €1,600–1,800
$2,000–2,250 ⊞ CHA

Tiffany & Co

A Tiffany Favrile glass flower bowl, decorated with a band of leaves, engraved mark, American, early 20thC, 12½in (32cm) wide.
£1,300–1,550 / €1,900–2,250
$2,350–2,800 ⚒ S(O)

A Tiffany Favrile glass and bronze box, decorated with grapevines, damaged, American, c1900, 6¾in (17cm) wide.
£280–330 / €400–480
$500–600 ⚒ JAA

A Tiffany bronze box, American, New York, c1915, 5in (12.5cm) wide.
£570–640 / €830–930
$1,000–1,150 ⊞ TDG

◄ A Tiffany silver and metal Japanese-style creamer, by Edward C. Moore, with applied gold and copper fruit and insects, pierced handle, marked, American, c1878, 4¼in (11cm) high.
£10,600–12,700
€15,500–18,500
$19,200–23,000 ⚒ S(NY)

A Tiffany copper and silver two-handled cup, etched with poppies, marked, American, c1900, 9¾in (25cm) high.
£4,300–5,100 / €6,300–7,500
$7,700–9,200 ⚒ S(NY)

A Tiffany silver photograph frame, engraved with daisy heads and tied ribbons, American, 1907–47, 9in (23cm) high.
£1,400–1,650
€2,000–2,400
$2,500–3,000 ⚒ S(O)

A Tiffany patinated bronze and leaded glass table lamp, stamped mark, American, c1890, 23¾in (60.5cm) high.
£9,200–11,000
€13,400–16,100
$16,700–19,900 ⚒ S(NY)

A Tiffany Favrile glass and patinated-bronze counter-balance table lamp, engraved and stamped marks, American, c1900, 14¾in (37.5cm) high.
£5,300–6,300
€7,700–9,200
$9,600–11,400 ⚒ S(NY)

A Tiffany patinated-bronze and glass counter-balance table lamp, stamped marks, American, early 20thC, 17in (43cm) high.
£1,500–1,800
€2,200–2,650
$2,700–3,250 ⚒ LHA

A Tiffany glass and bronze lamp, decorated with poinsettias, with later pulls, stamped marks, American, early 20thC, 22in (56cm) high.
£25,900–31,000
€38,000–45,000
$47,000–56,000 ⚒ SK

◄ **A Tiffany Favrile glass and bronze lamp shade,** applied and impressed marks, American, c1900, 24in (61cm) diam.
£11,400–13,600
€16,600–19,900
$20,600–24,600 ⚒ S

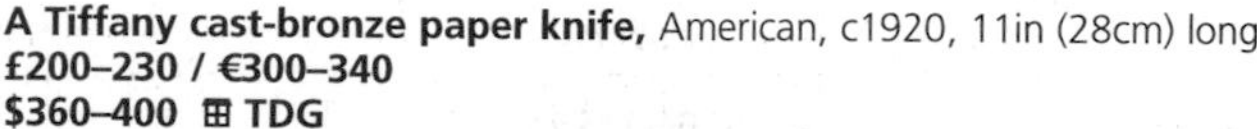

A Tiffany cast-bronze paper knife, American, c1920, 11in (28cm) long.
£200–230 / €300–340
$360–400 ⊞ TDG

A Tiffany cast-bronze pen tray, decorated with entwined tendrils, signed, American, c1920, 10in (25.5cm) long.
£340–380 / €500–550
$620–690 ⊞ TDG

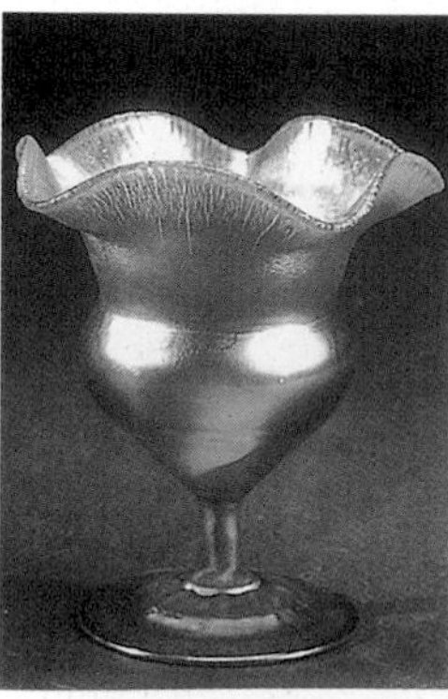

A Tiffany Favrile iridescent glass vase, inscribed mark, American, c1900, 4¾in (12cm) high.
£410–490 / €600–720
$740–890 ⚒ JAA

A Tiffany silver scent bottle, American, c1907, 4¼in (11cm) high.
£850–950 / €1,250–1,400
$1,500–1,700 ⊞ SHa

◄ **A Tiffany Favrile iridescent glass vase,** moulded with vertical bands and incised with a wavy line, engraved mark, American, early 20thC, 19in (48.5cm) high.
£3,100–3,700
€4,550–5,400
$5,600–6,700 ⚒ S(O)

A Tiffany Favrile glazed earthenware vase, decorated with poppies, incised and engraved marks, American, c1910, 8½in (21.5cm) high.
£11,200–13,400
€16,400–19,600
$20,300–24,300 ⚒ S(NY)

Art Nouveau Metalware

A silver-plated and glass biscuit barrel, by Barrett of Piccadilly, with a Japanese-style carved ivory knop, signed, c1900, 7½in (19cm) high.
£580–650 / €850–950
$1,050–1,200 ⊞ JSG

A WMF silver-plated and etched-glass biscuit barrel, German, c1906, 6in (15cm) high.
£310–350 / €450–510
$560–630 ⊞ NAW

A silver bowl, in the form of an orchid, American, c1900, 3in (7.5cm) wide.
£120–135 / €175–195
$210–240 ⊞ ANO

A silver bowl, embossed with stylized tulips, maker's mark HE, Sheffield 1902, 7in (18cm) diam.
£240–280 / €350–400
$430–500 ⚒ SWO

► A WMF silver-plated bowl, with glass liner, c1905, 9in (23cm) diam.
£630–700 / €900–1,000
$1,100–1,250 ⊞ TDG

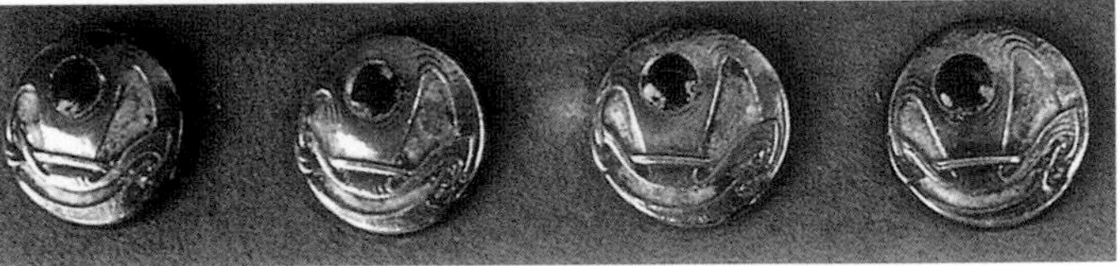

A set of six Liberty & Co silver and enamel buttons, by W. H. Haseler, each decorated with a stylized motif, Birmingham 1905, cased.
£470–560 / €690–820
$850–1,000 ⚒ RTo

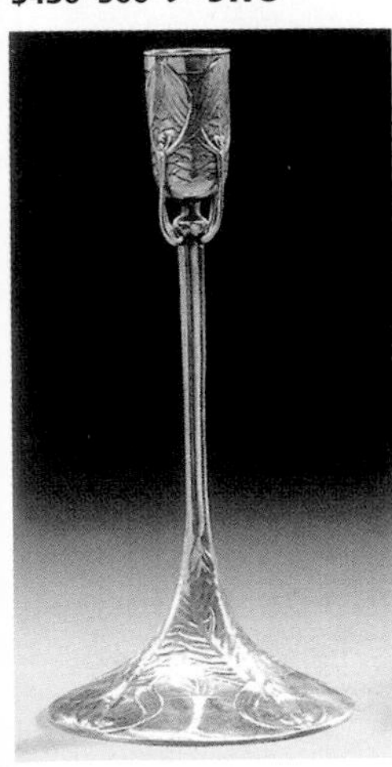

A pair of Gallia silvered-metal candlesticks, designed by Emile Gallé, cast with foliage, stamped mark, French, c1906, ½in (24cm) high.
£1,300–1,550
€1,900–2,250
$2,350–2,800 ⚒ S(O)

► A pair of Kayserzinn pewter candlesticks, possibly by Hugo Leven, with later sconces, marked, German, c1902, 16½in (42cm) high.
£660–790 / €960–1,150
$1,200–1,450 ⚒ S(O)

Kayserzinn was established in 1896 at Krefeld-Bochum near Düsseldorf in Germany by J. P. Kayser & Söhn. The company produced art pewter but unlike WMF they did not electroplate their wares, so they were more akin to ordinary pewter. They used a strong, malleable alloy of tin, copper and antimony to achieve a high standard of casting, which gave a fine silvery shine when polished. The majority of wares were in Jugendstil (German 'youth art' style) and were in turn the inspiration for Liberty & Co's Tudric range.

► A pair of silver candlesticks, Chester 1902 and 1904, maker's mark JMB, 5¾in (14.5cm) high.
£300–360 / €440–530
$540–650 ⚒ SWO

A pair of Liberty & Co pewter candlesticks, c1905, 5in (12.5cm) high.
£540–600 / €760–860
$980–1,100 ⊞ HABA

A silver card case, embossed with poppies, seed pods and swirling foliage, with leather compartments, marked H&A, Birmingham 1900, 4in (10cm) wide.
£165–195 / €240–290
$300–360 ⚒ DN

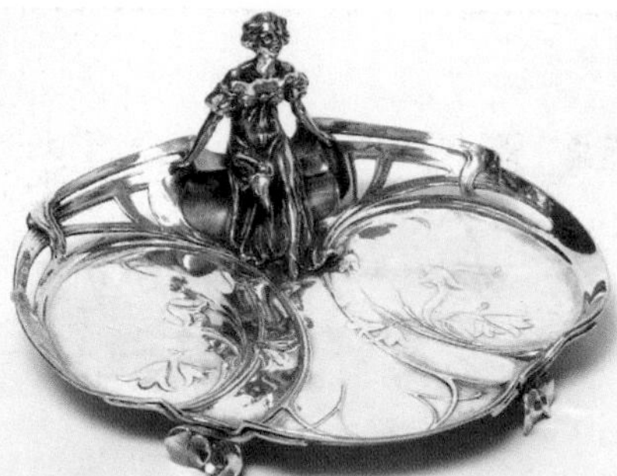

A WMF polished pewter card tray, German, c1900, 10in (25.5cm) wide.
£520–580 / €760–850
$940–1,050 ⊞ WAC

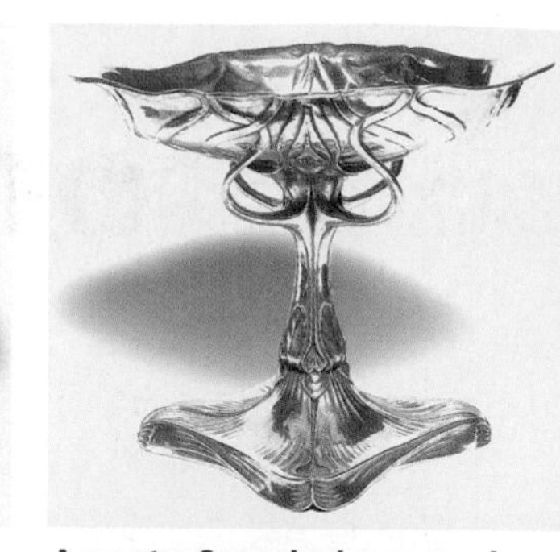

A pewter Secessionist centrepiece, Austrian, c1900, 8in (20.5cm) high.
£300–330 / €430–480
$540–600 ⊞ NAW

A WMF pewter and glass figural centrepiece, the vase and dish engraved with foliage, the stem in the form of a maiden, stamped marks, German, early 20thC, 24in (61cm) high.
£3,100–3,700
€4,550–5,400
$5,600–6,700 ⚒ S(O)

A silver cigarette case, with relief decoration of a woman and waves, marked '925', 1900, 2¾in (7cm) wide.
£260–310 / €380–450
$470–560 ⚒ DuM

A silver tea and coffee service, comprising five pieces, by the Mauser Manufacturing Co, New York, decorated with repoussé spiral gadroons and pansies, American, c1900, coffee pot 11in (28cm) high, 82oz.
£1,250–1,500 / €1,850–2,200
$2,250–2,700 ⚒ NOA

► A Liberty & Co pewter crumb scoop, by Archibald Knox, c1905, 9in (23cm) wide.
£260–290 / €380–420
$470–520 ⊞ HABA

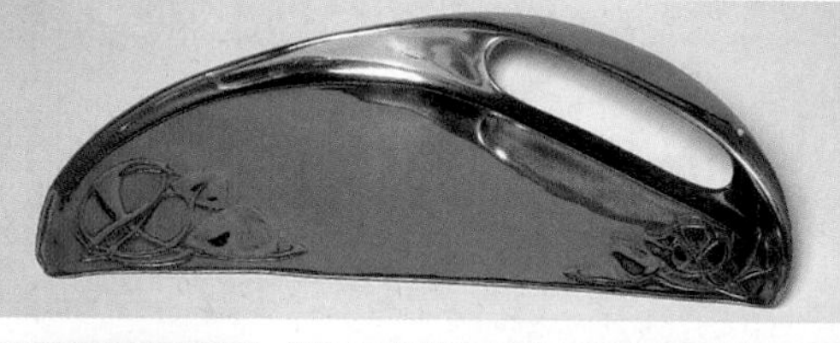

A silver-gilt-mounted glass decanter, with etched decoration, French, c1900, 10in (25.5cm) high, with six matching glasses.
£760–860 / €1,100–1,250
$1,400–1,550 ⊞ ANO

A bronze dish, by Auguste Ledru, cast with a naked female reclining on the moon, signed, stamped marks, French, 1894, 20in (51cm) wide.
£1,300–1,550 / €1,900–2,250
$2,350–2,800 ⚒ S(O)

A silver-mounted oak photograph frame, by Charles Green & Co, embossed with a girl picking apples from a tree, Birmingham 1903, 9½in (24cm) high.
£1,050–1,250 / €1,550–1,850
$1,900–2,250 ⚒ G(L)

► A Liberty & Co silver photograph frame, by William Hutton & Sons, London 1903, 7¼in (18.5cm) wide.
£1,600–1,800
€2,350–2,650
$2,900–3,250 ⊞ RICC

An Orivit pewter and glass inkwell, German, c1905, 12in (30.5cm) wide.
£180–200 / €260–310
$320–360 ⊞ NAW

A Kayserzinn silvered-pewter inkwell, in the form of a speeding car with a hinged boot, the inkwell under the bonnet, German, early 20thC, 16in (40.5cm) wide.
£2,400–2,850 / €3,500–4,150
$4,350–5,200 ⚒ S

► A copper jardinière and stand, c1870, 44in (112cm) high.
£1,400–1,600 / €2,100–2,350
$2,600–2,900 ⊞ DaM

A Orivit pewter-mounted ceramic jardinière, impressed marks, slight damage, c1900, 12½in (32cm) diam.
£590–700 / €840–1,000
$1,050–1,250 ⚒ RTo

A pewter plaque, signed 'A. M. Peche', c1910, 9in (23cm) wide.
£100–115 / €145–175
$180–210 ⊞ LBr

A Liberty & Co Tudric pewter jug and cover, by Archibald Knox, 1900–03, 5in (12.5cm) high.
£320–360 / €470–530
$580–650 ⊞ STRA

► A cast-iron panel, by Hector Guimard, cast with stylized foliage and whiplash motifs, early 20thC, 32¾in (83cm) high.
£5,400–6,400
€7,900–9,300
$9,800–11,600 ⚒ S

Hector Guimard (1867–1942) was a member of the Paris School, an architect and a craftsman who is perhaps most famous for his designs in iron for entrances to the Paris Metro stations. He also designed the interiors of some of his buildings. His furniture was rather more sculptural in form than that of the other Paris designers.

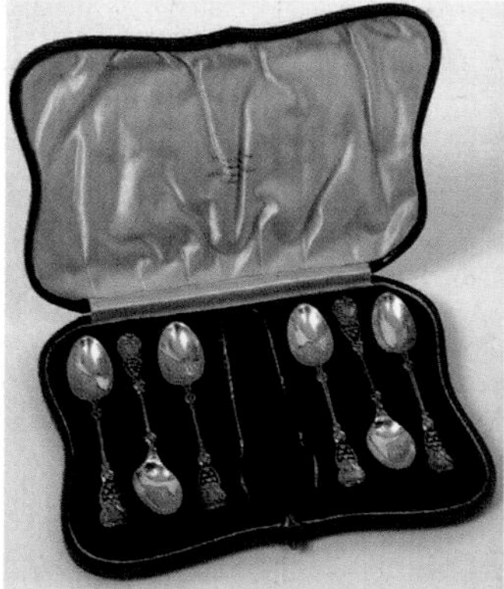

A set of six silver teaspoons, pierced and decorated with stylized tulips, with a pair of matching sugar tongs, Sheffield 1905, cased.
£105–125 / €155–185
$190–220 ⚒ CHTR

A Clement Massier enamel vase, French, c1900, 28in (71cm) high.
£850–950
€1,250–1,400
$1,500–1,700
⊞ ANO

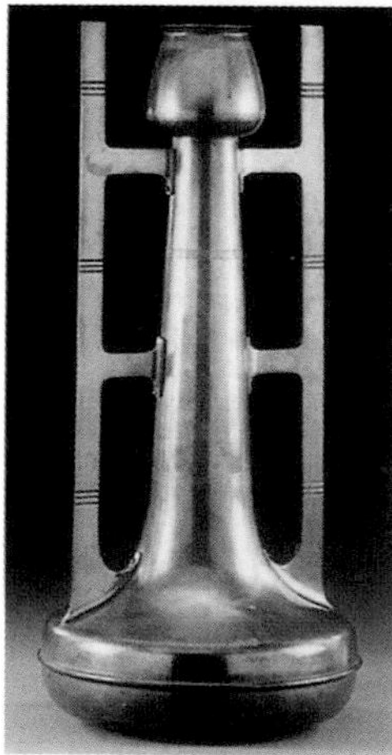

◄ A brass vase, by Gustave Serrurier-Bovy, Belgian, c1905, 21¼in (54cm) high.
£1,050–1,250
€1,550–1,850
$1,900–2,250 ⚒ S(O)

► A Liberty & Co Tudric pewter vase, by Archibald Knox, c1910, 12in (30.5cm) high.
£1,250–1,400
€1,850–2,050
$2,250–2,550
⊞ HTE

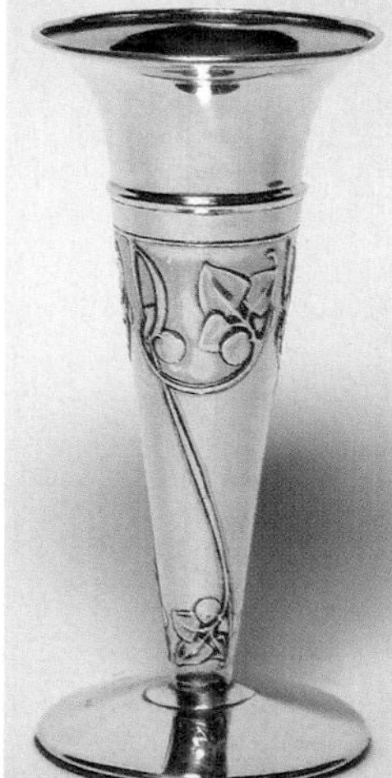

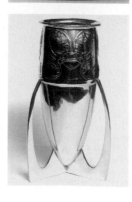

A Liberty & Co silver flower vase, by Archibald Knox, embossed with stylized foliage and berries, 1907, 6in (15cm) high.
£810–900 / €1,200–1,350
$1,450–1,650 ⊞ DAD

A WMF Secessionist hammered-brass vase, with incised banding and stylized enamel flowerheads, slight damage, stamped stork mark, German, early 20thC, 6½in (16.5cm) high.
£105–125 / €155–185
$190–210 ⚒ PFK

Art Deco Ceramics

A Boch Frères pottery vase, French, c1930, 14½in (37cm) high.
£5,100–6,100
€7,400–8,900
$9,200–11,000 SK

A Burleigh ware pottery charger, by Charlotte Rhead, c1930, 14in (35.5cm) diam.
£3,650–4,350 / €5,300–6,400
$6,600–7,900 AH
This is a very strong price for Charlotte Rhead and it shows that collectors are keen to acquire a rare design.

A Carlton Ware jardinière, decorated with Mikado pattern, printed mark, painted No. 2881, 1920s, 8½in (21.5cm) high.
£165–195 / €240–280
$300–360 PFK
Standard Carlton patterns are inexpensive when compared to the rarities

◄ A Carter, Stabler & Adams vase, decorated with YT pattern, shape No. 769, late 1920s, 11in (28cm) high.
£940–1,050 / €1,350–1,550
$1,700–1,900 MMc

A Susie Cooper tea cup and saucer, decorated with Sea Anemone pattern, c1930, cup 2¼in (5.5cm) high.
£70–80 / €100–110
$125–140 RH
Pink colourways are very popular with Japanese collectors.

► A Goldscheider wall mask, Austrian, mid-1930s, 13in (33cm) high.
£580–650 / €850–950
$1,050–1,200 LLD
Wall masks, popular in the Art Deco period, were made by many companies, those by Goldscheider being the most desirable. This Viennese firm was founded in 1885 for the manufacture of porcelain, faïence and terracotta. Their output was prolific, and they mass-produced a whole range of figures in mainstream Art Nouveau style.

A pair of Ram earthenware Dun beaker vases, designed by T. A. C. Colenbrander and painted by W. Elstrodt, model No. 8, stamped, incised and painted marks, Dutch, 1923, 3¼in (8.5cm) high, with original factory boxes.
£2,250–2,700 / €3,300–3,950
$4,100–4,900 S(Am)

An Emile Lenoble pottery vase, artist's cypher to base, French, c1930, 9½in (24cm) high.
£1,150–1,350
€1,700–2,000
$2,100–2,450 SK

A Teco Art Pottery vase, by William Day Gates, model No. 431, stamped mark, American, c1910, 10¼in (26cm) high.
£8,600–10,300
€12,600–15,000
$15,600–18,600 S(NY)

A Wedgwood Fairyland lustre plate, by Daisy Makeig-Jones, decorated with Imps on Bridge pattern, c1920, 10½in (26.5cm) diam.
£3,950–4,400
€5,700–6,400
$7,100–8,000 POW
The market for Fairyland lustre wares is currently very strong in America.

A Wiener Keramik jar and cover, model No. 310, finial repaired, impressed marks, Austrian, 1910–12, 4¼in (11cm) high.
£760–910 / €1,100–1,300
$1,400–1,650 DORO

Clarice Cliff

A Clarice Cliff Bizarre biscuit barrel, decorated with Autumn pattern, with a cane handle, 1930–34, 6¼in (16cm) high.
£540–640 / €790–930
$980–1,150 L&E

A Clarice Cliff Bizarre bowl, decorated with Rhodanthe pattern, No. 55, c1934, 9in (23cm) diam.
£175–210 / €260–310
$320–380 DA

A Clarice Cliff jam pot, decorated with Blue Chintz pattern, c1930, 4in (10cm) high.
£500–550 / €720–800
$900–1,000 TDG

A Clarice Cliff Fantasque Bizarre bowl, decorated with Oasis pattern, printed mark, c1933, 9in (23cm) diam.
£280–330 / €410–480
$510–600 Bea

A Clarice Cliff Fantasque box and cover, decorated with Bobbins pattern, 1931–33, 5¾in (14.5cm) wide.
£300–360 / €440–530
$540–650 G(L)

◄ **A pair of Clarice Cliff Bizarre coffee cans and saucers,** 1930s, cans 3in (7.5cm) high.
£270–300 / €390–440
$490–540 NAW

A Clarice Cliff Lotus jug, decorated with Latona Bouquet pattern, painted and printed marks, c1930, 12in (30.5cm) high.
£1,900–2,250 / €2,750–3,300
$3,350–4,000 S(O)

A Clarice Cliff Fantasque fruit bowl, with silver-plated mounts, decorated with Tree and House pattern, c1930, 8in (20.5cm) diam.
£350–420 / €510–610
$630–760 GIL

A Clarice Cliff cake stand, decorated with Idyll pattern, on a metal stem, 1930s, 9in (23cm) diam.
£175–210 / €260–310
$320–380 PFK

A Clarice Cliff jam pot, decorated with Crocus pattern, c1930, 4in (10cm) diam.
£310–350 / €450–510
$560–630 TDG

A Clarice Cliff Bizarre Lotus jug, decorated with Rhodanthe pattern, printed mark, c1930, 7¾in (19.5cm) high.
£230–270 / €340–400
$420–500 DMC

A Clarice Cliff Biarritz plate, decorated with Aurea pattern, printed marks and facsimile signature, c1930, 9in (23cm) wide.
£175–210 / €260–310
$320–380 ⚒ SWO

A Clarice Cliff Bizarre plate, decorated with Melon pattern, printed and impressed marks, c1930, 8¾in (22cm) diam.
£230–270 / €340–400
$420–500 ⚒ CHTR

A Clarice Cliff Biarritz charger, decorated with Rhodanthe pattern, No. 6315, 1930s, 16¼in (41.5cm) wide.
£300–330 / €430–480
$540–600 ⊞ NAW

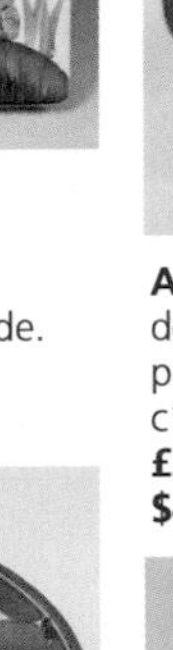

Further reading

Miller's Twentieth-Century Ceramics, 1999

◄ **A Clarice Cliff tazza,** decorated with Sunrise pattern, c1932, 9in (23cm) diam.
£900–1,000 / €1,300–1,450
$1,600–1,800 ⊞ MI

A Clarice Cliff Fantasque coffee service, comprising 12 pieces, decorated with Umbrella pattern, 1929–30.
£2,200–2,600 / €3,200–3,800
$4,000–4,700 ⚒ DD

A Clarice Cliff Bizarre Stamford tea-for-two, comprising ten pieces, decorated with Windbells pattern, one cup damaged, 1933–34.
£2,450–2,900 / €3,600–4,250
$4,400–5,200 ⚒ AG

A Clarice Cliff tea-for-two, decorated with Cowslip pattern, printed marks, 1933–34, teapot 5½in (14cm) high.
£2,400–2,850 / €3,500–4,150
$4,350–5,200 ⚒ S(O)

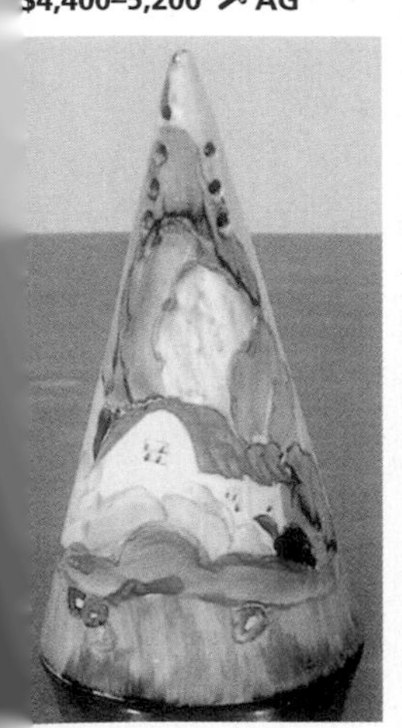

\ Clarice Cliff sugar aster, decorated with orest Glen pattern, narked, c1930, ½in (14cm) high.
560–670 / €820–980
1,000–1,200 ⚒ E

A Clarice Cliff Bizarre sugar caster, decorated with Alton pattern, c1934, 5¼in (13.5cm) high.
£560–670 / €820–980
$1,000–1,200 ⚒ HYD

A Clarice Cliff Bizarre vase, decorated with Geometric pattern, c1930, 6in (15cm) high.
£175–210 / €260–310
$320–380 ⚒ DMC

A Clarice Cliff vase, decorated with Newlyn pattern, c1934, 5in (12.5cm) high.
£1,000–1,100
€1,450–1,600
$1,800–2,000 ⊞ TDG

Art Deco Clocks & Watches

A spelter and onyx figural mantel clock, on a slate base, 1910–20, 25½in (65cm) wide.
£430–510 / €630–740
$780–920 ⚒ CHTR

A Wiener Werkstätte brass table clock, by Josef Hoffmann, with an enamel dial, movement by M. & Sohn, marked, Austrian, c1928, 9¾in (25cm) high.
£8,200–9,800 / €12,000–14,300
$14,800–17,700 ⚒ DORO

An Asprey & Co silver-mounted tortoiseshell clock, with an inscribed plaque, London 1915, 4in (10cm) high.
£900–1,050
€1,300–1,550
$1,600–1,900 ⚒ S(O)

An enamel clock, c1920, 4¾in (12cm) wide.
£580–650 / €850–950
$1,050–1,200 ⊞ SHa

► A platinum watch, set with onyx and diamonds, with a silvered dial, the two onyx panels each set with a diamond, the rope-twist strap joined by a row of diamonds to either side, c1925, 1in (2.5cm) wide.
£1,300–1,550
€1,900–2,250
$2,350–2,800
⚒ S

◄ A bronze figural clock, by Josef Lorenzl, on an onyx plinth, signed, Austrian, c1930, 11¼in (28.5cm) high.
£8,400–10,000 / €12,300–14,600
$15,000–18,100 ⚒ S(O)

Art Deco Furniture

A pair of bedside cabinets, 25in (63.5cm) high.
£880–980 / €1,300–1,450
$1,600–1,800 ⊞ DOA

► A chrome and leather armchair, with carved wooden armrests, with *faux* veneer and inlay, c1925.
£230–270 / €340–400
$420–500 ⚒ PFK

◄ An Asprey & Co mahogany drinks cabinet, c1930, 23in (58.5cm) high.
£1,200–1,350
€1,750–1,950
$2,150–2,450 ⊞ TDG

An oak kitchen cabinet, the upper section with three cupboards with etched glazed doors, the base with three cupboards and drawers and an enamel work surface, 1930s, 40in (101.5cm) wide.
£630–700 / €900–1,000
$1,100–1,250 ⊞ B&R

A pair of bird's-eye maple-veneered side cabinets, each with an inset marble top above a door set with a carved owl and enclosing adjustable shelves, French, c1930, 26½in (67.5cm) wide.
£3,600–4,300
€5,300–6,300
$6,500–7,800 ⚒ S(O)

DECORATIVE ARTS

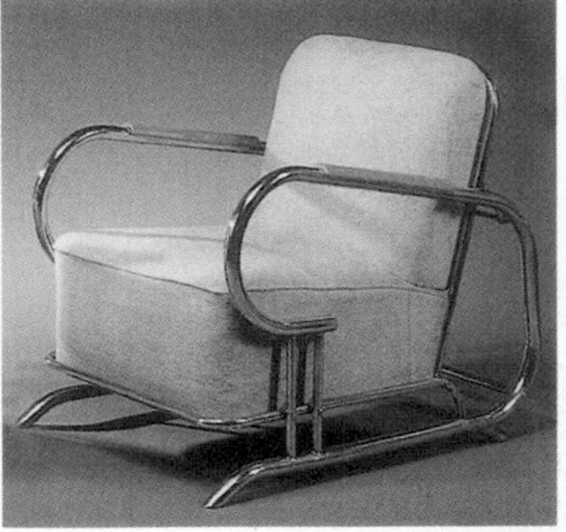

A chrome-plated tubular steel and upholstery armchair, with wooden arm rests and adjustable back rest, 1930s.
£1,750–2,100 / €2,550–3,050
$3,150–3,800 S(Am)

A walnut desk, with leather top and ebonized handles, c1930, 47in (119.5cm) wide.
£1,650–1,850 / €2,400–2,700
$3,000–3,350 ⊞ TDG

An oak dressing table and stool, c1930, 49in (124.5cm) wide.
£450–500 / €660–730
$810–910 ⊞ HEM

A sycamore and glass dressing table and stool, by Betty Joel, with articulated mirrored drawers, c1932, 59in (150cm) wide.
£4,300–4,800
€6,300–7,000
$7,800–8,700 ⊞ DeP

A vellum-covered dressing table and stool, French School, the dressing table with glass shelves and three drawers, c1930, 46¾in (119cm) wide.
£4,300–5,100
€6,300–7,400
$7,800–9,200 S

For further information on
Furniture see page 460

A chrome mirror, 1920s, 36in (91.5cm) wide.
£310–350 / €450–510
$560–630 ⊞ MARK

A satin-birch sideboard, inlaid with mother-of-pearl and mounted with three gilt-bronze stylized female figures, the two doors with parquetry inlay flanked by two further doors enclosing a sycamore interior and chequer-inlaid shelves, French, c1940, 91in (231cm) wide.
£3,800–4,550 / €5,500–6,600
$6,900–8,200 S(O)

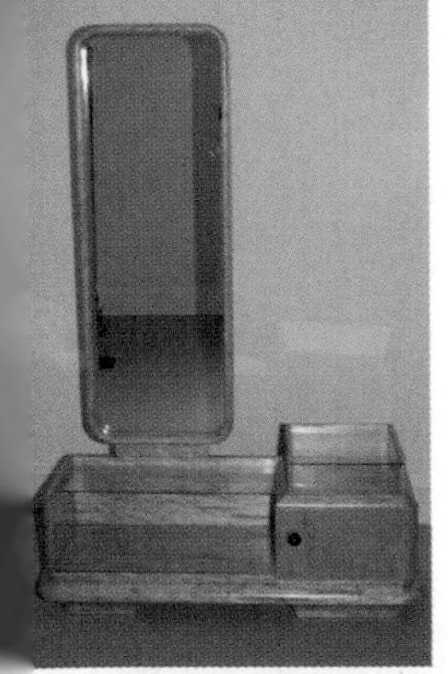

◄ **A birch-veneered cheval mirror,** Continental, c1930, 68in (172.5cm) high.
£990–1,100
€1,450–1,600
$1,800–2,000 ⊞ WAA

◄ **A leather and nickel-plated metal sofa and two lacquered-wood end tables,** probably by Paul T. Frankl for Frankl Galleries, American, New York, 1930s, 96¼in (244.5cm) wide.
£6,600–7,900
€9,600–11,500
$11,900–14,300 S(NY)

An ebonized oak and parcel-gilt dining room suite, by Restol, comprising a court cupboard, draw-leaf table, four chairs and two carvers, 1930s, table 78in (198cm) wide.
£440–520 / €640–760
$800–940 DN

A walnut coffee table, with an undertier, 1930s, 27in (68.5cm) wide.
£640–760 / €930–1,100
$1,200–1,400 SWO

A walnut nest of four tables, c1930, 30in (76cm) diam.
£1,300–1,450 / €1,900–2,100
$2,350–2,600 ⊞ TDG

A walnut drinks table, the rising central section with a bottle holder, c1930, 30in (76cm) diam.
£1,000–1,150
€1,450–1,650
$1,800–2,100 ⊞ TDG

For further information on Twentieth-Century Design see pages 491–502

A burr-elm-veneered coffee table, stamped '14 7 37B', Swedish, c1930, 21¾in (55.5cm) wide.
£360–430 / €530–630
$650–780 ⚒ S(O)

A burr-maple extending dining table, by Hille, each twin support with scroll legs, ivorine label for S. Hille & Co, c1935, 97¼in (247cm) extended.
£1,800–2,150 / €2,650–3,150
$3,250–3,900 ⚒ S(O)

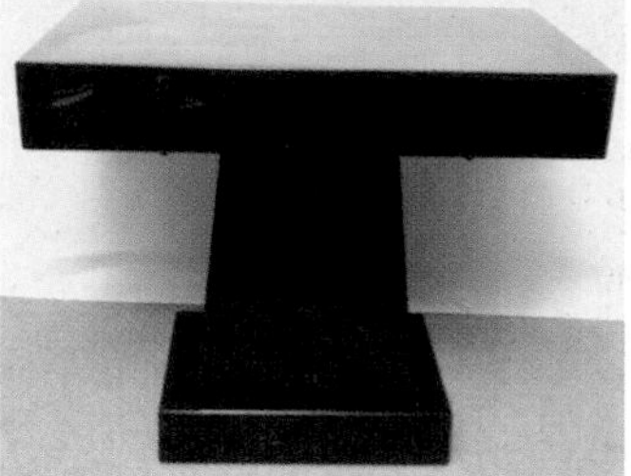

A mahogany Champagne table, the interior with a stained mahogany bucket, c1935, 30in (76cm) wide.
£1,350–1,500 / €1,950–2,200
$2,450–2,700 ⊞ TDG

◄ **A pair of acacia and burrwood console tables,** marked 'Sans Epoque/Robsjohn-Gibbings', American, c1937, 30in (76cm) wide.
£3,300–3,950 €4,800–5,700
$6,000–7,100 ⚒ S(NY

A leather and Lucite writing table, by Jansen, with three frieze drawers, c1940, 71in (180.5cm) wide.
£39,000–44,000 / €57,000–64,000
$71,000–80,000 ⊞ NART

Jansen was a French design house established in the mid-19th century that produced glamorous furniture. Lucite is a type of solid, transparent plastic, often used instead of glass. This piece would be of particular appeal to an interior designer, with its unusual appearance and good size.

Art Deco Glass

◄ **An Argy-Rousseau *pâte-de-verre* bowl,** decorated with a band of running gazelles, moulded mark, French, post-1928, 3¾in (9.5cm) diam.
£7,800–9,300
€11,400–13,600
$14,100–16,800 ⚒ S(O)

A Daum glass vase, with acid-etched decoration, France, Nancy, 1920s, 13½in (34.5cm) high.
£1,800–2,000
€2,600–2,900
$3,250–3,600 ⊞ TDG

A Daum glass vase, damaged, signed, cross of Lorraine, French, Nancy, c1930, 13in (33cm) high.
£1,350–1,500
€1,950–2,200
$2,450–2,700 ⊞ MI

A Daum glass vase, signed, cross of Lorraine, French, Nancy, c1930, 16in (40.5cm) high.
£2,150–2,400
€3,150–3,500
$3,900–4,350 ⊞ MI

A Degué cameo glass vase, with etched decoration, signed, French, early 20thC, 19½in (49.5cm) high.
£840–1,000 / €1,250–1,500
$1,500–1,800 ⚒ SK

► **A P. Gaillard *pâte-de-cristal* car mascot,** in the form of a stylized bird, on a lacquered wood base, signed, moulded mark, French, c1930, 9½in (24cm) high.
£2,850–3,400
€4,150–4,950
$5,200–6,200 ⚒ S

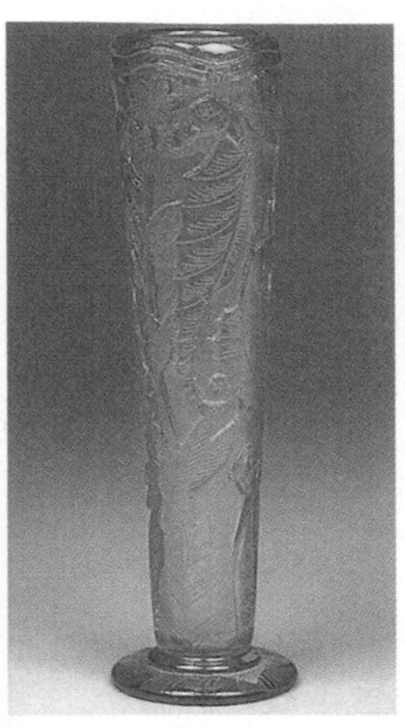

A Ludwig Moser & Söhne glass vase, by Heinrich Hussmann, decorated with seahorses, floral motifs and a snail, artist's monogram, factory mark, Czechoslovakian, Karlsbad, c1927, 9¾in (25cm) high.
£640–760 / €930–1,100
$1,200–1,400 DORO

A glass vase, designed by Michael Powolny and Otto Prutscher, decorated with bands and dots, Austrian, c1925, 8in (20.5cm) high.
£2,550–3,050
€3,700–4,450
$4,600–5,500 DORO

A Schneider glass vase, signed 'Le Verre Français', French, 1920, 13in (33cm) high.
£1,700–1,900
€2,500–2,750
$3,100–3,450 SAT

Charles Schneider founded the Verrerie Schneider in Epinay-sur-Seine near Paris in 1913. Many wares are signed 'Le Verre Français' or 'Charder'.

A Schneider cameo glass vase, signed 'Le Verre Français', French, c1925, 22in (56cm) high.
£4,850–5,400
€7,100–7,900
$8,800–9,800 MI

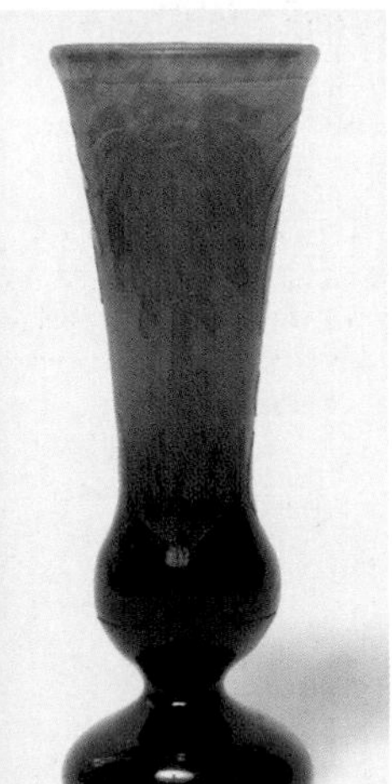

A Schneider glass, with acid-etched decoration, signed 'Le Verre Français', French, c1925, 7in (18cm) high.
£940–1,050 / €1,350–1,550
$1,700–1,900 MI

A Schneider glass vase, overlaid and etched with flowerheads and thorny fronds, signed 'Charder', cameo mark, incised Le Verre Français mark, French, c1928, 26¾in (68cm) high.
£3,600–4,300
€5,300–6,300
$6,500–7,800 S(O)

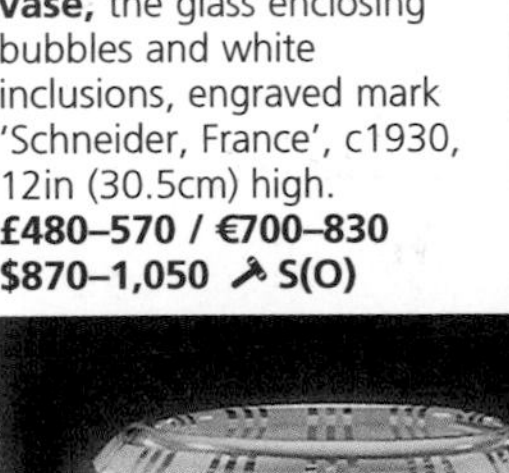

► **A Schneider glass vase,** the glass enclosing bubbles and white inclusions, engraved mark 'Schneider, France', c1930, 12in (30.5cm) high.
£480–570 / €700–830
$870–1,050 S(O)

◄ **A Schneider glass vase,** etched and polished with a stylized basket of fruit, with two handles, engraved mark 'Schneider', French, 1930s, 7in (18cm) high.
£840–1,000
€1,200–1,450
$1,500–1,800
S(O)

A Schneider glass vase, with inclusions and bubbles and two clear glass handles, etched mark 'Schneider, France', post-1930, 12in (30.5cm) high.
£840–1,000 / €1,200–1,450
$1,500–1,800 S(O)

A Verlys opalescent glass dish, moulded with three naked female figures and waves, moulded 'A. Verlys', French, c1930, 15½in (39.5cm) diam.
£660–790 / €960–1,150
$1,200–1,450 S(O)

A frosted glass charger, moulded with birds, French, c1903, 14in (35.5cm) diam.
£220–250 / €330–370
$400–450 NAW

Lalique

The career of René Lalique spanned both the Art Nouveau and Art Deco periods. He began designing jewellery in the 1890s and his reputation peaked in 1900 at the Universal Exhibition in Paris. His display of jewellery captured the style of Art Nouveau with its sinuous lines, imagery from nature and sensual portrayal of the female form. Lalique amazed some of his design contemporaries by using semi-precious stones and enamels in many of his designs rather than expensive diamonds and other precious stones.

By 1907, his attention had turned to the design of mass-produced glassware. He started with commercial scent bottles for François Coty and enlarged his repertoire in the 1920s to encompass vases, bowls, light fittings, car mascots, drinking wares and timepieces – in fact, any area in which commercial glassware was in demand. Nearly all his designs depicted organic form and the suggestion of movement, and his genius was being able to produce these designs in polished, opalescent and coloured glass that dazzled the eye when exposed to light.

René Lalique glass became popular again in the mid-1960s with the revival of interest in Art Nouveau and Art Deco. By the early 1970s, the London auction houses were holding specialist sales to showcase these two periods of design, and a strong international demand for discontinued Lalique was established. New collectors could start by buying a commonly available Coquilles design bowl, a drinking glass or a side plate. Virtually all the pre-1945 designs are marked 'R. Lalique' or 'R. Lalique France', and therefore it was easy to date pieces. Vases became the most popular collecting area with coloured glass, particularly black and electric blue, selling at a premium. A very strong market was also established for the glass car mascots that had once graced the front of stylish automobiles.

By the mid-1980s, prices for Lalique glass were spiralling to new heights. One London auction room held prestigious evening sales of Lalique glass, with phone lines catering to largely American and Japanese clients. Unique pieces of *cire-perdue* glass, often with Lalique's own fingerprints preserved on the surface, were making £25,000–50,000 / €37,000–73,000 / $45,000–91,000.

The bubble burst in the early 1990s when the Japanese economy took a downturn and many collectors pulled out of the market, but momentum picked up again and today demand is as strong as ever. A modest Chinon pattern tumbler can still be bought for around £120 / €175 / $220 while a very rare example of the master's work may reach in excess of £100,000 / €145,000 / $181,000.

Mark Oliver

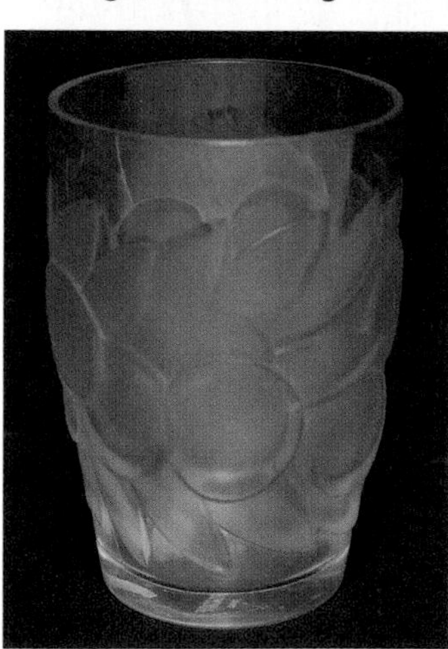

A Lalique frosted and stained glass beaker, 'Blidah', French, 1930s, 5in (12.5cm) high.
£220–250 / €320–360
$400–450 ⊞ MiW

A set of six Lalique glass fruit bowls, each moulded with a band of birds, etched 'R. Lalique', French, c1920, 4¾in (12cm) diam.
£280–330 / €410–480
$510–600 ⚒ SWO

A Lalique glass bowl, 'Perruches', moulded with opalescent budgerigars, French, 1920s, 9in (23cm) diam.
£1,900–2,250 / €2,750–3,300
$3,450–4,050 ⚒ BWL

◄ A Lalique glass finger bowl, 'Raisins', moulded with grapes and foliage, French, c1930, 4in (10cm) diam.
£190–220 / €280–320
$350–400 ⊞ GGD

A Lalique glass bowl, 'Pissenlit' moulded with 12 leaves, moulded signature, incised No. 3215, French, early 1920s, 9½in (24cm) diam.
£175–210 / €260–310
$320–380 ⚒ PFK

A Lalique glass dressing table box and cover, 'Dahlia', French, c1930, 4in (10cm) diam.
£175–195 / €260–290
$310–350 ⊞ GGD

A Lalique glass box and cover, 'Festoons', French, 1930s, 7in (18cm) diam.
£430–480 / €630–700
$780–870 ⊞ MiW

Marcilhac Numbers

Marcilhac numbers were devized by Felix Marcilhac and he used this system for his reference work *R. Lalique Catalogue Raisonne de l'Oeuvre de Verre,* published by Les Editions de l'Amateur, 1989.

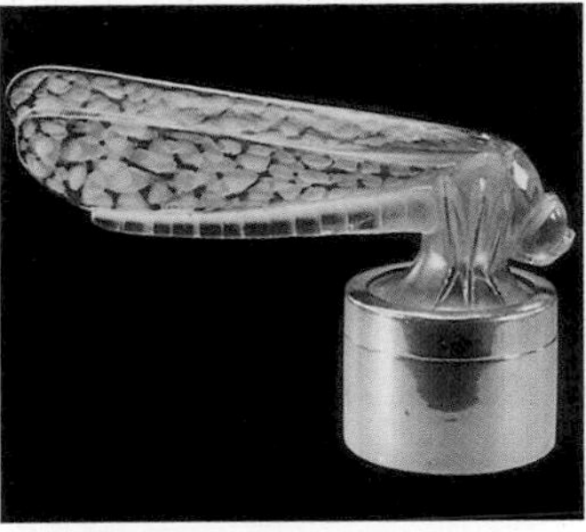

A Lalique frosted and polished glass car mascot, 'Libellule', modelled as a dragonfly with folded wings, Marcilhac No. 1144, moulded marks 'Lalique' and 'France', French, c1928, 6¼in (16cm) wide.
£4,300–5,100 / €6,300–7,400
$7,800–9,200 ⚒ S(O)
Nearly all pre-war Lalique models are marked 'R. Lalique' but a few exist with just the 'Lalique' mark.

A Lalique frosted and clear glass clock, 'Roitelets', the Omega movement in a chromium-plated case, Marcilhac No. 731, etched mark 'R. Lalique' and 'France', French, post-1931, 8in (20.5cm) high.
£2,150–2,550
€3,150–3,700
$3,900–4,600 ⚒ S(O)

DECORATIVE ARTS

A Lalique glass decanter, 'Boules', with a moulded stopper, French, 1935–40, 8¼in (21cm) high.
£210–250 / €310–370
$380–450 ⚒ G(L)

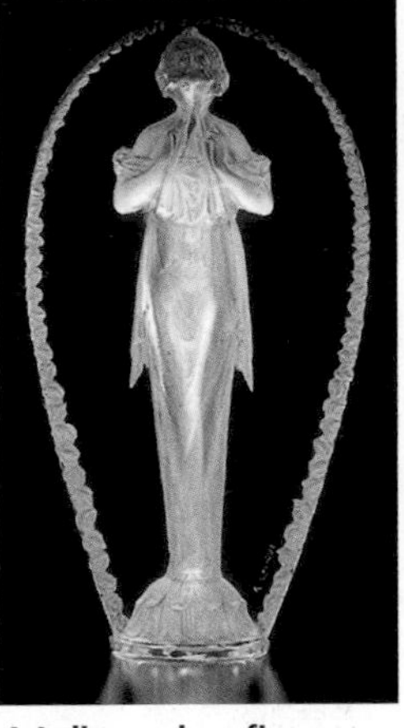

A Lalique glass figure, 'Grande Ovale Joyeuse de Flute', moulded as a classical figure playing pipes, Marcilhac No. 826, engraved mark 'R. Lalique, France', French, designed 1919, 14½in (37cm) high.
£7,200–8,600
€10,500–12,600
$13,000–15,600 ⚒ S

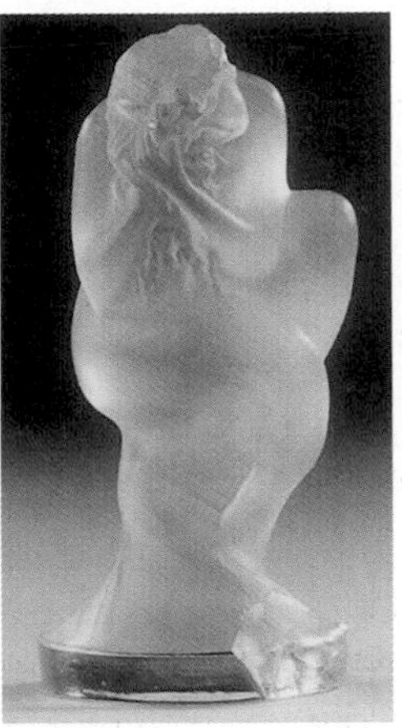

A Lalique frosted glass figure, 'Sirene', modelled as a crouching mermaid, Marcilhac No. 831, engraved mark 'R. Lalique', French, post-1920, 4in (10cm) high.
£720–860 / €1,050–1,250
$1,300–1,550 ⚒ S(O)
This model is listed in Marcilhac's book as a car mascot and also as a paperweight.

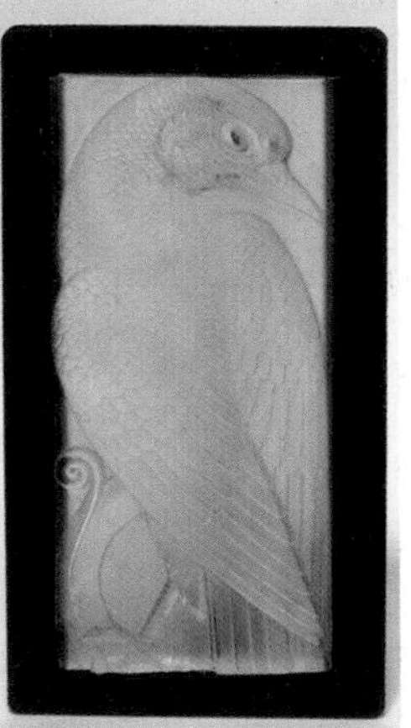

A pair of Lalique frosted glass panels, 'Oiseaux', French, designed 1929, 14in (35.5cm) high.
£7,200–8,000
€10,500–11,700
$13,000–14,500 ⊞ MiW
These were designed to form part of the architectural panel 'Oiseaux et Spirales'.

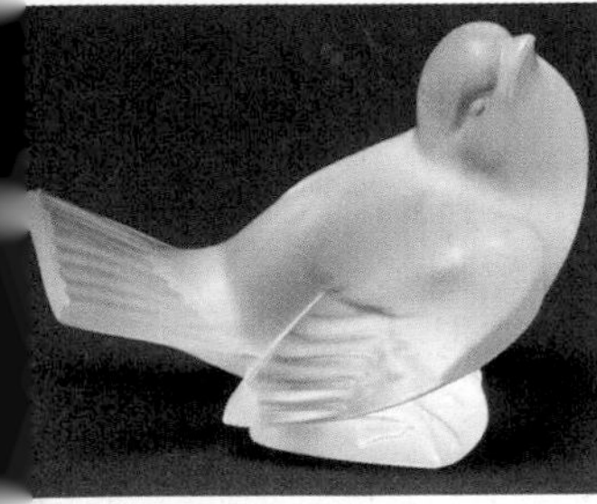

A Lalique frosted glass paperweight, 'Moineau Moqueur', French, c1950, 3½in (9cm) high.
£190–220 / €280–320
$340–400 ⊞ GGD

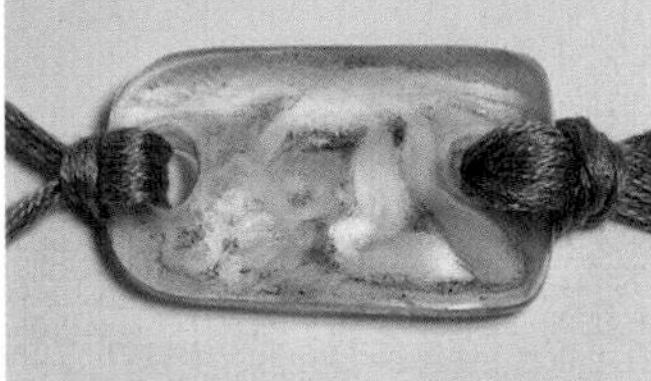

◄ A Lalique frosted and stained glass pendant, 'Colombes', French, 1920s, 1½in (4cm) long.
£540–600 / €790–880
$980–1,100 ⊞ MiW

► A Lalique glass and chromium-plated metal photograph frame, with an easel support, engraved mark 'Lalique, France', French, 1940s, 15in (38cm) high.
£6,600–7,900 / €9,600–11,500
$11,900–14,100 ⚒ S

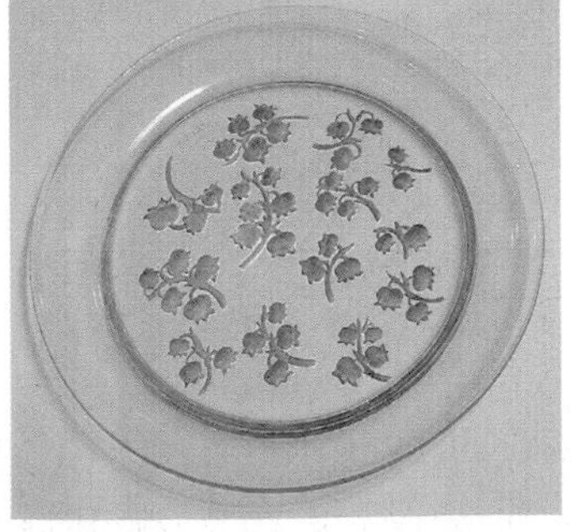

A Lalique stained glass plate, 'Muguets', French, 1920s, 8½in (21.5cm) diam.
£200–220 / €290–320
$360–400 ⊞ MiW

A Lalique glass tumber, 'Chinon', on a stained and frosted stem, French, 1930s, 4in (10cm) high.
£105–120 / €155–175
$190–220 ⊞ MiW

◀ **A Lalique opalescent glass vase,** 'Ormeaux', moulded with overlapping foliage, mould No. 984, signed 'R. Lalique, France', 1926–30, 6½in (16.5cm) high.
£760–910
€1,100–1,300
$1,400–1,650
⚒ TEN

A René Lalique vase, 'Charmilles', decorated in relief with a floral pattern, raised signature 'R. Lalique', French, designed 1926, 14¼in (36cm) high.
£5,600–6,700 / €8,200–9,800
$10,100–12,100 ⚒ DORO

A Lalique opalescent glass vase, 'Beautreillis', French, 1930s, 7in (18cm) high.
£1,250–1,400 / €1,800–2,000
$2,250–2,550 ⊞ MiW

◀ **A Lalique glass vase,** 'Acacia', French, 1930s, 8in (20.5cm) high.
£1,800–2,000 / €2,600–2,900
$3,250–3,600 ⊞ MiW

A Lalique glass vase, 'Esterel', moulded with overlapping foliage, moulded mark, c1930, 6in (15cm) high
£640–760 / €930–1,100
$1,250–1,400 ⚒ G(L)

A Lalique opalescent glass vase, 'Violettes', French, 1930s, 6¼in (16cm) high.
£3,150–3,500 / €4,600–5,100
$5,700–6,300 ⊞ MiW

A Lalique stained glass vase, 'Bagatelle', etched mark 'R. Lalique, France', French, c1939, 6½in (16.5cm) high.
£560–670 / €820–980
$1,000–1,200 ⚒ DN(BR)

A Lalique glass vase, 'Six Figurines', with stained glass panels, French, 1930s, 7½in (19cm) high.
£2,700–3,000
€3,950–4,400
$4,900–5,400 ⊞ MiW

▶ **A Lalique opalescent glass vase,** 'Laurier', pattern No. 947, moulded with leaves and berries, engraved mark 'R. Lalique, France', French, pre-1945, 7in (18cm) high.
£730–870 / €1,050–1,250
$1,300–1,550 ⚒ SWO

◀ **A Lalique glass vase,** moulded with doves, marked, French, early 20thC, 7in (18cm) high
£280–320
€410–470
$510–580 ⊞ L

Art Deco Jewellery

A platinum, diamond and Burma ruby bracelet, c1925, 6½in (16.5cm) long.
£12,600–14,000 / €18,400–20,400
$22,800–25,300 ⊞ NBL

A pearl and enamel bracelet, French, c1930, 7½in (19cm) long.
£3,850–4,300 / €5,600–6,300
$7,000–7,800 ⊞ NBL

An opal and diamond brooch, with a ribbon setting, c1920.
£470–560 / €690–820
$850–1,000 ⚒ DD

A silver, *faux* pearl and paste bow brooch, c1925, 1½in (4cm) wide.
£130–145 / €190–210
$230–260 ⊞ TDG

A platinum and diamond envelope brooch, c1925, 2in (5cm) wide.
£5,400–6,000 / €7,900–8,800
$9,800–10,900 ⊞ WIM

◄ **A platinum, lapis lazuli, rock crystal and diamond brooch,** by Shreve, Treat & Eacret, American, San Francisco, c1925, 1¾in (4.5cm) wide.
£1,750–1,950 / €2,550–2,850
$3,150–3,550 ⊞ NBL

A silver and paste brooch, probably French, c1925, 2in (5cm) wide.
£165–185 / €240–270
$300–330 ⊞ TDG

A silver and paste bar brooch, French, c1925, 2¼in (5.5cm) wide.
£115–130 / €170–190
$210–240 ⊞ TDG

For further information on
Jewellery see pages 532-546

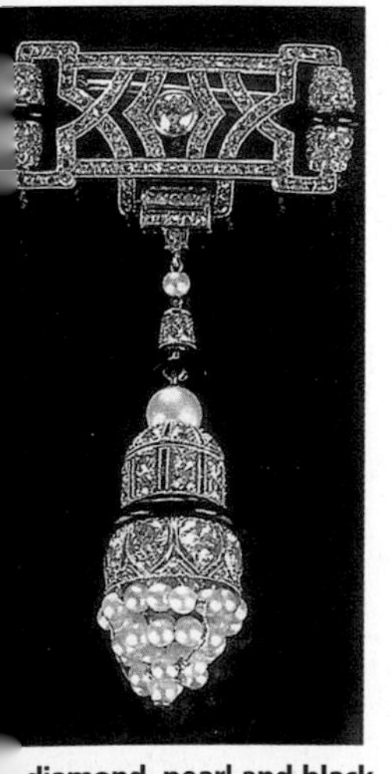

A diamond, pearl and black onyx pendant brooch, in a fitted Hennell leather case inscribed 'Nina 1930'.
£6,100–7,300
€8,900–10,700
$11,000–13,200 ⚒ DN

A carved coral, amber and jet necklace, c1925, 48in (122cm) long.
£230–260 / €340–380
$420–470 ⊞ TDG

◄ **A platinum, sapphire and diamond ring,** c1920, ¾in (2cm) wide.
£2,450–2,750
€3,600–4,000
$4,450–5,000
⊞ WIM

► **A platinum, diamond and sapphire calibré ring,** c1925, ¾in (2cm) wide.
£11,900–13,300
€17,400–19,400
$21,500–24,100
⊞ NBL

DECORATIVE ARTS

Art Deco Lighting

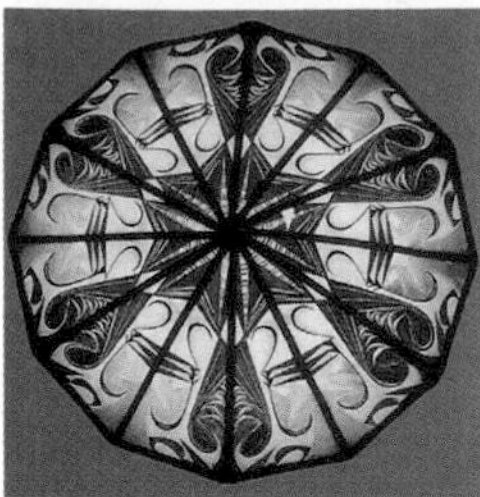

A stained and leaded glass hanging lamp, Amsterdam School, with a turned wood finial, with chains and ceiling rose, Dutch, c1920, 22¾in (58cm) diam.
£1,750–2,100
€2,550–3,050
$3,200–3,800 S(Am)

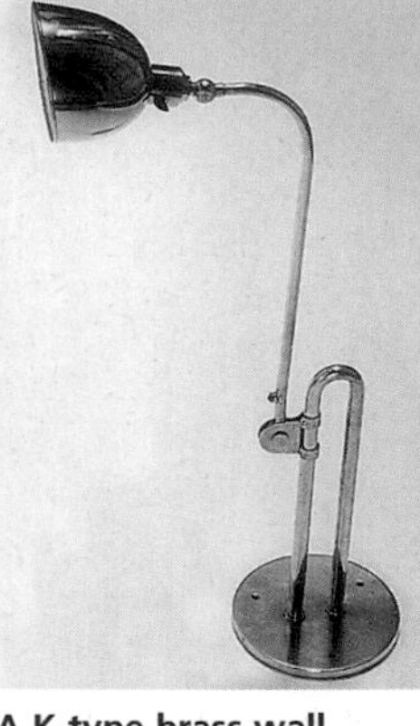

A K-type brass wall lamp, by Christian Dell for Belmag, Swiss, Zurich, c1928, 41in (104cm) long.
£6,600–7,900
€9,600–11,500
$11,900–14,300 S(NY)
This lamp is one of only two wall-mounted lamps of this model known to exist, and the only one in solid brass.

◄ **A Handel reverse-painted table lamp,** the shade decorated with a woodland scene, maker's mark, artist's initial and No. 6159, American, Connecticut, c1920, shade 15½in (39.5cm) diam.
£3,550–4,250
€5,200–6,200
$6,400–7,700 SK

A glass and metal ceiling light, by Marianne Brandt and Hin Bredendieck, 1930, German, Leipzig, 7¼in (18.5cm) diam.
£450–540 / €660–790
$810–980 SK

A Handel bronze and glass two-light table lamp, impressed mark, American, New York, 1910–20, 18½in (47cm) high.
£4,000–4,800 / €5,800–7,000
$7,200–8,700 DORO

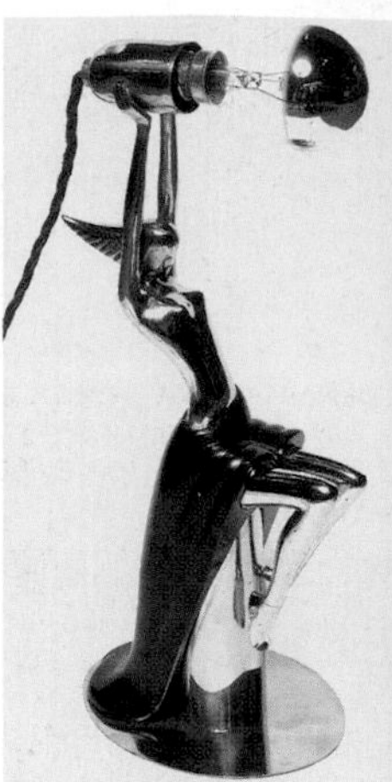

A Hagenauer nickel-plated figural table lamp, Austrian, 1930s, 15in (38cm) high.
£1,600–1,800
€2,350–2,650
$2,900–3,250 JSG

A brass and glass PH table lamp, by Poul Hennigsen for Louis Poulse[n], with three graduated glass shades, stamped 'Pat. App[l.]', Danish, c1927, 17¾in (45cm) high.
£3,350–4,000
€4,900–5,800
$6,100–7,200 S(O)
Hennigsen began to design lighting for Louis Poulsen in 1924. The first lamp from his PH series was exhibited to great acclaim and won a gold medal at the 1925 Paris Exposition Internationale des Arts Décoratifs et Industriels Modernes. The lamps were the result of ten years of scientific study and were designed to eliminate glare and produce soft, warm light. By 1926, Hennigsen had developed three types of shade: metal, matt glass and opaque glass. This lamp can be dated to the first series of PH lamp production of 1927–28 due to the 'Patent Applied' stamp to the shade. Pieces after this date were marked 'Patented'.

Handel Glass

The Handel Company was founded in Meriden, Connecticut in 1885 as a partnership between Phil Handel and Adolph Eyden. Handel initially began to manufacture vases, bottles and globular lamp shades with an opalescent quality to the glass, but once the company had established their showroom on Fifth Avenue, New York, it was decorative table lamps that became their most sought-after commodity. Handel's lamps are usually signed with the firm's name so they are easily identified today. Many incorporated a decorative cast-pewter or copper base with a leaded glass shade which would often be internally decorated to suggest parchment or rippling water. Some of the more exotic lamps have shades in the form of glass panels internally decorated with fish swimming as though in an aquarium, while the outside of the shade is heightened with enamel to add depth to the glass when illuminated. These lamps are usually signed by the decorator, and this adds to the value. Handel also used a Greek Key design on many of his shades, but at present there is less demand for these among collectors.

► **A brass two-light table lamp,** by Melzer & Neuhardt, slight damage, Austrian, Vienna, c1925, 21¾in (55.5cm) high.
£1,600–1,900
€2,350–2,750
$2,900–3,450
DORO

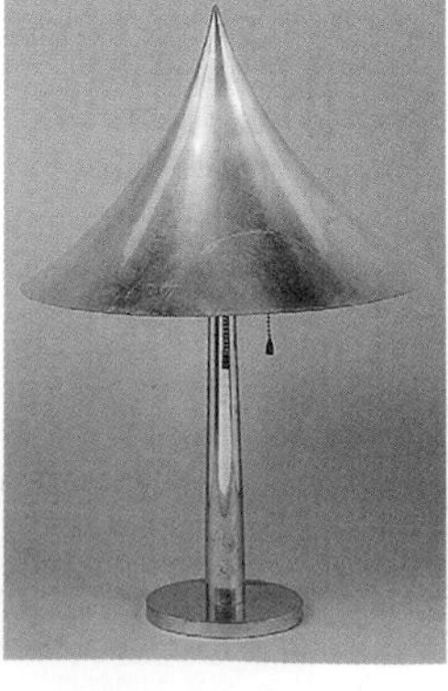

A Muller Frères glass lampshade, French, 1930s, 14in (35.5cm) diam.
£180–200 / €260–290
$320–360 MARK

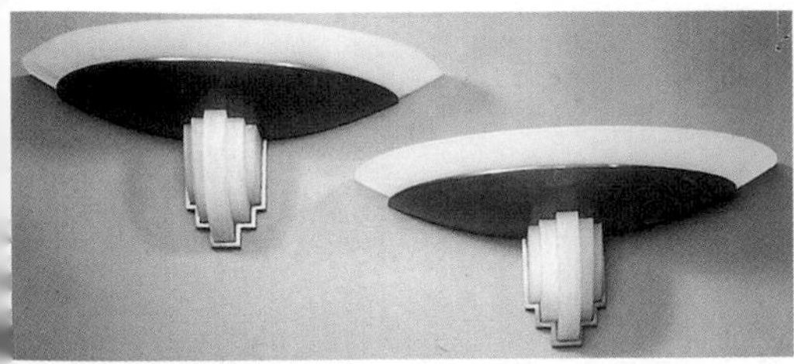

A pair of patinated-brass and frosted glass wall lamps, by Jean Perzel, signed, French, c1930, 21¾in (55.5cm) wide.
£3,800–4,550 / €5,500–6,600
$6,900–8,200 ⚒ S

A bronze, ivory and Lötz glass figural table lamp, by P. Tereszczuk, inscribed 'P. Tereszczuk' and 'AR', Austrian, c1920, 13½in (34.5cm) high.
£3,600–4,300
€5,300–6,300
$6,500–7,800 ⚒ S(O)

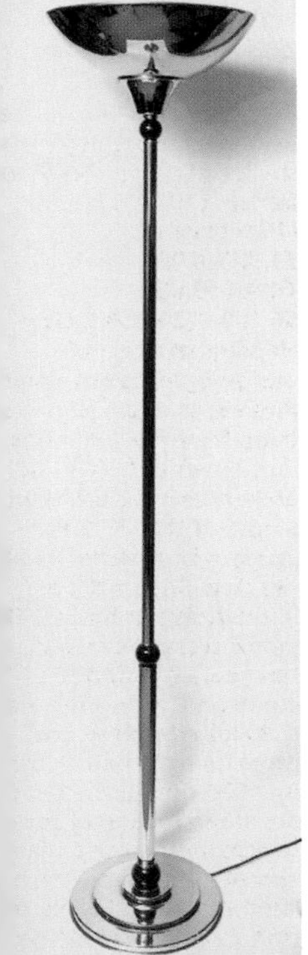

A chrome standard lamp, c1930, 72in (183cm) high.
£650–730 / €950–1,050
$1,200–1,350 ⊞ TDG

A brass and painted glass ceiling light, by XRay, American, Chicago, c1930.
£105–120 / €155–175
$200–220 ⊞ OLA

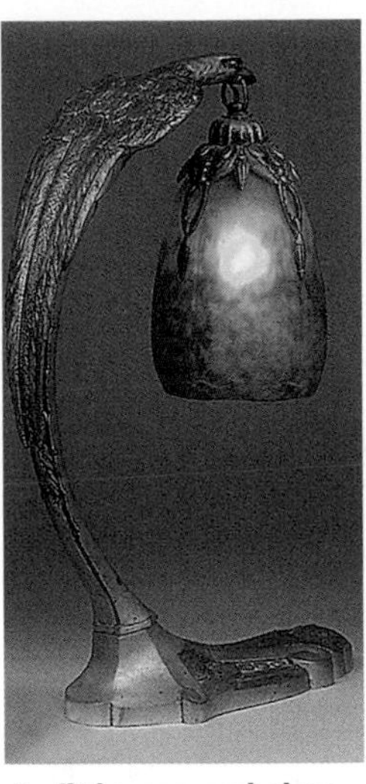

A gilt-bronze and glass table lamp, by C. Ranc, moulded as a bird of prey, the shade by Daum, carved 'Daum, Nancy', the base inscribed 'C. Ranc', French, c1925, 14½in (37cm) high.
£2,050–2,450
€3,000–3,600
$3,700–4,450 ⚒ DORO

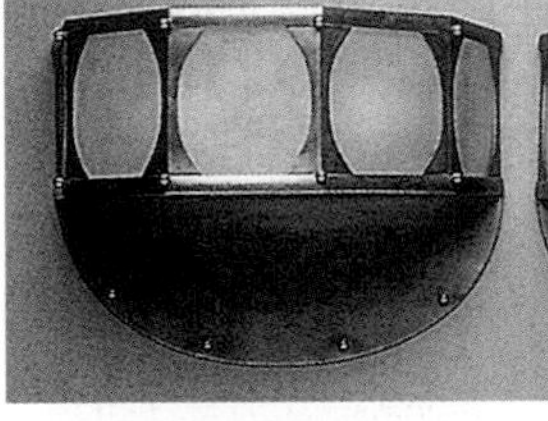

A pair of brass and glass two-light wall lamps, 1920s, 17in (43cm) wide.
£1,900–2,250 / €2,750–3,300
$3,450–4,050 ⚒ S(Am)

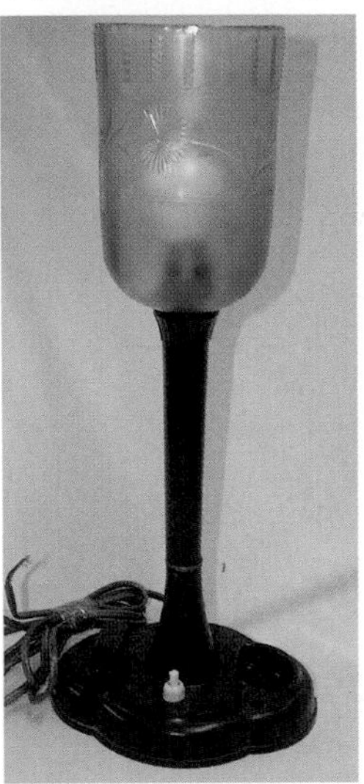

A Bakelite table lamp, with etched glass shade, 1930s, 16in (40.5cm) high.
£45–50 / €65–75
$85–95 ⊞ HEI

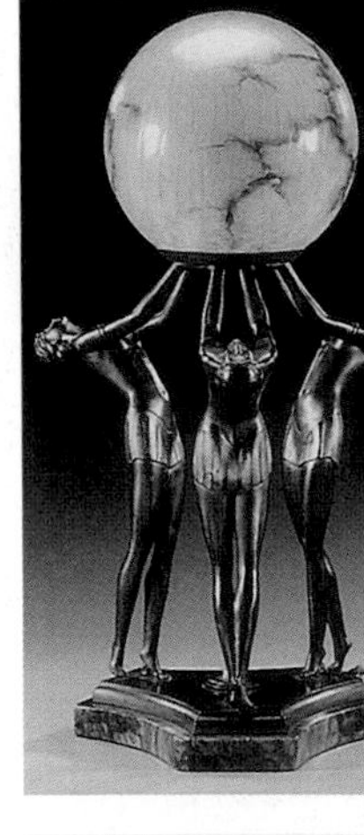

► A chrome and amber phenolic table lamp, c1930, 14in (35.5cm) diam.
£470–530 / €690–770
$850–960 ⊞ TDG

A Schneider glass Eucalyptus hanging lamp, with metal mounts and suspension chains, inlaid ingot mark, French, designed 1925, 15½in (39.5cm) diam.
£2,400–2,850
€3,500–4,150
$4,350–5,200 ⚒ S(O)

An alabaster and gilt-bronze ceiling light, the ceiling rose, chains and mounts cast with foliage, c1930, 17¾in (45cm) diam.
£1,900–2,250
€2,750–3,300
$3,450–4,050 ⚒ S(O)

◄ A spelter and glass figural table lamp, the glass globe painted to simulate alabaster, c1930, 20¼in (51cm) high.
£2,150–2,550
€3,150–3,700
$3,900–4,600 ⚒ S(O)

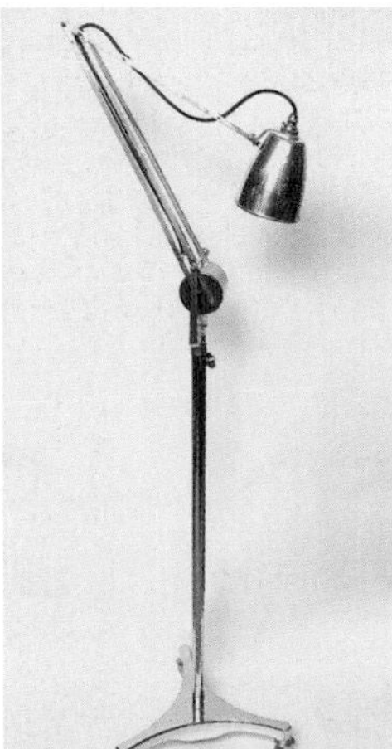

A chrome counterpoise trolley lamp, c1930, 64in (162.5cm) high.
£630–700 / €900–1,000
$1,100–1,250 ⊞ TDG

Metalware

A pair of marble and silvered-bronze bookends, by Charles, with fan-tailed doves, signed, French, c1930, 7in (18cm) high.
£1,800–2,150
€2,650–3,150
$3,250–3,900 S(O)

A silver fruit bowl, by Walker & Hall, with ivory handles, maker's mark, Birmingham 1930, 11½in (29cm) diam.
£330–390 / €480–570
$600–710 DN

► A Hagenauer brass two-light candelabrum, the column composed of two stylized horses and a dog, marked, 'WHW', Austrian, designed c1930, 15½in (39.5cm) high.
£4,000–4,800
€5,800–7,000
$7,200–8,700 DORO

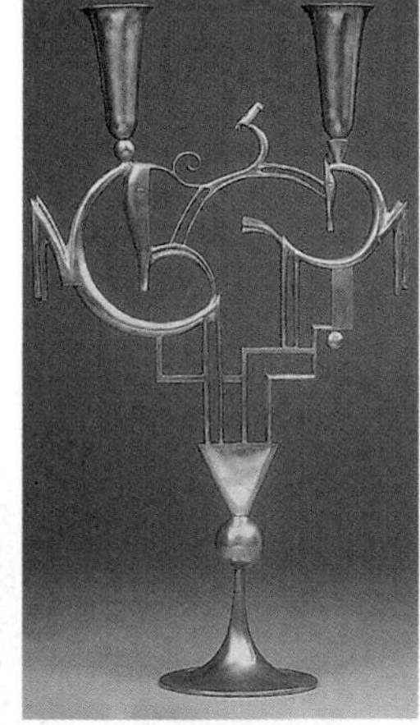

A pair of silver-plated candelabra, by Jean Després, each with three sconces on a hammered support, the reeded stems with a stylized chain motif, signed, French, c1930, 8¼in (21cm) high.
£4,300–5,100
€6,300–7,400
$7,800–9,200 S

A silver cocktail pitcher, by the Durgin division of Gorham Manufacturing Co, with a corked cover and stopper, American, Rhode Island, 1929, 14in (35.5cm) high.
£570–680 / €830–990
$1,050–1,250 NOA

A gilt cast-alloy Golden Arrow record model car, with rubber tyres, integral metal driver and Perspex windscreen, tyres marked 'Dunlop Cord Racing, Made in England', 1930s, 34in (86.5cm) long.
£9,600–11,500 / €14,000–16,800
$17,400–20,800 S

Designed by Captain Irving, the Golden Arrow was driven by Major Sir Henry Seagrave, Kt, on Daytona Beach, Florida, 11 March 1929, to create a World Land Speed Record of 231.352mph. It is said that this model was used to represent the full-sized machine at the 1929 Olympia Exhibition and, to keep it unique, the mould from which it was cast was destroyed. At the end of the exhibition, the model went to Brough Engineering, in whose offices it remained, housed in a glass case, for a period of over 40 years.

◄ A silver cocktail shake[r,] by Mappin & Webb, make[r's] mark, Sheffield 1919, 9in (23cm) high.
£630–700 / €900–1,000
$1,150–1,300 DAD

A silver cocktail pitcher, by Sigvard Bernadotte for Georg Jensen, chased with a diamond design, the spout with a chained cap, stamped 'Sterling', maker's mark, No. 819, Danish, 1930s, 6¾in (17cm) high.
£1,900–2,250
€2,750–3,300
$3,450–4,050 M

A pewter cup, by Cartier, French, c1920, 4in (10cm) high.
£340–380 / €500–550
$620–690 SHa

A silver cutlery set, by J. C. Klinkosch, comprising 61 pieces, monogrammed, Austrian, Vienna, c1930, 95oz.
£2,250–2,700 / €3,300–3,950
$4,050–4,900 DORO

A silver dressing table set, comprising three pieces, with engine-turned decoration, Birmingham 1935, mirror 9in (23cm) long.
£85–100 / €120–145
$150–180 TMA

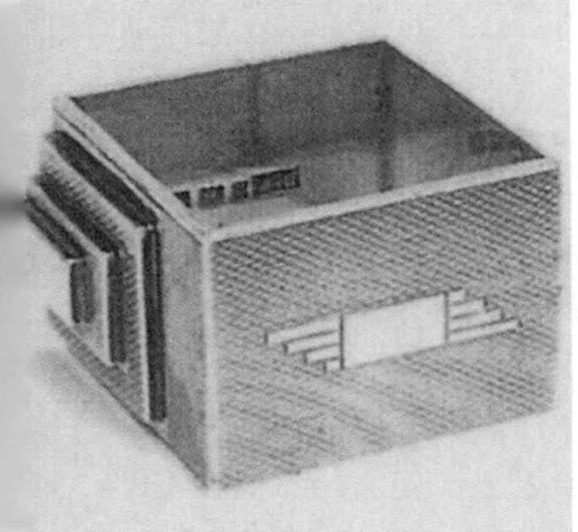

A pair of silver napkin rings, by Mappin & Webb, with engine-turned decoration and applied stepped motifs, London 1933, 1¾in (4.5cm) wide.
£340–400 / €500–580
$610–720 DN

A set of six silver spoons, Sheffield 1935, 4¼in (10cm) long, cased.
£135–150 / €195–220
$240–270 TDG

A silver and enamel vanity case, retailed by Cartier, the cover mounted with a Cartier watch on a gilt ribbon mounted with emeralds, the mirrored interior with two hinged compartments and a lipstick holder, French, c1930, 4¾in (12cm) wide.
£1,650–1,950 / €2,400–2,850
$3,000–3,550 S(O)

► **A silver-mounted cut-glass inkwell,** Birmingham 1930, 2½in (6.5cm) wide.
£90–100 / €130–145
$160–180 FOX

An enamelled metal napkin holder, by Marianne Brandt for Ruppelwerk, German, c1930, 6in (15cm) wide.
£360–400 / €520–580
$650–720 JSG
Marianne Brandt joined Bauhaus, the German school of architecture and applied arts, in 1923 to work in the metal workshop. In 1929 she moved to Berlin to work in the studio of Walter Gropius.

► **A cast-aluminium plaque,** by Réne P. Chambellan, depicting lovebirds, the reverse with an inscription, signed, American, c1930, 12 x 9in (30.5 x 23cm).
£500–600 / €730–880
$910–1,100 JAA

A silver four-piece tea and coffee service, by Jean E. Puiforcat, with hardwood handles and finials, French, c1930, coffee pot 7in (18cm) high.
£4,800–5,700 / €7,000–8,300
$8,700–10,300 S(O)

A patinated copper vase, by Marie Zimmermann, stamped with artist's monogram and name, c1920, 16½in (42cm) wide.
£3,600–4,300 / €5,300–6,300
$6,500–7,800 S(NY)

A silver-plated Diament tea service, by Gene Theobald for the Wilcox Silver Plate Co of the International Silver Co, comprising teapot, creamer and covered sugar bowl, all with Bakelite handles, and a tray, stamped marks and numbers, American, Connecticut, c1928, tray 13¼in (33.5cm) wide.
£10,600–12,700 / €15,500–18,500
$19,200–23,000 S(NY)

◄ **A silver three-piece tea service,** by Wakely & Wheeler, the teapot with an ivory finial, London 1932, 39oz.
£440–520 / €640–760
$800–940 HYD

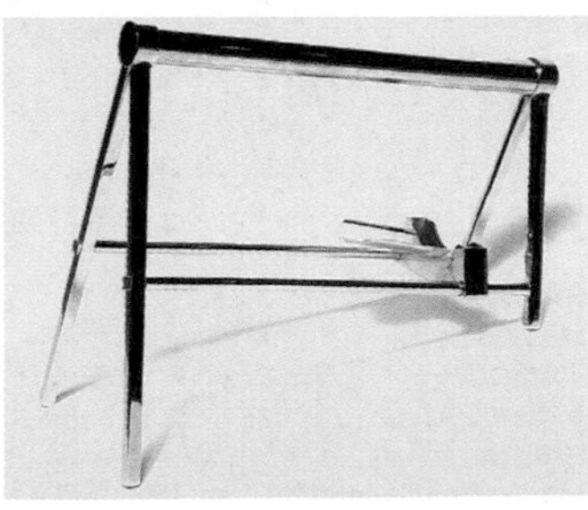

A chrome-plated wine carrier, by Jacques Adnet, French, c1930, 12in (30.5cm) wide.
£450–500 / €660–730
$810–910 JSG

Art Deco Models

◄ **A rosewood figural group of a dancing couple,** by Jacques Adnet, stamped '2A, Made in France', French, c1930, 12¾in (32.5cm) high.
£5,000–6,000
€7,300–8,800
$9,100–10,900 ⚒ S(O)

► **An Ashtead figure,** by Phoebe Stabler, entitled 'Buster Boy', c1930, 5½in (14cm) high.
£710–790 / €1,000–1,150
$1,300–1,450 ⊞ MMc

A Bechyne porcelain figure of a running female with two dogs, Czechoslovakian, c1925, 21in (53.5cm) high.
£670–750 / €980–1,100
$1,200–1,350 ⊞ LLD

A bronze figure, by Marcel Bouraine, entitled 'Penthesilia: Queen of the Amazons', signed and inscribed 'Susse Fres Edts Paris', French, c1930, 18in (45.5cm) wide.
£7,800–9,300 / €11,400–13,600
$14,100–16,800 ⚒ S(O)

A gilt-bronze and ivory figural group, by Demêtre Chiparus, on a marble base, signed, French, c1925, 11¾in (30cm) wide.
£3,550–4,250 / €5,200–6,200
$6,400–7,700 ⚒ LJ

A bronze and ivory figure, by Demêt Chiparus, entitled 'Tanara', on an ony plinth, signed, French, c1925, 12½in (32cm) wide.
£8,100–9,700 / €11,800–14,200
$14,700–17,600 ⚒ S

◄ **A spelter figural group of Diana and a dog,** by H. Fugère, on a marble base, slight damage, base inscribed 'H. Fugère', French, 1920s, 17¾in (45cm) high.
£640–760
€930–1,100
$1,200–1,400
⚒ S(Am)

◄ **A Goldscheider ceramic figure of a dancer,** printed and impressed marks, Austria c1930, 16½in (42cm) high.
£1,200–1,400
€1,750–2,050
$2,150–2,550 ⚒ S(O)

A Goldscheider ceramic figure of a traveller seated on a trunk, by Stefan Dakon, legs restored, marked, impressed model No. 7364/42/19, Austrian, c1935, 10in (25.5cm) high.
£1,350–1,600
€1,950–2,350
$2,450–2,900 ⚒ DORO

A Goldscheider ceramic model of a dancer, by Josef Lorenzl, entitled 'Butterfly Girl', restored, signed, factory mark, Austrian, c1937, 16in (40.5cm) high.
£1,450–1,700
€2,100–2,500
$2,600–3,100 ⚒ SK

A Goldscheider porcelain model of a female nude, by Josef Lorenzl, factory mark, impressed model No 8493/22/7, Austrian, 1938–39, 16¾in (42.5cm) high.
£1,750–2,100
€2,550–3,050
$3,150–3,800 ⚒ DORO

An ivory and gilt-bronze figure, by Affortunato Gory, entitled 'Danseuse Orientale', on a marble base, French, early 20thC, 18in (45.5cm) high.
£5,400–6,400
€7,900–9,300
$9,800–11,600 ⚒ WILK

Specialist in Art Nouveau & Art Deco
AUDREY STERNSHINE
Antique Galleries
26 Broad St, Pendleton, Salford
Manchester M6 5BY
Tel: 0161 737 5938 • Fax: 0161 737 6626
as@artnouveau-artdeco.com
www.artnouveau-artdeco.com

A bronze figure of a woman holding an onyx ball, by Maurice Guiraud-Rivière, entitled 'Stella', on a marble base, signed, French, c1930, 26in (66cm) high.
£8,600–10,300
€12,600–15,000
$15,600–18,600 S

A Hagenauer bronze figure of a kneeling woman, on a stained oak plinth, with seal mark and stamped 'Hagenauer, Wien', Austrian, c1930, 10½in (26.5cm) high.
£4,300–5,100
€6,300–7,400
$7,800–9,200 S(O)

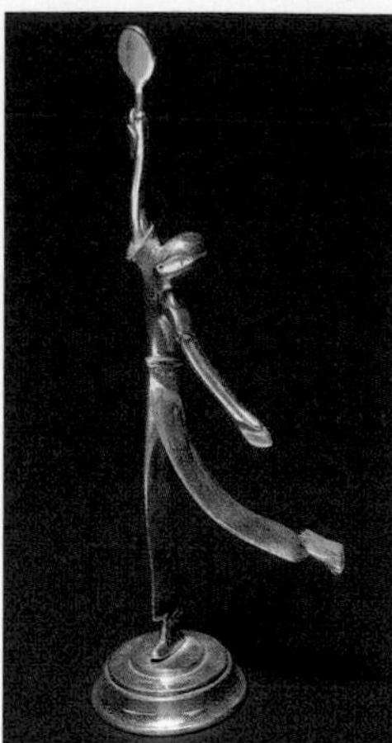

A Hagenauer nickel figure of a tennis player, Austrian, 1930s, 10½in (26.5cm) high.
£1,050–1,200
€1,550–1,750
$1,900–2,150 JSG
The tennis subject matter increases the value of this piece.

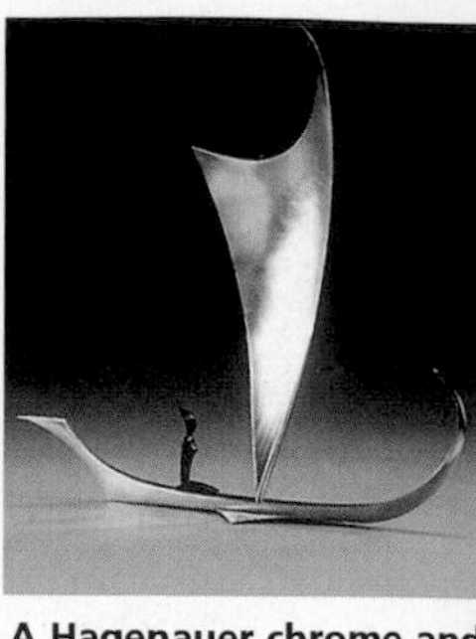

A Hagenauer chrome and patinated-bronze model of a boat, with a stylized female figure, stamped, seal mark, Austrian, c1930, 17¼in (44cm) high.
£1,800–2,150
€2,650–3,150
$3,250–3,900 S(O)

A patinated-bronze figure of a javelin thrower, by P. Hugonnet, on an inscribed, stone socle, French, c1935, 37½in (95.5cm) wide.
£2,050–2,450 / €3,000–3,600
$3,700–4,450 DORO

► **A bronze model of a leaping stag,** by Georges Laurent, on a marble plinth, marked and stamped, French, c1930, 22¾in (58cm) wide.
£2,850–3,400
€4,150–4,950
$5,200–6,200
S(O)

An Ilmenau porcelain figure of a woman, probably designed by G. Schliepstein, German, 1920s, 8in (20.5cm) high.
£360–400 / €520–580
$650–720 LLD

A Katzhütte porcelain figure of a lady with a fan, German, c1935, 20in (51cm) high.
£900–1,000
€1,300–1,450
$1,600–1,800 LLD

A painted bronze figure of a female, by Pierre Le Faguays, entitled 'Vertal', on an onyx base, losses, painted later, marked, French, c1930, 13¾in (35cm) high.
£1,400–1,650
€2,050–2,400
$2,550–3,000 S(O)

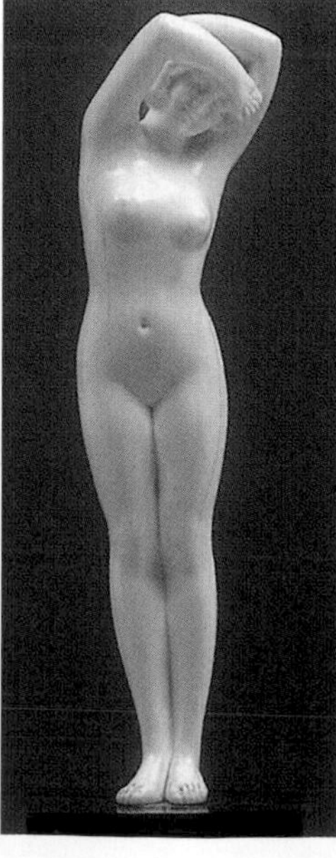

◄ **An ivory figure of a female nude,** by Samuel Lipszyk, on a stone socle, signed, Austrian, 1910–20, 8in (20.5cm) high.
£1,750–2,100 / €2,550–3,050
$3,150–3,800 DORO

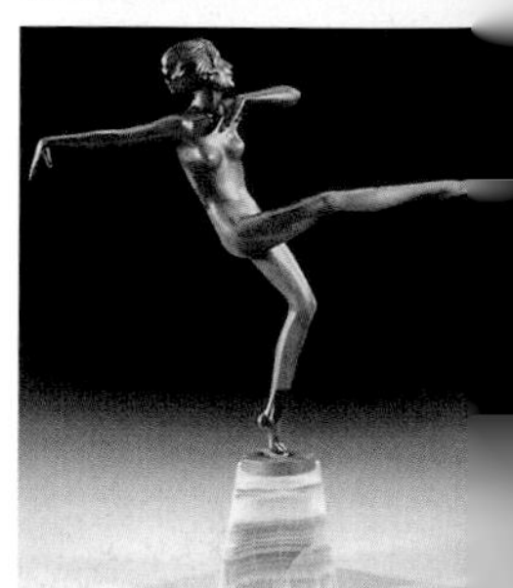

A bronze figure of a female nude, by Josef Lorenzl, on an onyx base, slight damage, signed, Austrian, c1930, 14¾in (37.5cm) high.
£1,400–1,650
€2,050–2,400
$2,550–3,000 S(O)

◄ **A bronze figure of a female nude,** by Josef Lorenzl, on an onyx socle, signed, Austrian, 1920s, 11in (28cm) high.
£1,050–1,200
€1,550–1,750
$1,850–2,100 TDG

A bronze bust of a young woman, by Josef Lorenzl, on an onyx base, signed, Austrian, c1930, 14½in (37cm) high.
£5,000–6,000
€7,300–8,800
$9,100–10,900 S

A patinated-bronze figure of a dancing woman with two birds, by L. Lormier, on a marble base, slight damage, signed, French, c1925, 14¼in (36cm) high.
£1,400–1,650
€2,050–2,400
$2,500–3,000 BUK

A bronze and ivory figure of a matador, by Roland Paris, on a marble base, signed, French, c1930, 14½in (37cm) high.
£1,650–1,950
€2,400–2,850
$3,000–3,550 S(O)

A carved ivory figure of a dancer holding cymbals, on an onyx pedestal, inscribed 'Oliviore OnII(?)', c1930, 12¼in (31cm) high.
£1,050–1,250
€1,550–1,850
$1,900–2,250 S(O)

A painted gilt-bronze and ivory figure of a dancer, by Karl Perl, on an onyx base, signed, Austrian, c1930, 19in (48.5cm) high.
£5,400–6,400
€7,900–9,300
$9,800–11,600 S(O)

A bronze and ivory figure, by Ferdinand Preiss, entitled 'The Archer', on an onyx plinth with four ivory feet, inscribed mark, German, c1925, 8½in (21.5cm) high.
£10,200–12,200
€14,900–17,800
$18,500–21,900 S(O)

◄ A Primavera ceramic figure of a harlequin, French, c1930, 13in (33cm) high.
£450–500 / €660–730
$810–910 ⊞ MI

A pair of bronze figural bookends, by Riedl, modelled as dancers with feathers, signed, c1930, 7in (18cm) high.
£960–1,150
€1,450–1,700
$1,750–2,100 S(O)

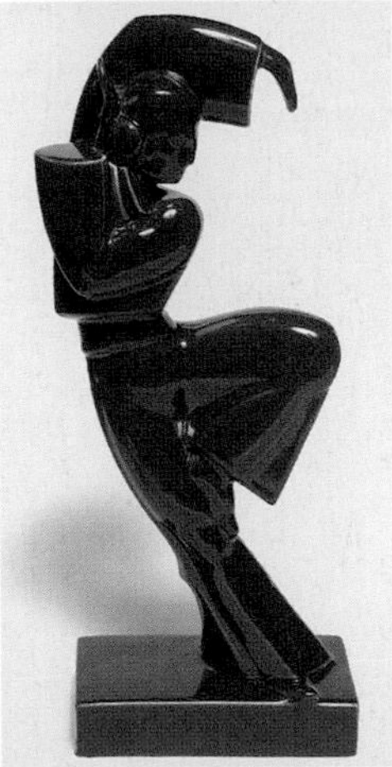

◄ A Robj ceramic figure of a dancer, French, c1930, 19in (48.5cm) high.
£540–600 / €790–880
$980–1,100 ⊞ JSG

A Royal Dux porcelain figure of a girl with a discus, Bohemian, c1935, 9in (23cm) high.
£450–500 / €660–730
$810–910 ⊞ LLD

A Royal Dux porcelain figure of a Spanish dancer, Bohemian, 1930s, 14in (35.5cm) high.
£360–400 / €520–580
$650–720 ⊞ LLD

A bronze model of a running goose, by Edouard Marcel Sandoz, modelled with a snail on its beak, signed, with Susse seal, French, c1930, 8in (20.5cm) wide.
£4,550–5,400 / €6,600–7,900
$8,200–9,800 S(O)

A pair of Susse Frères patinated-bronze figural book ends, by Paul Silvestre, signed, maker's mark, French, Paris, c1930, 7in (18cm) high.
£1,600–1,800 / €2,350–2,650
$2,900–3,250 ⊞ MI

► An Alméric Walter *pâte de verre* figure of a reclining woman, by A. Houillon, a cat at her feet, signed, moulded marks, French, Nancy, c1920, 7½in (19cm) wide.
£2,400–2,850
€3,500–4,150
$4,350–5,200
⚒ S(O)

◄ A bronze figure of a kneeling woman, on a wooden base, c1925, 4½in (11.5cm) high.
£220–250 / €320–370
$400–450 ⊞ LBr

► A bronze figure of a dancer, on a marble base, Continental, c1930, 34¾in (88.5cm) high.
£2,250–2,700
€3,300–3,950
$4,000–4,800 ⚒ S(O)

► A ceramic model of a deer, c1930, 20in (51cm) wide.
£60–70
€90–100
$110–125
⊞ ASP

◄ A bronze and ivory figure of a dancing bather, in the style of Ferdinand Preiss, with gilded and painted decoration, on an alabaster socle, c1930, 16in (40.5cm) high.
£4,450–5,300
€6,500–7,700
$8,100–9,600 ⚒ TEN

► A bronze figure of a harlequin, with a *faux* ivory face, on a marble base, French, c1930, 4½in (11.5cm) high.
£110–130 / €160–190
$200–240 ⚒ JAA

A ceramic trial figure, attributed to Phoebe Stabler, c1935, 9in (23cm) high.
£1,100–1,250
€1,600–1,800
$2,000–2,250 ⊞ MMc
This figure is from the collection of Freda Doughty, one of the premier modellers at the Royal Worcester factory in the mid-20th century.

A patinated-bronze and ivory pierrot and pierrette, by Peter Tereszczuk, on an onyx socle, inscribed, Austrian, Vienna, 1925–30, 14½in (37cm) high.
£1,500–1,800
€2,200–2,650
$2,700–3,250 ⚒ DORO

A bronze and alabaster figural dragonfly group, on a carved alabaster frog, c1930, 9¾in (25cm) high.
£2,000–2,400
€2,900–3,500
$3,600–4,350 ⚒ S(O)

A gilded spelter figure of a woman, on a stepped marble plinth, early 20thC, 16¼in (41.5cm) high.
£175–210 / €260–310
$320–380 ⚒ L&E

Twentieth-Century Design

Ceramics

A St Ives redware mug, by Michael Cardew, inscribed, slight damage, impressed marks, 1925–26, 4¼in (11cm) high.
£230–270 / €340–400
$420–500 SWO

A Gray's Pottery lustre plate, by Gordon Forsyth, c1927, 11in (28cm) diam.
£140–155 / €200–220
$250–280 JFME

◄ **A Ruskin Pottery crystalline table lamp,** stamped marks, dated 1927, 12in 930.5cm) high.
£330–390 €480–570
$600–710 CHTR

► **A Ruskin Pottery bowl,** with three feet, 1928–29, 3½in (9cm) diam.
£195–220
€280–320
$350–400
SAT

A Ruskin Pottery jar and cover, c1926, 8in (20.5cm) high.
£1,300–1,450
€1,900–2,100
$2,350–2,600 MMc

► **A porcelain plate,** commemorating Russian Suprematists, painted with a factory, sickle and an ear of wheat, with Cyrillic script, hammer and sickle mark, painted artist's signature, Russian, early 20thC, 9½in (24cm) diam.
£440–520 / €640–760
$800–940 RTo

A bowl and cover, by Jessie Marion King, 1930s, 5½in (14cm) diam.
£580–650 / €850–950
$1,050–1,200 SDD

A Wedgwood earthenware mug, by Eric Ravilious, commemorating the coronation of King George VI and Queen Elizabeth, 1937, 4in (10cm) high.
£1,150–1,300 / €1,700–1,900
$2,100–2,350 H&G

A San Ildefonso plate, by Maria and Santana Martinez, decorated with a stylized snake, signed, American, 1943–56, 13in (33cm) diam.
£1,900–2,250 / €2,750–3,300
$3,450–4,100 JDJ

◄ **A Gamboni bowl,** Italian, 1940s–50s, 4½in (11.5cm) diam.
£400–450 / €580–660
$720–810 EMH

► **A Midwinter Stylecraft sugar pot and cover,** by Hugh Casson, decorated with Riviera pattern, c1954, 5in (12.5cm) diam.
£40–45 / €55–65
$70–80 CHI

An earthenware bowl, by James Tower, with cross-hatched decoration, signed, dated 1954, 13¼in (33.5cm) wide.
£470–560 / €690–820
$850–1,000 DN

◄ **A Gustavberg Studio Pottery stoneware vase,** by Stig Lindberg, signed, Swedish, 1950s, 9in (23cm) high.
£3,200–3,800
€4,650–5,500
$5,800–6,900 BUK

A Höganäs glazed vase, Swedish, 1960s, 6½in (16.5cm) high.
£105–120 / €155–175
$190–220 MARK

An earthenware teapot and cover, by Alan Caiger-Smith, decorated with stylized calligraphy, painted monogram and date code for 1961, 9¾in (25cm) high.
£290–340 / €420–500
$520–620 Bea

A stoneware vase, by Bernard Rooke, decorated with raised dragonflies, 1960s, 14in (35.5cm) high.
£200–230 / €300–340
$360–410 MARK

► **A Poole Pottery Aegean fruit bowl,** 1968, 13in (33cm) diam.
£95–110
€140–155
$170–200
FRD

A Poole Pottery Delphis vase, 1960s, 16in (40.5cm) high.
£310–350 / €450–510
$560–630 CHI

A Troika double-sided mask, painted mark, artist's initials 'M. M.',1970s, 10in (25.5cm) high.
£2,600–3,100
€3,800–4,550
$4,700–5,600 S(O)

An Arabia stoneware dish, by Birger Kaipiainen, signed, Finnish, 1970s–80s, 15¼in (38.5cm) wide.
£1,300–1,550 / €1,900–2,250
$2,350–2,800 BUK

The Arabia factory in Helsinki was set up in 1873 by the Swedish company Rörstrand as a means of exporting, to Russia in particular, where there was a ready market. Soon the factory was producing half of Sweden's ceramics and in 1916 it separated from Rörstrand. From the mid-1920s Arabia was producing work of importance and shortly after WWII a separate design-planning studio was set up. By the end of the century, due to expansions and amalgamations, Arabia and Rörstrand were once more part of the same umbrella group.

An Aldermaston Pottery jug and cover, by Alan Caiger-Smith, painted marks, date code for 1974, 10in (25.5cm) high.
£100–120 / €145–175
$185–220 DN

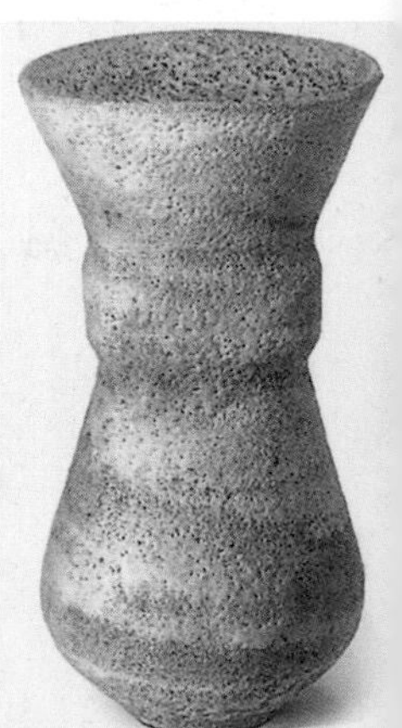

A stoneware vase, by Lucie Rie, stamped artist's monogram, c1980, 12¼in (31cm) high.
£3,150–3,750
€4,600–5,500
$5,700–6,800 S(NY)

Furniture

A plywood and laminated beech armchair, by Alvar Aalto, Finnish, 1932.
£2,000–2,400 / €2,900–3,500
$3,600–4,350 ⚒ BUK(F)

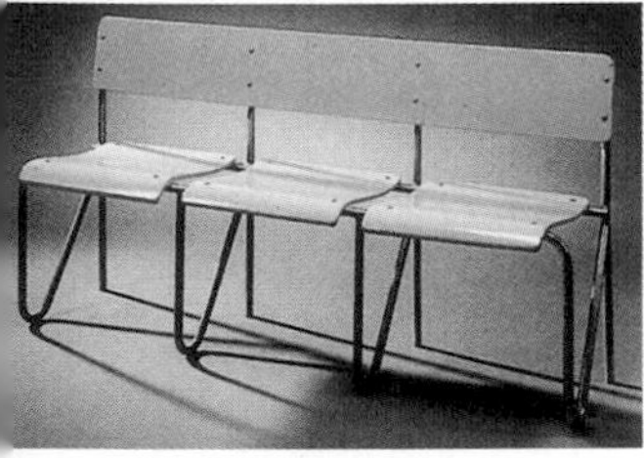

A steel and plywood bench, by G. Th. Rietveld for Metz & Co, slight damage, Dutch, Amsterdam, c1935, 59½in (151cm) wide.
£1,350–1,600 / €1,950–2,350
$2,450–2,900 ⚒ S(Am)

An upholstered aluminium 304 armchair, by Marcel Breuer, with ebonized wood armrests, German, 1932–33.
£3,600–4,300
€5,300–6,300
$6,500–7,800 ⚒ S
In the early 1930s, Breuer experimented with flat aluminium in his design for seating. There were three basic side chair designs by Breuer, which also came in armchair versions. Model 304 was the middle-sized of the three, with a more fully articulated back, and was used for restaurants, living rooms and dining rooms.

A pair of chrome and leather armchairs, by PEL, 1936.
£810–900 / €1,150–1,300
$1,450–1,650 ⊞ FRD

An oak and leather stool, by 'Rabbit Man', 1945, 20in (51cm) wide.
£450–500 / €660–730
$810–910 ⊞ TDG
'Rabbit Man' was one of Robert 'Mouseman' Thompson's apprentices.

◄ **An aluminium and upholstery BA chair,** by Ernest Race, 1945.
£400–450 / €580–660
$720–810 ⊞ EMH
Wood was in short supply after WWII so Ernest Race concentrated on using metal in his designs, particularly aluminium. His highly innovative BA chair was made from sandblasted aluminium scrap which, with its refined, tapering legs and elegant curved back, combined strength with lightness and visual minimalism.

A birch and hemp Pernilla chaise longue, by Bruno Mathsson for Karl Mathsson, with label, stamped, Swedish, c1934.
£840–1,000 / €1,250–1,500
$1,500–1,800 ⚒ SWO

A birch-veneered and lacquer coffee table, by Greta Magnusson Grossman for Studio, slight damage, Swedish, 1930s, 49¼in (125cm) diam.
£4,550–5,400 / €6,600–7,900
$8,200–9,800 ⚒ BUK
Greta Magnusson Grossman (1906–99) was a student of industrial design in Stockholm, with a particular interest in furniture, textiles and metalwork. After graduating, she worked with a cabinet-maker for a year before opening her own shop and furniture upholstery workshop named Studio. While she ran the business she also attended the Royal Academy of Technology in Stockholm to obtain her architecture degree. Around 1939 she and her husband moved to Los Angeles where she soon became established as a designer and an interior decorator.

► **A steel and vinyl Standard chair,** by Jean Prouvé, model No. 4, French, Nancy, c1940.
£2,450–2,900
€3,550–4,250
$4,350–5,200
⚒ S(NY)

A walnut and glass occasional table, by Gio Ponti, with brass supports, the sections stamped 1, 2, 3, 4, Italian, 1940s, 37½in (95.5cm) diam.
£3,350–4,000 / €4,900–2,350
$6,100–7,200 ⚒ S(O)

◄ **A jacaranda and mahogany-veneered cupboard,** by Carl Malmsten, with two doors over four drawers, enclosing shelves and drawers, inlaid with vases of flowers, branded mark, Swedish, 1949, 43¼in (110cm) wide.
£3,300–3,950
€4,800–5,800
$6,000–7,200
⚒ BUK

A wrought-iron and glass patio bar, by Salterini, with a variegated marble top and a wire mesh bottle/plant holder, American, New York, c1950, 48in (122cm) wide.
£640–760 / €930–1,100
$1,200–1,400 ⚒ SK

An iron and fabric DKR-2 chair, by Charles Eames for Herman Miller, 1951.
£270–300 / €390–440
$490–540 ⊞ HSR

A Lady chair, by Marco Zanuso, Italian, 1951.
£1,350–1,500 / €1,950–2,200
$2,450–2,700 ⊞ MARK

A pair of fruitwood and leatherette chairs, French, 1950s.
£1,050–1,200
€1,550–1,750
$1,900–2,150 ⊞ DeP

An enamel Pepsi Cola bench, mid-20thC, 86in (218.5cm) wide.
£1,950–2,150 / €2,850–3,150
$3,500–3,900 ⊞ DRU

A moulded plywood cabinet, by Cees Braakman, Dutch, 74in (188cm) wide.
£760–850 / €1,100–1,250
$1,400–1,550 ⊞ BOOM

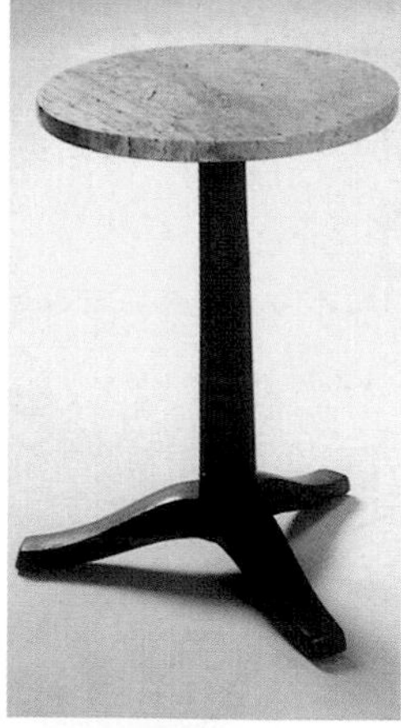

A beech and mirrored glass table, Italian, 1950s, 36½in (92.5cm) wide.
£580–650 / €850–950
$1,050–1,200 ⊞ DeP

◄ **A pair of mahogany and stone side tables,** by Edward Wormley for Dunbar, maker's metal tag, American, Indiana, c1951, 21½in (54.5cm) diam.
£1,800–2,150 / €2,650–3,150
$3,250–3,900 ⚒ SK

A set of six stained beech chairs, possibly by Ray Komai, American, 1950s.
£1,050–1,200 / €1,550–1,750
$1,900–2,150 ⊞ EMH

A beech and cherrywood-laminate Hillestack chair, by Robin Day for Hille, 1954.
£90–100 / €130–145
$160–180 ⊞ FRD

A pair of fruitwood low tables, by Willy van der Meeren, with laminate lower drawers, Belgian, c1954, 20½in (52cm) high.
£1,650–1,850 / €2,400–2,700
$3,000–3,350 ⊞ DeP

A printed screen, by Piero Fornasetti, entitled 'Reflecting City', printed with classical buildings, the reverse depicting a wooded landscape, Italian, designed 1955, 81¼in (206.5cm) high.
£11,700–14,000
€17,100–20,400
$21,200–25,300 S

A sapelewood cabinet, by Thomas Appleby, with two satinwood sliding doors enclosing shelves and drawers, c1955, 54in (137cm) wide.
£1,100–1,250 / €1,600–1,800
$2,000–2,250 BOOM

A table, by Robert Picault, probably in collaboration with Roger Capron, French, Vallauris, c1955, 18½in (47cm) wide.
£1,050–1,200 / €1,550–1,750
$1,900–2,150 EMH

A Hayward Wakefield armchair, coffee table and two side tables, American, mid-20thC.
£190–220 / €280–330
$340–410 JAA

◀ **A bentwood and upholstery chair,** by Norman Cherner for Plycraft, American, Massachusetts, c1955.
£350–420 / €510–610
$630–760 SK

A Heal's rosewood and Formica cocktail cabinet, the illuminated interior with bottle rack and drawer, Heal's mark, c1957, 38in (96.5cm) wide.
£420–500 / €610–2730
$760–910 SWO

TWENTIETH-CENTURY DESIGN

A Vanson satinwood and sapelewood cabinet, Danish, 1957, 54in (137cm) wide.
£1,550–1,750 / €2,200–2,500
$2,800–3,100 ⊞ BOOM

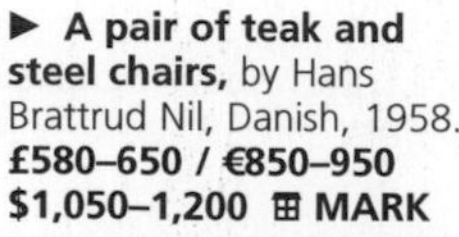

► A pair of teak and steel chairs, by Hans Brattrud Nil, Danish, 1958.
£580–650 / €850–950
$1,050–1,200 ⊞ MARK

► An oak, walnut and mahogany cupboard, by Josef Frank for Svenskt Tenn, model No. 2237, with 13 drawers, the sides with amboyna veneer, on a walnut stand, slight damage, Swedish, designed 1957, 35in (90cm) wide.
£6,000–7,200 / €8,800–10,500
$10,900–13,000 ⚒ BUK

A birch and teak table, by Alvar Aalto, Finnish, c1959, 27½in (70cm) diam.
£3,200–3,800 / €4,650–5,500
$5,800–6,900 ⚒ BUK(F)

A Gucci leather, parchment and metal wine rack, 1950s, 15¾in (40cm) high.
£3,300–3,950 / €4,800–5,800
$6,000–7,200 ⚒ S(NY)

A chromed-steel and leather B-35 lounge chair, by Marcel Breuer, paper label, American, c1960.
£900–1,050 / €1,300–1,550
$1,600–1,900 ⚒ SK

An aluminium and leather Oxford chair, by Arne Jacobsen, Danish, c1960.
£670–750 / €980–1,100
$1,200–1,350 ⊞ DeP

A plywood stool, by Riko Tanabe for Tendo Moko, Japanese, 1960, 14in (35.5cm) high.
£1,050–1,200 / €1,550–1,750
$1,900–2,150 ⊞ EMH

A sapelewood Hexagon cabinet, by David Booth for Gordon Russell, c1961, 44in (112cm) wide.
£1,100–1,250 / €1,600–1,800
$2,000–2,250 ⊞ BOOM

A chrome and leather PK41 folding stool, by Poul Kjaerholm, Danish, 1961, 24in (61cm) wide.
£1,500–1,650 / €2,150–2,400
$2,700–3,000 ⊞ DeP

A Stag teak side cabinet, on metal supports, 1960s, 36in (91.5cm) wide.
£210–250 / €310–370
$380–450 ⚒ CHTR

A set of four Ercol beech and elm chairs, 1960s.
£220–250 / €320–370
$400–450 ⊞ NWE

A rosewood dining suite, by Archie Shine, comprising an extending dining table with one extra leaf, a set of six chairs and a sideboard, 1960s, table 84in (213.5cm) extended.
£2,600–3,100 / €3,800–4,550
$4,700–5,600 ⚒ S(O)

A wood and rope Harp chair, by Jorgen Hovelskov, Danish, 1968.
£1,200–1,400 / €1,750–2,050
$2,150–2,550 ⚒ SK

A pair of Lucite armchairs, covers replaced, American, c1970.
£1,300–1,450 / €1,900–2,100
$2,350–2,600 ⊞ AGO

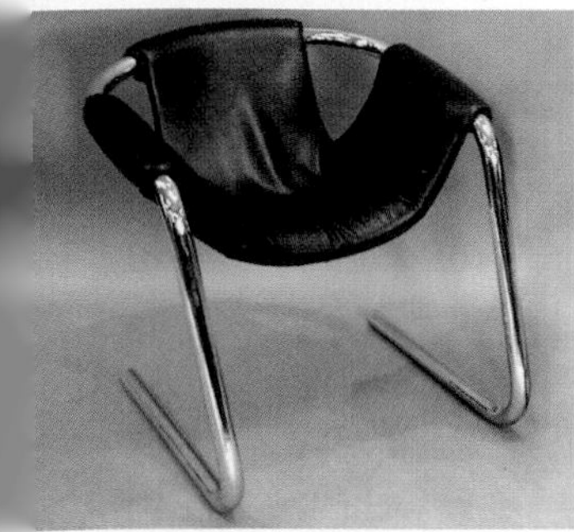

A pair of Arkana aluminium armchairs, 1970s.
£230–270 / €340–400
$420–500 ⚒ SWO

A Seagull chair and footstool, by Gösta Berg and Stenerik Erikson for Fritz Hansen, Danish, 1968.
£4,250–4,750 / €6,200–6,900
$7,700–8,600 ⊞ MARK

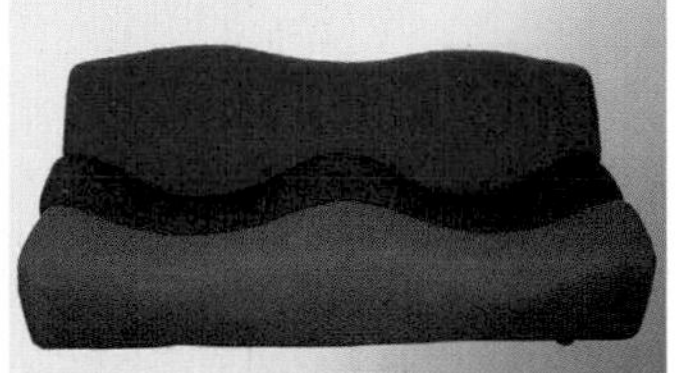

A foam ABCD sofa, by Pierre Paulin for Artifort, Dutch, 1968, 63in (160cm) wide.
£2,900–3,250 / €4,250–4,750
$5,200–5,900 ⊞ MARK

A plaster occasional table, by John Dickinson, model No. 111, c1972, 19in (48.5cm) high.
£4,600–5,500 / €6,700–8,000
$8,300–10,000 ⚒ S(NY)

A chrome and leather Mandarin armchair, by Pieff for Conran, 1974.
£1,100–1,250 / €1,600–1,800
$2,000–2,250 ⊞ BOOM

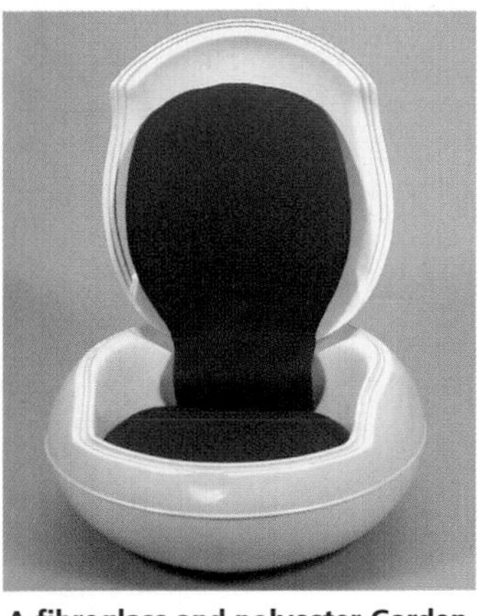

A fibreglass and polyester Garden Egg chair, by Peter Ghyczy for Reuter Products, 1968.
£590–700 / €850–1,000
$1,050–1,250 ⚒ WW

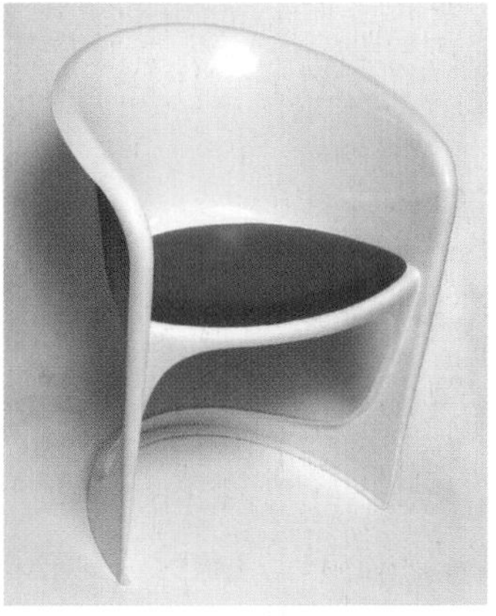

A pair of plastic Cado armchairs, by Steen Ostergaard, Danish, 1969.
£180–200 / €260–290
$320–360 ⊞ FRD

A rosewood-veneered and mahogany sofa table, by John Makepeace, with two frieze drawers and laminated legs, 1975–2000, 64in (162.5cm) wide.
£6,600–7,900 / €9,600–11,500
$11,900–14,300 ⚒ S

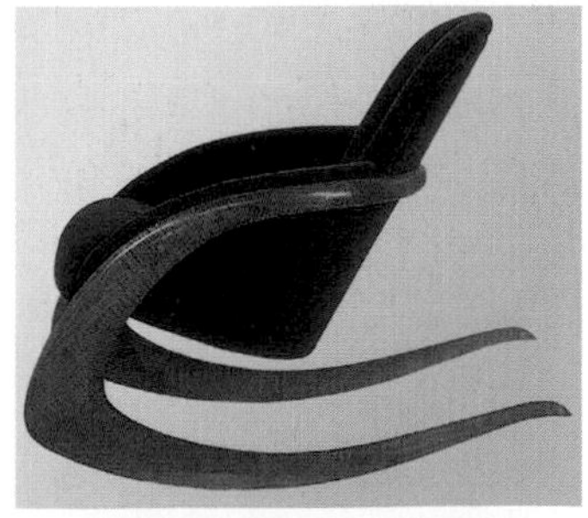

A maple and velvet upholstery Crescent Rocker chair, by Wendell Castle, incised mark, American, 1982.
£9,200–11,000 / €13,400–16,100
$16,700–19,900 ⚒ S(NY)

Glass

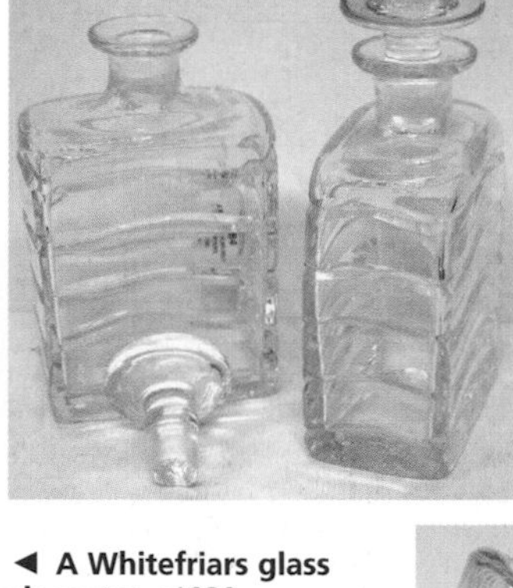

◄ **A pair of Stevens & Williams glass decanters,** by Keith Murray, etched marks, 1930s, 8½in (21.5cm) high.
£300–360
€440–530
$540–650
G(L)

◄ **A Whitefriars glass decanter,** c1930, 9in (23cm) high.
£150–170 / €220–250
$270–300 JHa

A Royal Brierley Cactus glass vase, by Keith Murray, etched signature, c1935, 14in (35.5cm) high.
£1,050–1,250
€1,550–1,850
$1,900–2,250 G(L)

For further information on glass see pages 313–334

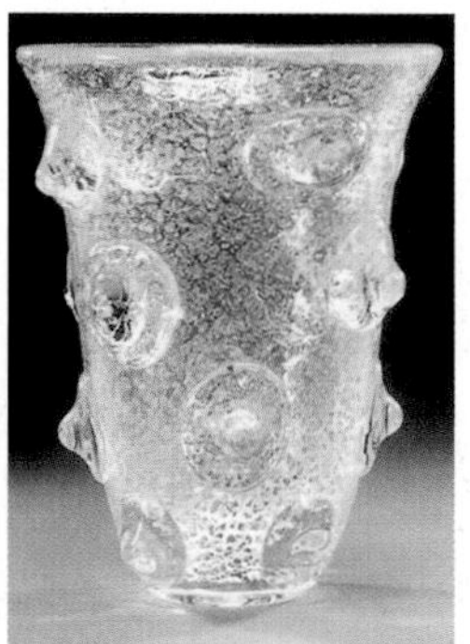

A Barovier & Toso glass vase, with gilt inclusions, engraved marks, Italian, c1940, 12½in (32cm) high.
£3,100–3,700
€4,550–5,400
$5,600–6,700 S(O)

◄ **A Hartil glass vase,** Czechoslovakian, c1950, 5½in (14cm) high.
£70–80 / €100–110
$125–140 JHAa

A Kosta Abstracta glass dish, by Vicke Lindstrand, signed, Swedish, 1950s, 11½in (29cm) wide.
£400–480 / €580–700
$720–870 BUK

A Kosta glass vase, by Vicke Lindstrand, Swedish, c1935, 6in (15cm) high.
£230–260 / €340–380
$420–470 JHa

► **An Orrefors Graal glass vase,** by Edward Hald, decorated with fish, slight damage, Swedish, 1953, 5¼in (13.5cm) diam.
£420–500
€610–730
$760–910
BUK

◄ **A Venini Corroso glass vase,** Italian, Murano, 1955–65, 8½in (21.5cm) high.
£960–1,150
€1,450–1,700
$1,750–2,100
DORO

A Whitefriars Cow Parsley glass vase, by Geoffrey Baxter, 1954, 9in (23cm) high.
£220–250 / €320–360
$400–440 COO

A Nuutajärvi Notsjö Kremlin Bells glass decanter, by Kaj Franck, engraved mark, Finnish, dated 1959, 13¾in (35cm) high.
£600–720 / €880–1,050
$1,100–1,300 S(O)

TWENTIETH-CENTURY DESIGN

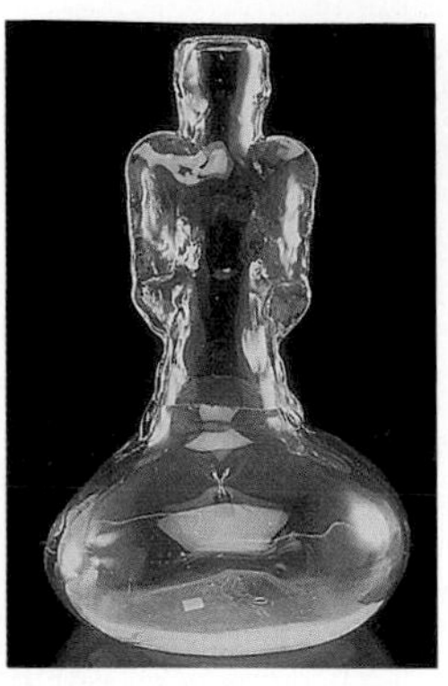

A Nuutajärvi Notsjö glass vase, by Oiva Toikka, engraved mark, Finnish, 1966, 15½in (39.5cm) high.
£1,000–1,200
€1,450–1,750
$1,800–2,150 BUK(F)

A Mdina glass bottle, by Michael Harris, Maltese, 1969, 12in (30.5cm) high.
£135–150 / €195–220
$240–270 COO

A Whitefriars basket-weave slab glass vase, by Geoffrey Baxter, 1970s, 6in (15cm) high.
£130–155 / €200–240
$240–290 DN

A Whitefriars studio range glass vase, 1974, 8in (20.5cm) high.
£220–250 / €320–360
$400–450 COO

◄ **A Memphis Sol glass tazza,** by Ettore Sottsas, engraved mark, Italian, Milan, 1980s, 10¾in (27.5cm) wide.
£1,000–1,200 / €1,450–1,750
$1,800–2,150 S(O)

► **A Barovier & Toso Intarsio glass vase,** by Ercole Barovier, signed, Italian, 1980s, 9½in (24cm) high.
£1,100–1,300 / €1,600–1,900
$2,000–2,350 BUK

Jewellery

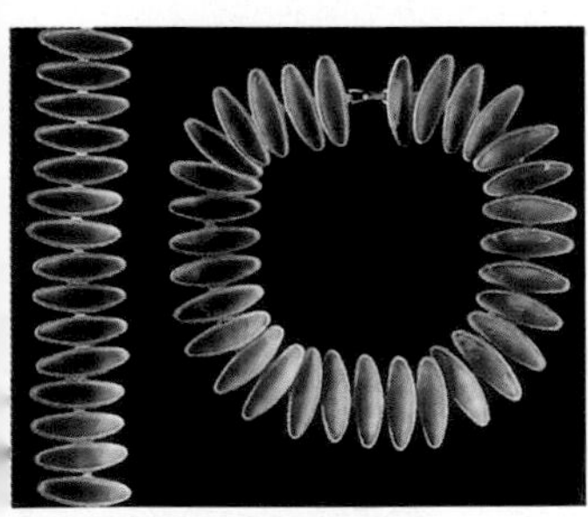

A Borgila Studio silver and enamel bracelet and necklace, Swedish, Stockholm 1957, necklace 14½in (37cm) long.
£520–620 / €760–910
$940–1,100 BUK

A gold and ruby ring, by Francis Beck, with a peacock feather motif, London 1970.
£370–440 / €540–640
$670–800 DN

An 18ct gold Kinetic brooch, by Pol Bury, with moveable spherules, marked and numbered 2/30, 1970s.
£3,250–3,900 / €4,750–5,700
$5,900–7,100 SK(B)

TWENTIETH-CENTURY DESIGN

A bronze amulet pendant, by Pentti Sarpaneva, Finnish, c1966, 3in (7.5cm) long.
£300–340 / €440–500
$540–600 BOOM

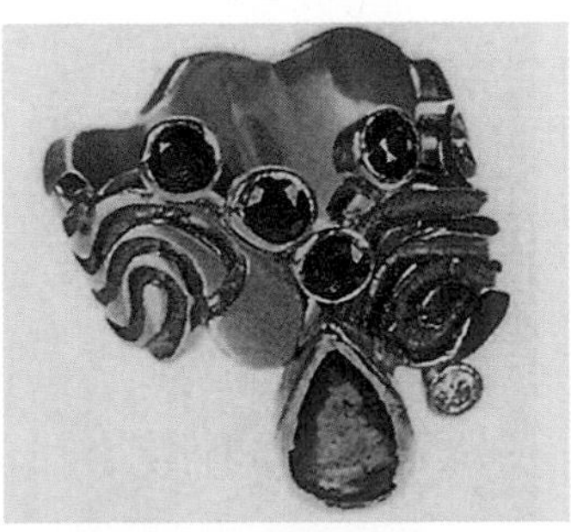

An 18ct gold ring, by Francis Beck and Ernest Blyth, set with an emerald, diamond and four rubies, marked, London 1977.
£440–520 / €640–760
$800–950 DN

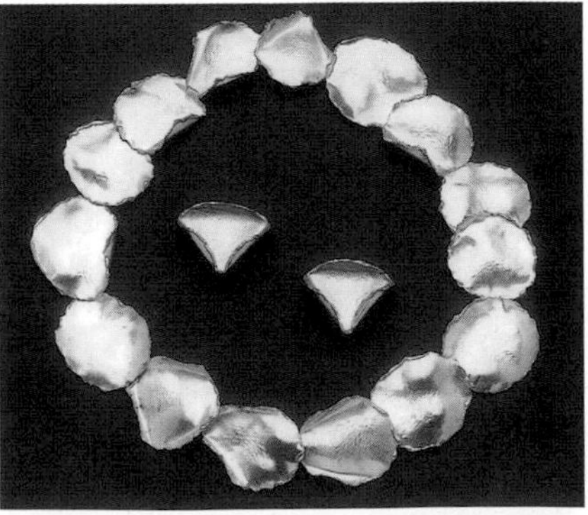

A Tiffany & Co 18ct gold Rose Petal necklace, by Angela Cummings, signed, American, 1979–80, 15½in (39.5cm) long, with matching earrings.
£3,550–4,250 / €5,200–6,200
$6,400–7,700 SK(B)

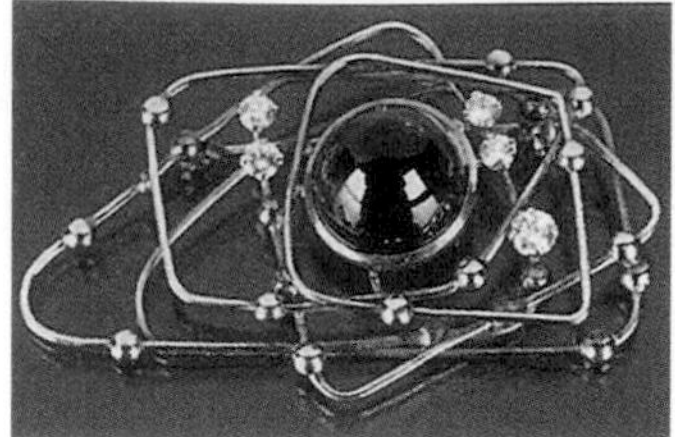

An 18ct gold brooch, by Andrew Grima, set with tourmaline and diamonds, marked, London 1986, 2in (5cm) wide.
£1,500–1,800 / €2,200–2,650
$2,700–3,250 ⚒ DN

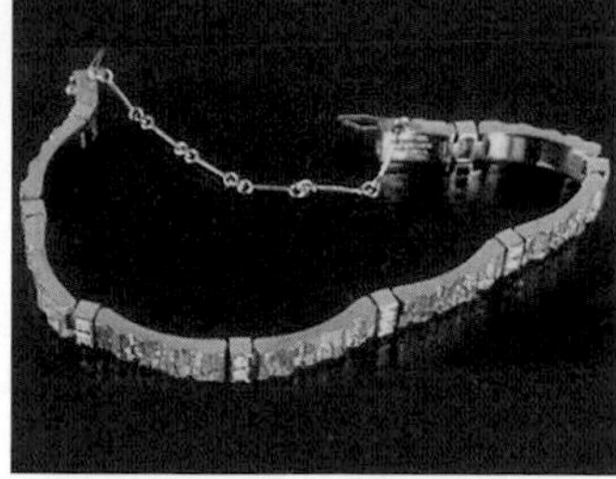
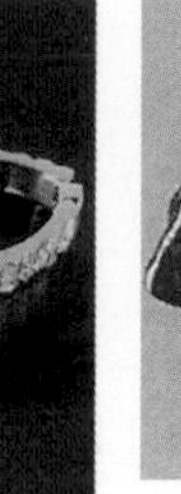

A Lapponia 18ct gold bracelet, with diamond-set collet spacers, Finnish, 1987.
£350–420 / €570–680
$630–760 ⚒ DN

A Lapponia 18ct gold ring, set with a diamond collet, marked, Finnish, dated 1989.
£165–195 / €240–290
$300–360 ⚒ DN

Lighting

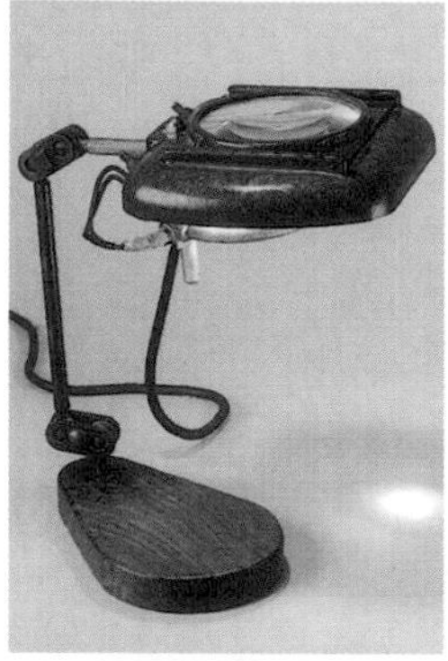

A Bakelite desk lamp, with a magnifier, on a wooden base, American, c1930, 13½in (34.5cm) high.
£210–250 / €310–370
$380–450 ⚒ SK

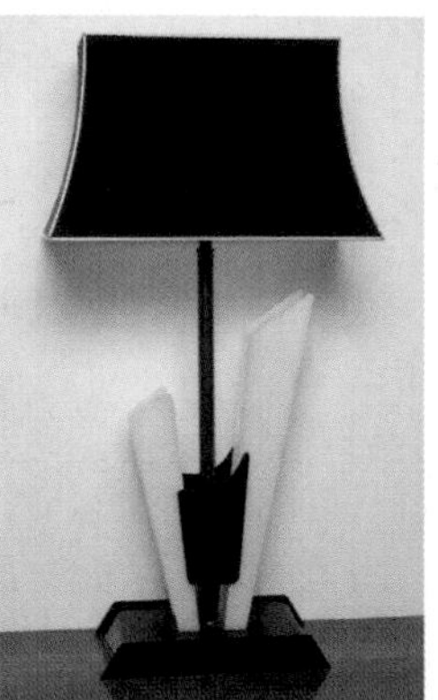

A pair of Lucite table lamps, American, 1930s, 29½in (75cm) high.
£850–950 / €1,250–1,400
$1,500–1,700 ⊞ DeP

A Murano glass table lamp, with bronze mounts, Italian, c1940, 38in (96.5cm) high.
£3,000–3,400
€4,400–4,950
$5,400–6,100 ⊞ DeP

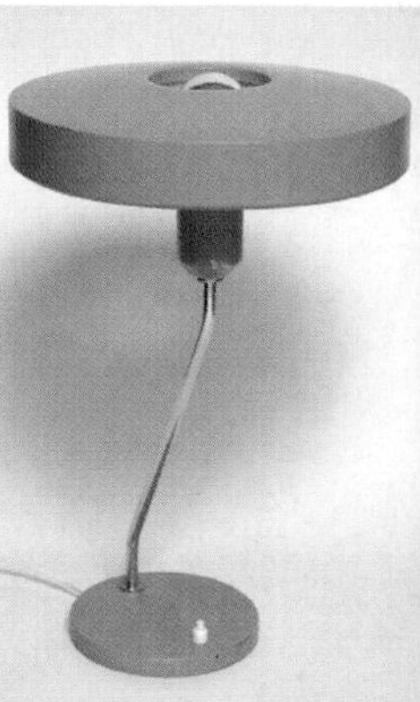

A pair of Phillips enamelled-metal and chrome table lamps, Dutch, c1955, 16in (40.5cm) high.
£450–500 / €660–730
$810–910 ⊞ BOOM

A Venini glass and brass lamp, by Massimo Vignelli for Olivetti Gallery, Italian, mid-1950s, 5in (12.5cm) high.
£2,200–2,500
€3,200–3,600
$4,000–4,500 ⊞ EMH

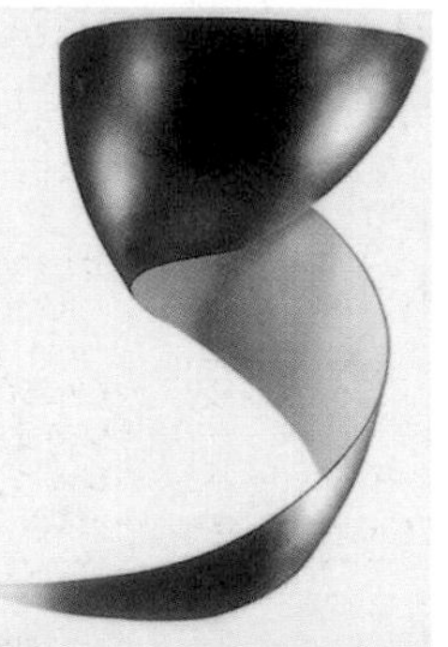

A pair of painted aluminium Flamme ceiling lights, by Serge Mouille, edition of 300, French, c1958, 15½in (39.5cm) high.
£3,350–4,000 / €4,900–5,800
$6,100–7,200 ⚒ S

◄ **A Boda glass and wrought-iron chandelier,** by Erik Höglund, Swedish, 1960s, 35½in (90cm) high.
£1,550–1,850
€2,250–2,700
$2,800–3,350 ⚒ BUK

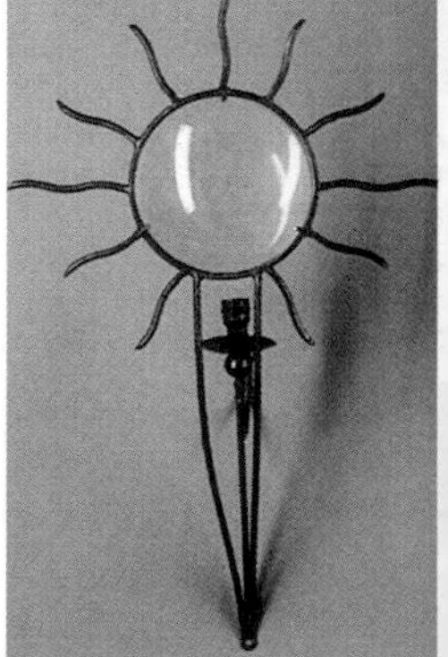

A pair of iron and copper Sunburst wall sconces, by André Dubreuil, with lenses, c1980, 26¾in (68cm) high.
£5,400–6,400
€7,900–9,300
$9,800–11,600 ⚒ S(O)

► **A pair of Fontana Arte glass floor lamps,** Italian, 1970s, 28in (71cm) high.
£850–950 / €1,250–1,400
$1,500–1,700 ⊞ DeP

◄ **A Lucite table lamp,** American, c1975, 17½in (44.5cm) high.
£630–700 / €900–1,000
$1,100–1,250 ⊞ AGO

Metalware

A Georg Jensen silver and glass preserve jar and spoon, import marks for London 1928, Danish, 3in (7.5cm) diam.
£580–650 / €850–950
$1,050–1,200 ⊞ SHa

A Georg Jensen silver dish, by Harald Nielsen, import marks for London 1930, Danish, 6in (15cm) diam.
£400–450 / €580–650
$720–820 ⊞ SAT

A pair of Georg Jensen silver candlesticks, Danish, c1950, 3in (7.5cm) diam.
£1,550–1,750 / €2,250–2,550
$2,800–3,150 ⊞ SHa

A silver centrepiece, by William de Matteo, American, Virginia, c1960, 6½in (16.5cm) high.
£2,850–3,200 / €4,150–4,650
$5,200–5,800 ⊞ KK

A silver bread basket, by Tapio Wirkkala, signed, Finnish, 1961, 9¾in (25cm) square.
£1,550–1,850 / €2,250–2,700
$2,800–3,350 ⚒ BUK

A silver bowl, by Tapio Wirkkala, signed, Finnish, 1967, 8½in (21.5cm) diam.
£1,300–1,550 / €1,900–2,250
$2,350–2,800 ⚒ BUK

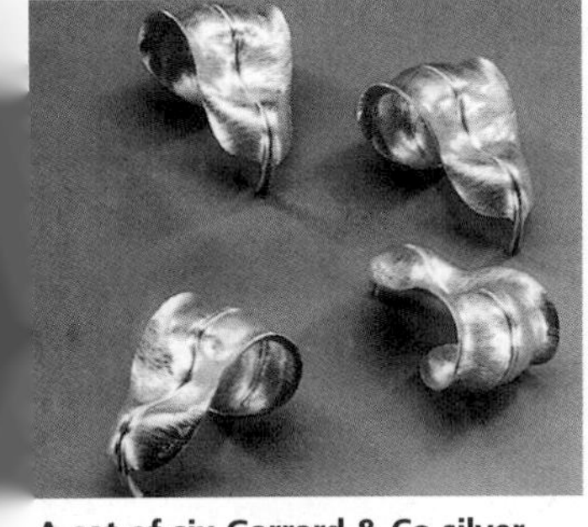

A set of six Garrard & Co silver napkin rings, each in the form of a feather, London 1968–69, 3¼in (8.5cm) wide.
£2,250–2,700 / €3,300–3,950
$4,050–4,900 ⚒ S(O)

A pair of Robert Welch parcel-gilt silver candlesticks, Birmingham 1970, 9½in (24cm) high.
£3,600–4,300 / €5,300–6,300
$6,500–7,800 ⚒ S(O)

A parcel-gilt silver centrepiece, by Stuart Devlin, with a trumpet-shaped vase and a parcel-gilt table lighter, marked, London 1970, 16¼in (41.5cm) wide.
£4,050–4,850 / €5,900–7,100
$7,300–8,800 ⚒ S(O)

Stuart Devlin has exhibited his work in many countries and is represented in important public and private collections worldwide. In 1982 he received the Royal Warrant as Goldsmith and Jeweller to Her Majesty the Queen.

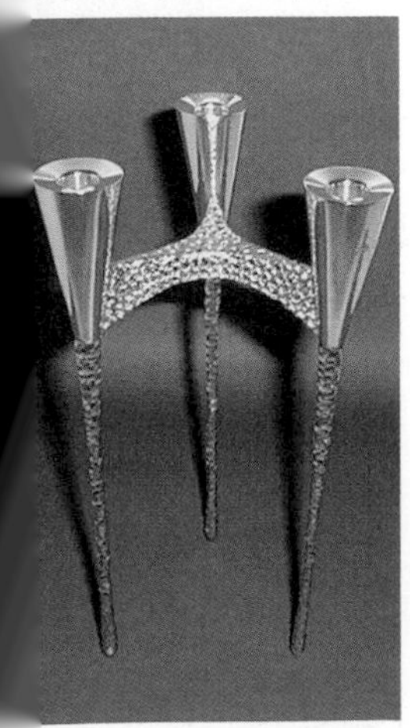

◄ **A silver candelabra,** by Stuart Devlin, London 1971, 8¾in (22cm) high.
£1,450–1,650
€2,100–2,400
$2,600–3,000
⊞ BEX

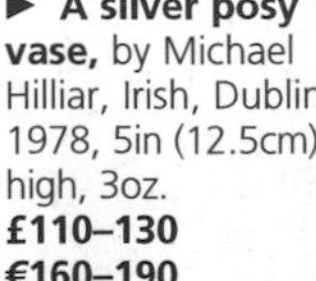

► **A silver posy vase,** by Michael Hilliar, Irish, Dublin 1978, 5in (12.5cm) high, 3oz.
£110–130
€160–190
$200–240 ⚒ JAd

A pair of iron and glass Fleur candlesticks, by André Dubreuil, c1982, 24in (61cm) high.
£9,600–11,500 / €14,000–16,800
$17,400–20,800 ⚒ S(O)

Sculpture

A bronze figure, by Walter Spitzer, entitled 'The Water Carrier', signed, c1940, 12in (30.5cm) high.
£3,000–3,350
€4,400–4,900
$5,400–6,100 ⊞ MI

A bronze mask, by Hagenauer, stamped maker's mark, Austrian, mid-20thC, 3½in (9cm) high.
£480–570 / €700–830
$870–1,050 ⚒ S(O)

▶ **A bronze figure,** by Rudolf Schwaiger, dated 1974, 8¾in (22cm) high.
£720–860 / €1,050–1,250
$1,300–1,550 ⚒ DORO

◀ **A polished steel sculpture,** by James Prestini, entitled 'Untitled Construction #174', stamped mark, 1967, 21¾in (55.5cm) high.
£2,500–3,000
€3,650–4,400
$4,550–5,400 ⚒ S(NY)

Textiles

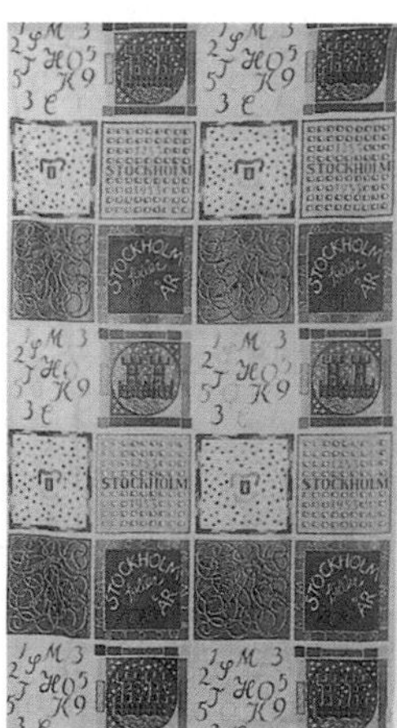

◀ **A cotton fabric panel,** by Josef Frank for Svenskt Tenn, depicting 28 handkerchiefs commemorating Stockholm's 700th anniversary, 1953, 47¼ x 94½in (120 x 240cm).
£150–180 / €220–260
$270–320 ⚒ BUK

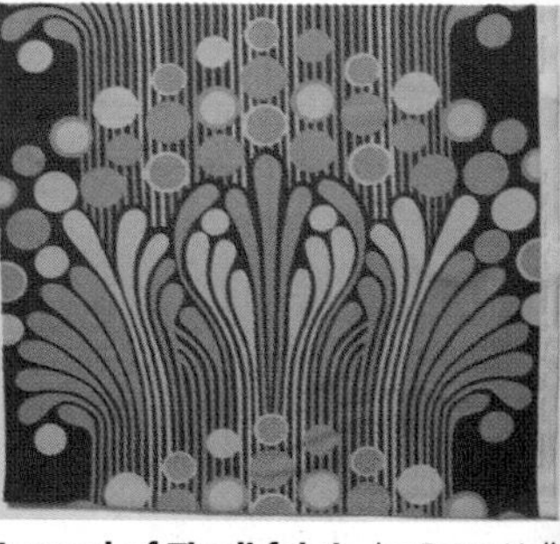

A panel of Tivoli fabric, by Peter Hall for Heal's, 1968, 157½in (400cm) long.
£105–120 / €155–175
$190–210 ⊞ FRD

◀ **A panel of Larch fabric,** by Lucienne Day for Heal's, 1961, 157½in (400cm) long.
£120–140 / €180–200
$220–250 ⊞ FRD

Wireless & Television

A Philco Bakelite 444 People's wireless, c1936, 17in (43cm) wide.
£310–350 / €450–500
$560–630 ⊞ OTA

A Bush Bakelite Dac90A wireless, c1950, 12½in (32cm) wide.
£155–185 / €230–270
$280–330 ⚒ S(P)

▶ **A plastic Mirror television,** by Stig Lindberg for Luxor, Swedish, 1960s, 23¾in (60.5cm) wide.
£175–210
€260–310
$320–380 ⚒ BUK

▶ **A plastic Aphelion television,** 1981, 36in (91.5cm) high.
£1,550–1,750 / €2,250–2,550
$2,800–3,150 ⊞ BOOM

Lamps & Lighting

Ceiling & Wall Lights

A brass four-branch chandelier, Dutch, 18thC, 11½in (29cm) high.
£810–970 / €1,200–1,400
$1,450–1,750 S(Am)

A brass and glass six-light chandelier, Swedish, c1800, 34in (86.5cm) high.
£4,000–4,800
€5,800–7,000
$7,200–8,700 BUK

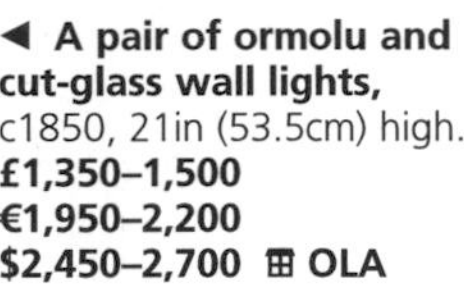

◄ **A pair of ormolu and cut-glass wall lights,** c1850, 21in (53.5cm) high.
£1,350–1,500
€1,950–2,200
$2,450–2,700 OLA

A brass two-branch gas lamp, with an opaque glass shade, c1880, 15in (38cm) diam.
£210–240 / €310–350
$380–430 EAL

◄ **A Victorian brass wall lantern,** with cut-glass panels, 43in (109cm) high.
£490–580 / €720–850
$890–1,050 BWL

pair of brass wall gas lights, with glass shades, 1880, 16in (40.5cm) wide.
720–800 / €1,000–1,150
1,300–1,450 CHA

► **A wrought-iron ceiling lantern,** c1830, 26in (66cm) high.
£500–550 / €720–800
$900–1,000 OLA

A pair of gilt-bronze three-branch wall lights, c1850, 20in (51cm) high.
£450–500 / €660–730
$810–910 EAL

► **A pair of brass wall lights,** Dutch, 19thC, 15¾in (40cm) wide.
£650–780 / €960–1,150
$1,200–1,400 S(P)

A Victorian bronze three-branch gas lamp, with acid-etched glass shades, lozenge mark, pre-1883, 32in (81.5cm) high.
£1,000–1,100
€1,450–1,600
$1,800–2,000 ⊞ CHA

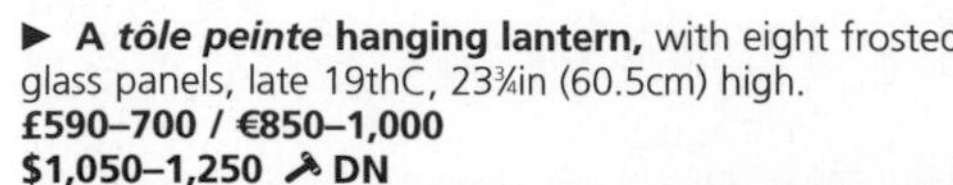

► **A *tôle peinte* hanging lantern,** with eight frosted-glass panels, late 19thC, 23¾in (60.5cm) high.
£590–700 / €850–1,000
$1,050–1,250 ⚒ DN

A painted wood and antler four-branch chandelier, one branch detached, German, late 19thC, 33¾in (85.5cm) wide.
£2,600–3,100 / €3,800–4,550
$4,700–5,600 ⚒ S(Am)

A late Victorian cut-glass eight-branch chandelier, damaged, 28¼in (72cm) diam.
£1,050–1,250
€1,550–1,850
$1,900–2,250 ⚒ S(O)

A pair of gilt-brass wall lamps, with cut-glass shades, c1900, 15in (38cm) high.
£320–360 / €470–530
$580–650 ⊞ EAL

A brass three-branch ceiling light, with cut-glass shades, c1900, 27in (68.5cm) wide.
£450–500 / €660–730
$810–910 ⊞ JeH

A painted and carved wood ceiling light, Austrian, Tyrol, early 20thC, 15¾in (40cm) high.
£760–910 / €1,100–1,300
$1,400–1,650 ⚒ DORO

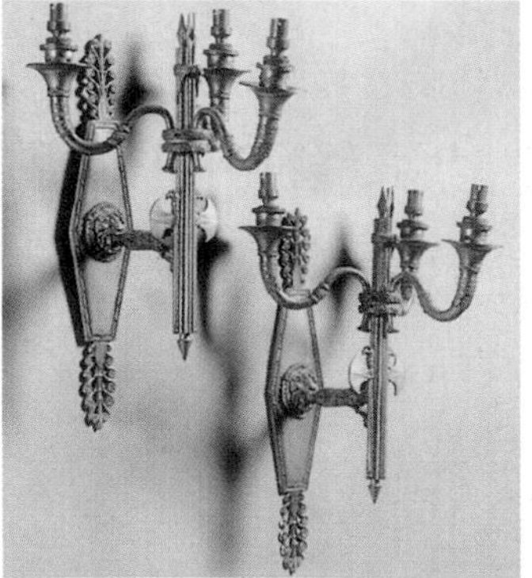

A pair of Empire-style gilt-bronze three-branch wall lights, French, c1900, 11¾in (30cm) wide.
£3,350–4,000 / €4,900–5,800
$6,100–7,200 ⚒ S(O)

A brass five-branch ceiling light, c1910, 30in (76cm) high.
£1,050–1,200 / €1,550–1,750
$1,900–2,100 ⊞ CHA

A pair of wall lights, with mica glass shades, fitted for electricity, c1910, 9in (23cm) high.
£155–175 / €230–260
$280–320 ⊞ JeH

An ormolu ceiling light, with facet-cut glass beads, French, c1910, 23¾in (60.5cm) diam.
£820–980 / €1,200–1,450
$1,500–1,800 ⚒ TEN

A pair of gilt-bronze wall lights, in the French Empire style, early 20thC, 23¾in (60.5cm) diam.
£2,200–2,600 / €3,200–3,800
$4,000–4,700 ⚒ S(O)

A pair of gilt-bronze wall sconces, by E. F. Caldwell & Co, each in the form of a cornucopia issuing from the mouth of a satyr mask, fitted for electricity, marked, American, New York, early 20thC, 13in (33cm) high.
£3,300–3,950
€4,800–5,700
$6,000–7,100 S(NY)

A pair of cast-brass wall lights, c1920, 10in (25.5cm) high.
£105–120 / €155–175
$190–210 JeH

A spelter ceiling light, in the form of flying cherubs, French, 1920s, 16in (40.5cm) wide.
£360–400 / €520–580
$650–720 JPr

Always check that electric lighting conforms to the current safety regulations before using.

A gilt-bronze five-branch chandelier, restored and rewired, French, 1920s, 12in (30.5cm) wide.
£270–300 / €390–440
$490–540 JPr

Table & Standard Lamps

A Regency mahogany and brass colza oil table lamp, fitted for electricity, 24½in (62cm) high,
£260–310 / €380–450
$470–560 PFK

A brass and *pâte-sur-pâte* two-branch table lamp, decorated with plaques of classical figures, 19thC, 30in (76cm) high.
£140–165 / €200–240
$250–300 G(L)

A pair of *tôle peinte* and gilt-bronze lamps, fitted for electricity, 19thC, 27½in (70cm) high.
£2,450–2,900
€3,600–4,250
$4,400–5,200 S(P)

◄ **A pair of candlesticks,** restored, French, 19thC, 16in (40.5cm) high.
£370–420 / €540–620
$670–760 CHES

◄ **A Victorian brass and frosted glass oil lamp,** with embossed decoration, on a slag base, 22in (56cm) high.
£115–135 / €170–200
$210–240 GAK

► **A Victorian enamelled oil lamp,** decorated with birds and flowers, with an opaque glass shade and a clear glass chimney, 23¾in (60.5cm) diam.
£80–95 / €120–140
$145–170 WilP

A miniature gas lamp, with a cranberry glass shade, c1880, 9in (23cm) high.
£670–750 / €980–1,100
$1,200–1,350 TOL

◄ **A wooden figural lamp,** in the form of a woman, on a carved column, Continental, c1900, 89in (226cm) high.
£4,000–4,450
€5,700–6,500
$7,200–8,100
⊞ MTay

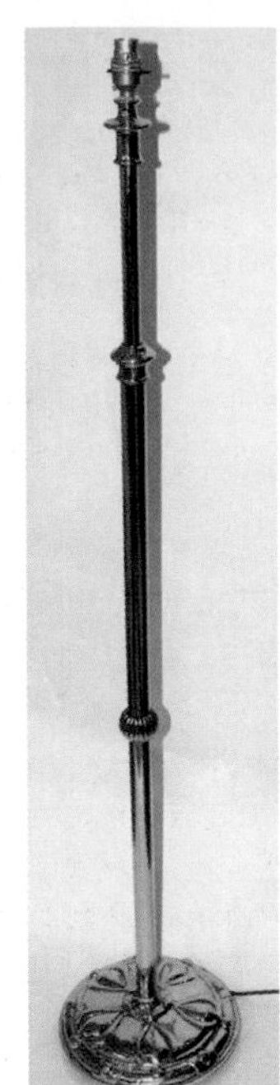

► **A brass adjustable standard lamp,** c1900, 52in (132cm) high.
£220–250
€330–370
$400–450
⊞ OLA

A cast-brass table lamp, with a cut-glass shade, c1905, 17in (43cm) high.
£800–900 / €1,100–1,300
$1,450–1,650 ⊞ TOL

A pair of cast-brass desk lamps, c1910, 13in (33cm) high.
£300–330 / €430–480
$540–600 ⊞ JeH

A pair of milkglass table lamps, rewired, c1910, 17in (43cm) high.
£310–350 / €460–510
$560–630 ⊞ GLAS

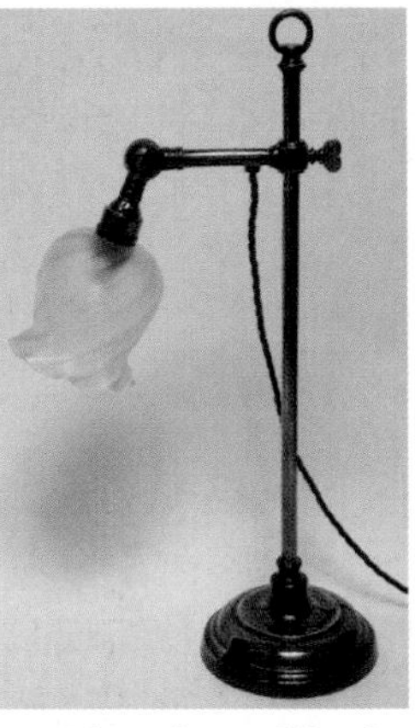

An Edwardian oxidized metal adjustable table lamp, with an etched-glass shade, 18in (45.5cm) high.
£150–165 / €210–240
$270–300 ⊞ JeH

A pair of brass desk lamps, with glass shades, c1910, 16in (40.5cm) high.
£800–900 / €1,150–1,300
$1,450–1,650 ⊞ CHA

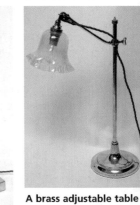

A brass adjustable table lamp, with a vaseline glass shade, c1910, 17in (43cm) high.
£300–330 / €430–480
$540–600 ⊞ JeH

An oxidized cast-brass table lamp, the glass shade decorated with pansies, c1920, 16in (40.5cm) high.
£430–480 / €630–700
$780–870 ⊞ TOL

An oxidized copper table lamp, with an etched and painted glass shade, c1920, 20in (51cm) high.
£135–150 / €195–220
$240–270 ⊞ JeH

A cast-brass desk lamp, c1925, 19in (48.5cm) high.
£810–900 / €1,200–1,350
$1,450–1,650 ⊞ TOL

► **A parcel-gilt and painted bronze lamp,** by E. F. Caldwell & Co, with ivory mounts, American, New York, c1925, 29¾in (75.5cm) high.
£4,600–5,500
€6,700–8,000
$8,300–10,000 ⚒ S(NY)

Rugs & Carpets

The market for antique rugs and carpets can simply be described as multi-faceted. It might be useful to begin by defining the various collecting areas. The term 'carpet' generally refers to pieces over 144 x 96in (366 x 241.5cm) and they are usually regarded as decorative furnishing. Weavings that are smaller than this are defined as rugs and these can fall into the decorative furnishing category as well as that of the collector. The term 'runner' refers to long narrow weavings which again tend to fall into the decorative furnishing category. Apart from rugs, carpets and runners, functional artefacts such as bags and trappings are popular with collectors.

In recent years, the decorative furnishing market has been dramatically affected by decorating trends, especially those prevalent in the US, where the trend is for oversize carpets such as Ziegler carpets from west Persia, Ushak carpets from Turkey and Tabriz carpets from northwest Persia. The desire for a minimalist approach towards decorating and the popularity of pastel colour tones has had a deleterious affect on this area of the market, which predominantly consists of items that display traditional strong colours and dense patterning. To counter this, examples that have pastel colours, mostly tones of ivory, terracotta and pale blues, have increased dramatically in value. Similar trends apply to smaller rugs, although finely made examples in good condition are still sought after and values remain consistent whatever the colour. Examples that are worn or damaged are not as desirable, and prices compared with recent years have not shown significant increase. The production of well-made modern rugs and carpets specifically geared to the furnishing market, and constantly adapting to current market trends in design and colour, has also had a significant impact on the antique furnishing market.

The collectors' market in rugs and artefacts from the Caucasian, Turkoman and southwest Persian groups remains consistent, with the accent very much on condition which, for the seasoned collector, has to be close to perfect and of good colour, which means no chemical dyes. Examples in lesser condition, and of a slightly later date (that is around 1900 to 1920) tend to be ignored by collectors and represent a good buy in today's market. Rugs recognized to have rare designs,or particularly unusual designs or colour combinations to the respective group, command higher values even if the condition leaves something to be desired.

Jonathan Wadsworth

A Savonnerie-style carpet, probably Spanish, Madrid, 1900–25, 266 x 138in (677 x 351.5cm).
£3,050–3,650 / €4,450–5,300
$5,500–6,600 ⚒ BUK
Most Spanish carpets of this date were made in Madrid by the Real Fabrique Manufactury and often, but not always, bear the mark 'RFM', accompanying a date.

An Aubusson carpet, French, c1860, 124 x 101in (310 x 258cm).
£2,150–2,550
€3,150–3,700
$3,900–4,600 ⚒ S(O)

An Aubusson carpet, slight damage, French, c1920, 141 x 114in (358 x 289.5cm).
£2,800–3,350
€4,100–4,900
$5,100–6,100 ⚒ S(NY)

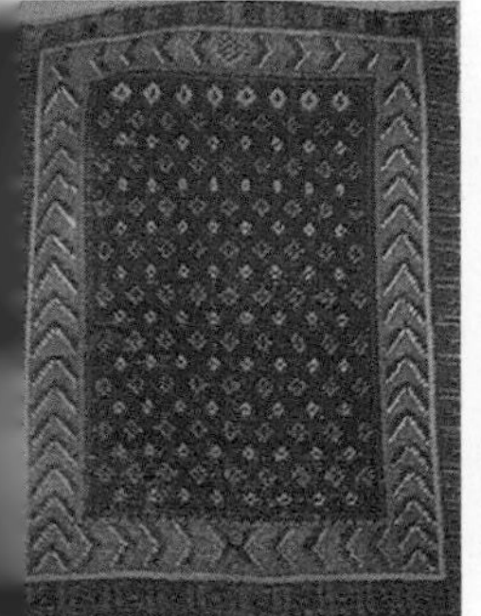

A Rya rug, damaged and repaired, Finnish, 19thC, 75 x 53in (190.5 x 134.5cm).
£190–220 / €280–330
$340–400 ⚒ NSal

A Bessarabian silk miniature kilim, Ukrainian, 1850–1900, 15 x 11in (38 x 28cm).
£120–140 / €170–200
$220–260 ⚒ NSal

The rugs in this section have been arranged in geographical sequence from west to east, in the following order: Europe, Turkey, Anatolia, Caucasus, Persia, Turkestan, India and China.

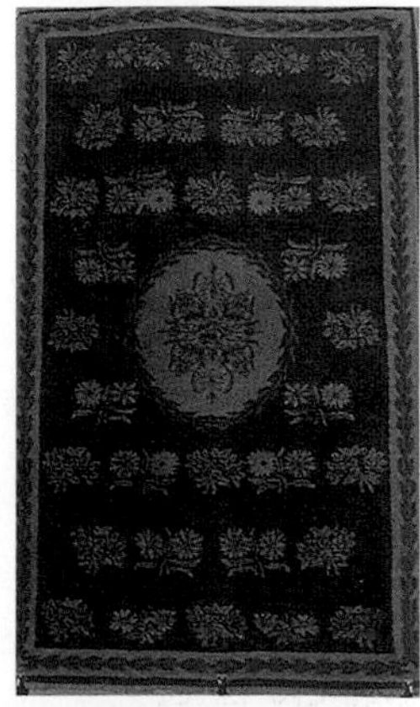

▶ **A rug,** Moldavian, c1930, 77 x 48in (195.5 x 122cm).
£540–640 / €790–930
$980–1,150 ⚒ NSal

A rug, probably Bergama, Turkish, c1900, 74 x 47in (188 x 119.5cm).
£720–800 / €1,000–1,150
$1,300–1,450 ⊞ DNo

An Ushak carpet, Turkish, c1920, 187 x 109½in (476 x 278cm).
£2,250–2,700 / €3,300–3,950
$4,050–4,900 ⚒ RTo
The bold pattern on this carpet is a desirable feature.

An Erivan rug, Caucasian, c1900, 57 x 45in (145 x 114.5cm).
£2,000–2,200
€2,900–3,200
$3,600–4,000 ⊞ KW

A Gendje rug, southwest Caucasian, c1890, 61 x 46in (155 x 117cm).
£1,550–1,750
€2,250–2,550
$2,700–3,100 ⊞ DNo

A Kazak rug, southwest Caucasian, c1890, 80 x 62in (203 x 157.5cm).
£2,000–2,250 / €2,900–3,300
$3,600–4,050 ⊞ DNo

A Melas rug, Turkish, c1880, 53¼ x 39in (135.5 x 99cm).
£1,700–1,900
€2,500–2,750
$3,100–3,450 ⊞ KW

A Kayseri prayer rug, central Anatolian, c1900, 67 x 50in (170 x 127cm).
£670–750 / €980–1,100
$1,200–1,350 ⊞ DNo

An Ushak carpet, Turkish, c1910, 187 x 149in (475 x 378.5cm).
£3,600–4,300
€5,300–6,300
$6,500–7,800 ⚒ S(O)

A Derbend rug, Caucasian, c1910, 68 x 43in (172.5 x 109cm).
£670–750 / €980–1,100
$1,200–1,350 ⊞ WADS

◄ **A Gendje long rug,** southwest Caucasian, c1890 88 x 43in (223.5 x 109cm).
£1,350–1,500
€2,000–2,200
$2,450–2,700 ⊞ WADS

A Karabakh kilim, small repair, south Caucasian, c1900, 130 x 56in (330 x 142cm).
£350–420 / €510–610
$630–760 ⚒ NSal

◄ **A Kazak Fachralo rug,** southwest Caucasian, c1910 61¾ x 41¼in (157.5 x 105cm
£860–1,000 / €1,250–1,50
$1,500–1,800 ⚒ S(O)

A Kazak Loripambak rug, southwest Caucasian, early 20thC, 89 x 70in (226 x 178cm).
£1,250–1,500
€1,850–2,200
$2,250–2,700 LHA
Loripambak rugs frequently incorporate an octagonal medallion, seen in ivory here, enclosing the hooked cruciform motif.

Caucasian carpets

The Caucasian mountain range between the Black Sea and the Caspian Sea is home to many ethnic groups whose weaving traditions go back centuries. Little is known of the type of carpet produced before the middle of the 17th century, but then a clearly identifiable group of carpets based on a nomadic and semi-nomadic way of weaving begin to appear. Pre-1900 examples are particularly sought after as they possess great individuality and charm. Caucasian rug designs incorporate both bold and finely drawn geometric motifs in bright vivid colours, often contrasting, and characteristically depict intensely stylized fauna and floral forms. Carpets from the west and south Caucasus, (Kazak and Karabagh districts) use bold geometric motifs, and the pile is long and lustrous. Examples from the East and North, (Shirvan and Kuba districts) tend to be finely woven with great detail and often display a huge range of jewel-like colours. Caucasian carpets are highly prized by collectors and, if the colours and condition are good, they will command high prices.

A Moghan rug, south Caucasian, indistinctly dated 1304 (1887), 113 x 51in (287 x 126.5cm).
£1,650–1,950
€2,400–2,850
$3,000–3,550 S(O)

A Shirvan rug, east Caucasian, c1880, 58¾ x 46¾in (149 x 119cm).
£4,650–5,200
€6,800–7,600
$8,300–9,400 KW

A Shirvan rug, east Caucasian, late 19thC, 62 x 46in (157.5 x 117cm).
£340–400 / €500–590
$600–720 NSal

A Shirvan rug, east Caucasian, c1890, 57 x 39in (145 x 99cm).
£1,550–1,750
€2,250–2,550
$2,800–3,150 DNo

A Shirvan rug, east Caucasian, c1890, 73 x 49in (185.5 x 124.5cm).
£580–650 / €850–950
$1,050–1,200 DNo

◄ **A Shirvan rug,** east Caucasian, c1900, 62¼ x 44in (158 x 112cm).
£1,750–2,100
€2,550–3,050
$3,150–3,800 RTo

► **A Shirvan rug,** east Caucasian, 1900, 120 x 46in (305 x 117cm).
£8,200–9,200
€12,000–13,400
$14,800–16,700 KW

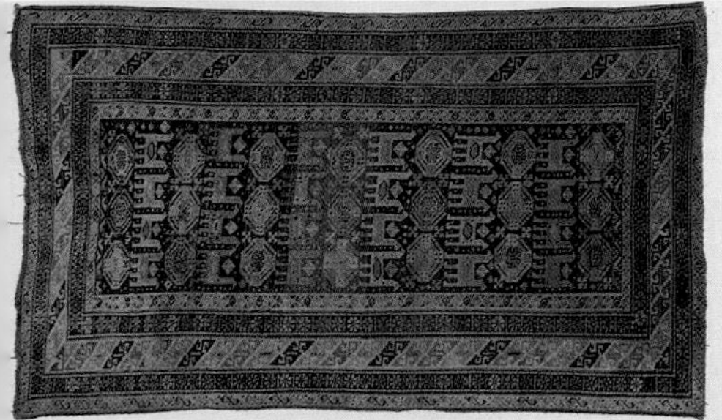

A Shirvan rug, east Caucasian, c1900, 76 x 57in (193 x 229.5cm).
£2,000–2,250 / €2,900–3,300
$3,600–4,050 DNo

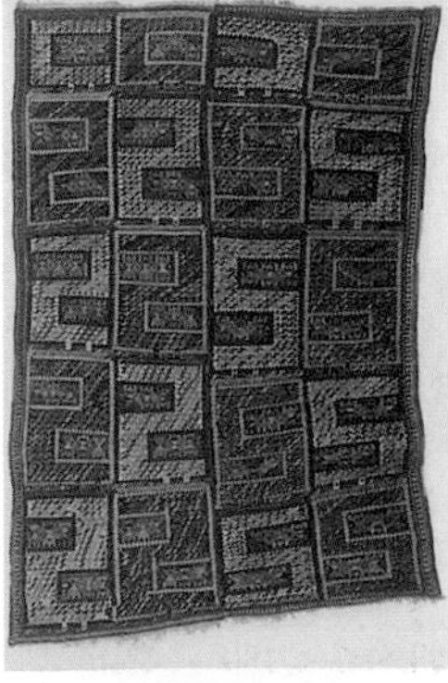

► **A Sileh embroidered flatweave rug,** south Caucasian, c1920, 111½ x 77½in (283 x 197cm).
£1,050–1,250
€1,550–1,850
$1,900–2,250 S(O)
The date of this rug may have had a bearing on the price it realized. Late 19th-century pieces are more desirable as they have no chemical colours whereas this rug clearly shows bright orange chemical colour.

Miller's Compares

I. An Afshar rug, southwest Persian, Shiraz Province, c1900, 61 x 50in (155 x 127cm).
£2,550–2,850
€3,700–4,150
$4,600–5,200 ⊞ DNo

II. An Afshar rug, southwest Persian, c1890, 53 x 42in (134.5 x 106.5cm).
£580–650 / €850–950
$1,050–1,200 ⊞ DNo

Item I displays a much more detailed and rare design that Item II, which is of a type frequently seen from this tribal group. The design on Item I is also normally found on larger rugs than this one. In addition, Item I is less worn and faded than Item II, which is invariably a desirable factor.

A Bidjar runner, northwest Persian, c1890, 200 x 39in (508 x 99cm).
£1,550–1,750
€2,250–2,550
$2,800–3,150 ⚒ S(O)

A Bidjar rug, northwest Persian, c1910, 77 x 55in (195.5 x 139.5cm).
£720–800
€1,050–1,200
$1,300–1,450 ⊞ WADS

A Gabbeh rug, south Persian, c1920, 88 x 54in (223.5 x 137cm).
£430–480 / €630–700
$780–870 ⊞ DNo

An Afshar rug, southwest Persian, Shiraz Province, c1890, 72 x 53in (183 x 134.5cm).
£3,350–3,750
€4,900–5,500
$6,100–6,800 ⊞ DNo

An Afshar rug, southwest Persian, Shiraz Province, c1920, 72 x 61in (183 x 155cm).
£810–900 / €1,150–1,300
$1,450–1,650 ⊞ DNo

A Fereghan carpet, west Persian, c1870, 215 x 161in (546 x 410cm).
£2,400–2,850
€3,500–4,150
$4,350–5,200 ⚒ S(O)
Plain field carpets currently do not sell well, particularly with a 'floating' diamond medallion such as that shown in this example, hence the relatively low price for the size of the carpet.

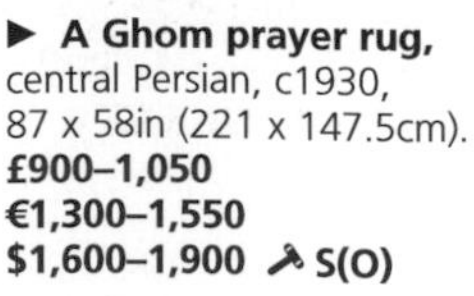

▶ A Ghom prayer rug, central Persian, c1930, 87 x 58in (221 x 147.5cm).
£900–1,050
€1,300–1,550
$1,600–1,900 ⚒ S(O)

An Afshar rug, southwest Persian, c1920, 81 x 59in (205.5 x 150cm).
£2,000–2,250
€2,900–3,300
$3,600–4,050 ⊞ DNo

A Bakhtiyari rug, northwest Persian, c1900, 55 x 45in (139.5 x 114.5cm).
£880–980 / €1,300–1,450
$1,600–1,800 ⊞ WADS

A Feraghan rug, west Persian, c1900, 78 x 50in (198 x 127cm).
£1,550–1,750
€2,250–2,550
$2,800–3,150 ⊞ DNo

A Gorevan runner, northwest Persian, c1900, 88¼ x 28in (224 x 71cm).
£700–780 / €1,000–1,100
$1,250–1,400 ⊞ KW

A Hamadan rug, west Persian, c1920, 61 x 47in (155 x 119.5cm).
£760–850 / €1,100–1,250
$1,400–1,550 ⊞ DNo

A Hamadan rug, northwest Persian, c1890, 82 x 50in (208.5 x 127cm).
£880–980 / €1,300–1,450
$1,600–1,800 ⊞ WADS

A Hamadan rug, west Persian, 1900–20, 79 x 44in (200.5 x 112cm).
£290–340 / €420–500
$520–620 ⚒ NSal

A Heriz carpet, northwest Persian, c1910, 130 x 97in (330 x 246.5cm).
£1,350–1,500 / €1,950–2,200
$2,450–2,700 ⊞ WADS

What to look for

Each antique carpet is an individual work of art in its own right. In order to establish whether a carpet is handmade, turn it over – the pattern should be as clear to read on the reverse. The fringe ends should be an integral part of the rug and run all the way through the carpet. By reversing the carpet, any repairs that might have been undertaken will become more visible. Particularly look out for repairs that might indicate that the carpet has been cut and rejoined to reduce it in size. This has a very serious impact on the value. If the colours on the reverse side of a carpet are stronger than on the front then it is likely that the surface has been chemically washed to tone the original colours down. Although this may make a rug look more attractive, it is a negative characteristic as dyes that fade and respond to this washing are always chemical dyes.

A Hamadan rug, west Persian, c1920, 66 x 48in (167.5 x 122cm).
£340–380 / €500–550
$620–690 ⊞ DNo

◄ **A Heriz rug,** northwest Persian, c1880, 55in x 36¾in (139.5 x 93.5cm).
£1,500–1,700
€2,200–2,500
$2,700–3,000 ⊞ KW

A Heriz carpet, northwest Persian, c1900, 142 x 70½in (360.5 x 179cm).
£6,600–7,900
€9,600–11,500
$11,900–14,300 ⚒ LHA

A Heriz carpet, northwest Persian, 1900–25, 90 x 70in (228.5 x 178cm).
£1,200–1,400
€1,750–2,050
$2,150–2,550 ⚒ S(O)

► **A Heriz runner,** northwest Persian, c1915, 132 x 32in (335.5 x 81.5cm).
£1,500–1,700
€2,200–2,500
$2,700–3,000 ⊞ KW

A Heriz rug, northwest Persian, c1920, 50 x 32in (127 x 81.5cm).
£280–320 / €420–470
$510–580 ⊞ DNo

An Isfahan rug, central Persian, c1880, 59¾ x 41in (152 x 104cm).
£1,300–1,450
€1,900–2,100
$2,350–2,600 ⊞ KW

A Kashan pictorial rug, central Persian, c1900, 59 x 42in (150 x 106.5cm).
£2,700–3,000
€3,950–4,400
$4,900–5,400 ⊞ KW

A Kashgai rug, southwest Persian, c1880, 85 x 53in (216 x 134.5cm).
£880–980 / €1,300–1,450
$1,600–1,800 ⊞ WADS

A Kashgai rug, southwest Persian, c1890, 50 x 36in (127 x 91.5cm).
£390–440 / €570–640
$700–800 ⊞ WADS

◄ **A Kashgai bag face,** southwest Persian, c1890, 24½ x 23¼in (62 x 59cm).
£400–450
€580–660
$720–810 ⊞ KW

► **A Kashgai bag,** southwest Persian, c1890, 25 x 24in (63.5 x 61cm).
£490–550
€720–800
$890–1,000
⊞ WADS

A Kashgai rug, southwest Persian, c1900, 88 x 58in (223.5 x 147.5cm)
£2,000–2,250 / €2,900–3,300
$3,600–4,050 ⊞ WADS

A Kashgai kilim, slight damage, southwest Persian, late 19thC, 96 x 63in (244 x 160cm).
£410–490 / €600–720
$740–890 ⚒ NSal

LOCATE THE SOURCE

The source of each illustration in Miller's can be found by checking the code letters below each caption with the Key to Illustrations, pages 778–784.

A Kashgai Kashkuli rug, southwest Persian, c1910, 77 x 44in (195.5 x 112cm).
£1,300–1,450 / €1,900–2,100
$2,350–2,600 ⊞ WADS

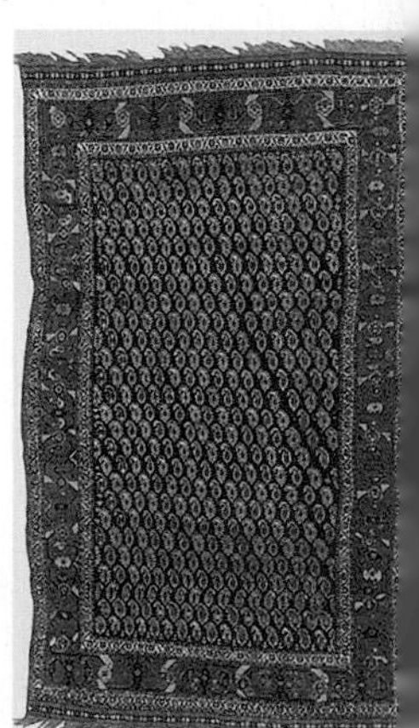

A Khamseh rug, southwest Persian, c1880, 115 x 69in (292 x 175.5cm).
£1,800–2,150
€2,650–3,150
$3,250–3,900 ⚒ S(O)

A Khorasan rug, some wear, northeast Persian, c1900, 66 x 46in (167.5 x 117cm).
£360–400 / €530–590
$650–720 ⊞ DNo

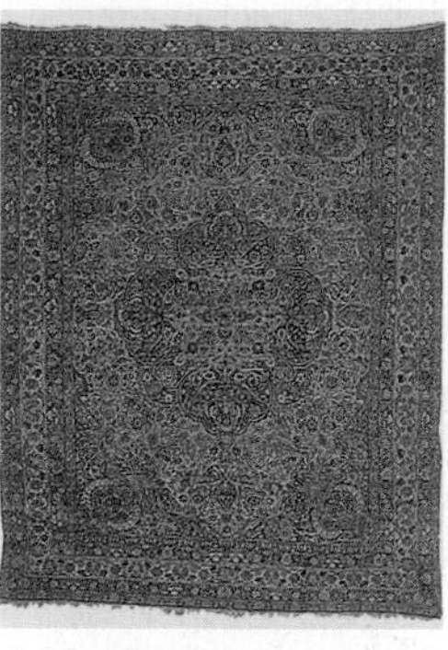

A Kirman carpet, southeast Persian, c1900, 159 x 121in (404 x 307.5cm).
£3,000–3,600
€4,400–5,300
$5,400–6,500 ⚒ S(O)

A Kirman rug, southeast Persian, c1920, 61 x 32in (155 x 81.5cm).
£500–550 / €720–800
$900–1,000 ⊞ DNo

► A Kurdish bag face, northwest Persian, c1880, 30 x 27in (76 x 68.5cm).
£490–550
€720–800
$890–1,000
⊞ WADS

A Kurdish rug, northwest Persian, c1890, 70 x 49in (178 x 124.5cm).
£360–400 / €520–580
$650–720 DNo

A Kurdish rug, northwest Persian, c1920, 74 x 49in (188 x 124.5cm).
£670–750 / €980–1,100
$1,200–1,350 ⊞ DNo

A Kurdish rug, northwest Persian, c1920, 75 x 55in (190.5 x 139.5cm).
£900–1,000 / €1,300–1,450
$1,600–1,800 ⊞ DNo

A Kurdish rug, northwest Persian, c1920, 87 x 56in (221 x 142cm).
£1,100–1,250
€1,600–1,800
$2,000–2,200 ⊞ DNo

A Mahal carpet, central Persian, c1890, 157 x 114in (399 x 289.5cm).
£4,300–4,800 / €6,300–7,000
$7,800–8,700 ⊞ WADS

A Mahal carpet, central Persian, c1900, 161 x 127in (409 x 322.5cm).
£3,600–4,300
€5,300–6,300
$6,500–7,800 ⚒ S(O)
Carpets with a terracotta ground are popular in today's market

A Maslaghan rug, northwest Persian, c1920, 80 x 56in (203 x 142cm).
£760–850 / €1,100–1,250
$1,400–1,550 ⊞ DNo

A Sarouk rug, west Persian, c1890, 48½ x 28¾in (123 x 73cm).
£1,400–1,600 / €2,050–2,300
$2,550–2,900 ⊞ KW

A Sarouk Hamadan rug, west Persian, c1900, 56 x 43in (142 x 109cm).
£670–750 / €980–1,100
$1,200–1,350 ⊞ DNo

A Sarouk rug, west Persian, c1920, 60 x 42in (152.5 x 106.5cm).
£850–950 / €1,250–1,400
$1,500–1,700 ⊞ DNo

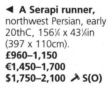

A Serabend runner, west Persian, c1890, 92 x 39in (233.5 x 99cm).
£1,000–1,150
€1,500–1,700
$1,850–2,100 ⊞ DNo

► A Teheran rug, central Persian, c1910, 78 x 56in (198 x 142cm).
£1,800–2,000
€2,600–2,900
$3,250–3,600 ⊞ WADS

A Sarouk rug, west Persian, c1920, 84 x 51in (213.5 x 129.5cm).
£850–950 / €1,250–1,400
$1,500–1,700 ⊞ WADS

A Sarouk rug, west Persian, c1920, 60 x 41¼in (152.5 x 105cm).
£2,250–2,500 / €3,300–3,650
$4,050–4,550 ⊞ KW

A Senneh rug, west Persian, c1900, 77 x 54in (195.5 x 137cm).
£180–210 / €260–310
$320–380 ⚒ NSal

◄ A Serapi runner, northwest Persian, early 20thC, 156¼ x 43¼in (397 x 110cm).
£960–1,150
€1,450–1,700
$1,750–2,100 ⚒ S(O)

► A Ziegler Mahal carpet, reduced, northwest Persian, late 19thC, 170 x 138in (432 x 350.5cm).
£880–1,050
€1,300–1,550
$1,600–1,900
⚒ WW

A Senneh kilim, slight damage, west Persian, c192 83 x 53in (211 x 134.5cm).
£500–550 / €720–800
$900–1,000 ⊞ DNo

A Tabriz rug, northwest Persian, c1920, 34 x 24in (86.5 x 61cm).
£195–220 / €280–320
$360–400 ⊞ DNo

◄ A Shiraz rug, with depictions of animals in th borders and field, southwes Persian, c1920, 71 x 51in (180.5 x 129.5cm).
£580–650 / €850–950
$1,050–1,200 ⊞ DNo

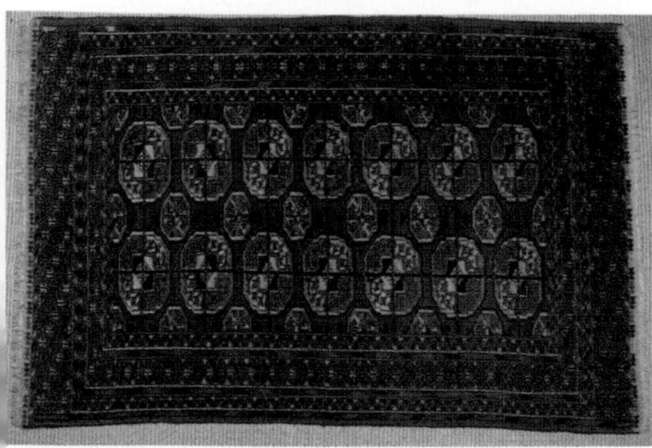

A Bokhara Turkoman rug, Turkestani, c1920, 45¼ x 31½in (115 x 80cm).
£1,050–1,200 / €1,550–1,750
$1,900–2,150 ⊞ KW

A Salor rug, west Turkestani, c1930, 81 x 46in (205.5 x 117cm).
£760–850 / €1,100–1,250
$1,400–1,550 ⊞ DNo

A Tekke Turkoman rug, west Turkestani, c1880, 42in (106.5cm) square.
£850–950 / €1,250–1,400
$1,500–1,700 ⊞ DNo

A Tekke rug, west Turkestani, c1900, 58¼ x 39½in (148 x 100.5cm).
£3,750–4,200 / €5,500–6,100
$6,800–7,600 ⊞ KW

A Tekke Turkoman rug, west Turkestani, c1900, 50 x 46in (127 x 117cm).
£760–850 / €1,100–1,250
$1,400–1,550 ⊞ DNo

A Tekke *chuval*, west Turkestani, c1900, 42¼ x 24¾in (107.5 x 63cm).
£1,500–1,700 / €2,200–2,500
$2,800–3,100 ⊞ KW

◄ A Turkoman *hatchli*, Turkestani, c1910, 55 x 48in (139.5 x 122cm).
£1,450–1,600
€2,100–2,350
$2,600–2,900
⊞ KW

A Tekke Turkoman rug, west Turkestani, 1900–20, 59 x 49¼in (150 x 125cm).
£470–560 / €690–820
$850–1,000 ⚒ DORO

A Yomut Turkoman *ensi*, slight damage, northwest Turkestani, late 19thC, 73 x 54in (185.5 x 137cm).
£460–550 / €670–800
$830–1,000 ⚒ NSal

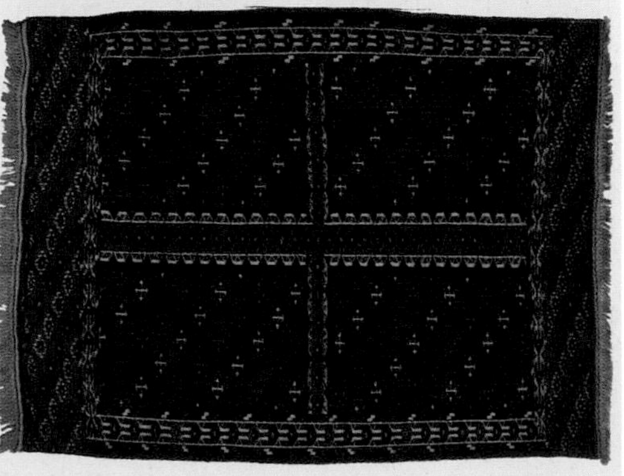

A Yomut Turkoman *hatchli*, northwest Turkestani, c1920, 69 x 49in (175.5 x 124.5cm).
£950–1,100 / €1,450–1,600
$1,800–2,000 ⊞ DNo

A Balouch rug, Afghani, c1880, 90 x 45in (228.5 x 114.5cm).
£1,550–1,750
€2,250–2,550
$2,800–3,150 ⊞ WADS

A Balouch rug, Afghani, Khorasan, late 19thC, 59 x 37in (150 x 94cm).
£350–420 / €510–610
$630–760 ⚒ NSal

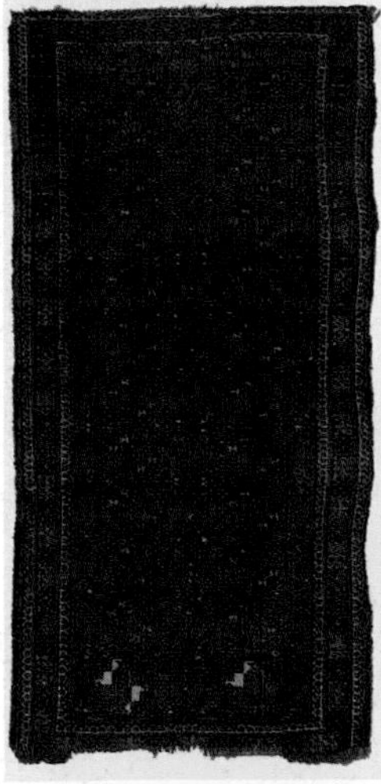

A Chob Bash rug, Afghani, c1900, 81 x 40in (205.5 x 101.5cm).
£500–550 / €720–800
$900–1,000 ⊞ DNo

A Balouch prayer rug, Afghani, c1880, 55¼ x 30¾in (140.5 x 78cm).
£630–700 / €900–1,000
$1,100–1,250 ⊞ KW

A Balouch rug, Afghani, c1890, 50½ x 27½in (128.5 x 70cm).
£1,800–2,000
€2,600–2,900
$3,250–3,600 ⊞ KW

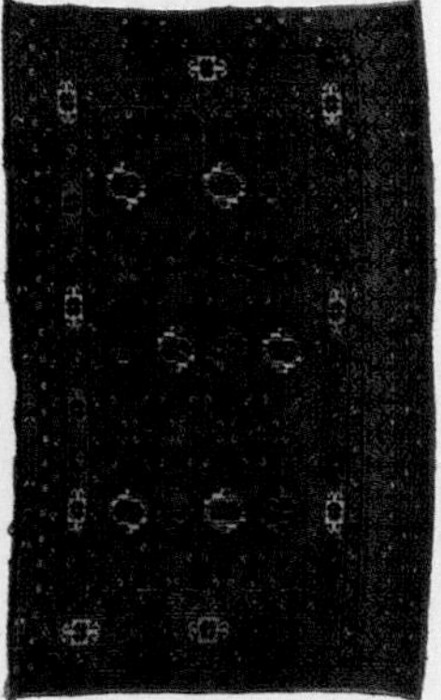

An Ersari *chuval*, northwest Afghani, c1900, 66 x 40in (167.5 x 101.5cm).
£760–850 / €1,100–1,250
$1,400–1,550 ⊞ DNo

A Balouch rug, Afghani, c1880, 59 x 37in (150 x 94cm).
£490–550 / €720–800
$890–1,000 ⊞ WADS

A Balouch prayer rug, Afghani, c1900, 56 x 29in (142 x 73.5cm).
£400–450 / €580–660
$720–810 ⊞ DNo

An Ersari *chuval*, northwest Afghani, c1900, 67 x 39in (170 x 99cm).
£670–750 / €1,000–1,100
$1,200–1,350 ⊞ DNo

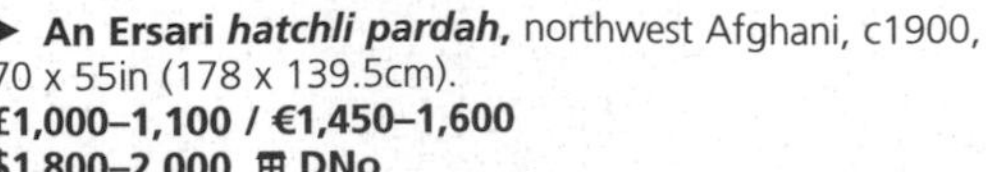

► An Ersari *hatchli pardah*, northwest Afghani, c1900, 70 x 55in (178 x 139.5cm).
£1,000–1,100 / €1,450–1,600
$1,800–2,000 ⊞ DNo

A Balouch rug, Afghani, c1890, 70 x 39½in (178 x 100.5cm).
£600–720 / €880–1,050
$1,100–1,300 ⚒ S(O)
This very attractive rug is a good example of Balouch weaving. The background colour is of natural camel hair with white used sparingly.

A Balouch rug, Afghani, c1920, 73 x 41in (185.5 x 104cm).
£580–650 / €850–950
$1,050–1,200 ⊞ DNo

A Salor Turkoman rug, Afghani, c1950, 65¾ x 47¼in (167 x 120cm).
£550–620 / €800–910
$1,000–1,100 ⊞ KW

◄ **An Agra rug,** Indian, c1880, 47 x 43in (119.5 x 109cm).
£520–580
€760–850
$940–1,050 ⊞ **DNo**

An Amritsar carpet, c1920, 151½ x 111in (385 x 282cm).
£3,600–4,300
€5,300–6,300
$6,500–7,800 ⚒ **S(O)**

A *dhurrie*, Indian, c1900, 82¼ x 50¾in (209 x 129cm).
£780–930 / €1,150–1,350
$1,450–1,700 ⚒ **S(O)**

An Imperial silk and metal thread carpet, Chinese, 18th–19thC, 97¾ x 61½in (248.5 x 156cm).
£21,600–25,900
€32,000–38,000
$39,000–47,000 ⚒ **S**
The five-character inscription woven at the top of the carpet can be translated as 'For the use of the Hall of Great Benevolence'. This was one of the Six Eastern Halls in the Forbidden City in Beijing. During the Qing Dynasty they served as the living quarters of the imperial wives and concubines.

An Imperial silk and metal thread rug, Chinese, 1850–1900, 116¼ x 96in (295.5 x 244cm).
£4,750–5,700
€6,900–8,300
$8,600–10,300 ⚒ **WcH**

Antique Chinese carpets

Weaving techniques reached China via trade with neighbouring Turkestan during the 17th century. These early Chinese weavings are especially associated with Ningshia in northwest China, situated on the silk route between Beijing and eastern Turkestan, and were made here well into the 19th century. Other significant provinces, particularly for 19th-century production, include Xinjiang, Gansu and inner Mongolia. The designs are broadly similar, illustrating religious influences including Buddhism and Daoism.

◄ **A Ninghsia rug,** northwest Chinese, c1880, 47 x 23in (119.5 x 58.5cm).
£880–980 / €1,300–1,450
$1,600–1,800 ⊞ **WADS**

A rug, slight wear, northwest Chinese, c1900, 80 x 48in (203 x 122cm).
£230–270 / €340–400
$420–500 ⚒ **NSal**

A rug, Chinese, c1920, 48½ x 28¾in (123 x 73cm).
£450–500 / €660–730
$810–910 ⊞ **KW**

Textiles

Covers & Quilts

A silk bedspread, embroidered in floss silks with birds, deer, mythological heads and pineapples, made for the Portuguese market, Chinese, Macao, 17thC, 89 x 65in (226 x 165cm).
£5,200–5,800 / €7,600–8,500
$9,400–10,500 ⊞ MGa

A quilt, signed and dated 'SBD' and 'SBD IHB', slight damage and repair, Swedish, Skåne, dated 1828, 80 x 48½in (203 x 123cm).
£1,400–1,650 / €2,050–2,400
$2,550–3,000 ⚒ BUK

A velvet and silk patchwork and embroidered quilt, 1870–80, 54 x 45in (137 x 114.5cm).
£170–190 / €250–280
$310–350 ⊞ JPr

A patchwork coverlet, by Elizabeth Capes, dated 1816, the reverse initialled 'SC 1809', early 19thC, 108 x 112in (274.5 x 284.5cm).
£490–580 / €720–850
$890–1,050 ⚒ WW

A cotton and chintz Grandmother's Garden patchwork quilt, c1840, 56in (142cm) square.
£180–200 / €260–310
$320–360 ⊞ JPr

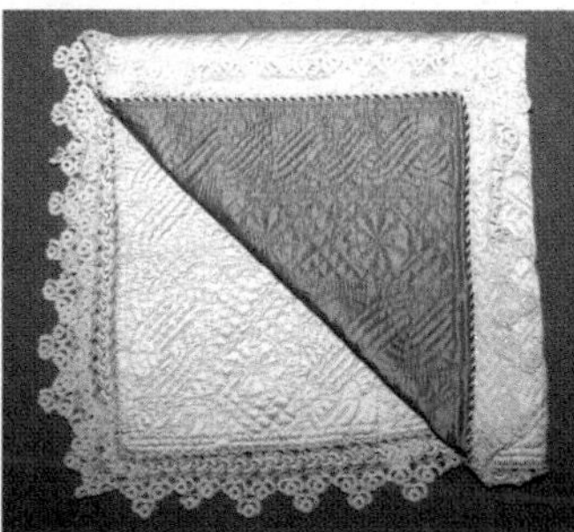

A silk Durham quilt, with crochet edging, 1860–70, 60in (152.5cm) square.
£150–170 / €220–250
$270–310 ⊞ JPr

A Victorian wool tapestry bedcover, with a patchwork border, 88in (223.5cm) square.
£270–300 / €390–440
$490–540 ⊞ Ech

A cotton patchwork coverlet, by Elizabeth Hill, applied with assorted motifs including household objects and animals within a block-printed floral border, 1820–30, 106¾ x 102½in (271 x 260.5cm).
£4,700–5,600 / €6,800–8,200
$8,500–10,100 ⚒ KTA

An early Victorian silk patchwork quilt, 94in (239cm) square.
£310–350 / €470–520
$570–630 ⊞ Ech

An appliqué quilt, worn, losses, American, mid-19thC.
£320–380 / €470–550
$580–690 ⚒ JDJ

A Victorian patchwork coverlet, embroidered with flowers, the corners with eight-pointed star motifs, 90¼ x 89½in (229 x 227.5cm
£240–280 / €350–410
$430–510 ⚒ PFK

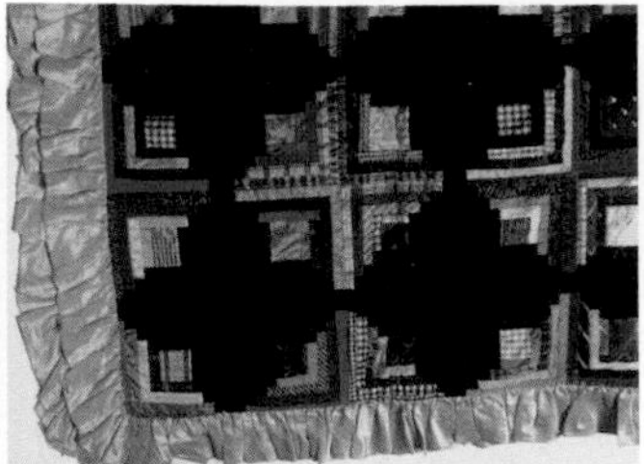

A Victorian silk and velvet log cabin patchwork quilt, 80 x 66in (203 x 167.5cm).
£300–330 / €440–490
$540–600 ⊞ Ech

A wool and cotton log cabin quilt, American, Pennsylvania, c1900, 73 x 81in (185.4 x 205.5cm).
£220–260 / €320–380
$400–470 ⚒ JDJ

► **A basket pattern coverlet,** with squares of diagonal strips within a lattice framework, American, early 20thC, 91½ x 81½in (232.5 x 207cm).
£150–180 / €220–260
$270–320 ⚒ PFK

A Victorian cotton patchwork quilt, with a central medallion, 88 x 82in (223.5 x 208.5cm).
£340–380 / €500–550
$620–690 ⊞ Ech

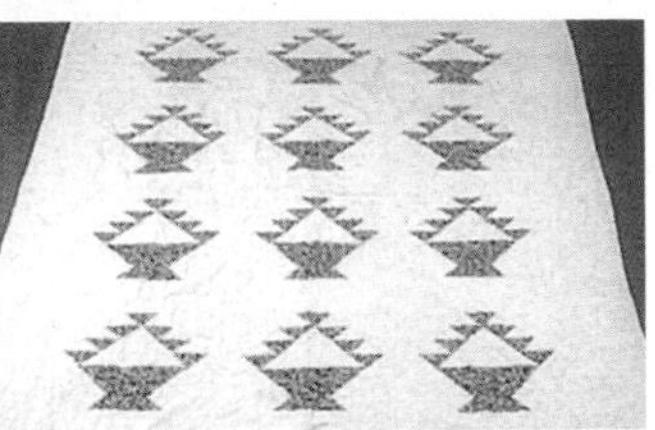

A coverlet, worked in tessellating triangles with a basket pattern, the back with hand stitching, American, early 20thC, 73 x 58in (185.5 x 147.5cm).
£150–180 / €220–260
$270–320 ⚒ PFK

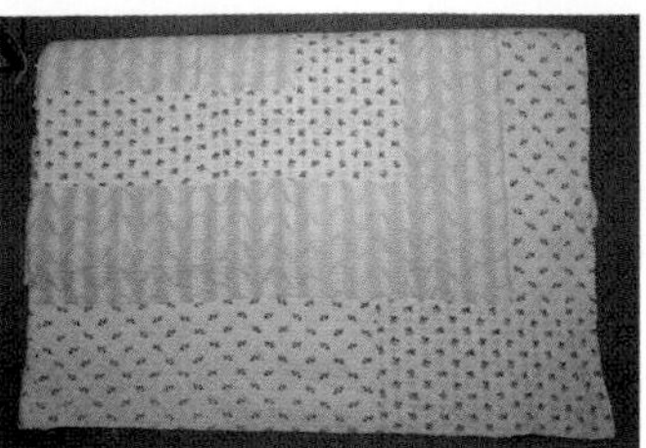

A cotton Durham quilt, decorated with rosebuds, c1890, 90 x 82in (228.5 x 208.5cm).
£350–390 / €510–570
$630–710 ⊞ JPr

A cotton *susani*, Uzbekistan, 1900–20, 90½ x 63¾in (230 x 162cm).
£440–520 / €640–760
$800–940 ⚒ DORO

Embroidery & Needlework

A stumpwork panel, depicting a woman gathering flowers, flanked by a leopard, deer, insects, flowers and foliage, 17thC, 11½ x 9in (29 x 23cm).
£2,350–2,800 / €3,450–4,050
$4,250–5,100 G(L)

An embroidered panel, worked in tent stitch with Rebecca and Eliezer at the well, with animals, flowers and insects, late 17thC, in a later frame, 13 x 17in (33 x 43cm).
£1,400–1,650 / €2,050–2,400
$2,550–3,000 S

A needlework panel, worked in tent stitch with a shepherdess holding a staff and flowers, flanked by trees, sheep, a dog and deer, 1675–1700, in a later ebonized and parcel-gilt frame, 15¼ x 16½in (38.5 x 42cm).
£900–1,050 / €1,300–1,550
$1,600–1,900 S

An embroidered silk panel, worked with silk and metal threads, early 18thC, 59 x 72in (150 x 183cm).
£3,450–3,800 / €5,000–5,500
$6,200–6,900 JPr

An embroidered runner, with velvet border, French, 17thC, 13 x 41½in (33 x 105.4cm).
£1,500–1,700 / €2,200–2,500
$2,700–3,100 MGa

An embroidered picture, worked in tent stitch with Noah's Ark, c1660, 16 x 12in (40.5 x 30.5cm).
£7,200–8,000 / €10,500–11,700
$13,000–14,500 HIS

An embroidered altar cloth, the central panel worked with the Assumption of the Virgin, 17thC, on a 19thC silk ground, 39½ x 119in (100.5 x 302.5cm).
£820–980 / €1,200–1,450
$1,500–1,800 KTA

A wool and silk cushion front, depicting an official coat-of-arms, flanked with two ribbon-tied palm leaves and the coat-of-arms of the seven provinces, Dutch, 1675–1700, 28¼ x 33¼in (72 x 84.5cm).
£2,400–2,850 / €3,500–4,150
$4,350–5,200 S(Am)

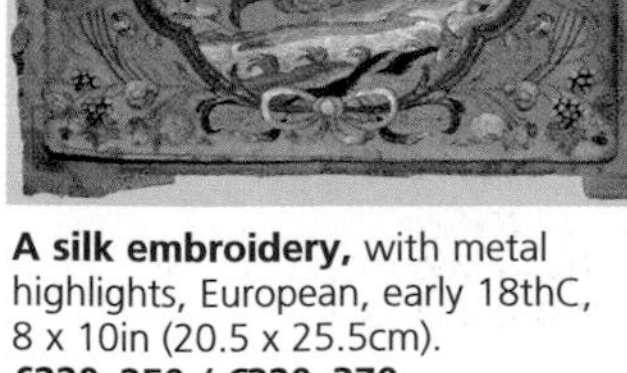

A silk embroidery, with metal highlights, European, early 18thC, 8 x 10in (20.5 x 25.5cm).
£220–250 / €320–370
$400–450 JPr

▶ **A crewelwork embroidery fragment,** worked on linen, 18thC, 21 x 20in (53.5 x 51cm).
£310–350 / €450–510
$560–630 MGa

An embroidered border, from a bedcover, worked with polychrome silks and silver thread on a quilted ground, with modern backing, c1700, 60 x 11in (152.5 x 28cm).
£1,050–1,200 / €1,550–1,750
$1,900–2,150 MGa

An embroidered linen cope, worked with floral slips, edged in gold braid and fringes, lined with linen, French, early 18thC, 106in (269cm) long.
£700–840 / €1,000–1,200
$1,250–1,500 KTA

An embroidered hanging, worked in wools and silks on a canvas ground with vases of flowers, the corners with heraldic devices, probably French, 1740–50, 94 x 98in (239 x 249cm).
£4,450–5,300 / €6,500–7,700
$8,000–9,600 KTA

A silkwork picture, depicting a woman standing on the foreshore, within a garlanded border, 18thC, framed, 17 x 15in (43 x 38in).
£130–155 / €190–220
$240–280 TMA

An embroidered linen panel, worked in wools and silks with an image of Christ within a 'jewelled' halo, probably Armenian or Russian, 18thC, 12¼ x 9½in (31 x 24cm).
£350–420 / €510–610
$630–760 KTA

An embroidered panel, worked in tent stitch with a traveller surrounded by animals, foliage and a tree within a floral border, with a later velvet surround, c1750, framed, 32¼ x 22in (82 x 56cm).
£2,050–2,450 / €3,000–3,550
$3,700–4,400 S(O)

A needlepoint panel, depicting a gardener holding two water buckets, French, 18thC, 21 x 16in (53.5 x 40.5cm).
£670–750 / €980–1,100
$1,200–1,350 MGa

◄ **A beadwork card case,** decorated with pansies within a wrigglework border, c1770, 4in (10cm) wide.
£410–460 / €600–670
$740–830 SiA

An embroidered map of the world, c1800, framed, 18 x 16in (45.5 x 40.5cm).
£1,800–2,000 / €2,600–2,900
$3,250–3,600 HIS

► **An embroidered map of England and Wales,** by Amelia Jordan, c1809, framed, 17 x 21in (43cm x 53.5cm).
£800–900 / €1,150–1,300
$1,450–1,650 VHA

A needlework picture, depicting a shepherd and shepherdess sitting among sheep and wild animals, 18thC, 10½ x 8¾in (26.5 x 22cm).
£5,000–5,500 / €7,200–8,000
$9,000–10,000 MGa

An embroidered linen skirt panel, worked in silks with a crowned figure emerging from a vase between urns, Cretan, 18thC, 15 x 22in (38 x 56cm).
£640–760 / €930–1,100
$1,150–1,350 KTA

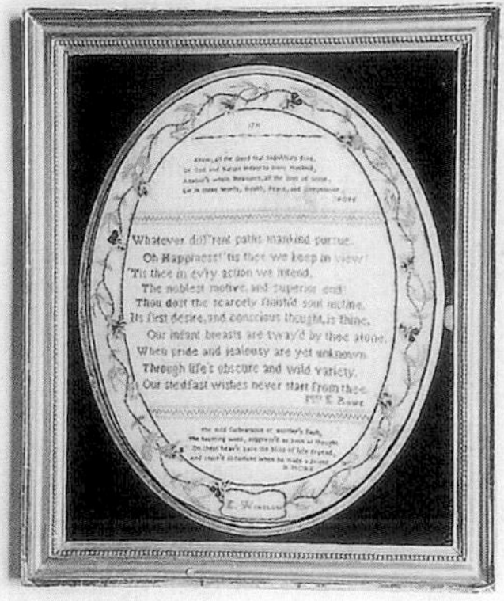

A silk embroidered picture, by E. Winslow, worked with a verse, c1791, framed, 14 x 11in (35.5 x 28cm).
£1,650–1,850 / €2,400–2,700
$3,000–3,350 HIS

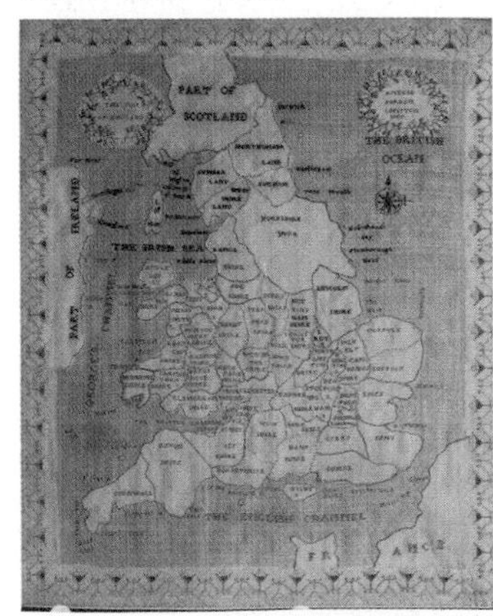

A late Georgian needlework picture, by Alice Wardle, depicting a child feeding a dog, 9 x 7in (23 x 18cm).
£440–530 / €640–770
$800–960 LAY

A pair of cushions, embroidered with initials 'L. T. S', damaged and repaired, Swedish, Skåne, dated 1825, 19¾ x 19in (50 x 48.5cm).
£320–380 / €460–550
$580–690 BUK

A pair of needlepoint seat covers, worked in wool and silk with cherries, flowers and foliage, French, 19thC, 21 x 23in (53.5 x 58.5cm).
£1,000–1,100 / €1,450–1,600
$1,800–2,000 MGa

A silkwork picture, worked in silk with a Great Northern Railway 2–2–2 locomotive No. 201 with tender and passenger carriages, mid-19thC, 22¾ x 27½in (58 x 70cm).
£1,150–1,350 / €1,650–1,950
$2,050–2,450 Bea

A needlework picture, by Jane Wright, worked in wools on a linen ground, entitled 'On the Pleasures of Benevolence', 1820, 18 x 24½in (45.5 x 62cm), in a gilt frame.
£470–560 / €690–810
$850–1,000 KTA

An embroidered picture, by Elizabeth Hart, worked in silk on linen with a verse, house, trees and animals, 1833, framed, 20¾ x 20¼in (52.5 x 51.5cm).
£470–560 / €690–810
$850–1,000 KTA

A feltwork picture, depicting fruit in a basket, 19thC, 10¾ x 13in (27.5 x 33cm).
£410–490 / €600–720
$740–880 CHTR

An embroidered picture, by Margeret Bell, entitled 'The Asia Cock', c1842, 12 x 13in (30.5 x 33cm).
£2,250–2,500 / €3,300–3,650
$4,050–4,550 HIS

► **A pair of embroidered satin curtains,** early 20thC, 24 x 50in (61 x 127cm).
£125–140 / €180–200
$220–250 JPr

A late Georgian silk and woolwork picture, depicting a lady and a dog, damaged, 15½in (39.5cm) square.
£170–200 / €250–290
$300–360 PFK

A pair of embroidered pictures, one depicting a tabby cat, the other a King Charles Spaniel, 1800–50, in moulded giltwood frames, 8in (20.5cm) wide.
£2,750–3,300 / €4,000–4,800
$5,000–6,000 S(O)

A woolwork tapestry, entitled 'Mad Bull', inscribed 'Under what my oud coo ud got in that tree, best see I spose',19thC, framed, 17 x 12½in (43 x 32cm).
£150–180 / €220–260
$270–320 TMA

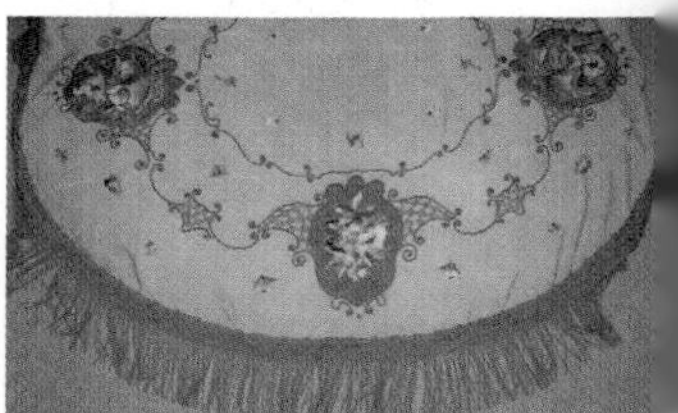

An embroidered tablecloth, late 19thC, 68in (173cm) wide.
£270–300 / €390–440
$490–540 JPr

Lace

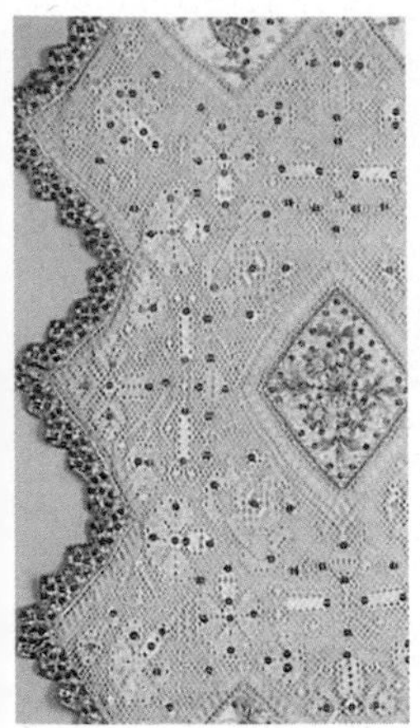

A lace cover, worked with filet carnations interspersed with linen panels, embroidered with gold silk and decorated with sequins, Italian, 17thC, on a 19thC cotton backing cloth, 66 x 43in (167.5 x 109cm).
£290–340 / €420–490
$520–610 ⚒ KTA

A whitework sampler, mid-17thC, 17 x 6in (43 x 15cm).
£1,450–1,600
€2,100–2,350
$2,600–2,900 ⊞ HIS

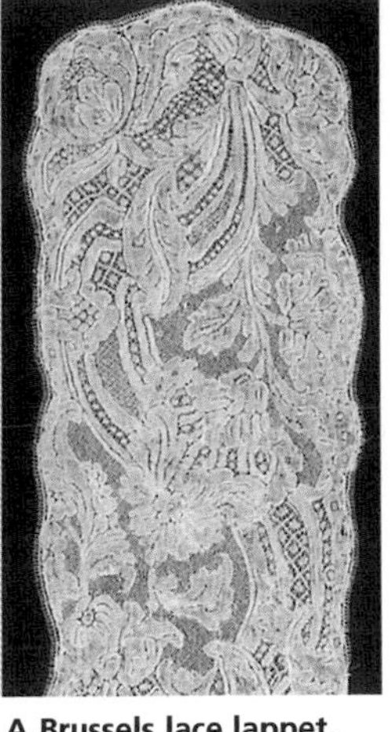

A Brussels lace lappet, with exotic blooms, shadework and *oeil de perdrix* fillings, c1730, 44in (112cm) long.
£410–490 / €600–720
$740–890 ⚒ KTA

◄ **A lace sampler,** with bands of whitework, pulled and drawn threadwork, filet lace and reticella, 1650–1700, 30 x 8¾in (76 x 22cm), framed.
£4,700–5,600
€6,900–8,200
$8,500–10,100 ⚒ KTA

◄ **A lace sampler,** by Sophie Raben, dated 1826, in a later wood and gesso frame, 8 x 10¼in (20.5 x 26cm).
£890–1,050
€1,300–1,550
$1,600–1,900
⚒ JDJ

Two flounces of Brussels lace, with floral swags and strapwork, c1860, 14¼ x 216½in (36 x 550cm).
£730–870 / €1,050–1,250
$1,300–1,550 ⚒ KTA

◄ **A flounce of Brussels lace,** worked in *point-de-gaze*, with duchesse bobbin lace, with appliquéd roses, ribbon swags and flower sprays, slight damage, c1870, 170in (432cm) long.
£590–700 / €860–1,000
$1,050–1,250 ⚒ F&C

◄ **A chemical lace stole/dresser scarf,** 1920s, 82in (208.5cm) long.
£65–75 / €95–110
$120–135 ⊞ DHa

\ lacework picture, depicting
ı castle, within three borders, 19thC,
3 x 27in (58.5 x 68.5cm), framed.
:130–155 / €190–220
;240–280 ⚒ TMA

An embroidered net stole/ vedding veil, 1900–10,
12in (284.5cm) long.
'135–150 / €200–220
240–270 ⊞ DHa

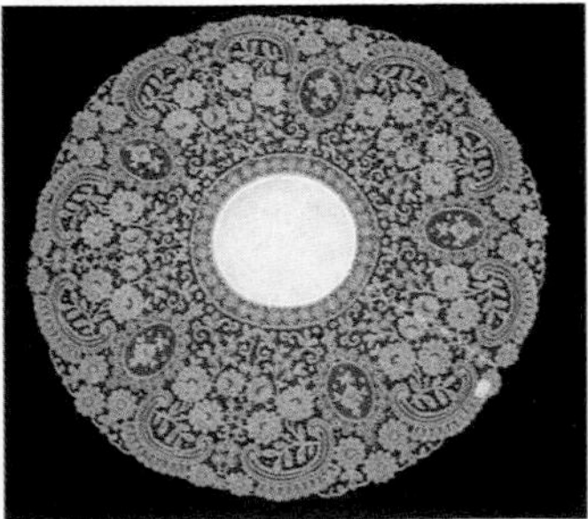

A chemical lace table centre, 1920s, 34in (86.5cm) diam.
£50–55 / €70–80
$90–100 ⊞ DHa

TEXTILES

Samplers

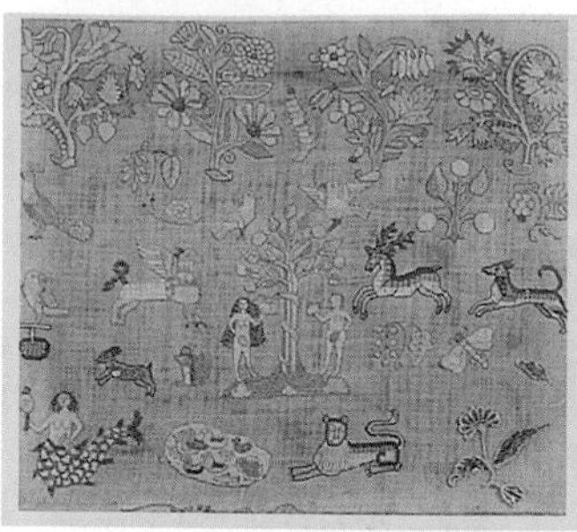

A spot sampler, worked in silk and silver thread on a linen ground with Adam and Eve, animals, birds and flowering plants, 1600–50, 14½ x 16in (37 x 40.5cm), framed.
£3,300–3,950 / €4,800–5,800
$5,900–7,100 ⚒ KTA

An alphabet sampler, by Elizabeth Walklett, worked with the alphabet and an inscription, dated 1802, framed, 11½in (29.5cm) square.
£200–240 / €290–350
$360–430 ⚒ CHTR

A sampler, worked with text, Adam and Eve, birds, animals and trees, within a flowerhead border, 1809, framed, 15½ x 12in (39.5 x 30.5cm).
£1,150–1,300 / €1,700–1,900
$2,100–2,350 ⊞ HIS

► **A sampler,** by Elizabeth Brooks, worked in cross and running stitches with verses, flanked by a church, a house, Adam and Eve, animals and foliage, within a flowerhead and vine border, dated 1817, 19½ x 16¼in (49.5 x 41cm).
£560–670 / €820–980
$1,000–1,200 ⚒ RTo

An alphabet sampler, by Joice Hope, worked in cross-stitch, dated 1791, 14¼ x 13¾in (36 x 35cm).
£300–360 / €440–520
$540–650 ⚒ RTo

A linen sampler, by Rachel Withy Downend, worked with the alphabet and numbers, dated 1806, in a rosewood frame, 12in (30.5cm) square.
£230–270 / €330–390
$410–480 ⚒ Mal(O)

An embroidered sampler, worked on a wool ground, early 19thC, 13 x 12½in (33 x 32cm), in original gilt frame.
£1,750–2,100 / €2,550–3,050
$3,150–3,800 ⚒ KTA

A sampler, by Phebe Carter, American, dated 1793, 9 x 13in (23 x 33cm).
£840–940 / €1,250–1,400
$1,500–1,700 ⊞ HCFA

A needlework sampler, by Mary Moller, dated 1808, in a stained wood frame, 15½ x 13¼in (39.5 x 33.5cm).
£700–840 / €1,000–1,200
$1,250–1,500 ⚒ AH

A sampler, by Agnes Wyllie, worked with a verse, Adam and Eve, animals and birds, dated 1815, in a mahogany frame, 20½ x 17in (52 x 43cm).
£1,100–1,300 / €1,600–1,900
$2,000–2,350 ⚒ G(L)

A sampler, by Margaret Hyndman, worked with the alphabet and a verse within a border, Irish, dated 1817, framed, 7 x 8in (18 x 20.5cm).
£1,200–1,450 / €1,750–2,100
$2,150–2,600 ⊞ HIS

A sampler, by Margaret Burt, worked with the alphabet and numbers, flanked by flowers and birds, dated 1819, 16 x 12½in (40.5 x 32cm), framed.
£1,650–1,950 / €2,400–2,850
$3,000–3,550 HYD

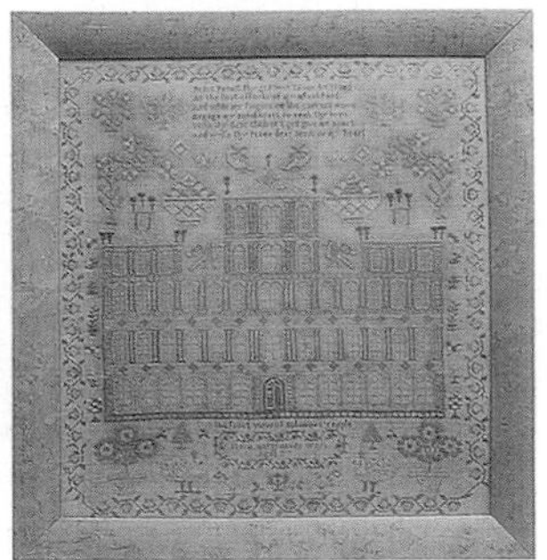

A sampler, by Maria Hargreaves, worked with 'The Front View of Solomon's Temple', early 19thC, 22 x 21in (56 x 53cm), in a bird's-eye maple frame.
£260–310 / €380–450
$470–560 DD

A linen sampler, decorated with a verse, a coat-of-arms, the alphabet, numbers and foliage, dated 1826, 7½in x 5½in (19 x 14cm), framed and glazed.
£145–170 / €200–240
$260–300 Mit

A sampler, by Jane Wake Parsons, worked with a verse, house and animals, dated 1822, in an ebonized frame, 15½ x 11½in (39.5 x 29cm).
£350–410 / €510–600
$630–740 Mal(O)

A sampler, by Mary Boaler, dated 1824, 23½ x 19½in (59.5 x 49.5cm).
£730–870 / €1,050–1,250
$1,300–1,550 G(L)

A sampler, by M. Fuller, worked with the alphabet and dated 1827, 3in (7.5cm) square, framed.
£540–600 / €790–880
$980–1,100 HIS

◄ **A linen sampler,** by Elizabeth Godwin, worked in silk with Adam and Eve, a house and trees, American, Pennsylvania, dated 1828, 16¼ x 17in (41 x 43cm), framed.
£1,650–1,950 / €2,400–2,850
$3,000–3,550 S(NY)

► **A sampler,** by Emily Hannam, dated 1828, in a later frame, 15 x 13in (38 x 223cm).
£1,250–1,500 / €1,850–2,200
$2,250–2,700 JDJ

An embroidered sampler, by Mary Laycock, worked with silk in cross-stitch, dated 1822, in a gilt gesso frame, 16 x 13in (40.5 x 33cm).
£1,150–1,350 / €1,700–2,000
$2,100–2,450 F&C

A sampler, by Bessy Coulta, worked with a verse and motifs, dated 1826, 25½ x 19¼in (65 x 49cm), in a moulded rosewood frame.
£1,050–1,250 / €1,550–1,850
$1,900–2,250 DD

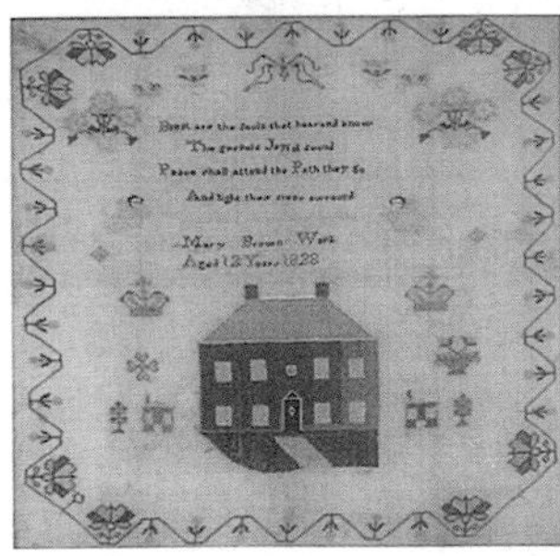

A sampler, by Mary Brown, worked mainly in cross-stitch, dated 1828, 16½ x 17½in (42 x 44.5cm).
£145–170 / €210–250
$260–310 RTo

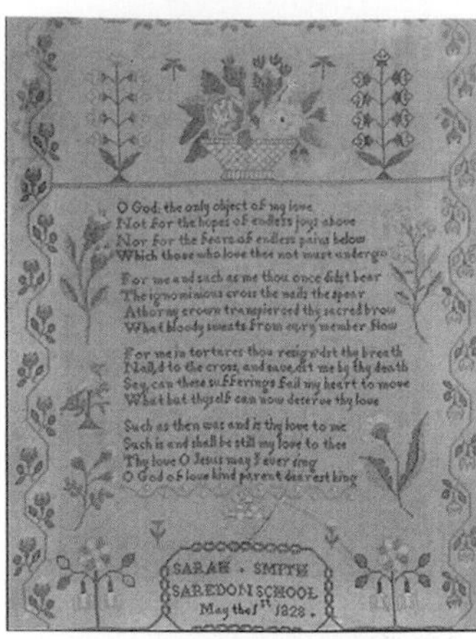

A sampler, by Sarah Smith, dated 1828, 17¼ x 21¼in (44 x 54cm).
£390–460 / €570–670
$700–830 WL

A needlework sampler, by Frances Paull Jewell, worked in satin stitch with a verse and angels, dated 1834, framed, 17 x 12in (43 x 30.5cm).
£420–500 / €610–730
$760–910 LAY

A sampler, by Sarah Guy, dated 1836, framed, 15 x 12½in (38 x 32cm).
£260–310 / €380–450
$470–560 HYD

A sampler, by Eleanor Amelia Brixey, worked in silks, dated 1831, in an oak frame, 16½ x 12in (42 x 30.5cm).
£350–420 / €510–610
$630–760 Hal

A silkwork sampler, by Elizabeth Jackson, dated 1836, 21¾ x 17¾in (55.5 x 45cm).
£1,250–1,450 / €1,800–2,100
$2,250–2,600 DA

A sampler, by Mary Woodbury, worked in silks with Adam and Eve in the Garden of Eden, dated 1837, 12¼ x 11½in (31 x 29cm).
£350–410 / €510–600
$630–740 Bea

◄ **A sampler,** by Ann Culmer, dated 1841, framed, 13 x 12in (33 x 30.5cm).
£140–160 / €200–230
$250–290 G(L)

► **A needlework sampler,** by Margarett Campbell, dated 1844, 13½ x 13¾in (34 x 35cm).
£1,900–2,250 / €2,750–3,250
$3,450–4,050 L

A sampler, by Ann Margaret Broad, dated 1832, 17½ x 13in (44.5 x 33cm), framed.
£2,000–2,200 / €2,900–3,200
$3,600–4,000 HIS

A linen sampler, by Maria Imboden, worked in silks, American, Pennsylvania, dated 1836, 16½ x 15in (42 X 38cm), in a frame.
£990–1,150 / €1,450–1,700
$1,800–2,100 S(NY)

A sampler, by Mary Jones, dated 1839, in a maple frame, 17½ x 16½in (44.5 x 42cm).
£600–720 / €870–1,050
$1,100–1,300 JDJ

► **A sampler,** by Hannah Banbam, dated 1844, framed, 12in (30.5cm) square.
£700–840 / €1,000–1,200
$1,250–1,500 JDJ

A sampler, by E. E. C. Hood, worked in silks on wool gauze with Raine's Asylum, dated 1848, 19¼ x 17¼in (49 x 44cm), in a later maple frame.
£9,400–11,300 / €13,700–16,500
$17,000–20,500 KTA
Samplers from asylums, schools and orphanages are particularly sought after.

A wool sampler, by Anne Nelson, decorated with the alphabet, numbers and motifs, dated 1849, framed, 15 x 13in (38 x 33cm).
£540–600 / €790–880
$980–1,100 JPr

A sampler, by Emma Susannah Holman, damaged, dated 1848, 18¾ x 19in (47.5 x 48.5cm).
£260–310 / €380–450
$470–560 CHTR

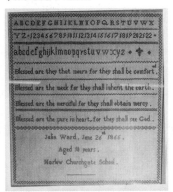

A sampler, by Julie Ward, dated 1865, 11¾ x 10¼in (30 x 26cm).
£80–90 / €115–130
$145–165 AMB

◄ **A woolwork sampler,** by Esther Bambridge, worked with a biblical verse and Westminister Abbey, c1865, 24½ x 16¼in (61.5 x 41.5cm), in a rosewood frame.
£400–480
€580–700
$720–860 AH

A sampler, by Mabel ane Pugh, dated 1885, 17¾ x 14in (45 x 35.5cm).
£120–140 / €175–200
$220–250 L&E

A silkwork sampler, by Susan Ann Wheeler, dated 1885, 13in (33cm) square, framed.
£1,550–1,750
€2,250–2,550
$2,800–3,150 SEA

► **A sampler,** by Edith . Gilbert, dated 1894, ¼in (16cm) square, framed.
180–200 / €260–290
320–360 HIS

TEXTILES

Tapestries

A tapestry panel, depicting Artmesia and the Tomb of Mausolus, Belgian, Brussels, early 17thC, 97 x 81in (246.5 x 205.5cm).
£3,000–3,600 / €4,400–5,200
$5,400–6,500 ⚒ S(NY)

A tapestry, depicting the arrival of Mark Antony at the court of Cleopatra, probably Flemish, 1600–50, 84 x 130in (213.5 x 330cm).
£9,600–11,500 / €14,000–16,700
$17,400–20,800 ⚒ S

A tapestry, depicting a biblical scene of Esther and Ahasuerus, German, 17thC, 100½ x 116¼in (255.5 x 295.5cm).
£6,000–7,200 / €8,800–10,500
$10,900–13,000 ⚒ S(Am)

An Aubusson tapestry fragment, French, late 17thC, 39 x 8in (99 x 20.5cm).
£135–150 / €195–220
$240–270 ⊞ JPr

A wool and silk tapestry, depicting a monarch and retainers looking at the Trojan horse, reduced and altered, Flemish, 17thC, 98 x 84in (249 x 213.5cm).
£2,450–2,900 / €3,550–4,250
$4,400–5,200 ⚒ BUK

A Brussels tapestry panel, made into a runner with modern border and trim, late 17thC, 48 x 12in (122 x 30.5cm).
£580–650 / €850–950
$1,050–1,200 ⊞ MGa

A tapestry, depicting three classical maidens in a landscape, Flemish, 17th–18thC, 115 x 111in (292 x 282cm).
£5,900–7,000 / €8,600–10,200
$10,700–12,700 ⚒ JNic

A Mortlake tapestry, depicting August, woven with harvesters in a cornfield, late 17thC, 98½ x 105in (250 x 267cm).
£12,000–14,300 / €17,500–20,900
$21,700–25,900 ⚒ S

Several other English series of the Months and Seasons are known but are based on different designs. The Metropolitan Museum in New York has panels entitled 'Spring' and 'Autumn'.

A wool verdure tapestry, depicting a pavillion and fountains in a landscape, flanked by trees and flowering bushes, with cotton backing, Flemish, 17th–18thC, 95 x 99in (241.5 x 251.5cm).
£2,750–3,300 / €4,000–4,800
$5,000–6,000 ⚒ SK

► **An Aubusson verdure tapestry,** depicting a wooded landscape, French, c1700, 90¼ x 48in (229 x 122cm).
£2,800–3,350 / €4,100–4,900
$5,100–6,100 ⚒ S(Am)

A tapestry, depicting female figures, possibly representing the Toilet of Venus, beside a lake, flanked by trees, gardens, a waterfall and flowers, reduced, restored, the border associated, Flemish, probably Oudenaarde, early 18thC, 116¼in (295cm) high.
£6,900–8,200 / €10,100–12,000
$12,500–14,800 ⚒ S(Am)

► A tapestry fragment, depicting flowers and foliage flanked by birds, probably Soho, mid 18thC, 22¾ x 48in (58 x 122cm), on a wooden support.
£1,900–2,250 / €2,750–3,300
$3,450–4,050 ⚒ S(O)

An Aubusson tapestry, depicting figures in a landscape, French, 18thC, 106 x 91in (269 x 231cm).
£2,950–3,550 / €4,300–5,100
$5,300–6,400 ⚒ S(NY)

An Aubusson tapestry panel, depicting two flying ducks holding a turtle, French, 18thC, 21½ x 20in (54.5 x 51cm).
£1,250–1,400 / €1,800–2,000
$2,250–2,550 ⊞ MGa

A verdure tapestry, woven in wool and silk with a woodland and lake, altered, Franco/Flemish, 18thC and later, 105 x 69in (266.5 x 175.5cm).
£2,400–2,850 / €3,500–4,150
$4,350–5,200 ⚒ S(O)

A wool verdure tapestry, Flemish, 19thC, 85 x 64¼in (216 x 163cm).
£1,500–1,800 / €2,200–2,600
$2,700–3,250 ⚒ SK

An Aubusson-style tapestry, 19thC, 78½ x 101½in (199.5 x 258cm).
£840–1,000 / €1,250–1,500
$1,500–1,800 ⚒ SK

Condition

The condition is absolutely vital when assessing the value of an antique. Damaged pieces on the whole appreciate much less than perfect examples. However, a rare desirable piece may command a high price even when damaged.

A tapestry panel, woven with Mercury and attendants, 19thC, 57 x 81in (145 x 205.5cm).
£3,000–3,600 / €4,400–5,300
$5,400–6,500 ⚒ S(O)

An Aubusson tapestry, French, late 19thC, 18 x 21in (45.5 x 53.5cm).
£160–180 / €230–260
$290–320 ⊞ JPr

A rococo-style tapestry, French, late 19thC, 71¾ x 93in (182 x 236cm).
£1,900–2,250 / €2,750–3,300
$3,450–4.050 ⚒ S(O)

Costume

◄ **A pair of brocaded silk shoes and pattens,** 1715–20.
£2,350–2,800
€3,450–4,050
$4,250–5,100
KTA

► **A silk gauze petticoat,** embroidered with silk and sequins, underskirt later, French, 18thC.
£2,700–3,000
€3,950–4,400
$4,900–5,400
MGa

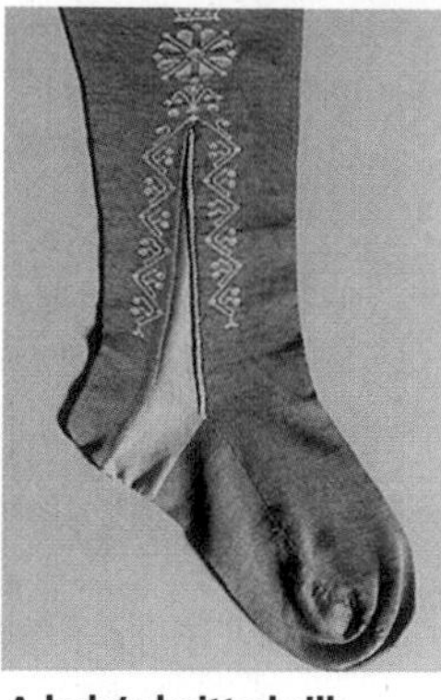

A lady's knitted silk stocking, with contrasting decoration and ankle panels, early 18thC.
£350–420 / €510–610
$630–760 KTA

A brocaded silk open robe, c1770.
£1,500–1,800
€2,200–2,600
$2,700–3,250 KTA

A gentleman's wool mix undress coat, printed with tiny blooms, c1830.
£940–1,100
€1,350–1,600
$1,700–2,000 KTA

A Victorian beaded evening bag, with brass clasp, 7in (18cm) high.
£145–165 / €210–240
$270–300 Ech

A pair of Victorian leather lace-up boots.
£145–165 / €210–240
$270–300 Ech

A Victorian silk day dress, with lace trim.
£500–550 / €720–800
$900–1,000 Ech

A Victorian silk taffeta wedding dress, with flowers.
£580–650 / €850–950
$1,050–1,200 Ech

◄ **A Worth satin and cut velvet ball gown,** with boned bodice and woven signature label, later alterations, c1900.
£760–910
€1,100–1,300
$1,400–1,650
KTA

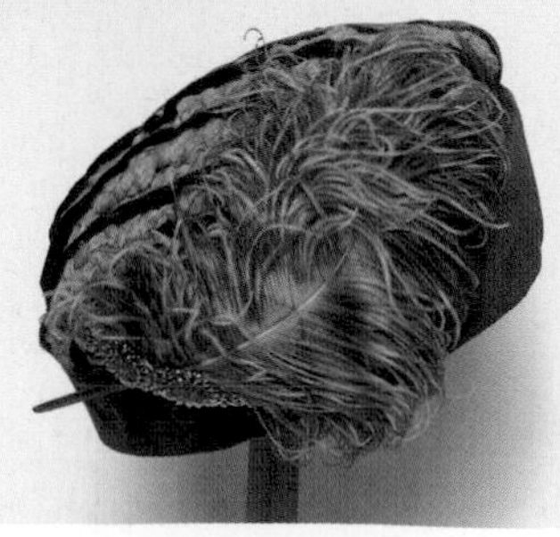

► **An Edwardian velvet hat,** with cut steel and feather decoration.
£130–145
€190–210
$230–260 Ech

An Edwardian muslin dress
£230–270 / €330–390
$410–490 GH

Fans

◄ **An ivory fan,** the leaf decorated with a classical scene, the gilt and painted sticks carved with figures of lovers and putti, slight damage, c1760, 10½in (26.5cm) high.
£420–500
€610–730
$760–910 ⚒ F&C

An ivory fan, the silk leaf decorated with Kaufmann-style engravings, on pierced and gilt sticks, late 18thC, 20½in (52cm) wide, framed.
£300–360 / €440–530
$540–650 ⚒ WW

A mother-of-pearl fan, the leaf painted with a lady and gentleman at a well with a cherub above, on pierced gilt sticks carved with figures, urns and foliage, late 18thC, 20in (51cm) wide, framed.
£330–390 / €480–570
$600–710 ⚒ WW

A fan, the leaf painted with a scene depicting the myth of Perseus, possibly Italian, c1800, 19¼in (49cm) wide, framed.
£970–1,150 / €1,450–1,700
$1,750–2,100 ⚒ DN(BR)

An ivory fan, the leaf decorated with romantic scenes, the pierced ivory sticks with inlaid silver and gilt decoration, early 19thC, 19½in (49.5cm) wide, framed.
£370–440 / €540–640
$670–800 ⚒ WW

Fans were introduced in the 15th century to western Europe from China and Japan by the Portuguese, who had strong trading connections with the East. The most sought-after examples date from the 18th century when the fashion for fans was at its height. These examples are hand-painted and often of the most superb quality. By the 19th century, fans with leaves of satin, silk, gauze and lace had become popular and feathers were increasingly used from the 1880s. Many fans from the late 19th century commemorate great events or advertise hotels, scents or restaurants.

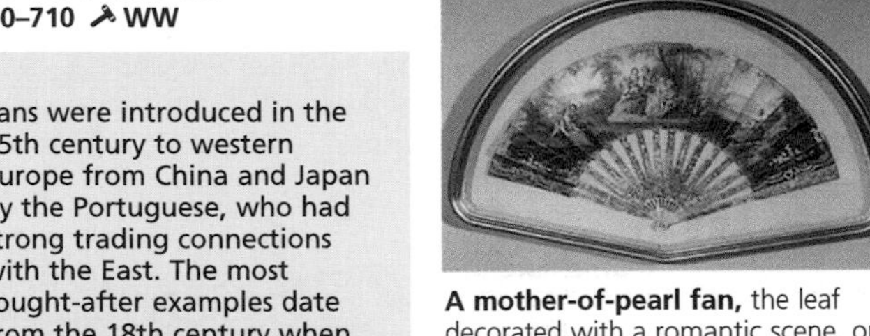

A mother-of-pearl fan, the leaf decorated with a romantic scene, on pierced parcel-gilt sticks decorated with figures and foliage, repaired, early 19thC, 20in (51cm) wide, framed.
£190–220 / €280–330
$340–400 ⚒ WW

A mother-of-pearl fan, decorated with figures on a quay and simulated lace, on pierced parcel-gilt sticks, 19thC, 21in (53.5cm) wide, framed.
£230–270 / €340–400
$420–500 ⚒ WW

► **A mother-of-pearl fan,** the leaf decorated on either side with ladies, the sticks with silver-mounted ivory inserts, slight damage, French, c1860, 11½in (29cm) high.
£350–420
€510–610
$630–760 ⚒ F&C

A blonde tortoiseshell fan, by Duvelleroy, the painted silk leaf depicting lovers, the sticks inset with steel, French, c1890, 9in (23cm) high.
£360–400 / €520–580
$640–710 ⊞ VK

An ivory fan, the silk leaf painted with a Watteauesque scene, on pierced and painted sticks, 19thC, 20in (51cm) wide, framed.
£190–220 / €280–330
$340–400 ⚒ WW

A paper fan, 'The Violet Calendar', by Arthur Day & Sons, Sheffield, issued as a free gift, 1897, 8in (20.5cm) high.
£340–380 / €500–550
$610–680 ⊞ Qua

Jewellery

Bangles & Bracelets

A silver and gold bracelet, set with paste stones, c1800, 6¾in (17cm) long.
£540–640 / €790–930
$980–1,150 ⚒ F&C

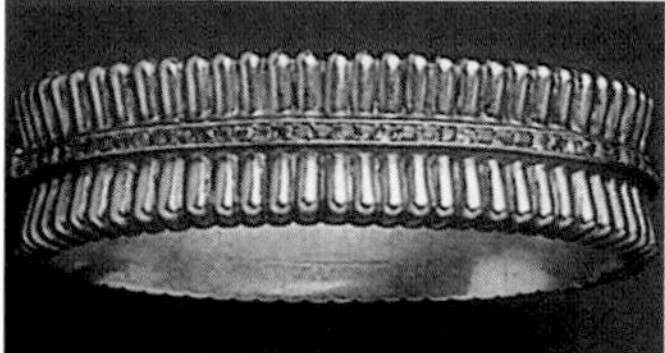

A 15ct gold bracelet, set with alternating emeralds and rubies, with a hidden interior compartment, c1820, 6¼in (16cm) diam.
£1,900–2,250 / €2,750–3,300
$3,450–4,050 ⚒ SK(B)

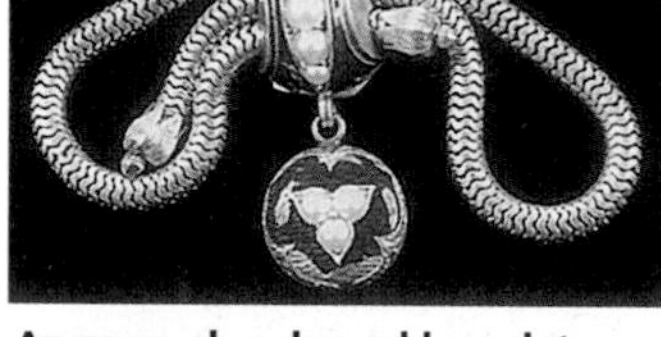

An enamel and pearl bracelet, with a locket, French, 19thC.
£300–360 / €440–530
$540–650 ⚒ JAA

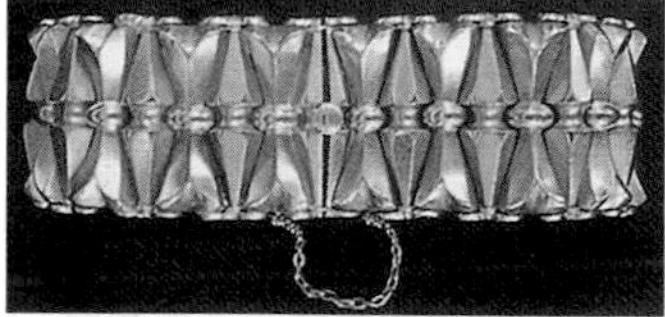

A Victorian Etruscan-style gold bracelet, with spear-shaped links.
£470–560 / €690–820
$850–1,000 ⚒ HYD

A Victorian 15ct gold buckle bracelet, inset with enamel, 2½in (6.5cm) wide.
£1,800–2,000 / €2,600–2,900
$3,250–3,600 ⊞ WIM

A Berlin ironwork bracelet, with scrolled panels, German, early 19thC.
£370–440 / €540–640
$670–800 ⚒ DN

A gold bracelet, with four bronzed silhouette panels depicting neo-classical gods in mother-of-pearl surrounds, the links with glass spacers and trace interlinks, early 19thC.
£560–670 / €820–980
$1,000–1,200 ⚒ DN

A gilt-metal-mounted micro-mosaic bracelet, the seven panels depicting buildings of ancient Rome, Italian, mid-19thC, 6½in (16.5cm) long.
£330–390 / €480–570
$600–710 ⚒ PFK

A 15ct gold and *pietra dura* bracelet, the six plaques depicting floral bouquets, the settings with wirework decoration, c1860, 7in (18cm) long.
£980–1,150 / €1,450–1,700
$1,750–2,100 ⚒ LJ

A Victorian gold curb-link bracelet, set with three cultured pearls and two diamonds.
£230–270 / €340–400
$420–500 ⚒ G(L)

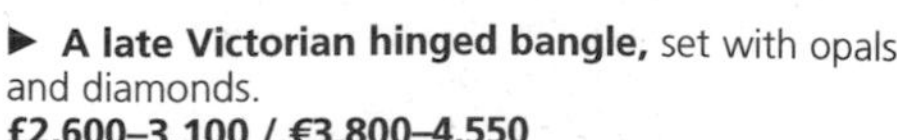

► **A late Victorian hinged bangle,** set with opals and diamonds.
£2,600–3,100 / €3,800–4,550
$4,700–5,600 ⚒ Mal(O)

A gold bracelet, set with natural pearls and diamonds, c1880, 2½in (6.5cm) wide.
£6,000–6,600 / €8,800–9,700
$10,800–11,900 ⊞ SGr

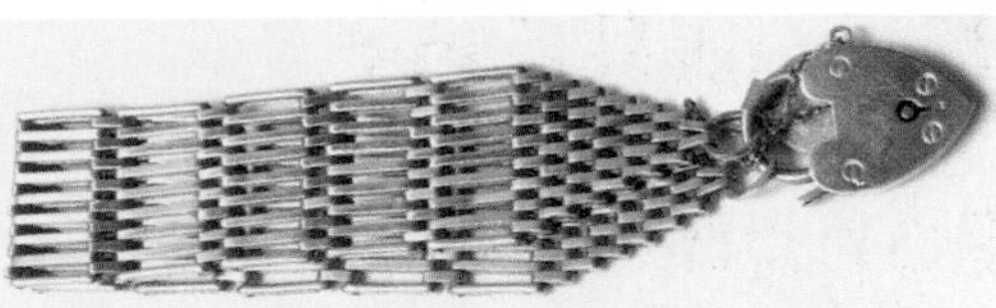

A 9ct gold gate bracelet, c1900, 5in (12.5cm) long.
£720–800 / €1,000–1,150
$1,300–1,450 ⊞ TGL

An Edwardian silver and gold bangle, set with a pearl and diamonds.
£640–760 / €930–1,100
$1,200–1,400 ⚒ DN

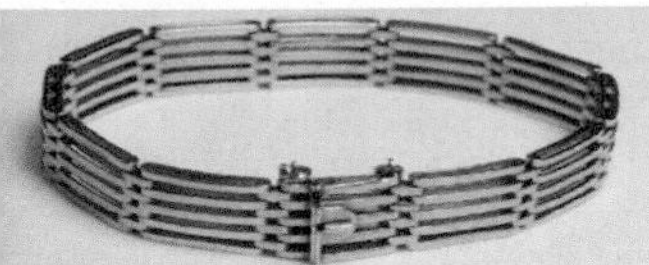

A 15ct gold gate bracelet, c1910, 3½in (9cm) wide.
£720–800 / €1,000–1,150
$1,300–1,450 ⊞ WIM

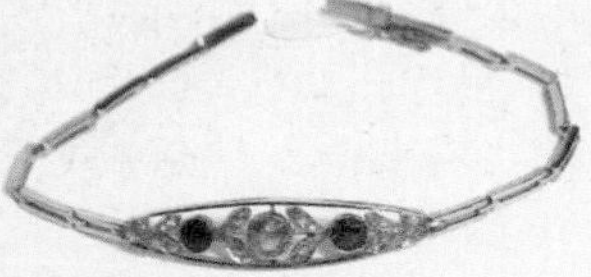

A gold bracelet, set with demantoid garnets and red garnets, Russian, c1905, ½in (1cm) wide.
£2,000–2,250 / €2,900–3,300
$3,600–4,050 ⊞ SHa

A 15ct gold gate bracelet, c1920, 3¾in (9.5cm) wide.
£810–900 / €1,200–1,350
$1,450–1,650 ⊞ WIM

A 9ct rose gold double-curb bracelet, with engraved decoration and heart padlock, Chester 1908, 7½in (19cm) long.
£350–420 / €510–610
$630–760 ⚒ SWO

Items in the Jewellery section have been arranged in date order within each sub-section.

Brooches

A brooch, set with seed pearls, diamonds and a lock of hair, c1780.
£2,200–2,450 / €3,200–3,600
$4,000–4,450 ⊞ SAY

A gold snake brooch, set with emerald eyes, the pendent drop set with a diamond in an enamelled surround, the hinged crystal back enclosing plaited hair, c1835.
£530–630 / €770–920
$960–1,150 ⚒ PFK

A gold brooch, set with jet, the central locket containing plaited hair, with an inscription to the reverse, c1820, ¾in (2cm) wide.
£130–145 / €190–210
$230–260 ⊞ Aur

Further reading
Miller's Costume Jewellery: A Collector's Guide, Miller's Publications, 2002

A carved coral brooch, depicting the three Muses of Literature, Theatre and Music, c1840.
£1,050–1,250 / €1,550–1,850
$1,900–2,250 ⚒ HAM

A brooch, in the form of a reindeer, set with diamonds, possibly Turkish, c1830, 2in (5cm) wide.
£3,550–3,950 / €5,100–5,700
$6,400–7,100 ⊞ NBL

An 18ct gold brooch, set with three amethysts and diamonds within scrolled motifs, with an amethyst drop, 19thC, pendent amethyst 1in (2.5cm) long.
£1,000–1,200 / €1,450–1,750
$1,800–2,150 ⚒ WEBB

A 15ct gold brooch, set with a citrine surrounded by natural pearls, c1840, 1in (2.5cm) wide.
£310–350 / €450–510
$560–630 ⊞ EXC

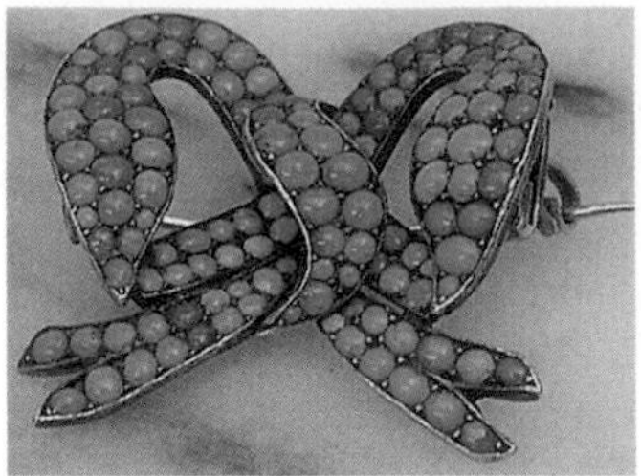

A Victorian bow brooch, set with turquoises, inscribed and dated 1851.
£175–210 / €260–310
$320–380 ⚒ DD

A silver brooch, the reverse with a locket, c1850, 2in (5cm) wide.
£145–165 / €210–240
$260–290 ⊞ Aur

An 18ct gold and enamel brooch, set with pearls and two diamonds, c1860, 1¼in (3cm) wide.
£1,150–1,300 / €1,650–1,900
$2,100–2,300 ⊞ SGr

A gold fringe brooch, with filigree decoration, c1860, 3in (7.5cm) high.
£880–980 / €1,300–1,450
$1,600–1,800 ⊞ WIM

A Victorian gold, silver and enamel brooch, set with diamonds, with a ribbon-tied surmount, the reverse with a glazed compartment.
£820–980 / €1,200–1,450
$1,500–1,750 ⚒ G(L)

A tortoiseshell brooch, in the form of a butterfly inlaid with silver and gold, c1860, 2in (5cm) wide.
£720–800 / €1,000–1,150
$1,300–1,450 ⊞ SGr

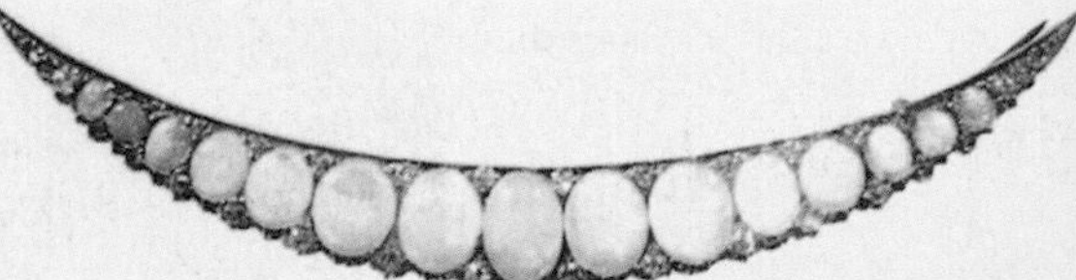

A Victorian gold brooch, set with 15 graduated opals surrounded by diamonds, 3¼in (8.5cm) wide.
£590–700 / €850–1,000
$1,050–1,250 ⚒ F&C

► **A Victorian gold brooch,** set with a floral micro-mosaic.
£140–165 / €200–240
$250–300 ⚒ G(L)

A Victorian brooch, set with half-pearls and diamonds.
£940–1,100 / €1,350–1,600
$1,700–2,000 ⚒ TEN

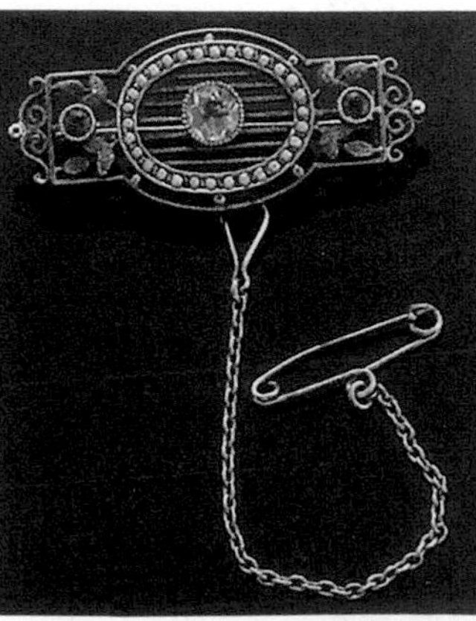

A Victorian 15ct gold brooch, set with seed pearls, an aquamarine and garnets, 1½in (4cm) wide.
£220–260 / €320–380
$400–470 ⚒ SWO

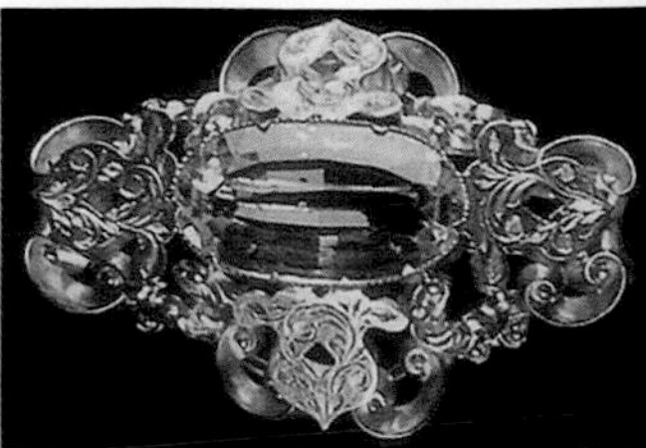

A Victorian 15ct gold brooch, set with an aquamarine within a floral mount.
£430–510 / €630–740
$780–920 ⚒ L

A gold brooch, set with a banded agate, with an inscription and a modelled lock of hair, 19thC, 1½in (4cm) diam.
£530–590 / €770–860
$960–1,100 ⊞ Aur

An 18ct gold and enamel brooch, set with a diamond, c1880, 1¼in (3cm) wide.
£400–450 / €580–660
$720–810 ⊞ SGr

A late Victorian 18ct gold brooch, depicting a fox mask.
£120–140 / €170–200
$210–250 ⚒ GAK

A gold and *guilloche* enamel Fabergé-style brooch, set with seed pearls, c1900, 1in (2.5cm) diam.
£260–290 / €380–420
$470–520 ⊞ TDG

A gold brooch, set with plaidwork agates, with an agate back, Scottish, c1880, 2in (5cm) wide.
£1,000–1,100 / €1,450–1,600
$1,800–2,000 ⊞ Aur

A gold and glass brooch, set with seed pearls, French, c1880, 1½in (4cm) diam.
£240–270 / €350–390
$430–490 ⊞ Aur

A late Victorian silver and gold brooch, set with diamonds within a foliate scroll.
£1,400–1,650 / €2,050–2,400
$2,550–3,000 ⚒ WW

► A garnet and diamond brooch, in the form of an ostrich, c1900.
£1,400–1,650 / €2,050–2,400
$2,550–3,000 ⚒ S

◄ An enamel and diamond brooch, c1900, 1½in (4cm) high.
£400–440
€580–640
$720–800
⊞ SGr

An 18ct gold brooch, in the form of a bee, the body and wings set with diamonds, the abdomen set with an opal, the eyes set with rubies, c1880.
£700–840 / €1,000–1,200
$1,250–1,500 ⚒ LJ

A gold and bog oak brooch, Irish, c1880, 2in (5cm) high.
£240–270 / €350–390
$430–490 ⊞ SIL

An 18ct gold brooch, in the form of a winged Medusa's head, set with a ruby, with a hairpin attachment, c1890, 4½in (11.5cm) wide.
£3,600–4,000 / €5,300–5,900
$6,500–7,200 ⊞ NBL

An 18ct gold brooch, set with opals, sapphires and diamonds, c1900, 3in (7.5cm) wide.
£2,700–3,000 / €3,950–4,400
$4,900–5,400 ⊞ EXC

A gold brooch, by Ivanoff, Russian, c1900, 1½in (4cm) wide, with original case.
£2,000–2,250 / €2,900–3,300
$3,600–4,050 ⊞ SHa

An Edwardian platinum and gold brooch, set with enamel and diamonds and an applied pearl.
£440–520 / €640–760
$800–940 DN

An Edwardian enamel brooch, depicting Venus, surrounded by a border of diamonds.
£230–270 / €340–400
$420–500 L

An Edwardian gold brooch/ pendant, set with a pink topaz and diamonds.
£2,900–3,450 / €4,250–5,000
$5,200–6,200 G(L)

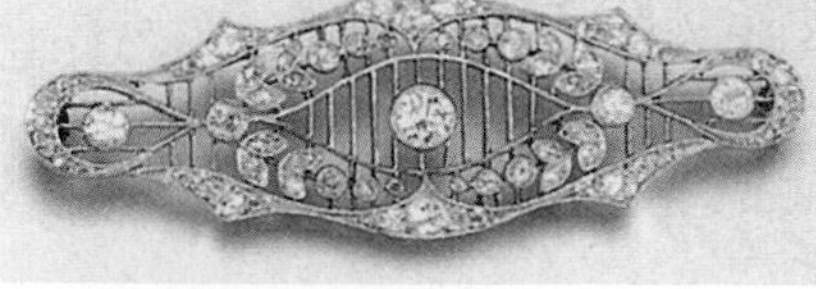

◄ **A brooch,** set with diamonds, c1910.
£1,400–1,650
€2,050–2,400
$2,550–3,000 S

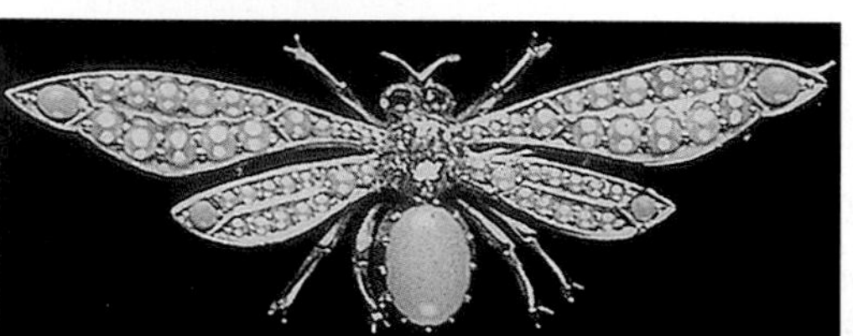

An Edwardian 15ct gold brooch, in the form of an insect set with a diamond, turquoises and seed pearls, the eyes set with garnets.
£700–840 / €1,050–1,250
$1,250–1,500 L

A platinum brooch, by Boucheron, in the form of an arrow, set with onyx and diamonds, c1910, 3¾in (9.5cm) wide.
£6,900–7,700 / €10,100–11,200
$12,500–13,900 ⊞ NBL

A gold and enamel brooch, in the form of a butterfly, the wings decorated with gilt fleur-de-lys and set with diamonds, with a diamond body and thorax and ruby eyes, early 20thC.
£440–520 / €640–760
$800–940 DN

A silver-topped 14ct gold butterfly brooch, set with opals, diamonds, sapphires, emeralds and rubies, slight damage, c1910.
£970–1,150 / €1,450–1,700
$1,750–2,100 SK(B)

A platinum and velvet brooch, set with a rose diamond, French, 1910–15, 1¼in (3cm) wide.
£2,250–2,500 / €3,300–3,650
$4,050–4,550 ⊞ WIM

LOCATE THE SOURCE

The source of each illustration in Miller's can be found by checking the code letters below each caption with the Key to Illustrations, pages 778–784.

A panel brooch, the diamonds set in stylized flower and leaf openwork, one diamond missing, early 20thC.
£490–580 / €720–850
$890–1,050 DN

◄ **A silver and cornelian brooch,** set with marcasite, c1915, 2in (5cm) long.
£145–165 / €210–240
$270–300 ⊞ TDG

► **A brooch,** in the form of a lizard set with seed pearls and green stones, with ruby eyes, early 20thC.
£540–640
€790–930
$970–1,150
DD

Cameos

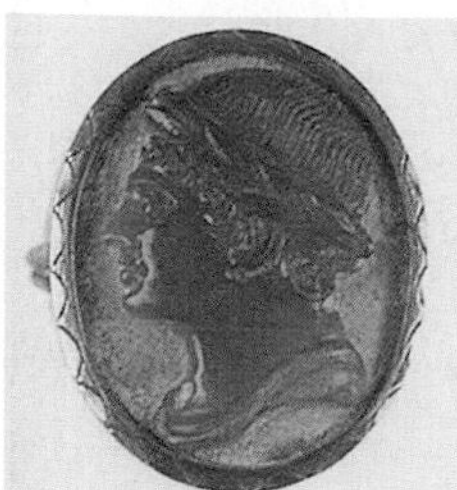

A carnelian cameo ring, carved with the head of Julius Caesar, mount later, c1780.
£470–560 / €690–820
$850–1,000 L

An agate cameo ring, carved with a young Roman woman, mount and shank possibly later, c1820.
£800–960 / €1,200–1,400
$1,450–1,750 L

An agate cameo ring, carved with the head of Bacchus, later mount and shank, c1820.
£900–1,050
€1,300–1,550
$1,600–1,900 L

A shell cameo brooch, carved with an allegory of Spring in a scalloped gold mount, 19thC.
£280–330 / €410–480
$500–600 HAM

An early Victorian cameo brooch, carved with a mother and child, in a gold scroll mount, 2¼in (5.5cm) high.
£720–800 / €1,000–1,150
$1,300–1,450 AMC

A shell cameo brooch and earring suite, the brooch carved with a lady in profile, set in an 18ct gold frame with a rope-twist border and fleur-de-lys mounts, the lower hinged section with chased and engraved decoration and graduated fringing, earrings damaged, c1860, boxed.
£420–500 / €610–730
$760–910 LJ

A cameo brooch, carved with Romeo and Juliet and set in a gold chased mount with leaves and scrolls, c1870, 2¼in (5.5cm) high.
£500–550 / €730–810
$900–1,000 AMC

A Victorian hardstone cameo brooch, carved with a female portrait profile, within bead borders set with clusters of graduated half-pearls, 2in (5cm) high.
£700–840 / €1,000–1,200
$1,250–1,500 L&T

A shell cameo, depicting Night and Day, within a metal filigree mount and border, 19thC.
£640–760 / €930–1,100
$1,150–1,350 G(B)

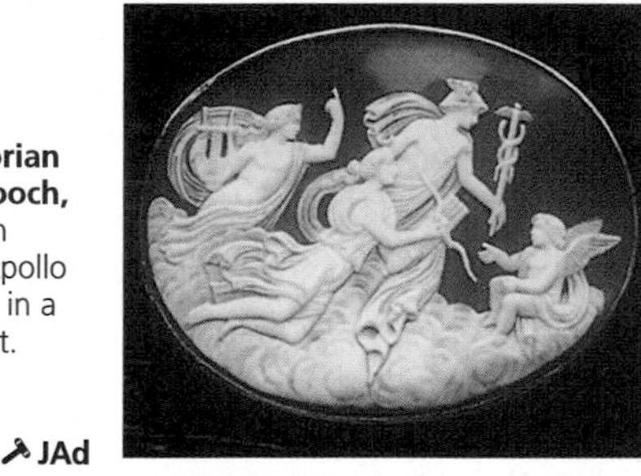

► **A Victorian cameo brooch,** carved with Mercury, Apollo and Diana, in a gold mount.
£200–240
€290–350
$360–430 JAd

A lava cameo bracelet, with eight graduating plaques, each depicting a female classical head in profile, with bead link spacers, c1880.
£230–270 / €340–400
$420–500 TEN

A stone cameo, carved with a male profile, in a gold setting, c1890, ¾in (2cm) high.
£170–190 / €250–280
$300–340 AMC

Items in the Jewellery section have been arranged in date order within each sub-section.

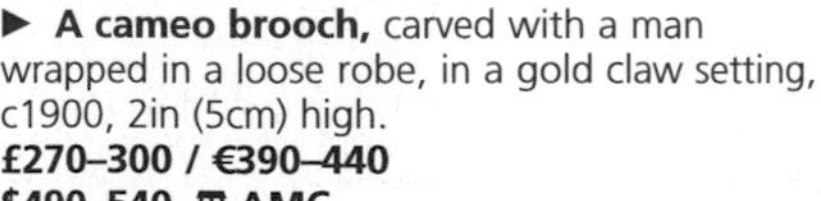

► **A cameo brooch,** carved with a man wrapped in a loose robe, in a gold claw setting, c1900, 2in (5cm) high.
£270–300 / €390–440
$490–540 AMC

Cufflinks

A pair of Georgian paste cufflinks, set in white metal.
£190–220 / €280–330
$340–400 G(L)

A pair of late Victorian gold and enamel cufflinks, by Carlo Giuliano, maker's mark, in original fitted case.
£7,000–8,400
€10,200–12,300
$12,700–15,200 DN

◄ A pair of carved amethyst and pearl cufflinks, 1919.
£95–110 / €140–160
$175–200 Aur

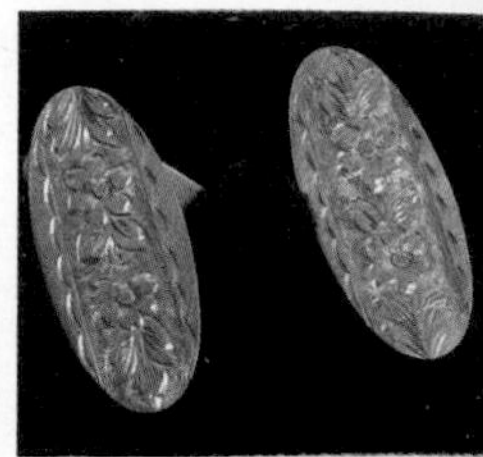

A pair of gold cufflinks, engraved with flowers, 1919.
£140–155 / €200–220
$250–280 Aur

A pair of 9ct gold cufflinks, the panels with engine-turned bands within a wrigglework border, Birmingham 1928, cased.
£220–260 / €320–380
$400–470 DN

Earrings

A pair of cannetille gold and garnet earrings, adapted to pendant earrings, early 19thC.
£530–630 / €770–920
$960–1,150 DN

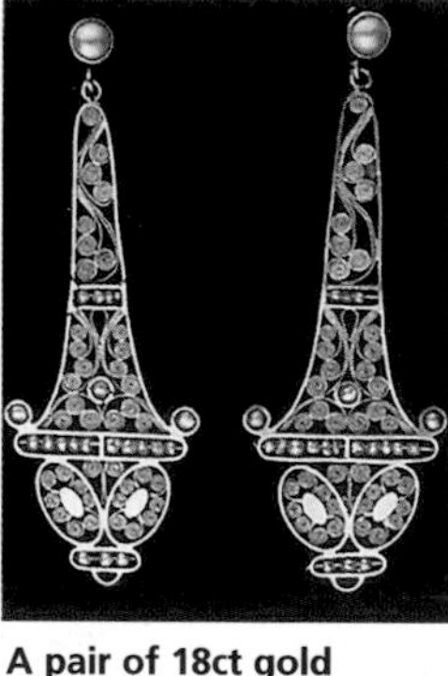

A pair of 18ct gold filigree earrings, set with pearls, with later screw fittings, early 19thC.
£680–810 / €1,000–1,200
$1,250–1,500 BUK

A pair of Etruscan-style gold earrings, with tassel fringing and beaded borders, c1860, with a fitted case.
£880–1,050
€1,300–1,550
$1,600–1,900 TEN

A pair of ivory earrings, carved with flowerheads and leaves, c1860.
£190–220 / €280–330
$340–400 TEN

A pair of 18ct gold and enamel earrings, c1860, 2in (5cm) long.
£580–650 / €850–950
$1,050–1,200 EXC

A pair of Victorian 15ct gold and garnet earrings, 2in (5cm) long.
£1,050–1,200
€1,550–1,750
$1,900–2,150 WIM

► A pair of Victorian gold earrings, 1¾in (4.5cm) long.
£720–800 / €1,000–1,150
$1,300–1,450 WIM

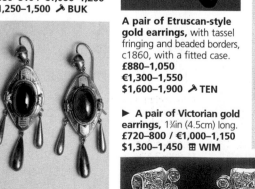

◄ A pair of diamond-set scroll-and-ribbon panel earrings, adapte early 20thC.
£440–520
€640–760
$800–940 D

Necklaces

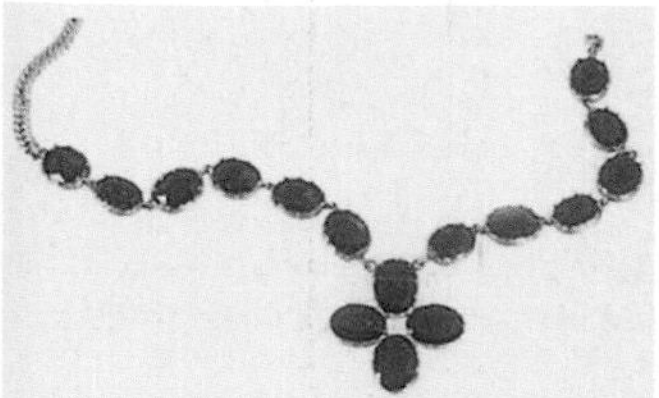

A gold and garnet necklace, with a pendant, 18thC, on a later chain.
£470–560 / €690–820
$850–1,000 DN

A gold and silver graduated paste rivière necklace, French, 1837–47.
£630–750 / €920–1,100
$1,150–1,350 F&C

A George III gold necklace, the links embossed with beads, with a ruby, emerald and turquoise clasp decorated with burr-beads.
£1,400–1,650 / €2,050–2,400
$2,550–3,000 DN

A garnet necklace, with a cross pendant, c1850.
£880–1,050 / €1,300–1,550
$1,600–1,900 TEN

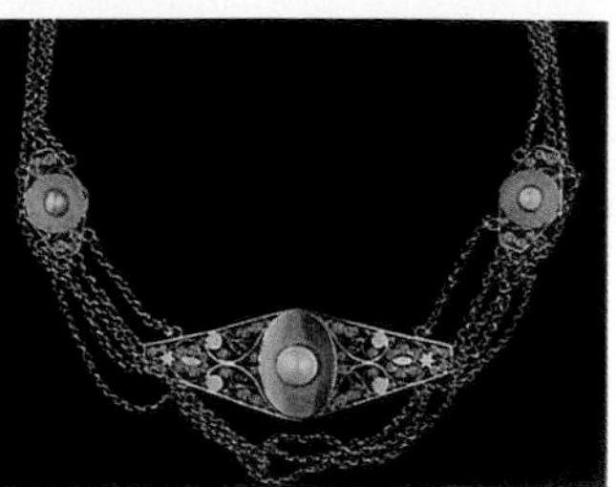

An 18ct gold and freshwater pearl necklace, with a later clasp, Swedish, Gothenburg, early 19thC.
£700–840 / €1,000–1,200
$1,250–1,500 BUK

A Whitby jet necklace, with three carved pendants, 1850–90.
£400–450 / €580–660
$720–810 TDG

A Victorian enamel and half-pearl necklace, with three pendant drops and two divisions, with original case.
£820–980 / €1,200–1,450
$1,500–1,800 RTo

► **A Victorian jet necklace,** the front two rows with graduated faceted beads on a single back row of matching beads.
£140–165
€200–240
$250–300 G(L)

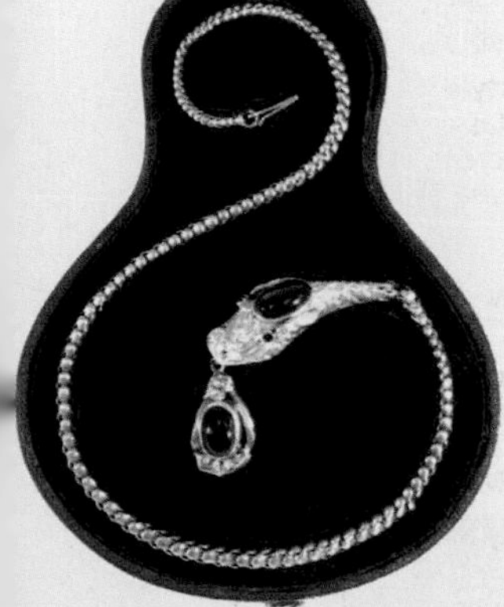

A Victorian gold snake necklace, the head set with a garnet, a similar set foliate pendant hanging from its mouth, with case.
£770–920 / €1,100–1,300
$1,400–1,650 AH

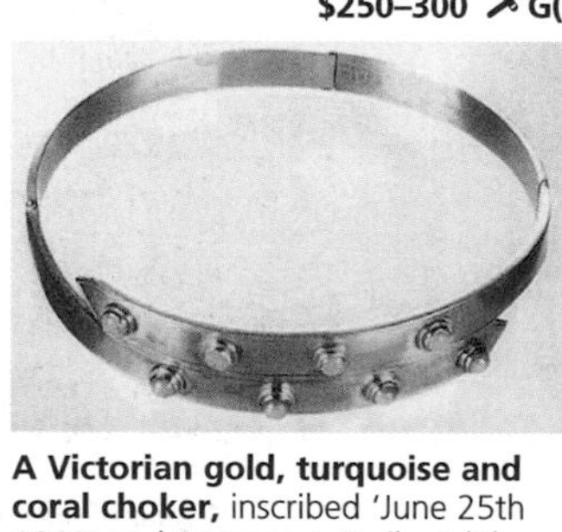

A Victorian gold, turquoise and coral choker, inscribed 'June 25th 1868' and 'Margaret, Emily, Edith, Florence, Kate, Ada, May and Evelyn'.
£1,000–1,200 / €1,450–1,750
$1,800–2,150 DN

A gold and agate necklace, Scottish, c1880.
£360–400 / €520–580
$650–720 Aur

► **An amethyst and seed pearl necklace,** with a 15ct gold clasp, c1880.
£770–920 / €1,100–1,300
$1,400–1,650 LJ

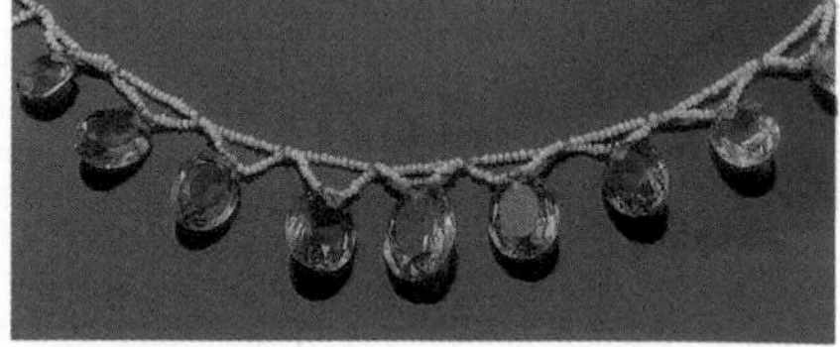

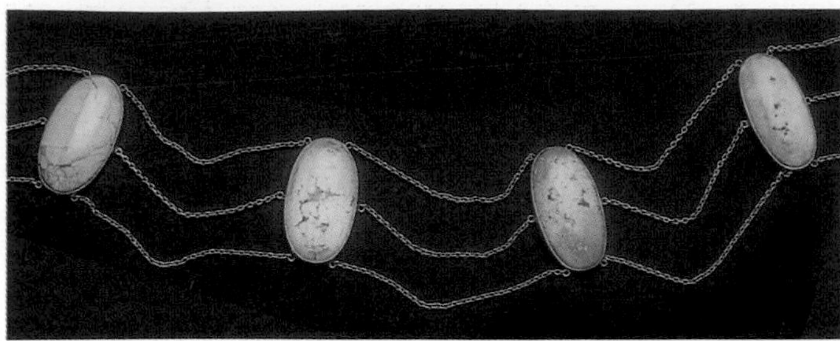

A 14ct gold and turquoise choker, the six turquoises joined by a trace link chain, c1900.
£420–500 / €610–730
$760–910 SK(B)

A gold, diamond and enamel necklace, in the form of seven pansies, each set with a diamond, early 20thC.
£1,950–2,300 / €2,850–3,350
$3,550–4,200 DN

A pearl and base metal choker, c1910, with original D. J. Wellby, London, case.
£380–450 / €550–660
$690–810 JAA

A silver, enamel, diamond and pearl necklace, c1910, with original Kirby & Bunn, London, case.
£500–600 / €730–880
$910–1,100 JAA

A platinum and diamond necklace, c1920.
£5,000–5,500 / €7,200–8,000
$9,000–10,000 EXC

Parures & Sets

A jet pendant and earrings, set with porcelain plaques decorated with putti, mid-19thC.
£320–380 / €470–550
$580–690 Bea

A Victorian pearl and amethyst necklace and earring set, set with seed pearls, in a fitted case.
£590–700 / €850–1,000
$1,050–1,250 TEN

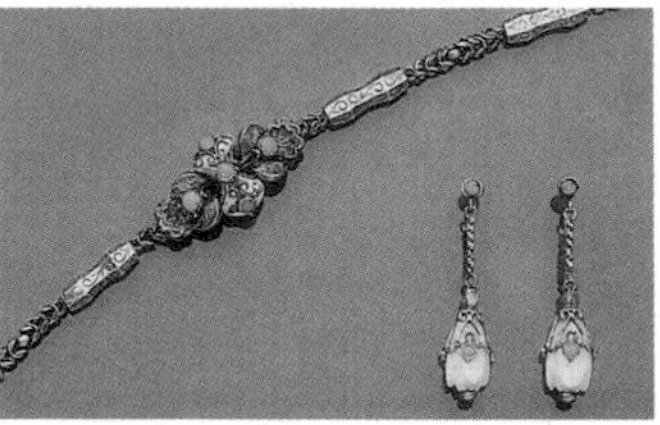

A gold and turquoise demi-parure, comprising bracelet, brooch and earrings, c1870.
£410–490 / €600–720
$740–890 TEN

A 15ct gold and pearl brooch and earring set, in original fitted case, c1870.
£2,250–2,500 / €3,300–3,650
$4,050–4,550 WIM

A Victorian Etruscan-style gold and white coral demi-parure, comprising a hinged bangle, brooch and earrings.
£940–1,100 / €1,350–1,600
$1,700–2,000 WW

An 18ct gold, ruby and seed pearl brooch and earring set, French, c1880.
£2,000–2,250 / €2,900–3,300
$3,600–4,050 EXC

◄ **An Edwardian gold necklace and brooch set,** set with amethysts and seed pearls.
£630–750 / €920–1,100
$1,150–1,350 L&E

Pendants

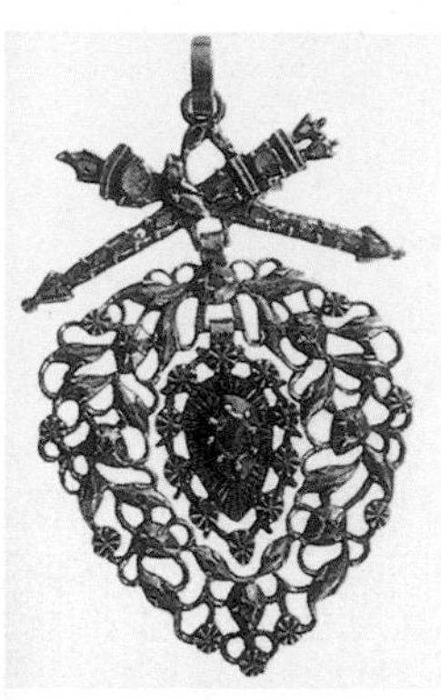

A silver and gold pendant, set with diamonds, the suspension loop in the form of a quiver and arrows, 18thC, 2¼in (5.5cm) high.
£370–440 / €540–640
$670–800 F&C

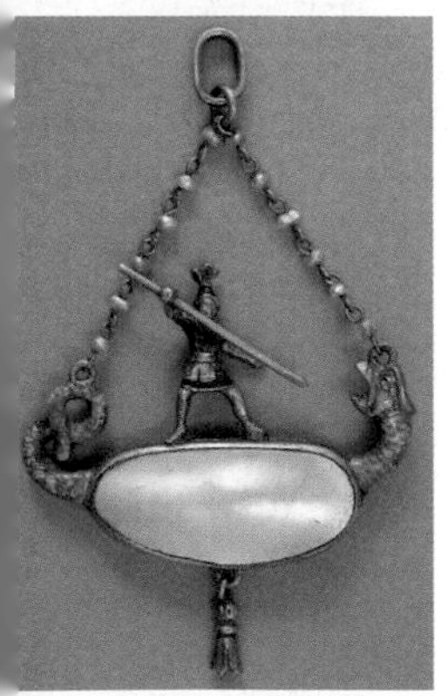

A silver-gilt, enamel and mother-of-pearl pendant, depicting St George and the Dragon, suspended on a chain set with seed pearls, 19thC.
£140–165 / €200–240
$250–300 G(L)

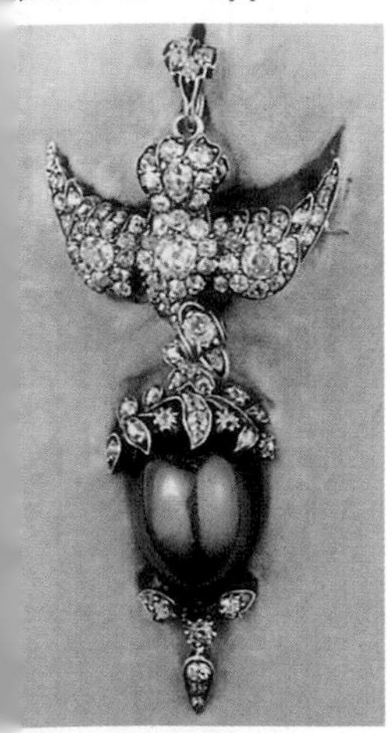

A gold and silver pendant/ brooch, set with diamonds and a garnet, 1850–1900, in original case.
£5,500–6,600
€8,000–9,600
$10,000–11,900 BUK

A Bilston enamel and gilt-metal locket, painted with a portrait of a girl, c1760, 1in (2.5cm) high.
£280–330 / €410–480
$510–600 WW

A gold filigree pendant, French, 19thC, 4¼in (11cm) high.
£190–220 / €280–330
$340–410 F&C

A 18ct gold pendant, decorated in micro-mosaic, with a locket compartment and a 9ct gold chain, c1860, in a box.
£790–940 / €1,150–1,350
$1,450–1,700 LJ

A Regency gold pendant, set with seed pearls and pink stones.
£750–900 / €1,100–1,300
$1,400–1,650 HYD

An enamel, diamond and pearl locket, c1850, 1¾in (4.5cm) high.
£8,100–9,000
€11,800–13,100
$14,700–16,300 NBL

A blister pearl pendant, set in a diamond mount, c1860.
£2,700–3,000
€3,950–4,400
$4,900–5,400 NBL

◀ **A gold memorial locket,** decorated with a pedestal and flowers, c1860, 1½in (4cm) high.
£170–195 / €250–280
$310–350 Aur

▶ **A Victorian gold and silver pendant,** set with diamonds, 2in (5cm) high, with a later silver chain.
£1,500–1,800
€2,200–2,650
$2,700–3,250 SWO

A Renaissance-style silver-gilt pendant, mounted with an emerald, enamelled flowerheads set with garnets and pearls, with a pearl-suspension loop and emerald drop, Austro-Hungarian, 19thC, 3¼in (8.5cm) high.
£470–560 / €680–820
$830–1,000 F&C

A 15ct pendant, in the form of a birdcage, set with coral and turquoise in a malachite base, with a slide-out locket compartment, c1850, 1¾in (4.5cm) high.
£3,600–4,000
€5,200–5,800
$6,500–7,200 NBL

A Victorian opal and diamond pendant, with a white-metal chain set with pearls.
£1,100–1,300
€1,600–1,900
$2,000–2,350 HYD

A 15ct gold pendant, set with amethysts and seed pearls, late 19thC.
£710–850 / €1,050–1,250
$1,300–1,550 WEBB

An Edwardian 18ct gold pendant, set with an aquamarine, four garnets and five pearls, 3¼in (8.5cm) high.
£1,450–1,700
€2,100–2,500
$2,600–3,100 SWO

A Victorian 15ct gold floral scroll, on a rope chain.
£220–260 / €320–380
$400–470 SWO

An opal and diamond pendant/brooch, late 19thC.
£1,550–1,850
€2,250–2,700
$2,800–3,350 Bea

An Edwardian 15ct gold pendant, set with a green tourmaline and seed pearls, with a pink tourmaline drop.
£700–840 / €1,000–1,200
$1,250–1,500 G(L)

An Edwardian gold and silver pendant, set with diamonds.
£370–440 / €540–640
$670–800 G(L)

A silver and gold pendant, set with diamonds and an opal, c1880, 1in (2.5cm) high.
£3,150–3,500
€4,600–5,100
$5,700–6,300 ⊞ EXC

A late Victorian silver locket, embossed with a horseshoe, on a matching chain.
£120–140 / €170–200
$210–250 G(L)

An Edwardian platinum pendant, set with a garnet and diamonds, 2in (5cm) high, with a platinum chain.
£3,150–3,500
€4,600–5,100
$5,700–6,300 ⊞ EXC

A silver locket, with a rope-twist chain, Birmingham 1882, cased.
£200–240 / €290–350
$360–430 L&E

An Edwardian 15ct gold pendant/brooch, set with diamonds and half-pearls, with a gold chain.
£1,450–1,700
€2,100–2,500
$2,600–3,100 L

An Edwardian 9ct gold pendant, set with seed pearls and a garnet, with a 9ct gold chain, 18½in (47cm) long.
£280–330 / €400–480
$500–600 DA

Rings

◄ **A gold and sapphire ring,** decorated with scrollwork, 16thC.
£2,150–2,550
€3,100–3,700
$3,850–4,600
S

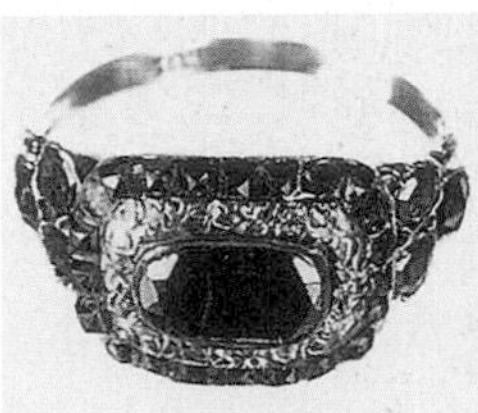

A gold and garnet ring, 18thC.
£210–250 / €310–370
$380–450 DN

An 18ct gold mourning ring, 1782.
£2,450–2,750
€3,550–4,000
$4,450–5,000 CVA

A George III rose gold ring, inset with a portrait of a maiden, inscribed 'Lord Gray OB. 17th December 1786 AE 35'.
£320–380 / €470–560
$580–690 DD

An 18ct gold mourning ring, set with hair and pearls, c1795.
£400–450 / €580–660
$720–810 WELD

A gold, ruby and diamond ring, early 19thC.
£210–250 / €310–370
$380–450 DN

A diamond cluster ring, damaged, 19thC.
£440–520 / €640–760
$800–950 SWO

◄ **An 18ct gold ring,** set with amethysts and diamonds, 19thC.
£260–310
€380–450
$470–560
G(L)

A Victorian ring, set with rubies, amethysts, turquoise and a diamond, with a glazed locket back.
£130–155 / €200–230
$240–290 DD

A Victorian peridot and diamond cluster ring/pendant, one diamond missing.
£2,100–2,500
€3,050–3,650
$3,800–4,550 F&C

An 18ct gold, ɩiamond and ɛmerald eternity ɩing, c1880.
'800–890
ɩ1,150–1,300
ɩ1,450–1,600
SGr

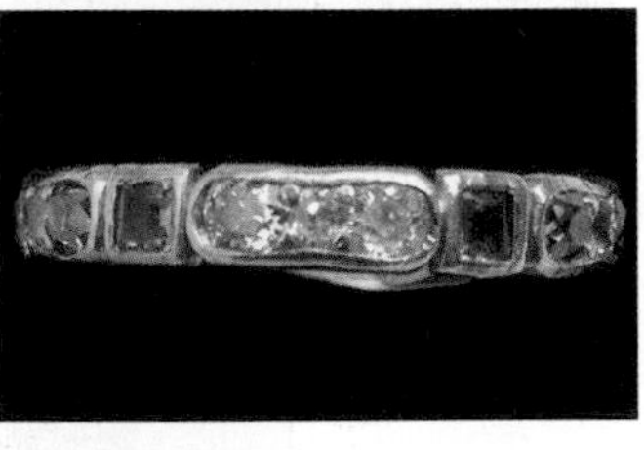

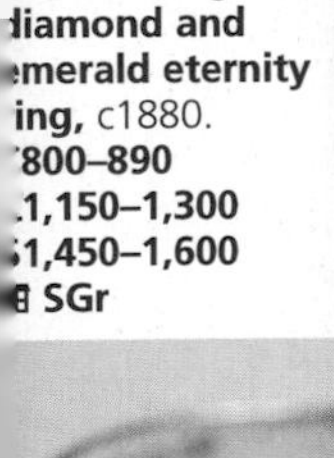

◄ **A late Victorian gold, diamond and ruby ring.**
£1,250–1,400
€1,850–2,050
$2,250–2,550
WIM

A Victorian white gold and diamond ring.
£1,300–1,550
€1,900–2,250
$2,350–2,800 DN(BR)

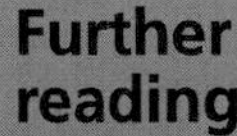

Further reading

Miller's Antiques Checklist: Jewellery, Miller's Publications, 1998

. gold and diamond cluster ring, 1890.
11,000–12,200
16,100–17,800
29,100–32,200 NBL

A sapphire and diamond ring, the white-metal shank set with diamonds, c1905.
£4,450–5,300 / €6,500–7,700
$8,100–9,600 HYD

A platinum and diamond ring, c1910.
£3,400–3,800 / €4,950–5,500
$6,200–6,900 EXC

Enamel

An Imperial cloisonné beaker, Russian, 1896–1907, 2in (5cm) high.
£490–550 / €720–800
$890–1,000 ⊞ SHa

An enamel box, with a hinged mirror cover, painted with birds, inscribed 'Keep This For My Sake', late 18thC, 1¾in (4.5cm) wide.
£300–360 / €440–530
$540–650 ⚒ WW

An enamel card case, painted with a garden scene, possibly Italian, c1890, 4in (10cm) wide.
£380–430 / €560–630
$690–780 ⊞ SiA

An enamel and ormolu inkstand and pen, with 'jewelled' decoration, late 19thC, 8½in (21.5cm) wide.
£280–330 / €410–490
$500–600 ⚒ G(L)

A cloisonné bowl, decorated with scrolling bands of flowers and lunettes, with a swing handle, stamped mark, Russian, late 19thC, 5¼in (13.5cm) diam.
£500–600 / €730–880
$900–1,050 ⚒ DN

An enamel snuff box, inset with a watercolour of a carriage crossing a bridge, the interior with a carriage in a village, Swiss, probably Geneva, late 18thC, 3¼in (8.5cm) wide.
£2,900–3,450 / €4,200–5,000
$5,200–6,200 ⚒ L

A rock crystal and enamel comport, the support in the form of a stork, Continental, early 19thC, 5in (12.5cm) high.
£2,000–2,400 / €2,900–3,500
$3,600–4,300 ⚒ BWL

A Bilston enamel patch box, decorated with flowers and a bird, inscribed 'Forget Me Not', 18thC, 1½in (4cm) diam.
£420–470 / €610–690
$760–850 ⊞ LBr

A Staffordshire enamel box, decorated with a view entitled 'Harwood House', the interior inscribed 'A Trifle From Harrogate', slight damage, late 18thC, 3½in (9cm) wide
£520–620 / €760–910
$920–1,100 ⚒ RTo

An enamel bonbon dish, by Rudolf Linke, with silver-gilt mounts, painted with nymphs and putti, Austrian, Vienna, late 19thC, 5in (12.5cm) wid
£1,400–1,650 / €2,000–2,400
$2,500–3,000 ⚒ S

An enamel and topaz seal, Swiss, c1850, 3in (7.5cm) high.
£3,150–3,500 / €4,600–5,100
$5,700–6,300 ⊞ SHa

◀ **A set of six silver and enamel menu card holders,** signed 'Serge Lemaitre', stamped mark, French, Paris, c1900, 1½in (4cm) wide, with original leather Mappin & Webb box
£1,550–1,850 / €2,250–2,700
$2,800–3,350 ⚒ DORO

Fabergé

A Fabergé carved bowenite model of a bulldog puppy, with ruby eyes, Russian, St Petersburg, late 19thC, 1½in (4cm) wide.
£7,800–9,300 / €11,400–13,600
$14,100–16,800 ⚒ S

A Fabergé candelabra/ lamp, with a marble base, workmaster Johan Viktor Aarne, Russian, St Petersburg, 1896–1907, 22¾in (58cm) high.
£16,800–20,100
€24,500–29,300
$30,000–36,000 ⚒ BUK(F)

A Fabergé silver and gem-set guilloche enamel cigarette case, by August Hollming, marked, Russian, St Petersburg, 1908–17, 1½in (4cm) wide.
£4,150–4,950 / €6,100–7,200
$7,500–9,000 ⚒ JAA

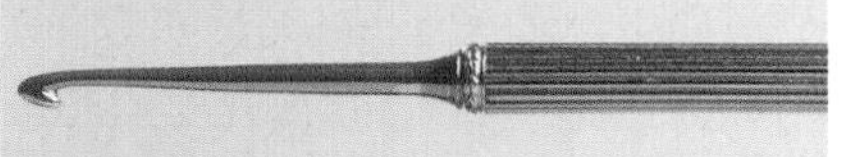

A Fabergé gold and nephrite crotchet hook, Russian, c1900, 7in (18cm) long.
£2,550–2,850 / €3,700–4,150
$4,600–5,200 ⊞ ICO

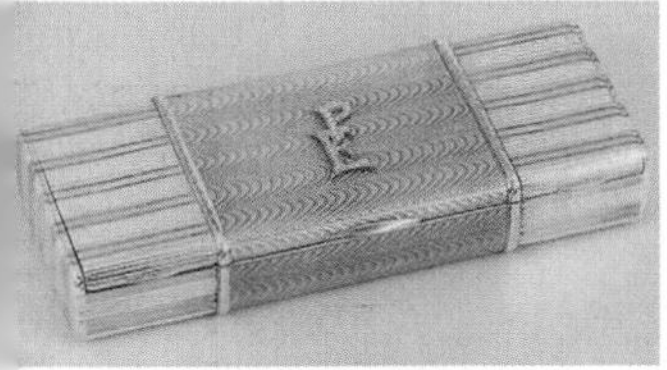

A Fabergé two-colour gold, silver and enamel cosmetics box, with a diamond-set monogram 'PE', the interior with a mirror, workmaster's mark 'AH', Russian, St Petersburg, early 20thC, 4¼in (11cm) wide.
£8,900–10,600 / €13,000–15,500
$16,100–19,200 ⚒ DORO

◄ A Fabergé two-colour gold and enamel-mounted nephrite dish, by H. Wigström, the handles formed from gold coins depicting Catherine the Great, Russian, St Petersburg, 1904–08, 4in (10cm) wide.
£6,600–7,900
€9,600–11,500
$11,900–14,300 ⚒ S

FABERGE

► A Fabergé carved rock crystal model of an elephant, with ruby eyes, Russian, late 19thC, 1½in (4cm) wide.
£6,000–6,800
€8,800–9,900
$10,900–12,300
⚒ S

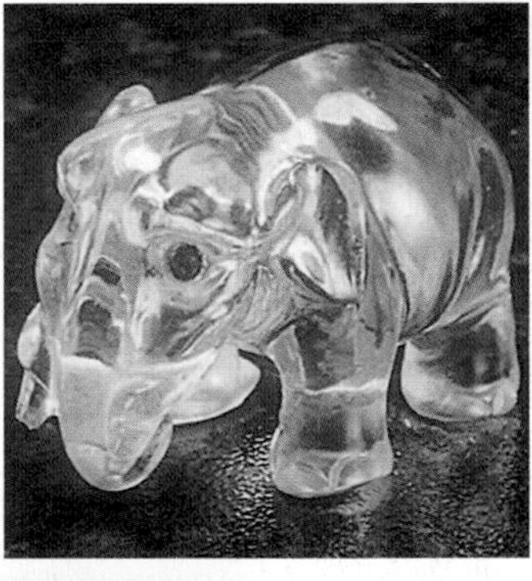

◄ A Fabergé silver and enamel photograph frame, by Anders Nevalainen, slight damage, Russian, 1896–1907, 8¼in (21cm) wide.
£16,800–20,100
€24,500–29,300
$30,000–36,000
⚒ BUK(F)

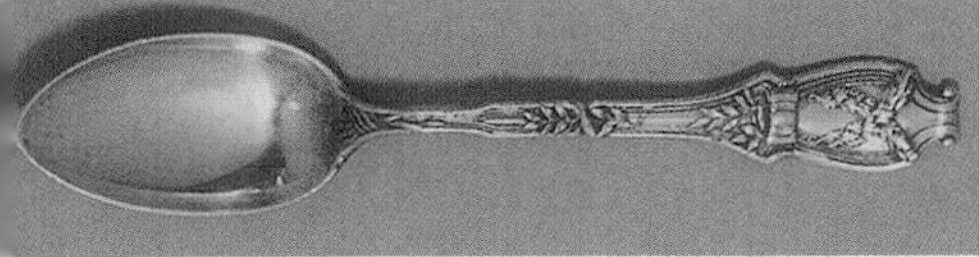

A pair of Fabergé Louis XVI-style silver-gilt spoons, Russian, Moscow, 1896–1908.
£570–680 / €830–990
$1,050–1,250 ⚒ BUK

Gold

A gold and heliotrope *aide mémoire*, containing a miniature portrait of a young nobleman, the clasp formed by a pencil in a gold case, the original leather outer case lined in silk, French, probably Paris, late 18thC, 3in (7.5cm) wide.
£4,100–4,900
€6,000–7,200
$7,400–8,900 ⚒ S(Am)

An 18thC-style gold-mounted hardstone *aide mémoire*, the cagework mounts chased with formal scrollwork and enclosing agate panels, containing a pencil and an ivory memorandum slip, marked, 19thC, 3½in (9cm) high.
£660–790 / €960–1,150
$1,200–1,450 ⚒ S

► A gold compact, by Vacheron Constantin, Swiss, c1935, 2½in (6.5cm) wide.
£1,100–1,250
€1,600–1,800
$2,000–2,200
⊞ SHa

► A gold-mounted coral desk seal, carved in the form of a bust of a classical woman, the gold mount chased with acanthus, mid-19thC, 2½in (6.5cm) high.
£2,600–3,100
€3,800–4,550
$4,700–5,600
⚒ Bea

A Victorian gold-mounted citrine fob, the mount cast with hounds chasing a fox, 2¼in (5.5cm) long.
£700–840 / €1,000–1,200
$1,250–1,500 ⚒ L&T

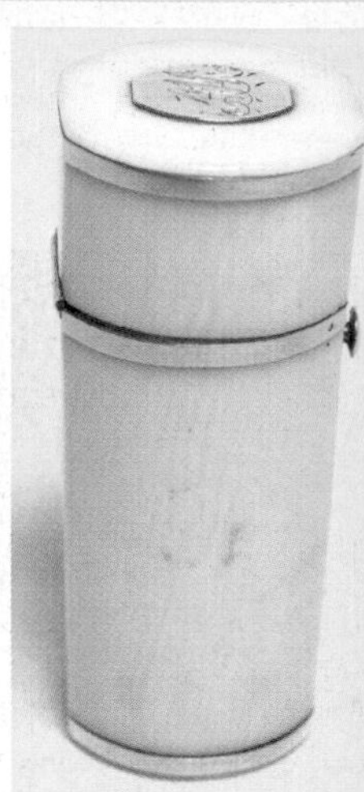

A gold-mounted ivory scent bottle case, the hinged cover with press-button to release, c1800, 5½in (14cm) high.
£360–400 / €520–580
$650–720 ⊞ LBr

An 18ct gold snuff box, by William Currie, Irish, 1752, 3in (7.5cm) diam.
£46,000–52,000 / €67,000–76,000
$83,000–94,000 ⊞ WELD
This box was presented to the Duke of Leinster on his being given the Freedom of the City of Dublin.

◄ A three-colour gold snuff box, with engine-turned decoration, engraved with the crest and motto o Bryce, with chased borders and floral thumbpiece, the interior with presentation inscription, maker's mark, probably German, c1825, 3¼in (8.5cm) wide.
£1,050–1,250 / €1,550–1,850
$1,900–2,250 ⚒ S

Insurance values

Always insure your valuable antiques for the cost of replacing them with similar items, regardless of the original price paid. Both dealers and auctioneers can provide a valuation service for a fee.

A gold snuff box, by John Norwood, with chased decoration of a sportsman and his dog, the surround decorated with swans, cranes, exotic birds and squirrels, with three maker's marks, 18thC, 2¾in (7cm) wide.
£6,300–7,500 / €9,200–11,000
$11,400–13,600 ⚒ G(B)

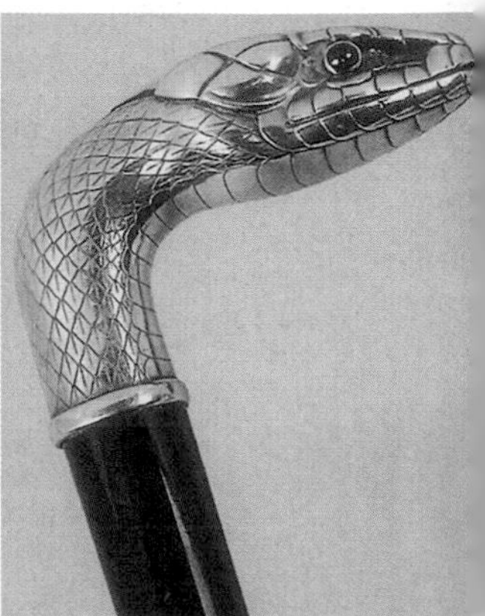

A gold-mounted thuyawood walking cane, the handle in the fo of a snake's head, set with ruby eye French, c1900, 37in (94cm) long.
£2,400–2,850 / €3,500–4,150
$4,350–5,200 ⚒ DORO

Asian Works of Art

Cloisonné & Enamel

A Canton enamel bowl, with *famille rose* Buddhist emblems, Chinese, 19thC, 5¼in (13.5cm) diam.
£310–350 / €450–500
$560–630 G&G

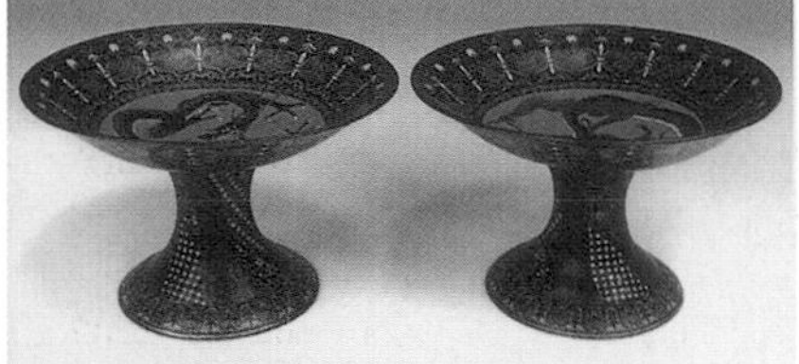

A pair of cloisonné comports, each decorated with a dragon within a geometric border, Japanese, Meiji period, 1868–1911, 9¾in (25cm) diam.
£330–390 / €480–570
$600–700 RTo

A cloisonné ewer and cover, moulded with *taotie* masks between stylized bands, the spout and handle with dragon heads, the cover surmounted by a *qilin*, slight damage, stylized mark, Chinese, 18thC, 12½in (32cm) high.
£1,300–1,550
€1,900–2,250
$2,350–2,800 S(Am)

A pair of cloisonné moon flasks, decorated with a phoenix curled around a peony bloom, flanked by gilt-metal dragon handles, Chinese, 18thC, 15½in (39.5cm) high.
£3,350–4,000 / €4,900–5,800
$6,100–7,200 S(O)

A cloisonné incense burner, with floral decoration and scroll handles, Chinese, 18thC, 3¼in (8.5cm) diam.
£4,250–5,100 / €6,200–7,400
$7,700–9,200 G(L)
Although catalogued as 18th-century, this piece may well be 17th-century, which would explain the high price it realized.

A cloisonné eating set sheath, with gilt-engraved mounts, decorated with florets and scrolls, containing ivory chopsticks, Chinese, 1750–1800, 9½in (24cm) long.
£760–910 / €1,100–1,300
$1,400–1,650 SWO

LOCATE THE SOURCE
The source of each illustration in Miller's can be found by checking the code letters below each caption with the Key to Illustrations, pages 778–784.

A pair of Ginbari vases, enamel-decorated with goldfish, one vase repaired, Japanese, 1890, 9¾in (25cm) high.
£420–500 / €610–730
$760–900 SWO

A pair of cloisonné bottle vases, decorated with cranes and lotus, bases formerly drilled, Chinese, 19thC, 21in (53.5cm) high.
£700–840 / €1,000–1,200
$1,250–1,500 DN

A cloisonné vase, decorated with birds and blossoms, Chinese, 19thC, 58in (147.5cm) high, with a carved wood stand.
£7,000–8,400
€10,200–12,300
$12,600–15,200 JNic

Glass

A pair of glass bowls, Chinese, Beijing, 19thC, 2¼in (5.5cm) diam.
£790–880 / €1,150–1,300
$1,450–1,600 ⊞ G&G

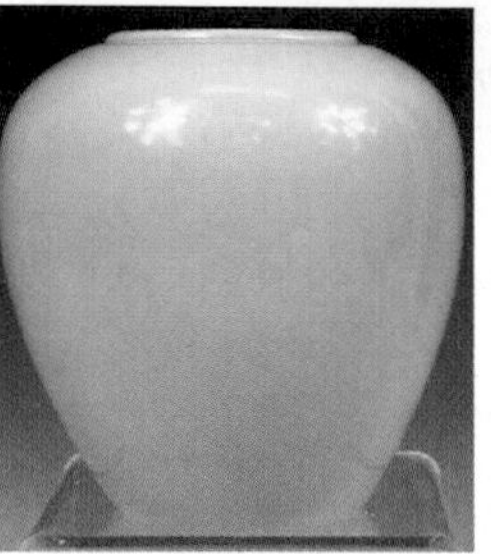

A glass vase, four-character marks, Chinese, Beijing, Qianlong period, 1736–95, 4½in (11.5cm) high.
£4,100–4,900
€6,000–7,200
$7,400–8,900 ⚒ SWO

A pair of glass vases, with tall necks, Chinese, Beijing, probably 19thC, 8½in (21.5cm) high.
£330–390 / €480–570
$600–700 ⚒ WW

A pair of reverse paintings on glass, depicting a lady splitting oysters and two ladies walking, in moulded giltwood frames, Chinese, early 19thC, 9 x 10½in (23 x 26.5cm).
£7,300–8,700
€10,600–12,700
$13,000–15,700 ⚒ WW

A pair of reverse paintings on mirrors, depicting figures on terraces and Immortals in the sky, mirror degrading, Chinese, c1920, with later frames, 25¼ x 17¾in (64 x 45cm).
£120–145 / €175–210
$220–260 ⚒ SWO

Further reading

Miller's Chinese & Japanese Buyers Guide, Miller's Publications, 2004

Jade

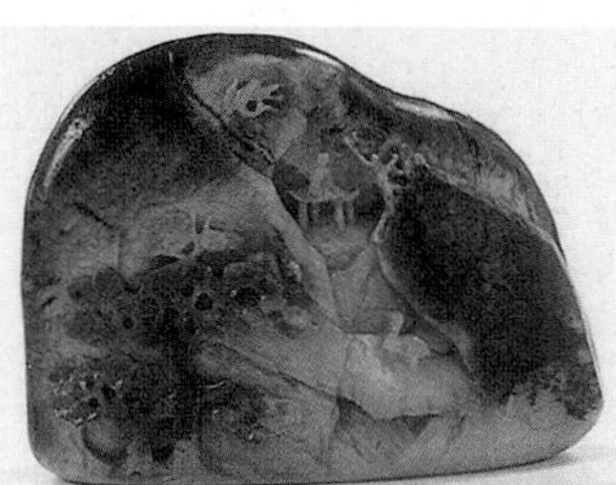

A nephrite boulder carving, depicting a mountain scene, Chinese, Kangxi period, 1662–1722, 3¼in (8.5cm) wide.
£26,000–31,000 / €38,000–45,000
$47,000–56,000 ⚒ JNic
This is a superb natural boulder jade with exceptional carving, making full use of the natural colour.

A spinach jade bowl, carved with bats and scrolls, Chinese, Kangxi period, 1662–1722, 6¼in (16cm) diam.
£34,000–41,000 / €50,000–60,000
$62,000–74,000 ⚒ JNic
This bowl was made for the Imperial court and is of exceptional quality, both in the carving and the colour.

A jade bowl and cover, carved wit[h] a bird perched on a prunus branch, c1800, 4½in (11.5cm) high.
£1,400–1,650 / €2,050–2,400
$2,550–2,950 ⚒ WW

Items in the Asian Works of Art section have been arranged in alphabetical order within each sub-section.

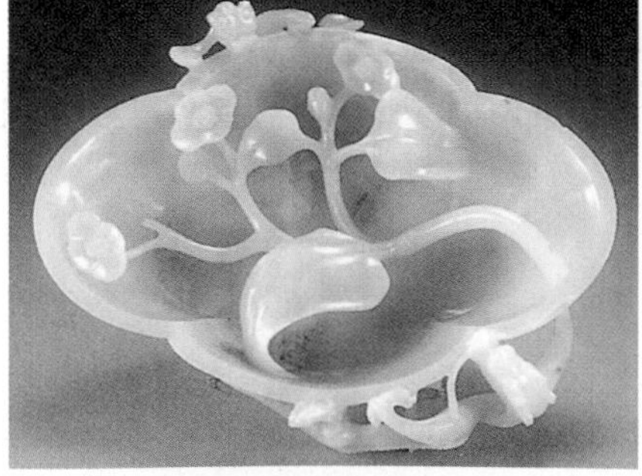

A celadon jade bowl, carved with a sprig of prunus flanked by two *chilong,* Qing Dynasty, 19thC, 7½in (19cm) high.
£4,200–5,000 / €6,100–7,300
$7,600–9,000 ⚒ S(O)

A pair of jade bowls, with gilt decoration of figures in gardens, the interior with a bird among flowers, Chinese, 19thC, 5in (12.5cm) diam.
£840–1,000
€1,250–1,450
$1,500–1,800 ⚒ S(O)

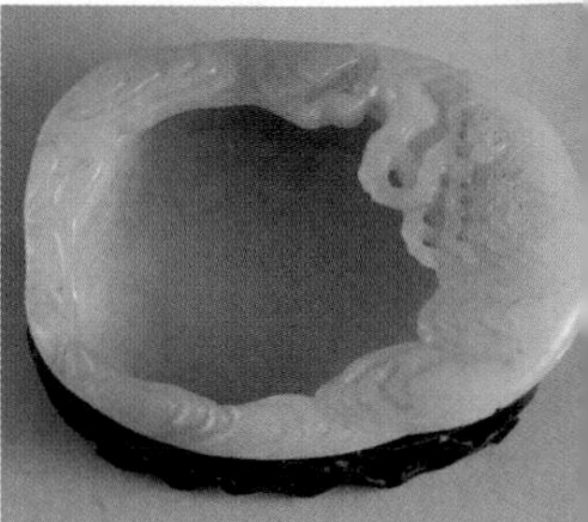

A jade brush washer, carved with pine tree growing from rocks aroun[d] a pool, Chinese, 18th–19thC, 3¾in (9.5cm) high, with a carved stand.
£760–910 / €1,100–1,300
$1,400–1,650 ⚒ WW

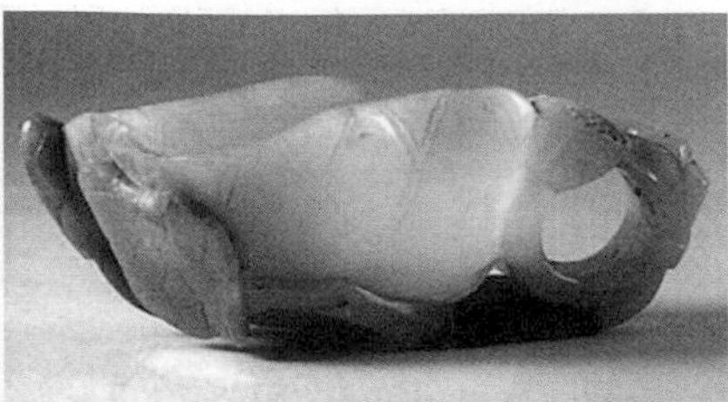

A white jade brush washer, in the form of a lotus leaf, the branch and pod forming the handle, Chinese, 18th/19thC, 4½in (11.5cm) wide.
£440–520 / €640–760
$800–940 WW

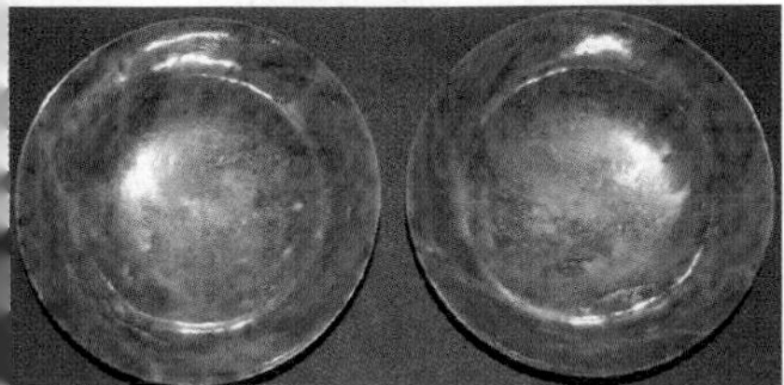

A pair of jade dishes, Chinese, 18thC, 7in (18cm) diam.
£2,150–2,400 / €3,150–3,500
$3,900–4,350 G&G

► **A carved jade brush washer,** in the form of a leaf with a frog and snails, Chinese, 19thC, 3½in (9cm) wide.
£200–240 / €300–350
$360–430 JAA

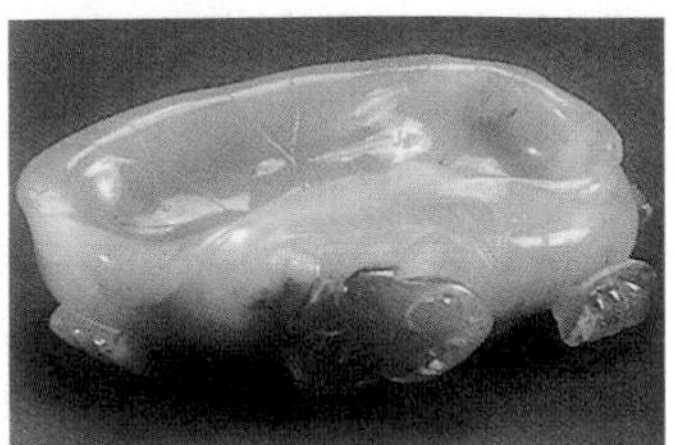

A jade carving of a peach, encased by branches, leaves and fruit bats, slight damage, Chinese, 19thC, 4¾in (12cm) high.
£7,600–9,100
€11,100–13,300
$13,800–16,500 WW

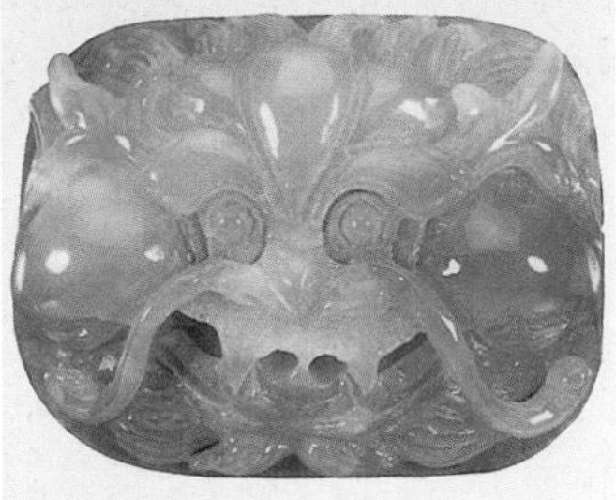

A jadeite plaque, carved with a dragon's head, mounted on a stone base, Chinese, Qing Dynasty, 19thC, 1¾in (4.5cm) wide.
£1,350–1,600 / €2,000–2,350
$2,450–2,900 S

Lacquer

A lacquer card case, Indian, Kashmiri, c1880, 3¼in (8.5cm) wide.
£250–280 / €360–400
$450–500 SiA

◄ **A lacquer tiered container (*jubako*),** decorated in gilt and silver with flowers and foliage, one tier missing, slight damage, Japanese, 19thC, 14¼in (36cm) high.
£140–165
€200–240
$250–300
WW

A cinnabar lacquer dish, carved with dragons amid *ruyi* clouds encircling a *Shou* character medallion in seal script, the reverse with a border of scrolling camellia, inscribed and gilded with a six-character mark, Chinese, Jiajing period, 1522–66, 6¼in (16cm) diam.
£7,600–9,100 / €11,100–13,300
$13,800–16,500 S(HK)
***Shou* is the Chinese character for longevity and is often used as decoration in Chinese applied arts.**

◄ **A lacquered metal tray,** decorated in coloured mother-of-pearl with two pheasants among flowering cherry and peony, Japanese, Nagasaki, early 19thC, 29in (73.5cm) wide.
£1,300–1,550 / €1,900–2,250
$2,350–2,800 S

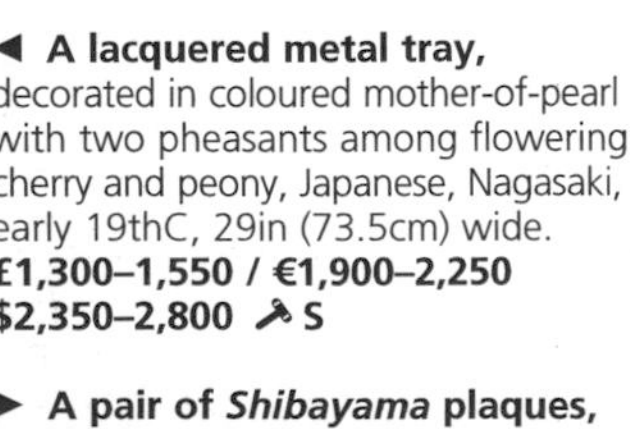

► **A pair of *Shibayama* plaques,** decorated with bone and mother-of-pearl birds in branches, Japanese, Meiji period, 1868–1911, in lacquered frames, 13 x 12½in (33x 22cm).
£230–270 / €330–390
$410–490 L&E

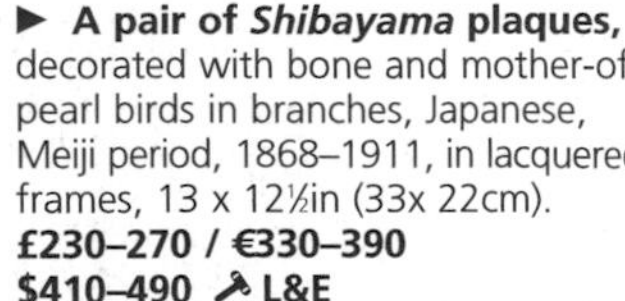

A lacquered food carrier, in the form of a *stupa*, Burmese, late 19thC, 27in (68.5cm) high.
£450–500 / €660–730
$810–900 SOO
This is a ceremonial item from a monastery.

Metalware

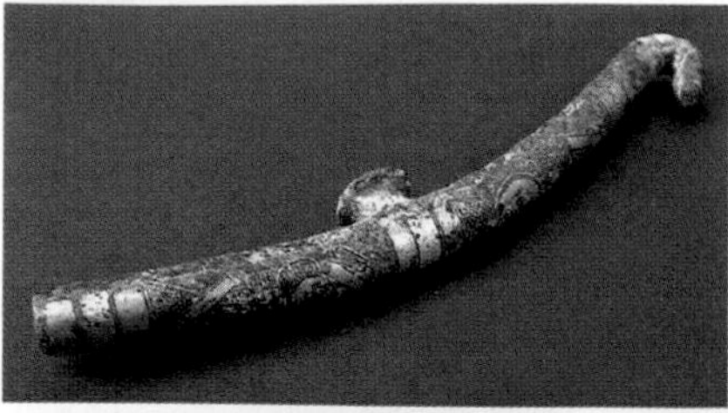

◄ **A bronze belt hook (*daigou*),** inlaid with silver and gold, Chinese, Warring States period, 480–222 BC, 5½in (14cm) long.
£580–650 / €850–950
$1,050–1,200 ⊞ G&G

A silver bowl and cover, chased with dragons, on dragon-head supports, the cover hung with bells, slight damage, Chinese character mark, Chinese, c1900, 17in (43cm) high, 76oz.
£1,650–1,950 / €2,400–2,850
$2,900–3,500 ⚒ S

A parcel-gilt and bronze censer, decorated with eight Buddhist emblems and auspicious objects, on three *ruyi* feet, Hu Wenming seal mark, Chinese, 17thC, 3¼in (8.5cm) high.
£1,400–1,650 / €2,050–2,400
$2,550–3,000 ⚒ S(O)
Hu Wenming was a celebrated 17th-century metalworker.

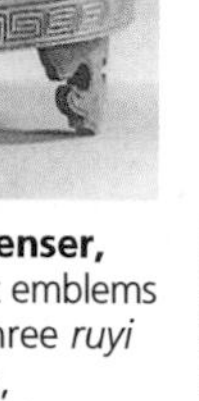

A Chinese export silver and mother-of-pearl dish, by Wang Hing, c1890, 6½in (16.5cm) wide.
£410–470 / €600–680
$740–850 ⊞ BEX

A pair of silver dishes, each in the form of a lotus leaf, the stem and bud forming the foot, enamel-decorated with insects, Japanese, Meiji period, 1868–1911, 3in (7.5cm) diam.
£1,050–1,250 / €1,550–1,850
$1,900–2,250 ⚒ S

► **A silver ewer and cover,** the cover with a gold knop in the form of a lion dog, the body decorated with panels of figures and animals, Chinese, 18th–19thC, 6¾in (17cm) high.
£8,400–10,100 / €12,300–14,700
$15,200–18,300 ⚒ WW

◄ **A silver-inlaid *huqqa* base,** decorated with flowering shrubs, Indian, early 19thC, 6½in (16.5cm) high.
£700–840 / €1,000–1,200
$1,250–1,500 ⚒ F&C
A *huqqa* is an Oriental smoking device.

A bronze jardinière, relief-decorated with exotic birds and foliage, on mask-and-paw feet, Japanese, late 19thC, 15in (38cm) high.
£350–420 / €510–610
$640–760 ⚒ DD

A pair of bronze jars and covers, each in the form of tied sacks, the cover surmounted by a seated boy musician, the cover and body cast with *ho-o* birds and clouds, on three feet in the form of kneeling boys, Japanese, Meiji period, 1868–1911, 9in (23cm) high.
£350–420 / €510–610
$640–760 ⚒ RTo

◄ **A gilt-bronze mirror,** relief-decorated with Chinese characters and gilt hunting dogs, Chinese, Tang Dynasty, 618–907, 5¼in (13.5cm) diam.
£2,450–2,950 / €3,600–4,300
$4,450–5,350 ⚒ BUK

Sets/pairs

Unless otherwise stated, any description which refers to 'a set' or 'a pair' includes a guide price for the entire set or the pair, even though the illustration may show only a single item.

A copper tea kettle, with applied decoration of crickets, with simulated bamboo handle, Japanese, Meiji period, 1868–1911, 4¾in (12cm) high.
£720–860 / €1,050–1,250
$1,300–1,550 ⚒ DORO

► A Chinese export silver tea service, Chinese, c1900, teapot 4½in (1.5cm) high.
£1,100–1,250
€1,600–1,800
$2,000–2,250
⊞ BLm

A hammered-silver tray, the rim cast and applied with dragons, impressed seal mark, three-character mark, Japanese, Meiji period, 1868–1911, 22½in (57cm) wide, 80oz.
£1,600–1,900 / €2,350–2,750
$2,900–3,450 ⚒ LHA

A pair of mixed metal vases, by Ikodo, decorated with bands of birds in flight and swimming carp, signed, Japanese, Meiji period, 1868–1911, 7¾in (19.5cm) high.
£330–390 / €480–570
$600–720 ⚒ HOLL

A Chinese export silver vase, Chinese, c1880, 6in (15cm) high, 6oz.
£1,150–1,300
€1,700–1,900
$2,100–2,350 ⊞ BEX

A pair of bronze vases, inlaid with silver- and gold-coloured metal cockerels on blossoming branches, signed, Japanese, late 19thC, 8¼in (21cm) high.
£590–710 / €860–1,000
$1,100–1,300 ⚒ SWO

A bronze water trough, cast with dragons and waves, with inscriptions on both sides, the four feet in the form of demons, Chinese, 19thC, 51in (129.5cm) wide.
£3,200–3,850 / €4,650–5,600
$5,800–7,000 ⚒ SWO

Wood

A bamboo brushpot, engraved with a pak-choi plant and two-line poem to the reverse, Chinese, 18th–19thC, 5in (12.5cm) high.
£1,550–1,850
€2,250–2,700
$2,800–3,350 ⚒ S(O)

A pair of wooden doors, Chinese, Shanxi Province, 19thC, 83in (211cm) high.
£2,700–3,000
€3,950–4,350
$4,900–5,400 ⊞ LOP

For further information on Architectural Antiques see pages 569–580

A bamboo and bronze opium pipe, with a leather pouch, late 19thC, 17in (43cm) long.
£230–260 / €340–380
$410–470 ⊞ SOO

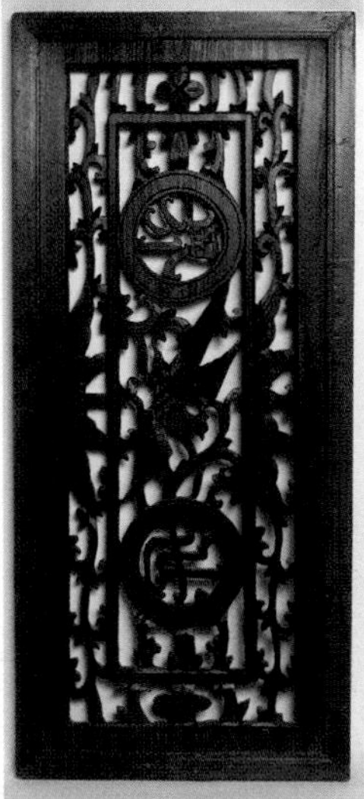

A pair of carved wood screens, northern Chinese, c1900, 41in (104cm) high.
£430–480 / €630–700
$780–870 ⊞ QM

Arms & Armour

◄ **A suit of lacquered iron and leather armour,** Japanese, Edo period, 18thC, 68in (173cm) high.
£12,800–14,300 / €18,700–20,900
$23,200–25,900 ⊞ TLA

Four body armour plates, decorated with silver and gold damascene, with buckles, Indian, late 19thC.
£1,350–1,600 / €1,950–2,350
$2,450–2,900 ⚒ WEBB

A lacquered mask (*mempo*), with a natural hair moustache and chin tuft and a neck guard, Japanese, Edo period, 18thC.
£1,200–1,400 / €1,750–2,050
$2,150–2,550 ⚒ S

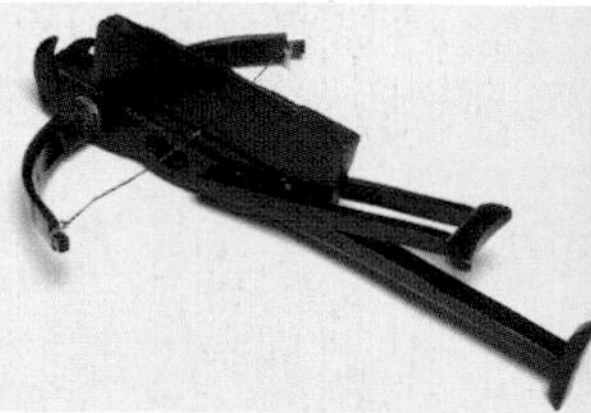

A hardwood repeating crossbow, Chinese, Manchurian, c1800, 26in (66cm) long.
£580–650 / €850–950
$1,050–1,200 ⊞ TLA

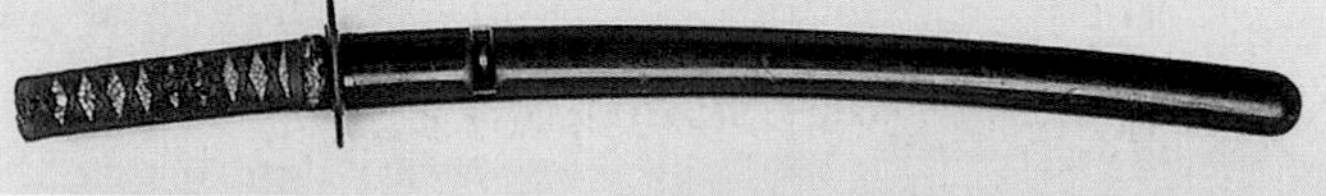

A *wakizashi*, the hilt decorated with dragons in gold, the engraved iron *tsuba* in a lacquered scabbard, *kozuka* missing, slight damage, Japanese, c1600, blade 17¾in (45cm) long.
£560–670 / €820–980
$1,000–1,200 ⚒ WAL

A ivory-cased short dagger, the handle carved as a dragon, the sheath carved with figures at a market, Japanese, Meiji period, 1868–1911, 15¼in (38.5cm) long.
£820–980 / 1,200–1,450
$1,500–1,800 ⚒ TEN

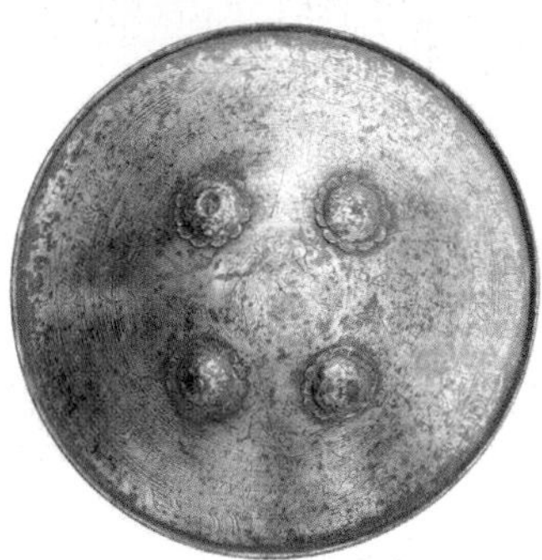

◄ **A steel shield,** with rolled edge and four scalloped-edge bosses, the body etched with seated nobles and dignitaries surrounded by foliage, slight damage, arm bands and pads missing, Indian, 19thC, 18½in (47cm) diam.
£150–165 / €210–240
$270–300 ⊞ FAC

Tsuba

A brass *tsuba*, decorated with a wedding procession, the reverse with rats, signed 'Jagetsusai Hiro Yoshi', Japanese, c1840, 2½in (6.5cm) high.
£860–1,000 / €1,250–1,500
$1,550–1,800 ⚒ BUK

An iron *mokko*-form *tsuba*, decorated with cloisonné enamel *shikishi*, Japanese, Edo period, 19thC, 2¾in (7cm) high.
£900–1,050 / €1,300–1,550
$1,600–1,900 ⚒ S
***Shikishi* are decorative papers for poems.**

An iron, gold and copper *tsuba*, by Soten, carved, pierced and inlaid with Taira Atsumori at the battle of Ichi no Tani, signed, Japanese, Edo period, 19thC, 3in (7.5cm) high.
£1,200–1,400 / €1,750–2,050
$2,150–2,550 ⚒ S

Boxes

A parcel-gilt and paste seal box and cover, Hu Wenming mark, Chinese, 17thC, 3¼in (8.5cm) high.
£8,000–9,600 / €11,700–14,000
$14,500–17,400 ⚒ S(HK)

An ebony writing slope, inlaid with an ivory pomegranate tree and palm trees, c1740, Indian, Vizagapatam, 16¾in (42.5cm) wide.
€4,950–5,500 / €7,200–8,000
$9,000–10,000 ⊞ MANO

A leather and camphor wood trunk, 1830–63, 34½in (87.5cm) wide.
£630–700 / €920–1,050
$1,150–1,300 ⊞ ChC

These cases were mostly made in the East for European travellers. Camphor wood was used because of its pungent smell which would discourage moths and other pests.

A carved tortoiseshell snuff box, decorated with figures within landscapes, the cover with a gilt disc inscribed 'AC to HJL', Chinese, 19thC, 3¼in (8.5cm) diam.
£290–340 / €420–500
$520–620 ⚒ WW

A cloisonné box and cover, decorated with stylized chrysanthemum flowerheads, the cover with a *shou* character, Chinese, Qianlong period, 1736–95, 2¾in (7cm) diam.
£500–550 / €720–800
$1,300–1,450 ⊞ G&G

► **A painter's leather case,** with bronze clasp, the interior decorated with figures, Chinese, 18thC, 21in (53.5cm) wide.
£175–210 / €250–300
$320–380 ⚒ WW

A carved mother-of-pearl games counter box, the interior lined with silk and enclosing four boxes containing games counters, Chinese, 19thC, 7¼in (18.5cm) wide.
£1,650–1,950 / €2,400–2,850
$3,000–3,550 ⚒ S(O)

► **A carved ivory casket,** Chinese, Canton, 19thC, 9¾in (25cm) wide.
£440–520 / €640–760
$800–950 ⚒ CHTR

An enamel sweetmeat box and cover, decorated with a *shou* medallion surrounded by five bats within a border of the Eight Buddhist Emblems, the interior with nine compartments, Chinese, Canton, 19thC, 13½in (34.5cm) diam.
£2,650–3,150 / €3,850–4,600
$4,800–5,700 ⚒ S(NY)

An enamel box, decorated with a lady and an attendant in a walled garden, Chinese, Qianlong period, 1736–95, 5in (12.5cm) diam.
£1,100–1,250 / €1,600–1,800
$2,000–2,250 ⊞ G&G

A mother-of-pearl and tortoiseshell tea caddy, inlaid with ivory, the hinged cover enclosing two compartments, Indian, c1800, 9½in (24cm) wide, with an associated pair of Chinese canisters.
£760–910 / €1,100–1,300
$1,400–1,650 ⚒ L&E

A carved *huanghuali* box, the sliding cover enclosing an interior with a lidded till, Chinese, 19thC, 14½in (37cm) wide.
£540–640 / €790–940
$970–1,150 ⚒ S(O)

A tortoiseshell snuff box, carved with figures and pagodas, Chinese, Canton, 19thC, 3¾in (9.5cm) diam.
£350–420 / €510–610
$630–760 G(L)

A lacquer box and cover, decorated with a boy riding a buffalo, slight damage, Japanese, 19thC, 5¼in (13.5cm) high.
£175–210 / €250–300
$320–380 WW

A lacquer box and cover, decorated with butterflies, Chinese, mid-19thC, 14in (35.5cm) diam.
£310–350 / €450–500
$560–630 SOO

A Chinese export lacquer games box, the interior with compartments containing mother-of-pearl and bone counters, c1860, 14½in (37cm) wide.
£1,100–1,250 / €1,600–1,800
$2,000–2,250 HAA

A lacquer box and cover, Chinese, c1870, 7in (18cm) wide.
£90–100 / €130–145
$160–180 MB

A *Komai* box, the hinged cover inlaid with mount Fuji and a river scene, the gilt interior engraved with a tree and birds, signed, Japanese, Meiji period, 1868–1911, 8¼in (21cm) wide.
£800–960 / €1,150–1,400
$1,450–1,750 RTo
***Komai* was a lacquer studio which has also given its name to this style of lacquerwork.**

A lacquer box and cover, Chinese, late 19thC, 14in (35.5cm) wide.
£290–320 / €420–470
$520–580 SOO

◄ **A pair of artist's lacquer carrying boxes,** Chinese, late 19thC, 17in (43cm) wide.
£770–860 / €1,100–1,250
$1,400–1,550 SOO

Clocks

A table clock, the gilt dial above a three-tier gilt movement striking on a bell, encased in a pierced and engraved silver sleeve, on an ivory stand, Japanese, c1820, in a glazed mulberry wood case, 4in (10cm) wide.
£12,300–13,800
€18,000–20,100
$22,300–25,000 PT

◄ **An ivory-mounted sandalwood clock case,** the interior with a watch recess, Indian, Vizagapatam, 19thC, 8in (20.5cm) high.
£590–700 / €850–1,000
$1,050–1,250 TEN

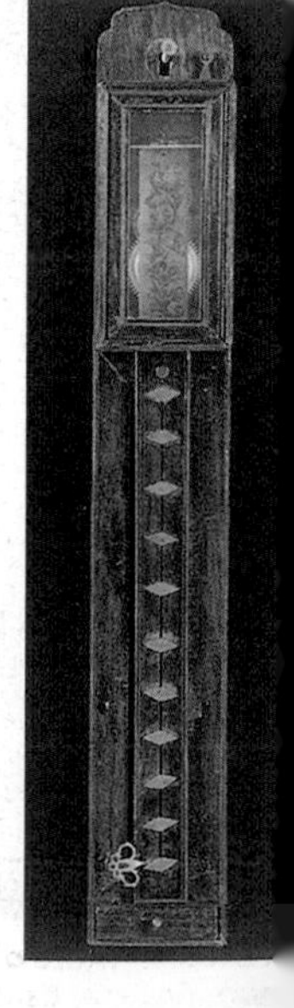

► **A wisteria pillar timepiece,** the brass weight-driven movement engraved with chrysanthemums, with verge and balance escapement, the trunk with adjustable hour plaques, the pointer attached to the concealed weight, the base with a key drawer, Japanese, 19thC, 18½in (47cm) high.
£1,300–1,550 / €1,900–2,250
$2,350–2,800 S(Am)

For more clocks
see pages 371–424

◄ **A brass verge watch,** the brass movement with verge escapement, fusee with Harrison's maintaining power, Japanese, in a wisteria case, 1850–1900, 3¼in (8.5cm) high.
£1,200–1,450 / €1,750–2,100
$2,150–2,600 S

Figures & Models

A bronze *chilong* group, formerly a knop, on a later marble base, Chinese, Western Han Dynasty, 296 BC–AD 220, 2¾in (7cm) high.
£330–390 / €480–570
$600–710 SWO

A carved stone figure of a crowned Buddha, ndian, 11thC, 12½in 32cm) high.
€4,000–4,800
€5,900–7,000
$7,300–8,700 S(NY)

bronze figure of a nan, Chinese, Kangxi eriod, 1662–1722, 2¼in (31cm) high.
2,500–2,800
3,650–4,100
4,550–5,100 G&G

A terracotta figure of a dancing man, Chinese, Sichuan Province, Eastern Han Dynasty, AD 89–198, 17in (43cm) high.
£1,450–1,650
€2,100–2,400
$2,650–3,000 SOO

A Khmer Angkor Wat-style carved sandstone head of a male divinity, possibly Vishnu, 12thC, 7in (18cm) high.
£1,350–1,500
€1,950–2,200
$2,450–2,700 LOP

A carved sandstone figure of an attendant deity, Indian, Rajasthan, 9thC, 27in (68.5cm) high.
£4,300–5,100
€6,300–7,500
$7,800–9,300 S(NY)

► A gilt lacquered wood figure of Buddha, damaged and repaired, Japanese, Edo period, 1600–1868, 14¼in (36cm) high.
£650–770 / €950–1,100
$1,200–1,400 S(Am)

A carved sandstone figure of an Apsaras, Indian, 10th–11thC, 49in (124cm) high.
£6,700–7,500
€9,800–11,000
$12,100–13,600 MANO
An Apsaras is a nature spirit, usually a water nymph.

◄ A carved soapstone figure of a seated Luohan, 17thC, 3¼in (8.5cm) high.
£8,500–10,200
€12,400–14,900
$15,400–18,500 S(HK)

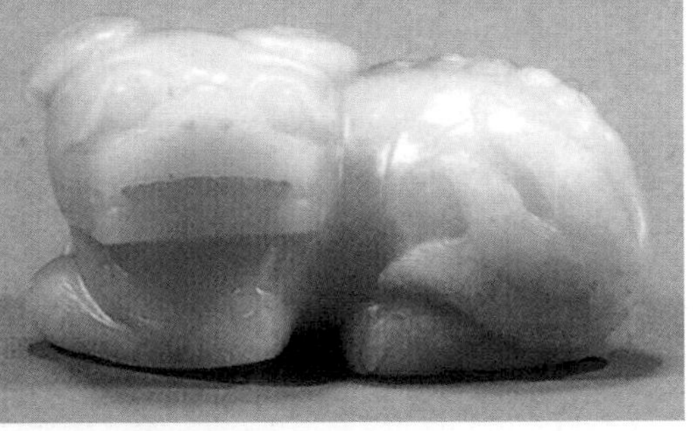

A carved celadon jade model of a mythical beast, 18thC, 2¾in (7cm) high.
£960–1,150 / €1,400–1,650
$1,750–2,100 S

► A carved teak figure of a prince, wood weathered, Burmese, 18thC, 27in (68.5cm) high.
£8,000–8,900 / €11,700–13,000
$14,500–16,100 SOO

◀ **A gilt-copper figure of Garuda,** Tibeto-Chinese, 18thC, 16in (40.5cm) high.
£3,300–3,950
€4,800–5,800
$6,000–7,200 **S(NY)**

A bronze figure of Ganesh, Indian, 18thC, 2¼in (5.5cm) high.
£195–220 / €290–320
$360–400 ⊞ HEL

A bronze figure of Buddha Laotian, 18th–19thC, 15½in (39.5cm) high.
£580–650 / €850–950
$1,050–1,200 ⊞ LOP

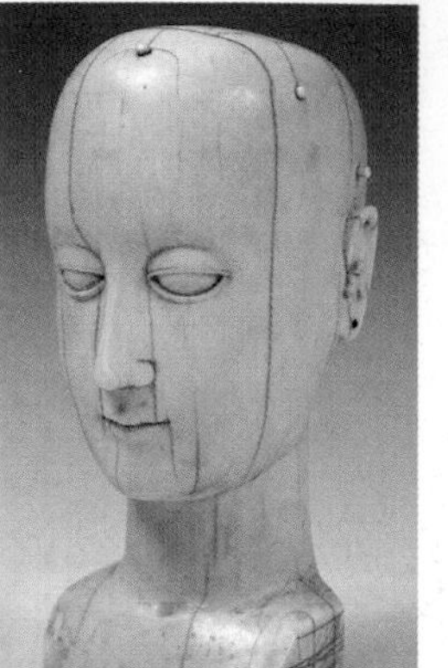

◀ **A carved ivory bust of a young lady,** southeast Asian, c1800, 5½in (14cm) high.
£1,700–2,000
€2,500–3,000
$3,100–3,650 SWO

A pair of carved sandstone models of mythological beasts, Indonesian, 19thC, 24in (61cm) wide.
£1,800–2,150 / €2,650–3,150
$3,250–3,900 S(S)

A bronze head of Buddha, Burmese, Mandalay, 19thC 17¼in (44cm) high.
£6,300–7,000
€9,200–10,200
$11,400–12,700 ⊞ LOP

A pair of Bai carved wood ancestor worship figures, Chinese, Yunnan Province, 19thC, 33in (84cm) high.
£4,300–4,800
€6,300–7,000
$7,800–8,700 ⊞ Wai

A carved ivory figural group of Lan Caihe and a dragon, Chinese, 19thC, 8¼in (21cm) high.
£1,700–2,000
€2,500–3,000
$3,100–3,650 WW
Lan Caihe is one of Eight Immortals

A glass figure, Chinese, Beijing, 19thC, 10in (25.5cm) high.
£900–1,000
€1,300–1,450
$1,600–1,800 ⊞ BOW

A carved ivory figure of a grape seller, signed 'Gyokudo', Japanese, Meiji period, 1868–1911, 8in (20.5cm) high.
£1,650–1,850
€2,400–2,700
$3,000–3,350 ⊞ LBO

◀ **A pair of carved wood figures of Fujian ancestors,** Chinese, 19thC, 20in (51cm) high.
£1,250–1,400
€1,850–2,050
$2,250–2,550
⊞ SOO

A carved horn model of a stallion, Chinese, 19thC, 3in (7.5cm) high.
£530–630 / €770–920
$960–1,150 WW

An ivory *okimono* of a farm labourer, signed, Japanese, Meiji period, 1868–1911, 13in (33cm) high.
£6,200–7,400
€9,100–10,800
$11,200–13,400 ⚒ HYD

► A carved ivory figural group of a mother and her children, signed 'Shinsai', Japanese, Meiji period, 1868–1911, 4in (10cm) high.
£2,900–3,200
€4,200–4,650
$5,200–5,800
⊞ LBO

◄ A lacquered wood and ivory model of a Tatebina doll, maker's signature Juraku?, Japanese, 19thC, 2¼in (5.5cm) high.
£1,300–1,550
€1,900–2,200
$2,350–2,800 ⚒ S

An ivory *okimono* of a *bijin*, slight damage, Japanese, Meiji period, 1868–1911, 5¾in (14.5cm) high.
£470–560 / €690–820
$850–1,000 ⚒ WW

A pair of giltwood kneeling disciples, Burmese, Mandalay, 19thC, 11in (28cm) high.
£1,050–1,200 / €1,550–1,750
$1,900–2,150 ⊞ LOP

\ carved ivory *okimono* ›f a drum seller, with *'hibayama*-style inlay, signed, ıpanese, Meiji period, 868–1911, 4in (10cm) high.
760–850 / €1,100–1,250
1,400–1,550 ⊞ G&G

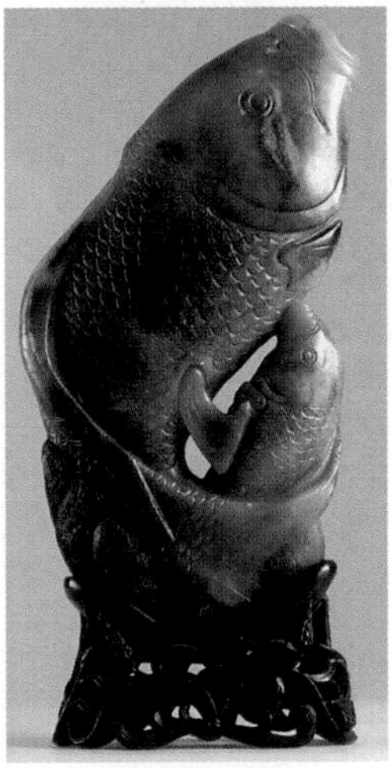

A carved jade model of two carp, on a carved wood stand, Chinese, 19thC, 8¾in (22cm) high.
£22,500–27,000
€33,000–39,000
$41,000–49,000 ⚒ WW
This is a superb example of Chinese carving.

A bronze incense burner, in the form of a mythical beast, repaired, Burmese, 19thC, 14in (35.5cm) high.
£120–140 / €170–200
$210–250 ⚒ NSal

A carved coral figure of a warrior, on a carved ivory base, slight damage, Chinese, 19thC, 6½in (16.5cm) high.
£940–1,100
€1,350–1,600
$1,700–2,000 ⚒ WW

. silver model of a rane, with an enamelled rest and patinated lumage, on a later base, ight damage, Japanese, leiji period, 1868–1911, in (15cm) high.
470–560 / €690–820
850–1,000 ⚒ DN

A carved ivory model of an egret, by Gyokushu, with bronze legs and mother-of-pearl eyes, signed, Japanese, Meiji period, 1868–1911, 7in (18cm) high.
£2,250–2,700
€3,300–3,950
$4,050–4,900 ⚒ S

◄ A bronze and ivory group of an elderly man and a child feeding chickens, on a hardwood base, Japanese, Meiji period, 1868–1911, 14½in (37cm) high.
£1,200–1,400
€1,750–2,050
$2,150–2,550 ⚒ G(B)

A bronze figural group of a monkey trainer and a monkey, with copper and gilt decoration, the box with an opening drawer, on a wooden stand, Japanese, Meiji period, 1868–1911, 9in (23cm) high.
£1,000–1,200
€1,450–1,750
$1,800–2,150 S

A carved wood *okimono* of the Seven Gods of Good Fortune, in a boat, signed, Japanese, 19thC, 6in (15cm) high.
£1,000–1,150
€1,450–1,700
$1,800–2,150 K&M

A carved ivory figural group of a father and son playing Go, signed 'Kosai To', Japanese, Meiji period, 1868–1911, 5½in (14cm) high.
£2,850–3,200
€4,150–4,650
$5,200–5,800 LBO

For further information on
Japanese antiques see pages 308–311

► **A bronze figural group of two Sumo wrestlers,** with gilded belts, signed 'Miyo', Japanese, late 19thC, 11in (28cm) high.
£6,300–7,500 / €9,200–11,000
$11,400–13,600 AH

A bronze model of an elephant, with ivory tusks, signed 'Mitsumoto', Japanese, Meiji period, 1868–1911, 6¼in (16cm) high.
£380–450 / €550–660
$690–820 LHA

A bronze group of two geese, with silver eyes, on a rootwood base, Japanese, Meiji period, 1868–1911, 12in (30.5cm) wide.
£3,750–4,200 / €5,500–6,100
$6,800–7,600 LBO

A Hida School carved wood *okimono* of three toads, signed 'Sukeyuki' and 'Kao', Japanese, late 19thC, 2in (5cm) wide.
£1,050–1,250 / €1,550–1,850
$1,900–2,250 Mal(O)

► **A bronze figure of a beggar and a dog of *Fo*,** Chinese, c1900, 14in (35.5cm) wide.
£380–450 / €550–660
$690–820 DuM

A carved ivory *okimono* of a *Sennin*, standing on a stylized toad made of antler, slight damage, incised signature, Japanese, c1900, 4½in (11.5cm) high.
£1,250–1,500
€1,850–2,200
$2,250–2,700 MAR

A carved ivory figure of a gardener, signed, Japanese, Meiji period, 1868–1911, 5½in (14cm) high.
£240–280 / €350–410
$430–510 DD

A carved ivory figure of a gold prospector and a dog, signed with inset seal, Japanese, early 20thC, 8¼in (21cm) high.
£610–730 / €880–1,050
$1,100–1,300 WW

A carved wood and gilt figure of a female deity figure, with mirror-glass decoration, southeast Asian, early 20thC, 45½in (115.5cm) high.
£165–195 / €240–290
$300–360 DMC

-urniture

.n ebony four-poster bed, canopy eplaced, Ceylonese, 19thC, 2¾in (185cm) wide.
26,000–31,000 / €38,000–45,000
47,000–56,000 S
his bed is an example of superb raftsmanship and it is rare to nd ebony being used to make ırge items of furniture.

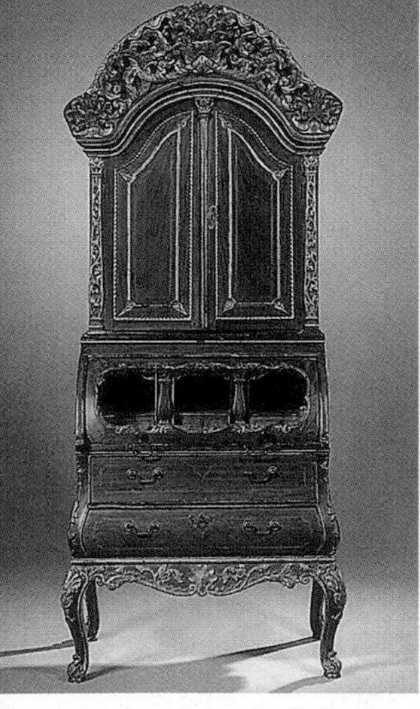

. hardwood and parcel-gilt bureau abinet, the glazed cylinder enclosing fitted interior, altered and restored, ıdonesian, probably Batavian, 18thC nd later, 30¾in (78cm) wide.
3,450–4,100 / €5,000–6,000
6,200–7,400 S(Am)

A rosewood four-poster bed, with carved decoration, Chinese, 19thC, 85¾in (218cm) wide.
£1,750–1,950 / €2,550–2,850
$3,150–3,550 ⊞ LOP

A Namban lacquer cabinet, decorated with foliage, flowering shrubs and pavilions in gold lacquer within mother-of-pearl frames, with ten drawers, front flap and handles missing, repaired, Japanese, early 17thC, 20½in (52cm) wide.
£820–980 / €1,200–1,450
$1,500–1,800 TEN
Namban are black lacquer items. They were made for export, principally to Portugal.

A lacquer cabinet, on a later European giltwood and gesso stand, Japanese, 18thC, 35¾in (91cm) wide.
£5,400–6,400 / €7,900–9,500
$9,800–11,600 S(O)

◄ **A lacquer cabinet,** with carved and pierced gilt decoration, the late 18thC-panels depicting court scenes, Chinese, 19thC, 49in (124.5cm) wide.
£1,000–1,200 / €1,450–1,750
$1,800–2,200 NSal

A burr-elm bureau, with a fitted interior, Chinese, mid-19thC, 40in (101.5cm) wide.
£950–1,100 / €1,400–1,650
$1,700–2,000 JDJ

An elm cabinet, Chinese, 18thC, 46½in (118cm) wide.
£1,050–1,200 / €1,550–1,750
$1,900–2,150 ⊞ QM

A lacquered elm cabinet, Chinese, early 19thC, 47in (119.5cm) wide.
£1,650–1,850 / €2,400–2,700
$3,000–3,350 ⊞ QM

Condition

The condition is absolutely vital when assessing the value of an antique. Damaged pieces on the whole appreciate much less than perfect examples. However, a rare desirable piece may command a high price even when damaged.

A Chinese export lacquer cabinet-on-stand, painted with figures and buildings in Oriental landscapes, the two panelled doors enclosing six drawers, two recesses and a pocket watch holder, the removable work box enclosing a fitted lift-out tray, 19thC, 24½in (62cm) wide.
£2,350–2,800
€3,450–4,100
$4,250–5,100
DN

A Chinese export lacquer bureau cabinet-on-stand, the two doors enclosing a fitted interior and a pocket barometer, the desk with a pen tray and hinged slope enclosing a well and a drawer, 19thC, 28in (71cm) wide.
£1,200–1,400
€1,750–2,100
$2,150–2,550 TEN

An elm and fruitwood food cabinet, Chinese, 19thC, 41in (104cm) wide.
£1,250–1,400
€1,850–2,050
$2,250–2,500 QM

A lacquer table cabinet, decorated with leaves, the two doors enclosing six graduated long drawers, Chinese, 19thC, 15¾in (40cm) wide.
£360–430 / €530–630
$650–780 CHTR

► A pair of lacquer cabinets, with hardstone decoration, on later stands, Chinese, early 20thC, 19in (48.5cm) wide.
£1,200–1,400
€1,750–2,050
$2,150–2,550
S(O)

A hardwood display cabinet, decorated with raised gilt, mother-of-pearl and ivory-inlaid birds and flowers, with an arrangement of sliding doors, open shelves, cupboard doors and drawers, Japanese, Meiji period, 1868–1911, 53¼in (135.5cm) high.
£590–700 / €850–1,000
$1,050–1,250 RTo

A lacquer miniature bureau cabinet, inlaid with abalone birds and flowers, with engraved gilt-metal mounts, Japanese, Nagasaki, late 19thC, 17¾in (45cm) wide.
£12,000–14,400
€17,500–21,000
$21,700–26,100 S
The trade in lacquer wares of this kind appears to have been established towards the end of the 18th century when the Dutch East India Company chartered American ships to maintain their monopoly at Nagasaki, Japan.

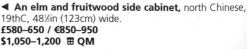

◄ An elm and fruitwood side cabinet, north Chinese, 19thC, 48½in (123cm) wide.
£580–650 / €850–950
$1,050–1,200 QM

A carved *Shibayama* lacquer table cabinet, inlaid with mother-of-pearl and coral flowers, the cupboard doors enclosing three drawers, losses, Japanese, Meiji period, 1868–1911, 10½in (26.5cm) wide.
£220–260 / €320–380
$400–480 Hal

A *komai* perfume cabinet (*kodansu*), each side decorated with cartouches of dragons, birds and buildings within landscapes, the door enclosing three drawers, signed 'Fujisei', Japanese, Meiji period, 1868–1911, 6in (15cm) wide.
£4,700–5,600 / €6,900–8,200
$8,500–10,100 G(L)

A lacquer table cabinet, decorated in *hiramakie* and *takamakie* with cranes, *minogame* and trees, damaged, Japanese, 19thC, 21¾in (55.5cm) wide.
£530–630 / €770–920
$960–1,150 S(Am)

A pair of elm and fruitwood chairs, Chinese, 19thC.
£720–800 / €1,000–1,150
$1,300–1,450 ⊞ QM

A pair of wooden chairs, Chinese, 19thC.
£1,350–1,500
€1,950–2,200
$2,450–2,700 ⊞ LOP

An elm and fruitwood chair, Chinese, 19thC.
£400–450 / €580–660
$720–810 ⊞ QM

An elm chair, with carved backsplat above a rattan seat, Chinese, mid-19thC.
£220–250 / €330–370
$400–450 ⊞ OE

A pair of bamboo armchairs, Chinese, late 19thC.
£540–600 / €790–880
$980–1,100 ⊞ SOO

► **A carved hardwood armchair,** Indian, 19thC.
£220–260 / €320–380
$400–480 ⚒ SWO

A carved hardwood chair, the back and arms in the form of dragons, Chinese, late 19thC.
£350–420 / €510–610
$630–760 ⚒ Mit

A lacquer chest-on-stand, with gilded decoration, 19thC, 30in (76cm) wide.
£3,150–3,500 / €4,600–5,100
$5,700–6,300 ⊞ DOA

A Dutch Colonial brass-mounted teak chest, Indonesian, probably Batavian, c1800, 58in (147.5cm) wide.
£1,300–1,550 / €1,900–2,250
$2,350–2,800 ⚒ S(Am)

An elm coffer, with two drawers above hidden storage space, Chinese, late 19thC, 40in (101.5cm) wide.
£720–800 / €1,000–1,100
$1,300–1,450 ⊞ OE

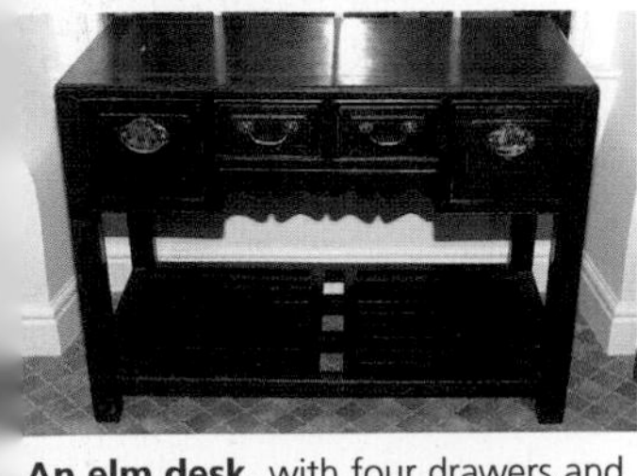

An elm desk, with four drawers and a secret compartment, Chinese, 19thC, 44in (112cm) wide.
£1,100–1,250 / €1,600–1,800
$2,000–2,250 ⊞ OE

A lacquer desk, Chinese, 19thC, 39½in (100.5cm) wide.
£990–1,100 / €1,450–1,600
$1,800–2,000 ⊞ LOP

A lacquer screen, decorated with domestic scenes in a rural landscape, the reverse with flowers and birds, comprising six panels, Chinese, early 18thC, each panel 76¾ x 19in (195 x 48.5cm).
£1,750–2,100 / €2,550–3,050
$3,200–3,800 ⚒ TEN

A hardwood vase stand, carved with irises, Chinese, c1900, 30in (76cm) high.
£190–220 / €280–330
$340–400 PFK

A pair of wooden folding stools, with woven seats, Chinese, mid-19thC.
£370–420 / €540–610
$670–760 ⊞ SOO

An elm stool, Chinese, c1850, 40in (101.5cm) wide.
£490–550 / €720–800
$890–1,000 ⊞ WAA

A hardwood silver table, with satinwood and chequered banding, Anglo-Colonial, c1740, 30in (76cm) wide.
£14,900–16,500 / €21,800–24,100
$27,000–29,900 ⊞ RGa

A padouk games table, the fold-over top with a suede interior, on claw-and-ball feet, Portuguese Colonial, c1750, 32in (81.5cm) wide.
£14,400–16,000
€21,000–23,400
$26,100–29,000 ⊞ HA

A mahogany and cane footstool, Anglo-Indian, c1850, 16in (40.5cm) wide.
£220–250 / €320–360
$400–450 ⊞ CRU

▶ **A lacquer altar table,** with gilt panels, Chinese, 19thC, 63in (160cm) wide.
£230–270 / €340–400
$420–490 NSal

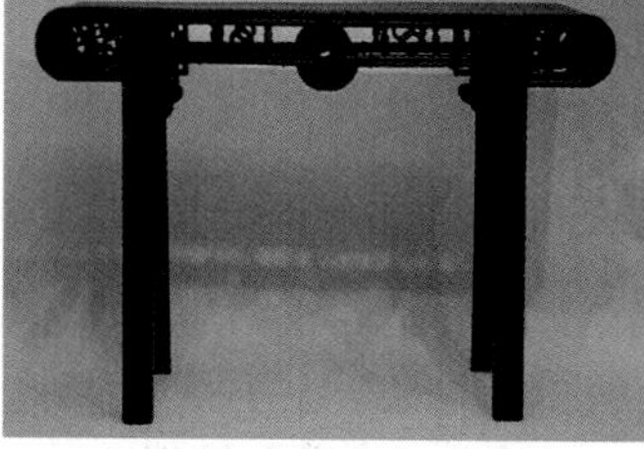

A carved Jichiwood altar table, Chinese, 19thC, 43¼in (110cm) wide.
£760–850 / €1,100–1,250
$1,400–1,550 ⊞ LOP
Jichiwood (chicken-wing wood) belongs to the *Ormosia* family. The grain forms patterns suggesting the feathers near the neck and wings of a bird.

◀ **A rosewood centre table,** the marble top within a moulded border with shell, floral and acanthus-leaf carved frieze, Anglo-Chinese, 19thC, 57in (145cm) diam.
£5,300–6,300 / €7,700–9,200
$9,600–11,400 HYD

An ivory-inlaid ebony folding games board table, with shakers and pieces, on a later stand, Anglo-Indian, c1840, 20½in (52cm) wide.
£3,600–4,000
€5,200–5,800
$6,500–7,200 ⊞ RGa

A carved rosewood serpentine side table, Indian, c1860, 47in (119.5cm) wide.
£640–760 / €930–1,100
$1,200–1,400 Hal

A Chinese export lacquer work table, with fitted interior, c1880, 26in (66cm) wide.
£340–400 / €500–590
$620–740 WL

Inro

A gold lacquer *inro*, by Toju, decorated in *takamakie* with a lobster and seabream, the interior of *nashiji*, signed, Japanese, c1800, 1¾in (4.5cm) wide
£3,350–4,000 / €4,900–5,800
$6,100–7,200 ⚒ S

◄ A Kajikawa School four-case *inro*, decorated with *takamakie* and *togidashi* maple and pine trees in a landscape, the interior of rich *nashiji*, Japanese, 19thC, 3¼in (8.5cm) high.
£840–1,000
€1,250–1,450
$1,500–1,800
⚒ S

A lacquer five-case *inro*, decorated in relief with pagodas, waterfalls and fishermen, Japanese, Meiji period, 1868–1911, 3¼in (8.5cm) high.
£340–400 / €500–590
$610–720 ⚒ DN(BR)

Netsuke

An ivory *netsuke* of a *shishi* and cub, Japanese, Kyoto, 18thC, 2¼in (5.5cm) high.
£1,400–1,650 / €2,000–2,400
$2,500–3,000 ⚒ S

A boxwood *netsuke* of a deer, by Issen, signed, Japanese, 19thC, 1½in (4cm) high.
£1,400–1,650 / €2,000–2,400
$2,500–3,000 ⚒ S

A boxwood *netsuke* of fungus, by Masanao, Japanese, 19thC, 1¼in (3cm) high.
£1,050–1,200 / €1,550–1,750
$1,900–2,150 ⊞ BOW

An ivory *netsuke* of Ashinaga and Tenaga, Japanese, 19thC, 3½in (9cm) high.
£2,300–2,600 / €3,350–3,800
$4,150–4,700 ⊞ BOW
Ashinaga and Tenaga are often shown together. They are mythical people who live upon fish which Tenaga catches with his long arms.

A Tamba School wood *netsuke* of carp and crayfish, by Toyomasa, signed, Japanese, mid-19thC, 2¼in (5.5cm) wide.
£1,750–2,100 / €2,550–3,050
$3,150–3,800 ⚒ SWO

An ivory and *shakudo kamibuta netsuke*, Japanese, Meiji period, 1868–1911, 1½in (4cm) diam.
£190–220 / €280–330
$340–400 ⚒ DN(BR)
***Shakudo kamibuta* is an alloy of copper with a small percentage of gold, patinated to a lustrous blue-black.**

A wood *netsuke* of an *oni* repairing a sandal, Japanese, 19thC, 1½in (4cm) high.
£520–580 / €760–850
$940–1,050 ⊞ K&M

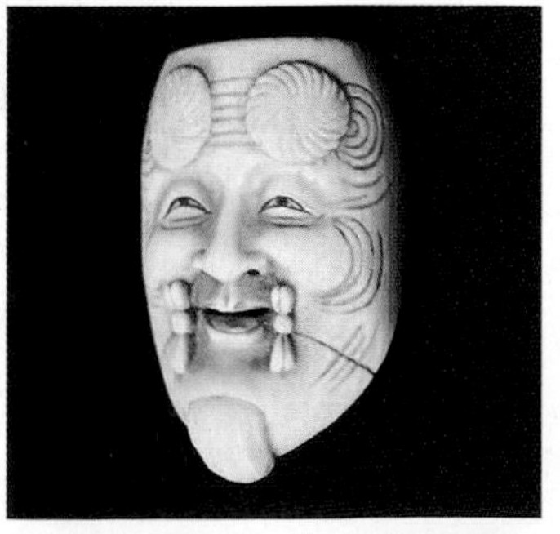

An ivory *netsuke* of a Noh mask, signed, Japanese, early 20thC, 2in (5cm) high.
£290–330 / €430–480
$540–600 ⊞ AMC

Robes & Costume

A *kudzu*, cotton and human hair two-piece costume, Chinese, Jin Ping County, Yunnan, 19thC.
£2,000–2,250
€2,900–3,300
$3,600–4,100 ⊞ Wai
This costume is for a village priest (Shaman). The hat is made of thread of *kudzu*, a type of hemp, and human hair, which represents experience and importance. The long clothes have a dragon design on the front piece and pilgrimage pictures on the back and the eight Chinese characters mean long life and exorcism. This costume is typically worn by the priest officiating at the Adult Ceremony for the youth of Yao.

A Hongtou woman's three-piece costume, early 20thC.
£4,300–4,800
€6,300–7,000
$7,800–8,700 ⊞ Wai
This is a costume for the wife of the tribal chief of the ethnic group Yao. The black jacket is decorated with six silver pendant buttons to show high rank and the embroidery symbolizes good fortune. The silver coin dated 1907 shows wealth and status.

A pair of silk ear muffs, Chinese, late 19thC, 4in (10cm) wide.
£65–75 / €100–110
$120–135 ⊞ JCH

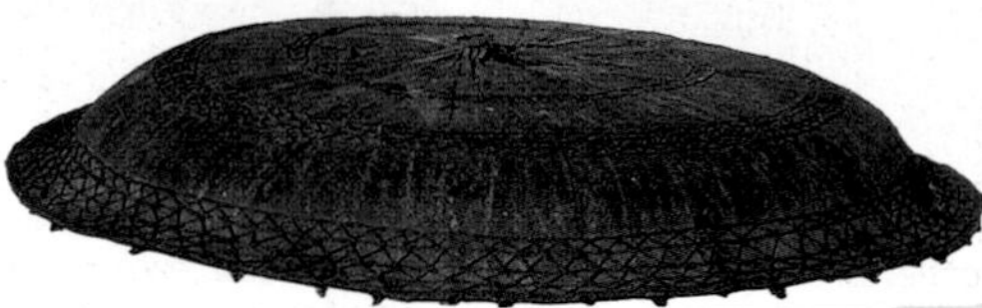

A bamboo and mulberry bark peasant's hat, Japanese, c1800.
£220–250 / €320–360
$400–450 ⊞ FAC

A child's hat, Chinese, late 19thC.
£135–150 / €195–220
$240–270 ⊞ JCH

A cotton tiger hat, Chinese, Yunnan, early 20thC.
£195–220 / €290–320
$360–400 ⊞ Wai
The tiger hat has its origins in the tiger totem of the ancient Bai group and is a symbol of driving away evil. The ears and eyes of the tiger are found on the original hat. Later, colourful embroidery was added. With the emergence of Buddhism, this symbol of the ancient religion was combined with the figure of Buddha signifying a wish for life-long security.

A Mandarin's fur-trimmed winter hat, Chinese, c1900.
£960–1,150 / €1,400–1,650
$1,750–2,100 ⚒ WW

A gauze informal robe, with counted stitch medallions of butterflies, precious emblems and flowers, above a border of crashing and rolling waves and the Eight Treasures above a *lishui* border, Chinese, late 19thC.
£1,850–2,200 / €2,700–3,200
$3,350–4,000 ⚒ S(NY)
The colour orange, known as apricot yellow, was kept for the exclusive use of the consort of the heir apparent.

A lady's embroidered satin robe, Chinese, c1900.
£110–130 / €160–190
$200–240 ⚒ NSal

► A hand-woven paisley shawl, Indian, Kashmir, early 19thC, 69in (175.5cm) square.
£1,800–2,000 / €2,600–2,900
$3,250–3,600 ⊞ JPr

An embroidered silk shawl, with a macramé fringe, Chinese, c1880, 59in (150cm) wide.
£580–650 / €850–950
$1,050–1,200 ⊞ JPr

Snuff Bottles

A rock crystal snuff bottle, with carved decoration, Chinese, c1800, 2½in (6.5cm) high.
£1,000–1,200
€1,450–1,750
$1,800–2,150 WW

Miller's Compares

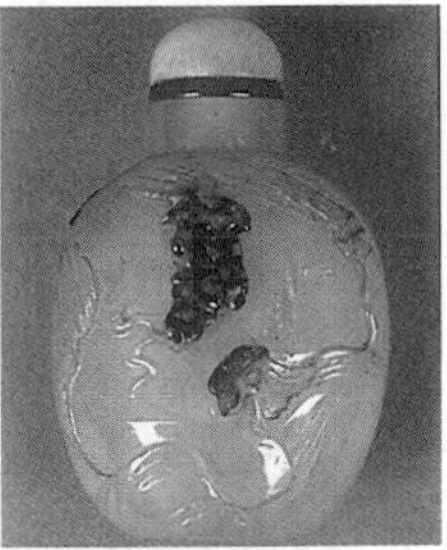

I. A Suzhou chalcedony snuff bottle, each side carved with a lion dog, rockwork and pine trees, with a jade stopper, Chinese, c1800, 2½in (6.5cm) high.
£3,750–4,500
€5,500–6,600
$6,800–8,200 HYD

II. A chalcedony snuff bottle, carved with a cockerel, butterfly and plant, with a silver and jade stopper, Chinese, early 19thC, 2¼in (5.5cm) high.
£700–840
€1,000–1,200
$1,250–1,500 HYD

The standard of craftsmanship and design are very important to a snuff bottle collector who is prepared to a pay a high price for the best. In this case, the coloured stone in the earlier Item I has been fully incorporated into the overall superior carving and design. However, Item II has only used the coloured stone in the relief decoration on a flat ground making it less desirable to a collector.

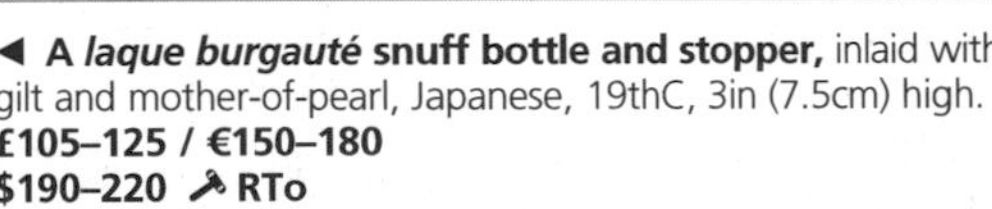

◄ **A *laque burgauté* snuff bottle and stopper,** inlaid with gilt and mother-of-pearl, Japanese, 19thC, 3in (7.5cm) high.
£105–125 / €150–180
$190–220 RTo

A realgar snuff bottle, Chinese, 19thC, 2½in (6.5cm) high.
£1,600–1,800
€2,350–2,600
$2,900–3,250 ⊞ BOW
Realgar is a soft mineral consisting of arsenic sulphide in crystaline form.

A turquoise matrix snuff bottle and stopper, carved in the form of a cat looking up at a vase and butterfly, Chinese, 19thC, 2½in (6.5cm) high.
£210–250 / €310–370
$380–450 RTo

Textiles

A *kesi* panel of a *meiren*, in a wood frame, Chinese, Qing Dynasty, c1800, 61½in (156cm) high.
£5,100–6,100
€7,400–8,900
$9,200–11,000 S(HK)
***Kesi* is a silk tapestry weaving and *meiren* is a beautiful, elegant lady.**

A Chinese export embroidered panel from a bed cover, with satin embroidery, early 19thC, 15½ x 17½in (39.5 x 44.5cm), framed.
£310–350 / €450–500
$560–630 ⊞ ACAN

A silk panel, depicting figures in an emperor's garden, Chinese, 19thC, 85¾ x 98½in (218 x 250cm).
£1,950–2,300 / €2,850–3,400
$3,550–4,200 Bea

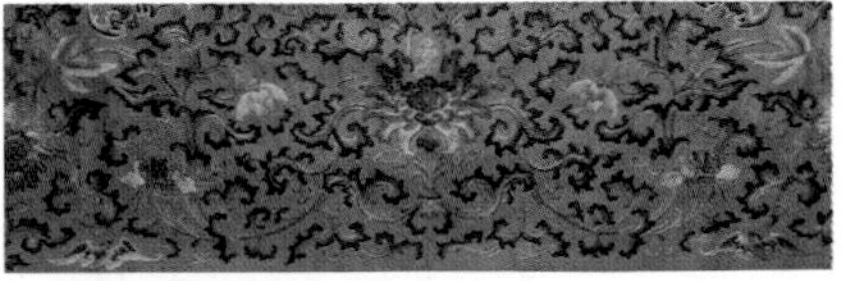

A silk embroidery panel, Chinese, c1875, 72in (183cm) long.
£150–165 / €210–240
$260–300 ⊞ JPr

◄ **A 5th civil rank badge,** decorated with a pheasant, Chinese, c1860, 12 x 11½in (30.5 x 28cm).
£340–380 / €500–550
$620–690 ⊞ JCH

Islamic Works of Art

Arms & Armour

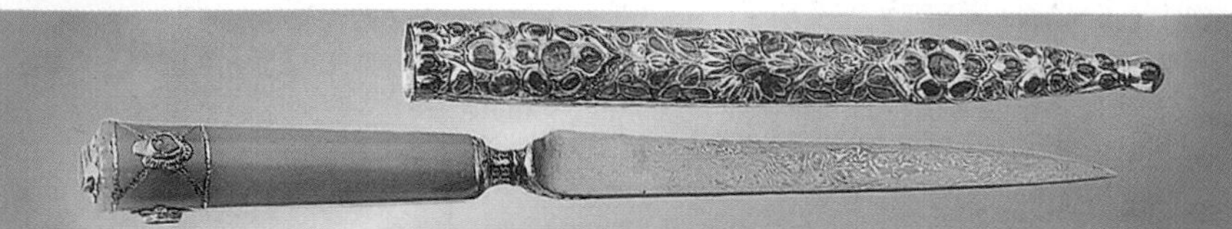

A knife, the jade grip inlaid with gold and rubies, the gold scabbard with embossed and enamel decoration set with rubies and emeralds, grip possibly associated, damage and repair, Ottoman, 17thC, 7½in (19cm) long.
£7,400–8,800 / €10,800–12,800
$13,400–15,700 ⚒ Herm

► **A silver-mounted *pesh kabz*,** with an ivory hilt, the silver hilt-mounts engraved with traditional patterns, with a leather-covered scabbard, Persian, dagger 18thC, refurbished in 1934, blade 8½in (21.5cm) long.
£790–880 / €1,150–1,300
$1,450–1,600 ⊞ FAC

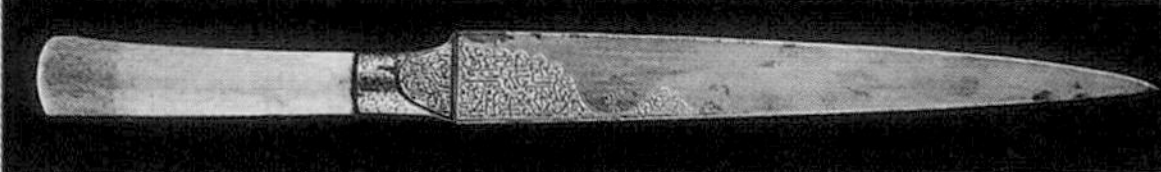

A watered-steel dagger (*kard*), decorated with gold-inlaid inscriptions, the reverse with chiselled and inlaid cartouches and palmettes, the hilt with gold-inlaid calligraphy and marine ivory facings, Persian, c1800, 15¼in (38.5cm) long.
£4,800–5,700 / €7,000–8,300
$8,700–10,300 ⚒ S

► **A steel helmet *khula khud*,** with foliate decoration, chain mail guard and matching shield, Persian, 19thC, 18½in (47cm) diam.
£490–580 / €720–850
$880–1,050 ⚒ L&E

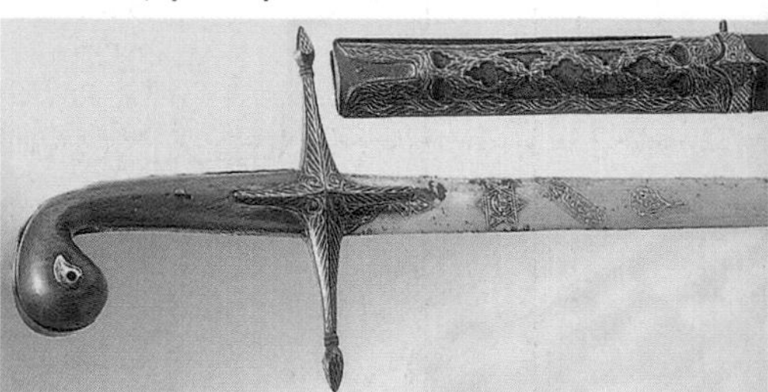

A watered-steel dagger (*shamshir*), with gold-inlaid decoration, the grip with two rhinoceros horn scales, the carved wood scabbard covered with chamois leather, the openwork locket and chape backed with velvet, slight damage, Ottoman, dated 1819, 36¼in (92cm) long.
£3,200–3,800 / €4,650–5,500
$5,800–6,900 ⚒ Herm

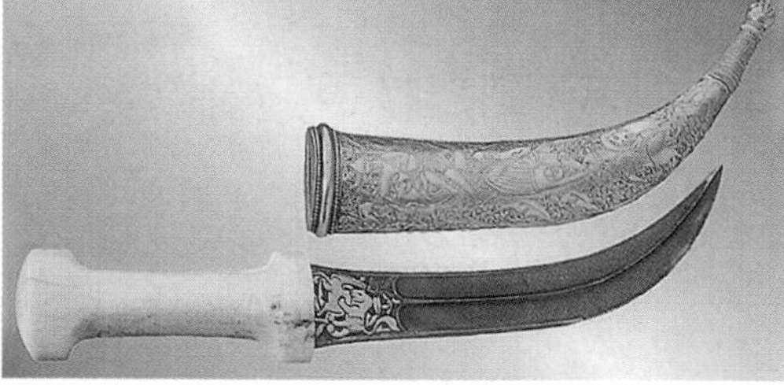

A walrus ivory and gilded *kandjar*, the grip set with turquoises in gold, the blade decorated with a gilded lion attacking an antelope, with a silver-covered and later gilded wood scabbard with embossed decoration, Persian, 1800–50, 13½in (34.5cm) long.
£2,800–3,350 / €4,100–4,900
$5,100–6,100 ⚒ Herm

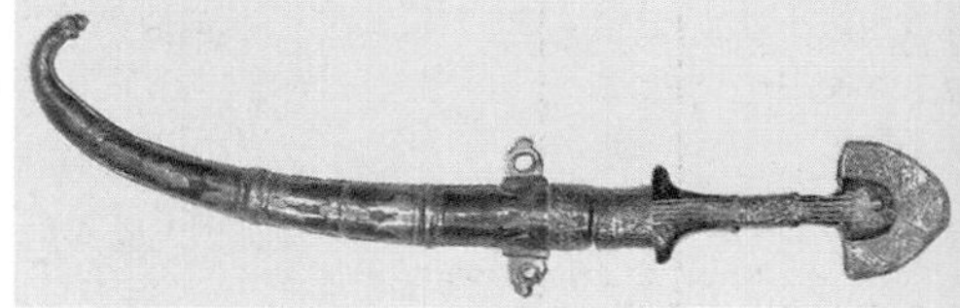

A wood, copper and brass dagger (*jambiya*), the wood grip with wire inlay, with an embossed brass medial and faceted crest, copper and brass scabbard, worn and repaired, Moroccan, early 20thC, blade 9½in (24cm) long.
£175–195 / €250–280
$310–350 ⊞ FAC

Ceramics

◄ **A Nishapur pottery bowl,** with slip-painted and incised decoration, east Persian/Transoxianan, 10thC, 9in (23cm) diam.
£6,000–7,200
€8,800–10,500
$10,900–13,000
⚒ S

A pottery jug and bowl, the jug with a strap handle and unglazed foot, Persian, 12thC, jug 6¾in (17cm) high.
£3,600–4,300 / €5,300–6,300
$6,500–7,800 ⚒ S

A Bamiyan jug, with incised and glazed decoration, the interior decorated with swags, on an unglazed foot, east Persian, 12th–13thC, 7in (18cm) high.
£6,000–7,200 / €8,800–10,500
$10,900–13,000 S
Bamiyan stonepaste wares are associated with the find site of Bamiyan and are typically covered in a greenish glaze that has a tendency to gather in drips and droplets. The muted palette is restricted to cobalt blue, copper turquoise and manganese black or deep purple.

An Iznik pottery dish, decorated with stylized flowers within an ammonite scroll border, damaged, Turkish, 17thC, 11¾in (30cm) diam.
£730–870 / €1,050–1,250
$1,300–1,550 SWO

► A Kütahya pottery bowl, painted with foliate decoration, Turkish, 18thC, 5in (12.5cm) diam.
£3,600–4,300 / €5,300–6,300
$6,500–7,800 S

A pottery tile, relief-moulded, overglazed and gilt, depicting a scene from the *Shahnama* with Bahram Gur on horseback with an attendant and a dog, northwest Iranian, late 13thC, 11¼in (28.5cm) wide.
£2,150–2,550 / €3,150–3,700
$3,900–4,600 S(NY)
This tile probably comes from the interior wall decoration of Takht-i Sulayman, the summer royal palace of the Mongol ruler Abakha from 1265 to 1282 in northwest Iran.

An Iznik pottery dish, with chequerboard and dot decoration, slight damage, Turkish, west Anatolian, c1640, 11¾in (30cm) diam.
£7,600–8,500 / €11,100–12,400
$13,800–15,400 MANO

An Arista pottery tile, decorated with an eight-pointed star, Spanish, Seville, 1520–38, 5¼in (13.5cm) square.
£2,400–2,850 / €3,500–4,150
$4,350–5,200 S

An Iznik pottery tankard, painted with bands of keyfret, wave scrolls and interlocking prunus blossoms, Turkish, 17thC, 7½in (19cm) high.
£4,800–5,700 / €7,000–8,300
$8,700–10,300 S

Three Qajar pottery tiles, depicting riders on horseback, Persian, 19thC, framed, 9½ x 26¼in (24 x 66.5cm).
£1,450–1,700 / €2,100–2,500
$2,600–3,100 TRM(E)

Furniture

A carved walnut serpentine chest-on-stand, with two long drawers flanked by two short drawers, the sides inlaid with a minaret with sides enclosing two secret drawers to either side, stand later, Turkish, c1750, 36¼in (92cm) wide.
£5,000–6,000 / €7,300–8,800
$9,100–10,900 S

Two Ottoman ivory, mother-of-pearl and tortoiseshell-inlaid tables, Turkish, 18thC, 21in (53.5cm) diam.
£14,400–17,200 / €21,000–25,100
$26,100–31,000 S

A parquetry-inlaid games table, with a fitted interior, Syrian, Damascus, late 19thC, 33in (84cm) wide.
£1,050–1,250 / €1,550–1,850
$1,900–2,250 S(O)

Jewellery

An Ottoman gilt-metal belt buckle, the relief decoration of rocaille and flowers inlaid with silver and coloured glass stones, Turkish, 1800–50, 11in (28cm) wide.
£820–980 / €1,200–1,450
$1,500–1,800 DORO

A pair of gold earrings, with wire decoration, Persian, 12th–13thC, 2in (5cm) diam.
£2,400–2,850 / €3,500–4,150
$4,350–5,200 S

An Ottoman Greek gilt-brass hair ornament, with incised and repoussé decoration, surmounted by a pair of birds, 18thC, 3½in (9cm) wide.
£360–400 / €520–580
$650–720 MANO

Metalware

A silver and niello amulet case, Persian, 12thC, 4¼in (11cm) wide.
£3,000–3,600 / €4,400–5,300
$5,400–6,500 S

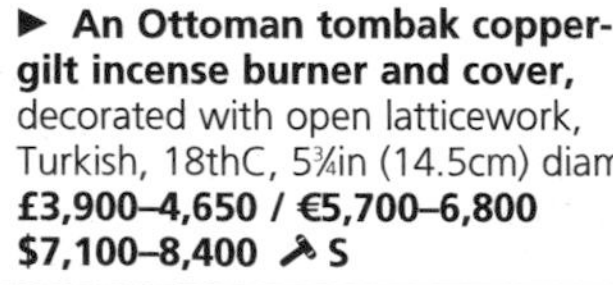

A silver snuff box, chased with figural scenes, birds and flowers, Persian, 1850–1900, 3½in (9cm) wide, 2½oz.
£140–165 / €200–240
$250–300 WW

A pair of Ottoman silver and silver-gilt rosewater bottles, part of one foot missing, 19thC, 9¼in (23.5cm) high.
£2,600–3,100 / €3,800–4,550
$4,700–5,600 S(P)

► **An Ottoman tombak copper-gilt incense burner and cover,** decorated with open latticework, Turkish, 18thC, 5¾in (14.5cm) diam.
£3,900–4,650 / €5,700–6,800
$7,100–8,400 S

A copper bowl, slight damage and restoration, Islamic, 18thC, 15½in (39.5cm) diam.
£1,400–1,650 / €2,050–2,400
$2,550–3,000 S(Mi)

Miscellaneous

A pen box, the sides and cover painted with figures in landscapes, Persian, c1860, 8¾in (22cm) long.
£175–210 / €260–310
$320–380 SWO

◄ **A pair of Qajar lacquer manuscript covers,** the floral panel surrounded by a border with a scrolling floral motif, Persian, 19thC, 8¼ x 5½in (21 x 14cm).
£960–1,150 / €1,450–1,700
$1,750–2,100 S

An embroidered ceremoni saddle, saddle cloth and bridle, with silver-inlaid iro stirrups, fabric breaststrap, crupper and headpiece wit an iron bit, stirrups slightly damaged, Moroccan, c190C saddle 23¾in (60.5cm) long
£2,700–3,200
€3,950–4,650
$4,900–5,800 Herm

Architectural Antiques

Bronze

A bronze base, by Elkington & Co, cast with wheatsheaves, maker's stamp, c1900, 48in (122cm) wide.
£1,800–2,150 / €2,650–3,150
$3,250–3,900 ⚒ S(S)

► **A bronze heliochronometer,** with a stone base and associated marble column, early 20thC, 61in (155cm) high.
£1,200–1,400 / €1,750–2,050
$2,150–2,550 ⚒ S(S)

A bronze swan-neck tap, French, c1900, 18in (45.5cm) high.
£1,600–1,800
€2,350–2,650
$2,900–3,250 ⊞ DRU

Ceramics

A set of three terracotta roof finials, by Dennis Ruabon, c1900, 27in (68.5cm) high.
£4,500–5,000
€6,600–7,300
$8,100–9,100 ⊞ HOP

A pair of saltglaze fireclay planters, in the form of treetrunks, Scottish, c1900, 24in (61cm) high.
£500–600 / €730–880
$910–1,100 ⚒ S(S)

A stoneware urn and pedestal, late 19thC, 45½in (115.5cm) high.
£1,600–1,900
€2,350–2,750
$2,900–3,450 ⚒ S(S)

A terracotta urn and pedestal, by Gibbs & Canning, the pedestal cast with laurel leaves, maker's stamp, late 19thC, 44½in (113cm) high.
£530–630 / €770–920
$960–1,150 ⚒ DN

Iron

◄ **A wrought-iron bell assembly and bell pull,** 18thC, 44in (112cm) high.
£1,350–1,500
€1,950–2,200
$2,450–2,700
⊞ OLA

A pair of wrought-iron gates, c1900, 132in (335.5cm) wide.
£2,700–3,000 / €3,950–4,400
$4,900–5,400 ⊞ WRe

◄ **A wrought-iron kissing gate,** with cast-iron post and side frame, mid-19thC, 64½in (164cm) high.
£2,600–3,100 / €3,800–4,500
$4,700–5,600 ⚒ S(S)

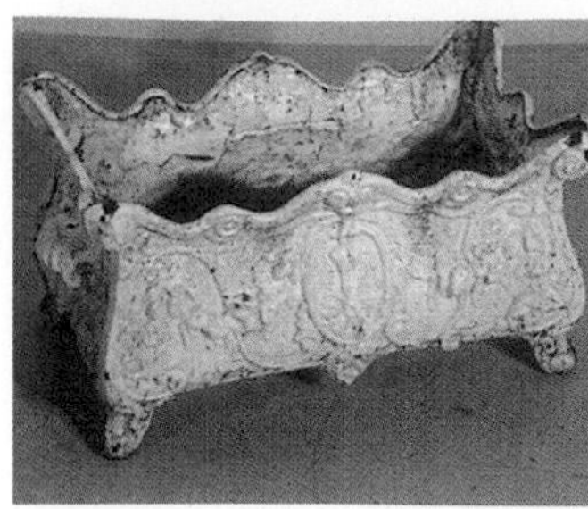

◄ **A pair of cast-iron planters,** c1900, 19in (48.5cm) wide.
£350–420
€510–610
$630–760 Hal

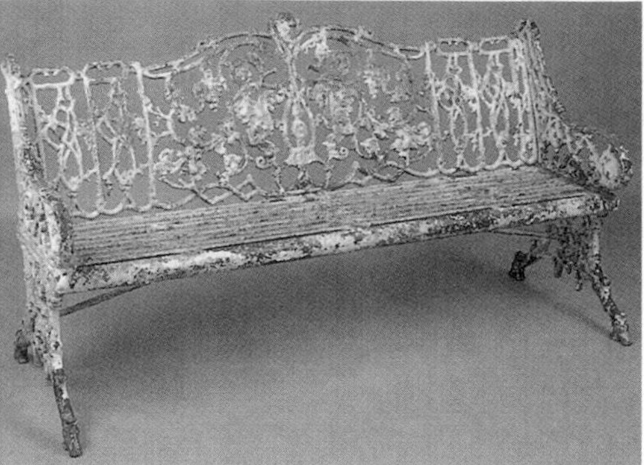

A cast-iron garden seat, the back cast with trailing vines, 19thC, 61½in (156cm) wide.
£1,100–1,300 / €1,600–1,900
$2,000–2,350 L

A large range of cast-iron garden furniture and ornament was produced in the 19th century by Coalbrookdale Iron Foundry, based at Ironbridge, Shropshire. The Carron Foundry, the Falkirk Iron Foundry and the French Val d'Osne Foundry were other main producers of cast-iron seating, and many smaller foundries proliferated to fulfil the enormous demand for garden furniture in the late 19th and early 20th centuries.

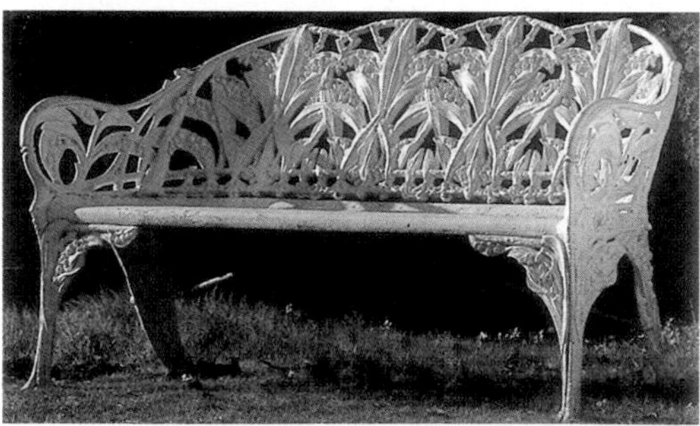

A Coalbrookdale cast-iron garden seat, the sides and back with lily-of-the-valley decoration, c1870, 62in (157.5cm) wide.
£2,600–3,100 / €3,800–4,550
$4,700–5,600 S(S)

A Victorian wrought-iron tree seat, in two sections, 74in (188cm) diam.
£1,900–2,250 / €2,750–3,250
$3,450–4,100 Gam

A wrought-iron garden seat, with original paint, c1825, 56in (142cm) wide.
£6,700–7,500 / €9,800–11,000
$12,100–13,600 ⊞ RYA

A neo-classical painted cast-iron garden seat, after Karl Friedrich Schinkel, the back splat with pierced decoration, the arms terminating in rams' heads, with a wooden seat, German, 19thC, 31½in (80cm) high.
£1,400–1,650 / €2,000–2,400
$2,550–3,000 S(Am)

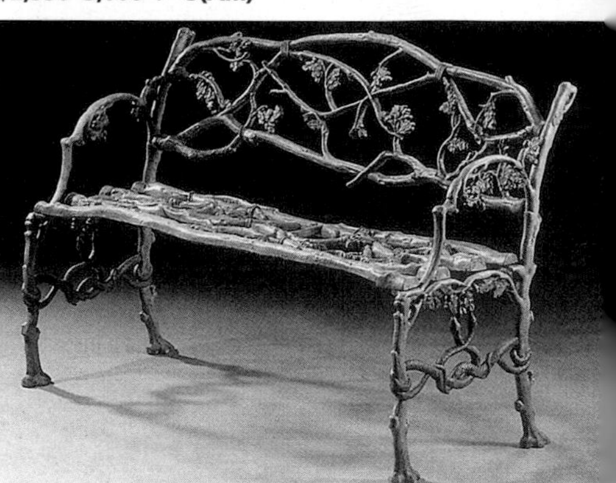

A cast-iron garden seat, by James Haywood, cast with oak branch pattern, stamped 'J. Haywood, Phoenix Foundry, Derby', c1870, 51in (129.5cm) wide.
£3,100–3,700 / €4,550–5,400
$5,600–6,700 S(S)

A pair of wrought-iron window seats, with upholstered cushions, c1900, 59in (150cm) wide.
£1,200–1,400 / €1,750–2,050
$2,150–2,550 S(S)

A ceramic and cast-iron stove, damaged, 19thC, 73¾in (187.5cm) high.
£3,450–4,100
€5,000–6,000
$6,200–7,400 S(P)

A cast-iron table, probably by L. I. Enthoven & Co, Dutch, 1850–1900, 29½in (75cm) diam.
£1,300–1,550
€1,900–2,250
$2,350–2,800 S(S)

► **A pair of cast-iron uprights,** c1840, 87in (221cm) high.
£4,200–5,000
€6,100–7,300
$7,600–9,100 S(S)

A pair of cast-iron urns, after the antique Medici and Borghese urns, 1850–1900, 31in (78.5cm) high.
£1,200–1,400 / €1,750–2,050
$2,150–2,550 S(S)

◄ **A pair of cast-iron campana urns,** paint later, 19thC, 16in (40.5cm) diam.
£410–490
€600–720
$740–890
Hal

A cast-iron water hopper, c1880, 23in (58.5cm) high.
£220–250 / €320–360
$400–450 WRe

ARCHITECTURAL ANTIQUES

Lead

A lead cistern, with strapwork decoration and a bronze tap, dated 1763, 39in (99cm) wide.
£3,350–4,000 / €4,900–5,800
$6,100–7,200 S(S)

Items in the Architectural Antiques section have been arranged in alphabetical order.

A pair of Georgian-style lead cisterns, with strapwork decoration, inscribed 1717, early 20thC, 37in (94cm) wide.
£3,600–4,300 / €5,300–6,300
$6,500–7,800 S(S)

A lead Newcastle fire mark, cast with three castles within a wreath, 18thC, 7½in (19cm) high.
£550–660 / €800–960
$1,000–1,200 JRA

◄ **A lead planter,** with applied lion masks, 19thC, 17in (43cm) diam.
£290–340 / €420–500
$520–620 Hal

► **A pair of lead garden urns,** with raised decoration depicting sailing ships, shells and dolphins, dated 1757, mid-18thC, 18½in (47cm) high.
£2,350–2,800
€3,450–4,100
$4,250–5,100 G(L)

Marble

A pair of marble brackets, late 19thC, 13in (33cm) high.
£200–230 / €300–340
$360–410 ⊞ NEW

► **A marble pedestal,** with a rotating top, Italian, late 19thC, 79in (200.5cm) high.
£3,100–3,700 / €4,550–5,400
$5,600–6,700 ⚒ S(S)

As marble is an expensive material it was used in moderation as an architectural decoration. Marble troughs are found, but in general marble fittings will often have come from a church, and therefore the quality of the carving is likely to be of superior quality.

► **A Victorian marble and cast-iron conservatory stand,** by Parnall & Sons, with three shelves, 36¼in (92cm) wide.
£440–520
€640–760
$800–940 ⚒ SWO

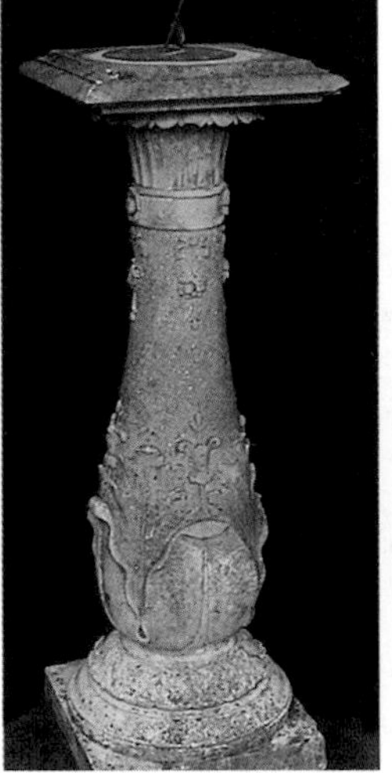

A carved marble pedestal, with a later sundial, 19thC, 48½in (123cm) high.
£5,900–7,000
€8,600–10,200
$10,700–12,700 ⚒ WW

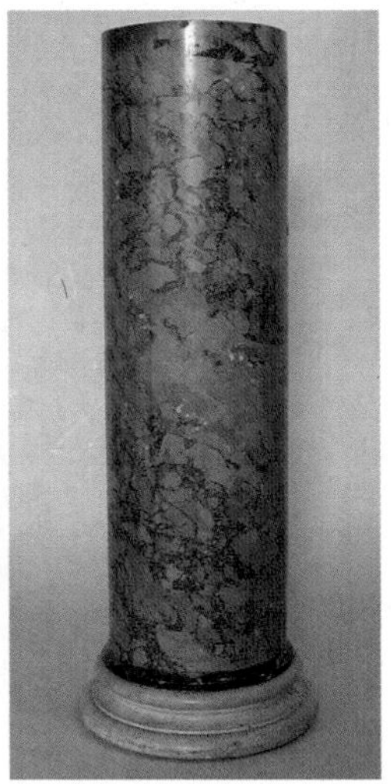

A reconstituted marble pillar, with a spreading base, 19thC, 46in (117cm) high.
£910–1,050
€1,350–1,600
$1,650–1,950 ⚒ BWL

A pair of marble urns, each in the form of a Roman bath, carved with ring handles, Italian, 19thC, 13in (33cm) wide.
£1,050–1,250 / €1,550–1,850
$1,900–2,250 ⚒ DN

Stone

A set of ten Victorian granite baluster columns, 26in (66cm) high.
£1,800–2,150
€2,650–3,150
$3,250–3,900 ⚒ Mal(O)

A pair of carved Portland stone gate finials, 19thC, 48in (122cm) high.
£2,600–3,100
€3,800–4,550
$4,700–5,600 ⚒ S(S)

A carved stone finial and pedestal, French, 19thC, 51in (129.5cm) high.
£2,150–2,550
€3,150–3,700
$3,900–4,600 ⚒ S(S)

A granite Kasuge lantern, Japanese, Meiji period, 1868–1911, 60in (152.5cm) high.
£1,900–2,250
€2,750–3,300
$3,450–4,100 ⚒ S(S)

A carved stone wall plaque, Low Countries, 19thC, 33in (84cm) wide.
£1,400–1,650 / €2,000–2,400
$2,550–3,000 ⚒ S(S)

A pair of carved limestone garden stools, each with lion-mask ring handles, one pair of handles studded with florettes and tied with ribbon, the other pair imitating bamboo, both with nail-head bosses around the top and foot, 17thC, 14½in (37cm) high.
£2,300–2,750 / €3,350–4,000
$4,150–5,000 ⚒ S(NY)

A Louis XV-style stone plinth, with a sundial and a later wrought-iron and copper armillary sphere, Dutch, 18thC, 71in (180.5cm) high.
£9,700–11,600
€14,200–16,900
$17,600–21,000 ⚒ S(Am)

A Portland stone sundial, with a bronze dial, late 19thC, 34in (86.5cm) high.
£1,550–1,850
€2,250–2,700
$2,800–3,350 ⚒ S(S)

◄ A baroque-style carved stone sundial pillar, the column carved with compass points, mason's mark, sundial missing, 19thC, 60in (152.5cm) high.
£4,250–5,100
€6,200–7,400
$7,700–9,200 ⚒ PFK

Further reading

Miller's Garden Antiques, Miller's Publications, 2003.

A carved stone thistle, on an associated stone base, Scottish, 19thC, 35in (89cm) high.
£1,050–1,250
€1,550–1,850
$1,900–2,250 ⚒ S(S)

Wood

A walnut carving, Flemish, c1615, 49in (124.5cm) wide.
£1,800–2,000 / €2,600–2,900
$3,200–3,600 ⊞ SEA

A carved oak caryatid, 19thC, 42in (106.5cm) high.
£2,650–2,950
€3,850–4,300
$4,800–5,300 ⊞ WAA

► A carved oak overmantel, c1640, 54in (137cm) wide.
£1,050–1,250
€1,550–1,850
$1,900–2,250 ⚒ S(O)

◄ A painted wood ceiling panel, Italian, 17thC, 90in (228.5cm) wide.
£2,850–3,200
€4,150–4,650
$5,200–5,800 ⊞ DOA

Bathroom Fittings

A copper bath, c1890, 58in (147.5cm) long.
£760–850 / €1,100–1,250
$1,400–1,550 ⊞ JUN

A cast-iron slipper bath, on feet, restored, c1900, 65in (165cm) long.
£3,000–3,300 / €4,400–4,900
$5,400–6,000 ⊞ C&R

An iron bateau bath, c1900, 61in (155cm) long.
£900–1,000 / €1,300–1,450
$1,600–1,800 ⊞ C&R

A cast-iron plunger bath, on feet, restored, c1900, 73in (185.5cm) wide.
£2,250–2,500 / €3,300–3,650
$4,050–4,550 ⊞ C&R

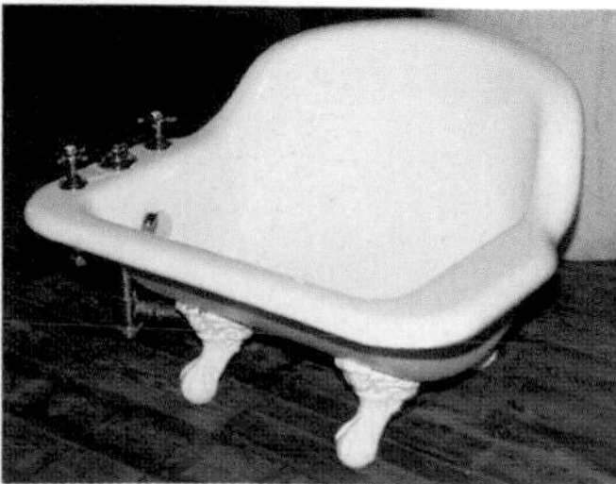

► An enamel plunger hip bath, on feet, c1900, 35in (89cm) wide.
£1,900–2,150
€2,800–3,150
$3,450–3,900
⊞ DRU

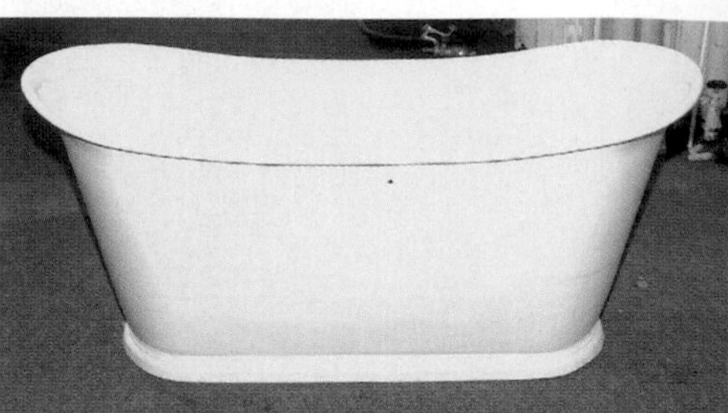

A cast-iron bateau bath, c1900, 61in (155cm) long.
£3,000–3,300 / €4,400–4,900
$5,400–6,000 ⊞ C&R

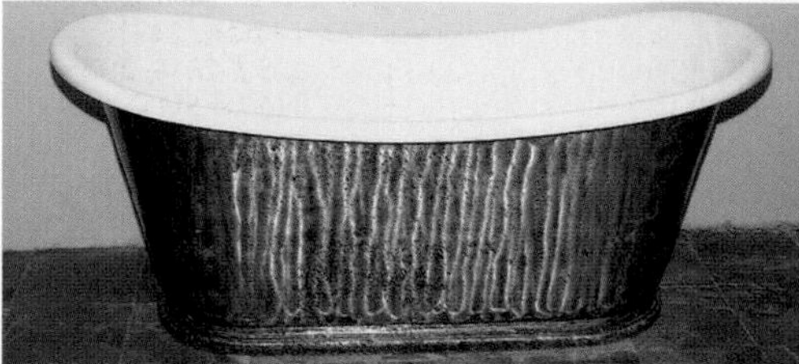

An iron bateau bath, with a polished metal exterior, restored, c1900, 65in (165cm) long.
£3,200–3,600 / €4,650–5,300
$5,800–6,500 ⊞ C&R

A carved marble bath, c1900, 69in (175.5cm) long.
£8,000–8,900 / €11,700–13,000
$14,500–16,100 ⊞ DRU

A John Bolding cast-iron plunger bath, on feet, restored, c1900, 60in (152cm) long.
£3,600–4,000 / €5,300–5,900
$6,500–7,200 ⊞ C&R

An Edwardian plunger bath, with built-in soap trays and nickel fittings, on feet, 85in (216cm) long.
£4,050–4,500 / €5,900–6,600
$7,200–8,100 ⊞ WRe

A Victorian Shanks & Co mahogany lever cistern and lavatory pan, 41in (104cm) wide.
£4,750–5,300
€6,900–7,700
$8,600–9,600 ⊞ DRU

A Victorian Dent & Hellyer porcelain lavatory pan, 21¾in (55.5cm) high.
£165–195 / €240–290
$300–360 ⚒ SWO

A pair of Cauldon Pottery Rotterdam lavatory pans, c1900, 16in (40.5cm) high.
£4,000–4,500 / €5,800–6,600
$7,200–8,100 ⊞ C&R

A ceramic Excelsior lavatory pan, c1900, 16in (40.5cm) high.
£810–900 / €1,200–1,350
$1,450–1,650 ⊞ OLA

A chrome tap outlet, restored, French, c1900, 16in (40.5cm) high.
£1,750–1,950 / €2,550–2,850
$3,150–3,550 ⊞ DRU

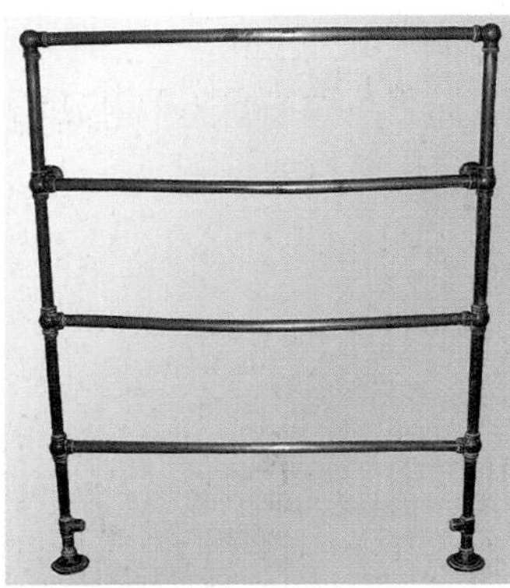

An Edwardian copper heated towel rail, with nickel joints, 76in (193cm) wide.
£1,700–1,900 / €2,500–2,750
$3,100–3,450 ⊞ WRe

◄ **A pedestal washbasin,** restored, c1900, 33in (84cm) high.
£3,500–4,200 / €5,100–6,100
$6,300–7,600 ⊞ C&R

► **An Edwardian marble washstand,** on chrome legs, 50in (127cm) high.
£1,400–1,600 / €2,050–2,300
$2,550–2,900 ⊞ WRe

Doors & Door Furniture

◄ **A Gothic arch pitch pine door and frame,** 19thC, 49in (124.5cm) wide.
£1,250–1,400
€1,850–2,050
$2,250–2,550 ⊞ DRU

► **An oak panelled door and frame,** 19thC, 37in (94cm) wide.
£940–1,050
€1,400–1,550
$1,700–1,900 ⊞ DRU

A Victorian oak panelled door and frame, with a twin column pierced opening, 38¼in (97cm) wide.
£400–480 / €580–700
$720–860 ⚒ SWO

A set of 18 brass door handles and escutcheons, late 19thC, handle 3in (7.5cm) high.
£760–850 / €1,100–1,250
$1,400–1,550 ⊞ OLA

A pair of brass pull handles, c1910, 18½in (47cm) high.
£560–630 / €820–920
$1,000–1,100 ⊞ Penn

A cast-iron door knocker, 19thC, 7in (18cm) high.
£650–730 / €950–1,050
$1,150–1,300 ⊞ DRU

A painted cast-iron door knocker, with a ram's head 19thC, 9in (23cm) high.
£420–470 / €610–690
$760–850 ⊞ DRU

A pair of brass door locks, French, c1800, 21in (53.5cm) high.
£900–1,000 / €1,300–1,450
$1,600–1,800 ⊞ OLA

A Victorian Gothic-style cast-iron door knocker, 9in (23cm) high.
£160–180 / €230–260
$290–330 ⊞ OLA

A bronze door knocker and letterbox, surmounted with a bat, c1870, 9½in (24cm) high.
£350–390 / €510–570
$630–710 ⊞ Penn

A pair of steel and brass door locks, 19thC, 7in (18cm) wide.
£340–380 / €500–550
$620–690 ⊞ DRU

◄ **A steel and brass door lock,** early 20thC, 7in (18cm) wide.
£100–110
€145–160
$180–200
⊞ DRU

A carved oak and parcel-gilt overdoor, carved with the words from a psalm, mid-19thC, 53½in (136cm) wide
£1,050–1,250 / €1,550–1,850
$1,900–2,250 ⚒ S

Fireplaces

A Jacobean-style carved oak fire surround, c1720, 71in (180.5cm) wide.
£2,450–2,750 / €3,600–4,000
$4,450–5,000 ⊞ OLA

A gesso fire surround, moulded with a pair of female heads, 18thC, 80¾in (205cm) wide.
£400–450 / €580–660
$720–810 ⚒ SWO

A pine fire surround, mounted on later boards, mid-18thC, 58in (147.5cm) wide.
£2,250–2,700 / €3,300–3,950
$4,100–4,900 ⚒ S(S)

A carved pine and composition fire surround, c1770, 70½in (179cm) wide.
£6,400–7,600 / €9,300–11,100
$11,600–13,800 ⚒ S

A Louis XVI-style marble fire surround, with ormolu decoration, French, c1850, 57in (145cm) wide.
£6,700–7,500 / €9,800–11,000
$12,100–13,600 ⊞ OLA

A Victorian oak fire surround, with Corinthian column supports, 63¾in (162cm) wide.
£630–750 / €920–1,100
$1,150–1,350 ⚒ DD

Further reading

Miller's Buying Affordable Antiques Price Guide,
Miller's Publications, 2005

A Victorian carved stone fire surround, c1860, 56in (142cm) wide.
£1,800–2,150 / €2,650–3,150
$3,250–3,900 ⚒ S(S)

An Edwardian cast-iron fireplace, with moulded beaded decoration, with grate, firebox and adjustable hood, 50in (127cm) high.
£160–190 / €230–270
$290–340 ⚒ JRA

An Edwardian carved oak fire surround, by Shoolbred & Co, opening 35¾in (91cm) wide.
£370–440 / €540–640
$670–800 ⚒ SWO

A George III steel dog grate, decorated with a rieze of pierced anthemia, with baluster finials, on Doric column supports, 7in (68.5cm) wide.
1,650–1,950 / €2,400–2,850
2,900–3,500 ⚒ HOLL

A Coalbrookdale cast-iron range, late 19thC, 61in (155cm) wide.
£2,850–3,200
€4,150–4,650
$5,200–5,800 ⊞ DRU

Regency cast-iron fire rate, 17in (43cm) wide.
550–660 / €800–960
1,000–1,200 ⚒ PBA

A George III-style cast-iron and polished steel fire grate, the back plate decorated with a woman in a landscape, 19thC, 29¼in (74.5cm) wide.
£1,400–1,650
€2,050–2,400
$2,550–3,000 ⚒ JAd

Fireplace Accessories

A brass ash bucket, with copper rivets, Dutch, c1780, 12in (30.5cm) high.
£400–450 / €580–660
$720–810 ⊞ SEA

► **A toleware coal bin,** with a hinged lid, painted with hunting scenes, c1900, 19in (48.5cm) wide.
£1,100–1,300 / €1,600–1,900
$2,000–2,350 ⚒ SK

A polished steel fender, pierced with scrolling foliage, 18thC, 56in (142cm) wide.
£370–440 / €540–640
$670–800 ⚒ DA

A brass fender, designed by William Chambers, late 18thC, 59in (150cm) wide.
£2,250–2,700 / €3,300–3,950
$4,050–4,900 ⚒ HOK

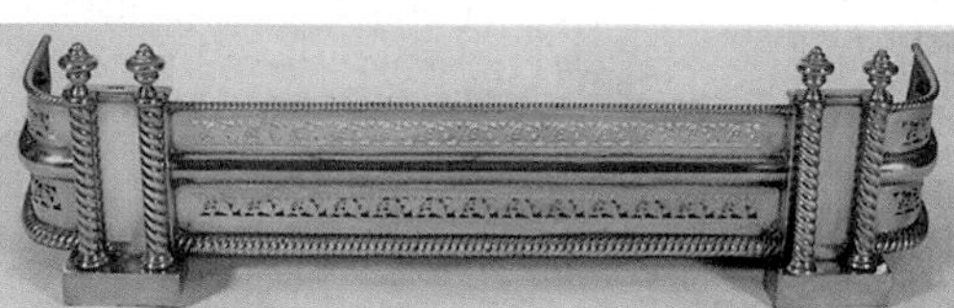

A brass fender, with rope-twist and pierced decoration, early 19thC, 48in (122cm) wide.
£210–250 / €310–370
$380–450 ⚒ DMC

► **A George II painted and gilded cast-iron fireback,** dated 1737, 36in (91.5cm) wide.
£520–620
€760–910
$940–1,100
⚒ G(L)

A set of polished steel fire irons, c1850, 29in (73.5cm) high.
£540–600 / €790–880
$980–1,100 ⊞ NEW

A Regency brass fender, with pierced floral decoration, 44½in (113cm) wide.
£300–360 / €440–530
$540–650 ⚒ Mit

A cast-iron and brass fender, French, c1880, 40½in (103cm) wide.
£780–930 / €1,150–1,350
$1,400–1,650 ⚒ S(O)

A cast-iron fire front, cast with five gnomes, c1880, 16in (40.5cm) wide.
£135–150 / €195–220
$240–270 ⊞ SMI

A Federal wire mesh firescreen, with brass finials, American, 1786–1810, 34½in (87.5cm) wide.
£1,650–1,950 / €2,400–2,850
$3,000–3,550 ⚒ SGA

Fountains

A marble fountain, carved in the form of a dolphin above a scallop-shaped bowl, Dutch, 18thC, 19¾in (50cm) wide.
£6,000–7,200
€8,800–10,500
$10,900–13,000 S(Am)

A cast-iron two-tier fountain, Continental, c1880, 52in (132cm) high.
£2,700–3,000
€3,950–4,400
$4,900–5,400 ⊞ CHES

A stoneware fountain, attributed to Doulton, in the form of a boy and a dolphin, c1900, 27in (68.5cm) high.
£1,550–1,850
€2,250–2,700
$2,800–3,350 S(S)

A lead fountain, cast as a boy holding a duck, early 20thC, 31½in (80cm) high.
£1,400–1,650
€2,050–2,400
$2,550–3,000 S(S)

Statuary

marble bust of Minerva, ow Countries, 1700–50, 9in (73.5cm) high.
2,500–3,000
3,650–4,400
4,550–5,400 S(S)

A carved stone mastiff, 18thC, 33in (84cm) high.
£1,200–1,400
€1,750–2,050
$2,150–2,550 S(S)

A pair of lead gate finials, in the form of eagles, on later-carved Vicenza stone bases, c1900, 29in (73.5cm) high.
£2,400–2,850 / €3,500–4,150
$4,350–5,200 S(S)

pair of spelter busts, Miroy Bros, Paris, picting Bacchus and be, French, c1860, in (53.5cm) high.
,500–5,000
,600–7,300
,100–9,100 ⊞ OIA

A pair of early Victorian cast-iron garden statues, by John Crowley, Sheffield, one a lion, the other a unicorn, stamped marks, dated December 1847, each 28in (71cm) wide.
£400–480 / €580–700
$720–870 Mit

◄ A bronze figure of the Venus de Milo, after the antique, French, late 19thC, 42in (106.5cm) high.
£5,200–6,200
€7,600–9,100
$9,400–11,200
S(S)

A pair of carved stone lions, on plinths, c1880, 34in (86.5cm) wide.
£2,000–2,400 / €2,900–3,500
$3,600–4,350 TEN

◀ **A pair of painted cast-iron whippets,** probably by J. W. Fiske Foundry, New York, one late 19thC, one early 20thC, American, 51¼in (130cm) long.
£7,200–8,600 / €10,500–12,600
$13,000–15,600 ⚒ S(Am)

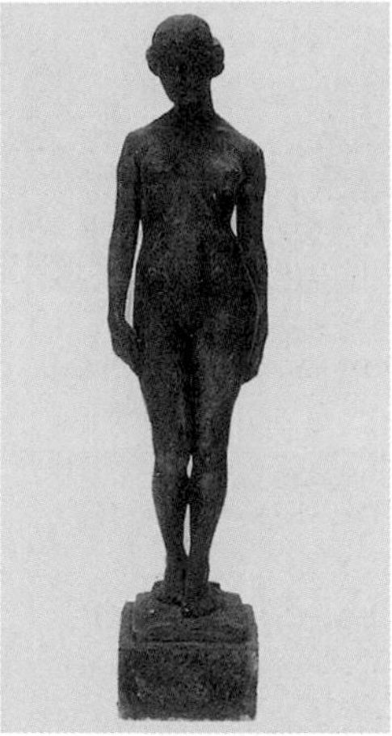

A cast-plaster sculpture of a woman, early 20thC, 32½in (82.6cm) high.
£290–340 / €420–500
$520–610 ⚒ HOLL

A bronze garden statue of a man and a dog, c1920, 30in (76cm) wide.
£1,050–1,200
€1,550–1,750
$1,900–2,150 ⊞ OLA

A pair of stone lions, c1930, 14in (35.5cm) high.
£175–195 / €260–290
$310–350 ⊞ TOP

A composition stone figure of a boy, on a pedestal, 1930s, 70in (178cm) high.
£1,600–1,800
€2,350–2,650
$2,900–3,250 ⊞ PAS

Windows

A fan light, c1790, 57in (145cm) wide.
£810–900 / €1,200–1,350
$1,450–1,650 ⊞ OLA

▶ **A fan light,** c1790, 64in (162cm) wide.
£810–900 / €1,200–1,350
$1,450–1,650 ⊞ OLA

▶ **A pair of Victorian stained glass and leaded window panels,** each with a panel decorated with a bird, 78¼in (199cm) high.
£460–550 / €670–800
$830–1,000 ⚒ SWO

Miscellaneous

A pair of copper lanterns, c1900, 36in (91.5cm) high.
£5,700–6,800
€8,300–9,900
$10,300–12,300 ⚒ S(S)

▶ **Two pairs of acid-etched glass panels,** c1890, 33¼in (84.5cm) high.
£2,650–2,950
€3,850–4,300
$4,800–5,400
⊞ DREW

A painted plaque, probably coppe cast with mythical figures, German, late 19thC, 24in (61cm) diam.
£470–560 / €680–810
$850–1,000 ⚒ SWO

Sculpture

A gilt and painted carved wood figure of St James, paint refreshed, French, 15thC, 39in (99cm) high.
£6,600–7,900
€9,600–11,500
$11,900–14,300 S(NY)

A carved marble bust of a young man, attributed to Christopher Hewetson, on a turned socle, 18thC, 24in (61cm) high.
£5,600–6,700
€8,200–9,800
$10,100–12,100 WW

A bronze allegory of Music, by Albert Carrier-Belleuse, later converted to a table lamp, signed, French, 19thC, 14¾in (37.5cm) wide.
£1,300–1,550
€1,900–2,250
$2,350–2,800 WEBB

A parcel-gilt and painted carved wood figure of St Mary Magdalene, on a later giltwood stand, Netherlands, c1500, 18in (45.5cm) high.
£5,600–6,700
€8,200–9,800
$10,100–12,100 TEN

► **A pair of carved wood busts of Charles I and Charles II,** early 18thC, 13in (33cm) high.
£3,050–3,400
€4,450–4,950
$5,500–6,200 KEY

A bronze model of a bull, after Giambologna, on a wooden plinth, Italian, 17thC, bronze 3¾in (9.5cm) high.
£1,400–1,650
€2,050–2,400
$2,550–3,000 S(O)

A marble bust of a woman, 17th–18thC, 32¼in (82cm) high.
£1,750–2,100
€2,550–3,050
$3,150–3,800 HOK

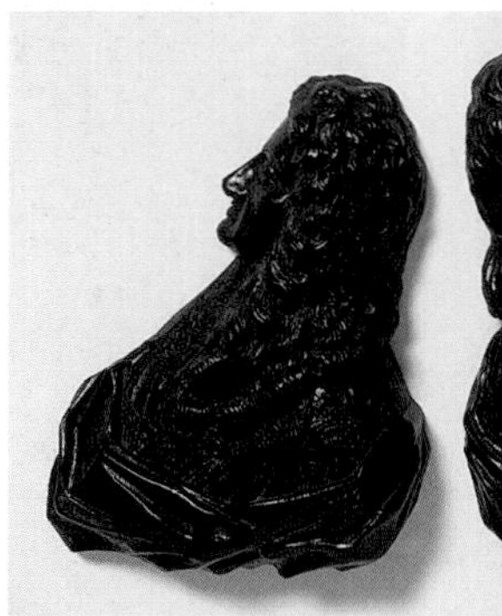

A bronze model of two horses, by Pierre Jules Mêne, entitled 'L'Accolade', French, signed, 1865, 27in (68.5cm) wide.
£31,000–35,000 / €45,000–51,000
$56,000–63,000 RGa

This large version of Mêne's model is rarely seen.

A terracotta bust of a young woman, after Jean Jacques Pradier, French, c1819, 20½in (52cm) high.
£1,850–2,100
€2,700–3,050
$3,400–3,800 G&H

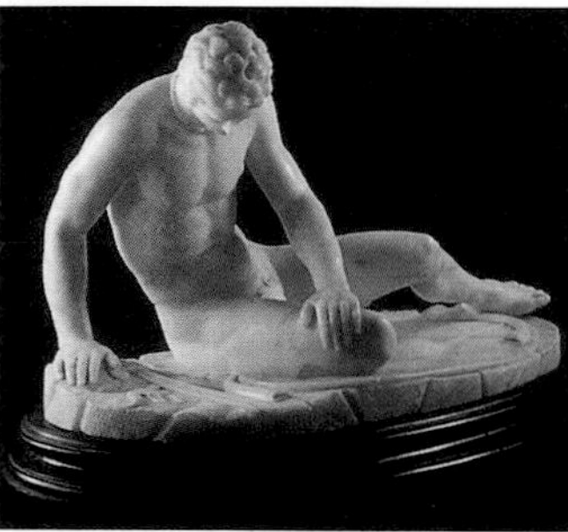

► **A carved marble figure of an athlete,** on a carved base, 19thC, 26¾in (68cm) wide.
£2,650–3,150
€3,850–4,600
$4,800–5,700
LJ

► **A terracotta bust of a young woman,** on a turned marble socle, 19thC, 21½in (54.5cm) high.
£540–640 / €790–930
$980–1,150 WW

A set of six carved bone figures of street musicians, each playing different instruments and standing on oak barrels, early 19thC, 6in (15cm) high.
£1,250–1,500 / €1,850–2,200
$2,250–2,700 ⚒ BWL

◀ **A carved oak figure of a standard bearer,** 19thC, 14in (35.5cm) high.
£460–520 / €670–760
$830–940 ⊞ KEY

A parcel-gilt, stained and carved wood figure of an angel, 19thC, 22in (56cm) wide.
£620–740 / €910–1,100
$1,100–1,300 ⚒ BERN

► **A bronze figure of a classical woman,** by Jean Baptiste Clesinger, entitled 'Standing Sappho', foundry mark, signed, French, dated 1857, 26½in (67.5cm) high.
£1,900–2,250
€2,750–3,300
$3,450–4,050 ⚒ JAA

A bronze figure of a classical woman, plinth stamped 'F. Barbedienne', French, Paris, 19thC, 34in (86.5cm) high.
£1,300–1,550
€1,900–2,250
$2,300–2,700 ⚒ HOK

A marble bust of Sir Robert Peel, by M. Noble, with inscription, 1850, 17½in (44.5cm) high.
£530–630 / €770–920
$960–1,150 ⚒ TEN

A bronze model of a cow and suckling calf, by Pierre Jules Mêne, French, c1860, 19in (48.5cm) wide.
£6,600–7,300 / €9,600–10,700
$11,900–13,200 ⊞ RGa

◀ **A bronze figure of Narcissus,** by Chiurazzi, marked, Italian, 19thC, 24½in (62cm) high.
£1,050–1,250 / €1,550–1,850
$1,900–2,250 ⚒ WEBB
Chiurazzi set up and ran an art school and foundry in Naples c1840. He was often permitted to take moulds directly from antique originals, his bronzes providing the closest, most faithful and exact casts. Succeeded by his sons in 1895, the foundry continued until the outbreak of war in 1939.

A marble figure of a Native American woman in a canoe, by Duchoiselle, 19thC, 17in (43cm) high.
£4,300–5,100 / €6,300–7,400
$7,800–9,200 ⚒ S(NY)
Little is known about the sculptor Duchoiselle except that he supplied ceiling reliefs for the Louvre and Garnier's Opera House in 1882. Other examples of this model, which Duchoiselle probably created in the 1860s, were produced in marble by the Frilli Gallery, Florence The idealized American Native female, representing the artistic personification of the country itself, was a popular subject for bot American and European sculptors.

◀ **A bronze model of a panther and its prey,** by Antoine-Louis Barye, entitled 'Panthère surprenant un zibeth', signed, foundry mark, French, c1870, 17in (43cm) wide.
£10,800–12,000 / €15,800–18,000
$19,500–22,000 ⊞ RGa

A marble bust of a woman, on a socle base, c1870, 26in (66cm) high.
£940–1,100
€1,350–1,600
$1,700–2,000 SWO

A bronze figural group, by Süsse Frères, entitled 'The Discovery of Moses', foundry mark, French, c1870, 16¼in (41.5cm) high.
£1,650–1,850
€2,400–2,700
$3,000–3,350 BeF

A Black Forest carved wood model of a standing bear, holding a begging bowl, German, 1880, 39in (99cm) high.
£2,350–2,800
€3,450–4,100
$4,250–5,100 F&C

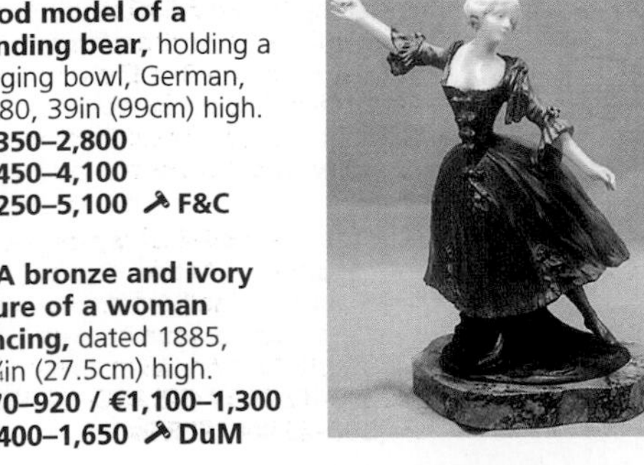

A bronze and ivory figure of a woman dancing, dated 1885, 10¾in (27.5cm) high.
£770–920 / €1,100–1,300
$1,400–1,650 DuM

A bronze model of a frog playing a mandolin, by Auguste Nicolas Cain, signed, French, c1870, 4½in (11.5cm) high.
£1,100–1,250
€1,600–1,800
$2,000–2,250 BeF

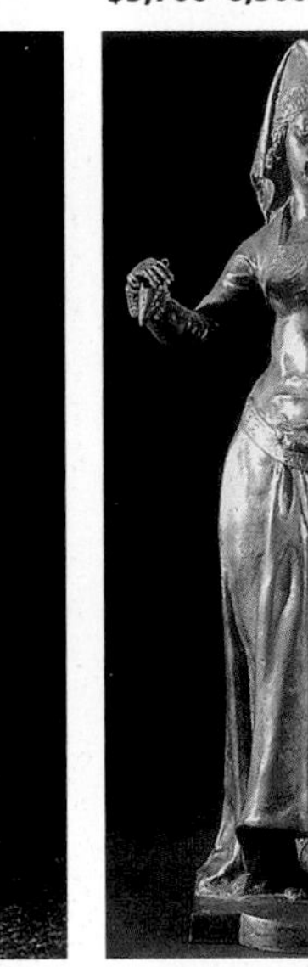

A carved ivory figure of Paris, by Emile Philippe Scailliet, with a bronze drape, on a marble stand, signed and dated 1874, French, 14¼in (36cm) high.
£3,700–4,400
€5,400–6,400
$6,700–8,000 S
Emile Scailliet (1846–1911) was born in Paris and studied under Jouffroy and Moreau-Vauthier. He exhibited at the Salon from 1866 to 1910 and was considered one of the finest ivory carvers of his time.

A pair of silvered-bronze figures of young women, by Jean Baptiste Germain, signed, French, c1870, 12½in (32cm) high.
£3,150–3,500
€4,600–5,100
$5,700–6,300 BeF

A silvered-bronze figure of a woman, by Charles Veeck, entitled 'La Fileuse', silver worn, signed, Belgian, 19thC, 15½in (39.5cm) high.
£60–70 / €90–105
$110–130 JAA

A bronze group of deer, by Antoine Louis Barye, entitled 'Cerf, Biche et Faon', gold seal mark, French, c1877, 10in (25.5cm) wide.
£11,200–12,500
€16,400–18,300
$20,300–22,600 RGa
This model is of the highest quality and therefore stamped with a gold seal by the Barbedienne Foundry.

A bronze model of a chamois goat, by Jules Moigniez, entitled 'Chamois Seul', signed, French, c1870, 10½in (26.5cm) wide.
£1,300–1,450
€1,900–2,100
$2,350–2,600 BeF

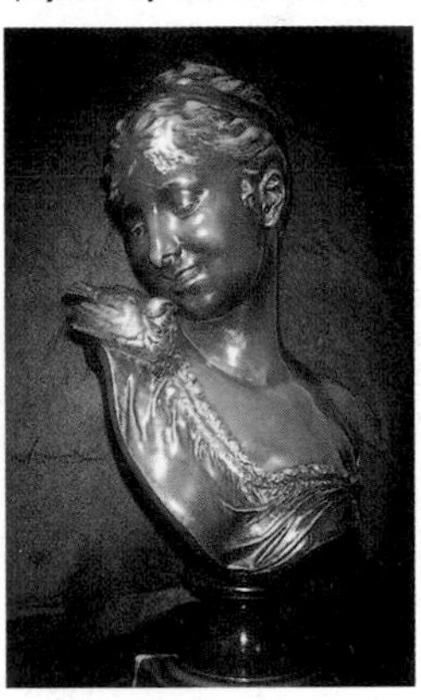

A bronze bust of a young woman, by Albert Carrier-Belleuse, French, c1880, 20½in (52cm) high.
£3,500–3,900
€5,100–5,700
$6,300–7,100 G&H
Carrier-Belleuse studied in Paris under David d'Angers at the Ecole de Beaux Arts from 1840, and exhibited at the Salon in 1851. He was highly regarded by Napoleon III who referred to him as 'Our Clodion'. He worked in every medium and his assistants at one time included Rodin and Mathurin Moreau.

A bronze group of Cupid and the Maiden, by A. Piquemal, signed, c1880, 16½in (42cm) high.
£410–490 / €600–720
$740–890 TEN

◀ **A bronze model of two horses,** by Jules Moigniez, entitled 'L'Accolade', French, c1880, 16½in 942cm) wide.
£6,300–7,000
€9,200–10,200
$11,400–12,600
⊞ G&H

A bronze figural group, by Louis Barrias, entitled 'Les Deux Soeurs', French, c1885, 10¾in (27.5cm) high.
£2,600–2,900
€3,800–4,200
$4,700–5,200 ⊞ G&H

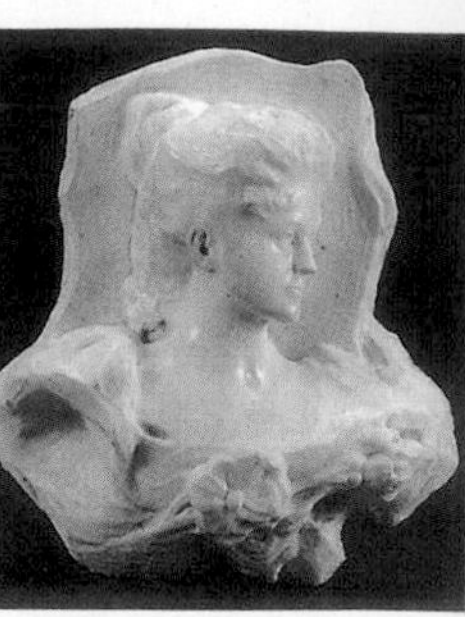

A relief-carved marble plaque, entitled 'Young Beauty', c1890, 8¼in (21cm) high.
£75–90 / €110–130
$135–160 ⚒ JAA

A bronze figure of a fisherwoman, by E. Picault, signed, French, late 19thC, 32½in (82.5cm) high.
£2,100–2,500
€3,050–3,650
$3,800–4,550 ⚒ NSal

A gilt-bronze figure of a girl seated on the head of a Sphinx, by Bofill, Spanish, c1890, 12in (30.5cm) high.
£1,450–1,650
€2,100–2,400
$2,650–3,000 ⊞ ANO

A bronze figure of a man, by Alfred Boucher, entitled 'Terrassier', French, c1890, 16¼in (41.5cm) high.
£5,800–6,400
€8,400–9,300
$10,500–11,600 ⊞ G&H

A bronze group of a girl with a dog and cat, by Fél Pierre Richard, entitled 'Une Mascotte', signed, French, c1890, 21in (53.5cm) high.
£3,400–3,800
€4,950–5,500
$6,200–6,900 ⊞ BeF

A bronze figure of a female Olympian, by A. E. Lewis, dated 1898, on a polished marble base, 19in (48.5cm) high.
£440–520 / €640–760
$800–940 ⚒ Bea

A marble figure of Joan of Arc, by Henri Michel Antoine Chapu, inscribed 'H. Chapu' and 'F. Barbedienne Editeur Paris', French, late 19thC, 12½in (32cm) high.
£1,550–1,850
€2,250–2,700
$2,800–3,350 ⚒ S(O)

◀ **A bronze group,** by Alfred Dubucand, entitled 'The Ostrich Hunt', French, c1894, 15in (38cm) high
£4,800–5,300
€7,000–7,700
$8,500–9,400
⊞ RGa

▶ **A pair of bronze figures,** entitled 'Harmonie' and 'Peinture', after Albert Ernest Carrier-Belleuse and Jean Paul Aube, on *faux* marble columns, French, c1900, 25½in (65cm) high.
£7,300–8,700
€10,700–12,700
$13,200–15,700
⚒ DN(BR)

◀ **A Carrara marble bust of a young woman,** c1900, 24in (61cm) high.
£1,300–1,550 / €1,900–2,250
$2,350–2,800 ⚒ WILK

A bronze figure of a girl on a seashell, by Emmanuel Villanis, entitled 'Jeune Femme sur un Coquillage', French, c1900.
£10,800–12,000
€15,800–17,500
$19,500–21,700 ⊞ G&H

◀ A bronze figure of a girl, by Georges Recipon, entitled 'Porte Bonheur', French, c1900, 6in (15cm) high.
£2,600–2,900
€3,800–4,200
$4,700–5,200
⊞ G&H

A bronze bust of Abraham Lincoln, by George Edwin Bissell, American, 1904, 31in (78.5cm) high.
£4,500–5,400
€6,600–7,900
$8,100–9,800 ⚒ DuM

▶ A gold-patinated-bronze figural group, by Mathurin Moreau, entitled 'Immortality', on a marble base, French, c1904, 41in (104cm) high.
£7,000–8,400
€10,200–12,300
$12,700–15,200 ⚒ WILK

A marble and alabaster bust of a young woman, by V. Mariani, c1910, 15in (38cm) high.
£440–520 / €640–760
$800–940 ⚒ TEN

▶ A bronze figure, by Dominique Alonzo, entitled 'The Newspaper Boy', Etling-Paris foundry mark, French, early 20thC, 13¾in (35cm) high.
£1,350–1,600
€1,950–2,350
$2,450–2,900 ⚒ Bea

A bronze group, by L. Graefner, entitled 'The Eagle Bearer', on a marble plinth, slight damage, signed, German, c1910, 22¾in (58cm) high.
£3,150–3,750
€4,600–5,500
$5,700–6,800 ⚒ Herm

An alabaster figural group of a woman carrying her slain son, after the model by Stephan-Abel Sinding, signed, German, 1900–25, 17¼in (44cm) high.
£1,550–1,850
€2,250–2,700
$2,800–3,350 ⚒ S(O)

A bronze figure of a seated man, by David McGill, entitled 'The Victor', 1920, 11¼in (28.5cm) high.
£3,000–3,300
€4,400–4,900
$5,400–6,000 ⊞ BeF

▶ A terracotta bust of a young man, by Ortis, signed, French, c1930, 15in (38cm) high.
£450–500 / €660–730
$810–910 ⊞ ASP

SCULPTURE

Metalware

Brass

A brass candlestick, c1475, 9in (23cm) high.
£1,350–1,500
€1,950–2,200
$2,400–2,700 ⊞ SEA

A pair of brass candlesticks, late 17thC, 7in (18cm) high.
£6,800–7,600
€9,900–11,100
$12,300–13,800 ⊞ KEY

A pair of brass candlesticks, c1820, 9¾in (25cm) high.
£100–115 / €150–170
$180–200 ⊞ F&F

◀ **A brass candlestick,** with a drip pan, c1670, 9in (23cm) high.
£630–700 / €900–1,000
$1,100–1,250 ⊞ F&F

A pair of gilt-brass candlesticks, by Abbott, modelled as ostriches with coronets, cast mark to bases, 19thC, 15¼in (38.5cm) high.
£470–560 / €690–820
$850–1,000 ⚒ DN(BR)

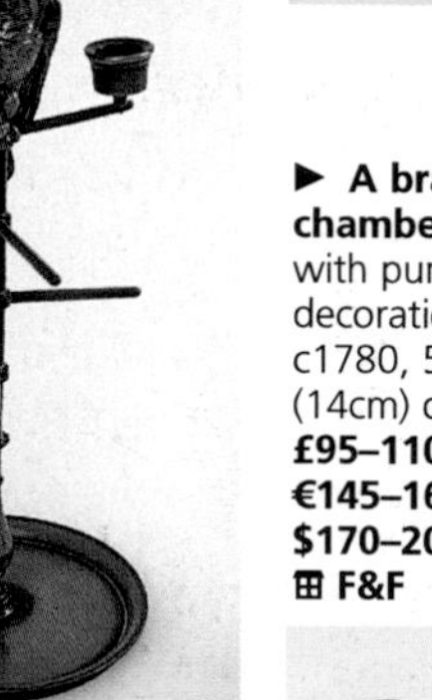

A Victorian brass candelabrum, modelled as a parrot on a perch, the hinged head match tidy flanked by a pair of sconces, 13in (33cm) high.
£190–220 / €280–330
$340–400 ⚒ G(L)

▶ **A brass chamberstick,** with punched decoration, c1780, 5½in (14cm) diam.
£95–110
€145–160
$170–200
⊞ F&F

◀ **A brass taper chamberstick,** c1820, 2¾in (7cm) diam.
£75–85
€110–125
$135–150
⊞ F&F

A Victorian brass doorstop, modelled as a gamekeeper and his dog, 17in (43cm) high.
£130–145 / €190–210
$235–260 ⊞ TOP

◀ **A brass oil lamp,** engraved 'Buckingham Palace' and 'No. 43', feet missing, 19thC, 4½in (11.5cm) diam.
£105–125
€155–185
$195–230 ⚒ G(L)

A brass urn, with repousée decoration, scrolled handles and three taps, on three feet, Dutch, early 18thC, 13¾in (335cm) high.
£230–270 / €340–400
$420–500 ⚒ WilP

◀ **An iron and brass warming pan,** c1650, 41in (104cm) long.
£880–980 / €1,300–1,450
$1,600–1,800 ⊞ SEA

Bronze

A pair of bronze figural bookends, by Edna I. Spencer, Gorham foundry, American, Rhode Island, c1920, 11¼in (28.5cm) high.
£1,600–1,900 / €2,350–2,750
$2,900–3,400 ⚒ DuM

► **A gilt-bronze étui,** with chased decoration, the hinged cover revealing a fitted interior including scissors, fruit knife and other items, the chased chatelaine belt clip hung with a pair of hinged thimble cases, possibly French or Dutch, mid-18thC, 7½in (19cm) long.
£700–840 / €1,000–1,200
$1,250–1,500 ⚒ HOLL

◄ **A bronze urn,** after the antique, the body set with masks, with entwined handles, 19thC, 17¼in (44cm) wide.
£890–1,050
€1,300–1,550
$1,600–1,900 ⚒ HOK

Copper

A copper jug, c1860, 15in (38cm) high.
£360–400 / €530–590
$650–720 ⊞ NEW

A copper kettle, 18thC, 12in (30.5cm) high.
£310–350 / €450–500
$560–630 ⊞ SEA

A pair of copper mantel ornaments, modelled as swans, 19thC, 7in (18cm) wide.
£135–150 / €195–220
$240–270 ⊞ SEA

◄ **A copper ale mug,** with a brass seam, c1790, 4½in (11.5cm) high.
£85–95
€125–140
$150–170
⊞ F&F

A Victorian copper and brass samovar, 17¼in (44cm) high.
£120–140 / €175–200
$220–250 ⚒ SWO

A copper tea canister, with crocodile-skin effect decoration, c1900, 7in (18cm) high.
£120–135 / €175–195
$210–240 ⊞ BS

A copper and brass tobacco box, engraved with a hunting scene and verse, the reverse with a boy fishing from a coracle, Dutch, 18thC, 7in (18cm) long.
£230–270 / €340–400
$420–500 ⚒ F&C

► **An embossed copper wine cooler,** Dutch, mid-18thC, 23¼in (59cm) wide.
£1,900–2,250
€2,750–3,300
$3,400–4,000
⚒ S(O)

Iron

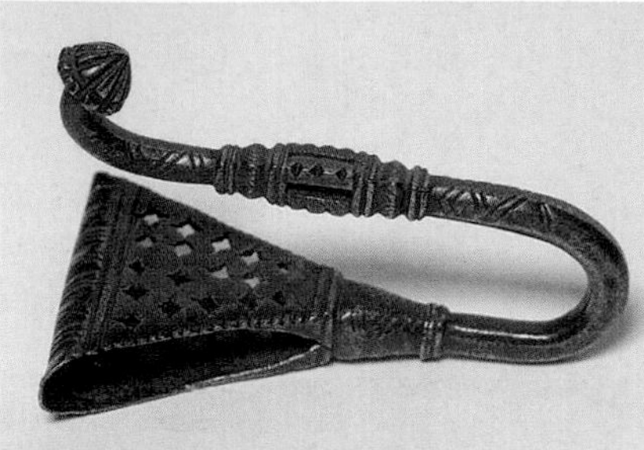

An iron belt hook, c1770, 4in (10cm) wide.
£250–280 / €370–410
$450–510 ⊞ SEA

◀ **A wrought-iron cross,** applied with fruiting vines, flowers and foliate scrolls, with Christ crucified, on a stone socle, Austrian, 18thC, 85½in (217cm) high.
£2,100–2,500
€3,050–3,650
$3,800–4,450
⚒ S(Am)

A wrought-iron hanging lamp, c1775, 16in (40.5cm) high.
£135–150
€195–220
$240–270
⊞ SEA

A sheet-iron and horn lantern, c1790, 12in (30.5cm) high.
£270–300 / €390–440
$490–540 ⊞ MMA

A cast-iron mortar, with initials, dated 1689, 7in (18cm) high.
£340–380 / €500–550
$620–690 ⊞ KEY

A cast-iron rush light holder, with an ash base, c1760, 8½in (21.5cm) high.
£430–480 / €630–700
$780–870 ⊞ MMA

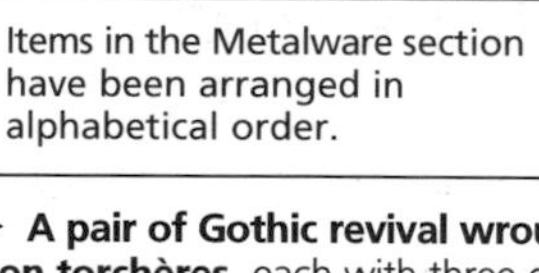

Items in the Metalware section have been arranged in alphabetical order.

▶ **A pair of Gothic revival wrought-iron torchères,** each with three candle sconces on a spiral-twist stem with stylized foliate scrolls, each base with two further candle holders, each with an iron snuffer and a wick trimmer, late 19thC, 63½in (161.5cm) high.
£2,250–2,700 / €3,300–3,950
$4,050–4,900 ⚒ S(O)

▶ **A wrought-iron floor-standing rush light,** late 18thC, 44in (112cm) high.
£650–720 / €950–1,050
$1,150–1,300 ⊞ KEY

Ormolu

A pair of ormolu six-light candelabra, the stems formed as cherubs seated on swagged columns, French, 19thC, 24in (61cm) high.
£1,750–2,100 / €2,550–3,050
$3,150–3,800 ⚒ HOK

An alabaster and ormolu centrepiece, the turned alabaster bowl with a gilt collar and lion-mask mounts with ring handles, on a cast base with four claw feet, 19thC, 11½in (29cm) high.
£820–980 / €1,200–1,450
$1,500–1,800 ⚒ WILK

An ormolu tazza, decorated with figures, putti and mythical beasts, Russian, late 19thC, 10in (27.5cm) high
£2,200–2,600 / €3,200–3,800
$4,000–4,700 ⚒ BUK(F)

Pewter

A pewter half-pint beaker, with ribbed decoration and engraved inscription, 19thC, 3½in (9cm) high.
£60–70 / €85–100
$110–125 ⚒ TMA

A pair of pewter candlesticks, 19thC, 9in (23cm) high.
£85–100 / €125–145
$155–180 ⚒ TMA

A pewter cup, c1800, 3½in (9cm) high.
£180–200 / €260–290
$320–360 ⊞ DML

► A pewter flagon, Continental, c1780, 10in (25.5cm) high.
£230–260 / €340–380
$420–470 ⊞ HWK

◄ A pewter cream jug, by James Dixon & Sons, 1842–51, 4½in (11.5cm) high.
£80–90 / €115–130
$145–165 ⊞ DML

A pewter jug, probably by W. Scott, Edinburgh, Scottish, c1800, 7½in (19cm) high.
£900–1,000 / €1,300–1,450
$1,650–1,800 ⊞ DML

► A pewter flagon, by John Brown, touchmark, Scottish, Edinburgh, late 18thC, 11in (28cm) high.
£1,300–1,450
€1,900–2,100
$2,350–2,600 ⊞ HWK

A pewter tappit hen measure, Scottish, c1800, 11in (28cm) high.
£1,250–1,400
€1,850–2,050
$2,250–2,550 ⊞ HWK

A pewter half-gill measure, by R. Mister, 1802–39, 2½in (6.5cm) high.
£50–60 / €75–85
$90–105 ⊞ DML

A pewter gill measure, the cover with a thumbpiece, early 18thC, 4in (10cm) high.
£540–600 / €790–880
$980–1,100 ⊞ DML

LOCATE THE SOURCE

The source of each illustration in Miller's can be found by checking the code letters below each caption with the Key to Illustrations, pages 778–784.

A pewter tappit hen measure, Scottish, 18thC, 7½in (19cm) high.
£610–680 / €890–990
$1,100–1,250 ⊞ KEY

A 'tappit hen' or Scots pint is equal to three Imperial pints. The shape resembles pewter measures from Normandy, and the name may be derived from the French quart measure 'Topynett'. Tappit hens are seldom found with makers' marks.

A pewter gill measure, by L. & R. Merry, Irish, Dublin, 1845–80, 3½in (9cm) high.
£70–80 / €100–110
$125–140 ⊞ DML

A pair of pewter measures, Irish, c1880, larger 6in (15cm) high.
£260–290 / €380–420
$470–520 ⊞ MFB

A pewter footed half-pint mug, by Boulton & Wilde, Wigan, early 19thC, 4½in (11.5cm) high.
£135–150 / €195–220
$240–270 ⊞ DML

A set of six Victorian pewter pint mugs, inscribed 'R. Adams Viper's Castle', some damage.
£120–140 / €180–200
$220–250 ⚒ WW

A pewter plate, by Jonas Durand, early 18thC, 9¾in (25cm) diam.
£900–1,000 / €1,300–1,450
$1,600–1,800 ⊞ DML

A pewter porringer, c1700, 7½in (19cm) wide.
£720–800 / €1,050–1,200
$1,300–1,450 ⊞ DML

A pewter spoon, with a baluster knop, Dutch, 16th–17thC, 7in (18cm) long.
£135–150 / €195–220
$240–270 ⊞ DML

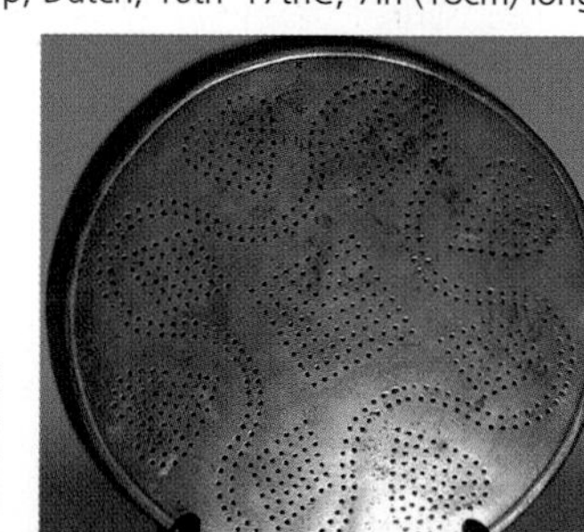

► A pewter straining plate, by Alexander Cleeve, London, c1730, 10¾in (27.5cm) diam.
£540–600 / €790–880
$1,000–1,100 ⊞ DML

A pewter quart tankard, with a domed cover, c1690, 10¾in (27.5cm) high.
£3,600–4,000 / €5,300–5,900
$6,500–7,200 ⊞ DML

A pewter tankard, with a domed cover, stamped 'S', c1710, 8in (20.5cm) high.
£1,350–1,550 / €2,000–2,250
$2,350–2,800 ⊞ KEY

◄ A pewter tankard, by James Kinnieburgh, the cover with a twin-cusped thumbpiece, inscribed with owner's initials, makers mark 'IK', touchmark, Scottish, Glasgow, c1800, 10in (25.5cm) high.
£1,300–1,450 / €1,900–2,100
$2,350–2,600 ⊞ HWK

Toleware

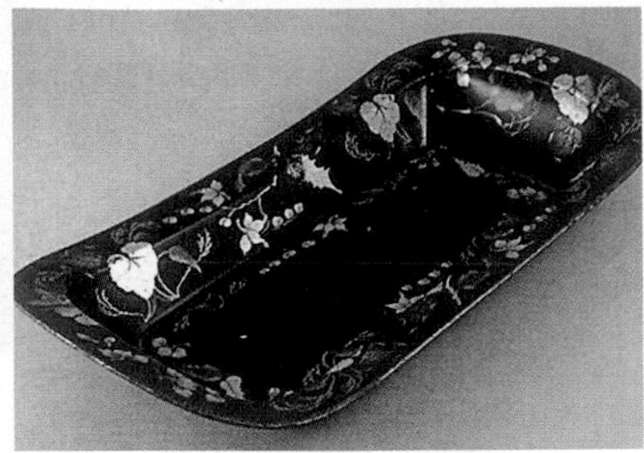

A toleware bread dish, decorated with gilt insects and foliage, 19thC, 15¾in (40cm) wide.
£70–80 / €100–110
$125–140 WW

A pair of toleware figures, Austrian, c1850, 13½in (34.5cm) high.
£470–560 / €690–820
$850–1,000 SWO

A toleware tea canister, c1900, 16in (40.5cm) high.
£135–150 / €195–220
$240–270 JUN

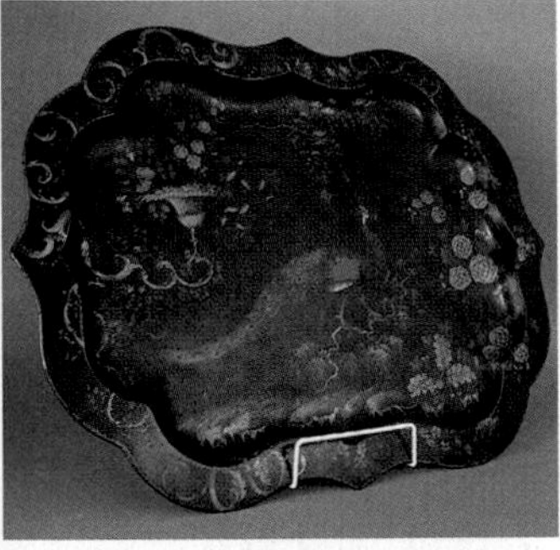

A toleware tray, painted with birds and flowers, 19thC, 25½in (65cm) wide.
£200–240 / €290–350
$360–430 BWL

A toleware tray, the pierced gallery with integral handles, painted and gilt-decorated with a view of a stately house and parkland, 19thC, 19½in (49.5cm) wide.
£120–140 / €180–200
$220–250 PFK

A toleware tray, painted with a pair of *ho-o* birds and scattered floral sprays, late 19thC, 31½in (80cm) wide.
£970–1,100 / €1,400–1,600
$1,750–2,000 SK

Miscellaneous

A gilt-metal door stop, in the form of a horse, late 19thC, 12in (30.5cm) wide.
£320–360 / €470–530
$580–650 RGa

A tin tobacco box, the cover painted with a Napoleonic battle scene, c1810, 4¾in (12cm) wide.
£135–150 / €195–220
$240–270 MB

A pair of Victorian gilt-metal three-light girandoles, each mirror back within a cast leaf, twig and berry border, with three naturalistic branches, 17¾in (45cm) high.
£420–500 / €610–730
$760–910 RTo

A gilt-metal posy holder, with a mother-of-pearl handle, probably French, late 19thC, 7in (18cm) long.
£290–340 / €420–500
$520–620 MAR

A lead tobacco jar, the cover with a knop in the form of a man's head, c1760, 5in (12.5cm) diam.
£130–145 / €190–210
$230–260 F&F

◄ **A bell metal tobacco jar,** c1840, 6in (15cm) high.
£400–450 / €580–660
$720–810 RGe

Papier-Mâché

A papier-mâché box, decorated with a boy serenading a spinner, Russian, c1882, 4in (10cm) diam.
£270–300 / €390–440
$490–540 ⊞ RdeR

A pair of papier-mâché coasters, with gilt decoration, c1840, 5½in (14cm) diam.
£380–430 / €560–630
$690–780 ⊞ CB

A papier-mâché snuff box, the cover painted with a character in a wig, 18thC, 4in (10cm) diam.
£360–400 / €530–590
$650–720 ⊞ RdeR

A papier-mâché snuff box, by Stobwasser, decorated with a young woman in a landscape, the interior with an inscription and numbered 8681, German, 19thC, 3½in (9cm) wide.
£470–560 / €690–820
$850–1,000 ⚒ CHTR

A papier-mâché box, the cover decorated with a framed painted scene of a balloon in a crowded town square, with a tortoiseshell interior, French, 19thC, 3in (7.6cm) diam.
£200–240 / €290–350
$360–430 ⚒ G(L)

A papier-mâché and lacquer cruet frame, with a brass handle and seven later bottles, c1800, 8½in (21.5cm) wide.
£175–210 / €260–310
$320–380 ⚒ WW

A papier-mâché snuff box, with a painted cover, early 19thC, 4in (10cm) wide.
£500–560 / €730–820
$900–1,000 ⊞ WAA

A papier-mâché snuff box, the hinged cover painted with a woman in her dressing room, the interior inscribed 'Corset', c1850, 3½in (9cm) wide.
£300–360 / €440–530
$540–650 ⚒ WW

A papier-mâché box, decorated with a horse at a graveside, Russian, c1913, 5½in (14cm) wide.
£270–300 / €390–440
$490–540 ⊞ RdeR

A papier-mâché matchbox cover, by Lukutin, Russian, c1860, 2½in (6.5cm) wide.
£270–300 / €390–440
$490–540 ⊞ RdeR

A papier-mâché snuff box, engraved and painted with a face, c1850, 3in (7.5cm) wide.
£380–430 / €550–630
$690–780 ⊞ RdeR

A Victorian papier-mâché tea caddy, japanned and gilt-decorated in rococo-style with birds and exotic flowers, the hinged cover revealing two lidded compartments, on bun feet, 9½in (24cm) wide.
£430–510 / €630–740
$780–920 ⚒ L&E

A papier-mâché tea caddy, the cover decorated with a girl by a fence, Russian, c1860, 5½in (14cm) wide.
£310–350 / €470–520
$570–630 ⊞ RdeR

A papier-mâché tea caddy, with painted and gilt decoration, c1880, 8in (20.5cm) wide.
£370–420 / €540–610
$670–760 ⊞ WAA

A papier-mâché tray, painted with a scene of a ruined abbey, with gilt and lacquer decoration, c1840, 32in (81.5cm) wide.
£1,050–1,200 / €1,550–1,750
$1,900–2,150 ⊞ GGD

A papier-mâché tray, by Jennens & Bettridge, painted with a peacock on a balustrade and a *ho-o* bird in flight in a wooded landscape, late 19thC, 31½in (80cm) wide.
£1,200–1,400 / €1,750–2,050
$2,100–2,500 ⚒ SK

A papier-mâché tea caddy, decorated with children, Russian, c1860, 6in (15cm) wide.
£450–500 / €660–730
$810–910 ⊞ RdeR

A papier-mâché tea caddy, the cover decorated with a winter scene, Russian, c1885, 4in (10cm) wide.
£360–400 / €530–590
$650–720 ⊞ JTS

A Victorian papier-mâché tray, by Jennens & Bettridge, painted with roses and flowers in a gilt-scrolled border, stamped mark, 31¼in (79cm) wide.
£880–1,050 / €1,300–1,550
$1,600–1,900 ⚒ DN

A papier-mâché writing slope, the gilt and mother-of-pearl decoration with three painted plaques of cherubs, the interior with a velvet writing tablet and inkwells, c1865, 13in (33cm) wide.
£1,800–2,000 / €2,600–2,900
$3,250–3,600 ⊞ JTS

A papier-mâché double tea caddy, with mother-of-pearl and gilt decoration, c1875, 8¼in (21cm) wide.
£900–1,000 / €1,300–1,450
$1,600–1,800 ⊞ JTS

A George III papier-mâché tray, by Clay, London, painted with a Claudesque scene, impressed mark, 28½in (72.5cm) wide.
£1,300–1,550 / €1,900–2,250
$2,350–2,800 ⚒ SWO

A Victorian papier-mâché tray, with rococo-style gilt foliate scroll decoration with exotic birds and an urn of flowers, 30½in (77.5cm) wide.
£175–210 / €260–310
$320–380 ⚒ PFK

A papier-mâché tray, by Vishniakov, painted with romantic scenes, marked with six Medals of Merit, Russian, c1887, 7½in (19cm) square.
£400–450 / €580–660
$720–810 ⊞ RdeR
The most talented artists were awarded Medals of Merit for their wares. Items with six Medals of Merit were of the highest quality.

Insurance values

Always insure your valuable antiques for the cost of replacing them with similar items, regardless of the original price paid. Both dealers and auctioneers can provide a valuation service for a fee.

Treen

A fruitwood apple corer, c1770, 6in (15cm) long.
£430–480 / €630–700
$780–870 ⊞ SEA

A George III satinwood table-top book carrier, inlaid with boxwood stringing, 18in (45.5cm) wide.
£2,250–2,700 / €3,300–3,950
$4,100–4,900 ⚒ L

An arbutus wood inlaid book slide, Irish, c1870, 15in (38cm) wide.
£360–400 / €520–580
$650–720 ⊞ STA

A Shaker wood-gathering basket, American, early 20thC, 18in (45.5cm) high.
£260–310 / €380–450
$470–560 ⚒ DuM

A Victorian rosewood book stand, the pierced three-quarter gallery above a surface inlaid with various woods, on bun feet, 17¾in (45cm) wide.
£470–560 / €690–820
$850–1,000 ⚒ RTo

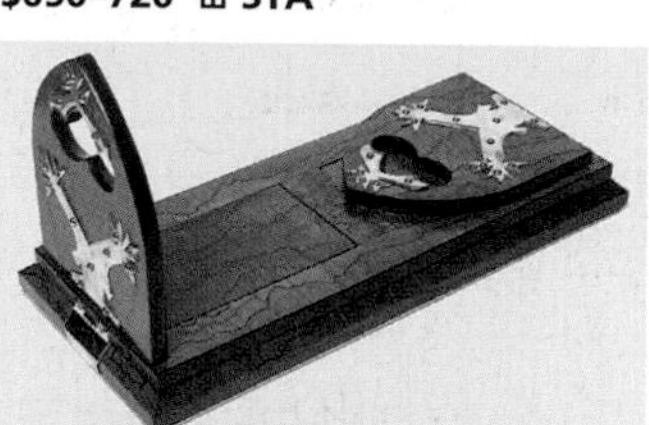

A Betjeman's patent self-closing walnut book slide, with maker's name and patent number, c1900, 13in (33cm) wide.
£250–280 / €370–410
$450–510 ⊞ PEZ

A lignum vitae wassail bowl, with ring-turned decoration, on a spreading foot, 17th/18thC, 7¾in (19.5cm) high.
£2,700–3,200
€3,950–4,650
$4,900–5,800 ⚒ HYD

A carved fruitwood box, French, 17thC, 8in (20.5cm) wide.
£430–480 / €630–700
$780–870 ⊞ SEA

A walnut trinket box, in the form of a house with a crenellated roof, with two drawers, Continental, 19thC, 9in (23cm) wide.
£350–420 / €510–610
$630–760 ⚒ DN(BR)

A pair of rosewood adjustable candle stands, c1835, 9¾in (25cm) high.
£2,150–2,550
€3,150–3,700
$3,900–4,600 ⚒ S(O)

A pair of painted, carved and turned limewood pricket candle stands, converted for use as electric table lamps, early 19thC, 14in (35.5cm) high.
£260–310 / €380–450
$470–560 ⚒ TMA

An arbutus wood card case, decorated with scenes of Blarney Castle and Muchloss Abbey, Irish, c1860, 4in (10cm) wide.
£145–160 / €210–240
$260–290 ⊞ SiA

► **A carved wood and horn coat rack,** carved as a rabbit in shooting dress with a shotgun on his shoulder, the legs formed from antelope horns, German, Bavarian, 19thC, 10¾in (27.5cm) high.
£590–700
€850–1,000
$1,050–1,250
⚒ AH

◄ **A mahogany church collection box,** c1830, 31in (79cm) long.
£220–250
€340–380
$400–450 ⊞ **WAA**

A wooden container, in the form of a portly gentleman, c1860, 5in (12.5cm) high.
£200–230 / €290–340
$360–410 ⊞ **SAT**

A carved coconut and turned lignum vitae commemorative goblet, the bowl carved with portraits of William and Mary, their cyphers and a stylized coat-of-arms, c1700, 7in (18cm) high.
£4,550–5,400
€6,600–7,900
$8,200–9,800 ⚒ **S**

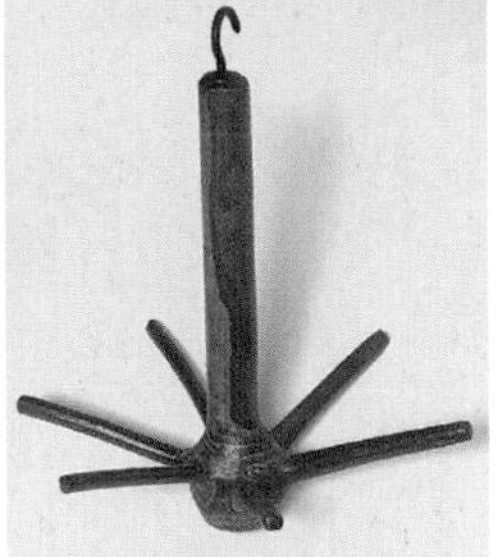

A larch-wood hanger, Continental, 19thC, 16in (40.5cm) long.
£430–480 / €630–700
$780–870 ⊞ **SEA**

► **A pair of walnut knife urns,** c1860, 28in (71cm) high.
£7,600–8,500
€11,100–12,400
$13,800–15,400 ⊞ **HAA**

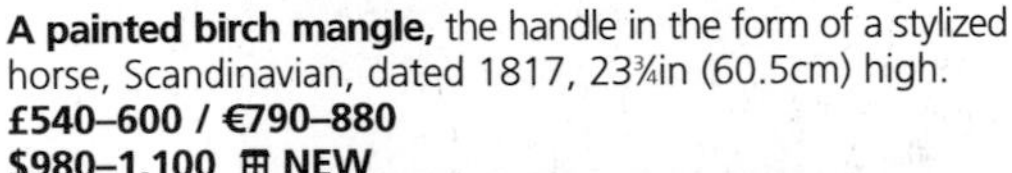

A painted birch mangle, the handle in the form of a stylized horse, Scandinavian, dated 1817, 23¾in (60.5cm) high.
£540–600 / €790–880
$980–1,100 ⊞ **NEW**

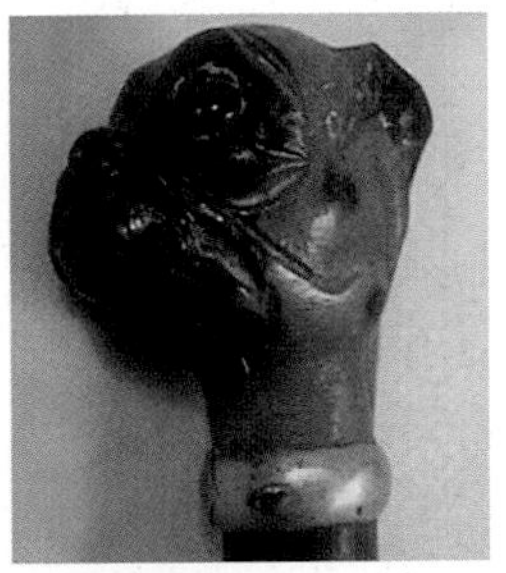

A carved blonde wood paper knife, the terminal in the form of a pug's head with glass eyes and a plated collar, c1900, 10¾in (27.5cm) long.
£130–155 / €185–220
$240–280 ⚒ **DN(BR)**

A fruitwood pestle and mortar, 19thC, 8in (20.5cm) high.
£240–270 / €350–390
$430–490 ⊞ **DOA**

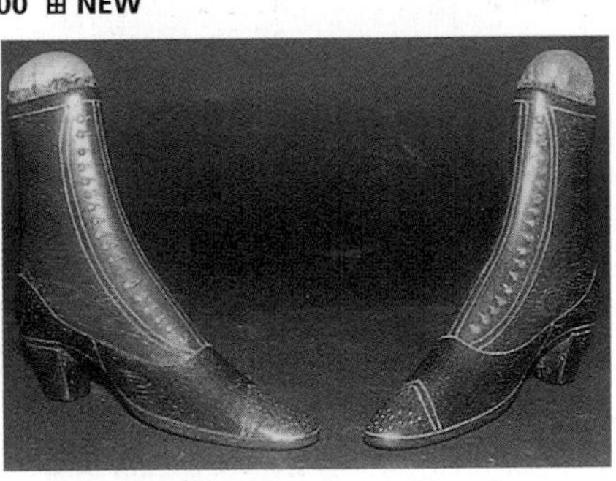

A pair of late Victorian hardwood padded pin cushions, in the form of high-buttoned boots, the two different woods simulating different leathers, with brass piqué details, 3½in (9cm) high.
£230–270 / €340–400
$420–500 ⚒ **PFK**

A fruitwood pocket watch holder, carved as a longcase clock, c1810, 9¾in (25cm) high.
£450–500 / €660–730
$810–910 ⊞ **F&F**

A fruitwood sewing casket, in the form of a piano, some sewing accessories missing, c1820, 12in (30.5cm) wide.
£900–1,000 / €1,300–1,450
$1,600–1,800 ⊞ **RdeR**

◄ **A rosewood sewing compendium,** the turned handle with a reel support, with two pincushions and a thimble, 19thC, 5in (12.5cm) high.
£150–180 / €220–260
$280–330 ⚒ **WW**

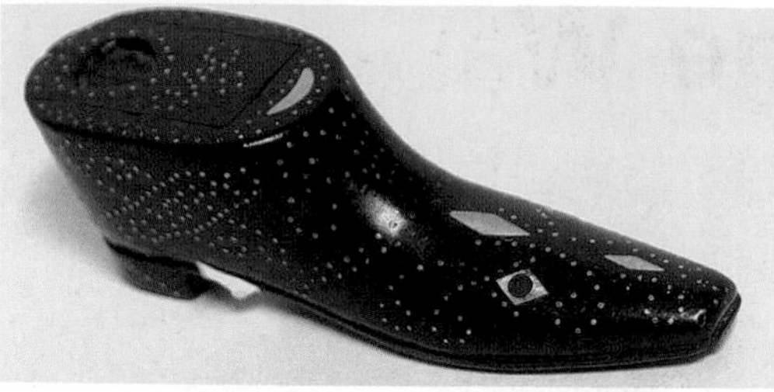

A mahogany snuff box, in the form of a shoe inlaid with mother-of-pearl, dated 1840, 4in (10cm) wide.
£360–400 / €530–590
$650–720 ⊞ NEW

◄ A Jacobite silver-mounted laburnum snuff mull, the domed cover with a chain attachment and silver snuff spoon inscribed 'God Save the King 1705, I. R. VII', and depicting crossed swords and sceptre with a crown, early 18thC, 3½in (9cm) high.
£1,400–1,650 / €2,050–2,400
$2,550–3,000 ⚒ F&C

A burr-vine or rootwood staff, the terminal carved with a male head with inset glass or porcelain eyes, possibly Irish, 19thC, 63in (160cm) long.
£500–600 / €730–870
$900–1,050 ⚒ PFK

◄ A walnut staybust, with carved decoration, dated 1786, 14in (35.5cm) long.
£1,050–1,200
€1,550–1,750
$1,900–2,150 ⊞ NEW

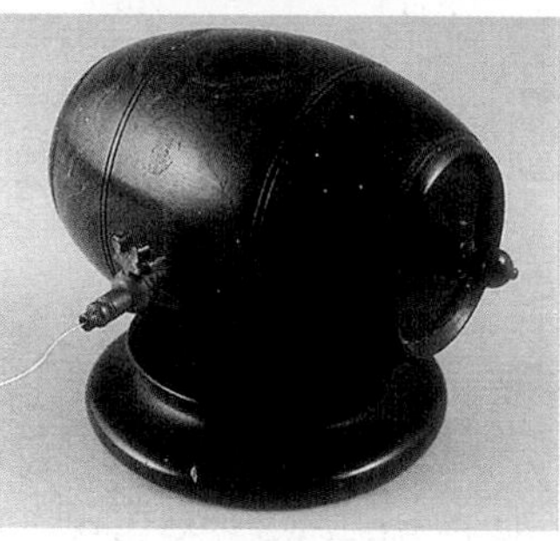

A turned lignum vitae string barrel, the brass tap with a cutter, 19thC, 3½in (9cm) high.
£165–195 / €240–290
$300–360 ⚒ WW

A lignum vitae beehive string box, c1880, 4in (10cm) high.
£155–175 / €230–260
$280–320 ⊞ SAT

A pair of stained lacewood tea caddies, banded throughout with chequer stinging and zigzag inlay, with a foil-lined interior, finials later, restored, damaged, late 18thC, 9¾in (25cm) high.
£5,400–6,500 / €7,900–9,500
$9,800–11,800 ⚒ S
Lacewood is the timber of the plane tree.

A fruitwood tea canister, in the form of an apple, c1820, 5in (12.5cm) high.
£3,150–3,500 / €4,600–5,100
$5,700–6,300 ⊞ RdeR

An inlaid mahogany tray, with a piecrust edge, crossbanded top and carved shell handles, c1780, 30in (76cm) wide.
£720–800 / €1,000–1,150
$1,300–1,450 ⊞ WAA

A mahogany tray, with a scalloped edge, c1810, 21in (53.5cm) wide.
£300–340 / €440–500
$540–620 ⊞ WAA

A burr-walnut tray, with a brass gallery, c1880, 22in (56cm) wide.
£610–680 / €890–990
$1,100–1,250 ⊞ GEO

An inlaid mahogany tray, with brass handles, c1900, 24in (61cm) wide.
£310–350 / €450–510
$560–630 ⊞ GGD

An oak writing box, in the form of a book, c1840, 17in (43cm) wide.
£340–380 / €500–550
$620–690 ⊞ PeN

Tunbridge Ware

A Tunbridge ware basket, with bird's-eye maple veneer and floral mosaic, c1870, 8½in (21.5cm) diam.
£720–800 / €1,000–1,150
$1,300–1,450 ⊞ AMH

A Tunbridge ware box, inlaid with a print of Chain Pier and Marine Parade, Brighton, c1820, 7in (18cm) wide.
£270–300 / €390–440
$490–540 ⊞ RdeR

A Tunbridge ware box, with velvet lining, c1880, 4in (10cm) wide.
£260–290 / €380–420
$470–520 ⊞ PrB

A Tunbridge ware cribbage board, decorated with foliate and geometric bands on a rosewood ground, late 19thC, 10in (25.5cm) wide.
£280–330 / €410–480
$510–600 ⚒ G(L)

A Tunbridge ware jewellery box, decorated with a view of Eridge Castle, 19thC, 7in (18cm) wide.
£260–310 / €380–450
$470–560 ⚒ G(L)

A Tunbridge ware Chalybeate stained bird's-eye maple Besique box, with a divided interior for four packs of cards, 19thC, 9in (23cm) wide.
£290–340 / €420–500
$520–620 ⚒ DN(BR)

Veneers used in Tunbridge ware were sometimes immersed in Chalybeate spring water taken from the well at The Pantiles, Tunbridge Wells. This changed the colour of veneers such as maple or ash from yellow/brown to grey, although time and repolishing usually removes the grey effect.

A Tunbridge ware rosewood box, by Robert Russell, with stylized oak leaf marquetry, the base with tartan paper and maker's label, slight damage, 19thC, 8½in (21.5cm) wide.
£1,600–1,900 / €2,350–2,750
$2,900–3,450 ⚒ DN(BR)

A Tunbridge ware bracelet, c1870, 3¾in (9.5cm) diam.
£300–330 / €440–490
$540–600 ⊞ AMH

A Tunbridge ware coromandel jewellery box, possibly by Nye, the lid with an anemone spray mosaic within mosaic banding, 19thC, 3¼in (8.5cm) wide.
£230–270 / €340–400
$420–500 ⚒ DN(BR)

A Tunbridge ware bookmark, in the form of a teardrop, c1880, 3½in (9cm) long.
£220–250 / €320–360
$400–450 ⊞ AMH

A Victorian Tunbridge ware and rosewood box, decorated with floral sprays within geometric banded reserves, 8in (20.5cm) wide.
£300–360 / €440–530
$540–650 ⚒ G(B)

A pair of Tunbridge ware cloak buttons, c1860, 1in (2.5cm) wide.
£360–400 / €530–590
$650–720 ⊞ AMH

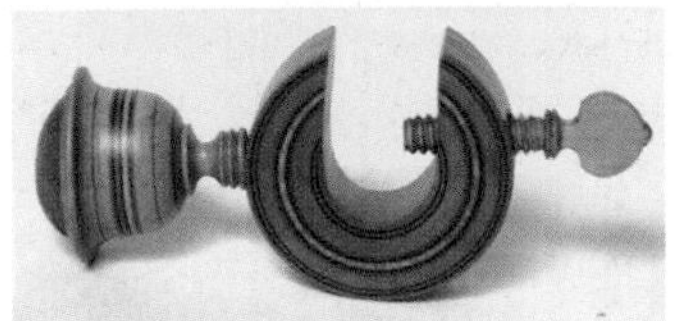

A Tunbridge ware clamp, with painted decoration, c1820, 6in (15cm) high.
£90–100 / €130–145
$160–180 ⊞ RdeR

A Tunbridge ware coromandel jewellery cabinet, by T. Barton late Nye, the top with a mosaic of roses, the hinged doors with similar flower sprays enclosing three mosaic-banded drawers with tesserae knobs, feet missing, 19thC, 7in (18cm) high.
£1,050–1,250 / €1,550–1,850
$1,900–2,250 ⚒ DN(BR)

A Tunbridge ware tatting box, inlaid with the word 'Tatting' within mosaic borders, c1870, 4in (10cm) wide.
£220–250 / €320–360
$400–450 ⊞ VB

Tatting is a type of lace made by looping threads of cotton or linen with a hand shuttle.

A Tunbridge ware match box holder, in the form of a book, with three drawers, 19thC, 3¾in (9.5cm) wide.
£230–270 / €340–400
$420–500 ⚒ DN(BR)

A Tunbridge ware needle case, in the form of a knife box, c1880, 2¼in (5.5cm) high.
£175–195 / €260–290
$310–350 ⊞ VB

◄ A Tunbridge ware needle case, inlaid with a mosaic butterfly, c1860, 3¼in (8.5cm) wide.
£155–175 / €230–260
$280–310 ⊞ AMH

A Tunbridge ware propelling pencil, c1850, 4¼in (11cm) long.
£175–195 / €260–290
$310–350 ⊞ VB

A Tunbridge ware rosewood pen tray, by T. Barton late Nye, the sides with a mosaic flower band, the base with a paper label, 19thC, 9¾in (25cm) wide.
£640–760 / €930–1,100
$1,200–1,400 ⚒ DN(BR)

A Tunbridge ware picture, attributed to Henry Hollamby, depicting a view of The Pantiles, Tunbridge Wells, c1870, 9 x 10½in (23 x 26.5cm), in an Oxford-style Tunbridge ware frame.
£1,000–1,100 / €1,450–1,600
$1,800–2,000 ⊞ PGO

A Tunbridge ware picture, depicting Shakespeare's birthplace, c1870, 8 x 9½in (20.5 x 24cm), in an Oxford-style Tunbridge ware frame.
£720–800 / €1,000–1,150
$1,300–1,450 ⊞ AMH

A Tunbridge ware pin cushion, in the form of a coffee pot, c1840, 1in (2.5cm) diam.
£180–200 / €260–290
$320–360 ⊞ VB

A Tunbridge ware pin holder, in the form of a miniature table, marked 'Weymouth 1859', 1¾in (4.5cm) diam.
£145–165 / €210–240
$270–300 ⊞ VB

A Tunbridge ware pin cushion, in the form of a kettle, c1840, 2in (5cm) diam.
£180–200 / €260–290
$320–360 ⊞ VB

A Tunbridge ware scent box, attributed to Thomas Barton, with three bottles, c1870, 6½in (16.5cm) wide.
£810–900 / €1,200–1,350
$1,450–1,650 ⊞ AMH

► A Tunbridge ware stamp box, decorated with a stag, c1860, 1½in (4cm) wide.
£220–250 / €320–360
$400–450 ⊞ VB

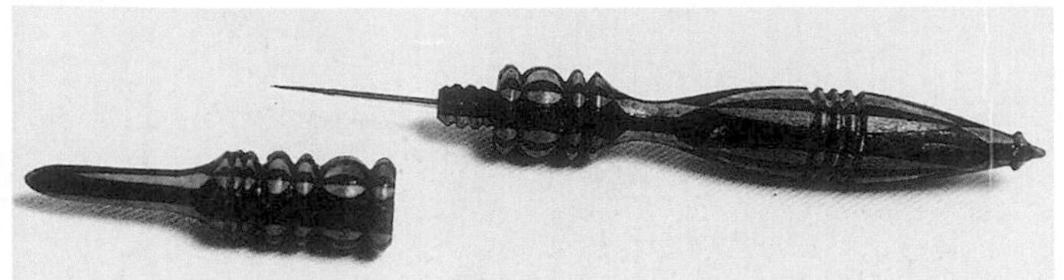

A Tunbridge ware stiletto, c1850, 3¼in (8.5cm) long.
£155–175 / €230–260
$280–310 ⊞ VB
This type of Tunbridge ware was also known as stickware.

A Tunbridge ware tape measure, in the form of a cottage with painted decoration, c1800, 1½in (4cm) high.
£220–250 / €320–360
$400–450 ⊞ VB

A Tunbridge ware tape measure, with painted decoration, c1820, 2½in (6.5cm) high.
£180–200 / €260–290
$320–360 ⊞ RdeR

A Tunbridge ware tea caddy, decorated with Van Dyke veneers, c1825, 12in (30.5cm) wide.
£1,700–1,900 / €2,500–2,750
$3,100–3,450 ⊞ HAA

A Tunbridge ware rosewood tea caddy, the top with a cube pattern within a mosaic flower band, the interior decorated with a mosaic band and fitted with two caddies, sugar bowl missing, 19thC, 12½in (32cm) wide.
£560–670 / €820–980
$1,000–1,200 ⚒ DN(BR)

► **A Tunbridge ware tea caddy,** with stick marquetry, decorated with a view of Eridge Castle and floral banding, c1860, 10¾in (27.5cm) wide.
£1,650–1,850
€2,400–2,700
$3,000–3,350 ⊞ JTS

A Tunbridge ware rosewood trinket box, with a lift-out tray, c1855, 4½in (11.5cm) wide.
£250–280 / €370–410
$450–510 ⊞ AMH

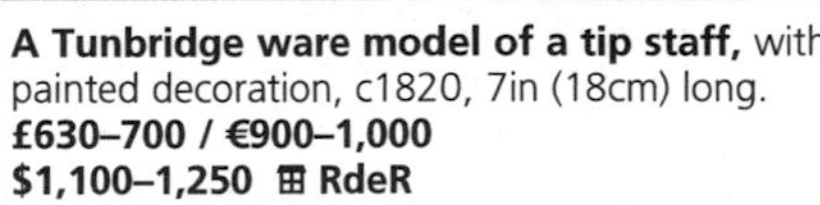

A Tunbridge ware model of a tip staff, with painted decoration, c1820, 7in (18cm) long.
£630–700 / €900–1,000
$1,100–1,250 ⊞ RdeR

Items in the Tunbridge Ware section have been arranged in alphabetical order.

A Tunbridge ware coromandel thermometer stand, by Edmund Nye, the ivory scale engraved 'E. Nye Tunbridge Wells', slight damage, 19thC, 6¼in (16cm) high.
£330–390 / €480–570
$600–710 ⚒ DN(BR)

A Tunbridge ware waxer, with stickware marquetry, c1850, 1in (2.5cm) high.
£85–95 / €125–140
$150–170 ⊞ VB

A Victorian Tunbridge ware writing slope, depicting Hever Castle within floral borders, the interior with two lidded glass bottles, a pen tray, a lidded compartment and slopes, with a hinged velvet-lined surface, 18½in (47cm) wide.
£1,000–1,200 / €1,450–1,750
$1,800–2,150 ⚒ WW

Boxes

A walnut lace box, with oyster-veneered cover, c1695, 19in (48.5cm) wide.
£1,050–1,200 / €1,550–1,750
$1,900–2,150 ⊞ PeN

A mahogany tea caddy, with brass fittings, c1775, 11in (28cm) wide.
£210–250 / €310–370
$380–450 ⊞ SAT

A shagreen knife box, with 16 pieces of silver cutlery, by Sykes & Co, 1784, 12½in (32cm) high.
£1,100–1,250 / €1,600–1,850
$2,000–2,250 ⊞ JTS

A satinwood tea caddy, with tulipwood crossbanding and ebony and boxwood stringing, inlaid with a floral panel, c1785, 5½in (14cm) wide.
£360–400 / €520–580
$650–720 ⊞ SAT

A mahogany tea caddy, with three compartments, mid-18thC, 9in (23cm) wide.
£610–680 / €890–990
$1,100–1,250 ⊞ WAA

A mahogany tea caddy, with brass fittings, c1780, 9in (23cm) wide.
£270–300 / €390–440
$490–540 ⊞ DEB

A mahogany tea caddy, the quarter-veneered panels with purple heart crossbanding and inlaid with oval floral inlays, c1785, 8in (20.5cm) wide.
£290–330 / €420–480
$520–600 ⊞ SAT

An ivory snuff box, decorated with an enamel miniature, French, c1790, 2½in (6.5cm) diam.
£220–250 / €320–370
$400–450 ⊞ MB

A George III silver-mounted tortoiseshell *bombé* tea caddy, the fitted interior with silver braid, enclosing two canisters and a sugar box by Samuel Taylor, London 1770, slight damage, 10in (25.5cm) wide.
£11,200–13,400 / €16,400–19,600
$20,300–24,300 ⚒ F&C

A harewood tea caddy, with satinwood panels and tulipwood crossbanding, c1780, 5in (12.5cm) high.
£1,700–1,900 / €2,500–2,750
$3,100–3,450 ⊞ HAA

A harewood tea caddy, inlaid with burr-yew, with a removable canister and later glass sugar bowl, c1785, 9in (23cm) wide.
£1,150–1,300 / €1,700–1,900
$2,100–2,350 ⊞ JTS

A mahogany box, inlaid with ivory, satinwood, kingwood, ebony and boxwood banding, c1790, 9in (23cm) wide.
£140–160 / €200–230
$250–290 ⊞ GGD

A mother-of-pearl tea caddy, French, c1790, 4in (10cm) high.
£2,000–2,250 / €2,900–3,300
$3,600–4,050 ⊞ JTS

A japanned box, worn, Italian, Venice, 1750–1800, 14¼in (36cm) wide.
£5,300–6,300 / €7,700–9,200
$9,600–11,400 ⚒ S(Mi)

A George III tortoiseshell and *piqué* toothpick case, with floral decoration and brass thumbpiece, 3½in (9cm) long.
£190–220 / €280–320
$340–400 ⚒ WW

A satin-birch tea caddy, with two compartments, c1790, 5in (12.5cm) high.
£1,500–1,700 / €2,200–2,500
$2,700–3,100 ⊞ HAA

A George III mahogany tea caddy, inlaid with a shell patera, 4¾in (12cm) wide.
£1,050–1,250 / €1,550–1,850
$1,900–2,250 ⚒ CHTR

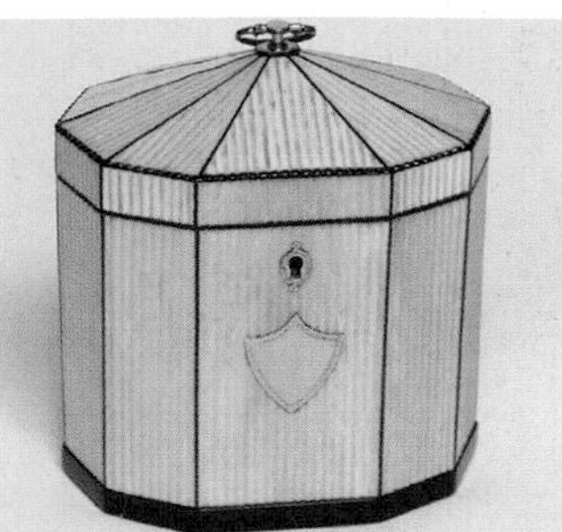

A gold-mounted ivory tea caddy, c1790, 5in (12.5cm) high.
£5,400–6,000 / €7,900–8,800
$9,800–11,000 ⊞ BBo

◄ **A George III silver-mounted shagreen tea caddy,** the velvet-lined interior with two glass jars and stoppers, 6in (15cm) wide.
£2,800–3,350 / €4,100–4,900
$5,100–6,100 ⚒ LFA

A mahogany knife box, with painted decoration, c1810, 23in (58.5cm) high.
£720–800 / €1,050–1,150
$1,300–1,450 ⊞ PeN

A burr-yew sewing box, with boxwood inlay and rosewood stringing, c1810, 11in (28cm) wide.
£210–250 / €310–370
$380–450 ⊞ SAT

A Regency mother-of-pearl tea caddy, with two compartments, 8in (20.5cm) wide.
£260–310 / €380–450
$470–560 ⚒ L&E

A brass-bound morocco leather document box, c1820, 15in (38cm) wide.
£210–240 / €310–350
$380–430 ⊞ DEB

A parquetry tea caddy, inlaid with boxwood and ebonized stringing, the interior with two compartments and a secret drawer, early 19thC, 9½in (24cm) wide.
£940–1,100 / €1,350–1,600
$1,700–2,000 ⚒ GAK

A satin-maple tea caddy, c1835, 9in (23cm) wide.
£1,100–1,250 / €1,600–1,850
$2,000–2,250 ⊞ JTS

A Regency penwork paintbox, with fitted interior, 10¾in (27.5cm) wide.
£400–480 / €580–700
$720–870 ⚒ GH

A rosewood sewing box, with boxwood inlay, fitted drawer and pincushion top, on gilt claw-and-ball feet, c1815, 9in (23cm) wide.
£180–200 / €260–290
$320–360 ⊞ SAT

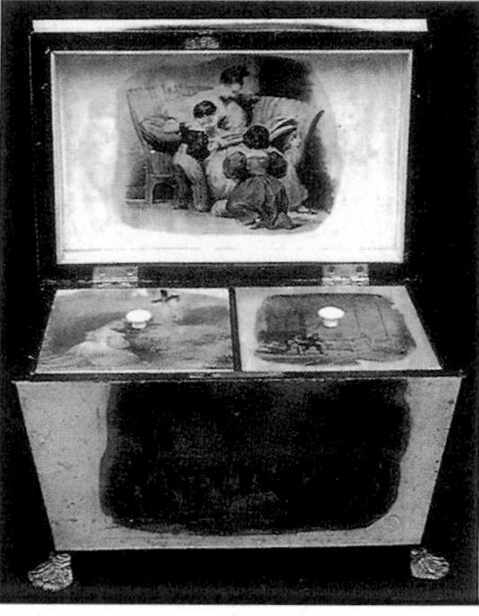

A late Regency painted tea caddy, applied with engravings, on gilt paw feet, 8¾in (22cm) wide.
£680–810 / €1,000–1,200
$1,250–1,450 ⚒ GH

A penwork box, decorated with a harbour scene, early 19thC, 11in (28cm) wide.
£140–165 / €200–240
$250–300 ⚒ G(L)

► **A gold-mounted tortoiseshell snuff box,** with micro-mosaic decoration, repaired, 19thC, 3½in (9cm) wide.
£7,300–8,700 / €10,700–12,700
$13,200–15,700 ⚒ SPF

A Regency penwork tea caddy, with two divisions, decorated with scrolling foliage and masks, on gilt-metal claw-and-ball feet, 8¾in (22cm) wide.
£280–330 / €410–480
$510–600 ⚒ G(L)

A tortoiseshell and mother-of-pearl tea caddy, with two compartments, c1820, 7½in (19cm) wide.
£1,900–2,250 / €2,750–3,300
$3,450–4,050 ⚒ S(O)

A mahogany writing desk, the hinged leather writing surface with ratchet, with brass fittings, early 19thC, 16¾in (42.5cm) wide.
£490–550 / €720–800
$890–1,000 ⊞ ChC

A porphyry butter box, with gilt-brass knop, Swedish, early 19thC, 5in (12.5cm) diam.
£1,450–1,700 / €2,100–2,500
$2,600–3,100 ⚒ BUK

A marquetry-inlaid tea caddy, decorated with figures within parquetry borders, Italian, 19thC, 4½in (11.5cm) wide.
£300–360 / €440–530
$540–650 WW

A satinwood tea caddy, with cut-steel beading and inlaid with a medallion depicting a classical Greek figure, French, c1840, 4¼in (11cm) wide.
£1,450–1,650 / €2,100–2,400
$2,600–3,000 JTS

A tiger-maple box, American, 19thC, 4½in (11.5cm) wide.
£50–60 / €75–90
$90–105 DuM

A burr-walnut and marquetry *bombé* tea caddy, with ebony mouldings, the fitted interior with two caddies and a cut-glass bowl, mid-19thC, 14in (35.5cm) wide.
£2,100–2,500 / €3,050–3,650
$3,800–4,550 PFK

An early Victorian gilt-metal-mounted burrwood writing box, the coromandel fitted interior with an inkwell, 14in (35.5cm) wide.
£610–730 / €890–1,050
$1,100–1,300 BWL

A leather-covered drinks box, in the form of a stack of books, the interior with two gilded decanters and four glasses, French, c1840, 7in (18cm) wide.
£900–1,000 / €1,300–1,450
$1,600–1,800 JTS

A mahogany and gilt-inlaid box, the interior with a mirror, French, c1850, 17in (43cm) wide.
£1,400–1,600 / €2,050–2,350
$2,550–2,900 ⊞ Man

A Victorian oak stationery cabinet, the folding fall-front inset with leather skivers, with a fitted interior, 12½in (32cm) high.
£210–250 / €310–370
$380–450 ⚒ DA

A Victorian leather vanity case, the hinged cover enclosing fitted compartments with scent bottles, ring caskets and jars, each with an initialled gold mount and coral beads, above a fitted tray with manicure items and a mirror, signed 'Asprey & Son', 8¼in (21cm) wide.
£760–910 / €1,100–1,300
$1,400–1,650 ⚒ Bea

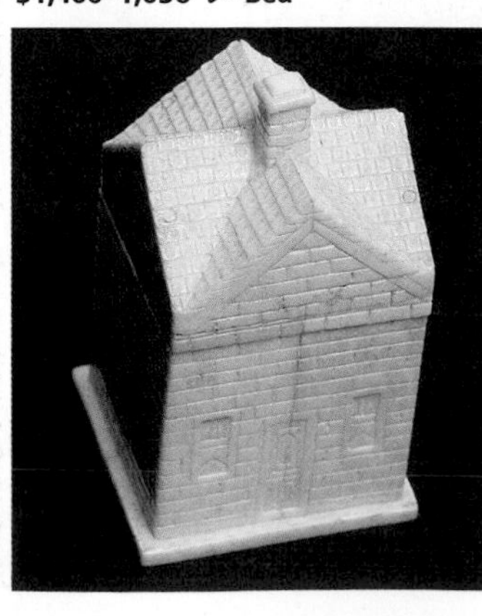

A coromandel writing box, with mother-of-pearl inlay, the hinged cover enclosing a tooled-leather writing surface and a satinwood lift-out tray, Irish, 1850–1900, 15¼in (38.5cm) wide.
£370–440 / €540–640
$670–800 ⚒ AH

A Victorian burr-walnut and mahogany travelling writing desk, 14in (35.5cm) high.
£380–430 / €550–630
$690–780 ⊞ GEO

A walnut tea caddy, with two compartments and brass and ivorine strapping, c1875, 7in (18cm) wide.
£760–850 / €1,100–1,250
$1,400–1,550 ⊞ JTS

An ivory box, decorated with a portrait miniature of King George IV by M. Segun, French, late 19thC, 4in (10cm) diam.
£850–950 / €1,250–1,400
$1,500–1,700 ⊞ RdeR

◄ **A carved bone box,** in the form of a house, c1880, 3in (7.5cm) high.
£155–175 / €230–260
$280–320 ⊞ MB

A lacquer box, depicting a troika and passengers, Russian, c1860, 9in (23cm) wide.
£630–700 / €920–1,050
$1,150–1,300 ⊞ RdeR

A Victorian ebonized and brass-inlaid tea caddy, with a fitted interior, 10in (25.5cm) wide.
£190–220 / €280–320
$340–400 ⚒ SWO

A Mauchline ware snuff box, the to decorated with a penwork coaching scene, Scottish, c1880, 4in (10cm) wid
£430–480 / €630–700
$780–870 ⊞ GAU

An ormolu-mounted and blood-stone jewellery casket, the hinged cover inset with a miniature painted with bacchanalian figures, Continenta late 19thC, 5¼in (13.5cm) wide.
£560–670 / €820–980
$1,000–1,200 ⚒ DN(BR)

A brass-mounted oak letter box, with glazed panels and a Bramah lock, c1900, 12in (30.5cm) wide.
£190–220 / €280–320
$340–400 ⚒ G(L)

Music

Cylinder Musical Boxes

◀ **A cylinder musical box,** playing eight airs, in a rosewood case, Swiss, early 19thC, 17in (43cm) wide.
£400–480
€580–700
$720–870
G(L)

A key-wound cylinder musical box, by Nicole Frères, playing six airs, Swiss, c1859, 20in (51cm) wide.
£3,600–4,000 / €5,300–5,800
$6,500–7,200 ⊞ KHW

► **A two-per-turn cylinder musical box,** by Nicole Frères, playing 12 airs, movement overhauled, case repolished, Swiss, c1860, 22in (56cm) wide.
£4,700–5,300
€6,900–7,700
$8,500–9,600
⊞ PGO

A crank-wound cylinder musical box, playing nine airs, the rosewood case with inlaid decoration, Swiss, c1860, 24in (61cm) wide.
£2,150–2,400 / €3,150–3,500
$3,900–4,350 ⊞ WAA

◀ **A cylinder musical box,** by Baptiste Antoine Bremond, Geneva, playing 8 airs, in a mahogany case, Swiss, c1865, 18in (45.5cm) wide.
£2,250–2,500
€3,300–3,650
$4,050–4,550
⊞ VHA

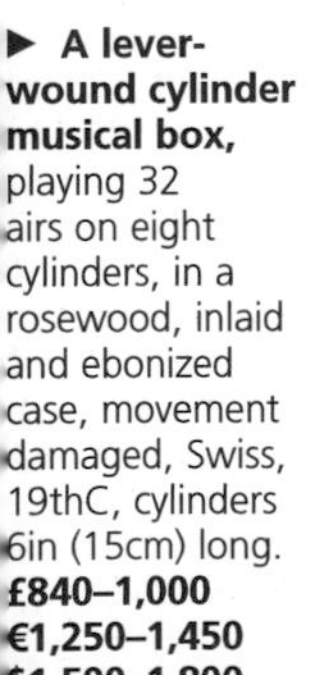

► **A lever-wound cylinder musical box,** playing 32 airs on eight cylinders, in a rosewood, inlaid and ebonized case, movement damaged, Swiss, 19thC, cylinders 6in (15cm) long.
£840–1,000
€1,250–1,450
$1,500–1,800
Bea

A cylinder musical box, in a marquetry-inlaid and crossbanded walnut case, Continental, 19thC, 30¼in (77cm) wide.
£440–520 / €640–760
$800–940 WilP

A cylinder musical box, by Paillard Vaucher & Fils, Ste Croix, playing eight airs, Swiss, c1875, 18in (45.5cm) wide.
£2,000–2,250 / €2,900–3,300
$3,600–4,050 ⊞ VHA

A crank-wound cylinder musical box, by Mermod Frères, playing eight airs, the case with a transfer-decorated cover, Swiss, late 19thC, 17in (43cm) wide.
£480–570 / €700–830
$870–1,050 ⚒ SK

A cylinder musical box, playing eight airs, the walnut case with inlaid stringing, Swiss, c1890, 17in (43cm) wide.
£1,050–1,200 / €1,550–1,750
$1,900–2,150 ⊞ K&D

Disc Musical Boxes

► A Polyphon disc musical box, with 14 8in (20.5cm) discs, in a walnut case, German, late 19thC, 10½in (26.5cm) wide.
£640–760
€750–1,100
$1,200–1,400
⚒ G(L)

◄ A Regina disc musical box, playing 15½in (39.5cm) discs on a duplex comb arrangement, No. 33245, American, c1898, 10in (25.5cm) wide.
£5,400–6,000
€7,900–8,800
$9,800–10,900
⊞ VHA

► A Stella disc musical box, with two combs, speed moderator, with 75 17in (43cm) discs, in a mahogany case with oak-leaf carving, No. 3969, Swiss, late 19thC, 29in (73.5cm) wide.
£2,400–2,800
€3,500–4,100
$4,350–5,100 ⚒ SK

A Regina Corona nickelodeon, with 25 21in (53.5cm) discs, in an oak cabinet with gilt-bonze mounts and a turned gallery, American, c1899, 68in (172.5cm) high.
£9,500–11,400
€13,900–16,600
$17,200–20,600 ⚒ JAA

A Fortuna disc musical box, with 15 discs, in a walnut case with glazed doors painted with waterlilies and flowers, signed, German, c1900, 51¼in (130cm) high.
£4,050–4,850
€5,900–7,100
$7,300–8,800 ⚒ S(Am)

A Kalliope disc musical box, the coin-operated mechanism with side wind handle, with 18 discs, in a moulded walnut case, pediment replaced, signed, German, c1900, 44½in (113cm) high.
£2,400–2,800
€3,500–4,100
$4,350–5,100 ⚒ S(Am)

A Polyphon disc musical box, with 53 discs, the walnut and burrwood-veneered case inlaid with a floral spray, the interior with a print of cherubs playing musical instruments, No. 10120, damaged, German, c1900, 26½in (67.5cm) wide.
£3,000–3,600
€4,400–5,300
$5,400–6,500 ⚒ S

◄ A Polyphon disc musical box, with ratchet-wind, single comb and grained case, with a quantity of discs, No. 71, German, c1900, 12½in (32cm) wide.
£350–420 / €510–610
$630–760 ⚒ SK

Gramophones

◄ **A mahogany gramophone,** early 20thC, 40in (101.5cm) high.
£300–360 / €440–530
$540–650 SWO

► **An HMV mahogany gramophone,** model No. 203, with oxidized-brass fittings, c1930, 28in (71cm) wide.
£1,900–2,250
€2,750–3,300
$3,450–4,050 GH

An HMV wind-up portable gramophone, model No. 99, c1930, 14in (35.5cm) wide.
£90–100 / €130–145
$160–180 OTA

Mechanical Music

A Regency mahogany chamber pipe barrel organ, probably by J. Hicks, with 92 pipes, restored, 36in (92cm) wide.
£2,450–2,900
€2,750–3,300
$3,450–4,050 BWL

A piano barrel organ, playing six tunes, in an ebonized case, late 19thC, 22¾in (58cm) wide.
£230–270 / €340–390
$420–490 CHTR

Items in the Mechanical Music section have been arranged in object order.

A cabinet roller organ, by Autophone Co, with 20 extra rolls, American, Ithaca, New York, 19thC, 15¾in (40cm) wide.
£840–1,000 / €1,250–1,450
$1,500–1,800 JBe

► **An Improved Celestina organette,** with five music rolls and 20 notes, in a mahogany case, American, c1880, 15in (38cm) wide.
£720–800 / €1,050–1,200
$1,300–1,450 VHA

A musical picture, by Ami Rivenc, Geneva, playing three airs, with maker's plaque, Swiss, 1875, 23in (58.5cm) wide.
£1,050–1,200 / €1,550–1,750
$1,900–2,150 VHA

◄ **A singing bird in a cage automaton,** by Bontems, Paris, restored, French, c1880, 17in (43cm) high.
£4,300–4,800 / €6,300–7,000
$7,800–8,700 AUTO

A sterling silver singing bird musical box, European, c1900, 4in (10cm) wide.
£2,900–3,250 / €4,250–4,750
$5,200–5,900 SHa

Musical Instruments

A rosewood bassoon, by Buffet-Grampon & Cie, No, 4943, French, late 19thC, 50in (127cm) long, cased.
£280–330 / €410–480
$510–600 GH

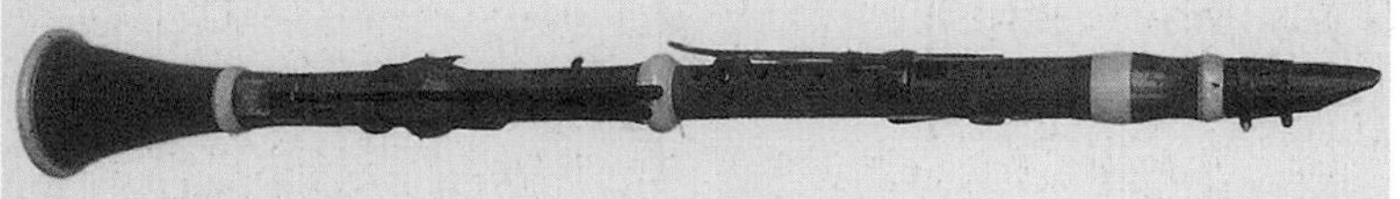

A boxwood clarinet, by Key, London, with turned ivory mounts, the brass keys with covers, slight damage, 19thC, 26½in (67.5cm) long.
£190–220 / €280–320
$340–400 F&C

A cello, possibly by Edward Pamphilon, head later, late 17thC, length of back 29½in (75cm).
£7,000–8,400
€10,200–12,200
$12,700–15,200 S

Miller's Compares

I. A pierced metal Anglo-system Linota concertina, by Wheatstone & Co, with 37 metal buttons, six-fold bellows and steel reeds, No. 34966, c1938, 7in (18cm) diam, cased.
£2,900–3,450 / €4,250–5,000
$5,200–6,200 GH

II. A pierced and brass-inlaid rosewood English-system concertina, by Wheatstone & Co, with 48 metal buttons and six-fold bellows, c1910, 8in (20.5cm) diam.
£520–620 / €760–910
$940–1,100 GH

Both Item I and Item II are by Wheatstone & Co and are attractive in appearance, but Item I realized more than five times the amount of Item II. Item I is the more desirable piece because it is an Anglo-system example. It produces a better sound and is more versatile than Item II as it gives a different note on the inward and outward movement of the bellows. Item II is an English-system example and gives the same note on the inward and outward movement.

A boxwood and ivory flageolet, by E. P. Williams, London, c1820, 15½in (39.5cm) long.
£850–950 / €1,250–1,400
$1,500–1,700 ⊞ ANGE

A rosewood acoustic guitar, by C. F. Martin, repaired, American, c1880, 38in (96.5cm) long.
£820–980 / €1,200–1,450
$1,500–1,750 JAA

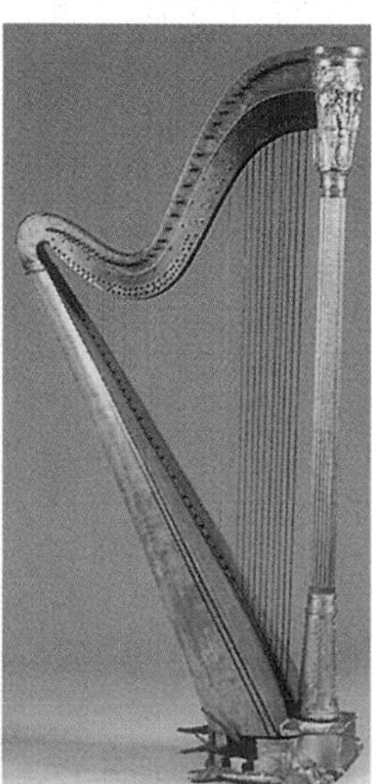

◄ **A Victorian gilt harp,** by P. F. Browne & Co, London and New York, with animal-paw feet, the column surmounted by a capital carved with a winged woman, damaged, 67½in (171.5cm) high.
£2,500–3,000
€3,650–4,400
$4,550–5,400 JDJ

► **A carved giltwood, gilt-brass, fruitwood and satinwood harp,** by Lyon & Healy, signed, American, Chicago, c1900, 70in (178cm) high.
£3,150–3,750
€4,600–5,500
$5,700–6,800 NOA

A Bardie harp, by James McFall, with a brass plaque, Irish, Belfast, c1910, 48in (122cm) high
£760–910 / €1,100–1,30
$1,400–1,650 GH

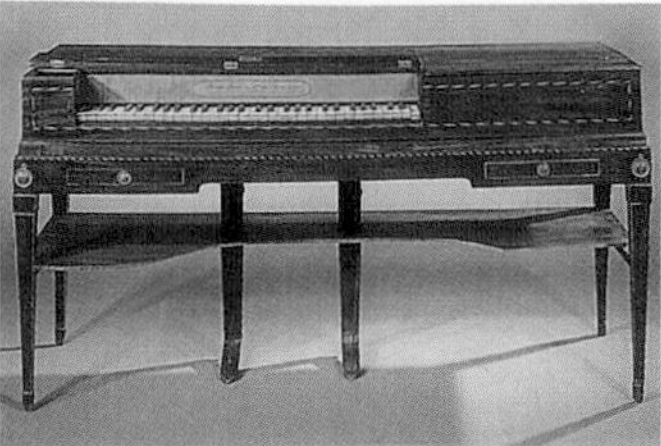

A mahogany, satinwood, ebonized and fruitwood table piano, by Meincke & Pieter Meyer, the keyboard above a frieze with one dummy and one short drawer, Dutch, Amsterdam, c1780, 61in (155cm) wide.
£7,000–8,400 / €10,200–12,300
$12,700–15,200 ⚒ S(Am)

A mahogany square piano, by Card & Co, c1835, 67¾in (172cm) wide.
£3,350–3,800 / €4,900–5,500
$6,100–6,900 ⊞ RBM

A Victorian rosewood grand piano, by John Broadwood & Sons, London, 54¾in (139cm) wide.
£1,050–1,250 / €1,550–1,850
$1,900–2,250 ⚒ PFK

A rosewood grand piano, by Blüthner, c1895, 75in (190.5cm) wide.
£4,250–5,100 / €6,200–7,400
$7,700–9,200 ⚒ BWL

► **A model IV grand piano,** by Bechstein, c1897, 80in (203cm) wide.
£7,900–8,800 / €11,500–12,800
$14,300–16,000 ⊞ RBM

A mahogany square piano, by Adam Beyer, London, 1788, 60in (152.5cm) wide.
£7,900–8,800 / €11,500–12,800
$14,300–15,900 ⊞ WAA

A William IV mahogany square piano, by John Broadwood & Sons, London, the rosewood-banded hinged top above a brass marquetry and trellis panel, 67¾in (172cm) wide.
£440–520 / €640–760
$800–940 ⚒ WW

A satinwood piano, by Ernst Munck, painted with scrolling foliate designs, Continental, 1875–1900, 82in (208.5cm) wide.
£3,850–4,600 / €5,600–6,700
$7,000–8,300 ⚒ LHA

A mahogany fortepiano, by John Broadwood & Sons, London, c1807, 93in (236cm) wide.
£3,400–3,750 / €5,000–5,500
$6,100–6,800 ⊞ RBM

A walnut and marquetry upright piano, by Erard, London, with gilt-bronze mounts, manufacturer's label, c1855, with a Victorian piano stool.
£4,550–5,400 / €6,600–7,900
$8,200–9,800 ⚒ S(O)

A rosewood square grand piano, by Steinway & Sons, style VII, c1879, 81in (205.5cm) wide.
£760–910 / €1,100–1,300
$1,400–1,650 ⚒ JAA

A rosewood grand piano, by Bechstein, c1900, 78¾in (200cm) wid
£1,500–1,800 / €2,200–2,650
$2,700–3,250 ⚒ DD

A rosewood grand piano, by Blüthner, c1900, 76in (193cm) wide.
£8,900–9,900 / €13,000–14,400
$16,100–18,000 ⊞ RBM

A rosewood model V upright piano, by Bechstein, c1902, 58in (147.5cm) wide.
£3,850–4,300 / €5,600–6,300
$6,900–7,800 ⊞ RBM

An inlaid mahogany upright piano, by Broadway & Sons, c1910, 58¼in (148cm) wide.
£2,850–3,400 / €4,150–4,950
$5,200–6,200 ⚒ S(O)

A walnut spinet, by Stephanus Keene, London, 1690–1710, 60in (152.5cm) wide.
£17,100–19,000 / €25,000–27,800
$31,000–34,400 ⊞ WAA

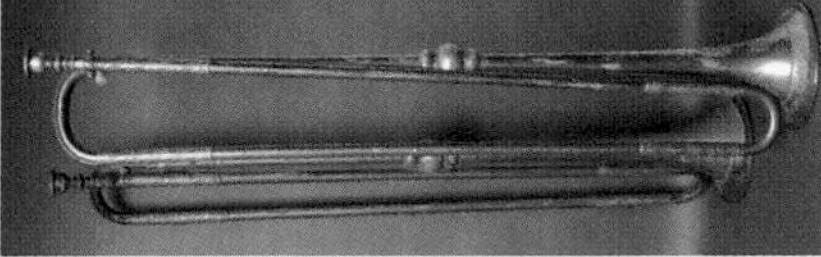

A pair of plated ceremonial trumpets, used at the Angelsey Assizes, 1902, 36in (91.5cm) long.
£370–440 / €540–640
$670–800 ⚒ BWL

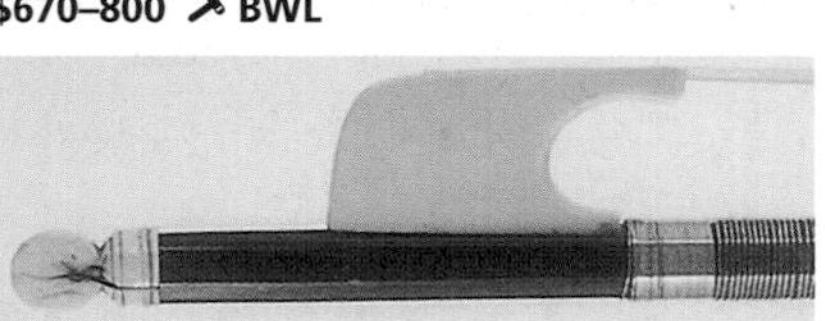

An ivory-mounted viola bow, Dodd School, c1780, 69g.
£1,050–1,250 / €1,550–1,850
$1,900–2,250 ⚒ S

A mahogany-banded ukulele, labelled 'Jose Fernandez, Made in Saxony', German, 1920s, 27in (68.5cm) long, cased.
£280–330 / €410–480
$510–600 ⚒ GH

◄ **A viola,** German, Dresden, c1900, 15¼in (38.5cm) long.
£470–560 / €690–820
$850–1,000 ⚒ GH

A violin, probably by Jacques Bocquay, French, Paris, length of back 14in (35.5cm), cased.
£5,400–6,400
€7,900–9,400
$9,800–11,600 ⚒ S

◄ **A violin,** by Leonhard Maussiell, maker's label, German, Nuremberg, c1740, length of back 14in (35.5cm), cased.
£7,200–8,600
€10,500–12,500
$13,000–15,600 ⚒ S

◀ **A violin,** probably by Georg Kloz II, c1760, length of back 14in (35cm).
£2,200–2,600
€3,200–3,800
$4,000–4,700 GH

A violin, by William Smith, Sheffield, maker's mark, late 18thC, length of back 14in (35.5cm), cased.
£4,550–5,400
€6,600–7,900
$8,200–9,800 S

◀ **A violin,** by J. T. L., French, c1900, length of back 14¼in (36cm).
£280–330 / €400–480
$500–600 MAR

A violin, by Martin Stoss, labelled, Austrian, Vienna, dated 1835, length of back 14in (35.5cm), cased.
£400–480 / €580–700
$720–870 GH

A violin, inscribed 'Grandjon', French, c1890, 24in (61cm) long.
£800–960 / €1,200–1,400
$1,450–1,750 GH

A violin, by W. E. Hill & Sons, labelled, London, dated 1907, length of back 14in (35.5cm), cased.
£4,550–5,400
€6,600–7,900
$8,200–9,800 S

A violin, by Colin Mezin, French, c1920, length of back 14in (35.5cm), cased, with two bows.
£1,500–1,800
€2,200–2,650
$2,700–3,250 PBA

A silver-mounted violin bow, by François Nicolas Voirin, French, Paris, c1880, 53.5g.
£3,800–4,550 / €5,500–6,600
$6,900–8,200 S

A nickel-mounted violin bow, stamped 'C. H. Buthod Paris', French, c1910, 29in (73.5cm) long.
£210–250 / €310–370
$380–450 GH

A silver-mounted mahogany violin case, converted to a jewellery box, French, c1840, 30in (76cm) wide.
£400–450 / €580–660
$720–810 JTS

Icons

A pair of carved wooden icons of the Nativity and Visit of the Magi and the Presentation of Christ in the Temple, Russian, 16thC, largest 4¾ x 4¼ (12 x 11cm).
£6,600–7,400 / €9,600–10,800
$11,900–13,400 ⊞ RKa

An icon of the Saints Zossim and Savatii, Russian, 17thC, 12½ x 10¾in (32 x 27.5cm).
£800–900 / €1,150–1,300
$1,450–1,650 ⊞ TeG

An icon of Archangel Michael Voyevoda, Russian, c1650, 13½ x 11½in (34.5 x 29cm).
£6,700–7,500 / €9,800–11,000
$12,100–13,600 ⊞ TeG

An icon of Saint Paul of the Oborna River, Russian, late 16thC, 12½ x 10¼in (32 x 26cm).
£2,200–2,500 / €3,200–3,650
$4,000–4,550 ⊞ TeG
The monastic Saint Paul of the Oborna River was born in Moscow in 1317 and died, aged 112, in 1429. He spent a large period of his life as a hermit.

An icon of the Last Judgement, Russian, 17thC, 15½ x 12½in (39.5 x 32cm).
£6,300–7,000 / €9,200–10,200
$11,400–12,700 ⊞ RKa

An icon of Saint John in Silence, Russian, late 17thC, 12½ x 10½in (32 x 26.5cm).
£2,200–2,500 / €3,200–3,600
$4,000–4,500 ⊞ TeG

◄ **An icon of Saint George,** Greek, early 18thC, 8¾ x 7in (22 x 18cm).
£400–450 / €580–660
$720–810 ⊞ TeG

An icon of the Mother of God Galaktotrophousa, Italo/Cretan, c1625, 8 x 6¼in (20.5 x 16cm).
£1,100–1,300 / €1,600–1,900
$2,000–2,350 ⚒ JAA

A pair of carved wooden sanctuary doors painted with icons, Greek Islands, 17thC, 51¼ x 29¾in (130 x 75.5cm).
£20,000–22,000 / €29,000–32,000
$36,000–40,000 ⊞ RKa

An icon of the Protecting Veil, Russian, late 17thC, 11½ x 10¼in (29 x 26cm).
£1,600–1,800 / €2,350–2,650
$2,900–3,250 ⊞ TeG
In this icon the Mother of God, accompanied by archangels, the 12 apostles, bishops, holy women, monks and martyrs, spreads her veil in protection over the congregation.

An icon of the Mother of God Enthroned, Greek, Ionian Islands, 18thC, 12¼ x 9¼in (31 x 23.5cm).
£1,700–1,900 / €2,500–2,750
$3,100–3,450 ⊞ RKa

An icon of the Tikhvin Mother of God, Russian, 18thC, 13½ x 11¾in (34.5 x 30cm).
£440–520 / €640–760
$800–940 ⚒ JAA

Items in the Icons section have been arranged in date order.

An icon of Blessed Silence, Russian, c1750, 12¼ x 10¾in (31 x 27.5cm).
£1,800–2,000 / €2,600–2,900
$3,250–3,600 ⊞ TeG

► An icon of the Virgin and Child, Russian, late 18thC, 12 x 10¾in (30.5 x 27.5cm).
£810–900 / €1,200–1,350
$1,450–1,650 ⊞ TeG

A carved wood icon of Saint Nil Stolbenski, Russian, 18thC, 9¾ x 5¾in (25 x 14.5cm).
£2,500–2,800 / €3,650–4,100
$4,550–5,100 ⊞ TeG
Saint Nilus of Stolbny (d1555) was a monk and miracle worker of Novgorod. He founded a monastery on the island of Stolbny on Lake Seliger.

A quadripartite icon, of the Archangel Michael, The Holy Wisdom, the Beheading of Saint John and various Saints, Russian, 18thC, 14 x 12in (35.5 x 30.5cm) wide.
£2,500–2,800 / €3,650–4,100
$4,550–5,100 ⊞ ICO

An icon of the three Hierarchs of Orthodoxy, Saints John Chrysostom, Basil and Gregory, Russian, 18thC, 12 x 10½in (30.5 x 26.5cm).
£2,700–3,000 / €3,950–4,400
$4,900–5,400 ⊞ ICO

An icon of Christ Pantocrator, Greek, c1750, 4¼ x 3¼in (11 x 8.5cm).
£180–200 / €260–290
$320–360 ⊞ TeG

An icon of the Virgin Hodegitria, Russian, late 18thC, 12½ x 10½in (32 x 26.5cm).
£1,100–1,250 / €1,600–1,800
$2,000–2,200 ⊞ TeG
Legend tells that the original work was a portrait of the Mother of God painted by Saint Luke during her lifetime. The historical origins are obscure but the type was known in the period before iconoclasm. The Tuesday procession of the Hodegitria icon kept in the Hodegon monastery in Constantinople was one of the memorable events of the city recorded by medieval visitors and pilgrims. The prototype for this icon would have been one of the 11th-century copies made in Constantinople of the Hodegitria Virgin.

An icon of St John the Theologian, Greek, 18th–19thC, 9½ x 7in (24 x 18cm).
£350–420 / €510–610
$630–760 JAA

n icon of Saint Nicholas, Russian, arly 19thC, 10¼ x 8½in (26 x 21.5cm).
900–1,000 / €1,300–1,450
1,600–1,800 TeG
he full title is Saint Nicholas the Vonderworker and Holy Bishop of Ayra. Saint Nicholas is the most videly revered saint in Orthodoxy. he Russians have a saying 'If nything happens to God, we ave always got St Nicholas'.

n icon of the Kiev Saints, Russian, 9thC, 5¼ x 4½in (13.5 x 11.5cm).
520–580 / €760–850
940–1,050 TeG
1670, celebrations were stablished in memory of the aints buried over a period of any hundreds of years in the ercherski Caves Monastery at iev. Such icons were made there r pilgrims visiting the shrines of e miracle workers.

An icon of the Mother of God Joy to All Who Suffer, Russian, c1800, 13½ x 10½in (34.5 x 26.5cm).
£190–220 / €280–330
$340–400 JAA

An icon of the Union of Love, Russian, early 19thC, 10¼ x 8¾in (26 x 22cm).
£1,350–1,500 / €1,950–2,200
$2,450–2,700 TeG
The design is a continuous 'renaissance knot'. At the centre is the Crucifixion surrounded by the 12 Apostles. In the four corners of the design are the Evangelists represented by their symbols. Above is a representation of God, with miniature icons either side depicting Christ the Blessed Silence and the Virgin and Child.

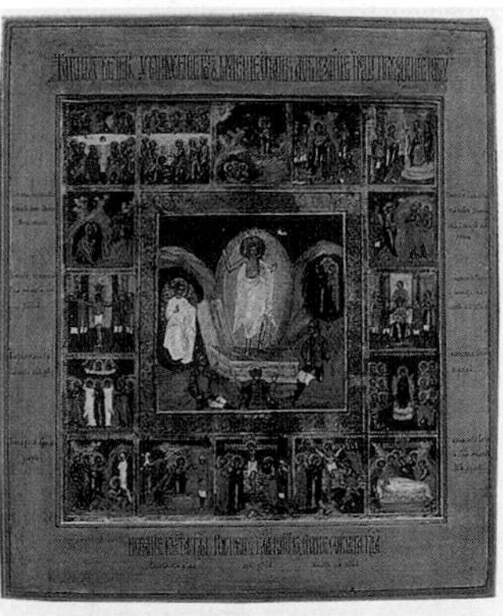

An icon of The Passion, the central panel of Christ surrounded by 16 scenes related to the Crucifixion and Resurrection, Russian, 19thC, 14 x 12in (35.5 x 30.5cm).
£1,300–1,550 / €1,900–2,250
$2,350–2,800 JAA

An icon of Saint Anna Kashinskaya, Russian, early 19thC, 8¾ x 7in (22 x 18cm).
£1,250–1,400 / €1,850–2,050
$2,250–2,550 TeG
Saint Anna Kashinskaya was famous for her role in the liberation of the town of Kashin, near Tver, from Lithuanians in the 17th century.

An icon of the Virgin of Kazan, Russian, Palekh, early 19thC, 14¼ x 12in (36 x 30.5cm).
£3,150–3,500 / 4,600–5,100
$5,700–6,300 TeG
This is one of the many icons after the famous prototype of the Virgin, which dates from the mid-16th century when Ivan the Terrible captured Kazan, the ancient Tartar capital. The original icon, considered miraculous by the Church and believers, was brought to St Petersburg in the 17th century by Peter the Great, who became patron of the Romanovs.

An icon of the Archangel Michael, Russian, 19thC, 14 x 12in (35.5 x 30.5cm).
£1,450–1,700 / €2,100–2,500
$2,600–3,100 JAA

An icon of the Virgin of the Burning Bush, Russian, 19thC, 8¾ x 7½in (22 x 19cm).
£670–750 / €980–1,100
$1,200–1,350 ⊞ TeG

A brass-coloured metal icon of the Crucifixion and Selected Feasts, Russian, 19thC, 15¼ x 9½in (38.5 x 24cm).
£810–900 / €1,200–1,350
$1,450–1,650 ⊞ RKa

An icon of a Holy face, by A. A. Muchin, in a silver-gilt oklad, Russian, Moscow 1880, 11½ x 9¾in (29 x 25cm), framed.
£1,750–2,100 / €2,550–3,050
$3,150–3,800 ⚒ BUK

LOCATE THE SOURCE

The source of each illustration in Miller's can be found by checking the code letters below each caption with the Key to Illustrations, pages 778–784.

A brass icon of Saints Boris and Gleb, Russian, 19thC, 5¼ x 3¼in (13.5 x 8.5cm).
£400–450 / €580–660
$720–810 ⊞ RKa

An Icon of the Miracle of the Icon of the Mother of God Hodegitria, Russian, 19thC, 10¾ x 8¾in (27.5 x 22cm).
£190–220 / €270–320
$340–400 ⚒ SWO

An icon of the Selected Saints, depicting Saints Timothy and Evdokia beneath an image of Christ, Russian, c1890, 9 x 7in (23 x 18cm).
£200–240 / €290–350
$360–430 ⚒ JAA

► **An icon of Saint Minas,** with a metal oklad, Greek, c1900, 8½ x 7½in (21.5 x 19cm).
£95–110 / €140–165
$170–200 ⚒ JAA

A painted icon of The Mother of God of the Passion, Russian, 19thC, 12 x 10½in (30.5 x 26.5cm).
£630–750 / €920–1,100
$1,150–1,350 ⚒ JAA

An icon of the Three-Handed Virgin, Russian, c1850, 11¼ x 9in (28.5 x 23cm).
£610–680 / €890–990
$1,100–1,250 ⊞ TeG
The story of the Virgin with three hands is related to the miraculous healing of John of Damascus, whose hand was severed by the Khalif of Damascus because of the dispute between John and the 8th-century Byzantine emperor Leo the Isaurion. John of Damascus made a hand of silver and put it on the Virgin's icon. When he uttered a prayer in front of the icon his hand was healed. The icon – with three hands – became a cult 'miracle working' image. In time painters forgot the origins of the story and the third hand became the Virgin's.

Portrait Miniatures

Without doubt the most significant recent event in the field of portrait miniatures was the auction of the Albion Collection at Bonhams. To emphasize its importance, the collection was accorded a hardback catalogue and an evening sale – unprecedented in the world of miniatures. Such treatment paid off and produced some remarkable prices. Nonetheless, the results were consistent with the general mood of the miniatures market and as such can be used as an indicator of current trends.

Miniatures by the masters of the late 16th and early 17th centuries that have survived unscathed are scarcely seen and, when they do appear, the prices are invariably high. A notable sitter will further force the figure. The late 18th and early 19th centuries have long been favoured by collectors and the triumvirate of Richard Cosway, John Smart and George Engleheart were generously represented in the Albion Collection. Assuming an even standard of accomplishment, prices are dependent on certain factors that are universally applicable, whatever the miniature: the period within an artist's oeuvre; the attractiveness of the sitter and an identified subject – biography can make a significant impact. The frame would ideally be contemporary, enamelled and jewelled. When all these requirements are met, records are broken. In contrast, prices for the humble and often anonymous miniatures of the mid-18th century have remained unchanged at low three-figure sums.

Generally the criteria cited above are applicable to the Continental Schools. However, there is greater emphasis on blue-chip artists, such as François Dumont or Moritz Daffinger, and the importance of history is evident in the many portraits of the Royal Houses of Savoy and Naples and the Imperial House of Russia.

For a long time out of fashion, enamel miniatures are the focus of revived interest, albeit concentrated on a few artists. Henry Bone's large works consistently attain high prices and similar levels are paid for the works of Jean Petitot. Nonetheless, most enamel miniatures, even signed examples, still hover between three and four figures.

Oil miniatures have been equally unmodish – predominantly early in date (17th century) they have suffered from being mostly unattributable. Now it seems collectors are waking up to the virtues of this neglected field and will buy works by unknown painters, provided the quality is evident and the condition good. When an oil miniature is signed the price can soar, as proved by the five-figure sum paid for a Cornelius Jonson from the Albion Collection.

Haydn Williams

A portrait miniature, oil on copper, Anglo-Dutch, 1640–50, 5in (12.5cm) high.
£2,700–3,000
€3,950–4,400
$4,900–5,400 ⊞ BHa

Items in the Portrait Miniatures section have been arranged in date order.

▸ A portrait miniature of a gentleman, attributed to Noah Seeman, c1720, in a gilt-metal frame, 1½in (4cm) high.
£780–930 / €1,150–1,350
$1,450–1,700 ⚒ S

A portrait miniature of Lady Mary Wortley Montagu, Modest School, watercolour on ivory, 1689–1762, 1½in (4cm) high.
£4,000–4,500
€5,800–6,600
$7,200–8,100 ⊞ EFA
Modest School is a term established by Graham Reynolds c1952 to describe a certain group of mid-18th century English miniaturists.

A portrait miniature of a young lady, by Christian Richter, watercolour on vellum, c1710, 2in (5cm) high.
£1,350–1,500
€1,950–2,200
$2,450–2,700 ⊞ EFA

A portrait miniature of a gentleman, studio of Christian Friedrich Zincke, enamel, c1720, in a gilt-metal frame, 1½in (4cm) high.
£780–930 / €1,150–1,350
$1,450–1,700 ⚒ S
Zincke was born in Dresden, but moved to England in his twenties where he remained for the rest of his life. Highly successful, he is considered part of the British School.

◂ A portrait miniature of a gentleman, by R. Haskins, plumbago on card, signed and dated 1745, 4¾in (12cm) high.
£2,150–2,400
€3,150–3,500
$3,900–4,350 ⊞ EFA

A portrait miniature of a gentleman, by Jean André Rouquet, enamel, signed and dated 1748, 1¾in (4.5cm) high.
£4,050–4,500 / €5,800–6,600 $7,200–8,100 ⊞ EFA
Rouquet was born in Switzerland to French parents. He spent most of his working life in England and his last years in Paris, where he died deranged.

A portrait miniature of an officer, by Simon Pine, signed 'SP', Irish, Dublin, c1760, in a gold bracelet-clasp frame, 1½in (4cm) high.
£1,700–1,900 / €2,500–2,750 $3,100–3,450 ⊞ SIL

Enamel Miniatures

The technique of painting on enamel evolved in France during the second quarter of the 17th century and within a remarkably short period works of exceptional quality were produced, notably in the hands of Jean Petitot. The base was either copper or, more exclusively, gold upon which a white enamel ground was laid and fired. This surface was then painted with colours, the sequence being determined by the melting point of the individual pigments. Usually a minimum of six firings in a kiln of gradually diminishing temperature was required to achieve the desired effect. Unlike the colours of most miniatures painted in watercolour, those in enamel remain as bright and fresh as the day they left the artist's studio.

Miller's Compares

I. A portrait miniature of Anne Countess of Chesterfield, by Samuel Cotes, the reverse with the Earl's coronet and initials 'AC', signed and dated 1778, in a split-pearl and enamel frame, the reverse with a hair panel, 3in (7.5cm) high.
£7,200–8,000 / €10,500–11,700 $13,000–14,500 ⊞ BHa

II. A portrait miniature of a young officer, by Samuel Cotes, signed with initials, 1779, in a gold locket frame, 2in (5cm) high.
£1,650–1,850 / €2,400–2,700 $3,000–3,350 ⊞ BHa

Items I and II are by the same artist and painted at a similar time, but Item I is more desirable because female portraits are invariably more popular than male, and it is of a known subject. Item I is also larger than Item II and in an attractive ornate frame.

A portrait miniature of a young lady, by James Scouler, watercolour on ivory, signed and dated 1778 on the reverse, 1½in (4cm) high.
£3,150–3,500 €4,600–5,100 $5,700–6,300 ⊞ EFA

A portrait miniature of Lieutenant Colonel Buckland, English School, on ivory, 18thC, 3in (7.5cm) high.
£880–1,050 €1,300–1,550 $1,600–1,900 ⚒ HYD

► A portrait miniature of Sir Archibald Hope, by John Smart, watercolour on ivory, signed with initials and dated 1780, 1½in (4cm) high.
£9,000–10,000 / €13,100–14,600 $16,300–18,100 ⊞ EFA

◄ A portrait miniature of a gentleman, circle of Richard Cosway, the reverse with a blue glass and glazed hair compartment with beaded initials, c1780, in a gold frame, 2in (5cm) high.
£600–720 / €880–1,050 $1,100–1,300 ⚒ S

A portrait miniature of a gentleman, by George Engleheart, in a gilt-metal frame, c1785, 1¾in (4.5cm) high.
£2,500–3,000 €3,650–4,400 $4,550–5,400 ⚒ S

PORTRAIT MINIATURES

A portrait miniature of Mr Ginkel, by Richard Cosway, the reverse with a plait of hair surrounding blue glass and a gold monogram, c1790, in a gold locket frame, 3¼in (8.5cm) high.
£9,000–10,000 / €13,100–14,600
$16,300–18,100 ⊞ BHa

► A portrait miniature of a young lady, by Edward Miles, watercolour on ivory, c1790, 2in (5cm) high.
£2,700–3,000 / €3,950–4,400
$4,900–5,400 ⊞ EFA

A portrait miniature of a lady, after George Engleheart, c1790, 3in (7.5cm) high.
£990–1,100 / €1,450–1,600
$1,800–2,000 ⊞ PSC

A portrait miniature of a young lady, by Samuel Shelley, watercolour on ivory, c1790, 2½in (6.5cm) high.
£3,600–4,000 / €5,200–5,800
$6,500–7,200 ⊞ EFA

Two portrait miniatures of the Reverend and Mrs Charles Fiennes-Clinton, English School, c1775, one mounted as a brooch, the other as a bracelet with a plaited hair band, in chased and foliate frames, possibly later, 1¾in (4.3cm) high, in a leather presentation case.
£2,100–2,500 / €3,050–3,650
$3,800–4,550 ⚒ Bea

◄ A portrait miniature of a young officer, by Frederick Buck, the reverse with a lock of hair and a monogram, Irish, c1795, in a gold locket frame, 2in (5cm) high.
£1,800–2,000
€2,600–2,900
$3,250–3,600
⊞ BHa

The various grounds used for watercolour miniatures

Until c1700, miniaturists who painted in either watercolour or gouache (opaque watercolour) worked on vellum. Around this date, and probably originating in Venice, ivory was introduced as an alternative ground. In spite of the technical difficulties it presented, ivory quickly gained favour in most countries and eventually artists learned how to exploit its translucency to convey flesh tones. During the late 18th century, some miniaturists began to work on card which, unlike ivory, was not limited by the shape of the tusk and did not present constraints of size. Miniatures on card were fashionable in the early 19th century, popularized by the French artist Jean-Baptiste Isabey whose influence assured its use for several decades. At the end of the 19th century, another ground was made available in the form of a man-made composition, known as ivorine. This sought to replicate the quality of ivory but had the advantage of not cracking as a result of fluctuations of heat.

A portrait miniature of a lady, by Frederick Buck, Irish, c1795, 4in (10cm) square.
£1,000–1,150
€1,450–1,650
$1,800–2,100 ⊞ SIL

A portrait miniature of a gentleman, by Henry Jacob Burch, watercolour on ivory, c1800, 2½in (6.5cm) high.
£1,250–1,400
€1,850–2,050
$2,250–2,550 ⊞ EFA

A portrait miniature of a young girl, by Andrew Plimer, the reverse with a hair panel, c1805, in a gilt locket frame, 2in (5cm) high.
£9,000–10,000
€13,100–14,600
$16,300–18,100 ⊞ BHa

A portrait miniature of a gentleman, English School, watercolour on ivory, the reverse with an enamel panel with a seed-pearl monogram on a plaited hair ground, c1800, in a gilt-metal frame, 2¾in (7cm) high, with a leather case.
£490–580 / €720–850
$890–1,050 ⚒ RTo

◄ A portrait miniature of a lady, by Charles Jagger, the reverse with an opaline glass and hair panel, c1800, in a gilt locket frame, 3in (7.5cm) high.
£3,200–3,600
€4,650–5,300
$5,800–6,500 ⊞ BHa

A portrait miniature of a young gentleman, by William Wood, the reverse with a hair panel and initials, c1800, in a gold locket frame, 3in (7.5cm) high.
£7,000–7,800
€10,200–11,400
$12,700–14,100 ⊞ BHa

A portrait miniature of Napoleon, by Peter Mayr, signed, c1805, in a turned wood frame, 4in (10cm) high.
£2,700–3,000
€3,950–4,400
$4,900–5,400 ⊞ BHa

A portrait miniature of a young man, attributed to Edward Miles, c1790, 2¼in (5.5cm) high.
£530–630 / €770–920
$960–1,150 ⚒ Bea

A portrait miniature of a gentleman, English School, on ivory, c1800, 1½in (4cm) high.
£165–195 / €240–290
$300–360 ⚒ HOLL

A portrait miniature of a gentleman, in an enamelled and jewelled frame, c1800, 1½in (4cm) high.
£530–630 / €770–920
$960–1,150 ⚒ WW

A portrait miniature of a young gentleman, by George Engleheart, signed and initialled, the reverse with a hair panel, c1805, in a gilt-metal frame, 3¼in (8.5cm) high.
£3,500–4,200
€5,100–6,100
$6,300–7,600 ⚒ G(B)

A portrait miniature of Dr Bealey, by Louis Ami Arlaud-Jurine, the reverse with a hair panel, signed with monogram, c1800, 4in (10cm) high.
£3,150–3,500
€4,600–5,100
$5,700–6,300 ⊞ BHa
Arlaud was a Swiss painter of portrait miniatures. This example dates from the period he spent in London between 1792 and 1802.

A portrait miniature of Mrs J. A. Ramsay, follower of George Engleheart, the reverse with a hair panel and inscribed 'Mrs. J. A. Ramsay, 25 August 1804', in a gold locket frame, 3in (7.5cm) high.
£1,200–1,400
€1,750–2,050
$2,150–2,550 ⚒ TEN

A portrait miniature of a young man, English School, watercolour on ivory, the reverse with an enamel panel with a seed pearl monogram and a hair and gold thread arrangement, c1805, in a gilt-metal frame, 2½in (6.5cm) high, with a leather case.
£610–730 / €890–1,050
$1,100–1,300 ⚒ RTo

A portrait miniature of a gentleman, watercolour on ivory, c1810, 3in (7.5cm) high, framed.
£400–450 / €580–660
$720–810 ⊞ PSC

A portrait miniature of Sir Robert Carr-Porter, by Thomas Hazelhurst, watercolour on ivory, c1810, 3in (7.5cm) high, framed.
£760–850 / €1,100–1,250
$1,400–1,550 ⊞ PSC

A portrait miniature of Roderick MacDonald, English School, early 19thC, in a gold metal frame, 4½in (11.5cm) high, with a case and letter written by the sitter.
£760–910 / €1,100–1,300
$1,400–1,650 ⚒ TEN

A portrait miniature of a gentleman, by Thomas Snelgrove, labelled, c1810, 3in (7.5cm) high.
£310–350 / €450–510
$560–630 ⊞ PSC

◄ **A portrait miniature of Sarah Tibbatt,** English School, watercolour on ivory, initialled 'MJH', early 19thC, 4in (10cm) high.
£440–520 / €640–760
$800–940 ⚒ G(L)

A pair of portrait miniatures of the Reverend Higgins and his wife, watercolour on ivory, 1819, 2in (5cm) high, framed.
£250–280 / €370–410
$450–510 ⊞ PSC

◄ **A portrait miniature of a young lady,** English School, watercolour on ivory, 19thC, 3in (7.5cm) high, framed.
£140–165 / €200–240
$250–300 ⚒ G(L)

A portrait miniature of a lady, by William Marshall Craig, c1810, 4in (10cm) high.
£1,400–1,600 / €2,050–2,350
$2,550–2,950 ⊞ BHa

A portrait miniature of a young boy, by Isaac Wane Slater, signed and dated 1813, 3in (7.5cm) high.
£1,800–2,000 / €2,600–2,900
$3,250–3,600 ⊞ BHa

A portrait miniature of a young man, oil on ivory, the reverse with enamel and hair inset, damaged, early 19thC, 2¼in (5.5cm) high.
£180–210 / €260–310
$320–380 ⚒ L&E

Sets/pairs

Unless otherwise stated, any description which refers to 'a set' or 'a pair' includes a guide price for the entire set or the pair, even though the illustration may show only a single item.

A portrait miniature of a military gentleman, English School, on ivory, early 19thC, 2¼in (5.5cm) high.
£165–195 / €240–290
$300–360 HOLL

A portrait miniature of a young man, by J. V. C. Way, signed and dated 1829, in a composition frame, 2in (5cm) high.
£600–720 / €880–1,050
$1,100–1,300 S

A portrait miniature of a lady, by F. T. Rochard, c1835, 4in (10cm) high.
£2,700–3,000 / €3,950–4,400
$4,900–5,400 BHa
Rochard was born in France but came to England in his twenties and made a career here. He is therefore considered a British miniaturist.

► A portrait miniature of a gentleman, by Horatio Nelson, Irish, Dublin, signed and dated 1846, 4in (10cm) square, framed.
£520–580 / €760–850
$940–1,050 SIL

A portrait miniature of Annibale Carracci as a young man, on enamel, inscribed on the reverse 'Annibale Carracci after a picture of himself, London April 1824, painted by Henry Bone RA enamel painter to His Majesty and enamel painter to His RH the Duke of York', in a gilt-metal frame, 3½in (9cm) diam.
£2,350–2,800 / €3,450–4,100
$4,250–5,100 G(B)

A portrait miniature of a young lady, English School, c1835, in a pierced gilt rococo frame, 4½in (11.5cm) high, with a leather case.
£490–580 / €720–850
$890–1,050 HYD

A portrait miniature of a young lady, by John Cox Dillman Engleheart, signed and dated 1829, in a gilt-metal frame, 5½in (14cm) high.
£4,500–5,000 / €6,600–7,300
$8,100–9,100 BHa

A portrait miniature of a lady, by Emma Eleanora Kendrick, c1835, in a gold locket frame, 4in (10cm) high.
£1,800–2,000 / €2,650–2,950
$3,250–3,600 BHa

◄ A portrait miniature of Alice and Minnie Squarey, possibly by Reginald Easton, the reverse inscribed 'painted about 1846', 5½in (14cm) high.
£3,000–3,600 / €4,400–5,300
$5,400–6,500 HYD

A portrait miniature of a lady, by Richard Schwager, Austrian, Vienna, c1850, in a diamond and jewel frame, 4in (10cm) high.
£4,050–4,500 / €5,900–6,600
$7,300–8,100 BHa

A portrait miniature of a lady, on ivory, c1850, in a silver brooch frame set with diamonds, with a gold back, 1¼in (3cm) high.
£1,000–1,100
€1,450–1,600
$1,800–2,000 ⊞ EXC

A portrait miniature of James II, by Henry Pierce Bone RA, after Sir Peter Lely, the reverse inscribed 'James, 2 May 1852', in a stiff-leaf gilt-metal frame, 4½in (11.5cm) high.
£2,350–2,800
€3,450–4,100
$4,250–5,100 ⚒ G(B)

A portrait miniature of Marie Anne de la Trémoille, Princesse des Ursins, on enamel, probably French, 19thC, 3½in (9cm) high.
£370–440 / €540–640
$670–800 ⚒ HYD

A portrait miniature of Charles I, English School, after Van Dyck, enamel on copper, 19thC, in a gilt-metal frame, 3in (7.5cm) high.
£1,000–1,200
€1,450–1,750
$1,800–2,150 ⚒ G(B)

A portrait miniature of a lady in late 18thC costume, on ivory, 19thC, 2¾in (7cm) high.
£90–105 / €130–155
$160–190 ⚒ TMA

A portrait miniature of a gentleman, English School, the reverse inscribed 'Algernon Sidney', 19thC, 1½in (4cm) high.
£300–360 / €440–530
$540–650 ⚒ HOLL

'Revival' Miniatures

Visitors to art galleries in the 19th century would have been familiar with the sight of professional copyists painting souvenir miniatures of celebrated works. This vestige of Grand Tour memorabilia was succeeded later on in the century by a more industrial production. Taking advantage of the developments in photography, sepia-toned images of large-scale paintings were projected onto a ground, often the man-made composition ivorine, and then hand-coloured. Replicating famous portraits of, among others, Marie-Antoinette, Napoleon and Nelson, these copies were frequently given spurious signatures. The names of artists such as Gainsborough and Vigée-LeBrun, neither of whom worked in miniature, occur regularly in this context. More deceptively, the names of Smart, Cosway and Plimer were also applied – however, the mistake made was to use the name in full, when in reality these artists only ever signed the front of their miniatures with initials and, in the case of Cosway and Plimer, only in their early periods.

◄ A portrait miniature of an elderly lady, 19thC, in a later yellow-metal mount on a velvet cushion, glazed and framed, 2½in (6.5cm) high.
£120–140 / €175–210
$220–260 ⚒ L&E

A pair of portrait miniatures of Louisa and Frederick Fisher, by Alexander Fisher, watercolour on ivory, c1900, 3½in (9cm) high.
£1,050–1,200
€1,550–1,750
$1,900–2,150 ⊞ EFA

A portrait miniature of a lady, 19thC, on ivory, in a brass frame, 2¾in (7cm) high.
£110–130 / €160–190
$200–240 ⚒ TMA

◄ A portrait miniature of Princess Victoria Mary of Teck, by Alyn Williams, signed and dated 1895, in an ormolu frame, 3in (7.5cm) high.
£2,850–3,200
€4,150–4,650
$5,200–5,800 ⊞ BHa

► A portrait miniature of a lady, by Pauline Appert, French School, on ivory, signed, 19thC, in a palisander and gilt-bronze frame, 4½in (11.5cm) high.
£450–540 / €660–790
$810–980 ⚒ S(P)

A portrait miniature of a lady, English School, watercolour on ivory, c1900, 3in (7.5cm) high.
£100–120 / €145–175
$175–210 ⚒ G(L)

Silhouettes

A pair of hollow cut silhouettes of a lady and a gentleman, by Mrs Harrington, labelled, c1790, 4in (10cm) high.
£315–350 / €470–520
$570–630 ⊞ PSC

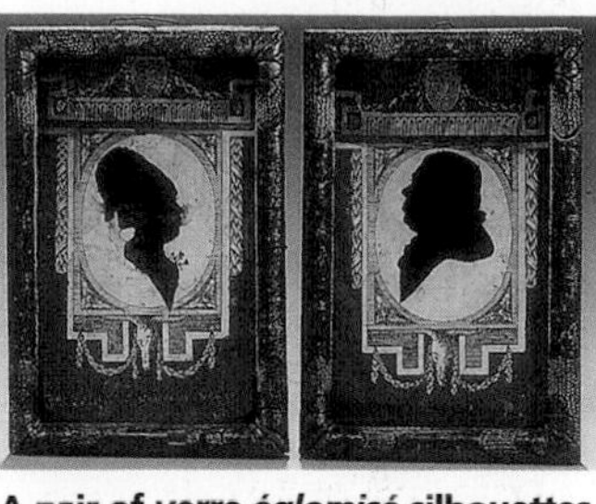

A pair of *verre églomisé* silhouettes of a lady and a gentleman, dated 1793, in moulded wooden frames, 7½in (19cm) high.
£1,100–1,300 / €1,600–1,900
$2,000–2,350 ⚒ S(Am)

A silhouette of a lady, by John Field, painted on paper, signed, c1800, in an ormolu frame, 3in (7.5cm) high.
£490–580 / €720–850
$890–1,050 ⚒ G(L)

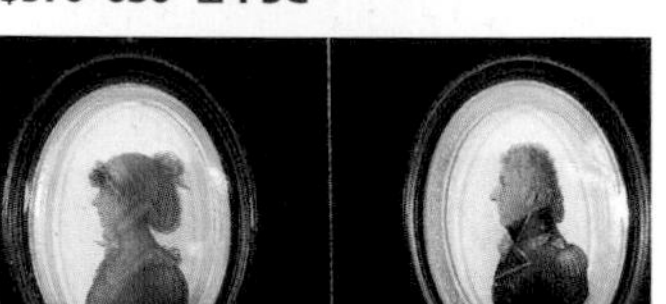

A pair of reverse-painted silhouettes of a Naval Officer and a Lady, by Arthur Lea, c1800, in *verre églomisé* frames, 3¾in (9.5cm) high.
£1,300–1,550 / €1,900–2,250
$2,350–2,800 ⚒ G(L)

A pair of painted plaster silhouettes, by M. R. Wall, c1800, in pearwood and *verre églomisé* frames, 5¼in (13.5cm) high.
£760–910 / €1,100–1,300
$1,400–1,650 ⚒ G(L)

A silhouette of an officer, by John Buncombe, painted on card, c1800, in a hammered-brass frame, 3½in (9cm) high.
£1,000–1,200
€1,450–1,750
$1,800–2,150 ⚒ MEA

A silhouette of Reverend Joseph Coltman MA with a bicycle, cut paper, early 19thC, in an ebonized frame, 10¼in (26cm) square.
£150–180 / €220–260
$270–320 ⚒ DA
The Reverend Joseph Coltman was curate of Beverley Minster, Yorkshire for 24 years. He died in 1837, weighing 37 stone 8lbs and is buried in Minster Yard.

A silhouette of Henrietta Theed and Mrs Theed dancing before Mrs Cuningham, by Augustin Edouart, cut on paper, inscribed and dated 1st March 1829, 9¾ x 13¼in (25 x 33.5cm).
£490–580 / €720–850
$890–1,050 ⚒ AH

A silhouette of a gentleman, by John Field, on card, signed, c1830, 3in (7.5cm) high.
£220–250 / €340–380
$400–450 ⊞ PSC

A silhouette group of Samuel and Bennet Whitaker with Alfred and Emily Agnes Whitaker and Mrs Ann Lord, attributed to the Royal Victorian Gallery, cut paper, bronzed, on a wash background, 1840–50, in a rosewood frame, 13¾ x 18¼in (35 x 46.5cm).
£500–600 / €730–880
$910–1,100 ⚒ L

A silhouette of a deer hunt, by Sanders K. G. Nellis, cut paper, inscribed 'Executed for the Honourable D. B. Viger by S. K. G. Nellis, Born Without Arms', dated 27 September 1845, Canadian, Montreal, 5¼ x 10in (13.5 x 25.5cm).
£380–450 / €550–660
$690–810 ⚒ RIT
Attached to the reverse is a copy of an 1836 newspaper article describing the nature of Master S. K. G. Nellis' travelling performances which delighted audiences across North America. His long list of talents included cutting silhouette portraits 'with scissors in toes', playing the violoncello and shooting targets with a bow and arrow.

An embossed and hand-painted silhouette of a cadet, by W. H. Brown, 1841, 9½ x 7in (24 x 18cm).
£450–540 / €660–790
$810–980 ⚒ DuM

Antiquities

A faïence offering cup, decorated with heiroglyphs, Egyptian, New Kingdom, 1400–1200 BC, 2in (5cm) high.
£175–195 / €260–290
$310–350 ⊞ MIL

A limestone stele, incised with figures and inscriptions, Egyptian, 19th Dynasty, 1305–1196 BC, 17¼in (44cm) high.
£3,950–4,700
€5,800–6,900
$7,100–8,500 ⚒ S(NY)

A composition amulet, in the form of Anubis, the god of embalming, Egyptian, Late Period, c600 BC, 1½in (4cm) high.
£110–125 / €160–180
$200–220 ⊞ MIL

A glazed composition funerary scarab, Egyptian, Late Period, c600 BC, 2¼in (5.5cm) high.
£170–190 / €250–280
$300–340 ⊞ MIL

◄ **A faïence shabti,** impressed with hieroglyphs, Egyptian, 6th–4thC BC, 4¼in (11cm) high.
£175–195 / €260–290
$310–350 ⊞ A&O

► **A pottery vessel,** Holy Land, 3000–2500 BC, 4½in (11.5cm) high.
£70–80 / €100–110
$125–140 ⊞ HEL

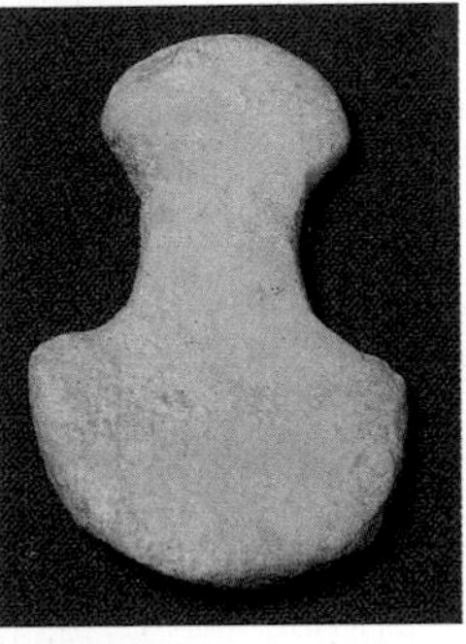

A marble idol, Anatolian, possibly from Troy, c2500 BC, 2½in (6.5cm) high.
£720–800 / €1,050–1,200
$1,300–1,450 ⊞ HEL

The items in this section have been arranged chronologically in sequence of civilizations, namely Egyptian, Near Eastern, Greek, Roman, Byzantine, western Europe, British, Anglo-Saxon and Medieval.

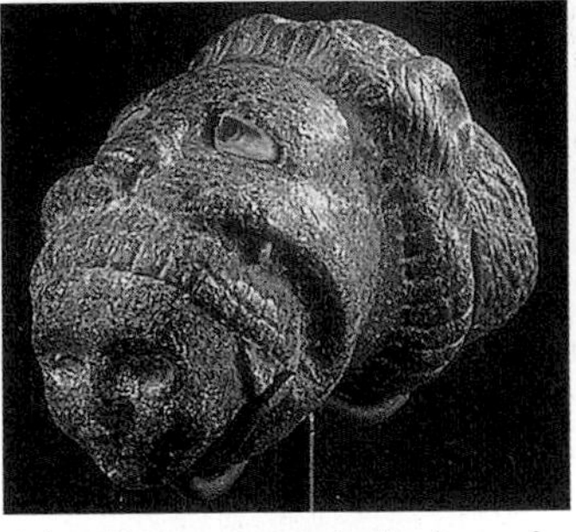

A lazulite protome, in the form of a lion's head holding a human head in its jaws, Syrian, 1100–700 BC, 2½in (6.5cm) high.
£3,300–3,950 / €4,800–5,700
$6,000–7,100 ⚒ S(NY)

A gold vase, Near East, 1100–900 BC, 2½in (6.5cm) high.
£3,300–3,950 / €4,800–5,700
$6,000–7,100 ⚒ S(NY)

A bronze model of a stag, Anatolian, c800 BC, 5in (12.5cm) high.
£580–650 / €850–950
$1,050–1,200 ⊞ A&O

◄ **A steatite mirror handle,** in the form of Bes holding a pair of serpents, Egypto-Phoenician, 3rdC BC, 4in (10cm) high.
£2,650–3,150
€3,850–4,600
$4,800–5,700
⚒ S(NY)

A bronze amphora, each handle in the form of a rampant feline, Parthian, 2nd–3rdC AD, 15¼in (38.5cm) high.
£2,650–3,150 / €3,850–4,600
$4,800–5,700 ⚒ S(NY)

A Mycenaean pottery stirrup jar, Greek, c1200 BC, 4in (10cm) diam.
£130–145 / €190–210
$230–260 ⊞ ANG

A pottery bowl, with geometric decoration, damaged and repaired, Cypriot, Iron Age, 11th–8thC BC, 6in (15cm) diam.
£130–145 / €190–210
$230–260 ⊞ ANG

A painted pottery amphora, Cypriot, Iron Age, 1050–650 BC, 5in (12.5cm) high.
£190–220 / €280–330
$360–400 ⊞ HEL

A painted pottery bowl, Cypriot, 1050–650 BC, 5¼in (13.5cm) diam.
£160–180 / €230–260
$290–330 ⊞ HEL

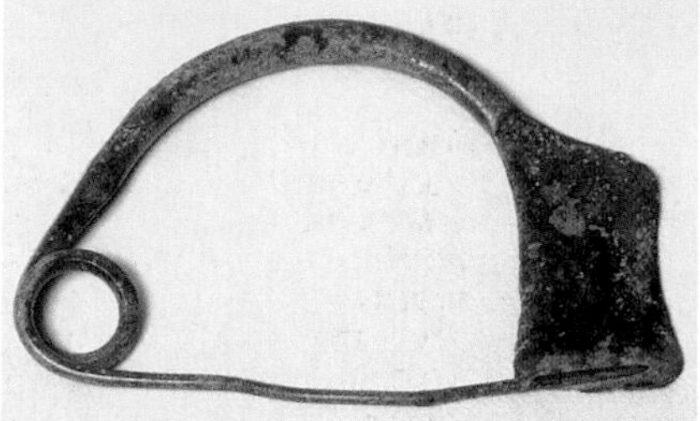

A bronze bow brooch, Greek, 8thC BC, 4¼in (11cm) long.
£110–125 / €160–180
$200–220 ⊞ ANG

An Etruscan terracotta votive profile portrait head, damaged, 6thC BC, 11in (28cm) high.
£900–1,000 / €1,300–1,450
$1,600–1,800 ⊞ MIL

A Daunian terracotta olla, decorated with olive branches, with two handles, Greek South Italy, 6th–4thC BC, 9½in (24cm) high.
£460–520 / €670–760
$830–940 ⊞ MIL

An Attic Black-Figure cup, painted with eyes flanking a rooster, Greek, 520–510 BC, 8¾in (22cm) diam.
£2,950–3,500 / €4,300–5,100
$5,300–6,300 ⚒ S(NY)

A terracotta figure of a votary, holding a piglet, Greek, early 5thC BC, 10½in (26.5cm) high.
£5,300–6,300
€7,700–9,200
$9,600–11,400 ⚒ S(NY)

◀ **A terracotta figure of a man,** slight damage, Greek, Boeotian, 5thC BC, 6in (15cm) high.
£270–310 / €400–450
$490–550 ⊞ MIL

► **A bronze greave,** Greek, 5th–4thC BC, 16½in (42cm) long.
£2,950–3,500
€4,300–5,100
$5,300–6,300 ⚒ Herm

Votaries

Ancient civilizations took the business of life after death very seriously and a good deal of communication took place between the living and their ancestors or the gods, both publicly and privately. Votive objects were left as sacrificial offerings, frequently in the form of small figures that represented the person making the offering or a deity who could make the offering in their stead.

A moulded pottery head of Demeter, Greek, 4thC BC, 3¾in (9.5cm) high.
£160–180 / €230–260
$290–330 ⊞ HEL

A glazed pottery oinochoe, with a trefoil mouth and ribbed body, Greek South Italy, 4thC BC, 4in (10cm) high.
£180–200 / €260–290
$320–360 ⊞ HEL

◄ A pottery cup, Greek South Italy, 4thC BC, 3¾in (9.5cm) diam.
£85–95
€125–140
$150–170
⊞ ANG

► A Red-Figure lekythos, decorated with a palmette, Greek South Italy, chipped, 4thC BC, 3½in (9cm) high.
£110–125 / €160–185
$200–230 ⊞ ANG

A Gnathian ware lekythos, the ribbed body with slipware decoration to the neck and shoulder, Greek South Italy, 4thC BC, 4in (10cm) high.
£160–180 / €230–260
$290–330 ⊞ ANG

► A glazed pottery guttus, with vertical spout and ring handle, decorated with a relief mask of Demeter, surrounded by ribbing, Greek South Italy, 4thC BC, 4¼in (11cm) high.
£220–250 / €320–360
$400–450 ⊞ ANG

◄ A Red-Figure dish, slip-decorated with a Lady of Fashion, rim chips, Greek South Italy, 4th–3rdC BC, 4½in (11.5cm) diam.
£230–270
€340–390
$420–490
⊞ A&O

A terracotta figure of a votary, some slip decoration remaining, Boeotian, 4th–3rdC BC, 6½in (16.5cm) high.
£580–650 / €850–950
$1,050–1,200 ⊞ HEL

► A glass footed bowl, with lathe-cut grooved decoration, Hellenistic, late 3rd–early 2ndC BC, 7¼in (18.5cm) high.
£4,600–5,500
€6,700–8,000
$8,400–10,000
⚒ S(NY)

A terracotta figure of a woman, probably Myrina, some gesso and pigment remaining, Hellenistic, 3rd–2ndC BC, 7in (18cm) high.
£2,500–3,000
€3,650–4,400
$4,550–5,400 ⚒ S(NY)

Buying Ancient Pottery

Before you buy an object always ask the provenance and, if you are buying from a dealer, ask for a certificate of authenticity. Wherever possible buy an item with as little restoration as possible, as this does have a detrimental affect on value, although less so on more elaborate and rare pieces. Always ask about the condition of the object before you buy. Items that have only been repaired have a greater value than those that have been repaired and restored.

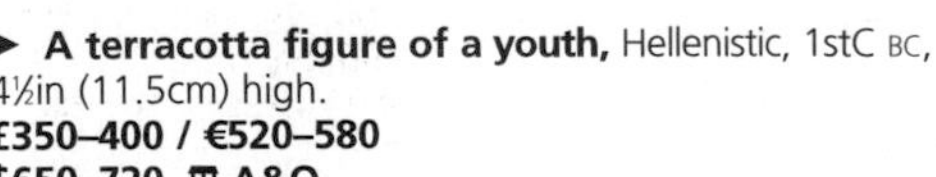

► A terracotta figure of a youth, Hellenistic, 1stC BC, 4½in (11.5cm) high.
£350–400 / €520–580
$650–720 ⊞ A&O

A brooch, in the form of two addorsed lions, Roman, late 1stC BC, 1¼in (3cm) wide.
£85–95 / €120–140
$150–170 ⊞ ANG

A pottery jug, slight damage, Roman, 1stC AD, 5¼in (13.5cm) high.
£100–115 / €145–170
$180–210 ⊞ CrF

A bronze figure of a votary, on a presentation base, Roman, 1stC AD, 3¼in (8.5cm) high.
£400–450 / €580–660
$720–810 ⊞ MIL

A bronze patera handle terminal, in the form of a ram's head, with lead infill, Roman, 1stC AD, 2in (5cm) long.
£85–95 / €120–140
$150–170 ⊞ ANG

A marble figure of the Knidian Aphrodite, after the statue by Praxiteles, Roman, 1st–2ndC AD, 12¼in (31cm) high.
£4,000–4,800
€5,800–7,000
$7,200–8,700 ⚒ S(NY)

A glass jug, with applied handle, Roman, 1st–2ndC AD, 5¼in (13.5cm) high.
£490–550 / €720–800
$890–1,000 ⊞ G&G

A brooch, in the form of a lion, Roman Gaul, 1st–2ndC AD, 1½in (4cm) wide.
£120–135 / €175–195
$220–250 ⊞ ANG

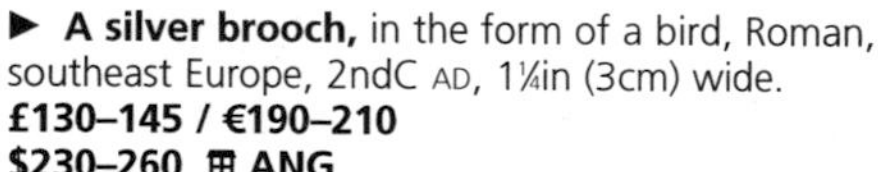

► **A silver brooch,** in the form of a bird, Roman, southeast Europe, 2ndC AD, 1¼in (3cm) wide.
£130–145 / €190–210
$230–260 ⊞ ANG

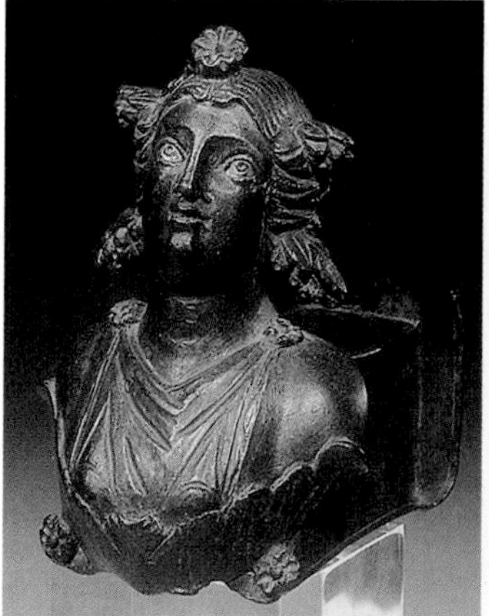

A bronze protome bust of a maenad, Roman, 2nd–3rdC AD, 5¼in (13.5cm) high.
£4,300–5,100 / €6,300–7,400
$7,800–9,200 ⚒ S(NY)

A terracotta equestrian group, Roman, Eastern Empire, 2nd–3rdC AD, 5¼in (13.5cm) high.
£530–590 / €770–860
$960–1,200 ⊞ A&O

A glass flask, with trailing zigzag decoration to the lip and shoulder, slight damage, Roman, 3rdC AD, 1¾in (4.5cm) high.
£400–450 / €580–660
$720–810 ⊞ G&G

A bronze lamp and stand, the lamp handle surmounted by a bird, the swivel cover in the form of a scallop shell, on tripod claw feet, Byzantine, 5th–6thC AD, 11¼in (28.5cm) high.
£2,500–3,000
€3,650–4,400
$4,550–5,400 S(NY)

A stone bas relief, depicting a man on horseback, probably an Emperor, bearing a cross, with a Greek cross below, Byzantine, losses and restoration, 12th–13thC, 36 x 26½in (91.5 x 67.5cm).
£6,600–7,900
€9,600–11,500
$11,900–14,300 S(NY)

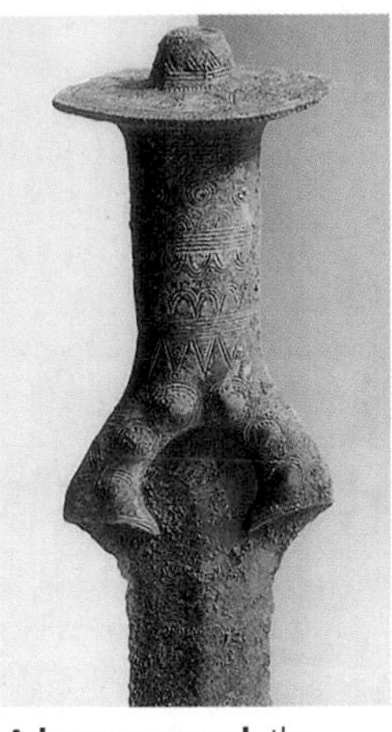

A bronze sword, the blade mount decorated with six false rivets, the grip and domed pommel with geometric decoration, central European, c1500 BC, 23¾in (60.5cm) long.
£4,050–4,850
€5,900–7,100
$7,300–8,800 Herm

A bronze sickle, Ancient Gaul, c900 BC, 7½in (19cm) long.
£85–95 / €125–140
$150–170 ANG

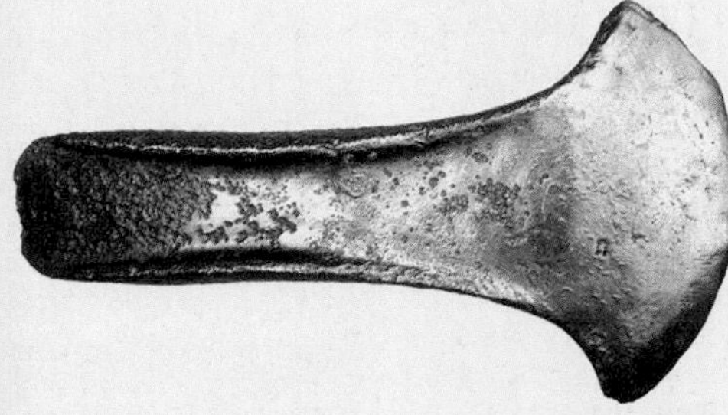

◄ **A bronze axe,** slight pitting, 1600–1400 BC, 5in (12.5cm) wide.
£300–340 / €440–500
$540–620 A&O

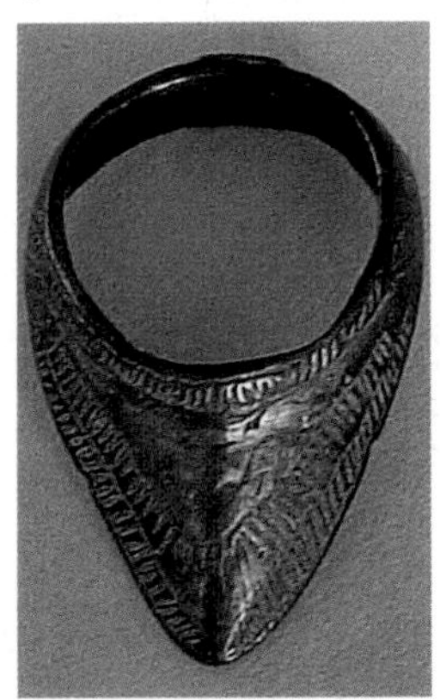

► **An archer's silvered-bronze thumb ring,** with engraved design, 14thC.
£90–100 / €130–145
$160–180 MIL

Tribal Art

A Northwest Coast wooden box, lid missing, Canadian, British Columbia, 17in (43cm) wide.
£2,300–2,750
€3,300–4,000
$4,200–5,000 S(P)
Such coffers were used to store ancestral treasures such as crest hats. The sides of these chests were constructed from a single piece of steamed bent wood.

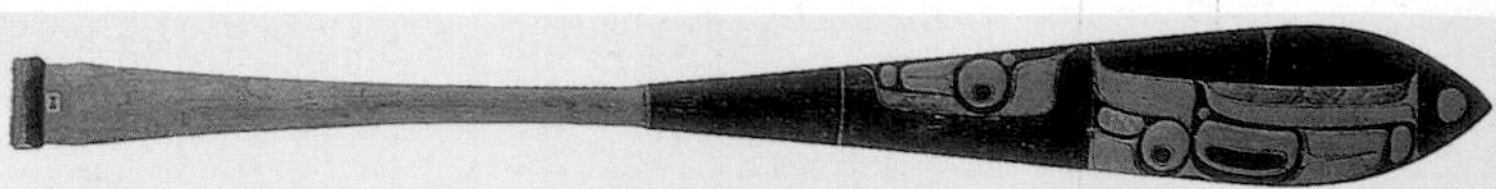

A Northwest Coast wooden paddle, both sides with painted decoration, Canadian, British Columbia, 58½in (148.5cm) long.
£4,500–5,400 / €6,600–7,900
$8,200–9,800 S(P)

► **A pair of Cheyenne lady's beaded leggings,** Native American, c1890, 11in (28cm) long.
£480–570 / €700–830
$870–1,050 JAA

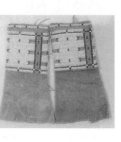

► **A Cheyenne beaded hide, cloth and wood miniature cradle,** boards damaged, Native American, late 19thC, 8in (20.5cm) high.
£1,250–1,450
€1,850–2,100
$2,250–2,600 SK

► **A Crow/Blackfoot beaded knife case,** Native American, c1890, 13in (33cm) long.
£1,250–1,500
€1,850–2,200
$2,250–2,700 JAA

◄ **An Iroquois man's beaded cap,** Native American, late 19thC, 9in (23cm) long.
£175–210
€250–300
$320–380 JAA

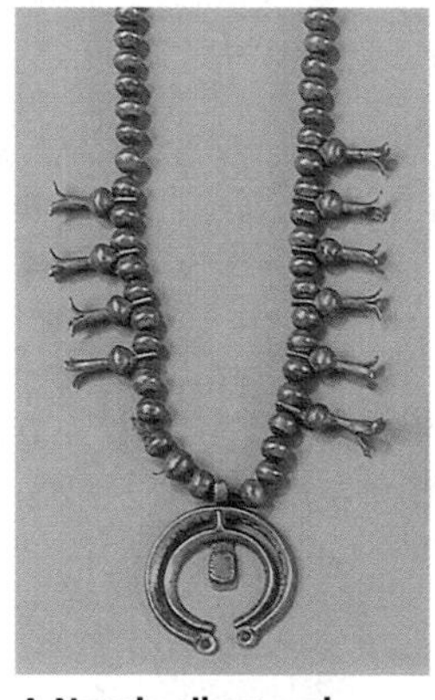

A Navajo silver and turquoise necklace, with 12 squash blossoms, the double-barred Naja set with a turquoise in a serrated bezel, damaged, Native American, c1900, 13½in (34.5cm) long.
£1,300–1,550
€1,900–2,250
$2,350–2,800 SK

A Navajo saddle blanket, repaired, tassels later, Native American, c1900, 71½ x 52in (181.5 x 132cm).
£410–490 / €600–720
$740–880 WcH

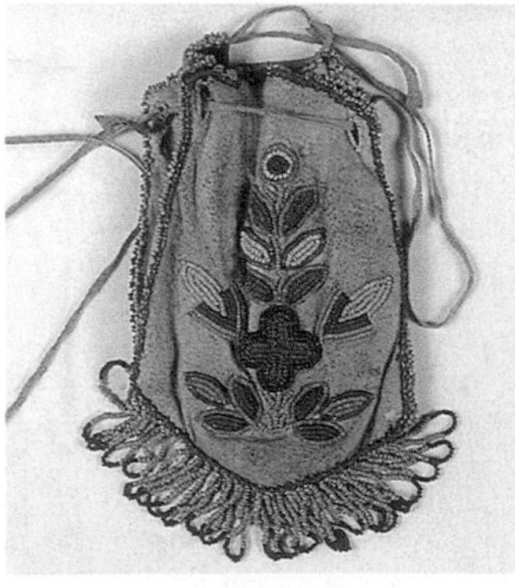

A Prairie beaded pouch, Native American, c1910, 5¾in (14.5cm) long.
£125–150 / €180–220
$230–270 JAA
Note the bright orange and red shades of some of the beadwork on this pouch. Harsher coloured beads are a good indicator that an artefact is of later date, ie 1910–20. When looking for older beadwork avoid items sewn with cotton. Earlier examples of beadwork will be strung on beige-coloured gut or sinew.

◄ **A carved wood totem pole,** the front carved with human and animal forms, Native American, c1900, 20in (51cm) high.
£580–690
€840–1,000
$1,050–1,250
SK

A Sioux boy's beaded vest, Native American, c1890, 17in (43cm) long.
£1,650–1,950 / €2,400–2,850
$3,000–3,550 JAA

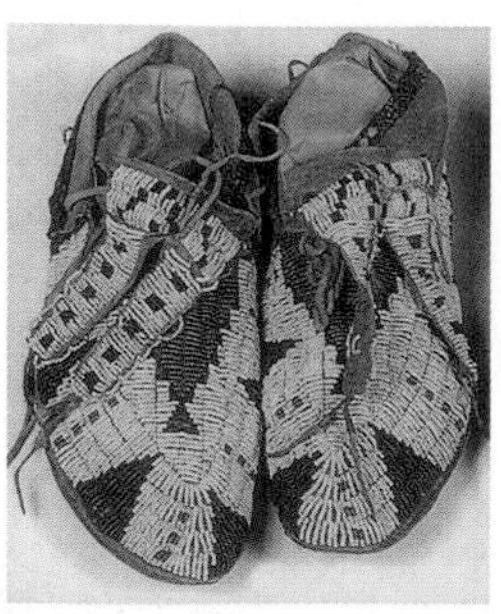

A pair of Sioux men's beaded moccasins, Native American, c1900, 10¼in (26cm) long.
£700–830 / €1,000–1,150
$1,250–1,450 JAA

A Sioux beaded pipe bag, Native American, c1900, 30in (76cm) long, with fringe.
£890–1,050 / €1,300–1,550
$1,600–1,900 JAA

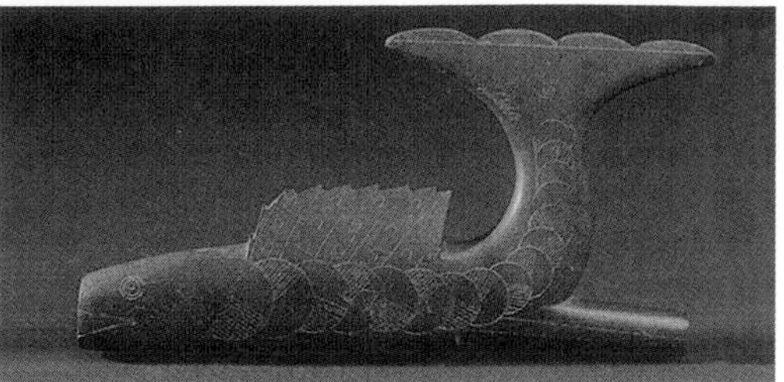

A catlinite pipe bowl, in the form of a fish, Native American, c1900, 8¼in (21cm) wide.
£350–410 / €510–600
$630–740 JAA

Catlinite is a red stone composed of compressed clay which, due to its soft character, is ideal for carving pipes. Such pipes are typically smooth and plastic in their modelling and in the case of this example it is also intricately incised. More commonly, simple angular catlinite pipes may be inlaid with sparse lead designs.

A Lobi wooden maternity figure, losses and damage, African, Burkina Faso, 4¼in (11cm) high.
£2,150–2,550
€3,150–3,700
$3,900–4,600 S(P)

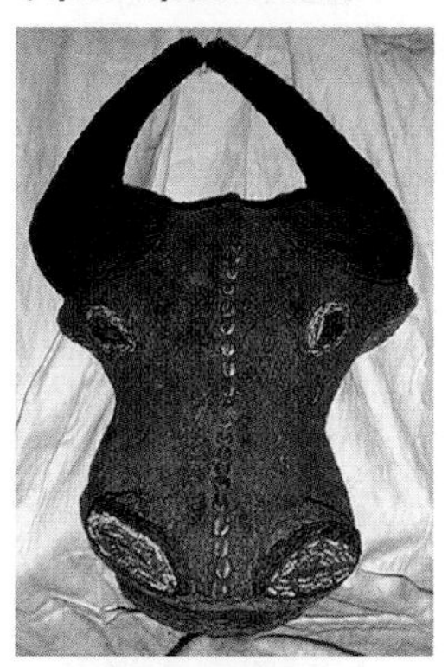

► A carved wood chair, African, Cameroon, 31¾in (80.5cm).
£1,900–2,250
€2,750–3,250
$3,450–4,050 S(O)

◄ A Bamum wood, bead and fabric royal icon helmet mask, in the form of a buffalo head, African, Cameroon, c1965, 26in (66cm) high.
£350–390 / €510–570
$630–700 ⊞ ARTi

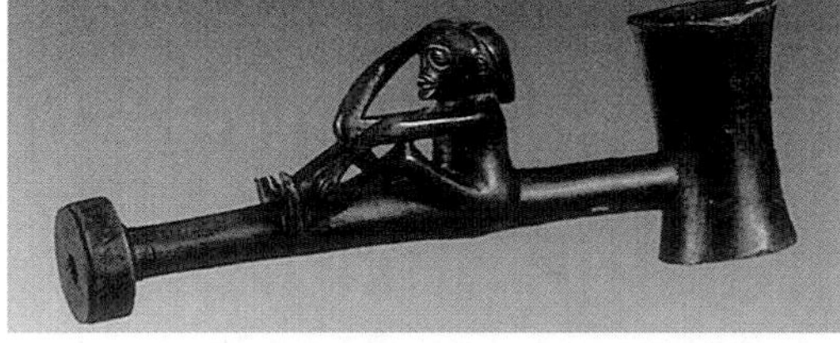

A Luena wood pipe, the stem carved with the form of a woman, damaged, African, Democratic Republic of Congo, 10¾in (27.5cm) long.
£1,900–2,250 / €2,750–3,250
$3,450–4,050 S(P)

A chief's Venetian glass and leopard's tooth necklace, slight damage, African, Democratic Republic of Congo, collected 1972, 16½in (42cm) long.
£2,050–2,450
€3,000–3,600
$3,700–4,450 S(P)

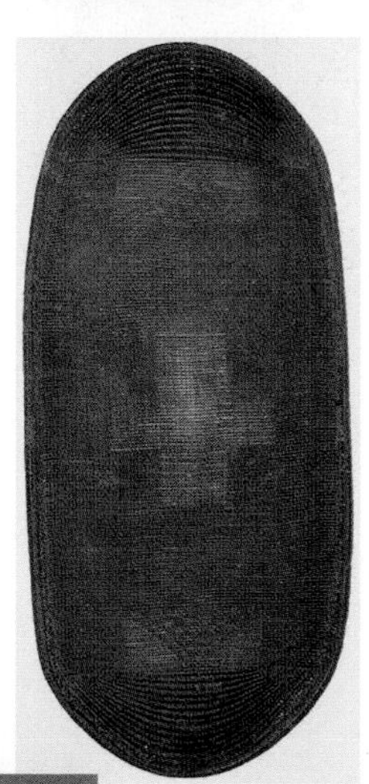

◄ An Azande rattan and wood shield, the reverse with a carved panel, slight damage, African, Democratic Republic of Congo, 19thC, 40½in (103cm) high.
£1,450–1,650
€2,100–2,400
$2,600–3,000
⊞ FAC

An Ashanti carved wood stool, with pierced and punched decoration, African, Ghana, early 20thC, 17in (43cm) wide.
£120–140 / €175–200
$220–250 F&C

Although Ashanti stools are relatively common, there is something very appealing about their solid and often geometric construction. Originally, the stools were made for Ashanti chiefs and each different pattern represented a proverb or symbol of authority. They are both practical and collectable.

An ivory bracelet, with pokerwork decoration, damaged, African, Ethiopia, 19thC or earlier, 5¼in (13.5cm) diam.
£1,500–1,750 / €2,200–2,550
$2,700–3,150 S(P)

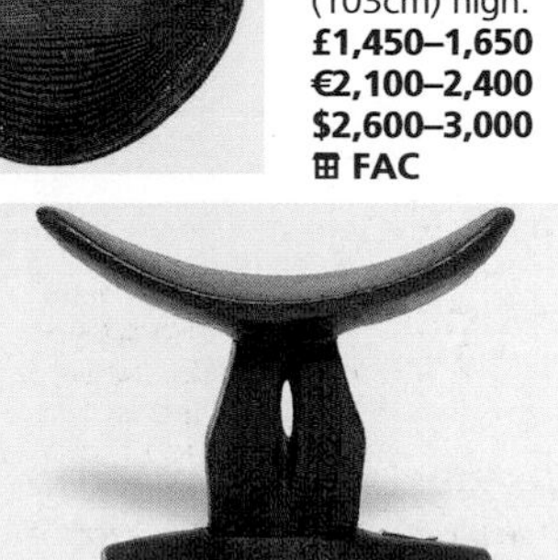

A wood headrest, African, Ethiopia, early 20thC, 9in (23cm) wide.
£140–160 / €200–230
$250–290 ⊞ Trib

An Ashanti carved wood stool, with incised decoration, African, Ghana, 21½in (54.5cm) wide.
£210–250 / €310–370
$380–450 ⚒ WW

Items in the Tribal Art section have been arranged in geographical sequence from west to east starting with Native American artefacts.

A Pende carved ivory necklace, decorated with 11 graduated stylized heads with glass trade bead spacers, African, Gabon, largest head 2¼in (5.5cm) long.
£550–650 / €800–950
$1,000–1,150 ⚒ SK

A Tsogho carved wood figure, African, Gabon, 5in (12.5cm) high.
£1,650–1,950
€2,400–2,850
$3,000–3,550
⚒ S(P)

A Dan Gunyeya wooden mask, with a plaited fibre beard, the crest with an iron nail and traces of kaolin, African, Ivory Coast, 5in (12.5cm) wide.
£940–1,100
€1,350–1,600
$1,700–2,000
⚒ F&C

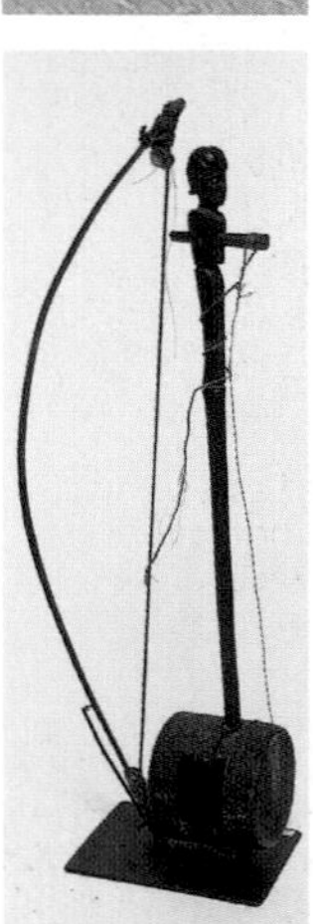

A Bambara carved wood Tji-Wara headdress, in the form of an antelope, African, Mali, 13½in (34.5cm) wide.
£900–1,050 / €1,300–1,550
$1,650–1,900 ⚒ S(O)
Bambara headdresses such as this were worn in dance ceremonies by the Tji-Wara society in order to increase crop fertility.

◄ **A Senufo carved wood model of a hornbill,** African, Ivory Coast, c1970, 42in (106.5cm) high.
£350–390 / €510–570
$630–700 ⊞ ARTi
The hornbill is a symbol of fertility and the mythological Senufo creator.

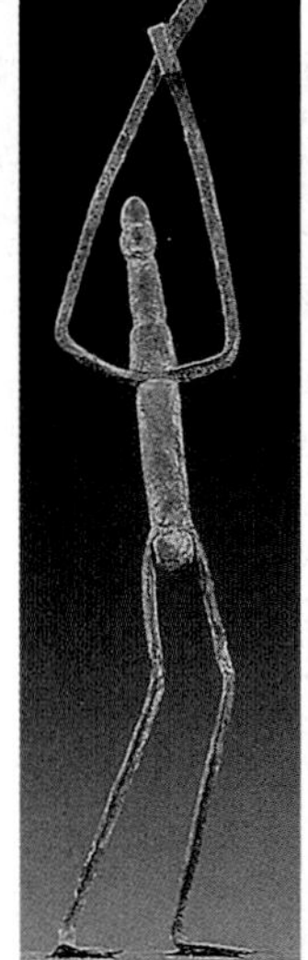

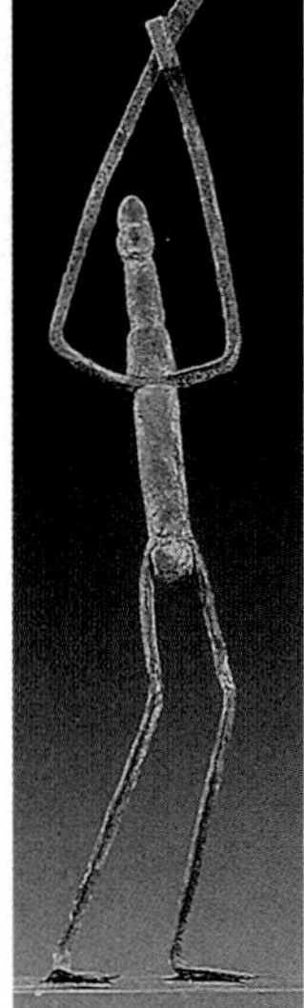

◄ **A Dogon bronze figure,** African, Mali, 4½in (11.5cm) high.
£1,650–1,950
€2,400–2,850
$3,000–3,500
⚒ S(P)

A Makonde wood musical instrument, African, Mozambique, early 20thC, 25in (63.5cm) high.
£490–540
€710–790
$890–980
⊞ Trib

An Ekoi wood and antelope skin dance headdress, carved as a stylized human head, on a basketwork base, evidence of hair attachment, African, Nigeria, Cross River region, 10¼in (26cm) high.
£230–270 / €330–390
$410–490 ⚒ F&C

An ivory side-blown trumpet, carved with warrior figures and scroll devices, slight damage, Nigerian, Benin, 28in (71cm) long.
£3,250–3,850
€4,750–5,600
$5,900–7,000 ⚒ SK

A Yoruba carved wood offering cup, loss and damage, African, Nigeria, Ikiti region, 11¼in (28.5cm) wide.
£2,950–3,550 / €4,300–5,200
$5,600–6,400 ⚒ S(P)
Such ceremonial cups were used to store objects of divination such as palm nuts or a metal chain.

A Yoruba carved wood divination tray, African, Nigeria, 17¾in (45cm) wide.
£900–1,050 / €1,300–1,550
$1,650–1,900 S(O)
Divination trays are covered with sawdust while the diviner uses a *tapa* to communicate with the spirits. He then throws 16 palm nuts or a chain which provides answers to the questions asked by his client.

A Zulu ceramic beer pot, South African, early 20thC, 10in (25.5cm) diam.
£520–580 / €760–850
$940–1,050 Trib
These pots were used for serving beer during rituals.

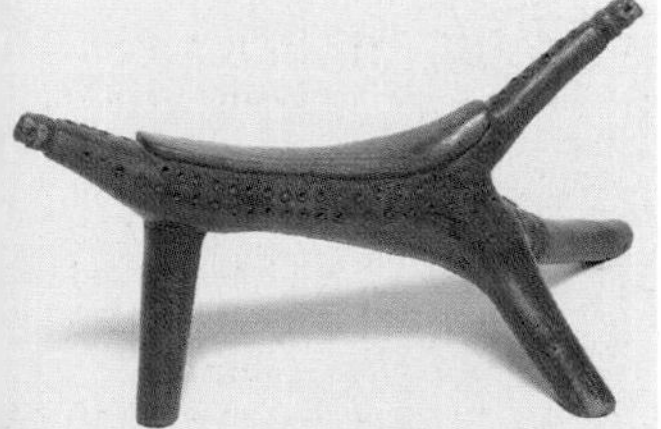

A Dinka wooden headrest, decorated with brass roundels, African, south Sudan, early 20thC, 18in (45.5cm) wide.
£770–850 / €1,100–1,250
$1,400–1,550 Trib

► **A pair of Yoruba wood and cowri shell *ibeji* figures,** African, Nigeria, 10¼in (26cm) high.
£1,000–1,150 / €1,450–1,700
$1,800–2,100 S(O)
The Yoruba tribe has the highest incidence of twin births in the world, and they are considered a blessing. If one of them died, a figure would be commissioned for the mother to care for as if it were living, to look after its soul and prevent it from taking the surviving twin. If both the twins died, a pair of figures was carved.

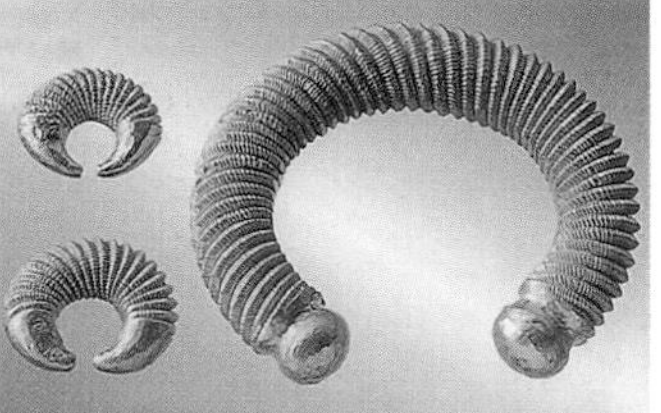

A Peulh 22ct gold bracelet and earrings, West African, c1900, bangle 3½in (9cm) wide.
£7,600–9,100 / €11,100–13,300
$13,800–16,500 Herm
The Peulh or Fulani are a nomadic people spread across West Africa from Nigeria to Senegal on the Atlantic coast. Most of the objects made by the Peulh are for practical uses. The women, however, are renowned for their elaborate gold jewellery including large earrings.

A Tutsi wicker shield, African, Rwanda, early 20thC, 31in (78.5cm) high.
£770–850 / €1,100–1,250
$1,400–1,550 Trib

◄ **A Bongo wooden staff,** the carved female figure terminal with copper marks to the face, African, Sudan, early 20thC, 38in (96.5cm) high.
£400–450 / €580–660
$720–810 Trib

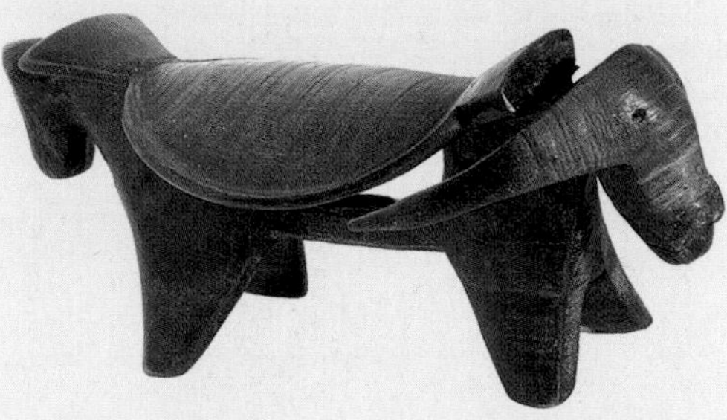

A Nguni wood neckrest, one end carved as a bull with horns, the other end carved as a cow, slight damage, African, Tanzania, c1900, 19in (48.5cm) wide.
£8,200–9,800 / €11,800–14,200
$14,800–17,700 F&C

◄ **A Sukuma leather shield,** African, Tanzania, c1925, 24in (61cm) high.
£770–850
€1,100–1,250
$1,400–1,550
Trib

A padouk wood dhow chest, with brass-studded decoration, lock and corner plates, African, Zanzibar, 19thC, 74in (188cm) wide.
£2,900–3,450 / €4,250–5,000
$5,200–6,200 BWL

A carved wood window shutter, depicting masks and oxen heads, the eyes picked out in bone, the handle carved with a crouching figure, Indonesian, Sulawesi, 38in (96.5cm) high.
£210–250 / €310–370
$380–450 ⚒ NSal

A carved wood Igorot figure, Philippino, 14in (35.5cm) high.
£3,100–3,700
€4,550–5,400
$5,600–6,700 ⚒ S(P)

► A Kunwinjku Aboriginal bark painting, Australian, western Arnhemland, c1950, 27in (68.5cm) high.
£450–530 / €660–780
$810–960 ⚒ S(P)
This bark painting was collected in the 1950s and represents Borlung, the Serpent Rainbow, with the head of a kangaroo, the body of a snake and the tail of a crocodile.

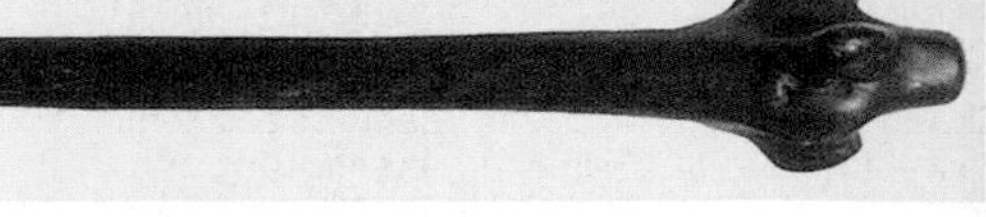

A rootwood club, with chip-carved decoration, slight damage and repair, Fijian, early 19thC, 44in (112cm) long.
£230–270 / €330–390
$420–490 ⚒ F&C

Miller's Compares

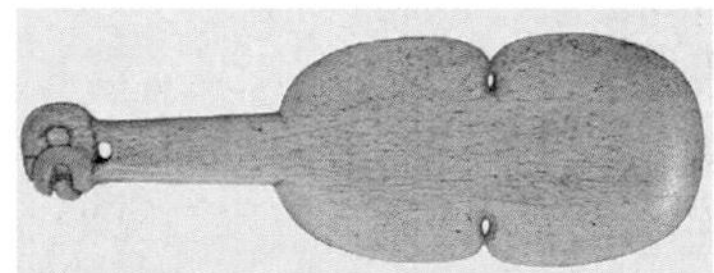

I. A Maori whalebone hand club (*kotiate*), with a pierced sinus to each side, the grip with perforation for a wrist thong, with a carved *tiki* head finial, New Zealand, 1800–50, 14in (35.5cm) long.
£4,850–5,800 / €7,100–8,500
$8,800–10,500 ⚒ F&C

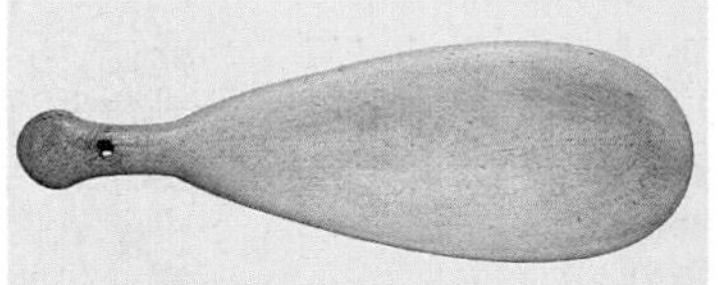

II. A Maori whalebone hand club (*patu paroa*), the waisted grip with perforation for a wrist thong, New Zealand, 1800–50, 18½in (47cm) long.
£1,200–1,400 / €1,750–2,050
$2,150–2,550 ⚒ F&C

Item I, the violin-shaped *kotiate* hand club is a rarer type than Item II, the more simply carved spatulate *patu paroa* club. The more elaborate *tiki* head carved at the base of the handle of Item I provides additional decorative appeal and value.

A Maori wood staff, New Zealand, 19thC, 67¾in (172cm) long.
£1,800–2,100
€2,650–3,050
$3,250–3,800 ⚒ S(P)
During the 19th century quarter staffs, *taiaha*, were popular weapons among the Maoris. These weapons were used for thrusting and parrying while staffs such as the one illustrated which were decorated with flax, feathers and dog hair became symbols of authority used by orators. *Taiaha* survive in some abundance and their value is dependent on age, quality and condition.

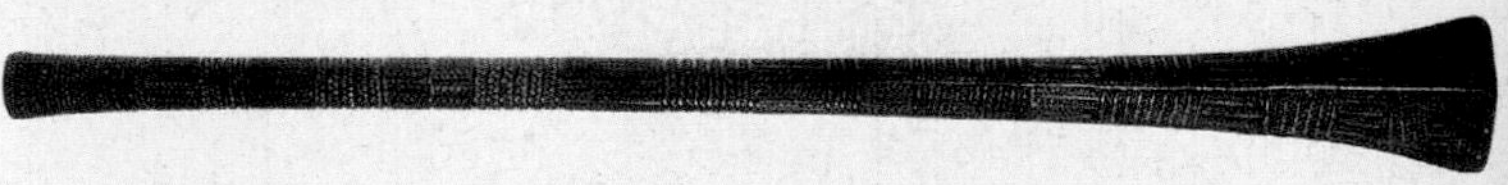

A wood palm leaf club (*apa apai*), with a diamond section blade, the grip carved with zigzag decoration, slight damage, Tongan, 1800–50, 39¼in (99.5cm) long.
£1,500–1,750 / €2,200–2,550
$2,700–3,150 ⚒ F&C

A wood war club, with a tooth-form head, damaged, Samoan, 19thC, 31½in (80cm) long
£230–270 / €340–390
$420–490 ⚒ CHTR

A casuarina-wood pole club, carved with panels of zigzag and spiral patterned decoration, one panel depicting a primitive axe, slight loss and damage, Tongan, 1800–50, 39¾in (101cm) long.
£1,100–1,300 / €1,600–1,900
$2,000–2,350 ⚒ F&C

Books & Book Illustrations

Charles Aleyn, *The Historie of That Wise and Fortunate Prince, Henrie of that Name the Seventh, King of England..*, printed by Tho. Cotes for William Cooke, 1638, 8°, sheepskin, worn.
£440–520 / €640–760
$800–960 RTo

Items in the Books & Book Illustrations section have been arranged in alphabetical order.

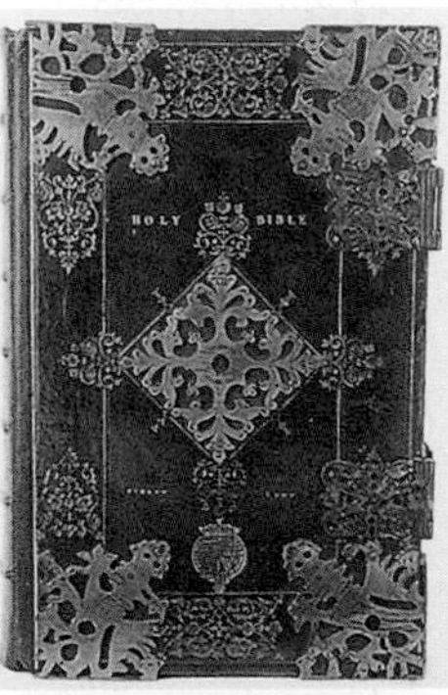

▶ The Holy Bible, printed by Robert Barker, London, 1602, 17¾in (45cm) high, gilt leather, brass armorial corner pieces, cover with royal coat-of-arms.
£3,500–4,200
€5,100–6,100
$6,300–7,600 GIL

J. M. Barrie, *Peter Pan in Kensington Gardens*, illustrated by Arthur Rackham, published by Hodder & Stoughton, London, 1906, No. 2 of edition of 500, 11 x 9in (28 x 23cm).
£2,250–2,500
€3,300–3,800
$4,050–4,500 BAY

Pierre Bernard (and others), *Le Jardin des Plantes, Description complète, historique et pittoresque de Muséum d'Histoire Naturelle, de la Ménagerie, des Serres, des Galeries de Minérologie et d'Anatomie, et de la Vallée Suisse*, 2 vols, Paris, 1842–43, large 8°, 183 engraved plates, 32 hand-coloured plates, wood engravings, gilt half morocco, slight wear.
£290–350 / €430–510
$530–630 DW

◀ *Old English Ballads,* illustrated by Birkett Foster, Joseph Nash and others, c1870, 9in (23cm) high.
£95–105 / €140–155
$170–190 TDG

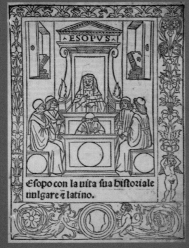

Pierre Boitard, *Le jardin des Plantes description et Moeurs des Mammifères de la Ménagerie et du Muséum d'Histoire Naturelle*, Paris, 1842, 4°, 4 hand-coloured engravings, 51 plates, folding aquatint plan and two tinted litho plates, gilt half morocco.
£80–95 / €115–135
$145–170 ⚒ DW

► Miguel de Cervantes Saavedra, *Vida y Hechos del Ingenioso Cavallero Don Quixote de la Mancha*, published by Acosta de Francisco Laso Mercader de Libros, Madrid, 1714, 16 engraved illustrations, vellum, string ties, minor loss.
£300–360 / €440–520
$800–960 ⚒ BBA

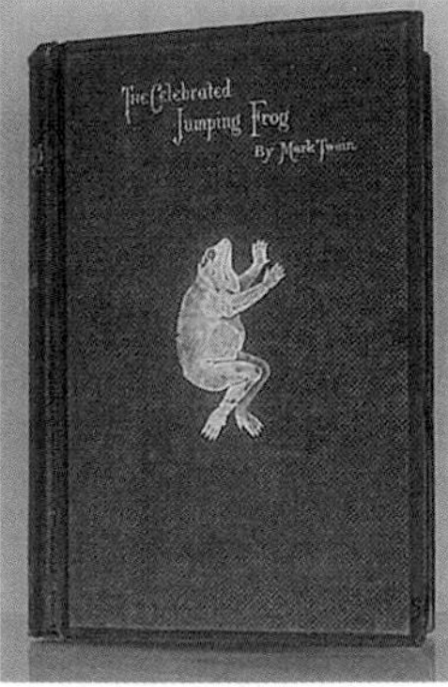

Samuel L. Clemens (Mark Twain), *The Celebrated Jumping Frog of Calaveras County, and Other Stories*, edited by John Paul, published by Charles Henry Webb, New York, first edition, 1867, 12°, gold-stamped cloth, morocco-tipped slipcase, wear, repaired.
£5,300–6,300
€7,700–9,200
$9,600–11,400 ⚒ S(NY)

► Arthur Crichton *The Festival of Flora*, published by N. Hailes, London, second edition, 1818, 8°, 7 plates, cloth-backed marbled boards.
£175–210 / €260–310
$320–380 ⚒ DW

James Bolton, *Harmonia Ruralis; or, an Essay towards a Natural History of British Song Birds*, published by W. T. Gilling, London, 1824, 4°, 1 vol of 2, 40 hand-coloured engraved plates, half morocco, worn, damaged.
£680–810 / €990–1,150
$1,200–1,450 ⚒ RTo

OBSERVATIONS
UPON THE
ANTIQUITIES
Of the TOWN of
HERCULANEUM,
Difcovered at the Foot of
MOUNT VESUVIUS.
With fome Reflections on the PAINTING and SCULPTURE of the Ancients.
And a fhort Defcription of the ANTIQUITIES in the Neighbourhood of NAPLES.
By Mr. BELLICARD, Architect, Member of the Academies of BOLOGNA and FLORENCE.
Enriched with Forty-two PLATES, defigned and engraved by the Author.
LONDON:
Printed for D. WILSON, and T. DURHAM, at Plato's Head, in the Strand.
MDCCLIII.

THE
FESTIVAL
OF
FLORA.
LONDON:
PRINTED FOR N. HAILES,
PICCADILLY
1819.

Book of Hours, 'Agony in the Garden', a full-page miniature on vellum, Belgium or north France, mid-15thC, 4 x 3¼in (10.5 x 8cm).
£2,350–2,800
€3,450–4,050
$4,250–5,000 ⚒ BBA

◄ Charles Nicolas Cochin and Jerome Charles Bellicard, *Observations Upon the Antiquities of the Town of Herculaneum*, printed for D. Wilson and T. Durham, London, 1753, 8°, 42 etched plates, full calf.
£260–310 / €380–450
$470–560 ⚒ DW

Edward Curtis, *The North American Indian*, Cambridge, Massachusetts, foreword signed by Theodore Roosevelt, 1907, 4°, vol 1, gilt half morocco.
£8,600–10,300
€12,600–15,000
$15,600–18,600 ⚒ S(NY)

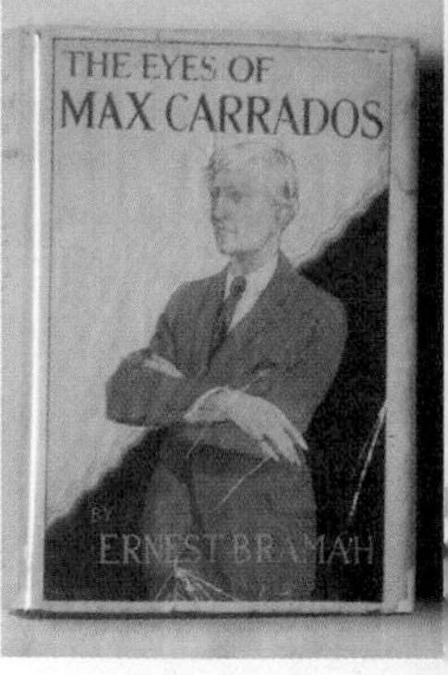

Ernest Bramah, *The Eyes of Max Carrados*, published by Grant Richards, London, first edition, 1932, 9 x 5in (23 x 12.5cm).
£1,350–1,500
€1,950–2,200
$2,450–2,700 ⊞ NW

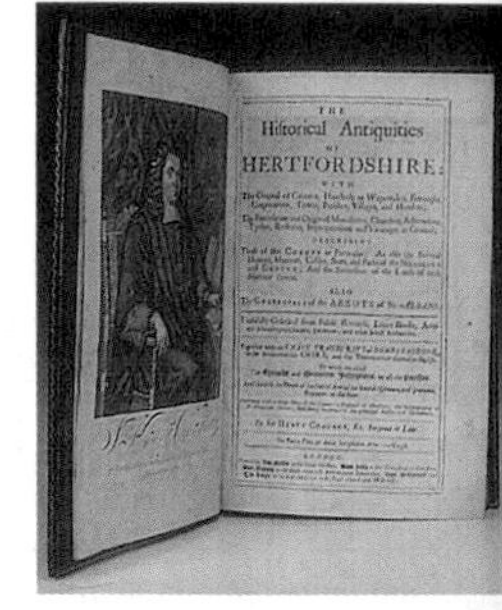

Sir Henry Chauncy, *The Historical Antiquities of Hertfordshire*, London, 1700, 2°, engraved frontispiece and folding county map by H. Moll, 46 double-page engraved plates, 19thC gilt morocco, slight damage.
£2,250–2,700
€3,300–3,950
$4,050–4,850 ⚒ RTo

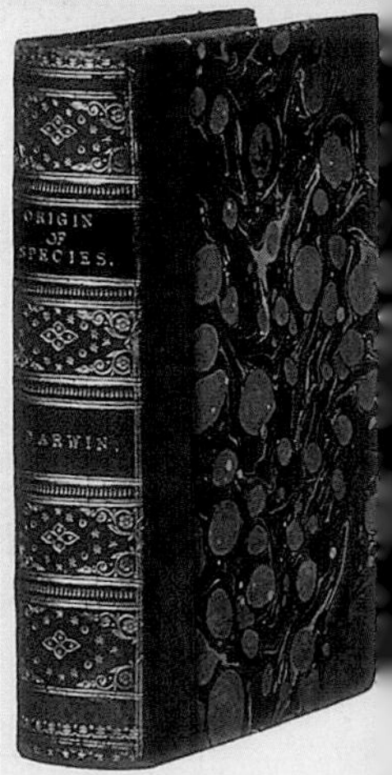

Charles Darwin, *Origin of the Species*, published by Freeman, 1861, 8°, third edition with additions and corrections, later half morocco, gilt spine.
£910–1,100
€1,350–1,600
$1,650–1,950 ⚒ DW

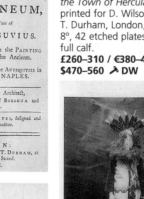

Sir Arthur Conan Doyle, *The Adventures of Sherlock Holmes*, published by George Newnes Ltd, London, first edition, 1892, 8°, original cloth.
£590–700 / €860–1,000
$1,050–1,250 ⚒ RTo

Paul Gauguin, *Letters to Ambroise Vollard and André Fontainas*, edited by John Rewald, published by Grabhorn Press, San Francisco, 1943, 2°, edition of 250, 10 woodcut reproductions, original cloth-backed paper boards.
£350–420 / €510–610
$630–760 ⚒ BBA

Eugene Grasset (editor), *Plants and their Application to Ornament*, published by Chapman & Hall, London, 1896–97, 2°, 72 stencil coloured plates, 12 monthly parts with cloth case.
£1,450–1,700
€2,100–2,500
$2,600–3,100 ⚒ DW

Sir Arthur Conan Doyle, *The Sign of Four*, published by George Newnes, London, 1892, 8 x 5½in (20.5 x 14cm).
£310–350 / €450–510
$560–630 ⊞ BAY

Edmund Dulac (illustrator), *Stories from Arabian Nights*, retold by Laurence Housman, published by Hodder & Stoughton, 1907, edition of 350, 11 x 9in (28 x 23cm).
£1,600–1,800
€2,350–2,650
$2,900–3,250 ⊞ BAY

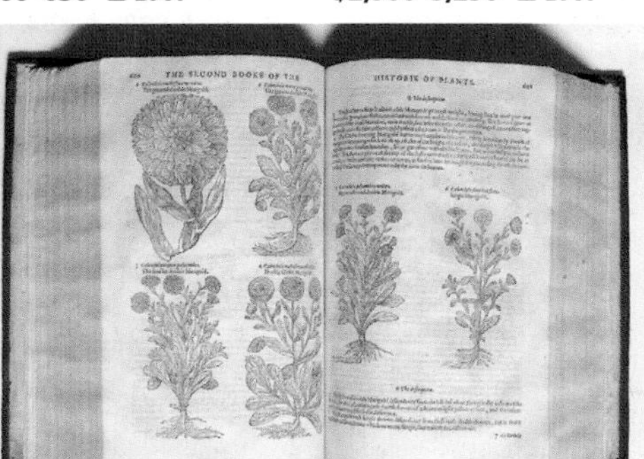

John Gerarde, *The Herball, or Generall Historie of Plants*, printed by John Norton, London, 1597, 13 x 9in (33 x 23cm).
£2,700–3,000 / €3,950–4,350
$4,900–5,400 ⊞ BIB

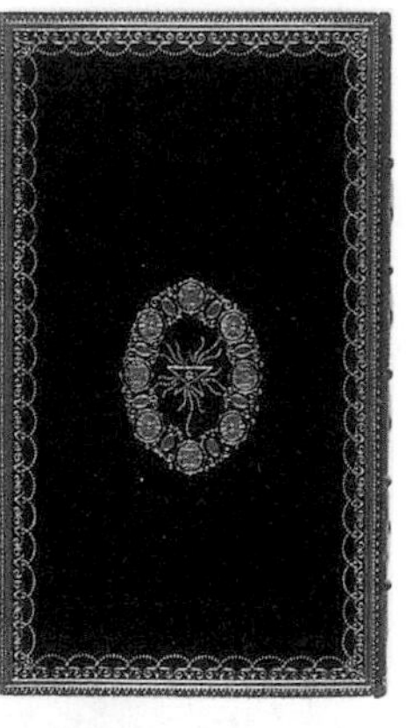

Johann Wolfgang von Goethe, *Faust*, published by Ernst Engel Offenbach, 1924, 8°, edition of 120 hand-printed with silk end-papers, gilt morocco and slip case by Paul Kersten.
£470–560 / €690–820
$850–1,000 ⚒ BBA
Paul Kersten (1865–1943) was a pioneer of new modern German binding, working for much of his career in Leipzig. He created a distinctive style of his own, later going on to Berlin where he taught and influenced Otto Dorfner.

Oliver Goldsmith, *The Vicar of Wakefield*, illustrated by Arthur Rackham, published by George G. Harrap & Co, London, first edition, 1929, 10 x 8in (25.5 x 20.5cm).
£220–250 / €320–370
$400–450 ⊞ NW

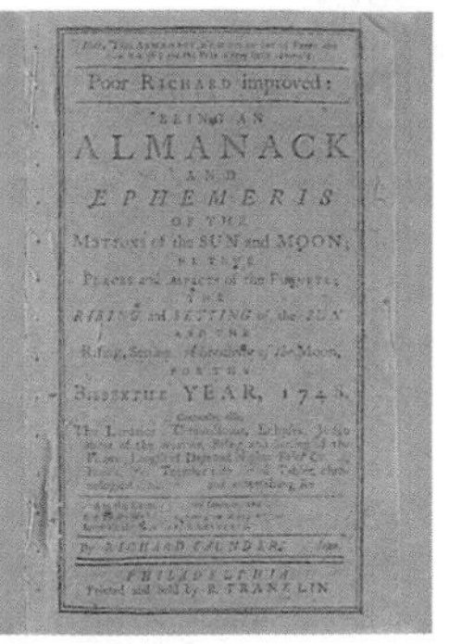

Benjamin Franklin, *Poor Richard Improved: Being an Almanack and Ephemeris of the Motions of the Sun and Moon*, printed by B. Franklin, Philadelphia, 1747, 12°, later whipstitching, modern protective paper wrapper, morocco folding case.
£10,600–12,700
€15,500–18,500
$19,200–23,000 ⚒ S(NY)
This is a first edition of *Franklin's Almanack for the Year 1748*, and the first use of the title *Poor Richard Improved*. The almanack appeared in three different issues in an attempt by Franklin to customize it for regional markets. The Pennsylvania issue had a list of the governors for Pennsylvania, the Southern issue had a court schedule for Virginia, North Carolina and South Carolina and the New England issue had a New England court schedule. The experiment was apparently unsuccessful since Franklin reverted to a single edition the following year.

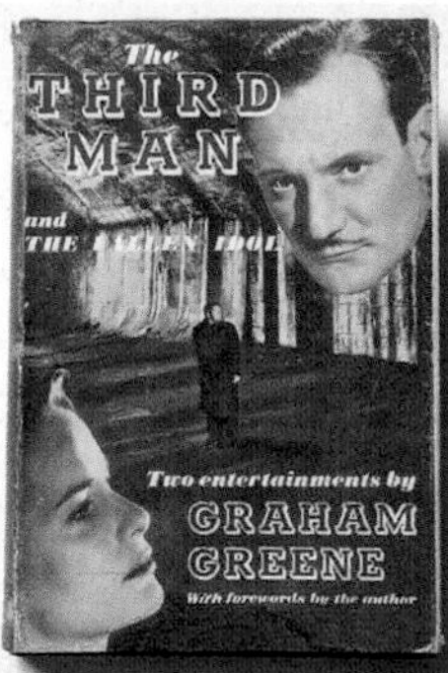

Graham Greene, *The Third Man* and *The Fallen Idol*, published by William Heinemann, London, first edition, 1950, 7½ x 5in (19 x 12.5cm).
£155–175 / €220–250
$280–310 ⊞ BAY

◄ **Graham Greene,** *The Quiet American*, published by William Heinemann, London, first edition, 1955, dust jacket.
£670–750 / €980–1,100
$1,200–1,350 ⊞ BIB

Jan van der Groen, *Le Jardinier Hollandois*, Amsterdam, 1669–70, small 4°, 5 parts in 1 vol, 15 copper engravings, 57 woodcuts, 19thC morocco with marbled boards.
£670–800 / €980–1,150
$1,200–1,450 DW

Clive Holland, *Unknown Hampshire*, illustrated by Douglas Snowdon, 1926, 4°, later morocco with gilt decoration.
£240–280 / €350–410
$430–510 BBA

Wallace Irwin, *Letters of a Japanese Schoolboy*, illustrated by Rollin Kirb, published by Doubleday Page & Co, New York, 1909, 8 x 5½in (20.5 x 14cm).
£65–75 / €95–110
$120–135 BAY

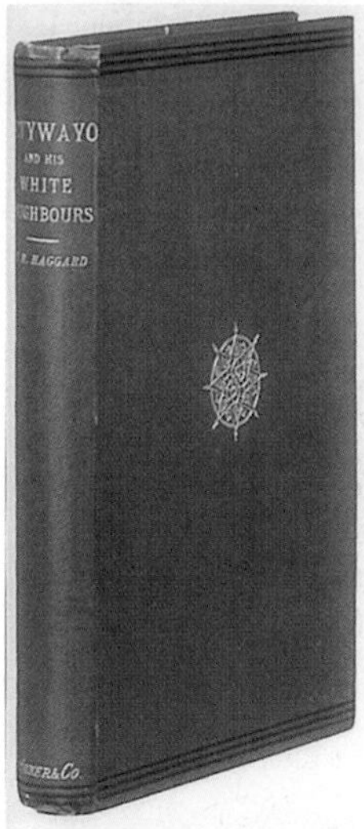

H. Rider Haggard, *Cetywayo and his White Neighbours*, published by Trubner & Co, first edition, 1882, 8°, edition of 750, gilt cloth.
£800–960 / €1,200–1,400
$1,450–1,750 DW

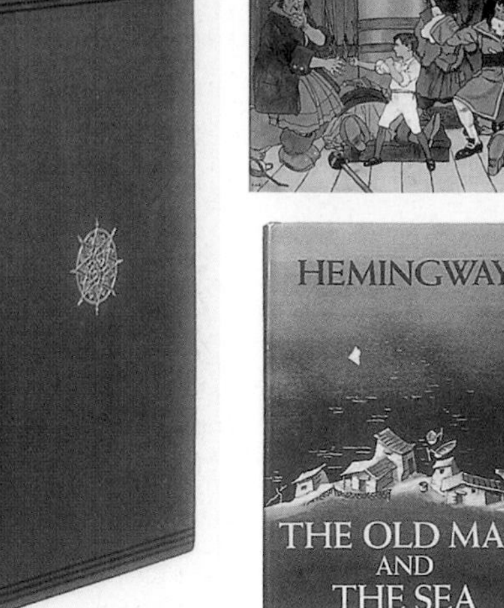

John Hassall (illustrator), *Peter Pan*, a set of 6 chromolithographs, c1920, 10¼ x 28in (26 x 71cm).
£2,450–2,900
€3,600–4,250
$4,450–5,200 DW

Ernest Hemingway, *The Old Man and the Sea*, published by Charles Scribner's Sons, New York, first edition, 1952, 8°, cloth, dust jacket.
£650–780 / €950–1,100
$1,200–1,400 BBA

Mrs Charles Hetley, *The Native Flowers of New Zealand*, first edition, 1888, 2°, 36 chromolithographed plates, pictorial cloth gilt.
£440–520 / €640–760
$800–940 DW

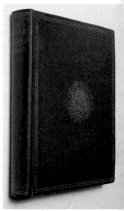

Victor Hugo, *Les Misérables*, published by Lacroix ver Boeckhoven & Co, Brussels, 1862, 8°, 10 vols, half cat's paw calf, spines gilt, morocco lettering pieces.
£560–670 / €820–980
$1,000–1,200 RTo

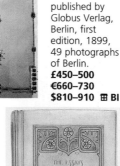

◄ **Jessie Marion King (illustrator),** *Album von Berlin*, published by Globus Verlag, Berlin, first edition, 1899, 49 photographs of Berlin.
£450–500
€660–730
$810–910 BI

Charles Kingsley, *The Water Babies*, illustrated by J. Noel Paton, published by Macmillan & Co, 1863, 8 x 7in (20.5 x 18cm).
£540–600 / €790–880
$980–1,100 NW

► **Charles Lamb,** *The Essays and the Last Essays of Elia*, illustrated by Charles E. Brock, 1902, 8°, bound by Cedric Chivers, vellum with watercolour insert.
£410–490 / €600–720
$740–890 BBA

◄ **Rudyard Kipling,** *Just So Stories*, published by Macmillan & Co, London, first edition, 1902, 9 x 7in (23 x 18cm).
£540–600 / €790–880
$980–1,100 BAY

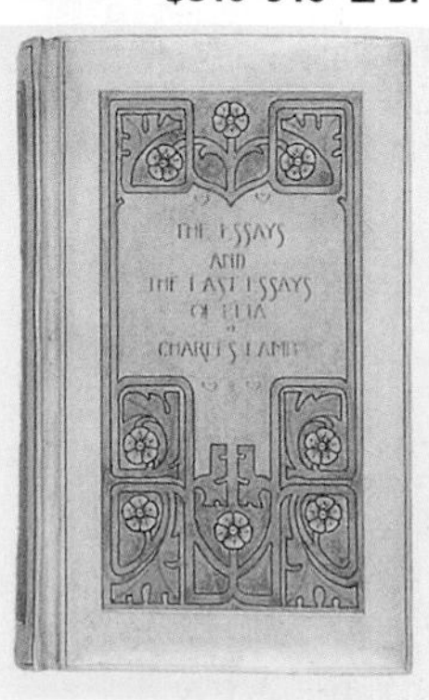

Laudes Beatae Mariae Virginis, printed and published by the Kelmscott Press, 1896, 8°, edition of 250 copies, cloth boards.
£330–390 / €480–570
$600–710 RTo

Mrs R. Lee, *Trees, Plants and Flowers, their Beauties, Uses and Influences*, published by Griffith & Farran, 1859, 8°, 8 hand-coloured plates.
£120–140 / €175–200
$220–250 DW

Les Modes Parisiennes, Paris, 1846–47, 4°, 2 vols, 103 hand-coloured plates, quarter sheepskin.
£560–670 / €820–980
$1,000–1,200 DW

Items in the Books & Book Illustrations section have been arranged in alphabetical order.

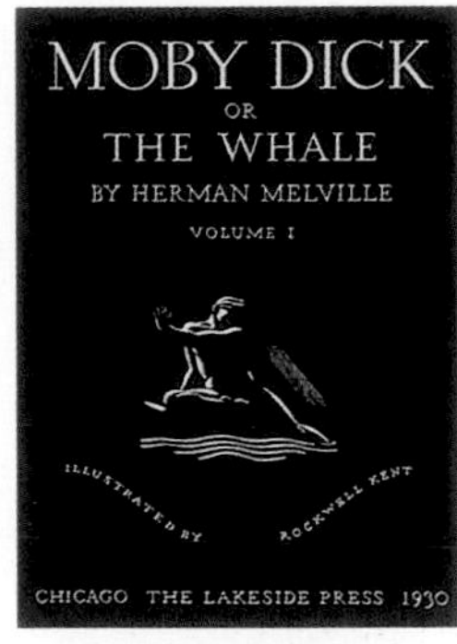

Herman Melville, *Moby Dick or The Whale*, illustrated by Rodwell Kent, published by Lakeside Press, Chicago, 1930, 4°, 3 vols, edition of 1,000, pictorial cloth.
£1,550–1,850
€2,250–2,700
$2,800–3,350 BBA

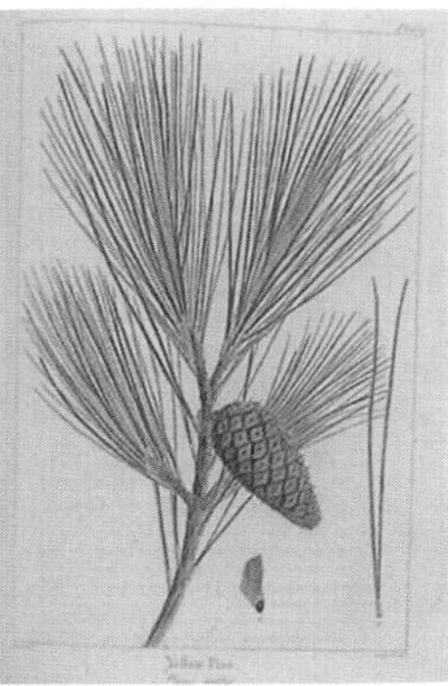

François André Michaux and Thomas Nuttall, *The North American Sylva*, published by Rice & Hart, Philadelphia, 1857–59, 8°, 5 vols, hand-coloured engraved and lithographed plates after Redouté, Bessa and others, gilt morocco.
£1,650–1,950
€2,400–2,850
$3,000–3,550 S(NY)
This was the standard reference book on American trees until Charles Singer Sargent's *Silva of North America* was published from 1891 to 1902. Michaux spent more than two years travelling throughout western New England, New York, Pennsylvania and Ohio, gathering seeds and taking careful notes of the natural history. He later toured all the Atlantic states. The first American edition was published in Philadelphia in 1841, with three supplementary volumes by Thomas Nuttall, giving descriptions of trees from California, Oregon and the Rocky Mountains. Nuttall emigrated to the United States from England specifically to study ornithology and botany. He served as curator for the Botanical Garden of Harvard for over ten years.

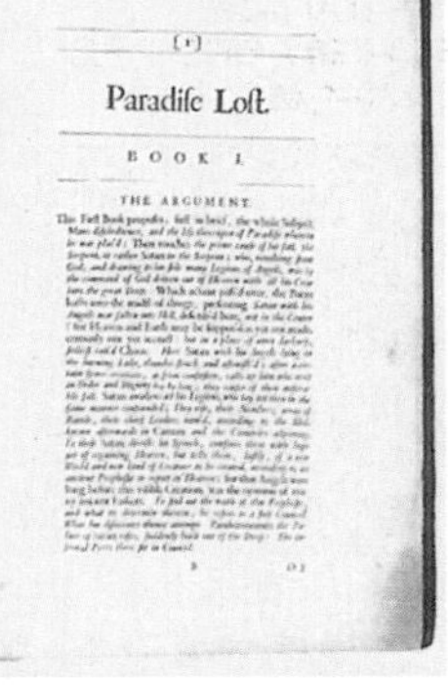

John Milton, *Paradise Lost*, first illustrated edition, 1688, 2°, frontispiece by R. White after Faithorne, 12 engraved plates, mostly after J. B. Medina, calf, gilt, list of subscribers at end, rebacked and repaired.
£1,150–1,350 / €1,650–1,950
$2,050–2,450 BBA
As well as being the first illustrated edition of *Paradise Lost,* this is one of the earliest examples of financing a publication through subscription. The list of subscribers includes John Dryden, Sir Paul Rycaut, Charles Sackville, Dr Robert Uvedale and the bookseller Awnsham Churchill.

Alphonse Mucha (illustrator), *Ilsée, Prinzessin von Tripolis*, by Robert de Flers, published by B. Koci, Prague, 1901, 4°, 132 chromolithographed plates, printed wrappers, morocco portfolio.
£1,050–1,250
€1,550–1,850
$1,900–2,250 S(NY)

William Nicholson, *Twelve Portraits*, first series, 1899, 2°, 12 colour illustrations, loose as issued in cloth portfolio, silk ties.
£880–1,050
€1,300–1,550
$1,600–1,900 BBA

Thomas Moore, *The Ferns of Great Britain and Ireland*, edited by John Lindley, 1855, full 2°, 51 nature-printed plates, half morocco gilt.
£3,750–4,500
€5,500–6,600
$6,800–8,100 DW

Naturalist's Pocket Magazine, c1798, 8°, 18 parts bound in 1 vol, 54 hand-coloured plated, half calf, worn, repaired.
£145–170 / €210–250
$260–310 DW

LOCATE THE SOURCE
The source of each illustration in Miller's can be found by checking the code letters below each caption with the Key to Illustrations, pages 778–784.

Baroness Orczy, *Leather-face*, published by Hodder & Stoughton, London, first edition, 1916, 8 x 5in (20.5 x 12.5cm), dust jacket.
£260–290 / €380–420
$470–520 NW

William Oughtred, *Mathematical Recreations or a Collection of Sundrie Excellent Problems*, printed by Leake & Leake, London, 1674, 6 x 4in (15 x 10cm), bound in marbled card, worn.
£300–360 / €440–530
$540–650 WL

John Piper, *Paintings, Drawings and Theatre Designs 1932–54*, published by Faber & Faber, London, first edition, 1955, 4°, introduction by S. John Woods, hand-coloured aquatint frontispiece numbered and signed by Piper, cloth gilt, dust jacket, slipcase.
£960–1,150 / €1,400–1,650
$1,750–2,100 DW

James Cowles Pritchard, *The Natural History of Man*, 1845, large 8°, 45 plates, 40 hand-coloured, wood engravings, gilt morocco.
£300–360 / €440–530
$540–650 DW

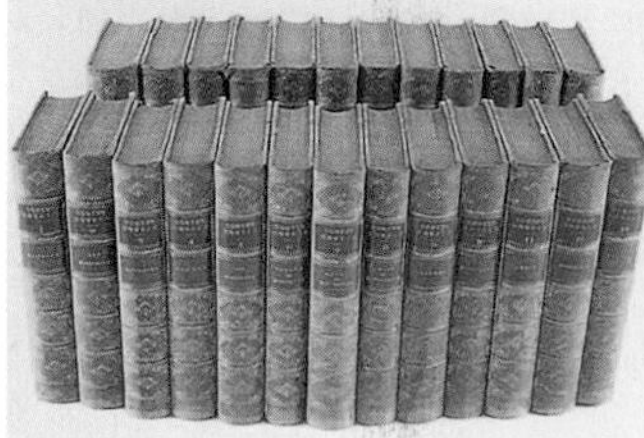

Victor Petit, *Parcs et Jardins dans Environs de Paris*, published by Monrocq Frères, Paris, c1865, 2°, 50 coloured litho plates, morocco, some wear.
£340–400 / €500–580
$620–720 DW

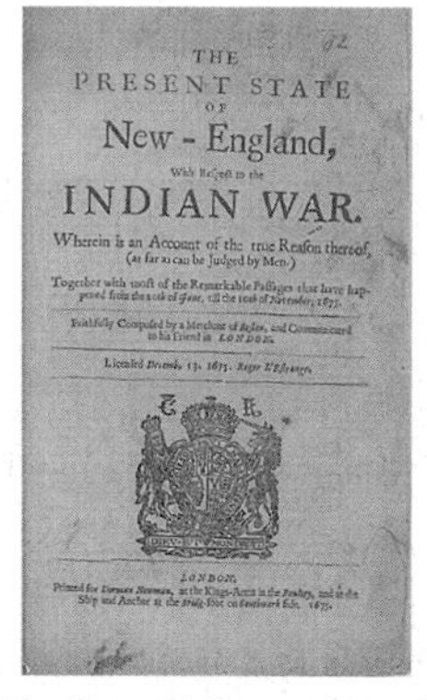

The Present State of New-England with Respect to the Indian War, printed for Dorman Newman, London, 1675, 2°, woodcut royal seal on title, spine with gilt letting, probably a made-up copy, quire B possibly from another copy.
£2,150–2,550
€3,150–3,700
$3,900–4,600 S(NY)

Arthur Rackham (illustrator), *The Romance of King Arthur*, text by Alfred W. Pollard, signed by Rackham, published by Macmillan & Co, 1917, 11½ x 9½in (29 x 24cm), edition of 500.
£1,600–1,800
€2,350–2,650
$2,900–3,250 BI

◄ **Walter Scott,** *Waverley, or, 'Tis Sixty Years Since*, published by Adam & Charles Black, Edinburgh, 1871, 8°, 25 vols, frontispieces, title vignettes, marbled boards.
£730–870 / €1,050–1,250
$1,300–1,550 DW

The Piccaninnies Library, published by Sands & Co, 1904, 12°, 5 vols, illustrated by Louis Wain, M. York Shuter, Cecil Aldin, Percy J. Billinghurst and John Hassall, cloth, in original box.
£1,450–1,700 / €2,100–2,500
$2,600–3,100 F&C

Edward Pretty, *A Practical Essay on Flower Painting in Water Colours*, printed by D. N. Shury for S. and J. Fuller, 1810, oblong 2°, 25 aquatint plates, 15 hand-coloured, boards with morocco label.
£610–730 / €890–1,050
$1,100–1,300 DW

W. H. Pyne, *The History of the Royal Residence of Windsor Castle, St James's Palace, Carlton House, Kensington House, Hampton Court, Buckingham House and Frogmore*, first edition 1819, 4°, 3 vols, 100 hand-coloured aquatints, later half morocco gilt, one volume damaged.
£2,100–2,500 / €3,050–3,650
$3,800–4,500 DW

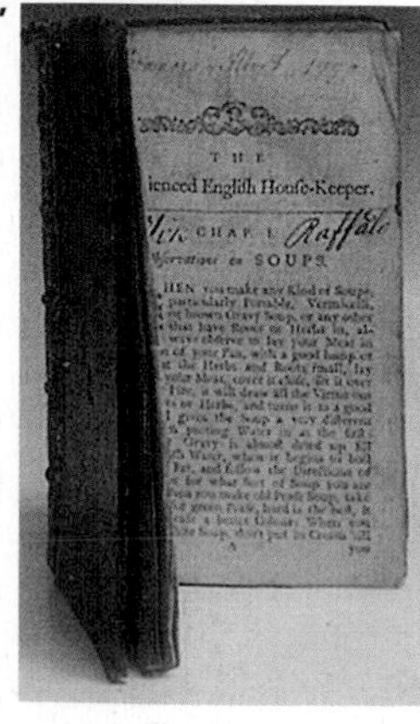

◄ **Elizabeth Raffald,** *The Experienced Engl[ish] House-keeper; f[or] the Use and Eas[e] of Ladies, House keepers and Coo[ks]*, printed for the author by J. Harr[op], Manchester, firs[t] edition, signed b[y] the author, 176[9], 8°, two folding plates, sheepski[n] worn.
£440–520
€640–760
$800–940 R[…]

BOOKS & BOOK ILLUSTRATIONS

Gabriel Setoun, *The Child World*, illustrated by Charles Robinson, published by John Lane, London, 1896, 7½ x 5½in (19 x 14cm).
£135–150 / €195–220
$240–270 ⊞ BAY

Vero Shaw, *The Illustrated Book of the Dog*, published by Cassell, Petter, Galpin & Co, (1881), 4°, 28 chromo-lithographed plates, half roan gilt.
£540–640 / €790–930
$980–1,150 ⚒ L

► Stephen Spender, *Poems*, published by Faber & Faber, London, first edition, 1933, 9 x 6in (23 x 15cm).
£100–115
€145–170
$180–210 ⊞ BIB

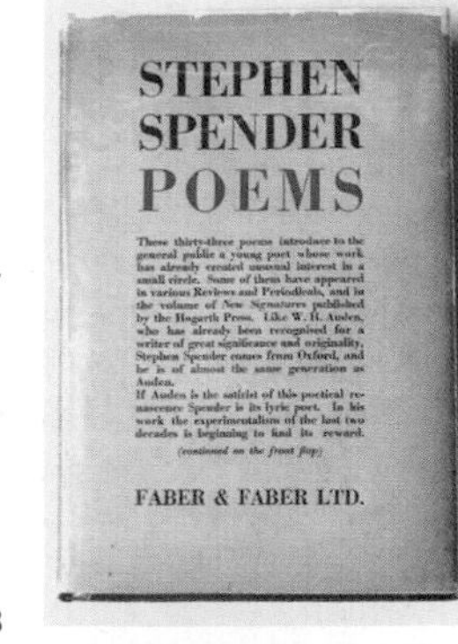

► John Stephenson and James Morss Churchill , *Medical Botany*, new edition edited by Gilbert T. Burnett, 1834–36, 8°, 185 hand-coloured engravings, later half morocco gilt.
£1,750–2,100
€2,550–3,050
$3,150–3,800 ⚒ DW

Robert Louis Stevenson, *Treasure Island*, illustrated by Rowland Hilder, published by Humphrey Milford, Oxford University Press, London, first edition, 1929, 9 x 7in (23 x 18cm).
£160–180 / €230–260
$290–330 ⊞ BAY

Harriet Beecher Stowe, *Uncle Tom's Cabin; or, Life Among the Lowly*, published by J. P. Jewett, Boston and Cleveland, first edition, 1852, 8°, 2 vols, 6 plates, half morocco slipcase.
£4,300–5,100
€6,300–7,400
$7,800–9,200 ⚒ S(NY)
This is the first edition of Stowe's passionate anti-slavery novel. *Uncle Tom's Cabin* first appeared in serial form in the abolitionist periodical *National Era*. J. P. Jewett published this two-volume work before the appearance of the last two serial instalments.

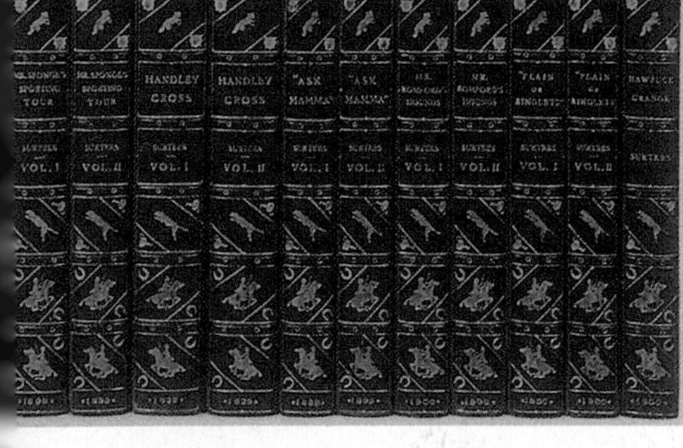

Robert Surtees, *The Sporting Novels*, illustrated by John Leech, 1900, large 8°, 11 vols, half morocco gilt, repaired.
£560–670 / €820–980
$1,000–1,200 ⚒ DW

Further reading

Miller's Collecting Modern Books, Miller's Publications, 2003

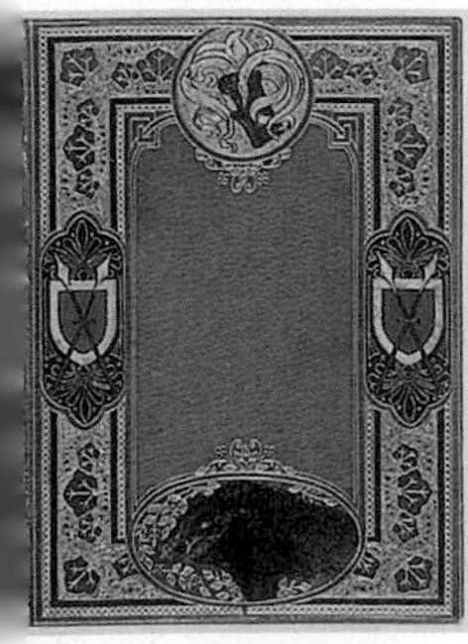

Algernon Charles Swinburne, *Atalanta in Calydon*, printed and published by the Kelmscott Press, 1894, 4°, edition of 285, morocco with gilt and silver.
£2,900–3,450
€4,250–5,000
$5,200–6,200 ⚒ BBA

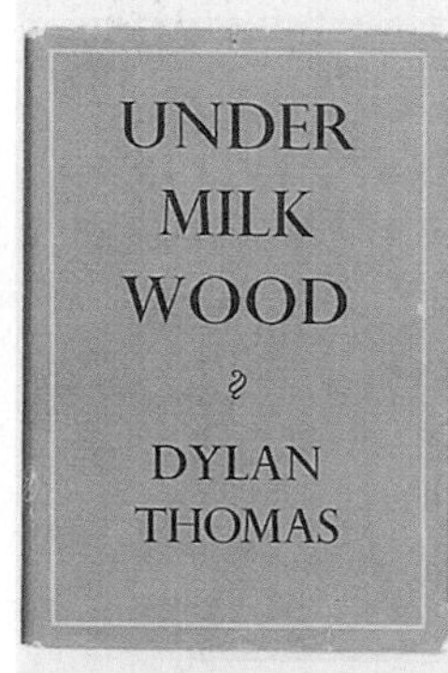

Dylan Thomas, *Under Milk Wood*, published by J. M. Dent, London, first edition, 1954, 8°, dust jacket.
£230–270 / €330–390
$420–490 ⚒ BBA

Henri de Toulouse-Lautrec (illustrator), *Au Pied de Sinai*, by Georges Clemenceau, published by Chamerot & Renouard for Henri Floury, 1898, 4°, edition of 380, 10 lithographed plates, later morocco, original wrappers bound in, slipcase.
£4,300–5,100
€6,300–7,400
$7,800–9,200 ⚒ S(NY)

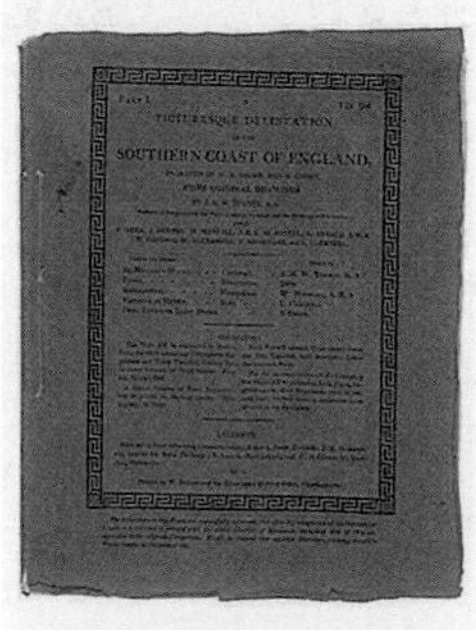

J. M. W. Turner (illustrator), *A Picturesque Delineation of the Southern Coast of England*, 1814–26, 4°, 48 engravings by W. B. Cooke and G. Cooke from Turner's original drawings, 16 parts bound in printed wrappers, in two morocco solander cases.
£2,200–2,600
€3,200–3,800
$4,000–4,700 ⚒ DW

Emeric Essex Vidal, *Picturesque Illustrations of Buenos Ayres and Monte Video*, first edition, published by R. Ackermann, London, 1820, 4°, edition of 750, 24 hand-coloured plates after Vidal, later morocco panelled gilt.
£3,650–4,350 / €5,300–6,400
$6,600–7,900 S(NY)
This is one of the few colour-plate books depicting Argentina and Uruguay. Born c1788, Vidal joined the Royal Navy in 1808, and from 1820 to 1821 he served as secretary to Admiral Lambert at St Helena. The engraved plates of his sketches formed part of Ackermann's plan to offer Spanish and South American views to Engish buyers. By 1824, over 3,000 British subjects had settled in Buenos Aires.

George Walker, *The Costume of Yorkshire*, printed by T. Bensley, 1814, first edition, 2°, 40 engravings, text in English and French, later half morocco.
£1,600–1,900 / €2,250–2,750
$2,900–3,450 DW

Evelyn Waugh, *Men at Arms*, published by Chapman & Hall, London, first edition, 1952, 7½ x 5in (19 x 12.5cm).
£220–250 / €320–370
$400–450 BAY

Stanley J. Weyman, *Shrewsbury*, illustrated by C. A. Shepperson, published by Longmans Green & Co, London, first edition, 1898, 8 x 5½in (20.5 x 14cm).
£135–150 / €195–220
$240–270 BAY

Thomas Wolfe, *Look Homeward, Angel*, published by Charles Scribner's Sons, New York, first edition, 1929, 7¾ x 5¼in (19.5 x 13.5cm), cloth, dust jacket.
£3,650–4,350
€5,300–6,400
$6,600–7,900 S(NY)
This was Wolfe's first published book.

Virginia Woolf, *Orlando*, published by the Hogarth Press, first edition, 1928, 8°, cloth, dust jacket.
£540–640 / €790–930
$980–1,150 BBA

Ellen Willmott, *The Genus Rosa*, published by John Murray, London, 1914, 2°, 2 vols, 132 chromolithographed plates, 84 uncoloured plates, quarter morocco gilt, printed wrappers.
£1,300–1,550
€1,900–2,250
$2,350–2,800 DW

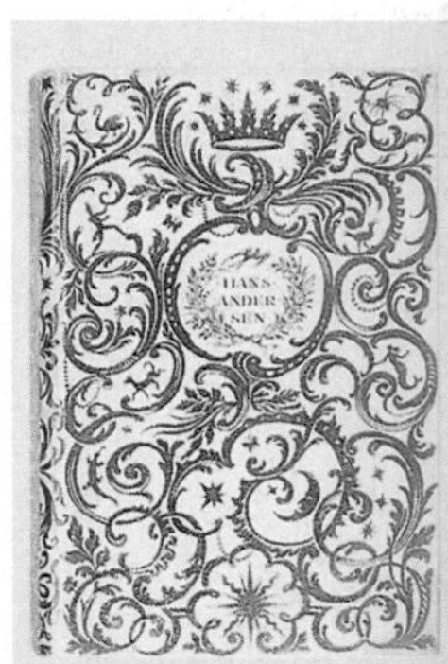

Rex Whistler (illustrator), *Fairy Tales and Legends*, by Hans Christian Andersen, signed by the artist, 1935, 8°, edition of 200, buckram decorated in gilt.
£490–580 / €720–850
$890–1,050 BBA

Prices

The price ranges quoted in this book reflect the average price a purchaser might expect to pay for a similar item. The price will vary according to the condition, rarity, size, popularity, provenance, colour and restoration of the item, and this must be taken into account when assessing values. Don't forget that if you are selling it is quite likely that you will be offered less than the price range.

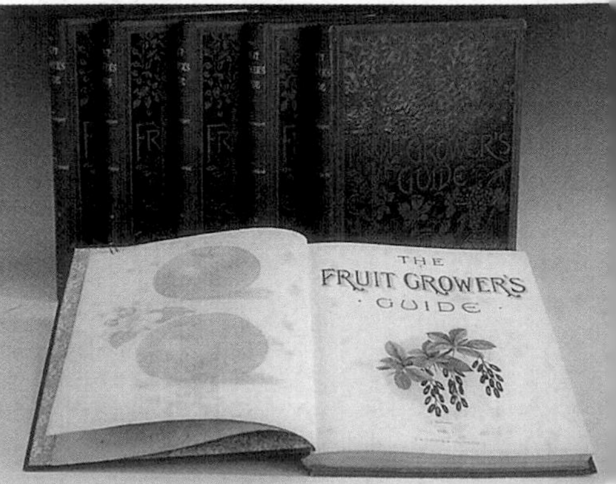

John Wright, *The Fruit Grower's Guide*, published by J. S. Virtue & Co, London, 1891–94, 6 vols, 4°, 43 chromolithographed plates, decorated cloth.
£440–520 / €640–760
$800–960 RTo

Maps & Atlases

Celestial Maps

Andreas Cellarius, a coloured copperplate celestial map, Dutch, Amsterdam, 1660, 17 x 20in (43 x 51cm).
£3,600–4,000 / €5,200–5,800
$6,500–7,200 ⊞ JOP

Vincenzo Maria Coronelli, a set of two coloured copperplate celestial maps, Italian, Venice, 1691, 18 x 24in (45.5 x 61cm).
£2,200–2,500 / €3,200–3,600
$4,000–4,500 ⊞ JOP

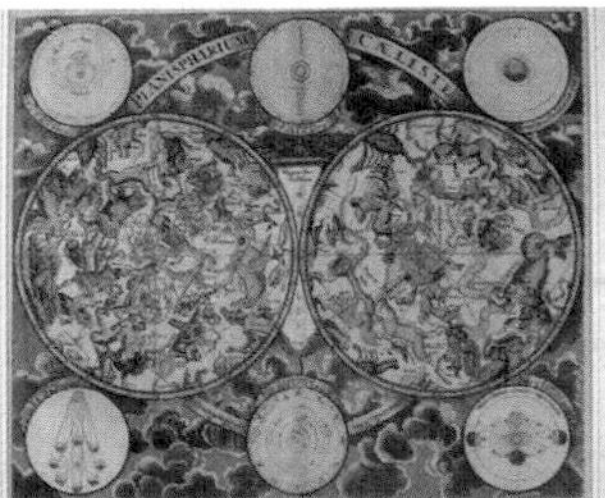

Georg Christoph Eimmart and Johann Baptist Homann, a coloured copperplate celestial map, German, Nuremberg, 1705–30, 19 x 22in (48.5 x 56cm).
£1,450–1,650 / €2,100–2,400
$2,700–3,000 ⊞ JOP

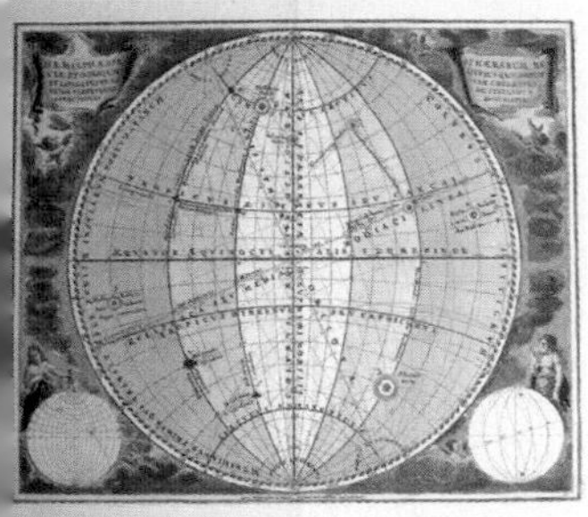

◀ **Andreas Cellarius,** a celestial chart, 1705, 20 x 24in (51 x 61cm).
£1,500–1,700 / €2,200–2,500
$2,800–3,100 ⊞ APS

▶ **Tobias Conrad Lotter,** a copper-engraved celestial chart, with original colouring, 1760, 19 x 22in (48.5 x 56cm).
£3,400–3,800 / €4,950–5,500
$6,200–6,900 ⊞ APS

World

Claudius Ptolemy ?and Sebastian Munster, *La Seconde Table Générale Selon Ptol(emaeus),* a woodcut map of the world bordered with 12 named windheads, hand-coloured, French text verso, c1540, 13½ x 9¾in (34.5 x 25cm).
£420–500 / €610–730
$760–910 ⚒ BBA

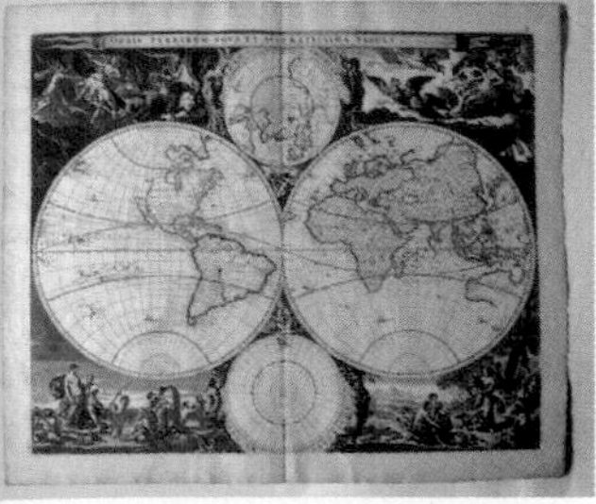

Nicolaus Visscher, a hand-coloured twin-hemisphere map, 1693, 21 x 24in (53.5 x 61cm).
£8,500–9,500 / €12,400–13,900
$15,400–17,200 ⊞ VHA

Robert Walton, a coloured copperplate map of the world, London, 1656–59, 16 x 20in (40.5 x 51cm).
£6,600–7,400 / €9,600–10,800
$11,900–13,400 ⊞ JOP

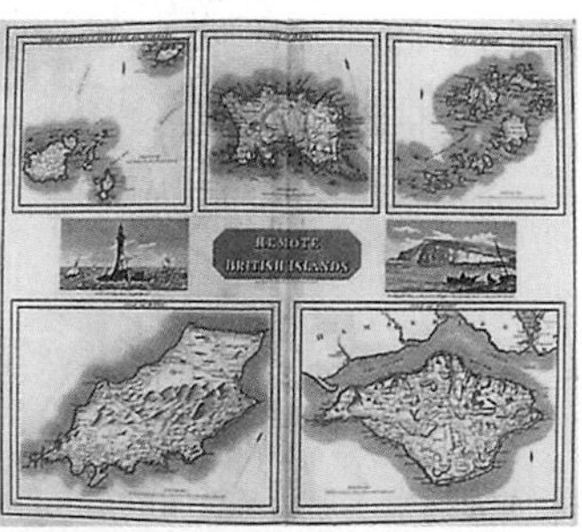

John Thomson, *A New General Atlas,* published by John Thomson & Co, Edinburgh, with 74 hand-coloured engraved maps, losses and damage, 1817, large 2°.
£1,750–2,100 / €2,550–3,050
$3,150–3,800 ⚒ BBA

Pieter Goos, *Orbis Terrarum Nova et Accuratissima Tabula*, double-page engraved twin-hemispherical world map with two smaller spheres depicting the north and south poles, hand-coloured, slight wear, Dutch, Amsterdam, 1666, 17½ x 21½in (44.5 x 54.5cm).
£4,550–5,400 / €6,600–7,900
$8,200–9,800 ⚒ S

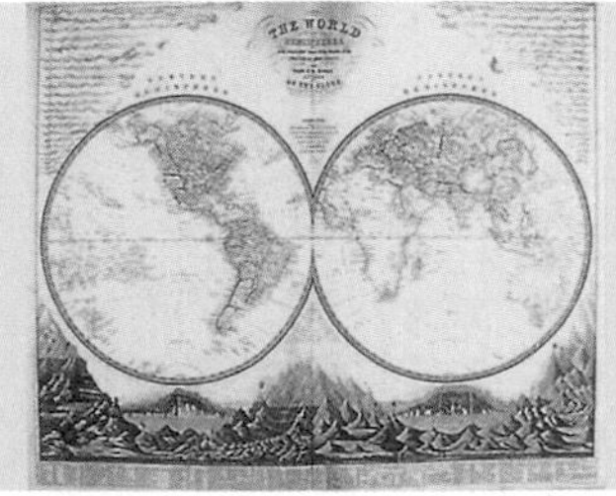

Alexander Keith Johnston, *The National Atlas of Historical, Commercial, and Political Geography*, published by J. Johnstone and W. & A. K. Johnston, Edinburgh, 46 double-page engraved maps, the majority with hand-coloured outlining, some losses and damage, 1843, 2°.
£840–1,000 / €1,250–1,500
$1,500–1,800 ⚒ BBA

Africa & Arabia

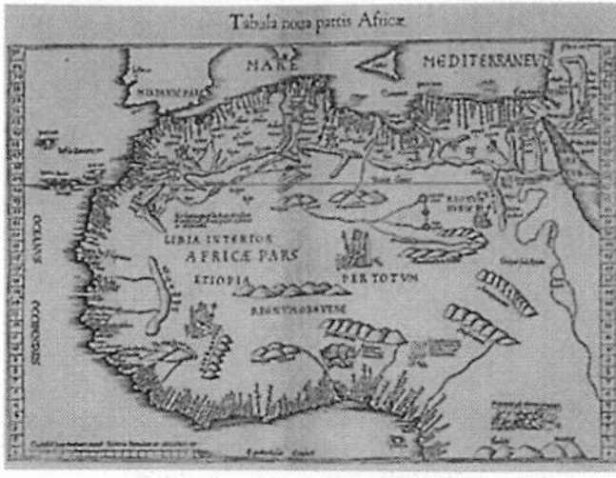

Martin Waldseemüller and Laurent Fries, *Tabula Nova Partis Africae,* an engraved map of Africa above the equator with fantastical figures and animals, slight damage and repair, 1541, 11 x 15¾in (28 x 40cm).
£420–500 / €610–730
$760–910 DW

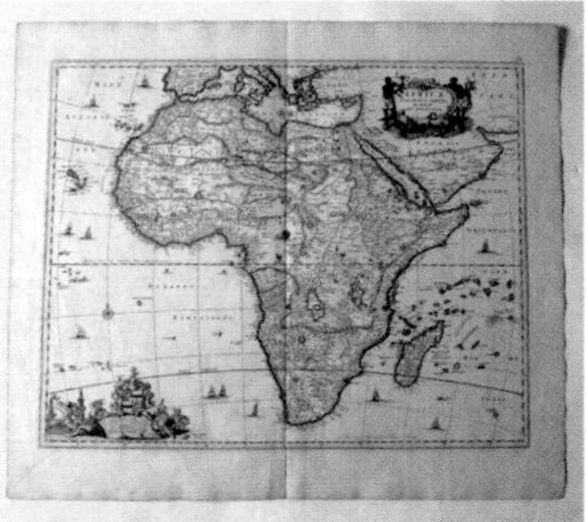

Nicolaus Visscher, a hand-coloured map of Africa, 1693, 21 x 24in (53.5 x 61cm).
£900–1,000 / €1,300–1,450
$1,650–1,800 ⊞ VHA

Claudius Ptolemy and Gerard Mercator, a coloured copperplate map of Arabia, Dutch, Amsterdam, 1578–1720, 14 x 19in (35.5 x 48.5cm).
£1,050–1,200 / €1,550–1,750
$1,900–2,150 ⊞ JOP

Georg Matthäus Seutter, *Africa Juxta Navigationes et Observationes Recentissimas,* a hand-coloured engraved map with an uncoloured ornamental title cartouche surrounded by figures and animals, German, 1730s, 19¾ x 22½in (50 x 57cm).
£320–380 / €470–550
$580–690 DW

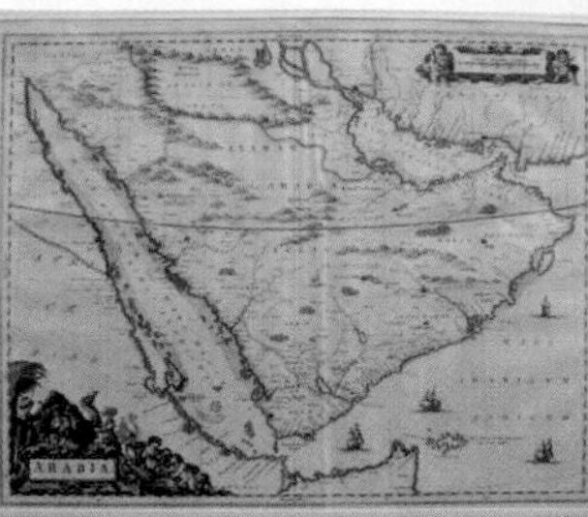

Joan Blaeu, a copperplate map of Arabia with outline colour, Dutch, Amsterdam, 1662, 17 x 21in (43 x 53.5cm).
£1,950–2,200 / €2,850–3,200
$3,550–4,000 ⊞ JOP

George Philip, a steelplate map of Arabia, Egypt and Abyssinia, London, 1852, 20 x 24in (51 x 61cm).
£270–300 / €390–440
$490–540 ⊞ JOP

Items in the Maps & Atlases section have been arranged in date order within each sub-section.

Americas

Nicolas Sanson, *Amérique Septentrionale,* an engraved map with outline colour, slight damage, French, Paris, 1650, 15½ x 21¾in (39.5 x 55.5cm).
£1,900–2,250 / €2,750–3,300
$3,450–4,100 S

Nicolaus Visscher, a hand-coloured map of the Americas showing California as an island, 1693, 21 x 24in (53.5 x 61cm).
£2,250–2,500 / €3,300–3,650
$4,050–4,550 ⊞ VHA

◄ **Tobias Conrad Lotter,** *Mappa Geographica Regionem Mexicanam et Floridam,* an engraved map of the southern states of America, Latin America and the West Indies, with four inset maps, some hand-coloured, vignette view of figures on the shore, slight damage, German, Augsburg, c1780, 19¼ x 22½in (49 x 57cm).
£1,100–1,300 / €1,600–1,900
$2,000–2,400 BBA

Henri Abraham Châtelain, *Map of New France,* a coloured copperplate map, Dutch, Amsterdam, 1719, 16 x 19in (40.5 x 48.5cm).
£900–1,000 / €1,300–1,450
$1,600–1,800 ⊞ JOP

John Thomson, *America,* a copperpla map with outline colour, Scottish, Edinburgh, c1816, 20 x 24in (51 x 61cm).
£280–320 / €420–470
$510–580 ⊞ JOP

Asia & Australia

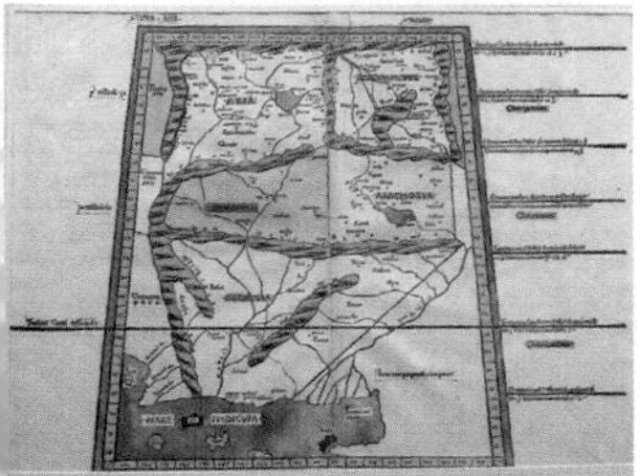

Claudius Ptolemy and Nicolaus Germanus, *Nona Asie Tabula*, a coloured woodblock map of Pakistan and Afghanistan, slight damage, 1482–86, German, Ulm, 16¼ x 21¾in (41.5 x 55.5cm).
£2,700–3,000 / €3,950–4,400
$4,900–5,400 ⊞ JOP

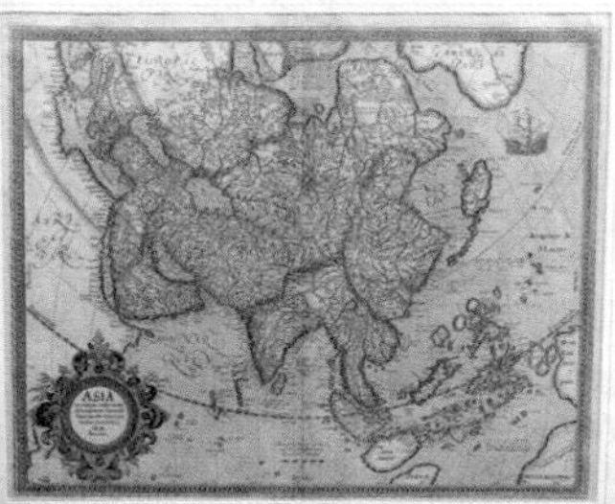

Gerard Mercator and Henricus Hondius, a copperplate map of Asia with outline colour, Dutch, Amsterdam, 1595–1628, 15½ x 19in (39.5 x 48.5cm).
£1,350–1,500 / €1,950–2,200
$2,450–2,700 ⊞ JOP

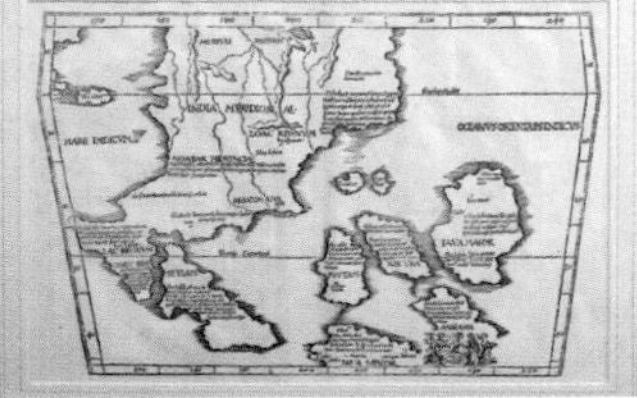

Laurent Fries, a woodblock map of South East Asia and the East Indies, French, Strasbourg, 1522–25, 11½ x 17¼in (29 x 44cm).
£1,050–1,200 / €1,550–1,750
$1,900–2,150 ⊞ JOP

Joannes Jansson, *Indiae Orientalis Nova Descriptio,* an engraved hand-coloured map of the East Indies with a decorative cartouche, Latin text verso, some damage, Dutch, Amsterdam, c1640, 15½ x 20in (39.5 x 51cm).
£300–360 / €440–530
$540–650 ⚒ BBA

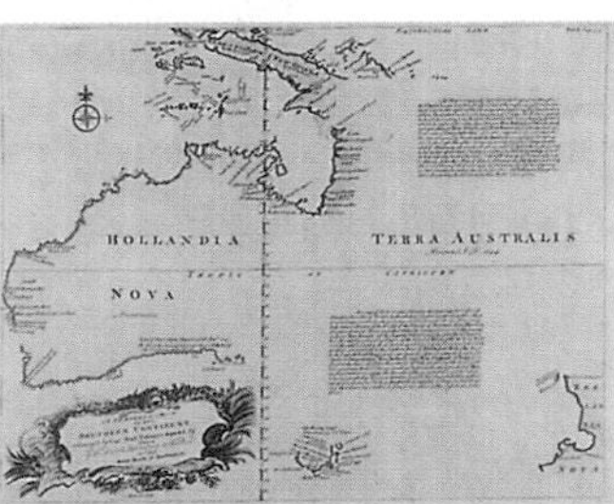

Abel Tasman, *A Complete Map of the Southern Continent,* a hand-coloured folding map of Australia and New Guinea, engraved by Bowen after Thevenot, London, 1744, 14½ x 18¾in (37 x 47.5cm).
£1,900–2,250 / €2,750–3,300
$3,450–4,050 ⚒ S

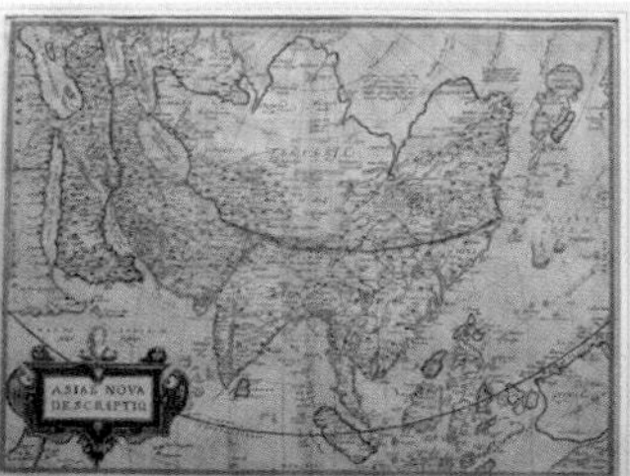

Abraham Ortelius, *Asiae Nova*, a coloured copperplate map, Belgian, Antwerp, 1570, 15 x 20in (38 x 51cm).
£1,250–1,400 / €1,850–2,050
$2,250–2,550 ⊞ JOP

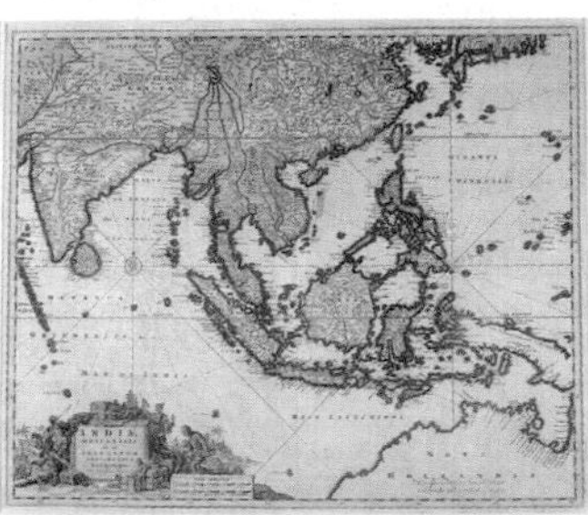

Nicolaus Visscher and Pieter Schenk, *Indiae Orientalis*, a coloured copperplate map, Dutch, Amsterdam, c1715, 18 x 22in (45.5 x 56cm).
£1,450–1,650 / €2,100–2,400
$2,600–3,000 ⊞ JOP

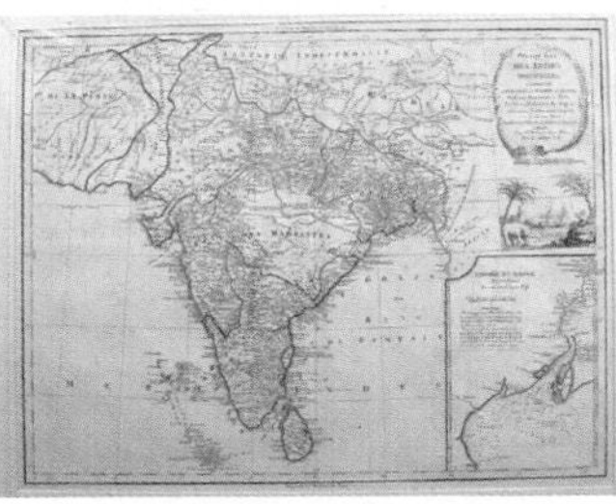

C. F. Delamarche, a coloured copperplate map of India, French, Paris, 1785–1820, 19½ x 25in (49.5 x 63.5cm).
£400–450 / €580–660
$720–810 ⊞ JOP

Europe & the Middle East

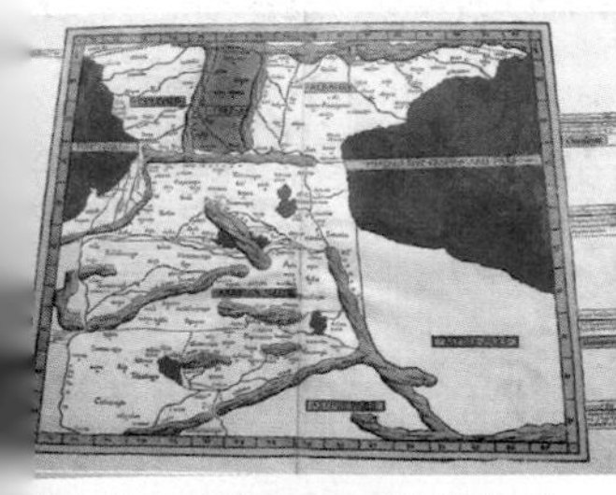

Claudius Ptolemy and Leinhart Holle, a coloured woodblock map of Armenia and Georgia, German, Ulm, 1482, 15½ x 21in (39.5 x 53.5cm).
£4,300–4,800 / €6,300–7,000
$7,800–8,700 ⊞ JOP

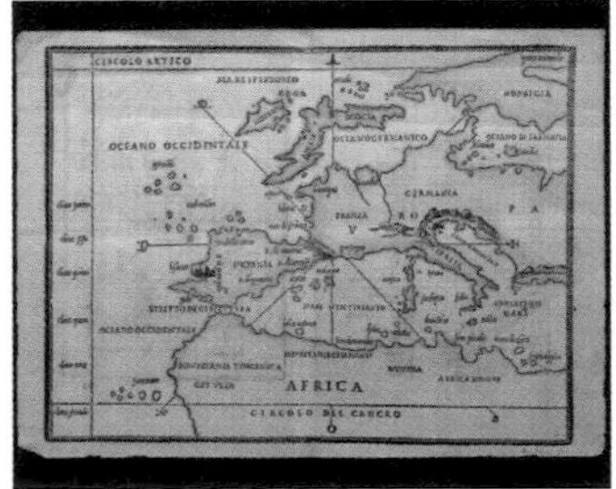

Benedetto Bordone, a woodblock map of Europe with later colouring, Italian, 1528, 11 x 15in (28 x 38cm).
£1,600–1,800 / €2,350–2,650
$2,900–3,250 ⊞ APS

Abraham Ortelius, *Germaniae Veteris Typus*, hand-coloured engraved map of ancient Germany with ornamental cartouche, Belgian, Antwerp, 1587, 14½ x 18½in (37 x 47cm).
£220–260 / €320–380
$400–480 ⚒ BBA

Abraham Ortelius, a coloured copperplate map of Persia, Belgian, Antwerp, 1570–79, 14 x 20in (35.5 x 51cm).
£430–480 / €630–700
$780–870 ⊞ JOP

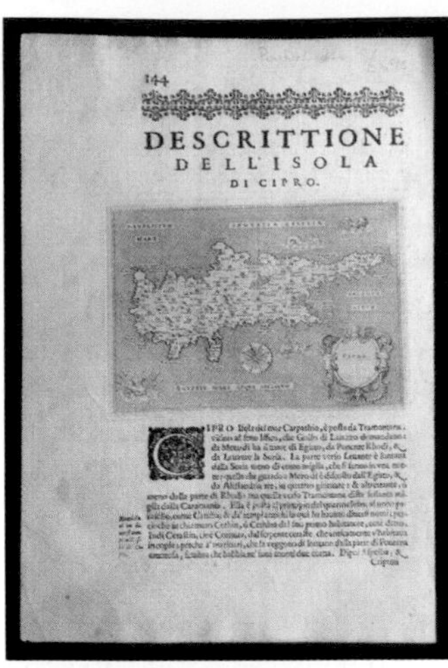

Tomaso Porcacchi, a copper-engraved map of Cyprus, Italian, 1620, 11 x 9in (28 x 23cm).
£630–700 / €900–1,000
$1,100–1,250 ⊞ APS

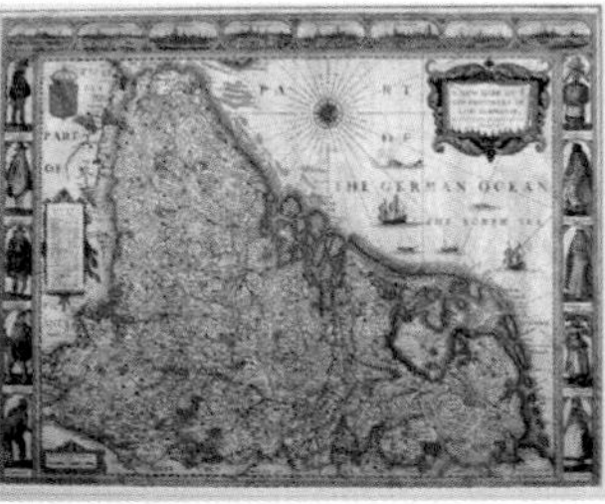

John Speed and George Humble, *A New Mape of Ye XVII Provinces of Low Germanie*, a coloured copperplate map of the Low Countries, 1626–50, 17 x 21in (43 x 53.5cm).
£3,150–3,500 / €4,600–5,100
$5,700–6,300 ⊞ JOP

Willem Blaeu, *Svecia*, a copperplate map of Scandinavia with outline colour, Dutch, Amsterdam, 1634–43, 17½ x 21½in (44.5 x 54.5cm).
£670–750 / €980–1,100
$1,200–1,350 ⊞ JOP

Matthäus Merians, *Tvrcicvm Imperivm*, a coloured copperplate map, German, Frankfurt, c1650, 11 x 14in (28 x 35.5cm).
£450–500 / €660–730
$810–910 ⊞ JOP

Jodocus Hondius Jr and Henricus Hondius, a copperplate map of Europe with outline colour, Dutch, Amsterdam, 1625–43, 15 x 20in (38 x 51cm).
£900–1,000 / €1,300–1,450
$1,600–1,800 ⊞ JOP

John Speed, a coloured copperplate map of Europe, London, 1627, 15 x 20in (38 x 51cm).
£2,500–2,800 / €3,650–4,100
$4,550–5,100 ⊞ JOP

Willem Blaeu, a copperplate map of Europe with outline colour, Dutch, Amsterdam, 1630–60, 17½ x 22in (44.5 x 56cm).
£3,150–3,500 / €4,600–5,100
$5,700–6,300 ⊞ JOP

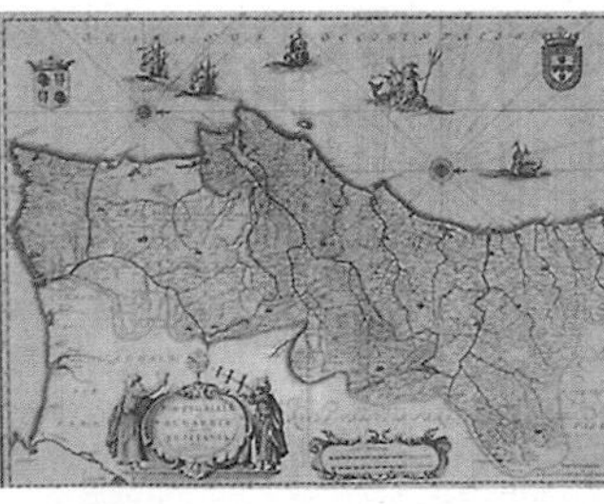

Jan Jansson, *Portugallia et Algarbia quae olim Lusitania*, after Vernando Alvero Secco, a hand-coloured engraved map of Portugal and the Algarve, English text verso, slight damage, Dutch, Amsterdam, 1636, 15½ x 19½in (39.5 x 49.5cm).
£320–380 / €470–550
$580–690 ⚒ BBA

John Speed, a coloured copperplate map of Europe, 1626–76, 16 x 20in (40.5 x 51cm).
£2,000–2,200 / €2,900–3,200
$3,600–4,000 ⊞ JOP

Jodocus Hondius Jr and Willem Blaeu, a copperplate map of the Holy Land with outline colour, Dutch, Amsterdam, c1629, 15 x 20in (38 x 51cm).
£760–850 / €1,100–1,250
$1,400–1,550 ⊞ JOP

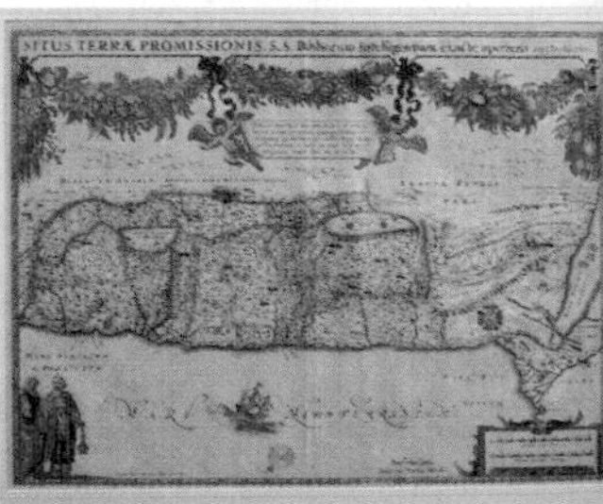

Henricus Hondius and Jan Jansson, a copperplate map of the Holy Land with outline colour, Dutch, Amsterdam 1633–47, 14½ x 20in (37 x 51cm).
£580–650 / €850–950
$1,050–1,200 ⊞ JOP

Joan Blaeu, *Regno di Napoli,* a hand-coloured engraved map of Southern Italy with ornamental title cartouche and armorials to the side margins, two compass roses and rhumb lines, German text verso, c1650, 15¼ x 19½in (38.5 x 49.5cm).
£410–490 / €600–720
$740–890 ⚒ DW

◄ **Abraham Ortelius and Pieter van den Keere,** a coloured copperplate map of Europe, Dutch, Amsterdam, c1652, 14½ x 20in (37 x 51cm).
£520–580 / €760–850
$940–1,050 ⊞ JOP

Frederic de Wit, a coloured copperplate map of Italy, Dutch, Amsterdam, 1671, 20 x 22in (51 x 56cm).
£520–580 / €760–850
$940–1,050 ⊞ JOP

Nicolaus Visscher, *Map of Sweden and Norway,* a hand-coloured map, Dutch, Amsterdam, 1693, 21 x 24in (53.5 x 61cm).
£720–800 / €1,000–1,150
$1,300–1,450 ⊞ VHA

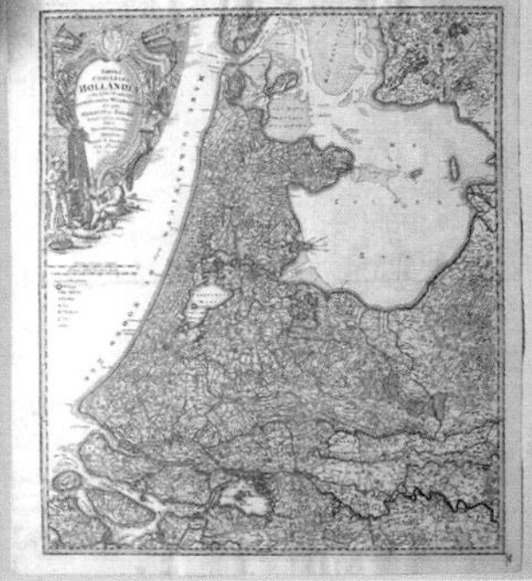

Johann Homann, a hand-coloured map of Holland, 1723, 23 x 19in (58.5 x 48.5cm).
£870–970 / €1,250–1,400
$1,550–1,750 ⊞ APS

Tobias Conrad Lotter, a coloured copperplate map of the eastern Mediterranean and the Middle East, German, Augsburg, c1760, 20 x 23in (51 x 58.5cm).
£460–520 / €670–760
$830–940 ⊞ JOP

▸ **Mahmoud Raif,** *The King of Great Britain's Dominions in Germany,* a coloured copperplate map, with Arabic text, Turkish, Usküdar, c1804, 23 x 21in (58.5 x 53.5cm).
£520–580 / €760–850
$940–1,050 ⊞ JOP

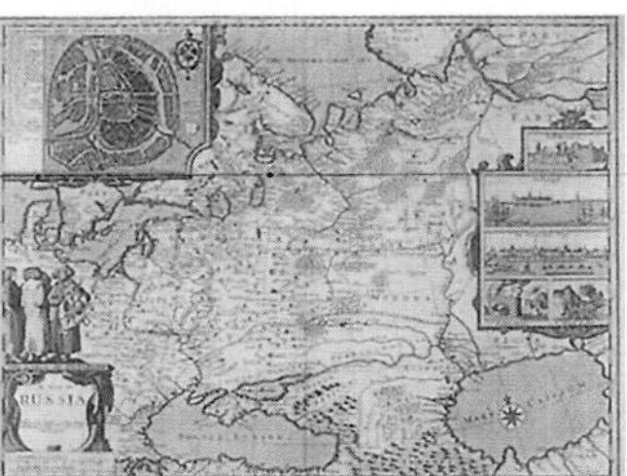

John Speed, *A Map of Russia,* a hand-coloured engraved map with ornamental cartouche surmounted by Russian figures and incorporating a scale of distance, with inset plan of Moscow and five topographical engravings, English text verso, 1676, 15¾ x 20in (40 x 51cm).
£410–490 / €600–720
$740–890 ⚒ DW

▸ **Nicolaus Visscher,** a hand-coloured map of Greece, 1693, 21 x 24in (53.5 x 61cm).
£720–800 / €1,000–1,150
$1,300–1,450 ⊞ VHA

An engraved and coloured map of the Netherlands, *De XVII Nederlandsche Provincien,* a depiction of the 17 Provinces as 'Leo Belgicus', early 18thC, 7 x 9in (18 x 23cm).
£820–980 / €1,200–1,450
$1,500–1,800 ⚒ BERN

Georg Matthäus Seutter, a coloured copperplate map of the Middle East, German, Augsburg, 1730, 20 x 23in (51 x 58.5cm).
£410–460 / €600–670
$740–830 ⊞ JOP

Nicolaus Visscher and Pieter Schenk, a coloured copperplate map of Italy, Dutch, Amsterdam, 1682–1726, 18 x 22in (45.5 x 56cm).
£580–650 / €850–950
$1,050–1,200 ⊞ JOP

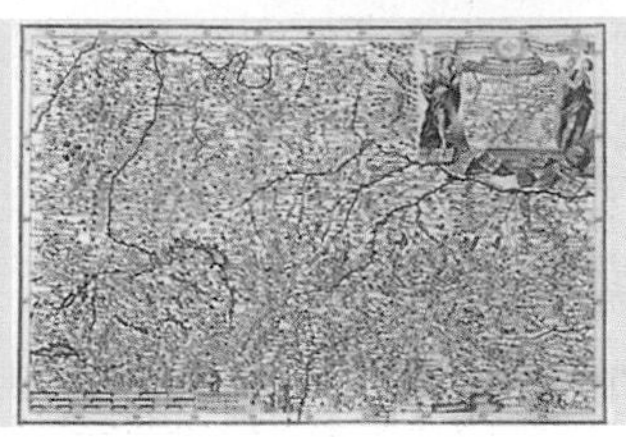

Heinrich Scherer, *Jesuit Map of Germany, Switzerland and Austria,* a partly-coloured copperplate map, German, c1700, 9 x 9½in (23 x 24cm).
£270–320 / €390–470
$490–580 ⚒ DORO

Johann Homann, a hand-coloured copper-engraved map of Catalonia, 1740, 19 x 22in (48.5 x 56cm).
£830–930 / €1,200–1,350
$1,500–1,700 ⊞ APS

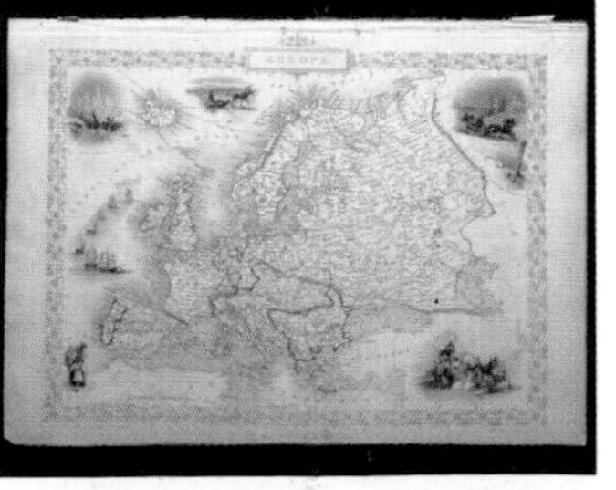

John Tallis, a steel-engraved map of Europe with outline colouring, 1851, 10 x 12in (25.5 x 30.5cm).
£270–300 / €390–440
$490–540 ⊞ APS

Great Britain & Ireland

Abraham Ortelius, a hand-coloured copper-engraved map of Wales, 1572, 18 x 20in (45.5 x 51cm).
£1,600–1,800 / €2,350–2,650
$2,900–3,250 ⊞ APS

Abraham Ortelius, a copper-engraved map of Scotland, 1580, 14 x 18in (35.5 x 45.5cm).
£1,250–1,400 / €1,850–2,050
$2,250–2,550 ⊞ APS

John Speed, a copper-engraved map of Essex with later hand-colouring, 1623, 15 x 20in (38 x 51cm).
£1,600–1,800 / €2,350–2,650
$2,900–3,250 ⊞ APS

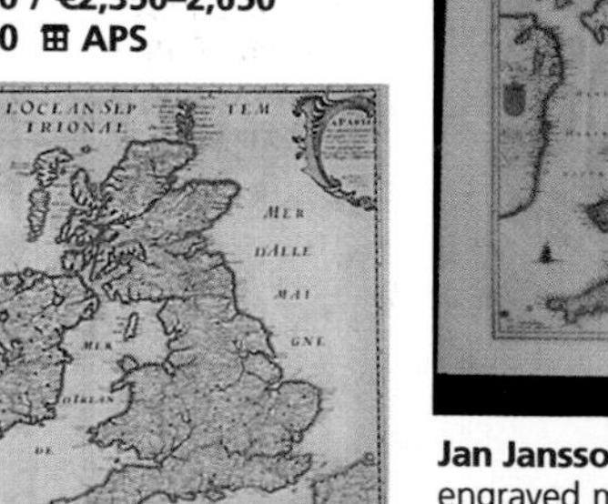

Nicolas Sanson, *Carte Generale des Royaume, d'Angleterre Ecosse et Irlande,* published by Pierre Mariette, engraved by Melchior Tavernier, with an inset map of the Shetlands, outline colour, slight damage, French, Paris, 1640, 16 x 21in (40.5 x 53.5cm).
£440–520 / €640–760
$800–950 ⚒ BBA

▶ Joan Blaeu, *Wiltonia*, a hand-coloured map of Wiltshire, c1646, 16 x 20in (40.5 x 51cm).
£450–500 / €660–730
$810–910 ⊞ VHA

Christopher Saxton and Philip Lea, a copperplate map of Cornwall, London, 1576–1694, 15½ x 20in (39.5 x 51cm).
£2,300–2,600 / €3,350–3,800
$4,150–4,700 ⊞ JOP

Abraham Ortelius, *Britannicarvm Insvlarvm Typvs*, a coloured map, dated 1595, 20 x 18½in (51 x 47cm).
£300–360 / €440–530
$540–650 ⚒ SWO

Jan Jansson, a hand-coloured copper-engraved map of England and Wales, 1645, 15 x 20in (38 x 51cm).
£1,100–1,250 / €1,600–1,800
$2,000–2,200 ⊞ APS

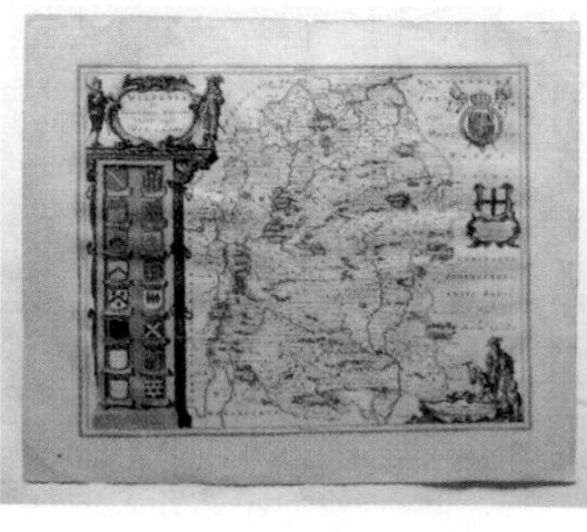

Christopher Saxton, a coloured copperplate map of Shropshire, London, 1579, 15½ x 20in (39.5 x 51cm).
£3,400–3,800 / €4,950–5,500
$6,200–6,900 ⊞ JOP

John Speed, *The Countie of Leinster with the Citie Dublin Described*, after Jodocus Hondius, published by Sudbury and Humble, an engraved map with outline colour, the plan coloured, English text verso, slight damage, c1610, 15¼ x 20in (38.5 x 51cm).
£350–420 / €510–610
$630–760 ⚒ BBA

◀ John Speed, a hand-coloured engraved map of Westmorland, 1600–50, 15½ x 20½in (39.5 x 52cm), mounted and framed.
£230–270 / €340–400
$420–500 ⚒ PFK

Humphrey Lhuyd and Gerard Mercator, *Cambriae Typus*, an engraved map of Wales, with ornamental cartouche, ship and sea monsters, Latin text verso, Belgian, Antwerp, c1630, 14½ x 19¾in (37 x 50cm).
£350–420 / €510–610
$630–760 ⚒ BBA

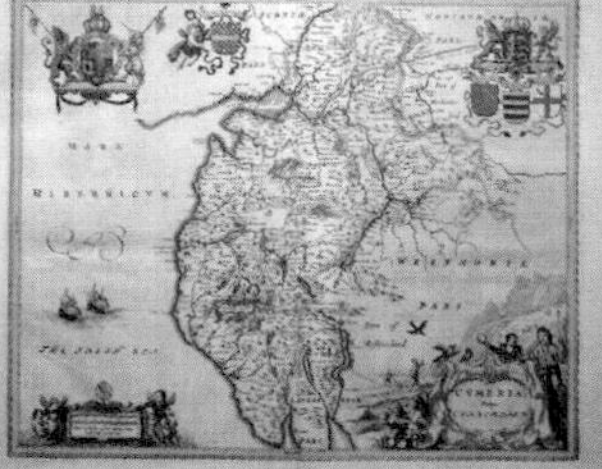

Joan Blaeu, a hand-coloured copper-engraved map of Cumbria, 1646, 13 x 20in (33 x 51cm).
£700–780 / €1,000–1,100
$1,250–1,400 ⊞ APS

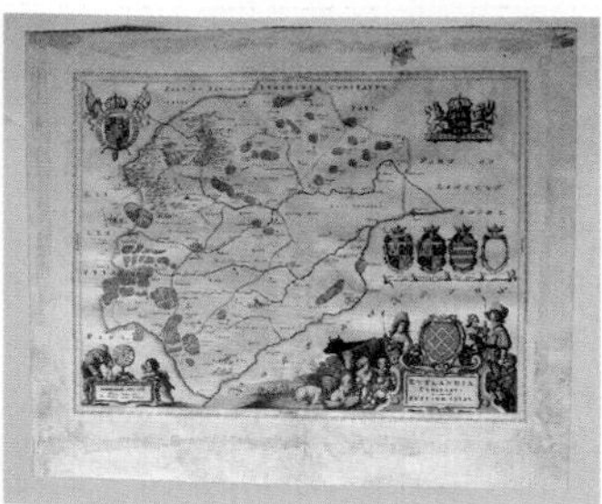

Joan Blaeu, a hand-coloured map of Rutland, c1648, 15 x 20in (38 x 51cm).
£450–500 / €660–730
$810–910 ⊞ VHA

Robert Morden, a hand-coloured engraved map of Westmorland, late 17thC, 14 x 16½in (35.5 x 42cm).
£130–155 / €200–230
$240–290 ⚒ PFK

Herman Moll, a copper-engraved map of Norfolk, 1728, 8 x 12in (20.5 x 30.5cm).
£250–280 / €370–410
$450–510 ⊞ APS

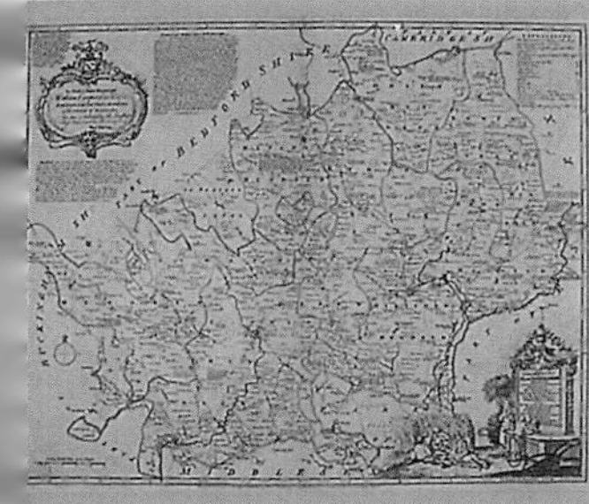

Thomas Kitchin, *A New Improved Map of Hartfordshire*, published by R. Sayer, T. and J. Bowles and J. Tinney, an engraved map with outline colour and pictorial cartouche, slight damage, 1760, 21¼ x 26½in (54 x 67.5cm).
£230–270 / €340–400
$420–500 ⚒ BBA

John Speed, *Somersetshire Described and the citie of Bathe*, a hand-coloured engraved map with colour outline and coloured arms and plan of Bath, 1668, 14¾ x 19½in (37.5 x 49.5cm).
£420–500 / €610–730
$760–910 ⚒ L

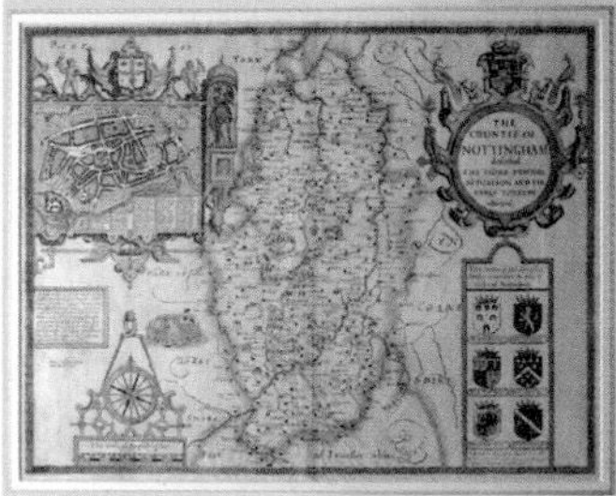

John Speed, *The Countie of Nottingham*, 1676, 16 x 21in (40.5 x 53.5cm).
£540–600 / €790–880
$980–1,100 ⊞ VHA

◄ **Henry Overton,** a coloured copperplate map of Suffolk, London, 1713, 13½ x 19¼in (34.5 x 49cm).
£1,050–1,200 / €1,500–1,700
$1,900–2,150 ⊞ JOP

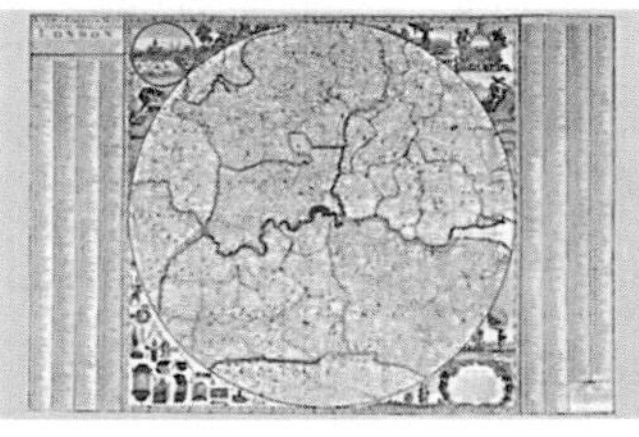

George Willdey, *A New & Correct Map of Thirty Miles Round London shewing all the Towns, Villages, Roads, etc*, a hand-coloured engraved map of London flanked by an index of places within eight columns, some restoration, c1720, 15 x 25½in (38 x 65cm).
£630–750 / €920–1,100
$1,150–1,350 ⚒ DW

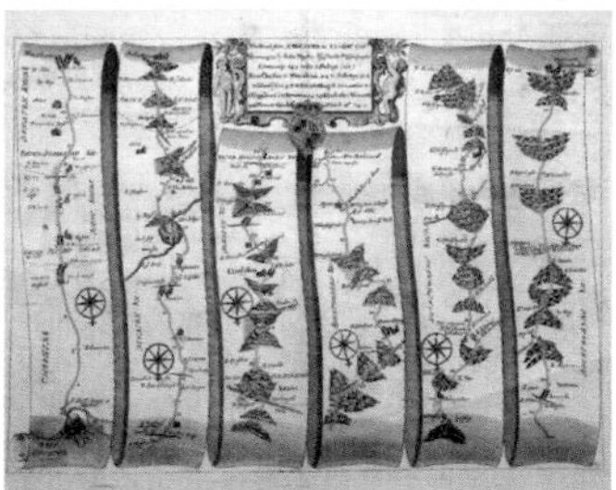

John Ogilby, a copper-engraved map of Chester to Cardiff, 1675, 13 x 17in (33 x 43cm).
£370–420 / €540–610
$670–760 ⊞ APS

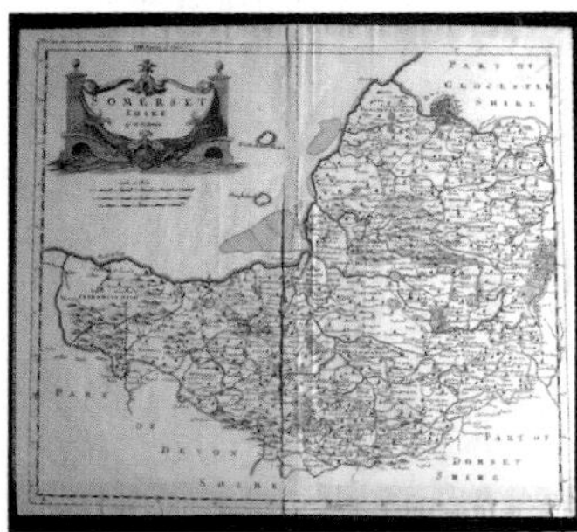

Robert Morden, a copper-engraved map of Somerset, 1695, 15 x 17in (38 x 43cm).
£270–300 / €390–440
$490–540 ⊞ APS

Robert Morden, a map of the West Riding of Yorkshire, London, 1722, 17 x 15in (43 x 38in).
£270–300 / €390–440
$490–540 ⊞ VHA

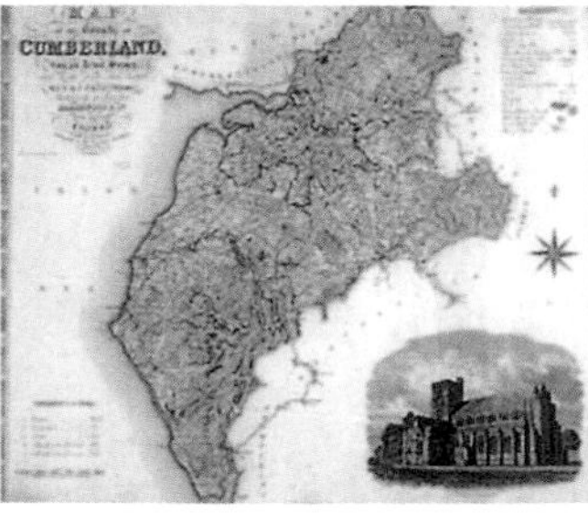

A hand-coloured engraved map of Cumberland, published by Greenwood & Co, engraved by J. Dower, with a vignette of Carlisle Cathedral, 1830, 24 x 27in (61 x 68cm).
£90–105 / €130–155
$160–190 ⚒ PFK

◄ **Carrington Bowles,** *Bowles New Pocket Guide Through England and Wales,* London, 1780, 23 x 19in (58.5 x 48.5cm).
£360–400 / €530–590
$650–720 ⊞ VHA

Polar Maps

Gerard Mercator, *Septentrionalium Terrarum Descriptio*, a hand-coloured engraved map of the North Pole extending to the northern tip of Scotland, the border inset with maps of the Shetland Isles, The Faroes and 'Frisland', Latin text verso, some damage and repair, Dutch, Amsterdam, c1606, 14¾ x 15½in (37.5 x 39.5cm).
£540–640 / €790–940
$980–1,150 BBA

Willem Blaeu, a hand-coloured map of the Arctic, 1793, 21 x 24in (53.5 x 61cm).
£900–1,000 / €1,300–1,450
$1,600–1,800 VHA

For further information on
Marine see pages 695–697

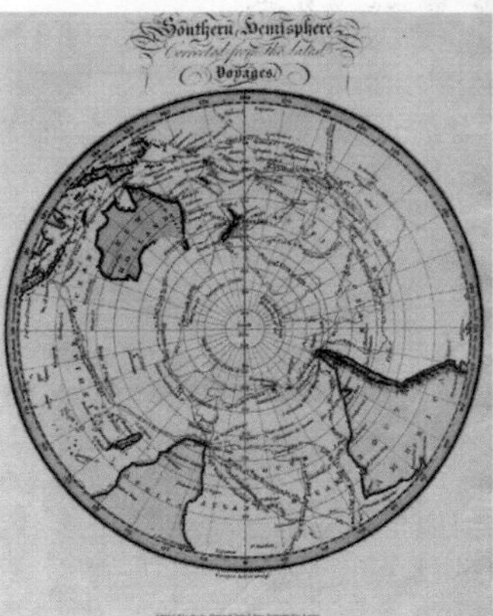

H. Cooper, J. Sherwood and Neely, *The Southern Hemisphere Corrected from the Latest Voyages*, a lithographic map of the southern hemisphere, depicts the tracks of a number of pre-eminent explorers including Cook, Carteret and Wallis, London, 1809, 9¾ x 7¾in (25 x 19.5cm).
£145–160 / €210–230
$260–290 JOP

Town & City Plans

Georg Braun and Frans Hogenberg, a hand-coloured copper-engraved map of Cambridge, 1575, 13 x 17in (33 x 43cm).
£1,400–1,600 / €2,050–2,300
$2,450–2,900 APS

Nicholas de Fer, a copperplate map of Paris, 1717, 18 x 24in (45.5 x 61cm).
£450–500 / €660–730
$810–910 JOP

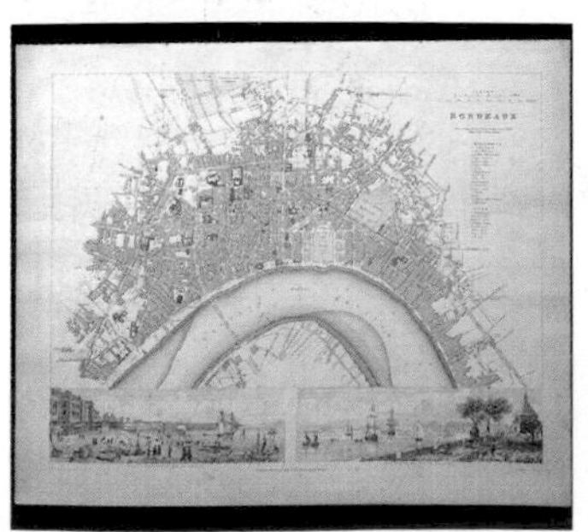

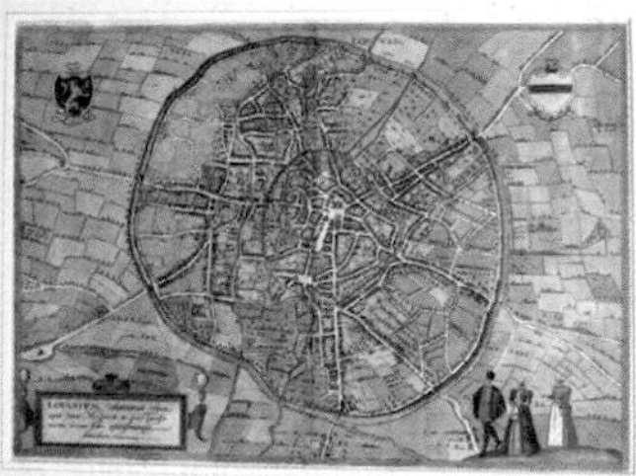

Georg Braun and Frans Hogenberg, a coloured copperplate map of Leuven in Belgium, German, Cologne, 1581, 13½ x 19½in (34.5 x 49.5cm).
£460–520 / €670–760
$830–940 JOP

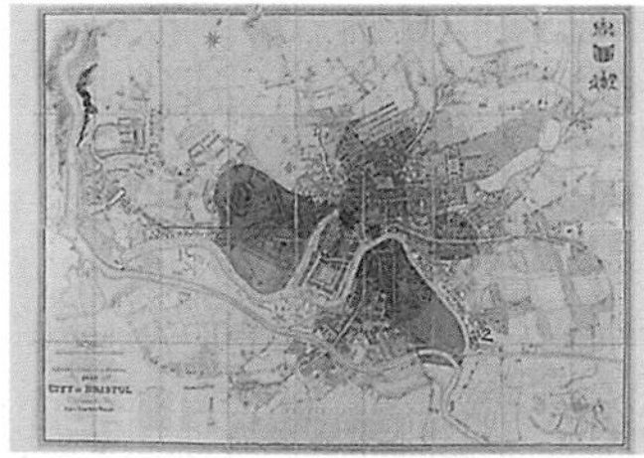

A Plan of the City of Bristol and its Suburbs, published by George C. Ashmead, a part hand-coloured engraved map with an inset map of Bristol showing its original boundaries, three coats-of-arms, reference tables, 2°, slight damage, 1828, 79½ x 30in (202 x 76cm).
£1,050–1,250 / €1,550–1,850
$1,900–2,250 BBA

◄ **Society for the Diffusion of Useful Knowledge,** a steel-engraved map of Bordeaux, 1836, 12 x 16in (30.5 x 40.5cm).
£120–135 / €175–195
$210–240 APS

An Exact Survey of the Mannr of Killmainhambegg in the Barony of Kels and County of East Meath, a watercolour over ink on paper backed with cloth, slight damage, c1625, 15½ x 23¾in (39.5 x 60.5cm).
£5,200–6,200 / €7,600–9,100
$9,400–11,200 HOK

LOCATE THE SOURCE

The source of each illustration in Miller's can be found by checking the code letters below each caption with the Key to Illustrations, pages 778–784.

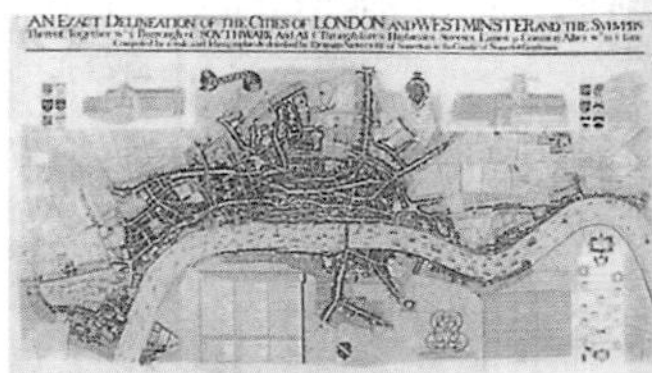

Richard Newcourt, *An Exact Delineation of the Cities of London and Westminster and the Suburbs thereof, together with ye Burrough of Southwark and all ye Through-fares, Highwaies, Streetes, Lanes and Common Allies*, published by A. E. Evans & Sons, four hand-coloured engraved mapsheets joined, showing individual buildings and ships, two architectural elevations of St Peter's and St Paul's, coats-of-arms and a genealogical table, slight damage, 1857, 40¼ x 71¾in (102 x 182.5cm).
£1,250–1,500 / €1,850–2,200
$2,150–2,550 BBA

Dolls

A C. M. Bergmann/ Simon & Halbig doll, with sleeping eyes, c1920, 23¼in (59cm) high.
£450–500 / €660–730
$810–910 ⊞ BaN

A Porzellanfabrik Burggrub Princess Elizabeth doll, with open mouth, sleeping eyes, mohair wig and five-piece toddler body, head marked, German, c1930, 17in (43cm) high.
£390–460 / €570–670
$710–830 ⚒ BWL

A Bru Jeune girl doll, with cork pate and wig, jointed leather and wood body, impressed mark, restored, French, c1890, 11in (28cm) high.
£7,000–8,400
€10,200–12,200
$12,700–15,200 ⚒ BWL

A Bru Jeune kiss-throwing walking doll, French, c1890, 22in (56cm) high.
£2,500–2,800
€3,650–4,100
$4,550–5,100 ⊞ GLEN

Items in the Dolls section have been arranged in maker order with unknown makers at the end.

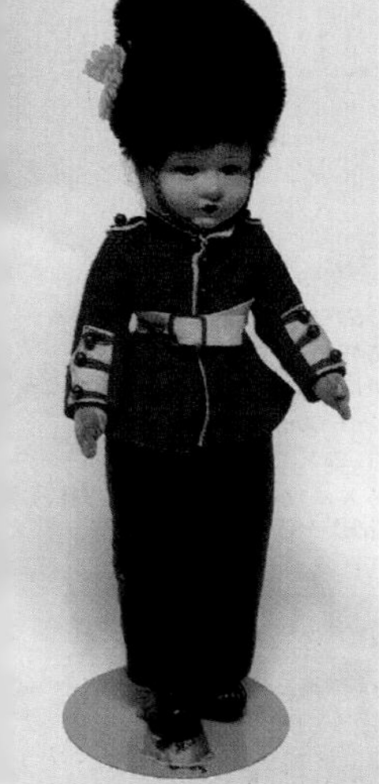

◀ A Chad Valley cloth doll, c1930, 17in (43cm) high.
£220–250 / €320–360
$400–450 ⊞ GLEN

◀ A pair of Deans Rag Book dolls, c1930, 18in (45.5cm) high.
£310–350
€450–510
$560–630
⊞ GLEN

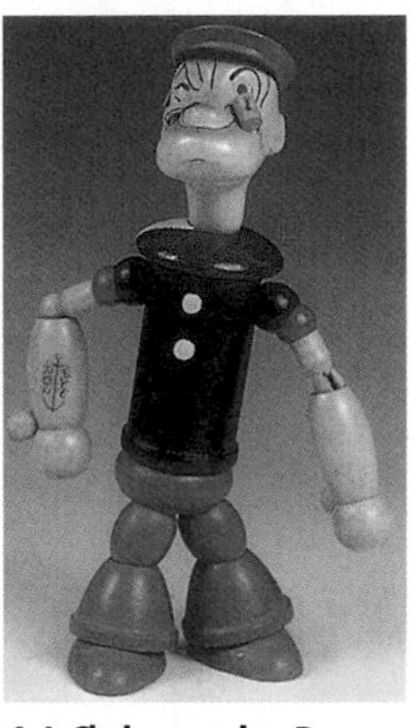

A J. Chein wooden Popeye doll, with jointed body, losses, American, dated 1932, 8in (20.5cm) high.
£125–150 / €185–220
$230–270 ⚒ JAA

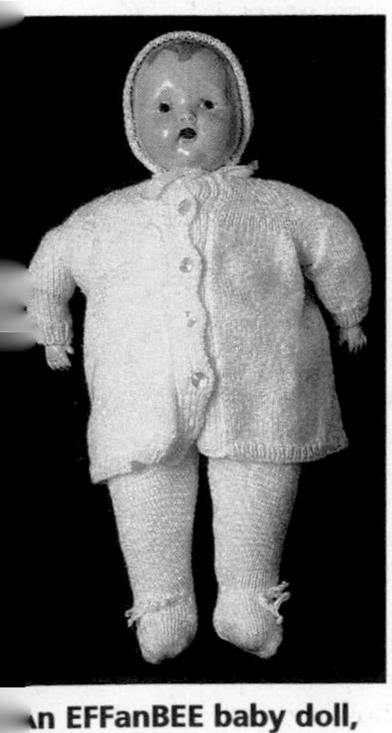

An EFFanBEE baby doll, with painted eyes, composite head, arms and legs and soft body, 1930s, 24in (61cm) high.
£110–125 / €160–180
$200–230 ⊞ POLL

A Gaultier Frères bisque-headed doll, with weighted glass eyes, mohair wig, composition and wood jointed body, marked, French, c1888, 29in (73.5cm) high.
£2,900–3,500
€4,250–5,100
$5,300–6,300 ⚒ THE

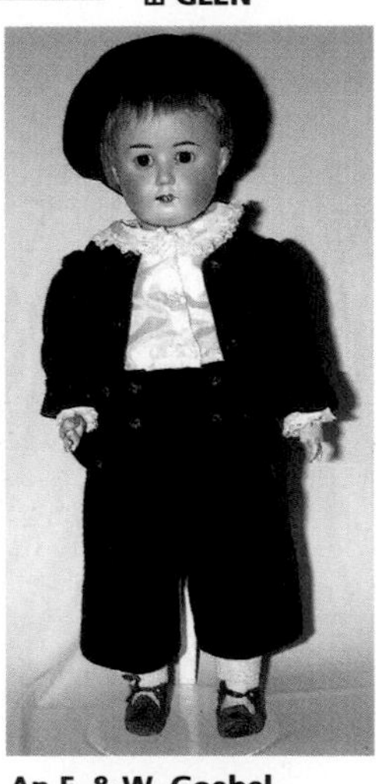

An F. & W. Goebel bisque-headed doll, mould No. 120, with sleeping eyes and original wig, German, c1920, 24¾in (63cm) high.
£430–480 / €630–700
$780–870 ⊞ BaN

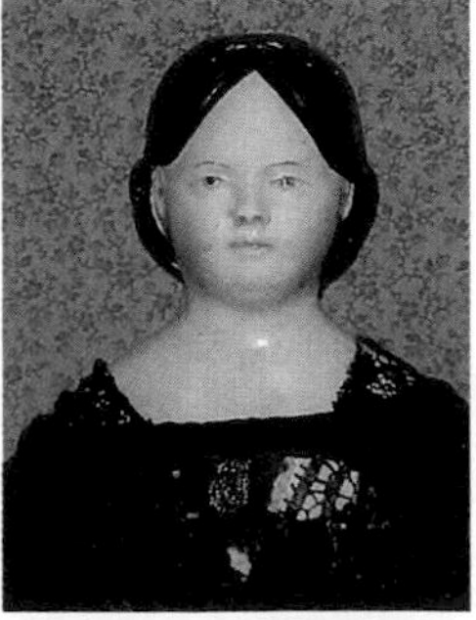

A Greiner doll, with cloth body and leather lower arms, with original clothes, American, 1858, 18in (45.5cm) high.
£470–530 / €690–770
$850–960 ⊞ SaB

A Max Handwerc Baby Elite doll, German, c1920, 15in (38cm) high.
£310–350 / €450–510
$560–630 ⊞ GLEN

An Ernst Heubach porcelain-headed doll, marked, German, 1926, 24¾in (63cm) high.
£600–720 / €880–1,050
$1,100–1,300 ⚒ Bern

► A Gebrüder Heubach bisque-headed doll, with sleeping glass eyes, jointed composition body, wearing original felt coat and hat, impressed mark, c1920, 16in (40.5cm) high.
£200–240 / €290–350
$360–430 ⚒ BWL

A Pierre-François Jumeau bisque-headed poupée doll, with glass eyes, mohair wig, kid jointed body, French, c1875, 25in (63.5cm) high.
£3,150–3,750
€4,600–5,500
$5,700–6,800 ⚒ THE

A Hertel & Schwab Googly-eyed bisque-headed doll, with sleeping eyes, moulded hair and jointed composition body, the socket head impressed '163 2/0', German, 1920s, 11¼in (28.5cm) high.
£2,900–3,450
€4,250–5,000
$5,400–6,200 ⚒ SK(B)

An Emile Jumeau bisque-headed *bébé* doll, with weighted glass eyes, pierced ears, mohair wig, Kestner body, impressed mark, French, c1885, 16in (40.5cm) high.
£1,600–1,900
€2,350–2,750
$2,900–3,450 ⚒ SK(B)

An Ernst Heubach bisque-headed doll, with original wig, German, c1900, 16½in (42cm) high.
£450–500 / €660–730
$810–910 ⊞ BaN

A Mary Hoyer hard plastic doll, with sleeping eyes, synthetic wig, one sleeve torn, embossed maker's mark, American, 1950s, 14in (35.5cm) high.
£220–260 / €320–380
$400–470 ⚒ SK(B)

An Ernst Heubach bisque-headed doll, German, c1920, 20in (51cm) high.
£310–350 / €450–510
$560–630 ⊞ GLEN

A Jullien bisque-headed *bébé* doll, marked, French, c1890, 19in (48.5cm) high.
£990–1,100 / €1,450–1,60
$1,800–2,000 ⊞ GLEN

◄ A Jumeau bisque-headed doll, with cloth body, one bisque arm damaged, French, 1870s, 21½in (54.5cm) high, with wardrobe and trunk.
£2,300–2,750
€3,350–4,000
$4,150–5,000
⚒ SK(B)

► A Jumeau bisque-headed doll, with weighted glass eyes, mohair wig, jointed composition and wood body, slight wear, impressed, French, early 20thC, 10in (25.5cm) high.
£1,100–1,300
€1,600–1,900
$2,000–2,350
⚒ SK(B)

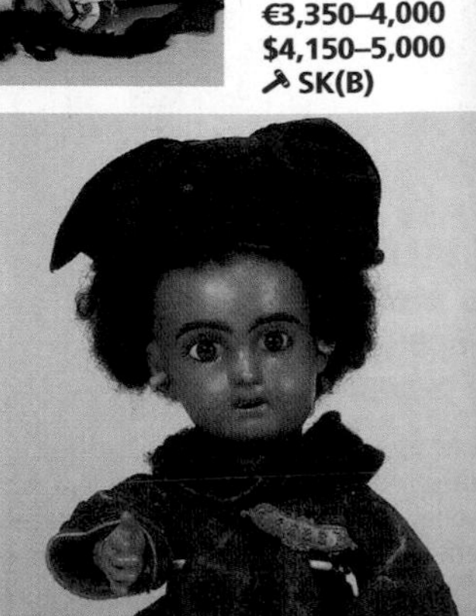

A Jumeau doll, with a Simon & Halbig head, original wig, sleeping eyes and a pullstring voice box, c1905, 24¾in (63cm) high.
£1,050–1,200
€1,550–1,750
$1,900–2,150 ⊞ BaN

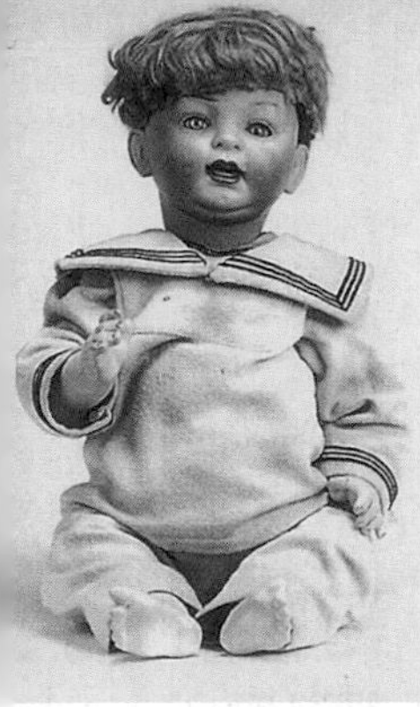

A J. D. Kestner bisque-headed doll, with leather body, marked, German, 1897, 15¾in (40cm) high.
£560–670 / €820–980
$1,000–1,200 ⚒ Bern

Madame Alexander omposition doll, with a ohair wig, marked, merican, New York, 1935, 14in (35.5cm) high.
260–310 / €380–450
470–560 ⚒ THE

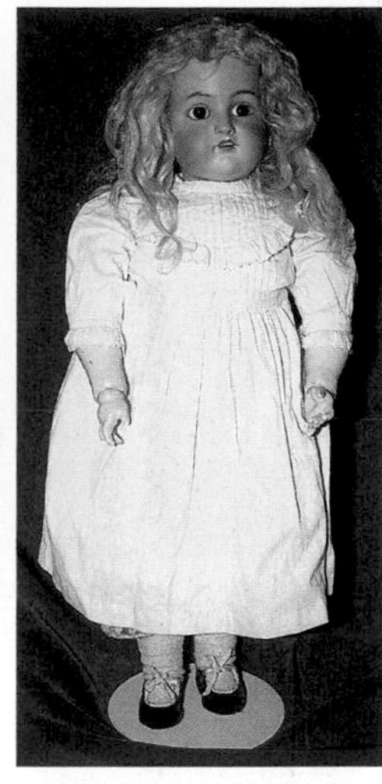

A Kämmer & Reinhardt doll, with a Simon & Halbig bisque head and sleeping eyes, German, 1880s, 28¼in (72cm) high.
£720–800 / €1,000–1,150
$1,300–1,450 ⊞ BaN

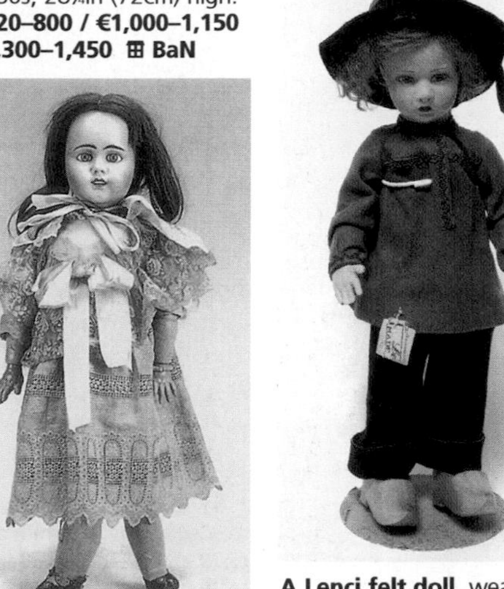

A J. D. Kestner bisque-headed doll, marked, German, 1910, 23¼in (59cm) high.
£450–540 / €660–790
$810–980 ⚒ Bern

An Armand Marseille porcelain-headed doll, marked, German, late 19thC, 23¾in (60.5cm) high.
£560–670 / €820–980
$1,000–1,200 ⚒ Bern

A J. D. Kestner bisque-headed doll, marked, German, 1897, 23¾in (60cm) high.
£640–760 / €930–1,100
$1,200–1,400 ⚒ Bern

A Lenci felt doll, wearing Dutch costume, with labels, Italian, c1930, 20in (51cm) high.
£360–400 / €520–580
$650–720 ⊞ GLEN

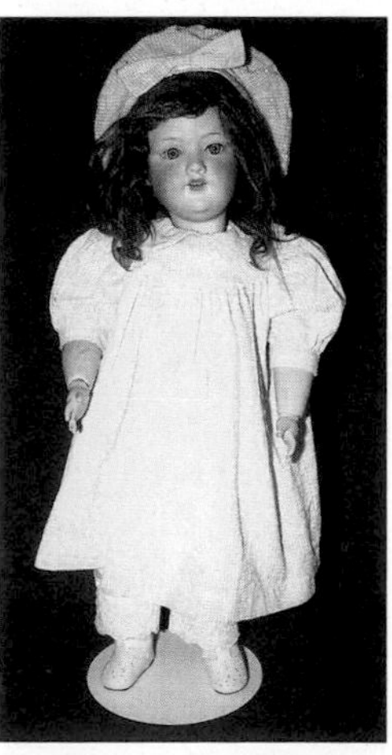

An Armand Marseille doll, mould No. 390, with sleeping eyes, original wig and composition body, German, c1910, 24½in (62cm) high.
£310–350 / €450–510
$560–630 ⊞ BaN

A J. D. Kestner bisque-headed doll, with leather body, marked, German, 1897, 26½in (67.5cm) high.
£370–440 / €540–640
$670–800 ⚒ Bern

A Lenci cloth doll, model No. 300/12, with a wooden rake, marked, Italian, c1935, 17in (43cm) high.
£1,500–1,800
€2,200–2,600
$2,700–3,250 ⚒ THE

An Armand Marseille doll, mould No. 390, with sleeping eyes, German, c1910, 25¼in (64cm) high.
£230–260 / €340–380
$420–470 ⊞ BaN

An Armand Marseille Dream Baby doll, mould No. 341, with sleeping eyes and composition body, German, 1920s, 11¾in (30cm) high.
£210–240 / €310–350
$380–430 ⊞ BaN

An Armand Marseille bisque-headed baby doll, German, c1920, 20in (51cm) high.
£340–380 / €500–550
$620–690 ⊞ GLEN

An Armand Marseille pillow baby doll, German, c1920, 10in (25.5cm) high.
£270–300 / €390–440
$490–540 ⊞ GLEN

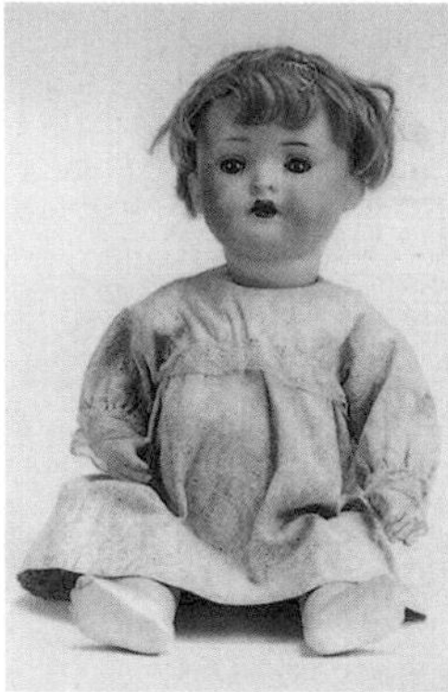

A bisque-headed doll, marked 'PM', German, 1920, 10¼in (26cm) high.
£160–190 / €240–280
$290–340 ⚒ Bern

An S. F. B. J. bisque-headed Poulbot doll, with glass eyes, marked, French, c1910, 14in (35.5cm) high.
£3,500–3,900
€5,100–5,700
$6,300–7,100 ⊞ SaB
This rare doll was designed by the artist Francisque Poulbot. It is representative of the Parisian street urchins depicted in his paintings.

► A Simon & Halbig bisque-headed doll, mould No. 1079, with original wig, composition body, original clothes and shoes, German, 1890s, 19in (48.5cm) high.
£400–450 / €580–660
$710–810 ⊞ BaN

A Lucy Peck wax doll, c1910, 20in (51cm) high.
£360–400 / €520–580
$650–720 ⊞ GLEN

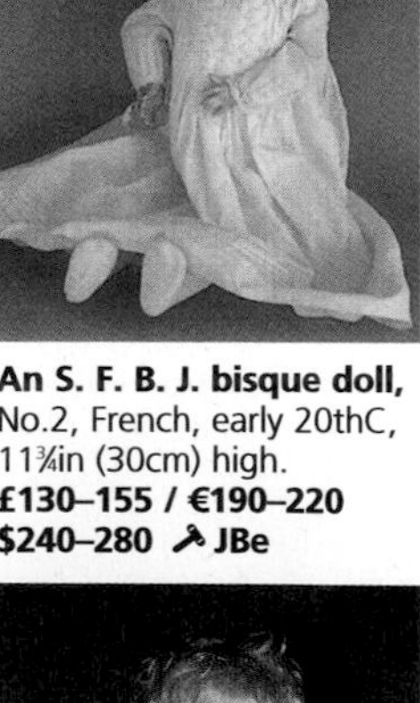

An S. F. B. J. bisque doll, No.2, French, early 20thC, 11¾in (30cm) high.
£130–155 / €190–220
$240–280 ⚒ JBe

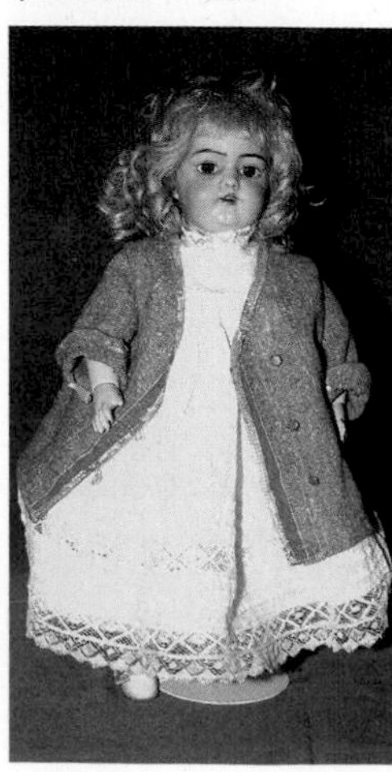

A Schoenhut wooden doll, model No. 102, with carved hair, American, c1914, 16in (40.5cm) high.
£2,350–2,800
€3,450–4,100
$4,250–5,100 ⚒ THE

A Simon & Halbig doll, mould No. 1079, with original wig, composition body, German, 1890s, 38¼in (97cm) high.
£1,600–1,800
€2,350–2,650
$2,900–3,250 ⊞ BaN

An S. F. B. J. bisque-headed *bébé* doll, with weighted glass eyes, marked, French, c1890, 28in (71cm) high.
£850–950 / €1,250–1,400
$1,500–1,700 ⊞ GLEN

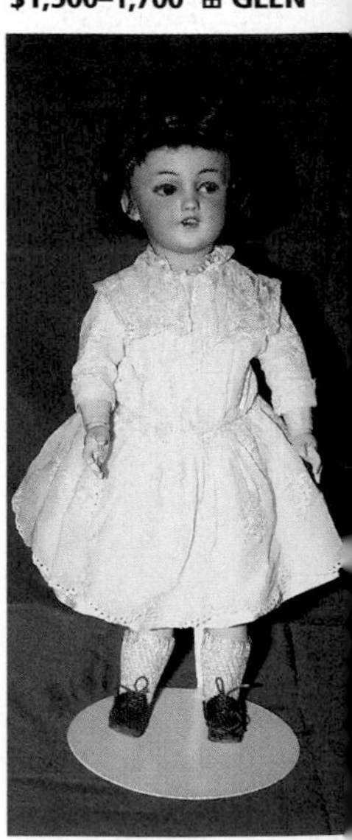

A Simon & Halbig doll, mould No. 1248, with flirty eyes, original wig and composition body, German, c1900, 19¾in (50cm) high.
£670–750 / €980–1,100
$1,200–1,350 ⊞ BaN

◄ **A Simon & Halbig bisque-headed doll,** with sleeping eyes, earrings, wig and a jointed wood and composition body, impressed 'S&H1249DEP', German, c1910, 19in (48.5cm) high.
£350–420 / €510–610
$630–760 ⚒ F&C

A Jules Steiner bisque-headed *bébé parlant* doll, with weighted glass eyes, human hair wig, fabric-covered cardboard torso containing mechanism to move hands and limbs and to cry, with composition body, paper label, lower teeth missing, French, 1880s, 22in (56cm) high.
£1,600–1,900 / €2,350–2,750
$2,900–3,450 ⚒ SK(B)

Condition

The condition is absolutely vital when assessing the value of an antique. Damaged pieces on the whole appreciate much less than perfect examples. However, a rare desirable piece may command a high price even when damaged.

A Simon & Halbig bisque-headed doll, mould No. 1079, c1910, 22in (56cm) high.
£450–500 / €660–730
$810–910 ⊞ GLEN

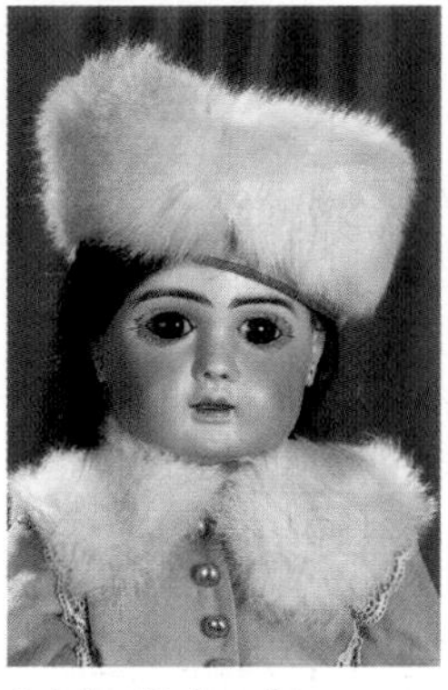

A Jules Steiner bisque-headed *bébé* doll, with glass eyes, painted eyelashes, human hair, composition and wood jointed body, French, c1890, 28in (71cm) high.
£2,850–3,400
€4,150–4,950
$5,200–6,200 ⚒ THE

A Simon & Halbig bisque-headed walking doll, with flirty eyes and original clothes, German, c1910, 18in (45.5cm) high.
£490–550 / €720–800
$890–1,000 ⊞ GLEN

A Norah Wellings cloth South Sea Islander doll, with glass eyes, c1930, 13in (33cm) high.
£85–95 / €125–140
$150–170 ⊞ GLEN

A Norah Wellings cloth Mountie doll, 1930s, 9in (23cm) high.
£70–80 / €100–115
$125–140 ⊞ GLEN

◄ **A bisque-headed doll,** with glass eyes, leather body and mohair wig, c1870, 17in (43cm) high.
£2,650–3,150
€3,850–4,600
$4,800–5,700
⚒ THE

► **A bisque-headed doll,** No. 192, with sleeping eyes and pierced ears, German, c1910, 27¼in (69cm) high.
£720–800 / €1,000–1,150
$1,300–1,450 ⊞ BaN

A poured wax doll, with mohair wig, pierced ears and cloth body, wearing original clothes, stamped, German, c1875, 21in (53.5cm) high.
£410–490 / €600–720
$740–890 ⚒ BWL

◄ **A composition doll,** wearing original clothes, 1930s, 18in (45.5cm) high.
£180–200 / €260–290
$320–360 ⊞ GLEN

Dolls' Clothes & Furniture

A silk and lace baby doll outfit, on a wood and cloth tailor's dummy, c1920–30,
£900–1,000 / €1,300–1,450
$1,600–1,800 ⊞ Beb

◄ A doll's dress and bonnet, made from 19thC fabric, 1950s,
£310–350 / €450–510
$560–630 ⊞ JPr

► A doll's dress and bonnet, made from 19thC fabric, 1950s,
£310–350 / €450–510
$560–630 ⊞ JPr

◄ A doll's metal and silk parasol, attributed to Huret, with an ivory tip, French, c1860, 9in (23cm) high.
£420–500
€610–730
$1,100–900
⚒ THE

A doll's *faux* bamboo armoire, c1900, 18in (45.5cm) high.
£135–150 / €195–220
$240–270 ⊞ MLL

A doll's ebonized beech armchair, c1900, 11in (28cm) high.
£90–100 / €130–145
$160–180 ⊞ MLL

► A doll's wooden desk, with a tooled leather writing surface, French, early 19thC, 9in (23cm) wide.
£480–570
€700–830
$870–1,050
⚒ THE

A miniature woven grocery box, containing miniature *faux* food, French, c1890, 3½in (9cm) wide.
£145–170 / €210–250
$260–310 ⚒ THE

A G. F. Filley miniature stove, entitled 'Charter Oak No. 103', with cast-iron cookware and ashtray, front grille broken, American, late 19thC, 19¾in (50cm) wide.
£270–320 / €390–470
$490–580 ⚒ Bert

A Kenton nickel-plated cast-iron miniature stove, entitled 'Zenda', with burner lids and warmer tray, restored, American, c1900, 17¾in (45cm) wide.
£360–430 / €530–630
$650–780 ⚒ Bert

◄ A Kenton cast-iron and pressed steel miniature stove, entitled 'Venus', with cast-iron cookware, lid lifter and tray, shelf repainted, American, c1920, 8½in (21.5cm) wide.
£45–50 / €65–75
$75–90 ⚒ Bert

► A doll's mahogany sofa, in the manner of George Smith, c1835, 30in (76cm) wide.
£780–930 / €1,150–1,350
$1,400–1,650 ⚒ S(O)

Teddy Bears

A Bing mechanical teddy bear, with boot-button eyes and a walking stick, tag to right ear and patent button under arm, German, c1907, 8in (20.5cm) high.
£1,350–1,500 / €1,950–2,200
$2,450–2,700 ⊞ BaN

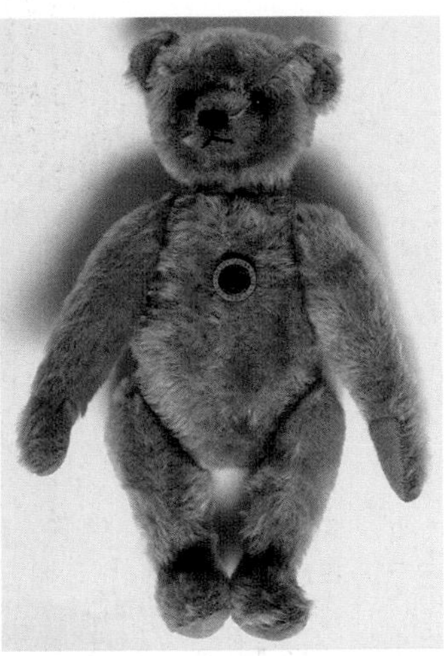

A Bing mohair teddy bear, with boot-button eyes and button under arm, German, c1910, 14in (35.5cm) high.
£2,250–2,500 / €3,300–3,650
$4,050–4,550 ⊞ BaN

A Bing teddy bear, with boot-button eyes and all-in-one ears, German, c1910, 20in (51cm) high.
£1,950–2,200 / €2,850–3,200
$3,550–4,000 ⊞ BaN

A Chad Valley mohair teddy bear, with glass eyes and button in ear, 1930s, 12in (30.5cm) high.
£450–500 / €660–730
$810–910 ⊞ BBe

A Chad Valley mohair teddy bear, 1930s, 21in (53.5cm) high.
£180–200 / €260–290
$320–360 ⊞ BaN

A Chad Valley teddy bear, 1950s, 18in (45.5cm) high.
£135–150 / €195–220
$240–270 ⊞ NAW

A Chiltern musical mohair Hugmee teddy bear, 1950s, 24in (61cm) high.
£500–550 / €730–810
$900–1,000 ⊞ BBe

A Chiltern mohair Ting-a-ling teddy bear, with glass eyes, c1953, 16in (40.5cm) high.
£450–500 / €660–730
$810–910 ⊞ BBe

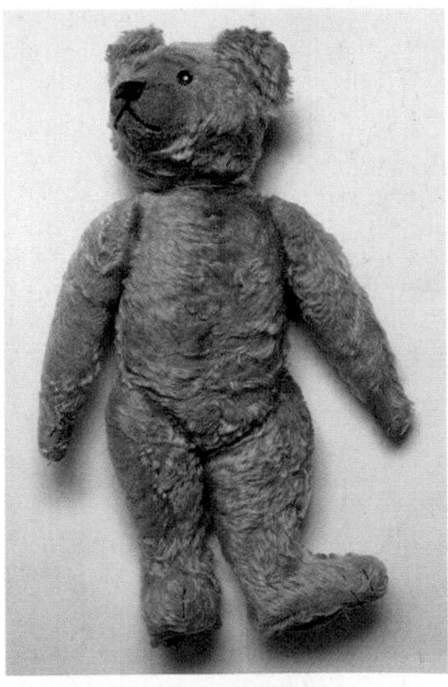

A Farnell mohair teddy bear, with glass eyes, worn, 1915–20, 19in (48.5cm) high.
£1,100–1,250 / €1,600–1,800
$2,000–2,250 ⊞ BBe

A Farnell mohair teddy bear, with cotton pads, 1920s, 14in (35.5cm) high.
£2,000–2,250
€2,900–3,300
$3,600–4,050 ⊞ BBe

A Farnell teddy bear, c1930, 12in (30.5cm) high.
£120–135 / €175–195
$220–250 ⊞ NAW

► A Farnell mohair Cuddle teddy bear, with glass eyes and Rexine pads, 1930s, 11in (28cm) high.
£290–330
€430–480
$530–600
⊞ BBe

◄ A Merrythought mohair Bingie teddy bear, with label, 1930s, 10in (25.5cm) high.
£175–195
€250–280
$310–350
⊞ BBe

◄ A Merrythought teddy bear, with limited edition label, c1930, 17in (43cm) high.
£320–360
€470–530
$580–650
⊞ NAW

A Schuco Yes/No teddy bear, German, 1920s–30s, 18in (45.5cm) high.
£900–1,000
€1,300–1,450
$1,600–1,800 ⊞ BBe

A Steiff teddy bear, with original muzzle, pads replaced, German, 1908–19, 12in (30.5cm) high.
£1,800–2,000
€2,600–2,900
$3,250–3,600 ⊞ BBe

A Merrythought mohair Cheeky teddy bear, with glass eyes, label on foot, late 1950s, 11in (28cm).
£330–370 / €480–540
$600–670 ⊞ BBe

A Pedigree teddy bear, 1920s, 20in (51cm) high.
£180–200 / €260–290
$320–360 ⊞ GLEN

► A Steiff mohair rod teddy bear, with button eyes, shaved muzzle, embroidered mouth and claws, felt pads and a metal rod connecting the limbs and head, feet initialled and dated, German, early 20thC, 16in (40.5cm) high.
£9,700–11,600
€14,200–16,900
$17,600–21,000 SK(B)

A Steiff miniature teddy bear, German, 1930s, 4in (10cm) high.
£175–195 / €250–280
$310–350 ⊞ NAW

A Steiff teddy bear, German, 1930s, 12in (30.5cm) high.
£430–480 / €630–700
$780–870 ⊞ NAW

A Steiff silk plush teddy bear, German, 1930–40, 13in (33cm) high.
£580–650 / €850–950
$1,050–1,200 ⊞ NAW

► **A Steiff mohair Teddy Baby bear,** with felt mouth, German, 1950s, 12in (30.5cm) high.
£630–700 / €900–1,000
$1,100–1,250 ⊞ BBe

A Steiff teddy bear, German, c1950, 10in (25.5cm) high.
£250–280 / €370–410
$450–510 ⊞ NAW

◄ **A Tara Toys mohair teddy bear,** Irish, 1950s, 23in (58.5cm) high.
£145–165 / €210–240
$260–300 ⊞ BBe

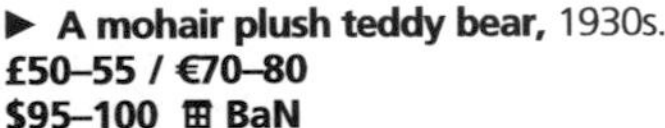

► **A mohair plush teddy bear,** 1930s.
£50–55 / €70–80
$95–100 ⊞ BaN

Soft Toys

A Deans Bonzo dog, with jointed limbs and printed detail, 1920s, 12½in (32cm) high.
£400–480 / €580–700
$720–860 ⚒ G(L)

A Schuco Piccalo miniature panda, c1949, 5in (12.5cm) high.
£120–135 / €175–195
$220–250 ⊞ BBe

A Steiff dog, German, 1930s, 8in (20.5cm) wide.
£165–185 / €240–270
$300–330 ⊞ NAW

A Steiff frog, German, 1950s, 12in (30.5cm) long.
£130–145 / €190–210
$230–260 ⊞ NAW

A Farnell Alpha Toys spaniel, c1930, 14in (35.5cm) high.
£130–145 / €190–210
$230–260 ⊞ NAW

A Schuco Yes/No monkey, 1950s, 8in (20.5cm) high.
£160–180 / €230–260
$290–330 ⊞ NAW

A Steiff mohair plush Bully Yale bulldog, with jointed head, glass eyes, button nose, velveteen muzzle and mouth, button in ear, with felt blanket and leather collar, slight wear, German, c1950, 10½in (26.5cm) wide.
£290–340 / €420–490
$520–620 ⚒ SK(B)

A Steiff wild boar, German, 1950s, 10in (25.5cm) long.
£65–75 / €95–110
$120–135 ⊞ GLEN

A Merrythought Granpops monkey pyjama case, c1949, 25in (63.5cm) long.
£50–60 / €80–90
$100–110 ⊞ NAW

A Steiff Rattler dog, German, c1920, 4½in (11.5cm) high.
£220–250 / €320–360
$400–450 ⊞ BaN

A Steiff Dally Dalmation, German, 1950s, 10in (25.5cm) high.
£160–180 / €230–260
$290–330 ⊞ NAW

A Steiff Nikili rabbit, German, 1950s, 11in (28cm) high.
£200–230 / €290–340
$360–420 ⊞ NAW

Toys

Aeroplanes

A Dinky Toys 60R Empire Flying Boat, 'Caledonia', with gliding clip and instruction sheet, slight wear, c1937, 5in (12.5cm) wide, with box.
£140–165 / €200–240
$250–300 SAS

A Dinky Avro Vulcan delta wing bomber, damaged, losses.
£350–420 / €510–610
$630–760 WAL

Items in the Toys section have been arranged alphabetically in factory order

A Joustra Super G Constellation battery-powered tinplate airliner, finished in Air France livery, F-B HBB, slight wear and damage, French, 1950s, 19in (48.5cm) long.
£120–140 / €170–200
$210–250 WAL

Boats

◄ **A Freidag cast-iron motorboat,** on three wheels, 1920s, 10¼in (26cm) long.
£3,000–3,600 / €4,400–5,300
$5,400–6,500 Bert

A Sutcliffe clockwork cruiser, 'Commodore', with key, slight wear, 1970s, with box, 10½in (26.5cm) wide.
£70–80 / €100–120
$125–150 WAL

A Hornby tinplate clockwork speed boat, 'Swift', No. 2, with instructions, slight damage, dated 1936, 12in (30.5cm) long, with box.
£120–140 / €170–200
$210–250 VEC

◄ **A set of Tremo Famous Fighting Ships of the British Navy,** No. 2, comprising HMS *Resolution*, *Defender*, *Dauntless*, Grimsby Escort Vessel and Shark Class submarine, 1930s, with box, 6in (15cm) long.
£330–390 / €480–570
$600–710 SAS

Figures & Models

A Britains diecast zoo set, No. 3Z, with palm trees, a dromedary, polar bear, two penguins, two pelicans, a chimpanzee, monkey, gorilla, lion, lioness and zebra, 1950s, with box, 15in (38cm) wide.
£230–270 / €340–400
$410–490 WAL

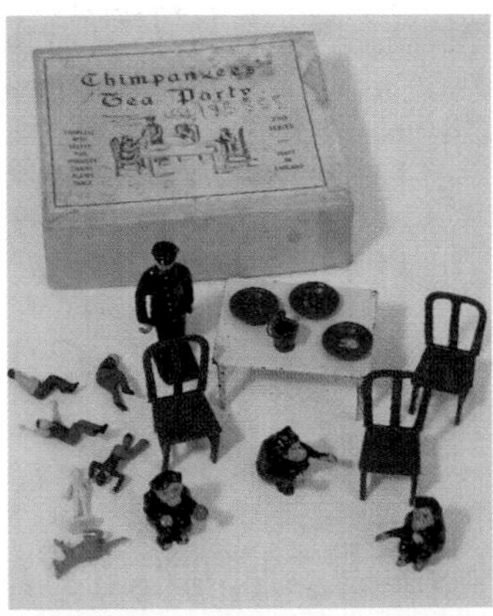

An F. G. T. & Sons hollowcast lead Chimpanzees' Tea Party set, late 1930s, with box, 4in (10cm) wide.
£120–140 / €170–200
$210–250 G(L)

A Phillip Segal Toys Old Woman in the Shoe set, from the Nursery Rhyme and Fairy Tale series, comprising a shoe and four figures, mid-1950s, shoe 2½in (6.5cm) wide, with box.
£1,800–2,150 / €2,650–3,150
$3,250–3,900 VEC

LOCATE THE SOURCE
The source of each illustration in Miller's can be found by checking the code letters below each caption with the Key to Illustrations, pages 778–784.

Meccano

A Meccano Electrical Outfit, with manual, 1920, with box.
£700–840 / €1,000–1,200
$1,250–1,500 VEC

A Meccano Aero set, No. 2, Spanish issue, slight damage, one storage tin missing, 1930s.
£230–270 / €340–400
$420–500 WAL

◄ **A Meccano set,** c1950, with box, 16in (40.5cm) wide.
£70–80 / €100–115
$125–145 ⊞ JUN

A Meccano aeroplane set, No. 00, struts and tailplane repainted, some parts missing.
£120–140 / €170–200
$210–250 WAL

A Meccano Showman's Engine motorized display model, with illumination, on a wooden plinth, slight damage, 1950s, 20in (51cm) wide.
£420–500 / €610–730
$760–910 VEC

Mechanical Toys

A pair of American Mechanical Toy Co clockwork dancing dolls, American, New York, late 19thC, 9¾in (25cm) high.
£1,050–1,200 / €1,550–1,750
$1,900–2,150 ⊞ ET

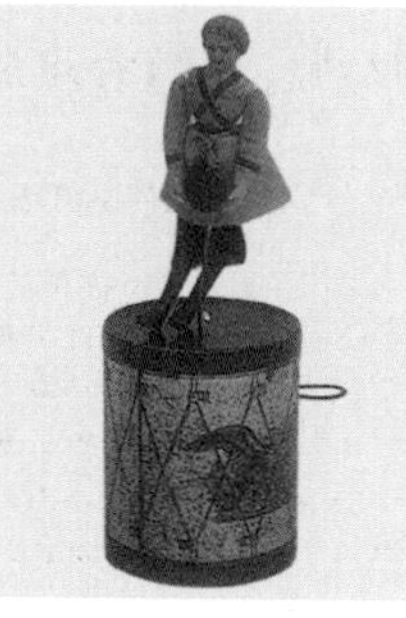

An Ives Centennial clockwork tinplate Drum Dancer, the base decorated with an eagle and '1776', the dancer with a composite head, American, 1876, with key and remains of box, 9½in (24cm) high.
£400–480 / €580–700
$720–870 BWL

► **A Fernand Martin tinplate clockwork L'Artiste Capillaire toy,** the barber dispensing hair tonic to the bald head of his client, some wear and losses, French, early 20thC, 8in (20.5cm) high, with box.
£1,850–2,200
€2,700–3,200
$3,350–4,000 SK(B)

◄ **A Louis Marx tinplate clockwork motorcycle,** American, c1940, 8in (20.5cm) wide
£190–220
€280–330
$350–400
⊞ TNS

◄ **A Schuco clockwork musical monkey,** German, c1935, 5in (12.5cm) high.
£140–160 / €200–220
$250–280 ⊞ HAL

► **A Schuco tinplate and felt clockwork pig band,** comprising drummer, flautist and violinist, German, late 1930s, 4in (10cm) high.
£350–420 / €510–610
$630–760 G(L)

A Suzuki & Edwards tinplate battery-powered Teddy Manager, retailed by Cragstan, slight wear, Japanese, 1960s, with box, 9in (23cm) square.
£220–260 / €320–380
$400–470 WAL
The bear lifts the ringing illuminated telephone and talks, with a wire to a larger telephone for use by a child.

A Wells-Brimtoy clockwork Mickey Mouse Handcar, with composition figures of Mickey and Minnie, a handcar, two card buildings and ten sections of track, 1930s, with fitted box, 13¾in (35cm) wide.
£590–700 / €850–1,000
$1,050–1,250 SWO

A papier-mâché and flock clockwork nodding duck, with a four-hour wind duration, c1900, 12in (30.5cm) wide.
£1,100–1,250
€1,600–1,800
$2,000–2,250 AUTO

A wooden clockwork girl and rocking horse, the doll with a bisque head, in a glass and wood case, early 20thC, 24in (61cm) wide.
£3,150–3,500 / €4,600–5,100
$5,700–6,300 Beb

A set of three clockwork monkey musicians, mid-20thC, 6½in (16.5cm) high.
£120–140 / €175–200
$210–250 MCA

Money Banks

◄ **A metal mechanical money bank,** in the form of a southern-style shack, American, 1882, 2¼in (5.5cm) wide.
£290–340
€420–490
$520–610
DuM

A cast-iron mechanical money bank, in the form of a man in a top hat, c1910, 8in (20.5cm) high.
£105–120 / €155–175
$200–220 JUN

A Spalheimer Strauss tinplate mechanical money bank, German, c1935, 7in (18cm) high.
£360–400 / €520–580
$640–710 HAL

Noah's Arks

◄ **A painted wood Noah's Ark,** with carved wooden animals, c1900, 18in (45.5cm) wide.
£580–650
€850–950
$1,050–1,200
⊞ JUN

A painted wood Noah's Ark, with carved wood animals, c1900, 12in (30.5cm) wide.
£130–145 / €190–210
$230–260 ⊞ JUN

◄ **A painted wood Noah's Ark,** with hinged roof and carved animals and figures, and three further carved wood models, c1920, 24in (61cm) wide.
£270–320 / €390–470
$490–580 ⚒ Mal(O)

► **A painted wood Noah's Ark,** with carved and painted wood animals, 1920s, 30¾in (78cm) wide.
£210–250 / €310–370
$380–450 ⚒ SWO

Rocking Horses

A wooden rocking horse, damaged, 19thC, 71in (180.5cm) long.
£1,600–1,900 / €2,350–2,750
$2,900–3,450 ⚒ DORO

A wooden rocking horse, on a pine safety rocker, early 20thC, 39in (100cm) high at shoulder.
£410–490 / €600–720
$750–890 ⚒ CHTR

A carved wood rocking horse, on a safety rocker, 1950s, 52in (132cm) high.
£4,100–4,900 / €6,000–7,200
$7,400–8,800 ⚒ BWL

Soldiers

A Britains Indian Mountain Battery, No. 2013, comprising a mounted officer, six soldiers and four loaded mules, 1950s, with box, 12½in (32cm) wide.
£1,900–2,250 / €2,750–3,300
$3,450–4,050 ⚒ WAL

A King's Troop Royal Horse Artillery set, comprising mounted officer, six gun horses, limber and field gun, 1950s, 18in (45.5cm) long.
£190–220 / €280–330
$340–400 ⚒ WAL

Further reading

Miller's Toys & Games: Buyer's Guide,
Miller's Publications, 2004

A Maison Lucotte First Empire Fusiliers of the Line set, comprising drummer, officer, standard bearers and marching fusiliers, French, c1890, figures 4in (10cm) high, with box.
£590–700 / €860–1,000
$1,050–1,250 ⚒ BWL

Trains

A Bassett-Lowke gauge 0 clockwork 4–4–0 BR locomotive and tender, No. 62453, 'Prince Charles', with 6-wheel tender, type 2 3-lever controls to cab, key and instruction sheet, 1950s, with box.
£400–480 / €580–700
$720–870 ⚒ WAL

► **A Hornby No. 1 Milk Traffic Van,** coded RS701, in an Export No. 0 Wagon box with Danish labels, c1932.
£130–155
€190–220
$240–290 ⚒ VEC

A Hornby gauge 0 locomotive and tender, Eton, c1938, with boxes.
£2,700–3,000 / €3,950–4,400
$4,900–5,400 ⊞ MDe

This was a popular toy in its day but expensive when first issued in 1937. There is no bulb holder in the smoke box door on this model, unlike the majority of electric locomotives in the pre-war Hornby range. The tender is the standard No. 2 type with the number 900 on the sides. It was sold separately and only issued in the red box shown.

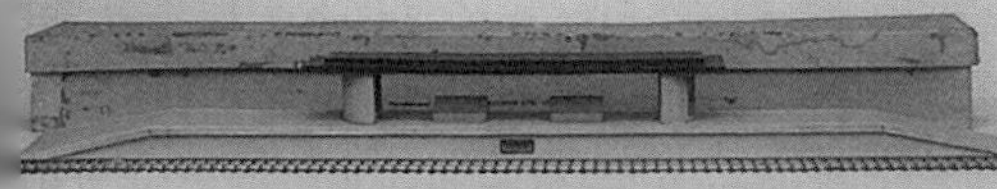

A Hornby island platform, 1938, 18in (45.5cm) long, with box.
£210–250 / €310–370
$380–450 ⚒ VEC

► **A Hornby Carr's Biscuits wagon,** c1938, 7in (18cm) long, with box.
£450–500
€660–730
$810–910
⊞ MDe

A Hornby gauge 0 clockwork train set, c1930, with box.
£200–220 / €290–320
$360–400 ⊞ HAL

◄ **A Hornby No. 2 gauge 0 Special LMS clockwork 4–4–0 locomotive and tender,** No. 1185, with key, slight damage, some wheels replaced, mid-1930s, with boxes.
£410–490 / €600–720
$740–890 ⚒ WAL

◀ **A Hornby-Dublo three-rail locomotive and tender,** Bristol Castle, 1950s, with box.
£115–130 / €170–190
$210–240 ⊞ HAL

A Hornby-Dublo three-rail locomotive, Mallard, with nickel-plated drive wheels, c1958.
£125–140 / €180–200
$220–250 ⊞ HAL

A Hornby-Dublo three-rail Co-Bo diesel-electric locomotive, No. D5702, 1950s, with box.
£135–150 / €195–220
$240–270 ⊞ HAL

◀ **A Hornby-Dublo two-rail class A4 4–6–2 streamline locomotive and tender,** No. 60030, Golden Fleece, with test label and spanner, minor wear, early 1960s, with box.
£150–180 / €220–260
$270–320 ⚒ WAL

A Hornby-Dublo ER restaurant car, No. E1939, with plastic wheels, slight wear, early 1960s, with box.
£140–165 / €200–240
$250–300 ⚒ WAL

A Märklin gauge 1 PO Series electric locomotive/ steeple cab, the sliding roof revealing the cab interior and electric motor, with two four-wheeled bogie units, one with power and side brushing for three-rail operation, one without power, slight paint loss, German, early 1920s.
£1,400–1,650 / €2,050–2,400
$2,550–3,000 ⚒ VEC

▶ **A Tri-ang T5 Suburban Passenger Train set,** comprising 0–6–0 3F Jinty tank locomotive, two coaches, with track, Tri-ang TT catalogue and instructions dated 1959, with box.
£105–125
€155–185
$195–230 ⚒ VEC

A gauge 2 steam locomotive, Winifred, 1960s.
£2,250–2,500 / €3,300–3,650
$4,050–4,550 ⊞ JUN

A model train station, German, c1920, 22in (56cm) wide.
£590–660 / €860–960
$1,050–1,200 ⊞ TNS

A Wrenn gauge 00 train set, freight No. WF200, comprising a 2–8–0 8f locomotive RN 48073 and eight assorted wagons, each marked Hornby Dublo, with paperwork and box.
£360–430 / €530–630
$650–780 ⚒ WAL

Vehicles

An AGL Bakelite clockwork Runlite Austin, 1930s, 9in (23cm) long.
£720–800 / €1,000–1,100
$1,300–1,450 ⊞ HAL

An Arcade pressed-steel and wood runabout model car, with cast-iron driver and spoke wheels, American, c1908, 9in (23cm) long.
£480–570 / €700–830
$870–1,050 ⚒ Bert

An Arcade cast-iron Studebaker ice truck, with ice and tongs, American, 1938, 6¾in (17cm) long, with box.
£1,350–1,600 / €1,950–2,350
$2,450–2,900 ⚒ Bert

A Bing clockwork taxi, damaged, c1925, 11in (28cm) high.
£220–250 / €320–380
$400–470 ⚒ BWL

A Buddy L steel hydraulic dump truck, No. 201, slight damage, c1928, 24½in (62cm) long.
£610–730 / €890–1,050
$1,100–1,300 ⚒ SK(B)

A Chad Valley tinplate Fordson tractor, c1950, 6in (15cm) long.
£220–250 / €320–360
$400–450 ⊞ JUN

A Chad Valley tinplate Fordson Dexta Tractor, c1955, 6in (15cm) long, with box.
£370–440 / €540–640
$670–800 ⚒ SAS

A Corgi Toys die-cast Rover 90 Saloon, No. 204, 1959, 3in (7.5cm) long, with box.
£140–165 / €200–240
$250–300 ⚒ SAS

A Corgi Toys die-cast gift set, set No. 25, comprising forecourt, No. 224 Bentley Continental, No. 419 Ford Zephyr, No. 225 Austin 7, No. 229 Chevrolet Corvair, missing No. 234 Ford Consul, 1960s, with box.
£590–700 / €850–1,000
$1,050–1,250 ⚒ SAS

A Corgi Toys die-cast Monte Carlo Mini-Cooper S, No. 339, 1960s, 3in (7.5cm) long, with box.
£125–140 / €180–200
$220–250 ⊞ HAL

◄ **A Corgi Toys die-cast MGA Sports Car,** No. 302, 1960s, 3½in (9cm) long.
£90–100
€130–145
$160–180
⊞ HAL

► **A Corgi Toys die-cast Chipperfields Menagerie transporter,** No. 1139, comprising two lions, two tigers and two bears, c1970, with box, 10in (25.5cm) long.
£270–300
€390–440
$490–550 ⊞ HAL

A Corgi Toys die-cast Batmobile, No. 267, 1972, 6½in (16.5cm) long, with box.
£200–230 / €300–340
$360–400 ⊞ GTM

A Corgi Toys die-cast RAC Rescue Land-Rover, No. 416, 1950s, 4in (10cm) long, with box.
£165–195 / €240–290
$300–360 ⚒ WAL

A Corgi Toys die-cast Carrimore Low-Loader, No. 1100, c1955, 9in (23cm) long, with box.
£165–195 / €240–290
$300–360 ⚒ WAL

Items in the Toys section have been arranged alphabetically in factory order.

A Corgi Toys die-cast Priestman Shovel and Machinery Carrier gift set, No. 27, 1960s, 11in (28cm) long, with box.
£125–140 / €180–200
$220–250 ⊞ HAL

A Dent cast-iron Lasalle sedan, American, 1934, 4¼in (11cm) long.
£390–460 / €570–670
$710–850 ⚒ Bert

A Dent cast-iron Lasalle wrecker, American, 1935, 4½in (11.5cm) long.
£660–790 / €960–1,150
$1,200–1,450 ⚒ Bert

◄ **A Dinky Toys die-cast 39 Series American Buick,** American, late 1940s, 4in (10cm) long.
£140–155 / €200–220
$250–280 ⊞ CBB

A Dinky Toys die-cast Foden Flat Truck with chains, No. 905, 2nd Type, 1950s, 8in (20.5cm) long, with box.
£220–250 / €320–370
$400–450 ⊞ HAL

◄ **A Dinky Supertoys die-cast Tank Transporter and Tank gift set,** No. 698, 1950s, 13in (33cm) long, with box.
£190–220
€290–320
$360–400
⊞ HAL

A Dinky Toys die-cast Bedford End Tipper truck, No. 410, 1950s, 4in (10cm) long, with box.
£150–170 / €220–250
$270–300 ⊞ HAL

A Girard Toys lithographed tin clockwork Overland Trail Bus Line bus, with driver, disc wheels, c1921, American, 13¾in (35cm) long, with box.
£1,200–1,400 / €1,750–2,050
$2,150–2,550 ⚒ Bert

A Hubley Manufacturing Co cast-iron Lincoln Zephyr taxi cab, American, c1939, 7¾in (19.5cm) long.
£330–390 / €480–570
$600–710 ⚒ Bert

A Dinky Toys die-cast *Joe 90* car, No. 102, 1960s, 6in (15cm) long, with box.
£220–250 / €320–360
$400–450 ⊞ HAL

A Hubley Manufacturing Co cast-iron Golden Arrow Racer, American, c1929, 8½in (21.5cm) long.
£1,150–1,350 / €1,700–2,000
$2,100–2,450 ⚒ Bert

An E. T. Co lithographed tin clockwork New Nash car, Japanese, 1932, 7½in (19cm) long.
£510–610 / €740–890
$920–1,100 ⚒ Bert

A Hubley Manufacturing Co Mack Ingersoll-Rand air compressor truck, American, c1933, 8¼in (21cm) long.
£5,100–6,100 / €7,400–8,900
$9,200–11,000 ⚒ Bert
This is a rare Hubley sample vehic and the only known example to be painted red.

◄ A Kenton cas iron Pontiac an house trailer, American, 1936, 9½in (24cm) long
£970–1,150
€1,400–1,650
$1,750–2,100
⚒ Bert

A Kenton cast-iron Texaco tanker truck, American, c1936, 7½in (19cm) long.
£660–790 / €960–1,150
$1,200–1,450 ⚒ Bert

A Kilgore policeman and motorcycle, American, c1933, 4¾in (12cm) long.
£570–680 / €830–990
$1,050–1,250 ⚒ Bert

A Lehmann tinplate clockwork autobus, German, c1910, 10in (25.5cm) long.
£720–800 / €1,000–1,100
$1,300–1,450 ⊞ HAL

A Louis Marx tinplate racing car, American, 1950s, 13½in (34.5cm) long.
£370–440 / €540–640
$670–800 ⚒ WAL

A Mettoy Wells-style tinplate clockwork tipping lorry, with balloon tyre wheels, 1930s, 9¾in (25cm) long.
£240–280 / €350–420
$420–500 ⚒ WAL

A Schuco clockwork Radio 4012 Car, German, c1950, 6in (15cm) long, with original box.
£190–220 / €280–330
$340–400 ⚒ SAS

A Showa tinplate battery-operated tractor, driver's hat missing, Japanese, 1960s, 10in (25.5cm) wide, with original box.
£135–150 / €195–220
$240–270 ⊞ HAL

A Toledo Metal Wheel Co Erskine pedal car, American, 1927–30, 37in (94cm) long.
£5,400–6,400 / €7,800–9,300
$9,800–11,600 ⚒ Bert
The full-size version of this car was produced by Studebaker from 1927 to 1930 and was named after Albert Russell Erskine, the President of the Studebaker Corporation.

A Vindex Toys cast-iron Packard club sedan, No. 53, American, c1929, 9½in (24cm) long, with later display box.
£10,900–13,100
€15,900–19,100
$19,700–23,700 ⚒ Bert
This is arguably one of the rarest of all Vindex Toys vehicles. There are reportedly only three or four other known examples.

An A. C. Williams cast-iron sedan, 1930s, 5in (12.5cm) long.
£240–280 / €350–420
$430–510 ⚒ Bert

An A. C. Williams cast-iron Shovel Nose Packard coupé, c1933, 4¼in (11cm) long.
£135–160 / €195–230
$250–300 ⚒ Bert

▶ An A. C. Williams cast-iron fire pumper, c1937, 6¾in (17cm) long.
£910–1,100
€1,350–1,600
$1,700–2,000
⚒ Bert
This is an extremely rare model.

A delivery wagon, with six glass milk bottles in a metal carrier, early 20thC, 21in (53.5cm) long.
£130–155 / €190–220
$230–270
⚒ SK(B)

A lithographed tin clockwork car and caravan, Japanese, c1930, 8in (20.5cm) long.
£300–360 / €440–530
$540–650 ⚒ Bert

▶ A cast-iron coupé, c1934, 8½in (21.5cm) long.
£1,150–1,350
€1,650–1,950
$2,050–2,450
⚒ Bert

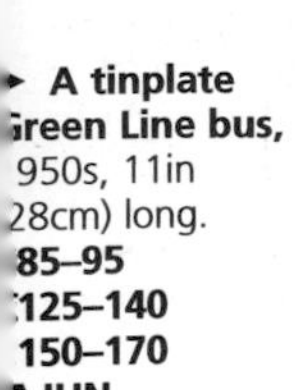

▶ A tinplate Green Line bus, 1950s, 11in (28cm) long.
£85–95
€125–140
$150–170
⊞ JUN

A battery-operated Ford 4000 tractor, Japanese, 1960s, 16in (40.5cm) long.
£320–360 / €470–520
$580–650 ⊞ HAL

Miscellaneous

An ivory alphabet, in a fitted mahogany case, 19thC, 6in (15cm) wide.
£340–400 / €500–600
$620–720 ⚒ G(B)

A painted wood chequerboard, initialled and dated, American, 1932, 18 x 25½in (45.5 x 65cm).
£260–310 / €380–450
$470–560 ⚒ SGA

A mahogany travelling chess set, by Jaques, London, with bone pieces, stamped mark, c1890, 9in (23cm) wide, with original leather case.
£400–450 / €580–660
$720–810 ⊞ TMi

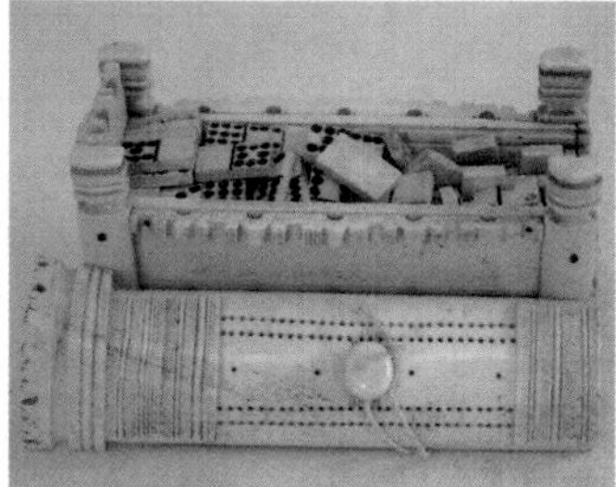

A carved bone domino box, with sliding top, containing miniature dominoes, 19thC, 7in (18cm) wide.
£280–330 / €410–480
$510–600 ⚒ G(L)

A carved teak mah jong set, 1920s, 10in (25.5cm) wide.
£210–240
€310–350
$380–430 ⊞ MB

A Pioneer doll's pram, 1930s, 34in (86.5cm) long.
£180–200 / €260–290
$320–360 ⊞ JUN

An N. N. Hill Brass Co cast-iron pull-along toy, in the form of Jonah and the Whale, worn, American, c1890, 6in (15cm) long.
£320–380 / €470–550
$580–690 ⚒ SK(B)

A Tower Guild pine sand toy, in the form of a miller cranking a paddle, with label, American, c1830, 9½in (24cm) long.
£260–310 / €380–450
$470–560 ⚒ SK(B)
This is one of the earliest commercial sand toys produced in America.

Further reading

Miller's American Insider's Guide to Toys & Games, Miller's Publications, 2002

A Victorian toy theatre, c1880, 28in (71cm) wide.
£630–700 / €920–1,050
$1,150–1,300 ⊞ OLA

Ephemera

Annuals, Books & Comics

Pip & Squeak Annual, 6th year, 1928, 10 x 8in (25.5 x 20.5cm).
£20–25 / €30–35
$35–40 ⊞ HTE

The Dandy Monster Comic, No. 2, slight damage and repair, 1940.
£420–500 / €610–730
$760–910 ⚒ CBP

Further reading
Miller's Collectables Price Guide, Miller's Publications, 2005

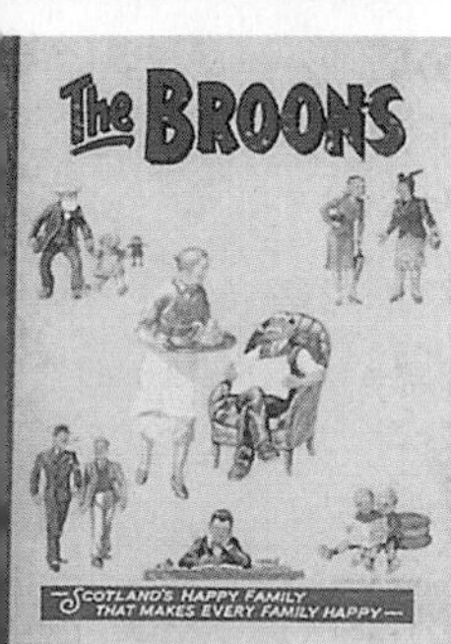

The Broons Book, No. 3, 1947.
£1,200–1,400
€1,700–2,050
$2,150–2,550 ⚒ CBP
D. C. Thomson printed some early hardback versions of *The Broons* books which were not generally distributed and this is one of them.

Mickey Mouse Annual, 1937, 8½in (21.5cm) high.
£310–350 / €450–510
$560–630 ⊞ NW

The New Rupert Book, 1946, 10 x 7in (25.5 x 18cm).
£180–200 / €260–290
$320–360 ⊞ UD

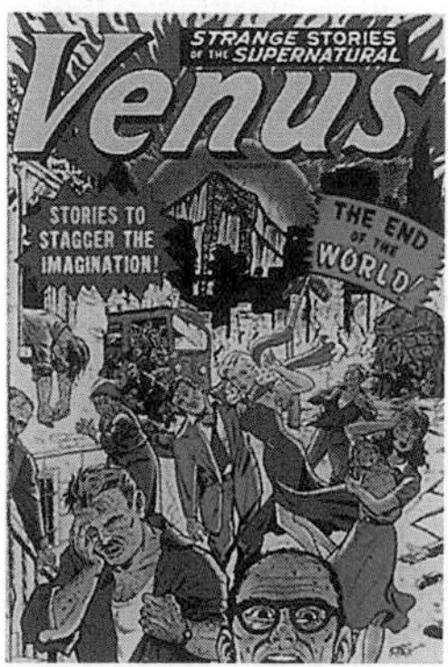

Venus, No. 11, 1950.
£120–140 / €175–210
$220–260 ⚒ CBP

The Beano Comic, No. 2, slight wear, 1938.
£2,050–2,450
€3,000–3,600
$3,700–4,450 ⚒ CBP
Only a handful of copies of this issue are known to exist.

◀ ***Superman,*** No. 6, slight damage, 1940.
£390–460 / €570–680
$710–840 ⚒ CBP

▶ ***Captain America Comic Book,*** No. 7, 1941.
£1,050–1,250
€1,550–1,850
$1,900–2,250 ⚒ JAA

The Dandy Comic, No. 20, first Easter issue, slight damage, 1938.
£100–120 / €145–175
$190–220 ⚒ CBP

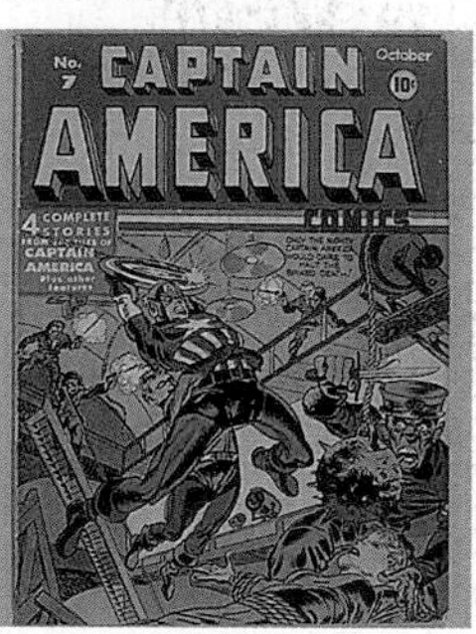

EPHEMERA

Autographs

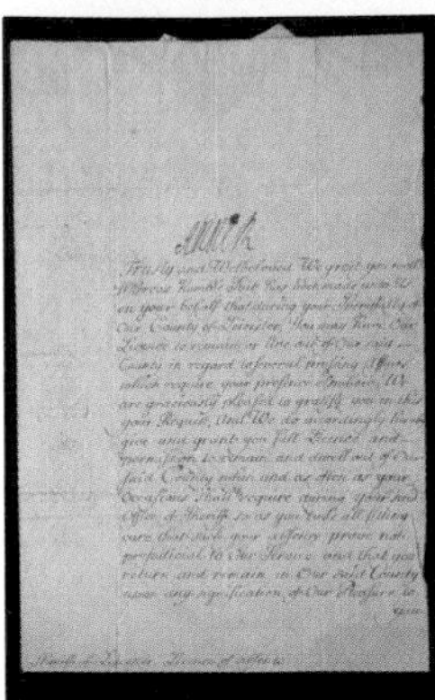

Anne, Queen of Great Britain and Ireland, a signed License of Absence addressed to George Burton, Sheriff of Leicester, countersigned by Lord Sunderland, dated 24 December 1709, 2°.
£1,350–1,500
€1,950–2,200
$2,450–2,700 ⊞ CFSD

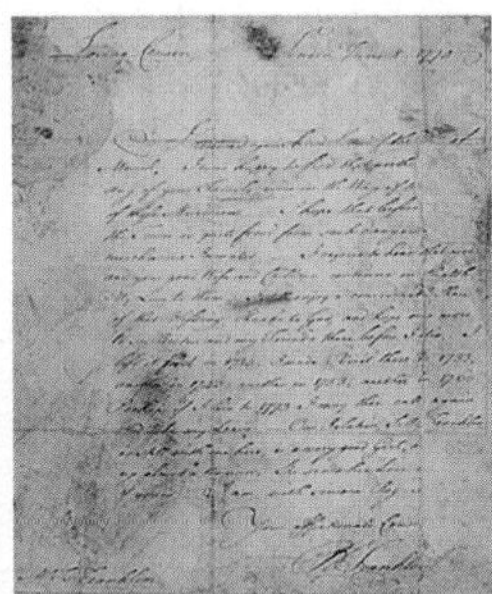

Benjamin Franklin, a signed letter to his cousin Thomas Franklin referring to the Boston Massacre, slight damage, dated 8 June 1770, 4°.
£15,000–18,000
€21,900–26,300
$27,400–33,000 ⚒ BBA

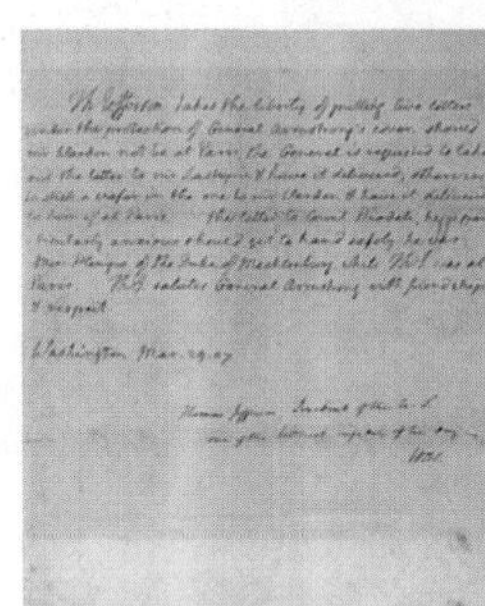

Thomas Jefferson, a signed letter to the Minister to France General John Armstrong Jr, slight damage, dated 29 March 1807, 9 x 7in (23 x 18cm).
£3,950–4,700
€5,750–6,900
$7,100–8,500 ⚒ S(NY)

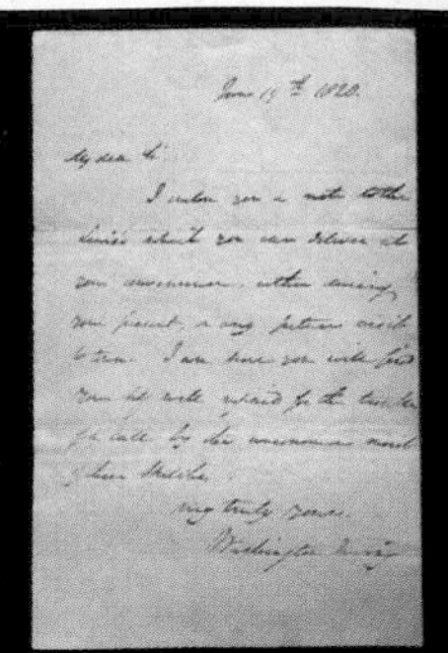

Washington Irving, a signed handwritten letter to an unnamed correspondent, dated 19 June 1820, 8°.
£430–480 / €630–700
$780–870 ⊞ CFSD

► General Robert E. Lee, a signed handwritten letter to Miss Nanny Campbell, 21 February 1866, with a print of Lee in a brass frame.
£1,400–1,650
€2,050–2,400
$2,550–3,000 ⚒ LHA

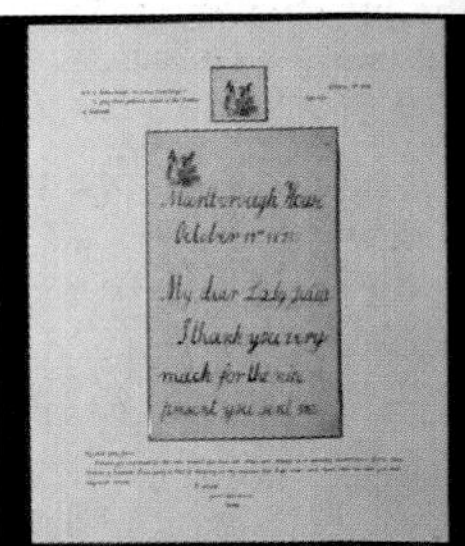

Prince George, aged eight, future King George V, a letter to Lady Julia Lockwood, sister of the Duchess of Inverness, dated October 1873, 8½ x 5½in (21.5 x 14cm).
£580–650 / €850–950
$1,050–1,200 ⊞ AEL

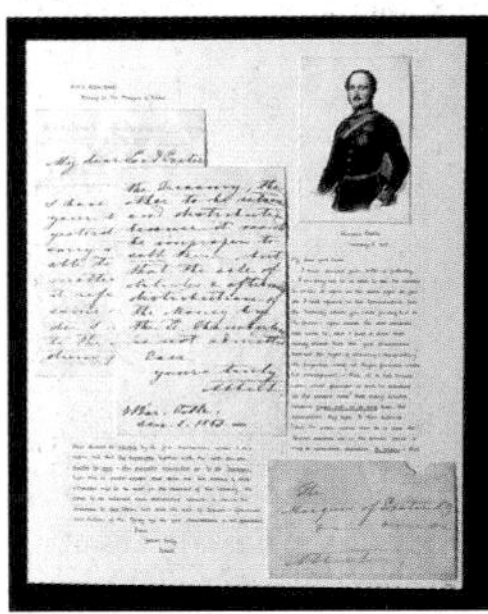

Prince Albert, a letter to the Marquis of Exeter, 1883, 7 x 4½in (18 x 11.5cm).
£850–950 / €1,250–1,400
$1,500–1,700 ⊞ AEL

◄ John Ruskin, a signed letter to the Editor of the *Daily Telegraph*, on lined paper, possibly a draft, some passages crossed out, slight damage, dated 9 January 1888, 2°.
£300–360 / €440–530
$540–650 ⚒ BBA

Princess Louise and her husband the Duke of Fife, a signed photograph, 1899, 7 x 4½in (18 x 11.5cm).
£340–380 / €500–550
$620–690 ⊞ AEL

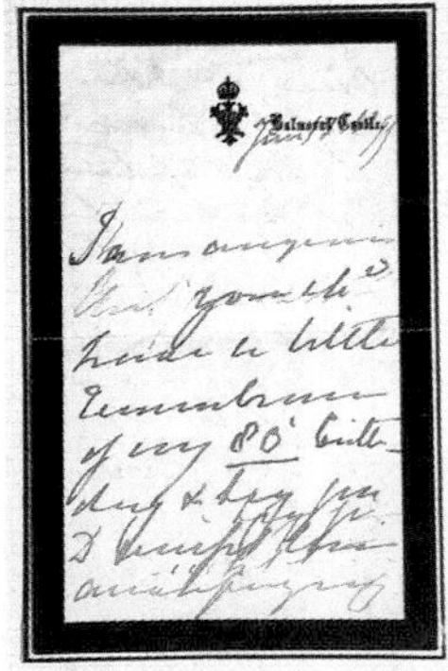

Queen Victoria, a letter written on Balmoral note-paper to Dr Cameron Lees, 1899, 7 x 5in (18 x 12.5cm).
£450–500 / €660–730
$810–910 ⊞ AEL

Theodore Roosevelt, a signed typewritten letter on White House stationery, framed with a photograph, April 1906.
£300–360 / €440–530
$540–650 ⚒ LHA

► Prince Henry, son of King George V and Queen Mary, a signed photograph, 1912, 9 x 6in (23 x 15cm).
£380–430 / €560–630
$690–780 ⊞ AEL

Henry Joseph Wood, a signed photograph laid on card, 1912, 13¾ x 9½in (35 x 24cm).
£140–165 / €200–240
$250–300 ⚒ SWO
Wood's real name was Paul Klenovsky. He was the principal figure in the popularization of orchestral music and was instrumental in starting the Promenade Concerts.

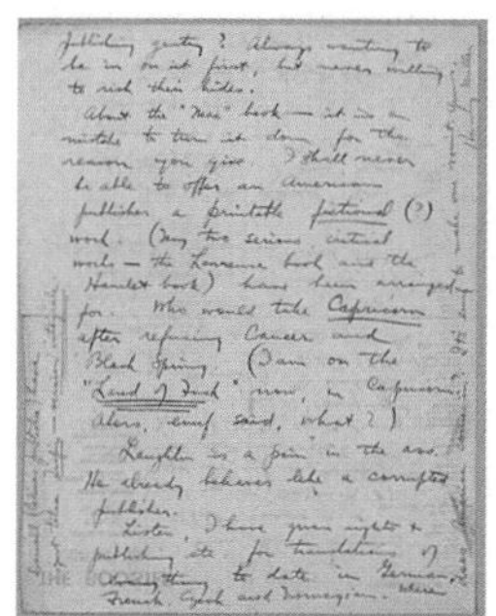

Items in the Autographs section have been arranged in date order.

◀ **Henry Miller,** a signed letter written on *The Booster* letterhead to American publisher Charles Pearce, in which Miller berates the publisher and blasts the United States for banning his fictional works, two pages, dated 12 December 1937, slight damage, 10 x 8in (25.5 x 20.5cm).
£530–630 / €770–920
$960–1,150 ⚒ S(NY)
The United States banned most of Miller's fictional work, claiming the moral integrity of many of his books was wanting. In response, Miller embarked on an extensive letter-writing campaign in the 1950s to defend his writing from censors. Finally, in 1961, *Tropic of Cancer* was published in America.

▶ **Stan Laurel and Oliver Hardy,** a signed photograph inscribed 'Thanks Pat! Good Luck!', early 1950s, 6 x 4in (15 x 10cm).
£400–480 / €580–700
$720–870 ⚒ AH

EPHEMERA

Cigarette Cards

V. A. & A. C. Churchman, Life on a
.iner, set of 25, 1930.
35–40 / €50–60
60–70 ⊞ SOR

Gallagher Ltd, Trains of the World,
et of 48, 1937.
45–50 / €65–75
80–90 ⊞ LCC

ohn Player & Sons, Film Stars, 3rd
eries, set of 50, 1938.
35–40 / €50–60
60–70 ⊞ SOR

W. A. & A. C. Churchman, The Story of London, set of 50, 1934.
£50–60 / €75–90
$100–110 ⊞ MUR

John Player & Sons, British Livestock, set of 25, 1915.
£50–60 / €75–90
$100–110 ⊞ MUR

▶ **W. D. & H. O. Wills,** Ships' Badges, set of 50, 1925.
£35–40 / €50–60
$60–70 ⊞ SOR

Edwards, Ringer and Brigg, British Trees and their Uses, set of 25, 1933.
£50–60 / €75–90
$100–110 ⊞ MUR

John Player & Sons, Footballers' Caricatures, by 'RIP', set of 50, 1926.
£50–60 / €75–90
$100–110 ⊞ SOR

Postcards

◄ **A postcard,** of General Grant and party at the Bonanza Mines, Virginia City, American, 1879.
£40–45 / €60–70
$70–80 JAA

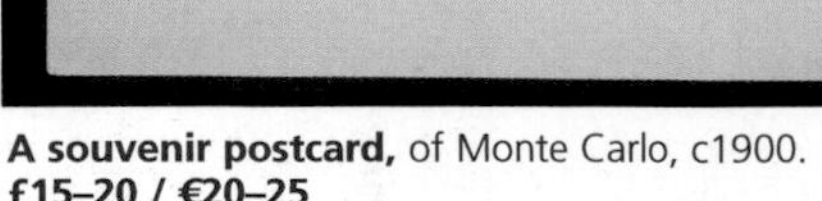

A souvenir postcard, of Monte Carlo, c1900.
£15–20 / €20–25
$25–30 S&D

◄ **A postcard,** of the accumulation of mail from a flood, American, c1900.
£20–25 / €35–40
$45–50 JAA

A postcard, depicting a covered wagon on the Old Oregon Trail Monument Expedition, American, 1906.
£105–125 / €155–185
$200–230 JAA

A postcard, depicting R.P. Willis's Café, Gravesend, Kent, 1906.
£55–65 / €80–95
$100–120 VS

A postcard, depicting the Sutton Tram Smash, Surrey, 1907.
£40–45 / €60–70
$70–80 VS

A postcard, depicting the launching of HMS *Defence*, Pembroke Dock, Wales, by Allen, 1907.
£35–40 / €50–60
$60–70 VS

◄ **A postcard,** depicting the fire at Godson & Dobson, Penge, Kent, by Bakes, 1907.
£35–40 / €50–60
$60–70 VS

A postcard, depicting the boiler explosion at Distington Ironworks, Cumberland, 1909.
£30–35 / €45–50
$55–65 VS

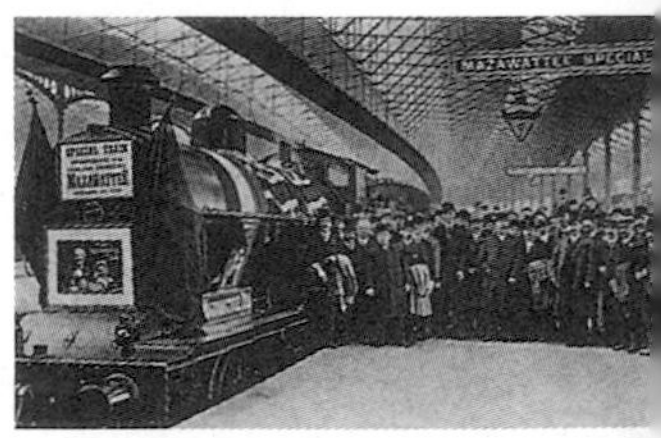

A postcard, depicting the Special Mazzawatte Train for the Birmingham Grocers, October, 1910.
£65–75 / €95–110
$120–135 VS

◄ **A political postcard,** French, c1908.
£20–25 / €35–40
$45–50 S&D

► **A postcard,** depicting the Vanderbilt Cup Race, Savannah, American, 1911.
£55–65 / €80–95
$100–120
JAA

An exhibition postcard, German, 1913.
£20–25 / €35–40
$45–50 S&D

Posters

An advertising poster, by Jules Chéret, 'Vin Mariani', French, 1894, 22½ x 15½in (57 x 39.5cm).
£510–610 / €740–890
$920–1,100 ⚒ VSP

A travel poster, by Solbach, 'Orient-Teppiche Geelhaar Bern', Swiss, c1910, 50½ x 35½in (128.5 x 90cm).
£490–580 / €720–850
$890–1,050 ⚒ VSP

A Boston, Copeland and Day poster, by Ethel Reed, 'Arabella and Araminta Stories', American, 1895, 27 x 15½in (68.5 x 39.5cm).
£2,100–2,500
€3,050–3,650
$3,800–4,550 ⚒ VSP

A poster, by Armand A. L. Rassenfosse, 'L'Art Indépendant', Belgian, 1896, 26 x 19¾in (66 x 50cm).
£450–540 / €660–790
$810–980 ⚒ VSP

► **A De Jong's Cacao poster,** German, c1910, 20 x 13in (51 x 33cm).
£780–930 / €1,150–1,350
$1,450–1,700 ⚒ VSP

◄ **A Hotel St Gotthard poster,** by Otto Baumberger, Swiss, 1917, 50½ x 35¾in (128.5 x 91cm).
£260–310 / €380–450
$470–560 ⚒ VSP

A poster, by J. Rosetti, 'La Raphaëlle, Liqueur Bonal', French, 1908, 63 x 47¼in (160 x 120cm).
£280–330 / €410–480
$510–600 ⚒ VSP

A Schaffer & Co poster, by J. S. Brandoly, 'The Sensation of Davos', on linen, German, c1920, 55½ x 37¼in (141 x 94.5cm).
£1,200–1,400 / €1,750–2,050
$2,150–2,550 ⚒ VSP

◄ **A Gilbey's Invalid Port poster,** 1920s, 29¼ x 39½in (74.5 x 100.5cm)
£240–280
€350–410
$430–510
⚒ DW

An LB&SCR poster, 'Seaford, at the foot of the South Downs', on linen, 1922, 40¼ x 25¼in (102 x 64cm).
£470–560 / €680–810
$850–1,000 ONS

◄ **A GWR poster,** by Barry Pittar, promoting the Cornish Riviera, limited edition, 1925, 40 x 50in (101.5 x 127cm).
£1,200–1,400
€1,750–2,050
$2,150–2,550
LAY

An Electric Railroad poster, advertising the service between Montreux and the Bernese Oberland, Switzerland, Swiss, 1926, 39½ x 30in (100.5 x 76cm).
£420–500 / €610–730
$760–900 ONS

► **A travel poster,** by William Ashton, featuring Sydney Harbour, Australia, 1935, 25 x 20in (63.5 x 51cm).
£700–840
€1,050–1,250
$1,250–1,500
VSP

◄ **A travel poster,** by Dwight Shepler, featuring New Hampshire, 1936, 24½ x 24in (62 x 61cm).
£340–400
€500–590
$610–720
VSP

A promotional poster, by John Atherton, for New York World's Fair, American, 1939, 20 x 30in (51 x 76cm).
£470–560 / €690–820
$850–1,000 VSP

A travel poster, for Verona, Italian, Milan, c1940, 39½ x 24½in (100 x 62cm).
£310–370 / €450–540
$560–670 VSP

A South African Railways poster, promoting Cape Town, South African, c1940, 40¼ x 26in (102 x 66cm).
£500–600 / €730–880
$910–1,100 VSP

A Monogram Pictures poster, *Wanderers of the West*, mounted on foam core, American, 1941, 78 x 41in (198 x 104cm).
£230–270 / €340–400
$420–500 JAA

An HMSO propaganda poster, by Lewitt-Him, 'The effects of over-cooking and keeping hot, vitamin value, goodness, taste "go up in smoke" – result is waste', c1945, 30 x 20in (76 x 51cm).
£230–270 / €330–390
$410–480 ONS

A Nassour Studios poster *African Screams*, starring Bud Abbott and Lou Costello, American, 1949, 36 x 14in (91.5 x 35.5cm).
£185–210 / €270–300
$330–370 Lim

Items in the Posters section have been arranged in date order.

◄ **An American Overseas Airlines poster,** American, c1950, 37½ x 24in (95.5 x 61cm).
£400–480 / €580–700
$720–870 DW

A 20th Century-Fox poster, *Monkey Business*, starring Cary Grant, Ginger Rogers and Marilyn Monroe, linen-backed, American, 1952, 41 x 27in (104 x 68.5cm).
£380–430 / €560–630
$700–780 ⊞ Lim

A Rank Organisation poster, *A Day to Remember*, starring Stanley Holloway, Joan Rice and Donald Sinden, 1953, 41 x 27in (104 x 68.5cm).
£155–175 / €230–260
$280–310 ⊞ Lim

A United Artists poster, *Love Happy*, starring the Marx Brothers, linen-backed, American, 1953, 41 x 27in (104 x 68.5cm).
£1,100–1,250
€1,600–1,800
$2,000–2,200 ⊞ Lim

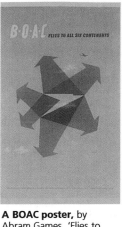

► **A shipping poster,** by Terence Cuneo, 'Port to Port', 1957, 40½ x 50in (102 x 127cm).
£640–760
€930–1,100
$1,200–1,400
⚒ ONS

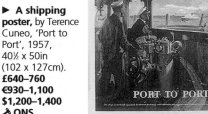

A BOAC poster, by Abram Games, 'Flies to all Six Continents', 1954, 39¾in x 21in (101 x 53.5cm).
£220–260 / €320–380
$400–470 ⚒ ONS

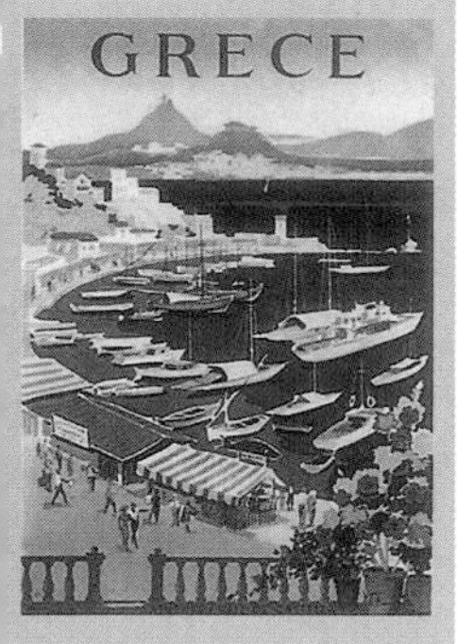

A travel poster, 'Grece', Greek, Athens, 1955, 31½ x 22¼in (80 x 56.5cm).
£240–280 / €350–410
$430–510 ⚒ VSP

A Rank Organisation poster, *Up in the World*, starring Norman Wisdom, 1956, 41 x 27in (104 x 68.5cm).
£110–125 / €160–180
$200–220 ⊞ Lim

A 20th Century-Fox poster, *Desk Set*, starring Spencer Tracy and Katharine Hepburn, American, 1957, 41 x 27in (104 x 68.5cm).
£180–200 / €260–290
$320–360 ⊞ Lim

An MGM poster, by Kapralyk, *Silk Stockings*, starring Fred Astaire and Cyd Charisse, American, 1957, 41 x 27in (104 x 68.5cm).
£400–450 / €580–660
$720–810 ⊞ Lim

A film poster, *The Great Dictator*, produced, written and directed by Charles Chaplin, American, 1958, 22 x 28in (56 x 71cm).
£270–300 / €390–440
$490–540 ⊞ Lim

► **An MGM poster,** *Some Came Running*, starring Frank Sinatra, Dean Martin and Shirley MacLaine, 1958, American, 41 x 27in (104 x 68.5cm).
£500–550 / €720–800
$900–1,000 ⊞ Lim

A United Artists poster, *La Parisienne*, starring Brigitte Bardot, American, 1958, 22 x 28in (56 x 71cm).
£145–165 / €210–240
$270–300 ⊞ Lim

Rock & Pop

◄ **A Selcol plastic Beatles New Sound Guitar,** printed with faces and signatures of John, Paul, George and Ringo, slight damage, c1964, 23in (58.5cm) high.
£100–120 / €145–175 $190–220 ⚒ RTo

A Beatles Christmas Show Programme, signed by all four members of the group, some wear, pages loose, 1963–64.
£940–1,100 / €1,450–1,600 $1,800–2,000 ⚒ CHTR

A film poster, *Roustabout*, starring Elvis Presley and Barbara Stanwyck, on linen, American, 1964, 28 x 22in (71 x 56cm).
£260–290 / €380–420 $470–520 ⊞ Lim

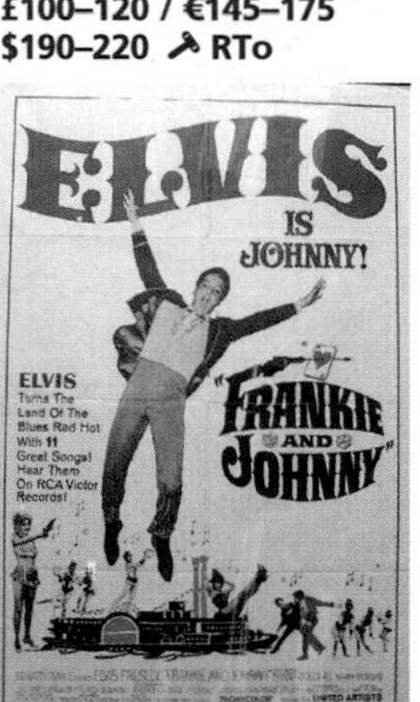

A film poster, *Frankie & Johnny*, starring Elvis Presley, American, 1965, 41 x 27in (104 x 68.5cm).
£120–135 / €175–195 $210–240 ⊞ Lim

Further reading

Miller's Movie Collectibles, Miller's Publications, 2002

ROCK & POP

► **A film poster,** advertising *Don't Look Back*, starring Bob Dylan and Joan Baez, 1967, 30 x 20in (76 x 51cm).
£500–550 €730–810 $900–1,000 ⊞ Lim

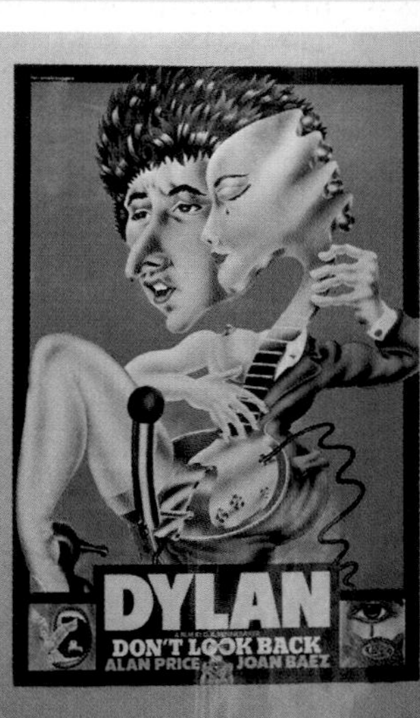

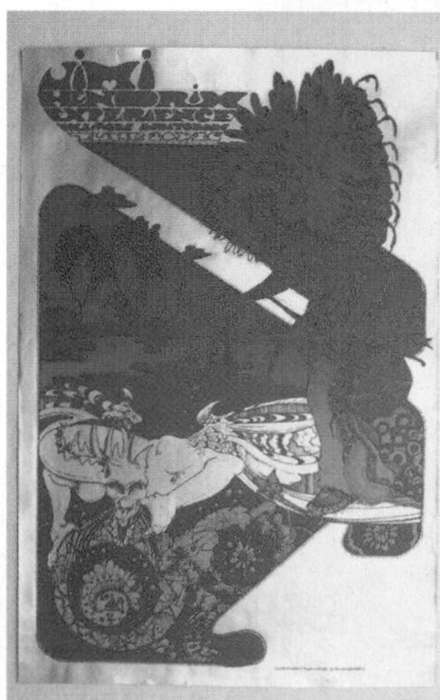

◄ **A silkscreen poster,** 'Jimi Hendrix at the Fillmore', by Hapshash and Th Coloured Coat, printed by Osiris, 1967, 30 x 20in (76 x 51cm).
£180–200 €260–290 $320–360 ⊞ AS

Hapshash and The Coloured Coat was the name used by the psychedelic design team founded in 196 by Nigel Weymouth and Michael English

Four Beatles pennants, Spanish, 1960s, 10in (25.5cm) long.
£220–250 / €320–370
$400–450 ⊞ CTO
The names on these pennants do not match the faces.

► **A Monkees concert programme and ticket,** London Empire Arena, 1967, programme 12in (30.5cm) square.
£70–80 / €100–115
$135–155 ⊞ CTO

A silkscreen poster, 'The Who/I Can See For Miles', by Hapshash and The Coloured Coat, 1967, 30 x 20in (76 x 51cm).
£180–200 / €260–290
$320–360 ⊞ ASC

An NBC poster, advertising an interview with Bob Dylan, American, 1968, 24 x 16in (61 x 40.5cm).
£330–380 / €480–550
$600–690 ⊞ Lim

A concert poster, advertising the Newport Festival, American, 1969, 33 x 23in (84 x 58.5cm).
£330–380 / €480–550
$600–690 ⊞ Lim

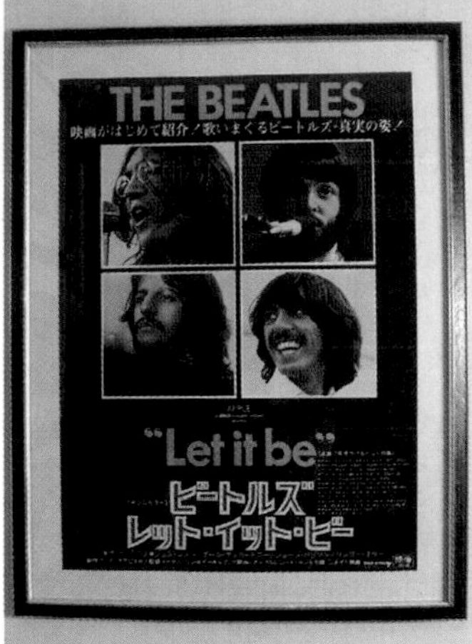

A poster, advertising 'Let It Be' by the Beatles, on linen, Japanese, 1970, 32 x 24in (81.5 x 61cm).
£360–400 / €530–580
$650–720 ⊞ Lim

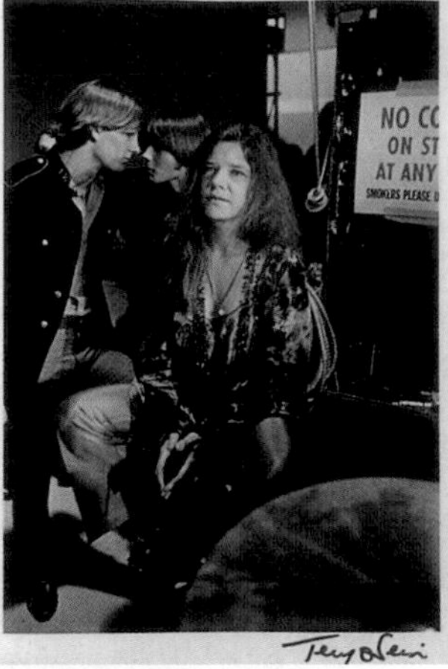

Terry O'Neill, Janis Joplin, a silver print, signed, with wetstamp, c1970, printed 1985, 16 x 12in (40.5 x 30.5cm).
£540–640 / €790–930
$980–1,150 ⚒ S

A poster, advertising Elvis on tour, American, 1972, 36 x 14in (91.5 x 35.5cm).
£240–270 / €350–390
$430–490 ⊞ Lim

◀ **David Bailey,** Charlie Watts, Ronnie Wood and Bill Wyman, a silver print, signed and dated, with wetstamp, 1977, 16 x 20in (40.5 x 51cm).
£540–640 / €790–930
$980–1,150 ⚒ S

An EMI poster, advertising 'Anarchy in the UK', by the Sex Pistols, signed by Jamie Reid, 1981, 17 x 24in (43 x 61cm).
£310–350 / €450–510
$560–630 ⊞ PLB

A poster, advertising 'Pretty Vacant' by the Sex Pistols, produced for Artificial, signed by Jamie Reid, edition of 200, 1997, 30 x 40in (76 x 101.5cm).
£490–550 / €720–800
$890–1,000 ⊞ PLB

Scientific Instruments

Calculating Instruments & Machines

A Thatcher's calculator, with paper scales, in an oak case, American, c1925, 24in (61cm) wide.
£2,250–2,500 / €3,300–3,650
$4,050–4,550 ⊞ ETO

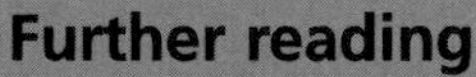

Further reading
Miller's Collecting Science & Technology, Miller's Publications, 2001

A Curta I aluminium calculator, Swiss, c1948, 5in (12.5cm) high, with original case.
£580–650 / €840–950
$1,050–1,200 ⊞ ETO

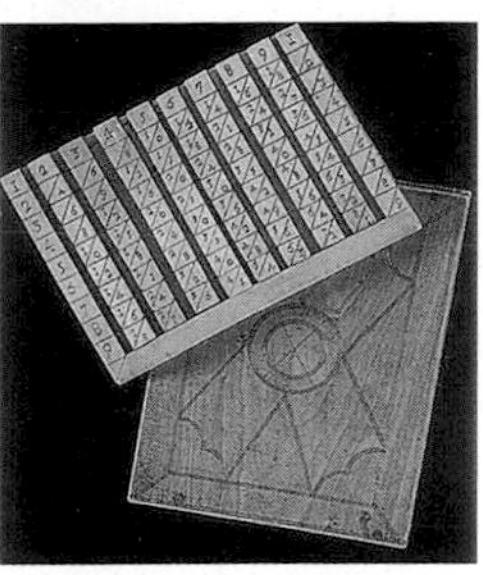

A satinwood Napier's Bones, the sliding cover revealing a boxwood tray with rods stamped with numbers, the case incised with geometric patterns, incomplete, late 18thC, 3½in (9cm) wide.
£1,200–1,400
€1,750–2,050
$2,150–2,550 ⚒ S

Compasses & Dials

A gilt-brass perpetual calendar, engraved with days of the week, planetary symbols, dates of the month, festivals and holidays, sun rising and setting times and zodiac signs, German, early 17thC, 1½in (4cm) diam.
£900–1,050 / €1,300–1,550
$1,650–1,900 ⚒ S

A bronze sundial, with scroll-pierced gnomon and calibrated with hours, minutes and compass points, signed 'John Potten, Londini', 1700–50, 17in (43cm) diam.
£1,200–1,400 / €1,750–2,050
$2,150–2,550 ⚒ S(S)

A Butterfield-style brass dial, with a hinged bird gnomon and engraved inset compass rose, the reverse engraved with European cities and their latitudes, within a velvet-lined fishskin-covered case, signed, French, early 18thC, 3in (7.5cm) wide.
£720–860 / €1,050–1,250
$1,300–1,550 ⚒ S

A bronze sundial, by Thomas Heath, signed, mid-18thC, 11¾in (30cm) diam.
£1,550–1,850 / €2,250–2,700
$2,800–3,350 ⚒ S

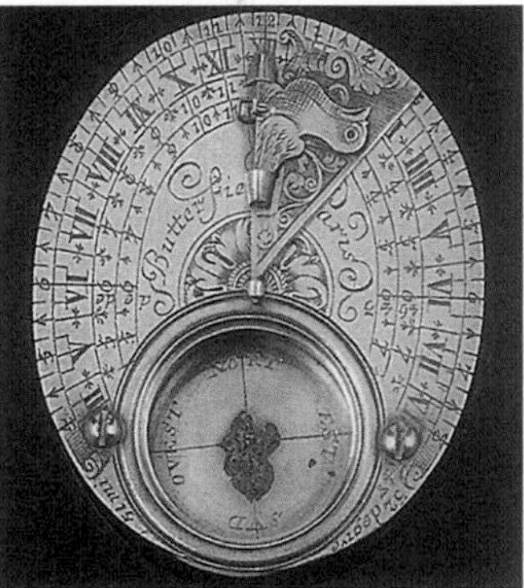

A silver Butterfield dial, fitted with a magnetic compass, applied folding gnomon and bird indicator, engraved with hours for different latitudes and a list of French towns, damaged, inscribed mark, French, Paris, c1720, 2in (5cm) wide.
£1,450–1,750 / €2,100–2,550
$2,650–3,150 ⚒ S(Am)

A gilt pocket compass, with hand-painted enamel dial, in a leather-covered wood and paper case, c1760, 1½in (4cm) diam.
£420–470 / €610–690
$760–850 ⊞ FOF

A brass universal equinoctial dial, with engraved markings, late 18thC, 6in (15cm) diam.
£480–570 / €700–830
$870–1,050 S

► **A silver fob compass,** with hand-painted gilt chapter ring and steel pointer, Birmingham 1898, ½in (1.5cm) diam.
£60–70 / €90–100
$110–125 FOF

A 9ct gold fob compass, with hand-painted gilt chapter ring and steel pointer, Chester 1912, ¾in (2cm) diam.
£130–145 / €190–210
$230–260 FOF
These pieces were produced as functional novelties to hang from chains.

► **An equinoctial compass/sundial,** French, early 19thC, 3½in (9cm) diam.
£280–330 / €410–480
$510–600 G(B)

A bronze sundial, by F. Barker & Son, London, engraved 'Light and Shadow by Turns but Love Always', 19thC, 7in (18cm) diam.
£150–180 / €220–260
$270–320 G(L)

A boxwood pocket sundial, mid-19thC, 2in (5cm) diam.
£200–230 / €290–340
$360–420 FOF

A United States Army hunter-cased tinned-brass compass, by Waltham Watch Co, with silvered dial and steel pointer, jewelled bearing and hinge-activated transit lock, American, 1914–18, 1¾in (4.5cm) diam.
£75–85 / €110–125
$135–155 FOF
During WWI, a number of watch firms began making compasses and other instruments for the war effort. These were generally made by women in the factories as the men were conscripted and, as can be seen here, they utilized the case style that was already made for watches.

◄ **A Sun Watch pocket sundial,** by Ansonia, with original card sleeve and instructions, American, c1922, 3¼ x 2¼in (8.5 x 5.5cm).
£130–145 / €190–210
$230–260 FOF

Globes

A pocket globe, by John Senex, the hand-coloured printed paper gores applied to a papier-mâché sphere, contained within a fishskin-covered case, the interior applied with paper gores depicting a celestial map, c1730, 2¾in (7cm) diam.
£4,800–5,700 / €7,000–8,300
$8,700–10,300 S

A terrestrial pocket globe, by R. Cushee, contained within a snakeskin hinged outer case, lined with a celestial map of the heavens, entitled 'The New Globe of the Earth 1731', wooden access pins missing, 18thC, 3in (7.5cm) diam.
£5,400–6,400 / €7,900–9,300
$9,800–11,600 TMA

A celestial globe, by J. & W. Cary, with a later printed horizon, on a stop-fluted stem with scrolled legs, dated 1799, 21in (53.5cm) diam.
£5,400–6,400
€7,900–9,300
$9,800–11,600 WW

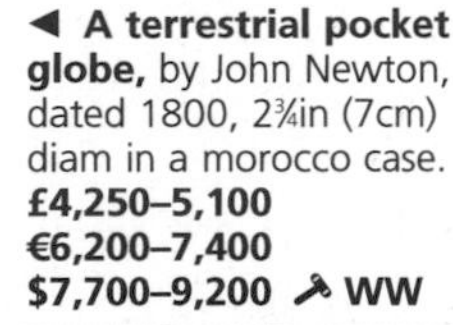

◄ **A terrestrial pocket globe,** by John Newton, dated 1800, 2¾in (7cm) diam in a morocco case.
£4,250–5,100
€6,200–7,400
$7,700–9,200 ⚒ WW

A pair of terrestrial and celestial globes, by Thomas M. Bardin, the terrestrial globe with printed paper gores applied to a papier-mâché sphere marked with Cook's tracks, with brass meridian ring, the celestial globe with printed paper gores depicting constellation figures, with brass meridian ring, the wooden horizontal ring printed with the zodiac calendar, c1817, 12 in (30.5cm) diam, on mahogany stands.
£3,600–4,300 / €5,300–6,300
$6,500–7,800 ⚒ S

A celestial globe, by Newton, with printed gores, calibrated brass meridian ring and printed horizontal ring with zodiac signs, damaged, on a mahogany stand, c1830, 19in (48.5cm) diam.
£2,100–2,500
€3,050–3,650
$3,800–4,550 ⚒ SK

► **A miniature terrestrial globe,** by Malby, with paper gores and brass fittings, varnish damaged, 19thC, 10in (25.5cm) diam, on a later mahogany stand.
£260–310 / €380–450
$470–560 ⚒ G(B)

A pocket globe, by Lane, with printed gores applied to a sphere with metal axis poles, c1800, 1½in (4cm) diam, in a morocco case.
£1,800–2,150 / €2,650–3,150
$3,250–3,900 ⚒ S

A celestial globe, by Cruchley, the printed paper gores depicting constellation figures on a papier-mâché sphere, with a graduated brass meridian ring, c1840, 9in (23cm) diam, on a wooden stand.
£900–1,050 / €1,300–1,550
$1,650–1,900 ⚒ S

A terrestrial pocket globe, by Cabel-Klinger, with paper gores on a wooden sphere, Dutch, 19thC, 3in (7.5cm) diam, with a paper case.
£1,050–1,250
€1,550–1,850
$1,900–2,250 ⚒ S(Am)

A terrestrial globe, by J. Forest, engraved by A. Soldan, slight damage, French, Paris, late 19thC, 3in (7.5cm) diam, on a later silver-plated stand.
£370–440 / €540–640
$670–800 ⚒ BBA

◄ **A terrestrial library globe,** by H. Kipert, German, Berlin, dated 1902, 39in (99cm) high.
£1,750–2,100
€2,550–3,050
$3,150–3,800 ⚒ S(Am)

◄ **A terrestrial globe,** entitled 'Geographica', depicting 'Railways, Steamer route distances in sea miles, Heights in English feet, British Possessions Red', with a brass meridian ring, c1900, 10in (25.5cm) diam, on a turned and ebonized stand.
£300–360 / €440–530
$540–650 ⚒ SWO

LOCATE THE SOURCE
The source of each illustration in Miller's can be found by checking the code letters below each caption with the Key to Illustrations, pages 778–784.

◄ **A terrestrial globe,** by Phillips, c1920, 19in (48.5cm) diam, on a carved and ebonized stand.
£700–840 / €1,000–1,200
$1,250–1,500 ⚒ DN

Medical & Dental

A mahogany apothecary box, the fitted interior with satinwood-veneered drug drawers, glass bottles and secret compartments, decorated with crossbanding, ebony stringing and parquetry banding, 19thC, 11in (28cm) high.
£1,400–1,650 / €2,050–2,400
$2,550–3,000 AH

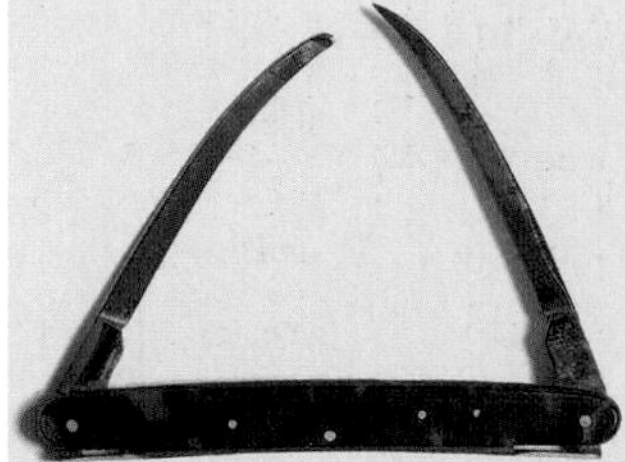

A tortoiseshell hernia bistoury knife, by T. Wood, c1850, 9½in (24cm) extended.
£200–230 / €290–340
$360–420 FOF
This piece was used for strangulated or irreducible hernias. The knop to the end of the blade enabled it to be used to push away the soft tissue without damage.

A Dutch Delft bleeding bowl, painted with stylized flowers, restored, c1720, 7¾in (19.5cm) diam.
£370–440 / €540–640
$670–800 SWO

A silver bleeding bowl, engraved 'Dr Miller', marked, c1790, 4¼in (11cm) diam.
£1,000–1,200 / €1,450–1,750
$1,800–2,150 L

Phlebotomy (Bloodletting)

This is one of the oldest procedures in medicine. There are two forms; wet and dry cupping. In wet cupping, the skin is broken with a fleam or a scarificator and the blood is drained away into a heated cup or bowl. In dry cupping, the skin is not broken. A cup or glass is gently heated and then applied to the skin. As the air inside cools it forms a vacuum and the blood is pulled to the surface of the skin where it leaves a bruise.

A set of mahogany chemist's drawers, late 19thC, 72½in (184cm) wide.
£680–800 / €990–1,150
$1,250–1,450 SWO

A travelling pocket fleam, possibly veterinary, with a bone handle and additional blades, c1820, case 4¼in (11cm) long.
£200–230 / €290–340
$360–420 FOF

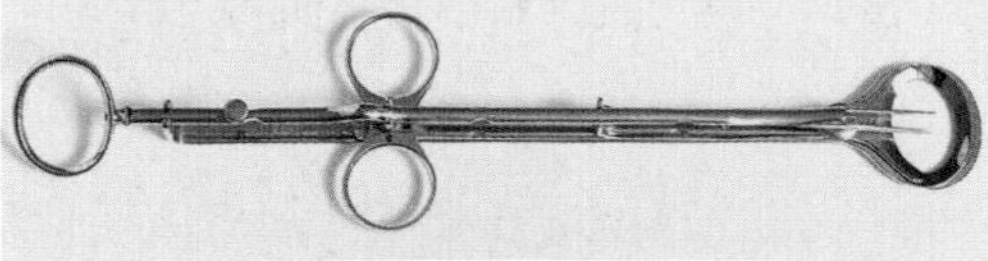

A stainless steel tonsil guillotine, by Jetter & Scheerer, c1915, 10¼in (26cm) long.
£135–150 / €195–220
$240–270 FOF

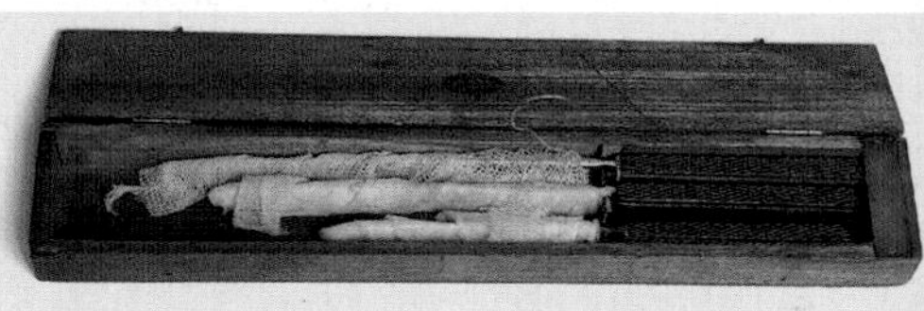

A set of three Liston amputation knives, by Henry Bigg, with ebony handles, in a mahogany case, c1860, 15½in (39.5cm) wide.
£260–290 / €380–420
$470–520 FOF

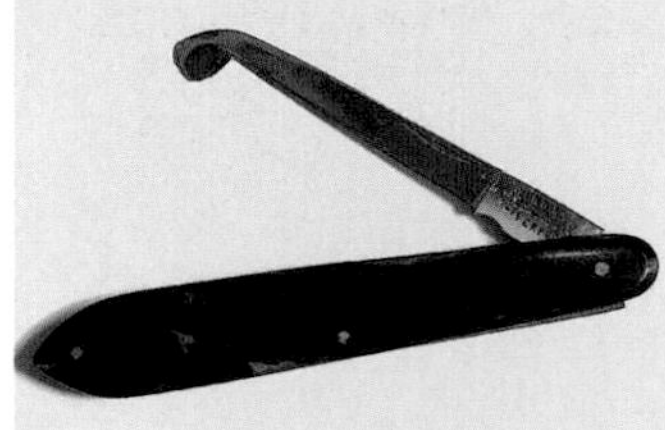

A tortoiseshell gum lancet, by John Wood, Liverpool, c1825, 3¼in (8.5cm) closed.
£130–145 / €190–210
$230–260 FOF

► **A Staffordshire earthenware jar and cover,** by Samuel Alcock, inscribed 'Leeches', moulded mark, mid-19thC, 12¼in (31cm) high.
£4,000–4,800 / €5,800–7,000
$7,200–8,700 SWO
From ancient times, it was believed that blood could be 'good' or 'bad' and, when a person was ill, the 'badness' could be removed either by bleeding or the application of leeches. It is interesting that leeches were still believed to be of benefit during the reign of Queen Victoria, but even more extraordinary is that they are now coming back into use in modern medicine.

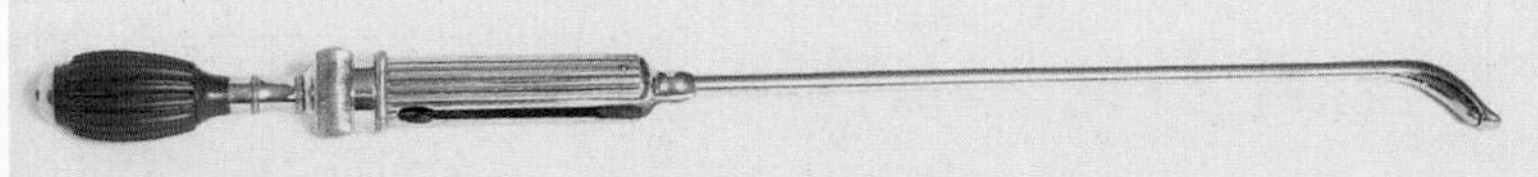

A stainless steel lithorite, by Thuerrigl, with a composite handle, 19thC, 19in (48.5cm) long.
£380–430 / €550–630
$690–780 FOF
This ingenious device was used to crush bladder stones. The closed jaws were passed into the bladder, the stones located by touch, held in the jaws and then crushed. This enabled the pieces to be made small enough to pass.

A Spode medicine spoon, printed with Two Figures pattern, mounted on a pedestal foot, 1800–05, 2¾in (7cm) high.
£1,000–1,200
€1,450–1,750
$1,800–2,150 DN

► A Spode medicine spoon, printed with Two Figures pattern, handle replaced, 1800–05, 4in (10cm) long.
£420–500 / €610–730
$760–910 DN

A pair of paintings on glass, entitled 'The Apothecary', one depicting a man holding scales, the other depicting a mortar and pestle and other equipment, 18thC, 20 x 15in (51 x 38cm), framed and glazed.
£730–870
€1,050–1,250
$1,300–1,550 TMA

Bloodletting instruments

The earliest bloodletting tool is the simple fleam or lancet with a single blade. In the early 19th century, spring-loaded multi-bladed examples known as scarificators appeared. These have rows of blades from four to 24 in number. Square-based examples tend to be German, octagonal-based examples are British or American and round examples are often French.

A scarificator, by Rein, London, with 12 blades, c1860, 2in (5cm) wide.
£270–300 / €390–440
$490–540 FOF

A surgeon's field set, comprising 14 instruments including scalpels, bone saw, retractors and tourniquet, some marked 'Bliss', some missing, American, 1861–65, in a brass-bound mahogany case, 16in (40.5cm) wide.
£1,250–1,500 / €1,850–2,200
$2,250–2,700 JAA
American Civil War sets of instruments often fetch more than their European counterparts.

A wooden vaginal speculum, c1850, 8½in (21.5cm) long.
£580–650 / €850–950
$1,050–1,200 CuS

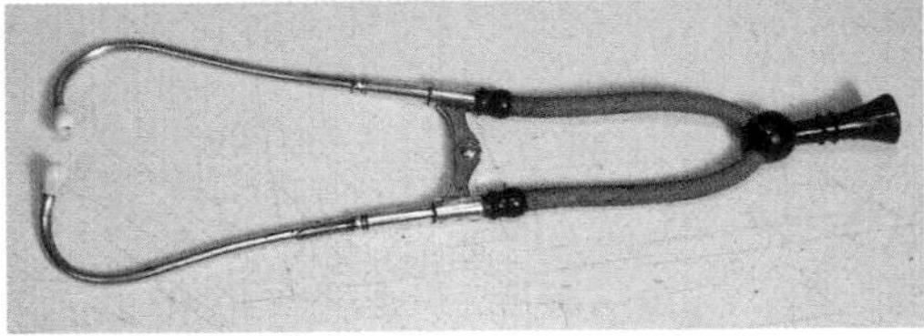

An ebony and turned ivory binaural stethoscope, c1860, 15¾in (40cm) long.
£590–650 / €860–950
$1,050–1,200 ET

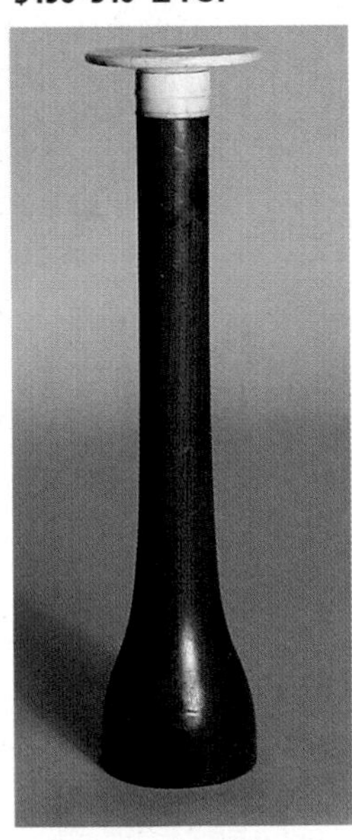

A fruitwood and ivory monaural stethoscope, c1840, 7in (18cm) long.
£310–350 / €450–510
$560–630 ET

◄ A silver Immisch's avitreous surface thermometer, by S. Maw, London, dial signed, patented 1881, 1in (2.5cm) diam.
£720–800 / €1,050–1,150
$1,300–1,450 FOF

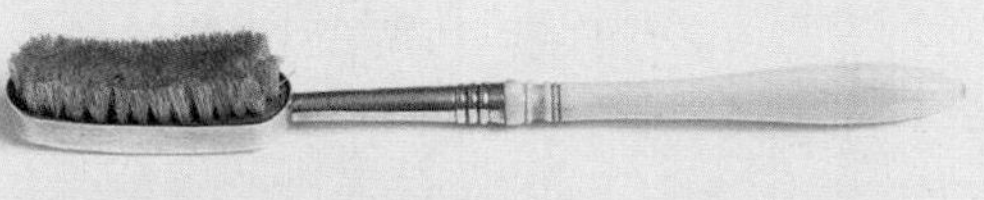

A silver and ivory toothbrush, Birmingham 1811, 4¾in (12cm) long.
£230–270 / €340–390
$420–490 FOF

Meteorological Instruments

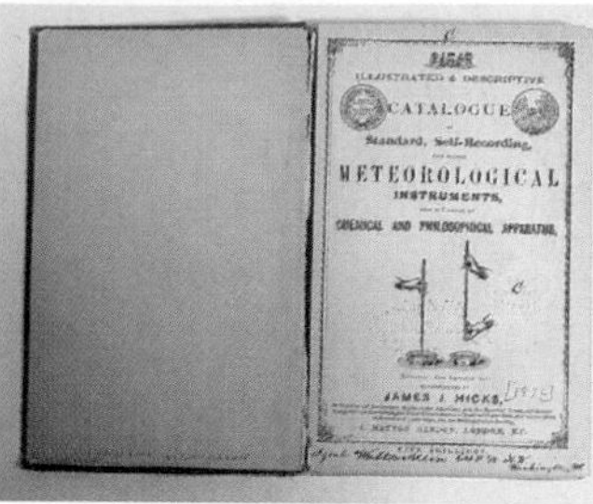

A meteorological instruments catalogue, by James J. Hicks, 1876, 9in (23cm) high.
£340–380 / €500–550
$620–690 ⊞ RTW

An automaton hygrometer, Italian, late 19thC, 12½in (32cm) wide.
£310–350 / €450–510
$560–630 ⊞ ET

► A sympiesometer, by Adie & Son, Edinburgh, with a thermometer, the silvered register plate signed, in a mahogany case, Scottish, mid-19thC, 24½in (61.5cm) high.
£2,200–2,600
€3,200–3,800
$4,000–4,700 ⚒ RTo

A sympiesometer uses gas and coloured oil to record air pressure.

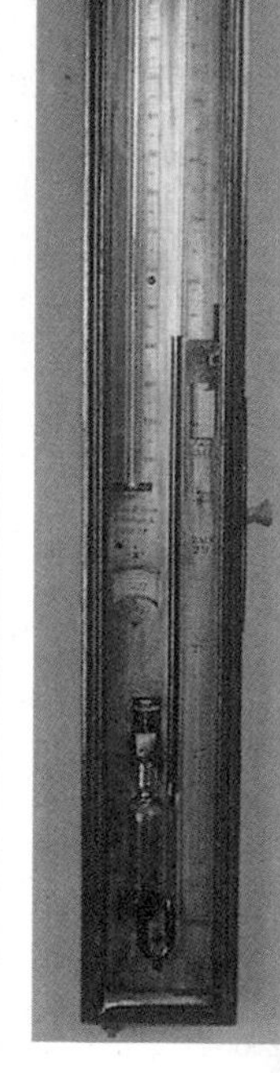

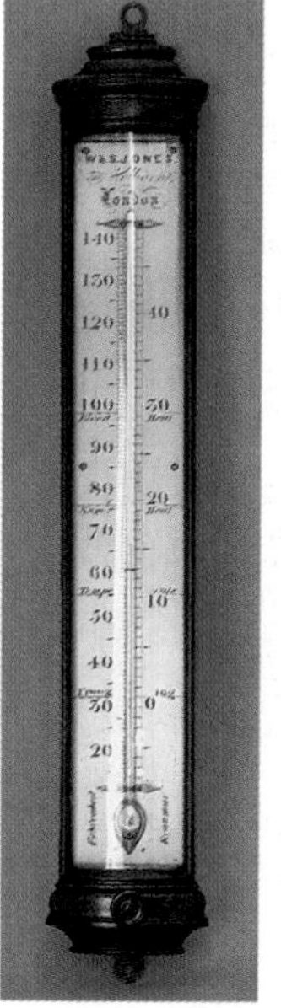

◄ A thermometer, by W. & S. Jones, Holborn, with engraved silvered dial, in a bowfronted rosewood case, signed, 18thC, 20in (51cm) high.
£3,300–3,950
€4,800–5,800
$6,000–7,200
⚒ G(L)

► A thermometer, with silvered scale and spiral spirit level, in an oak and mahogany case, French, c1860, 43in (109cm) high.
£2,250–2,500
€3,300–3,650
$4,050–4,550
⊞ RAY

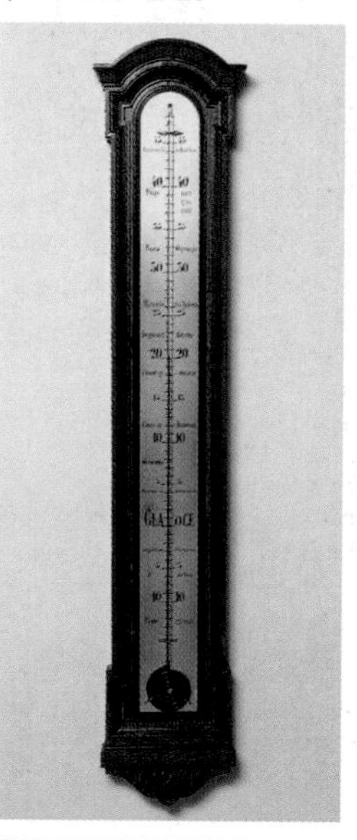

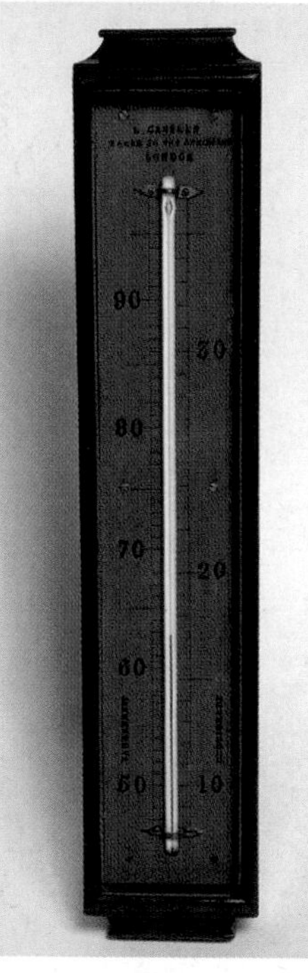

◄ A thermometer, by L. Casella, London, in a mahogany case, c1900, 16in (40.5cm) high.
£310–350
€450–510
$560–630
⊞ RTW

Microscopes

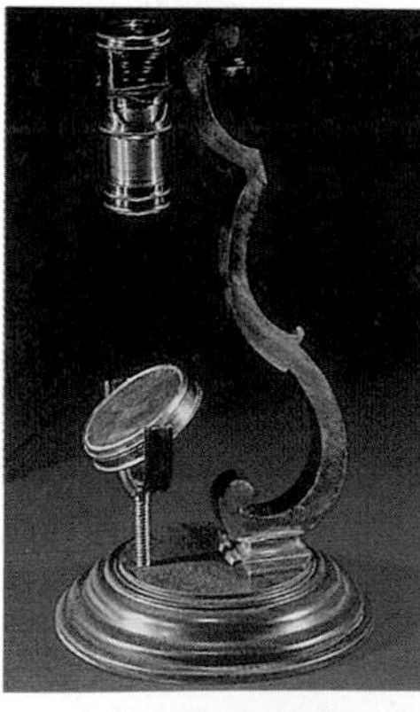

A scroll and screw-barrel microscope, attributed to John Cuff, on a lignum vitae stand with a mirror, accessories missing, c1740, 7¾in (19.5cm) high, with an oak case.
£1,500–1,800
€2,200–2,650
$2,700–3,250 ⚒ S

A brass box microscope, mounted on a kingwood-veneered box with accessories drawer, French, mid-18thC, 14in (35.5cm) high.
£8,500–10,200
€12,400–14,900
$15,400–18,500 ⚒ S

A Nuremberg compound monocular microscope, by François Jappertien, with a leather-covered outer tube, with accessories drawer, two accessories and two eyepieces without lenses, German, c1800, 15½in (39.5cm) high.
£9,500–11,400
€13,900–16,600
$17,200–20,600 ⚒ S

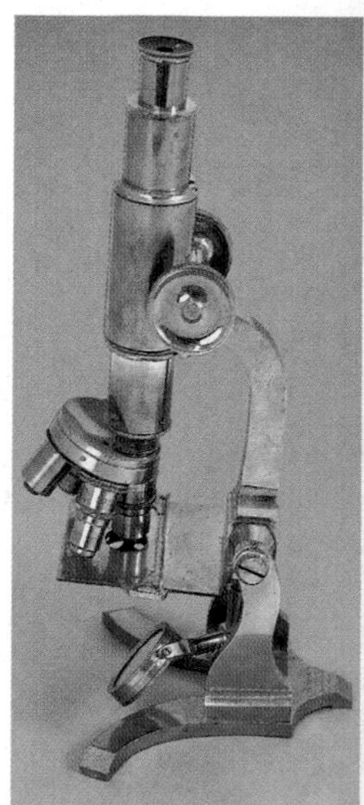

A lacquered-brass microscope, by William Salmon, London, with rotating lens, 19thC, 14in (35.5cm) high.
£230–270 / €340–390
$420–490 ⚒ G(L)

A brass monocular microscope, by Evans & Wormall, London, with specimen slides, signed, 19thC, 9in (23cm) high, with a mahogany case.
£210–250 / €310–370
$380–450 G(L)

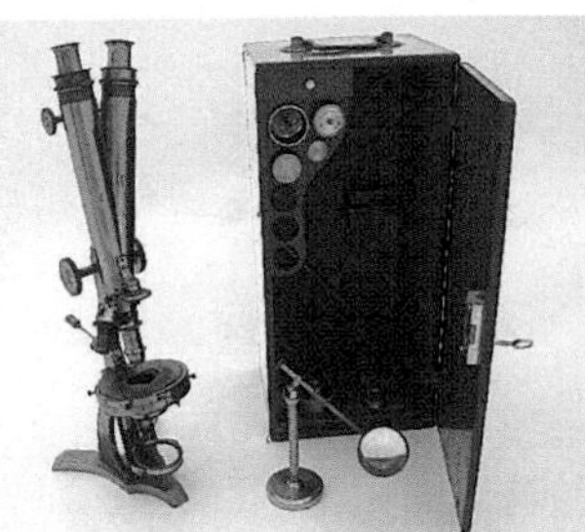

A Victorian lacquered-brass binocular microscope, by John Browning, London, No. 407, with lenses, 19in (48.5cm) high, with a fitted mahogany case.
£520–620 / €760–910
$940–1,100 G(B)

▶ **A Cuff-style microscope,** by Dollond, mounted on a mahogany base, with five numbered objectives, brass fish plate, ivory talc box, forceps, cylinder to carry a concave speculum, brass slide holder and six ivory specimen slides, signed, 1800–25, 14½in (37cm) high, with a deal case.
£2,400–2,850 / €3,500–4,150
$4,350–5,200 S

A lacquered-brass binocular microscope, by Henry Crouch, London, in a glazed mahogany case, with accessories, c1880, 19in (48.5cm) high.
£1,800–2,000 / €2,600–2,900
$3,250–3,600 TOM

A lacquered and oxidized-brass monocular microscope, in a fitted mahogany case, with accessories, French, c1880, 11in (28cm) high.
£135–150 / €195–220
$240–270 TOM

SCIENTIFIC INSTRUMENTS

A lacquered-brass and anodized monocular microscope, by Carl Zeiss, with separate objective lens and condenser and stand, German, late 19thC, with case, 12in (30.5cm) high.
£220–260 / €320–380
$400–470 ⚒ PFK

A lacquered-brass compound monocular microscope, by R. & J. Beck, London, c1890, 11in (28cm) high.
£160–180 / €230–260
$290–330 ⊞ TOM

A lacquered and oxidized brass binocular, monocular and petrological microscope, by W. Watson & Sons, London, in original case, with accessories, c1910, 17in (43cm) high.
£2,700–3,000 / €3,950–4,400
$4,900–5,400 ⊞ TOM

A walnut microscope slide cabinet, the 21 drawers with ivory pulls and containing 400 slides, c1870, 12in (30.5cm) wide.
£720–800 / €1,050–1,200
$1,300–1,450 ⊞ TOM

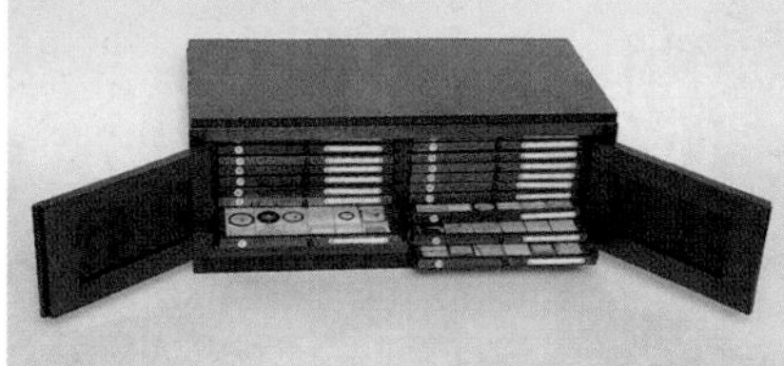

◄ A mahogany and rosewood microscope slide cabinet, the 20 drawers with ebony pulls and containing 200 microscope slides, c1910, 16in (40.5cm) wide.
£270–300 / €390–440
$490–540 ⊞ TOM

► A slide-maker's brass turntable, on a mahogany base, c1890, 7in (18cm) wide.
£25–30
€40–45
$50–55 ⊞ TOM

Surveying & Drawing Instruments

A brass beam compass, with two steel points, with floral and geometric engraving, probably German, c1700, 11in (28cm) long.
£1,050–1,250 / €1,550–1,850
$1,900–2,250 ⚒ S

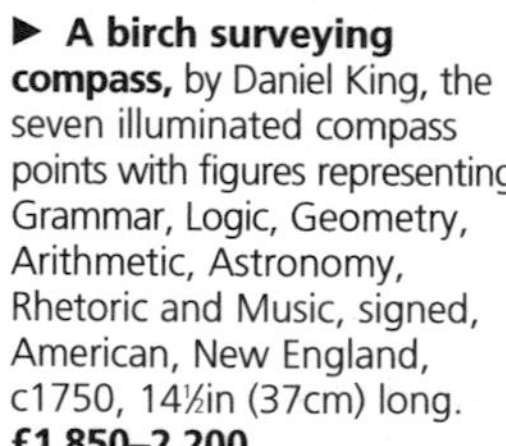

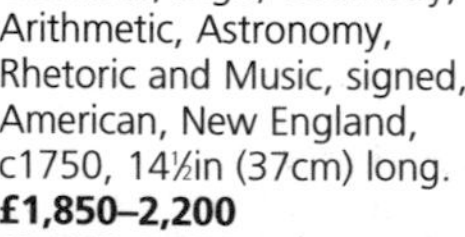

► A birch surveying compass, by Daniel King, the seven illuminated compass points with figures representing Grammar, Logic, Geometry, Arithmetic, Astronomy, Rhetoric and Music, signed, American, New England, c1750, 14½in (37cm) long.
£1,850–2,200
€2,700–3,200
$3,350–4,000 ⚒ SK

A mahogany surveyor's vernier compass, by George Leighton, with a brass needle clamp, the bone vernier with screw-thread adjustment, in a fitted box, American, New Hampshire, c1800, 14in (35.5cm) long.
£1,300–1,550 / €1,900–2,250
$2,350–2,800 ⚒ SK

A surveyor's brass compass, attributed to Grant, London, the silvered dial engraved with 360 degree and quadrant scales, inset with two levels, early 19thC, 6in (15cm) diam, with a later wooden box.
£190–220 / €280–320
$340–400 ⚒ DN(BR)

A surveyor's vernier compass, by W. & L. E. Gurley, with silvered dial and brass limbs, in a mahogany case with shipping instructions, American, Troy, N.Y., c1880, 6in (15cm) long.
£550–660 / €800–960
$1,000–1,200 ⚒ SK

An eidograph, by T. B. Winter, Newcastle-upon-Tyne, in a mahogany case, c1865, 35½in (90cm) long.
£790–880 / €1,150–1,300
$1,450–1,600 ⊞ FOF
The eidograph was invented in 1831 by William Wallace. It is used for the purpose of copying plans or drawings on the same or on different scales.

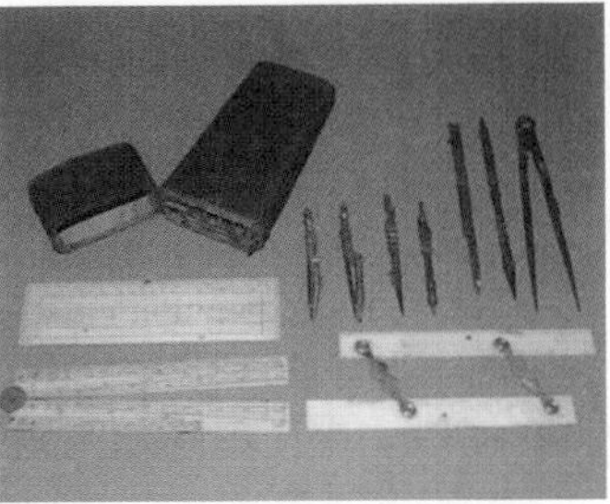

A set of mathematical instruments, comprising a bone protractor, bone sector with brass mount, bone and brass parallel rule and a variety of compasses, drawing pens and a penknife, in a rayskin case, c1800, 3in (7.5cm) long.
£300–360 / €440–530
$540–650 PFK

A set of draughtsman's instruments, the hinged cover revealing a fitted interior with nine brass and ivory drawing instruments, in a shagreen case, early 19thC, 6¾in (17cm) high.
£140–165 / €200–240
$250–300 WW

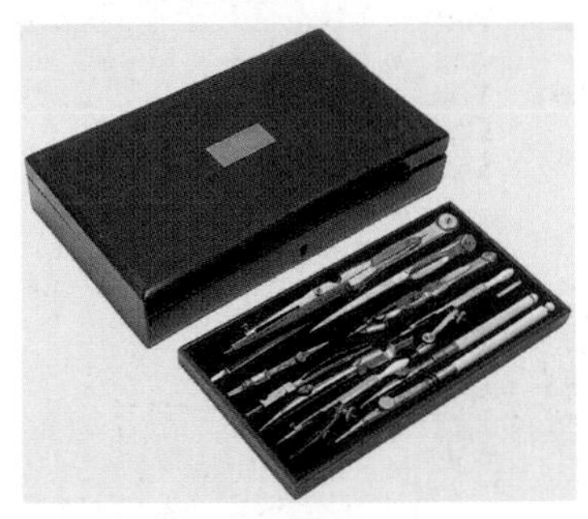

A set of drawing instruments, in a rosewood case, c1870, 8in (20.5cm) wide.
£105–120 / €155–175
$190–220 ⊞ MB

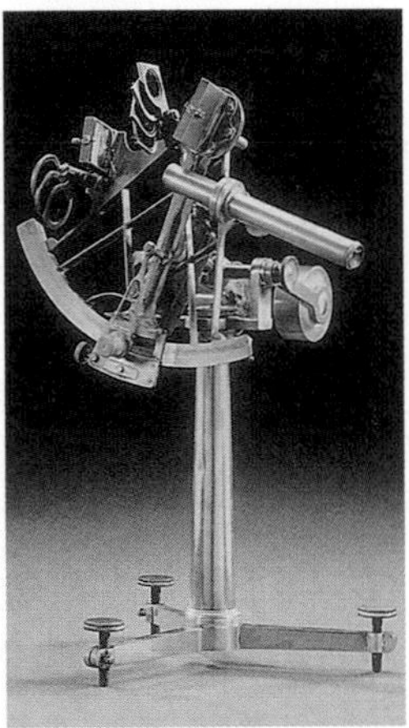

► **A brass pillar sextant,** by Troughton & Simms, London, with two sets of interchangeable filters, a mirror and a telescope attachment, with a mahogany handle, stamped mark, late 19thC, 19¾in (50cm) high.
£1,300–1,550 / €1,900–2,250
$2,350–2,800 S

A brass theodolite, by Yeates, with silvered scale, screw fitting and levels, inscribed marks, Irish, Dublin, 19thC, 12½in (32cm) long, with a mahogany box
£130–155 / €190–220
$240–280 WW

Telescopes

A 2¾in presentation brass refracting telescope, by Jesse Ramsden, signed, late 18thC, 19¾in (50cm) high, with a mahogany case and accessories including eyepieces and a lens cap.
£2,400–2,850
€3,500–4,150
$4,350–5,200 S

A 3in lacquered-brass telescope, with folding legs, inscribed 'G. Ledstone, Dartmouth', early 19thC, 16¾in (42.5cm) long.
£590–700 / €860–1,000
$1,050–1,250 WW

For further information on
Optical Instruments
see page 701

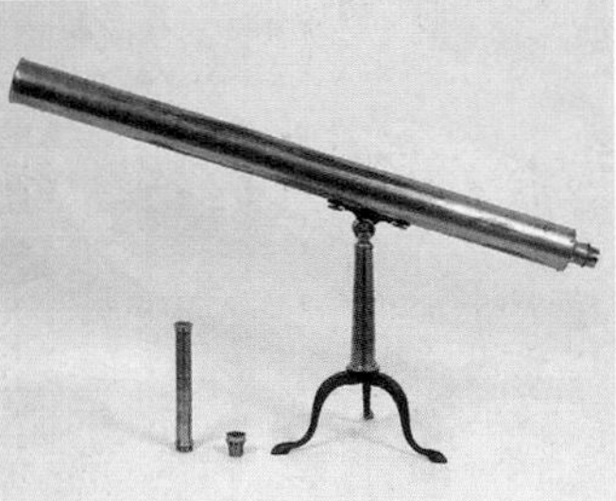

A late Victorian lacquered-brass telescope, signed 'J. Bateman, London', with a pine box, 52in (132cm) long.
£370–440 / €540–640
$670–800 CHTR

◄ **A 3½in refracting telescope,** by J. Dancer, Manchester, with a star finder, inscribed, late 19thC, 46¾in (119cm) long, with a mahogany case.
£1,500–1,800
€2,200–2,650
$2,700–3,250
DN

A late Victorian lacquered-brass and iron rack-and-pinion telescope, by Gardner & Lyle, Scottish, Glasgow, 39½in (100.5cm) long, with a fitted mahogany box.
£490–580 / €720–850
$890–1,050 HOLL

Weights & Measures

A burr-walnut miniature/pocket Sikes hydrometer, by Joseph Long, London, c1840, with case, 5in (12.5cm) long.
£200–230 / €290–340
$360–420 ⊞ FOF

In the 1740s, Custom and Excise and the London Brewers/Distillers began to use Clarke's hydrometer. In 1802, the Board of Excise held a competition to improve on this instrument for revenue purposes and 19 pieces were submitted for consideration. The winning design was that of Bartholemew Sikes, a London employee of the excise commissioners. Sike's hydrometer was enshrined in legislation in 1816 with the Sikes Hydrometer Act and remained the legal standard until 1907, although they remained in common use until 1980.

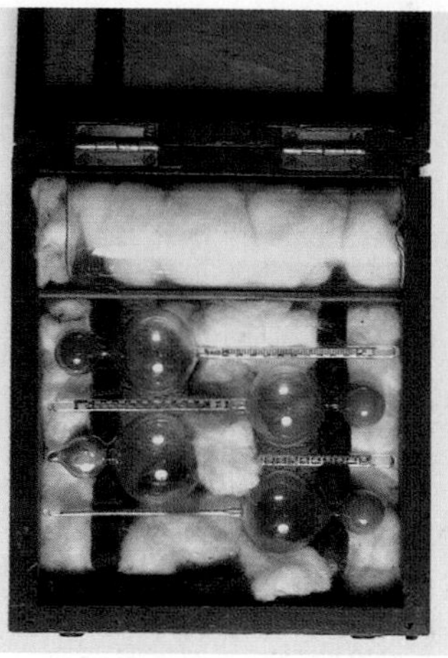

A five-piece Sikes hydrometer set, by Thomas Armstrong & Brothers, with four mercury bulbs and glass sample jar, in a mahogany case, signed, c1875, 5in (12.5cm) wide.
£260–290 / €380–420
$470–520 ⊞ FOF

A bronze standard half gallon measure, inscribed 'Potter, Poultry, London', 19thC, 6¼in (16cm) diam.
£230–270 / €340–390
$420–490 ⚒ F&C

► Ten brass county bushel measures, by Bate, London, each stamped 'Middlesex London County Council' and with royal crests, some with handles, peck measure missing, the replaced ¼ gill stamped 'County of Kent 1872', dated 1890, largest 20in (51cm) diam.
£3,600–4,300 / €5,300–6,300
$6,500–7,800 ⚒ S

A silver pedometer, by William Payne & Co, London, with an enamel dial, steel hand and engine-turned case, London 1863, 1½in (4cm) diam.
£220–250 / €320–370
$400–450 ⊞ FOF

A pedometer determines the distance walked by counting your footsteps. Leonardo Da Vinci identified this principle some 250 years before the first mechanical examples came into being. The device records angular displacement in a horizontal plane through a system of springs and gears to be recorded on a circular dial. Examples can be found in base metal as well as precious metal cases from about 1780 onwards.

Weights & Measures

Popular collecting areas are:

- Guinea Scales, introduced in 1774 by Anthony Wilkinson of Ormskirk and used to weigh new standard guinea and half guinea coins.
- Brass rocker or Sovereign scales (1817) complete with their close-fitting two-piece card case. These are found with various improvements to the patent including Harrison and Simpson's versions.
- Small boxed Georgian beam scales to weigh gold coins.
- Larger beam scales, which were used extensively. For example, bakers were required by law to carry them on their rounds until 1926 and were still required to have them in their shops until 1964, to determine the actual weight of each loaf of bread.

A silver pedometer, by Negretti & Zambra, in a morocco case, c1870, 1in (2.5cm) wide.
£180–200 / €260–290
$330–360 ⊞ RTW

► A set of Georgian brass travelling guinea scales, by A. Wilkinson, Ormskirk, 5in (12.5cm) long.
£210–240 / €310–350
$380–430 ⊞ FOF

◄ A 12in brass presentation sector, by J. Sisson, with a 3in gilt-brass miniature sector, signed, mid-18thC, in a hinged mahogany case, 13½in (34.5cm) wide.
£1,800–2,150
€2,650–3,150
$3,250–3,900 ⚒ S

Marine

Barometers

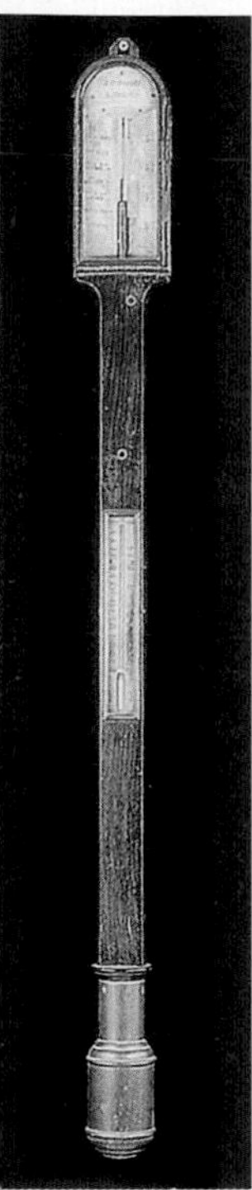

◄ **A rosewood marine barometer,** by Joseph Hughes, London, with signed ivory plates, inset with a mercury thermometer and brass cistern cover, gimbal missing, c1865, 37in (94cm) high.
£1,000–1,200
€1,450–1,750
$1,800–2,150 ⚒ S

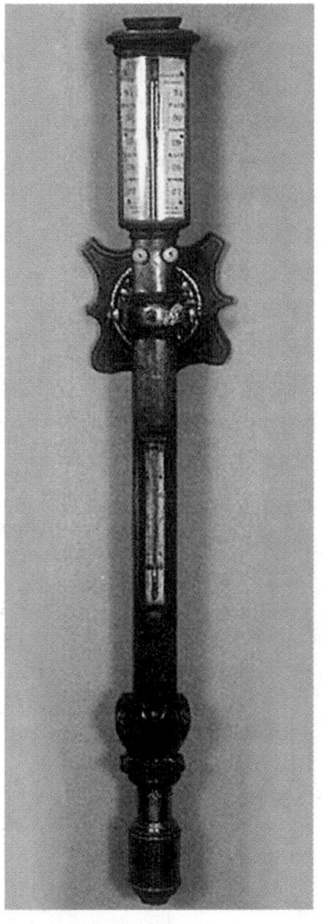

► **A Victorian walnut bowfronted marine stick barometer and gimbal,** by P. A. Feathers, Dundee, the ivory dials with vernier scales above two bone adjusters, the body with foliate carving and a brass well, on a brass and walnut bracket, Scottish, 37in (94cm) high.
£2,350–2,800
€3,450–4,100
$4,250–5,100 ⚒ WW
Peter Airth Feathers was at 26 Dock Street from 1853–63. During the 19th century Dundee was an important whaling port.

A Victorian brass aneroid barometer, set in a ship's wheel, with an anchor thermometer and a compass on a marble base, 6½in (16.5cm) wide.
£300–360 / €440–530
$540–650 ⚒ G(L)

Insurance values

Always insure your valuable antiques for the cost of replacing them with similar items, regardless of the original price paid. Both dealers and auctioneers can provide a valuation service for a fee.

Chronometers & Timekeepers

A two-day marine chronometer, by Parkinson & Frodsham, London, in a three-tier mahogany box, c1825, 7in (18cm) wide.
£5,000–5,500
€7,200–8,000
$9,100–10,000 ⊞ JeF

A mahogany one-day marine chronometer, by Joseph Simmons, London, No. 15, the fusee movement with maintaining power, Earnshaw's spring detent escapement, compensation balance, unusual count to train, the brass bowl gimbal-mounted in a brass-bound box, c1850, 6¾in (17cm) wide.
£2,200–2,600
€3,200–3,800
$4,000–4,700 ⚒ S

A mahogany marine chronometer, by Sutherland Davies & Co, Liverpool, the silvered dials with subsidiary seconds and adjustment dials, the case with brass side handles, late 19thC, 6¼in (16cm) wide.
£1,150–1,350
€1,700–2,000
$2,100–2,500
⚒ SK

A brass-plated and gilded clock, barometer and compass compendium, by Whytock & Sons, Paris, with an enamel dial, the top with a compass, the onyx plinth with enamel quartering on a cannon-ball-set ratchet, French, 19thC, 8in (20.5cm) wide.
£1,350–1,600
€1,950–2,350
$2,450–2,900 ⚒ NSal

◄ **A teak marine deck watch/chronometer,** by Waltham Watch Co, the watch case engraved 'US Navy No. 1156', the signed silvered dial with subsidiary power reserve and seconds dials, eight-day keyless movement, in a brass-bound case, American, early 20thC, 5in (12.5cm) wide.
£610–730 / €890–1,050
$1,100–1,300 ⚒ DN(BR)

A brass ship's bulkhead timepiece and matching barometer, by Sherman D. Neill, Belfast, on a later wood plinth, early 20thC, 23in (58.5cm) wide.
£230–270 / €340–400
$420–500 ⚒ NSal

Model Ships

◄ **A bone model of a three-masted sailing vessel,** 19thC, 15½in (39.5cm) wide, in a later case.
£1,500–1,800 / €2,200–2,650
$2,700–3,250 ⚒ E

A varnished pine pond yacht, with a planked hull, projecting fin and a simulated planked deck, early 20thC, 38½in (98cm) wide.
£350–420 / €510–610
$630–760 ⚒ DMC

◄ **A pond yacht,** with a planked hull, on a stand, early 20thC, hull 48in (122cm) wide.
£520–620 / €760–910
$940–1,100 ⚒ HOK

A sailor's model of a lightship, the hull inscribed 'Selker' to either side, with lifeboats and flying the Red Ensign, in a glazed wooden display case, late 19thC, 16½in (42cm) wide.
£175–210 / €260–310
$320–380 ⚒ PFK
Selker Bay is situated off the south Cumbrian coast (formerly Lancashire) near Millom.
The vessel broke away from its moorings during a storm in February 1903 and became grounded on the beach at Drigg.

Cross Reference
See Toys pages 661–672

Nautical Handicrafts

A scrimshaw whale's tooth, engraved with comical scenes, 19thC, 5¼in (13.5cm) high.
£430–510 / €630–740
$780–920 ⚒ TMA

◄ **A Victorian woolwork picture of two yachts at sea,** in a maple frame, 12 x 17½in (30.5 x 44.5cm).
£670–800 / €980–1,150
$1,200–1,450 ⚒ G(L)

A multi-media picture of the sailing boat *America*, attributed to Thomas H. Willis, worked with velvet and silk sails and silk thread embroidery on a painted canvas ground, American, c1900, 20¼ x 26in (51.5 x 66cm), framed.
£2,800–3,350 / €4,100–4,900
$5,100–6,100 ⚒ S(NY)

◄ **A scrimshaw whale's tooth,** engraved with a sailor beneath a flag, damaged, early 19thC, 4¾in (12cm) high.
£610–730 / €890–1,050
$1,100–1,300 ⚒ SWO

► **A sailor's scrimshaw whale's tooth watch stand,** the whalebone and tortoiseshell watch stand with a scrolled finial, flanked by whale's teeth engraved with portraits of a knight and a lady, on a whalebone tortoiseshell-veneered base with a key drawer, c1875, 8in (20.5cm) wide.
£3,350–4,000 / €4,900–5,800
$6,100–7,200 ⚒ S(O)

A shell ornament, in a mahogany frame, 19thC, 10¼in (26cm) wide.
£540–640 / €790–930
$980–1,150 ⚒ Mal(O)

Navigational Instruments

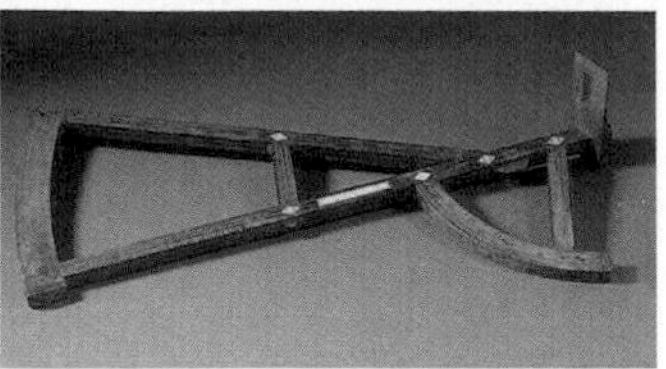

A boxwood and lignum vitae backstaff, the frame set with ivory inserts and joints, the arcs stamped and decorated with Tudor roses and stars, with an ivory name plaque stamped and dated 'Isaac Gorham 1763', with single sighting vane, 22in (56cm) overall.
£2,400–2,850 / €3,500–4,150
$4,350–5,200 ⚒ S
A backstaff was used for taking the altitude of the heavenly bodies, and is now superseded by the quadrant and sextant. It is so-called because the observer turned his back to the body observed.

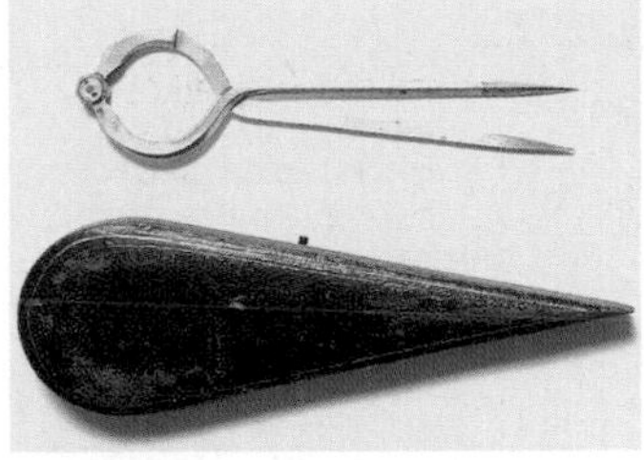

A pair of silver nautical dividers, with steel tips, German, c1800, 7in (18cm) long, in original leather case.
£200–230 / €290–340
$360–430 ⊞ FOF

A miniature sextant, by King & Son, Bristol, with a silvered scale, signed brass frame, two sets of interchangeable filters, index arm, magnifier, vernier and mirror, in a fitted mahogany case with an additional telescope, 1825–50, 5¼in (13.5cm) radius.
£500–600 / €730–880
$910–1,100 ⚒ S

► A double-frame sextant, by Cary, London, in a wooden box, with accessories, c1850, 11¾in (30cm) wide.
£1,800–2,000 / €2,600–2,900
$3,250–3,600 ⊞ ET

Ships' Fittings

A ship's bell, inscribed 'T.S.S. *Orcades* 1948 London', 16in (40.5cm) high.
£730–870 / €1,050–1,250
$1,300–1,550 ⚒ PF

◄ A carved and painted pine ship's figurehead, in the form of a dragoon officer, remains of iron mounting rod attached, right arm replaced, feet missing, American, c1850, 50in (127cm) high.
£13,300–16,000
€19,400–23,400
$24,000–29,000
⚒ S(NY)

A mahogany and brass ship's wheel, c1880, 55in (139.5cm) diam.
£450–500 / €660–730
$810–910 ⊞ JUN

Miscellaneous

A painted pine seaman's chest, with a hinged lid, the underside decorated with a tall ship, monogrammed 'G.T. 91', with rope handles to either side, late 19thC, 37in (94cm) wide.
£490–580 / €720–850
$890–1,050 ⚒ SWO

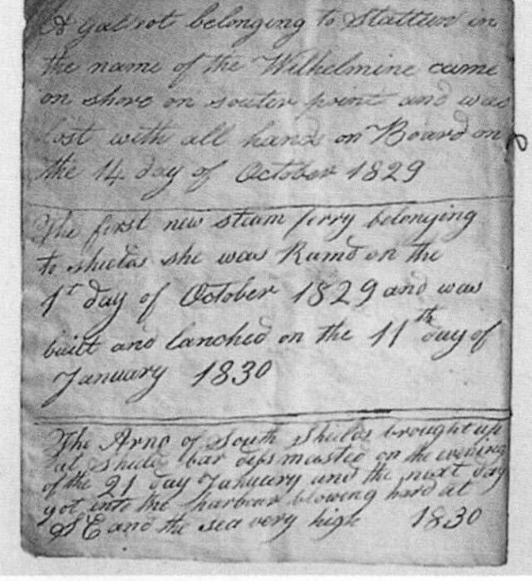

A galliot belonging to Stettin in the name of the Wilhelmine came on shore on souter point and was lost with all hands on Board on the 14 day of October 1829

The first new steam ferry belonging to shields she was Rund on the 1st day of October 1829 and was built and lanched on the 11th day of January 1830

The Arno of South Shields brought up at Shields bar dismasted on the evening of the 21 day January and the next day got into the harbour blowing hard at SE and the sea very high 1830

A manuscript record of employment of the South Shields Lifeboat 1814–46, 34 entries on 14 pages, slight damage, small 4°.
£240–280 / €350–410
$430–510 ⚒ F&C

A brass vesta case, with a copper plaque inscribed 'Copper from *Foudroyant*, launched 1798 and wrecked in 1897 at Blackpool', late 19thC, 2in (5cm) wide.
£90–100 / €130–145
$160–180 ⊞ MB
***Foudroyant* was Admiral Lord Nelson's flagship.**

Cameras

◄ **An Agfa Karat 12/2.8 camera,** with Karat-Xenar f2.8/5cm lens, the coupled rangefinder with 12 exposure Karat cassettes and case, German, 1948–50.
£330–370 / €480–540 $600–670 ⊞ CaH

A Berning Robot 11 motor-driven camera, German, c1940.
£135–150 / €195–220 $240–270 ⊞ APC

A Butcher Popular Prestman quarter-plate camera, with an Aldis Anastigmat f4.5/6in lens, 15 plate backs and a leather case, 1909–26.
£110–125 / €160–180 $200–230 ⊞ CaH

◄ **A Bradac-Prague camera,** Kamarad MII with Trioplan f2.9/7.5cm lens, Czechoslovakian, c1937.
£120–135 / €175–195 $220–250 ⊞ CaH

A Contessa-Nettel Sonnett Tropical teak camera, with a Carl Zeiss Jena Tessar f/3.5/7.5cm lens and leather bellows, c1915, in a leather case.
£210–250 / €310–370 $380–450 ⚒ SK

A Graflex Century Graphic camera, with a Kodak Ektar f4.5/101mm lens, No. 1 Kodak Supermatic shutter synch, Hugo Meyer Model 2PG Precision Rangefinder and three film holders, American, 1949–70.
£380–430 / €550–630 $690–780 ⊞ CaH

A George Hare quarter-plate tailboard camera, c1890.
£155–175 / €220–250 $280–310 ⊞ APC

A Graflex Speed Graphic press camera, American, 1930s.
£135–150 / €195–220 $240–270 ⊞ APC

Items in the Cameras section have been arranged in alphabetical order by maker.

A Kodak EKC No. 3 Cartridge camera, American, c1900.
£135–150 / €195–220 $240–270 ⊞ APC

A Kodak Regent camera, with a Xenar f4.5/10.5cm lens, American, 1935–39.
£120–135 / €175–195 $220–250 ⊞ CaH

A Lancaster mahogany Instantograph quarter-plate camera, c1895.
£200–230 / €300–340 $360–410 ⊞ ARP

A Lancaster mahogany Instantograph full-plate camera, c1900.
£360–400 / €520–580
$650–720 ⊞ ARP

A Leica IIIf camera, No. 66752, with an extra lens and instruction manuals, c1950, with a leather case.
£350–420 / €510–610
$630–760 ⚒ G(L)

A Lizars Tropical Dayspool roll film camera, c1905.
£360–400 / €520–580
$650–720 ⊞ APC

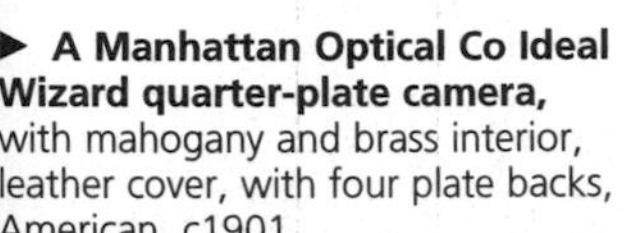

► A Manhattan Optical Co Ideal Wizard quarter-plate camera, with mahogany and brass interior, leather cover, with four plate backs, American, c1901.
£185–210 / €270–300
$340–380 ⊞ CaH

A Meagher mahogany stereo tailboard camera, c1885.
£630–700 / €920–1,050
$1,100–1,250 ⊞ APC

◄ A Newman & Guardia Special Pattern B camera, with a Zeiss patent 9in lens, the mahogany changing box with a doe-skin manipulating pouch, c1905.
£290–330 / €430–480
$520–580 ⊞ ARP

A Newman & Guardia Sibyl Imperial Model 8 quarter-plate camera, with a Carl Zeiss Tessar lens, film sheath, cable release, cased lens hood and case, 1912–13.
£290–330 / €430–480
$520–580 ⊞ CaH

A Victorian Perken, Son & Rayment brass-mounted mahogany half-plate camera, with a Rapid & Reddistart f.8 lens by Sands, Hutton & Co, London, with leather bellows and manual aperture adjustment and one darkslide.
£100–120 / €145–175
$185–220 ⚒ PFK

A Rochester Optical Co camera, with a Reko Bausch & Lomb f8-f128 lens and a leather-covered mahogany body with brass trim, c1899.
£100–115 / €150–170
$180–200 ⊞ CaH

A Tele Rolleiflex Type 1 camera, model No. 220, with a Zeiss Sonnar f4/135 lens, with associated external frame counter, cap and strap, German, 1959–75.
£840–940 / €1,250–1,400
$1,500–1,700 ⊞ CaH

LOCATE THE SOURCE

The source of each illustration in Miller's can be found by checking the code letters below each caption with the Key to Illustrations, pages 778–784.

► A Sanderson quarter-plate field camera, c1910.
£400–450 / €580–660
$720–810 ⊞ ARP

A Sanderson Junior Model Series V camera, with a No. 1 lens, the leather casewith a mahogany and brass interior, 1920–30.
£180–200 / €260–290
$320–360 ⊞ CaH

A Thornton Pickard mahogany Ruby half-plate field camera, c1900.
£290–330 / €430–480
$520–580 ⊞ ARP

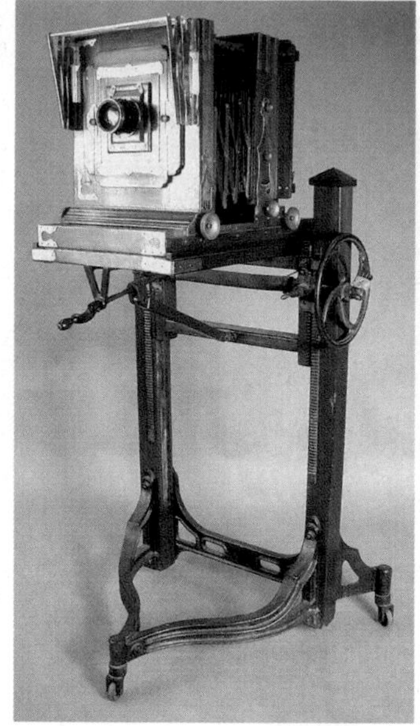

◄ A Victorian Taylor, Taylor & Hobson mahogany and cast-iron studio camera, with 460mm apochromatic lens and bellows action, 62¼in (158cm) high.
£700–840 / €1,000–1,200
$1,250–1,500 ⚒ SWO

◄ A Voigtländer Bergheil camera, with a Heliar f4.5/10.5cm lens, c1930.
£105–120
€155–175
$200–220
⊞ CaH

A Voigtländer Bessa RF camera, with a Helomar f3.5/10.5cm lens, the coupled rangefinder with filter, c1936, with case.
£210–240 / €310–350
$380–430 ⊞ CaH

◄ A Wray Stereo Graphic camera, with Wray Stereo f4/35mm lenses, American, 1959–62, with case.
£120–140 / €175–200
$220–250 ⊞ CaH

► A Zeiss Ikon A (520) camera, with a Tessar f3.5/7cm lens, German, 1933–40.
£95–110 / €140–160
$170–200 ⊞ CaH

A Zeiss Ikon Super Ikonta camera, Model 530/16, German, 1935.
£135–150 / €195–220
$240–270 ⊞ ARP

A Zeiss Ikon Okoflex Favourite twin lens reflex camera, German, c1957.
£165–185 / €240–270
$300–330 ⊞ ARP

A mahogany and brass half-plate field camera, c1900.
£155–175 / €220–250
$280–310 ⊞ APC

A mahogany and brass quarter-plate field camera, c1915.
£155–175 / €220–250
$280–310 ⊞ APC

Optical Devices & Viewers

A Rowsell's Patent walnut parlour graphoscope, c1875, 23¾in (60cm) wide.
£400–450 / €580–650
$720–810 ⊞ APC

A Brewster Patent kaleidoscope, with four phials, c1860, 6¼in (16cm) long, with fitted case.
£2,250–2,500 / €3,250–3,650
$4,000–4,500 ⊞ APC

A kaleidoscope, on a fruitwood base, French, c1880, 8in (20.5cm) long.
£270–300 / €390–440
$490–540 ⊞ APC

A mahogany magic lantern, c1880, 27½in (70cm) long.
£220–250 / €320–360
$400–450 ⊞ APC

An iron and brass magic lantern, Russian, c1900, 18in (45.5cm) long.
£160–180 / €230–260
$290–330 ⊞ ARP

A mahogany magic lantern, c1910, 26in (66cm) long.
£310–350 / €450–510
$560–630 ⊞ JUN

A Cosmorama-style stereoscope, on a stand, c1850, 14¼in (36cm) high.
£450–500 / €650–730
$810–900 ⊞ ET

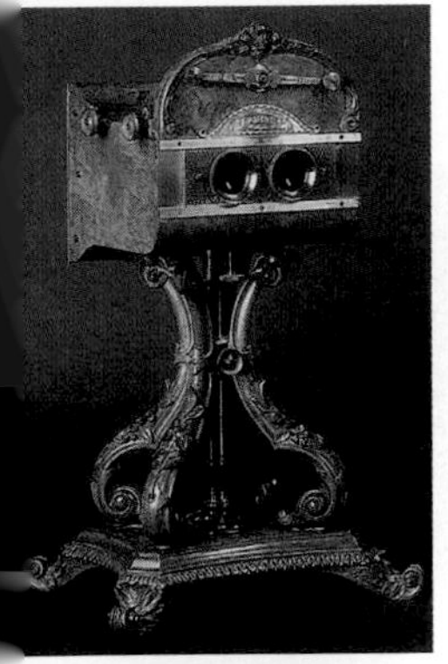

◄ **A figured walnut Natural Stereoscope,** by J. Wood, Huddersfield, with achromatic lens with lateral adjustment, slide holder with rack-and-pinion focusing, slide door, two double sets of rollers holding tinted tissue filters, on adjustable brass column, one set of rollers missing, 19thC, 22½in (57cm) high, with 14 topographical stereo positives in a stained wood box.
£11,000–13,200 / €16,000–19,200
$19,900–24,000 ⚒ SK

Patented in 1862, the Natural Stereoscope was designed by John Hirst and Joseph Wood of York. Several designs are known: a plain version, an Art Nouveau design and the deluxe model shown here. The decoration differed between examples of the same model, and the Royal feathers on the pediment is an unusual feature in this viewer.

A reversible Schneck-pattern stereoscope, with walnut lensboard, velvet-covered hood, focusing rack, card holder and adjustable pole holding magnifying lens, on a nickel-plated pillar and velvet-covered base, late 19thC, 17in (43cm) high, with 19 views.
£610–730 / €890–1,050
$1,100–1,300 ⚒ SK

A mahogany Le Taxiphote table-top stereoscopic slide viewer, with maker's label, instructions and 24 glass slides, 19thC, 24in (61cm) high.
£590–700 / €860–1,000
$1,050–1,250 ⚒ G(L)

A tinplate zoetrope, with 12 films, on a mahogany stand, c1860, 15¾in (40cm) high.
£540–600 / €790–870
$980–1,100 ⊞ APC

◄ **A fruitwood zograscope,** with ebony and boxwood-strung lens frame and mirror frame between turned uprights, adjustable stem, 19thC, 31in (78.5cm) high extended.
£410–490 / €600–720
$740–890 ⚒ PFK

Photographs

H. Agius, 'Panoramic View of the Great Harbour, Malta', albumen prints, four-part panorama, slight damage, c1880, 7¼ x 38¾in (18.5 x 98.5cm).
£175–210 / €260–310
$320–380 BBA

Manuel Álvarez Bravo, 'Instrumental (Instrumental)', silver print, matted, signed to reverse, inscribed 'Mexico', Mexican, 1931, printed later, 8 x 10in (20.5 x 25.5cm).
£2,150–2,550 / €3,150–3,700
$3,900–4,600 S

Diane Arbus, 'Two Ladies at the Automat, N.Y.C. 1966', later silver print by Neil Selkirk, signed, titled, numbered '52/75' by the photographer's daughter, Doon Arbus, stamped, American, 1980, 20 x 16in (51 x 40.5cm).
£9,000–10,800 / €13,100–15,800
$16,300–19,500 S

Emmy Andriesse, 'Children in the Kattenburg Neighbourhood, Amsterdam', silver print, mounted on card, stamp to reverse, Dutch, 1944–45, printed later, 7½ x 7in (19 x 18cm).
£980–1,150 / €1,450–1,700
$1,800–2,100 S(Am)

Eve Arnold, 'Marilyn Monroe, Arthur Miller, Nevada 1960', silver print, signed, titled and dated to reverse, American, 12 x 15¾in (30.5 x 40cm).
£1,650–1,950 / €2,400–2,850
$3,000–3,550 S

Felice Beato, 'Panorama of Kobe, from the hills above, shipping in the harbour', two-plate, albumen print, later overmount with original album caption 'Kobi, Japan 1872', 8 x 20in (20.5 x 51cm).
£400–480 / €580–700
$720–870 BBA

► **Cecil Beaton,** the Earl and Countess of Harewood, c1950, 10 x 7in (25.5 x 18cm).
£135–150 / €195–220
$240–270 AEL

Fratelli Alinari, 'Chiesa di S. Michelea Arcangelo, Lucca', albumen print, stamped, printed title, slight damage and repair, Italian, 1885, 17 x 22in (43.5 x 56cm).
£55–65 / €80–95
$100–120 DW

Thomas Annan, 'Old Vennel, Off High Street', Glasgow, carbon print, matted, printed title, Scottish, 1886–77, 10½ x 8¾in (26.5 x 22cm).
£1,000–1,200 / €1,450–1,750
$1,800–2,150 S

Eve Arnold, 'Marilyn, Nevada, 1960', cibachrome print, signed, titled and dated to reverse, American, 12 x 16in (30.5 x 40.5cm).
£720–860 / €1,050–1,250
$1,300–1,550 S

:va Besnyö, 'Boy with Bass, Hungary', ilver print, inscribed and stamped to everse, Dutch, 1931, printed later, 10¾ x 9in (27.5 x 23cm).
:3,250–3,900 / €4,750–5,700
,5,900–7,100 ⚒ S(Am)

ill Brandt, 'Co. Galway. Stone ottages near Kilkieran', silver print, natted, titled in ink, stamped to everse, before 1947, printed before 961, 9¾ x 7¾in (25 x 19.5cm).
:3,600–4,300 / €5,300–6,300
,6,500–7,800 ⚒ S

Brassaï (Gyula Halász), 'Picasso t Notre-Dame-de-Vie, 1966,' silver rint, signed, stamped to reverse, rench, printed later, 11¾ x 9¼in 30 x 23.5cm).
840–1,000 / €1,250–1,500
1,500–1,800 ⚒ S

Items in the Photographs section have been arranged in alphabetical order by photographer.

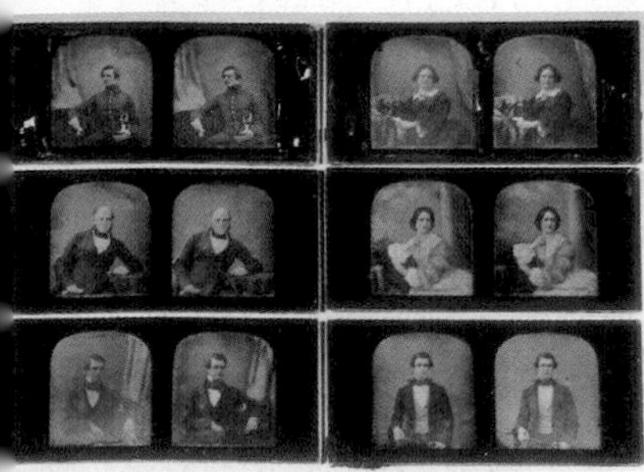

ntoine Claudet, a set of six daguerreotype ortrait frames, in a velvet-lined mahogany box vith an ivory keyplate, 7½in (19cm) wide.
1,450–1,700 / €2,100–2,500
2,600–3,100 ⚒ Mal(O)

Eva Besnyö, 'Starnberger Strasse, Berlin', silver print, signed to reverse, Dutch, 1931, printed later, 19¾ x 16in (50.5 x 40.5cm).
£3,700–4,400 / €5,400–6,400
$6,700–8,000 ⚒ S(Am)

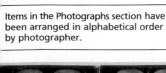

Bill Brandt, 'Connemara Landscape (Stream)', silver print, matted, before 1947, printed before 1961, 10 x 8in (25.5 x 20.5cm).
£840–1,000 / €1,250–1,500
$1,500–1,800 ⚒ S

Samuel Bourne, 'The Hanter Pass', albumen print from a collodion negative, 1868, 9¼ x 11½in (23.5 x 29cm).
£1,950–2,200 / €2,850–3,200
$3,550–4,000 ⊞ RHL

Brassaï (Gyula Halász), 'Matisse with a Bird in his Apartment, 132 Boulevard Montparnasse', silver print, signed, titled to reverse, stamped twice, French, 1933, printed later, 9 x 11in (23 x 28cm).
£600–720 / €880–1,050
$1,100–1,300 ⚒ S

Henri Cartier-Bresson, 'Mexico City', silver print, stamp to reverse, French, 1934, 8¾ x 11in (22 x 28cm).
£16,400–19,600 / €23,900–28,600
$29,700–35,000 ⚒ S(Am)

Patrick Demarchelier, 'Cindy Crawford, New York, '89', colour print, signed, titled and dated on overmount, French, 1989, 12 x 9¾in (30.5 x 25cm).
£1,050–1,250
€1,550–1,850
$1,900–2,250 ⚒ BBA

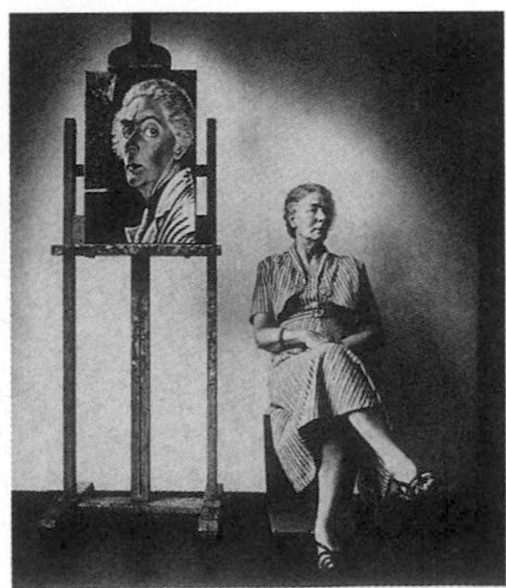

Ed van der Elsken, 'Portrait Charlie Toorop', silver print, mounted on card, signed in pencil to reverse, Dutch, 1955, 9½ x 9¼in (24 x 23.5cm).
£1,550–1,850 / €2,250–2,700
$2,800–3,350 ⚒ S(Am)

Karoly Escher, 'Budapest', silver print, printer labels to reverse, Hungarian, 1931, 6½ x 8¾in (16.5 x 22cm).
£5,400–6,400 / €7,900–9,300
$9,800–11,600 S(Am)

William Henry Fox Talbot, 'Bridge of Sighs, St John's College, Cambridge', salted paper print from a calotype negative, c1844, 7¼ x 9in (18.5 x 23cm).
£25,000–30,000 / €37,000–44,000
$45,000–54,000 RHL

Ralph Gibson, untitled, silver print, dated and numbered '8/25', American, 1976, 20 x 16in (51 x 40.5cm).
£600–720 / €880–1,050
$1,100–1,300 S

Thomas Höpker, 'Norwegian Tourists near Giza Pyramids, Egypt', c-print, mounted with Plexiglass, signed, titled and dated in ink, stamped and numbered 3/6 to reverse, 1962, printed later, 7 x 4½in (18 x 11.5cm).
£4,500–5,400
€6,600–7,900
$8,100–9,800 S(Am)

◄ **Horst P. Horst,** 'Helen Bennett with Cape Dress', silver print, stamped, signed, titled and dated 1936 in pencil, stamped to reverse 'This silver print comes from one of a set of three portfolios printed to date to commemorate Horst's 90th birthday' German, printed later, 19¾ x 15¾in (50 x 40cm).
£3,250–3,900
€4,750–5,700
$5,900–7,100 S(Am)

► **Aart Klein,** 'Wasvrouw Coimbra – Portugal', silver print, mounted, signed and inscribed, Dutch, dated 1949, printed later, 14¾ x 11¾in (37.5 x 30cm).
£740–880
€1,100–1,300
$1,350–1,600 S(Am)

Irina Ionesco, 'Izis', gelatin silver print, signed, titled and inscribed 'Tirage d'Epoque' to reverse, French, 1986, 15½ x 10½in (39.5 x 26.5cm).
£115–135 / €170–200
$210–250 BBA

William Lake Price, 'Portrait of the Painter, William Frith', albumen print from a collodion negative, c1855, 11¼ x 9½in (28.5 x 24cm).
£9,000–10,000
€13,100–14,600
$16,300–18,100 RHL

Robert Mapplethorpe, 'Tulip', dye transfer print, stamped and signed by Michael Ward Stout as executor, American, 1988, 24 x 20in (61 x 51cm).
£24,000–28,800 / €35,000–42,000
$43,000–52,000 S

Josiah Martin, 'Te Kooti's House', albumen print New Zealand, c1888, 6 x 8in (15 x 20.5cm).
£290–340 / €420–500
$520–620 WEBB

► **Nelly (Elli Seraidari),** 'The Dancer Nikolska in the Parthenon', silver bromide print, stamped, Greek, 1929, 6½ x 8¾in (16.5 x 22cm).
£6,600–7,900
€9,600–11,500
$11,900–14,300 S

Helmut Newton, 'Twiggy, August 1966', silver print, matted, inscribed 'To John, much love and best wishes, Twiggy' to reverse, stamped, 10¼ x 15in (26 x 38cm).
£1,000–1,200 / €1,450–1,750
$1,800–2,150 S

Terry O'Neill, 'Sean Connery and Brigitte Bardot', silver print signed and stamped to reverse, 1967, printed 1985, 16 x 12in (40.5 x 30.5cm).
£660–790 / €960–1,150
$1,200–1,450 S

Norman Parkinson, 'Fashion Study, Jill Kennington', silver print, matted, early 1960s, 19½ x 14½in (49.5 x 37cm).
£2,600–3,100
€3,800–4,550
$4,700–5,500 S

Ruth Orkin, 'Robert Capa', silver print, matted, stamp to reverse, American, 1952, printed later, 9¾ x 9¼in (24.5 x 23.5cm).
£1,450–1,700
€2,100–2,500
$2,600–3,100 S(Am)

Man Ray, 'Gertrude Stein 1924', silver print, titled, stamped and dated to reverse, 8¼ x 6½in (21 x 16.5cm).
£2,600–3,100
€3,800–4,550
$4,700–5,500 S

George W. Scott, 'Chief Gall', a cabinet card photograph, slight damage, American, 6½ x 4¼in (16.5 x 11.5cm).
£350–420 / €510–610
$630–760 SK

Norman Parkinson, 'The Young Look in the Theatre', silver print, signed, 1953, printed later, 16 x 20in (40.5 x 51cm).
£840–1,000 / €1,250–1,500
$1,500–1,800 S

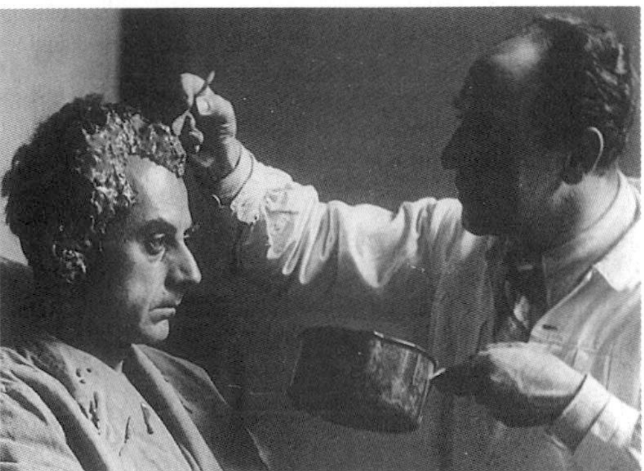

Man Ray, 'Paul Hamann making a life mask of Man Ray', silver print, titled and stamped to reverse, c1933, 4½ x 8¾in (11.5 x 22cm).
£3,200–3,800 / €4,650–5,500
$5,800–6,900 S

Art Shay, 'Madison Street with Algren', silver gelatin print, signed and titled, American, 1950, 10¾ x 17½in (27.5 x 44.5cm).
£450–540 / €660–790
$810–980 LHA

Roy Schatt, 'James Dean', from the Torn Sweater series, silver print, matted, signed and stamped to reverse, American, 1954, printed later, 17 x 13¾in (43 x 35cm).
£1,050–1,250
€1,550–1,850
$1,900–2,250 S

► **Art Shay,** 'Hugh Hefner at Mansion', silver gelatin print, signed and titled, American, 1968, 18¼ x 23½in (46.4 x 59.5cm).
£820–980 / €1,200–1,450
$1,500–1,800 LHA

Jeanloup Sieff, 'Ina', gelatin silver print, stamped to reverse, French, c1958, printed later, 15¼ x 10¼in (38.5 x 26cm).
£420–500 / €610–730
$760–910 ⚒ BBA

► **Christer Strömholm,** 'Boys with Handbags', silver gelatin print, signed and inscribed, Swedish, 1962, 17½ x 13¾in (44.5 x 35cm).
£1,800–2,150 / €2,650–3,150
$3,250–3,900 ⚒ BUK

Herbert Tobias, 'Allée Edgar Quinet, Paris - Montparnasse, 1952', silver print, signed and titled, stamped to reverse, framed and glazed, German, printed later, 19¾ x 15¾in (50 x 40cm).
£780–930 / €1,150–1,350
$1,450–1,700 ⚒ S

Anon, a one-sixth plate ambrotype of a seated Union NCO, American, c1865, 3¼ x 2¾in (8.5 x 7cm).
£110–130 / €160–190
$200–240 ⚒ JAA

Charles Spencer, 'Hot Baths, Pink Terrace', carbon print, New Zealand, c1884, 6 x 8in (15 x 20.5cm).
£240–280 / €350–410
$430–510 ⚒ WEBB

Peter Turnley, 'Café Lacour, Rue St Paul 1976', gelatin silver print, signed and dated, American, 14¼ x 9½in (36 x 24cm).
£640–760 / €930–1,100
$1,200–1,400 ⚒ BBA

For more photographs
see Ephemera pages 673–679

Bert Stern, 'Marilyn Monroe with Necklace', colour print, signed and stamped to reverse, American, 1962, printed 1982, 17 x 13¾in (43 x 35cm).
£1,900–2,250 / €2,750–3,300
$3,450–4,050 ⚒ S

Felix Teynard, 'Vue Générale Prise du Point 1, sur la Platforme du Premier Pylone', salted paper print by Fonteny, French, c1854, 9½ x 12¼in (24 x 31cm).
£19,800–22,000 / €28,900–32,000
$36,000–40,000 ⊞ RHL

Julien Vallou de Villeneuve, 'Nude Study', varnished salted paper print from a waxed paper negative, French, c1853, 6½ x 4¾in (16.5 x 12cm).
£15,700–17,500 / €22,900–25,600
$28,200–32,000 ⊞ RHL

► **Anon,** a black and white photograph of T. E. Lawrence on his Brough motorcycle, reverse inscribed by Lawrence 'Portrait of a contented airman', probably 1926, 4½ x 6¼in (11.5 x 16cm).
£630–750 / €920–1,100
$1,150–1,350 ⚒ DW

Arms & Armour

Armour

A cuirassier's armour, with 19thC arm and leg defences and backplate, German, c1620.
£7,700–9,200
€11,200–13,400
$13,900–16,700 Herm

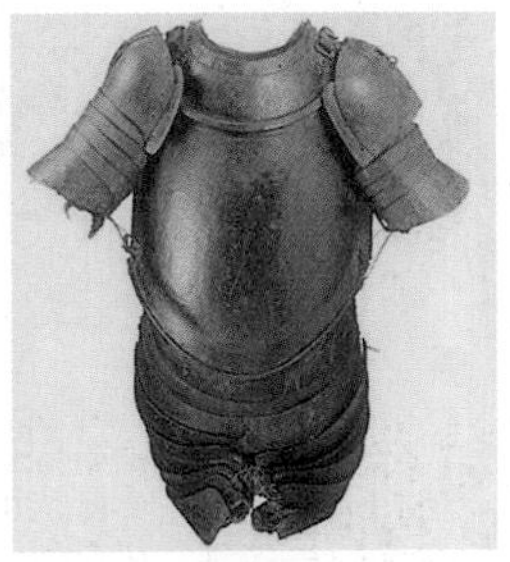

A sapper's siege armour, damaged, Continental, c1700.
£1,800–2,150
€2,650–3,150
$3,250–3,900 S(O)

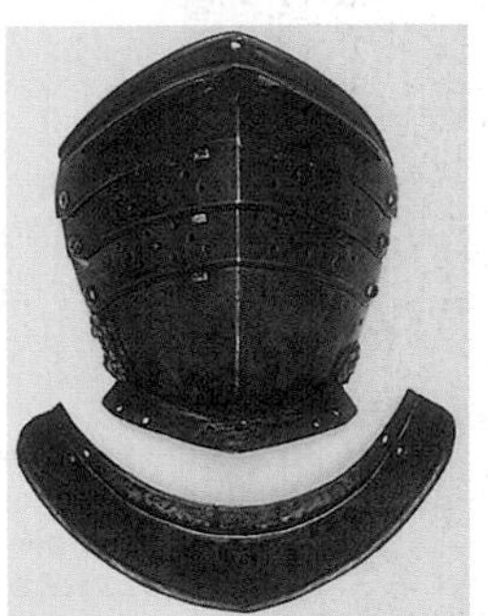

► A four-plate falling buffe, c1600, with two associated gorget plates.
£700–840 / €1,050–1,250
$1,250–1,500 WAL

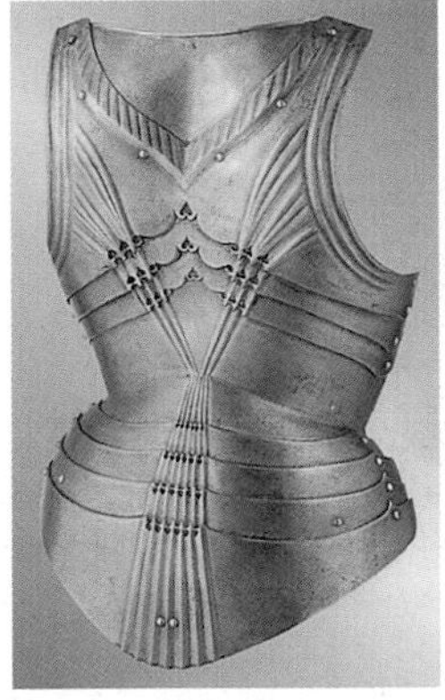

A backplate, minor repair, south German, 1480–90.
£9,200–11,000
€13,400–16,100
$16,700–19,900 Herm

A breastplate, with castle mark, north Italian, late 15thC.
£7,800–9,300
€11,400–13,600
$14,100–16,800 S(O)

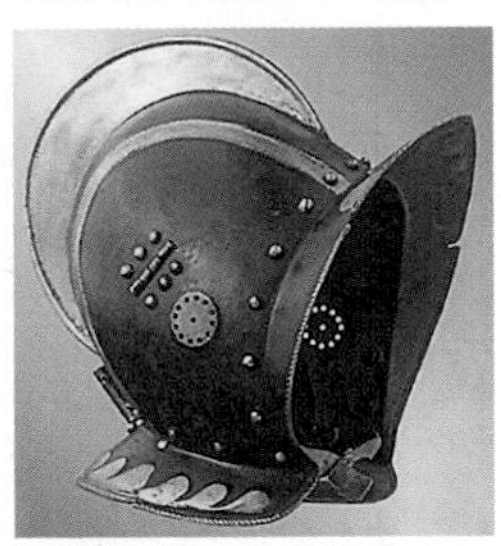

► A burgonet, with plume socket, stamped mark, German, Nuremberg, c1570.
£2,900–3,450
€4,250–5,000
$5,200–6,200 Herm

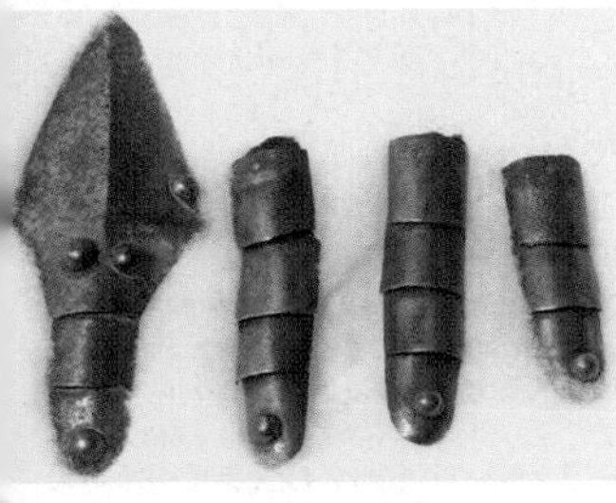

A chain-mail collar, late 15thC.
£9,600–11,500 / €14,000–16,800
$17,400–20,800 S(O)

A frontplate for a colletin, decorated with five coats-of-arms after Jan de Vries, probably French, 1620–40.
£1,800–2,150 / €2,650–3,150
$3,250–3,900 S(O)
The embossed trophies are inspired by a series of engravings entitled 'Panoplia', published in Antwerp by Jan Vredeman de Vries in 1572.

A pair of iron gauntlets, one with repair, German, 1550–1600.
£1,600–1,900 / €2,350–2,750
$2,900–3,450 Herm

A group of steel hand/finger guards, c1500.
£540–600 / €790–880
$980–1,100 ANG

A pair of sabatons, straps missing, German or Italian, probably 1450–1500.
£2,600–3,100 / €3,800–4,550
$4,700–5,600 S(O)

An officer's lobster-tail helmet, with an adjustable nose-piece and brass rivets, leather replaced, German, mid-17thC.
£3,550–4,250 / €5,200–6,200
$6,400–7,700 Herm

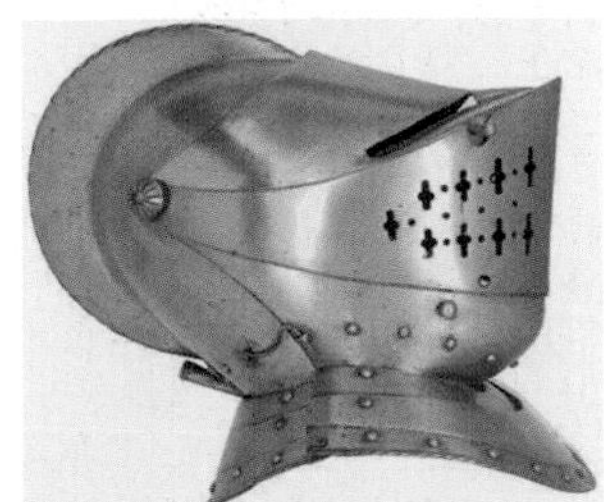

A close helmet, Italian, 1550–60.
£15,700–17,500 / €22,900–25,600
$28,400–32,000 FAC
The visor piercing on this helmet is executed in the German taste, suggesting that either the helmet was made for the German market or for an owner preferring the German form of ventilation. Armour of this quality was made to the specifications and taste of the owner and was influenced by a number of factors such as experience in battle or the advice of others.

Cannons

A pair of bronze saluting cannons, the lifting handles in the form of dolphins, each cast with a coat-of-arms and on a stepped wooden carriage, German or Dutch, dated 1638, barrels 19¾in (48.5cm) long.
£7,200–8,600 / €10,800–12,600
$13,000–15,600 ⚒ S(O)

► **A pair of bronze saluting cannons,** 18thC, 11¾in (30cm) long.
£1,850–2,200
€2,700–3,200
$3,350–4,000
⚒ BUK

◄ **A brass/bronze mortar,** on a later wooden base, c1840, 11in (28cm) long.
£1,200–1,400
€1,750–2,050
$2,200–2,550
⚒ WAL

Crossbows

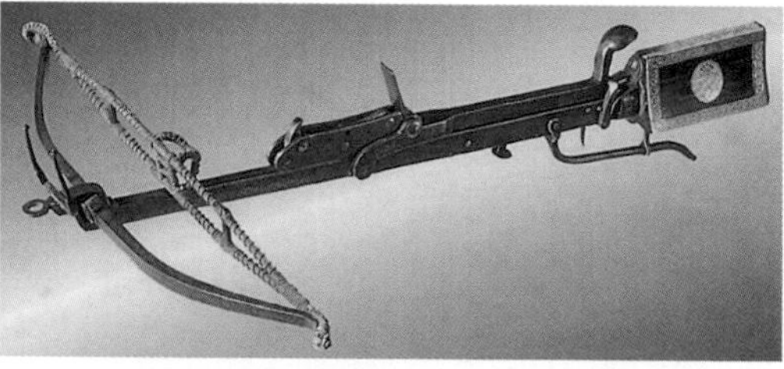

An iron stonebow, with twisted hemp cord, the ebonized stock with engraved decoration and inlaid with bone scrolls, the cheekpiece inlaid with mother-of-pearl coat-of-arms, c1580, 27½in (70cm) long.
£4,100–4,900 / €6,000–7,200
$7,400–8,900 ⚒ Herm

► **A steel stonebow,** by William Barker, Wigan, the figured walnut tiller inlaid with an engraved steel panel, No. 265, c1760, 30¼in (77cm) long.
£1,900–2,250 / €2,750–3,300
$3,450–4,050 ⚒ S(O)

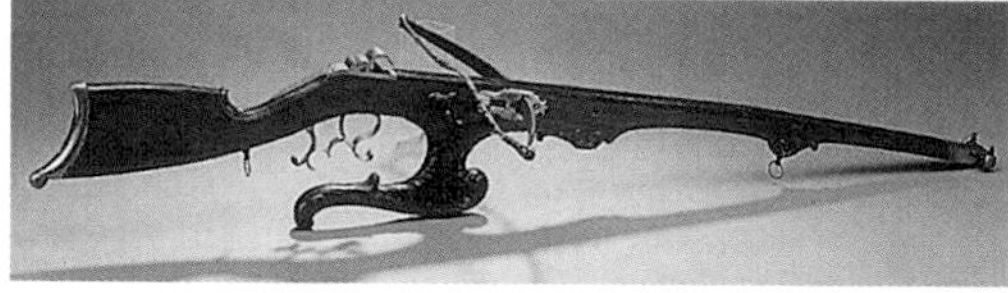

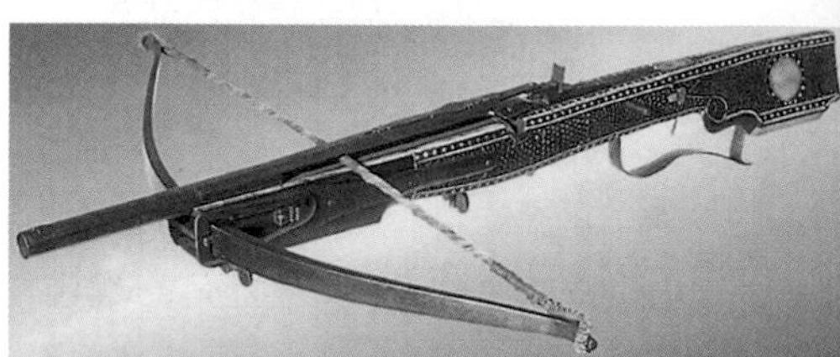

A steel crossbow, with an iron barrel and a later bow-string, the 16thC carved wood tiller with engraved plates and inlaid bone, German, 18thC, 33¼in (84.5cm) long.
£2,400–2,850 / €3,500–4,150
$4,350–5,200 ⚒ Herm

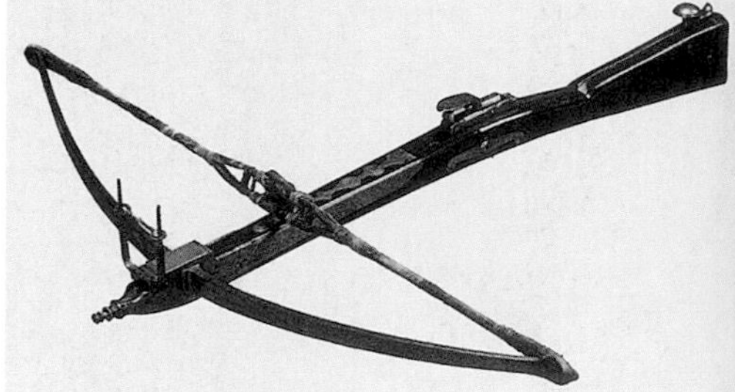

◄ **A carved fruitwood and mahogany crossbow,** with a foliate-carved support and brass and steel fire mechanism, German, 19thC, 47½in (121cm) long.
£890–1,050 / €1,300–1,550
$1,600–1,900 ⚒ S(Am)

Edged Weapons

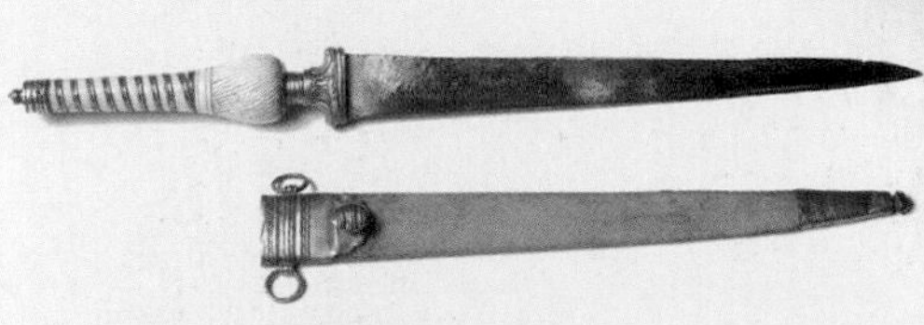

A silver-mounted hunting plug bayonet, with reversible grip scabbard, French, 18thC, 16in (40.5cm) long.
£1,800–2,000 / €2,600–2,900
$3,250–3,600 ⊞ WSA

► **A left-hand dagger,** with steel hilt, grip replaced, later scabbard, German, early 17thC, 16¾in (42.5cm) long.
£1,050–1,250 / €1,550–1,850
$1,900–2,250 ⚒ S(O)

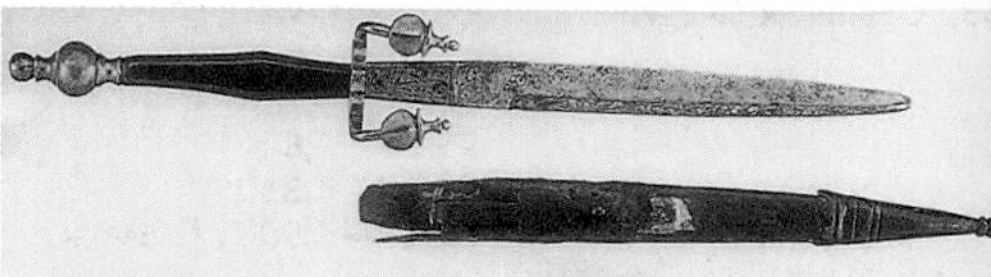

A dagger, with iron hilt, later wooden grip, the original fishskin-covered scabbard with iron mounts, scabbard damaged, Italian, probably Venetian, 1525–50, 12in (30.5cm) long.
£1,800–2,150 / €2,650–3,150
$3,250–3,900 ⚒ S(O)

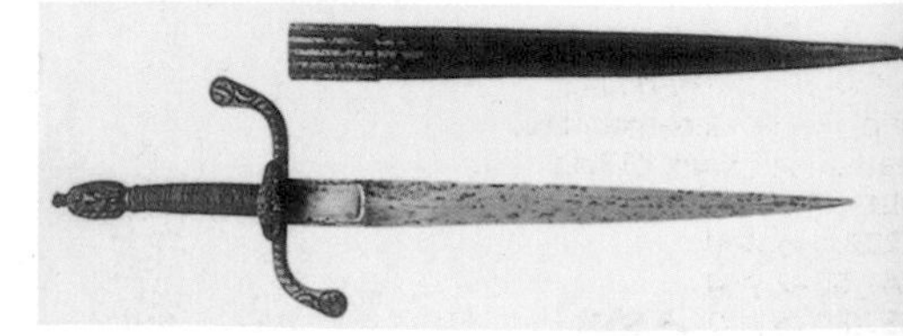

A Victorian military piper's dirk, by Robert Mole & Sons, etched with thistle leaves, with studded strapwork handle, stamped marks, with an iron-mounted leather scabbard, blade 11½in (29cm) long.
£330–390 / €480–570
$600–710 WAL

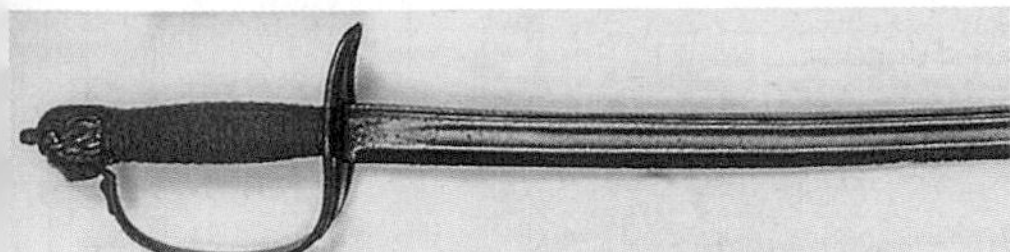

An officer's hanger, the brass knucklebow with a lion's head pommel, faint traces of gilt, with a simulated wire-bound copper grip, c1780, blade 26in (66cm) long.
£400–480 / €580–700
$720–870 WAL

A Bowie knife, by Barnes & Co, Sheffield, the bronze and brass grip cast with fish, with original scabbard, c1860, 16in (40.5cm) long.
£2,550–2,850 / €3,700–4,150
$4,600–5,200 MDL

A rapier, decorated with a bird, maker's mark, Spanish, c1660, blade 35in (89cm) long.
£1,700–1,900
€2,500–2,800
$3,100–3,450 FAC

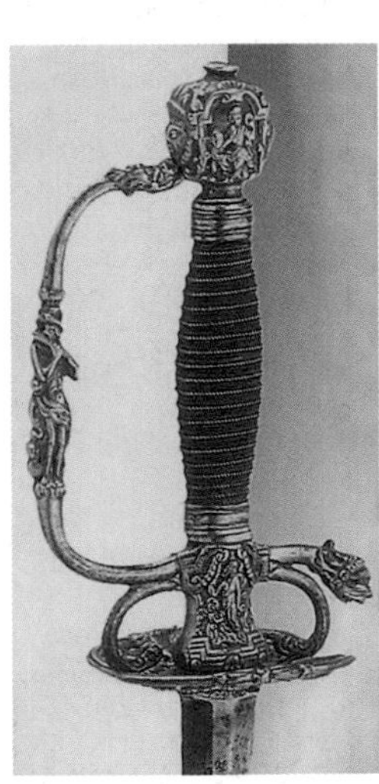

A court rapier, with gilt-brass hilt, the guard plate decorated with figures, with a copper wire grip, c1680, 37¼in (94.5cm) long.
£1,350–1,600
€1,950–2,350
$2,450–2,900 Herm

A sabre, the burnished steel hilt with an ivory-bound grip, with a steel-mounted leather scabbard, c1780, blade 26in (66cm) long.
£2,850–3,400
€4,150–4,950
$5,200–6,200 S(O)

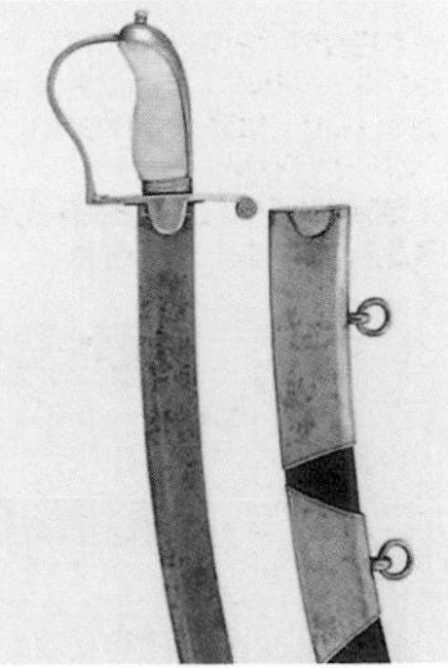

A Victorian regimental volunteer officer's dirk, set with extra pieces *en suite* with the hilt, in a leather-covered wooden scabbard, 15in (38cm) long.
£900–1,050 / €1,300–1,550
$1,650–1,900 S(O)

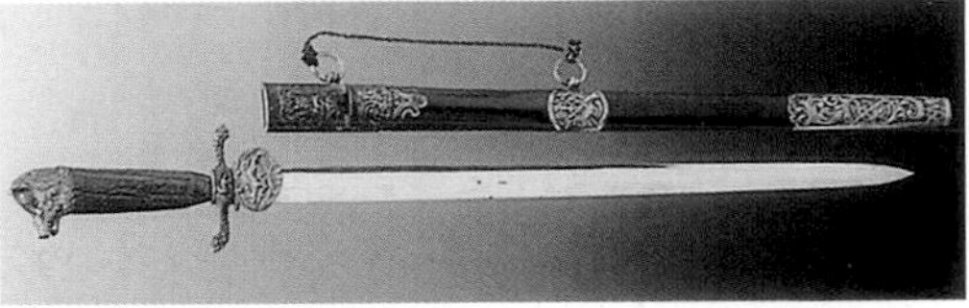

A hanger, the staghorn grip terminating in a carved wild boar, with a brass-mounted leather scabbard, 1850–1900, 30in (76cm) long.
£440–520 / €640–760
$800–940 DORO

A cup-hilt rapier, with steel hilt, engraved with bust medallions, the associated wooden grip bound with copper wire and riband, 1630–40, blade 39¾in (101cm) long.
£1,650–1,950
€2,400–2,850
$3,000–3,550 S(O)

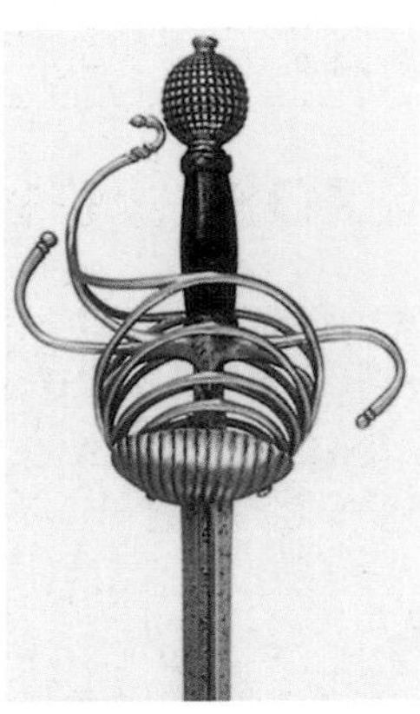

A rapier, with iron hilt, stamped 'Pietro' and 'Hernandez', binding to grip missing, one quillon replaced, Italian, 1630–40, blade 43½in (110.5cm) long.
£1,900–2,250
€2,750–3,300
$3,450–4,050 S(O)

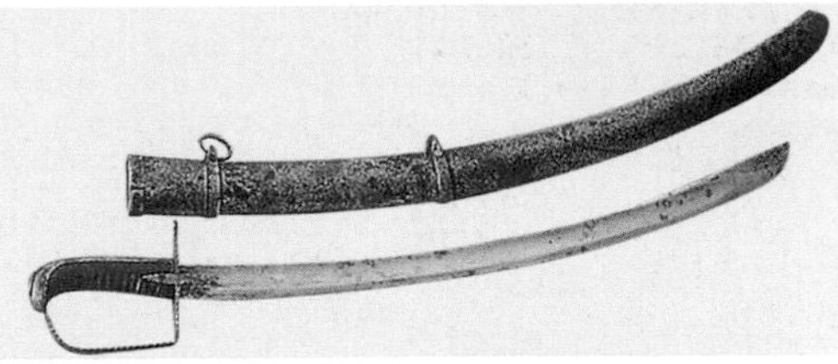

A hussar's sabre, with leather-covered wooden grip, crown mark, with scabbard, Austro-Hungarian, c1750, 36¾in (93.5cm) long.
£480–570 / €700–830
$870–1,050 DORO

► **A *schiavona*, Venetian,** 1700–50, blade 35in (89cm) long.
£1,950–2,150
€2,850–3,150
$3,500–3,900 FAC

◄ **An East India Company officer's silver-mounted sabre,** with silver hilt and bone grip, with inscription, scabbard damaged, early 19thC, blade 29in (73.5cm) long.
£2,400–2,850
€3,500–4,150
$4,350–5,200 S(O)

A sword, maker's mark, 14thC, 36½in (92.5cm) long.
£5,200–6,200
€7,600–9,100
$9,400–11,200 L

A broadsword, with iron hilt and moulded wooden grip, Italian, c1570, 40in (101.5cm) long.
£3,000–3,600
€4,400–5,300
$5,400–6,500 S(O)

A military backsword, with iron half-basket guard and fishtail pommel, with a leather-covered wooden grip, German, late 16thC, blade 31¼in (79.5cm) long.
£1,550–1,850
€2,250–2,700
$2,800–3,350 S(O)

A townguard's riding sword, with maker's mark of Wolfgang Stantler, German, Munich, late 16thC, blade 39½in (100.5cm) long.
£7,400–8,800
€10,800–12,800
$13,400–15,900 L

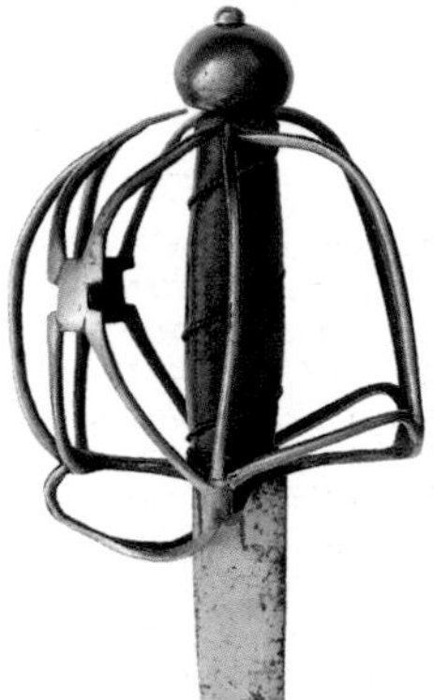

A horseman's basket-hilt sword, reduced from a broadsword, c1640, blade 34½in (87.5cm) long.
£1,500–1,700
€2,200–2,500
$2,700–3,100 ⊞ FAC

A cavalry officer's sword, c1645, 41in (104cm) long.
£3,150–3,550 / €4,600–5,100
$5,700–6,300 ⊞ ARB

A Civil War trooper's mortuary sword, with iron hilt, 18thC copper grip, running wolf and other marks, grip and scabbard later, c1645, blade 32¼in (82cm) long.
£970–1,150 / €1,400–1,650
$1,750–2,100 WEBB

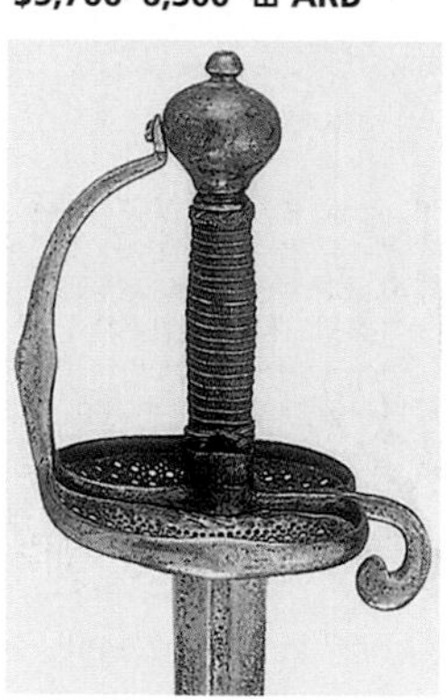

A cavalry sword, with iron 'Walloon' hilt, the wooden grip bound with wire, with running wolf mark and stamped 'Sachgom', Dutch, 1660–80, blade 36¾in (93.5cm) long.
£1,400–1,650
€2,050–2,400
$2,550–3,000 S(O)

◀ **A sword,** with a folding hilt and ivory grip, French, 18thC, blade 23in (58.5cm) long.
£350–420
€510–610
$630–760
GTH

A horseman's broadsword, with iron hilt, decorated with stylized foliage, the wooden grip carved with chevrons, south German, c1650, blade 30¼in (77cm) long.
£990–1,100
€1,450–1,600
$1,800–2,000 ⊞ FAC

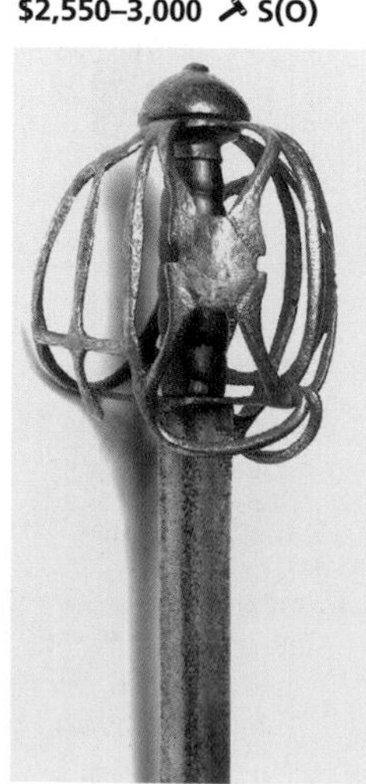

▶ **A backsword,** with running wolf mark and 'Ferrera', Scottish, 1720–40, 40in (101.5cm) long.
£1,800–2,000
€2,600–2,900
$3,250–3,600 ⊞ WSA

A broadsword, the steel basket hilt with panels pierced with hearts, the leather-covered wooden grip with brass ferrules, running wolf mark and 'XX', Scottish, mid-18thC, blade 31in (78.5cm) long.
£1,050–1,250
€1,550–1,850
$1,900–2,250 DNW

A smallsword, the silver hilt cast and chased with rococo decoration, marked, Flemish, Mons, c1770, blade 27¼in (69cm) long.
£2,000–2,400
€2,900–3,500
$3,600–4,300 S(O)

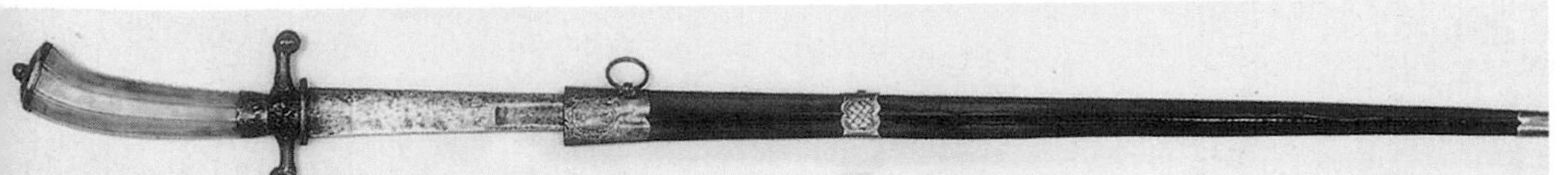

A silver-mounted hunting sword, with ivory grip, with a restored silver-mounted scabbard, grip cracked, 18thC, blade 20in (51cm) long.
£210–250 / €310–370
$380–450 WAL

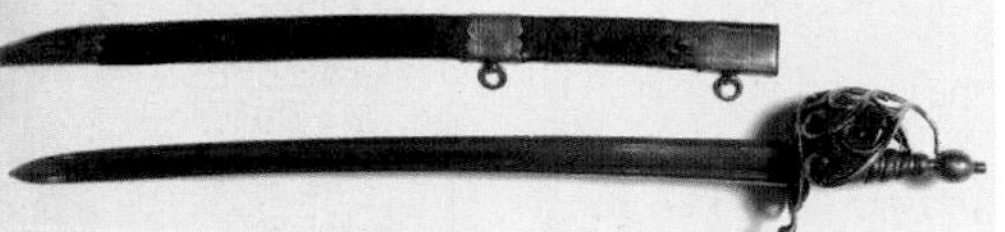

An officer's semi-basket-hilt sword, with original cloth basket liner and leather scabbard, c1775, 33½in (85cm) long.
£1,950–2,200 / €2,850–3,200
$3,550–4,000 TLA

A basket-hilt sword, blade bent and cracked, marked 'Andria Farara', Scottish, 18thC, blade 31¼in (79.5cm) long.
£490–580 / €720–850
$890–1,050 SWO

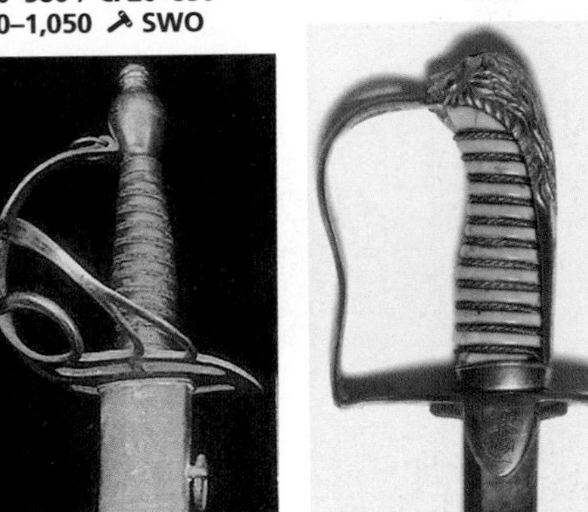

An officer's sword, the steel guard with scrolling side bars, the leather grip bound with silver wire, the steel-mounted leather scabbard with locket, marked with a shield and a crown, Order of the Thistle motto, engraved 'Woolley & Deakin's improved steel', damaged, Scottish, c1800,
£2,250–2,700
€3,300–3,950
$4,050–4,900 DNW

A Royal Navy captain's sword, c1805, 37in (94cm) long.
£740–830 / €1,100–1,200
$1,350–1,500 TLA

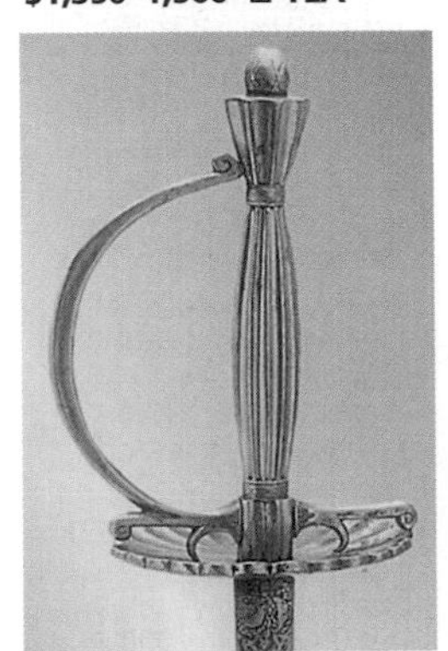

► **An infantry officer's sword,** with brass hilt, the blade with etched vine decoration and crowned 'FA', German, Saxony, c1800, 37¼in (94.5cm) long.
£1,450–1,700
€2,100–3,500
$2,650–3,100 Herm

A naval artillery sword, French, c1780, blade 22in (56cm) long.
£440–490 / €640–720
$790–890 FAC

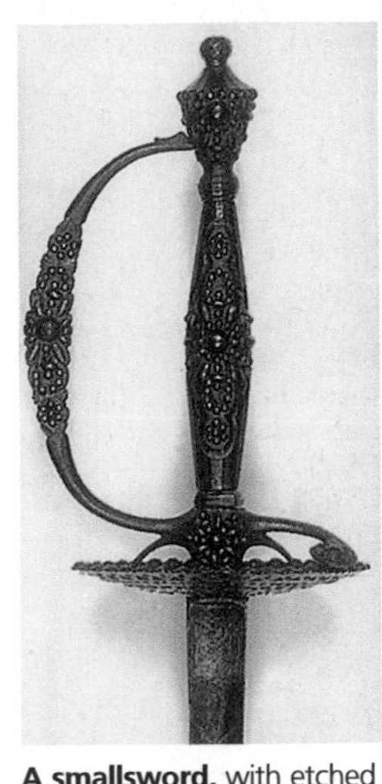

A smallsword, with etched decoration, the polished-steel hilt decorated with faceted studs, slight damage, late 18thC, blade 30½in (77.5cm) long.
£175–210 / €260–310
$320–380 WAL

◄ **A military smallsword,** decorated with panels of military motifs, French, c1780, blade 31¼in (79.5cm) long.
£660–740 / €960–1,050
$1,200–1,350 FAC

An officer's sword, French, c1803, 36in (91.5cm) long.
£1,100–1,250 / €1,600–1,850
$2,000–2,250 ⊞ TLA

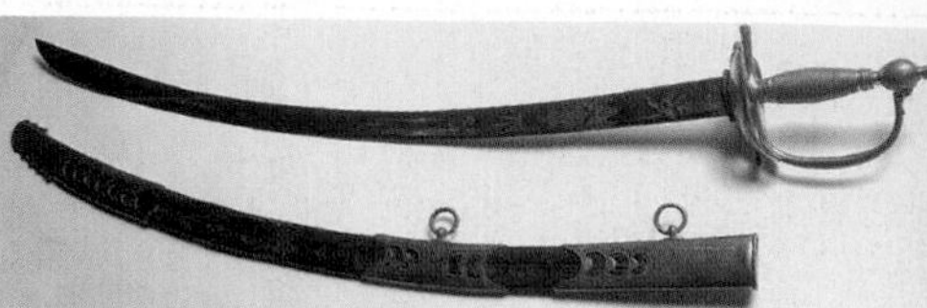

A sword, with inscription to Major John Hutcheson from the NCOs, Scottish, c1804, 40in (101.5cm) long.
£6,700–7,500 / €9,800–11,000
$12,100–13,600 ⊞ WSA

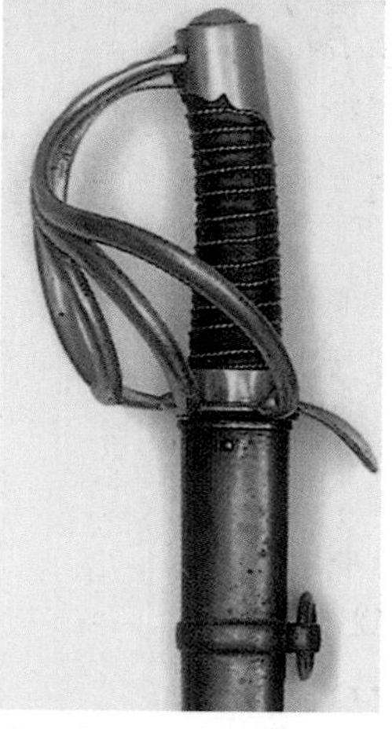

An AN XIII cuirassier's sword, with brass guard and leather-covered wire-bound grip, engraved 'Manufre Rle Du Klingenthal Obre 1814', in a steel scabbard, French, c1804, blade 38in (96.5cm) long.
£470–560 / €690–820
$850–1,000 ⚒ WAL

A Victorian 1827 pattern rifle volunteer's sword, by Prater & Co, London, with steel half-basket hilt and wire-bound fishskin grip, in a steel scabbard, blade 32in (81.5cm) long.
£240–280 / €350–410
$430–510 ⚒ WAL

► **An Edward VII pattern 1898 Mark I staff sergeant's sword,** by Wilkinson, with a steel hilt and a wire-bound fishskin grip, in a steel-mounted leather scabbard, blade 32½in (82.5cm) long.
£165–195 / €240–280
$300–350 ⚒ WAL

An officer's sword, the hilt with iron guard, the brass pommel in the form of an eagle's head, with reeded bone grip, American, c1812, blade 28in (71cm) long.
£570–640 / €830–930
$1,000–1,150 ⊞ FAC

A Victorian 1827 pattern rifle officer's sword, by Hobson & Sons, London, with steel hilt and wire-bound fishskin grip, in a steel scabbard, blade 32¼in (82cm) long.
£240–280 / €350–410
$430–510 ⚒ WAL

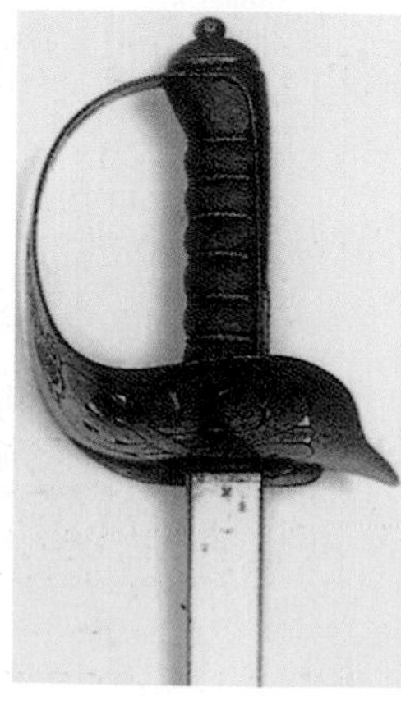

An officer's presentation sword, by Collins & Co, Connecticut, with gilt-brass half-basket hilt, in a gilt-brass mounted scabbard, American, dated 1862, blade 32in (81.5cm) long.
£1,900–2,250
€2,750–3,300
$3,450–4,050 ⚒ S(O)

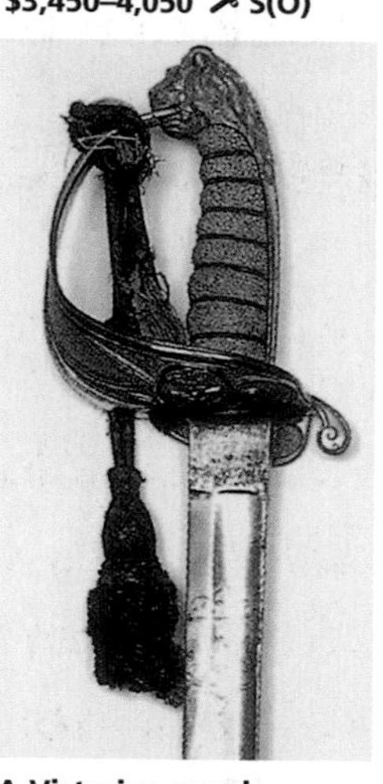

A Victorian naval officer's sword, by I. & E. Emanuel, with gilt-brass hilt and wire-bound fishskin grip with lion's head pommel, in a brass-mounted leather scabbard, 30½in (77.5cm) long.
£240–280 / €350–410
$430–510 ⚒ WAL

► **An officer's sword,** by Army & Navy Cooperative Co, Washington, D.C., with a japanned grip, scabbard damaged, American, c1902, blade 34½in (87.5cm) long.
£150–165 / €210–240
$270–300 ⊞ FAC

An early Victorian 1827 pattern rifle officer's sword, with steel half-basket hilt and wire-bound fishskin grip, in a steel scabbard, blade 32½in (82.5cm) long.
£230–270 / €340–400
$420–490 ⚒ WAL

A Victorian officer's basket-hilted broadsword, the steel hilt pierced with hearts and with a leather and cloth liner, in a steel scabbard, slight damage, Scottish, blade 32½in (82.5cm) long.
£470–560 / €690–820
$850–1,000 ⚒ WAL

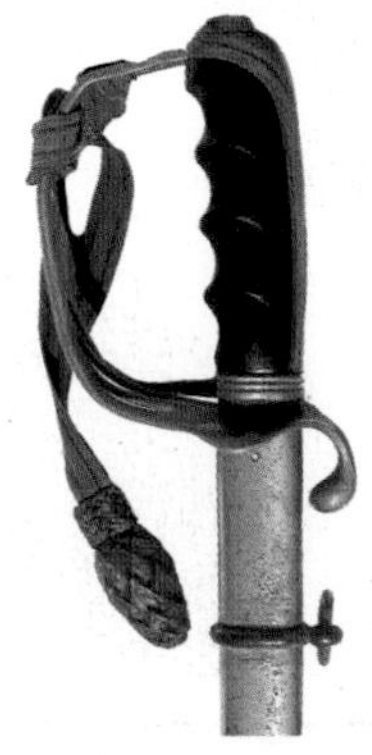

Firearms

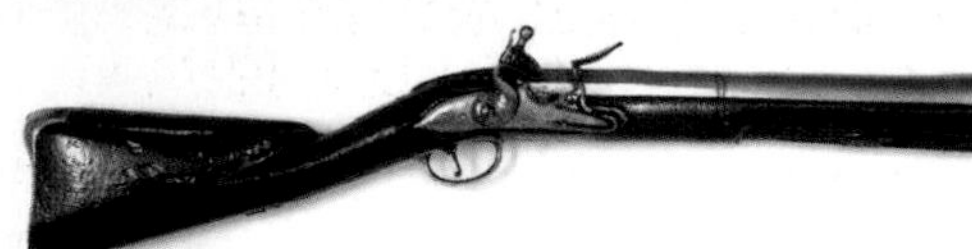

A flintlock blunderbuss, with leaf-chased barrel, the walnut full stock with brass mounts and wooden ram, early 18thC, barrel 14in (35.5cm) long.
£3,200–3,800 / €4,650–5,500
$5,800–6,900 AH

A flintlock blunderbuss, by Ketland & Co, with brass barrel, the walnut half stock with brass mounts and sideplate, ramrod pipes and steel ramrod, steel bayonet, c1775, barrel 15½in (39.5cm) long.
£3,300–3,900 / €4,800–5,700
$6,000–7,100 WAL

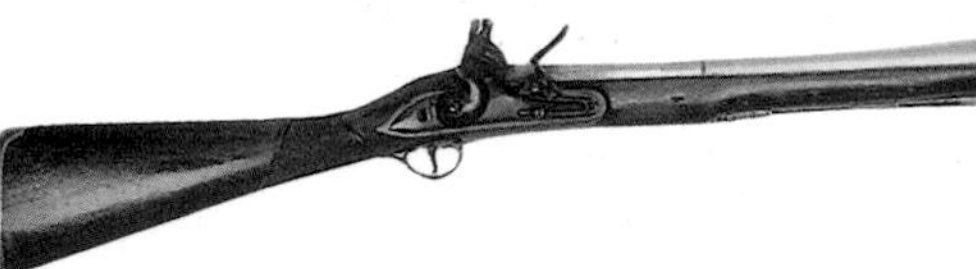

A flintlock ship's blunderbuss, with brass barrel and walnut full stock with chequered wrist, bone-tipped ramrod, repaired, some parts earlier, late 18thC, 32in (81.5cm) long.
£1,750–2,000 / €2,550–2,900
$3,150–3,600 WAL

A brass flintlock boxlock blunderbuss pistol, by Taylor & Mander, the barrel with London proofs, with walnut stock, the horn-tipped ramrod with worm, c1800, barrel 6in (15cm) long.
£2,250–2,500 / €3,300–3,650
$4,050–4,550 WSA

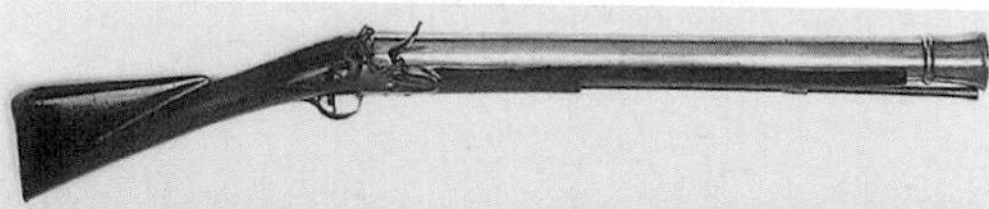

A flintlock boat's gun, the brass barrel with London and maker's proof marks and walnut full stock, with brass mounts and trigger guard with acanthus finial, slight damage and wear, repairs and restoration, c1740, 42½in (108cm) long.
£2,450–2,900 / €3,600–4,250
$4,450–5,200 WAL

► **A double-barrelled 16 bore flintlock coaching carbine,** by Walker, the walnut half-stock with chequered wrist, steel mounts and trigger guard, the brass-tipped ebony ramrod with worm, slight damage, c1815, 31½in (80cm) long.
£3,650–4,300 / €5,300–6,300
$6,600–7,800 WAL

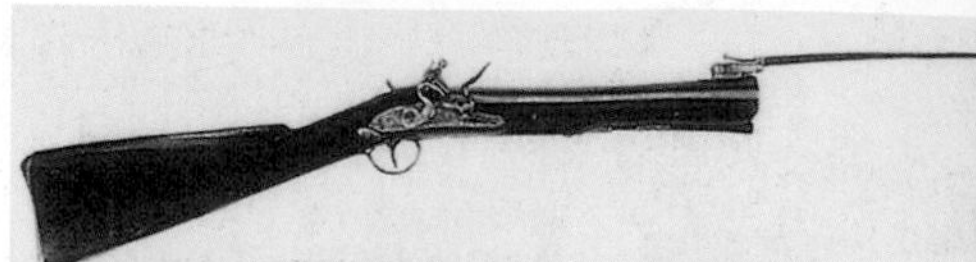

A flintlock blunderbuss, with figured walnut stock, engraved brass butt plate and trigger guard with acorn finial, the brass barrel with London proof marks, spring-loaded bayonet, steel lockplate signed 'Gamble Snr, Wisbeach', later ramrod, 18thC, 37¼in (94.5cm) extended.
£940–1,100 / €1,350–1,600
$1,700–2,000 F&C

A flintlock blunderbuss, by Clarke, with three-stage brass barrel, the figured walnut stock with brass buttplate, trigger-guard and ramrod pipes, stamped with Irish census marks on breech, later ramrod, slight damage, Irish, c1790, 30½in (77.5cm) long.
£2,650–3,150 / €3,850–4,600
$4,800–5,700 S(O)
Nicholas Clarke is recorded in Dublin 1788–1811.

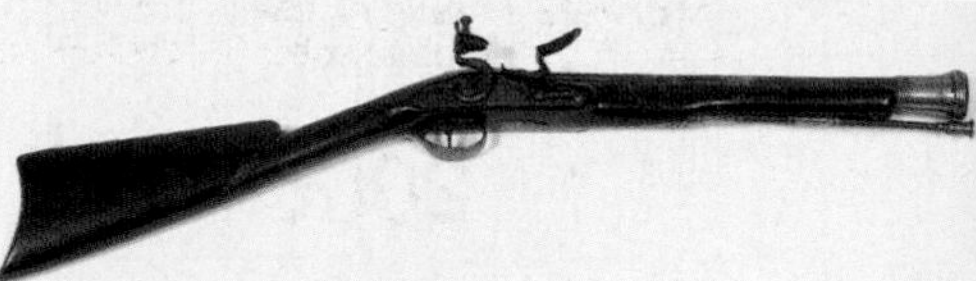

A flintlock blunderbuss, by Bourne & Hawkins, London, late 18thC, 30¼in (77cm) long.
£820–980 / €1,200–1,400
$1,500–1,750 CHTR

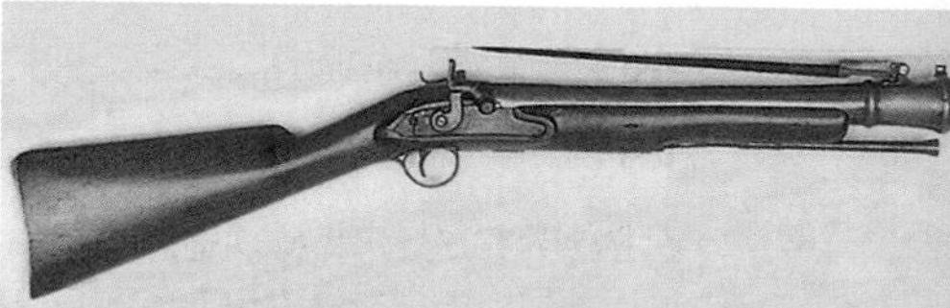

A percussion blunderbuss, by Nock, the brass barrel with spring bayonet, the walnut full stock with engraved brass mounts, the trigger guard with acorn finial, the brass-tipped ebony ramrod with worm, damage, alteration and repair, c1830, 31½in (80cm) long.
£760–910 / €1,100–1,300
$1,400–1,650 WAL

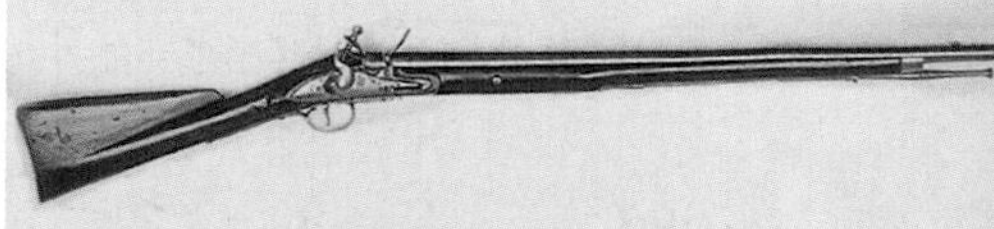

A .65 Elliotts flintlock cavalry carbine, the barrel with Tower proofs and Irish census mark, engraved Tower lock with inspector's stamp and crowned GR cypher, the full stock with brass furniture, steel ramrod, repaired and restored, mark for 1800, barrel 28in (71cm) long.
£3,650–4,300 / €5,300–6,300
$6,600–7,800 WAL

A percussion carbine, the walnut stock with a brass butt plate and furniture, swivel rammer, the side lock with Tower marks for 1844, 36in (91.5cm) long.
£440–520 / €640–760
$800–940 HOLL

A percussion carbine, the full stock with brass mounts, with adjustable rear sight, the lock with Tower marks for 1860, 40½in (103cm) long.
£470–560 / €690–820
$850–1,000 PFK

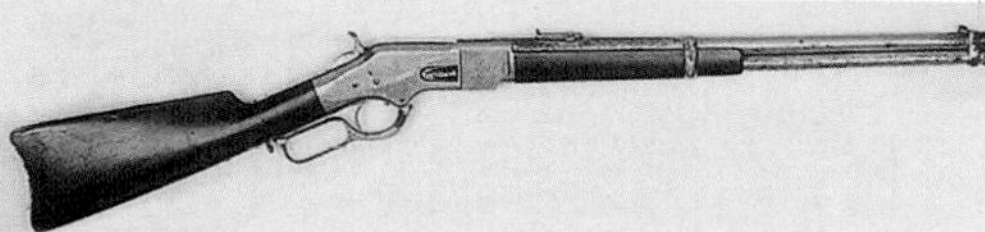

A nickel-plated .44 rim fire Winchester Model 1866 full tube magazine underlever carbine, No. 164512, the barrel with later type markings at breech, with walnut stock and saddle ring, the ladder rear sight dated 1873, 1866, 39½in (100.5cm) long.
£1,300–1,550 / €1,900–2,250
$2,350–2,800 WAL

A military matchlock musket, with sighted barrel, beechwood stock and iron mounts, the trigger lock with match-holder, damaged, ramrod missing, Austrian, 1650–60, barrel 38¼in (97cm) long.
£3,100–3,700 / €4,550–5,400
$5,600–6,700 S(O)

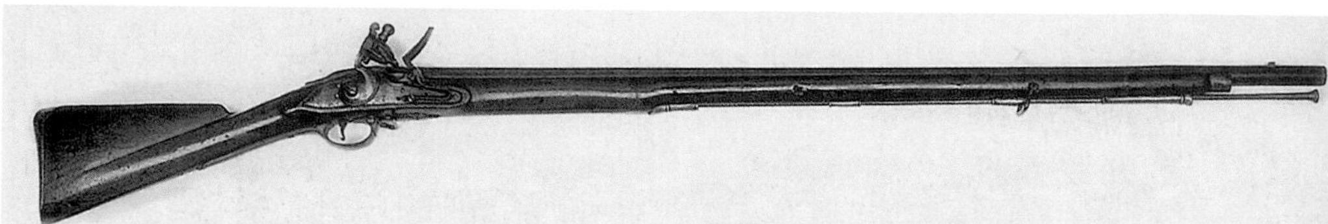

A .75 Tower Land Pattern Brown Bess flintlock musket, the walnut full stock with ordnance keeper's mark and brass mounts, with Tower proofs, the plate engraved with crowned 'GR' and 'Tower', steel ramrod, wear and repair, c1775, 58in (147.5cm) long.
£5,900–7,000 / €8,600–10,200
$10,700–12,700 WAL

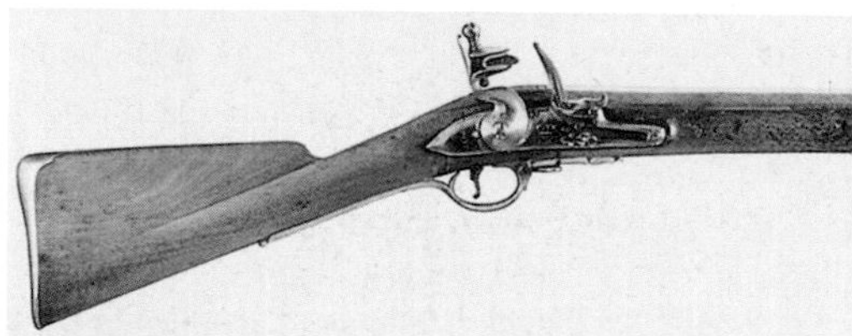

A .750 calibre New Land Pattern flintlock musket, the barrel engraved 'Glamorgan' and 'M', the lock engraved with crowned 'GR' and 'Tower', the stock impressed 'HM', with ramrod, damaged, c1815, 57¾in (146.5cm) long.
£3,100–3,700 / €4,550–5,400
$5,600–6,700 S(O)

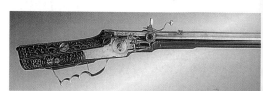

A wheel-lock rifle, the carved walnut full stock with bone and brass inlay, the muzzle, breech and tang engraved with a floral pattern, 'HK' struck on the breech, with front and rear folding sights, German, Saxony, c1670, 39¾in (101cm) long.
£5,900–7,000 / €8,600–10,200
$10,700–12,700 Herm

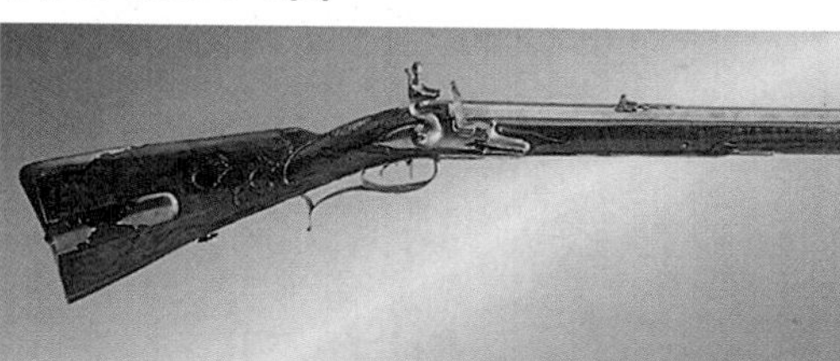

A flintlock rifle, by Joseph Hauer, the walnut full stock carved with rococo motifs and with brass furniture, the breech engraved with maker's name, later ramrod, repaired, German, Bamberg, c1750, 43¼in (110cm) long.
£1,600–1,900 / €2,350–2,750
$2,900–3,450 Herm

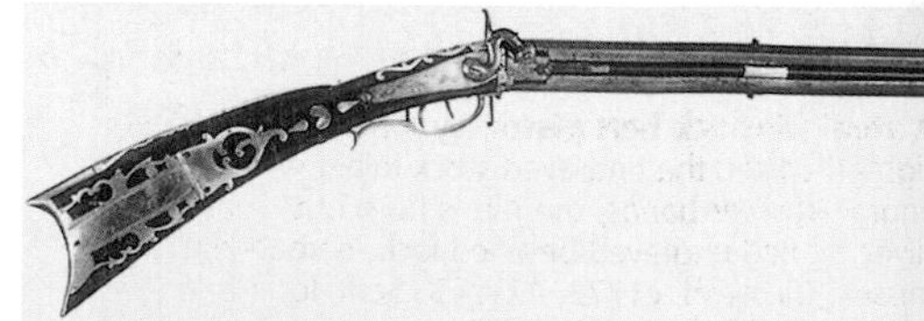

A percussion turnover plains rifle, by N. Ashmore, the hardwood quarter stock inlaid with silver plaques, with a brass trigger guard, butt-plate and ramrod pipes, the German silver patch box cover engraved with flowers and foliage, with two brass-tipped wooden ramrods, American, c1850, barrels 34in (86.5cm) long.
£2,400–2,800 / €3,500–4,100
$4,350–5,100 S(O)

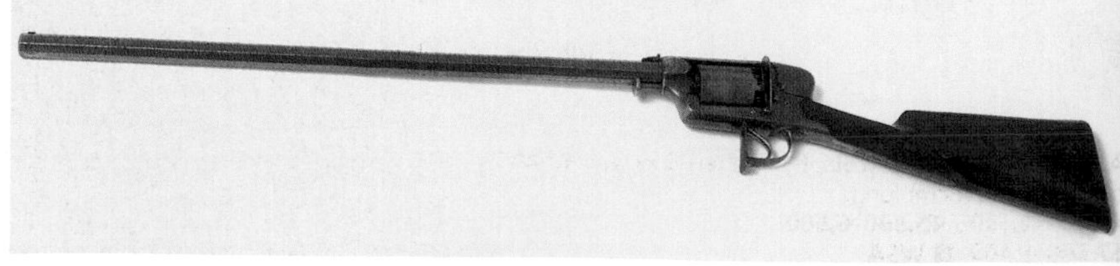

► **An Adams & Dean revolving rifle,** c1860, 45in (114.5cm) long.
£3,500–4,000
€5,100–5,800
$6,300–7,200
MDL

A .526 Jacob's double-barrelled percussion rifle, by Swinburn & Son, the barrels with folding rearsights and ladder rearsight, the walnut half stock with steel mounts, patch box engraved 'Jacob's Rifles', slight damage, repair, ramrod replaced, 1860, 40½in (103cm) long.
£2,450–2,900 / €3,600–4,250
$4,450–5,200 WAL

A .670 calibre Confederate import percussion rifle, signed 'Tanner & Cie', barrel with Liège proof marks, the figured walnut half stock with inspector's marks, iron trigger guard, American, c1865, 46½in (118cm) long.
£2,050–2,450 / €3,000–3,550
$3,700–4,400 S(O)

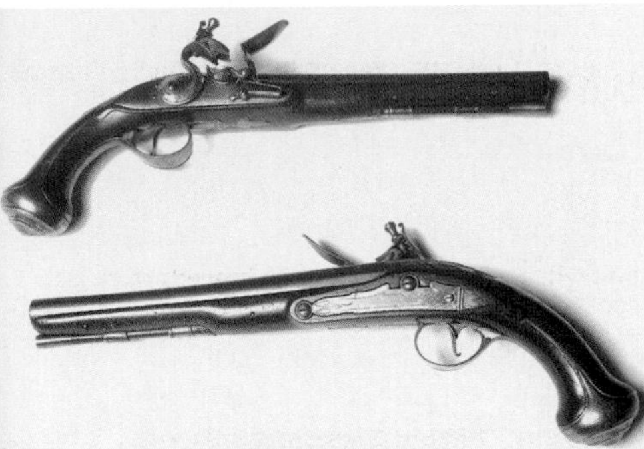

A pair of flintlock holster pistols, by David Wynn, London, with silver mounts, c1720, 16in (40.5cm) long.
£8,100–9,000 / €11,800–13,100
$14,700–16,300 WSA

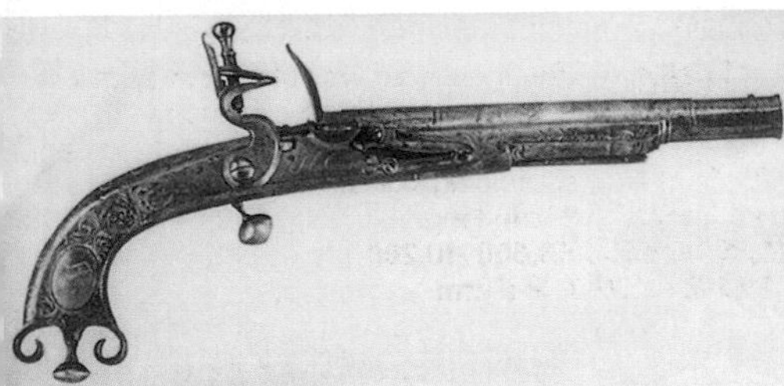

A steel flintlock belt pistol, by John Campbell, with sighted barrel, the engraved stock inlaid with three engraved silver bands, the ram's horn butt inlaid with silver, signed engraved bevelled lock, damaged, ramrod missing, Scottish, c1775, 12in (30.5cm) long.
£3,100–3,700 / €4,550–5,400
$5,600–6,700 S(O)

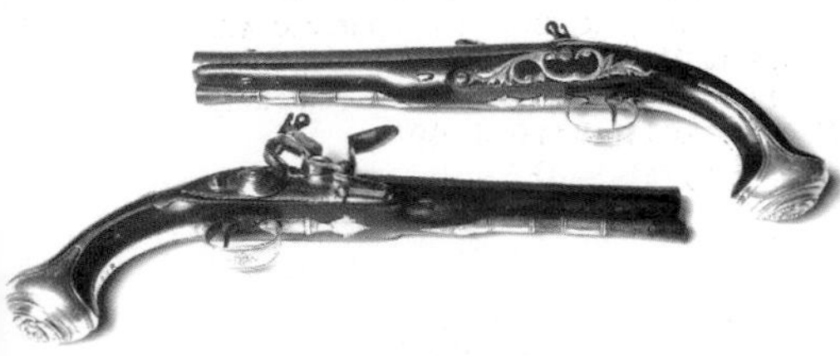

A pair of flintlock pistols, by Greffen & Tow, London, c1775, 15in (38cm) long.
£4,050–4,500 / €5,900–6,600
$7,300–8,100 WSA

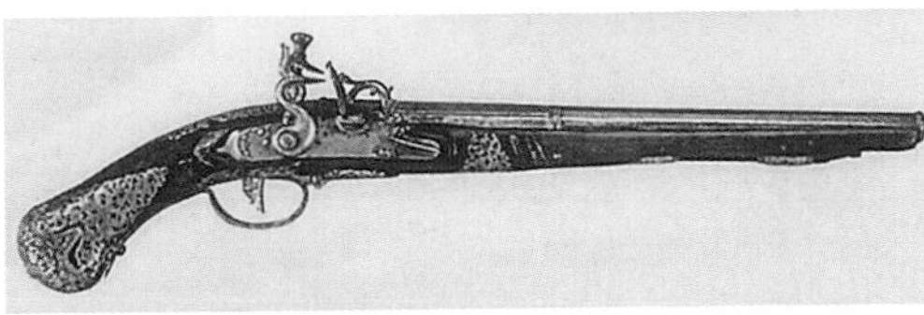

A Snapaunce belt pistol, by Lazarino Cominazo, the chiselled reeded breech with signature and barrelmaker's stamp, the figured walnut stock inset with steel plaques with pierced and engraved decoration, losses and repair, Italian, Brescia, 1650–60, 19in (48.5cm) long.
£2,400–2,800 / €3,500–4,100
$4,350–5,100 S(O)

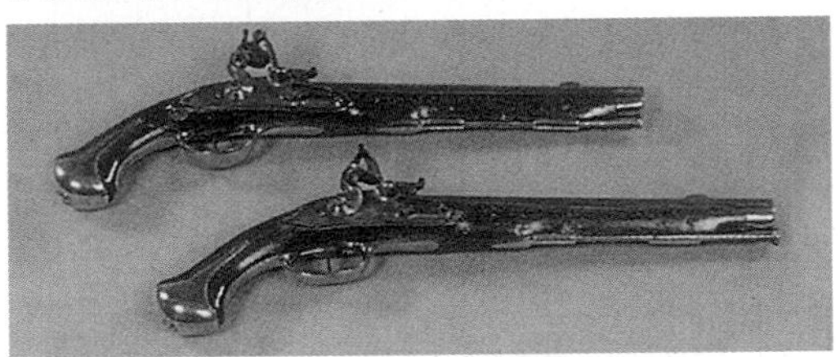

A pair of military flintlock holster pistols, the full stocks with brass furniture, butt caps numbered '21' and '29', Liège proof marks, Belgian, 18thC, 20in (51cm) long.
£1,500–1,750 / €2,200–2,500
$2,700–3,150 PFK

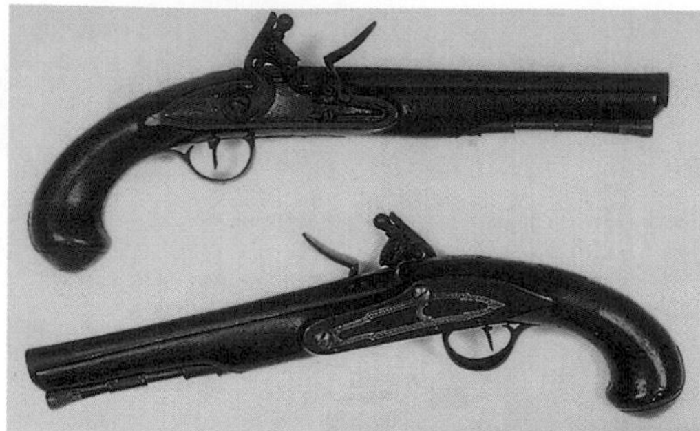

A pair of 20 bore flintlock holster pistols, by Thomas, with engraved teardrop panels, the walnut full stocks with silver wire inlay, horn-tipped ramrods, slight damage and losses, c1775, 13½in (34.5cm) long.
£2,250–2,500 / €3,300–3,650
$4,050–4,550 ⚒ WAL

A flintlock pistol, the walnut stock carved with flowers and leaves, damaged, late 18thC, 11in (28cm) long.
£150–175 / €220–260
$270–320 ⚒ CHTR

A George III pistol, with a chequered walnut grip, dolphin hammer and swing-out ramrod, hammer repaired, 8in (20.5cm) long.
£250–300 / €370–430
$450–540 ⚒ CHTR

A 1786 Pattern sea service pistol, by Manufacture Nationale du Tulle, French, c1804, 16in (40.5cm) long.
£2,600–2,900 / €3,800–4,250
$4,700–5,200 ⊞ TLA

A pair of officer's double-barrelled 24 bore flintlock holster pistols, by Twigg, London, the walnut half stocks with chequered butts, the engraved steel mounts with pineapple finials, with horn-tipped ramrods, one cock replaced, repaired, c1785, 14½in (37cm) long, in original fitted oak case with accessories.
£9,400–11,200 / €13,700–16,400
$17,000–20,300 ⚒ WAL

A pair of George III travelling flintlock pistols, by West & Richards, London, the turn-off barrels with spring bayonets, the walnut stocks with silver escutcheons, box lock action signed, barrel 2¼in (5.5cm) long.
£1,050–1,250 / €1,550–1,850
$1,900–2,250 ⚒ LAY

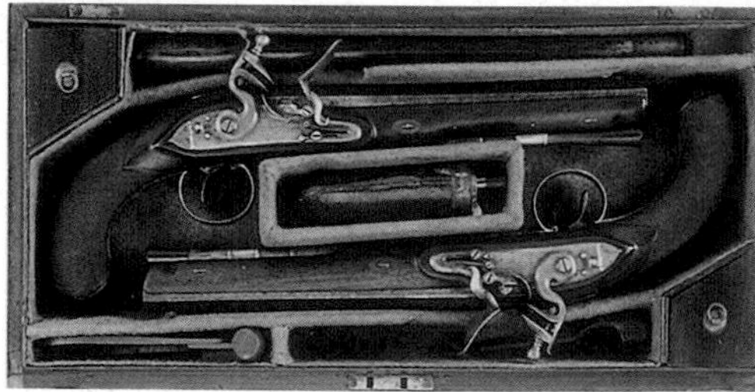

A pair of flintlock duelling pistols, by Philip Bond, London, each barrel signed and engraved, the figured walnut stocks with chequered butts, gold vent, engraved breech tang and steel trigger-guard with pineapple finial, with a horn-tipped wooden ramrod, reconverted, c1800, 14½in (37cm) long, with original fitted case and accessories.
£2,400–2,800 / €3,500–4,100
$4,350–5,100 ⚒ S(O)

A flintlock four-barrelled top-action pistol, by Twigg, London, c1805, 12in (30.5cm) long.
£4,050–4,500 / €5,900–6,600
$7,300–8,100 ⊞ WSA

◄ **A 16 bore flintlock overcoat pistol,** the full stock with engraved brass furniture, 'Kilkenny' engraved to the top flat, engraved lock, slight damage and alteration, Irish, c1810, 3¾in (9.5cm) long.
£560–670 / €810–980
$1,000–1,200 ⚒ WAL

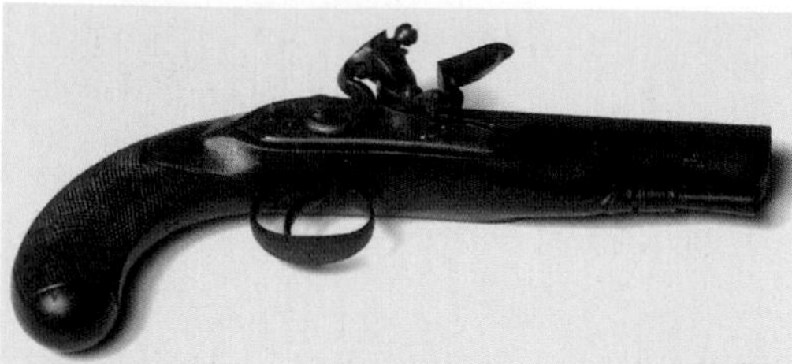

A pair of flintlock travelling pistols, by James Stevens, London, c1815, 10in (25.5cm) long.
£1,750–2,000 / €2,550–2,900
$3,150–3,600 ⊞ WSA

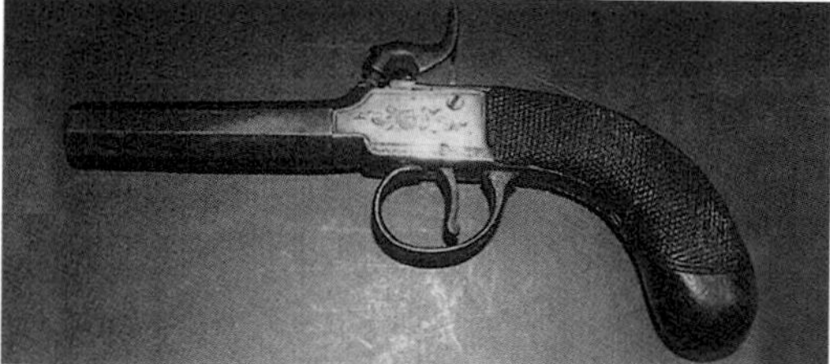

A boxlock percussion pocket pistol, by J. H. Timing & Son, London, the brass-sided lock engraved with scrollwork, the butt with chequered grip and nickel escutcheon, 1825–50, 7½in (19cm) long.
£200–230 / €290–340
$360–420 ⚒ PFK

A percussion holster pistol, by Richardson, Edinburgh, with sighted barrel and chequered half stock, engraved and signed bolted lock and foliate-engraved trigger guard, Scottish, 19thC, 8in (20.5cm) long.
£480–570 / €700–830
$870–1,000 ⚒ Bea

A flintlock duelling pistol, by Rosser, with a diamond-carved walnut stock, London marks, ramrod missing, 19thC, 11½in (29cm) long.
£280–330 / €410–480
$510–600 ⚒ TMA

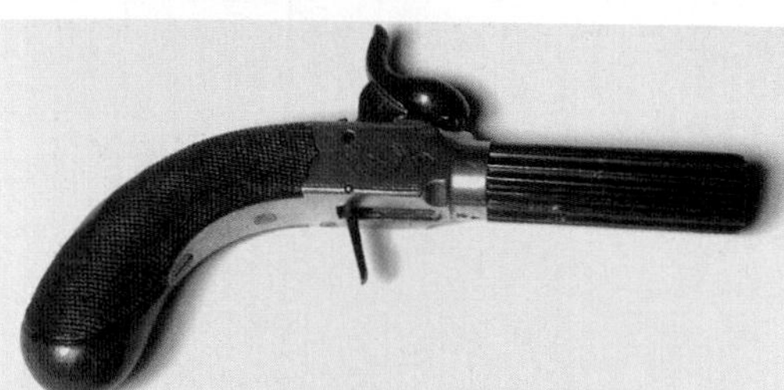

A pair of pocket pistols, with German silver frames and fluted barrels, c1840, 7in (18cm) long.
£540–600 / €790–880
$980–1,100 ⊞ WSA

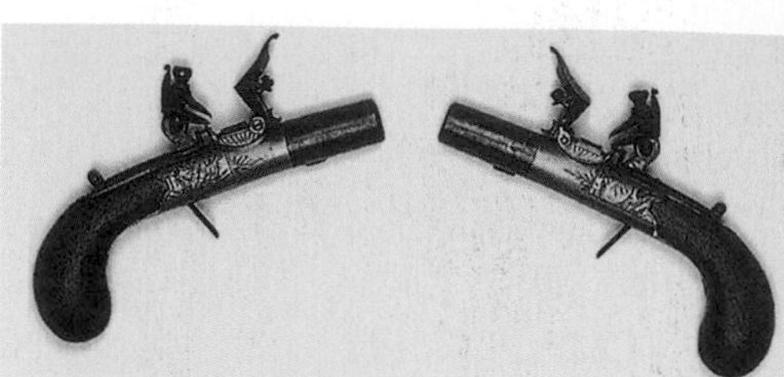

A pair of brass-framed flintlock boxlock pocket pistols, the barrels with Birmingham proofs engraved with the Union shield and flags, slight damage, c1820, 6in (15cm) long.
£760–900 / €1,100–1,300
$1,400–1,650 ⚒ WAL

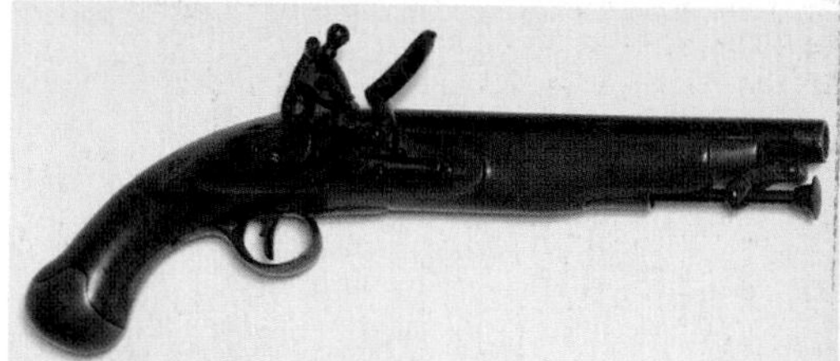

A William IV naval sea service pistol, with original blackened finish, Board of Ordnance mark, 15½in (39.5cm) long.
£1,700–1,900 / €2,500–2,750
$3,100–3,450 ⊞ TLA

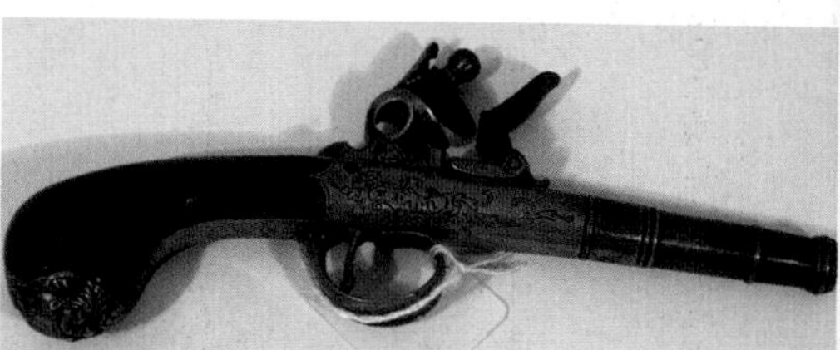

A pocket flintlock pistol, by F. Parr, with tapering steel barrel and walnut butt, engraved brass lockplate and trigger guard, 19thC, 8in (20.5cm) long.
£210–250 / €310–70
$380–450 ⚒ G(L)

A rifled Kentucky pistol, American, 19thC, 13in (33cm) long.
£1,250–1,400 / €1,850–2,050
$2,250–2,550 ⊞ TLA
A rifled pistol is a pistol with a rifled barrel with internal grooves for accuracy.

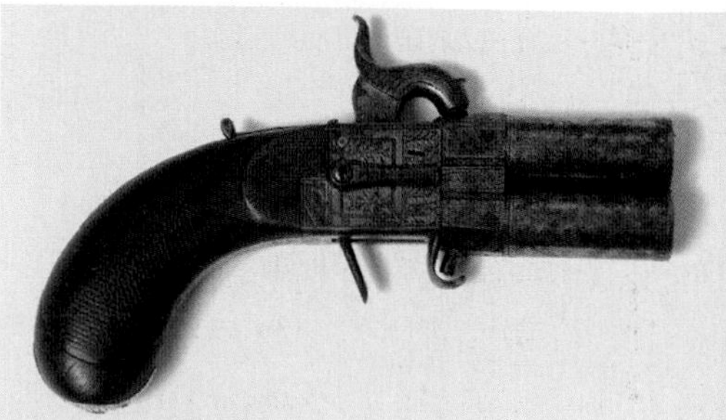

An over-and-under percussion pistol, by Lang, London, with chequered wood grips and folding trigger, with proof stamps, c1840, 6in (15cm) long.
£510–570 / €740–830
$920–1,050 ⊞ MDL

A pair of infantry officer's percussion pistols, by Peter Goltjakoff, barrels signed, Russian, c1850, 11½in (29cm) long.
£4,650–5,500 / €6,800–8,000
$8,400–10,000 BUK(F)

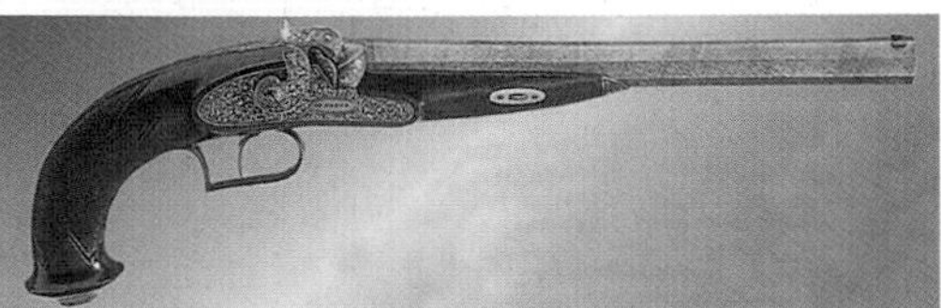

A percussion pistol, by A. Fent, top of barrel with carved cartouche and front sight, percussion lock inscribed, the walnut half stock with chequered grip and engraved iron furniture, German, Steyr, c1860, 15½in (39.5cm) long.
£1,350–1,600 / €1,950–2,300
$2,450–2,900 Herm

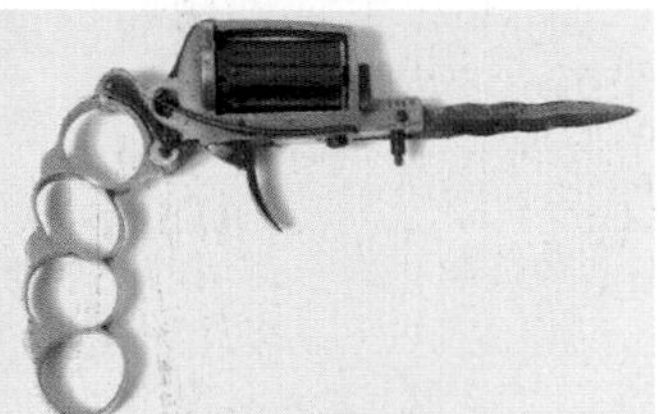

◀ **An Apache pistol,** French, c1885, 8in (20.5cm) long.
£1,450–1,650
€2,100–2,400
$2,600–3,000
MDL

A Remington revolver, American, 1860s, 14in (35.5cm) long.
£1,900–2,150 / €2,750–3,150
$3,450–3,900 TLA

A 36 calibre Colt revolver, No. 5282, 1862, barrel 6½in (16.5cm) long.
£3,150–3,500 / €4,600–5,100
$5,700–6,300 WSA

A Tranter double-trigger .50 percussion revolving rifle, by Alex Thomson & Sons, Edinburgh, No. 17712T, c1860, 45in (114.5cm) long, with original fitted wooden case with accessories.
£7,600–8,500 / €11,100–12,400
$13,800–15,400 MDL
Only five of this type of rifle are known.

A Colt pocket pistol, No. 171, model 1849, London proof marks, American, assembled in UK, 1853, barrel 6in (16cm) long.
£1,500–1,700 / €2,200–2,500
$2,700–3,100 SPA

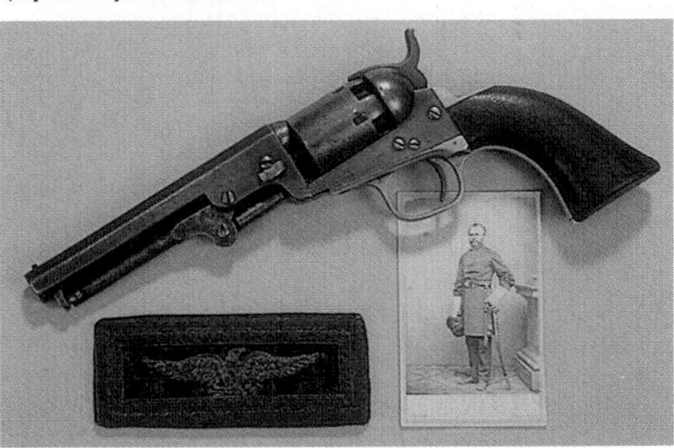

A Colt pocket pistol, No. 177142, the cylinder with an engraved stagecoach scene, the walnut grip with a brass butt plate inscribed 'Col Samuel W. Black Company D Pennsylvania Volunteers', American, c1861, 9¾in (25cm) long.
£3,900–4,650 / €5,700–6,800
$7,100–8,400 SK

A pair of flintlock pistols, by Fowler, Dublin, the walnut full stocks cut for shoulder stock, Irish, c1899, in a case with accessories, 9 x 17in (23 x 43cm).
£8,100–9,000 / €11,800–13,100
$14,700–16,300 WSA

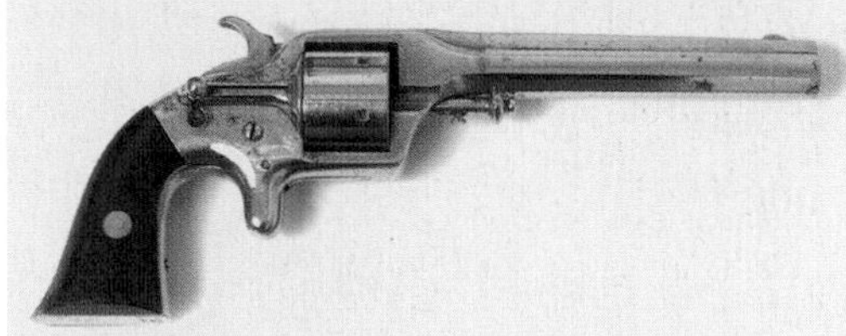

A Plants patent revolver, with nickel six-shot cylinder and walnut grips, original holster, American, c1870, 12in (30.5cm) long.
£900–1,000 / €1,300–1,450
$1,600–1,800 MDL
Only approximately two hundred and fifty of this type of revolver were made.

A Three Band British Snider rifle, the walnut full stock with ramrod, sling swivels and leather sling, brass trigger guard and butt plate, the percussion action breech inscribed 'London Armoury, Jas Kere & Co, 54 King William Street', storekeeper's stamp, dated 1868, 55in (139.5cm) long.
£1,000–1,200 / €1,450–1,750
$1,800–2,150 AH

Polearms

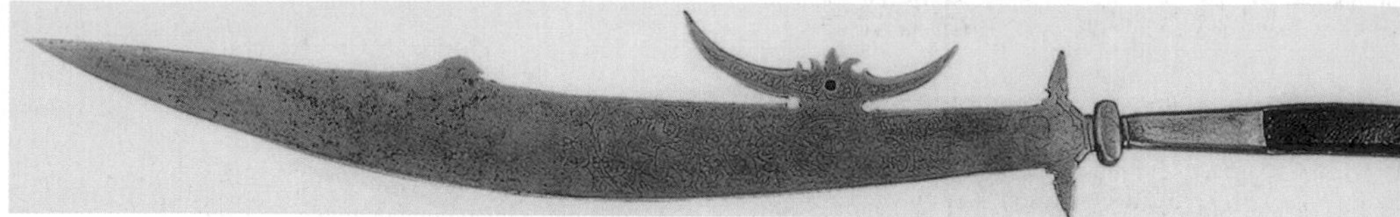

A processional glaive of the Guard of the Counts Giustiniani, the punch-etched blade engraved with scrolls, foliage, monsters and putti enclosing a cartouche with the arms of the Counts Giustiniani of Venice, repaired, Italian, Venice, early 17thC, 45¾in (116cm) long.
£2,900–3,400 / €4,250–4,950
$5,200–6,200 ⚒ S(O)

A wood and iron flail, the head with spikes, the haft carved with vertical and spiral fluting, one spike missing, German, 17thC, 25in (63.5cm) long.
£1,700–2,000 / €2,500–2,900
$3,100–3,600 ⚒ S(O)

A halberd, the blade stamped with smith's mark, repaired, softwood haft replaced, central/northern Europe, c1450, 78in (198cm) long.
£1,900–2,250 / €2,750–3,300
$3,450–4,050 ⚒ Herm

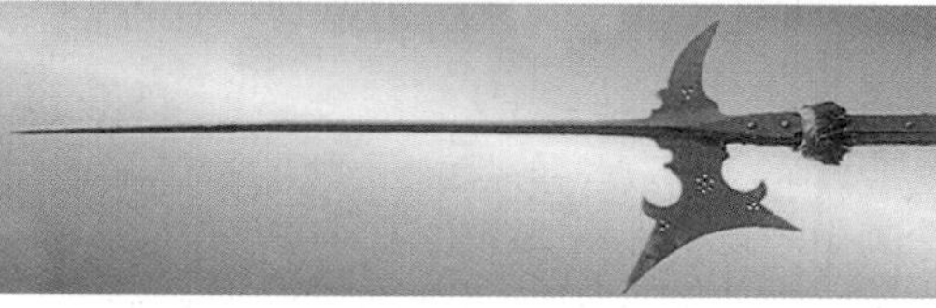

A halberd, the blade with dot decoration, the socket decorated with tassels and long sidestraps, ash haft, German, c1600, 102¾in (261cm) long.
£1,000–1,200 / €1,450–1,750
$1,800–2,150 ⚒ Herm

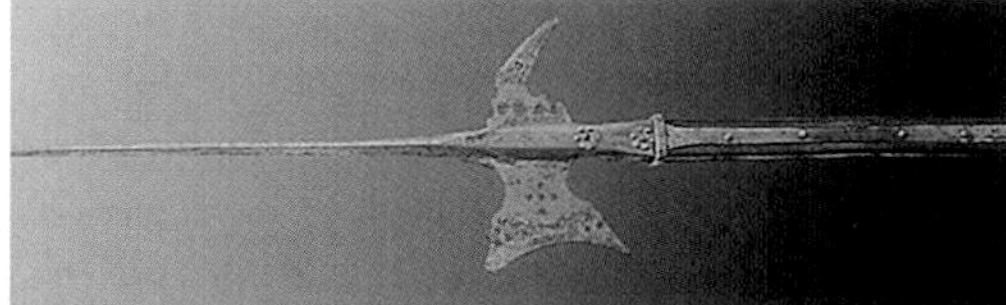

A halberd, back fluke stamped, Swiss, c1550, 113¾in (289cm) long.
£1,650–1,850 / €2,400–2,700
$3,000–3,300 ⊞ FAC

A halberd, by Pankraz Taller, the neck decorated with brass rosettes, wooden haft later, maker's mark, Austrian, 1575–1600, 100½in (255.5cm) long.
£720–860 / €1,050–1,250
$1,300–1,550 ⚒ DORO

A Saxon Electoral Guard state halberd, with etched decoration to the blade, one side with the arms of Saxony, the reverse with the arms of the Archmarshalship of the Holy Roman Empire, later wood haft with additional iron straps and tassel, German, early 17thC, head 20¼in (51.5cm) long.
£2,250–2,700 / €3,300–3,950
$4,050–4,850 ⚒ S(O)

◀ **A parade halberd,** the head decorated with etched flora and scrollwork, haft replaced, early 17thC, 84in (213.5cm) long.
£440–520 / €640–760
$800–940 ⚒ DA

▶ **A mace,** the head with seven flanges, damaged, wooden grip missing, German, 1500–50, 19¼in (49cm) long.
£1,200–1,400 / €1,750–2,050
$2,150–2,550 ⚒ Herm

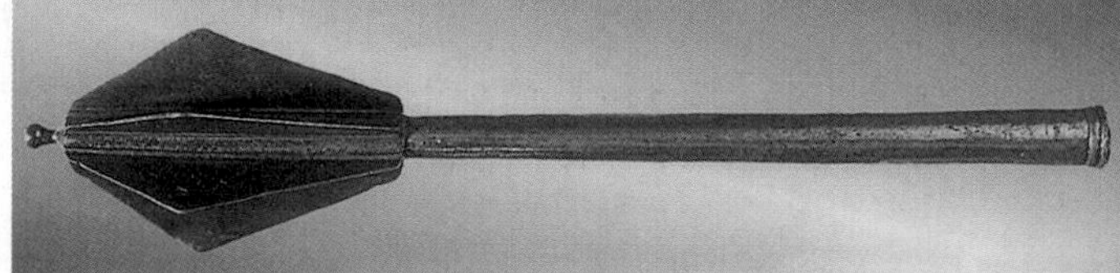

A horseman's gilt-bronze and leather mace, the moulded gilt-bronze head with button finial, the haft covered in leather with gilt-bronze terminals at either end, 1620–50, 36¾in (93.5cm) long.
£3,000–3,600 / €4,400–5,200
$5,400–6,500 ⚒ S(O)

Militaria

Badges & Plates

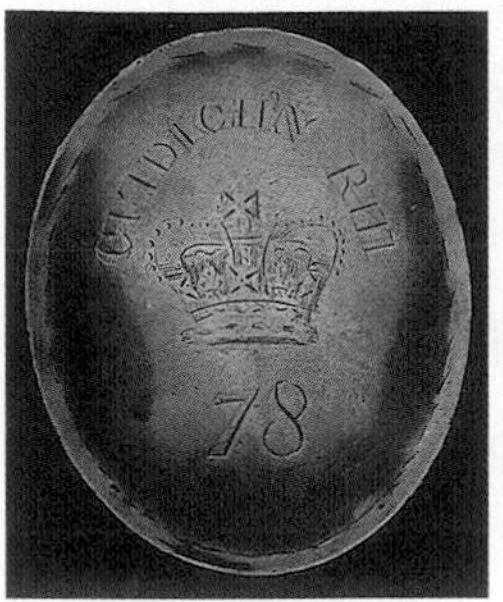

A 78th Highland Regiment officer's gilt-copper shoulder belt plate, engraved 'Cuidich'n Rhi' above a crown and '78', Scottish, 1797–1807.
£640–760 / €930–1,100
$1,200–1,400 ⚒ DNW

A 1st Royal Lancashire Militia officer's silver, copper and enamel shoulder belt plate, by J. & Co, Birmingham 1852.
£590–700 / €850–1,000
$1,050–1,250 ⚒ DNW

A Hereford Militia silver-plated helmet plate, with inscription and county arms and crest mounted on leather, 1878–81.
£440–520 / €640–760
$800–940 ⚒ DNW

An Aberdeenshire Local Militia 2nd Regiment officer's silver shoulder belt plate, with inscribed decoration, maker's mark 'G. MH.' for George McHattie, Scottish, Edinburgh, 1809–16.
£940–1,100
€1,350–1,600
$1,700–2,000 ⚒ DNW

A Victorian Devonshire Regiment officer's gilt and silver-plated forage cap badge.
£140–165 / €200–240
$250–300 ⚒ WAL

A Cameronians (Scottish Rifles) officer's metal pouch belt plate, with a Guelphic crown over thistle sprays enclosing a mullet and a bugle, Scottish, 1881–1901.
£175–210 / €260–310
$320–380 ⚒ DNW

◄ A Victorian Queen's Body Guard for Scotland headdress badge, with enamel decoration, Scottish.
£130–155 / €200–230
$240–290 ⚒ WAL

A 25th King's Own Regiment officer's special pattern gilt and silver-plated shoulder belt plate, with enamel decoration, slight damage, pre-1855, with matching belt slide with battle honours and ornamental tip.
£1,900–2,250
€2,750–3,300
$3,450–4,050 ⚒ WAL

A Victorian Flintshire Rifle Corps officer's silver-plated pouch belt badge, with Prince of Wales feathers in a wreath on a crowned Maltese Cross with title, Welsh.
£190–220 / €280–330
$340–400 ⚒ WAL

A 44th Regiment Indian Army officer's gilt and silver-plated shoulder belt plate, with leather liner, pre-1855.
£470–560 / €690–820
$850–1,000 ⚒ WAL

A Victorian Norfolk Regiment officer's gilt and silver-plated glengarry badge.
£135–160 / €195–230
$240–290 ⚒ WAL

A Victorian Royal Army Medical Corps NCO's gilt helmet plate, with enamel decoration.
£140–165 / €200–240
$250–300 ⚒ WAL

◄ A King's Shropshire Light Infantry officer's gilt, silver and enamel helmet plate, 1902–14.
£190–220 / €280–330
$340–400 ⚒ DNW

Costume

A pair of Army Medical Staff officer's gilt lace epaulettes, c1850.
£260–310 / €380–450
$470–560 WAL

A Victorian Royal Artillery officer's full dress sabretache, embroidered with the Royal coat-of-arms, foliate sprays and motto scrolls, with foul weather cover.
£670–800 / €980–1,150
$1,200–1,450 WAL

A copper-gilt gorget, with engraved decoration, slight gilt loss, 1801–30.
£410–490 / €600–720
$740–890 DNW

◄ **A Victorian Cinque Ports Volunteer Rifles officer's leather shoulder belt and pouch,** with silver-plated badges, lion boss, whistle and chains.
£300–360 / €440–530
$540–650 WAL

A Victorian East Lothian Yeomanry Cavalry officer's velvet pouch, with lace and embroidered decoration, containing a wooden block drilled for five cartridges, Scottish.
£120–140 / €170–200
$210–250 WAL

A United States Army leather pouch, American, c1865, 7in (18cm) wide.
£145–170 / €210–250
$260–310 DuM

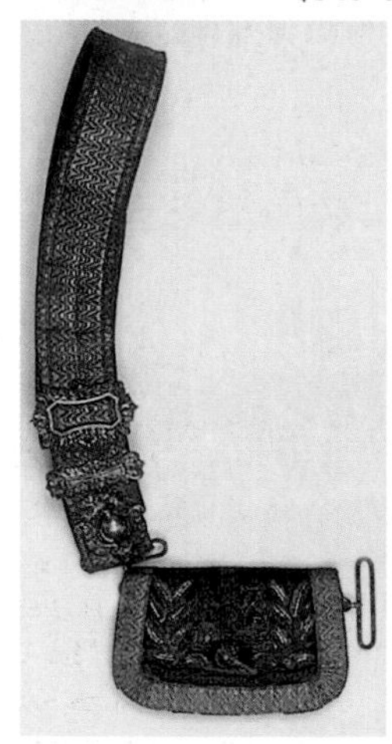

► **A Victorian First Northumberland Artillery Volunteers officer's full dress shoulder belt and pouch,** the belt with a silver-plated buckle, tip and slide, the pouch with embroidered decoration, with foul weather cover, slight damage.
£260–310 / €380–450
$470–560 WAL

A Victorian 4th Brigade South Irish Division Royal Garrison Artillery officer's shoulder belt and pouch, the belt with gilt buckle and slide, the cloth pouch embroidered with Royal Arms and supporters, Irish.
£320–380 / €470–550
$580–690 WAL

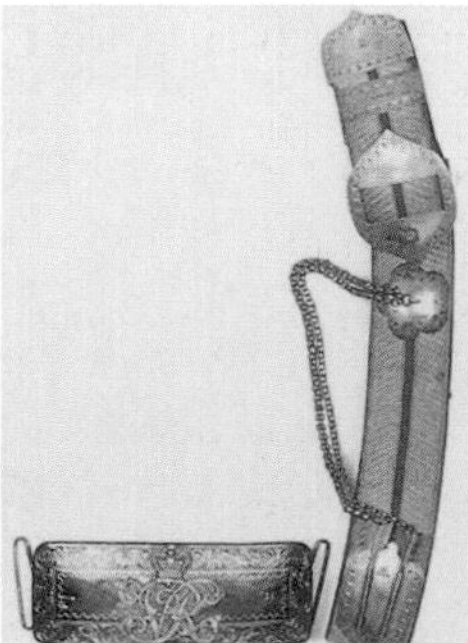

A 3rd/4th Hussars officer's silver-mounted shoulder belt and pouch, the pouch with embroidered decoration and silver mounts, with a crowned brass 'VR' cypher flap badge, slight damage, with helmet plate *en suite*, Birmingham 1898.
£550–660 / €800–960
$1,000–1,200 WAL

A pilot's uniform, German, 1914–18.
£370–440 / €540–640
$670–800 SWO

► **A Victorian South Devon Regiment of Militia officer's 1855 pattern leather belt,** worn.
£190–220 / €280–330
$340–400 DNW

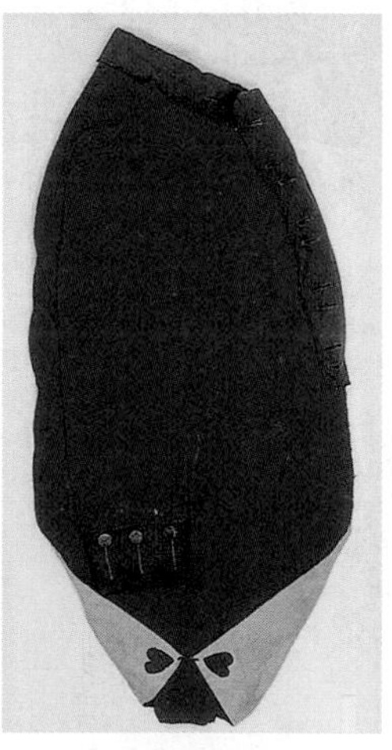

An other ranks' uniform tailcoat, some cast-metal buttons missing, c1765.
£1,000–1,200
€1,450–1,750
$1,800–2,150 WAL

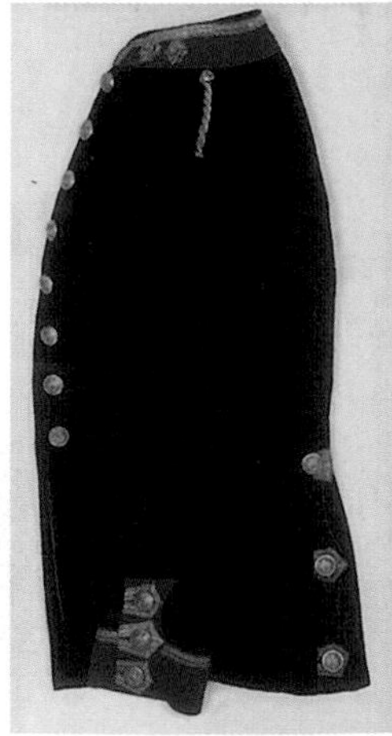

A Victorian Assistant Superintendant of the Military Stores Staff full dress tunic, with gilt buttons, slight repairs.
£220–260 / €320–380
$400–470 WAL

Helmets & Headdresses

An 11th Regiment other ranks' worsted forage cap, numbered '11', damaged, c1800.
£590–700 / €850–1,000
$1,050–1,250 ⚒ WAL

◄ A Prussian Cavalry officer's model 1808 mohair and silk hat, with a leather sweatband, in a wooden storage case, German, c1830.
£1,650–1,950
€2,400–2,850
$3,000–3,550
⚒ Herm

A Victorian 1st Life Guards officer's gilt-mounted white metal helmet, with silver-plated helmet plate, hair plume and brass ball, slight damage, lining restored.
£550–660 / €800–960
$1,000–1,200 ⚒ WAL

◄ A Victorian Northamptonshire Regiment officer's gilt-mounted cloth helmet, with gilt and silver-plated helmet plate, leather and padded silk lining.
£610–730 / €890–1,050
$1,200–1,300 ⚒ WAL

A 5th Royal Irish Lancers *tchapka*, with chin strap, plume missing, c1860.
£890–1,050
€1,300–1,550
$1,600–1,900 ⚒ HOK

◄ A Leicestershire Regiment 1st Volunteer Battalion officer's 1878 pattern cloth helmet, with silver-plated fittings and helmet plate, late 19thC.
£530–630 / €770–920
$960–1,150 ⚒ DNW

► A Victorian Norfolk Regiment 2nd Volunteers Batallion officer's cloth helmet, with white-metal mounts, leather and silk lining, the headband padded with a newspaper dated 1892.
£1,050–1,250
€1,550–1,850
$1,850–2,200 ⚒ WAL

◄ An officer's helmet, by J. Haslett, Woolwich, 1914–18, with a metal case.
£490–580
€720–850
$890–1,050
⚒ SWO

► A 2nd Reiter Bavarian Heavy Cavalry officer's *Pickelhaube*, German, 1914–18.
£1,600–1,800
€2,350–2,650
$2,900–3,250 ⊞ TLA

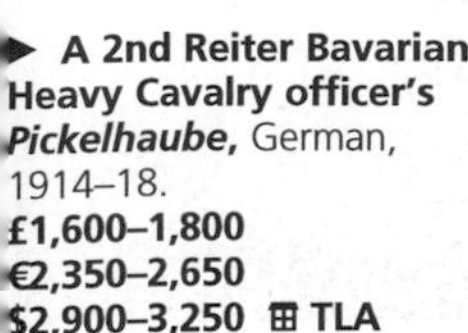

MILITARIA

Orders & Medals

A pair, awarded to Corporal Robert Pocock, 40th Foot: Military General Service medal 1793–1814, with nine bars, Egypt, Vimiera, Talavera, Busaco, Badajoz, Salamanca, Vittoria, Pyrenees and Toulouse; Waterloo 1815 medal, silver clip and bar suspension replaced, with related paperwork.
£9,400–11,200
€13,700–16,400
$17,000–20,300 DNW

► **A group of six,** awarded to General Lawrenson of the 13th Hussars and 17th Lancers: Crimea medal 1845–55, with two bars; Turkish Crimea; three Turkish Orders of the Medjidie; Sardinian War medal.
£5,000–5,500
€7,300–8,000
$9,000–10,000 JBM

A Crimea medal, awarded to J. Pine, 1st Battalion, Rifles, with four bars, Alma, Balaklava, Inkermann and Sebastopol.
£670–800 / €980–1,150
$1,200–1,450 WAL

► **A silver Challenge Cup medal,** awarded to Private William Joseph Birks, 1st Manchester Rifles, 1862, 2in (5cm) diam.
£140–165 / €200–240
$250–300 DNW

The Most Honourable Order of the Bath KCB Knight Commander's 22ct gold and enamel neck badge, London 1815.
£1,650–1,950
€2,400–2,850
$3,000–3,550 DNW

A group of four medals, awarded to Private J. Nash: Crimea medal 1854, with one bar Sebastopol; Crimea 1855; Long Service and Good Conduct; Canada, with one bar Fenian Raid 1866, mounted in a glazed case.
£960–1,150
€1,400–1,650
$1,750–2,100 WW

A group of five, awarded to Admiral's Coxswain J. Garland, Royal Navy: China 1842; Baltic 1854–55; Crimea 1854–55; Royal Navy Long Service and Good Conduct; Turkish Crimea, 1855.
£2,250–2,700 / €3,300–3,950
$4,050–4,900 DNW

A pair, awarded to General H. G. Rainey, 61st Foot, late 49th Foot: China 1842, with replacement bar suspension and bar; Indian Mutiny 1857–59, with one bar, Delhi.
£2,000–2,400
€2,900–3,500
$3,600–4,350 DNW

A New Zealand medal, awarded to Commander J. C. Hoseason, HMS *Inflexible*, 1845–66, reverse dated 1847.
£3,000–3,600
€4,400–5,300
$5,400–6,500 WW
Only 20 medals were issued to the Royal Navy with this reverse date, and all to HMS *Inflexible*.

An India General Service medal, awarded to Private T. Swain, 1st Battalion Rifle Brigade, with one bar, Burma 1887–89.
£410–490 / €600–720
$740–890 WAL

An India General Service medal, awarded to Captain C. E. Boodle, Land Transport Corps, with one bar, Persia.
£530–630 / €770–920
$960–1,150 CHTR

LOCATE THE SOURCE

The source of each illustration in Miller's can be found by checking the code letters below each caption with the Key to Illustrations, pages 778–784.

A gold Rajah of Kolapore's Prize medal, Gunner James Shand, 1st Brigade, Garrison Artillery, 1872.
£330–390 / €480–570
$600–710 ⚒ DNW
In 1870 the Rajah of Kolapore presented £100 / €145 / $180 to the National Rifle Association as a prize. He also sent his £10 / €15 / $18 subscription but died suddenly a few months later. The N. R. A. Council decided to invest the whole amount in a trophy – a pair of challenge vases to be named after the Rajah and to be competed for by teams from Great Britain, India, Canada and other colonies. The first shooting match was held in 1872 and was won by Canada.

Items in the Orders & Medals section have been arranged in date order.

A British North Borneo Company silver medal, awarded to Private 42 Bahadur, with one bar, Rundum, 1897–1916.
£1,050–1,250
€1,550–1,850
$1,900–2,250 ⚒ DNW
Approximately 100 medals were issued for the Rundum rebellion of 1915–16.

A group of three, awarded to Lieutenant-Sergeant Charles Albert Baskett, 2/21st Royal Scots Fusiliers: South Africa medal 1877–79 with one bar 1879; India General Service medal with one bar, Burma 1885–7 and Long Service and Good Conduct medal.
£910–1,050 / €1,350–1,600
$1,600–1,900 ⚒ GTH

A group of four, awarded to Lieutenant A. H. Thomson, Royal Navy, HMS *Himalaya* and HMS *Superb*: South Africa 1877–79; Egypt and Sudan 1882–89 with one bar, Alexandria 11th July; British War medal 1914–20; Khedive's Star 1882.
£590–700 / €850–1,000
$1,050–1,250 ⚒ DNW

A group of four, awarded to Lieutenant-Commander F. Garland, Royal Navy; Egypt and Sudan 1882–89: British War Medal 1914–20; Khedive's Star 1882; Royal Humane Society bronze medal.
£360–430 / €530–630
$650–780 ⚒ DNW

A pair, awarded to R. J. M. MacLeod: Egypt and Sudan 1882–89; Khedive's Star 1884, with photographs, documents and certificates.
£1,200–1,400 / €1,750–2,050
$2,150–2,550 ⚒ JBe

MILITARIA

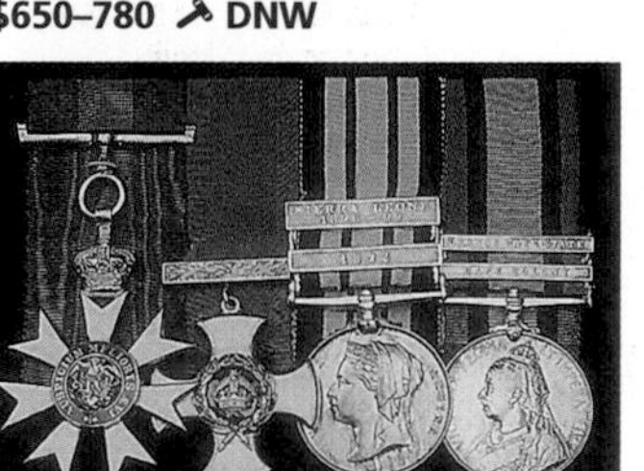

A group of four, awarded to Major Alexander Tarbet, Lagos Hausa Force and South Lancashire Regiment: The Most Distinguished Order of St Michael and St George; Distinguished Service Order; East and West Africa 1887–1900 with two bars, 1892; Sierra Leone 1898–99; Queen's South Africa 1899–1902 with two bars, Orange Free State and Cape Colony.
£4,700–5,600
€6,900–8,200
$8,500–10,100 ⚒ DNW

A group of seven, awarded to Brigadier General E. N. Stockley, Royal Engineers: Distinguished Service Order with second award bar; India General Service medal 1895 with one bar, Punjab Frontier 1897–98; 1914–15 Star; British War and Victory medals; Légion d'Honneur; Croix de Guerre.
£2,450–2,750 / €3,600–4,000
$4,450–5,000 ⊞ JBM

A group of six, awarded to G. Ault, 7th London Regiment: India General Service medal with one bar, Relief of Chitral 1895; Queen's South Africa with five bars, Cape Colony, Paardeberg, Driefontein, Transvaal, Wittebergen; King's South Africa with two bars, 1901 and 1902; 1914–15 Star; British War and Victory medals.
£700–780 / €1,000–1,150
$1,250–1,400 ⊞ GBM

◄ **A Canada General Service medal,** awarded to Private G. Walker, Rifle Brigade, 1899, with two bars, Fenian Raid 1866 and Fenian Raid 1870.
£530–630 / €770–920
$960–1,150 ⚒ WAL

A group of eight, awarded to Brigadier-General A. H. C. James, South Staffs Regiment: Distinguished Service Order; Member of the Order of the Royal Victorian Order 4th Class; Queen's South Africa with three bars, Cape Colony, Transvaal and Wittebergen; King's South Africa with two bars, South Africa 1901 and 1902; 1914–15 Star; British War and Victory Medals with Oak Leaf; Légion d'Honneur.
£2,900–3,450 / €4,250–5,000
$5,200–6,200 L

A silver Delhi Durbar medal, 1903.
£150–180 / €220–260
$270–320 WAL

A group of five, awarded to R. Atkinson, Vol. Coy. Border Regiment: Military Cross, Queen's South Africa with four bars, Cape Colony, Orange Free State, Transvaal and South Africa 1901; 1914–15 Star; British War and Victory medals, with photograph.
£5,600–6,700 / €8,200–9,800
$10,100–12,100 PFK

A group of four, awarded to Major Warde, Royal Engineers: Military Cross, 1914–15 Star with one bar, Mons; British War and Victory medals with MID oak leaf.
£1,100–1,250 / €1,600–1,800
$2,000–2,250 GBM
The recipient of this group attached two oak leaves to the ribbon of the Victory to indicate that he was mentioned twice in dispatches, although an oak leaf in reality denotes any number of mentions.

A group of six, awarded to F. Zanelli, HMS *Blanche*: 1914–15 Star; British War and Victory medals; Defence medal 1939–45; War medal 1939–45; Navy Long Service and Good Conduct medal, with photographs and related paperwork, with a wooden box.
£190–220 / €280–330
$340–400 JBe

A group of five, awarded to Colonel Thomas Lindsay, Irish Guards: OBE; 1939–45 Star; France and Germany Star; War medal with oak leaf; Defence Medal, with related paperwork.
£350–420 / €510–610
$630–760 G(L)

A group of four medals, awarded to Lance Corporal A. W. C. Jones, Northants Regiment: Military medal; 1914–15 Star; British War and Victory medals, with press release and further research.
£800–950 / €1,150–1,350
$1,450–1,700 GAK

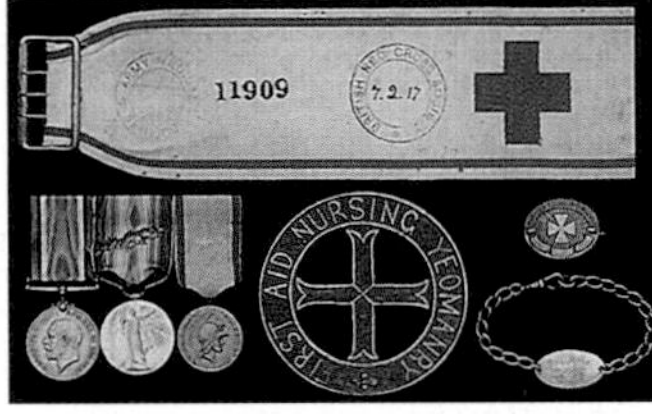

A group of three, awarded to Miss D. M. Paynter, First Aid Nursing Yeomanry: British War and Victory medals with MID oak leaf; First Aid Nursing Yeomanry 1914–18; with a British Red Cross Society armband, silver identity bracelet, bronze badge and carved wood badge.
£550–660 / €800–960
$1,000–1,200 DNW
Miss D. M. Paynter was one of just 15 members of the First Aid Nursing Yeomanry to be mentioned in dispatches during WWI.

A Thailand Order of the Crown neck medal and breast star, 1940s.
£270–300 / €390–440
$490–540 GBM

A group of four, awarded to Private D. Taylor: 1914–15 Star; British War and Victory medals; Long Service and Good Conduct medal with one bar, India, with miniatures and a Royal Scots Greys badge, mounted on a pad.
£260–310 / €380–450
$470–560 WW

A group of six, awarded to Fireman W. F. Mitchell, HMS *Queen of Thanet*: Distinguished Service medal; 1939–45 Star; Atlantic Star; 1939–45 Defence medal; 1939–45 War Medal; 1940 Dunkirk Medal.
£1,400–1,650 / €2,050–2,400
$2,550–3,000 E

A group of six, awarded to Squadron Leader G. Wood, Royal Air Force: Distinguished Flying Cross; 1939–45 Star; Air Crew Europe Star; Defence and War medals; American Silver Star; with miniatures.
£1,750–2,100 / €2,550–3,050
$3,150–3,800 DNW
Only 29 American Silver Star medals were awarded to the RAF during WWII.

Powder Flasks & Horns

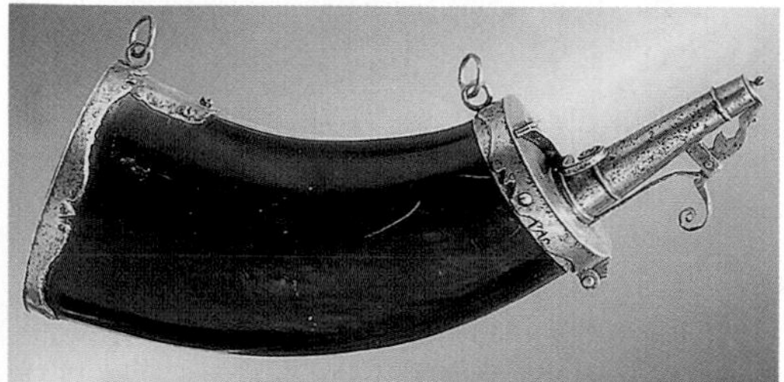

◄ **A powder horn,** incised with ornamental lines, with an iron belt hook, two suspension rings and measuring spout with spring-loaded valve, German, c1630, 14¼in (36cm) long.
£1,000–1,200
€1,450–1,750
$1,800–2,150 ⚒ Herm

An iron-mounted powder flask, with turned decoration, two suspension rings and measuring spout with spring-loaded valve, c1650, 6¾in (17cm) high.
£1,200–1,400
€1,750–2,050
$2,150–2,550 ⚒ Herm

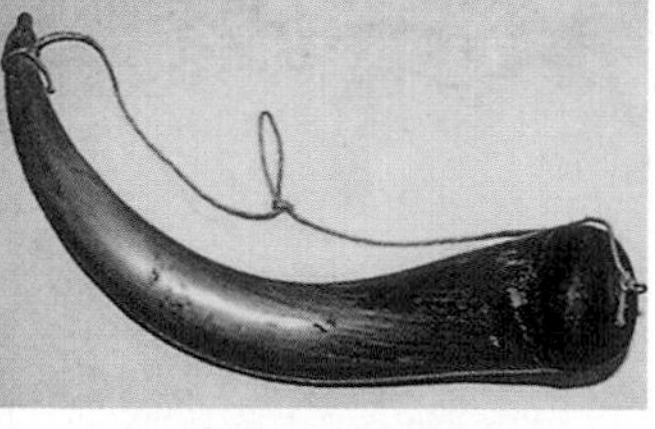

A hand-painted wood butt powder horn, c1800, 17in (43cm) long.
£130–155 / €190–220
$240–280 ⚒ DuM

► **A United States Military Dragoon brass powder flask,** c1860, 9in (23cm) long.
£260–310 / €380–450
$470–560 ⚒ DuM

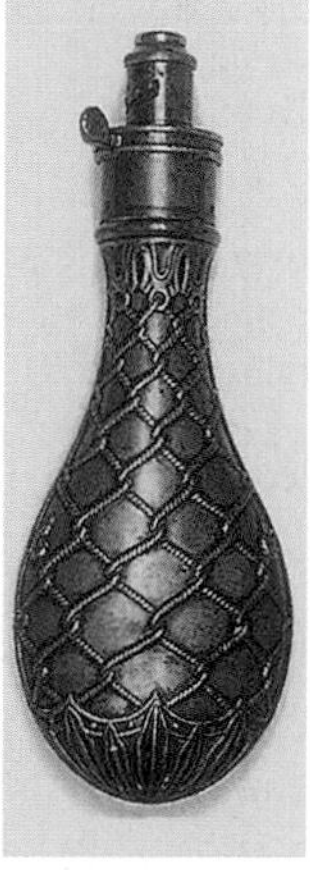

◄ **An embossed copper powder flask,** decorated with entwined ropework, with Hawksley patent top, c1860, 8in (20.5cm) high.
£120–140 / €170–200
$210–250 ⚒ WAL

Miscellaneous

A Boer War horn beaker, engraved with the figure of a soldier and inscription, c1900, 3½in (9cm) high.
£210–250 / €310–370
$380–450 ⚒ G(L)

◄ **A bronze box,** by I. Porter & E. Orme, containing 13 discs depicting the Duke of Wellington and the victories of the Peninsular War, in a leather case, two discs later, 1815, 3in (7.5cm) diam.
£620–690
€900–1,000
$1,100–1,250
⊞ TML

A brass dinner gong, made from a WWI 14in shell, in a mahogany stand with felt-ended striker, 22in (56cm) high.
£910–1,100
€1,350–1,600
$1,700–2,000 ⚒ DW
This shell case was brought from France by 2nd Lieutenant Eric Clowes Pashley who was mentioned in a dispatch for gallant and distinguished service in the field and accounted for ten aeroplanes in five months. He was killed in active service with the B. E. Force in 1917, aged 24.

► **A painted wood military manoeuvres game,** with a sliding cover, damaged, c1775, box 6½ x 4½in (16.5 x 11.5cm).
£940–1,100
€1,350–1,600
$1,700–2,000
⚒ WAL

A Victorian painted drum, decorated with the Royal coat-of-arms, on later bun feet, damaged, 18in (45.5cm) high.
£230–270 / €340–400
$420–490 ⚒ NSal

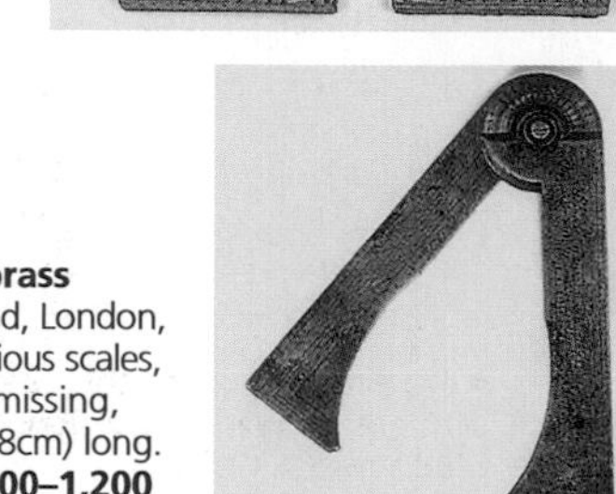

► **A gunner's brass caliper,** by Dollond, London, engraved with various scales, signed, iron tips missing, late 18thC, 7in (18cm) long.
£700–840 / €1,000–1,200
$1,250–1,500 ⚒ WAL

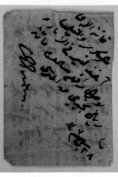

A letter from General Gordon, written on Arabic tissue paper, sent during the siege of Khartoum, 1884, 1¾ x 1¼in (4.5 x 3cm).
£700–840 / €1,000–1,200
$1,250–1,500 ⚒ SWO

A cast-silver menu holder, by W. Gibson & J. Langman, in the form of the badge of the 13th Hussars, bearing the motto 'Viret in Aeternum', London 1899, 2¼in (5.5cm) high.
£270–320 / €400–470
$490–580 ⚒ WW

An appliqué quilt/ prayer mat, early 20thC, 80in (203cm) wide.
£200–240 / €290–350
$360–430 ⚒ PF
This mat is thought to have been made by a WWI Turkish prisoner-of-war.

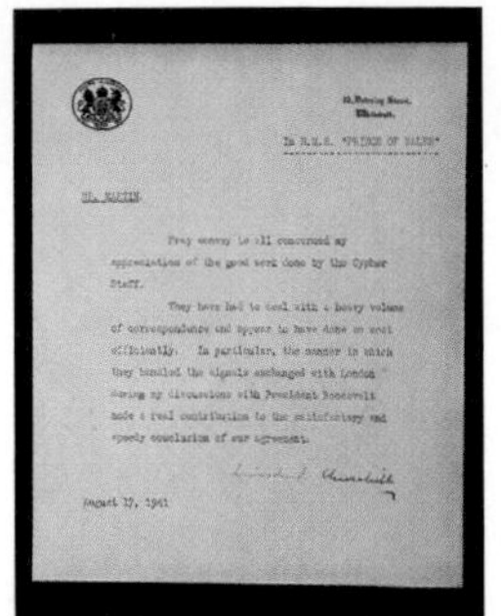

A letter from Sir Winston Churchill, to Mr Martin asking him to 'convey to all concerned my appreciation of the good work done by the Cypher Staff,' complimenting them particularly on 'the manner in which they handled the signals exchanged with London during my discussions with President Roosevelt made a real contribution to the satisfactory and speedy conclusion of our agreement,' dated 17 August 1941, 4°.
£3,350–3,750
€4,900–5,500
$6,100–6,800 ⊞ CFSD
Churchill worked tirelessly to get the Americans to join forces with the Allies. His first success in persuading the Americans away from neutrality was to begin a sustained correspondence with President Roosevelt in 1940. In August 1941, Churchill and Roosevelt had their long-postponed meeting at Argentia in Placentia Bay off the Newfoundland coast. Churchill arrived in the *Prince of Wales*, the newest battleship, just refitted after the successful sinking of the *Bismarck*. The Atlantic Charter resulted from this meeting, but more important than this statement of principles was the assumption by the American navy of the task of convoying fast merchant ships as far east as Iceland, which Churchill visited on his way back to England.

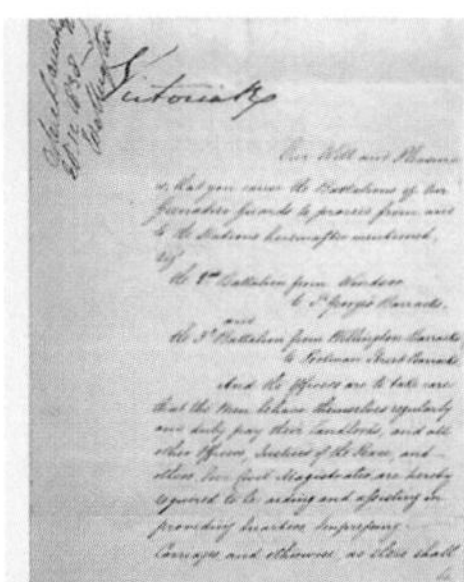

A signed manuscript, with an order to the Duke of Wellington from Queen Victoria dated 8 February 1838.
£230–270 / €340–400
$420–490 ⚒ BBA

A map of the Battle of Belgrade, coloured copper engraving, inscribed 'Chr: Weigel excudit, 1717', 16¼ x 13½in (41.5 x 34.5cm), glazed and framed.
£250–300 / €370–440
$450–540 ⚒ DORO

An engraved picture of the Siege of Bergen-op-Zoom, by Dolondeo, mid-17thC, 9 x 12½in (23 x 32cm), framed.
£160–190 / €220–280
$290–340 ⚒ BERN

A terracotta tobacco jar and cover, in the form of a bust of a soldier wearing Boer War uniform, c1900, 6in (15cm) high.
£280–330 / €410–480
$510–600 ⚒ WL

A military officer's mahogany travelling box, containing scent bottles, inkwells, porcelain cups, saucers, sugar bowls, an eye bath, funnel, boot pulls, coffee pot, glass containers, corkscrew, razors, spoon, strop, silver washing bowl and moustache brush, French, c1825, 15in (38cm) wide.
£6,300–7,000
€9,200–10,200
$11,400–12,700 ⊞ JTS

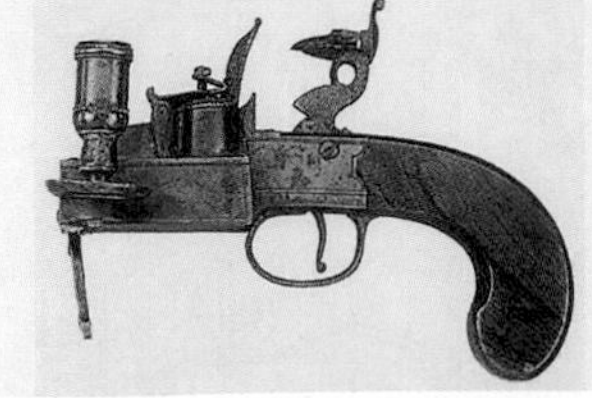

A brass flintlock tinder lighter, with compartment for tinder and candle holder, with a figured walnut butt, jaw screw missing, one foot incomplete, early 19thC, 7in (18cm) long.
£900–1,050 / €1,300–1,550
$1,600–1,900 ⚒ S(O)

A silver trophy cup, by James Kenzie, with later floral decoration and inscription to the 6th Royal Lancashire Militia, Irish, Dublin 1817, 11in (28cm) high.
£190–220 / €280–320
$340–400 ⚒ G(L)

A tureen holder, made from three bayonet grips, 1914–18, 6½in (16.5cm) high.
£135–150 / €195–220
$240–270 ⊞ GBM

Sport

Billiards

A rosewood billiard ball holder, by William Morton, New York, with a marble top, needlework panel and open shelves to the reverse, American, c1840, 26¾in (68cm) wide.
£320–380 / €470–550
$580–690 ⚒ SK

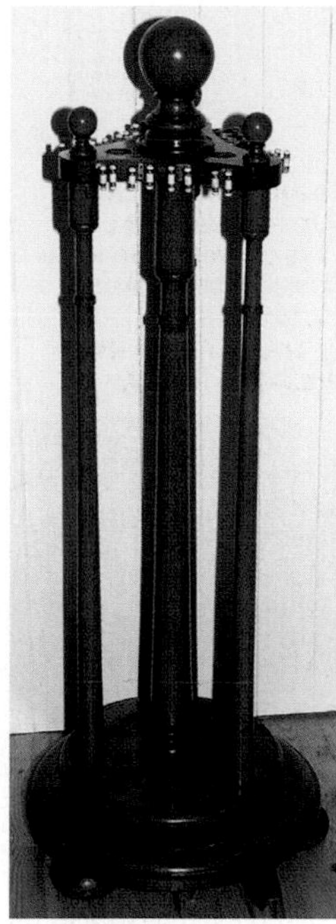

A revolving oak snooker cue stand, c1870, 46in (117cm) high.
£1,150–1,300
€1,700–1,900
$2,100–2,350 ⊞ MTay

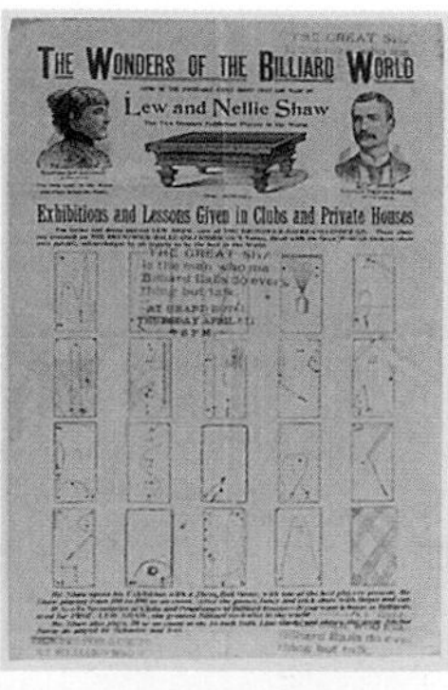

◄ A billiard poster, illustrating Lew & Nellie Shaw's trick shot billiard exhibition at the Grand Hotel, c1895, 18 x 12in (45.5 x 30.5cm).
£310–370 / €450–540
$560–670 ⚒ JAA

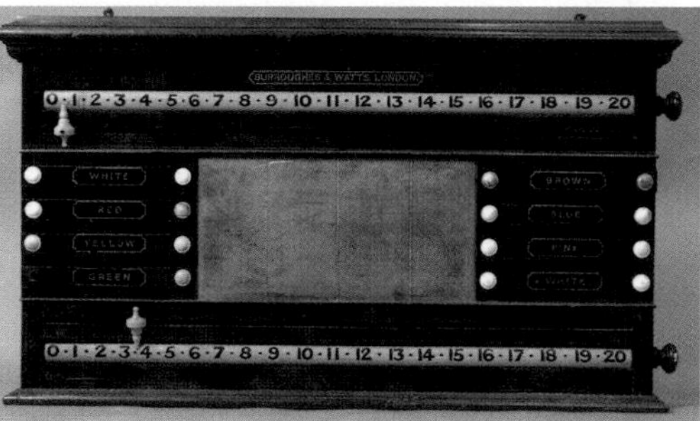

A Burroughs & Watts billiard scoreboard, with a blackboard, two revolving score indicators and ten slides, late 19thC, 35in (89cm) wide.
£350–420 / €510–610
$630–760 ⚒ SWO

A mahogany folding bagatelle table, 1880s, 84in (213.5cm) long.
£2,250–2,500 / €3,300–3,650
$4,050–4,550 ⊞ MSh

A Victorian miniature table-top snooker table, by H. Spiers & Co, London, with slate bed and adjustable supports, 52in (132cm) wide.
£90–100 / €130–145
$160–180 ⊞ HEM

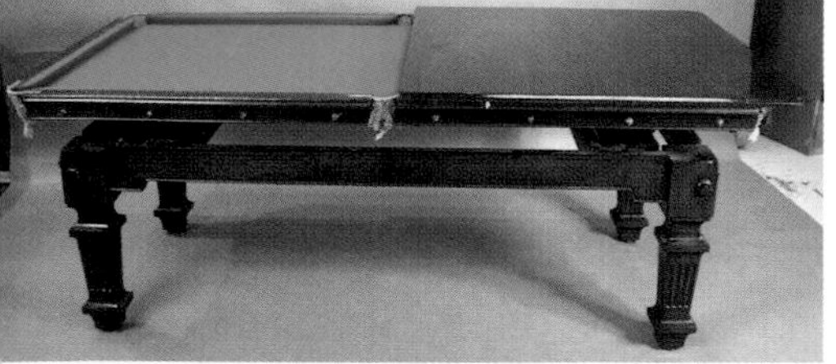

A mahogany snooker/dining table, with four leaves and adjustable slate bed, stamped No. 1353 and 2264212, early 20thC, 91in (231cm) long.
£800–960 / €1,150–1,350
$1,450–1,750 ⚒ SWO

Insurance values

Always insure your valuable antiques for the cost of replacing them with similar items, regardless of the original price paid.
Both dealers and auctioneers can provide a valuation service for a fee.

► A tinplate clockwork billiard player mechanical toy, by Güntherman, German, c1905, 11in (28cm) long.
£630–700 / €920–1,050
$1,150–1,300 ⊞ HAL

Boxing

A silver-gilt and enamel Lord Lonsdale Challenge boxing belt, by Mappin & Webb, Sheffield, awarded to Bunny Sterling in 1967, set with an enamel portrait of Lord Lonsdale, the reverse inscribed 'This belt is the sole property of Bunny Sterling who has won the Middleweight Championship of Gt Britain three times', with four plaques decorated with a rose, thistle, daffodil and shamrock, two enamelled plaques depicting boxing scenes and six presentation plaques inscribed with details of contests, with a copy of John Harding's book *Lonsdale's Belt*, 36in (91.5cm) long.
£4,750–5,700 / €6,900–8,300
$8,600–10,300 BUDD
Bunny Sterling was the first West Indian immigrant boxer to hold a British professional boxing title, when crowned Middleweight Champion in 1970.

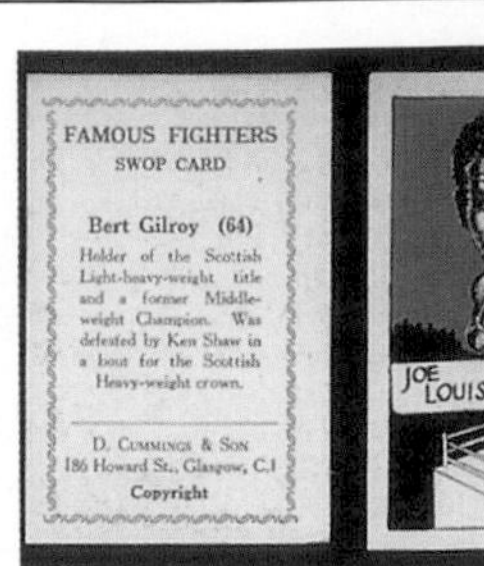

D. Summings & Son, Famous Fighters, set of 64, c1949.
£100–120 / €145–175
$180–220 RTo

For more cigarette cards
see Ephemera pages 673–679

A postcard of Jessie Willard and Jack Johnson, posted in Havana, Cuba, American, 1916.
£75–90 / €110–130
$140–165 JAA

Henry Alken, 'A Prize Fight', from The National Sports of Great Britain series, hand-coloured aquatint by I. Clark, 1820, 10¾ x 14½in (27.5 x 37cm).
£175–210 / €260–310
$320–380 BBA

An Einfalt tinplate clockwork boxing toy, the boxers with swinging arms, facing each other on two-wheel trolleys that move forwards and backwards, German, 1930s.
£130–155 / €190–220
$240–280 WAL

Cricket

A silver rose bowl, by Atkins Bros, inscribed 'Yorkshire County Cricket Club, presented to T. Hunter, to commemorate the record season of 1900', Sheffield 1900, 6¾in (17cm) diam, 12½oz.
£700–840 / €1,050–1,250
$1,250–1,500 DD

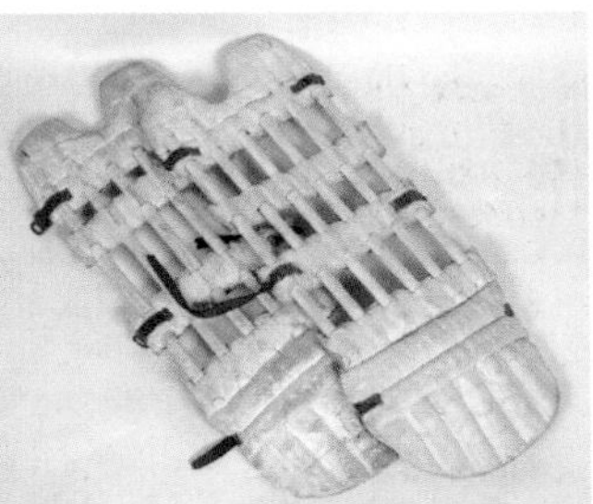

A pair of leather skeleton cricket pads, c1900, 24in (61cm) high.
£145–160 / €200–230
$260–290 MSh

An albumen photograph of the England Cricket Team, on board a sailing vessel, presumably on the way to play in America, late 19thC, 7 x 10¼in (18 x 26cm), framed.
£240–280 / €350–410
$430–510 DW

A monochrome print, 'Play', depicting a Gentlemen v Players Day at Lord's, 19thC, 18½ x 38½in (47 x 98cm).
£470–560 / €690–820
$850–1,000 GTH

A pair of pottery side plates, each inscribed and depicting Syd F. Barnes, 1908, 8in (20.5cm) diam.
£360–430 / €530–630
$650–780 SAS

◄ **A colour print,** 'Cricket 1885', 19thC English School, 17 x 14in (43 x 35.5cm).
£120–140 / €175–200
$220–250 GTH

SPORT

Croquet

An ivory croquet mallet, with an ash shaft, c1870, 34in (86.5cm) long.
£360–400 / €520–580
$650–720 ⊞ MSh

A wooden table croquet set, with original pine box, 1920s, 15in (38cm) wide.
£135–150 / €195–220
$240–270 ⊞ MSh

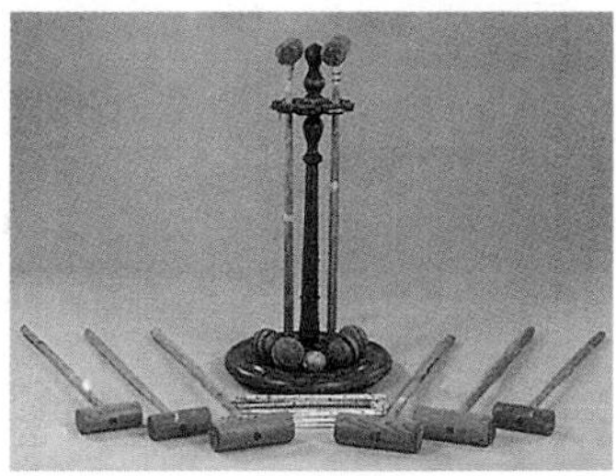

A wooden croquet set, by Jaques & Son, comprising eight mallets, four striped wooden balls and a marble ball with maker's mark, 12 iron hoops, with a wooden stand with maker's stamp, early 20thC.
£290–340 / €420–500
$520–620 ⚒ PFK

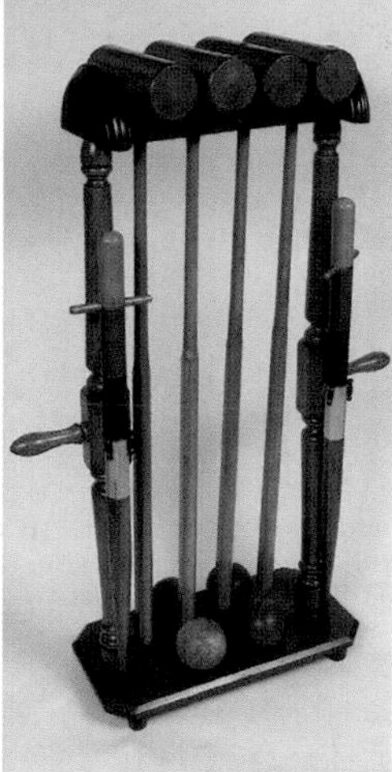

A boxwood and ash croquet set, by George Bussey & Co, with an elm and mahogany stand, c1900, 40in (35.5cm) high.
£760–850 / €1,100–1,250
$1,400–1,550 ⊞ MSh

Curling

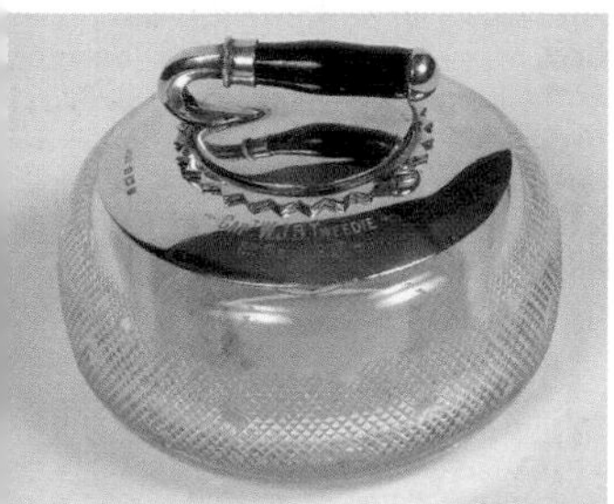

A glass and silver inkwell, in the form of a curling stone, inscribed, 1904, 5in (12.5cm) diam.
£760–850 / €1,100–1,250
$1,400–1,550 ⊞ MSh

A granite curling stone, mid-20thC, 11in (28cm) diam.
£90–100 / €130–145
$160–180 ⊞ OLA

A silver curling trophy, on an ebonized shield, 1907, 30in (76cm) high.
£2,850–3,200 / €4,150–4,650
$5,200–5,800 ⊞ MSh

Equestrian

A horn beaker, engraved with a hunting scene, late 18thC, 5in (12.5cm) high.
£450–500 / €660–730
$810–910 ⊞ SEA

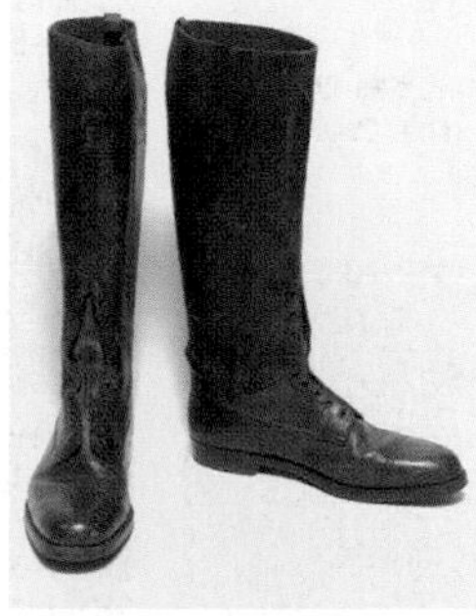

◄ **A pair of leather polo boots,** 1920s.
£135–150
€195–220
$240–270
⊞ OH

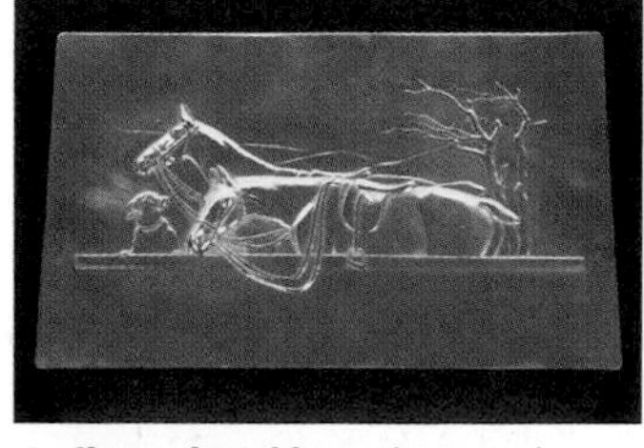

A silver-plated box, decorated with two horses and a dog, c1900, 9in (23cm) wide.
£1,250–1,400 / €1,850–2,050
$2,250–2,550 ⊞ RGa

► **A silver-plated hunting sandwich box,** by James Dixon & Sons, with original leather case, c1930, 6in (15cm) wide.
£140–160 / €200–230
$250–290 ⊞ MSh

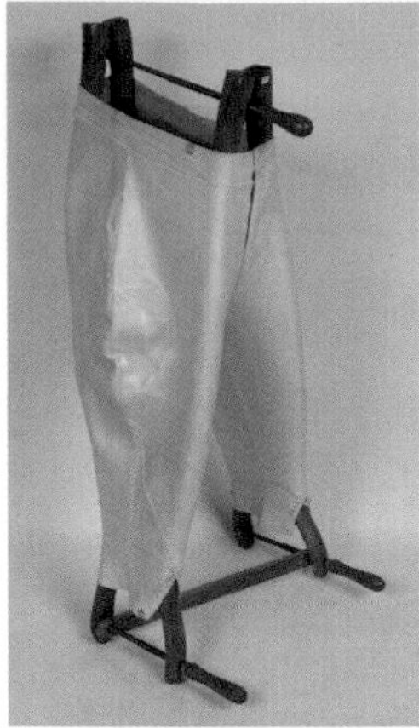

A pair of leather hunting breeches, with original beech stretchers, c1920, 43in (109cm) high.
£670–750 / €950–1,100
$1,200–1,350 ⊞ MSh

A Victorian glass claret jug, the silver-plated mount chased and embossed with fox masks, riding hats and whips, the hinged cover with a finial in the form of a dog at a gate, 11in (28cm) high.
£320–380 / €470–550
$580–690 ⚒ HOLL

A silver-gilt horse racing trophy cup, by Benjamin Smith, inscribed 'Newcastle Races, 1807', decorated with bands of trailing vine and foliate scrolls, with scrolled loop handles, London 1806, on an ebonized plinth, 16¼in (41.5cm) high.
£4,600–5,500
€6,700–8,000
$8,300–10,000 ⚒ AH

A set of six Bilston buttons, enamelled with scenes of the care and schooling of horses, with gilt-metal backs, 18thC, 1¼in (3cm) diam.
£4,100–4,900 / €6,000–7,200
$7,400–8,900 ⚒ HOLL

A silver-plated cruet set, the salt and pepper modelled as a pair of boots, the mustard as a cap with two crop spoons, on a stand, lozenge mark, c1869, 3½in (9cm) high.
£240–280 / €350–410
$430–510 ⚒ WL

A silver-gilt two-handled cup, by Messrs Hutton, for the 1948 Royal Hunt, Ascot, won by Master Vote, one side engraved with the results, the reverse with a Royal crest, on an ebony plinth, London 1908, 15in (38cm) high, 60oz.
£940–1,100 / €1,350–1,600
$1,700–2,000 ⚒ JNic

A silver and enamel cigarette case, decorated with two steeplechasers, Austrian, c1900, 2in (5cm) wide.
£1,300–1,450 / €1,900–2,100
$2,350–2,600 ⊞ SHa

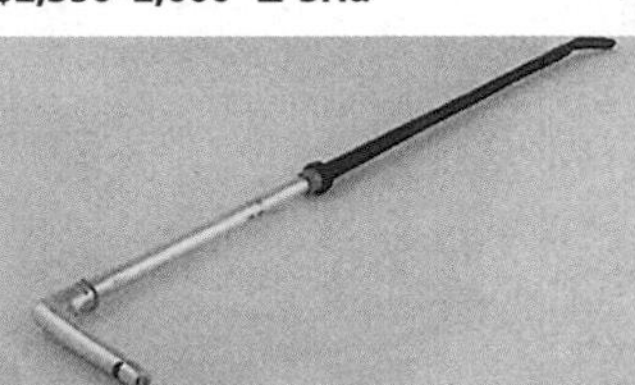

A late Victorian riding crop with a whistle terminal, by G. W. White & Co, London, retailed by Asprey, London, 22¼in (56.5cm) long.
£610–730 / €890–1,050
$1,100–1,300 ⚒ WW

◄ A leather-cased hunting crop, with a white-metal surmount in the form of a bust of a jockey, late 19thC, 22¼in (56.5cm) long.
£150–180 / €220–260
$270–320 ⚒ BUDD

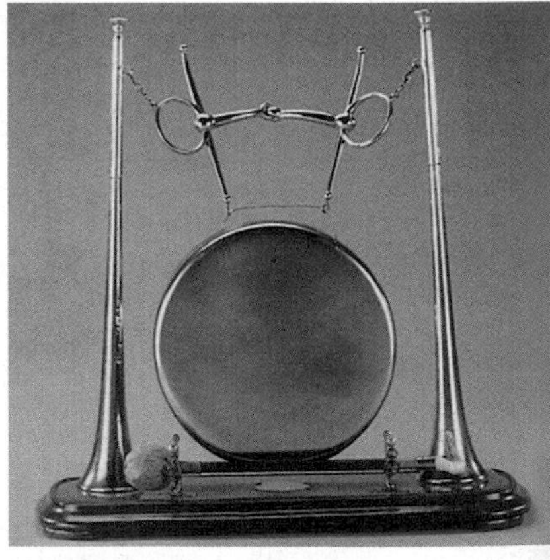

A Victorian white-metal dinner gong, by Henry Keat & Sons, London, the gong suspended from a horse's bit between two copper hunting horns, the striker converted from a cane and bone hunting crop, on an oak base, 23¾in (60.5cm) high.
£500–600 / €730–880
$910–1,100 ⚒ BUDD

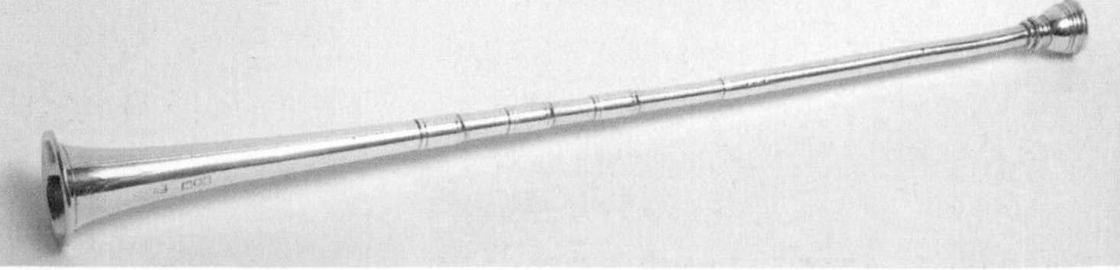

A silver hunting horn, by Sampson Mordan & Co, London 1897, 12in (30.5cm) long.
£210–240 / €310–350
$380–430 ⊞ CoHA

◄ **An ivory knife,** decorated with a riding hat and whip, c1890, 15in (38cm) long.
£500–560 / €730–820
$900–1,000 ⊞ RGa

► **A set of four silver menu holders,** by Sampson Mordan & Co, two mounted with a fox's mask, two with a hound's mask, Chester 1909, in a fitted case.
£1,000–1,200
€1,450–1,750
$1,800–2,150 ⚒ RTo

A pair of silver menu holders, in the form of a horsewoman and horseman jumping fences, maker's mark SJ, London 1899, 3in (7.5cm) wide, 2½oz.
£1,000–1,200
€1,450–1,750
$1,800–2,150 ⚒ TEN

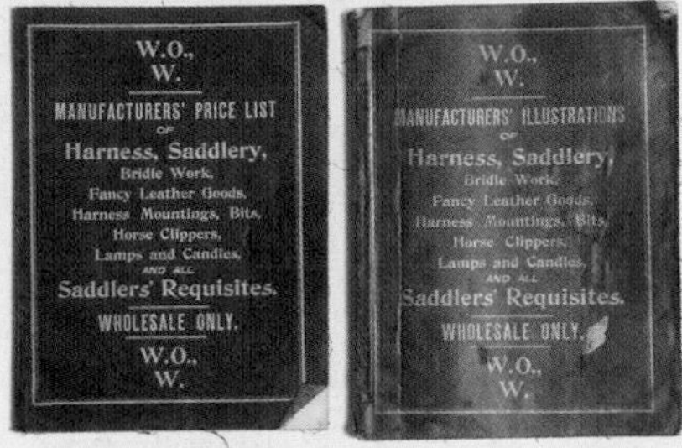

A William Overton manufacturers' price list, 1904, 10in (25.5cm) high.
£135–150 / €200–220
$240–270 ⊞ JUN

► **An ormolu silhouette of a horse,** mounted on velvet, in a glazed case, 19thC, 16in (40.5cm) wide.
£175–210 / €260–310
$320–380 ⚒ G(L)

A Coalbrookdale bronze figure of a polo player, by W. Roche, signed, dated 1882, 13in (33cm) high.
£2,700–3,000 / €3,900–4,650
$4,900–5,800 ⊞ MSh

Fishing

► **A fishing guide barometer,** by Short & Mason, 1950s, 9in (23cm) diam.
£105–120
€155–175
$190–220 ⊞ RTW
This barometer was made for export to North America.

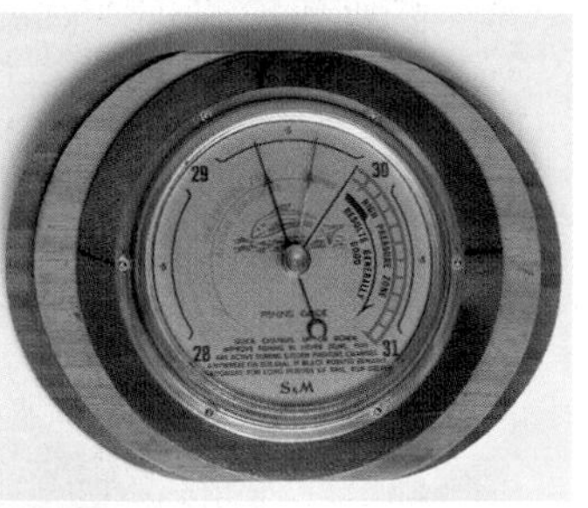

Items in the Fishing section have been arranged in alphabetical order.

◄ **A glass bowl,** engraved with a fishing scene, c1880, 10in (25.5cm) high.
£180–200 / €260–290
$320–360 ⊞ SPA

A pair of stuffed and mounted perch, in glass-fronted cases, c1860, 11in (28cm) wide.
£670–750 / €980–1,100
$1,200–1,350 ⊞ MSh

SPORT

A stuffed and mounted tench, in a bowfronted glazed case, caught by Mr Bailey on the river Stour, January 1898, weight 1lb 3oz, case 15¾in (40cm) wide.
£290–340 / €420–500
$520–620 ⚒ SWO

Three stuffed and mounted perch, in a display case inscribed 'caught by D. Green, River Ouse, 30 July 1935, weight 8lbs 3oz', case 31in (78.5cm) wide.
£1,050–1,200 / €1,550–1,750
$1,900–2,150 ⊞ MSh

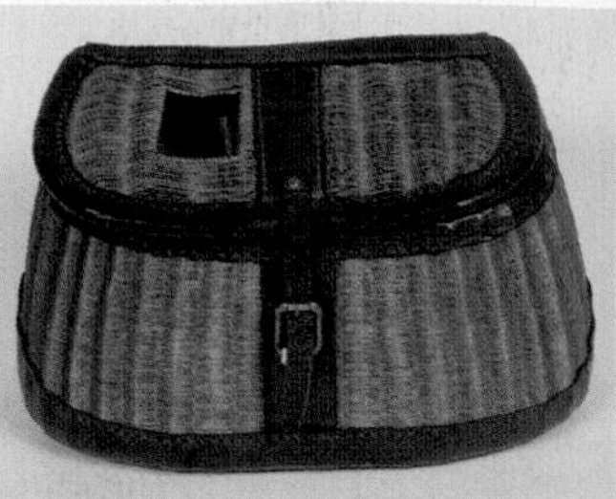

A wicker and leather fishing creel, c1900, 14in (35.5cm) wide.
£195–220 / €280–320
$350–450 ⊞ MSh

A silver presentation cup, with inscription for St Leonard's Sea Anglers, 1928, 15in (38cm) high.
£95–110 / €140–160
$170–200 ⊞ SPA

A pigskin fly wallet, by P. D. Malloch, Scottish, Perth, c1920, 8in (20.5cm) wide.
£105–120 / €155–175
$200–230 ⊞ OTB

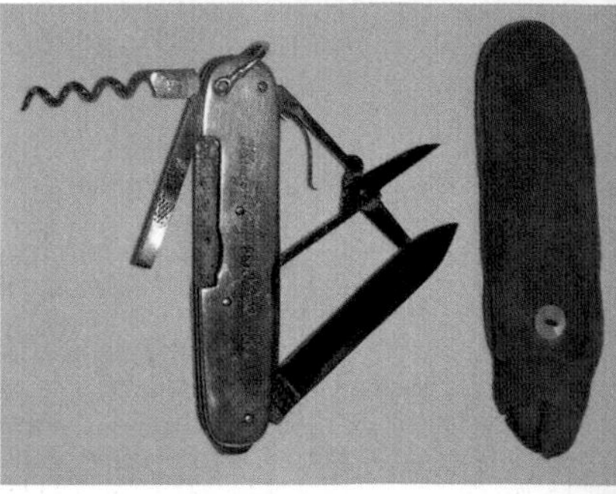

A Hardy No.4 angler's knife, with nine tools, engraved marks, c1930, 4in (10cm) long, with original chamois case.
£310–350 / €450–510
$560–630 ⊞ OTB

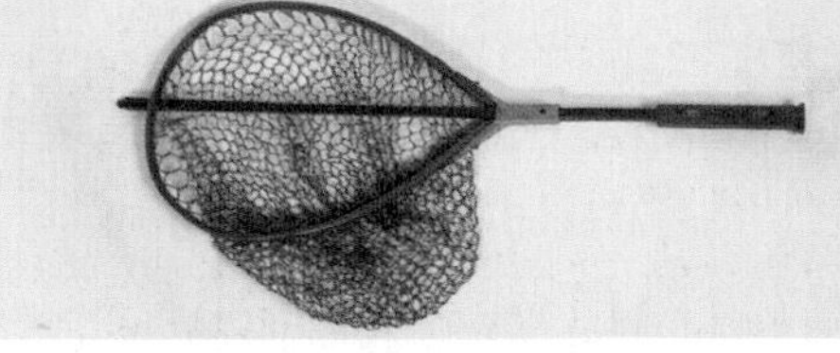

An extending trout landing net, c1920, 12in (30.5cm) dia
£105–120 / €155–175
$190–220 ⊞ MSh

► **A pottery dessert plate,** transfer-printed with Fishing Party pattern, c1830, 8in (20.5cm) diam.
£210–250
€310–370
$380–450
⚒ DN

Denton, six chromolithographs of North American fish, American, 1896, 8 x 10in (20.5 x 25.5cm).
£420–500 / €610–730
$760–910 ⚒ LHA

A Hardy 4½in salmon reel, with a horn handle, 1890.
£360–400 / €530–580
$650–720 ⊞ MSh

A Slater brass 3in reel, with a zipped case, c1900.
£180–200 / €260–290
$320–360 ⊞ SPA

An Eaton & Deller 2½in trout fly wheel, with revolving plate, engraved maker's name, c1900.
£50–60 / €75–85
$90–105 ⊞ OTB

A Mullock brass 4½in sidecasting reel, Scottish, Perth, c1910.
£195–220 / €280–320
$350–400 ⊞ MSh

A Hardy Uniqua alloy 3¼in trout fly reel, c1920.
£180–200 / €260–290
$320–360 ⊞ MSh

A brass skeleton reel, with a horn handle, c1930.
£75–85 / €110–125
$135–155 ⊞ MSh

A Hardy split cane trout rod, c1954, 105in (255.5cm) long.
£220–250 / €320–370
$400–450 ⊞ MSh

LOCATE THE SOURCE
The source of each illustration in Miller's can be found by checking the code letters below each caption with the Key to Illustrations, pages 778–784.

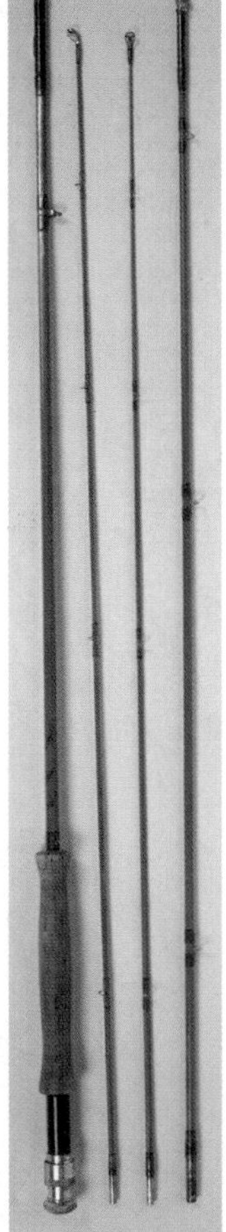

► A Hardy split cane trout rod, c1975, 105in (255.5cm) long.
£310–350 / €450–510
$560–630 ⊞ MSh

A silver trout fly winch, by Alfred, London, engraved with flowers, c1880, 2½in (6.5cm) diam.
£9,000–10,000 / €13,100–14,600
$16,300–18,100 ⊞ OTB
Solid silver presentation winches made to special order are very rare: Alfred was one of the few London makers to include them routinely in their sales catalogue.

Football

An England v Belgium friendly International cap, worn by Bobby Moore, 1969–70.
£1,500–1,800 / €2,200–2,600
$2,700–3,250 BUDD
This cap was a gift to the vendor from Bobby Moore's father-in-law.

A leather football, c1930, 9in (23cm) diam.
£75–85 / €110–125
$135–155 MSh

A hat box, by Battersby, London, decorated with the Cup Final at Wembley and the Test Match at Lord's Cricket Ground, slight damage, probably 1930s, 12in (30.5cm) wide.
£370–440 / €540–640
$670–800 VS

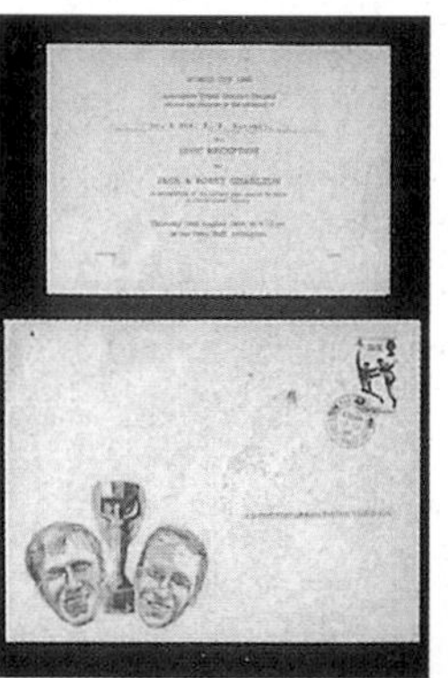

◄ **A postal cover and invitation,** to a civic reception for World Cup team brothers Bobby and Jack Charlton, issued by Ashington Urban Council, 18 August 1966.
£150–180 / €220–260
$270–320 BUDD

► **A players' itinerary booklet,** for the 1930 FA Cup Final at Huddersfield Town.
£280–330 / €410–480
$510–600 VS

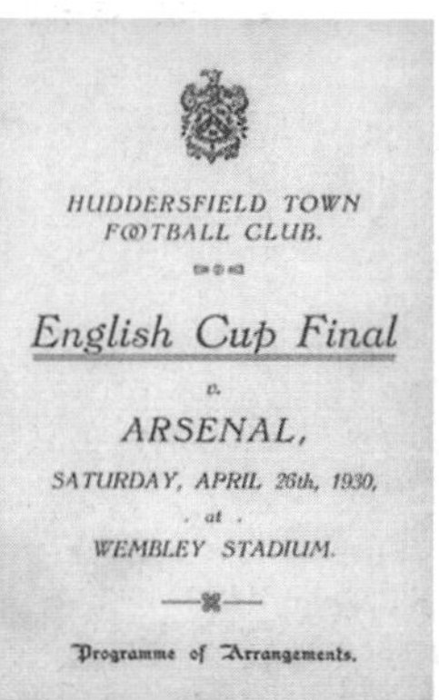

HUDDERSFIELD TOWN FOOTBALL CLUB.

English Cup Final

v.

ARSENAL,

SATURDAY, APRIL 26th, 1930,

at

WEMBLEY STADIUM.

Programme of Arrangements.

A 9ct gold Southern League Division II Championship medal, with inscription, 1898–99.
£1,000–1,200
€1,450–1,750
$1,800–2,100 BUDD

TOTTENHAM HOTSPUR FOOTBALL CLUB

Chairman FRED J. BEARMAN

BANQUET

In Celebration of the Final Tie of the Football Association Challenge Cup Competition

SEASON 1960-61

SATURDAY, MAY 6th, 1961
SAVOY HOTEL, LONDON

A Tottenham Hotspur FA Cup Final banquet menu, from the 1960–61 double-winning season, 6 May 1961.
£150–180 / €220–260
$270–320 BUDD

Preston North End 'Invincibles', a chromo-lithograph print, 1886, 12¼ x 10in (31 x 25.5cm).
£800–960 / €1,200–1,400
$1,450–1,750 BUDD

► **A World Cup souvenir programme,** signed by all 22 members of the England team, 1966.
£1,500–1,800
€2,200–2,650
$2,700–3,250 BUDD
These signatures were obtained after an England training session at Wembley FC during the World Cup.

SPORT

Golf

A lacquered feather golf ball, inscribed in ink 'Presented to Rev. H. M. Lamont by J. W. Inglis C. B. (?), an old student in St Andrews, 18??', and 'This ball was made by Wil. Robertson, 1790, Father (?) of Allan, the famous golfer'.
£24,000–28,800 / €35,000–42,000
$43,000–52,000 ⚒ L&T

A silver punchbowl, by Hamilton & Inches, embossed and chased with golfers and caddies, Scottish, Edinburgh 1885, 11½in (29cm) diam, 42½oz.
£16,500–19,800 / €24,100–29,100
$29,900–36,000 ⚒ DN(BR)

A silver matchbox holder, by Calmon & Neate, the top with an applied model of a golf club, London 1908, 3in (7.5cm) wide.
£350–420 / €510–610
$630–760 ⚒ TEN

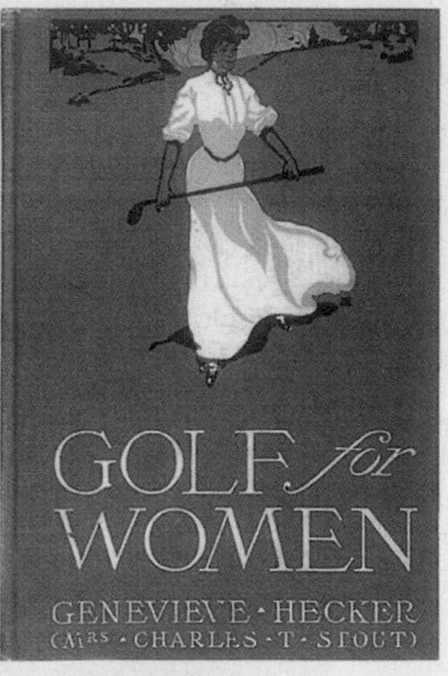

◄ Genevieve Hecker (Mrs Charles T. Stout), *Golf for Women*, published by The Baker & Taylor Co, New York, first edition, 1904, illustrated with photographs and drawings, pictorial cloth cover.
£490–580 / €720–850
$890–1,050 ⚒ L&T

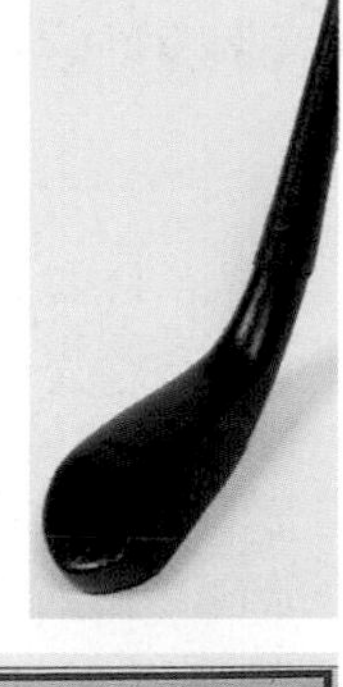

► A long-nose driver, by Forrester of Elie, Scottish, c1870.
£2,500–2,800
€3,650–4,100
$4,550–5,100
⊞ MSh

An LNER lithographic poster, by H. G. Gawthorn, 'St Andrews: The Home of the Royal & Ancient Game', 1930s, 38 x 48in (96.5 x 122cm).
£8,200–9,800 / €12,000–14,300
$14,800–17,700 ⚒ AG

A silver salt, by John Newton Mappin, in the form of a golf ball, with three golf clubs on the base, London 1888, 2½in (6.5cm) diam.
£400–440 / €580–640
$720–800 ⊞ BEX

SPORT

A lady's composition mannequin golf prize, inscribed 'Westward Ho! Golf Club, Ladies Championship, 1907', on a wooden stand, 53in (134.5cm) high.
£550–660 / €800–960
$1,000–1,200 ⚒ BUDD

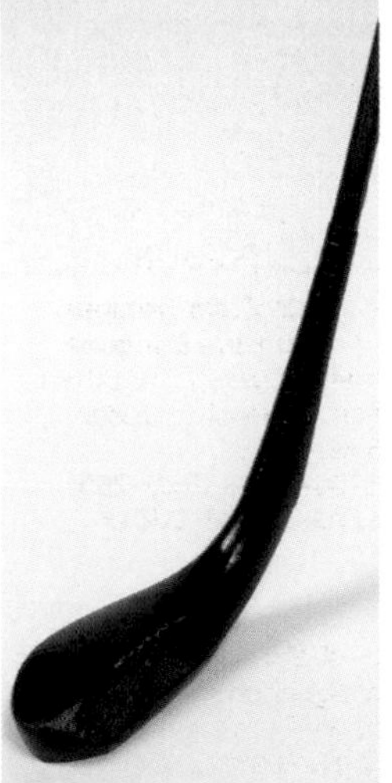

A long-nose short spoon, by McEwan of Musselburgh, with sheepskin grip, c1875.
£1,550–1,750
€2,250–2,550
$2,800–3,150 ⊞ MSh

A silver and enamel vesta case, by Sampson Mordan & Co, with an enamel portrait of Old Tom Morris, 1891, 2¼in (5.5cm) long.
£2,600–3,100
€3,800–4,550
$4,700–5,600 ⚒ BUDD

A silver and enamel vesta case, by Henry Charles Freeman, the engine-turned ground applied with a roundel enamelled with a scene of golfers, Birmingham 1910, 2¼in (5.5cm) high.
£910–1,050
€1,350–1,600
$1,600–1,800 ⚒ TEN

Rowing & Sailing

A Metropolitan Amateur Regatta silver prize medal, by J. Pinches, inscribed 'Metropolitan Eight Oared Challenge Cup' surrounding a presentation cup, the reverse with a legend within a wreath border, slight damage, c1866, 2¾in (7cm) diam.
£110–125 / €160–180
$200–220 ⊞ TML

A silver yachting prize tankard, by Whiting Manufacturing Co, New York, the body applied with a nymph on a hippocamp, with chased seaweed and an applied ribbon, the cover chased with shells, seaweed and swags of pearls, marked and numbered 5171, American, c1895, 12in (30.5cm) high, 70oz.
£6,600–7,900
€9,600–11,500
$11,900–14,100 ⚒ S(NY)

A commemorative glass mug, moulded with a portrait and inscribed 'Edward Hanlan, Champion of the World, Nov 15th 1880, beat Trickett of NSW', flanked by crossed oars, registration mark for December 1880, 4¼in (11cm) high.
£140–165 / €200–240
$250–300 ⚒ DN

A silver rowing trophy cup, London 1912, 10in (25.5cm) high.
£400–450 / €580–660
$720–810 ⊞ MSh

A Wadham College, Oxford Scratch Fours silver blade, by R. Rowell, monogrammed and engraved '2nd prize', in the original case with a silver plaque to the lid inscribed 'Wadh. Coll. Scratch Fours 1853, H. M. Clifford–Bow, D. A. Williams–2, G. R. Gilling–3, G. H. Pratt–Stroke, R. Walker–Cox', 1853, 5¼in (13.5cm) wide.
£400–450 / €580–660
$720–810 ⊞ TML

A silver model sculling oar, by S. J. Philips, the case with two inscribed silver plaques, London 1907, 18in (45.5cm) wide, 6½oz.
£590–700 / €850–1,000
$1,050–1,250 ⚒ WW

A pair of photographs, depicting Pembroke College, Cambridge rowing team, 1923, 16 x 29in (40.5 x 73.5cm), framed.
£90–100 / €130–145
$160–180 ⊞ MINN

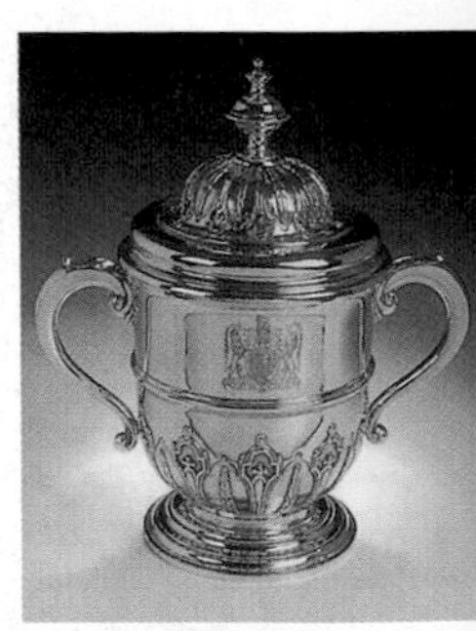

► **A silver twin-handled trophy cup and cover,** by Heming & Co Ltd, the cover inscribed 'Royal Yacht Squadron Regatta, The King's Cup, 1938, Presented by King George VI', with ebonized wooden plinth and a fitted wooden case, London 1937, 19in (48.5cm) high, 102½oz.
£1,300–1,550
€1,900–2,250
$2,350–2,800 ⚒ L&T

SPORT

Rugby

A velvet rugby football cap, with a tassel and braids, 1927–28.
£105–120 / €150–175
$190–220 ⊞ MSh

◄ **A spelter figure of a rugby player,** on a later marble base, c1920, 23in (58.5cm) high.
£1,400–1,600
€2,050–2,300
$2,550–2,900
⊞ MSh

A Royal Doulton Lambeth ware jug, decorated with rugby and football scenes, 1883, 7¼in (18.5cm) high.
£850–950 / €1,250–1,400
$1,500–1,700 ⊞ MSh

Shooting

◄ **A leather cartridge case,** with brass and copper fittings, 1920s, 13in (33cm) wide.
£380–430
€560–630
$690–780
⊞ MCa

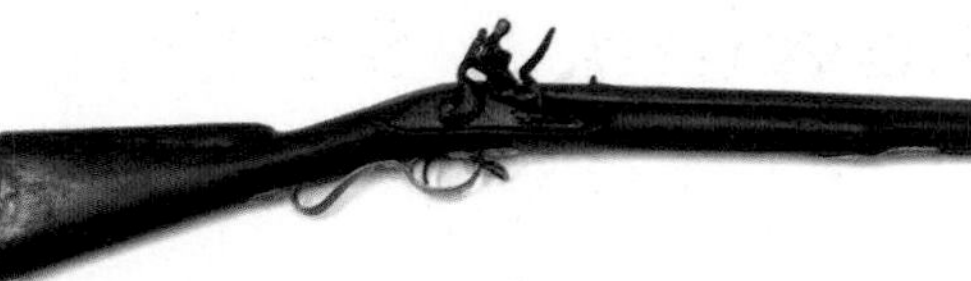

A flintlock fowling piece, with damascus barrel, the half stock with steel butt plate, chased action, 19thC, 46in (117cm) long.
£420–500 / €610–730
$760–910 ⚒ AH

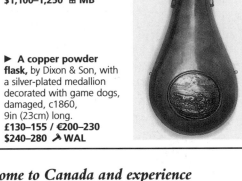

A stoneware jug, possibly by Edward Walley, relief-moulded with a hunting scene, 1845–50, 3½in (21.5cm) high.
£70–80 / €100–120
$125–150 ⚒ DN

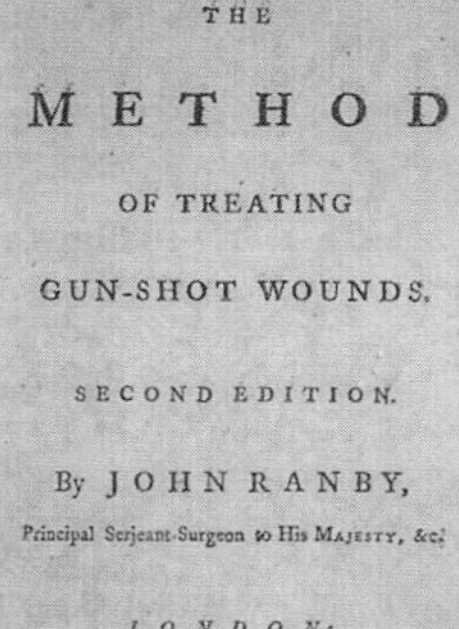

THE

METHOD

OF TREATING

GUN-SHOT WOUNDS.

SECOND EDITION.

By JOHN RANBY,

Principal Serjeant-Surgeon to His MAJESTY, &c.

LONDON:

Printed for ROBERT HORSFIELD, at the Crown, in *Ludgate-street*, 1760.

John Ranby, *The Method of Treating Gun-Shot Wounds,* second edition, 1760, 8°.
£240–280 / €350–410
$430–510 ⚒ DW

A wood and canvas gun case, by Watson Brothers, London, inscribed 'Lord Louis Mountbatten', c1925, 41in (104cm) long.
£630–700 / €900–1,000
$1,100–1,250 ⊞ MB

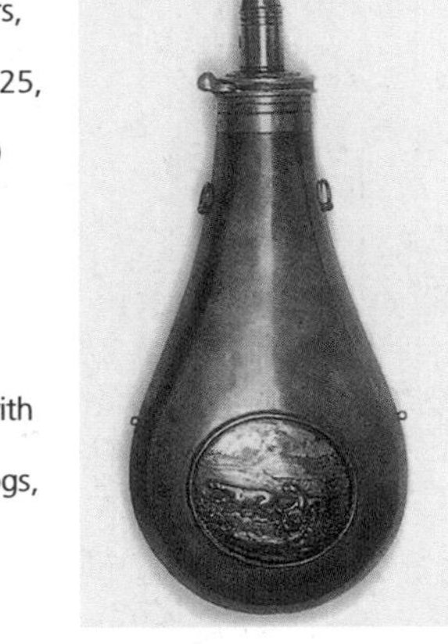

► **A copper powder flask,** by Dixon & Son, with a silver-plated medallion decorated with game dogs, damaged, c1860, 9in (23cm) long.
£130–155 / €200–230
$240–280 ⚒ WAL

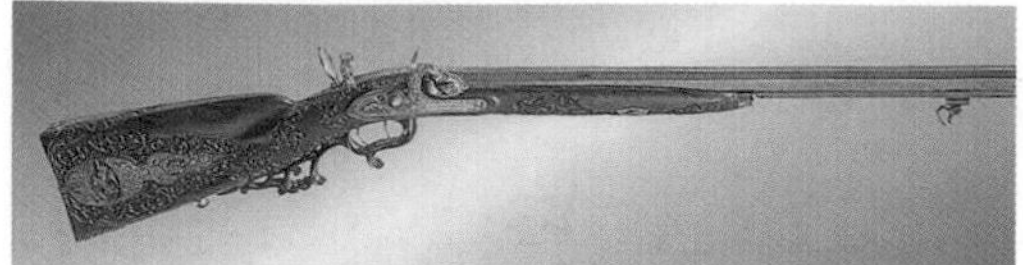

A 9mm calibre target rifle, by Joseph Bauer, the barrel with an inlaid silver signature, ramrod missing, German, 1840–50, 44½in (113cm) long.
£3,200–3,850 / €4,650–5,600
$5,800–7,000 Herm

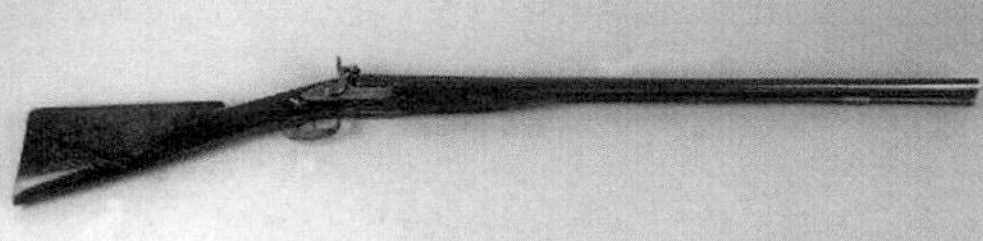

A muzzle-loading double-barrelled shotgun, with damascus barrels, engraved lock plate and tang, the figured walnut stock with a chequered grip, with ramrod, 19thC, 48¾in (124cm) long.
£280–330 / €410–480
$510–600 PFK

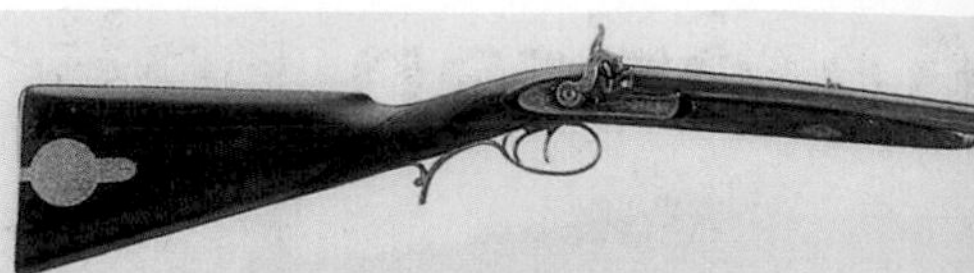

A 40 bore percussion sporting rifle, by J. Purdey, London, No. 5597, the breeches with platinum line and engraved platinum plugs, figured walnut half stock with chequered grip and fore-end, brass-tipped wooden ramrod, signed, slight damage, 1859, barrels 30in (76cm) long.
£4,200–5,000 / €6,100–7,300
$7,600–9,100 S(O)

► **A tin tobacco box,** the cover printed with a shooting scene, c1810, 4¾in (12cm) wide.
£160–180
€230–260
$290–330 MB

Skiing

A pair of spelter figures of skiers, on marble bases, signed, French, c1930, 5in (12.5cm) high.
£320–360 / €470–530
$580–650 PEZ

► **A brass ornament,** in the form of skis and a stick, c1900, 7in (18cm) high.
£220–250 / €320–360
$400–450 MSh

A glass plaque, relief-decorated with a cross-country skier, c1910, 6 x 5in (15 x 12.5cm).
£270–300 / €390–440
$490–540 MSh

A silver and enamel matchbox holder, the front enamelled with a skier, maker's mark 'JC', Sheffield 1895, 1½in (3.5cm) wide.
£260–310 / €380–450
$470–560 TEN

SPORT

Tennis

A Kleenball boxwood tennis ball cleaner, the interior lined with brushes, 19thC, 6in (15cm) high.
£360–430 / €530–630
$650–780 BWL

An oak and brass tennis trophy, the brass gong suspended between crossed rackets, 1890s, 13in (33cm) wide.
£800–900 / €1,150–1,300
$1,450–1,650 MSh

► **A film poster,** *The Art of Tennis*, printed on linen for The Parkstone Film Co, Lytham, c1920, 29½ x 19¼in (75 x 49cm).
£330–390
€480–570
$600–710 VSP

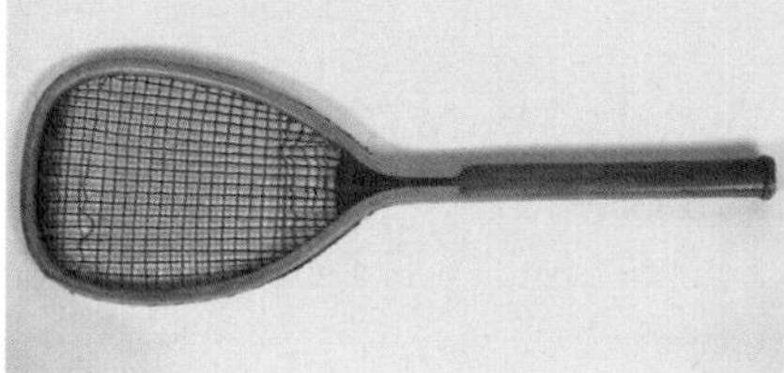

◄ **A lawn tennis racket,** by F. H. Ayres, c1885, 27in (68.5cm) long.
£360–400
€520–580
$650–720 MSh

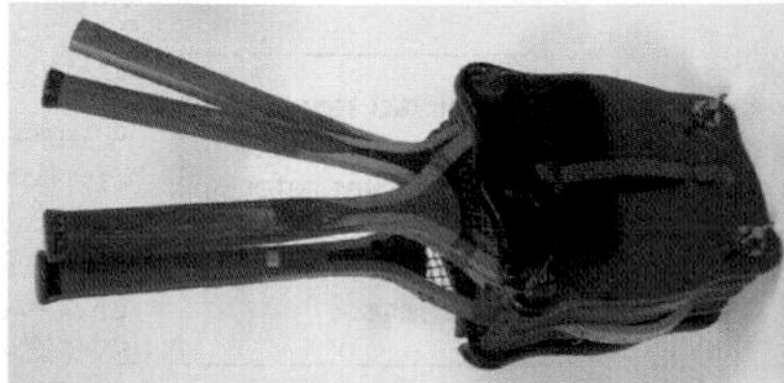

A lacquered wood tennis racket press, 'The Compactum', with steel and brass fittings, c1900, 12 x 11in (30.5 x 28cm).
£220–250 / €320–360
$400–450 MSh

American Folk Art

A toleware covered basket, mid-19thC, 11in (28cm) wide.
£160–190 / €230–270
$290–340 ⚒ DuM

A pine and tin footwarmer, with punched decoration of an eagle, New England, 1800–25, 9½in (24cm) wide.
£3,150–3,750 / €4,600–5,500
$5,700–8,800 ⚒ S(NY)

A Federal carved giltwood eagle pendant, with metal hanging ring, c1800, 13in (33cm) wide.
£290–340 / €420–500
$520–610 ⚒ SGA

Folk Art is a very broad term, encompassing many collecting areas. For other examples refer to the sections on kitchenware, Marine, Metalware, Treen, Boxes, Textiles and Toys.

A carved and painted Cigar Store Indian, small hole at waist holding a carved flower bud, 19thC, 65in (165cm) high.
£1,650–1,950
€2,400–2,850
$2,900–3,500 ⚒ LHA

A painted wood and cast-iron pump, by A. Y. McDonald, c1900, 77in (195.5cm) high.
£570–680 / €830–990
$1,050–1,250 ⚒ JAA

A goldeneye drake decoy, by Amos Wheaton, with original paint, New Jersey, South Seaville, c1900, 16in (40.5cm) long.
£11,900–14,300 / €17,400–21,000
$22,000–26,000 ⚒ S(NY)

A wooden Temperance panel, painted with four scences, with applied moulding, losses, late 19thC, 25¼ x 37½in (64 x 95.5cm).
£4,850–5,800 / €7,100–8,500
$8,800–10,500 ⚒ SK

A wool and cotton hooked rug, mounted on a wood frame, slight wear, late 19thC, 31½ x 62½in (80 x 159cm).
£2,400–2,850 / €3,500–4,150
$4,350–5,200 ⚒ SK(B)

A carved wood trade sign, in the form of a horse, with bottle-cap eyes and traces of original paint, with threaded mounting rod, 1900–50, 38in (96.5cm) wide.
£1,000–1,200 / €1,450–1,750
$1,800–2,150 ⚒ JAA

► **A gilt cast- and sheet-iron weather vane,** by Rochester Iron Works, in the form of a rooster, on a metal stand, losses, New Hampshire, Rochester, late 19thC, 35½in (90cm) wide.
£4,550–5,500 / €6,700–8,000
$8,200–9,900 ⚒ SK(B)

Glossary

Below are explanations of some of the terms that you will come across in the book.

agate ware: 18thC pottery, veined or marbled to resemble the mineral agate.

***albarello*:** Drug jar, usually of waisted cylindrical form, used in most major European countries from the 15thC.

anchor escapement: Said to have been invented c1670 by Robert Hooke or William Clement. A type of escape mechanism shaped like an anchor, which engages at precise intervals with the toothed escape wheel. The anchor permits the use of a pendulum (either long or short), and gives greater accuracy than was possible with the verge escapement.

***anhua*:** Hidden decoration on Chinese porcelain.

argyle: Silver gravy-warmer shaped like a coffee pot with a central well for the gravy and an outer casing for hot water, said to have been invented by one of the Dukes of Argyll.

associated: Term used in antiques, in which one part of an item is of the same design but not originally made for it. See *marriage* and *made up*.

automaton: Any moving toy or decorative object, usually powered by a clockwork mechanism.

aventurine: Usually brownish-coloured glass flecked with gold-coloured mica or other metals.

barbotine: Painting on pottery using coloured kaolin pastes, invented in 1865 by Ernest Chaplet.

bezel: Ring, usually brass, surrounding the dial of a clock, and securing the glass dial cover.

***bianco-sopra-bianco*:** Literally white-on-white. Used in ceramics to describe an opaque white pattern painted on an off-white background.

Biedermeier: Style of furniture made principally in the 1820s and '30s in Austria, Germany and parts of Scandinavia and characterized by simple, heavy Classical forms. It is named after a fictional character who symbolized the German bourgeoisie of the early 19thC.

biggin: Form of coffee percolator invented c1799 by George Biggin.

***bijin*:** Japanese term for a beautiful woman.

bisque: French term for biscuit ware, or unglazed porcelain.

***blanc-de-Chine*:** Translucent white Chinese porcelain, unpainted and with a thick glaze, made in kilns in Dehua in the Fujian province from the Song Dynasty and copied in Europe.

Bodhisattva: Attendant of Buddha.

***bombé*:** Bulbous, curving form, a feature often seen on wares produced during the rococo period.

***bonbonnière*:** Sweet jar or box.

bordalou: Lady's portable commode.

***boteh*:** Stylized design of a floral bush found on rugs, similar to a Paisley design.

Britannia Standard: Higher standard of silver required between 1697 and 1720. Denoted by Britannia and a lion's head in profile on the hallmark.

***bureau de dame*:** Writing desk of delicate appearance and designed for use by ladies. Usually raised above slender cabriole legs and with one or two external drawers.

***bureau plat*:** French writing table with a flat top and drawers in the frieze.

cabaret set: Tea set on a tray for three or more people.

calamander: Hardwood, imported from Sri Lanka (of the same family as ebony), used in the Regency period for making small articles of furniture, as a veneer and for crossbanding.

cameo glass: Two or more layers of coloured glass in which the top layers are then cut or etched away to create a multi-coloured design in relief. An ancient technique popular with Art Nouveau glassmakers in the early 20thC.

cannetille: Extremely thin gold wirework decoration.

cartouche: Ornate tablet or shield surrounded by scrollwork and foliage, often bearing an inscription, monogram or coat-of-arms.

celadon: Chinese stoneware with an opaque grey-green glaze, first made in the Song Dynasty and still made today, principally in Korea.

cellaret: Lidded container on legs designed to hold wine. The interior is often divided into sections for individual bottles.

***champlevé*:** Enamelling on copper or bronze, similar to cloisonné, in which a glass paste is applied to the hollowed-out design, fired and ground smooth.

character doll: One with a naturalistic face, especially laughing, crying, pouting, etc.

***chilong*:** Small lizard, often portrayed on Chinese ceramics.

Chinese Imari: Chinese imitations of Japanese blue, red and gold painted Imari wares, made from the early 18thC.

chinoiserie: The fashion, prevailing in the late 18thC, for Chinese-style ornamentation on porcelain, wall-papers, fabrics, furniture and garden architecture.

***chuval*:** Turkic word meaning bag.

cistern tube: Mercury tube fitted into stick barometers, the lower end of which is sealed into a boxwood cistern.

clock garniture: Matching group of clock and vases or candelabra made for the mantel shelf. Often highly ornate.

cloisonné: Enamelling on metal with divisions in the design separated by lines of fine metal wire. A speciality of the Limoges region of France in the Middle Ages, and of Chinese craftsmen to the present day.

close-concentric paperweight: One which consists of concentric circles of canes arranged tightly together so that the clear glass cannot be seen between the rings of canes.

close-pack paperweight: One which is characterized by canes closely packed together without a pattern.

***coiffeuse*:** French dressing table.

coin silver: Silver of the standard used for coinage, ie .925 or sterling.

***coffor bach*:** Small Welsh coffer.

coromandel: Imported wood from the Coromandel coast of India, of similar blackish appearance to calamander and used from c1780 for banding, and for small pieces of furniture.

countwheel: Wheel with segments cut out of the edge or with pins fitted to one face, which controls the striking of a clock. Also known as a locking plate.

***craquelé* glass:** Technique used to decorate some Venetian glass in the 17thC and revived in the 19thC, particularly in Britain and France. A fine network of cracks was created on the surface of a vessel during the process of blowing, by plunging it into cold water. The resulting finish resembled the cracks on the surface of ice and so it is also known as 'ice glass' in England.

***crespina*:** Shallow Italian dish with a fluted border.

***cuerda seca*:** Technique of tile-making, developed in Iran in the 15thC, whereby the colours of the design were separated by an oily substance which leaves a brownish outline.

***cwpwrdd deuddarn*:** Welsh variety of the press cupboard with two tiers.

***cwpwrdd tridarn*:** Welsh variety of the press cupboard with three tiers.

cyma: Double-carved moulding. Cyma recta is concave above and convex below; cyma reversa the other way round. Also known as ogee and reverse ogee moulding. Popular with 18thC cabinet makers.

Cymric: Trade-name used by Liberty & Co for a mass-produced range of silverware inspired by Celtic art, introduced in 1899 and often incorporating enamelled pictorial plaques.

deadbeat escapement: Type of anchor escapement, possibly invented by George Graham and used in precision pendulum clocks.

Delft: Dutch tin-glazed earthenwares named after the town of Delft, the principal production centre, from the 16thC onwards. Similar pottery made in England from the late 16thC is also termed 'delft' or 'delftware'.

dentils: Small rectangular blocks applied at regular intervals as a decorative feature.

***dhurrie*:** Cotton flatweave rug or carpet from India.

diaper: Surface decoration composed of repeated diamonds or squares, often carved in low relief.

dog of *Fo*: Buddhist guardian lion.

***doucai*:** Decoration on Chinese porcelain using five colours.

***duchesse brisée*:** Type of chaise longue of French origin, consisting of one or two tub-shaped chairs and a stool to extend the length. Popular in Britain during the late 18thC.

***encre-de-Chine*:** Indian Ink.

***en grisaille*:** Painted decoration using a mainly black and grey palette and resembling a print.

***ensi*:** Rug used as a tent door by Turkoman tribes.

escapement: Means or device which regulates the release of the power of a timepiece to its pendulum or balance.

***façon de Venise*:** Literally 'in the Venetian style', used to describe high quality, Venetian-influenced glassware made in Europe during the 16th to 17thC.

faïence: Tin-glazed earthenware named after the town of Faenza in Italy, but actually used to describe products made anywhere but Italy, where they are called maiolica.

***famille jaune/noire/rose/verte*:** Chinese porcelain in which yellow, black, pink or green respectively are the predominant ground colours.

***fauteuil*:** French open-armed drawing room chair.

fielded panel: Panel with bevelled or chamfered edges.

flambé: Glaze made from copper, usually deep crimson, flecked with blue or purple, and often faintly crackled.

flatware (1): Collective name for flat pottery and porcelain, such as plates, dishes and saucers.

flatware (2): Cutlery.

flow blue: Process used principally after 1840 in which powder is added to the dye used in blue and white transfer-printed ceramics so that the blue flows beyond the edges of the transfer, making the pattern less sharply defined. Items using this process were made primarily for the American market.

fluted: Border that resembles a scalloped edge, used as a decoration on furniture, glass, silver and porcelain items.

***fuku*:** Chinese term for happiness.

***fu shou*:** Chinese decorative motif meaning happiness and longevity.

fusee: 18thC clockwork invention; a cone-shaped drum, linked to the spring barrel by a length of gut or chain. The shape compensates for the declining strength of the mainspring thus ensuring constant timekeeping.

gadroon: Border or ornament comprising radiating lobes of either curbed or straight form. Used from the late Elizabethan period.

girandole: Carved and gilt candle sconce incorporating a mirror.

***guéridon*:** Small circular table designed to carry some form of lighting.

***guilloche*:** Decorative motif of interlacing circles forming a continuous figure-of-eight pattern.

***gul*:** From the Persian word for flower – usually used to describe a geometric flowerhead on a rug.

***guttus*:** Ancient Greek closed vessel with a spout and handle for pouring oil into lamps.

halberd: Spear fitted with a double axe.

hard paste: True porcelain made of china stone (petuntse) and kaolin; the formula was long known to, and kept secret by, Chinese potters but only discovered in the 1720s at Meissen, Germany, from where it spread to the rest of Europe and the Americas. Recognized by its hard, glossy feel.

***hatchli*:** Rug used as a door by Turkomans on their tents.

***hiramakie*:** Japanese term for sponged gold applied level with the surface.

***ho-o*:** Mythical Chinese bird, similar to a phoenix, symbolizing wisdom and energy.

***huanghuali*:** Type of Oriental wood, much admired for its colour.

Imari: Export Japanese porcelain of predominantly red, blue and gold decoration which, although made in Arita, is called Imari after the port from which it was shipped.

impasto: Technique of applying paint thickly to ceramics so that the brush or palette knife marks are visible.

***inro*:** Japanese multi-compartmental medicine or seal container, carried suspended from the sash of a kimono.

ironstone: Stoneware, patented 1813 by Charles James Mason, containing ground glassy slag, a by-product of iron smelting, for extra strength.

Kakiemon: Family of 17thC Japanese porcelain decorators who produced wares decorated with flowers and figures on a white ground in distinctive colours: azure, yellow, turquoise and soft red. Widely imitated in Europe.

***katana*:** Long Japanese sword.

***kelleh*:** Long narrow carpets which are wider than runners.

***kendi*:** Chinese or Japanese globular drinking vessel which is filled through the neck, the liquid being drunk through the spout.

kilim: Flat woven rug without a pile.

***klapmuts*:** Chinese dish with rounded wall and flattened rim, said to resemble a type of woollen hat of this name worn by the Dutch in the 16th and 17th centuries.

knop: Knob, protuberance or swelling in the stem of a wine glass, of various forms which can be used as an aid to dating and provenance.

***Komai*:** Style of Japanese lacquerwork made famous by the Komai family.

***koro*:** Japanese incense burner.

***kotile*:** Ancient Greek vessel in the form of a bowl.

***kovsh*:** Russian vessel used for measuring drink, often highly decorated for ornamental purposes.

***kozuka*:** Small Japanese utility knife.

kraak porselein: Dutch term for porcelain raided from Portuguese ships, used to describe the earliest Chinese export porcelain.

krater: Ancient Greek vessel for mixing water and wine in which the mouth is always the widest part.

***laque burgauté*:** Asian lacquer wares, inlaid with mother-of-pearl, gold or precious stones.

***latticinio*:** Fine threads of white or clear glass forming a filigree mesh effect enclosed in clear glass.

***lattimo*:** from the Italian *latte* meaning milk; an opaque white glass made by adding bone ash or tin oxide to the glass batch.

lekythos: Ancient Greek flask used for oil or perfume.

***lingzhi*:** Type of fungus or mushroom, used as a motif on Chinese works of art.

***lishui*:** Chinese term for vertical water. A traditional border design normally used on Imperial Chinese garments.

loaded: Term used for a silver candlestick with a hollow stem filled with pitch or sand for weight and stability.

made up: Piece of furniture that has been put together from parts of other pieces of furniture. See *associated* and *marriage*.

maiolica: Tin-glazed earthenware produced in Italy from the 15thC to the present day.

majolica: Heavily-potted, moulded ware covered in transparent glazes in distinctive, often sombre colours, developed by the Minton factory in the mid-19thC.

marriage: Joining together of two unrelated parts to form one piece of furniture. See *associated* and *made up*.

***martelé*:** Term for silverware with a fine, hammered surface, first produced in France and later revived by the American silversmiths Gorham Manufacturing Co during the Art Nouveau period.

matched pair: Two items that are very similar in appearance and give the appearance of being a pair.

***meiping*:** Chinese for cherry blossom, used to describe a tall vase with high shoulders, small neck and narrow mouth, used to display flowering branches.

merese: Flat disc of glass which links the bowl and stem, and sometimes the stem and foot, of a drinking glass.

***mihrab*:** Prayer niche with a pointed arch; the motif which distinguishes a prayer rug from other types.

milk glass: (*milchglass*) Term for glass made with tin oxide, which turns it an opaque white. Developed in Venice in the late 15thC.

millefiori: Italian term meaning 'thousand flowers'. A glassmaking technique whereby canes of coloured glass are arranged in bundles so that the cross-section creates a pattern. Commonly used in paperweights.

***minogame*:** Mythical Japanese character, half turtle, half beast.

***mon*:** Japanese crest or coat-of-arms.

monteith: Large bowl with detachable collar and scalloped rim from which wine glasses were suspended to cool over iced water.

***nashiji*:** Multitude of gold flakes in Japanese lacquer.

near pair: Two items that are very similar in appearance and give the appearance of being a pair. Also known as a matched pair.

***netsuke*:** Japanese carved toggles made to secure *sagemono* (hanging things) to the *obi* (waist belt) from a cord; usually of ivory, lacquer, silver or wood, from the 16thC.

niello: Black metal alloy or enamel used for filling in engraved designs on silverware.

nulling (knulling): Decorative carving in the form of irregular fluting, usually found on early oak furniture.

ogee: Double curve of slender S shape.

oinochoe: Ancient Greek small jug with handles.

***ojime*:** Japanese word meaning bead.

***okimono*:** Small, finely carved Japanese ornament.

oklad: Silver or gold icon cover, applied as a tribute or in gratitude for a prayer answered. Also known as a riza or basma.

olla: Ancient earthenware pot for cooking or carrying water.

***oni*:** Chinese devil.

opaline: Semi-translucent glass.

ormolu: Strictly, gilded bronze but used loosely for any yellow metal. Originally used for furniture handles and mounts but, from the 18thC, for inkstands, candlesticks etc.

overlay: In cased glass, the top layer, usually engraved to reveal a different coloured layer beneath.

palmette: Stylized palm-leaf motif.

***pardah*:** A rug which is suspended in a tent doorway.

***pâte-de-cristal*:** Glass that is crushed into fine crystals and then bound together so that it can be moulded rather than having to be worked in its molten state.

***pâte-sur-pâte*:** 19thC Sèvres porcelain technique, much copied, of applying coloured clay decoration to the body before firing.

penwork: Type of decoration applied to japanned furniture, principally in England in the late 18th/early 19thC. Patterns in white japan were applied to a piece which had already been japanned black, and then the details and shading were added using black Indian ink with a fine quill pen.

pier glass: Mirror designed to be fixed to the pier, or wall, between two tall window openings, often partnered by a matching pier table. Made from the mid-17thC.

***pietra dura*:** Italian term for hardstone, applied to a mosaic pattern of semi-precious stones and marble.

***piqué*:** Technique in which a material such as tortoiseshell is inlaid with metal decoration.

plumbago: Another word for graphite.

plum pudding: Type of figuring in some veneers, produced by dark oval spots in the wood. Found particularly in mahogany.

pole screen: Small adjustable screen mounted on a pole and designed to stand in front of an open fire to shield a lady's face from the heat.

***poudreuse*:** French dressing table.

powder flask: Device for measuring out a precise quantity of priming powder, suspended from a musketeer's belt or bandolier and often ornately decorated. Sporting flasks are often made of antler and carved with hunting scenes.

powder horn: Cow horn hollowed out, blocked at the wide end with a wooden plug and fitted with a measuring device at the narrow end, used by musketeers for dispensing a precise quantity of priming powder.

prie-dieu: Chair with a low seat and a tall back designed for prayer. Usually dating from the 19thC.

printie: Circular or oval hollow cut into glass for decorative effect, sometimes called a lens.

protome: Ancient Greek head and shoulders bust, often with a flat back.

prunt: Blob of glass applied to the stem of a drinking vessel both as decoration and to stop the glass from slipping in the hand.

***punchong*:** Style of 15th-century Korean ceramics.

***qilin*:** Chinese mythical beast. Also spelt *kilin*.

Qingbai: White ware produced by potters in the Jingdezhen area of China throughout the Song Dynasty.

quarter-veneered: Four consecutively cut, and therefore identical, pieces of veneer laid at opposite ends to each other to give a mirrored effect.

***ruyi* clouds:** Cloud-like decorative feature often used as a design in Chinese art.

register plate: Scale of a barometer against which the mercury level is read.

regulator: Clock of great accuracy, thus sometimes used for controlling or checking other timepieces.

repoussé: Relief decoration on metal made by hammering on the reverse so that the decoration projects.

rocaille: Shell and rock motifs found in rococo work.

rummer: 19thC English low drinking goblet.

***sancai*:** Three-colour decoration on Chinese porcelain.

S. F. B. J.: *Société de Fabrication de Bébés et Jouets*; association of doll makers founded 1899 by the merger of Jumeau, Bru and others.

***sang-de-bouef*:** Bright red glaze used extensively on Chinese ceramics during the Qing Dynasty.

***Sennin*:** Japanese immortal.

sgraffito: Form of ceramic decoration incised through a coloured slip, revealing the ground beneath.

shabti: Answerer. Ancient Egyptian ceramic figure placed in a tomb to work in the afterworld in the place of the dead person they represented.

***Shibayama*:** Japanese term for lacquer applied with semi-precious stones and ivory.

***shishi*:** Japanese mythical beast, a lion-dog.

***shou* symbol:** Chinese decorative motif, symbolizing longevity.

shoulder-head: Term for a doll's head and shoulders below the neck.

shoulderplate: Area of a doll's shoulder-head below the neck.

silver resist: Decorative technique normally found on pearlware ceramics c1800–20, whereby a design is painted in wax onto an object and then silver lustre is applied to the surface. When the wax is burnt off in the kiln, the painted design appears on a silver lustre ground.

siphon tube: U-shaped tube fitted into wheel barometers where the level of mercury in the short arm is used to record air pressure.

soft paste: Artificial porcelain made with the addition of ground glass, bone-ash or soap-stone. Used by most European porcelain manufacturers during the 18thC. Recognized by its soft, soapy feel.

spadroon: Cut-and-thrust sword.

spandrel: Element of design, closing off a corner.

spelter: Zinc treated to look like bronze and much used as an inexpensive substitute in Art Nouveau appliqué ornament and Art Deco figures.

strapwork: Repeated carved decoration suggesting plaited straps.

stuff-over: Descriptive of upholstered furniture where the covering extends over the frame of the seat.

stumpwork: Embroidery which incorporates distinctive areas of raised decoration, formed by padding certain areas of the design.

***sugán*:** Twisted lengths of straw: referring to a type of Irish country chair that has a seat of this type.

***susani*:** Central Asian hand-embroidered bridal bed-cover.

***table ambulante*:** French term for a small, portable occasional table.

***takamakie*:** Technique used in Japanese lacquerware in which the design is built up and modelled in a mixture of lacquer and charcoal or clay dust, and then often gilded.

***taotie*:** Chinese mythical animal that devours wrong-doers.

tazza: Wide but shallow bowl on a stem with a foot; ceramic and metal tazzas were made in antiquity and the form was revived by Venetian glassmakers in the 15thC. Also made in silver from the 16thC.

teapoy: Piece of furniture in the form of a tea caddy on legs, with a hinged lid opening to reveal caddies, mixing bowl and other tea drinking accessories.

tear: Tear-drop-shaped air bubble in the stem of an early 18thC wine glass, from which the air-twist evolved.

tête-à-tête: Tea set for two people.

thuyawood: Reddish-brown wood with distinctive small 'bird's-eye' markings, imported from Africa and used as a veneer.

***tiki*:** Symbol of the procreative power of the Maori god Tane.

timepiece: Clock that does not strike or chime.

tin glaze: Glassy opaque white glaze of tin oxide; re-introduced to Europe in the 14thC by Moorish potters; the characteristic glaze of delftware, faïence and maiolica.

***togidashi*:** Japanese lacquer technique in which further layers of lacquer are added to *hiramake* (qv) then polished flush with the original surface.

toleware: Items made from tinplated sheet iron which is varnished and then decorated with brightly coloured paints.

tombak: Alloy of copper and zinc.

touch: Maker's mark stamped on much, but not all, early English pewter. Their use was strictly controlled by the Pewterer's Company of London: early examples consist of initials, later ones are more elaborate and pictorial, sometimes including the maker's address.

Trafalgar chair: Type of dining chair with sabre legs and a ropetwist bar, made during the Regency period to commemorate the Battle of Trafalgar

trumeau: Section of wall between two openings; a pier mirror.

***tsuba*:** Guard of a Japanese sword, usually consisting of an ornamented plate.

Tudric: Range of Celtic-inspired Art Nouveau pewter of high quality, designed for mass-production by Archibald Knox and others, and retailed through Liberty & Co.

tyg: Three-handled mug.

verge escapement: Oldest form of escapement, found on clocks as early as 1300 and still in use in 1900. Consisting of a bar (the verge) with two flag-shaped pallets that rock in and out of the teeth of the crown or escape wheel to regulate the movement.

vernier scale: Short scale added to the traditional 3in (7.5cm) scale on stick barometers to give more precise readings than had previously been possible.

***vernis Martin*:** Type of japanning or imitation lacquerwork invented by the Martin family in Paris in the 18th century.

***verre églomisé*:** Painting on glass. Often the reverse side of the glass is covered in gold or silver leaf through which a pattern is engraved and then painted black.

vesta case: Ornate flat case of silver or other metal for carrying vestas, an early form of match. Used from the mid-19thC.

vitrine: French display cabinet which is often of *bombé* or serpentine outline and ornately decorated with marquetry and ormolu.

***wakizashi*:** Short Japanese sword.

WMF: Short for Württembergische Metallwarenfabrik, a German foundry that was one of the principal producers of Art Nouveau metalware.

***wucai*:** Type of five-colour Chinese porcelain decoration, executed in vigorous style.

***wufu*:** Chinese term meaning 'the five happinesses' (long life, riches, tranquility, love of virtue and a good end to one's life).

Directory of Specialists

If you wish to be included in next year's directory, or if you have a change of address or telephone number, please contact Miller's Advertising Department on +44 (0) 1580 766411 by April 2006. We advise readers to make contact by telephone before visiting a dealer, therefore avoiding a wasted journey.

UNITED KINGDOM & REPUBLIC OF IRELAND

20TH CENTURY DESIGN

Essex
20th Century Marks, Whitegates, Rectory Road, Little Burstead, Near Billericay, CM12 9TR
Tel: 01268 411 000
info@20thcenturymarks.co.uk
www.20thcenturymarks.co.uk
20th century furniture and design.

ANTIQUE DEALERS ASSOCIATIONS

London
Portobello Antiques Dealers Association, 223a Portobello Road, W11 1LU
Tel: 020 7229 8354
info@portobelloroad.co.uk
www.portobelloroad.co.uk

Oxfordshire
T.V.A.D.A., The Old College, Queen Street, Dorchester-on-Thames, OX10 7HL
Tel: 01993 882420
tamesis@tvada.co.uk
www.tvada.co.uk

ANTIQUITIES

Dorset
Ancient & Gothic, P O Box 5390, Bournemouth, BH7 6XR
Tel: 01202 431721
Antiquities from before 300,000 BC to about 1500 AD.

ARCHITECTURAL ANTIQUES

Cheshire
Nostalgia, Hollands Mill, 61 Shaw Heath, Stockport, SK3 8BH
Tel: 0161 477 7706
www.nostalgia-uk.com

Gloucestershire
Minchinhampton Architectural Salvage Company, Cirencester Road, Chalford, Stroud, GL6 8PE
Tel: 01285 760886
masco@catbrain.com
www.catbrain.com
Architectural antiques, garden statuary, bespoke chimney pieces and traditional flooring. MASCo specialises in large architectural features and garden ornaments. The company also carries extensive stocks of hard and soft wood flooring as well as reclaimed building materials. Call or email for further details. Subscribers to the SALVO code. We also offer a Garden Design service.

Wales
Drew Pritchard Ltd, St Georges Church, Church Walks, Llandudno, LL30 2HL
Tel: 01492 874004
enquiries@drewpritchard.co.uk
www.drewpritchard.co.uk

ARMS & MILITARIA

Cheshire
Armourer - The Militaria Magazine, Published by Beaumont Publishing Ltd, 1st floor Adelphi Mill, Bollington, SK10 5JB
Tel: 01625 575700
editor@armourer.co.uk
www.armourer.co.uk
A bi-monthly magazine for military antique collectors and military history enthusiasts offering hundreds of contacts for buying and selling, articles on all aspects of militaria collecting plus the dates of UK militaria fairs and auctions. Available on subscription.

Gloucestershire
Q & C Militaria, 22 Suffolk Road, Cheltenham, GL50 2AQ
Tel: 01242 519815
qcmilitaria@btconnect.com
www.qcmilitaria.com

Lincolnshire
Garth Vincent, The Old Manor House, Allington, Nr Grantham, NG32 2DH
Tel: 01400 281358
garthvincent@aol.com
www.guns.uk.com

Surrey
West Street Antiques, 63 West Street, Dorking, RH4 1BS Tel: 01306 883487 weststant@aol.com
www.antiquearmsandarmour.com

East Sussex
Wallis & Wallis, West Street Auction Galleries, Lewes, BN7 2NJ Tel: 01273 480208
auctions@wallisandwallis.co.uk
grb@wallisandwallis.co.uk
www.wallisandwallis.co.uk
Auctioneers of militaria, arms and armour and medals.

Warwickshire
London Antique Arms Fairs Ltd, 35 Rosefield Street, Leamington Spa, CV32 4HE
Tel: 01432 355416 & 01926 883665
info@antiquearmsfairsltd.co.uk
www.antiquearmsfairsltd.co.uk

Yorkshire
Andrew Spencer Bottomley, The Coach House, Thongsbridge, Holmfirth, HD9 3JJ
Tel: 01484 685234
andrewbottomley@compuserve.com

BAROGRAPHS

Somerset
Twort, Richard
Tel: 01934 641900 or 07711 939789

Berkshire
Alan Walker, Halfway Manor, Halfway, Newbury, RG20 8NR
Tel: 01488 657670
www.alanwalker-barometers.com

Wiltshire`
P A Oxley Antique Clocks & Barometers, The Old Rectory, Cherhill, Calne, SN11 8UX
Tel: 01249 816227
info@paoxley.com
www.british-antiqueclocks.com

BEDS

Worcestershire
S.W. Antiques, Newlands (road), Pershore, WR10 1BP
Tel: 01386 555580
catchall@sw-antiques.co.uk
www.sw-antiques.co.uk

BOOKS

Surrey
David Aldous-Cook, PO Box 413, Sutton, SM3 8SZ
Tel: 020 8642 4842
office@davidaldous-cook.co.uk
www.davidaldous-cook.co.uk
Reference books on antiques and collectables.

Wiltshire
Winter Book Auctions, The Old School, Maxwell Street, Swindon, SN1 5DR
Tel: 01793 611340
info@dominicwinter.co.uk
www.dominicwinter.co.uk
Specialist book auctions.

BOXES & TREEN

Berkshire
Mostly Boxes, 93 High Street, Eton, Windsor, SL4 6AF Tel: 01753 858470

London
Gerald Mathias, Antiquarius, 135–142 Kings Road, Chelsea, SW3 4PW
Tel: 020 7351 0484
info@geraldmathias.com
www.geraldmathias.com

BRITISH ANTIQUE FURNITURE RESTORERS' ASSOCIATION

BAFRA Head Office,
The Old Rectory, Warmwell, Dorchester, Dorset DT2 8HQ
Tel: 01305 854822
headoffice@bafra.org.uk
www.bafra.org.uk

Berkshire
Ben Norris & Co., Knowl Hill Farm, Knowl Hill, Kingsclere, Newbury, RG20 4NY
Tel: 01635 297950
Gilding, carving & architectural woodwork. Antique furniture restorer

Devon
Tony Vernon, 15 Follett Road, Topsham, Exeter, EX3 0JP Tel: 01392 874635
tonyvernon@antiquewood.co.uk
www.antiquewood.co.uk
All aspects of conservation and restoration including gilding, carving, upholstery, veneering and polishing. Accredited member of BAFRA; the British Antique Furniture Restorers' Association.

Gloucestershire
Stuart Bradbury, M & S Bradbury, The Barn, Hanham Lane, Paulton, Bristol, BS39 7PF
Tel: 01761 418910
enquiries@mandsbradbury.co.uk
www.mandsbradbury.co.uk
Antique furniture conservation and restoration.

Alan Hessel, The Old Town Workshop, St George's Close, Moreton-in-Marsh, GL56 0LP
Tel: 01608 650026
Our skilled craftsmen have restored fine furniture since 1976. We accept commissions from galleries and private collections. Our specialism is from the late 17thC to early 19thC furniture.

Hertfordshire
John B Carr, Charles Perry Restorations Ltd, Praewood Farm, Hemel Hempstead Road, St Albans, AL3 6AA
Tel: 01727 853487
cperry@praewood.freeserve.co.uk
Specialists in restoration and conservation of all types of antique furniture.

Kent
Timothy Akers, The Forge, 39 Chancery Lane, Beckenham, BR3 6NR
Tel: 020 8650 9179
enquiries@akersofantiques.co.uk
www.akersofantiques.co.uk
Longcase and bracket clocks, cabinet-making, French polishing. Dealers of selected fine English furniture.

Benedict Clegg, Rear of 20 Camden Road, Tunbridge Wells, TN1 2PT
Tel: 01892 548095
All aspects of 17th–19th century furniture.

Lancashire
Eric Smith, Antique Restorations The Old Church, Park Road, Darwen, BB3 2LD
Tel: 01254 776222
eric.smith@restorations.ndo.co.uk
www.ericsmithrestorations.co.uk
Accredited member of the British Antique Furniture Restorers Association. Consultant to Galway Claire Castle Galway Ireland. Workshop is included on the Conservation register maintained by the United Kingdom Institute for Conservation in London.

Lincolnshire
Michael Czajkowski BSc, E. Czajkowski & Son, 96 Tor O Moor Road, Woodhall Spa, LN10 6SB
Tel: 01526 352895
michael.czajkowski@ntlworld.com
Conservation and restoration of antique furniture, clocks (dials, movements and cases) and barometers. Skills include: marquetry Buhle and inlay work; carving & gilding; lacquer work, re-upholstery and upholstery conservation; clockwork & associated metal work. Regular collection service to the East Midlands and London. Member of BAFRA and Accredited Member United Kingdom Institute of Conservation.

London
Rodrigo Titian, Titian Studio, 32 Warple Way, Acton, W3 0DJ
Tel: 020 8222 6600
enquiries@titianstudios.co.uk
www.titianstudios.co.uk
Carving, gilding, lacquer, painted furniture and French polishing. Caning & rushing.

Norfolk
Michael Dolling, Church Farm Barns, Glandford, Holt, NR25 7JR
Tel: 01263 741115
Also at: 44 White Hart Street, East Harling NR16 2NE. Tel: 01953 718658. Restoration of antique and fine furniture including marquetry, carving, gilding, upholstery and caning.

North Somerset
Robert P Tandy, Lake House Barn, Lake Farm, Colehouse Lane, Kenn, Clevedon, BS21 6TQ
Tel: 01275 875014
robertptandy@hotmail.com
Traditional antique furniture restoration & repairs.

Scotland
Jeremy Gow, Gow Antique Restoration, Pitscandly Farm, Forfar, Angus, DD8 3NZ Tel: 01307 465342
jeremy@knowyourantiques.com
www.knowyourantiques.com
17th & 18thC marquetry English & continental.

Staffordshire
Stefan Herberholz, Middleton Hall, Middleton, B78 2AE
Tel: 01827 282858
www.herberholz.co.uk

Surrey
Hedgecoe & Freeland Antique Furniture Restoration and Upholstery, 21 Burrow Hill Green, Chobham, Woking, GU24 8QP Tel: 01276 858206/07771 953870
hedgecoefreeland@aol.com

Timothy Naylor, 24 Bridge Road, Chertsey, KT16 8JN
Tel: 01932 567129
tim@timothynaylor.com
www.timothynaylor.com

West Midlands
Phillip Slater, 93 Hewell Road, Barnt Green, Birmingham, B45 8NL
Tel: 0121 445 4942
Inlay work, marquetry.

CARD CASES
Gloucestershire
Simply Antiques, Windsor House, High Street, Moreton-in-Marsh, GL56 0AD
Tel: 07710 470877
info@callingcardcases.com
www.callingcardcases.com
Visiting card cases. Small 18th/19th century furniture. Objects of vertu. Search/seek service.

CHESS
Cornwall
T. J. Millard Antiques, 59 Lower Queen Street, Penzance, TR18 4DF
Tel: 01736 333454 or 07773 776086
chessmove@btinternet.com
Antique chess sets, chess and backgammon boards.

CLOCKS
Cheshire
Coppelia Antiques, Holford Lodge, Plumley Moor Road, Nr Knutsford, Plumley, WA16 9RS
Tel: 01565 722197
www.coppeliaantiques.co.uk

Devon
Musgrave Bickford Antiques, 15 East Street, Crediton, EX17 3AT
Tel: 01363 775042
Antique clocks and barometers.

Gloucestershire
The Grandfather Clock Shop, Styles of Stow, The Little House, Sheep Street, Stow-on-the-Wold, GL54 1JS
Tel: 01451 830455
info@stylesofstow.co.uk
www.stylesofstow.co.uk

Woodward Antique Clocks, 21 Suffolk Parade, Cheltenham, GL50 2AE
Tel: 01242 245667
woodwardclocks@onetel.com
www.woodwardclocks.com

Greater Manchester
Northern Clocks, Boothsbank Farm, Worsley, Manchester, M28 1LL
Tel: 0161 790 8414
info@northernclocks.co.uk
www.northernclocks.co.uk

Hampshire
The Clock-Work-Shop (Winchester), 6A Parchment Street, Winchester, SO23 8AT
Tel: 01962 842331
www.clock-work-shop.co.uk

Kent
Gaby Gunst, 140 High Street, Tenterden, TN30 6HT
Tel: 01580 765818

The Old Clock Shop, 63 High Street, West Malling, ME19 6NA
Tel: 01732 843246
theoldclockshop@tesco.net
www.theoldclockshop.co.uk

Derek Roberts Antiques, 25 Shipbourne Road, Tonbridge, TN10 3DN
Tel: 01732 358986
drclocks@clara.net
www.qualityantiqueclocks.com

London
The Clock Clinic Ltd, 85 Lower Richmond Road, Putney, SW15 1EU
Tel: 020 8788 1407
clockclinic@btconnect.com
www.clockclinic.co.uk

Pendulum, King House, 51 Maddox Street, W1S 2PH
Tel: 020 7629 6606
www.pendulumofmayfair.co.uk

Roderick Antique Clocks, 23 Vicarage Gate, W8 4AA
Tel: 020 7937 8517
rick@roderickantiqueclocks.com
www.roderickantiqueclocks.com

W. F. Turk, 355 Kingston Road, Wimbledon Chase, SW20 8JX
Tel: 020 8543 3231
sales@wfturk.com
www.wfturk.com

North Yorkshire
Brian Loomes, Calf Haugh Farm, Pateley Bridge, HG3 5HW
Tel: 01423 711163
clocks@brianloomes.com
www.brianloomes.com

Oxfordshire
Craig Barfoot Antique Clocks, Tudor House, East Hagbourne, OX11 9LR
Tel: 01235 818968
craig.barfoot@tiscali.co.uk

Scotland
John Mann Antique Clocks, The Clock Showroom, Canonbie, Near Carlisle, Galloway, DG14 0SY
Tel: 013873 71337
jmannclock@aol.com
www.johnmannantiqueclocks.co.uk

Somerset
Kembery Antique Clocks Ltd, George Street Antique Centre, 8 Edgar Buildings, George Street, Bath, BA1 2EH
Tel: 0117 956 5281
kembery@kdclocks.co.uk
www.kdclocks.co.uk

Surrey
Antique Clocks by Patrick Thomas, 62a West Street, Dorking, RH4 1BS
Tel: 01306 743661
patrickthomas@btconnect.com
www.antiqueclockshop.co.uk

The Clock House, 75 Pound Street, Carshalton, SM5 3PG
Tel: 020 8773 4844
markcocklin@theclockhouse.co.uk
www.theclockhouse.co.uk

The Clock Shop, 64 Church Street, Weybridge, KT13 8DL
Tel: 01932 840407/855503
www.theclockshopweybridge.co.uk

West Sussex
Samuel Orr Antique Clocks, 34–36 High Street, Hurstpierpoint, Nr Brighton, BN6 9RG
Tel: 01273 832081
clocks@samorr.co.uk
www.samorr.co.uk

Wiltshire
P A Oxley Antique Clocks & Barometers, The Old Rectory, Cherhill, Calne, SN11 8UX
Tel: 01249 816227

info@paoxley.com
www.british-antiqueclocks.com

Allan Smith Clocks, Amity Cottage, 162 Beechcroft Road, Upper Stratton, Swindon, SN2 7QE
Tel: 01793 822977
allansmithclocks@lineone.net
www.allansmithantiqueclocks.co.uk

COMICS
London
Comic Book Postal Auctions Ltd, 40–42 Osnaburgh Street, NW1 3ND
Tel: 020 7424 0007
comicbook@compalcomics.com
www.compalcomics.com

DECORATIVE ARTS
Greater Manchester
A. S. Antique Galleries, 26 Broad Street, Pendleton, Salford, M6 5BY
Tel: 0161 737 5938
as@artnouveau-artdeco.com
www.artnouveau-artdeco.com

London
Crafts Nouveau, 112 Alexandra Park Road, Muswell Hill, N10 2AE
Tel: 0208 444 3300
lauriestrange@craftsnouveau.co.uk
www.craftsnouveau.co.uk

Republic of Ireland
Mitofsky Antiques, 8 Rathfarnham Road, Terenure, Dublin 6
Tel: 00 353 1492 0033
info@mitofskyantiques.com
www.mitofskyantiques.com

Worcestershire
Art Nouveau Originals, The Bindery Gallery, 69 High Street, Broadway, WR12 7DP
Tel: 01386 854645
cathy@artnouveauoriginals.com
www.artnouveauoriginals.com

EPHEMERA
Nottinghamshire
T Vennett-Smith, 11 Nottingham Road, Gotham, NG11 0HE
Tel: 0115 983 0541
info@vennett-smith.com
www.vennett-smith.com
Ephemera auctions.

EXHIBITION & FAIR ORGANISERS
Devon
Trident Exhibitions - Buxton Antiques Fair, West Devon Business Park, Tavistock, PL19 9DP Tel: 01822 614671 info@trident-exhibitions.co.uk
www.tridentexhibitions.co.uk
www.interfine.co.uk
www.surreyantiquesfair.co.uk
www.buxtonantiquesfair.co.uk

Nottinghamshire
DMG Fairs, PO Box 100, Newark, NG24 1DJ
Tel: 01636 702326
www.dmgantiquefairs.com

Warwickshire
London Antique Arms Fairs Ltd, 15 Burbury Court, Emscote Road, Warwick, CV34 5LD
Tel: 01432 355416 & 01926 883665
info@antiquearmsfairsltd.co.uk
www.antiquearmsfairsltd.co.uk

West Midlands
Antiques for Everyone Fair, NEC House, National Exhibition Centre, Birmingham, B40 1NT
Tel: 0121 780 4141
antiques@necgroup.co.uk

EXPORTERS
Gloucestershire
Piano-Export, Bridge Road, Kingswood, Bristol, BS15 4FW
Tel: 0117 956 8300

Staffordshire
Acorn G.D.S. Ltd, 1 83 Queens Road, Penkhull, Stoke-on-Trent, ST4 7LF
Tel: 01782 817700 or 01782 845051
acorn@acorn-freight.co.uk
www.acorn-freight.co.uk
Export shipping.

East Sussex
International Furniture Exporters Ltd, Old Cement Works, South Heighton, Newhaven, BN9 0HS
Tel: 01273 611251
ife555@aol.com
www.int-furniture-exporters.co.uk

The Old Mint House Antiques, High Street, Pevensey, BN24 5LF
Tel: 01323 762337
antiques@minthouse.co.uk
www.minthouse.co.uk

Wiltshire
North Wilts. Exporters, Farm Hill House, Brinkworth, SN15 5AJ
Tel: 01666 510876
mike@northwilts.demon.co.uk
www.northwiltsantiqueexporters.com

FABERGÉ
London
Shapiro & Co, Stand 380, Gray's Antique Market, 58 Davies Street, W1Y 5LP
Tel: 020 7491 2710

Hampshire
Evans & Partridge, Agriculture House, High Street, Stockbridge, SO20 6HF
Tel: 01264 810702
Sporting auctions.

Kent
The Old Tackle Box, PO Box 55, High Street, Cranbrook, TN17 3ZU
Tel: 01580 713979
tackle.box@virgin.net

London
Angling Auctions, P O Box 2095, W12 8RU
Tel: 020 8749 4175 or 07785 281349
neil@anglingauctions.demon.co.uk

FURNITURE
Cumbria
Anthemion, Cartmel, Near Grange-Over-Sands, LA11 6QD
Tel: 01539 536295

Derbyshire
Spurrier-Smith Antiques, 28, 39 Church Street, Ashbourne, DE6 1AJ
Tel: 01335 342198/343669
ivan@spurrier-smith.fsnet.co.uk

Devon
Pugh's Antiques, Pugh's Farm, Monkton, Nr Honiton, EX14 9QH
Tel: 01404 42860
sales@pughsantiques.com
www.pughsantiques.com
Relocating to: Portley House, Old Ludlow Road, Leominster H36 0AA Tel: 01568 616546

Essex
Junior Antiques, Longcroft Farm, Dowsetts Lane, Ramsden Heath, Billericay, CM11 1JN
Tel: 01268 711 777
info@juniorantiques.com
www.juniorantiques.com
Specialising in bars.

Kent
Flower House Antiques, 90 High Street, Tenterden, TN30 6JB
Tel: 01580 763764

Pamela Goodwin, 11 The Pantiles, Royal Tunbridge Wells, TN2 5TD
Tel: 01892 618200
mail@goodwinantiques.co.uk
www.goodwinantiques.co.uk
Antique furniture, clocks, oil lamps, mirrors, decorative items.

London
Oola Boola Antiques, 139–147 Kirkdale, SE26 4QJ
Tel: 020 8291 9999
oola.boola@telco4u.net

Northamptonshire
Lorraine Spooner Antiques, 211 Watling Street, West Towcester, NN12 6BX
Tel: 01327 358777
lorraine@lsantiques.com
www.lsantiques.com
Period furniture, clocks, silver, porcelain, glass, paintings & prints, linens, books.

Oxfordshire
Georg S. Wissinger Antiques, Georgian House Antiques, 2, 21 & 44 West Street, Chipping Norton, OX7 5EU Tel: 01608 641369

Surrey
Dorking Desk Shop, J.G. Elias Antiques Limited, 41 West Street, Dorking, RH4 1BU Tel: 01306 883327/880535
info@dorkingdeskshop.co.uk
www.desk.uk.com

J Hartley Antiques Ltd, 186 High Street, Ripley, GU23 6BB
Tel: 01483 224318

East Sussex
The Old Mint House Antiques, High Street, Pevensey, BN24 5LF
Tel: 01323 762337
antiques@minthouse.co.uk
www.minthouse.co.uk

Patrick Moorhead Antiques, Spring Gardens, 76 Church Street, Brighton, BN1 1RL
Tel: 01273 779696
info@patrickmoorhead.co.uk
18th & 19thc English and continental furniture, oriental and continental ceramics, bronzes, clocks and works of art.

Northiam Antiques & Interiors, Station Road, Northiam, TN31 6QT
Tel: 01797 252523
robert.bingham2@btconnect.com

West Sussex
British Antique Replicas, 22 School Close, Queen Elizabeth Avenue, Burgess Hill, RH15 9RX
Tel: 01444 245577
www.1760.com
Antique replica furniture.

Warwickshire
Coleshill Antiques & Interiors, 12–14 High Street, Coleshill, B46 1AZ
Tel: 01675 467416
enquiries@coleshillantiques.com
www.coleshillantiques.com
Dealers in fine antiques and exclusive interiors.

West Midlands
Yoxall Antiques, 68 Yoxall Road, Solihull, B90 3RP
Tel: 0121 744 1744
sales@yoxallantiques.co.uk
www.yoxall-antiques.co.uk

Wiltshire
Cross Hayes Antiques, Units 6–8 Westbrook Farm, Draycot Cerne, Chippenham, SN15 5LH
Tel: 01249 720033
david@crosshayes.co.uk
www.crosshayes.co.uk
Shipping furniture.

FURNITURE PRODUCTS
Kent
Liberon Ltd, Mountfield Industrial Estate, New Romney, TN28 8XU
Tel: 01797 361 136

GLASS
Staffordshire
Gordon Litherland, 25 Stapenhill Road,

Burton on Trent, DE15 9AE
Tel: 01283 567213
gordon@jmp2000.com
Bottles, breweriana and pub jugs, advertising ephemera and commemoratives.

ICONS
London
The Temple Gallery, 6 Clarendon Cross, Holland Park, W11 4AP
Tel: 020 7727 3809
info@templegallery.com
www.templegallery.com

LIGHTING
Devon
The Exeter Antique Lighting Co., Cellar 15, The Quay, Exeter, EX2 4AP
Tel: 01392 490848
www.antiquelighting company.com
Antique lighting and stained glass specialists.

MARKETS & CENTRES
Bedfordshire
Woburn Abbey Antiques Centre, Woburn, MK17 9WA
Tel: 01525 290666
antiques@woburnabbey.co.uk
www.discoverwoburn.co.uk

Derbyshire
Chappells Antiques Centre - Bakewell, King Street, Bakewell, DE45 1DZ
Tel: 01629 812496
ask@chappellsantiques centre.com
www.chappellsantiques centre.com
30 established dealers inc LAPADA members. Quality period furniture, ceramics, silver, plate, metals, treen, clocks, barometers, books, pictures, maps, prints, textiles, kitchenalia, lighting and furnishing accessories from the 17th–20thC. Open Mon–Sat 10–5pm Sun 12–5pm. Closed Christmas Day, Boxing Day & New Year's Day. Please ring for brochure, giving location and parking information.

Matlock Antiques, Collectables & Riverside Café, 7 Dale Road, Matlock, DE4 3LT
Tel: 01629 760808
bmatlockantiques@aol.com
www.matlock-antiques-collectables.cwc.net
Proprietor W. Shirley. Over 70 dealers. Open 7 days a week 10am–5pm. Sun 11am–5pm. Call in to buy, sell or browse. We have a centre with a warm and friendly atmosphere, selling a wide range of items. Including collectables, mahogany, pine, oak, pictures, books, linen, kitchenalia, china, clocks, clothes and jewellery.

Devon
Colyton Antiques Centre, Dolphin Street, Colyton, EX24 6LU
Tel: 01297 552339
colytonantiques@model garage.co.uk
www.modelgarage.co.uk

Essex
Debden Antiques, Elder Street, Debden, Saffron Walden, CB11 3JY
Tel: 01799 543007
info@debden-antiques.co.uk
debden-antiques.co.uk
Tues–Sat 10am–5.30pm Sundays and Bank Hols 11am–4pm. 30 quality dealers in a stunning 17th century Essex barn. Large selection of 16th–20th century oak, mahogany and pine furniture, watercolours and oil paintings, rugs, ceramics, silver and jewellery. Plus garden furniture and ornaments in our lovely courtyard.

Flintshire
Afonwen Craft & Antique Centre, Afonwen, Nr Caerwys, Nr Mold, CH7 5UB
Tel: 01352 720965
www.afonwen.co.uk
The largest antique & craft centre in north Wales and the Borders. 14,000 sq.ft. 40 dealers, fabulous selection of antiques, china, silver, crystal, quality collectables. Fine furniture, oak, walnut, mahogany and pine from around the world. Open all year Tues–Sun, 9.30am–5.30pm. Closed Mondays, except open all Bank Holiday Mondays. Free parking, free entrance.

Gloucestershire
Durham House Antiques, Sheep Street, Stow-on-the-Wold, GL54 1AA
Tel: 01451 870404
30+ dealers. Town and country furniture, metalware, books, ceramics, sewing implements, samplers, needlework, silver and jewellery. Mon–Sat 10am–5pm, Sunday 11am–5pm. Stow-on-the-Wold, Cotswold home to over 40 antique shops, galleries and bookshops.

Jubilee Hall Antiques Centre, Oak Street, Lechlade on Thames, GL7 3AY Tel: 01367 253777
sales@jubileehall.co.uk
www.jubileehall.co.uk

The Top Banana Antiques Mall, 1 New Church Street, Tetbury, GL8 8DS
Tel: 0871 288 1102
info@topbananaantiques.com
www.topbananaantiques.com

The Top Banana Antiques Mall, 32 Long Street, Tetbury, GL8 8AQ
Tel: 0871 288 1110
info@topbananaantiques.com
www.topbananaantiques.com

The Top Banana Antiques Mall, 48 Long Street, Tetbury, GL8 8AQ
Tel: 0871 288 3058
info@topbananaantiques.com
www.topbananaantiques.com

Kent
Malthouse Arcade, High Street, Hythe, CT21 5BW
Tel: 01303 260103
Open Fridays and Saturdays Bank holiday Mondays 9.30am–5.30pm. 37 Stalls and cafe. Furniture, china and glass, jewellery, plated brass, picture postcards, framing.

Lancashire
GB Antiques Centre, Lancaster Leisure Park, (the former Hornsea Pottery), Wyresdale Road, Lancaster, LA1 3LA Tel: 01524 844734
Over 140 dealers in 40,000 sq. ft. of space. Showing porcelain, pottery, Art Deco, glass, books and linen. Also a large selection of mahogany, oak and pine furniture. Open 7 days a week 10am–5pm.

Kingsmill Antique Centre, Queen Street, Harle Syke, Burnley, BB10 2HX
Tel: 01282 431953
antiques@kingsmill.demon.co.uk
www.kingsmill.demon.co.uk
Open 7 days 10am–5pm, 8pm Thurs. 8,500 sq ft. Trade welcome.

Leicestershire
Oxford Street Antique Centre, 16–26 Oxford Street, Leicester, LE1 5XU
Tel: 0116 255 3006
Vast selection of clean English furniture ideal for home and overseas buyers, displayed in fourteen large showrooms on four floors, covering 30,000 sq feet. Reproduction furniture and accessories also stocked.

Lincolnshire
Hemswell Antique Centres, Caenby Corner Estate, Hemswell Cliff, Gainsborough, DN21 5TJ
Tel: 01427 668389
info@hemswell-antiques.com
www.hemswell-antiques.com

London
Antiquarius Antiques Centre, 131/141 King's Road, Chelsea, SW3 5ST
Tel: 020 7351 5353
neiljackson@atlantic100.freeserve.co.uk
www.antiquarius.co.uk

Atlantic Antiques Centres, Chenil House, 181–183 Kings Road, SW3 5EB
Tel: 020 7351 5353
antique@dial.pipex.com

Bond Street Antiques Centre, 124 New Bond Street, W1Y 9AE
Tel: 020 7351 5353
antique@dial.pipex.com

Northamptonshire
Trinity Collections Ltd, Unit 5, Wakefield Country Courtyard, Wakefield Lodge Estate, Potterspury, Towcester, NN12 7QX
Tel: 01327 8118822
steve@trinitycollections.co.uk
www.trinitycollections.co.uk

Nottinghamshire
Newark Antiques Warehouse Ltd, Old Kelham Road, Newark, NG24 1BX Tel: 01636 674869/07974 429185
enquiries@newarkantiques.co.uk
www.newarkantiques.co.uk

Scotland
Scottish Antique and Arts Centre, Carse of Cambus, Doune, Perthshire, FK16 6HG Tel: 01786 841203
sales@scottish-antiques.com
www.scottish-antiques.com
Over 100 dealers. Huge gift & collectors sections. Victorian & Edwardian furniture. Open 7 days 10am–5pm.

Scottish Antique Centre, Abernyte, PH14 9SJ
Tel: 01828 686401
sales@scottish-antiques.com
www.scottish-antiques.com
Over 100 dealers. Huge gift & collectors sections. Victorian & Edwardian furniture. Open 7 days 10am–5pm.

Surrey
Great Grooms Antiques Centre, 51/52 West Street, Dorking, RH4 1BU
Tel: 01306 887076
dorking@greatgrooms.co.uk
www.greatgrooms.co.uk

East Sussex
Antiques Warehouse Ltd, 54 High Street, Old Town, Hastings, TN34 3EN
Tel: 01424 433142
aw54@btconnect.com

Church Hill Antiques Centre, 6 Station Street, Lewes, BN7 2DA
Tel: 01273 474 842
churchhilllewes@aol.com
www.church-hill-antiques.com

Wales
Offa's Dyke Antique Centre, 4 High Street, Knighton, Powys, LD7 1AT
Tel: 01547 528635/520145
Open Mon–Sat 10am–5pm. Wide ranging stock. Specialists in ceramics and glass, fine art of the 19th & 20th centuries. Country antiques and collectables.

Warwickshire
Barn Antiques Centre, Station Road, Long Marston, Nr Stratford-upon-Avon, CV37 8RB
Tel: 01789 721399
www.barnantique.co.uk
Huge old barn crammed full of affordable antiques. Over 13,000 sq ft and 50 established dealers. Open daily 10am–5pm, Sun 12pm–6pm. Large free car park. Licensed bistro.

Yorkshire
Cavendish Antique & Collectors Centre, 44 Stonegate, York, YO1 8AS Tel: 01904 621666
sales@cavendishantiques.com
www.cavendishantiques.com
Open 7 days 9am–6pm. Browse at leisure. Over 70 dealers on three floors. Jewellery, silver, porcelain, glass engravings and prints, furniture, oils & watercolours, watches, collectables.

The Court House, 2–6 Town End Road, Ecclesfield, Sheffield, S35 9YY Tel: 0114 257 0641
thecourthouse@email.com
www.courthouseantiques.co.uk

MONEY BOXES
Yorkshire
John & Simon Haley, 89 Northgate, Halifax, HX1 1XF Tel: 01422 822148/360434
toysandbanks@aol.com

MUSIC
Kent
Stephen T. P. Kember, Pamela Goodwin, 11 The Pantiles, Royal Tunbridge Wells, TN2 5TD
Tel: 01959 574067
steve.kember@btinternet.com www.antique-music boxes.co.uk
Antique cylinder & disc musical boxes.

MUSICAL INSTRUMENTS
Gloucestershire
Piano-Export, Bridge Road, Kingswood, Bristol, BS15 4FW
Tel: 0117 956 8300

London
Robert Morley & Co Ltd, Piano and Harpsicord Showroom & Workshop, 34 Engate Street, SE13 7HA
Tel: 020 8318 5838
jvm@morley-r.u-net.com
www.morleypianos.com
Harpsichords, spinets, clavichords, virginals, upright, grand, square & forte pianos with musical stools, cabinets, metronomes and other accessories. Sale, restoration and repair. Antique and modern. Brochures available on request.

Nottinghamshire
Turner Violins, 1–5 Lily Grove, Beeston, NG9 1QL
Tel: 0115 943 0333
info@turnerviolins.co.uk

West Midlands
Turner Violins, 1 Gibb Street, Digbeth High Street, Birmingham, B9 4AA
Tel: 0121 772 7708
info@turnerviolins.co.uk

OAK & COUNTRY
Surrey
The Refectory, 38 West Street, Dorking, RH4 1BU
Tel: 01306 742111
www.therefectory.co.uk
Oak & country - refectory table specialist.

London
Robert Young Antiques, 68 Battersea Bridge Road, SW11 3AG
Tel: 020 7228 7847
office@robertyoungantiques.com
www.robertyoungantiques.com
Country furniture & Folk Art.

Northamptonshire
Paul Hopwell Antiques, 30 High Street, West Haddon, NN6 7AP
Tel: 01788 510636
paulhopwell@antiqueoak.co.uk
www.antiqueoak.co.uk

Surrey
Anthony Welling, Broadway Barn, High Street, Ripley, GU23 6AQ
Tel: 01483 225384
ant@awelling.freeserve.co.uk
www.antique-oak-furniture.com

PACKERS & SHIPPERS
Gloucestershire
The Shipping Company, Bourton Industrial Park, Bourton on the Water, Cheltenham, GL54 2HQ
Tel: 01451 822451
enquiries@theshippingcompanyltd.com
www.theshippingcompanyltd.com

Kent
Alex Flood & son, 41 Highstreet, Rolvenden, Kent TN17 4LP
Tel/Fax: 01580 241637 or 07711 391315
alex@frenchremovals.co.uk
www.frenchremovals.co.uk
Specialist carrier service, antiques & fine art, UK, France, Spain.

PAPERWEIGHTS
Cheshire
Sweetbriar Gallery Paperweights Ltd, 3 Collinson Court, off Church Street, Frodsham, WA6 6PN
Tel: 01928 730064
sales@sweetbriar.co.uk
www.sweetbriar.co.uk

PHOTOGRAPHS
London
Jubilee Photographica, 10 Pierrepoint Row, Camden Passage, N1 8EE Tel: 07860 793707
meara@btconnect.com
Specialist shop and gallery dealing in rare and collectable photographs from the 19th & 20th centuries. We sell and hold a large and constantly changing stock of cartes de visite, stereocards, daguerreotypes and ambrotypes, albums of travel, tpopgraphical and ethic photgraphs, art photographs and a range of books on the art and history of photography. We also have magic lanterns and lantern slides, and stereoscopic viewers. the shop is open on Wednesdays and Saturdays 10am–4pm.

PINE
Cornwall
Julie Strachey, Trevaskis Barn, Gwinear Road, Nr Hayle, TR27 5JQ
Tel: 01209 613750
Antique farm & country furniture in pine, oak, etc. Ironwork & interesting pieces for the garden (no repro). By appointment. Junction 9 M40 2 miles. Established 27 years.

Hampshire
Pine Cellars, 39 Jewry Street, Winchester, SO23 8RY Tel: 01962 867014/777546

Republic of Ireland
Ireland's Own Antiques, Alpine House, Carlow Road, Abbeyleix, Co Laois
Tel: 353 502 31348
Ireland's own antiques have a fine stock of original country furniture, which for years has been collected from country cottages and mansions all over Ireland by Peter & Daniel Meaney. Years of experience in the art of packing and shipping, and have many customers. This is a well worthwhile call for overseas buyers.

Somerset
Gilbert & Dale Antiques, The Old Chapel, Church Street, Ilchester, Nr Yeovil, BA22 8ZA
Tel: 01935 840464
roy@roygilbert.com
Painted pine & country furniture.

Wiltshire
North Wilts. Exporters, Farm Hill House, Brinkworth, SN15 5AJ
Tel: 01666 510876
mike@northwilts.demon.co.uk
www.northwiltsantiqueexporters.com

PORCELAIN
Essex
Barling Porcelain
Tel: 01621 890058
stuart@barling.uk.com
www.barling.uk.com

Hampshire
The Goss & Crested China Club & Museum, incorporating Milestone Publications, 62 Murray Road, Horndean, PO8 9JL
Tel: (023) 9259 7440
info@gosschinaclub.demon.co.uk
www.gosscrestedchina.co.uk

Shropshire
Harvey Antiques
Tel: 01584 876375
christopher-harvey@tesco.net
By appointment only.

East Sussex
Tony Horsley, PO Box 3127, Brighton, BN1 5SS
Tel: 01273 550770
Candle extinguishers, Royal Worcester and other fine porcelain

Warwickshire
Coleshill Antiques & Interiors, 12–14 High Street, Coleshill, B46 1AZ
Tel: 01675 467416
enquiries@coleshillantiques.com
www.coleshillantiques.com

Wiltshire
Andrew Dando, 34 Market Street, Bradford on Avon, BA15 1LL
Tel: 01225 865444
andrew@andrewdando.co.uk
www.andrewdando.co.uk
English, oriental and continental porcelain.

East Yorkshire
The Crested China Co, Highfield, Windmill Hill, Driffield, YO25 5YP
Tel: 0870 300 1 300
dt@thecrestedchinacompany.com
www.thecrestedchinacompany.com

PORTRAIT MINIATURES
Gloucestershire
Judy & Brian Harden, PO Box 14, Bourton on the Water, Cheltenham, GL54 2YR
Tel: 01451 810684
harden@portraitminiatures.co.uk
www.portraitminiatures.co.uk

POTTERY
Berkshire
Special Auction Services, Kennetholme, Midgham, Reading, RG7 5UX
Tel: 0118 971 2949
www.invaluable.com/sas/
Specialist auctions of commemoratives, pot lids & Prattware, Fairings, Goss & Crested, Baxter & Le Blond prints.

Buckinghamshire
Gillian Neale Antiques,
PO Box 247,
Aylesbury, HP20 1JZ
Tel: 01296 423754/
07860 638700
gillianneale@aol.com
www.gilliannealeantiques.co.uk
Blue & white transfer printed pottery 1780–1860.

Dorset
Greystoke Antiques,
4 Swan Yard, (off Cheap Street), Sherborne,
DT9 3AX
Tel: 01935 812833
Established 28 years. Adjacent to town centre car park. 10am–4.30pm daily, closed Wednesday. Also blue transfer printed pottery 1800–50 Always some 200 to 300 pieces in stock.

London
Jonathan Horne,
66c Kensington
Church Street, W8 4BY
Tel: 020 7221 5658
JH@jonathanhorne.co.uk
www.jonathanhorne.co.uk
Early English pottery

Rogers de Rin, 76 Royal Hospital Road, SW3 4HN
Tel: 020 7352 9007
rogersderin@rogersderin.co.uk
www.rogersderin.co.uk
Wemyss.

Oxfordshire
Winson Antiques, Unit 11, Langston Priory Workshops, Kingham, OX7 6UR
Tel: 01608 658856 or
07764 476776
clive.payne@virgin.net
www.clivepayne.co.uk
Mason's Ironstone china and period furniture.

Surrey
Judi Bland Antiques
Tel: 01276 857576 or
01536 724145
18th & 19th century English Toby jugs.

Julian Eade
Tel: 01865 300349 or
07973 542971
Doulton Lambeth stoneware and Burslem wares, also Royal Worcester, Minton and Derby.

Wiltshire
Andrew Dando,
34 Market Street, Bradford on Avon, BA15 1LL
Tel: 01225 865444
andrew@andrewdando.co.uk
www.andrewdando.co.uk
English, oriental and continental pottery.

PUBLICATIONS
Cheshire
Armourer - The Militaria Magazine, Published by Beaumont Publishing Ltd, 1st floor Adelphi Mill, Bollington, SK10 5JB
Tel: 01625 575700
editor@armourer.co.uk
www.armourer.co.uk
A bi-monthly magazine for military antique collectors and military history enthusiasts offering hundreds of contacts for buying and selling, articles on all aspects of militaria collecting plus the dates of UK militaria fairs and auctions. Available on subscription.

Essex
Antique Dealer and Collectors Guide,
PO Box 935, Finchingfield, Braintree, CM7 4LJ
Tel: 01371 810433
marypayne@esco.co.uk
www.antiquecollectorsguide.co.uk

West Midlands
Antiques Magazine,
H.P. Publishing, 2 Hampton Court Road, Harborne, Birmingham, B17 9AE
Tel: 0121 681 8000
Subs 01562 701001

RESTORATION
Northamptonshire
Leather Conservation Centre, University College Campus, Boughton Green Road, Moulton Park, Northampton, NN2 7AN
Tel: 01604 719766
lcc@northampton.ac.uk
www.leatherconservation.org
Conservation and restoration of leather screens, wall hangings, car, carriage and furniture upholstery, saddlery, luggage, firemens' helmets and much, much more. The centre is included on the register maintained by the United Kingdom Institute for Conservation.

ROCK & POP
Cheshire
Collector's Corner, PO Box 8, Congleton, CW12 4GD
Tel: 01260 270429
dave.popcorner@ukonline.co.uk

Lancashire
Tracks, PO Box 117,
Chorley, PR6 0UU
Tel: 01257 269726
sales@tracks.co.uk
www.tracks.co.uk
Beatles and rare pop memorabilia.

RUGS & CARPETS
Oxfordshire
Rugmark of Henley,
The Rug Gallery,
14 Reading Road,
Henley-on-Thames, RG9 1AN
Tel: 01491 412322
www.rugmark.co.uk

West Sussex
Wadsworth's, Marehill,
Pulborough, RH20 2DY
Tel: 01798 873555
info@wadsworthsrugs.com
www.wadsworthsrugs.com

SCIENTIFIC INSTRUMENTS
Cheshire
Charles Tomlinson, Chester
Tel: 01244 318395
charlestomlinson@tiscali.co.uk

Scotland
Early Technology,
Monkton House,
Old Craighall, Musselburgh, Midlothian, EH21 8SF
Tel: 0131 665 5753
michael.bennett-levy@virgin.net
www.earlytech.com
www.rare78s.com
www.tvhistory.tv

SCULPTURE
East Sussex
Garret & Hazlehurst,
PO Box 138,
Hailsham, BN27 1WX
Tel: 01323 848824
margendygarret@btinternet.com
www.garretandhazlehurst.co.uk

SECURITY SERVICES
Kent
Security CCTV, Brook House, Cranbrook Road, Hawkhurst, TN18 5EE
Tel: 0808 173 0069
Protecting people, possessions and property. Quality closed circuit television systems, discreet cameras, digital recorders, remote monitoring, professional installation, systems to meet your requirements.

SILVER
Dorset
Greystoke Antiques,
4 Swan Yard, (off Cheap Street), Sherborne,
DT9 3AX
Tel: 01935 812833
Adjacent to town centre car park. 10am–4.30pm daily, closed wednesday. Georgian, Victorian and later silver.

London
Daniel Bexfield Antiques,
26 Burlington Arcade,
W1J 0PU Tel: 020 7491 1720
antiques@bexfield.co.uk
www.bexfield.co.uk

Lyn Bloom & Jeffrey Neal, Vault 27, The London Silver Vaults, Chancery Lane, WC2A 1QS Tel: 0207 242 6189 or 07768 533055
bloomvault@aol.com
www.bloomvault.com
We stock fine quality silver items ranging from £70 to £20,000 which includes anything from silver napkin rings and flatware to large centrepieces. Our speciality is a range of over 200 antique miniature silver toys.

Shropshire
Harvey Antiques
Tel: 01584 876375
christopher-harvey@tesco.net
By appointment only.

SPORTS & GAMES
Nottinghamshire
T Vennett-Smith,
11 Nottingham Road,
Gotham, NG11 0HE
Tel: 0115 983 0541
info@vennett-smith.com
www.vennett-smith.com
Sporting auctions.

STAINED GLASS
Wales
Drew Pritchard Ltd,
St Georges Church,
Church Walks,
Llandudno, LL30 2HL
Tel: 01492 874004
enquiries@drewpritchard.co.uk
www.drewpritchard.co.uk

TEDDY BEARS
Oxfordshire
Teddy Bears of Witney,
99 High Street,
Witney, OX28 6HY
Tel: 01993 706616
www.teddybears.co.uk

TEXTILES
London
Erna Hiscock & John Shepherd, Chelsea Galleries, 69 Portobello Road,
W11 Tel: 01233 661407
erna@ernahiscockantiques.com
www.ernahiscockantiques.com
Antique samplers.

TOYS
Berkshire
Special Auction Services,
Kennetholme, Midgham,
Reading, RG7 5UX
Tel: 0118 971 2949
www.invaluable.com/sas/
Specialist auctions of toys for the collector including Dinky, Corgi, Matchbox, lead soldiers and figures, tinplate and model railways, etc.

East Sussex
Wallis & Wallis, West Street Auction Galleries, Lewes,
BN7 2NJ Tel: 01273 480208
auctions@wallisandwallis.co.uk
grb@wallisandwallis.co.uk
www.wallisandwallis.co.uk
Auctioneers of diecast toys, model railways, tin plate toys and models

Yorkshire
John & Simon Haley,
89 Northgate, Halifax,
HX1 1XF Tel: 01422
822148/360434
toysandbanks@aol.com

TUNBRIDGE WARE
Kent
Dreweatt Neate, The Auction Hall, The Pantiles, Tunbridge Wells, TN2 5QL
Tel: 01892 544500
tunbridgewells@dnfa.com
www.dnfa.com/tunbridgewells
Tunbridge ware auctioneers.

WATCHES

Kent

Tempus
Tel: 01344 874007
www.tempus-watches.co.uk

Lancashire

Brittons Jewellers, 4 King Street, Clitheroe, BB7 2EP
Tel: 01200 425555
sales@brittonswatches.com
www.internetwatches.co.uk
www.antique-jewelry.co.uk

London

Pieces of Time, 1–7 Davies Mews, W1K 5AB
Tel: 020 7629 2422
info@antique-watch.com
www.antique-watch.com
www.cufflinksworld.com

Yorkshire

Harpers Jewellers Ltd, 2/6 Minster Gates, York, YO1 7HL Tel: 01904 632634
york@harpersjewellers.co.uk
www.vintage-watches.co.uk
Vintage and modern wrist and pocket watches.

U.S.A.

AMERICANA

American West Indies Trading Co. Antiques & Art
Tel: 001 305 872 3948
awindies@att.net
www.goantiques.com/members/awindiestrading
Ethnographic, Folk, Tribal, Spanish Colonial, Santos & Retablos, American Indian, Indonesian Keris, southeast Asian antiquities, orientalia, Art Deco, Floridiana.

George and Debbie Spiecker, PO Box 40, North Hampton, NH 03862
Tel: 603 964 4738
g.spiecker@attbi.com
www.fineamericana.com
Specialising in 18th and early 19th century American furniture, weathervanes, nautical and New England paintings.

ANTIQUITIES

Hurst Gallery, 53 Mt. Auburn Street, Cambridge, MA 02138
Tel: 617 491 6888
manager@hurstgallery.com
www.hurstgallery.com

ARMS & MILITARIA

Faganarms, Box 425, Fraser, MI 48026
Tel: 00 1 586 465 4637
info@faganarms.com
www.faganarms.com

CLOCKS

R. O. Schmitt Fine Art, Box 1941, Salem, New Hampshire 03079
Tel: 603 893 5915
bob@roschmittfinearts.com
www.antiqueclockauction.com
Specialist antique clock auctions.

Setniks In Time Again, 815 Sutter Street, Suite 2, Folsom, California 95630
Tel: 916 985 2390
Toll Free 888 333 1715
setniks@pacbell.net
setniksintimeagain.com

DOLLS

Theriault's, PO Box 151, Annapolis, MD 21404
Tel: 410 224 3655
info@theriaults.com
www.theriaults.com
Doll auctions.

FURNITURE

Antiquebug, Frank & Cathy Sykes, 85 Center Street, Wolfeboro, New Hampshire 03894
Tel: 603 569 0000
dragonfly@antiquebug.com
www.antiquebug.com
Also Folk Art, mahogany speed boat models, maps and antiquarian books.

Marion Atten, 498 N. Farwell Bridge Road, Pecatonica, IL 61063
Tel: 815 239 2421
hillwood@aeroinc.net
17th, 18th and early 19th century furniture.

Douglas Hamel Antiques, 56 Staniels Road, Chichester, New Hampshire 03234 Tel: 603 798 5912
doughamel@shakerantiques.com
www.shakerantiques.com

GLASS

AllAntiqueGlass.com, PO Box 3515, Norfolk, VA 23514 Tel: 757 625 1888
webmaster@allantiqueglass.com
www.allantiqueglass.com
Early American pattern glass.

MARKETS & CENTRES

Chesapeake Antique Center, Inc., Rt. 301, PO Box 280 Queenstown, MD 21658
Tel: 00 1 410 827 6640
admin@chesapeakeantiques.com
www.chesapeakantiques.com

ORIENTAL

Mimi's Antiques
Tel: 410 381 6862/ 443 250 0930
mimisantiques@comcast.net
www.mimisantiques.com
www.trocadero.com/mimisantiques
18th and 19th century Chinese export porcelain, American and English furniture, continental porcelain, paintings, sterling, oriental rugs.

PAPERWEIGHTS

The Dunlop Collection, P.O. Box 6269, Statesville, NC 28687
Tel: 704 871 2626 or Toll Free (800) 227 1996

SCULPTURE

Steve Newman, 468 E. Boca Raton Road, Boca Raton, FL 33432
Tel: 561 338 6339
info@s-newman.com
www.s-newman.com
19th and 20th century American and European sculpture.

SERVICES

Go Antiques, 94 North Street, Suite 300, Dublin, Ohio 43017
Tel: 614 923 4250
kathy@goantiques.com
www.goantiques.com

SILVER

Antique Elegance
Tel: 617 484 7556
gloriab415@aol.com

Imperial Half Bushel, 831 North Howard Street, Baltimore, Maryland 21201
Tel: 410 462 1192
www.imperialhalfbushel.com

Silver Magazine, PO Box 9690, Rancho Santa Fe, CA 92067
Tel: 858 756 1054
silver@silvermag.com
www.silvermag.com
Specialising in the entire field of fine silver, featuring researched articles on antique English, continental and Colonial American silver and 20th century and contemporary works.

TEXTILES

Antique European Linens & Decadence Down, PO Box 789, Gulf Breeze, Florida 32562-0789
Tel: 850 432 4777
sales@antiqueeuropeanlinens.com
www.antiqueeuropeanlinens.com
Hungarian goose down pillows & european duvets.

M. Finkel & Daughter, 936 Pine Street, Philadelphia, Pennsylvania 19107-6128
Tel: 215 627 7797
mailbox@finkelantiques.com
www.finkelantiques.com

The Old Linen and Lace Shop, Inc., 1841 SW 67th Ave, Plantation, FL 33317
Tel: 954 327 3330
Cell: 954 258 2274
Antique linens and clothing, including lace and accessories from Europe, Britain and America.

CANADA

ARCHITECTURAL

507 Home and Garden Ltd, 50 Carroll St, Toronto, ON M5R 1J2
Tel: 416 462 0046
Antique garden furnishings and associated architectural artefacts

FISHING

Juniper Fishing Camps Ltd, The Old River Lodge, 40 Green Bye Road, Blissfield, Nr Doaktown, New Brunswick, E9C 1L4
Tel: 001 506 365 7277
Mob/cell 001 902 233 7777
Jon@theoldriverlodge.net
www.theoldriverlodge.net

FURNITURE

Bruce Howard & Co, 158 Davenport Rd, Toronto, ON Tel: 416 922 7966
BHOWARD@on.aibn.com
English 18th century furniture.

J. W. Humphries Antiques Ltd., 9 Glenelg Street East, Lindsay, ON K9V 1Y5
Tel: 705 324 5050
19th century English and Canadian furniture.

R.H.V. Tee & Son (England) Ltd., 7963 Granville Street, Vancouver, BC V6P 4Z3
Tel: 604 263 2791
17th/18th century English furniture.

JEWELLERY

Fraleigh Jewellers, 1977 Yonge St, Toronto, ON M4S 1Z6
Tel: 416 483 1481
rfraleigh@sympatico.ca
Antique and estate jewellery and silver.

Fiona Kenny Antiques
Tel: 905 682 0090
merday@cogeco.ca
www.trocadero.com/merday
www.fionakennyantiques.com
18th–20thC jewellery and antiques, sterling and silver plate, china and pottery, 20thC modern, collectibles and advertising.

ORIENTAL

Pao and Moltke Ltd, Oriental Art, 21 Avenue Rd (Four Seasons Hotel), Toronto, ON M5R 2G1
Tel: 416 925 6197
paoandmoltke@mail.com
Oriental art, early Chinese Neolithic period to Ming and Qing period. Chinese ceramics and works of art.

POTTERY

Staffordshire House, 1 Chestnut Park Rd, Toronto, ON M4W 1W4
Tel: 416 929 3258
JJD@aol.com
www.staffordshirehouse.ca
19th century English pottery, transferware and ironstone.

RUGS & CARPETS

Turco Persian Rug Co, 452 Richmond St E, Toronto, ON M5A 1R2
Tel: 416 366 0707
greg@turcopersian.com
www.turcopersian.com

SCIENTIFIC INSTRUMENTS

Paul Murray Antiques, 11-700 Glasgow Street, Kitchener, ON N2N 2N8
Tel: 519 743 4851
Scientific instruments, militaria and telescopes.

SILVER

Donohue & Bousquet, 27 Hawthorne Avenue, Ottawa, ON K1S 0A9
Tel: 613 232 5665
bousquet@rogers.com
Antique silver and old Sheffield plate.

Directory of Auctioneers

Auctioneers who hold frequent sales should contact us on +44 (0) 1580 766411 by April 2006 for inclusion in the next edition.

UNITED KINGDOM

BEDFORDSHIRE

W&H Peacock, 26 Newnham Street, Bedford, MK40 3JR Tel: 01234 266366

BERKSHIRE

Cameo Auctions, Kennet Holme Farm, Bath Road, Midgham, Reading, RG7 5UX Tel: 01189 713772 office@cameo-auctioneers.co.uk www.cameo-auctioneers.co.uk

Dreweatt Neate, Donnington Priory, Donnington, Newbury, RG14 2JE Tel: 01635 553553 donnington@dnfa.com www.dnfa.com/donnington

Law Fine Art Tel: 01635 860033 info@lawfineart.co.uk www.lawfineart.co.uk

Padworth Auctions, 30 The Broadway, Thatcham, RG19 3HX Tel: 01734 713772

Shiplake Fine Art, 31 Great Knollys Street, Reading, RG1 7HU Tel: 01734 594748

Special Auction Services, Kennetholme, Midgham, Reading, RG7 5UX Tel: 0118 971 2949 www.invaluable.com/sas/

BUCKINGHAMSHIRE

Amersham Auction Rooms, Station Road, Amersham, HP7 0AH Tel: 01494 729292 info@amershamauctionrooms.co.uk

Bourne End Auction Rooms, Station Approach, Bourne End, SL8 5QH Tel: 01628 531500

Dickins Auctioneers Ltd, The Claydon Saleroom, Calvert Road, Middle Claydon, MK18 2EZ Tel: 01296 714434 info@dickins-auctioneers.com www.dickins-auctioneers.com

CAMBRIDGESHIRE

Cheffins, Clifton House, 1 & 2 Clifton Road, Cambridge, CB1 7EA Tel: 01223 271966 www.cheffins.co.uk

Rowley Fine Art, The Old Bishop's Palace, Little Downham, Ely, CB6 2TD Tel: 01353 699177 mail@rowleyfineart.com www.rowleyfineart.com

Willingham Auctions, 25 High Street, Willingham, CB4 5ES Tel: 01954 261252 info@willinghamauctions.com www.willinghamauctions.com

CHESHIRE

Bonhams, New House, 150 Christleton Road, Chester, CH3 5TD Tel: 01244 313936 www.bonhams.com

Halls Fine Art Auctions, Booth Mansion, 30 Watergate Street, Chester, CH1 2LA Tel: 01244 312300/312112

Frank R Marshall & Co, Marshall House, Church Hill, Knutsford, WA16 6DH Tel: 01565 653284

Maxwells of Wilmslow inc Dockree's, 133A Woodford Road, Woodford, SK7 1QD Tel: 0161 439 5182 www.maxwells-auctioneers.co.uk

Wright Manley, Beeston Castle Salerooms, Tarporley, CW6 9NZ Tel: 01829 262150 www.wrightmanley.co.uk

CLEVELAND

Vectis Auctions Ltd, Fleck Way, Thornaby, Stockton-on-Tees, TS17 9JZ Tel: 01642 750616 admin@vectis.co.uk www.vectis.co.uk

CO. DURHAM

Addisons Auctions, The Auction Rooms, Staindrop Road, Barnard Castle, DL12 8TD Tel: 01833 690545 enquiries@addisons-auctions.co.uk www.addisons-auctioneers.co.uk

CORNWALL

Bonhams, Cornubia Hall, Eastcliffe Road, Par, PL24 2AQ Tel: 01726 814047 www.bonhams.com

Lambrays, Polmorla Walk Galleries, The Platt, Wadebridge, PL27 7AE Tel: 01208 813593

W H Lane & Son, Jubilee House, Queen Street, Penzance, TR18 2DF Tel: 01736 361447 graham.bazlet@excite.com

David Lay ASVA, Auction House, Alverton, Penzance, TR18 4RE Tel: 01736 361414 david.lays@btopenworld.com

Martyn Rowe, The Truro Auction Centre, Triplets Business Park, Poldice Valley, Nr Chacewater, Truro, TR16 5PZ Tel: 01209 822266 www.invaluable.com/martynrowe

CUMBRIA

Bonhams, 48 Cecil Street, Carlisle, CA1 1NT Tel: 01228 542422 www.bonhams.com

Kendal Auction Rooms, Sandylands Road, Kendal, LA9 6EU Tel: 01539 720603 www.kendalauction.co.uk/furniture

Mitchells Auction Company, The Furniture Hall, 47 Station Road, Cockermouth, CA13 9PZ Tel: 01900 827800 info@mitchellsfineart.com

Penrith Farmers' & Kidd's plc, Skirsgill Salerooms, Penrith, CA11 0DN Tel: 01768 890781 info@pfkauctions.co.uk www.pfkauctions.co.uk

Thomson, Roddick & Medcalf Ltd, Coleridge House, Shaddongate, Carlisle, CA2 5TU Tel: 01228 528939 www.thomsonroddick.com

DEVON

Bearnes, St Edmund's Court, Okehampton Street, Exeter, EX4 1DU Tel: 01392 207000 enquiries@bearnes.co.uk www.bearnes.co.uk

Bonhams, Dowell Street, Honiton, EX14 1LX Tel: 01404 41872 www.bonhams.com

Bonhams, 38/39 Southernhay East, Exeter, EX1 1PE Tel: 01392 455 955 www.bonhams.com

Michael J Bowman, 6 Haccombe House, Nr Netherton, Newton Abbott, TQ12 4SJ Tel: 01626 872890

Dreweatt Neate, 205 High Street, Honiton, EX14 1LQ Tel: 01404 42404 honiton@dnfa.com www.dnfa.com/honiton

Eldreds Auctioneers & Valuers, 13-15 Ridge Park Road, Plympton, Plymouth, PL7 2BS Tel: 01752 340066

S.J. Hales, 87 Fore Street, Bovey Tracey, TQ13 9AB Tel: 01626 836684

The Plymouth Auction Rooms, Edwin House, St John's Road, Cattedown, Plymouth, PL4 0NZ Tel: 01752 254740

Rendells, Stonepark, Ashburton, TQ13 7RH Tel: 01364 653017 stonepark@rendells.co.uk www.rendells.co.uk

G S Shobrook & Co, 20 Western Approach, Plymouth, PL1 1TG Tel: 01752 663341

John Smale & Co, 11 High Street, Barnstaple, EX31 1BG Tel: 01271 42000/42916

Martin Spencer-Thomas, Bicton Street, Exmouth, EX8 2SN Tel: 01395 267403

DORSET

Chapman, Moore & Mugford, 9 High Street, Shaftesbury, SP7 8JB Tel: 01747 822244

Charterhouse, The Long Street Salerooms, Sherborne, DT9 3BS Tel: 01935 812277 enquiry@charterhouse-auctions.co.uk www.charterhouse-auctions.co.uk

Cottees of Wareham, The Market, East Street, Wareham, BH20 4NR Tel: 01929 552826 www.auctionsatcottees.co.uk

Hy Duke & Son, The Dorchester Fine Art Salerooms, Weymouth Avenue, Dorchester, DT1 1QS Tel: 01305 265080 www.dukes-auctions.com

Onslow's Auctions Ltd, The Coach House, Manor Road, Stourpaine, DT8 8TQ Tel: 01258 488838

Riddetts of Bournemouth, 1 Wellington Road, Bournemouth, BH8 8JQ Tel: 01202 555686 auctions@riddetts.co.uk www.riddetts.co.uk

Semley Auctioneers, Station Road, Semley, Shaftesbury, SP7 9AN Tel: 01747 855122/855222

ESSEX

Ambrose, Ambrose House, Old Station Road, Loughton, IG10 4PE Tel: 020 8502 3951

Cooper Hirst Auctions, The Granary Saleroom, Victoria Road, Chelmsford, CM2 6LH Tel: 01245 260535

Leigh Auction Rooms, John Stacey & Sons, 88-90 Pall Mall, Leigh-on-Sea, SS9 1RG Tel: 01702 477051

Saffron Walden Auctions, 1 Market Street, Saffron Walden, CB10 1JB Tel: 01799 513281 www.saffronwaldenauctions.com

Sworders, 14 Cambridge Road, Stansted Mountfitchet, CM24 8BZ Tel: 01279 817778 auctions@sworder.co.uk www.sworder.co.uk

FLINTSHIRE

Dodds Property World, Victoria Auction Galleries, 9 Chester Street, Mold, CH7 1EB Tel: 01352 752552

GLOUCESTERSHIRE

Bruton, Knowles & Co, 111 Eastgate Street, Gloucester, GL1 1PZ Tel: 01452 880000

Clevedon Salerooms, The Auction Centre, Kenn Road, Kenn, Clevedon, Bristol, BS21 6TT Tel: 01934 830111 clevedon.salerooms@blueyonder.co.uk www.clevedon-salerooms.com

The Cotswold Auction Company Ltd, incorporating Short Graham & Co and Hobbs and Chambers Fine Arts, The Coach House, Swan Yard, 9-13 West Market Place, Cirencester, GL7 2NH Tel: 01285 642420 info@cotswoldauction.co.uk www.cotswoldauction.co.uk

The Cotswold Auction Company Ltd, incorporating Short Graham & Co and Hobbs and Chambers Fine Arts, Chapel Walk Saleroom, Cheltenham, GL50 3DS Tel: 01242 256363 info@cotswoldauction.co.uk www.cotswoldauction.co.uk

The Cotswold Auction Company Ltd, incorporating Short Graham & Co and Hobbs and Chambers Fine Arts, 4–6 Clarence Street, Gloucester, GL1 1DX Tel: 01452 521177 info@cotswoldauction.co.uk www.cotswoldauction.co.uk

Dreweatt Neate, St John's Place, Apsley Road, Clifton, Bristol, BS8 2ST Tel: 0117 973 7201 bristol@dnfa.com www.dnfa.com/bristol

Dreweatt Neate, Bristol Saleroom Two, Baynton Road, Ashton, Bristol, BS3 2EB Tel: 0117 953 1603 bristol@dnfa.com www.dnfa.com/bristol

Mallams, 26 Grosvenor Street, Cheltenham, GL52 2SG Tel: 01242 235712

Moore, Allen & Innocent, The Salerooms, Norcote, Cirencester, GL7 5RH Tel: 01285 646050 fineart@mooreallen.co.uk www.mooreallen.co.uk

Specialised Postcard Auctions, 25 Gloucester Street, Cirencester, GL7 2DJ Tel: 01285 659057

Tayler & Fletcher, London House, High Street, Bourton-on-the-Water, Cheltenham, GL54 2AP Tel: 01451 821666 bourton@taylerfletcher.com www.taylerfletcher.com

Wotton Auction Rooms, Tabernacle Road, Wotton-under-Edge, GL12 7EB Tel: 01453 844733 info@wottonauctionrooms.co.uk www.wottonauctionrooms.co.uk

GREATER MANCHESTER

Bonhams, The Stables, 213 Ashley Road, Hale, WA15 9TB Tel: 0161 927 3822 www.bonhams.com

Capes Dunn & Co, The Auction Galleries, 38 Charles Street, Off Princess Street, M1 7DB Tel: 0161 273 6060/1911 capesdunn@yahoo.co.uk

HAMPSHIRE

Bonhams, 54 Southampton Road, Ringwood, BH24 1JD Tel: 01425 473333 www.bonhams.com

Evans & Partridge, Agriculture House, High Street, Stockbridge, SO20 6HF Tel: 01264 810702

Jacobs & Hunt, 26 Lavant Street, Petersfield, GU32 3EF Tel: 01730 233933 www.jacobsandhunt.co.uk

George Kidner, The Lymington Saleroom, Emsworth Road, Lymington, SO41 9BL Tel: 01590 670070 info@georgekidner.co.uk www.georgekidner.co.uk

May & Son, The Auctioneers & Valuers, Delta Works, Salisbury Road, Shipton Bellinger, SP9 7UN Tel: 01980 846000 enquiries@mayandson.com www.mayandson.com

D M Nesbit & Co, Fine Art and Auction Department, Southsea Salerooms, 7 Clarendon Road, Southsea, PO5 2ED Tel: 023 9286 4321 auctions@nesbits.co.uk www.nesbits.co.uk

Odiham Auction Sales, Unit 4, Priors Farm, West Green Road, Mattingley, RG27 8JU Tel: 01189 326824 Tel: 07836 201764 auction@dircon.co.uk

HEREFORDSHIRE

Brightwells Fine Art, The Fine Art Saleroom, Easters Court, Leominster, HR6 0DE Tel: 01568 611122 fineart@brightwells.com www.brightwells.com

Morris Bricknell, Stroud House, 30 Gloucester Road, Ross-on-Wye, HR9 5LE Tel: 01989 768320 morrisbricknell@lineone.net www.morrisbricknell.com

Williams & Watkins, Ross Auction Rooms, Ross-on-Wye, HR9 7QF Tel: 01989 762225

Nigel Ward & Co, The Border Property Centre, Pontrilas, HR2 0EH Tel: 01981 240140 www.nigel-ward.co.uk

HERTFORDSHIRE

Sworders, The Hertford Saleroom, 42 St Andrew Street, Hertford, SG14 1JA Tel: 01992 583508 auctions@sworder.co.uk www.sworder.co.uk

Tring Market Auctions, The Market Premises, Brook Street, Tring, HP23 5EF Tel: 01442 826446 sales@tringmarketauctions.co.uk www.tringmarketauctions.co.uk

KENT

Bonhams, 49 London Road, Sevenoaks, TN13 1AR Tel: 01732 740310 www.bonhams.com

Calcutt Maclean Standen, The Estate Office, Stone Street, Cranbrook, TN17 3HD Tel: 01580 713828

The Canterbury Auction Galleries, 40 Station Road West, Canterbury, CT2 8AN Tel: 01227 763337 auctions@thecanterburyauctiongalleries.com www.thecanterburyauctiongalleries.com

Mervyn Carey, Twysden Cottage, Scullsgate, Benenden, Cranbrook, TN17 4LD Tel: 01580 240283

Dreweatt Neate, The Auction Hall, The Pantiles, Tunbridge Wells, TN2 5QL Tel: 01892 544500 tunbridgewells@dnfa.com www.dnfa.com/tunbridgewells

Gorringes, 15 The Pantiles, Tunbridge Wells, TN2 5TD Tel: 01892 619670 www.gorringes.co.uk

Ibbett Mosely, 125 High Street, Sevenoaks, TN13 1UT Tel: 01732 456731 auctions@ibbettmosely.co.uk www.ibbettmosely.co.uk

Lambert & Foster, 102 High Street, Tenterden, TN30 6HT Tel: 01580 762083 saleroom@lambertandfoster.co.uk www.lambertandfoster.co.uk

Lambert & Foster, 77 Commercial Road, Paddock Wood, TN12 6DR Tel: 01892 832325

B J Norris, The Quest, West Street, Harrietsham, Maidstone, ME17 1JD Tel: 01622 859515

Wealden Auction Galleries, Desmond Judd, 23 Hendly Drive, Cranbrook, TN17 3DY Tel: 01580 714522

LANCASHIRE

Smythes Fine Art, Chattel & Property Auctioneers & Valuers, 174 Victoria Road West, Cleveleys, FY5 3NE Tel: 01253 852184 smythes@btinternet.com www.smythes.net

Tony & Sons, 4-8 Lynwood Road, Blackburn, BB2 6HP Tel: 01254 691748

LEICESTERSHIRE

Gilding's Auctioneers and Valuers, 64 Roman Way, Market Harborough, LE16 7PQ Tel: 01858 410414 sales@gildings.co.uk www.gildings.co.uk

LINCOLNSHIRE

Batemans Auctioneers, The Exchange Hall, Broad Street, Stamford, PE9 1PX Tel: 01780 766466 www.batemans-auctions.co.uk

DDM Auction Rooms, Old Courts Road, Brigg, DN20 8JD Tel: 01652 650172 www.ddmauctionrooms.co.uk

Golding Young, Old Wharf Road, Grantham, NG31 7AA Tel: 01476 565118

Thomas Mawer & Son, Dunston House, Portland Street, Lincoln, LN5 7NN Tel: 01522 524984 mawer.thos@lineone.net

Marilyn Swain Auctions, The Old Barracks, Sandon Road, Grantham, NG31 9AS Tel: 01476 568861

Walter's, No 1 Mint Lane, Lincoln, LN1 1UD Tel: 01522 525454

LONDON

Angling Auctions, PO Box 2095, W12 8RU Tel: 020 8749 4175 or 07785 281349 neil@anglingauctions.demon.co.uk

Bloomsbury Auctions Ltd, Bloomsbury House, 24 Maddox Street, W1S 1PP Tel: 020 7495 9494 info@bloomsburyauctions.com www.bloomsburyauctions.com

Bonhams, 65-69 Lots Road, Chelsea, SW10 0RN Tel: 020 7393 3900 www.bonhams.com

Bonhams, 101 New Bond Street, W1S 1SR Tel: 020 7629 6602 www.bonhams.com

Bonhams, Montpelier Street, Knightsbridge, SW7 1HH Tel: 020 7393 3900 www.bonhams.com

Graham Budd Auctions Ltd, Auctioneers & Valuers gb@grahambuddauctions.co.uk

Christie's, 8 King Street, St James's, SW1Y 6QT Tel: 020 7839 9060 www.christies.com

Christie's, 85 Old Brompton Road, SW7 3LD Tel: 020 7930 6074 www.christies.com

Comic Book Postal Auctions Ltd, 40-42 Osnaburgh Street, NW1 3ND Tel: 020 7424 0007 comicbook@compalcomics.com www.compalcomics.com

Cooper Owen, 21 Denmark Street, WC2H 8NP Tel: 020 7240 4132 www.CooperOwen.com

Criterion Salerooms, 53 Essex Road, Islington, N1 2BN Tel: 020 7359 5707

Dix-Noonan-Webb, 16 Bolton Street, W1J 8BQ Tel: 020 7016 1700 auctions@dnw.co.uk www.dnw.co.uk

Harmers of London, 111 Power Road, Chiswick, W4 5PY Tel: 020 8747 6100 auctions@harmers.demon.co.uk www.harmers.com

Lloyds International Auction Galleries, Lloyds House, 9 Lydden Road, SW18 4LT Tel: 020 8788 7777 valuations@lloyds-auction.co.uk www.lloyds-auction.co.uk

Lots Road Auctions, 71-73 Lots Road, Chelsea, SW10 0RN Tel: 020 7351 7771 marketing@lotsroad.com www.lotsroad.com

Morton & Eden Ltd, in association with Sotheby's, 45 Maddox Street, W1S 2PE Tel: 020 7493 5344 info@mortonandeden.com

Phillips, de Pury & Co., 25-26 Albermarle Street, W1S 4HX Tel: 020 7318 4010 www.phillipsdepury.com

Piano Auctions Ltd, Sale room: Conway Hall, 25 Red Lion Square, Holborn, WC1 R4RL Tel: 01234 831742 www.pianoauctions.co.uk

Proud Oriental Auctions, Proud Galleries, 5 Buckingham St, WC2N 6BP Tel: 020 7839 4942

Rosebery's Fine Art Ltd, 74/76 Knights Hill, SE27 0JD Tel: 020 8761 2522 auctions@roseberys.co.uk

Sotheby's, 34-35 New Bond Street, W1A 2AA Tel: 020 7293 5000 www.sothebys.com

Sotheby's Olympia, Hammersmith Road, W14 8UX Tel: 020 7293 5555 www.sothebys.com

Spink & Son Ltd, 69 Southampton Road, Bloomsbury, WC1B 4ET Tel: 020 7563 4000

Kerry Taylor Auctions in Association with Sotheby's, St George Street Gallery, Sotheby's New Bond Street, W1A 2AA Tel: 07785 734337 fashion.textiles@sothebys.com

MERSEYSIDE

Cato Crane & Company, Antiques & Fine Art Auctioneers, 6 Stanhope Street, Liverpool, L8 5RF Tel: 0151 709 5559 johncrane@cato-crane.co.uk www.cato-crane.co.uk

Outhwaite & Litherland, Kingsway Galleries, Fontenoy Street, Liverpool, L3 2BE Tel: 0151 236 6561

MIDDLESEX

West Middlesex Auction Rooms, 113-114 High Street, Brentford, TW8 8AT Tel: 020 8568 9080

NORFOLK

Garry M. Emms & Co. Ltd., Auctioneers, Valuers & Agents, Great Yarmouth Salerooms, Beevor Road (off South Beach Parade), Great Yarmouth, NR30 3PS Tel: 01493 332668 garry@greatyarmouthauctions.com www.greatyarmouthauctions.com

Thomas Wm Gaze & Son, Diss Auction Rooms, Roydon Road, Diss, IP22 4LN Tel: 01379 650306 sales@dissauctionrooms.co.uk www.twgaze.com

Horners Professional Valuers & Auctioneers, incorporating Howlett & Edrich and Jonathan Howlett, North Walsham Salerooms, Midland Road, North Walsham, NR28 9JR Tel: 01692 500603

Keys, Off Palmers Lane, Aylsham, NR11 6JA Tel: 01263 733195 www.aylshamsalerooms.co.uk

Knight's, Cuckoo Cottage, Town Green, Alby, Norwich, NR11 7HE Tel: 01263 768488

NORTHAMPTONSHIRE

Denise E. Cowling FGA, Northampton Tel: 01604 686219 or 0781 800 3786 northants@peacockauction.co.uk

J. P. Humbert Auctioneers Ltd, The Salerooms, Unit 2A, Burcote Road Estate, Towcester, NN12 6TF Tel: 01327 359595 www.invaluable.com/jphumbert www.jphumbertauctioneers.co.uk

NORTHERN IRELAND

Anderson's Auction Rooms Ltd, Unit 7, Prince Regent Business Park, Prince Regent Road, Castereagh, Belfast, BT5 6QR Tel: 028 9040 1888

NORTHUMBERLAND

Jim Railton, Nursery House, Chatton, Alnwick, NE66 5PY Tel: 01668 215323 office@jimrailton.com www.jimrailton.com

NOTTINGHAMSHIRE

Bonhams, 57 Mansfield Road, Nottingham, NG1 3PL Tel: 0115 947 4414 www.bonhams.com

Arthur Johnson & Sons Ltd, The Nottingham Auction Centre, Meadow Lane, Nottingham, NG2 3GY Tel: 0115 986 9128 antiques@arthurjohnson.co.uk

Mellors & Kirk, The Auction House, Gregory Street, Lenton Lane, Nottingham, NG7 2NL Tel: 0115 979 0000

Neales, Nottingham Salerooms, 192 Mansfield Road, Nottingham, NG1 3HU Tel: 0115 962 4141 fineart@neales-auctions.com www.dnfa.com/nottingham

C B Sheppard & Son, The Auction Galleries, Chatsworth Street, Sutton-in-Ashfield, NG17 4GG Tel: 01623 556310

T Vennett-Smith, 11 Nottingham Road, Gotham, NG11 0HE Tel: 0115 983 0541 info@vennett-smith.com www.vennett-smith.com

OXFORDSHIRE

Bonhams, 39 Park End Street, Oxford, OX1 1JD Tel: 01865 723524 www.bonhams.com

Holloway's, 49 Parsons Street, Banbury, OX16 5NB Tel: 01295 817777 nwilliams@hollowaysauctioneers.co.uk www.hollowaysauctioneers.co.uk

Mallams, Bocardo House, 24 St Michael's Street, Oxford, 0X1 2EB Tel: 01865 241358 oxford@mallams.co.uk

Jones & Jacob, The Barn, Ingham Lane, Watlington OX49 5EJ www.jonesandjacob.com

Soames County Auctioneers, Pinnocks Farm Estates, Northmoor, OX8 1AY Tel: 01865 300626

SCOTLAND

Bonhams, 65 George Street, Edinburgh, EH2 2JL Tel: 0131 225 2266 www.bonhams.com

Bonhams, 176 St Vincent Street, Glasgow, G2 5SG Tel: 0141 223 8866 www.bonhams.com

William Hardie Ltd, 15a Blythswood Square, Glasgow, G2 4EW Tel: 0141 221 6780

Loves Auction Rooms, 52 Canal Street, Perth, PH2 8LF Tel: 01738 633337

Lyon & Turnbull, 33 Broughton Place, Edinburgh, EH1 3RR Tel: 0131 557 8844 info@lyonandturnbull.com

Macgregor Auctions, 56 Largo Road, St Andrews, Fife, KY16 8RP Tel: 01334 472431

Shapes Fine Art Auctioneers & Valuers, Bankhead Avenue, Sighthill, Edinburgh, EH11 4BY Tel: 0131 453 3222 auctionsadmin@shapesauctioneers.co.uk www.shapesauctioneers.co.uk

L S Smellie & Sons Ltd, Within the Furniture Market, Lower Auchingramont Road, Hamilton, ML10 6BE Tel: 01698 282007 or 01357 520211

Sotheby's, 112 George Street, Edinburgh, EH2 4LH Tel: 0131 226 7201 www.sothebys.com

Thomson, Roddick & Medcalf Ltd, 60 Whitesands, Dumfries, DG1 2RS Tel: 01387 279879 trmdumfries@btconnect.com www.thomsonroddick.com

Thomson, Roddick & Medcalf Ltd, 20 Murray Street, Annan, DG12 6EG Tel: 01461 202575 www.thomsonroddick.com

Thomson, Roddick & Medcalf Ltd, 43/4 Hardengreen Business Park, Eskbank, Edinburgh, EH22 3NX Tel: 0131 454 9090 www.thomsonroddick.com

SHROPSHIRE

Halls Fine Art Auctions, Welsh Bridge, Shrewsbury, SY3 8LA Tel: 01743 231212

McCartneys, Ox Pasture, Overture Road, Ludlow, SY8 4AA Tel: 01584 872251

Mullock & Madeley, The Old Shippon, Wall-under-Heywood, Nr Church Stretton, SY6 7DS Tel: 01694 771771 auctions@mullockmadeley.co.uk www.mullockmadeley.co.uk

Nock Deighton, Livestock & Auction Centre, Tasley, Bridgnorth, WV16 4QR Tel: 01746 762666

Walker, Barnett & Hill, Cosford Auction Rooms, Long Lane, Cosford, TF11 8PJ Tel: 01902 375555 wbhauctions@lineone.net www.walker-barnett-hill.co.uk

Welsh Bridge Salerooms, Welsh Bridge, Shrewsbury, SY3 8LH Tel: 01743 231212

SOMERSET

Aldridges, Newark House, 26-45 Cheltenham Street, Bath, BA2 3EX Tel: 01225 462830

Bonhams, 1 Old King Street, Bath, BA1 2JT Tel: 01225 788 988 www.bonhams.com

Greenslade Taylor Hunt Fine Art, Magdelene House, Church Square, Taunton, TA1 1SB Tel: 01823 332525

Lawrence Fine Art Auctioneers, South Street, Crewkerne, TA18 8AB Tel: 01460 73041 www.lawrences.co.uk

Tamlyn & Son, 56 High Street, Bridgwater, TA6 3BN Tel: 01278 458241

Gardiner Houlgate, The Bath Auction Rooms, 9 Leafield Way, Corsham, Nr Bath, SN13 9SW Tel: 01225 812912 auctions@gardiner-houlgate.co.uk www.invaluable.com/gardiner-houlgate

STAFFORDSHIRE

Louis Taylor Auctioneers & Valuers, Britannia House, 10 Town Road, Hanley, Stoke on Trent, ST1 2QG Tel: 01782 214111

Potteries Specialist Auctions, 271 Waterloo Road, Cobridge, Stoke on Trent, ST6 3HR Tel: 01782 286622

Wintertons Ltd, Lichfield Auction Centre, Fradley Park, Lichfield, WS13 8NF Tel: 01543 263256 enquiries@wintertons.co.uk www.wintertons.co.uk

SUFFOLK

Abbotts Auction Rooms, Campsea Ashe, Woodbridge, IP13 0PS Tel: 01728 746323

Boardman Fine Art Auctioneers, PO Box 99, Haverhill, CB9 7YF Tel: 01440 730414

Bonhams, 32 Boss Hall Road, Ipswich, IP1 5DJ Tel: 01473 740494 www.bonhams.com

Diamond Mills & Co, 117 Hamilton Road, Felixstowe, IP11 7BL Tel: 01394 282281

Dyson & Son, The Auction Room, Church Street, Clare, CO10 8PD Tel: 01787 277993 info@dyson-auctioneers.co.uk www.dyson-auctioneers.co.uk

Lacy Scott and Knight, Fine Art Department, The Auction Centre, 10 Risbygate Street, Bury St Edmunds, IP33 3AA Tel: 01284 763531

Neal Sons & Fletcher, 26 Church Street, Woodbridge, IP12 1DP Tel: 01394 382263

Olivers, Olivers Rooms, Burkitts Lane, Sudbury, CO10 1HB Tel: 01787 880305 oliversauctions@btconnect.com

Vost's, Newmarket, CB8 9AU Tel: 01638 561313

SURREY

Bonhams, Millmead, Guildford, GU2 4BE Tel: 01483 504030 www.bonhams.com

Clarke Gammon, The Guildford Auction Rooms, Bedford Road, Guildford, GU1 4SJ Tel: 01483 880915

Dreweatt Neate formerly Hamptons Fine Art Auctioneers, Baverstock House, 93 High Street, Godalming, GU7 1AL Tel: 01483 423567 godalming@dnfa.com www.dnfa.com/godalming

Ewbank Auctioneers, Burnt Common Auction Rooms, London Road, Send, Woking, GU23 7LN Tel: 01483 223101 antiques@ewbankauctions.co.uk www.ewbankauctions.co.uk

Lawrences Auctioneers Limited, Norfolk House, 80 High Street, Bletchingley, RH1 4PA Tel: 01883 743323 www.lawrencesbletchingley.co.uk

John Nicholson, The Auction Rooms, Longfield, Midhurst Road, Fernhurst, GU27 3HA Tel: 01428 653727 sales@johnnicholsons.com

P F Windibank, The Dorking Halls, Reigate Road, Dorking, RH4 1SG Tel: 01306 884556/876280 sjw@windibank.co.uk www.windibank.co.uk

Richmond & Surrey Auctions Ltd, Richmond Station, Kew Road, Old Railway Parcels Depot, Richmond, TW9 2NA Tel: 020 8948 6677 rsatrading.richmond@virgin.net

EAST SUSSEX

Burstow & Hewett, Abbey Auction Galleries, Lower Lake, Battle, TN33 0AT Tel: 01424 772374 www.burstowandhewett.co.uk

Dreweatt Neate, 46-50 South Street, Eastbourne, BN21 4XB Tel: 01323 410419 eastbourne@dnfa.com www.dnfa.com/eastbourne

Gorringes Auction Galleries, Terminus Road, Bexhill-on-Sea, TN39 3LR Tel: 01424 212994 bexhill@gorringes.co.uk www.gorringes.co.uk

Gorringes inc Julian Dawson, 15 North Street, Lewes, BN7 2PD Tel: 01273 478221 clientservices@gorringes.co.uk www.gorringes.co.uk

Raymond P Inman, 98a Coleridge Street, Hove, BN3 5AA Tel: 01273 774777 www.invaluable.com/raymondinman

Rye Auction Galleries, Rock Channel, Rye, TN31 7HL Tel: 01797 222124 sales@ryeauction.fsnet.co.uk

Scarborough Perry Fine Art, Hove Auction Rooms, Hove Street, Hove, BN3 2GL Tel: 01273 735266

Wallis & Wallis, West Street Auction Galleries, Lewes, BN7 2NJ Tel: 01273 480208 auctions@wallisandwallis.co.uk grb@wallisandwallis.co.uk www.wallisandwallis.co.uk

WEST SUSSEX

Henry Adams Fine Art Auctioneers, Baffins Hall, Baffins Lane, Chichester, PO19 1UA Tel: 01243 532223 enquiries@henryadamsfineart.co.uk

John Bellman Auctioneers, New Pound Business Park, Wisborough Green, Billingshurst, RH14 PAZ Tel: 01403 700858 hbeves@bellmans.co.uk

Peter Cheney, Western Road Auction Rooms, Western Road, Littlehampton, BN17 5NP Tel: 01903 722264 & 713418

Denham's, The Auction Galleries, Warnham, Nr Horsham, RH12 3RZ Tel: 01403 255699 enquiries@denhams.com www.denhams.com

R H Ellis & Sons, 44-46 High Street, Worthing, BN11 1LL Tel: 01903 238999

Sotheby's Sussex, Summers Place, Billingshurst, RH14 9AD Tel: 01403 833500 www.sothebys.com

Stride & Son, Southdown House, St John's Street, Chichester, PO19 1XQ Tel: 01243 780207

Rupert Toovey & Co Ltd, Spring Gardens, Washington, RH20 3BS Tel: 01903 891955 auctions@rupert-toovey.com www.rupert-toovey.com

Worthing Auction Galleries Ltd, Fleet House, Teville Gate, Worthing, BN11 1UA Tel: 01903 205565 info@worthing-auctions.co.uk www.worthing-auctions.co.uk

TYNE & WEAR

Anderson & Garland (Auctioneers), Marlborough House, Marlborough Crescent, Newcastle-upon-Tyne, NE1 4EE Tel: 0191 232 6278

Boldon Auction Galleries, 24a Front Street, East Boldon, NE36 0SJ Tel: 0191 537 2630

Bonhams, 30-32 Grey Street, Newcastle Upon Tyne, NE1 6AE Tel: 0191 233 9930 www.bonhams.com

Sneddons, Sunderland Auction Rooms, 30 Villiers Street, Sunderland, SR1 1EJ Tel: 0191 514 5931

WALES

Anthemion Auctions, 2 Llandough Trading Park, Penarth Road, Cardiff, CF11 8RR Tel: 029 2071 2608

Peter Francis, Curiosity Sale Room, 19 King Street, Carmarthen, SA31 1BH Tel: 01267 233456 nigel@peterfrancis.co.uk www.peterfrancis.co.uk

Morgan Evans & Co Ltd, 30 Church Street, Llangefni, Anglesey, LL77 7DU Tel: 01248 723303/ 421582 gaerwen.auction@morganevans.i12.com www.morganevans.com

Rogers Jones & Co, The Saleroom, 33 Abergele Road, Colwyn Bay, LL29 7RU Tel: 01492 532176 www.rogersjones.co.uk

J. Straker, Chadwick & Sons, Market Street Chambers, Abergavenny, Monmouthshire, NP7 5SD Tel: 01873 852624

Wingetts Auction Gallery, 29 Holt Street, Wrexham, Clwyd, LL13 8DH Tel: 01978 353553 auctions@wingetts.co.uk www.wingetts.co.uk

WARWICKSHIRE

Bigwood Auctioneers Ltd, The Old School, Tiddington, Stratford-upon-Avon, CV37 7AW Tel: 01789 269415

Locke & England, 18 Guy Street, Leamington Spa, CV32 4RT Tel: 01926 889100 info@leauction.co.uk www.auctions-online.com/locke

WEST MIDLANDS

Biddle and Webb Ltd, Ladywood, Middleway, Birmingham, B16 0PP Tel: 0121 455 8042 antiques@biddleandwebb.freeserve.co.uk www.biddleandwebb.co.uk

Bonhams, The Old House, Station Road, Knowle, Solihull, B93 0HT Tel: 01564 776151 www.bonhams.com

Fellows & Sons, Augusta House, 19 Augusta Street, Hockley, Birmingham, B18 6JA Tel: 0121 212 2131 info@fellows.co.uk www.fellows.co.uk

Weller & Dufty Ltd, 141 Bromsgrove Street, Birmingham, B5 6RQ Tel: 0121 692 1414 sales@welleranddufty.co.uk www.welleranddufty.co.uk

WILTSHIRE

Henry Aldridge & Son Auctions, Unit 1, Bath Road Business Centre, Devizes, SN10 1XA Tel: 01380 729199 andrew@henry-aldridge.co.uk www.henry-aldridge.co.uk

Dreweatt Neate formerly Hamptons Fine Art Auctioneers, Hilliers Yard, High Street, Marlborough, SN8 1AA Tel: 01672 515161 marlborough@dnfa.com www.dnfa.com/marlborough

Finan & Co, The Square, Mere, BA12 6DJ Tel: 01747 861411 post@finanandco.co.uk www.finanandco.co.uk

Kidson Trigg, Estate Office, Friars Farm, Sevenhampton, Highworth, Swindon, SN6 7PZ Tel: 01793 861000

Netherhampton Salerooms, Salisbury Auction Centre, Netherhampton, Salisbury, SP2 8RH Tel: 01722 340 041

Dominic Winter Book Auctions, The Old School, Maxwell Street, Swindon, SN1 5DR Tel: 01793 611340 info@dominicwinter.co.uk www.dominicwinter.co.uk

Woolley & Wallis, Salisbury Salerooms, 51-61 Castle Street, Salisbury, SP1 3SU Tel: 01722 424500/411854 enquiries@woolleyandwallis.co.uk www.woolleyandwallis.co.uk

WORCESTERSHIRE

Andrew Grant, St Mark's House, St Mark's Close, Cherry Orchard, Worcester, WR5 3DL Tel: 01905 357547 www.andrew-grant.co.uk

Philip Laney, The Malvern Auction Centre, Portland Road, off Victoria Road, Malvern, WR14 2TA Tel: 01684 893933 philiplaney@aol.com

Philip Serrell, The Malvern Saleroom, Barnards Green Road, Malvern, WR14 3LW Tel: 01684 892314 serrell.auctions@virgin.net www.serrell.com

YORKSHIRE

BBR, Elsecar Heritage Centre, Elsecar, Barnsley, S74 8HJ Tel: 01226 745156 sales@onlinebbr.com www.onlinebbr.com

Boulton & Cooper, St Michael's House, Market Place, Malton, YO17 7LR Tel: 01653 696151 antiques@boultoncooper.co.uk www.boultoncooper.co.uk

H C Chapman & Son, The Auction Mart, North Street, Scarborough, YO11 1DL Tel: 01723 372424

Cundalls, 15 Market Place, Malton, YO17 7LP Tel: 01653 697820

Dee, Atkinson & Harrison, The Exchange Saleroom, Driffield, YO25 6LD Tel: 01377 253151 info@dahauctions.com www.dahauctions.com

David Duggleby, The Vine St Salerooms, Scarborough, YO11 1XN Tel: 01723 507111 auctions@davidduggleby.com www.davidduggleby.com

ELR Auctions Ltd, The Nichols Building, Shalesmoor, Sheffield, S3 8UJ Tel: 0114 281 6161

Andrew Hartley, Victoria Hall Salerooms, Little Lane, Ilkley, LS29 8EA Tel: 01943 816363 info@andrewhartleyfinearts.co.uk www.andrewhartleyfinearts.co.uk

Lithgow Sons & Partners, The Auction Houses, Station Road, Stokesley, Middlesbrough, TS9 7AB Tel: 01642 710158 info@lithgowsauctions.com www.lithgowsauctions.com

Malcolm's No. 1 Auctioneers & Valuers Tel: 01977 684971 info@malcolmsno1auctions.co.uk www.malcolmsno1auctions.co.uk

Christopher Matthews, 23 Mount Street, Harrogate, HG2 8DQ Tel: 01423 871756

Morphets of Harrogate, 6 Albert Street, Harrogate, HG1 1JL Tel: 01423 530030

Paul Beighton, Woodhouse Green, Thurcroft, Rotherham, S66 9AQ Tel: 01709 700005 www.paulbeightonauctioneers.co.uk

Sheffield Railwayana Auctions, 43 Little Norton Lane, Sheffield, S8 8GA Tel: 0114 274 5085 ian@sheffrail.freeserve.co.uk www.sheffieldrailwayana.co.uk

Tennants, The Auction Centre, Harmby Road, Leyburn, DL8 5SG Tel: 01969 623780 enquiry@tennants-ltd.co.uk www.tennants.co.uk

Tennants, 34 Montpellier Parade, Harrogate, HG1 2TG Tel: 01423 531661 enquiry@tennants-ltd.co.uk www.tennants.co.uk

Wilkinson & Beighton Auctioneers, Woodhouse Green, Thurcroft, Rotherham, SY3 8LA Tel: 01709 700005

Wilkinson's Auctioneers Ltd, The Old Salerooms, 28 Netherhall Road, Doncaster, DN1 2PW Tel: 01302 814884 sid@wilkinsons-auctioneers.co.uk www.wilkinsons-auctioneers.co.uk

Wombell's Antiques & General Auction, The Auction Gallery, Northminster Business Park, Northfield Lane, Upper Poppleton, York, YO26 6QU Tel: 01904 790777 www.invaluable.com/wombell

AUSTRALIA

Leonard Joel Auctioneers, 333 Malvern Road, South Yarra, Victoria 3141 Tel: 03 9826 4333 decarts@ljoel.com.au or jewellery@ljoel.com.au www.ljoel.com.au

Shapiro Auctioneers, 162 Queen Street, Woollahra, Sydney NSW 2025 Tel: 612 9326 1588

CANADA

Bailey's Auctioneers & Appraisers Tel: 001 519 823 1107 www.BaileyAuctions.com

Robert Deveau Galleries Fine Art Auctioneers, 297-299 Queen Street, Toronto, Ontario, M5A 1S7 Tel: 416 364 6271

Ritchies Inc. Auctioneers & Appraisers of Antiques & Fine Art, 288 King Street East, Toronto, Ontario, M5A 1K4 Tel: (416) 364 1864 auction@ritchies.com www.ritchies.com

Sotheby's, 9 Hazelton Avenue, Toronto, Ontario, M5R 2EI Tel: (416) 926 1774 www.sothebys.com

A Touch of Class Auction & Appraisal Service Tel: 705 726 2120 info@atouchofclassauctions.com www.atouchofclassauctions.com

Waddington's Auctions, 111 Bathurst Street, Toronto, M5V 2R1 Tel: 001 416 504 9100 info@waddingtons.ca www.waddingtons.ca

When the Hammer Goes Down, 440 Douglas Avenue, Toronto, Ontario, M5M 1H4 Tel: 001 416 787 1700 TOLL FREE 1 (866) BIDCALR (243 2257) BIDCALR@rogers.com www.bidcalr.com

FRANCE

Sotheby's France SA, 76 rue du Faubourg, Saint Honore, Paris 75008 Tel: 33 1 53 05 53 05 www.sothebys.com

GERMANY

Auction Team Koln, Postfach 50 11 19, 50971 Koln Tel: 00 49 0221 38 70 49 auction@breker.com

Hermann Historica OHG, Postfach 201009, 80010 Munchen Tel: 00 49 89 5237296

Sotheby's Berlin, Palais anmFestungsgraben, Unter den Linden, Neue Wache D-10117 Tel: 49 (30) 201 0521 www.sothebys.com

Sotheby's Munich, Odeonsplatz 16, D-80539 Munchen Tel: 49 (89) 291 31 51 www.sothebys.com

ITALY

Christie's, Palazzo Massimo, Lancellotti, Piazza Navona 114, 00186 Rome Tel: 39 06 686 3333 www.christies.com

Sotheby's, Palazzo Broggi, Via Broggi, 19, Milan 20129 Tel: 39 02 295 001 www.sothebys.com

Sotheby's Rome, Piazza d'Espana 90, Rome 00186 Tel: 39(6) 69941791/6781798 www.sothebys.com

NETHERLANDS

Christie's, Cornelis Schuystraat 57, 1071 JG Amsterdam Tel: 020 575 5255 www.christies.com

Sotheby's Amsterdam, De Boelelaan 30, Amsterdam 1083 HJ Tel: 31 20 550 2200 www.sothebys.com

Van Sabben Poster Auctions, PO Box 2065, 1620 EB Hoorn Tel: 31 229 268203 uboersma@vsabbenposterauctions.nl www.vsabbenposterauctions.nl

NEW ZEALAND

Webb's, 18 Manukau Rd, Newmarket, PO Box 99251, Auckland Tel: 09 524 6804 auctions@webbs.co.nz www.webbs.co.nz

REPUBLIC OF IRELAND

James Adam & Sons, 26 St Stephen's Green, Dublin 2 Tel: 00 3531 676 0261 www.jamesadam.ie/

Hamilton Osborne King, 4 Main Street, Blackrock, Co. Dublin Tel: 353 1 288 5011 blackrock@hok.ie www.hok.ie

Mealy's, Chatsworth Street, Castle Comer, Co Kilkenny Tel: 00 353 564 441 229 info@mealys.com www.mealys.com

Whyte's Auctioneers, 38 Molesworth Street, Dublin 2 Tel: 00 353 1 676 2888 info@whytes.ie www.whytes.ie

SINGAPORE

Sotheby's (Singapore) Pte Ltd, 1 Cuscaden Road, 01-01 The Regent, 249715 Tel: 65 6732 8239 www.sothebys.com

SOUTH AFRICA

Rudd's Auctioneers, 87 Bree Street, Cape Town, 8001 Tel: (021) 426 0384/6/7 info@rudds.co.za

SWITZERLAND

Bonhams, 7 Av. Pictet-de-Rochemont, 1207 Geneva Tel: (0) 22 300 3160

Christie's, 8 Place de la Taconnerie, 1204 Geneva Tel: 022 319 1766 www.christies.com

Phillips, Kreuzstrasse 54, 8008 Zurich Tel: 00 41 1 254 2400

Phillips Geneva, 9 rue Ami-Levrier, CH-1201 Geneva Tel: 00 41 22 738 0707

Sotheby's, 13 Quai du Mont Blanc, Geneva CH-1201 Tel: 41 22 908 4800 www.sothebys.com

Sotheby's Zurich, Gessneralee 1, CH-8021 Zurich www.sothebys.com

U.S.A.

Bertoia Auctions, 2141 DeMarco Drive, Vineland, New Jersey 08360 Tel: 856 692 1881 bill@bertoiaauctions.com www.bertoiaauctions.com

Bloomington Auction Gallery, 300 East Grove St, Bloomington, Illinois 61701 Tel: 309 828 5533 joyluke@verizon.net www.joyluke.com

Bonhams & Butterfields, 220 San Bruno Avenue, San Francisco, CA 94103 Tel: 415 861 7500

Bonhams & Butterfields, 7601 Sunset Boulevard, Los Angeles, CA 90046 Tel: 323 850 7500

Bonhams & Butterfields, 441 W. Huron Street, Chicago, IL 60610 Tel: 312 377 7500

Frank H Boos Gallery, 420 Enterprise Court, Bloomfield Hills, Michigan 48302 Tel: 248 332 1500 artandauction@boosgallery.com www.boosgallery.com

Christie's, 20 Rockefeller Plaza, New York, NY 10020 Tel: 212 636 2000 www.christies.com

The Cobbs Auctioneers LLC, Noone Falls Mill, 50 Jaffrey Rd, Peterborough, NH 03458 Tel: 603 924 6361 info@thecobbs.com www.thecobbs.com

Copake Auction, Inc., 266 RT. 7A, Copake, NY 12516 Tel: 518 329 1142 info@copakeauction.com www.copakeauction.com

Doyle New York, 175 East 87th Street, New York, NY 10128 Tel: 212 427 2730 info@doylenewyork.com www.doylenewyork.com

Du Mouchelles, 409 East Jefferson, Detroit, Michigan 48226 Tel: 313 963 6255

Eldred's, Robert C Eldred Co Inc, 1475 Route 6A, East Dennis, Massachusetts 0796 Tel: 508 385 3116 www.eldreds.com

Freeman Fine Art Of Philadelphia Inc., 1808 Chestnut Street, Philadelphia, PA 19103 Tel: 215 563 9275

The Great Atlantic Auction Company, 2 Harris & Main Street, Putnam, CT 06260 Tel: 860 963 2234 www.thegreatatlanticauction.com

Green Valley Auctions, Inc., 2259 Green Valley Lane, Mt. Crawford, VA 22841 Tel: 540 434 4260 gvai@shentel.net www.greenvalleyauctions.com

Gene Harris, Antique Auction Center, 203 S. 18th Avenue, PO Box 476, Marshalltown, Iowa 50158 Tel: 641 752 0600 geneharris@geneharrisauctions.com geneharrisauctions.com

Leslie Hindman Inc., 122 North Aberdeen Street, Chicago, Illinois 60607 Tel: 312 280 1212 www.lesliehindman.com

Hunt Auctions, 75 E. Uwchlan Avenue, Suite 130, Exton, Pennsylvania 19341 Tel: 610 524 0822 info@huntauctions.com www.huntauctions.com

Randy Inman Auctions Inc., PO Box 726, Waterville, Maine 04903-0726 Tel: 207 872 6900 inman@inmanauctions.com www.inmanauctions.com

Jackson's International Auctioneers & Appraisers of Fine Art & Antiques, 2229 Lincoln Street, Cedar Falls, IA 50613 Tel: 319 277 2256/800 665 6743 sandim@jacksonsauctions.com www.jacksonsauction.com

James D Julia, Inc., P O Box 830, Rte.201, Skowhegan Road, Fairfield, ME 04937 Tel: 207 453 7125 www.juliaauctions.com

Mastronet, 660 Kingery HWY, Willowbrook, Illinois 60527 Tel: 630 472 1200 www.mastronet.com

Paul McInnis Inc., Auction Gallery, 21, Rockrimmon Road, Northampton, New Hampshire Tel: 603 964 1301

New Orleans Auction Galleries, Inc., 801 Magazine Street, AT 510 Julia, New Orleans, Louisiana 70130 Tel: 504 566 1849

Northeast Auctions, 93 Pleasant St, Portsmouth, NH 03810-4504 Tel: 603 433 8400 neacat@ttlc.net

Phillips New York, 406 East 79th Street, New York, NY10021 Tel: 212 570 4830

Phillips, de Pury & Co., 450 West 15th Street, New York, NY 10011 Tel: 212 940 1200 www.phillipsdepury.com

R. O. Schmitt Fine Art, Box 1941, Salem, New Hampshire 03079 Tel: 603 893 5915 bob@roschmittfinearts.com www.antiqueclockauction.com

Skinner Inc., 357 Main Street, Bolton, MA 01740 Tel: 978 779 6241

Skinner Inc., The Heritage On The Garden, 63 Park Plaza, Boston, MA 02116 Tel: 617 350 5400

Sloan's & Kenyon, 4605 Bradley Boulevard, Bethesda, Maryland 20815 Tel: 301 634 2330 info@sloansandkenyon.com www.sloansandkenyon.com

Sotheby's, 1334 York Avenue at 72nd St, New York, NY 10021 Tel: 212 606 7000 www.sothebys.com

Sotheby's, 9665 Wilshire Boulevard, Beverly Hills, California 90212 Tel: 310 274 0340 www.sothebys.com

Sotheby's, 215 West Ohio Street, Chicago, Illinois 60610 Tel: 312 670 0010 www.sothebys.com

Sprague Auctions, Inc., Route 5, Dummerston, VT 05301 Tel: 802 254 8969 bob@spragueauctions.com www.spragueauctions.com

Stair Galleries, P O Box 418, 33 Maple Avenue, Claverack, NY 12513 Tel: 212 860 5446/518 851 2544 rebecca.hoffmann@stairgalleries.com www.stairgalleries.com

Strawser Auctions, Michael G. Strawser, 200 North Main Street, Wolcottville, Indiana 46795 Tel: 260 854 2859 info@strawserauctions.com www.strawserauctions.com www.majolicaauctions.com

Theriault's, PO Box 151, Annapolis, MD 21404 Tel: 410 224 3655 info@theriaults.com www.theriaults.com

Treadway Gallery, Inc., 2029 Madison Road, Cincinnati, Ohio 45208 Tel: 513 321 6742 www.treadwaygallery.com

TreasureQuest Auction Galleries, Inc., 2690 S.E.Willoughby Blvd, Stuart, Florida 34994 Tel: 772 781 8600 customerservice@TQAG.com/TIM@TQAG.com www.TQAG.com

Weschler's Auctioneers & Appraisers, 909 E Street, NW, Washington DC2004 Tel: 202 628 1281/800 331 1430 karen@weschlers.com www.weschlers.com

Wolfs Gallery, 1239 W 6th Street, Cleveland, OH 44113 Tel: 216 575 9653

Swann, 104 East 25th Street, New York 10010 Tel: 212 254 4710 swann@swanngalleries.com

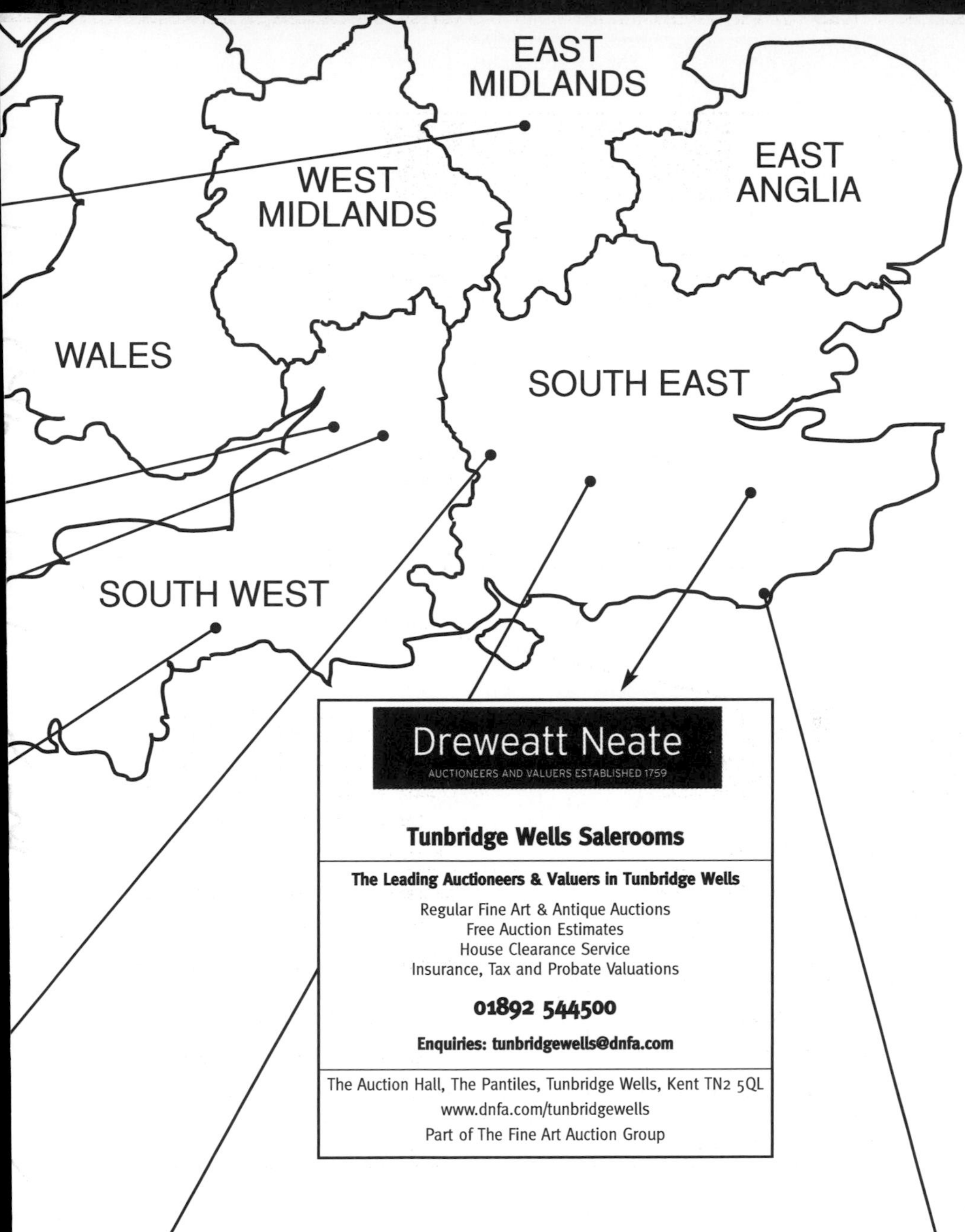
EAST
MIDLANDS
EAST
ANGLIA
WEST
MIDLANDS
WALES
SOUTH EAST
SOUTH WEST

The Barn, Ingham Lane, Watlington, Oxfordshire
Tel: 01491 612810
Fax: 01491 614564

www.jonesandjacob.com

AUCTIONEERS & VALUERS OF

ANTIQUES, FINE ART & CHATTELS

MAY & SON

(Established 1925)

Monthly catalogued auctions of Antiques & Collectables
Periodical Specialist Sales
Invaluable Auction Contributor – House Clearances

Good friendly Auctions with fascinating and interesting items

For information on viewing & catalogues
Tel: 01980 846000 Fax: 01980 846600
Email: office@mayandson.com Website: www.mayandson.com

1964
LAWRENCES

AUCTIONEERS LIMITED

Regular Sales of Fine Art & Chattels
Single Items or Complete House Contents
Free Auction Estimates
Valuation for Probate & Insurance
Collection & Delivery Available
30 years experience in Auctions

Norfolk House, 80 High Street
Bletchingley, Surrey RH1 4PA

Telephone: 01883 743323

www.lawrencesbletchingley.co.uk

A Regular Programme of Sales

of Antique, Victorian and Edwardian Furniture, Works of Art, Silver, Glass, Watches, China, Musical Instruments, Jewellery, etc. etc.

Held in our Saleroom at Otford, Nr. Sevenoaks, Kent

Also valuations carried out for Probate, Insurance and Family Division

Complete house clearances undertaken with personal supervision

Storage facilities available for short periods pending sale

125 High Street, Sevenoaks, Kent TN13 1UT

Telephone: 01732 456731 Fax: 01732 740910
Email: auctions@ibbettmosely.co.uk Website: www.ibbettmosely.co.uk

WALES
SOUTH EAST
SOUTH WEST

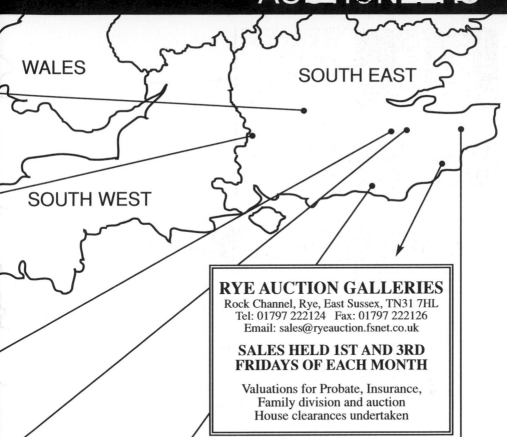

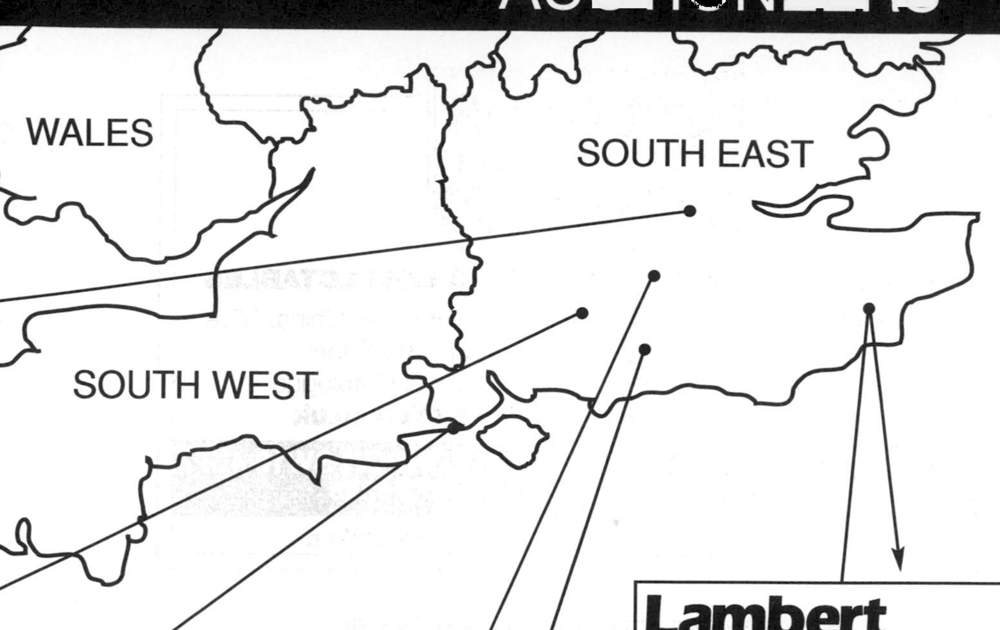
WALES
SOUTH EAST
SOUTH WEST

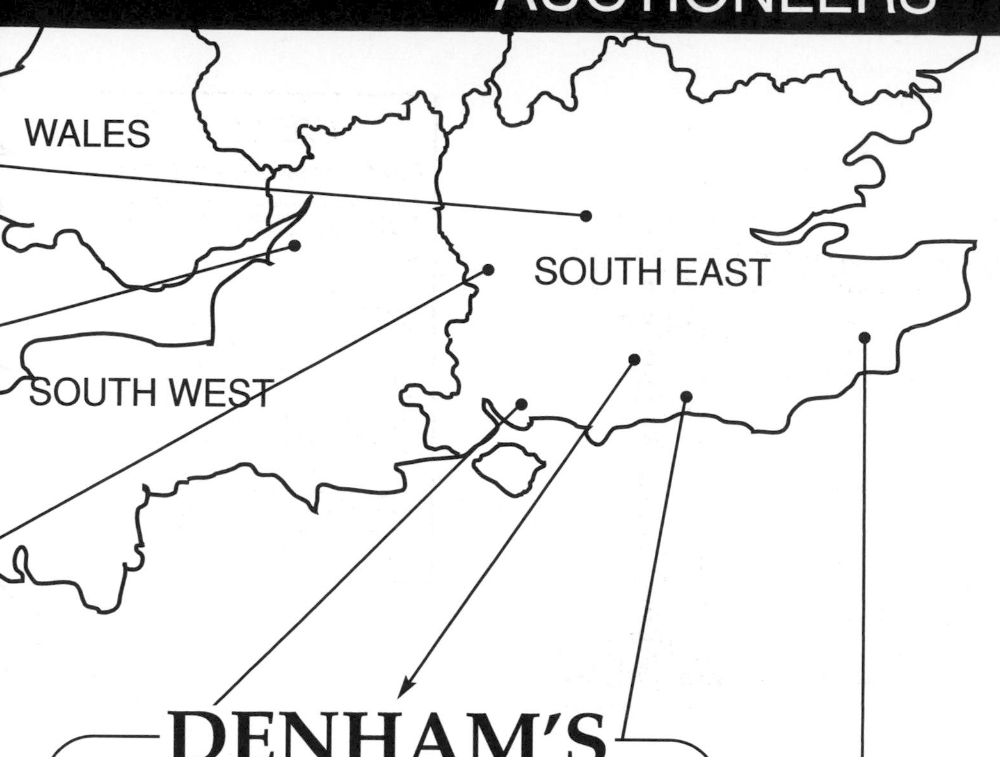
WALES
SOUTH EAST
SOUTH WEST

www.twgaze.com

- **Leading Provincial Auction House - Established 1857**
- **Over 2000 Lots every Week - Fridays & many Saturdays**
- Fine Furniture & Collectables
- Architectural Salvage
- Modern Design
- Pop Memorabilia
- 19th & 20th Century Paintings
- Rural & Domestic Bygones
- Decorative Arts
- Shipping Goods
- Valuation Department
- Buyer's Premium 10%

DISS AUCTION ROOMS
ROYDON ROAD DISS
NORFOLK IP22 4LN
tel 01379 650306

sales@dissauctionrooms.co.uk

Thos.Wm.
GAZE & SON
Chartered Surveyors Est.1857

OLIVERS
AUCTIONEERS & VALUERS

REGULAR SALES OF
ANTIQUES & WORKS OF ART

FORTNIGHTLY SALES OF
VICTORIAN & LATER FURNITURE
& HOUSEHOLD EFFECTS

VALUATIONS FOR INSURANCE
PROBATE AND FAMILY DIVISION

SPECIALISTS IN HOUSE CLEARANCES
FOR DECEASED ESTATES

Members of the society SOFAA of Fine Art Auctioneers

The Saleroom, Burkitts Lane, Sudbury, Suffolk CO10 1HB
Telephone 01787 880305 Fax 01787 883107
Email: oliversauctions@btconnect.com

SWORDERS
FINE ART AUCTIONEERS

G E Sworder & Sons
14 Cambridge Road
Stansted Mountfitchet
Essex CM24 8BZ

01279 817778
Fax 01279 817779
auctions@sworder.co.uk

www.sworder.co.uk

Regular Fine Art & Antique Sales, Weekly Auctions of 19th & 20th Century Furniture and Decoration with a First Class Valuation Department covering the whole of East Anglia.

PETER CHENEY

Auctioneers & Valuers

MONTHLY AUCTION SALES
ANTIQUES, FURNITURE, PICTURES, SILVER,
PORCELAIN AND COLLECTORS ITEMS
NO BUYERS PREMIUM
VALUATIONS FOR INSURANCE & PROBATE

Western Road Auction Rooms, Western Road,
Littlehampton, West Sussex BN17 5NP
Tel: 01903 722264 & 713418
Fax: 01903 713418

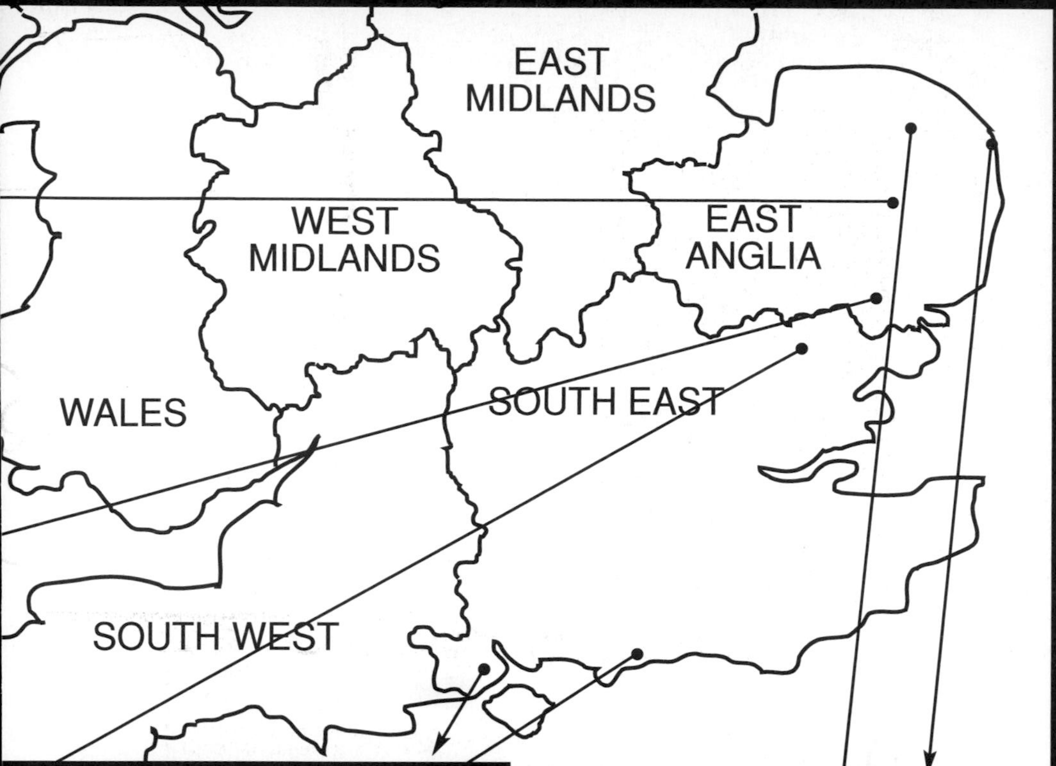

EAST
MIDLANDS
WEST
MIDLANDS
EAST
ANGLIA
WALES
SOUTH EAST
SOUTH WEST

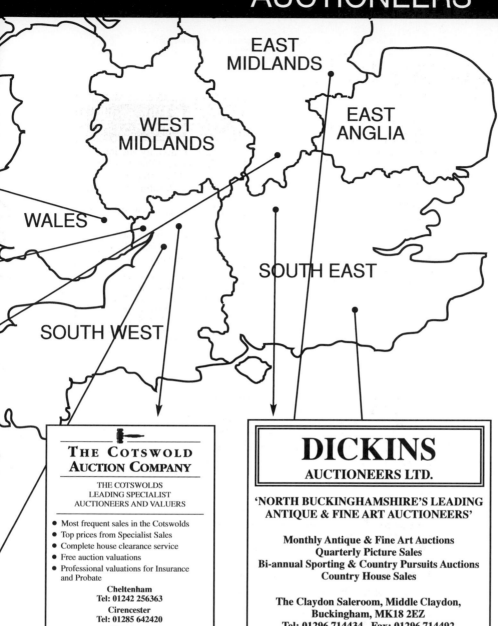

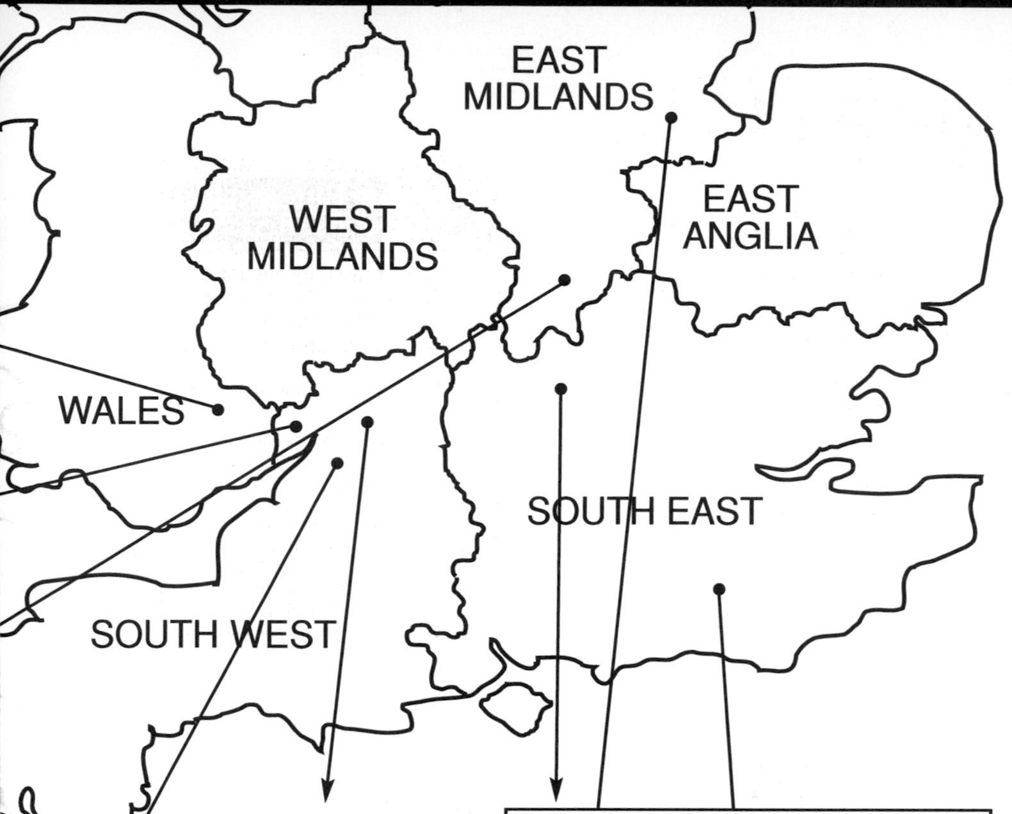

EAST MIDLANDS

EAST ANGLIA

WEST MIDLANDS

WALES

SOUTH EAST

SOUTH WEST

THE COTSWOLD AUCTION COMPANY

THE COTSWOLDS
LEADING SPECIALIST
AUCTIONEERS AND VALUERS

- Most frequent sales in the Cotswolds
- Top prices from Specialist Sales
- Complete house clearance service
- Free auction valuations
- Professional valuations for Insurance and Probate

Cheltenham
Tel: 01242 256363
Cirencester
Tel: 01285 642420
Gloucester
Tel: 01452 521177

www.cotswoldauction.co.uk
email: info@cotswoldauction.co.uk

RICS

DICKINS
AUCTIONEERS LTD.

'NORTH BUCKINGHAMSHIRE'S LEADING ANTIQUE & FINE ART AUCTIONEERS'

Monthly Antique & Fine Art Auctions
Quarterly Picture Sales
Bi-annual Sporting & Country Pursuits Auctions
Country House Sales

The Claydon Saleroom, Middle Claydon,
Buckingham, MK18 2EZ
Tel: 01296 714434 Fax: 01296 714492
info@dickins-auctioneers.com
www.dickins-auctioneers.com

BI-MONTHLY ANTIQUE & FINE ART SALES
INTERNET LISTED & COLOUR ILLUSTRATED
REGULAR COLLECTIVE SALES WITH HOUSE CLEARANCE CONTENTS
VALUATIONS FOR ALL PURPOSES
Members of the Society of Fine Art Auctioneers
THE OLD BARRACKS,
SANDON ROAD, GRANTHAM, LINCS
TEL: 01-476-568861

EWBANK
FINE ART
AUCTIONEERS & VALUERS

Antiques and Fine Art Auctioneers

Valuations for Probate, Insurance and Family Division

House clearances arranged

Burnt Common Auction Rooms,
London Road, Send, Woking GU23 7LN
Tel: 01483 223101 · Fax: 01483 222171
www.ewbankauctions.co.uk

Out of town location fronting the A3 halfway between Guildford and M25

CHARTERED ART AND ANTIQUES SURVEYORS

MEMBERS OF THE SOCIETY OF FINE ART AUCTIONEERS

Peter Francis
The Auctioneers in Wales

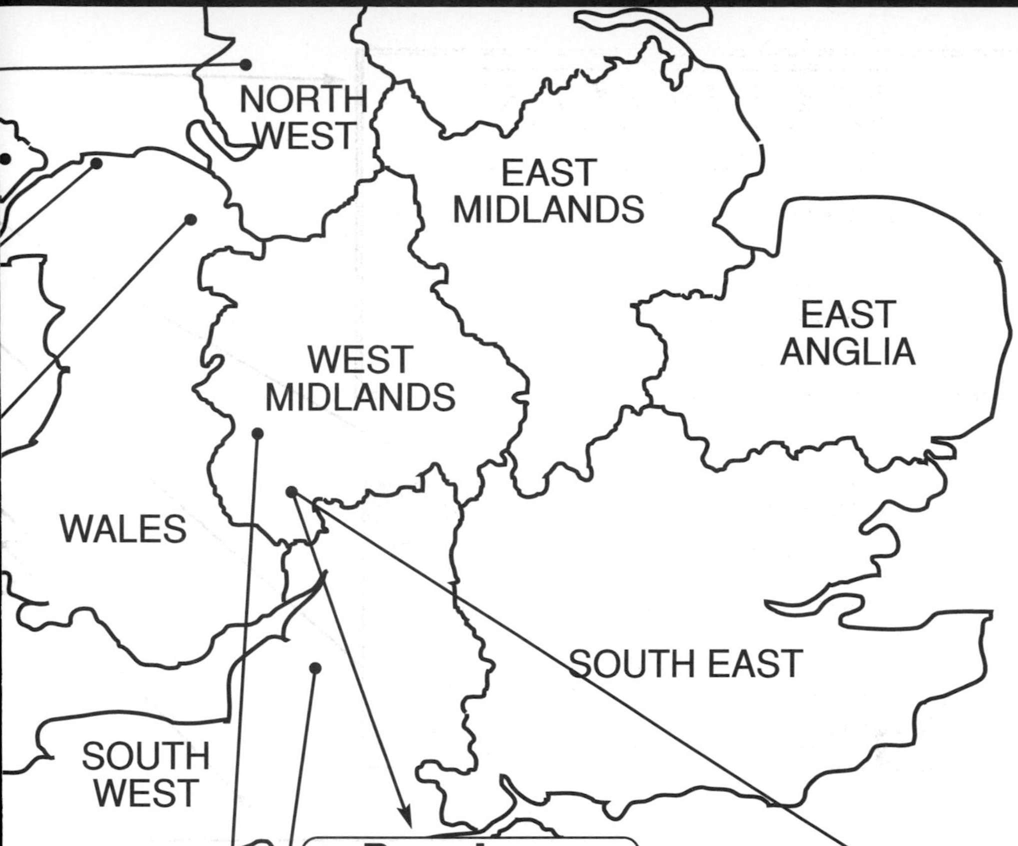
NORTH WEST
EAST MIDLANDS
EAST ANGLIA
WEST MIDLANDS
WALES
SOUTH EAST
SOUTH WEST

PHILIP LANEY

Chartered Surveyor

THE MALVERN AUCTION CENTRE

REGULAR SALES OF ANTIQUES, WORCESTER AND OTHER PORCELAIN AND COLLECTABLES

Portland Road, off Victoria Road, Malvern Worcestershire WR14 2TA. Tel: 01684 893933

PHILIP **SERRELL**

auctioneers & valuers

REGULAR SALES OF ANTIQUES & FINE ART

TWO SALES EACH MONTH OF VICTORIAN, EDWARDIAN, CONTEMPORARY FURNITURE & EFFECTS

FREE SALES ESTIMATES FOR A SINGLE ITEM OR COMPLETE HOUSE CONTENTS, INCLUDING FULL HOUSE CLEARANCE SERVICE

VALUATIONS FOR PROBATE & INSURANCE PURPOSES

SPECIALISTS IN THE SALE OF WORCESTER PORCELAIN

MORE SALES, MORE LOTS, MORE OFTEN...

SALEROOM
The Malvern Saleroom
Barnards Green Road, Malvern WR14 3LW
Tel: 01684 892314 Fax: 01684 569832
www.serrell.com

Henry Aldridge & Son Auctions

DEVIZES AUCTION ROOMS
Unit 1, Bath Road Business Centre, Devizes, Wiltshire SN10 1XA Tel: 01380 729199
Website: www.henry-aldridge.co.uk

Auctioneers of Antique & General Furniture, Specialist Sales, Collectors Items

***Titanic*, White Star & Maritime Specialists**

Brightwells
FINE ART
Established 1846

The Fine Art Saleroom
Easters Court, Leominster, Herefordshire HR6 0DE

FINE NEW SALEROOMS - with on site parking & café
Monthly catalogue sales of ANTIQUES

Regular Specialist Sales of:
- PICTURES
- SILVER & JEWELLERY
- SPORTING ITEMS
- PORCELAIN, POTTERY & GLASS
- CLASSIC & VINTAGE CARS & AUTOMOBILIA
- TOYS & TEXTILES
- ROCK, POP & 20TH CENTURY DESIGN
- BOOKS & STAMPS

Sales fixtures list on request

VALUATIONS for ALL PURPOSES
Tel: 01568 611122 Fax: 01568 610519
E-mail: fineart@brightwells.com Website: www.brightwells.com

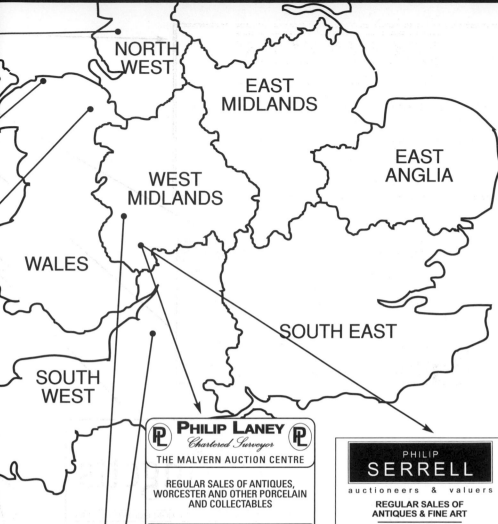

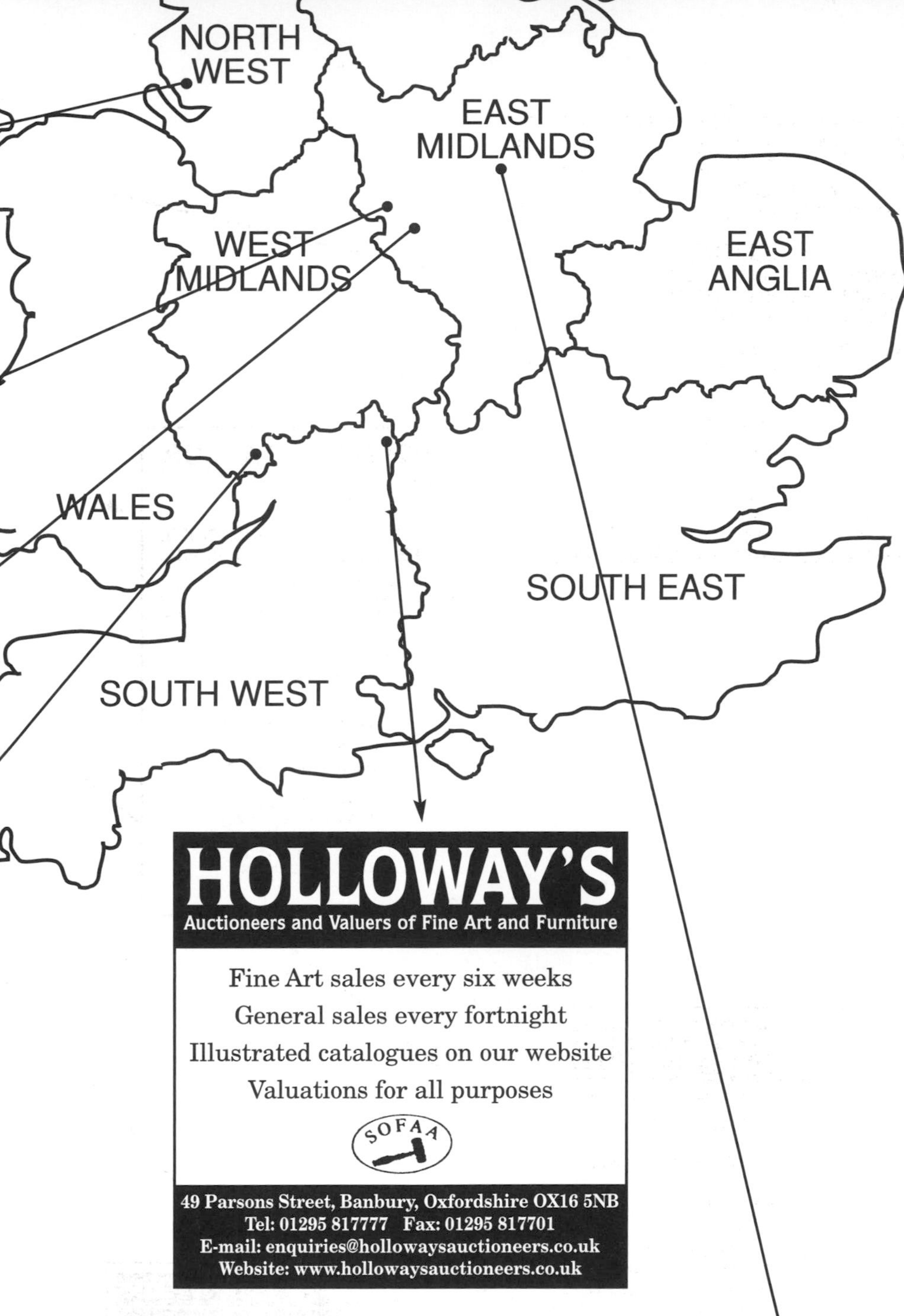
NORTH WEST
EAST MIDLANDS
WEST MIDLANDS
EAST ANGLIA
WALES
SOUTH EAST
SOUTH WEST

SOFAA

Founded in 1801

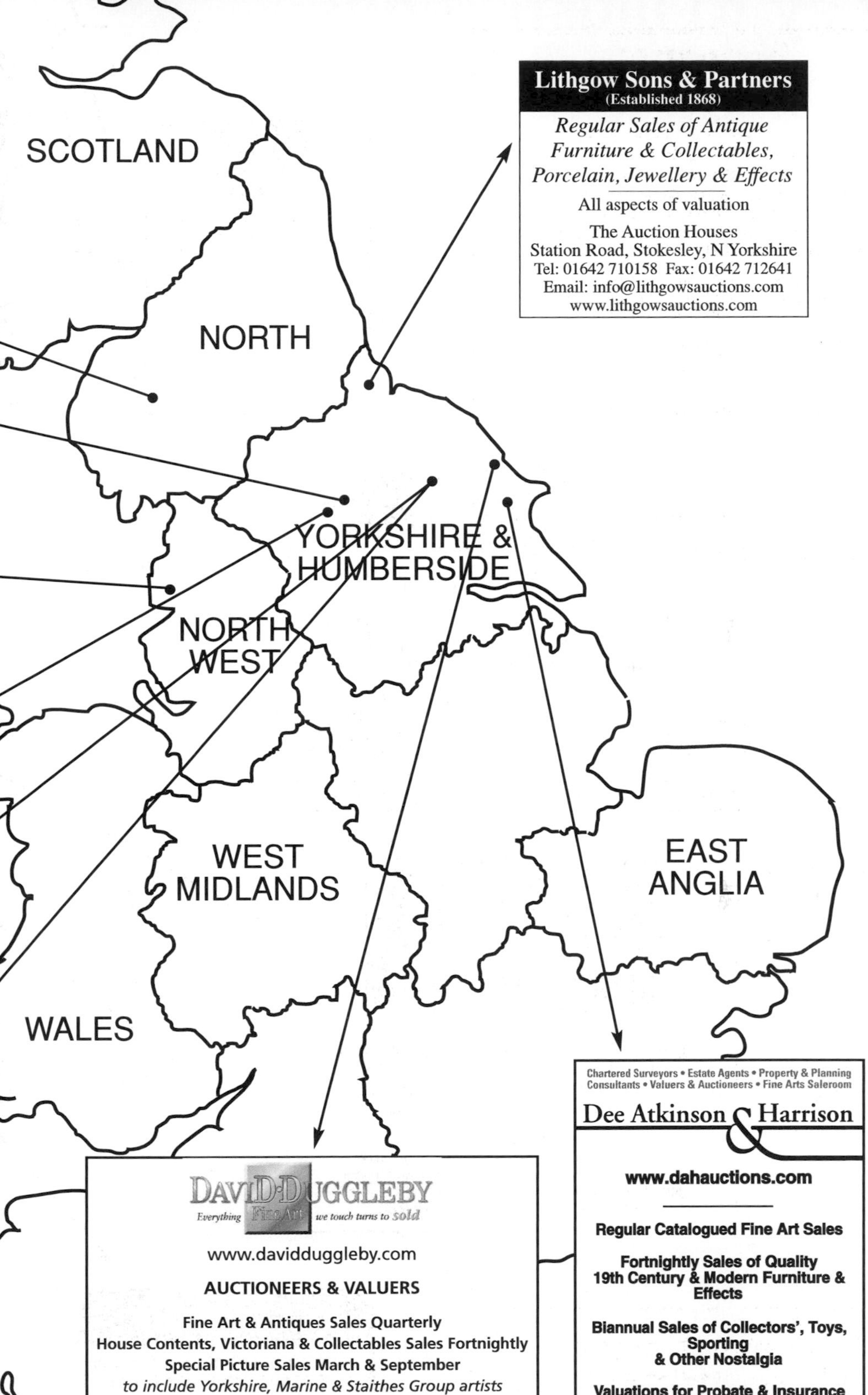
SCOTLAND
NORTH
YORKSHIRE & HUMBERSIDE
NORTH WEST
WEST MIDLANDS
EAST ANGLIA
WALES

Key to Illustrations

Each illustration and descriptive caption is accompanied by a letter code. By referring to the following list of auctioneers (denoted by ⚒) and dealers (⊞) the source of any item may be immediately determined. Inclusion in this edition in no way constitutes or implies a contract or binding offer on the part of any of our contributors to supply or sell the goods illustrated, or similar articles, at the prices stated. Advertisers in this year's directory are denoted by †.

If you require a valuation for an item, it is advisable to check whether the dealer or specialist will carry out this service and if there is a charge. Please mention Miller's when making an enquiry. Having found a specialist who will carry out your valuation it is best to send a photograph and description of the item to the specialist together with a stamped addressed envelope for the reply. A valuation by telephone is not possible.

Most dealers are only too happy to help you with your enquiry; however, they are very busy people and consideration of the above points would be welcomed.

A&O ⊞ Ancient & Oriental Ltd Tel: 01664 812044 alex@antiquities.co.uk www.antiquities.co.uk

ACAN ⊞ Acanthus, Chipping Norton, Oxfordshire OX7 7WB Tel: 01869 340009 www.acanthusonline.co.uk

AEL ⊞ Argyll Etkin Ltd, 1–9 Hills Place, Oxford Circus, London W1F 7SA Tel: 020 7437 7800 philatelists@argyll-etkin.com www.argyll-etkin.com

AFD ⊞ Afford Decorative Arts Tel: 01827 330042 afforddecarts@fsmail.net

AG ⚒ Anderson & Garland (Auctioneers), Marlborough House, Marlborough Crescent, Newcastle-upon-Tyne, Tyne & Wear NE1 4EE Tel: 0191 232 6278

AGO ⊞ Ashton Gower Antiques, 9 Talbot Court, Market Square, Stow-on-the-Wold, Gloucestershire GL54 1BQ Tel: 01451 870699 ashtongower@aol.com

AH ⚒† Andrew Hartley, Victoria Hall Salerooms, Little Lane, Ilkley, Yorkshire LS29 8EA Tel: 01943 816363 info@andrewhartleyfinearts.co.uk www.andrewhartleyfinearts.co.uk

ALS ⊞† Allan Smith Clocks, Amity Cottage, 162 Beechcroft Road, Upper Stratton, Swindon, Wiltshire SN2 7QE Tel: 01793 822977 allansmithclocks@lineone.net www.allansmithantiqueclocks.co.uk

AMB ⚒ Ambrose, Ambrose House, Old Station Road, Loughton, Essex IG10 4PE Tel: 020 8502 3951

AMC ⊞ Amelie Caswell Tel: 0117 9077960

AMH ⊞ Amherst Antiques, Monomark House, 27 Old Gloucester Street, London WC1N 3XX Tel: 01892 725552 info@amherstantiques.co.uk www.amherstantiques.co.uk

ANAn ⊞ Angel Antiques, Church Street, Petworth, West Sussex GU28 0AD Tel: 01798 343306 swansonantiques@aol.com www.angel-antiques.com

ANG ⊞† Ancient & Gothic, P O Box 5390, Bournemouth, Dorset BH7 6XR Tel: 01202 431721

ANGE ⊞ Angelo Tel: 01753 864657

ANO ⊞† Art Nouveau Originals, The Bindery Gallery, 69 High Street, Broadway, Worcestershire WR12 7DP Tel: 01386 854645 cathy@artnouveauoriginals.com www.artnouveauoriginals.com

APC ⊞ Antique Photographic Company Ltd, Lincolnshire Tel: 01949 842192 alpaco47@aol.com

APO ⊞ Apollo Antiques Ltd, The Saltisford, Birmingham Road, Warwick, CV34 4TD Tel: 01926 494746/494666 mynott@apolloantiques.com

APS ⊞ The Antique Print Shop, 11 Middle Row, East Grinstead, West Sussex RH19 3AX Tel: 01342 410501 printsandmaps@www.theantiqueprintshop.com

ARB ⊞ Arbour Antiques Ltd, Poet's Arbour, Sheep Street, Stratford-on-Avon, Warwickshire CV37 6EF Tel: 01789 293453

ARCA ⊞ Arcadia Antiques, 30 Long Street, Tetbury, Gloucestershire GL8 8AQ Tel: 01666 500236 jackharness1@aol.com www.arcadiaantiques.co.uk

ARP ⊞ Arundel Photographica, The Arundel Antiques and Collectors Centre, 51 High Street, Arundel, West Sussex BN18 9AJ Tel: 01903 885540 cameras@arundel-photographica.co.uk www.arundel-photographica.co.uk

ARTi ⊞ Artifactory, 641 Indiana Ave. NW, Washington DC 20004, U.S.A. Tel: 202 393 2727 artifactorydc@msn.com www.artifactorydc.com

ASC ⊞ Andrew Sclanders, 32 St Paul's View, 15 Amwell Street, London EC1R 1UP Tel: 020 7278 5034 sclanders@beatbooks.com www.beatbooks.com

ASP ⊞ Aspidistra Antiques, 51 High Street, Finedon, Wellingborough, Northamptonshire NN9 9JN Tel: 01933 680196 info@aspidistra-antiques.com www.aspidistra.antiques.com

AUC ⊞ Aurea Carter, PO Box 44134, London SW6 3YX Tel: 020 7731 3486 aureacarter@englishceramics.com www.englishceramics.com

Aur ⊞ Aurum, 310/311 Grays Antique Market, 58 Davies Street, London W1K 5LP Tel: 020 7409 0215 aurum@tinyworld.co.uk www.graysantiques.com

AUTO ⊞ Automatomania, Stands 23 & 24, 284 Westbourne Grove (corner of Portobello road), London W11 2QA Tel: 07790 719097 magic@automatomania.com www.automatomania.com

AW ⊞† Alan Walker, Halfway Manor, Halfway, Newbury, Berkshire RG20 8NR Tel: 01488 657670 www.alanwalker-barometers.com

B&R ⊞ Bread & Roses, Warwickshire Tel: 01926 817342

B2W ⊞ Back 2 Wood, The Old Goods Shed, Station Road, Appledore, Ashford, Kent TN26 2DF Tel: 01233 758109 pine@back2wood.com www.back2wood.com

BaN ⊞ Barbara Ann Newman Tel: 07850 016729

BAY ⊞ George Bayntun, Manvers Street, Bath, Somerset BA1 1JW Tel: 01225 466000 EBayntun@aol.com

BBA ⚒ Bloomsbury, Bloomsbury House, 24 Maddox Street, London W1S 1PP Tel: 020 7495 9494 info@bloomsburyauctions.com www.bloomsburyauctions.com

BBe ⊞ Bourton Bears, Oxfordshire Tel: 01993 824756 help@bourtonbears.co.uk www.bourtonbears.com

BBo ⊞ Bazaar Boxes Tel: 01992 504 454 bazaarboxes@hotmail.com commerce.icollector.com/BazaarBoxes/

Bea ⚒ Bearnes, St Edmund's Court, Okehampton Street, Exeter, Devon EX4 1DU Tel: 01392 207000 enquiries@bearnes.co.uk www.bearnes.co.uk

Beb ⊞ Bebes et Jouets, c/o Post Office, Edinburgh, Scotland EH7 6HW Tel: 0131 332 5650 bebesetjouets@u.genie.co.uk www.you.genie.co.uk/bebesetjouets

BeF ⊞ Bevan Fine Art, PO Box 60, Uckfield, East Sussex TN22 1ZD Tel: 01825 766649 bevanfineart@quista.net

BELL ⊞ Bellhouse Antiques, Chelmsford, Essex Tel: 01268 710415 Bellhouse.Antiques@virgin.net

BERN ⚒ Bernaerts, Verlatstraat 18–22, 2000 Antwerpen/Anvers, Belgium Tel: +32 (0)3 248 19 21 edmond.bernaerts@ping.be www.auction-bernaerts.com

Bert ⚒† Bertoia Auctions, 2141 DeMarco Drive, Vineland, New Jersey 08360, U.S.A. Tel: 856 692 1881 bill@bertoiaauctions.com www.bertoiaauctions.com

BEX ⊞† Daniel Bexfield Antiques, 26 Burlington Arcade, London W1J 0PU Tel: 020 7491 1720 antiques@bexfield.co.uk www.bexfield.co.uk

BHa ⊞† Judy & Brian Harden, PO Box 14, Bourton on the Water, Cheltenham, Gloucestershire GL54 2YR Tel: 01451 810684 harden@portraitminiatures.co.uk www.portraitminiatures.co.uk

BI ⊞ Books Illustrated Tel: 0777 1635 777 booksillustrated@aol.com www.booksillustrated.com

BIB ⊞ Biblion, Grays Antique Market, 1–7 Davies Mews, London, W1K 5AB Tel: 020 7629 1374 info@biblion.com www.biblion.com www.biblionmayfair.com

BLm ⊞ Lyn Bloom & Jeffrey Neal, Vault 27, The London Silver Vaults, Chancery Lane, London WC2A 1QS Tel: 0207 242 6189 bloomvault@aol.com www.bloomvault.com

Bns ⊞† Brittons Jewellers, 4 King Street, Clitheroe, Lancashire BB7 2EP Tel: 01200 425555 sales@brittonswatches.com www.internetwatches.co.uk www.antique-jewelry.co.uk

BoC ⊞ Bounty Antiques Centre, 76 Fore Street, Topsham, Devon EX3 0HQ Tel: 01392 875007

BOOM ⊞ Boom Interiors, 115–117 Regents Park Road, Primrose Hill, London NW1 8UR Tel: 020 7722 6622 info@boominteriors.com www.boominteriors.com

BOW ⊞ David Bowden, 304/306 Grays Antique Market, 58 Davies Street, London W1K 5LP Tel: 020 7495 1773

BP ⊞† Barling Porcelain Tel: 01621 890058 stuart@barling.uk.com www.barling.uk.com

BROW ⊞ David Brower, 113 Kensington Church Street, London W8 7LN Tel: 0207 221 4155 David@davidbrower-antiques.com www.davidbrower-antiques.com

BRT ⊞ Britannia, Grays Antique Market, Stand 101, 58 Davies Street, London W1Y 1AR Tel: 020 7629 6772 britannia@grays.clara.net

BrW ⊞ Brian Watson Antique Glass, Foxwarren Cottage, High Street, Marsham, Norwich, Norfolk NR10 5QA Tel: 01263 732519 brian.h.watson@talk21.com BY APPOINTMENT ONLY

BS ⊞ Below Stairs, 103 High Street, Hungerford, Berkshire RG17 0NB Tel: 01488 682317 hofgartner@belowstairs.co.uk www.belowstairs.co.uk

BUDD ⚒ Graham Budd Auctions Ltd, London gb@grahambuddauctions.co.uk

BUK ⚒ Bukowskis, Arsenalsgatan 4, Stockholm, Sweden Tel: +46 (8) 614 08 00 info@bukowskis.se www.bukowskis.se

BUK(F) ⚒ Bukowskis, Horhammer, Iso Roobertink, 12 Stora Robertsg, 00120 Helsinki Helsingfors, Finland Tel: 358 9 668 9110 www.bukowskis.fi

BWL ⚒† Brightwells Fine Art, The Fine Art Saleroom, Easters Court, Leominster, Herefordshire HR6 0DE Tel: 01568 611122 fineart@brightwells.com www.brightwells.com

C&R ⊞ Catchpole & Rye, Saracens Dairy, Jobbs Lane, Pluckley, Ashford, Kent TN27 0SA Tel: 01233 840840 info@crye.co.uk www.crye.co.uk

CaH ⊞ The Camera House, Oakworth Hall, Colne Road, Oakworth, Keighley, Yorkshire BD22 7HZ Tel: 01535 642333 colin@the-camera-house.co.uk www.the-camera-house.co.uk

CAL ⊞ Cedar Antiques Ltd, High Street, Hartley Wintney, Hampshire RG27 8NY Tel: 01252 843222 or 01189 326628

CANI ⊞ Caniche Decorative Arts, PO Box 350, Watford, Hertfordshire WD19 4ZX Tel: 01923 251 206

CAu ⚒† The Cotswold Auction Company Ltd, incorporating Short Graham & Co and Hobbs and Chambers Fine Arts, The Coach House, Swan Yard, 9–13 West Market Place, Cirencester, Gloucestershire GL7 2NH Tel: 01285 642420 info@cotswoldauction.co.uk www.cotswoldauction.co.uk

CAV ⊞ Rupert Cavendish Antiques, 610 King's Road, London SW6 2DX Tel: 020 7731 7041 www.rupertcavendish.co.uk

CB ⊞ Christine Bridge Antiques, 78 Castelnau, London SW13 9EX Tel: 07000 445277 christine@bridge-antiques.com www.bridge-antiques.com www.antiqueglass.co.uk

CBB ⊞ Colin Baddiel, Gray's Mews, 1–7 Davies Mews, London W1Y 1AR Tel: 020 7408 1239/ 020 8452 7243

CBP ⚒† Comic Book Postal Auctions Ltd, 40–42 Osnaburgh Street, London NW1 3ND Tel: 020 7424 0007 comicbook@compalcomics.com www.compalcomics.com

CCO ⊞ Collectable Costume, Showroom South, Gloucester Antiques Centre, 1 Severn Road, Gloucester, GL1 2LE Tel: 01989 562188

CFSD ⊞ Clive Farahar & Sophie Dupre, Horsebrook House, XV The Green, Calne, Wiltshire SN11 8DQ Tel: 01249 821121 post@farahardupre.co.uk www.farahardupre.co.uk

CHA ⊞ Chislehurst Antiques, 7 Royal Parade, Chislehurst, Kent BR7 6NR Tel: 020 8467 1530

CHAC ⊞† Church Hill Antiques Centre, 6 Station Street, Lewes, East Sussex BN7 2DA Tel: 01273 474 842 churchhilllewes@aol.com www.church-hill-antiques.com

ChC ⊞ Christopher Clarke (Antiques) Ltd, The Fosseway, Stow-on-the-Wold, Gloucestershire GL54 1JS Tel: 01451 830476 cclarkeantiques@aol.com www.campaignfurniture.com

Che ⊞ Chevertons of Edenbridge Ltd, 71–73 High Street, Edenbridge, Kent TN8 5AL Tel: 01732 863196 chevertons@msn.com www.chevertons.com

CHES ⊞† Chesapeake Antique Center, Inc., Rt. 301, PO Box 280, Queenstown, MD 21658, U.S.A. Tel: 410 827 6640 admin@chesapeakeantiques.com www.chesapeakantiques.com

CHI ⊞ Chinasearch, Ltd, 4 Princes Drive, Kenilworth, Warwickshire CV8 2FD Tel: 01926 512402 helen.rush@chinasearch.co.uk jackie@chinasearch.co.uk www.chinasearch.uk.com

CHTR ⚒ Charterhouse, The Long Street Salerooms, Sherborne, Dorset DT9 3BS Tel: 01935 812277 enquiry@charterhouse-auctions.co.uk www.charterhouse-auctions.co.uk

COF ⊞ Cottage Farm Antiques, Stratford Road, Aston Subedge, Chipping Campden, Gloucestershire GL55 6PZ Tel: 01386 438263 info@cottagefarmantiques.co.uk www.cottagefarmantiques.co.uk

CoHA ⊞ Corner House Antiques and Ffoxe Antiques, Gardners Cottage, Broughton Poggs, Filkins, Lechlade-on-Thames, Gloucestershire GL7 3JH Tel: 01367 252007 jdhis007@btopenworld.com enquiries@corner-house-antiques.co.uk www.corner-house-antiques.co.uk

COO ⊞ Graham Cooley Tel: 07968 722269

Cot ⊞ Cottage Collectibles, Long Street Antiques, 14 Long Street, Tetbury, Gloucestershire G18 8AQ Tel: 01666 500850 sheila@cottagecollectibles.co.uk

CPC ⊞ Carnegie Paintings & Clocks, 15 Fore Street, Yealmpton, Plymouth, Devon PL8 2JN Tel: 01752 881170 info@paintingsandclocks.com www.paintingsandclocks.com

CrF ⊞ Crowdfree Antiques, PO Box 395, Bury St Edmunds, Suffolk IP31 2PG Tel: 0870 444 0791 info@crowdfree.com www.crowdfree.com

CRU ⊞ Mary Cruz Antiques, 5 Broad Street, Bath, Somerset BA1 5LJ Tel: 01225 334174

CTO ⊞† Collector's Corner, PO Box 8, Congleton, Cheshire CW12 4GD Tel: 01260 270429 dave.popcorner@ukonline.co.uk

CuS ⊞ Curious Science, 319 Lillie Road, Fulham, London SW6 7LL Tel: 020 7610 1175 curiousscience@medical-antiques.com

CVA ⊞ Courtville Antiques, Powerscourt Townhouse Centre, South William Street, Dublin 2, Republic of Ireland Tel: 01 679 4042 courtville@eircom.net

DA ⚒† Dee, Atkinson & Harrison, The Exchange Saleroom, Driffield, East Yorkshire YO25 6LD Tel: 01377 253151 info@dahauctions.com www.dahauctions.com

DAD ⊞ decorative arts @ doune, Scottish Antique & Arts Centre, By Doune, Stirling, Scotland FK16 6HD Tel: 01786 834401/07778 475974 decorativearts.doune@btinternet.com www.decorativearts-doune.com

DaM ⊞ Martin's Antiques & Collectibles, The Shed Antiques Collectibles Centre, West Midlands Tel: 01386 438387/0795 1600573 Jackiem743710633@aol.com www.martinsantiquescollectibles.co.uk

DAN ⊞ Andrew Dando, 34 Market Street, Bradford on Avon, Wiltshire BA15 1LL Tel: 01225 865444 andrew@andrewdando.co.uk www.andrewdando.co.uk

DAP ⊞ David Phillips Antiques, Westbank, Pontypridd, Mid Glamorgan, Wales, CF37 2HS Tel: 01443 404646

DAV ⊞ Hugh Davies, The Packing Shop, 6–12 Ponton Road, London, SW8 5BA Tel: 020 7498 3255

DD ⚒† David Duggleby, The Vine St Salerooms, Scarborough, Yorkshire YO11 1XN Tel: 01723 507111 auctions@davidduggleby.com www.davidduggleby.com

DeA ⊞ Delphi Antiques, Powerscourt Townhouse Centre, South William Street, Dublin 2, Republic of Ireland Tel: 353 679 0331

DEB ⊞ Debden Antiques, Elder Street, Debden, Saffron Walden, Essex CB11 3JY Tel: 01799 543007 info@debden-antiques.co.uk debden-antiques.co.uk

DeP ⊞ De Parma, Core One, The Gasworks, 2 Michael Road, London SW6 2AN Tel: 0207 736 3384 info@deparma.com www.deparma.com

DFA ⊞ Delvin Farm Antiques, Gormonston, Co Meath, Republic of Ireland Tel: 353 1 841 2285 info@delvinfarmpine.com john@delvinfarmpine.com www.delvinfarmpine.com

DHA ⊞ Durham House Antiques, Sheep Street, Stow-on-the-Wold, Gloucestershire GL54 1AA Tel: 01451 870404

DLP ⊞† The Dunlop Collection, P.O. Box 6269, Statesville, NC 28687, U.S.A. Tel: 704 871 2626 or Toll Free Telephone (800) 227 1996

DMa ⊞ David March, Abbots Leigh, Bristol, Gloucestershire BS8 Tel: 0117 937 2422

DMC ⚒ Diamond Mills & Co, 117 Hamilton Road, Felixstowe, Suffolk IP11 7BL Tel: 01394 282281

DML ⊞ David Moulson, The Gorralls, Cold Comfort Lane, Alcester, Warwickshire B49 5PU Tel: 01789 764092 dmoulson@hotmail.com

DN ⚒† Dreweatt Neate, Donnington Priory, Donnington, Newbury, Berkshire RG14 2JE Tel: 01635 553553 donnington@dnfa.com www.dnfa.com/donnington

DN(BR) ⚒† Dreweatt Neate, The Auction Hall, The Pantiles, Tunbridge Wells, Kent TN2 5QL Tel: 01892 544500 tunbridgewells@dnfa.com www.dnfa.com/tunbridgewells

DN(HAM) ⚒† Dreweatt Neate formerly Hamptons Fine Art Auctioneers, Baverstock House, 93 High Street, Godalming, Surrey GU7 1AL Tel: 01483 423567 godalming@dnfa.com www.dnfa.com/godalming

DNo ⊞ Desmond & Amanda North, The Orchard, 186 Hale Street, East Peckham, Kent TN12 5JB Tel: 01622 871353

DNW ⚒ Dix-Noonan-Webb, 16 Bolton Street, London W1J 8BQ Tel: 020 7016 1700 auctions@dnw.co.uk www.dnw.co.uk

DOA ⊞ Dorchester Antiques, 3 High Street, Dorchester-on-Thames, Oxfordshire OX10 7HH Tel: 01865 341 373

DORO ⚒ Dorotheum, Palais Dorotheum, A-1010 Wien, Dorotheergasse 17, 1010 Vienna, Austria Tel: 515 60 229 client.services@dorotheum.at

DRA ⊞† Derek Roberts Antiques, 25 Shipbourne Road, Tonbridge, Kent TN10 3DN Tel: 01732 358986 drclocks@clara.net www.qualityantiqueclocks.com

DREW ⊞ Drew Pritchard Ltd, St Georges Church, Church Walks, Llandudno, Wales LL30 2HL Tel: 01492 874004 enquiries@drewpritchard.co.uk www.drewpritchard.co.uk

DRU ⊞ Drummonds Architectural Antiques Ltd, The Kirkpatrick Buildings, 25 London Road (A3), Hindhead, Surrey GU26 6AB Tel: 01428 609444 www.drummonds-arch.co.uk

DuM ⚒ Du Mouchelles, 409 East Jefferson, Detroit, Michigan 48226, U.S.A. Tel: 313 963 6255

E ⚒† Ewbank Auctioneers, Burnt Common Auction Rooms, London Road, Send, Woking, Surrey GU23 7LN Tel: 01483 223101 antiques@ewbankauctions.co.uk www.ewbankauctions.co.uk

EAL ⊞† The Exeter Antique Lighting Co., Cellar 15, The Quay, Exeter, Devon EX2 4AP Tel: 01392 490848 www.antiquelightingcompany.com

Ech ⊞ Echoes, 650a Halifax Road, Eastwood, Todmorden, Yorkshire OL14 6DW Tel: 01706 817505

EFA ⊞ Claudia Hill at Ellison Fine Art BY APPOINTMENT ONLY Tel: 01494 678880 www.ellisonfineart.com

EHCS The European Honeypot Collectors' Society, John Doyle, The Honeypot, 18 Victoria Road, Chislehurst, Kent BR7 6DF Tel: 020 8289 7725 johnhoneypot@hotmail.com www.geocities.com/tehcsuk

EMH ⊞ Eat My Handbag Bitch, 37 Drury Lane, London WC2B 5RR Tel: 020 7836 0830 contact@eatmyhandbagbitch.co.uk www.eatmyhandbagbitch.co.uk

ERA ⊞ English Rose Antiques, 7 Church Street, Coggeshall, Essex CO6 1TU Tel: 01376 562683 & 0049 (0)1719 949541 englishroseantiques@hotmail.com www.englishroseantiques.co.uk www.Delta-Line-Trading.com

ET ⊞† Early Technology, Monkton House, Old Craighall, Musselburgh, Midlothian, Scotland EH21 8SF Tel: 0131 665 5753 michael.bennett-levy@virgin.net www.earlytech.com www.rare78s.com www.tvhistory.tv

ETO ⊞ Eric Tombs, 62a West Street, Dorking, Surrey RH4 1BS Tel: 01306 743661 ertombs@aol.com www.dorkingantiques.com

EXC ⊞ Excalibur Antiques, Taunton Antique Centre, 27–29 Silver Street, Taunton, Somerset TA13DH Tel: 01823 289327/07774 627409 pwright777@btopenworld.com www.excaliburantiques.com

F ⊞ Freshfords, High Street, Freshford, Bath, Somerset BA3 6EF Tel: 01225 722111 antiques@freshfords.com www.freshfords.com

F&C ⚒ Finan & Co, The Square, Mere, Wiltshire BA12 6DJ Tel: 01747 861411 post@finanandco.co.uk www.finanandco.co.uk

F&F ⊞ Fenwick & Fenwick, 88–90 High Street, Broadway, Worcestershire WR12 7AJ Tel: 01386 853227/841724

FAC ⊞† Faganarms, Box 425, Fraser, MI 48026, U.S.A. Tel: 586 465 4637 info@faganarms.com www.faganarms.com

FOF ⊞ Fossack & Furkle, PO Box 733, Abington, Cambridgeshire CB1 6BF Tel: 01223 894296 fossack@btopenworld.com www.fossackandfurkle.freeservers.com

FOX ⊞ Fox Cottage Antiques, Digbeth Street, Stow on the Wold, Gloucestershire GL54 1BN Tel: 01451 870307

FRD ⊞ Fragile Design, 8 The Custard Factory, Digbeth, Birmingham, West Midlands B9 4AA Tel: 0121 693 1001 info@fragiledesign.com www.fragiledesign.com

G(B) ⚒ Gorringes Auction Galleries, Terminus Road, Bexhill-on-Sea, East Sussex TN39 3LR Tel: 01424 212994 bexhill@gorringes.co.uk www.gorringes.co.uk

G(L) ⚒ Gorringes inc Julian Dawson, 15 North Street, Lewes, East Sussex BN7 2PD Tel: 01273 478221 clientservices@gorringes.co.uk www.gorringes.co.uk

G&G ⊞ Guest & Gray, 1–7 Davies Mews, London W1K 5AB Tel: 020 7408 1252 info@chinese-porcelain-art.com www.chinese-porcelain-art.com

G&H ⊞† Garret & Hazlehurst, PO Box 138, Hailsham, East Sussex BN27 1WX Tel: 01323 848824 margendygarret@btinternet.com www.garretandhazlehurst.co.uk

GAK ⚒† Keys, Off Palmers Lane, Aylsham, Norfolk NR11 6JA Tel: 01263 733195 www.aylshamsalerooms.co.uk

Gam ⚒ Clarke Gammon, The Guildford Auction Rooms, Bedford Road, Guildford, Surrey GU1 4SJ Tel: 01483 880915

GAU ⊞ Becca Gauldie Antiques, The Old School, Glendoick, Perthshire, Scotland PH2 7NR Tel: 01738 860 870 becca@scottishantiques.freeserve.co.uk

GBM ⊞ GB Military Antiques, 17–18 The Mall, 359 Upper Street, Islington, London N1 0PD Tel: 0207 354 7334 info@gbmilitaria.com www.gbmilitaria.com

GBr ⊞ Geoffrey Breeze Antiques Tel: 01225 466499 antiques@geoffreybreeze.co.uk www.antiquecanes.co.uk

GD ⊞† Gilbert & Dale Antiques, The Old Chapel, Church Street, Ilchester, Nr Yeovil, Somerset BA22 8ZA Tel: 01935 840464 roy@roygilbert.com

GDB ⊞ G D Blay Antiques, 56 West Street, Dorking, Surrey RH4 1BS Tel: 07785 767718 gdblay@gdblayantiques.com www.gdblayantiques.com

GEO ⊞ Georgian Antiques, 10 Pattinson Street, Leith Links, Edinburgh, Scotland EH6 7HF Tel: 0131 553 7286 info@georgianantiques.net JDixon7098@aol.com www.georgianantiques.net

GGD ⊞† Great Grooms Antiques Centre, 51/52 West Street, Dorking, Surrey RH4 1BU Tel: 01306 887076 dorking@greatgrooms.co.uk www.greatgrooms.co.uk

GH ⚒ Gardiner Houlgate, The Bath Auction Rooms, 9 Leafield Way, Corsham, Nr Bath, Somerset SN13 9SW Tel: 01225 812912 auctions@gardiner-houlgate.co.uk www.invaluable.com/gardiner-houlgate

GIL ⚒† Gilding's Auctioneers and Valuers, 64 Roman Way, Market Harborough, Leicestershire LE16 7PQ Tel: 01858 410414 sales@gildings.co.uk www.gildings.co.uk

GIR ⊞ Helen Girton Antiques, PO Box 2022, Buckingham, MK18 4ZH Tel: 01280 815012

GLAS ⊞ Glasstastique BY APPOINTMENT ONLY Tel: 0113 287 9308 or 07967 337795/07967 345952 glasstastique@aol.com www.glasstastique.com

GLB ⊞ Glebe Antiques, Scottish Antique Centre, Doune, Scotland FK16 6HG Tel: 01259 214559 rrglebe@aol.com

GLD ⊞ Glade Antiques, PO Box 873, High Wycombe, Buckinghamshire HP14 3ZQ Tel: 01494 882818 sonia@gladeantiques.com www.gladeantiques.com

GLEN ⊞ Glenda - Antique Dolls, A18–A19 Grays Antique Market, Davies Mews, London W1Y 2LP Tel: 020 8367 2441/020 7629 7034 glenda@glenda-antiquedolls.com www.glenda-antiquedolls.com

GN ⊞† Gillian Neale Antiques, PO Box 247, Aylesbury, Buckinghamshire HP20 1JZ Tel: 01296 423754/07860 638700 gillianneale@aol.com www.gilliannealeantiques.co.uk

GOv ⊞ Glazed Over Tel: 0773 2789114

GRe ⊞ Greystoke Antiques, 4 Swan Yard, (off Cheap Street), Sherborne, Dorset DT9 3AX Tel: 01935 812833

GS ⊞ Ged Selby Antique Glass BY APPOINTMENT Tel: 01756 799673

GTH ⚒ Greenslade Taylor Hunt Fine Art, Magdelene House, Church Square, Taunton, Somerset TA1 1SB Tel: 01823 332525

GTM ⊞ Gloucester Toy Mart, Ground Floor, Antique Centre, Severn Road, Old Docks, Gloucester GL1 2LE Tel: 07973 768452

H&G ⊞ Hope & Glory, 131A Kensington Church Street, London W8 7LP Tel: 020 7727 8424

HA ⊞ Hallidays, The Old College, Dorchester- on-Thames, Oxfordshire OX10 7HL Tel: 01865 340028/68 antiques@hallidays.com www.hallidays.com

HAA ⊞ Hampton Antiques, The Crown Arcade, 119 Portobello Road, London W11 2DY Tel: 01604 863979 info@hamptonantiques.co.uk www.hamptonantiques.co.uk

HABA ⊞ Hall-Bakker Decorative Arts at Heritage, 6 Market Place, Woodstock, Oxfordshire OX20 1TA Tel: 01993 811332

HAL ⊞† John & Simon Haley, 89 Northgate, Halifax, Yorkshire HX1 1XF Tel: 01422 822148/360434 toysandbanks@aol.com

Hal ⚒ Halls Fine Art Auctions, Welsh Bridge, Shrewsbury, Shropshire SY3 8LA Tel: 01743 231212

HAM See DN(HAM)

HCFA ⊞ Henry T. Callan, 162 Quaker Meeting House Road, East Sandwich, MA 02537-1312, U.S.A. Tel: 508 888 5372

HEI No longer trading

HEL ⊞ Helios Gallery, 292 Westbourne Grove, London W11 2PS Tel: 077 11 955 997 info@heliosgallery.com www.heliosgallery.com

HEM ⊞† Hemswell Antique Centres, Caenby Corner Estate, Hemswell Cliff, Gainsborough, Lincolnshire DN21 5TJ Tel: 01427 668389 info@hemswell-antiques.com www.hemswell-antiques.com

Herm ⚒ Hermann Historica OHG, Postfach 201009, 80010 Munchen, Germany Tel: 00 49 89 5237296

HIS ⊞† Erna Hiscock & John Shepherd, Chelsea Galleries, 69 Portobello Road, London W11 Tel: 01233 661407 erna@ernahiscockantiques.com www.ernahiscockantiques.com

HKW ⊞ Hawkswood Antiques, PO Box 156, Goole DN14 7FW Tel: 01757 638630 jenny@hawkswood.fsbusiness.co.uk

HO ⊞ Houghton Antiques, Houghton, Cambridgeshire Tel: 01480 461887 or 07803 716842

HOK ⚒ Hamilton Osborne King, 4 Main Street, Blackrock, Co. Dublin, Republic of Ireland Tel: 353 1 288 5011 blackrock@hok.ie www.hok.ie

HOLL ⚒† Holloway's, 49 Parsons Street, Banbury, Oxfordshire OX16 5NB Tel: 01295 817777 enquiries@hollowaysauctioneers.co.uk www.hollowaysauctioneers.co.uk

HOM ⊞ Home & Colonial, 134 High Street, Berkhamsted, Hertfordshire HP4 3AT Tel: 01442 877007 homeandcolonial@btinternet.com www.homeandcolonial.co.uk

HOP ⊞ The Antique Garden, Grosvenor Garden Centre, Wrexham Road, Belgrave, Chester, Cheshire CH4 9EB Tel: 01244 629191/07976 539 990 antigard@btopenworld.com

HOW ⊞ John Howard at Heritage, 6 Market Place, Woodstock, Oxfordshire OX20 1TA Tel: 01993 811332/0870 4440678 john@johnhoward.co.uk www.antiquepottery.co.uk www.atheritage.co.uk

HSR ⊞ High Street Retro, 39 High Street, Old Town, Hastings, East Sussex TN34 3ER Tel: 01424 460068

HTE ⊞ Heritage, 6 Market Place, Woodstock, Oxfordshire OX20 1TA Tel: 01993 811332/0870 4440678 dealers@atheritage.co.uk www.atheritage.co.uk

HUN ⊞ The Country Seat, Huntercombe Manor Barn, Henley-on-Thames, Oxfordshire RG9 5RY Tel: 01491 641349 wclegg@thecountryseat.com www.thecountryseat.com

HWK ⊞ H W Keil Ltd, Tudor House, Broadway, Worcestershire WR12 7DP Tel: 01386 852408 hans@hwkeil.co.uk

HYD ⚒ Hy Duke & Son, The Dorchester Fine Art Salerooms, Weymouth Avenue, Dorchester, Dorset DT1 1QS Tel: 01305 265080 www.dukes-auctions.com

ICO ⊞ Iconastas, 5 Piccadilly Arcade, London SW1 Tel: 020 7629 1433 info@iconastas.com www.iconastas.com

IM ⚒† Ibbett Mosely, 125 High Street, Sevenoaks, Kent TN13 1UT Tel: 01732 456731 auctions@ibbettmosely.co.uk www.ibbettmosely.co.uk

JAA ⚒† Jackson's International Auctioneers & Appraisers of Fine Art & Antiques, 2229 Lincoln Street, Cedar Falls, IA 50613, U.S.A. Tel: 319 277 2256/800 665 6743 sandim@jacksonsauctions.com www.jacksonsauction.com

JAd ⚒ James Adam & Sons, 26 St Stephen's Green, Dublin 2, Republic of Ireland Tel: 353 1 676 0261 www.jamesadam.ie/

JAK ⊞ Clive & Lynne Jackson Tel: 01242 254375

JBe ⚒ John Bellman Auctioneers, New Pound Business Park, Wisborough Green, Billingshurst, West Sussex RH14 PAZ Tel: 01403 700858 hbeves@bellmans.co.uk

JBL ⊞† Judi Bland Antiques Tel: 01276 857576 or 01536 724145

JBM ⊞ Jim Bullock Militaria, PO Box 217, Romsey, Hampshire SO51 5XL Tel: 01794 516455 jim@jimbullockmilitaria.com www.jimbullockmilitaria.com

JC ⊞ J Collins & Son, PO Box No 119, Bideford, Devon EX39 1WX Tel: 01237 473103 biggs@collinsantiques.co.uk www.collinsantiques.co.uk

JCH ⊞ Jocelyn Chatterton, 126 Grays, 58 Davies St, London W1Y 2LP Tel: 020 7629 1971 jocelyn@cixi.demon.co.uk www.cixi.demon.co.uk

JDJ ⚒† James D Julia, Inc., P O Box 830, Rte.201 Skowhegan Road, Fairfield, ME 04937, U.S.A. Tel: 207 453 7125 www.juliaauctions.com

JE ⊞† Julian Eade Tel: 01865 300349 or 07973 542971

JeA ⊞ Jess Applin, 8 Lensfield Road, Cambridge, CB2 1EG Tel: 01223 315168

JeF ⊞ Jeffrey Formby, The Gallery, Orchard Cottage, East Street, Moreton-in-Marsh, Gloucestershire GL56 0LQ Tel: 01608 650558 www.formby-clocks.co.uk

JeH ⊞ Jennie Horrocks Tel: 07836 264896 info@artnouveaulighting.plus.net www.artnouveaulighting.co.uk

JFME ⊞ James Ferguson, Mark Evans Tel: 0141 950 2452 or 077 699 72935, 01388 768108 or 07979 0189214 james@dec-art.freeserve.co.uk mark@evanscollectables.co.uk www.evanscollectables.co.uk

JHa ⊞ Jeanette Hayhurst Fine Glass, 32a Kensington Church Street, London W8 4HA Tel: 020 7938 1539

JHo ⊞† Jonathan Horne, 66c Kensington Church Street, London W8 4BY Tel: 020 7221 5658 JH@jonathanhorne.co.uk www.jonathanhorne.co.uk

JIL ⊞ Jillings Antique Clocks, Croft House, 17 Church Street, Newent, Gloucestershire GL18 1PU Tel: 01531 822100 clocks@jillings.com www.jillings.com

JM ⚒† Maxwells of Wilmslow inc Dockree's, 133A Woodford Road, Woodford, Cheshire SK7 1QD Tel: 0161 439 5182 www.maxwells-auctioneers.co.uk

JNic ⚒ John Nicholson, The Auction Rooms, Longfield, Midhurst Road, Fernhurst, Surrey GU27 3HA Tel: 01428 653727 sales@johnnicholsons.com

JOP ⊞ Jonathan Potter Ltd. Antique Maps, 125 New Bond Street, London W1S 1DY Tel: 020 7491 3520 jpmaps@attglobal.net www.jpmaps.co.uk

JOR ⊞ John Rogers Tel: 01643 863170/07710 266136 johnrogers024@btinternet.com

JP ⊞ Janice Paull, PO Box 100, Kenilworth, Warwickshire CV8 1JX Tel: 07876 284647 janicepaull@yahoo.com www.janicepaull.com

JPr ⊞ Joanna Proops Antique Textiles & Lighting, 34 Belvedere, Lansdown Hill, Bath, Somerset BA1 5HR Tel: 01225 310795 antiquetextiles@aol.co.uk www.antiquetextiles.co.uk

JRA ⚒ Jim Railton, Nursery House, Chatton, Alnwick, Northumberland NE66 5PY Tel: 01668 215323 office@jimrailton.com www.jimrailton.com

JSG ⊞ James Strang Tel: 01334 472 566 or 07950 490088 jameslstrang@hotmail.com www.mod-i.com

JTS ⊞ June & Tony Stone Fine Antique Boxes, PO Box 106, Peacehaven, East Sussex BN10 8AU Tel: 01273 579333 rachel@boxes.co.uk www.boxes.co.uk

JUN ⊞ Junktion, The Old Railway Station, New Bolingbroke, Boston, Lincolnshire PE22 7LB Tel: 01205 480068/480087 junktionantiques@hotmail.com

JUP ⊞ Jupiter Antiques, P.O. Box 609, Rottingdean, East Sussex BN2 7FW Tel: 01273 302865

K&D ⊞† Kembery Antique Clocks Ltd, George Street Antique Centre, 8 Edgar Buildings, George Street, Bath, Somerset BA1 2EH Tel: 0117 956 5281 kembery@kdclocks.co.uk www.kdclocks.co.uk

K&M ⊞ K & M Antiques, 369–370 Grays Antique Market, 58 Davies Street, London W1K 5LP Tel: 020 7491 4310 Kandmantiques@aol.com

KET ⊞ Carol Ketley Antiques, PO Box 16199, London NW1 7WD Tel: 020 7359 5529

KEY ⊞ Key Antiques of Chipping Norton, 11 Horsefair, Chipping Norton, Oxfordshire OX7 5AL Tel: 01608 644992/643777 info@keyantiques.com www.keyantiques.com

KK ⊞ Karl Kemp & Assoc., Ltd. Antiques, 36 East 10th Street, New York 10003, U.S.A. Tel: 212 254 1877 info@karlkemp.com www.karlkemp.com

KTA ⚒ Kerry Taylor Auctions, in Association with Sotheby's, St George Street Gallery, Sotheby's New Bond Street, London W1A 2AA Tel: 07785 734337 fashion.textiles@sothebys.com

KW ⊞ Karel Weijand, Lion & Lamb Courtyard, Farnham, Surrey GU9 7LL Tel: 01252 726215 carpets@karelweijand.com

L ⚒ Lawrence Fine Art Auctioneers, South Street, Crewkerne, Somerset TA18 8AB Tel: 01460 73041 www.lawrences.co.uk

L&E ⚒ Locke & England, 18 Guy Street, Leamington Spa, Warwickshire CV32 4RT Tel: 01926 889100 info@leauction.co.uk www.auctions-online.com/locke

L&T ⚒ Lyon & Turnbull, 33 Broughton Place, Edinburgh, Scotland EH1 3RR Tel: 0131 557 8844 info@lyonandturnbull.com

LAY ⚒ David Lay ASVA, Auction House, Alverton, Penzance, Cornwall TR18 4RE Tel: 01736 361414 david.lays@btopenworld.com

LBO ⊞ Laura Bordignon Antiques, PO Box 6247, Finchingfield, Essex CM7 4ER Tel: 01371 811 791 or 07778 787929 laurabordignon@hotmail.com

LBr ⊞ Lynda Brine BY APPOINTMENT ONLY lyndabrine@yahoo.co.uk www.scentbottlesandsmalls.co.uk

LCC ⊞ The London Cigarette Card Co Ltd, Sutton Road, Somerton, Somerset TA11 6QP Tel: 01458 273452 cards@londoncigcard.co.uk www.londoncigcard.co.uk

LF ⚒ Lambert & Foster, 77 Commercial Road, Paddock Wood, Kent TN12 6DR Tel: 01892 832325

LFA ⚒† Law Fine Art Tel: 01635 860033 info@lawfineart.co.uk www.lawfineart.co.uk

Lfo ⊞ Lorfords, 57 Long Street, Tetbury, Gloucestershire GL8 8AA Tel: 01666 505111 toby@lorfordsantiques.co.uk www.lorfordsantiques.co.uk

LGr ⊞ Langton Green Antiques, Langton Road, Langton Green, Tunbridge Wells, Kent TN3 0HP Tel: 01892 862004 antiques@langtongreen.fsbusiness.co.uk www.langtongreenantiques.co.uk

LHA ⚒† Leslie Hindman, Inc, 122 North Aberdeen Street, Chicago, Illinois 60607, U.S.A. Tel: 312 280 1212 www.lesliehindman.com

Lim ⊞ Limelight Movie Art, N13–16 Antiquarius Antiques Centre, 131–141 King's Road, Chelsea, London SW3 4PJ Tel: 01273 206919 info@limelightmovieart.com www.limelightmovieart.com

LJ ⚒ Leonard Joel Auctioneers, 333 Malvern Road, South Yarra, Victoria 3141, Australia Tel: 03 9826 4333 decarts@ljoel.com.au jewellery@ljoel.com.au www.ljoel.com.au

LLD ⊞ Lewis & Lewis Deco Tel: 07739 904681 lewis_robin@hotmail.com

LOP ⊞ Lopburi Art & Antiques, 5/8 Saville Row, Bath, Somerset BA1 2QP Tel: 01225 322947 mail@lopburi.co.uk www.lopburi.co.uk

M ⚒ Morphets of Harrogate, 6 Albert Street, Harrogate, Yorkshire HG1 1JL Tel: 01423 530030

MAA ⊞ Mario's Antiques, 288 Westbourne Grove, London W11 2PS Tel: 020 8902 1600 marwan@barazi.screaming.net www.marios_antiques.com

Mal(O) ⚒ Mallams, Bocardo House, 24 St Michael's Street, Oxford, 0X1 2EB Tel: 01865 241358 oxford@mallams.co.uk

Man ⊞ Mansers, 31 Wyle Cop, Shrewsbury, Shropshire SY1 1XF Tel: 01743 240328 info@fineartdealers.co.uk www.fineartdealers.co.uk

MANO ⊞ Millner Manolatos, 2 Campden Street, Off Kensington Church Street, London W8 7EP Tel: 020 7229 3268 info@arthurmillner.com www.arthurmillner.com

MAR ⚒ Frank R Marshall & Co, Marshall House, Church Hill, Knutsford, Cheshire WA16 6DH Tel: 01565 653284

MARK ⊞† 20th Century Marks, Whitegates, Rectory Road, Little Burstead, Near Billericay, Essex CM12 9TR Tel: 01268 411 000 info@20thcenturymarks.co.uk www.20thcenturymarks.co.uk

MB ⊞† Mostly Boxes, 93 High Street, Eton, Windsor, Berkshire SL4 6AF Tel: 01753 858470

MCA ⚒† Mervyn Carey, Twysden Cottage, Scullsgate, Benenden, Cranbrook, Kent TN17 4LD Tel: 01580 240283

McP ⊞ R & G McPherson Antiques, 40 Kensington Church Street, London W8 4BX Tel: 020 7937 0812 rmcpherson@orientalceramics.com www.orientalceramics.com

MDe ⊞ Mike Delaney Tel: 01993 840064 or 07979 919760 mike@vintagehornby.co.uk www.vintagehornby.co.uk

MDL ⊞ Michael D Long Ltd, 96–98 Derby Road, Nottingham NG1 5FB Tel: 0115 941 3307 sales@michaeldlong.com www.michaeldlong.com

MEA ⚒ Mealy's, Chatsworth Street, Castle Comer, Co Kilkenny, Republic of Ireland Tel: 353 564 441 229 info@mealys.com www.mealys.com

MFB ⊞ Manor Farm Barn Antiques Tel: 01296 658941 or 07720 286607 mfbn@btinternet.com btwebworld.com/mfbantiques

MGa ⊞ Marilyn Garrow BY APPOINTMENT ONLY Tel: 01728 648671 or 07774 842074 marogarrow@aol.com www.antiquesweb.co.uk/marilyngarrow

MHA ⊞ Merchant House Antiques, 19 High Street, Honiton, Devon EX14 1PR Tel: 01404 42694/44406 antiquesmerchant@ndirect.co.uk

MI ⊞† Mitofsky Antiques, 8 Rathfarnham Road, Terenure, Dublin 6, Republic of Ireland Tel: 353 1492 0033 info@mitofskyantiques.com www.mitofskyantiques.com

MIL ⊞ Millennia Antiquities Tel: 01204 690175 or 07930 273998 millenniaant@aol.com www.AncientAntiquities.co.uk

MIN ⊞ Ministry of Pine, Timsbury Village Workshop, Unit 2, Timsbury Industrial Estate, Hayeswood Road, Timsbury, Bath, Somerset BA2 0HQ Tel: 01761 472297 ministryofpine.uk@virgin.net www.ministryofpine.com

MINN ⊞ Geoffrey T Minnis, Hastings Antique Centre, 59–61 Norman Road, St Leonards-on-Sea, East Sussex TN38 0EG Tel: 01424 428561

Mit ⚒ Mitchells Auction Company, The Furniture Hall, 47 Station Road, Cockermouth, Cumbria CA13 9PZ Tel: 01900 827800 info@mitchellsfineart.com

MiW ⊞ Mike Weedon, 7 Camden Passage, Islington, London N1 8EA Tel: 020 7226 5319 or 020 7609-6826 info@mikeweedonantiques.com www.mikeweedonantiques.com

MLa ⊞ Marion Langham Limited Tel: 028 895 41247 marion@ladymarion.co.uk www.ladymarion.co.uk

MLL ⊞ Millers Antiques Ltd, Netherbrook House, 86 Christchurch Road, Ringwood, Hampshire BH24 1DR Tel: 01425 472062 mail@millers-antiques.co.uk www.millers-antiques.co.uk

MMA ⊞ Martin Murray Antiques, East Finchley, London Tel: 020 8883 0755 martin@martin97.wannadoo.co.uk

MMc ⊞ Marsh-McNamara Tel: 07790 759162

MRW ⊞ Malcolm Russ-Welch, PO Box 1122, Rugby, Warwickshire CV23 9YD Tel: 01788 810 616 malcolm@rb33.co.uk

MSh ⊞ Manfred Schotten, 109 High Street, Burford, Oxfordshire OX18 4RG Tel: 01993 822302 www.antiques@schotten.com

MTay ⊞ Martin Taylor Antiques, 323 Tettenhall Road, Wolverhampton, West Midlands WV6 0JZ Tel: 01902 751166/07836 636524 enquiries@mtaylor-antiques.co.uk www.mtaylor-antiques.co.uk

MUR ⊞ Murray Cards (International) Ltd, 51 Watford Way, Hendon Central, London NW4 3JH Tel: 020 8202 5688 murraycards@ukbusiness.com www.murraycard.com/

NART ⊞ Newel Art Galleries, Inc., 425 East 53rd Street, New York 10022, U.S.A. Tel: 212 758 1970 info@newel.com www.Newel.com

NAW ⊞† Newark Antiques Warehouse Ltd, Old Kelham Road, Newark, Nottinghamshire NG24 1BX Tel: 01636 674869/07974 429185 enquiries@newarkantiques.co.uk www.newarkantiques.co.uk

NBL ⊞ N Bloom & Son (1912) Ltd, 12 Piccadilly Arcade, London SW1Y 6NH Tel: 020 7629 5060 nbloom@nbloom.com www.nbloom.com

NEW ⊞ Newsum Antiques, 2 High Street, Winchcombe, Gloucestershire GL54 5HT Tel: 01242 603446/ 07968 196668 mark@newsumantiques.co.uk www.newsumantiques.co.uk

NOA ⚒ New Orleans Auction Galleries, Inc., 801 Magazine Street, AT 510 Julia, New Orleans, Louisiana 70130, U.S.A. Tel: 504 566 1849

NS ⊞ Nicholas Shaw Antiques, Virginia Cottage, Lombard Street, Petworth, West Sussex GU28 0AG Tel: 01798 345146/01798 345147 silver@nicholas-shaw.com www.nicholas-shaw.com

NSal ⚒ Netherhampton Salerooms, Salisbury Auction Centre, Netherhampton, Salisbury, Wiltshire SP2 8RH Tel: 01722 340 041

NW ⊞ Nigel Williams Rare Books, 25 Cecil Court, London, WC2N 4EZ Tel: 020 7836 7757 nigel@nigelwilliams.com www.nigelwilliams.com

NWE ⊞† North Wilts. Exporters, Farm Hill House, Brinkworth, Wiltshire SN15 5AJ Tel: 01666 510876 mike@northwilts.demon.co.uk www.northwiltsantiqueexporters.com

OE ⊞ Orient Expressions, Landsdown Place East, Bath, Somerset BA1 5ET Tel: 01225 425446 www.orientexpressions.com

OH ⊞ Old Hat, 66 Fulham High Road, London SW6 3LQ Tel: 020 7610 6558

OIA ⊞ The Old Ironmongers Antiques Centre, 5 Burford Street, Lechlade, Gloucestershire GL7 3AP Tel: 01367 252397

OLA ⊞ Olliff's Architectural Antiques, 19–21 Lower Redland Road, Redland, Bristol, Gloucestershire BS6 6TB Tel: 0117 923 9232 marcus@olliffs.com www.olliffs.com

ONS ⚒ Onslow's Auctions Ltd, The Coach House, Manor Road, Stourpaine, Dorset DT8 8TQ Tel: 01258 488838

OTA ⊞ On The Air, 42 Bridge Street Row, Chester, Cheshire CH1 1NN Tel: 01244 348468

OTB ⊞† The Old Tackle Box, PO Box 55, High Street, Cranbrook, Kent TN17 3ZU Tel: 01580 713979 tackle.box@virgin.net

PAO ⊞ P A Oxley Antique Clocks & Barometers, The Old Rectory, Cherhill, Calne, Wiltshire SN11 8UX Tel: 01249 816227 info@paoxley.com www.british-antiqueclocks.com

PBA ⚒ Paul Beighton, Woodhouse Green, Thurcroft, Rotherham, Yorkshire S66 9AQ Tel: 01709 700005 www.paulbeightonauctioneers.co.uk

PeN ⊞ Peter Norden Antiques, 61 Long Street, Tetbury, Gloucestershire GL8 8AA Tel: 01666 503 854 peternorden_antiques@lineone.net www.peter-norden-antiques.co.uk

Penn ⊞ Penny Fair Antiques Tel: 07860 825456

PEZ ⊞ Alan Pezaro, 62a West Street, Dorking, Surrey RH4 1BS Tel: 01306 743661

PF ⚒† Peter Francis, Curiosity Sale Room 19 King Street, Carmarthen, Wales SA31 1BH Tel: 01267 233456 nigel@peterfrancis.co.uk www.peterfrancis.co.uk

PFK † Penrith Farmers' & Kidd's plc, Skirsgill Salerooms, Penrith, Cumbria CA11 0DN Tel: 01768 890781 info@pfkauctions.co.uk www.pfkauctions.co.uk

PGO † Pamela Goodwin, 11 The Pantiles, Royal Tunbridge Wells, Kent TN2 5TD Tel: 01892 618200 mail@goodwinantiques.co.uk www.goodwinantiques.co.uk

PICA Piccadilly Antiques, 280 High Street, Batheaston, Bath, Somerset BA1 7RA Tel: 01225 851494 piccadillyantiques@ukonline.co.uk

PLB Planet Bazaar, 149 Drummond Street, London NW1 2PB Tel: 020 7387 8326 info@planetbazaar.co.uk www.planetbazaar.co.uk

POLL Pollyanna, 34 High Street, Arundel, West Sussex BN18 9AB Tel: 01903 885198

POW Sylvia Powell Decorative Arts, Suite 400, Ceramic House, 571 Finchley Road, London NW3 7BN Tel: 020 8458 4543 dpowell909@aol.com

PrB Pretty Bizarre, 170 High Street, Deal, Kent CT14 6BQ Tel: 07973 794537

PSC Peter & Sonia Cashman, Bath, Somerset Tel: 01225 469497 pete@doubleflint.freeserve.co.uk soniacashman@hotmail.com www.cashman-antiques.co.uk

PT † Pieces of Time, 1–7 Davies Mews, London W1K 5AB Tel: 020 7629 2422 info@antique-watch.com www.antique-watch.com www.cufflinksworld.com

PTh Antique Clocks by Patrick Thomas, 62a West Street, Dorking, Surrey RH4 1BS Tel: 01306 743661 patrickthomas@btconnect.com www.antiqueclockshop.co.uk

PUGH † Pugh's Antiques, Pugh's Farm, Monkton, Nr Honiton, Devon EX14 9QH Tel: 01404 42860 sales@pughsantiques.com www.pughsantiques.com ***Relocating to: Portley House, Old Ludlow Road, Leominster H36 0AA Tel: 01568 616546***

QA Quayside Antiques, 9 Frankwell, Shrewsbury, Shropshire SY3 8JY Tel: 01743 360490 www.quaysideantiques.co.uk www.quaysideantiquesshrewsbury.co.uk

QM The Wyndham Gallery, Lafayette Antiques Center, 401E 110th Street, New York, U.S.A. Tel: 212 722 8400 john_cullis@hotmail.com

Qua Quadrille, 146 Portobello Road, London W11 2DZ Tel: 01923 829079/020 7727 9860

RAY Derek & Tina Rayment Antiques, Orchard House, Barton Road, Barton, Nr Farndon, Cheshire SY14 7HT Tel: 01829 270429/07860 666629 and 07702 922410 raymentantiques@aol.com www.antique-barometers.com

RBA Roger Bradbury Antiques, Church Street, Coltishall, Norfolk NR12 7DJ Tel: 01603 737444

RBB See BWL

RBM Robert Morley & Co Ltd, Piano and Harpsicord Showroom & Workshop, 34 Engate Street, London SE13 7HA Tel: 020 8318 5838 jvm@morley-r.u-net.com www.morleypianos.com

RdeR † Rogers de Rin, 76 Royal Hospital Road, London SW3 4HN Tel: 020 7352 9007 rogersderin@rogersderin.co.uk www.rogersderin.co.uk

RdV Roger de Ville Antiques Tel: 01629 812496 or 07798 793857 www.rogerdeville.co.uk

REF † The Refectory, 38 West Street, Dorking, Surrey RH4 1BU Tel: 01306 742111 www.therefectory.co.uk

ReN Rene Nicholls, 56 High Street, Malmesbury, Wiltshire SN16 9AT Tel: 01666 823089

RGa Richard Gardner Antiques, Swanhouse, Market Square, Petworth, West Sussex GU28 0AN Tel: 01798 343411

RGe Rupert Gentle Antiques, The Manor House, Milton Lilbourne, Nr Pewsey, Wiltshire SN9 5LQ Tel: 01672 563344

RH Rick Hubbard Art Deco, 3 Tee Court, Bell Street, Romsey, Hampshire SO51 8GY Tel: 01794 513133 rick@rickhubbard-artdeco.co.uk www.rickhubbard-artdeco.co.uk

RHa Robert Hall, 15c Clifford Street, London W1X 1RF Tel: 020 7734 4008

RHL Robert Hershkowitz Limited, Cockhaise, Monteswood Lane, Near Lindfield, Sussex RH16 2QP Tel: 01444 482240 prhfoto@hotmail.com

RICC Riccardo Sansoni

RIT Ritchies Inc., Auctioneers & Appraisers of Antiques & Fine Art, 288 King Street East, Toronto, Ontario M5A 1K4, Canada Tel: (416) 364 1864 auction@ritchies.com www.ritchies.com

ROH Roy C Harris 01283 520355 or 0771 8500961 rchclocks@aol.com rch-antique-clocks.com

ROSc † R. O. Schmitt Fine Art, Box 1941, Salem, New Hampshire 03079, U.S.A. Tel: 603 893 5915 bob@roschmittfinearts.com www.antiqueclockauction.com

RTo † Rupert Toovey & Co Ltd, Spring Gardens, Washington, West Sussex RH20 3BS Tel: 01903 891955 auctions@rupert-toovey.com www.rupert-toovey.com

RTW † Richard Twort Tel: 01934 641900 or 07711 939789

RYA † Robert Young Antiques, 68 Battersea Bridge Road, London SW11 3AG Tel: 020 7228 7847 office@robertyoungantiques.com www.robertyoungantiques.com

S Sotheby's, 34–35 New Bond Street, London W1A 2AA Tel: 020 7293 5000 www.sothebys.com

S(Am) Sotheby's Amsterdam, De Boelelaan 30, Amsterdam 1083 HJ, Netherlands Tel: 31 20 550 2200 www.sothebys.com

S(HK) Sotheby's, 5/F Standard Chartered Bank Building, 4–4A Des Voeux Road, Central Hong Kong, China Tel: 852 2524 8121 www.sothebys.com

S(Mi) Sotheby's, Palazzo Broggi, Via Broggi, 19, Milan 20129, Italy Tel: 39 02 295 001 www.sothebys.com

S(NY) Sotheby's, 1334 York Avenue at 72nd St, New York 10021, U.S.A. Tel: 212 606 7000 www.sothebys.com

S(O) Sotheby's Olympia, Hammersmith Road, London W14 8UX Tel: 020 7293 5555 www.sothebys.com

S(P) Sotheby's France SA, 76 rue du Faubourg, Saint Honore, Paris 75008, France Tel: 33 1 53 05 53 05 www.sothebys.com

S&D S&D Postcards, Bartlett Street Antique Centre, 5–10 Bartlett Street, Bath, Somerset BA1 2QZ Tel: 07979 506415 wndvd@aol.com

SaB Sara Bernstein Antique Dolls & Bears, Englishtown, New Jersey 07726, U.S.A. Tel: 732 536 4101 santiqbebe@aol.com www.sarabernsteindolls.com

SAS † Special Auction Services, Kennetholme, Midgham, Reading, Berkshire RG7 5UX Tel: 0118 971 2949 www.invaluable.com/sas/

SAT The Swan at Tetsworth, High Street, Tetsworth, Nr Thame, Oxfordshire OX9 7AB Tel: 01844 281777 antiques@theswan.co.uk www.theswan.co.uk

SAW Salisbury Antiques Warehouse Ltd, 94 Wilton Road, Salisbury, Wiltshire SP2 7JJ Tel: 01722 410634 kevin@salisbury-antiques.co.uk

SAY Charlotte Sayers, 360 Grays Antique Market, 58 Davies St, London W1K 5LP Tel: 020 7499 5478

SCO Peter Scott Tel: 0117 986 8468 or 07850 639770

SDD Sandra D Deas Tel: 01333 360 214 or 07713 897 482

SEA Mark Seabrook Antiques, PO Box 396, Huntingdon, Cambridgeshire PE28 0ZA Tel: 01480 861935 enquiries@markseabrook.com www.markseabrook.com

SER Serendipity, 125 High Street, Deal, Kent CT14 6BB Tel: 01304 369165/01304 366536 dipityantiques@aol.com

SGA † Stair Galleries, P O Box 418, 33 Maple Avenue, Claverack, NY 12513, U.S.A. Tel: 212 860 5446/ 518 851 2544 rebecca.hoffmann@stairgalleries.com www.stairgalleries.com

SGr Sarah Groombridge, Saturdays only: Silver Fox Gallery, 121 Portobello Road, London W11 2DY BY APPOINTMENT Tel: 07770 920277 sarah.groombridge@totalise.co.uk

SHa † Shapiro & Co, Stand 380, Gray's Antique Market, 58 Davies Street, London W1Y 5LP Tel: 020 7491 2710

SiA † Simply Antiques, Windsor House, High Street, Moreton-in-Marsh, Gloucestershire GL56 0AD Tel: 07710 470877 info@callingcardcases.com www.callingcardcases.com

SIL The Silver Shop, Powerscourt Townhouse Centre, St Williams Street, Dublin 2, Republic of Ireland Tel: 01 679 4147 ianhaslam@eircom.net

SJH S. J. Hales, 87 Fore Street, Bovey Tracey, Devon TQ13 9AB Tel: 01626 836684

SK Skinner Inc., The Heritage On The Garden, 63 Park Plaza, Boston, MA 02116, U.S.A. Tel: 617 350 5400

SK(B) Skinner Inc., 357 Main Street, Bolton, MA 01740, U.S.A. Tel: 978 779 6241

SMI Skip & Janie Smithson Antiques Tel: 01754 810265 or 07831 399180 smithsonantiques@hotmail.com

SOO Soo San, 598a Kings Road, London SW6 2DX Tel: 020 7731 2063 enquiries@soosan.co.uk www.soosan.co.uk

SOR Soldiers of Rye, Mint Arcade, 71 The Mint, Rye, East Sussex TN31 7EW Tel: 01797 225952 rameses@supanet.com chris@johnbartholomewcards.co.uk www.rameses.supanet.com

SOS Styles of Stow, The Little House, Sheep Street, Stow-on-the-Wold, Gloucestershire GL54 1JS Tel: 01451 830455 www.stylesofstow.co.uk

SPA Sporting Antiques, 10 Union Square, The Pantiles, Tunbridge Wells, Kent TN4 8HE Tel: 01892 522661

SPF Scarborough Perry Fine Art, Hove Auction Rooms, Hove Street, Hove, East Sussex BN3 2GL Tel: 01273 735266

STA George Stacpoole, Main Street, Adare, Co. Limerick, Republic of Ireland Tel: 6139 6409 stacpoole@iol.ie www.georgestacpooleantiques.com

STRA Strachan Antiques, 40 Darnley Street, Pollokshields, Glasgow, Scotland, G41 2SE Tel: 0141 429 4411 alex.strachan@btconnect.com www.strachanantiques.co.uk

SWA † S.W. Antiques, Newlands (road), Pershore, Worcestershire WR10 1BP Tel: 01386 555580 catchall@sw-antiques.co.uk www.sw-antiques.co.uk

SWB † Sweetbriar Gallery Paperweights Ltd., 3 Collinson Court, off Church Street, Frodsham, Cheshire WA6 6PN Tel: 01928 730064 sales@sweetbriar.co.uk www.sweetbriar.co.uk

SWO † Sworders, 14 Cambridge Road, Stansted Mountfitchet, Essex CM24 8BZ Tel: 01279 817778 auctions@sworder.co.uk www.sworder.co.uk

TDG The Design Gallery 1850–1950, 5 The Green, Westerham, Kent TN16 1AS Tel: 01959 561234 sales@thedesigngalleryuk.com www.thedesigngalleryuk.com

TeG The Temple Gallery, 6 Clarendon Cross, Holland Park, London W11 4AP Tel: 020 7727 3809 info@templegallery.com www.templegallery.com

TEM † Tempus Tel: 01344 874007 www.tempus-watches.co.uk

TEN † Tennants, The Auction Centre, Harmby Road, Leyburn, Yorkshire DL8 5SG Tel: 01969 623780 enquiry@tennants-ltd.co.uk www.tennants.co.uk

TGL The Gilded Lily, 145/146 Gray's, 58 Davies Street, London W1K 5LP Tel: 020 7499 6260 jewellery@gilded-lily.co.uk graysantiques.com

TH † Tony Horsley, PO Box 3127, Brighton, East Sussex BN1 5SS Tel: 01273 550770

THE † Theriault's, PO Box 151, Annapolis, MD 21404, U.S.A. Tel: 410 224 3655 info@theriaults.com www.theriaults.com

TIM S & S Timms, 2–4 High Street, Shefford, Bedfordshire SG17 5DG Tel: 01462 851051 info@timmsantiques.com www.timmsantiques.com

TLA The Lanes Armoury, 26 Meeting House Lane, The Lanes, Brighton, East Sussex BN1 1HB Tel: 01273 321357 enquiries@thelanesarmoury.co.uk www.thelanesarmoury.co.uk

TMA Tring Market Auctions, The Market Premises, Brook Street, Tring, Hertfordshire HP23 5EF Tel: 01442 826446 sales@tringmarketauctions.co.uk www.tringmarketauctions.co.uk

TMi † T. J. Millard Antiques, 59 Lower Queen Street, Penzance, Cornwall TR18 4DF Tel: 01736 333454 or 07773 776086 chessmove@btinternet.com

TML Timothy Millett Ltd, Historic Medals and Works of Art, PO Box 20851, London SE22 0YN Tel: 020 8693 1111 tim@timothymillett.demon.co.uk

TNS Toy's N Such Toy's - Antiques & Collectables, 437 Dawson Street, Sault Sainte Marie, MI 49783-2119, U.S.A. Tel: 906 635 0356

TOL Turn On Lighting, Antique Lighting Specialists, 116/118 Islington High St, Camden Passage, Islington, London N1 8EG Tel: 020 7359 7616

TOM † Charles Tomlinson Tel: 01244 318395 charlestomlinson@tiscali.co.uk

TOP † The Top Banana Antiques Mall, 1 New Church Street, Tetbury, Gloucestershire GL8 8DS Tel: 0871 288 1102 info@topbananaantiques.com www.topbananaantiques.com

TPC † Pine Cellars, 39 Jewry Street, Winchester, Hampshire SO23 8RY Tel: 01962 867014/01962 777546

Trib Tribal Gathering, No 1 Westbourne Grove Mews, Notting Hill, London W11 2RU Tel: 020 7221 6650 bryan@tribalgathering.com www.tribalgatheringlondon.com

TRM See TRM(C), TRM(D), TRM(E)

TRM(C) Thomson, Roddick & Medcalf Ltd, Coleridge House, Shaddongate, Carlisle, Cumbria CA2 5TU Tel: 01228 528939 www.thomsonroddick.com

TRM(D) Thomson, Roddick & Medcalf Ltd, 60 Whitesands, Dumfries, Scotland DG1 2RS Tel: 01387 279879 trmdumfries@btconnect.com www.thomsonroddick.com

TRM(E) Thomson, Roddick & Medcalf Ltd, 43/4 Hardengreen Business Park, Eskbank, Edinburgh, Scotland EH22 3NX Tel: 0131 454 9090 www.thomsonroddick.com

TSC The Silver Collection Ltd Tel: 01442 890954 or 07802 447813

TUR † W. F. Turk, 355 Kingston Road, Wimbledon Chase, London SW20 8JX Tel: 020 8543 3231 sales@wfturk.com www.wfturk.com

TYE Typically English Antiques Tel: 01249 721721 or 07818 000704 typicallyeng@aol.com

VB Variety Box Tel: 01892 531868

VEC Vectis Auctions Ltd, Fleck Way, Thornaby, Stockton-on-Tees, Cleveland TS17 9JZ Tel: 01642 750616 admin@vectis.co.uk www.vectis.co.uk

VHA Vanbrugh House Antiques, Park Street, Stow-on-the-Wold, Gloucestershire GL54 1AQ Tel: 01451 830797 johnsands@vanbrughhouse.co.uk www.vanbrughhouse.co.uk

VK Vivienne King of Panache Tel: 01934 814759 or 07974 798871 Kingpanache@aol.com

VS † T Vennett-Smith, 11 Nottingham Road, Gotham, Nottinghamshire NG11 0HE Tel: 0115 983 0541 info@vennett-smith.com www.vennett-smith.com

VSP Van Sabben Poster Auctions, PO Box 2065, 1620 EB Hoorn, The Netherlands Tel: 31 229 268203 uboersma@vsabbenposterauctions.nl www.vsabbenposterauctions.nl

WAA † Woburn Abbey Antiques Centre, Woburn, Bedfordshire MK17 9WA Tel: 01525 290666 antiques@woburnabbey.co.uk www.discoverwoburn.co.uk

WAC Worcester Antiques Centre, Reindeer Court, Mealcheapen Street, Worcester, Worcestershire WR1 4DF Tel: 01905 610680 WorcsAntiques@aol.com

WADS † Wadsworth's, Marehill, Pulborough, West Sussex RH20 2DY Tel: 01798 873555 info@wadsworthsrugs.com www.wadsworthsrugs.com

Wai Peter Wain, Mor Awel, Marine Terrace, Camaes Bay, Anglesey LL67 0ND Tel: 01407 710077 or 07860 302945 peterwain@supanet.com

WAL † Wallis & Wallis, West Street Auction Galleries, Lewes, East Sussex BN7 2NJ Tel: 01273 480208 auctions@wallisandwallis.co.uk grb@wallisandwallis.co.uk www.wallisandwallis.co.uk

WcH † Weschler's Auctioneers & Appraisers, 909 E Street, NW, Washington. DC2004, U.S.A. Tel: 202 628 1281/800 331 1430 karen@weschlers.com www.weschlers.com

WeA Wenderton Antiques Tel: 01227 720295 BY APPOINTMENT ONLY

WEBB Webb's, 18 Manukau Rd, Newmarket, PO Box 99251, Auckland, New Zealand Tel: 09 524 6804 auctions@webbs.co.nz www.webbs.co.nz

WELD J. W. Weldon, 55 Clarendon Street, Dublin 2, Republic of Ireland Tel: 353 1 677 1638

WeW West Wales Antiques, 18 Mansfield Road, Murton, Swansea, Wales, SA3 3AR Tel: 01792 234318/ 01639 644379 info@westwalesantiques.co.uk www.westwalesantiques.co.uk

WiB Wish Barn Antiques, Wish Street, Rye, East Sussex TN31 7DA Tel: 01797 226797

WILK Wilkinson's Auctioneers Ltd, The Old Salerooms, 28 Netherhall Road, Doncaster, Yorkshire DN1 2PW Tel: 01302 814884 sid@wilkinsons-auctioneers.co.uk www.wilkinsons-auctioneers.co.uk

WilP W&H Peacock, 26 Newnham Street, Bedford, Bedfordshire MK40 3JR Tel: 01234 266366

WIM Wimpole Antiques, Stand 349, Grays Antique Market, 58 Davies Street, London W1K 5LP Tel: 020 7499 2889 WimpoleAntiques@compuserve.com

WL † Wintertons Ltd, Lichfield Auction Centre, Fradley Park, Lichfield, Staffordshire WS13 8NF Tel: 01543 263256 enquiries@wintertons.co.uk www.wintertons.co.uk

WRe Walcot Reclamations, 108 Walcot Street, Bath, Somerset BA1 5BG Tel: 01225 444404 rick@walcot.com www.walcot.com

WSA † West Street Antiques, 63 West Street, Dorking, Surrey RH4 1BS Tel: 01306 883487 weststant@aol.com www.antiquearmsandarmour.com

WW Woolley & Wallis, Salisbury Salerooms, 51–61 Castle Street, Salisbury, Wiltshire SP1 3SU Tel: 01722 424500/411854 enquiries@woolleyandwallis.co.uk www.woolleyandwallis.co.uk

YOX † Yoxall Antiques, 68 Yoxall Road, Solihull, West Midlands B90 3RP Tel: 0121 744 1744 sales@yoxallantiques.co.uk www.yoxall-antiques.co.uk

Index to Advertisers

Index

Bold page numbers refer to information and pointer boxes

INDEX

INDEX

M

INDEX

INDEX

INDEX